PHILOSOPHY

The Quest for Truth

EIGHTH EDITION

PHILOSOPHY

The Quest for Truth

EIGHTH EDITION

Louis P. Pojman
Lewis Vaughn

New York • Oxford
OXFORD UNIVERSITY PRESS

Oxford University Press, Inc., publishes works that further Oxford University's
objective of excellence in research, scholarship, and education.

Oxford   New York
Auckland   Cape Town   Dar es Salaam   Hong Kong   Karachi
Kuala Lumpur   Madrid   Melbourne   Mexico City   Nairobi
New Delhi   Shanghai   Taipei   Toronto

With offices in
Argentina   Austria   Brazil   Chile   Czech Republic   France   Greece
Guatemala   Hungary   Italy   Japan   Poland   Portugal   Singapore
South Korea   Switzerland   Thailand   Turkey   Ukraine   Vietnam

For titles covered by Section 112 of the US Higher Education
Opportunity Act, please visit www.oup.com/us/he for the latest
information about pricing and alternate formats.

Published by Oxford University Press, Inc.
198 Madison Avenue, New York, New York 10016
http://www.oup.com

Oxford is a registered trademark of Oxford University Press

Library of Congress Cataloging-in-Publication Data

Philosophy : the quest for truth / [edited by] Louis P. Pojman, Lewis Vaughn. — 8th ed.
   p. cm.
  Includes bibliographical references.
  ISBN 978-0-19-975179-2
 1. Philosophy—Introductions.   I. Pojman, Louis P.   II. Vaughn, Lewis.
  BD21.P48 2012
  100—dc22   2010043587

Printing number: 9 8 7 6 5 4 3 2 1

Printed in the United States of America
on acid-free paper

Dedicated to Teachers
who themselves are dedicated
to opening the hearts of the young
to the love of wisdom and
the quest for truth

Contents

IV. Philosophy of Mind: The Mind-Body Problem   281

Introduction   282

V. Freedom of the Will and Determinism   399

Introduction   400

VI. Ethics   473

VII. Political Philosophy   557

Preface

I T IS DIFFICULT TO IMPROVE ON a good thing, but it is possible—as this new eighth edition of *Philosophy: The Quest for Truth* shows. The original aim of this text was to provide an anthology focused on the classic readings in the classic philosophical problems but firmly planted in the middle ground between texts that are rigorous but inaccessible and accessible but thin. This guiding principle lives on in this latest incarnation—but with higher-quality readings and greatly enhanced pedagogy.

Eighty-nine readings are arranged in a pro/con format around key philosophical questions. Each selection comes with explanatory headnotes plus questions before and after it, every major section has a substantial preface, Part I includes a logic and argument tutorial and a brief introduction to philosophy, and an Appendix offers helpful guidelines for reading and writing philosophy papers. All the traditional problems of philosophy are represented here, as well as some nontraditional ones: philosophy of religion, knowledge, philosophy of mind, free will and determinism, ethics, political philosophy, the meaning of life, and contemporary moral issues.

New to the Eighth Edition

- Eleven new readings:

    Plato: The Allegory of the Cave

    David Hume: Skeptical Doubts Concerning the Operations of the Understanding (expanded)

    Wesley C. Salmon: The Problem of Induction

    Ned Block: Troubles with Functionalism

    Buddhist Scripture: Questions to King Milinda

    Peter van Inwagen: The Powers of Rational Beings: Freedom of the Will

    Louis P. Pojman: Egoism and Altruism: A Critique of Ayn Rand

    Virginia Held: The Ethics of Care

    Julian Baggini: Living Life Forwards

    Peter Singer: Famine, Affluence, and Morality

    Garrett Hardin: Living on a Lifeboat

- Two new sections: "Induction" in Part III: Knowledge and "Do We Have Obligations to the Poor and Hungry?" in Part IX: Contemporary Moral Problems
- Expanded section on logic to include more help for students in identifying and evaluating arguments
- Expanded and revised section introductions for knowledge and philosophy of mind
- Revised Appendix to provide more detailed instruction in how to read and write philosophy papers
- Boldfaced Key Terms throughout the section introductions, listed at the end of each part, and gathered into the end-of-book glossary
- Time line highlighting the authors included in the text

Ancillaries

Along with the revised text come updated ancillaries.

- **The Instructor's Manual and Test Bank on CD includes:**
  - Sample Syllabi for planning courses
  - Summaries of every selection for easy reference
  - A list of Key Terms with definitions
  - Helpful Web Links that guide exploration of each philosophical problem
  - Lecture outlines in PowerPoint format for each chapter
  - A Test Bank that includes Multiple Choice, True/False, and Essay Questions on each reading
- **A Companion Website for Students and Instructors (www.oup.com/ pojman) includes:**
  - All the material contained in the Instructor's Manual
  - Essay Questions for review of every selection, to reaffirm main ideas and arguments
  - Interactive quizzes that test student knowledge of each selection
  - Flashcards for students that highlight Key Terms and concepts
  - Helpful Web Links for students for additional information

Acknowledgments

Over the years, dozens of astute reviewers have prompted improvements in *Quest*. For help with the eighth edition, I am grateful to many more: H. Scott Hestevold, The University of Alabama; Seung-Kee Lee, Drew University; Jack C. Lyons, University of Arkansas; Mark Packer, University of South Carolina, Upstate; William Ramsey, University of Nevada–Las Vegas; Bruce McGraw, Cuyamaca, Southwestern, and Palomar

Colleges; Timothy Quandt, Cal State Fullerton; Eric Sotnak, The University of Akron; Renée J. Smith, Coastal Carolina University; Keith Stanglin, Harding University; Andreas Teuber, Brandeis University; and Steven Vogel, Denison University. As always, many thanks are due the devoted and talented editors at Oxford University Press, especially Robert Miller, the guiding light of the project, and Christina Mancuso and Lauren Roth.

Lewis Vaughn

Time Line

THE ANCIENT PERIOD

Philosophers	Dates	Major Figures and Events
Socrates*	c. 470–399 B.C.	Trial and death of Socrates, 399 B.C.
Democritus	c. 460–370 B.C.	
Plato	c. 427–347 B.C.	Plato founds the Academy, c. 388 B.C.
Aristotle	384–322 B.C.	Aristotle founds the Lyceum, 334 B.C.
Pyrrho	c. 360–270 B.C.	Death of Alexander the Great, 323 B.C.
Epicurus	341–270 B.C.	Epicurus opens school in Athens, 306 B.C.
Zeno the Stoic	c. 336–264 B.C.	Zeno opens school at the Stoa, 301 B.C. Rome conquers the Greek world, 200–128 B.C. Caesar is dictator of Rome, 49–44 B.C. Jesus Christ, c. 4 B.C.–A.D. 30
Epictetus	c. 50–130	Romans destroy Temple in Jerusalem, 70
Marcus Aurelius	121–180	
Sextus Empiricus	c. 200	

THE MEDIEVAL PERIOD

Philosophers	Dates	Major Figures and Events
		Constantine grants tolerance to Christianity, 313
Augustine	354–430	Theodosius I makes Christianity the state religion of Rome, 392

*Philosophers whose names apperar in **boldface** appear in this volume.

THE MEDIEVAL PERIOD

Philosophers	Dates	Major Figures and Events
Boethius	c. 480–524	Fall of the Roman Empire in the West, 476
Avicenna	980–1037	
Anselm	1034–1109	
Averroës	1126–1198	University of Paris founded, 1160
Thomas Aquinas	1225–1274	
John Duns Scotus	c. 1266–1308	The Black Death ravages Europe, 1347–1351
William of Ockham	c. 1285–1349	

THE MODERN PERIOD

Philosophers	Dates	Major Figures and Events
		Johann Gutenberg invents the printing press, 1445 Leonardo da Vinci, 1452–1519
Thomas Hobbes	1588–1679	
René Descartes	1596–1650	The reign of Louis XIV in France, 1643–1715
Blaise Pascal	1623–1662	
Benedict (Baruch) Spinoza	1632–1677	Johann Sebastian Bach, 1685–1750
John Locke	1632–1704	*Two Treatises on Government*, 1689
Gottfried Wilhelm Leibniz	1646–1716	
George Berkeley	1685–1753	Wolfgang Amadeus Mozart, 1756–1791
David Hume	1711–1776	Ludwig van Beethoven, 1770–1827
Adam Smith	1723–1790	*The Wealth of Nations*, 1776
Immanuel Kant	1724–1804	*Critique of Pure Reason*, 1781
William Paley	1743–1805	
Jeremy Bentham	1748–1832	Industrial Revolution in England, c. 1790 Napoleon crowns himself emperor of France, 1804

THE MODERN PERIOD

Philosophers	Dates	Major Figures and Events
Mary Wollstonecraft	1759–1797	Charles Darwin, 1809–1882 Richard Wagner, 1813–1883
Georg W. F. Hegel	1770–1831	Fyodor Dostoevsky, 1821–1881 Leo Tolstoy, 1828–1910
Arthur Schopenhauer	1788–1860	Second French Revolution, 1830 Opium War in China, 1839
John Stuart Mill	1806–1873	*On Liberty*, 1859 Darwin's *Origin of Species*, 1859
Søren Kierkegaard	1813–1855	*Fear and Trembling*, 1841
Karl Marx	1818–1883	*The Communist Manifesto*, 1848 Sigmund Freud, 1856–1939
Friedrich Nietzsche	1844–1900	Pablo Picasso, 1881–1973 James Joyce, 1882–1941 Virginia Woolf, 1882–1941 The Dreyfus Affair (France), 1899

THE CONTEMPORARY PERIOD

Philosophers	Dates	Major Figures and Events
Charles S. Peirce	1839–1914	Albert Einstein presents theory of relativity, 1905
William James	1842–1910	
W. K. Clifford	1845–1879	
Alfred North Whitehead	1861–1947	Joseph Stalin becomes general secretary of the Communist party, 1922
Bertrand Russell	1872–1970	The Great Depression, 1929–1939 Spanish Civil War, 1936–1939
G. E. Moore	1873–1958	
Ludwig Wittgenstein	1889–1951	Second World War, 1939–1945
Martin Heidegger	1889–1976	Dropping of the atomic bomb on Hiroshima, August 6, 1945
Gilbert Ryle	1900–1976	Israel becomes a nation, 1949

THE CONTEMPORARY PERIOD

Philosophers	Dates	Major Figures and Events
Karl Popper	1902–1994	People's Republic of China under Mao Tse-tung established, 1949 Crick and Watson identify the structure of DNA, 1953
Jean-Paul Sartre	1905–1980	Cuban Missile Crisis, 1962
Simone de Beauvoir	1908–1986	
Willard V. O. Quine	1908–2000	War in Vietnam, 1954–1975
A. J. Ayer	1910–1989	Assassination of Martin Luther King, Jr., 1968
Philippa Foot	b. 1920	
John Rawls	1921–2002	*A Theory of Justice*, 1971
John Searle	b. 1932	
Thomas Nagel	b. 1937	Islamic terrorist attacks on U.S. World Trade Center and Pentagon, September 11, 2001

Part I

What Is Philosophy?

The unexamined life is not worth living.

SOCRATES

If God held all Truth in His right hand and in His left hand the eternal Quest for Truth, and said to me, "Choose!" I would with courage touch His left and say, "Father, Give me this! The pure Truth is fit for you alone."

G. E. LESSING, *Werke,* vol. X, p. 53; my translation.

PHILOSOPHY IS REVOLUTIONARY and vitally important to the good life. This book starts from an assumption that we hope you will be convinced of by the time you have completed this course: namely, that the unexamined life is not worth living and that while philosophy disturbs, it also consoles. Philosophy, as Aristotle said more than two thousand years ago, begins with wonder at the marvels and mysteries of the world. It begins in wonder, in the pursuit of truth and wisdom, and ends in life lived in passionate moral and intellectual integrity. At least this is the classical philosophical ideal. Of course, this thesis about the worth of philosophy is itself to be subject to rational scrutiny.

The term **philosophy** literally means the love of wisdom (etymologically from the Greek *philos* = love and *sophia* = wisdom), but it is a wisdom that results from a pursuit of knowledge of the most important parts of reality. Hence the title of this book, the quest for truth. The quest for truth is the contemplation or study of the most important questions in existence with the goal of promoting illumination and understanding, a vision of the whole. It uses reason, sense perception, the imagination, and intuitions in its activity of analyzing and constructing arguments and theories as possible answers to these perennial questions. It is revolutionary because its deliverances often disturb our common sense or our received tradition. Philosophy usually goes against the stream or the majority because the majority opinion is often a composite of past intellectual struggles or "useful" biases. There is often deeper truth, better and new evidence that disturbs the status quo and that forces us to revise or reject some of our beliefs. This experience can be as painful as it is exciting.

The pain may lead us to give up philosophical inquiry and may require a great deal of emotional health to persevere in it. We may retreat into unreason and obey the commandment of Ignorance, "Think not, lest Thou be confounded!" Truth (or what we seem justified in believing) may not always be edifying. But in the end, the philosopher's faith is that the Truth is good and worth pursuing for its own sake and for its secondary benefits. Intelligent inquiry, which philosophy promotes, is liberating, freeing us from prejudice, self-deceptive notions, and half-truths. As Bertrand Russell says in our fourth reading,

> The [person] who has no tincture of philosophy goes through life imprisoned in the prejudices derived from common sense, from the habitual beliefs of his age or his nation, and from convictions which have grown up in his mind without the co-operation or consent of his deliberate reason. . . . While diminishing our feeling of certainty as to what things are, [philosophy] greatly increases our knowledge as to what they may be; it removes the somewhat arrogant dogmatism of those who have never travelled into the region of liberating doubt, and it keeps alive the sense of wonder by showing familiar things in an unfamiliar light.

Philosophy should result in a wider vision of life in which the impartial use of reason results in an appreciation of other viewpoints and other people's rights and needs. There is no guarantee that this will occur. Some become radical skeptics with accompanied behavioral patterns, and some nasty people seem to be able to do philosophy quite well without being transformed by it. But for the most part those who have had the vision of a better life and have worked through arguments on substantive issues relating to the nature and destiny of humanity have been positively affected by the perennial pilgrimage. They march to a different drummer and show in their lives the fruits of their travail. This ability to live by reflective principle in spite of and in the midst of the noise of the masses is a special virtue of philosophy. It is illustrated by one of its heroes, Socrates (470–399 B.C.), in our first reading from Plato's work, *Apology.*

The hallmark of philosophy is centered in the argument. Philosophers clarify concepts, analyze, and test propositions and beliefs, but the major task is to analyze and construct arguments. At the end of Part I, we have added a section "A Little Bit of Logic" to help you understand the nature of arguments. Philosophical reasoning is closely allied to scientific reasoning in that both look for evidence and build hypotheses that are tested with the hope of coming closer to the truth. However, scientific experiments take place in laboratories and have testing procedures through which to record objective or empirically verifiable results. The laboratory of the philosopher is the domain of ideas: the mind, where imaginative thought-experiments take place; the study, where ideas are written down and examined; and wherever conversation or debate about the perennial questions takes place, where thesis and counter-example and counter-thesis are considered. A joke compares the equipment needs of the scientist, the mathematician, and the philosopher: The scientist needs an expensive laboratory with all sorts of experimental equipment. The mathematician needs only a pencil, paper, and a wastepaper basket. The philosopher needs only a pencil and paper! The truth embodied in this bit of humor is that it is not as easy to test philosophical theories as it is to test a mathematical theorem or a scientific hypothesis. Because philosophical questions are more speculative and metaphysical, one cannot prove or disprove most of the important theses. The relationship of philosophy to science is more complicated than this suggests, for some of what theoretical scientists do could with justice be called philosophy. In general, the sciences have one by one made their way out of the family fold of philosophy to independence as they systematized their decision-making procedures. In the words of Jeffrey Olen,

> The history of philosophy reads like a long family saga. In the beginning there were the great patriarch and matriarch, the searches for knowledge and wisdom, who bore a large number of children. Mathematics, physics, ethics, psychology, logic, political thought, metaphysics, . . . and epistemology . . .—all belonged to the same family. Philosophers were not *just* philosophers, but mathematicians and physicists and psychologists as well. Indeed, in the beginning of the family's history, no distinction was made between philosophy and these other disciplines. . . .
>
> In the beginning, then, all systematic search for knowledge was philosophy. This fact is still reflected in the modern university, where the highest degree granted in all of the sciences and humanities is the Ph.D.—the doctor of philosophy.
>
> But the children gradually began to leave home. First to leave were physics and astronomy, as they began to develop experimental techniques of their own. This exodus, led by Galileo (1564–1642), Isaac Newton (1642–1727), and Johannes Kepler (1571–1630), created the first of many great family crises. . . . Eventually, psychology left home. [*Persons and Their World,* Random House, 1983, p. 3f]

Although many of her children have left home, not all have, and some seem permanent residents. The major areas of philosophy today are metaphysics (regarding the nature of ultimate reality), epistemology (regarding the nature of knowledge and justification), logic, philosophy of religion, ethics, and political philosophy. But there are also secondary areas of philosophy that work on conceptual or theoretical problems arising within first-order nonphilosophical disciplines. Examples of these are philosophy of science, philosophy of psychology, philosophy of mathematics, philosophy of language, and philosophy of art. Wherever conceptual analysis or justification of a theoretical schema is needed, philosophical expertise is appropriate. More recently, as technology creates new possibilities and problems, applied ethics (for example, biomedical ethics, business ethics, environmental ethics, and legal ethics) has arisen. History plays a dialectical role relative to philosophy, for not only do philosophers do philosophy while teaching the history of philosophy, but they also critically examine the principles that underlie historical investigation itself, creating a philosophy of history.

We will touch on many of these areas in this work: philosophy of religion; epistemology; metaphysics, and within metaphysics the mind-body problem, personal identity, immortality, and free will and determinism; ethics; and political philosophy. These are more than enough for an introduction to philosophy.

Philosophical study is **dialectic**, proceeding as an intellectual conversation in which thesis and counter-thesis, hypothesis and counter-example continue in a way that exposes the weaknesses of proposed solutions to the puzzles of existence and leaves some answers as more or less plausible. In this conversation, all sides of an issue should receive a fair hearing, and then the reader is left to make up his or her own mind on the issue. Hence, in this work at least two opposing views are set forth on every issue.

Although a clearer understanding of the nature of philosophy will only emerge while you work through the arguments on the various issues you are going to study, we want to end this introduction with a set of guidelines for philosophical inquiry, "Ten Commandments of Philosophy," that will aid you in your own pilgrimage as you build your own philosophy of life. They embody what we take to be the classical philosophical perspective, but they are set forth as hypothetical. You should test them, refine them, and possibly reject some of them or add better ones as you proceed on your own Quest for Truth.

Ten Commandments of Philosophy

1. *Allow the spirit of Wonder to flourish in your breast.* Philosophy begins with deep wonder about the universe and about who we are and where we came from and where we are going. What is this life all about?

2. *Doubt every claim you encounter until the evidence convinces you of its Truth.* Be reasonably cautious, a moderate skeptic, suspicious of those who claim to have the Truth. Doubt is the soul's purgative. Do not fear intellectual inquiry. As Goethe said, "The masses fear the intellectual, but it is stupidity that they should fear, if they only realized how dangerous it really is."

3. *Love the Truth.* "Philosophy is the eternal search for truth, a search which inevitably fails and yet is never defeated; which continually eludes us, but which always guides us. This free, intellectual life of the mind is the noblest inheritance of the Western World; it is also the hope of our future." (W. T. Jones)

4. *Divide and Conquer.* Divide each problem and theory into its smallest essential components so you can analyze each unit carefully. This is the analytic method.

5. *Collect and Construct.* Build a coherent argument or theory from component parts. One should move from the simple, secure foundations to the complex and comprehensive. Bertrand Russell once said that the aim of philosophical argument was to move from simple propositions so obvious that no one would think of doubting them via a method of valid argument to conclusions so preposterous that no one could help but doubt them.

6. *Conjecture and Refute.* Make a complete survey of possible objections to your position, looking for counter-examples and subtle mistakes. As Karl Popper has insisted, philosophy is a system of conjecture and refutation. Seek bold hypotheses and seek to find disconfirmations of your favorite positions. In this way, by a process of elimination, you will negatively and indirectly and asymptotically approach the Truth.

7. *Revise and Rebuild.* Be willing to revise, reject, and modify your beliefs and the degree with which you hold any belief. Acknowledge that you probably have many false beliefs and be grateful to those who correct you. This is the **Principle of Fallibilism**, the thesis that we are very likely incorrect in many of our beliefs and have a tendency towards self-deception when considering objections to our position.

8. *Seek Simplicity.* Prefer the simpler explanation to the more complex, all things being equal. This is the **Principle of Parsimony**, sometimes known as "Occam's Razor." The simplest view is the one that makes the fewest assumptions.

9. *Live the Truth!* Appropriate your ideas in a personal way so that even as the Objective Truth is a correspondence of the thought to the world, this Lived Truth will be a correspondence of the life to the thought.

10. *Live the Good!* Let the practical conclusions of a philosophical reflection on the moral life inspire and motivate you to action. Let moral Truth transform your life so that you shine like a jewel in its light amidst the darkness of global ignorance.

We hope these guides will help you think about philosophy as you read the essays in this book. As we mentioned earlier, they are intended not as dogmatic pronouncements but as embodying the perennial values that have guided the classic vision of the goal of philosophy in pursuing the truth. Those who see philosophy only as technique would disagree with the tenth rule, but the classic vision, reflected in our first reading, holds that the pursuit of the Truth should result in living the morally good life. Truth is intrinsically good and leads to the good life.

We turn to our three readings on the nature and task of philosophy as the Quest for Truth.

I.1   Socratic Wisdom

PLATO

Plato (427–347 B.C.) is one of the most important philosophers who ever lived and the first to write systematically on philosophical subjects. He lived in Athens, the great Greek democratic city-state, in the aftermath of its glory under its illustrious leader, Pericles. During much of Plato's life, Athens was at war with Sparta, the Greek city-state to the south. He was Socrates' disciple, the founder of the first school of philosophy (the Academy in Athens), Aristotle's teacher, and an advisor to emperors. Among his important works are the *Republic*, the *Apology*, *Phaedo*, and *Timaeus*. Alfred North Whitehead calls the whole history of Western philosophy "a series of footnotes to Plato."

Socrates (470–399 B.C.) is one of the most impressive human beings to have lived, and a paradigm of a philosopher. He is considered the father of moral philosophy (see Part VI). Living in Athens under Pericles, he enjoyed the freedoms of a democratic society. Socrates spent much of his life in the marketplace of Athens, questioning and arguing with his contemporaries on philosophical issues (for example, what is justice, friendship, self-control, piety, virtue? how do we teach virtue? does anyone do evil voluntarily? and so forth). He saw himself as the gadfly of the Greek city-state, serving his fellow citizens without pay, but many of its leading citizens saw him as a nuisance and, eventually, brought him to trial. Our reading is about this trial. Three Athenians—Meletus, Anytus, and Lycon—have brought charges against Socrates that he has corrupted the youth and doesn't believe in the Greek gods. The real cause of the trial is probably that Socrates had made a number of enemies in high places. He defied the authorities when they ordered him to arrest naval officers against what Socrates took to be the law. He embarrassed many of the leading citizens, politicians, artisans, poets, and orators—often before their sons—in exposing their pretenses to knowledge. The accumulated ire erupted and caused one of the most famous trials of all time, if not the most famous trial of all time. The following reading is Plato's rendition of it.

Study Questions

1. What is the message of the Oracle of Delphi to Chaerephon about Socrates?
2. What is Socrates' response and how does he go about trying to disprove the oracle? What was the effect of his probing on his fellow citizens?
3. How does Socrates finally interpret the message of the oracle?
4. What are the charges brought against Socrates? What are Socrates' responses to the charges?
5. What should be our only concern when we deliberate on what to do?
6. Why doesn't Socrates plead for his life? What does he propose as the counter-penalty?
7. What penalty does the jury decide on? Do you notice anything peculiar when comparing the numbers voting for the original verdict and the numbers voting for the penalty? What accounts for this?

8. What kind of life does Socrates think is worth living?

9. Does Socrates believe that his fellow citizens are doing him enormous harm?

FROM THE APOLOGY

HOW YOU, O ATHENIANS, have been affected by my accusers, I cannot tell; but I know that they almost made me forget who I was—so persuasively did they speak; and yet they have hardly uttered a word of truth. But of the many falsehoods told by them, there was one which quite amazed me—I mean when they said that you should be upon your guard and not allow yourselves to be deceived by the force of my eloquence. To say this, when they were certain to be detected as soon as I opened my lips and proved myself to be anything but a great speaker, did indeed appear to me most shameless—unless by the force of eloquence they mean the force of truth; for if such is their meaning, I admit that I am eloquent. But in how different a way from theirs! Well, as I was saying, they have scarcely spoken the truth at all; but from me you shall hear the whole truth: not, however, delivered after their manner in a set oration duly ornamented with words and phrases. No, by heaven! but I shall use the words and arguments which occur to me at the moment; for I am confident in the justice of my cause*: at my time of life I ought not to be appearing before you, O men of Athens, in the character of a juvenile orator—let no one expect it of me. And I must beg of you to grant me a favour: If I defend myself in my accustomed manner, and you hear me using the words which I have been in the habit of using in the [market], at the tables of the money-changers, or anywhere else, I would ask you not to be surprised, and not to interrupt me on this account. For I am more than seventy years of age, and appearing now for the first time in a court of law, I am quite a stranger to the language of the place; and therefore I would have you regard me as if I were really a stranger, whom you would excuse if he spoke in his native tongue, and after the fashion of his country: Am I making an unfair request of you? Never mind the manner, which may or may not be good; but think only of the truth of my words, and give heed to that: let the speaker speak truly and the judge decide justly. . . .

Well, then, I must make my defence, and endeavor to clear away in a short time, a slander which has lasted a long time. May I succeed, if to succeed be for my good and yours, or likely to avail me in my cause! The task is not an easy one; I quite understand the nature of it. And so leaving the event with God, in obedience to the law I will now make my defence.

I will begin at the beginning, and ask what is the accusation which has given rise to the slander of me, and in fact has encouraged Meletus to prefer this charge against me. Well, what do the slanderers say? They shall be my prosecutors, and I will sum up their words in an affidavit: 'Socrates is an evil-doer, and a curious person, who searches into things under the earth and in heaven, and he makes the worse appear the better cause; and he teaches the aforesaid doctrines to others.' Such is the nature of the accusation: it is just what you have yourselves seen in the comedy of Aristophanes, who has introduced a man whom he calls Socrates, going about and saying that he walks in air, and talking a deal of nonsense concerning matters of which I do not pretend to know either much or little—not that I mean to speak disparagingly of any one who is a student of natural philosophy. I should be very sorry if Meletus could bring so grave a charge against me. But the simple truth is, O Athenians, that I have nothing to do with physical speculations. Very many of those here present are witnesses to the truth of this, and to them I appeal. Speak then, you who

---

*Or, I am certain that I am right in taking this course.

Reprinted from Dialogues of Plato, *trans. Benjamin Jowett, Oxford, 1896.*

have heard me, and tell your neighbours whether any of you have ever known me hold forth in few words or in many upon such matters. . . . You hear their answer. And from what they say of this part of the charge you will be able to judge of the truth of the rest.

As little foundation is there for the report that I am a teacher, and take money; this accusation has no more truth in it than the other. Although, if a man were really able to instruct mankind, to receive money for giving instruction would, in my opinion, be an honour to him. There is Gorgias of Leontium, and Prodicus of Ceos, and Hippias of Elis, who go the round of the cities, and are able to persuade the young men to leave their own citizens by whom they might be taught for nothing, and come to them whom they not only pay, but are thankful if they may be allowed to pay them. . . .

I dare say, Athenians, that some one among you will reply, 'Yes, Socrates, but what is the origin of these accusations which are brought against you; there must have been something strange which you have been doing? All these rumours and this talk about you would never have arisen if you had been like other men: tell us, then, what is the cause of them, for we should be sorry to judge hastily of you.' Now I regard this as a fair challenge, and I will endeavour to explain to you the reason why I am called wise and have such an evil fame. Please to attend then. And although some of you may think that I am joking, I declare that I will tell you the entire truth. Men of Athens, this reputation of mine has come of a certain sort of wisdom which I possess. If you ask me what kind of wisdom, I reply, wisdom such as may perhaps be attained by man, for to that extent I am inclined to believe that I am wise; whereas the persons of whom I was speaking have a superhuman wisdom, which I may fail to describe, because I have it not myself; and he who says that I have, speaks falsely, and is taking away my character. And here, O men of Athens, I must beg you not to interrupt me, even if I seem to say something

extravagant. For the word which I will speak is not mine. I will refer you to a witness who is worthy of credit; that witness shall be the God of Delphi—he will tell you about my wisdom, if I have any, and of what sort it is. You must have known Chaerephon; he was early a friend of mine, and also a friend of yours, for he shared in the recent exile of the people, and returned with you. Well, Chaerephon, as you know, was very impetuous in all his doings, and he went to Delphi and boldly asked the oracle to tell him whether—as I was saying, I must beg you not to interrupt—he asked the oracle to tell him whether any one was wiser than I was, and the Pythian prophetess answered, that there was no man wiser. Chaerephon is dead himself; but his brother, who is in court, will confirm the truth of what I am saying.

Why do I mention this? Because I am going to explain to you why I have such an evil name. When I heard the answer, I said to myself, What can the god mean? and what is the interpretation of his riddle? for I know that I have no wisdom, small or great. What then can he mean when he says that I am the wisest of men? And yet he is a god, and cannot lie; that would be against his nature. After long consideration, I thought of a method of trying the question. I reflected that if I could only find a man wiser than myself, then I might go to the god with a refutation in my hand. I should say to him, 'Here is a man who is wiser than I am; but you said that I was the wisest.' Accordingly I went to one who had the reputation of wisdom, and observed him—his name I need not mention; he was a politician whom I selected for examination—and the result was as follows: When I began to talk with him, I could not help thinking that he was not really wise, although he was thought wise by many, and still wiser by himself; and thereupon I tried to explain to him that he thought himself wise, but was not really wise; and the consequence was that he hated me, and his enmity was shared by several who were present and heard me. So I left him, saying to myself, as I went away: Well, although

I do not suppose that either of us knows anything really beautiful and good, I am better off than he is—for he knows nothing, and thinks that he knows; I neither know nor think that I know. In this latter particular, then, I seem to have slightly the advantage of him.

Then I went to another who had still higher pretensions to wisdom, and my conclusion was exactly the same. Whereupon I made another enemy of him, and of many others besides him. Then I went to one man after another, being not unconscious of the enmity which I provoked, and I lamented and feared this: But necessity was laid upon me,—the word of God, I thought, ought to be considered first. And I said to myself, Go I must to all who appear to know, and find out the meaning of the oracle. And I swear to you, Athenians, by the dog I swear!—for I must tell you the truth—the result of my mission was just this: I found that the men most in repute were all but the most foolish; and that others less esteemed were really wiser and better. I will tell you the tale of my wanderings and of the "Herculean" labours, as I may call them, which I endured only to find at last the oracle irrefutable. After the politicians, I went to the poets; tragic, dithyrambic, and all sorts. And there, I said to myself, you will be instantly detected; now you will find out that you are more ignorant than they are. Accordingly, I took them some of the most elaborate passages in their own writings, and asked what was the meaning of them—thinking that they would teach me something. Will you believe me? I am almost ashamed to confess the truth, but I must say that there is hardly a person present who would not have talked better about their poetry than they did themselves. Then I knew that not by wisdom do poets write poetry, but by a sort of genius and inspiration; they are like diviners or soothsayers who also say many fine things, but do not understand the meaning of them. The poets appeared to me to be much in the same case; and I further observed that upon the strength of their poetry they believed themselves to be the wisest of men in other things in which they were not wise. So I departed, conceiving myself to be superior to them for the same reason that I was superior to the politicians.

At last I went to the artisans, for I was conscious that I knew nothing at all, as I may say, and I was sure that they knew many fine things; and here I was not mistaken, for they did know many things of which I was ignorant, and in this they certainly were wiser than I was. But I observed that even the good artisans fell into the same error as the poets;—because they were good workmen they thought that they also knew all sorts of high matters, and this defect in them overshadowed their wisdom; and therefore I asked myself on behalf of the oracle, whether I would like to be as I was, neither having their knowledge nor their ignorance, or like them in both; and I made answer to myself and to the oracle that I was better off as I was.

This inquisition has led to my having many enemies of the worst and most dangerous kind, and has given occasion also to many calumnies. And I am called wise, for my hearers always imagine that I myself possess the wisdom which I find wanting in others: but the truth is, O men of Athens, that God only is wise; and by his answer he intends to show that the wisdom of men is worth little or nothing; he is not speaking of Socrates, he is only using my name by way of illustration, as if he said, He, O men, is the wisest, who, like Socrates, knows that his wisdom is in truth worth nothing. And so I go about the world, obedient to the god, and search and make enquiry into the wisdom of any one, whether citizen or stranger, who appears to be wise; and if he is not wise, then in vindication of the oracle I show him that he is not wise; and my occupation quite absorbs me, and I have no time to give either to any public matter of interest or to any concern of my own, but I am in utter poverty by reason of my devotion to the god.

There is another thing: Young men of the richer classes, who have not much to do, come about me of their own accord; they like to hear the pretenders examined, and they often imitate me, and proceed to examine others; there are plenty of persons, as they quickly discover, who think that they know something, but really know little or nothing; and then those who are examined by them instead of being angry with themselves are angry with me: This confounded Socrates, they say; this villainous misleader of youth!—and then if somebody asks them, Why, what evil does he practise or teach? they do not know, and cannot tell; but in order that they may not appear to be at a loss, they repeat the ready-made charges which are used against all philosophers about teaching things up in the clouds and under the earth, and having no gods, and making the worse appear the better cause; for they do not like to confess that their pretence of knowledge has been detected—which is the truth; and as they are numerous and ambitious and energetic, and are drawn up in battle array and have persuasive tongues, they have filled your ears with their loud and inveterate calumnies. And this is the reason why my three accusers, Meletus and Anytus and Lycon, have set upon me; Meletus, who has a quarrel with me on behalf of the poets; Anytus, on behalf of the craftsmen and politicians; Lycon, on behalf of the rhetoricians: and as I said at the beginning, I cannot expect to get rid of such a mass of calumny all in a moment. And this, O men of Athens, is the truth and the whole truth; I have concealed nothing, I have dissembled nothing. And yet, I know that my plainness of speech makes them hate me, and what is their hatred but a proof that I am speaking the truth?— Hence has arisen the prejudice against me; and this is the reason of it, as you will find out either in this or in any future enquiry.

I have said enough in my defence against the first class of my accusers; I turn to the second class. They are headed by Meletus, that good man and true lover of his country, as he calls himself. . . . He says that I am a doer of evil, and corrupt the youth; but I say, O men of Athens, that Meletus is a doer of evil, in that he pretends to be in earnest when he is only in jest, and is so eager to bring men to trial from a pretended zeal and interest about matters in which he really never had the smallest interest. And the truth of this I will endeavour to prove to you.

Come hither, Meletus, and let me ask a question of you. You think a great deal about the improvement of youth?

Yes, I do.

Tell the judges, then, who is their improver; for you must know, as you have taken the pains to discover their corrupter, and are citing and accusing me before them. Speak, then, and tell the judges who their improver is.—Observe, Meletus, that you are silent, and have nothing to say. But is not this rather disgraceful, and a very considerable proof of what I was saying, that you have no interest in the matter? Speak up, friend, and tell us who their improver is.

The laws.

But that, my good sir, is not my meaning. I want to know who the person is, who, in the first place, knows the laws.

The judges, Socrates, who are present in court.

What, do you mean to say, Meletus, that they are able to instruct and improve youth?

Certainly they are.

What, all of them, or some only and not others?

All of them.

By the goddess Herè, that is good news! There are plenty of improvers, then. And what do you say of the audience—do they improve them?

Yes, they do.

And the senators?

Yes, the senators improve them.

But perhaps the members of the assembly corrupt them?—or do they too improve them?

They improve them.

Then every Athenian improves and elevates them; all with the exception of myself; and I alone am their corrupter? Is that what you affirm?

That is what I stoutly affirm.

I am very unfortunate if you are right. But suppose I ask you a question: How about horses?

Does one man do them harm and all the world good? Is not the exact opposite the truth? One man is able to do them good, or at least not many—the trainer of horses, that is to say, does them good, and others who have to do with them rather injure them? Is not that true, Meletus, of horses, or of any other animals? Most assuredly it is; whether you and Anytus say yes or no. Happy indeed would be the condition of youth if they had one corrupter only, and all the rest of the world were their improvers. But you, Meletus, have sufficiently shown that you never had a thought about the young: your carelessness is seen in your not caring about the very things which you bring against me.

And now, Meletus, I will ask you another question—by Zeus I will: Which is better, to live among bad citizens, or among good ones? Answer, friend, I say; the question is one which may be easily answered. Do not the good do their neighbours good, and the bad do them evil?

Certainly.

And is there any one who would rather be injured than benefited by those who live with him? Answer, my good friend, the law requires you to answer—does any one like to be injured?

Certainly not.

And when you accuse me of corrupting and deteriorating the youth, do you allege that I corrupt them intentionally or unintentionally?

Intentionally, I say.

But you have just admitted that the good do their neighbours good, and evil do them evil. Now, is that a truth which your superior wisdom has recognized thus early in life, and am I, at my age, in such darkness and ignorance as not to know that if a man with whom I have to live is corrupted by me, I am very likely to be harmed by him; and yet I corrupt him, and intentionally, too—so you say, although neither I nor any other human being is ever likely to be convinced by you. But either I do not corrupt them, or I corrupt them unintentionally; and on either view of the case you lie. If my offence is unintentional, the law has no cognizance of unintentional

offences: you ought to have taken me privately, and warned and admonished me; for if I had been better advised, I should have left off doing what I only did unintentionally—no doubt I should; but you would have nothing to say to me and refused to teach me. And now you bring me up in this court, which is a place not of instruction, but of punishment.

It will be very clear to you, Athenians, as I was saying, that Meletus has no care at all, great or small, about the matter. But still I should like to know, Meletus, in what I am affirmed to corrupt the young. I suppose you mean, as I infer from your indictment, that I teach them not to acknowledge the gods which the state acknowledges, but some other new divinities or spiritual agencies in their stead. These are the lessons by which I corrupt the youth, as you say.

Yes, that I say emphatically.

Then, by the gods, Meletus, of whom we are speaking, tell me and the court, in somewhat plainer terms, what you mean! for I do not as yet understand whether you affirm that I teach other men to acknowledge some gods, and therefore that I do believe in gods, and am not an entire atheist—this you do not lay to my charge—but only you say that they are not the same gods which the city recognizes—the charge is that they are different gods. Or, do you mean that I am an atheist simply, and a teacher of atheism?

I mean the latter—that you are a complete atheist.

What an extraordinary statement! Why do you think so, Meletus? Do you mean that I do not believe in the godhead of the sun or moon, like other men?

I assure you, judges, that he does not: for he says that the sun is stone, and the moon earth.

Friend Meletus, you think that you are accusing Anaxagoras: and you have but a bad opinion of the judges, if you fancy them illiterate to such a degree as not to know that these doctrines are found in the books of Anaxagoras the Clazomenian, which are full of them. And so, forsooth, the youth are said to be taught them by Socrates, when there are not infrequently exhibitions of them at the theatre (price of admission one drachma at the most); and they might pay their money, and laugh at Socrates if he pretends to father these extraordinary views. And so, Meletus, you really think that I do not believe in any god?

I swear by Zeus that you believe absolutely in none at all.

Nobody will believe you, Meletus, and I am pretty sure that you do not believe yourself. I cannot help thinking, men of Athens, that Meletus is reckless and impudent, and that he has written this indictment in a spirit of mere wantonness and youthful bravado. Has he not compounded a riddle, thinking to try me? He said to himself: I shall see whether the wise Socrates will discover my facetious contradiction, or whether I shall be able to deceive him and the rest of them. For he certainly does appear to me to contradict himself in the indictment as much as if he said that Socrates is guilty of not believing in the gods, and yet of believing in them—but this is not like a person who is in earnest.

I should like you, O men of Athens, to join me in examining what I conceive to be his inconsistency; and do you, Meletus, answer. And I must remind the audience of my request that they would not make a disturbance if I speak in my accustomed manner:

Did ever man, Meletus, believe in the existence of human things, and not of human beings? . . . I wish, men of Athens, that he would answer, and not be always trying to get up an interruption. Did ever any man believe in horsemanship, and not in horses? or in flute-playing, and not in flute-players? No, my friend; I will answer to you and to the court, as you refuse to answer for yourself. There is no man who ever did. But now please to answer the next question: Can a man believe in spiritual and divine agencies, and not in spirits or demigods?

He cannot.

How lucky I am to have extracted that answer, by the assistance of the court! But then you swear in the indictment that I teach and believe in divine or spiritual agencies (new or old, no matter for that); at any rate, I believe in spiritual agencies—so you say and swear in the affidavit; and yet if I believe in divine beings, how can I help believing in spirits or demigods—must I not? To be sure I must; and therefore I may assume that your silence gives consent. Now what are spirits or demigods? are they not either gods or the sons of gods?

Certainly they are.

But this is what I call the facetious riddle invented by you: the demigods or spirits are gods, and you say first that I do not believe in gods, and then again that I do believe in gods; that is, if I believe in demigods. For if the demigods are the illegitimate sons of gods, whether by the nymphs or by any other mothers, of whom they are said to be the sons—what human being will ever believe that there are no gods if they are the sons of gods? You might as well affirm the existence of mules, and deny that of horses and asses. Such nonsense, Meletus, could only have been intended by you to make trial of me. You have put this into the indictment because you had nothing real of which to accuse me. But no one who has a particle of understanding will ever be convinced by you that the same men can believe in divine and superhuman things, and yet not believe that there are gods and demigods and heroes.

I have said enough in answer to the charge of Meletus: any elaborate defence is unnecessary; but I know only too well how many are the enmities which I have incurred, and this is what will be my destruction if I am destroyed—not Meletus, nor yet Anytus, but the envy and detraction of the world, which has been the death of many good men, and will probably be the death of many more; there is no danger of my being the last of them.

Some one will say: And are you not ashamed, Socrates, of a course of life which is likely to bring you to an untimely end? To him I may fairly answer: There you are mistaken: a man who is good for anything ought not to calculate the chance of living or dying; he ought only to consider whether in doing anything he is doing right or wrong—acting the part of a good man or of a bad. . . .

Strange, indeed, would be my conduct, O men of Athens, if I who, when I was ordered by the generals whom you chose to command me at Potidaea and Amphipolis and Delium, remained where they placed me, like any other man, facing death—if now, when, as I conceive and imagine, God orders me to fulfill the philosopher's mission of searching into myself and other men, I were to desert my post through fear of death, or any other fear; that would indeed be strange, and I might justly be arraigned in court for denying the existence of the gods, if I disobeyed the oracle because I was afraid of death, fancying that I was wise when I was not wise. For the fear of death is indeed the pretence of wisdom, and not real wisdom, being a pretence of knowing the unknown; and no one knows whether death, which men in their fear apprehend to be the greatest evil, may not be the greatest good. Is not this ignorance of a disgraceful sort, the ignorance which is the conceit that man knows what he does not know? And in this respect only I believe myself to differ from men in general, and may perhaps claim to be wiser than they are that whereas I know but little of the world below, I do not suppose that I know: but I do know that injustice and disobedience to a better, whether God or man, is evil and dishonourable, and I will never fear or avoid a possible good rather than a certain evil. And therefore if you let me go now, and are not convinced by Anytus, who said that since I had been prosecuted I must be put to death . . .—if you say to me, Socrates, this time we will not mind Anytus, and you shall be let off, but upon one condition, that you are not to enquire and speculate in this way any more, and that if you are caught doing so again you shall die—if this was the condition on which you let me go, I should reply: Men of Athens, I honour and love you; but I shall obey God rather than you, and while I have life and strength I shall never cease from the practice and teaching of philosophy, exhorting any one whom

I meet and saying to him after my manner: You, my friend—a citizen of the great and mighty and wise city of Athens—are you not ashamed of heaping up the greatest amount of money and honour and reputation, and caring so little about wisdom and truth and the greatest improvement of the soul, which you never regard or heed at all? And if the person with whom I am arguing, says: Yes, but I do care; then I do not leave him or let him go at once; but I proceed to interrogate and examine and cross-examine him, and if I think that he has no virtue in him, but only says that he has, I reproach him with undervaluing the greater, and overvaluing the less. And I shall repeat the same words to every one whom I meet, young and old, citizen and alien, but especially to the citizens, inasmuch as they are my brethren. For know that this is the command of God; and I believe that no greater good has ever happened in the state than my service to the God. For I do nothing but go about persuading you all, old and young alike, not to take thought for your persons or your properties, but first and chiefly to care about the greatest improvement of the soul. I tell you that virtue is not given by money, but that from virtue comes money and every other good of man, public as well as private. This is my teaching, and if this is the doctrine which corrupts the youth, I am a mischievous person. But if any one says that this is not my teaching, he is speaking an untruth. Wherefore, O men of Athens, I say to you, do as Anytus bids or not as Anytus bids, and either acquit me or not; but whichever you do, understand that I shall never alter my ways, not even if I have to die many times. . . .

And now, Athenians, I am not going to argue for my own sake, as you may think, but for yours, that you may not sin against the God by condemning me, who am his gift to you. For if you kill me you will not easily find a successor to me, who, if I may use such a ludicrous figure of speech, am a sort of gadfly, given to the state by God; and the state is a great and noble steed who is tardy in his motions owing to his very size, and requires to be stirred into life. I am that gadfly which God has attached to the state, and all day long and in all places am always fastening upon you, arousing and persuading and reproaching you. You will not easily find another like me, and therefore I would advise you to spare me. . . .

Perhaps it may seem strange to you that, though I go about giving this advice privately and meddling in others' affairs, yet I do not venture to come forward in the assembly and advise the state. You have often heard me speak of my reason for this, and in many places: it is that I have a certain divine sign, which is what Meletus has caricatured in his indictment. I have had it from childhood. It is a kind of voice which, whenever I hear it, always turns me back from something which I was going to do, but never urges me to act. It is this which forbids me to take part in politics. And I think it does well to forbid me. For, Athenians, it is quite certain that, if I had attempted to take part in politics, I should have perished at once and long ago without doing any good either to you or to myself. And do not be indignant with me for telling the truth. There is no man who will preserve his life for long, either in Athens or elsewhere, if he firmly opposes the multitude, and tries to prevent the commission of much injustice and illegality in the state. He who would really fight for justice must do so as a private citizen, not as an office-holder, if he is to preserve his life, even for a short time.

I will prove to you that this is so by very strong evidence, not by mere words, but by what you value highly, actions. Listen then to what has happened to me, that you may know that there is no man who could make me consent to do wrong from the fear of death, but that I would perish at once rather than give way. What I am going to tell you may be a commonplace in the law court; nevertheless it is true. The only office that I ever held in the state, Athenians, was that of Senator. When you wished to try the ten generals who did not rescue their men after the battle of Arginusae, as a group, which was illegal, as you all came to think afterwards, the tribe Antiochis, to which I belong, held the presidency. On that occasion I alone of all the presidents opposed your illegal action and gave my vote against you. The speakers were ready to suspend me and arrest me; and you were clamoring against me, and crying out to me to submit. But I thought that I ought to face the danger, with law and justice on my side, rather than join with you in your unjust proposal, from fear of imprisonment or death. That was when the state was democratic. When the oligarchy came in, the Thirty sent for me, with four others, to the council-chamber, and ordered us to bring Leon the Salaminian from Salamis, that they might put him to death. They were in the habit of frequently giving similar orders, to many others, wishing to implicate as many as possible in their crimes. But, then, I again proved, not by mere words, but by my actions, that, if I may speak bluntly, I do not care a straw for death; but that I do care very much indeed about not doing anything unjust or impious. That government with all its powers did not terrify me into doing anything unjust; but when we left the council-chamber, the other four went over to Salamis and brought Leon across to Athens; and I went home. And if the rule of the Thirty had not been destroyed soon afterwards, I should very likely have been put to death for what I did then. Many of you will be my witnesses in this matter.

Now do you think that I could have remained alive all these years if I had taken part in public affairs, and had always maintained the cause of justice like an honest man, and had held it a paramount duty, as it is, to do so? Certainly not, Athenians, nor could any other man. But throughout my whole life, both in private and in public, whenever I have had to take part in public affairs, you will find I have always been the same and have never yielded unjustly to anyone; no, not to those whom my enemies falsely assert to have been my pupils. But I was never anyone's teacher. I have never withheld myself from anyone, young or old, who was anxious to hear me discuss while I was making my investigation; neither do I discuss for payment, and refuse to discuss without payment. I am ready to ask questions of rich and poor alike, and if any man wishes to answer me, and then listen to what I have to say, he may. . . .

I believe in the gods as no one of my accusers believes in them: and to you and to God I commit my cause to be decided as is best for you and for me.

[The vote is taken and he is found guilty by 281 votes to 220.]

There are many reasons why I am not grieved, O men of Athens, at the vote of condemnation. I expected it, and am only surprised that the votes are so nearly equal; for I had thought that the majority against me would have been far larger; but now, had thirty votes gone over to the other side, I should have been acquitted. And I may say, I think, that I have escaped Meletus. I may say more; for without the assistance of Anytus and Lycon, any one may see that he would not have had a fifth part of the votes, as the law requires, in which case he would have incurred a fine of a thousand drachmae.

And so he proposes death as the penalty. And what shall I propose on my part, O men of Athens? Clearly that which is my due. And what is my due? What return shall be made to the man who has never had the wit to be idle during his whole life; but has been careless of what the many care for—wealth, and family interests, and military offices, and speaking in the assembly, and magistracies, and plots, and parties. Reflecting that I was really too honest a man to be a politician and live, I did not go where I could do no good to you or to myself; but where I could do the greatest good privately to every one of you, thither I went, and sought to persuade every man among you that he must look to himself, and seek virtue and wisdom before he looks to his private interests, and look to the state before he looks to the interests of the state; and that this should be the order which he observes in all his actions. What shall be done to such an one? Doubtless some good thing, O men of Athens, if he has his reward; and the good should be of a kind suitable to him. What would be a reward suitable to a poor man who is your benefactor, and who desires leisure that he may instruct you? There can be no

reward so fitting as maintenance in the Prytaneum, O men of Athens, a reward which he deserves far more than the citizen who has won the prize at Olympia in the horse or chariot race, whether the chariots were drawn by two horses or by many. For I am in want, and he has enough; and he only gives you the appearance of happiness, and I give you the reality. And if I am to estimate the penalty fairly, I should say that maintenance in the Prytaneum is the just return.

Perhaps you think that I am braving you in what I am saying now, as in what I said before about the tears and prayers. But this is not so. I speak rather because I am convinced that I never intentionally wronged any one, although I cannot convince you—the time has been too short; if there were a law at Athens, as there is in other cities, that a capital cause should not be decided in one day, then I believe that I should have convinced you. But I cannot in a moment refute great slanders; and, as I am convinced that I never wronged another, I will assuredly not wrong myself. I will not say of myself that I deserve any evil, or propose any penalty. Why should I? Because I am afraid of the penalty of death which Meletus proposes? When I do not know whether death is a good or an evil, why should I propose a penalty which would certainly be an evil? Shall I say imprisonment? And why should I live in prison, and be the slave of the magistrates of the year—of the Eleven? Or shall the penalty be a fine, and imprisonment until the fine is paid? There is the same objection. I should have to lie in prison, for money I have none, and cannot pay. And if I say exile (and this may possibly be the penalty which you will affix), I must indeed be blinded by the love of life, if I am so irrational as to expect that when you, who are my own citizens, cannot endure my discourses and words, and have found them so grievous and odious that you will have no more of them, others are likely to endure me. No indeed, men of Athens, that is not very likely. And what a life should I lead, at my age, wandering from city to city, ever changing my place of exile, and always being driven out! For I am quite sure that wherever I go, there, as here, the young men will flock to me; and if I drive them away, their elders will drive me out at their request; and if I let them come, their fathers and friends will drive me out for their sakes.

Some one will say: Yes, Socrates, but cannot you hold your tongue, and then you may go into a foreign city, and no one will interfere with you? Now I have great difficulty in making you understand my answer to this. For if I tell you that to do as you say would be a disobedience to the God, and therefore that I cannot hold my tongue, you will not believe that I am serious; and if I say again that daily to discourse about virtue, and of those other things about which you hear me examining myself and others, is the greatest good of man, and that the unexamined life is not worth living, you are still less likely to believe me. Yet I say what is true, although a thing of which it is hard for me to persuade you. Also, I have never been accustomed to think that I deserve to suffer any harm. Had I money I might have estimated the offence at what I was able to pay, and not have been much the worse. But I have none, and therefore I must ask you to proportion the fine to my means. Well, perhaps I could afford a mina, and therefore I propose that penalty: Plato, Crito, Critobulus, and Apollodorus, my friends here, bid me say thirty minae, and they will be the sureties. Let thirty minae be the penalty; for which sum they will be ample security to you.

[2nd vote: The jury decides for the death penalty by a vote of 360 to 141.]

Not much time will be gained, O Athenians, in return for the evil name which you will get from the detractors of the city, who will say that you killed Socrates, a wise man; for they will call me wise, even although I am not wise, when they want to reproach you. If you had waited a little while, your desire would have been fulfilled in the course of nature. For I am far advanced in years, as you may perceive, and not far from death. . . . The difficulty, my friends, is not to avoid death, but to avoid unrighteousness; for that runs faster than death. I am old and move slowly, and the slower runner has overtaken me, and my accusers are keen and quick, and the faster runner, who is

unrighteousness, has overtaken them. And now I depart hence condemned by you to suffer the penalty of death—they too go their ways condemned by the truth to suffer the penalty of villainy and wrong; and I must abide by my award—let them abide by theirs. I suppose that these things may be regarded as fated—and I think that they are well. . . .

Friends, who would have acquitted me, I would like also to talk with you about the thing which has come to pass, while the magistrates are busy, and before I go to the place at which I must die. Stay then a little, for we may as well talk with one another while there is time. You are my friends, and I should like to show you the meaning of this event which has happened to me. O my judges—for you I may truly call judges—I should like to tell you of a wonderful circumstance. Hitherto the divine faculty of which the internal oracle is the source has constantly been in the habit of opposing me even about trifles, if I was going to make a slip or error in any matter; and now as you see there has come upon me that which may be thought, and is generally believed to be, the last and worst evil. But the oracle made no sign of opposition, either when I was leaving my house in the morning, or when I was on my way to the court, or while I was speaking, at anything which I was going to say; and yet I have often been stopped in the middle of a speech, but now in nothing I either said or did touching the matter in hand has the oracle opposed me. What do I take to be the explanation of this silence? I will tell you. It is an intimation that what has happened to me is a good, and that those of us who think that death is an evil are in error. For the customary sign would surely have opposed me had I been going to evil and not to good.

Let us reflect in another way, and we shall see that there is great reason to hope that death is a good; for one of two things—either death is a state of nothingness and utter unconsciousness, or, as men say, there is a change and migration of the soul from this world to another. Now if you suppose that there is no consciousness, but a sleep like the sleep of him who is undisturbed even by dreams, death will be an unspeakable gain. For if a person were to select the night in which his sleep was undisturbed even by dreams, and were to compare with this the other days and nights of his life, and then were to tell us how many days and nights he had passed in the course of his life better and more pleasantly than this one, I think that any man, I will not say a private man, but even the great king will not find many such days or nights, when compared with the others. Now if death be of such a nature, I say that to die is gain; for eternity is then only a single night. But if death is the journey to another place, and there, as men say, all the dead abide, what good, O my friends and judges, can be greater than this? If indeed when the pilgrim arrives in the world below, he is delivered from the professors of justice in this world, and finds the true judges who are said to give judgment there, Minos and Rhadamanthus and Aeacus and Triptolemus, and other sons of God who were righteous in their own life, that pilgrimage will be worth making. What would not a man give if he might converse with Orpheus and Musaeus and Hesiod and Homer? Nay, if this be true, let me die again and again. I myself, too, shall have a wonderful interest in there meeting and conversing with Palamedes, and Ajax the son of Telamon, and any other ancient hero who has suffered death through an unjust judgment; and there will be no small pleasure, as I think, in comparing my own sufferings with theirs. Above all, I shall then be able to continue my search into true and false knowledge; as in this world, so also in the next; and I shall find out who is wise, and who pretends to be wise, and is not. What would not a man give, O judges, to be able to examine the leader of the great Trojan expedition; or Odysseus or Sisyphus, or numberless others, men and women too! What infinite delight would there be in conversing with them and asking them questions! In another world they do not put a man to death for asking questions: assuredly not. For besides being happier than we are, they will be immortal, if what is said is true.

Wherefore, O judges, be of good cheer about death, and know of a certainty, that no evil can happen to a good man, either in life or after death. He and his are not neglected by the gods; nor has my own approaching end happened by mere chance. But I see clearly that the time had arrived when it was better for me to die and be released from trouble; wherefore the oracle gave no sign. For which reason, also, I am not angry with my condemners, or with my accusers; they have done me no harm, although they did not mean to do me any good; and for this I may gently blame them.

Still I have a favour to ask of them. When my sons are grown up, I would ask you, O my friends, to punish them; and I would have you trouble them, as I have troubled you, if they seem to care about riches, or anything, more than about virtue; or if they pretend to be something when they are really nothing,—then reprove them, as I have reproved you, for not caring about that for which they ought to care, and thinking that they are something when they are really nothing. And if you do this, both I and my sons will have received justice at your hands.

The hour of departure has arrived, and we go our ways—I to die, and you to live. Which is better God only knows.

For Further Reflection

1. Describe Socrates. What kind of man was he? What were his deepest beliefs?
2. Some have found a note of arrogance and insensitivity in Socrates and argue that he deserved what he got. Does this reading lend any support to that thesis?
3. In the dialogue *Protagoras* Socrates identifies evil with ignorance. "My own opinion is more or less this: no wise man believes that anyone errs voluntarily or willingly does evil or any base act. They know very well that every base or evil act is committed involuntarily." If

people cannot do evil voluntarily, can we hold them responsible for their actions? Do you see this thesis in the *Apology*? Discuss this thesis.

4. Can the good be harmed by the bad? How do we harm ourselves?
5. What does Socrates mean when he says that "the unexamined life is not worth living"?

We will return to Socrates in Parts IV and VI.

I.2   The Allegory of the Cave

PLATO

In the *Republic*, Plato presents what is probably the most famous tale in Western philosophy: the "Allegory of the Cave." Through the persona of Socrates, Plato tells a story that works on many levels. Primarily the allegory represents facets of Plato's theories of knowledge and metaphysics, but it can also be seen as a metaphor for the search for the true and the good through philosophy. Imagine, Plato says, prisoners chained for life against a wall in a cave so that they can see only shadows on the opposite wall. The shadows appear because behind and above the wall to which the prisoners are chained there burns a fire, and between the fire and the prisoners is a raised walkway along which people pass carrying vessels, statues, and replicas of animals. The prisoners see the shadows of these artifacts on the wall and hear the people's voices echoing off of it, and they mistakenly believe that these sights and sounds are the real world. But the real world—the truth—lies above the darkened cave out in the bright sunlight. If a prisoner is released from his chains and is shown the true source of the shadows, he will not believe his eyes and will prefer to believe as he always has—just as people will often prefer comfortable commonplace assumptions to the deeper, sometimes unsettling understanding that philosophy can provide. If he is dragged into the light, his eyes will hurt, and he will be disoriented, just as the truths of philosophy can at first seem strange and frightening. If the prisoner finally sees things as they really are in the full sunlight, he will pity the prisoners he left behind and will return to the cave to enlighten them. But they will revile him as a ridiculous fool and might even put him to death for his heresies—a fate that has often befallen those who have dared speak unconventional truths (Socrates, for example).

Study Questions

1. What is the allegory of the cave?
2. What is likely to happen when a prisoner is forced to see how the shadows are actually produced? What happens when the prisoner is dragged into the sunshine?
3. What happens when the prisoner goes back into the cave to persuade the others of the true nature of reality? What does this part of the allegory represent?

4. How is the fate of the prisoner like that of Socrates? Does Plato condemn or commend the treatment of the enlightened prisoner at the hands of the other inmates in the cave?

5. Why do the other prisoners resist the enlightened prisoner's entreaties?

BOOK VII

And now, I said, let me show in a figure how far our nature is enlightened or unenlightened:— Behold! human beings living in an underground den, which has a mouth open towards the light and reaching all along the den; here they have been from their childhood, and have their legs and necks chained so that they can not move, and can only see before them, being prevented by the chains from turning round their heads. Above and behind them a fire is blazing at a distance, and between the fire and the prisoners there is a raised way; and you will see, if you look, a low wall built along the way, like the screen which marionette players have in front of them, over which they show the puppets.

I see.

And do you see, I said, men passing along the wall carrying all sorts of vessels, and statues and figures of animals made of wood and stone and various materials, which appear over the wall? Some of them are talking, others silent.

You have shown me a strange image, and they are strange prisoners.

Like ourselves, I replied; and they see only their own shadows, or the shadows of one another, which the fire throws on the opposite wall of the cave?

True, he said; how could they see anything but the shadows if they were never allowed to move their heads?

And of the objects which are being carried in like manner they would only see the shadows?

Yes, he said.

And if they were able to converse with one another, would they not suppose that they were naming what was actually before them?[1]

Very true.

And suppose further that the prison had an echo which came from the other side, would they not be sure to fancy when one of the passers-by spoke that the voice which they heard came from the passing shadow?

No question, he replied.

To them, I said, the truth would be literally nothing but the shadows of the images.

That is certain.

And now look again, and see what will naturally follow if the prisoners are released and disabused of their error. At first, when any of them is liberated and compelled suddenly to stand up and turn his neck round and walk and look towards the light, he will suffer sharp pains; the glare will distress him, and he will be unable to see the realities of which in his former state he had seen the shadows; and then conceive some one saying to him, that what he saw before was an illusion, but that now, when he is approaching nearer to being and his eye is turned towards more real existence, he has a clearer vision,— what will be his reply? And you may further imagine that his instructor is pointing to the objects as they pass and requiring him to name them,—will he not be perplexed? Will he not fancy that the shadows which he formerly saw are truer than the objects which are now shown to him?

Far truer.

And if he is compelled to look straight at the light, will he not have a pain in his eyes which

From The Republic, *Book 7, in* The Dialogues of Plato, *vol. 12, trans. Benjamin Jowett (1914), pp. 14–18.*
By permission of Oxford University Press, Inc.

will make him turn away to take refuge in the objects of vision which he can see, and which he will conceive to be in reality clearer than the things which are now being shown to him?

True, he said.

And suppose once more, that he is reluctantly dragged up a steep and rugged ascent, and held fast until he is forced into the presence of the sun himself, is he not likely to be pained and irritated? When he approaches the light his eyes will be dazzled, and he will not be able to see anything at all of what are now called realities.

Not all in a moment, he said.

He will require to grow accustomed to the sight of the upper world. And first he will see the shadows best, next the reflections of men and other objects in the water, and then the objects themselves; then he will gaze upon the light of the moon and the stars and the spangled heaven; and he will see the sky and the stars by night better than the sun or the light of the sun by day?

Certainly.

Last of all he will be able to see the sun, and not mere reflections of him in the water, but he will see him in his own proper place, and not in another; and he will contemplate him as he is.

Certainly.

He will then proceed to argue that this is he who gives the season and the years, and is the guardian of all that is in the visible world, and in a certain way the cause of all things which he and his fellows have been accustomed to behold?

Clearly, he said, he would first see the sun and then reason about him.

And when he remembered his old habitation, and the wisdom of the den and his fellow-prisoners, do you not suppose that he would felicitate himself on the change, and pity them?

Certainly, he would.

And if they were in the habit of conferring honors among themselves on those who were quickest to observe the passing shadows and to remark which of them went before, and which followed after, and which were together; and who were therefore best able to draw conclusions

as to the future, do you think that he would care for such honors and glories, or envy the possessors of them? Would he not say with Homer,

"Better to be the poor servant of a poor master,"

and to endure anything, rather than think as they do and live after their manner?

Yes, he said, I think that he would rather suffer anything than entertain these false notions and live in this miserable manner.

Imagine once more, I said, such an one coming suddenly out of the sun to be replaced in his old situation; would he not be certain to have his eyes full of darkness?

To be sure, he said.

And if there were a contest, and he had to compete in measuring the shadows with the prisoners who had never moved out of the den, while his sight was still weak, and before his eyes had become steady (and the time which would be needed to acquire this new habit of sight might be very considerable), would he not be ridiculous? Men would say of him that up he went and down he came without his eyes; and that it was better not even to think of ascending; and if any one tried to loose another and lead him up to the light let them only catch the offender, and they would put him to death.

No question, he said.

This entire allegory, I said, you may now append, dear Glaucon, to the previous argument; the prisonhouse is the world of sight, the light of the fire is the sun, and you will not misapprehend me if you interpret the journey upwards to be the ascent of the soul into the intellectual world according to my poor belief, which, at your desire, I have expressed—whether rightly or wrongly God knows. But, whether true or false, my opinion is that in the world of knowledge the idea of good appears last of all, and is seen only with an effort; and, when seen, is also inferred to be the universal author of all things beautiful and right, parent of light and of the lord of light in this visible world, and the immediate source of reason and truth in the intellectual; and that this is the power upon which he who would act rationally either in public or private life must have his eye fixed.

I agree, he said, as far as I am able to understand you.

Moreover, I said, you must not wonder that those who attain to this beatific vision are unwilling to descend to human affairs; for their souls are ever hastening into the upper world where they desire to dwell; which desire of theirs is very natural, if our allegory may be trusted.

Yes, very natural.

And is there anything surprising in one who passes from divine contemplations to the evil state of man, misbehaving himself in a ridiculous manner; if, while his eyes are blinking and before he has become accustomed to the surrounding darkness, he is compelled to fight in courts of law, or in other places, about the images or the shadows of images of justice, and is endeavoring to meet the conceptions of those who have never yet seen absolute justice?

NOTE

1. Reading παρόντα.

For Further Reflection

1. If this allegory is taken as a representation of the search for, and the impediments to, wisdom, what does the cave represent? What do the shadows on the wall represent?

2. The prisoners react with disdain and violence toward the enlightened one. Are there parallels in history to this sort of treatment for people with unconventional views?

3. What is the moral (or morals) of Plato's allegory?

Of Enthusiasm and the Quest for Truth　　　　I.3

JOHN LOCKE

John Locke (1632–1704) is considered the greatest English philosopher of the modern period. Educated at Christ Church, Oxford University, he was a tutor in Greek classics and philosophy. Later he was the administrative assistant and physician to the Earl of Shaftsbury. His work on representative government and human rights, *Two Treatises on Government* (1689), greatly influenced the founding fathers of the United States. His *Essay Concerning Human Understanding* (1689), from which this selection is taken, is considered a classic in the theory of knowledge. We will examine it more fully in Reading III.24.

Locke's value of philosophy as the search for truth is connected to his Christian faith, but the implications of his thought go beyond any particular religion. Locke held that since God was a God of Truth, he would never require that we believe anything, including in God, against or without the natural light of reason—although some mysteries (for example, immortality) are beyond our understanding. Religious people, who have ample grounds for believing in God, must beware lest they allow their imagination and passion ("enthusiasm") to run away with them. Reason and faith are compatible, so that every claim of faith must be supported with sufficient evidence. That is, we must be lovers of Truth, believing propositions in proportion to the strength of the evidence. In a letter to Anthony Collins, Locke wrote, "To love the truth for truth's sake is the principal part of human perfection in this world, and the seed-plot of all other virtues" (October 29, 1703). His friend, Lady Masham, wrote of him, "Locke was always, in the greatest and in the smallest affairs of human life, as well as in speculative opinions, disposed to follow reason, whosoever suggested it; he being ever a faithful servant, I had almost said a slave, to truth; never abandoning anything else, and following her for her own sake purely."*

Locke's use of *enthusiasm* contains the negative connotations that the word held for many philosophers and theologians of his day, including Bishop Butler, Jonathan Swift, Henry More, and Bishop Warburton. Leibniz, the German philosopher and Locke's friend, expressed the sentiment of these intellectuals when he wrote, "Enthusiasm was originally a good term. Just as *sophism* properly indicates an exercise of wisdom, so *enthusiasm* signifies that there is divinity in us. But these men having consecrated their passions, fancies, dreams, and even their anger, as something divine, *enthusiasm* began to signify a mental disturbance attributed to the influence of some divinity. . . . Since then, we attribute it to those who believe without foundation that their impulses come from God."

Study Questions

1. What is the first requirement in searching for Truth?
2. What is the one unerring mark of loving the Truth?
3. How does Locke characterize *enthusiasm*? What is its source?
4. How do reason and enthusiasm conflict?
5. How does enthusiasm cause us to go astray in our reasoning?
6. How can people distinguish a true revelation from God from a misguided claim of revelation?
7. How did God confirm his revelations to holy men of old?

1. HE THAT WOULD SERIOUSLY set upon the search of truth, ought in the first place to prepare his mind with a love of it. For he that loves it not, will not take much pains to get it, nor be much concerned when he misses it. There is nobody in the commonwealth of learning, who does not profess himself a lover of truth; and there is not a rational creature that would not take it amiss to be thought otherwise of. And yet for all this, one may truly say, that there are very few lovers of truth for truths sake, even amongst those who persuade themselves that they are so. How a man may know whether he be so in earnest, is worth inquiry: And I think there is one unerring mark of it, viz, the not entertaining any proposition with greater assurance than the proofs it is built upon will warrant. Whoever goes beyond this measure of assent, it is plain receives not the truth in the

---

Quoted in A. S. Pingle-Pattison's edition of Locke's An Essay Concerning Human Understanding *(Oxford University Press, 1924), p. 359.*

love of it; loves not truth for truths sake, but for some other bye end. For the evidence that any proposition is true (except such as are self-evident) lying only in the proofs a man has of it, whatsoever degrees of assent he affords it beyond the degrees of that evidence, it is plain that all the surplusage of assurance is owing to some other affection, and not to the love of truth: It being as impossible, that the love of truth should carry my assent above the evidence there is to me that it is true, as that the love of truth should make me assent to any proposition for the sake of that evidence, which it has not, that it is true; which is in effect to love it as a truth, because it is possible or probable that it may not be true. In any truth that gets not possession of our minds by the irresistible light of self-evidence, or by the force of demonstration, the arguments that gain it assent are the vouchers and gage of its probability to us; and we can receive it for no other, than such as they deliver it to our understandings. Whatsoever credit or authority we give to any proposition, more than it receives from the principles and proofs it supports itself upon, is owing to our inclinations that way, and is so far a derogation from the love of truth as such: Which, as it can receive no evidence from our passions or interests, so it should receive no tincture from them.

2. The assuming an authority of dictating to others, and a forwardness to prescribe to their opinions, is a constant concomitant of this bias and corruption of our judgments. For how almost can it be otherwise, but that he should be ready to impose on another's belief, who has already imposed on his own? Who can reasonably expect arguments and conviction from him, in dealing with others, whose understanding is not accustomed to them in his dealing with himself? Who does violence to his own faculties, tyrannizes over his own mind, and usurps the prerogative that belongs to truth alone, which is to command assent by only its own authority, i.e., by and in proportion to that evidence which it carries with it.

3. Upon this occasion I shall take the liberty to consider a third ground of assent [the first two are reason and revelation, ed.], which with some men has the same authority, and is as confidently relied on as either faith or reason; I mean enthusiasm: Which laying by reason, would set up revelation without it. Whereby in effect it takes away both reason and revelation, and substitutes in the room of it the ungrounded fancies of a man's own brain, and assumes them for a foundation both of opinion and conduct.

4. Reason is natural revelation, whereby the eternal father of light, and fountain of all knowledge, communicates to mankind that portion of truth which he has laid within the reach of their natural faculties: Revelation is natural reason enlarged by a new set of discoveries communicated by God immediately, which reason vouches the truth of, by the testimony and proofs it gives, that they come from God. So that he that takes away reason, to make way for revelation, puts out the light of both, and does much—what the same, as if he would persuade a man to put out his eyes, the better to receive the remote light of an invisible star by a telescope.

5. Immediate revelation being a much easier way for men to establish their opinions and regulate their conduct, than the tedious and not always successful labor of strict reasoning, it is no wonder that some have been very apt to pretend to revelation, and to persuade themselves that they are under the peculiar guidance of heaven in their actions and opinions, especially in those of them which they cannot account for by the ordinary methods of knowledge and principles of reason. Hence we see that in all ages, men, in whom melancholy has mixed with devotion, or whose conceit of themselves has raised them into an opinion of a greater familiarity with God, and a nearer admittance to his favor than is afforded to others, have often flattered themselves with a persuasion of an immediate intercourse with the Deity, and frequent communications from the Divine Spirit. God, I own, cannot be denied to

Reprinted from An Essay Concerning Human Understanding, *Book IV.19 (1689).*

be able to enlighten the understanding, by a ray darted into the mind immediately from the fountain of light; this they understand he has promised to do, and who then has so good a title to expect it as those who are his peculiar people, chosen by him, and depending on him?

6. Their minds being thus prepared, whatever groundless opinion comes to settle itself strongly upon their fancies, is an illumination from the spirit of God, and presently of divine authority: And whatsoever odd action they find in themselves a strong inclination to do, that impulse is concluded to be a call or direction from heaven, and must be obeyed; it is a commission from above, and they cannot err in executing it.

7. This I take to be properly enthusiasm, which, though founded neither on reason nor divine revelation, but rising from the conceits of a warmed or over-weening brain, works yet, where it once gets footing, more powerfully on the persuasions and actions of men, than either of those two, or both together: Men being most forwardly obedient to the impulses they receive from themselves; and the whole man is sure to act more vigorously, where the whole man is carried by a natural motion. For strong conceit, like a new principle, carries all easily with it, when got above common sense, and freed from all restraint of reason, and check of reflection, it is heightened into a divine authority, in concurrence with our own temper and inclination.

8. Though the odd opinions and extravagant actions enthusiasm has run men into, were enough to warn them against this wrong principle, so apt to misguide them both in their belief and conduct; yet the love of something extraordinary, the ease and glory it is to be inspired, and be above the common and natural ways of knowledge, so flatters many men's laziness, ignorance, and vanity, that when once they are got into this way of immediate revelation, of illumination without search, and of certainty without proof, and without examination, it is a hard matter to get them out of it. Reason is lost upon them, they are above it: They see the light infused into their understandings, and cannot be

mistaken; it is clear and visible there, like the light of bright sunshine; shows itself, and needs no other proof but its own evidence: They feel the hand of God moving them within, and the impulses of the spirit, and cannot be mistaken in what they feel. . . .

9. This is the way of talking of these men: They are sure, because they are sure: And their persuasions are right, because they are strong in them. For, when what they say is stripped of the metaphor of seeing and feeling, this is all it amounts to: And yet these similes so impose on them, that they serve them for certainty in themselves, and demonstration to others.

10. But to examine a little soberly this internal light, and this feeling on which they build so much. These men have, they say, clear light, and they see; they have awakened sense, and they feel; this cannot, they are sure, be disputed them. For when a man says he sees or feels, nobody can deny it him, that he does so. But here let me ask: This seeing, is it the perception of the truth of the proposition, or of this, that it is a revelation from God? This feeling, is it a perception of an inclination or fancy to do something, or of the spirit of God moving that inclination? These are two very different perceptions, and must be carefully distinguished, if we would not impose upon ourselves. I may perceive the truth of a proposition, and yet not perceive that it is an immediate revelation from God. I may perceive the truth of a proposition in Euclid, without its being or my perceiving it to be a revelation: Nay, I may perceive I came not by this knowledge in a natural way, and so may conclude it revealed, without perceiving that it is a revelation from God; because there be spirits, which, without being divinely commissioned, may excite those ideas in me, and lay them in such order before my mind, that I may perceive their connection. So that the knowledge of any proposition coming into my mind, I know not how, is not a perception that it is from God. Much less is a strong persuasion, that it is true, a perception that it is from God, or so much as true. But however it be called light and seeing, I suppose it is at most but belief and

assurance: And the proposition taken for a revelation, is not such as they know to be true, but take to be true. For where a proposition is known to be true, revelation is needless: And it is hard to conceive how there can be a revelation to any one of what he knows already. If therefore it be a proposition which they are persuaded, but do not know, to be true, whatever they may call it, it is not seeing, but believing. For these are two ways, whereby truth comes into the mind, wholly distinct, so that one is not the other. What I see I know to be so by the evidence of the thing itself: What I believe I take to be so upon the testimony of another: But this testimony I must know to be given, or else what ground have I of believing? I must see that it is God that reveals this to me, or else I see nothing. The question then here is, how do I know that God is the revealer of this to me; that this impression is made upon my mind by his Holy Spirit, and that therefore I ought to obey it? If I know not this, how great soever the assurance is that I am possessed with, it is groundless; whatever light I pretend to, it is but enthusiasm. For whether the proposition supposed to be revealed, be in itself evidently true, or visibly probable, or by the natural ways of knowledge uncertain, the proposition that must be well grounded, and manifested to be true, is this, that God is the revealer of it, and that what I take to be a revelation is certainly put into my mind by him, and is not an illusion dropped in by some other spirit, or raised by my own fancy. For if I mistake not, these men receive it for true, because they presume God revealed it. Does it not then stand them upon, to examine upon what grounds they presume it to be a revelation from God? or else all their confidence is mere presumption: And this light, they are so dazzled with, is nothing but an ignis fatuus that leads them constantly round in this circle; it is a revelation, because they firmly believe it, and they believe it, because it is a revelation.

11. In all that is of divine revelation, there is need of no other proof but that it is an inspiration from God: For he can neither deceive nor be deceived. But how shall it be known that any proposition in our minds is a truth infused by God; a truth that is revealed to us by him, which he declares to us, and therefore we ought to believe? Here it is that enthusiasm fails of the evidence it pretends to. For men thus possessed boast of a light whereby they say they are enlightened, and brought into the knowledge of this or that truth. But if they know it to be a truth, they must know it to be so, either by its own self-evidence to natural reason, or by the rational proofs that make it out to be so. If they see and know it to be a truth, either of these two ways, they in vain suppose it to be a revelation. For they know it to be true the same way, that any other man naturally may know that it is so without the help of revelation. For thus all the truths, of what kind soever, that men uninspired are enlightened with, came into their minds, and are established there. If they say they know it to be true because it is a revelation from God, the reason is good: But then it will be demanded how they know it to be a revelation from God. If they say, by the light it brings with it, which shines bright in their minds, and they cannot resist: I beseech them to consider whether this be any more than what we have taken notice of already, viz, that it is a revelation, because they strongly believe it to be true. For all the light they speak of is but a strong, though ungrounded persuasion of their own minds, that it is a truth. For rational grounds from proofs that it is a truth, they must acknowledge to have none; for then it is not received as a revelation, but upon the ordinary grounds that other truths are received: And if they believe it to be true because it is a revelation, and have no other reason for its being a revelation, but because they are fully persuaded without any other reason that it is true; they believe it to be a revelation, only because they strongly believe it to be a revelation; which is a very unsafe ground to proceed on, either in our tenets or actions. And what readier way can there be to run ourselves into the most extravagant errors and miscarriages, than thus to set up fancy for our supreme and sole guide, and to believe any proposition to be true, any action to be right, only because we believe it to be so? The strength of our persuasions is no evidence at all of their own

rectitude: Crooked things may be as stiff and inflexible as straight: And men may be as positive and peremptory in error as in truth. How come else the untractable zealots in different and opposite parties? For if the light, which every one thinks he has in his mind, which in this case is nothing but the strength of his own persuasion, be an evidence that it is from God, contrary opinions have the same title to be inspirations; and God will be not only the father of lights, but of opposite and contradictory lights, leading men contrary ways; and contradictory propositions will be divine truths, if an ungrounded strength of assurance be an evidence, that any proposition is a divine revelation.

12. This cannot be otherwise, whilst firmness of persuasion is made the cause of believing, and confidence of being in the right is made an argument of truth. St. Paul himself believed he did well, and that he had a call to it when he persecuted the Christians, whom he confidently thought in the wrong: But yet it was he, and not they, who were mistaken. Good men are men still, liable to mistakes; and are sometimes warmly engaged in errors, which they take for divine truths, shining in their minds with the clearest light.

13. Light, true light, in the mind is, or can be nothing else but the evidence of the truth of any proposition; and if it be not a self-evident proposition, all the light it has, or can have, is from the cleanness and validity of those proofs, upon which it is received. To talk of any other light in the understanding is to put ourselves in the dark, or in the power of the Prince of darkness, and by our own consent to give ourselves up to delusion to believe a lie. For if strength of persuasion be the light, which must guide us; I ask how shall any one distinguish between the delusions of Satan, and the inspirations of the Holy Ghost? He can transform himself into an angel of light. And they who are led by this son of the morning, are as fully satisfied of the illumination, i.e., are as strongly persuaded, that they are enlightened by the spirit of God, as any one who is so: They acquiesce and rejoice in it, are acted by it: And nobody can be more sure, nor more in the right (if their own strong belief may be judge) than they.

14. He therefore that will not give himself up to all the extravagancies of delusion and error, must bring this guide of his light within to the trial. God, when he makes the prophet, does not unmake the man. He leaves all his faculties in the natural state, to enable him to judge of his inspirations, whether they be of divine original or no. When he illuminates the mind with supernatural light, he does not extinguish that which is natural. If he would have us assent to the truth of any proposition, he either evidences that truth by the usual methods of natural reason, or else makes it known to be a truth which he would have us assent to, by his authority; and convinces us that it is from him, by some marks which reason cannot be mistaken in. Reason must be our last judge and guide in every thing. I do not mean that we must consult reason, and examine whether a proposition revealed from God can be made out by natural principles, and if it cannot, that then we may reject it: But consult it we must, and by it examine, whether it be a revelation from God or no. And if reason finds it to be revealed from God, reason then declares for it, as much as for any other truth, and makes it one of her dictates. Every conceit that thoroughly warms our fancies must pass for an inspiration, if there be nothing but the strength of our persuasions, whereby to judge of our persuasions: If reason must not examine their truth by something extrinsic to the persuasions themselves, inspirations and delusions, truth and falsehood, will have the same measure, and will not be possible to be distinguished.

15. Thus we see the holy men of old, who had revelations from God, had something else besides that internal light of assurance in their own minds, to testify to them that it was from God. They were not left to their own persuasions alone, that those persuasions were from God; but had outward signs to convince them of the author of those revelations. And when they were

to convince others, they had a power given them to justify the truth of their commission from heaven, and by visible signs to assert the divine authority of a message they were sent with. Moses saw the bush burn without being consumed, and heard a voice out of it. This was something besides finding an impulse upon his mind to go to Pharaoh, that he might bring his brethren out of Egypt: And yet he thought not this enough to authorize him to go with that message, till God, by another miracle of his rod turned into a serpent, had assured him of a power to testify his mission, by the same miracle repeated before them, whom he was sent to. Gideon was sent by an angel to deliver Israel from the Midianites, and yet he desired a sign to convince him that this commission was from God. These, and several the like instances to be found among the prophets of old, are enough to show that they thought not an inward seeing or persuasion of their own minds, without any other proof, a sufficient evidence that it was from God; though the scripture does not every where mention their demanding or having such proofs.

16. In what I have said I am far from denying that God can, or doth sometimes enlighten men's minds in the apprehending of certain truths, or excite them to good actions by the immediate influence and assistance of the holy spirit, without any extraordinary signs accompanying it. But in such cases too we have reason and scripture, unerring rules to know whether it be from God or no. Where the truth embraced is consonant to the revelation in the written word of God, or the action conformable to the dictates of right reason or holy writ, we may be assured that we run no risk in entertaining it as such; because though perhaps it be not an immediate revelation from God, extraordinarily operating on our minds, yet we are sure it is warranted by that revelation which he has given us of truth. . . .

For Further Reflection

1. Examine Locke's claim that the love of truth entails "not entertaining any proposition with greater assurance than the proofs it is built upon will warrant." Do you agree with this?

2. Discuss these questions. Do most people have a strong love of the Truth? How much do you value Truth?

3. How does Locke try to reconcile reason and revelation? Note how he thinks revelation was confirmed in the past. Is this the case today? What are the implications of this feature (confirmation) for the relationship of reason and religious belief?

The Value of Philosophy   I.4

BERTRAND RUSSELL

Bertrand Russell (1872–1970) is one of the most important philosophers of the twentieth century. His works cover almost every area of philosophy, from logic and philosophy of mathematics (*Principia Mathematica* [1910], written with Alfred North

Whitehead) to philosophy of religion ("Mysticism" and "Why I Am Not a Christian") and ethics ("Science and Ethics"). Russell's concern to live out his philosophy in his life led him to found a special school on his philosophy of education, become a leader in Britain's "Ban the Bomb" (the atom bomb) Movement, and speak out on moral and political issues, sometimes at personal risk.

In this reading, coming at the end of his brilliant essay *The Problems of Philosophy* (1912), Russell argues that the value of philosophy is not in any ability to produce material goods ("philosophy bakes no bread") or arrive at definitive conclusions about the nature of reality, but is its effect upon the lives of those who take it seriously. In its contemplation of the perennial questions of life, this essay enlarges our understanding of the task of philosophical reflection.

Study Questions

1. What do many scientific and practical people think of philosophy?
2. What is Russell's assessment of their views of philosophy? Why does he think that their prejudice occurs?
3. What are the aims of philosophy? Has it been successful in attaining them? Explain.
4. Where does Russell think that the value of philosophy is to be sought?
5. What effect can philosophy have on the instinctive person? What are the fruits of philosophical contemplation?
6. How does Russell define knowledge? What does he mean by this?
7. What does Russell think of the view that "man is the measure of all things"?

HAVING NOW COME TO THE END of our brief and very incomplete review of the problems of philosophy, it will be well to consider, in conclusion, what is the value of philosophy and why it ought to be studied. It is the more necessary to consider this question, in view of the fact that many men, under the influence of science or of practical affairs, are inclined to doubt whether philosophy is anything better than innocent but useless trifling, hair-splitting distinctions, and controversies on matters concerning which knowledge is impossible.

This view of philosophy appears to result, partly from a wrong conception of the ends of life, partly from a wrong conception of the kind of goods which philosophy strives to achieve. Physical science, through the medium of inven-

tions, is useful to innumerable people who are wholly ignorant of it; thus the study of physical science is to be recommended, not only, or primarily, because of the effect on the student, but rather because of the effect on mankind in general. Thus utility does not belong to philosophy. If the study of philosophy has any value at all for others than students of philosophy, it must be only indirectly, through its effects upon the lives of those who study it. It is in these effects, therefore, if anywhere, that the value of philosophy must be primarily sought.

But further, if we are not to fail in our endeavour to determine the value of philosophy, we must first free our minds from the prejudices of what are wrongly called "practical" men. The "practical" man, as this word is often used, is one

Reprinted from Bertrand Russell, The Problems of Philosophy *(New York: Oxford University Press, 1969), pp. 153–161, by permission of the publisher.*

who recognizes only material needs, who realizes that men must have food for the body, but is oblivious of the necessity of providing food for the mind. If all men were well off, if poverty and disease had been reduced to their lowest possible point, there would still remain much to be done to produce a valuable society; and even in the existing world the goods of the mind are at least as important as the goods of the body. It is exclusively among the goods of the mind that the value of philosophy is to be found; and only those who are not indifferent to these goods can be persuaded that the study of philosophy is not a waste of time.

Philosophy, like all other studies, aims primarily at knowledge. The knowledge it aims at is the kind of knowledge which gives unity and system to the body of the sciences, and the kind which results from a critical examination of the grounds of our convictions, prejudices, and beliefs. But it cannot be maintained that philosophy has had any very great measure of success in its attempts to provide definite answers to its questions. If you ask a mathematician, a mineralogist, a historian, or any other man of learning, what definite body of truths has been ascertained by his science, his answer will last as long as you are willing to listen. But if you put the same question to a philosopher, he will, if he is candid, have to confess that his study has not achieved positive results such as have been achieved by other sciences. It is true that this is partly accounted for by the fact that, as soon as definite knowledge concerning any subject becomes possible, this subject ceases to be called philosophy, and becomes a separate science. The whole study of the heavens, which now belongs to astronomy, was once included in philosophy; Newton's great work was called "the mathematical principles of natural philosophy." Similarly, the study of the human mind, which was a part of philosophy, has now been separated from philosophy and has become the science of psychology. Thus, to a great extent, the uncertainty of philosophy is more apparent than real: those questions which are already capable of definite answers are placed in the sciences, while those only to which, at present, no definite answer can be given, remain to form the residue which is called philosophy.

This is, however, only a part of the truth concerning the uncertainty of philosophy. There are many questions—and among them those that are of the profoundest interest to our spiritual life—which, so far as we can see, must remain insoluble to the human intellect unless its powers become of quite a different order from what they are now. Has the universe any unity of plan or purpose, or is it a fortuitous concourse of atoms? Is consciousness a permanent part of the universe, giving hope of indefinite growth in wisdom, or is it a transitory accident on a small planet on which life must ultimately become impossible? Are good and evil of importance to the universe or only to man? Such questions are asked by philosophy, and variously answered by various philosophers. But it would seem that, whether answers be otherwise discoverable or not, the answers suggested by philosophy are none of them demonstrably true. Yet, however slight may be the hope of discovering an answer, it is part of the business of philosophy to continue the consideration of such questions, to make us aware of their importance, to examine all the approaches to them, and to keep alive that speculative interest in the universe which is apt to be killed by confining ourselves to definitely ascertainable knowledge.

Many philosophers, it is true, have held that philosophy could establish the truth of certain answers to such fundamental questions. They have supposed that what is of most importance in religious beliefs could be proved by strict demonstration to be true. In order to judge of such attempts, it is necessary to take a survey of human knowledge, and to form an opinion as to its methods and its limitations. On such a subject it would be unwise to pronounce dogmatically; but if the investigations of our previous chapters have not led us astray, we shall be compelled to renounce the hope of finding philosophical proofs of religious beliefs. We cannot, therefore, include as part of the value of philosophy any definite set of answers to such questions. Hence, once more, the value of philosophy must not depend upon any supposed body of definitely ascertainable knowledge to be acquired by those who study it.

The value of philosophy is, in fact, to be sought largely in its very uncertainty. The man who has no tincture of philosophy goes through life imprisoned in the prejudices derived from common sense, from the habitual beliefs of his age or his nation, and from convictions which have grown up in his mind without the cooperation or consent of his deliberate reason. To such a man the world tends to become definite, finite, obvious; common objects rouse no questions, and unfamiliar possibilities are contemptuously rejected. As soon as we begin to philosophize, on the contrary, we find, as we saw in our opening chapters, that even the most everyday things lead to problems to which only very incomplete answers can be given. Philosophy, though unable to tell us with certainty what is the true answer to the doubts which it raises, is able to suggest many possibilities which enlarge our thoughts and free them from the tyranny of custom. Thus, while diminishing our feeling of certainty as to what things are, it greatly increases our knowledge as to what they may be; it removes the somewhat arrogant dogmatism of those who have never travelled into the region of liberating doubt, and it keeps alive our sense of wonder by showing familiar things in an unfamiliar aspect.

Apart from its utility in showing unsuspected possibilities, philosophy has a value—perhaps its chief value—through the greatness of the objects which it contemplates, and the freedom from narrow and personal aims resulting from this contemplation. The life of the instinctive man is shut up within the circle of his private interests: family and friends may be included, but the outer world is not regarded except as it may help or hinder what comes within the circle of instinctive wishes. In such a life there is something feverish and confined, in comparison with which the philosophic life is calm and free. The private world of instinctive interests is a small one, set in the midst of a great and powerful world which must, sooner or later, lay our private world in ruins. Unless we can so enlarge our interests as to include the whole outer world, we remain like a garrison in a beleaguered fortress, knowing that the enemy prevents escape and that ultimate surrender is inevitable. In such a life there is no peace, but a constant strife between the insistence of desire and the powerlessness of will. In one way or another, if our life is to be great and free, we must escape this prison and this strife.

One way of escape is by philosophic contemplation. Philosophic contemplation does not, in its widest survey, divide the universe into two hostile camps—friends and foes, helpful and hostile, good and bad—it views the whole impartially. Philosophic contemplation, when it is unalloyed, does not aim at proving that the rest of the universe is akin to man. All acquisition of knowledge is an enlargement of the Self, but this enlargement is best attained when it is not directly sought. It is obtained when the desire for knowledge is alone operative, by a study which does not wish in advance that its objects should have this or that character, but adapts the Self to the characters which it finds in its objects. This enlargement of Self is not obtained when, taking the Self as it is, we try to show that the world is so similar to this Self that knowledge of it is possible without any admission of what seems alien. The desire to prove this is a form of self-assertion and, like all self-assertion, it is an obstacle to the growth of Self which it desires, and of which the Self knows that it is capable. Self-assertion, in philosophic speculation as elsewhere, views the world as a means to its own ends; thus it makes the world of less account than Self, and the Self sets bounds to the greatness of its goods. In contemplation, on the contrary, we start from the not-Self, and through its greatness the boundaries of Self are enlarged; through the infinity of the universe the mind which contemplates it achieves some share in infinity.

For this reason greatness of soul is not fostered by those philosophies which assimilate the universe to Man. Knowledge is a form of union of Self and not-Self; like all union, it is impaired by dominion, and therefore by any attempt to force the universe into conformity with what we find in ourselves. There is a widespread philosophical tendency towards the view which tells us that Man is the measure of all things, that truth is man-made, that space and time and the world of universals are properties of the mind, and that, if there be anything not created by the mind, it is unknowable and of no account for us. This view, if our previous discussions were correct, is untrue; but in addition to being untrue, it has the effect of robbing philosophic contemplation of all that gives it value, since it fetters contemplation to Self. What it calls knowledge is not a union with the not-Self, but a set of prejudices, habits, and desires, making an impenetrable veil between us and the world beyond. The man who finds pleasure in such a theory of knowledge is like the man who never leaves the domestic circle for fear his word might not be law.

The true philosophic contemplation, on the contrary, finds its satisfaction in every enlargement of the not-Self, in everything that magnifies the objects contemplated, and thereby the subject contemplating. Everything, in contemplation, that is personal or private, everything that depends upon habit, self-interest, or desire, distorts the object, and hence impairs the union which the intellect seeks. By thus making a barrier between subject and object, such personal and private things become a prison to the intellect. The free intellect will see as God might see, without a *here* and *now,* without hopes and fears, without the trammels of customary beliefs and traditional prejudices, calmly, dispassionately, in the sole and exclusive desire of knowledge—knowledge as impersonal, as purely contemplative, as it is possible for man to attain. Hence also the free intellect will value more the abstract and universal knowledge into which the accidents of private history do not enter, than the knowledge brought by the senses, and dependent, as such knowledge must be, upon an exclusive and personal point of view and a body whose sense-organs distort as much as they reveal.

The mind which has become accustomed to the freedom and impartiality of philosophic contemplation will preserve something of the same freedom and impartiality in the world of action and emotion. It will view its purposes and desires as parts of the whole, with the absence of insistence that results from seeing them as infinitesimal fragments in a world of which all the rest is unaffected by any one man's deeds. The impartiality which, in contemplation, is the unalloyed desire for truth, is the very same quality of mind which, in action, is justice, and in emotion is that universal love which can be given to all, and not only to those who are judged useful or admirable. Thus contemplation enlarges not only the objects of our thoughts, but also the objects of our actions and our affections: it makes us citizens of the universe, not only of one walled city at war with all the rest. In this citizenship of the universe consists man's true freedom, and his liberation from the thraldom of narrow hopes and fears.

Thus, to sum up our discussion of the value of philosophy; philosophy is to be studied, not for the sake of any definite answers to its questions, since no definite answers can, as a rule, be known to be true, but rather for the sake of the questions themselves; because these questions enlarge our conception of what is possible, enrich our intellectual imagination and diminish the dogmatic assurance which closes the mind against speculation; but above all because, through the greatness of the universe which philosophy contemplates, the mind also is rendered great, and becomes capable of that union with the universe which constitutes its highest good.

For Further Reflection

1. Compare Russell's essay with Socrates' thought.

2. Evaluate Russell's contention: "The man who has no tincture of philosophy goes through life imprisoned in the prejudices derived from common sense, from the habitual beliefs of his age or his nation, and from convictions which have grown up in his mind without the cooperation or consent of his deliberate reason. . . . [T]hrough the greatness of the universe which philosophy contemplates, the mind also is rendered great, and becomes capable of that union with the universe which constitutes its highest good."

3. A particularly poignant vignette of his view of the significance of philosophy is recorded in his autobiography, where he relates the experience of seeing Mrs. Whitehead in severe pain. (See the last article in Part VIII.) What sort of view of philosophy do you see in this experience? Is it identical with what you read in Russell's essay, or does it add a new dimension? If you think it does bring in something new, what is that?

Suggestions for Further Reading

Audi, Robert. *The Cambridge Dictionary of Philosophy*. New York: Cambridge University Press, 1996.

Copleston, F. C. *History of Philosophy*. Westminster, MD: Newman, 1966. This eight-volume set is the most comprehensive contemporary work in the history of philosophy.

Cornman, James, and Keith Lehrer. *Philosophical Problems and Arguments*. New York: Macmillan, 1982. A contemporary paradigm of the analytic method.

Edwards, Paul, ed. *Encyclopedia of Philosophy*. New York: Macmillan, 1967. Many of the articles in this eight-volume set are excellent introductions to various aspects of philosophy.

Jones, W. T. *History of Western Philosophy*. New York: Harper & Row, 1976. A lucid, accessible five-volume set.

Miller, Ed. *Questions That Matter*. New York: McGraw-Hill, 1987.

Pojman, Louis. *Philosophy: The Pursuit of Wisdom*, 3rd ed. Belmont, CA: Wadsworth, 2001. A discussion of the topics included in this work.

Rachels, James. *Problems from Philosophy*. New York: McGraw-Hill, 2005.

Russell, Bertrand. *The Problems of Philosophy*. Oxford: Oxford University Press, 1912. Although the perspective is a little dated, this is a well-written, well-thought-out little book from which much can be learned.

Schick, Theodore, and Lewis Vaughn. *Doing Philosophy: An Introduction Through Thought Experiments*, 3rd ed. New York: McGraw-Hill, 2006.

Woodhouse, Mark. *A Preface to Philosophy*. Belmont, CA: Wadsworth, 1984. This little gem is useful in discussing the purposes and methods of philosophical inquiry. It contains lively discussions of informal logic, reading philosophy, and writing philosophical papers.

Excursus: A Little Bit of Logic

Philosophy is centered in the analysis and construction of **arguments**. We call the study of arguments **logic**. By argument we do not mean a verbal fight or quarrel. An argument is the supporting of a thesis (called the **conclusion**) with reasons (called **premises**). Both the conclusion and the premises are set forth in the form of statements—assertions that something is or is not the case (that is, statements that are either true or false). An argument, then, consists of at least two statements: a statement to be supported (the conclusion) and the statement (premise) meant to support it. This process of reasoning from premises to the conclusion is known as **inference**, which we can represent like this:

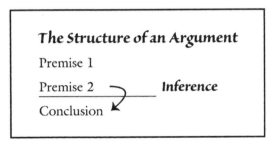

> **The Structure of an Argument**
>
> Premise 1
>
> Premise 2   **Inference**
> ———————
> Conclusion

In philosophy, arguments can be simple or complex, clearly expressed or muddy, neatly labeled or buried in an expanse of nonargumentative text. But they will all have a common structure: premises given to back up a conclusion. Identifying the premises and conclusion is not always easy, but **indicator words** can help. Indicator words frequently accompany arguments and alert you that a premise or conclusion may be nearby. Premise indicators include *because, since, due to the fact that, the reason being, for the reason that,* and *inasmuch as.* Some conclusion indicators are *therefore, it follows that, thus, so, it must be that, consequently,* and *we can conclude that.* In any case, probably the best technique for identifying the parts of an argument is to try to find the conclusion first.

Arguments can be good or bad. A good argument shows that its conclusion is worthy of acceptance; a bad argument fails to do this. In a good argument, the inference is solid *and* the premises are true. Bad arguments fail on one or both counts.

Deductive and Inductive Reasoning

Arguments are of two types—**deductive** and **inductive**. A deductive argument is supposed to give logically *conclusive* support to its conclusion. An inductive argument is supposed to give *probable* support to its conclusion. Both kinds of arguments are used not just in philosophy, but in every endeavor in life that calls for intelligent, reasoned inquiry.

Deductive Arguments

A deductive argument that succeeds in providing logically conclusive support for its conclusion is said to be *valid;* one that fails to provide such support is said to be *invalid.* In a valid argument, if the premises are true, the conclusion *must be true.* The logical structure of a valid argument (its pattern of inference) is such that *if* the premises are true, the conclusion cannot possibly be false. The logical structure *guarantees* the truth of the conclusion if the premises are true. Because of this guarantee, deductively valid arguments are said to be *truth-preserving.* Consider this classic valid argument:

1. Socrates is a man.
2. All men are mortal.
3. ∴ Socrates is mortal. (The symbol ∴ stands for *therefore.*)

And this valid argument:

1. If philosophy leads to wisdom, then it is worth studying.
2. Philosophy leads to wisdom.
3. ∴ Philosophy is worth studying.

In both arguments, you can see that *if* the premises are true, there is no way the conclusion can be false. This result is due to the argument's form, not its content. Thus, *valid* refers to the form and is not a synonym for *true.* We could set up many other arguments of the same inferential form and plug any statements we wanted into the form, and we would get the same result: If the premises are true, the conclusion will be true. Of course, the premises or conclusion of a valid argument may *not* be true. The only limit on the possible combinations is that a valid argument cannot possibly have true premises and a false conclusion.

In philosophy the form of an argument is sometimes indicated by using letters to represent the argument's statements. So we can signify, or symbolize, the form of the second argument tike this:

1. If *P,* then *Q.*
2. *P.*
3. ∴ *Q.*

Try substituting different statements into this form, and you will see the result is always a valid argument. (This form is known as a conditional, or hypothetical, argument because it contains at least one conditional, or if-then, premise. The first part of a conditional premise—the *if* part—is called the *antecedent;* the second—the *then* part—is called the *consequent.*)

Now consider this deductively *invalid* argument:

1. If Mary is sneezing, then she has a cold.
2. Mary is not sneezing.
3. ∴ She does not have a cold.

The conclusion certainly does not follow from the premises. It is possible for the premises to be true, and the conclusion false.

As we mentioned, a good deductive argument must not only be valid, but also have true premises. When an argument meets both these requirements, it is said to be *sound*. An argument that falls short of either requirement is not sound—it can be valid with false premises, or invalid with true premises, or invalid with false premises. Again, the quality of the reasoning is one thing; the truth of the premises another.

Here is an example of a sound argument:

1. If Mary is a mother, she must be a woman.

2. Mary is a mother (for she has just given birth to a baby).

3. ∴ Mary is a woman.

If Mary hasn't given birth, then premise 2 is false, and the argument is unsound.

$$\boxed{\text{Validity}} + \boxed{\text{All True Premises}} = \boxed{\text{Soundness}}$$

Some deductive argument forms are so common and so useful that they have been given names. They deserve special attention—and even memorization. Among the most famous ones are *modus ponens, modus tollens, disjunctive syllogism,* and *reductio ad absurdum*:

Modus Ponens (MP)
(*Affirming the Antecedent*)

1. If *P*, then *Q*.
2. *P*.
3. ∴ *Q*.

Modus Tollens (MT)
(*Denying the Consequent*)

1. If *P*, then *Q*.
2. Not *Q*.
3. ∴ Not *P*.

Both affirming the antecedent and denying the consequent are valid forms.

Disjunctive Syllogism (DS)
(*Denying the Disjunct*)

1. Either *P* or *Q*.

2. Not *Q*.

3. ∴ *P*.

Reductio ad Absurdum (RAA)
(*Reduce to a Contradiction*)

1. Assume *A* (*A* is the logical opposite of the conclusion you seek to prove).

2. Logically deduce a contradiction from *A*. (This shows that *A* implies a contradiction.)

3. This proves *A* is false, since a contradiction cannot be true. So not-*A* must be true.

We have already given examples of *modus ponens*, the last one being:

1. If Mary is a mother, she must be a woman.

2. Mary is a mother.

3. ∴ Mary is a woman.

Here is an example of *modus tollens*:

1. If Leslie is a mother, she is a woman.

2. Leslie is not a woman (but a man).

3. ∴ Leslie is not a mother.

Here is an example of a *disjunctive syllogism* (sometimes called "denying the disjunct"—a *disjunct* refers to a proposition with an "or" statement in it, such as "*P* or *Q*").

1. John is either a bachelor or a married man.

2. We know for certain that John is not married.

3. ∴ John is a bachelor.

We turn to *reductio ad absurdum* (RAA). This is an indirect method of proving or establishing a thesis. You assume the opposite of what you want to prove and show that it produces an absurd conclusion. Therefore, your thesis must be true. Here is an example of a *reductio ad absurdum*. It is a little more complicated than the other forms, but it is important especially in reference to the ontological argument (see Readings II.10 and II.11). Suppose that someone denies that there is such a thing as a self, and you want to refute the assertion. You might argue in the following manner:

1. Suppose that you're correct, and there is no such thing as a self (not *A*).

2. But if there is no such thing as a self, then no one ever acts (if not *A*, then not *B*).

3. But if no one ever acts, then no one can utter meaningful statements (if not *B*, then not *C*).

4. But you have purported to utter a meaningful statement in saying that there is no such thing as a self, so there is at least one meaningful statement (*C*).

5. According to your argument, there is and there is not at least one meaningful statement (*C* and not *C*).

6. ∴ It must be false that there is no such thing as a self (not, not *A*—which by double negation yields *A*). Thus, we have proved by *reductio ad absurdum* that there is such a thing as a self.

Before we leave the realm of deductive argument, we must point out two invalid forms that often give students trouble. To understand them, look back at forms MP and MT, which respectively argue by affirming the antecedent and denying the consequent. But notice that there are two other possible forms. You can also deny the antecedent and affirm the consequent in the following manner:

Denying the Antecedent (DA)	Affirming the Consequent (AC)
1. If *P*, then *Q*.	1. If *P*, then *Q*.
2. Not *P*.	2. *Q*.
3. ∴ Not *Q*.	3. ∴ *P*.

Are these valid forms? Remember a valid form must always yield true conclusions if the premises are true. Try to find a counterexample that will show that these two forms are invalid. You might let proposition 1 (if *P*, then *Q*) be represented by the previous proposition, "If Mary is a mother, then she is a woman." First, deny the antecedent. Does it necessarily yield a true conclusion? Not necessarily. The conclusion says that Mary is not a woman, but there are many women who are not mothers. So DA is an invalid form:

1. If Mary is a mother, she is a woman.

2. Mary is not a mother.

3. ∴ Mary is not a woman.

Take the same initial proposition and affirm the consequent "Mary is a woman." Does this in itself yield the conclusion that she is a mother? Of course not. She could be a woman without being a mother:

1. If Mary is a mother, she is a woman.

2. She is a woman.

3. ∴ Mary is a mother.

Thus, whereas MP and MT are valid forms, DA and AC are not. Be careful here. Many students slur over these distinctions. Work out your own examples of each form of argument.

These are just simple examples of deductive argument forms. Often, alas, it is difficult to state exactly what the author's premises are.

Inductive Arguments

Unlike deductive arguments, inductive arguments are not truth-preserving. An inductive argument cannot guarantee that if its premises are true, the conclusion will also be true. It is intended to provide only probable support to its conclusion—that is, support that renders the conclusion more likely to be true than not. An inductive argument that succeeds in providing such probable support is said to be *strong*. If its premises are true, then the conclusion is likely to be true. An inductive argument that fails to provide this level of support is said to be *weak*. A strong argument with true premises is considered *cogent*.

Inductive reasoning is the guiding light of scientific investigations and the primary means by which we come to know the workings of the empirical world. If we learn anything from experience, it likely comes by way of induction. Inductive arguments allow us to reason from the evidence we have in hand to new knowledge, to conclusions established by degrees of probability.

Inductive arguments take several familiar forms. Sometimes we reason inductively from premises about a group of things to a conclusion about a single member of the group. For example:

1. Ninety percent of the students attending this college are religious.

2. Maria attends this college.

3. ∴ Maria is probably religious.

1. Almost all the apples in the barrel are rotten.

2. ∴ The next apple I take out of the barrel will likely be rotten too.

Another common inductive argument form reasons from premises about a few members of a group to conclusions about the group as a whole—an argument pattern known as *enumerative induction*. Consider:

1. Half the students I've met at this college (ten students) are agnostics.

2. ∴ Half of all the students at this college are agnostics.

In enumerative induction the group generalized about is called the *target group* (all the students at the college, in the example). The observed or known members of the group are called the *sample* (the students met so far). To reach reliable conclusions about a target group, the sample must be large enough and representative of the whole target group. The agnostics argument is weak because the sample is much too small to reach reliable conclusions about the entire student population. Such an undersized sample is also unlikely to be representative of all the students. That is, it is unlikely to resemble the target group in all the relevant ways. Drawing conclusions about a target group based on a sample that is too small is a common error known as *hasty generalization*. Opinion polls—which are essentially enumerative inductions—usually avoid such errors by using large, representative samples. They can therefore reach reliable conclusions about the characteristics of all American adults, say, by using a representative sample of only 1,200 to 1,500 individuals.

When we should know better, generalizing about groups of people from inadequate samples is pure prejudice. If a child infers from only six bad experiences with people from Podunkville that all people in Podunkville are bad, that might be overlooked. However, if an adult who could easily have evidence that many good people live in Podunkville still makes such a faulty generalization and acts accordingly, we label that an irrational bias, a prejudice.

A special kind of induction reasoning is called *reasoning by analogy* (see the teleological argument Readings II.8 and II.9 for its use). Reasoning by analogy allows us to reason from the similarity of two things in some relevant respects to their similarity in an unexpected respect. For example, suppose I am lost in the forest and I want to determine whether to eat a certain mushroom, which my hungry stomach craves. I note that it is similar in shape, color, and constituency with other mushrooms that turned out to be edible. Thus, I infer that probably this mushroom will be edible too.

Inference to the Best Explanation

Another kind of inductive reasoning, both prevalent and powerful, is **inference to the best explanation** (or abduction). Here we reason from premises about a state of affairs to an explanation for that state of affairs. The premises are statements about the facts of a phenomenon or situation (usually based on observations or other kinds of evidence), and the explanation is a statement about why the facts are as they are. Arguments of this form are used widely in philosophy, science, ethics, the law, medicine, and everyday life. Consider this one, a typical line of reasoning in criminal trials:

1. The defendant was holding the murder weapon—a pistol—when the police entered the room.

2. The victim's blood was on the defendant's shirt.

3. An eyewitness saw the defendant enter the room holding a pistol and then heard a gunshot.

4. No one else was in the room at the time of the murder.

5. The best explanation of these facts is that the defendant committed the murder.

6. ∴ The defendant probably committed the murder.

As in all good inductive arguments, the conclusion here is shown to be only probable, and there is no guarantee of its truth. If the explanation given (statement 5) really is the best, then the argument is strong. If the premises are also true, then the argument is cogent.

Inference to the best explanation is especially important in science, where scientists advance their knowledge by positing theories or hypotheses to explain a set of data, then evaluating those explanations to see which is best. To explain the peculiarities of planetary motion, scientists proposed the heliocentric (sun-centered) theory as an alternative to the traditional earth-centered (Ptolemaic) view. The former turned out to be the better explanation, and the latter was discarded. Through this potent type of inference, scientists have plumbed great mysteries and discovered everything from vaccines to quarks to black holes.

One of the more famous and astute users of this kind of reasoning was none other than the fictional Sherlock Holmes:

> The portly client puffed out his chest with an appearance of some little pride and pulled a dirty and wrinkled newspaper from the inside pocket of his greatcoat. As he glanced down the advertisement column with his head thrust forward and the paper flattened out upon his knee, I took a good look at the man and endeavored, after the fashion of my companion, to read the indications which might be presented by his dress or appearance.
>
> I did not gain very much, however, by my inspection. Our visitor bore every mark of being an average commonplace British tradesman, obese, pompous, and slow. He wore rather baggy gray shepherd's check trousers, a not over-clean black frock-coat, unbuttoned in the front, and a drab waistcoat with a heavy brassy Albert chain, and a square pierced bit of metal dangling down as an ornament. A frayed top-hat and a faded brown overcoat with a wrinkled velvet collar lay upon a chair beside him. Altogether, look as I would, there was nothing remarkable about the man save his blazing red head and the expression of extreme chagrin and discontent upon his features.
>
> Sherlock Holmes's quick eye took in my occupation, and he shook his head with a smile as he noticed my questioning glances. "Beyond the obvious facts that he has at some time done manual labour, that he takes snuff, that he is a Freemason, that he has been in China, and that he has done a considerable amount of writing lately, I can *deduce* nothing else." Mr. Jabez Wilson started up in his chair, with his forefinger upon the paper, but his eyes upon my companion.

"How, in the name of good-fortune did you know all that, Mr. Holmes?" he asked. "How did you know, for example, that I did manual labour? It's as true as gospel, for I began as a ship's carpenter."

"Your hands, my dear sir. Your right hand is quite a size larger than your left. You have worked with it, and the muscles are more developed."

"Well, the snuff, then, and the Freemasonry?"

"I won't insult your intelligence by telling you how I read that, especially as, rather against the strict rules of your order, you use an arc-and-compass breastpin."

"Ah, of course, I forgot that. But the writing?"

"What else can be indicated by that right cuff so very shiny for five inches, and the left one with the smooth patch near the elbow where you rest it upon the desk?"

"Well, but China?"

"The fish which you have tattooed immediately above your right wrist could only have been done in China. I have made a small study of tattoo marks and have even contributed to the literature of the subject. That trick of staining the fishes' scales of a delicate pink is quite peculiar to China. When, in addition, I see a Chinese coin hanging from your watchchain, the matter becomes even more simple."

Mr. Jabez Wilson laughed heavily. "Well, I never!" said he. "I thought at first that you had done something clever, but I see that there was nothing in it, after all."[1]

Philosophers appreciate Mr. Wilson's final remark, that Holmes' explanation makes so much sense that one wonders why one didn't think of it oneself. Holmes often chided Watson: "You see, but you do not observe." A good philosopher, like a good detective or scientist, observes while he or she sees.

There is, however, a significant inaccuracy in Holmes' description of what he does. He claims to be deducing the conclusions about Mr. Wilson from the telltale signs. Strictly speaking, he is doing no such thing. What Holmes has really done is reason abductively, that is, reason to the best explanation of the facts. The best explanation of Mr. Wilson's wearing the arc-and-compass breastpin is his belonging to the Freemasons. The best explanation of a child's having a fever and red spots is that she has the measles. The best explanation of the puddles outside is that it has recently rained.

The notion of the best explanation is fascinating in its own right. How do we discover the best explanation? What characteristics does it have? How do we rank various virtues of a good explanation? There are no definite answers to these questions, but it is generally agreed that such criteria as predictability, coherence, simplicity, and fruitfulness are among the main yardsticks for judging theories. If a theory helps us predict future events, that is a powerful weapon. If it coheres well with everything or nearly everything else that we hold true in the field, that lends support to it. If it is simpler than its rivals, if it rests on fewer assumptions, that is a virtue. If it leads to new insight and discoveries, that is also a point in its favor. But what if explanatory theory A has more of one of these features and theory B more of another? Which should we prefer? There is no decision-making formula to decide the matter with any finality. Ultimately, applying the criteria and weighing theories comes down to reasoned judgment.

Inference to the best explanation has been neglected in philosophy, but it really is of the utmost importance. Consider the following questions: Why do you believe in God? Why do you believe in evolutionary theory? Why do you believe that there are universal moral principles? Why do you believe that all events are caused? In one way or another, the answer will probably be abductive: What you believe seems to you to be the best explanation among all the competitors of certain phenomena. We will have opportunity to use abductive reasoning at several points during our course of study.

Identifying Arguments

Consider these simple arguments:

1. Because banning assault rifles violates a constitutional right, the U.S. government should not ban assault rifles.
2. The *Wall Street Journal* says that people should invest heavily in stocks. Therefore, investing in stocks is a smart move.
3. When Judy drives her car, she's always late. Since she's driving her car now, she will be late.
4. Listen, any movie with clowns in it cannot be a good movie. Last night's movie had at least a dozen clowns in it. Consequently it was awful.
5. The war on terrorism must include a massive military strike on nation X because without this intervention, terrorists cannot be defeated. They will always be able to find safe haven and support in the X regime. Even if terrorists are scattered around the world, support from nation X will increase their chances of surviving and launching new attacks.
6. No one should buy a beer brewed in Canada. Old Guzzler beer is brewed in Canada, so no one should buy it.

Here are the same arguments laid out so the parts are easily identified:

1. [Premise] Because banning assault rifles violates a constitutional right, [Conclusion] the U.S. government should not ban assault rifles.
2. [Premise] The *Wall Street Journal* says that people should invest heavily in stocks.
   [Conclusion] Therefore, investing in stocks is a smart move.
3. [Premise] When Judy drives her car, she's always late.
   [Premise] Since she's driving her car now,
   [Conclusion] she will be late.
4. [Premise] Any movie with clowns in it cannot be a good movie.
   [Premise] Last night's movie had at least a dozen clowns in it.
   [Conclusion] Consequently it was awful.
5. [Premise] Without a military intervention in nation X, terrorists cannot be defeated.
   [Premise] They will always be able to find safe haven and support in the X regime.
   [Premise] Even if terrorists are scattered around the world, support from nation X will increase their chances of surviving and launching new attacks.

[Conclusion] The war on terrorism must include a massive military strike on nation X.

6. [Premise] No one should buy a beer brewed in Canada.
   [Premise] Old Guzzler beer is brewed in Canada.
   [Conclusion] So no one should buy it.

What all of these arguments have in common is that reasons (the premises) are offered to support or prove a claim (the conclusion). This logical link between premises and conclusion is what distinguishes arguments from all other kinds of discourse.

Now consider this passage:

> The cost of the new XJ fighter plane is $650 million. The cost of three AR21 fighter-bombers is $1.2 billion. The administration intends to fund such projects.

Is there an argument here? No. This passage consists of several claims, but no reasons are presented to support any particular claim (conclusion), including the last sentence. This passage can be turned into an argument, though, with some minor editing:

> The GAO says that any weapon that costs more than $50 million apiece will actually impair our military readiness. The cost of the new XJ fighter plane is $650 million dollars. The cost of three AR21 fighter-bombers is $1.2 billion. We should never impair our readiness. Therefore, the administration should cancel both these projects.

Now we have an argument because reasons are given for accepting a conclusion. Here's another passage:

> Allisha went to the bank to get a more recent bank statement of her checking account. The teller told her that the balance was $1725. Allisha was stunned that it was so low. She called her brother to see if he had been playing one of his twisted pranks. He hadn't. Finally, she concluded that she had been a victim of bank fraud.

Where is the conclusion? Where are the reasons? There are none. This is a little narrative hung on some descriptive claims. But it's not an argument. It could be turned into an argument if, say, some of the claims were restated as reasons for the conclusion that bank fraud had been committed.

Being able to distinguish between passages that do and do not contain arguments is a very basic skill—and an extremely important one. Many people think that if they have clearly stated their beliefs on a subject, they have presented an argument. But a mere declaration of beliefs is not an argument. Often such assertions of opinion are just a jumble of unsupported claims. Search high and low and you will not find an argument anywhere. A writer or speaker of these claims gives the readers or listeners no grounds for believing the claims. In writing courses, the absence of supporting premises is sometimes called "a lack of development."

Here are three more examples of verbiage sans argument:

> Attributing alcohol abuse by children too young to buy a drink to lack of parental discipline, intense pressure to succeed, and affluence incorrectly draws

attention to proximate causes while ignoring the ultimate cause: a culture that tolerates overt and covert marketing of alcohol, tobacco and sex to these easily manipulated, voracious consumers.—Letter to the editor, *New York Times*

[A recent column in this newspaper] deals with the living quarters of Bishop William Murphy of the Diocese of Rockville Centre. I am so disgusted with the higher-ups in the church that at times I am embarrassed to say I am Catholic. To know that my parents' hard-earned money went to lawyers and payoffs made me sick. Now I see it has also paid for a high-end kitchen. I am enraged. I will never make a donation again.—Letter to the editor, *Newsday*

I don't understand what is happening to this country. The citizens of this country are trying to destroy the beliefs of our forefathers with their liberal views. This country was founded on Christian beliefs. This has been and I believe still is the greatest country in the world. But the issue that we cannot have prayer in public places and on public property because there has to be separation of church and state is a farce.—Letter to the editor, *Douglas County Sentinel*

The passage on alcohol abuse in children is not an argument but an unsupported assertion about the causes of the problems. The passage from the disappointed Catholic is an expression of outrage (which may or may not be justified), but no conclusion is put forth, and no reasons supporting a conclusion are offered. Note the contentious tone in the third passage. This passage smells like an argument. But, alas, there is no argument. Each sentence is a claim presented without support.

Some Applications

Let us apply these brief lessons of logic to reading philosophy. Because the key to philosophy is the argument, you will want to concentrate and even outline the author's reasoning. Find his or her thesis or conclusion. Usually, it is stated early on. After this, identify the premises that support or lead to the conclusion. For example, Thomas Aquinas (1224–1274) holds the conclusion that God exists. He argues for this conclusion in five different ways. In the second argument, he uses the following premises to reach his conclusion: There is motion, and there cannot be motion without something initiating the motion.

It helps to outline the premises of the argument. For example, here's how we might set forth Aquinas' second argument:

1. Some things are in motion. (Premise)

2. Nothing in the world can move itself but must be moved by another. (Premise)

3. There cannot be an infinite regress of motions. (Premise)

4. There must be a First Mover who is responsible for all other motion. (Conclusion of premises 1–3, which in turn becomes a premise for the rest of the argument)

5. This First Mover is what we call God. (Explanation of the meaning of God) (Premise)

6. ∴ God exists. (Conclusion of second part of the argument, premises 4 and 5)

After you have identified the premises and conclusion, analyze them, looking for mistakes in the reasoning process. Sometimes arguments are faulty, but not obviously so. Then stretch your imagination and think of possible counter-examples to the claims of the author.

Because philosophical arguments are often complex and subtle (and because philosophers do not always write as clearly as they should), a full understanding of an essay is not readily available after a single reading. So read it twice or even thrice. Here is one good approach: the first time you read a philosophy essay, read it for understanding. After the first reading, leave the essay for some time, ruminating on it. Then go back a day or so later and read the essay a second time, this time, trying to determine its soundness.

A few pointers should be mentioned along the way. Some students find it helpful to keep a notebook on their reflections on the readings. If you own the book, you might want to make notes in the margins—initially in pencil because you may want to revise your impressions after a second reading.

Finally, practice charity. Give the author the best possible interpretation in order to see if the argument has merit. Always try to deal with the most generous version of the argument, especially if you don't agree with its conclusion. A position has not been seriously challenged unless the best arguments for it have been refuted. That's why it is necessary to construe all arguments, including those of your opponents, as charitably as possible. The exercise will broaden your horizons and help you develop sharper reasoning skills.

Fallacies of Reasoning

As we have seen, arguments can be defective either because their reasoning is faulty or their premises are false, or both. Certain kinds of faulty arguments are extremely common—and seductive—persuading many that they have hit solid truth when it is only thin air. These parodies of reasoning are known as *fallacies*. Studying them helps us identify them and avoid both being taken in by them and concocting them ourselves. Here are some of them, listed by their common names.

Ad Hominem Argument (or an argument against the man). This argument attacks the person instead of the position—for example, if someone says to you, "You can't trust what Joan says about abortion, she is an immoral person." But, of course, her argument for or against abortion might be sound on independent grounds. Even the devil has true beliefs. The character of the person is irrelevant to the soundness of the argument.

Argument from Authority Suppose you are arguing about the death penalty, and someone tells you that you should believe in the death penalty because Plato believed in it.

Since you don't know Plato's reasons, it is not sufficient grounds for you to believe in the death penalty. We need positive arguments, not simply authority. Advertisements are notorious for subtly and sometimes not so subtly using this device. In a beer commercial, a famous athlete (nicely remunerated for the exercise) can be seen gratifying his thirst, proclaiming the ecstasy of the beverage, as if that were proof of its quality.

Of course, authority might sometimes be the best we can get and sufficient for justified belief, as when a physicist tells us the conclusions of complicated physics research or a friend from Australia gives you pertinent information for your upcoming visit to that country. We sometimes do need to trust authority, but often it is an improper substitute for good reasoning.

Arguing in a Circle (sometimes referred to as "begging the question"). Suppose that someone argues that you should believe that God exists. You ask why. He says, "Because the Bible says so." You ask, "Why should I believe what the Bible says?" He replies, "Because it's the Word of God." That is, he argues in a circle, using his conclusion as a premise to prove the conclusion. Note that all valid deductive argument can appear as arguing in a circle, since the conclusion of such an argument is contained in the premises. The difference is that in a valid argument the conclusion brings out a nontrivial feature of the premises. Essentially, arguing in a circle is not invalid, just trivial and unconvincing, having no power to convince an opponent.

Appeal to Ignorance To use this fallacious ploy is to argue that a *lack of evidence* proves something. In one form of this fallacy, you argue that a conclusion must be true because no one has shown it to be false. For example:

1. Nobody has shown that God does not exist.

2. ∴ God exists.

Here a lack of evidence is supposed to prove something, but a lack of evidence alone can neither prove nor disprove a claim. If we have no evidence for a claim, then we have no reason for believing it. The lack does not prove the claim false.

In another form of the appeal to ignorance, you argue that a conclusion must be false because no one has shown it to be true:

1. Nobody has proven that God exists.

2. ∴ God does not exist.

If either version of this fallacy were credible, we could prove almost anything by citing a lack of evidence. For example: You cannot prove that gremlins are not hiding in this textbook, so gremlins must be hiding there. You cannot prove that Aristotle had blue eyes; therefore he did not have blue eyes.

False Dilemma This happens when we reduce several possibilities to two alternatives. Consider two travelers facing a swamp in which traveler A says to traveler B: "Since you admit you don't know the way through the swamp and there must be a way, follow me. I must know the way." Of course, neither might know the way. Likewise, someone can argue that since your answer to a problem isn't correct, his or hers must be. But, of course, both can be wrong.

Slippery Slope Fallacy This fallacy consists of arguing, without good reasons, that taking a particular step will inevitably lead to further, undesirable (usually catastrophic) steps. The basic form of the argument is "Doing action A will lead to action B, which will result in disastrous action C. Therefore you should not do action A." The argument is fallacious if there is no good reason to believe that doing action A will lead to action C. Robert Wright has argued that "once you buy the premise that animals can experience pain and pleasure, and that their welfare therefore deserves *some* consideration, you're on the road to comparing yourself with a lobster. There may be some exit ramps along the way—plausible places to separate welfare from rights—but I can't find any." Others have argued that if we allow voluntary euthanasia, we are on the slippery slope to involuntary euthanasia, even eventually to a holocaust. Still others have argued that if we pass a National Health Care bill, it will inevitably lead to socialism and communism. The slippery slope fallacy ignores the truth that very often wise policy is a moderate stance between two extremes and that rational people can hold to a rational position without going to an extreme.

Straw Man Argument This is an instance of misrepresenting an opponent's position. It occurs when someone ignores the evidence for a position and instead attacks an inferior version of the position. In the heat of debate on whether our nation should reduce its military spending, a militarist might argue that his opponent wants to leave our nation defenseless or a willing prey to communism. The straw man argument is often a distortion of the other person's position. There is a tendency in all of us to attack a weaker, less plausible version of our opponent's position. The *principle of charity* is the opposite of the straw man argument. It instructs us to give our opponent's position the very best form we can find—and then try to show it is unsound.

Genetic Fallacy This fallacy is arguing against a position or argument merely because its origins are suspect. Suppose someone tells you not to believe in the principles of chemistry because they originated in superstitious alchemy or that you should not believe in an astronomical theory because it arose from astrological sources. The fact that a theory or position originated in discredited circumstances is irrelevant if the theory is supported by the evidence. Chemistry and astronomy can produce impressive evidence for their theories that is independent of the authority of alchemy and astrology. It doesn't matter where the truth comes from, as long as it is true.

Fallacy of Composition This fallacy consists of an erroneous inference from the part to the whole. That is, because each part has an attribute, the whole is said to have the same attribute. For example sodium and chlorine are each deadly poisons, so that sodium chlorine must be a deadly poison. But it's not. It's ordinary table salt. The whole can have different properties from its parts. Here is another example: Each member of the football team is an excellent player, therefore the team must be excellent. But it might not be, for their individual excellences might not transfer into the right combination. For example, they might all be excellent halfbacks and quarterbacks, but none be good at blocking. Is the following an example of this fallacy: *Because every part of the world exhibits design, the whole must exhibit design?*

Inconsistency When we argue inconsistently, we argue from contradictory premises. Politicians, when trying to win votes from one constituency, sometimes contradict what they have said to other constituencies. For an illustration of this consider some statements made by former President Ronald Reagan at different periods of his political career:

On Civil Rights

1. I favor the Civil Rights Act of 1964 and it must be enforced at the point of a bayonet, if necessary (October 19, 1965).
2. I would have voted against the Civil Rights Act of 1964 (June 16, 1966).

On Redwood National Park

1. I believe our country can and should have a Redwood National Park in California (April 17, 1967).
2. There can be no proof given that a national park is necessary to preserve the redwoods. The state of California has already maintained a great conservation program (April 18, 1967—the next day).

On the Soviet Grain Embargo

1. I just don't believe the farmers should be made to pay a special price for our diplomacy, and I'm opposed to [the Soviet grain embargo] (January 7, 1980).
2. If we are going to do such a thing to the Soviet Union as a full grain embargo, which I support, first we have to be sure our own allies would join us on this (January 8, 1980, the next day).[2]

Of course, people change their minds and come to believe the opposite of what they formerly believed. That might show progress. But many of us are not aware of the inconsistencies in our own belief systems. For example, Fred might believe that morality entails universalizing principles (what's good for the goose is good for the gander), but fail to note that his view that premarital sex is morally permissible for men but not for women is inconsistent with that principle.

Exercises in Critical Reasoning

I. Analyze the following arguments and tell whether they are *valid* and *sound*:

1) 1. If Missy is a cat, then she is a mammal.
   2. Missy is not a mammal.
   3. Therefore she is not a cat.

2) 1. If Fido is a dog, then he is a mammal.
   2. Fido is a dog.
   3. Therefore he is a mammal.

3) 1. If nine hundred million people die of malnutrition each year, something needs to be done about the distribution of food.

   2. Nothing needs to be done about the distribution of food.

   3. Therefore [fill in the blank].

4) 1. If Fido is a dog, then he is a mammal.

   2. Fido is *not* a dog.

   3. Therefore Fido is not a mammal.

5) 1. If Fido is a dog, then he is a mammal.

   2. Fido is a mammal.

   3. Therefore he is a dog.

6) 1. If my boyfriend, John, is a dog, then he is a mammal.

   2. John is a mammal.

   3. Therefore John is a dog.

7) 1. If we keep burning so much coal and oil, the greenhouse effect will continue to get worse.

   2. But it will be a disaster if the greenhouse effect gets worse.

   3. Therefore, we have to cut down on these fossil fuels.

8) 1. If this wire is made of copper it will conduct electricity.

   2. This wire conducts electricity.

   3. Therefore this wire is made of copper.

9) 1. If a world government doesn't occur soon, then we're in for a lot more terrorism and war.

   2. A world government isn't going to occur soon.

   3. Therefore we're in for a lot more terrorism and war.

10) 1. Either the Yankees will win the American League pennant or their manager will get fired.

    2. The Yankees will not win the American League pennant.

    3. Therefore, the manager will get fired.

II. Indicate whether the following arguments are *strong* or *weak*.

1) The three fish that I caught in this stream were bass, so all the fish in this stream must be bass.

2) One thousand samples of water taken from sites all along the Miami river show unsafe concentrations of toxic chemicals. Therefore, the water in the river is unsafe.

3) Seventy percent of adults in Cincinnati and 90 percent of adults in Orange County, California, are conservatives. So a large majority of people in this country are conservatives.

4) All the evidence in this trial suggests that Mack the Knife committed the murder. There can be only one conclusion: He is guilty.

5) For the past year, every time Aziz left his apartment, he forgot to lock the door. He will probably forget this time, too.

6) Eighty percent of Americans believe in an afterlife, and 75 percent of Canadians do. Therefore the afterlife is a reality.

7) You should buy a Dell computer. They're great. I bought one last year and it has given me nothing but flawless performance.

8) All the celebrities highlighted on Fox TV have drug problems. Why are all the celebrities such stoners?

9) I have asked twenty undergraduates at this school if they believe in God, and ten of them have said yes. So half of the undergraduates at this school must be atheists.

10) Almost every Arabic-speaking person interviewed by CNN thinks that the United States is evil. Clearly, Arabic-speaking people throughout the world believe that the United States is evil.

III. *Fallacies of Reasoning.* Find an example of each of the following fallacies:

1. Ad Hominem Arguments
2. Arguments from Authority
3. Arguing in a Circle (Begging the Question)
4. Appeal to Ignorance
5. False Dilemma
6. Slippery Slope Fallacy
7. Straw Man Arguments
8. Genetic Fallacy
9. Fallacy of Composition
10. Inconsistency

IV. Symbolize the form of the following arguments and tell whether they are valid. Where possible, identify the form by name.

1) 1. If Mary gets the job, then she will be happy.
   2. Mary will get the job.
   3. Therefore, Mary will be happy.

2) 1. If Napoleon was born in Chicago, he was Emperor of France.
   2. Napoleon was not born in Chicago.
   3. Therefore Napoleon was not Emperor of France.

3) An Environmental Argument:
   1. If I wash, I'll pollute the water.

2. If I don't wash, I'll pollute the air.

3. Therefore whatever I do I will be a polluter.

4) 1. All cadets at military institutions are drug-free.

2. Timothy Leary was once a West Point cadet (a true statement).

3. Therefore Timothy was drug-free.

5) 1. If John is a bachelor, he is unmarried.

2. John is married.

3. Therefore [fill in blank].

6) 1. If Mary gets the job, she will be happy.

2. If she is happy, then her husband will be happy.

3. If her husband is happy, her mother-in-law will be happy.

4. If her mother-in-law is happy, her mother-in-law's boss, Bob, will be happy.

5. If Bob will be happy, his dog will be happy.

6. Therefore [fill in the blank].

7) 1. All dogs are animals.

2. All cats are animals.

3. Therefore all dogs are cats.

8) 1. If the fetus is a person, abortion is immoral.

2. Abortion is not immoral.

3. Therefore, the fetus is not a person.

Study and Discussion Questions

1. What is an argument? Using the argument forms discussed in this chapter, construct an argument of your own for each form shown.

2. Explain the difference between deductive, inductive, and abductive reasoning.

3. Explain the difference between validity and soundness.

4. Get a copy of your student newspaper or your local newspaper and analyze two arguments therein. Begin to look at the claims of others in argument form.

5. Philosophy can be seen as an attempt to solve life's perennial puzzles. Taking the material at hand, it tries to unravel enigmas by thought alone. See what you can do with the puzzles and paradoxes included here.

   a.   There is a barber in Barberville who shaves all and only those barbers who do not shave themselves. Does this barber shave himself?

   Who does shave him?

b. You are the sole survivor of a shipwreck and are drifting in a small raft parallel to the coast of an island. You know that on this island there are only two tribes of natives: Nobles, kind folk who *always* tell the truth, and Savages, cannibals who always lie. Naturally, you want to find refuge with the Nobles. You see a man standing on the shore and call out, "Are you a Noble or a Savage?" The man answers the question, but a wave breaks on the beach at that very moment, so you don't hear the reply. The boat drifts farther down along the shore when you see another man. You ask him the same question, and he replies, pointing to the first man, "He said he was a Noble." Then he continues, "I am a Noble." Your boat drifts farther down the shore where you see a third man. You ask him the same question. The man seems very friendly as he calls out, "They are both liars. I am a Noble. They are Savages."

The puzzle: Is the data given sufficient to tell you any man's tribe? Is it sufficient to tell you each man's tribe?

c. Mrs. Smith, a schoolteacher, announces to her class on Friday that there will be a surprise test during the following week. She defines "surprise test" as one that no one could reasonably predict on the day of the test. Johnny, one of her students, responds that she may not give the test on pain of contradicting herself. Mrs. Smith asks, "Why not?" Johnny replies, "You cannot give the test on Friday because on Friday everyone would know that the test would take place on that day, and so it would not be a surprise. So the test must take place on a day between Monday and Thursday. But it cannot take place on Thursday, for if it hasn't taken place by then, it would not be a surprise on Thursday. So the test must take place between Monday and Wednesday. But it cannot take place on Wednesday for the same reason that we rejected Friday and Thursday. Similarly, we can use the same reason to exclude Tuesday and Monday. On no day of the week can a surprise test be given. So the test cannot be given next week."

Mrs. Smith heard Johnny's argument and wondered what the solution was. She gave the test on Tuesday, and everyone was surprised, including Johnny.

How was this possible?

d. It is sometimes said that space is empty, which means presumably that there is nothing between two stars. But if there is nothing between stars, then they are not separated by anything, and, thus, they must be right up against one another, perhaps forming some peculiar sort of double star. We know this not to be the case, of course.[3]

What follows from this puzzle?

6. A good reason to be a critical thinker is to avoid getting cheated. Occasionally, you may be in danger of being duped by an unscrupulous salesperson. Thinking clearly may save you. Here is an example of such a situation that occurred after the Loma Prieta earthquake in the California Bay Area in 1989.

Last week the 55 year old [Eva] Davis was evicted from her . . . home of 22 years by San Francisco sheriff's deputies. Her troubles began in 1990 when a contractor offered to repair front steps damaged in the Loma Prieta earthquake. Two hours later came a disaster worse than an earthquake, a disaster with a smile, a representative of Congress Mortgage Co. of San Jose. Convinced that she was getting a federal loan that didn't have to be repaid until the house was sold, Davis signed a 15 percent loan with a 15 percent origination fee. The 15 points meant a $23,000 fee, instead of a usual $4,000 or so. Suddenly, Davis had $1,800 monthly payments instead of $459. It was only a matter of time before the house belonged to Congress Mortgage.

Congress Mortgage sold the home, valued at $225,000. The company makes some 400 loans a year and has scheduled 51 foreclosure sales in the next month alone. The bust business is booming. (Rob Morse, *San Francisco Chronicle* [Feb. 20, 1994])

Think of other examples of how critical thinking can save people from evil.

NOTES

1. Arthur Conan Doyle, *The Red-Headed League* (New York: Harper & Bros., 1892).
2. Marc Green and Gail MacCall, *There He Goes Again: Ronald Reagan's Reign of Error* (New York: Pantheon, 1983).
3. Jay Rosenberg, *The Practice of Philosophy* (Englewood Cliffs, NJ: Prentice Hall, 1978), p. 89.

Key Terms

philosophy	dialectic	principle of fallibilism
principle of parsimony	argument	logic
conclusion	premise	inference
indicator words	deductive	inductive
inference to the best explanation		

Suggestions for Further Reading

Bassham, Gregory, et al. *Critical Thinking: A Student's Introduction*, 3rd ed. New York: McGraw-Hill, 2008.
Copi, Irving. *Introduction to Logic*, 6th ed. New York: Macmillan, 1982. A widely used text, clear and concise.
Hurley, Patrick. *A Concise Introduction to Logic*, 4th ed. Belmont, CA: Wadsworth, 1991. An excellent work, clear and accessible.
Kahane, Howard. *Logic and Contemporary Rhetoric*, 7th ed. Wadsworth, 1995. An accessible introduction to critical thinking. Filled with interesting illustrations and examples.
Moore, Brooke, and Richard Parker. *Critical Thinking*. Mountain View, CA: Mayfield, 2007. A very good introduction to logical thinking.
Scriven, Michael. *Reasoning*. New York: McGraw-Hill, 1976. A rich presentation of the major topics in philosophical reasoning.
Vaughn, Lewis. *The Power of Critical Thinking*. New York: Oxford University Press, 2008.

Part II

~

Philosophy of Religion

If there is no God, then God is incalculably the greatest single creation of the human imagination. No other creation of the imagination has been so fertile of ideas, so great an inspiration to philosophy, to literature, to painting, sculpture, architecture, and drama. Set beside the idea of God, the most original inventions of mathematicians and the most unforgettable characters in drama are minor products of the imagination: Hamlet and the square root of minus one pale into insignificance by comparison.

ANTHONY KENNY, *Faith and Reason*, p. 59

QUESTIONS CONNECTED WITH THE EXISTENCE OF GOD may be the most important that we can ask and try to answer. If God, an omnibenevolent, supremely powerful being who interacts with the world, exists, then it is of the utmost importance that we come to know that fact and as much as possible about God and his plan. Implications follow that affect our understanding of the world and ourselves. If God exists, the world is not accidental, a product of mere chance and necessity, but a home which has been designed for rational and sentient beings. The universe is his handiwork, a place of personal purposefulness. We are not alone in the world to struggle for justice, but are working together with one whose plan is to redeem the world from evil. Most important, there is someone to whom we are responsible and to whom we owe absolute devotion and worship. Other implications follow for our self-understanding, the way we ought to live our lives, and prospects for continued life after death.

Of course, it may be false that a supreme being exists, and many people have lived well without believing in God. Pierre La Place, when asked about his faith, is reported to have replied, "I have no need of that hypothesis." But the testimony of humankind is against him. Millions have needed and been inspired by this notion. So great is the inspiration issuing from the idea of God that we could say that if God doesn't exist, the idea is the greatest invention of the human mind. What are all the world's works of literature, art, music, drama, architecture, science, and philosophy compared to this simple concept?

The field of philosophy of religion documents a significant part of the history of humanity's quest for a supreme being. Even if God does not exist, philosophy of religion retains importance for this documentation. The arguments centered around such a quest are interesting in their own right for their ingenuity and subtlety, even apart from their possible soundness. It may be argued that the Judeo-Christian tradition has informed our self-understanding to such a degree that it is imperative for every would-be well-informed person to come to grips with the arguments and counter-arguments surrounding its claims. Hence, even if the assertions of religion are rejected as misguided or superstitious leftovers from darker ages, an understanding of what is being rejected and why it is to be rejected is important.

The readings that follow center on three questions: (1) Are there arguments that demonstrate the existence of a supreme being? (2) Does the existence of evil provide evidence against the thesis that there is a God? and (3) What is the relationship between faith and reason? Is it rational to believe in God?

II.A   Is Belief in God Rationally Justified? Arguments for the Existence of God

Can the existence of God be demonstrated or made probable by argument? The debate between those who believe that reason can demonstrate that God exists and those who do not has an ancient lineage, going back to Protagoras (ca. 490–420 B.C.) and Plato (427–347 B.C.). The Roman Catholic Church has traditionally held that the existence of God is demonstrable by human reason. The strong statement of the First Vatican Council (1870) indicates that human reason is adequate to arrive at a state of knowledge of God's existence:

> If anyone says that the one and true God, our creator and Lord, cannot be known with certainty with the natural light of human reason by means of the things that have been made: Let him be anathema.

Many others—theists and nontheists, including Catholics—have denied that human reason is adequate to arrive at knowledge or demonstrate the existence of God.

Arguments for the existence of God divide into two main groups: *a priori* and *a posteriori* arguments. An **a posteriori argument** is based on premises that can be known only by means of experience of the world (for example, that there is a world, events have causes, and so forth). An **a priori argument** does not depend on such premises. Rather, it rests on premises that can be known to be true independently of experience of the world: One need only clearly conceive of the proposition to see that it is true.

In this section we shall consider two types of *a posteriori* arguments for the existence of God and one *a priori* argument. The *a posteriori* arguments are the cosmological argument and the teleological argument. The *a priori* argument is the ontological argument.

The questions before us are these: What do the arguments for the existence of God establish? Do any of them demonstrate beyond reasonable doubt the existence of a supreme being or deity? Do any of them make it probable (given the evidence at hand) that such a being exists?

The Cosmological Argument

All the versions of the **cosmological argument** begin with the *a posteriori* assumptions that the universe exists and that something outside the universe is required to explain its existence. That is, it is *contingent*, depending on something outside of itself for its existence. That "something else" is logically before the universe. It constitutes the reason for the existence of the universe. Such a being is God.

One version of the cosmological argument is called the "First Cause Argument." The first two arguments given by St. Thomas Aquinas in our readings serve as examples of it. The general outline goes something like this:

1. Everything in the universe has a cause. That is, for everything that exists (E), there is some other thing (C), which existed before E existed, and C produced E—that is, without C, E would not have existed. But C itself was caused by a prior cause, C_1, and C_1 by still another cause before it, C_2, and so on.

2. An infinite regress is impossible. The series of causes and effects cannot go on indefinitely but must have a beginning.

3. So there must be a first cause outside of the universe capable of producing everything besides itself (which is not produced but a necessary being).

4. Such a being must be an infinite, necessary being, that is, God.

This sort of argument can be challenged at every point, and you will find many of these challenges in Paul Edwards' article, "A Critique of the Cosmological Argument." You will decide whether the challenges are successful. First of all, we may challenge the first premise. Must everything have a cause? A significant number of physicists deny that the principle of causality applies to some behavior of subatomic particles. These particles seem to behave randomly and can be predicted only statistically. Their noncausal thesis has been confirmed by certain experiments, though the issue is controversial. Some physicists offer other explanations. In any case, the question should be raised: How do we know that everything must have a cause?

The second premise may be challenged with the question, how do we know that an infinite regress of causes is impossible? We have infinite series in mathematics, why not in physics too? Do we understand enough about the world to rule out such a series? If we can imagine an infinite series into the future, why not allow its possibility into the past?

Regarding the third premise, in using the notion of an infinite being to explain the world, have we really solved anything? For don't we still have to explain what an infinite being is? Isn't this simply a case of explaining the obscure with the even more obscure? And do we help our argument any by calling this unknown being God (the fourth premise)? Does the notion of a necessary being make any sense? We usually apply the notion of "necessity" to logically necessary propositions (such as that a contradiction is necessarily false or that it is necessarily true that 2 + 2 = 4). What sense does it make to say that a being must necessarily exist?

In "The *Kalam* Cosmological Argument and the Anthropic Principle," William Lane Craig attempts to develop a different form of the cosmological argument, the *kalam* argument first set forth by Arab philosophers in the Middle Ages. He then appeals to modern cosmology to develop an argument from the intricate complexity of the conditions for human life, called the anthropic principle.

The Teleological Argument

The **teleological argument** for the existence of God begins with the premise that the world exhibits intelligent purpose or order and proceeds to the conclusion that there must be or probably is a divine intelligence, a supreme designer to account for the observed or perceived intelligent purpose or order. Although the argument has been cited by Plato, by St. Paul in the Epistle to the Romans (Chapter 1), and by Cicero, the clearest sustained treatment is found in William Paley's *Natural Theology* (1802), provided in this section.

Paley argues that just as we infer an intelligent designer to account for the purpose-revealing watch, we must analogously infer an intelligent grand designer to account for the purpose-revealing world. "Every indication of contrivance, every manifestation of design, which existed in the watch, exists in the works of nature; with the difference, on the side of nature, of being greater and more, and that in a degree which exceeds all computation." The skeleton of the argument looks like this:

1. Human artifacts are products of intelligent design (purpose).
2. The universe resembles these human artifacts.
3. Therefore, the universe is (probably) a product of intelligent design (purpose).

4. But the universe is vastly more complex and gigantic than a human artifact.

5. Therefore, there probably is a powerful and vastly intelligent designer who designed the universe.

Ironically, Paley's argument was attacked even before Paley had set it down, for David Hume (1711–1776) had long before written his famous *Dialogues Concerning Natural Religion* (published posthumously in 1779), which constitutes the classic critique of the teleological argument. Paley seems to have been unaware of it. A selection of the *Dialogues* appears here. In it, the natural theologian, Cleanthes, debates the orthodox believer, Demea, and the skeptic or critic, Philo, who does most of the serious arguing.

Hume, through Philo, attacks the argument from several different angles. First, he argues that the universe is not sufficiently like the productions of human design to support the argument.

Philo's second objection is that the analogy from artifact to divine designer fails because we have no other universe with which to compare this one, which would be necessary to decide if it were the kind of universe designed or simply the kind that developed on its own. As C. S. Peirce put it, "Universes are not as plentiful as blackberries." There is only one of them, so we have no standard of comparison by which to judge it. Paley's answer to this would be that if we can find one clear instance of purposeness in nature (for example, the eye), we have a sufficient instance enabling us to conclude that there is probably an intelligent designer.

A third objection is that on the analogy from artifact to designer, we should infer a grand anthropomorphic designer, a human writ large, who has all the properties that we have. "Why not become a perfect anthropomorphite? Why not assert the Deity or Deities to be corporeal, and to have eyes, a nose, mouth, ears, and so on?"

Hume makes several other points against the design argument. The universe resembles in some ways an animal and in other ways a plant, in which case the argument fails because it depends on our seeing the world as a grand machine. The world might well be the result of mere chance. And, finally, the argument is weak because the world exhibits not merely order but much disorder. The question is whether the theist can answer enough of Hume's objections to make use of this argument.

The Ontological Argument

The **ontological argument** for the existence of God is the most intriguing of all the arguments for theism. It is one of the most remarkable arguments ever set forth. First set forth by St. Anselm (1033–1109) in the eleventh century, the argument has continued to puzzle and fascinate philosophers ever since.

The argument is not only important because it claims to be an *a priori* proof for the existence of God, but it also is the primary locus of such philosophical problems as whether existence is a property and whether the notion of necessary existence is intelligible. Furthermore, it has special religious significance because it is the only one of the traditional arguments which clearly concludes to the necessary properties of God, that is, his omnipotence, omniscience, omnibenevolence, and so on.

Although there are many versions of the ontological argument and many interpretations of some of these, most philosophers agree on the essential form of Anselm's version in the second chapter of his *Proslogium*. Anselm believes that God's existence is absolutely certain, so that only a fool would doubt or deny it. Yet he desires understanding to fulfill his faith.

The argument that follows can be treated as a *reductio ad absurdum* argument. That is, it begins with a supposition (S: suppose that the greatest conceivable being exists in the mind alone) that is contradictory to what one desires to prove and then one goes about showing that (S), together with other certain or self-evident assumptions (A_1 and A_2), yields a contradiction, which in turn demonstrates that the contradictory of (S) must be true. A greatest possible being must exist in reality; we shall leave it to you to work out the details of the argument.

Anselm's contemporary, Gaunilo, sets forth the first objection to Anselm's argument. Accusing Anselm of pulling rabbits out of hats, he tells the story of a delectable lost island, one that is more excellent than all lands. Because it is better that such a perfect island exists in reality rather than simply in the mind alone, this Isle of the Blest must necessarily exist. Anselm's reply is that the analogy fails for, unlike the greatest possible being, the greatest possible island can be conceived as not existing. Recently, Alvin Plantinga has clarified Anselm's point. There simply are some properties that do have intrinsic maximums, and some properties that don't have them. No matter how wonderful you make the Isle of the Blest, we can conceive of a more wonderful island. The greatness of islands is like the greatness of numbers in this respect. There is no greatest natural number, for no matter how large the number you choose, we can always conceive of one twice as large. On the other hand, the properties of God have intrinsic maximums. For example, we can define perfect knowledge this way: For any proposition an omniscient being knows whether it is true or false.

In one of our readings, William Rowe subjects the argument to close scrutiny and shows its major strengths and weakness.

II.5   The Five Ways

THOMAS AQUINAS

The Dominican monk Thomas Aquinas (1225–1274) is considered by many to be the greatest theologian in Western religion. The five arguments given here are *a posteriori* arguments, already described in the introduction. Put simply, their strategies are as follows. The first argument begins with the fact that there is change and argues that there must be an Unmoved Mover that originates all change (or motion) but itself is not moved. The second argument is from causation and argues that there must be a first cause to explain the existence of cause. The third argument is from contingency and argues that because there are dependent beings (for example, humans), there must be an independent or necessary being on whom the dependent beings rely for their subsistence. The fourth argument is from excellence, and it argues that because there are degrees of excellence, there must be a perfect being from whence come all excellences. The final argument is from the harmony of things: There is a harmony of nature that calls for an explanation. The only sufficient explanation is that there is a divine designer who planned such harmony.

Study Questions

1. What are the two objections that people give to deny the existence of God?
2. What are Aquinas' solutions to these two objections (stated at the end of his exposition)?
3. Identify the central idea in each of the five arguments.
4. Outline the second argument in your own words and analyze it. After this, try to sum up the other arguments.

[Aquinas first identifies two objections to the thesis that God exists]

OBJECTION 1. It seems that God does not exist, because if one of two contraries be infinite, the other would be altogether destroyed. But the name *God* means that He is infinite goodness. If, therefore, God existed, there would be no evil discoverable; but there is evil in the world. Therefore God does not exist.

OBJECTION 2. Further, it is superfluous to suppose that what can be accounted for by a few principles has been produced by many. But it seems that everything we see in the world can be accounted for by other principles, supposing God did not exist. For all natural things can be reduced to one principle, which is nature; and all voluntary things can be reduced to one principle, which is human reason, or will. Therefore there is no need to suppose God's existence.

On the Contrary, It is said in the person of God: *I am Who I am* (Ex. iii.14).

I answer that, The existence of God can be proved in five ways.

THE FIRST WAY: THE ARGUMENT FROM CHANGE

The first and clearest [way] is taken from the idea of motion. (1) Now it is certain, and our senses corroborate it, that some things in this world are in motion. (2) But everything which is in motion is moved by something else. (3) For nothing is in motion except insofar as it is potentiality in relation to that towards which it is in motion. (4) Now a thing causes movement in so far as it is in actuality. For to cause movement is nothing else than to bring something from potentiality to actuality; but a thing cannot be brought from potentiality to actuality except by something which exists in actuality, as, for example, that which is hot in actuality, like fire, makes wood, which is only hot in potentiality, to be hot in actuality, and thereby causes movement in it and alters it. (5) But it is not possible that the same thing should be at the same time in actuality and potentiality in relation to the same thing, but only in relation to different things; for what is hot in actuality cannot at the same time be hot in potentiality, though it is at the same time cold in potentiality. (6) It is impossible, therefore, that in relation to the same thing and in the same way anything should both cause movement and be caused, or that it should cause itself to move. (7) Everything therefore that is in motion must be moved by something else. If therefore the thing which causes it to move be in motion, this too must be moved by something else, and so on. (8) But we cannot proceed to infinity in this way, because in that cause there would be no first mover, and in

Reprinted from Thomas Aquinas, Summa Theologica, *translated by Laurence Shapcote (London: O. P. Benziger Brothers, 1911).*

consequence, neither would there be any other mover; for secondary movers do not cause movement except they be moved by a first mover, as, for example, a stick cannot cause movement unless it is moved by the hand. Therefore it is necessary to stop at some first mover which is moved by nothing else. And this is what we all understand God to be.

THE SECOND WAY: THE ARGUMENT FROM CAUSATION

The Second Way is taken from the idea of the Efficient Cause. (1) For we find that there is among material things a regular order of efficient causes. (2) But we do not find, nor indeed is it possible, that anything is the efficient cause of itself, for in that case it would be prior to itself, which is impossible. (3) Now it is not possible to proceed to infinity in efficient causes. (4) For if we arrange in order all efficient causes, the first is the cause of the intermediate, and the intermediate the cause of the last, whether the intermediate be many or only one. (5) But if we remove a cause the effect is removed; therefore, if there is no *first* among efficient causes, neither will there be a last or an intermediate. (6) But if we proceed to infinity in efficient causes there will be no first efficient cause, and thus there will be no ultimate effect, nor any intermediate efficient causes, which is clearly false. Therefore it is necessary to suppose the existence of some first efficient cause, and this men call God.

THE THIRD WAY: THE ARGUMENT FROM CONTINGENCY

The Third Way rests on the idea of the "contingent" and the "necessary" and is as follows: (1) Now we find that there are certain things in the Universe which are capable of existing and of not existing, for we find that some things are brought into existence and then destroyed, and consequently are capable of being or not being. (2) But it is impossible for all things which exist to be of this kind, because anything which is capable of not existing, at some time or other does not exist. (3) If therefore *all* things are capable of not existing, there was a time when nothing existed in the Universe. (4) But if this is true there would also be nothing in existence now; because anything that does not exist cannot begin to exist except by the agency of something which has existence. If therefore there was once nothing which existed, it would have been impossible for anything to begin to exist, and so nothing would exist now. (5) This is clearly false. Therefore all things are not contingent, and there must be something which is necessary in the Universe. (6) But everything which is necessary either has or has not the cause of its necessity from an outside source. Now it is not possible to proceed to infinity in necessary things which have a cause of their necessity, as has been proved in the case of efficient causes. Therefore it is necessary to suppose the existence of something which is necessary in itself, not having the cause of its necessity from any outside source, but which is the cause of necessity in others. And this "something" we call God.

THE FOURTH WAY: THE ARGUMENT FROM DEGREES OF EXCELLENCE

The Fourth Way is taken from the degrees which are found in things. (1) For among different things we find that one is more or less good or true or noble; and likewise in the case of other things of this kind. (2) But the words "more" or "less" are used of different things in proportion as they approximate in their different ways to something which has the particular quality in the highest degree—e.g., we call a thing hotter when it approximates more nearly to that which is hot in the highest degree. There is therefore something which is true in the highest degree, good in the highest degree and noble in the highest degree;

(3) and consequently there must be also something which has being in the highest degree. For things which are true in the highest degree also have being in the highest degree (see Aristotle, *Metaphysics,* 2). (4) But anything which has a certain quality of any kind in the highest degree is also the cause of all the things of that kind, as, for example, fire which is hot in the highest degree is the cause of all hot things (as is said in the same book). (5) Therefore there exists something which is the cause of being, and goodness, and of every perfection in all existing things; and this we call God.

THE FIFTH WAY:
THE ARGUMENT
FROM HARMONY

The Fifth Way is taken from the way in which nature is governed. (1) For we observe that certain things which lack knowledge, such as natural bodies, work for an End. This is obvious, because they always, or at any rate very frequently, operate in the same way so as to attain the best possible result. (2) Hence it is clear that they do not arrive at their goal by chance, but by purpose. (3) But those things which have no knowledge do not move towards a goal unless they are guided by someone or something which does possess knowledge and intelligence—e.g., an arrow by an archer. Therefore, there does exist something which possesses intelligence by which all natural things are directed to their goal; and this we call God.

Reply Obj. 1. As Augustine says: *Since God is the highest good, He would not allow any evil to exist in His works, unless His omnipotence and goodness were such as to bring good even out of evil.* This is part of the infinite goodness of God, that He should allow evil to exist, and out of it produce good.

Reply Obj. 2. Since nature works for a determinate end under the direction of a higher agent, whatever is done by nature must be traced back to God as to its first cause. So likewise whatever is done voluntarily must be traced back to some higher cause other than human reason and will, since these can change and fail; for all things that are changeable and capable of defect must be traced back to an immovable and self-necessary first principle, as has been shown.

For Further Reflection

1. Has Aquinas proved the existence of God? Why or why not? What do you think the value of these arguments is?

2. Do you agree that an infinite regress of causes is repugnant to reason?

3. Consider this question asked by John Stuart Mill: If God caused everything, what caused God? Is that a valid question? How would Aquinas respond to it? How would you respond to it?

The *Kalam* Cosmological Argument and the Anthropic Principle

II.6

WILLIAM LANE CRAIG

William Lane Craig is a research professor of philosophy at Talbot School of Theology in La Mirada, California. He received his Ph.D. in philosophy from the University of Birmingham (England) and a Th.D. from the University of Munich (Germany). He is the author of several works in philosophy of religion, including *The Kalam Cosmological Argument* (1979) and *Reasonable Faith* (1994), from which the following selection is taken. The *kalam* argument refers to a version of the cosmological argument developed by Arab Islamic scholars al-Kindi and al-Ghazali in the Middle Ages. The Arabic word *kalam* means "argument." In the first part of this essay Craig develops two versions of the *kalam* argument, both aiming to prove that the universe must have a cause of its existence. In the second part of this essay Craig describes the evidence from astronomy for the *kalam* cosmological argument for the existence of God. He argues that evidence for the Big Bang confirms the thesis that the universe began to exist and so must have had a cause. Toward the end of the article Craig introduces "the anthropic principle," which states that "if the universe were in fact different in any significant way from the way it is, we wouldn't be here to wonder why it is" (a definition given by Dewey Schwatzenburg). Finally, Craig argues that there is good reason to believe, on the basis of the anthropic principle, that the First Cause is the Personal Creator of Theism.

Study Questions

1. What are the premises of the *kalam* argument?
2. What do atheists like Quentin Smith say about our origins?
3. What does Hume say about causality? How do Mackie and Craig differ on their interpretations of Hume's theory?
4. What is Craig's first argument for the thesis that the universe began to exist?
5. What is the Hilbert's Hotel analogy?
6. What is the scientific evidence confirming the idea that the universe must have had a beginning?
7. What did Edwin Hubble discover in the 1920s?
8. What is a *singularity*?
9. When, according to some scientists, did the Big Bang take place?
10. Where did the Big Bang take place?
11. What are the alternative models to the Big Bang?
12. What is Stephen Hawking's view of the origins of the universe?
13. What is the anthropic principle?

I. DEFENSE OF THE *KALAM* ARGUMENT

I FIND QUITE A NUMBER of proffered theistic arguments to be sound and persuasive and together to constitute a powerful cumulative case for the existence of God. In particular, I find the *kalam* cosmological argument for a temporal first cause of the universe to be one of the most plausible arguments for God's existence. The argument shows that the universe began to exist. Anything that begins to exist must have a cause that brings it into being. So the universe must have a cause. Philosophical analysis reveals that such a cause must have several of the principal theistic attributes.

The argument may be formulated in three simple steps.

1. Whatever begins to exist has a cause.

2. The universe began to exist.

3. Therefore, the universe has a cause.

The logic of the argument is valid and very simple; the argument has the same logical structure as the argument: "All men are mortal; Socrates is a man; therefore, Socrates is mortal." So the question is, are there good reasons to believe that each of the steps is true? I think there are.

Whatever Begins to Exist Has a Cause

The first step is so intuitively obvious that I think scarcely anyone could sincerely believe it to be false. I therefore think it somewhat unwise to argue in favor of it, for any proof of the principle is likely to be less obvious than the principle itself. And as Aristotle remarked, one ought not to try to prove the obvious via the less obvious. The old axiom "out of nothing, nothing comes" remains as obvious today as ever. When I first wrote *The Kalam Cosmological Argument,* I remarked that I found it an attractive feature of this argument that it allows the atheist a way of escape: he can always deny the first premise and assert that the universe sprang into existence uncaused out of nothing. I figured that few would take this option, since I believed they would thereby expose themselves as persons interested only in an academic refutation of the argument and not in really discovering the truth about the universe. To my surprise, however, atheists seem to be increasingly taking this route. For example, Quentin Smith, commenting that philosophers are too often adversely affected by Heidegger's dread of "the nothing," concludes that "the most reasonable belief is that we came from nothing, by nothing, and for nothing"—a nice ending of a sort of Gettysburg Address of atheism, perhaps.

Similarly, the late J. L. Mackie, in refuting the *kalam* cosmological argument, turns his main guns on this first step: "there is a priori no good reason why a sheer origination of things, not determined by anything, should be unacceptable, whereas the existence of a god [*sic*] with the power to create something out of nothing is acceptable." Indeed, he believes *creatio ex nihilo* raises problems: (i) If God began to exist at a point in time, then this is as great a puzzle as the beginning of the universe. (ii) Or if God existed for infinite time, then the same arguments would apply to his existence as would apply to the infinite duration of the universe. (iii) If it be said that God is timeless, then this, says Mackie, is a complete mystery.

Now notice that Mackie never refutes the principle that whatever begins to exist has a cause. Rather, he simply demands what good reason there is a priori to accept it. He writes, "As Hume pointed out, we can certainly conceive an uncaused beginning-to-be of an object; if what we can thus conceive is nevertheless in some way impossible, this still requires to be shown." But, as many philosophers have pointed out, Hume's argument in no way makes it plausible to think that something could really come into being without a cause. Just because I can imagine an object, say a horse,

Reprinted from William Lane Craig, Reasonable Faith *(Crossway, 1994) by permission of the author; footnotes deleted.*

coming into existence from nothing, that in no way proves that a horse really could come into existence that way. The defender of the *kalam* argument is claiming that it is really impossible for something to come uncaused from nothing. Does Mackie sincerely believe that things can pop into existence uncaused, out of nothing? Does anyone in his right mind really believe that, say, a raging tiger could suddenly come into existence uncaused, out of nothing, in this room right now? The same applies to the universe: if prior to the existence of the universe, there was absolutely nothing—no God, no space, no time—how could the universe possibly have come to exist?

In fact, Mackie's appeal to Hume at this point is counterproductive. For Hume himself clearly believed in the causal principle. In 1754 he wrote to John Stewart, "But allow me to tell you that I never asserted so absurd a Proposition as that *anything* might arise without a cause. I only maintain'd, that our Certainty of the Falsehood of that Proposition proceeded neither from Intuition nor Demonstration, but from another source." Even Mackie confesses, "Still this [causal] principle has some plausibility, in that it is constantly confirmed in our experience (and also used, reasonably, in interpreting our experience)." So why not accept the truth of the causal principle as plausible and reasonable—at the very least more so than its denial?

Because, Mackie thinks, in this particular case the theism implied by affirming the principle is even more unintelligible than the denial of the principle. It makes more sense to believe that the universe came into being uncaused out of nothing than to believe that God created the universe out of nothing.

But is this really the case? Consider the three problems Mackie raises with *creatio ex nihilo*. Certainly, the proponent of the *kalam* argument would not hold (i) that God began to exist or (ii) that God has existed for an infinite number of, say, hours, or any other unit of time. But what is wrong with (iii), that God is, without creation, timeless? I would argue that God exists timelessly without creation and in time subsequent to creation. This

may be "mysterious" in the sense of "wonderful" or "awe-inspiring," but it is not, so far as I can see, unintelligible; and Mackie gives us no reason to think that it is. Moreover, there is also an alternative which Mackie failed to consider: (iv) prior to creation God existed in an undifferentiated time in which hours, seconds, days, and so forth simply do not exist. Because this time is undifferentiated, it is not incompatible with the *kalam* argument that an infinite regress of events cannot exist. It seems to me, therefore, that Mackie is entirely unjustified in rejecting the first step of the argument as not being intuitively obvious, plausible, and reasonable.

The Universe Began to Exist

If we agree that whatever begins to exist has a cause, what evidence is there to support the crucial second step in the argument, that the universe began to exist? I think that this step is supported by both philosophical arguments and scientific confirmation of those arguments.

PHILOSOPHICAL ARGUMENTS: (1) ARGUMENT FROM THE IMPOSSIBILITY OF AN ACTUALLY INFINITE NUMBER OF THINGS

An actually infinite number of things cannot exist because this would involve all sorts of absurdities, which I'll illustrate in a moment. And if the universe never had a beginning, then the series of all past events is actually infinite. That is to say, an actually infinite number of past events exists. Because an actually infinite number of things cannot exist, then an actually infinite number of past events cannot exist. The number of past events is finite; therefore, the series of past events had a beginning. Since the history of the universe is identical to the series of all past events, the universe must have begun to exist. This argument can also be formulated in three steps:

1. An actually infinite number of things cannot exist.

2. A beginningless series of events in time entails an actually infinite number of things.

3. Therefore, a beginningless series of events in time cannot exist.

Let's examine each step individually.

1. An actually infinite number of things cannot exist. In order to understand this first step, we need to understand what an actual infinite is. There is a difference between a potential infinite and an actual infinite. A potential infinite is a collection that is increasing toward infinity as a limit but never gets there. Such a collection is really indefinite, not infinite. For example, any finite distance can be subdivided into potentially infinitely many parts. You can just keep on dividing parts in half forever, but you will never arrive at an actual "infinitieth" division or come up with an actually infinite number of parts. By contrast, an actual infinite is a collection in which the number of members really is infinite. The collection is not growing toward infinity; it is infinite, it is "complete." This sort of infinity is used in set theory to designate sets that have an infinite number of members, such as {1, 2, 3 . . . }. Now I am arguing, not that a potentially infinite number of things cannot exist, but that an actually infinite number of things cannot exist. For if an actually infinite number of things could exist, this would spawn all sorts of absurdities.

Perhaps the best way to bring this home is by means of an illustration. Let me use one of my favorites, Hilbert's Hotel, a product of the mind of the great German mathematician David Hilbert. Let's imagine a hotel with a finite number of rooms. Suppose, furthermore, that all the rooms are full. When a new guest arrives asking for a room, the proprietor apologizes, "Sorry, all the rooms are full." But now let us imagine a hotel with an infinite number of rooms and suppose once more that *all the rooms are full.* There is not a single vacant room throughout the entire infinite hotel. Now suppose a new guest shows up, asking for a room. "But of course!" says the proprietor, and he immediately shifts the person in room #1 into room #2, the person in room #2 into room #3, the person in room #3 into room #4, and so on, out to infinity. As a result of these room

changes, room #1 now becomes vacant and the new guest gratefully checks in. But remember, before he arrived, all the rooms were full!

Equally curious, according to the mathematicians, there are now no more persons in the hotel than there were before: the number is just infinite. But how can this be? The proprietor just added the new guest's name to the register and gave him his keys—how can there not be one more person in the hotel than before? But the situation becomes even stranger. For suppose an infinity of new guests show up at the desk, asking for a room. "Of course, of course!" says the proprietor, and he proceeds to shift the person in room #1 into room #2, the person in room #2 into room #4, the person in room #3 into room #6, and so on out to infinity, always putting each former occupant into the room number twice his own. Because any natural number multiplied by two always equals an even number, all the guests wind up in even-numbered rooms. As a result, all the odd-numbered rooms become vacant, and the infinity of new guests is easily accommodated. And yet, before they came, all the rooms were full! And again, strangely enough, the number of guests in the hotel is the same after the infinity of new guests check in as before, even though there were as many new guests as old guests. In fact, the proprietor could repeat this process *infinitely many* times and yet there would never be one single person more in the hotel than before.

But Hilbert's Hotel is even stranger than the German mathematician made it out to be. For suppose some of the guests start to check out. Suppose the guest in room #1 departs. Is there not now one less person in the hotel? Not according to the mathematicians—but just ask the woman who makes the beds! Suppose the guests in rooms #1, 3, 5 . . . check out. In this case an infinite number of people have left the hotel, but according to the mathematicians, there are no less people in the hotel—but don't talk to that laundry woman! In fact, we could have every other guest check out of the hotel and repeat this process infinitely many times, and yet there would never be any less people in the hotel.

Now suppose the proprietor doesn't like having a half-empty hotel (it looks bad for business). No matter! By shifting occupants as before, but in reverse order, he transforms his half-vacant hotel into one that is jammed to the gills. You might think that by these manoeuvres the proprietor could always keep this strange hotel fully occupied. But you would be wrong. For suppose that the persons in rooms #4, 5, 6 . . . checked out. At a single stroke the hotel would be virtually emptied, the guest register would be reduced to three names, and the infinite would be converted to finitude. And yet it would remain true that the same number of guests checked out this time as when the guests in rooms #1, 3, 5 . . . checked out! Can anyone believe that such a hotel could exist in reality?

Hilbert's Hotel is absurd. As one person remarked, if Hilbert's Hotel could exist, it would have to have a sign posted outside: NO VACANCY GUESTS WELCOME. The above sorts of absurdities show that it is impossible for an actually infinite number of things to exist. There is simply no way to avoid these absurdities once we admit the possibility of the existence of an actual infinite. Students sometimes react to such absurdities as Hilbert's Hotel by saying that we really don't understand the nature of infinity and, hence, these absurdities result. But this attitude is simply mistaken. Infinite set theory is a highly developed and well-understood branch of mathematics, so that these absurdities result precisely because we do understand the notion of a collection with an actually infinite number of members. . . .

But does the possibility of an actual infinite really entail that such absurdities are possible, or could an actual infinite be possible, as Wainwright suggests, without thereby implying that such absurdities are possible? The answer to that question is simple: the possibility of the existence of an actual infinite *entails*, that is, necessarily implies, that such absurdities could exist. Hilbert's illustration merely serves to bring out in a practical and vivid way what the mathematics necessarily implies; for if an actually infinite number of things is possible, then a hotel with an actually infinite number of rooms must be possible. Hence, it logically follows that if such a hotel is impossible, then so is the real existence of an actual infinite.

These considerations also show how superficial Mackie's analysis of this point is. He thinks that the absurdities are resolved by noting that for infinite groups the axiom that the *whole is greater than its part* does not hold, as it does for finite groups. But far from being the solution, this is precisely the problem. Because in infinite set theory this axiom is denied, one gets all sorts of absurdities, like Hilbert's Hotel, when one tries to translate that theory into reality. And the contradictions that result when guests check out of the hotel are not even *prima facie* resolved by Mackie's analysis. (In trans-finite arithmetic, subtraction is against the rules because it leads to contradictions; but in reality, you can't stop people from checking out of the hotel if they want to!) Hence, I conclude that an actually infinite number of things cannot exist.

2. A beginningless series of events in time entails an actually infinite number of things. This second point is pretty obvious. If the universe never began to exist, then the series of events would be infinite. If the universe never began to exist, then prior to the present there have existed an actually infinite number of previous events. Thus, a beginningless series of events in time entails an actually infinite number of things, namely, events.

3. Therefore, a beginningless series of events in time cannot exist. If the above two premises are true, then the conclusion follows logically. The series of past events must be finite and have a beginning. Since, as I said, the universe is not distinct from the series of events, the universe therefore began to exist.

PHILOSOPHICAL ARGUMENTS: (2) ARGUMENT FROM THE IMPOSSIBILITY OF FORMING AN ACTUALLY INFINITE COLLECTION OF THINGS BY ADDING ONE MEMBER AFTER ANOTHER

It is very important to note that this argument is distinct from the foregoing argument, for it does not deny that an actually infinite number of things can exist. It denies that a collection containing an actually infinite number of things can be *formed by* adding one member after another. Basically, the argument goes like this: you cannot form an actually infinite collection of things by adding one member after another, because it would be impossible to get to infinity. The series of past events is a collection that has been formed by adding one event after another. Therefore, the series of past events up till now can only be finite, not infinite. Otherwise, it would be an actually infinite collection formed by adding one member after another. This argument, too, can be formulated in three steps:

1. The series of events in time is a collection formed by adding one member after another.

2. A collection formed by adding one member after another cannot be actually infinite.

3. Therefore, the series of events in time cannot be actually infinite.

Let's take a look at each step.

1. The series of events in time is a collection formed by adding one member after another. This is rather obvious. The past did not spring into being whole and entire but was formed sequentially, one event occurring after another. Notice, too, that the direction of this formation is "forward," in the sense that the collection grows with time. Although we sometimes speak of an "infinite regress" of events, in reality an infinite past would be an "infinite progress" of events with no beginning and its end in the present.

2. A collection formed by adding one member after another cannot be actually infinite. This is the crucial step. It's important to realize that this impossibility has nothing to do with the amount of time available: no matter how much time one has available, an actual infinite cannot be formed. No matter how many numbers you count, you can always add one more before arriving at infinity.

Now someone might say that while an infinite collection cannot be formed by beginning at a point and adding members, nevertheless an infinite collection could be formed by never beginning but ending at a point, that is to say, ending at a point after having added one member after another from eternity. But this method seems even more unbelievable than the first method. If one cannot count to infinity, how can one count down from infinity? If one cannot traverse the infinite by moving in one direction, how can one traverse it by moving in the opposite direction?

Indeed, the idea of a beginningless series ending in the present seems absurd. To give just one illustration: suppose we meet a man who claims to have been counting from eternity and who is now finishing: . . . , –3, –2, –1, 0. We could ask, why didn't he finish counting yesterday or the day before or the year before? By then an infinite time had already elapsed, so that he should already have finished. Thus, at no point in the infinite past could we ever find the man finishing his countdown, for by that point he should already be done! In fact, no matter how far back into the past we go, we can never find the man counting at all, for at any point we reach he will already have finished. But if at no point in the past do we find him counting, this contradicts the hypothesis that he has been counting from eternity. This illustrates that the formation of an actual infinite by never beginning but reaching an end is as impossible as beginning at a point and trying to reach infinity.

Hence, set theory has been purged of all temporal concepts; as Russell says, "classes which are infinite are given all at once by the defining properties of their members, so that there is no question of 'completion' or of 'successive synthesis.'" The only way an actual infinite could come to exist in the real world would be by being created all at once, simply in a moment. It would be a hopeless undertaking to try to form it by adding one member after another.

Mackie's objections to this step are off the target. He thinks that the argument illicitly assumes an infinitely distant starting point in the past and then pronounces it impossible to travel from that point to today. If we take the notion of infinity "seriously," he says, we must say that in the infinite past there would be no starting point whatever, not even an infinitely distant one. Yet from any given point in the past, there is only a finite distance to the present.

Now I know of no proponent of the *kalam* argument who assumed that there was an infinitely distant starting point in the past. On the contrary, the beginningless character of the series of past events only serves to underscore the difficulty of its formation by adding one member after another. The fact that there is *no beginning at all,* not even an infinitely distant one, makes the problem worse, not better. It is not the proponent of the *kalam* argument who fails to take infinity seriously. To say the infinite past could have been formed by adding one member after another is like saying someone has just succeeded in writing down all the negative numbers, ending at −1. And, we may ask, how is Mackie's point that from any given moment in the past there is only a finite distance to the present even relevant to the issue? The defender of the *kalam* argument could agree to this without batting an eye. For the issue is how the *whole* series can be formed, not a finite portion of it. Does Mackie think that because every *finite* segment of the series can be formed by adding one member after another the whole *infinite* series can be so formed? That is as logically fallacious as saying because every part of an elephant is light in weight, the whole elephant is light in weight. Mackie's point is therefore irrelevant. It seems that this step of the argument, that an actually infinite collection cannot be formed by adding one member after another, remains unrefuted.

3. Therefore, the series of events in time cannot be actually infinite. Given the truth of the premises, the conclusion logically follows. If the universe did not begin to exist a finite time ago, then the present moment would never arrive. But obviously it has arrived. Therefore, we know that the universe is finite in the past and began to exist.

We thus have two separate arguments to prove that the universe began to exist, one based on the impossibility of an actually infinite number of things and one on the impossibility of forming an actually infinite collection by successive addition. If one wishes to deny the beginning of the universe, he must refute, not one, but both of these arguments.

II. CONFIRMATION FROM THE BIG BANG MODEL OF THE UNIVERSE

Some people find philosophical arguments difficult to follow. They prefer empirical evidence. So I now turn to an examination of [a] remarkable scientific confirmation of the conclusion already reached by philosophical argument alone. This evidence comes from what is undoubtedly one of the most exciting and rapidly developing fields of science: astronomy and astrophysics.

Prior to the 1920s, scientists had always assumed that the universe was stationary. But in 1929 an alarming thing happened. An astronomer named Edwin Hubble discovered that the light from distant galaxies appears to be redder than it should. The startling conclusion to which Hubble was led was that the light is redder because the universe is growing apart; it is expanding! The light from the galaxies is affected because they are moving away from us. But this is the interesting part: Hubble not only showed that the universe is expanding, but that it is expanding the same in all directions.

To get a picture of this, imagine a balloon with buttons glued on its surface. As you blow up the balloon, the buttons get farther and farther apart. Now those buttons are just like the galaxies in space. Everything in the universe is expanding outward. The staggering implication of this is that at some point in the past the entire known universe was contracted down to a single mathematical point, from which it has been expanding ever since. The further back one goes in the past, the denser the universe becomes, so that one finally reaches a point of infinite density called the singularity from which the universe began to expand. That initial event has come to be known as the "Big Bang."

How long ago did the Big Bang occur? In a very important series of nine articles published over the course of three decades, two scientists, Allan Sandage and G. A. Tammann, estimated that the Big Bang occurred about 15 billion years ago. Therefore, according to the Big Bang theory the universe began to exist with a great explosion from a state of infinite density about 15 billion years ago. Four of the world's most famous astronomers describe that event in these words:

> The universe began from a state of infinite density. . . . Space and time were created in that event and so was all the matter in the universe. It is not meaningful to ask what happened before the Big Bang; it is like asking what is north of the North Pole. Similarly, it is not sensible to ask where the Big Bang took place. The point-universe was not an object isolated in space; it was the entire universe, and so the only answer can be that the Big Bang happened everywhere.

Thus, the term "Big Bang" and the terminology associated with an explosion can be misleading, because it is not correct to suppose that the expansion can be visualized from the outside. There is no external vantage point from which the expansion could be observed because what is expanding is the entire universe. Space itself is expanding in the sense that the separation between any two galaxies grows with time.

The event that marked the beginning of the universe becomes all the more amazing when one reflects on the fact that it implies the origin of the universe out of nothing. As the British physicist P. C. W. Davies explains,

> *If* we extrapolate this prediction to its extreme, we reach a point when all distances in the universe have shrunk to zero. An initial cosmological singularity therefore forms a past temporal extremity to the universe. We cannot continue physical reasoning, or even the concept of

space-time, through such an extremity. For this reason most cosmologists think of the initial singularity as the beginning of the universe. On this view the big bang represents the creation event; the creation not only of all the matter and energy in the universe, but also of space-time itself.

Similarly, another pair of physicists conclude, "At this singularity, space and time came into existence; literally nothing existed before the singularity, so, if the Universe originated in such a singularity, we would truly have a creation *ex nihilo*." Thus, as astronomer Fred Hoyle points out, the Big Bang theory requires the creation of the universe from nothing. This is because as one goes back in time, one reaches a point at which, in Hoyle's words, the universe was "shrunk down to nothing at all." So what the Big Bang model implies is that the universe had a beginning and was created out of nothing.

Now some people were deeply disturbed with the idea that the universe began from nothing. Einstein wrote privately, "This circumstance of an expanding universe irritates me. . . . To admit such possibilities seems senseless." Another scientist, Arthur Eddington, wrote, "I have no axe to grind in this discussion, but the notion of a beginning is repugnant to me. . . . I simply do not believe that the present order of things started off with a bang. . . . The expanding universe is preposterous . . . incredible. . . . It leaves me cold." The German chemist Walter Nernst declared, "To deny the infinite duration of time would be to betray the very foundations of science." Phillip Morrison of the Massachusetts Institute of Technology said, "I find it hard to accept the Big Bang theory; I would like to reject it, but I have to face the facts."

Alternative Models

But if one rejects the Big Bang model, the alternatives are not very convincing. Let's examine the major kinds of competing theories.

The *steady state model* holds that the universe never had a beginning, but has always existed in the same state. As the galaxies mutually recede, new matter comes into existence in the voids left by the retreating galaxies, so that the overall state of the universe remains the same. Ever since this model was first proposed in 1948, it has never been very convincing. According to S. L. Jaki, this theory never secured "a single piece of experimental verification." It always seemed to be trying to explain away the facts rather than explain them. According to Jaki, the proponents of this model were actually motivated by "openly anti-theological, or rather anti-Christian motivations."

Against this theory is the fact that a count of galaxies emitting radio waves indicates that there were once more radio sources than there are today. Therefore, the universe is not in a steady state after all. But the theory was decisively discredited when in 1965 two scientists working for the Bell Telephone Laboratory, A. A. Penzias and R. W. Wilson, discovered that the entire universe is bathed with a background of microwave radiation. This radiation background shows that the universe was once in a very hot and very dense state. In the steady state model no such state could have existed, since the universe is supposed to have been the same from eternity. Therefore, the steady state model has been abandoned by virtually everyone. According to Ivan King, "The steady-state theory has now been laid to rest, as a result of clear-cut observations of how things have changed with time."

A second alternative model is the *oscillating model.* John Gribbin describes this model:

> The biggest problem with the Big Bang theory of the origin of the universe is philosophical— perhaps even theological—what was there before the bang? This problem alone was sufficient to give a great initial impetus to the steady state theory; but with that theory now sadly in conflict with the observations, the best way round this initial difficulty is provided by a model in which the universe expands, collapses back again, and repeats the cycle indefinitely.

According to this model, the universe is sort of like a spring, expanding and contracting from

eternity. This model became a sort of "Great White Hope" for atheistic scientists, who terribly wanted it to be true so as to avoid an absolute beginning of the universe. You may have seen Carl Sagan, for example, in his popular *Cosmos* program on public television propounding this model and reading from the Hindu scriptures about cyclical Brahman years in order to illustrate the oscillating universe.

There are, however, at least two very well known difficulties with the oscillating model, which Sagan did not mention. First, the oscillating model is physically impossible. That is to say, for all the talk about such a model, the fact remains that it is only a theoretical possibility, not a real possibility. You can draft such models on paper, but they cannot be descriptive of the real universe, because they contradict the known laws of physics. As the late Professor Tinsley of Yale explains, in oscillating models "even though the mathematics says that the universe oscillates, there is no known physics to reverse the collapse and bounce back to a new expansion. The physics seems to say that those models start from the Big Bang, expand, collapse, then end." More recently, four other scientists, themselves obviously in sympathy with the oscillating model, admitted, in describing the contraction of the universe, "there is no understanding of how a bounce can take place. . . . We have nothing to contribute to the question of whether and/or how the universe bounces." In order for the oscillating model to be correct, the known laws of physics would have to be revised.

Second, the observational evidence is contrary to the oscillating model. Let me explain two respects in which the observational evidence does not support the oscillating model. The first is that there is no way to account for the observed even distribution of matter in the universe on the basis of an oscillating model. This is because as the universe contracts, black holes begin to suck everything up, so that matter becomes very unevenly distributed. But when the universe (supposedly) rebounds from its contracting phase, there is no mechanism to "iron out" these lumps and make the distribution smooth. Hence, the scientists cited above confess that even if there is some unknown mechanism that could cause the universe to bounce back to a new expansion, it is still not clear that it would prevent the unevenness that would result from the black holes formed during the contraction phase. The present evenness of matter distribution simply cannot be explained by using models in which the universe begins with matter unevenly distributed. The oscillating model therefore cannot satisfactorily account for the presently observed evenness of the distribution of matter in the universe. . . .

The observational evidence thus supports a low density universe destined to indefinite expansion. Sandage and Tammann conclude: "Hence, we are forced to decide that . . . it seems inevitable that the Universe will expand forever." This conclusion may be strengthened. For Sandage and Tammann in a later discussion go on to point out that in order to fit the observational evidence, even high density universes (which are typically thought to re-contract) may also have to expand forever. They conclude, "Hence, the one certain conclusion is that in all models of either high or low density, . . . the Universe will not stop its expansion. This means it has *happened only once.* The creation event was unique."

The oscillating model, therefore, is seriously flawed. It contradicts both the known laws of physics and the current observational evidence. It therefore provides no plausible escape from the beginning of the universe.

In recent years theoretical cosmology has become increasingly speculative, obscuring the boundary between physics and metaphysics. The marriage of the General Theory of Relativity (upon which the Big Bang model is based) to Quantum Theory (subatomic physics) has resulted in the conception of a third alternative to the standard Big Bang model: *quantum models* of the universe. One should say the "would be marriage," for the fact is that these two great theories of modern physics are mutually inconsistent, and nobody knows how to reconcile them. Quantum models grow out of the attempt at one such reconciliation. Prior to 10^{-43} seconds after the Big Bang (that's .0000000000000000000000000000000000000000001 of a second) quantum physics must be employed to describe the universe, and the goal of the union of Relativity Theory and Quantum Theory is to describe this brief moment. Unfortunately, this period is so poorly understood that one commentator has compared it with the regions on the maps of ancient cartographers marked "Here there be dragons!"—it can be filled with all sorts of fantasies. The fact is that these theories are as much speculation as science.

The first class of models appealing to quantum effects to explain the origin of the universe were vacuum fluctuation models. These theories hold that what we have thus far taken to be the expansion of the *whole* universe is really only the expansion of a part of it, or, in other words, that our observable universe is just a tiny part of a wider Universe-as-a-whole. The Universe-as-a-whole is itself a vacuum in a steady state. But throughout this vacuum subatomic energy fluctuations are conceived to be occurring, by means of which material particles are created out of the energy contained in the vacuum. These then grow into separate mini-universes within the whole. All we can observe is the expansion of our mini-universe, and we have no knowledge whatsoever of what is going on in other similar mini-universes.

Our universe thus never went back to an initial singularity, but emerged by an uncaused fluctuation from the vacuum of a wider background space—a view that is often expressed by saying that the universe is a "free lunch" because in this case we got something for nothing.

Such a congenial way of talking is, however, completely misleading. In popular presentations of these models it is often not explained that they require the postulation of some sort of specially fine-tuned, background space on the analogy of a quantum mechanical vacuum from which the universe emerges via a fluctuation. Thus, the origin of the observable universe out of this wider space-time is not at all a free lunch, but requires an elaborately set table in advance.

Such models face formidable theoretical difficulties which are so severe that even some of the original proponents of these models have now abandoned them. Brout and Spindel, for example, have moved beyond such models, commenting that the theoretical foundations of the particle production mechanisms as well as the instability of the background space to fluctuations "are flimsy at best."

In any case such models have been shown to be incompatible with observational cosmology. On such scenarios, there is no way to specify exactly when and where a fluctuation in the primordial vacuum will occur which will grow into a universe. Within any finite interval of time there is a positive probability of such a fluctuation occurring at any point in space. It follows that given infinite past time, universes will spring into being at every point in the vacuum and, as they expand, will begin to collide and coalesce with one another. But we do not observe anything of this sort happening in nature.

Isham comments that this problem is "fairly lethal" to vacuum fluctuation models and that they therefore "have not found wide acceptance." About the only way to avoid the difficulty of colliding universes is to postulate that the background vacuum space is itself expanding—but then we're forced to posit some origin of the wider Universe itself, and we're right back where we started from.

I mentioned that vacuum fluctuation models have been abandoned as plausible accounts of the origin of the universe by some of their original expositors and to that extent are already somewhat passé. Brout and Spindel now contend that an explanation of the origin of the universe "must await the yet-to-come quantum theory of gravity." That brings us to the second class of quantum models.

In addition to vacuum fluctuation models, there are also *quantum gravity* models. The particular quantum gravity model of the origin of the universe which has drawn the most attention in recent years is the Hartle-Hawking model, popularized by Stephen Hawking, the brilliant mathematical theorist of Cambridge University, who has received wide publicity of his views in the popular press. One of the most interesting features of Hawking's best-selling *Brief History of Time,* in which he expounds his views, is its overtly theological orientation. Although Hawking does not deny the existence of God, he does deny that there is a Creator in the sense of a temporal First Cause of the origin of the universe.

In discussing whether a Creator exists, Hawking admits that if the universe began to exist, then one could identify the Big Bang as the instant at which God created the universe. In fact, he thinks that a number of attempts to avoid the Big Bang were probably motivated by the feeling that a beginning of time "smacks of divine intervention." Although it is not clear if Hawking shares this same motivation, he does tout his model as preferable to the Big Bang, because there would be no edge of space-time at which one "would have to appeal to God."

Hawking's theory is perhaps most easily understood by contrasting it to the standard Big Bang model. In the standard model, the universe sprang from an initial singularity which marked the origin of all matter and energy, indeed, of physical space and time themselves. Nothing existed before this point; hence, the singularity cannot have any natural cause.

Hawking hopes that by introducing quantum physics into the description of the earliest stage of the universe, prior to 10^{-43} seconds after the Big Bang, one can eliminate the singularity. In order to accomplish this, however, Hawking must introduce imaginary numbers for the time variable in his equations, that is to say, numbers like $\sqrt{-1}$. Since any real number squared always equals a positive number, it is evident that there can be no real number which is the square root of -1. Therefore, mathematicians call such numbers "imaginary."

By using imaginary numbers for the time variable, one eliminates the singularity all right, but one also thereby eliminates the difference between time and space in the equations describing the universe. As Hawking says, "the distinction between time and space disappears completely." This is a very peculiar feature of the model, since in both the Special and General Theories of Relativity, time and space are distinct in virtue of their variables' having different mathematical signs ($+$ or $-$) in the equations. But in Hawking's model, this difference in sign disappears, because he is using imaginary numbers for the time variable. By means of this device, Hawking proposes a model in which time becomes imaginary prior to 10^{-43} seconds, so that the singularity is rounded off. Space-time in this early region is geometrically the four-dimensional analogue of the two-dimensional surface of a sphere. Any point on a sphere which one chooses to be an "initial" or "beginning" point, such as the North Pole, is really just like every other point on the sphere's surface. In particular, it does not constitute an edge or boundary to that surface. Thus, on Hawking's model, the past is finite, but boundless. Moreover, since imaginary time is not distinguishable from space, it would be improper to regard any point on this sphere-like surface as actually earlier than any other point on that surface, just as it would be improper to think of any point on the surface of a ball as earlier than any other similar point. Hawking comments,

> There would be no singularities at which the laws of science broke down and no edge of space-time at which one would have to appeal to God or some new law to set the boundary conditions for space-time. . . . The universe would be completely self-contained and not affected by anything outside itself. It would be neither created nor destroyed. It would just BE.

In saying that the universe on his theory would not begin to exist, but would just BE, Hawking expresses the timeless existence of this four-dimensional space-time in which time is imaginary. He is not at all reluctant to draw theological conclusions from his model:

> The idea that space and time may form a closed surface without boundary . . . has profound implications for the role of God in the affairs of the universe. . . . So long as the universe had a beginning, we could suppose it had a creator. But if the universe is really completely self-contained, having no boundary or edge, it would have neither beginning nor end. What place, then, for a creator?

In assessing Hawking's proposed model, one could criticize it effectively merely on the physical level alone. It is on the face of it highly speculative, and, according to Isham, it is most unlikely that it is even mathematically consistent. Moreover, it is now generally recognized that the Hartle-Hawking approach fails to predict uniquely our universe; consequently, why this universe exists rather than one of an infinite number of alternatives cannot be explained.

But I prefer to leave such criticisms aside; perhaps better, more consistent models can be devised. Rather my objections strike much deeper, at the philosophical or metaphysical foundations of such theories. Hawking's quantum cosmology is rife with unexamined philosophical assumptions which are, at best, unproven and, at worst, false. Given his claim to have eliminated the need for a Creator, it's evident that Hawking does not take his theory to be merely some mathematical model which is useful for facilitating scientific predictions but which makes no pretense to be a realistic description of the world. Such a non-realist (or instrumentalist) understanding of the theory would not be incompatible with the claim that in actual fact the universe began to exist in real time and was created. Hawking's model would in that case be a sort of symbolic description of the real origin of the universe using the mathematical formalism of quantum physics. The fact that there is no beginning of the universe *in the model* would do nothing to eliminate the beginning of the universe *in reality*. Since Hawking wants to avoid a beginning of the universe and the attendant need for a Creator, he must (and does) take his model to be a realistic description of the early universe. But this is precisely where the problems arise. It seems quite evident that

Hawking faces acute difficulties in commending his theory as a realistic account of the origin of the universe.

Take just one example: his use of so-called "imaginary time." Two problems arise in connection with this notion. First, it is physically unintelligible. If he is to commend his theory as a realistic description of the universe, then Hawking has the burden to explain what "imaginary time" means. Otherwise it is a meaningless combination of words. But it is no more evident what an imaginary interval of time is any more than, say, the imaginary volume of a box or the imaginary area of a field or the imaginary number of people in a room. Hawking insists that imaginary time is "a well-defined mathematical concept." But that's not the question; rather the question is whether that mathematical concept corresponds to any physical reality. The fact that something can be defined mathematically is no guarantee that any physical reality corresponds to it, as the late Sir Herbert Dingle so vividly illustrated.

> Suppose we want to find the number of men required for a certain job under certain conditions. Every schoolboy knows such problems, and he knows that he must begin by saying: "Let x = the number of men required." But that substitution introduces a whole range of possibilities that the nature of the original problem excludes. The mathematical symbol x can be positive, negative, integral, fractional, irrational, imaginary, complex, zero, infinite, and whatever else the fertile brain of the mathematician may devise. The number of men, however, must be simply positive and integral. Consequently, when you say, "Let x = the number of men required" you are making a quite invalid substitution, and the result of the calculation, though entirely possible for the symbol, might be quite impossible for the men.

Every elementary algebra book contains such problems that lead to quadratic equations, and these have two solutions, which might be 8 and −3 say. We accept 8 as the answer and ignore −3 because we know from experience that there are

no such things as negative men, and the only alternative interpretation—that we could get the work done by subtracting three men from our gang—is obviously absurd. . . .

So we just ignore [one] of the mathematical solutions, and quite overlook the significance of that fact—namely, that in the language of mathematics we can *tell lies as well as truths, and within the scope of mathematics itself there is no possible way of telling one from the other. We can distinguish them only by experience or by reasoning outside the mathematics, applied to the possible relation between the mathematical solution and its supposed physical correlate.*

The point is that a "well-defined mathematical concept" may in fact be a metaphysical impossibility and that the only way to determine this is by getting outside the mathematics to consult what experience or extra-mathematical reasoning tells us reality is like. Time is one of those aspects of reality with which we are most intimately acquainted by experience and which has received extensive philosophical analysis as well. We simply have no comprehension of what it would be for time to be "imaginary" in the mathematical sense. Putting in imaginary numbers for the time variable appears to make no more sense than using negative numbers for the number of men required to do a job. It is a mere mathematical artifice.

Such a use of imaginary numbers for the time coordinate is nothing new. Already in 1920, Sir Arthur Eddington said that readers who found it difficult to understand curved space-time could evade the difficulty by using the "dodge" of imaginary numbers. But, he said, it is "not very profitable" to speculate on the implications of this, because "it can scarcely be regarded as anything more than an analytical device." Imaginary time was only an illustrative tool, "which certainly does not correspond to any physical reality."

Imaginary numbers are useful as mathematical devices which help in the computation of certain equations; but one always converts back to real numbers at the end in order to have some physically meaningful result. Hawking himself admits, "As far as everyday quantum mechanics is concerned, we may regard our use of imaginary time . . . as a merely mathematical device (or trick) to calculate answers about real space-time." But Hawking in his model simply declines to take the final step of reconverting to real numbers. When you do that, the singularity suddenly reappears. Hawking states,

> Only if we could picture the universe in terms of imaginary time would there be no singularities. . . . When one goes back to the real time in which we live, however, there **will** still appear to be singularities.

Thus, Hawking does not really eliminate the singularity; he only conceals it behind the physically unintelligible artifice of imaginary time.

Secondly, the use of imaginary numbers for the time variable makes time a spatial dimension, which is just bad metaphysics. Space and time are essentially different. Space is ordered by a relation of *betweenness:* for three points x, y, and z on a spatial line, y is between x and z. But time is ordered in addition by a unique relation of earlier/later than: for two moments t1 and t2 in time, t1 is earlier than t2, and t2 is later than t1. Spatial points are not related by any such relation; but this relation is essential to the nature of time, as the philosopher George Schlesinger points out: "The relations 'before' and 'after' have generally been acknowledged as being the most fundamental temporal relations, which means that time deprived of these relations would cease to be time." Thus, it is impossible for time to be a dimension of space. Moreover, time is also ordered by the relations past/future with respect to the present. For example, my eating breakfast this morning was once present; but now it is past. There is nothing even remotely similar to this relation among points in space. Thus, space and time are essentially distinct.

But perhaps Hawking can be interpreted as holding, not that time in the earliest stage of the universe is a dimension of space, but that as one goes back in time, time ceases to exist and is replaced by a spatial dimension. But such an interpretation makes no sense. It would mean that the early history of the universe was timeless. But this assertion is contradictory to the claim that this era existed before the point that time began. For before/after is precisely a temporal relation, as we have seen. Thus, to say that this timeless segment existed *before time* is to presuppose a time before time, which is self-contradictory.

Hawking seems to realize the impossibility of having two successive stages of the universe, one timeless and the other temporal, and so he is driven to the position that our universe's existing in real time is just an illusion! He asserts,

> This might suggest that the so-called imaginary time is really the real time, and that what we call real time is just a figment of our imaginations. In real time, the universe has a beginning and an end at singularities that form a boundary to space-time and at which the laws of science break down. But in imaginary time, there are no singularities or boundaries. So maybe what we call imaginary time is really more basic, and what we call real is just an idea that we invent to help us describe what we think the universe is like.

But as Smith points out, such an interpretation is "preposterous . . . at least observationally, since it is perfectly obvious that the universe in which we exist lapses in real rather than imaginary time." If Hawking were right, we could not even correctly say, for example, that Lincoln's assassination occurred after his birth, since this is to assert a temporal relation between these two events.

Significantly, this philosophical critique applies not to the Hartle-Hawking model alone, but to all quantum gravitational models, since they all share the common feature of having real space-time originate in a quantum mechanical region which is a four-dimensional space involving imaginary time. The metaphysical inadequacy of such scenarios is not a deficiency which can be solved through scientific advance precisely because the deficit is metaphysical, not physical. Of course, if some such model is interpreted non-realistically, then no metaphysical objection arises. On a non-realist interpretation, the real beginning of the universe at an initial singularity can be re-described in the language of quantum physics as a non-singular point existing in imaginary time. But the advance here is scientific (in the instrumental sense), not metaphysical. Such a model would not abrogate the fact the universe really began to exist.

It seems evident, therefore, that quantum models of the origin of the universe avoid the beginning of the universe only at the expense of making enormous and unjustified metaphysical assumptions about reality, assumptions which in the end deny the reality of time and temporal becoming and thus vitiate the models based on them as realistic descriptions of the universe. Thus, it appears that none of the alternatives to the Big Bang model of the origin of the universe is plausible. The best scientific evidence available confirms that the universe began to exist. . . . Therefore, on the basis of both philosophical argument and scientific evidence, I think we are justified in accepting our second premiss, that the universe began to exist.

Therefore, the Universe Has a Cause of Its Existence

From the first premiss—that whatever *begins* to exist has a cause—and the second premiss—that the *universe began to exist*—it follows logically that *the universe has a cause.* This conclusion ought to stagger us, to fill us with awe, for it means that the universe was brought into existence by *something* which is greater than and beyond it.

But what is the nature of this first cause of the universe? It seems to me quite plausible that it is a personal being who created the universe. This thesis is supported by both philosophical argument and scientific confirmation.

Philosophical Argument

Consider the following puzzle: we've concluded that the beginning of the universe was the effect of a first cause. By the nature of the case that cosmic cause cannot have any beginning of its existence nor any prior cause. Nor can there have been any changes in this cause, either in its nature or operations, prior to the beginning of the universe. It just exists changelessly without any beginning, and a finite time ago it brought the universe into existence. Now this is exceedingly odd. The cause is in some sense eternal and yet the effect which it produced is not eternal, but began to exist a finite time ago. How can this be? If the necessary and sufficient conditions for the production of the effect are eternal, then why isn't the effect eternal? How can all the causal conditions sufficient for the production of the effect be changelessly existent and yet the effect not also be existent along with the cause? How can the cause exist without the effect?

Let me illustrate what I mean: Let's say the cause of water's freezing is sub-zero temperatures. Whenever the temperature falls below zero degrees Centigrade, the water freezes. Once the cause is given, the effect must follow, and if the cause exists from eternity, the effect must also exist from eternity. If the temperature were to remain below zero degrees from eternity, then any water around would be frozen from eternity. But this seems to *imply that* if the cause of the universe existed eternally, the universe would also have existed eternally. And this we know to be false.

One might say that the cause came to exist or changed in some way just prior to the first event. But then the cause's beginning or changing would be the first event, and we must ask all over again for its cause. And this cannot go on forever, for we know that a beginningless series of events cannot exist. There must be an absolutely first event, before which there was no change, no previous event. We know that this first event must have been caused. The question is: How can a first event come to exist if the cause of that event exists changelessly and eternally? Why isn't the effect as co-eternal as the cause?

It seems that there is only one way out of this dilemma, and that is to infer that the cause of the universe is a personal agent who chooses to create a universe in time. Philosophers call this type of causation "agent causation," and because the agent is free, he can initiate new effects by freely bringing about conditions which were not previously present. For example, a man sitting from eternity could will to stand up; thus, a temporal effect arises from an eternally existing agent. Similarly, a finite time ago a Creator endowed with free will could have willed to bring the world into being at that moment. In this way, God could exist changelessly and eternally but choose to create the world in time. By "choose" one need not mean that the Creator changes His mind about the decision to create, but that He freely and eternally intends to create a world with a beginning. By exercising his causal power, He therefore brings it about that a world with a beginning comes to exist. So the cause is eternal, but the effect is not. In this way, then, it is possible for the temporal universe to have come to exist from an eternal cause: through the free will of a personal Creator.

The Anthropic Principle

This purely philosophical argument for the personhood of the cause of the origin of the universe receives powerful scientific confirmation from the observed fine-tuning of the universe, which bespeaks intelligent design. Without wanting to go into a discussion of the teleological argument, let me simply say that in recent years the scientific community has been stunned by its discovery of how complex and sensitive a balance of initial conditions must be given in the Big Bang in order for the universe to permit the origin and evolution of intelligent life on Earth. The universe appears, in fact, to have been incredibly fine-tuned from the moment of its inception for the production of intelligent life on Earth at this point in cosmic history.

The incredibly complex and delicately balanced nexus of initial conditions necessary for intelligent life seems to be most plausibly explained if that nexus is the product of intelligent design, that is to say, if the cause of the beginning of the universe is a personal Creator. The scientific evidence thus serves to underscore the conclusion to which philosophical argument

has led us. More than that, however: the evidence also suggests a special relationship between the Creator and human beings. For man truly is the crown of creation. Though diminutive in size in comparison with the cosmos, a human being is nonetheless the most complex structure in the universe. After listing a minimum of ten crucial steps in the evolution of Homo sapiens, each of which is so improbable that the sun would have ceased to be a main sequence star and so incinerated the Earth before it would occur, Barrow and Tipler estimate that the odds against the assembly of the human genome are between 4–1800 (100,000) and 4–360 (110,000)! They also point out that far from showing the unimportance of human life, the vast size of the universe is a prerequisite of the natural production of just those elements which are necessary to life: "for there to be enough time to construct the constituents of living beings, the Universe must be at least ten billion years old and therefore, as a consequence of its expansion, at least ten billion light years in extent." That the entire universe should thus be so designed as to culminate in man as its most marvelous creation is highly suggestive of some special care of the Creator for human creatures in particular. Indeed, the Creator might be properly understood to be a Cosmic Parent of whom we are the children. The contemporary debate surrounding the Anthropic Principle thus not only confirms the personhood of the Creator, but is also quite suggestive theologically.

So we have both good philosophical and scientific reasons for regarding the cause of the universe as a personal Creator. What more can be known about his nature? On the basis of our philosophical arguments for the beginning of the universe, we know that He must be uncaused and changeless (since an infinite regress of events is impossible). Even if God was causally active prior to the creation of the universe in some sort of metaphysical time (say, creating spiritual realms), there must still be a beginning point to His activity and, hence to change; otherwise, one would have an infinite regress of events, which is impossible. Since we know nothing about God's having been active prior to physical creation, we may assume for simplicity's sake that time (or at least differentiated time) begins at creation and that God without creation is changeless. Since He is changeless without creation, He must be either timeless without creation, or at least "relatively timeless," to borrow the expression of one philosopher; that is, He exists in an undifferentiated time prior to creation. Since He is causally related to the world, He must be in time subsequent to creation (given that the "flow" of time is in some sense real). Since He is changeless without creation, He must be immaterial, since matter inherently involves change. Being immaterial, He must be spaceless as well as timeless. Since He created the universe from nothing, we know that He must be enormously powerful, if not omnipotent. Since He brought the universe into being without any antecedently determining conditions and fine-tuned it with a precision that literally defies comprehension, He must be both free and unimaginably intelligent, if not omniscient. Moreover, the fact that the entire known universe, from the smallest elementary particles to the most distant stars, was designed in such a way as to be a suitable environment for the existence of human life on Earth suggests the astounding conclusion that He may have some special concern for us. These properties constitute the central core of what theists mean by "God."

The book of Genesis declares, "In the beginning God created the heavens and the earth." For thousands of years, muses Robert Jastrow, people who have believed this statement have known the truth which scientists have discovered only within the last fifty years. For the rationalistic scientist (and, we may add, philosopher), the story ends, smiles Jastrow, like a bad dream:

> He has scaled the mountains of ignorance; he is about to conquer the highest peak; as he pulls himself over the final rock, he is greeted by a band of theologians who have been sitting there for centuries.

The beginning of the universe—declared by revelation, established by philosophy, and confirmed by science—thus points beyond itself to God, its Personal Creator.

Objections

Now certain thinkers have objected to the intelligibility of this conclusion. For example, Adolf Grunbaum, a prominent philosopher of space and time and a vociferous critic of theism, has marshaled a whole troop of objections against inferring God as the Creator of the universe. As these are very typical, a brief review of his objections should be quite helpful. Grunbaum's objections fall into three groups. Group I seeks to cast doubt upon the concept of "cause" in the argument for a cause of the universe. (1) When we say that everything has a cause, we use the word "cause" to mean something that transforms previously existing materials from one state to another. But when we infer that the universe has a cause, we must mean by "cause" something that creates its effect out of nothing. Since these two meanings of "cause" are not the same, the argument is guilty of equivocation and is thus invalid. (2) It does not follow from the necessity of there being a cause that the cause of the universe is a conscious agent. (3) It is logically fallacious to infer that there is a single conscious agent who created the universe.

But these objections do not seem to present any insuperable difficulties: (1) The univocal concept of "cause" employed throughout the argument is the concept of something which brings about or produces its effects. Whether this production involves transformation of already existing materials or creation out of nothing is an incidental question. Thus, the charge of equivocation is groundless. (2) The personhood of the cause does not follow from the cosmological argument proper, but from an analysis of the notion of a first cause of the beginning of the universe, confirmed by Anthropic considerations. (3) The inference to a single cause of the origin of the universe seems justified in light of the principle, commonly accepted in science, that one should not multiply causes beyond necessity. One is justified in inferring only causes such as are necessary to explain the effect in question; positing any more would be gratuitous. Since the universe is a single effect originating in the Big Bang event, we have no grounds for inferring a plurality of causes.

The objections of Group II relate the notion of causality to the temporal series of events: (1) Causality is logically compatible with an infinite, beginningless series of events. (2) If everything has a cause of its existence, then the cause of the universe must also have a cause of its existence.

Both of these objections, however, seem to be based on misunderstandings. (1) It is not the concept of causality which is incompatible with an infinite series of past events. Rather the incompatibility, as we have seen, is between the notion of an actually infinite number of things and the series of past events. That causality has nothing to do with it may be seen by reflecting on the fact that the philosophical arguments for the beginning of the universe would work even if the events were all spontaneous, causally non-connected events. (2) The argument does not presuppose that everything has a cause. Rather the operative causal principle is that whatever *begins to* exist has a cause. Something that exists eternally and, hence, without a beginning would not need to have a cause. This is not special pleading for God, since the atheist has always maintained the same thing about the universe: it is beginningless and uncaused. The difference between these two hypotheses is that the atheistic view has been shown to be untenable.

Group III objections are aimed at the alleged claim that creation from nothing surpasses all understanding: (1) If creation out of nothing is incomprehensible, then it is irrational to believe in such a doctrine. (2) An incomprehensible doctrine cannot explain anything.

But with regard to (1), creation from nothing is not incomprehensible in Grunbaum's sense. By "incomprehensible" Grunbaum appears to mean "unintelligible" or "meaningless." But the statement that a finite time ago a transcendent cause brought the universe into being out of nothing is clearly a meaningful statement, not mere gibberish, as is evident from the very fact that we are debating it. We may not understand how the cause brought the universe into being out of nothing, but then it is even more incomprehensible, in this sense, how the universe could have popped into being out of nothing without any cause, material or productive. One cannot avert the necessity of a cause by positing an absurdity. (2) The doctrine, being an intelligible statement, obviously does constitute a purported explanation of the origin of the universe. It may be a metaphysical rather than a scientific explanation, but it is no less an explanation for that.

Grunbaum has one final objection against inferring a cause of the origin of the universe: the cause of the Big Bang can be neither after the Big Bang (since backward causation is impossible) nor before the Big Bang (since time begins at or after the Big Bang). Therefore, the universe's beginning to exist cannot have a cause. But this argument pretty clearly confronts us with a false dilemma. For why couldn't God's creating the universe be simultaneous (or coincident) with the Big Bang? On the view I've defended, God may be conceived to be timeless or relatively timeless without creation and in time at and subsequent to the first moment of creation.

None of Grunbaum's objections, therefore, seems to undermine the credibility of our argument for God as the Personal Creator of the universe.

Hence, amazing as it may seem, the most plausible answer to the question of why something exists rather than nothing is that God exists.

For Further Reflection

1. Examine Craig's version of the *kalam* cosmological argument (the first part of this essay). Is it valid? Is it sound? Why or why not? Explain your answer.

2. Even if it is sound, what does it prove? Does it lend support to the theistic doctrine that a wholly Good, all-powerful being created the universe?

3. Examine the second part of Craig's argument, that dealing with the scientific confirmation evidence. Does that add significant support for a theistic conclusion?

4. How does the Big Bang support the idea that there is a God? Discuss whether the alternative theories which Craig rejects could find better support.

5. Craig argues that there is good reason to believe, on the basis of the anthropic principle, that the First Cause is the Personal Creator of Theism. Explain the anthropic principle and discuss whether it provides evidence for the existence of God.

6. Discuss Craig's brief treatment of the objections to his position.

II.7   A Critique of the Cosmological Argument

PAUL EDWARDS

Paul Edwards (1923–2004) was emeritus professor of philosophy at Brooklyn College, City University of New York, and the author of several books and articles, including *The Logic of Moral Discourse*. He was the editor of the *Encyclopedia of Philosophy*. In this article he attacks the cosmological argument, specifically Aquinas' second and third arguments, at several different points, holding that the argument fails at each of these points.

Study Questions

1. Even if the cosmological argument is sound, would it show that God is all-good or all-powerful? What is Edwards' view?

2. According to Aquinas, the idea of an infinite regress of causes would imply that nothing exists. Why does Aquinas hold this view? What mistake does Edwards accuse him of making?

3. Could there be more than one first cause?

4. Distinguish between causes *in fieri* and causes *in esse*. Give an illustration of this distinction.

5. Illustrate the difference between the cause of a whole series and the cause of individuals in the series.

6. State the argument from contingency.

7. What does Edwards say about the possibility of the universe being uncaused? What is his view about the universe being a "brute fact," something that is unexplainable?

INTRODUCTION

THE SO-CALLED "cosmological proof" is one of the oldest and most popular arguments for the existence of God. It was forcibly criticized by Hume, Kant, and Mill, but it would be inaccurate to consider the argument dead or even moribund. Catholic philosophers, with hardly any exception, appear to believe that it is as solid and conclusive as ever. Thus Father F. C. Copleston confidently championed it in his Third Programme debate* with Bertrand Russell, and in America, where Catholic writers are more sanguine, we are told by a Jesuit professor of physics that "the existence of an intelligent being as the First Cause of the universe can be established by *rational scientific inference.*"[1]

> I am absolutely convinced [the same writer continues] that any one who would give the same consideration to that proof (the cosmological argument), as outlined for example in William Brosnan's *God and Reason,* as he would give to a line of argumentation found in the *Physical Review* or the *Proceedings of the Royal Society* would be forced to admit that the cogency of this argument for the existence of God far outstrips that which is found in the reasoning which Chadwick uses to prove the existence of the neutron, which today is accepted as certain as any conclusion in the physical sciences.

Mild theists like the late Professor Dawes Hicks and Dr. [A. C.] Ewing, who concede many of Hume's and Kant's criticisms, nevertheless contend that the argument possesses a certain core of truth. In popular discussions it also crops up again and again—for example, when believers address atheists with such questions as "You tell me where the universe came from!" Even philosophers who reject the cosmological proof sometimes embody certain of its confusions in the formulation of their own position. In the light of all

*[BBC, 1948—ed. note]

this, it may be worthwhile to undertake a fresh examination of the argument with special attention to the fallacies that were not emphasized by the older critics.

ANALYSIS OF THE CAUSAL ARGUMENT

The cosmological proof has taken a number of forms, the most important of which are known as the "causal argument" and "the argument from contingency," respectively. In some writers, in Samuel Clarke for example, they are combined, but it is best to keep them apart as far as possible. The causal argument is the second of the "five ways" of Aquinas and roughly proceeds as follows: We find that the things around us come into being as the result of the activity of other things. These causes are themselves the result of the activity of other things. But such a causal series cannot "go back to infinity." Hence there must be a first member, a member which is not itself caused by any preceding member—an uncaused or "first" cause.

It has frequently been pointed out that even if this argument were sound it would not establish the existence of *God*. It would not show that the first cause is all-powerful or all-good or that it is in any sense personal. Somebody believing in the eternity of atoms, or of matter generally, could quite consistently accept the conclusion. Defenders of the causal argument usually concede this and insist that the argument is not in itself meant to prove the existence of God. Supplementary arguments are required to show that the first cause must have the attributes assigned to the deity. They claim, however, that the argument, if valid, would at least be an important step towards a complete proof of the existence of God.

Does the argument succeed in proving so much as a first cause? This will depend mainly on the soundness of the premise that an infinite series of

Reprinted from The Rationalist Annual, *1959, edited by Hector Hawton. Reprinted by permission of Paul Edwards. Notes [at end of reading] were edited.*

causes is impossible. Aquinas supports this premise by maintaining that the opposite belief involves a plain absurdity. To suppose that there is an infinite series of causes logically implies that nothing exists now; but we know that plenty of things do exist now; and hence any theory which implies that nothing exists now must be wrong. Let us take some causal series and refer to its members by the letters of the alphabet:

$$A \rightarrow B \ldots W \rightarrow X \rightarrow Y \rightarrow Z$$

Z stands here for something presently existing, e.g., Margaret Truman. Y represents the cause or part of the cause of Z, say Harry Truman. X designates the cause or part of the cause of Y, say Harry Truman's father, etc. Now, Aquinas reasons, whenever we take away the cause, we also take away the effect: if Harry Truman had never lived, Margaret Truman would never have been born. If Harry Truman's father had never lived, Harry Truman and Margaret Truman would never have been born. If A had never existed, none of the subsequent members of the series would have come into existence. But it is precisely A that the believer in the infinite series is "taking away." For in maintaining that the series is infinite he is denying that it has a first member; he is denying that there is such a thing as a first cause; he is in other words denying the existence of A. Since without A, Z could not have existed, his position implies that Z does not exist now; and that is plainly false. This argument fails to do justice to the supporter of the infinite series of causes. Aquinas has failed to distinguish between the two statements:

1. A did not exist, and

2. A is not uncaused.

To say that the series is infinite implies (2), but it does not imply (1). The following parallel may be helpful here: Suppose Captain Spaulding had said, "I am the greatest explorer who ever lived," and somebody replied, "No, you are not." This answer would be denying that the Captain possessed the exalted attribute he had claimed for

himself, but it would not be denying his existence. It would not be "taking him away." Similarly, the believer in the infinite series is not "taking A away." He is taking away the privileged status of A; he is taking away its "first causiness." He does not deny the *existence* of A or of any particular member of the series. He denies that A or anything else *is the first member* of the series. Since he is not taking A away, he is not taking B away, and thus he is also not taking X, Y, or Z away. His view, then, does not commit him to the absurdity that nothing exists now, or more specifically, that Margaret Truman does not exist now. It may be noted in this connection that a believer in the infinite series is not necessarily denying the existence of supernatural beings. He is merely committed to denying that such a being, if it exists, is uncaused. He is committed to holding that whatever other impressive attributes a supernatural being might possess, the attribute of being a first cause is not among them.

The causal argument is open to several other objections. Thus, even if otherwise valid, the argument, would not prove a *single* first cause. For there does not seem to be any good ground for supposing that the various causal series in the universe ultimately merge. Hence even if it is granted that no series of causes can be infinite, the possibility of a plurality of first members has not been ruled out. Nor does the argument establish the *present* existence of the first cause. It does not prove this, since experience clearly shows that an effect may exist long after its cause has been destroyed.

ORIGINATING VS. SUSTAINING CAUSES

Many defenders of the causal argument would contend that at least some of these criticisms rest on a misunderstanding. They would probably go further and contend that the argument was not quite fairly stated in the first place—or at any rate that if it was fair to some of its adherents it was not fair to others. They would in this connection distinguish between two types of causes—what they call "causes *in fieri*" and what they call "causes *in esse*." A cause *in fieri* is a factor which brought or helped to bring an effect into existence. A cause *in esse* is a factor which "sustains" or helps to sustain the effect "in being." The parents of a human being would be an example of a cause *in fieri*. If somebody puts a book in my hand and I keep holding it up, his putting it there would be the cause *in fieri,* and my holding it would be the cause *in esse* of the book's position. To quote Father [G. H.] Joyce:

> If a smith forges a horse-shoe, he is only a cause *in fieri* of the shape given to the iron. That shape persists after his action has ceased. So, too, a builder is a cause *in fieri* of the house which he builds. In both cases the substances employed act as causes *in esse* as regards the continued existence of the effect produced. Iron, in virtue of its natural rigidity, retains in being the shape which it has once received, and, similarly, the materials employed in building retain in being the order and arrangement which constitute them into a house.[2]

Using this distinction, the defender of the argument now reasons in the following way. To say that there is an infinite series of causes *in fieri* does not lead to any absurd conclusions. But Aquinas is concerned only with causes *in esse,* and an infinite series of *such* causes is impossible. In the words of the contemporary American Thomist, R. P. Phillips:

> Each member of the series of causes possesses being solely by virtue of the actual present operation of a superior cause. . . . Life is dependent, inter alia, on a certain atmospheric pressure, this again on the continual operation of physical forces, whose being and operation depends on the position of the earth in the solar system, which itself must endure relatively unchanged, a state of being which can only be continuously produced by a definite—if unknown—constitution of the material universe. This constitution, however, cannot be its own cause. That a thing should cause itself is impossible: for in order that it may cause it is necessary for it to exist,

which it cannot do, on the hypothesis, until it has been caused. So it must *be* in order to cause itself. Thus, not being uncaused nor yet its own cause, it must be caused by another, which produces and preserves it. It is plain, then, that as no member of this series possesses being except in virtue of the actual present operation of a superior cause, if there *be* no first cause actually operating none of the dependent causes could operate either. We are thus irresistibly led to posit a first efficient cause which, while itself uncaused, shall impart causality to a whole series. . . .

> The series of causes which we are considering is not one which stretches back into the past; so that we are not demanding a beginning of the world at some definite moment reckoning back from the present, but an actual cause now operating, to account for the present being of things.[3]

Professor Phillips offers the following parallel to bring out his point:

> In a goods train each truck is moved and moves by the action of the one immediately in front of it. If then we suppose the train to be infinite, i.e., that there is no end to it, and so no engine which starts the motion, it is plain that no truck will move. To lengthen it out to infinity will not give it what no member of it possesses of itself, viz. the power of drawing the truck behind it. If then we see any truck in motion we know there must be an end to the series of trucks which gives causality to the whole.[4]

Father Joyce introduces an illustration from Aquinas to explain how the present existence of things may be compatible with an infinite series of causes *in fieri* but not with an infinite series of causes *in esse.*

> When a carpenter is at work, the series of efficient causes on which his work depends is necessarily limited. The final effect, e.g., the fastening of a nail is caused by a hammer: the hammer is moved by the arm: and the motion of his arm is determined by the motor-impulses communicated from the nerve centres of the brain. Unless the subordinate causes were limited in number, and were connected with a starting-point of motion, the hammer must remain inert, and the

nail will never be driven in. If the series be supposed infinite, no work will ever take place. But if there is question of causes on which the work is not essentially dependent, we cannot draw the same conclusion. We may suppose the carpenter to have broken an infinite number of hammers, and as often to have replaced the broken tool by a fresh one. There is nothing in such a supposition which excludes the driving home of the nail.

The supporter of the infinite series of causes, Joyce also remarks, is

> . . . asking us to believe that although each link in a suspended chain is prevented from falling simply because it is attached to the one above it, yet if only the chain be long enough, it will, taken as a whole, need no support, but will hang loose in the air suspended from nothing.

This formulation of the causal argument unquestionably circumvents one of the objections mentioned previously. If Y is the cause *in esse* of an effect, Z, then it must exist as long as Z exists. If the argument were valid in this form it would therefore prove the present and not merely the past existence of a first cause. In this form the argument is, however, less convincing in another respect. To maintain that all "natural" or "phenomenal" objects—things like tables and mountains and human beings—require a cause *in fieri* is not implausible, though even here Mill and others have argued that strictly speaking only *changes* require a causal explanation. It is far from plausible, on the other hand, to claim that all natural objects require a cause *in esse*. It may be granted that the air around us is a cause *in esse* of human life and further that certain gravitational forces are among the causes *in esse* of the air being where it is. But when we come to gravitational forces or, at any rate, to material particles like atoms or electrons it is difficult to see what cause *in esse* they require. To those not already convinced of the need for a supernatural First Cause some of the remarks by Professor Phillips in this connection appear merely dogmatic and question-begging. Most people would grant that such particles as atoms

did not cause themselves, since, as Professor Phillips observes, they would in that event have had to exist before they began existing. It is not at all evident, however, that these particles cannot be uncaused. Professor Phillips and all other supporters of the causal argument immediately proceed to claim that there is something else which needs no cause *in esse*. They themselves admit thus, that there is nothing self-evident about the proposition that everything must have a cause *in esse*. Their entire procedure here lends substance to Schopenhauer's gibe that supporters of the cosmological argument treat the law of universal causation like "a hired cab which we dismiss when we have reached our destination."

But waiving this and all similar objections, the restatement of the argument in terms of causes *in esse* in no way avoids the main difficulty which was previously mentioned. A believer in the infinite series would insist that his position was just as much misrepresented now as before. He is no more removing the member of the series which is supposed to be the first cause *in esse* than he was removing the member which had been declared to be the first cause *in fieri*. He is again merely denying a privileged status to it. He is not denying the reality of the cause *in esse* labelled "A." He is not even necessarily denying that it possesses supernatural attributes. He is again merely taking away its "first causiness."

The advocates of the causal argument in either form seem to confuse an infinite series with one which is long but finite. If a book, Z, is to remain in its position, say 100 miles up in the air, there must be another object, say another book, Y, underneath it to serve as its support. If Y is to remain where it is, it will need another support, X, beneath it. Suppose that this series of supports, one below the other, continues for a long time, but eventually, say after 100,000 members, comes to a first book which is not resting on any other book or indeed on any other support. In that event the whole collection would come crashing down. What we seem to need is a first member of the series, a first support (such as the earth) which does not need another member as *its* support, which in other words is "self-supporting."

This is evidently the sort of picture that supporters of the First Cause argument have before their minds when they rule out the possibility of an infinite series. But such a picture is not a fair representation of the theory of the infinite series. A *finite* series of books would indeed come crashing down, since the first or lowest member would not have a predecessor on which it could be supported. If the series, however, were infinite this would not be the case. In that event every member *would* have a predecessor to support itself on and there would be no crash. That is to say: a crash can be avoided either by a finite series with a first self-supporting member or by an infinite series. Similarly, the present existence of motion is equally compatible with the theory of a first unmoved mover and with the theory of an infinite series of moving objects, and the present existence of causal activity is compatible with the theory of a first cause *in esse* as much as with the theory of an infinite series of such causes.

The illustrations given by Joyce and Phillips are hardly to the point. It is true that a carpenter would not, in a *finite* time-span, succeed in driving in a nail if he had to carry out an infinite number of movements. For that matter, he would not accomplish this goal in a finite time if he broke an infinite number of hammers. However, to make the illustrations relevant we must suppose that he has infinite time at his disposal. In that case he would succeed in driving in the nail even if he required an infinite number of movements for this purpose. As for the goods train, it may be granted that the trucks do not move unless the train has an engine. But this illustration is totally irrelevant as it stands. A relevant illustration would be that of engines, each moved by the one in front of it. Such a train would move if it were infinite. For every member of this series there would be one in front capable of drawing it along. The advocate of the infinite series of causes does not, as the original

illustration suggests, believe in a series whose members are not really causally connected with one another. In the series he believes in, every member is genuinely the cause of the one that follows it.

CAUSES OF SERIES AND OF INDIVIDUALS

No staunch defender of the cosmological argument would give up at this stage. Even if there were an infinite series of causes *in fieri* or *in esse,* he would contend, this still would not do away with the need for an ultimate, a first cause. As Father Copleston put it in his debate with Bertrand Russell:

> Every object has a phenomenal cause, if you insist on the infinity of the series. But the series of phenomenal causes is an insufficient explanation of the series. Therefore, the series has not a phenomenal cause, but a transcendent cause. . . .
> An infinite series of contingent beings will be, to my way of thinking, as unable to cause itself as one contingent being.

The demand to find the cause of the series as a whole rests on the erroneous assumption that the series is something over and above the members of which it is composed. It is tempting to suppose this, at least by implication, because the word "series" is a noun like "dog" or "man." Like the expression "this dog" or "this man," the phrase "this series" is easily taken to designate an individual object. But reflection shows this to be an error. If we have explained the individual members there is nothing additional left to be explained. Supposing I see a group of five Eskimos standing on the corner of Sixth Avenue and 50th Street and I wish to explain why the group came to New York. Investigation reveals the following stories:

- Eskimo No. 1 did not enjoy the extreme cold in the polar region and decided to move to a warmer climate.

- No. 2 is the husband of Eskimo No. 1. He loves her dearly and did not wish to live without her.

- No. 3 is the son of Eskimos 1 and 2. He is too small and too weak to oppose his parents.

- No. 4 saw an advertisement in the *New York Times* for an Eskimo to appear on television.

- No. 5 is a private detective engaged by the Pinkerton Agency to keep an eye on Eskimo No. 4.

Let us assume that we have now explained in the case of each of the five Eskimos why he or she is in New York. Somebody then asks: "All right, but what about the group as a whole; why is *it* in New York?" This would plainly be an absurd question. There is no group over and above the five members, and if we have explained why each of the five members is in New York we have *ipso facto* explained why the group is there. It is just as absurd to ask for the cause of the series as a whole as distinct from asking for the causes of individual members.

THE ARGUMENT FROM CONTINGENCY

It is most unlikely that a determined defender of the cosmological line of reasoning would surrender even here. He would probably admit that the series is not a thing over and above its members and that it does not make sense to ask for the cause of the series if the cause of each member has already been found. He would insist, however, that when he asked for the explanation of the entire series, he was not asking for its *cause*. He was really saying that a series, finite or infinite, is not "intelligible" or "explained" if it consists of nothing but "contingent" members. To quote Father Copleston once more:

> What we call the world is intrinsically unintelligible apart from the existence of God. The infinity of the series of events, if such an infinity

could be proved, would not be in the slightest degree relevant to the situation. If you add up chocolates, you get chocolates after all, and not a sheep. If you add up chocolates to infinity, you presumably get an infinite number of chocolates. So, if you add up contingent beings to infinity, you still get contingent beings, not a necessary being.

This last quotation is really a summary of the "contingency argument," the other main form of the cosmological proof and the third of the five ways of Aquinas. It may be stated more fully in these words: All around us we perceive contingent beings. This includes all physical objects and also all human minds. In calling them "contingent," we mean that they might not have existed. We mean that the universe can be *conceived* without this or that physical object, without this or that human being, however certain their actual existence may be. These contingent beings we can trace back to other contingent beings—e.g. a human being to his parents. However, since these other beings are also contingent, they do not provide a real or full explanation. The contingent beings we originally wanted explained have not yet become intelligible, since the beings to which they have been traced back are no more necessary than they were. It is just as true of our parents, for example, as it is of ourselves, that they might not have existed. We can then properly explain the contingent beings around us only by tracing them back ultimately to some necessary being, to something which exists necessarily, which has "the reason for its existence within itself." The existence of contingent beings, in other words, implies the existence of a necessary being.

This form of cosmological argument is even more beset with difficulties than the causal variety. In the first place, there is the objection, stated with great force by Kant, that it really commits the same error as the ontological argument in tacitly regarding existence as an attribute or characteristic. To say that there is a necessary being is to say that it would be a self-contradiction to deny its existence. This would mean that at least one existential statement is a necessary truth, and this in turn presupposes that in at least one case existence is contained in a concept. But only a characteristic can be contained in a concept and it has seemed plain to most philosophers since Kant that existence is not a characteristic, that it can hence never be contained in a concept, and that hence no existential statement can ever be a necessary truth. To talk about anything "existing necessarily" is in their view about as sensible as to talk about round squares, and they have concluded that the contingency-argument is quite absurd.

It would lead too far to discuss here the reasons for denying that existence is a characteristic. I will assume that this difficulty can somehow be surmounted and that the expression "necessary being," as it is intended by the champions of the contingency-argument, might conceivably apply to something. There remain other objections which are of great weight. I shall try to state these by first quoting again from the debate between Bertrand Russell and Father Copleston:

Russell: . . . It all turns on this question of sufficient reason, and I must say you haven't defined "sufficient reason" in a way that I can understand—what do you mean by sufficient reason? You don't mean cause?

Copleston: Not necessarily. Cause is a kind of sufficient reason. Only contingent beings can have a cause. God is his own sufficient reason, and he is not cause of himself. By sufficient reason in the full sense I mean an explanation adequate for the existence of some particular being.

Russell: But when is an explanation adequate? Suppose I am about to make a flame with a match. You may say that the adequate explanation of that is that I rub it on the box.

Copleston: Well for practical purposes—but theoretically, that is only a partial explanation. An adequate explanation must ultimately be a total explanation, to which nothing further can be added.

Russell: Then I can only say that you're looking for something which can't be got, and which one ought not to expect to get.

Copleston: To say that one has not found it is one thing; to say that one should not look for it seems to me rather dogmatic.

Russell: Well, I don't know. I mean, the explanation of one thing is another thing which makes the other thing dependent on yet another, and you have to grasp this sorry scheme of things entire to do what you want, and that we can't do.

Russell's main point here may be expanded in the following way. The contingency-argument rests on a misconception of what an explanation is and does, and similarly on what it is that makes phenomena "intelligible." Or else it involves an obscure and arbitrary redefinition of "explanation," "intelligible," and related terms. Normally, we are satisfied that we have explained a phenomenon if we have found its cause or if we have exhibited some other uniform or near-uniform connection between it and something else. Confining ourselves to the former case, which is probably the most common, we might say that a phenomenon, *Z*, has been explained if it has been traced back to a group of factors, *a*, *b*, *c*, *d*, etc., which are its cause. These factors are the full and real explanation of *Z*, quite regardless of whether they are pleasing or displeasing, admirable or contemptible, necessary or contingent. The explanation would not be adequate only if the factors listed are not really the cause of *Z*. If they are the cause of *Z*, the explanation would be adequate, even though each of the factors is merely a "contingent" being.

Let us suppose that we have been asked to explain why General Eisenhower won the elections of 1952. "He was an extremely popular general," we might answer, "while Stevenson was relatively little known; moreover there was a great deal of resentment over the scandals in the Truman Administration." If somebody complained that this was only a partial explanation we might mention additional antecedents, such as the widespread belief that the Democrats had allowed communist agents to infiltrate the State Department, that Eisenhower was a man with a winning smile, and that unlike Stevenson he had shown the good sense to say one thing on race relations in the North and quite another in the South. Theoretically, we might go further and list the motives of all American voters during the weeks or months preceding the elections. If we could do this we would have explained Eisenhower's victory. We would have made it intelligible. We would "understand" why he won and why Stevenson lost. Perhaps there is a sense in which we might make Eisenhower's victory even more intelligible if we went further back and discussed such matters as the origin of American views on Communism or of racial attitudes in the North and South. However, to explain the outcome of the election in any ordinary sense, loose or strict, it would not be necessary to go back to prehistoric days or to the amoeba or to a first cause, if such a first cause exists. Nor would our explanation be considered in any way defective because each of the factors mentioned was a "contingent" and not a necessary being. The only thing that matters is whether the factors were really the cause of Eisenhower's election. If they were, then it has been explained although they are contingent beings. If they were not the cause of Eisenhower's victory, we would have failed to explain it even if each of the factors were a necessary being.

If it is granted that, in order to explain a phenomenon or to make it intelligible, we need not bring in a necessary being, then the contingency-argument breaks down. For a series, as was already pointed out, is not something over and above its members, and every contingent member of it could in that case be explained by reference to other contingent beings. But I should wish to go further than this and it is evident from Russell's remarks that he would do so also. Even if it were granted, both that the phrase "necessary being" is meaningful and that all explanations are defective unless the phenomena to be explained are traced back to a necessary being, the conclusion would still not have been established. The conclusion follows from this premise together with the additional premise that *there are* explanations of phenomena in the special sense just mentioned. It is this further premise which Russell (and many other philosophers) would ques-

tion. They do not merely question, as Copleston implies, whether human beings can ever obtain explanations in this sense, but whether they *exist*. To assume without further ado that phenomena have explanations or an explanation in this sense is to beg the very point at issue. The use of the same word "explanation" in two crucially different ways lends the additional premise a plausibility it does not really possess. It may indeed be highly plausible to assert that phenomena have explanations, whether we have found them or not, in the ordinary sense in which this usually means that they have causes. It is then tempting to suppose, because of the use of the same word, that they also have explanations in a sense in which this implies dependence on a necessary thing. But this is a gross *non sequitur*.

COULD THE UNIVERSE BE UNCAUSED?

It is necessary to add a few words about the proper way of formulating the position of those who reject the main premise of the cosmological argument, in either of the forms we have considered. It is sometimes maintained in this connection that in order to reach a "self-existing" entity it is not necessary to go beyond the universe: the universe itself (or "Nature") is "self-existing." And this in turn is sometimes expanded into the statement that while all individual things "within" the universe are caused, the universe itself is uncaused. Statements of this kind are found in Büchner, Bradlaugh, Haeckel, and other freethinkers of the nineteenth and early twentieth century. Sometimes the assertion that the universe is "self-existing" is elaborated to mean that *it* is the "necessary being." Some eighteenth-century unbelievers, apparently accepting the view that there is a necessary being, asked why Nature or the material universe could not fill the bill as well or better than God.

"Why," asks one of the characters in Hume's *Dialogues,* "may not the material universe be the necessarily existent Being? . . . We dare not affirm that we know all the qualities of matter; and for aught we can determine, it may contain some qualities, which, were they known, would make its nonexistence appear as great a contradiction as that twice two is five."

Similar remarks can be found in d'Holbach and several of the Encyclopedists.

The former of these formulations immediately invites the question why the universe, alone of all "things," is exempted from the universal sway of causation. "The strong point of the cosmological argument," writes Dr. Ewing, "is that after all it does remain incredible that the physical universe should just have happened . . . It calls out for some further explanation of some kind." The latter formulation is exposed to the criticism that there is nothing any more "necessary" about the existence of the universe or Nature as a whole than about any particular thing within the universe.

I hope some of the earlier discussions in this article have made it clear that in rejecting the cosmological argument one is not committed to either of these propositions. If I reject the view that there is a supernatural first cause, I am not thereby committed to the proposition that there is a *natural* first cause, and even less to the proposition that a mysterious "thing" called "the universe" qualifies for this title. I may hold that there is no "universe" over and above individual things of various sorts, and, accepting the causal principle, I may proceed to assert that all these things are caused by other things, and these other things by yet other things, and so on, *ad infinitum*. In this way no arbitrary exception is made to the principle of causation. Similarly, if I reject the assertion that God is a "necessary being," I am not committed to the view that the universe is such an entity. I may hold that it does not make sense to speak of anything as a "necessary being" and that even if there were such a thing as the universe it could not be properly considered a necessary being.

However, in saying that nothing is uncaused or that there is no necessary being, one is not committed to the view that everything, or for that matter anything, is merely a "brute fact." Dr. Ewing laments that "the usual modern philosophical views opposed to theism do not try to give any rational explanation of the world at all, but just take it as a brute fact not to be explained." They thus fail to "rationalize" the universe. Theism, he concedes, cannot completely rationalize things either since it does not show "how God can be his own cause or how it is that he does not need a cause." Now, if one means by "brute fact" something for which there *exists* no explanation (as distinct from something for which no explanation is in our possession), then the theists have at least one brute fact on their hands, namely God. Those who adopt Büchner's formulation also have one brute fact on their hands, namely "the universe." Only the position I have been supporting dispenses with brute facts altogether. I don't know if this is any special virtue, but the defenders of the cosmological argument seem to think so.

NOTES

1. J. S. O'Connor, "A Scientific Approach to Religion," *The Scientific Monthly* (1940), p. 369; my italics.
2. *The Principles of Natural Theology*, p. 58.
3. *Modern Thomistic Philosophy*, Vol. II, pp. 284–285.
4. Ibid., p. 278.

For Further Reflection

1. Consider this question: "Why is there something rather than nothing?" Is it a question that we should try to answer? What would Aquinas say about this question? What does Edwards think? What do you think?
2. How successful has Edwards been in criticizing the two forms of the cosmological argument? How might a theist respond to him?

II.8   The Watch and the Watchmaker

WILLIAM PALEY

William Paley (1743–1805), archdeacon of Carlisle, was a leading evangelical apologist. His most important work is *Natural Theology, or Evidences of the Existence and Attributes of the Deity Collected from the Appearances of Nature* (1802), the first chapter of which is reprinted here. Paley argues that just as we infer an intelligent designer to account for the purpose-revealing watch, so we must infer an intelligent grand designer to account for the purpose-revealing world.

Study Questions

1. What does Paley think are the inherent differences between a stone and a watch? What inferences does each permit about its origins?
2. What is the analogy between the watch and the world, according to Paley? Describe his argument.
3. How does Paley respond to objections to the analogy?

STATEMENT OF THE ARGUMENT

IN CROSSING A HEATH, suppose I pitched my foot against a *stone*, and were asked how the stone came to be there, I might possibly answer, that, for anything I knew to the contrary, it had lain there forever; nor would it, perhaps, be very easy to show the absurdity of this answer. But suppose I found a *watch* upon the ground, and it should be inquired how the watch happened to be in that place, I should hardly think of the answer which I had given—that, for anything I knew, the watch might have always been there. Yet why should not this answer serve for the watch as well as for the stone? Why is it not as admissible in the second case as in the first? For this reason, and for no other; viz., that, when we come to inspect the watch, we perceive (what we could not discover in the stone) that its several parts are framed and put together for a purpose, e.g., that they are so formed and adjusted as to produce motion, and that motion so regulated as to point out the hour of the day; that, if the different parts had been differently shaped from what they are, if a different size from what they are, or placed after any other manner, or in any other order than that in which they are placed, either no motion at all would have been carried on in the machine, or none which would have answered the use that is now served by it. To reckon up a few of the plainest of these parts, and of their offices, all tending to one result: We see a cylindrical box containing a coiled elastic spring, which, by its endeavor to relax itself, turns round the box. We next observe a flexible chain (artificially wrought for the sake of flexure) communicating the action of the spring from the box to the fuse. We then find a series of wheels, the teeth of which catch in, and apply to, each other, conducting the motion from the fuse to the balance, and from the balance to the pointer, and, at the same time, by the size and shape of those wheels, so regulating that motion as to terminate in causing an index, by an equable and measured progression, to pass over a given space in a given time. We take notice that the wheels are made of brass, in order to keep them from rust; the springs of steel, no other metal being so elastic; that over the face of the watch there is placed a glass, a material employed in no other part of the work, but in the room of which, if there had been any other than a transparent substance, the hour could not be seen without opening the case. This mechanism being observed (it requires indeed an examination of the instrument, and perhaps some previous knowledge of the subject, to perceive and understand it; but being once, as we have said, observed and understood), the inference, we think, is inevitable, that the watch must have had a maker; that there must have existed, at some time, and at some place or other, an artificer or artificers who formed it for the purpose which we find it actually to answer; who comprehended its construction, and designed its use.

I. Nor would it, I apprehend, weaken the conclusion, that we had never seen a watch made; that we had never known an artist capable of making one; that we were altogether incapable of executing such a piece of workmanship ourselves, or of understanding in what manner it was performed; all this being no more than what is true of some exquisite remains of ancient art, of some lost arts, and, to the generality of mankind, of the more curious productions of modern manufacture. Does one man in a million know how oval frames are turned? Ignorance of this kind exalts our opinion of the unseen and unknown artist's skill, if he be unseen and unknown, but raises no doubt in our minds of the existence and agency of such an artist, at some former time, and in some place or other. Nor can I perceive that it varies at all the inference, whether the question arise concerning a human agent, or concerning an agent of a different species, or an agent possessing, in some respect, a different nature.

II. Neither, secondly, would it invalidate our conclusion, that the watch sometimes went wrong, or that it seldom went exactly right. The purpose of the machinery, the design, and the designer, might be evident, and, in the case supposed, would be evident, in whatever way we accounted for the irregularity of the movement, or whether we could account for it or not. It is not necessary that a machine be perfect, in order to show with what design it was made; still less necessary, where the only question is, whether it were made with any design at all.

III. Nor, thirdly, would it bring any uncertainty into the argument, if there were a few parts of the watch, concerning which we could not discover, or had not yet discovered, in what manner they conduced to the general effect; or even some parts, concerning which we could not ascertain whether they conduced to that effect in any manner whatever. For, as to the first branch of the case, if by the loss, or disorder, or decay of the parts in question, the movement of the watch were found in fact to be stopped, or disturbed, or retarded, no doubt would remain in our minds as to the utility or intention of these parts, although we should be unable to investigate the manner according to which, or the connection by which, the ultimate effect depended upon their action or assistance; and the more complex is the machine, the more likely is this obscurity to arise. Then, as to the second thing supposed, namely, that there were parts which might be spared without prejudice to the movement of the watch, and that he had proved this by experiment, these superfluous parts, even if we were completely assured that they were such, would not vacate the reasoning which we had instituted concerning other parts. The indication of contrivance remained, with respect to them, nearly as it was before.

IV. Nor, fourthly, would any man in his senses think the existence of the watch, with its various machinery, accounted for, by being told that it was one out of possible combinations of material forms; that whatever he had found in the place where he found the watch, must have

From William Paley, Natural Theology, or Evidences of the Existence and Attributes of the Deity Collected from the Appearances of Nature *(1802).*

contained some internal configuration or other; and that this configuration might be the structure now exhibited, viz., of the works of a watch, as well as a different structure.

V. Nor, fifthly, would it yield his inquiry more satisfaction, to be answered, that there existed in things a principle of order, which had disposed the parts of the watch into their present form and situation. He never knew a watch made by the principle of order; nor can he even form to himself an idea of what is meant by a principle of order, distinct from the intelligence of the watchmaker.

VI. Sixthly, he would be surprised to hear that the mechanism of the watch was no proof of contrivance, only a motive to induce the mind to think so.

VII. And not less surprised to be informed, that the watch in his hand was nothing more than the result of the laws of *metallic* nature. It is a perversion of language to assign any law as the efficient, operative cause of anything. A law presupposes an agent; for it is only the mode according to which an agent proceeds; it implies a power; for it is the order according to which that power acts. Without this agent, without this power, which are both distinct from itself, the *law* does nothing, is nothing. The expression, "the law of metallic nature," may sound strange and harsh to a philosophic ear; but it seems quite as justifiable as some others which are more familiar to him such as "the law of vegetable nature," "the law of animal nature," or, indeed, as "the law of nature" in general, when assigned as the cause of phenomena in exclusion of agency and power, or when it is substituted into the place of these.

VIII. Neither, lastly, would our observer be driven out of his conclusion, or from his confidence in its truth, by being told that he knew nothing at all about the matter. He knows enough for his argument: he knows the utility of the end: he knows the subserviency and adaptation of the means to the end. These points being known, his ignorance of other points, his doubts concerning other points, affect not the certainty of his reasoning. The consciousness of knowing little need not beget a distrust of that which he does know. . . .

APPLICATION OF THE ARGUMENT

Every indication of contrivance, every manifestation of design, which existed in the watch, exists in the works of nature; with the difference, on the side of nature, of being greater and more, and that in a degree which exceeds all computation. I mean that the contrivances of nature surpass the contrivances of art, in the complexity, subtlety, and curiosity of the mechanism; and still more, if possible, do they go beyond them in number and variety; yet in a multitude of cases, are not less evidently mechanical, not less evidently contrivances, not less evidently accommodated to their end, or suited to their office, than are the most perfect productions of human ingenuity. . . .

For Further Reflection

1. Do you think that Paley's argument is cogent? Do you think that the universe does reveal design or order? Is there a significant difference between the concepts of design and order?

2. Can you think of possible objections to Paley's argument? How might Paley respond to them?

A Critique of the Teleological Argument II.9

DAVID HUME

The Scottish empiricist and skeptic David Hume (1711–1776) is one of the most important philosophers in the history of philosophy. The *Dialogues Concerning Natural Religion* (published posthumously in 1779) contains the classic critique of the argument from design. Our reading is from Parts 2 and 5 of this dialogue. Cleanthes, who opens our selection, is a natural theologian, the Paley of his time, who opposes both the orthodox believer, Demea, and the skeptic, Philo. Philo puts forth the major criticisms against the argument from design.

Study Questions

1. How does the natural theologian Cleanthes argue for the existence of God?
2. What are (the orthodox believer) Demea's objections to Cleanthes' way of arguing for the existence of God?
3. What does the agnostic Philo say is his chief scruple about Cleanthes' argument?
4. In Philo's second main speech, what distinction does he make between order and arrangement, on the one hand, and design, on the other? What is his purpose in this?
5. What is Philo's contention about arguing from parts to wholes?
6. Why does Philo accuse Cleanthes of anthropomorphism?
7. List six objections that Philo makes to the design argument. Are they plausible objections?
8. What is Cleanthes' response to Philo's objections?

CLEANTHES: LOOK ROUND THE WORLD: Contemplate the whole and every part of it: You will find it to be nothing but one great machine, subdivided into an infinite number of lesser machines, which again admit of subdivisions to a degree beyond what human senses and faculties can trace and explain. All these various machines, and even their most minute parts, are adjusted to each other with an accuracy which ravishes into admiration all men who have ever contemplated them. The curious adapting of means to ends, throughout all nature, resembles exactly, though it much exceeds, the productions of human contrivance; of human design, thought, wisdom, and intelligence. Since therefore the effects resemble each other, we are led to infer, by all the rules of analogy, that the causes also resemble, and that the Author of Nature is somewhat similar to the mind of man, though possessed of much larger faculties, proportioned to the grandeur of the work which he has executed. By this argument *a posteriori*, and by this argument alone, do we prove at once the existence of a Deity and his similarity to human mind and intelligence.

Demea: I shall be so free, *Cleanthes,* said *Demea,* as to tell you that from the beginning I could not approve of your conclusion concerning the similarity of the Deity to men; still less can I approve of the mediums by which you endeavor to establish it. What! No demonstration of the

From David Hume, Dialogues Concerning Natural Religion *(1779).*

Being of God! No abstract arguments! No proofs *a priori!* Are these which have hitherto been so much insisted on by philosophers all fallacy, all sophism? Can we reach no farther in this subject than experience and probability? I will say not that this is betraying the cause of a Deity; but surely, by this affected candor, you give advantages to atheists which they never could obtain by the mere dint of argument and reasoning.

Philo: What I chiefly scruple in this subject, said *Philo,* is not so much that all religious arguments are by *Cleanthes* reduced to experience, as that they appear not to be even the most certain and irrefragable of that inferior kind. That a stone will fall, that fire will burn, that the earth has solidity, we have observed a thousand and a thousand times; and when any new instance of this nature is presented, we draw without hesitation the accustomed inference. The exact similarity of the cases gives us a perfect assurance of a similar event, and a stronger evidence is never desired nor sought after. But wherever you depart, in the least, from the similarity of the cases, you diminish proportionately the evidence, and may at last bring it to a very weak *analogy,* which is confessedly liable to error and uncertainty. After having experienced the circulation of the blood in human creatures, we make no doubt that it takes place in *Titius* and *Maevius;* but from its circulation in frogs and fishes it is only a presumption, though a strong one, from analogy that it takes place in men and other animals. The analogical reasoning is much weaker when we infer the circulation of the sap in vegetables from our experience that the blood circulates in animals; and those who hastily followed that imperfect analogy are found, by more accurate experiments to have been mistaken.

If we see a house, *Cleanthes,* we conclude, with the greatest certainty, that it had an architect or builder because this is precisely that species of effect which we have experienced to proceed from that species of cause. But surely you will not affirm that the universe bears such a resemblance to a house that we can with the same certainty infer a similar cause, or that the analogy is here entire and perfect. The dissimilitude is so striking that the utmost you can here pretend to is a guess, a conjecture, a presumption concerning a similar cause; and how that pretension will be received in the world, I leave you to consider.

Cleanthes: It would surely be very ill received, replied *Cleanthes;* and I should be deservedly blamed and detested did I allow that the proofs of a Deity amounted to no more than a guess or conjecture. But is the whole adjustment of means to ends in a house and in the universe so slight a resemblance? The economy of final causes? The order, proportion, and arrangement of every part? Steps of a stair are plainly contrived that human legs may use them in mounting, and this inference is certain and infallible. Human legs are also contrived for walking and mounting; and this inference, I allow, is not altogether so certain because of the dissimilarity which you remark; but does it, therefore, deserve the name only of presumption or conjecture?

Demea: Good God! cried *Demea,* interrupting him, where are we? Zealous defenders of religion allow that the proofs of a Deity fall short of perfect evidence! And you, *Philo,* on whose assistance I depended in proving the adorable mysteriousness of the Divine Nature, do you assent to all these extravagant opinions of *Cleanthes?* For what other name can I give them? or, why spare my censure when such principles are advanced, supported by such an authority, before so young a man as *Pamphilus?*

Philo: You seem not to apprehend, replied *Philo,* that I argue with *Cleanthes* in his own way, and, by showing him the dangerous consequences of his tenets, hope at last to reduce him to our opinion. But what sticks most with you, I observe, is the representation which *Cleanthes* has made of the argument *a posteriori;* and, finding that that argument is likely to escape your hold and vanish into air, you think it so disguised that you can scarcely believe it to be set in its true light. Now, however much I may dissent, in other respects, from the dangerous principle of *Cleanthes,* I must allow that he has fairly represented that argument, and I shall endeavor so to state the matter to you that you will entertain no further scruples with regard to it.

Were a man to abstract from everything which he knows or has seen, he would be altogether incapable, merely from his own ideas, to determine what kind of scene the universe must be, or to give the preference to one state or situation of things above another. For as nothing which he clearly conceives could be esteemed impossible or implying a contradiction, every chimera of his fancy would be upon an equal footing; nor could he assign any just reason why he adheres to one idea or system, and rejects the others which are equally possible.

Again, after he opens his eyes and contemplates the world as it really is, it would be impossible for him at first to assign the cause of any one event, much less of the whole of things, or of the universe. He might set his fancy a rambling, and she might bring him in an infinite variety of reports and representations. These would all be possible; but, being all equally possible, he would never of himself give a satisfactory account for his preferring one of them to the rest. Experience alone can point out to him the true cause of any phenomenon.

Now, according to this method of reasoning, *Demea*, it follows (and is, indeed, tacitly allowed by *Cleanthes* himself) that order, arrangement, or the adjustment of final causes, is not of itself any proof of design, but only so far as it has been experienced to proceed from that principle. For aught we can know *a priori*, matter may contain the source or spring of order originally within itself, as well as mind does; and there is no more difficulty in conceiving that the several elements, from an internal unknown cause, may fall into the most exquisite arrangement, than to conceive that their ideas, in the great universal mind, from a like internal unknown cause, fall into that arrangement. The equal possibility of both these suppositions is allowed. But, by experience, we find, according to *Cleanthes*, that there is a difference between them. Throw several pieces of steel together, without shape or form; they will never

arrange themselves so as to compose a watch. Stone and mortar and wood, without an architect, never erect a house. But the ideas in a human mind, we see, by an unknown, inexplicable economy, arrange themselves so as to form the plan of a watch or house. Experience, therefore, proves that there is an original principle of order in mind, not in matter. From similar effects we infer similar causes. The adjustment of means to ends is alike in the universe, as in a machine of human contrivance. The causes, therefore, must be resembling.

I was from the beginning scandalized, I must own, with this resemblance which is asserted between the Deity and human creatures, and must conceive it to imply such a degradation of the Supreme Being as no sound theist could endure. With your assistance, therefore, *Demea*, I shall endeavor to defend what you justly call the adorable mysteriousness of the Divine Nature, and shall refute this reasoning of *Cleanthes*, provided he allows that I have made a fair representation of it.

When *Cleanthes* had assented, *Philo*, after a short pause, proceeded in the following manner.

That all inferences, *Cleanthes*, concerning fact are founded on experience, and that all experimental reasonings are founded on the supposition that similar causes prove similar effects, and similar effects similar causes, I shall not at present much dispute with you. But observe, I entreat you, with what extreme caution all just reasoners proceed in the transferring of experiments to similar cases. Unless the cases be exactly similar, they repose no perfect confidence in applying their past observation to any particular phenomenon. Every alteration of circumstances occasions a doubt concerning the event; and it requires new experiments to prove certainly that the new circumstances are of no moment or importance. A change in bulk, situation, arrangement, age, disposition of the air, or surrounding bodies; any of these particulars may be attended with the most unexpected consequences. And unless the objects be quite familiar to us, it is the highest temerity to expect with assurance, after any of these changes, an event similar to that which before fell under our observation. The slow and deliberate steps of philosophers here, if anywhere, are distinguished from the precipitate march of the vulgar, who, hurried on by the smallest similitude, are incapable of all discernment or consideration.

But can you think, *Cleanthes,* that your usual phlegm and philosophy have been preserved in so wide a step as you have taken when you compared to the universe houses, ships, furniture, machines; and, from their similarity in some circumstances, inferred a similarity in their causes? Thought, design, intelligence, such as we discover in men and other animals, is no more than one of the springs and principles of the universe, as well as heat or cold, attraction or repulsion, and a hundred others which fall under daily observation. It is an active cause by which some particular parts of nature, we find, produce alterations on other parts. But can a conclusion, with any propriety, be transferred from parts to the whole? Does not the great disproportion bar all comparison and inference? From observing the growth of a hair, can we learn anything concerning the generation of a man? Would the manner of a leaf's blowing, even though perfectly known, afford us any instruction concerning the vegetation of a tree?

But allowing that we were to take the *operations* of one part of nature upon another for the foundation of our judgment concerning the *origin* of the whole (which never can be admitted), yet why select so minute, so weak, so bounded a principle as the reason and design of animals is found to be upon this planet? What peculiar privilege has this little agitation of the brain which we call "thought," that we must thus make it the model of the whole universe? Our partiality in our own favor does indeed present it on all occasions, but sound philosophy ought carefully to guard against so natural an illusion.

So far from admitting, continued *Philo,* that the operations of a part can afford us any just conclusion concerning the origin of the whole, I will not allow any one part to form a rule for another part if the latter be very remote from the former. Is there any reasonable ground to conclude that the inhabitants of other planets possess thought, intelligence, reason, or anything similar to these faculties in men? When nature has so extremely diversified her manner of operation in this small globe, can we imagine that she incessantly copies herself throughout so immense a universe? And if thought, as we may well suppose, be confined merely to this narrow corner, and has even there so limited a sphere of action, with what propriety can we assign it for the original cause of all things? The narrow views of a peasant who makes his domestic economy the rule for the government of kingdoms is in comparison a pardonable sophism.

But were we ever so much assured that a thought and reason resembling the human were to be found throughout the whole universe, and were its activity elsewhere vastly greater and more commanding than it appears in this globe; yet I cannot see why the operations of a world constituted, arranged, adjusted, can with any propriety be extended to a world which is in its embryostate, and is advancing towards that constitution and arrangement. By observation we know somewhat of the economy, action, and nourishment of a finished animal; but we must transfer with great caution that observation to the growth of a foetus in the womb, and still more to the formation of an animalcule in the loins of its male parent. Nature, we find, even from our limited experience, possesses an infinite number of springs and principles which incessantly discover themselves on every change of her position and situation. And what new and unknown principles would actuate her in so new and unknown a situation as that of the formation of a universe, we cannot, without the utmost temerity, pretend to determine.

A very small part of this great system, during a very short time, is very imperfectly discovered to us; and do we thence pronounce decisively concerning the origin of the whole?

Admirable conclusion! Stone, wood, brick, iron, brass, have not, at this time, in this minute globe of earth, an order or arrangement without human art and contrivance; therefore, the universe could not originally attain its order and arrangement without something similar to human art. But is a part of nature a rule for another part very wide of the former? Is it a rule for the whole? Is a very small part a rule for the universe? Is nature in one situation a certain rule for nature in another situation vastly different from the former?

And can you blame me, *Cleanthes,* if I here imitate the prudent reserve of *Simonides,* who, according to the noted story, being asked by *Hiero, What God was?* desired a day to think of it, and then two days more; and after that manner continually prolonged the term, without ever bringing in his definition or description? Could you even blame me if I had answered, at first, *that I did not know,* and was sensible that this subject lay vastly beyond the reach of my faculties? You might cry out skeptic and raillier, as much as you pleased; but, having found in so many other subjects much more familiar the imperfections and even contradictions of human reason, I never should expect any success from its feeble conjectures in a subject so sublime and so remote from the sphere of our observation. When two *species* of objects have always been observed to be conjoined together, I can *infer,* by custom, the existence of one wherever I see the existence of the other; and this I call an argument from experience. But how this argument can have place where the objects, as in the present case, are single, individual, without parallel or specific resemblance, may be difficult to explain. And will any man tell me with a serious countenance that an orderly universe must arise from some thought and art like the human because we have experience of it? To ascertain this reasoning it were requisite that we had experience of the origin of worlds; and it is not sufficient, surely, that we have seen ships and cities arise from human art and contrivance. . . .

Philo: But to show you still more inconveniences, continued *Philo,* in your anthropomorphism, please to take a new survey of your principles. *Like effects prove like causes.* This is the experimental argument; and this, you say too, is the sole theological argument. Now it is certain that the liker the effects which are seen and the liker the causes which are inferred, the stronger is the argument. Every departure on either side diminishes the probability and renders the experiment less conclusive. You cannot doubt of the principle; neither ought you to reject its consequences.

All the new discoveries in astronomy which prove the immense grandeur and magnificence of the works of nature are so many additional arguments for a Deity, according to the true system of theism; but, according to your hypothesis of experimental theism, they become so many objections, by removing the effect still farther from all resemblance to the effects of human art and contrivance. For if *Lucretius,* even following the old system of the world, could exclaim:

> Who is strong enough to rule the sum, who to hold in hand and control the mighty bridle of the unfathomable deep? who to turn about all the heavens at one time, and warm the fruitful worlds with ethereal fires, or to be present in all places and at all times.[1]

If Tully[2] esteemed this reasoning so natural as to put it into the mouth of his Epicurean:

> What power of mental vision enabled your master Plato to descry the vast and elaborate architectural process which, as he makes out, the deity adopted in building the structure of the universe? What method of engineering was employed? What tools and levers and derricks? What agents carried out so vast an understanding? And how were air, fire, water, and earth enabled to obey and execute the will of the architect?

If this argument, I say, had any force in former ages, how much greater must it have at present when the bounds of nature are so infinitely enlarged and such a magnificent scene is opened to us? It is still more unreasonable to form our idea of so unlimited a cause from our experience of the narrow productions of human design and invention.

The discoveries by microscopes, as they open a new universe in miniature, are still objections, according to you; arguments, according to me. The farther we push our researches of this kind, we are still led to infer the universal cause of all to be vastly different from mankind, or from any object of human experience and observation.

And what say you to the discoveries in anatomy, chemistry, botany? . . . *Cleanthes:* These surely are no objections, replied *Cleanthes;* they only discover new instances of art and contrivance. It is still the image of mind reflected on us from innumerable objects. *Philo:* Add a mind *like the human,* said *Philo. Cleanthes:* I know of no other, replied *Cleanthes. Philo:* And the liker, the better, insisted *Philo. Cleanthes:* To be sure, said *Cleanthes.*

Philo: Now, *Cleanthes,* said *Philo,* with an air of alacrity and triumph, mark the consequences. *First,* by this method of reasoning you renounce all claim to infinity in any of the attributes of the Deity. For, as the cause ought only to be proportioned to the effect, and the effect, so far as it falls under our cognizance, is not infinite: What pretensions have we, upon your suppositions, to ascribe that attribute to the Divine Being? You will still insist that, by removing him so much from all similarity to human creatures, we give in to the most arbitrary hypothesis, and at the same time weaken all proofs of his existence.

Secondly, you have no reason, on your theory, for ascribing perfection to the Deity, even in his finite capacity; or for supposing him free from every error, mistake, or incoherence, in his undertakings. There are many inexplicable difficulties in the works of Nature which, if we allow a perfect author to be proved *a priori,* are easily solved, and become only seeming difficulties from the narrow capacity of man, who cannot trace infinite relations. But according to your method of reasoning, these difficulties become all real; and, perhaps, will be insisted on as new instances of likeness to human art and contrivance. At least, you must acknowledge that it is impossible for us to tell, from our limited views, whether this system contains any great faults or deserves any considerable praise if compared to other possible and even real

systems. Could a peasant, if the *Aeneid* were read to him, pronounce that poem to be absolutely faultless, or even assign to it its proper rank among the productions of human wit, he who had never seen any other production?

But were this world ever so perfect a production, it must still remain uncertain whether all the excellences of the work can justly be ascribed to the workman. If we survey a ship, what an exalted idea must we form of the ingenuity of the carpenter who framed so complicated, useful, and beautiful a machine? And what surprise must we feel when we find him a stupid mechanic who imitated others, and copied an art which, through a long succession of ages, after multiplied trials, mistakes, corrections, deliberations, and controversies, had been gradually improving? Many worlds might have been botched and bungled, throughout an eternity, ere this system was struck out; much labor lost; many fruitless trials made; and a slow but continued improvement carried on during infinite ages in the art of world-making. In such subjects, who can determine where the truth, nay, who can conjecture where the probability lies, amidst a great number of hypotheses which may be proposed, and a still greater which may be imagined?

And what shadow of an argument, continued *Philo,* can you produce from your hypothesis to prove the unity of the Deity? A great number of men join in building a house or ship, in rearing a city, in framing a commonwealth; why may not several deities combine in contriving and framing a world? This is only so much greater similarity to human affairs. By sharing the work among several, we may so much further limit the attributes of each, and get rid of that extensive power and knowledge which must be supposed in one deity, and which, according to you, can only serve to weaken the proof of his existence. And if such foolish, such vicious creatures as man can yet often unite in framing and executing one plan, how much more those deities or demons, whom we may suppose several degrees more perfect?

To multiply causes without necessity is indeed contrary to true philosophy, but this principle applies not to the present case. Were one deity antecedently proved by your theory who were possessed of every attribute requisite to the production of the universe, it would be needless, I own (though not absurd), to suppose any other deity existent. But while it is still a question whether all these attributes are united in one subject or dispersed among several independent beings; by what phenomena in nature can we pretend to decide the controversy? Where we see a body raised in a scale, we are sure that there is in the opposite scale, however concealed from sight, some counterpoising weight equal to it; but it is still allowed to doubt whether that weight be an aggregate of several distinct bodies or one uniform united mass. And if the weight requisite very much exceeds anything which we have ever seen conjoined in any single body, the former supposition becomes still more probable and natural. An intelligent being of such vast power and capacity as is necessary to produce a universe, or, to speak in the language of ancient philosophy, so prodigious an animal, exceeds all analogy and even comprehension.

But further, *Cleanthes,* men are mortal, and renew their species by generation; and this is common to all living creatures. The two great sexes of male and female, says *Milton,* animate the world. Why must this circumstance, so universal, so essential, be excluded from those numerous and limited deities? Behold, then, the theogeny of ancient times brought back upon us.

And why not become a perfect anthropomorphite? Why not assert the deity or deities to be corporeal, and to have eyes, a nose, mouth, ears, etc.? *Epicurus* maintained that no man had ever seen reason but in a human figure; therefore, the gods must have a human figure. And this argument, which is deservedly so much ridiculed by *Cicero,* becomes, according to you, solid and philosophical.

In a word, *Cleanthes,* a man who follows your hypothesis is able, perhaps, to assert or conjecture that the universe sometime arose from something like design. But beyond that position he cannot ascertain one single circumstance and is left afterwards to fix every point of his theology by the utmost license of fancy and hypothesis. This world, for aught he knows, is very faulty and imperfect, compared to a superior standard, and was only the first rude essay of some infant deity who afterwards abandoned it, ashamed of his lame performance. It is the work only of some dependent, inferior deity, and is the object of derision to his superiors. It is the production of old age and dotage in some superannuated deity; and ever since his death has run on at adventures, from the first impulse and active force which it received from him. . . . You justly give signs of horror, *Demea,* at these strange suppositions; but these, and a thousand more of the same kind, are *Cleanthes'* suppositions, not mine. From the moment the attributes of the Deity are supposed finite, all these have place. And I cannot, for my part, think that so wild and unsettled a system of theology is, in any respect, preferable to none at all.

Cleanthes: These suppositions I absolutely disown. They strike me, however, with no horror, especially when proposed in that rambling way in which they drop from you. On the contrary, they give me pleasure when I see that, by the utmost indulgence of your imagination, you never get rid of the hypothesis of design in the universe, but are obliged at every turn to have recourse to it. To this concession I adhere steadily; and this I regard as a sufficient foundation for religion.

NOTES

1. *On the Nature of Things,* II, 1096–1099 (trans. by W. D. Rouse).

2. Tully was a common name for the Roman lawyer and philosopher Marcus Tullius Cicero, 106–43 B.C. The excerpt is from *The Nature of the Gods,* I, viii, 19 (trans. by H. Rackham).

For Further Reflection

1. The teleological argument has had a long and distinguished career, but is it plausible? How probable does it make the existence of a God?

2. How effective are Hume's criticisms? Consider his contention that we can't argue from the part to a whole. Is that always true? Can't we sometimes make valid inferences from a part to the whole? For example, if we discover that the saltwater from the Atlantic Ocean that is near our home is undrinkable, can't we infer that the rest of the water in the Atlantic Ocean is likely undrinkable? This may be a weak argument, but doesn't the part lend some probability to conclusions about the whole?

3. Examine each of Hume's objections to determine their strength. What might Paley reply to them?

II.10   The Ontological Argument

ST. ANSELM AND GAUNILO

St. Anselm (c. 1033–1109) was Abbot of Bec and later Archbishop of Canterbury. He wrote several important treatises on theological subjects, including *Cur Deus Homo* (*Why God Became Man*). In this selection from his *Proslogium,* he begins with the definition of God as "that than which nothing greater can be conceived." Today we might translate that as "the greatest possible being." From that definition he proceeds to argue for the necessary existence of God.

Gaunilo was an eleventh-century Benedictine monk who first criticized Anselm's argument. Little is known about him.

Study Questions

1. Note that St. Anselm begins his argument with a prayer to God. Is this significant for understanding the argument? What does his request show about Anselm's assumptions?
2. What is the significance of the analogy with the painter?
3. After an initial reading, attempt to outline the argument. Do you agree with Anselm that it proves the existence of God?
4. What is Gaunilo's criticism of the argument? Is it plausible?
5. Evaluate Anselm's rejoinder.

ST. ANSELM'S PRESENTATION

Truly there is a God, although the fool hath said in his heart, There is no God.

AND SO, LORD, DO THOU, who dost give understanding to faith, give me, so far as thou knowest it to be profitable, to understand that thou art as we believe; and that thou art that

These exerpts are from Anselm's Proslogium, Gaunilo's In Behalf of the Fool, *and Anselm's "Apologetic." Reprinted from St. Anselm,* Basic Writings, *trans. S. W. Deane, by permission of The Open Court Publishing Company, a division of Carus Publishing Company, Peru, IL. Copyright © 1903, 1962 by Open Court Publishing Company.*

which we believe. And, indeed, we believe that thou art a being than which nothing greater can be conceived. Or is there no such nature, since the fool hath said in his heart, there is no God? (Psalms xiv, 1). But, at any rate, this very fool, when he hears of this being of which I speak—a being than which nothing greater can be conceived—understands what he hears, and what he understands is in his understanding; although he does not understand it to exist.

For, it is one thing for an object to be in the understanding, and another to understand that the object exists. When a painter first conceives of what he will afterwards perform, he has it in his understanding, but he does not yet understand it to be, because he has not yet performed it. But after he has made the painting, he both has it in his understanding, and he understands that it exists, because he has made it.

Hence, even the fool is convinced that something exists in the understanding, at least, than which nothing greater can be conceived. For, when he hears of this, he understands it. And whatever is understood, exists in the understanding. And assuredly that, than which nothing greater can be conceived, cannot exist in the understanding alone. For, suppose it exists in the understanding alone: then it can be conceived to exist in reality; which is greater.

Therefore, if that, than which nothing greater can be conceived, exists in the understanding alone, the very being, than which nothing greater can be conceived, is one, than which a greater can be conceived. But obviously this is impossible. Hence, there is no doubt that there exists a being than which nothing greater can be conceived, and it exists both in the understanding and in reality.

God cannot be conceived not to exist.—God is that, than which nothing greater can be conceived.— That which can be conceived not to exist is not God.

And it assuredly exists so truly, that it cannot be conceived not to exist. For, it is possible to conceive of a being which cannot be conceived not to exist; and this is greater than one which can be conceived not to exist. Hence, if that, than which nothing greater can be conceived, can be conceived not

to exist, it is not that, than which nothing greater can be conceived. But this is an irreconcilable contradiction. There is, then, so truly a being than which nothing greater can be conceived to exist, that it cannot even be conceived not to exist; and this being thou art, O Lord, our God.

So truly, therefore, dost thou exist, O Lord, my God, that thou canst not be conceived not to exist; and rightly. For, if a mind could conceive of a being better than thee, the creature would rise above the Creator; and this is most absurd. And, indeed, whatever else there is, except thee alone, can be conceived not to exist. To thee alone, therefore, it belongs to exist more truly than all other beings, and hence in a higher degree than all others. For, whatever else exists does not exist so truly, and hence in a less degree it belongs to it to exist. Why, then, has the fool said in his heart, there is no God (Psalms xiv, 1), since it is so evident, to a rational mind, that thou dost exist in the highest degree of all? Why, except that he is dull and a fool?

How the fool has said in his heart what cannot be conceived.—A thing may be conceived in two ways: (1) when the word signifying it is conceived; (2) when the thing itself is understood. As far as the word goes, God can be conceived not to exist; in reality he cannot.

But how has the fool said in his heart what he could not conceive; or how is it that he could not conceive what he said in his heart? since it is the same to say in the heart, and to conceive.

But, if really, nay, since really, he both conceived, because he said in his heart; and did not say in his heart, because he could not conceive; there is more than one way in which a thing is said in the heart or conceived. For, in one sense, an object is conceived, when the word signifying it is conceived; and in another, when the very entity, which the object is, is understood.

In the former sense, then, God can be conceived not to exist; but in the latter, not at all. For no one who understands what fire and water are can conceive fire to be water, in accordance with the nature of the facts themselves, although this is possible according to the words. So, then, no one who understands what God is can conceive that

God does not exist; although he says these words in his heart, either without any or with some foreign, signification. For, God is that than which a greater cannot be conceived. And he who thoroughly understands this, assuredly understands that this being so truly exists, that not even in concept can it be non-existent. Therefore, he who understands that God so exists, cannot conceive that he does not exist.

I thank thee, gracious Lord, I thank thee; because what I formerly believed by thy bounty, I now so understand by thine illumination, that if I were unwilling to believe that thou dost exist, I should not be able not to understand this to be true.

GAUNILO'S CRITICISM

For example: it is said that somewhere in the ocean is an island, which, because of the difficulty, or rather the impossibility, of discovering what does not exist, is called the lost island. And they say that this island has an inestimable wealth of all manner of riches and delicacies in greater abundance than is told of the Islands of the Blest; and that having no owner or inhabitant, it is more excellent than all other countries, which are inhabited by mankind, in the abundance with which it is stored.

Now if some one should tell me that there is such an island, I should easily understand his words, in which there is no difficulty. But suppose that he went on to say, as if by a logical inference: "You can no longer doubt that this island which is more excellent than all lands exists somewhere, since you have no doubt that it is in your understanding. And since it is more excellent not to be in the understanding alone, but to exist both in the understanding and in reality, for this reason it must exist. For if it does not exist, any land which really exists will be more excellent than it; and so the island already understood by you to be more excellent will not be more excellent."

If a man should try to prove to me by such reasoning that this island truly exists, and that

its existence should no longer be doubted, either I should believe that he was jesting, or I know not which I ought to regard as the greater fool: myself, supposing that I should allow this proof; or him, if he should suppose that he had established with any certainty the existence of this island. For he ought to show first that the hypothetical excellence of this island exists as a real and indubitable fact, and in no wise as any unreal object, or one whose existence is uncertain, in my understanding.

ST. ANSELM'S REJOINDER

A criticism of Gaunilo's example, in which he tries to show that in this way the real existence of a lost island might be inferred from the fact of its being conceived.

But, you say, it is as if one should suppose an island in the ocean, which surpasses all lands in its fertility, and which, because of the difficulty, or rather the impossibility, of discovering what does not exist, is called a lost island; and should say that there can be no doubt that this island truly exists in reality, for this reason, that one who hears it described easily understands what he hears.

Now I promise confidently that if any man shall devise anything existing either in reality or in concept alone (except that than which a greater cannot be conceived) to which he can adapt the sequence of my reasoning, I will discover that thing, and will give him his lost island, not to be lost again.

But it now appears that this being than which a greater is inconceivable cannot be conceived not to be, because it exists on so assured a ground of truth; for otherwise it would not exist at all.

Hence, if any one says that he conceives this being not to exist, I say that at the time when he conceives of this either he conceives of a being than which a greater is inconceivable, or he does not conceive at all. If he does not conceive, he does not conceive of the non-existence of that of which he does not conceive. But if he does conceive, he certainly conceives of a being which cannot be even conceived not to exist. For if it could be conceived not to exist, it could be conceived to have a beginning and an end. But this is impossible.

He, then, who conceives of this being conceives of a being which cannot be even conceived not to exist; but he who conceives of this being does not conceive that it does not exist; else he conceives what is inconceivable. The nonexistence, then, of that than which a greater cannot be conceived is inconceivable.

For Further Reflection

1. Some philosophers have objected that Anselm misunderstands the concept of "being." Being is not an ordinary concept like "red" or "horse," but an instantiating concept which asserts that these other concepts are exemplified (for example, the concept unicorn is not exemplified, but the concept of horse is). It makes no sense, they contend, to say that being is exemplified. Are they correct?

2. Is it greater to exist than not to exist, as Anselm argues? Or is the term "greater" ambiguously or wrongly used here?

3. Could a similar argument as Anselm's be used to prove that a perfectly powerful devil exists as the supreme being and creator of all things?

An Analysis of the Ontological Argument   II.11

WILLIAM ROWE

William Rowe (1931–) is emeritus professor of philosophy at Purdue University and the author of several works in philosophy of religion, including *Philosophy of Religion: An Introduction* (1978), from which this selection is taken. Rowe begins by analyzing Anselm's version of the ontological argument and then considers Gaunilo's and Kant's criticisms of it, adding two criticisms of his own. He ends with an assessment of the value of the argument.

Study Questions

1. What are the basic concepts involved in the ontological argument?
2. What is the importance of the two concepts *existence in the understanding* and *existence in reality*?
3. What does Anselm mean by *greatness*?
4. With what term does Rowe advise substituting for "the being than which none greater exists"?
5. Who was Gaunilo and what is his objection to the ontological argument?
6. What is Kant's criticism of the ontological argument?
7. What are the other two criticisms of the ontological argument?

From Philosophy of Religion: An Introduction, *2nd ed., with permission of Wadsworth, a division of Thomson Learning: www.thomsonrights.com. Copyright © 1993.*

IT IS PERHAPS BEST to think of the Ontological Argument not as a single argument but as a family of arguments each member of which begins with a concept of God and, by appealing only to *a priori* principles, endeavors to establish that God actually exists. Within this family of arguments, the most important historically is the argument set forth by Anselm in the second chapter of his *Proslogium* (a discourse).[1] Indeed, it is fair to say that the Ontological Argument begins with Chapter Two of Anselm's *Proslogium*. In an earlier work, *Monologium* (a soliloquy), Anselm had endeavored to establish the existence and nature of God by weaving together several versions of the Cosmological Argument. In the preface to *Proslogium* Anselm remarks that after the publication of *Monologium* he began to search for a single argument which alone would establish the existence and nature of God. After much strenuous but unsuccessful effort, he reports that he sought to put the project out of his mind in order to turn to more fruitful tasks. The idea, however, continued to haunt him until one day the proof he had so strenuously sought became clear to his mind. It is this proof which Anselm sets forth in the second chapter of *Proslogium*.

BASIC CONCEPTS

Before setting forth Anselm's argument in step-by-step fashion, it will be useful to introduce a few concepts that will help us understand some of the central ideas which figure in the argument. Suppose we draw a vertical line in our imagination and imagine that on the left side of our line are all the things which exist, while on the right side of the line are all the things which don't exist. We might then set about to make a list of some of the things on both sides of our imaginary line, a list we might start as follows:

THINGS WHICH EXIST	THINGS WHICH DON'T EXIST
The Empire State Building	The Fountain of Youth
Dogs	Unicorns
The Planet Mars	The Abominable Snowman

Now, each of the things (or sort of things) listed thus far has the following feature: it logically might have been on the other side of the line. The Fountain of Youth, for example, is on the right side of the line but *logically* there is no absurdity in the idea that it might have been on the left side of the line. Similarly, although dogs do exist, we surely can imagine without logical absurdity that they might not have existed, that they might have been on the right side of the line. Let's then record this feature of the things thus far listed by introducing the idea of a *contingent thing* as a thing that logically might have been on the other side of the line from the side it actually is on. The planet Mars and the abominable snowman are contingent things even though the former happens to exist and the latter does not.

Suppose we add to our list by writing down the phrase "the object which is completely round and completely square at the same time" on the right side of our line. The round square, however, unlike the other things thus far listed on the right side of our line, is something that *logically could not* have been on the left side of the line. Noting this, let's introduce the idea of an *impossible thing* as a thing that is on the right side of the line and logically could not have been on the left side of the line.

Looking again at our list, the question arises as to whether there is anything on the left side of our imaginary line which is such that, unlike the things thus far listed on the left side, it *logically could not* have been on the right side of the line. At this point we don't have to answer this question. But it is useful to have a concept to apply to any such things should there be any. Accordingly, let's introduce the notion of a *necessary thing* as a thing that is on the left side of our imaginary line and logically could not have been on the right side of the line.

Finally, we may introduce the idea of a *possible thing* as any thing that is either on the left side of our imaginary line or logically might have been on the left side of the line. Possible things, then, will be all those things that are not impossible things—that is, all those things that are either contingent or necessary. If there are no necessary things then all possible things will be contingent and all contingent things will be possible. If there is a necessary thing, however, then there will be a possible thing which is not contingent.

Armed with the concepts just explained we can now proceed to clarify certain important distinctions and ideas in Anselm's thought. The first of these is his distinction between *existence in the understanding* and *existence in reality*. Anselm's notion of existence in reality is the same as our notion of existence, that is, being on the left side of our imaginary line. Since the Fountain of Youth is on the right side of the line it does not exist in reality. The things which exist are, to use Anselm's phrase, the things which exist in reality. Anselm's notion of existence in the understanding, however, is not the same as any idea we normally employ. But what Anselm means by "existence in the understanding" is not particularly mysterious. When we think of a certain thing, say the Fountain of Youth, then that thing, in Anselm's view, exists in the understanding. So some of the things on both sides of our imaginary line exist in the understanding, but only those on the left side of our line exist in reality. Are there any things that don't exist in the understanding? Undoubtedly there are. For there are things, both existing and nonexisting, of which we have not really thought. Now suppose I assert that the Fountain of Youth does not exist. Since to meaningfully deny the existence of something, I must have that thing in mind, it follows on Anselm's view that whenever someone asserts that some thing does not exist, that thing does exist in the understanding.[2] So in asserting that the Fountain of Youth does not exist I imply that the Fountain of Youth does exist in the understanding. And in asserting that it doesn't exist, I have asserted (on Anselm's view) that it doesn't exist in reality. This means that my simple assertion that the Fountain of Youth doesn't exist amounts to the somewhat more complex claim that the Fountain of Youth exists in the understanding but does not exist in reality—in short, that the Fountain of Youth exists *only* in the understanding.

In view of the above we can now understand why Anselm insists that anyone who hears of God, thinks about God, or even denies the existence of God is, nevertheless, committed to the view that God exists in the understanding. Also, we can understand why Anselm treats what he calls the fool's claim that God does not exist as the claim that God exists *only* in the understanding—that is, that God exists in the understanding but does not exist in reality.

In *Monologium* Anselm sought to prove that among those beings which do exist, there is one which is the greatest, highest, and the best. But in *Proslogium* he undertakes to prove that among those things which exist, there is one which is not just the greatest among existing beings, but is such that no conceivable being is greater. We need to distinguish these two ideas: (i) a being than which *no existing being* is greater, and (ii) a being than which *no conceivable being* is greater. If the only things in existence were a stone, a frog, and a human being, the last of these, the human being, would satisfy our first idea but not our second—for we can conceive of a being (an angel or God) greater than a human. Anselm's idea of God, as he expresses it in *Proslogium*, II, is the same as (ii) above; it is the idea of "a being than which nothing greater can be conceived." It will, I think, facilitate our understanding of Anselm's argument if we make two slight changes in the way he has expressed his idea of God. For his phrase I shall substitute the following: "*the* being than which none greater *is possible*."[3] What this idea says is that if a certain being is God, then no *possible* being can be greater than it; or conversely, if a certain being is such that it is even *possible* for there to be a being greater than it, then that being is not God. What Anselm proposes to prove, then, is that the being than which none greater is possible exists in reality. If he proves this he will have proved that God, as he conceives of him, exists in reality.

But what does Anselm mean by *greatness*? Is a building, for example, greater than a man? Anselm remarks: "But I do not mean physically great, as a material object is great, but that which, the greater it is, is the better or the more worthy—wisdom, for instance."[4] Contrast wisdom with size. Anselm is saying that wisdom is something that contributes to the greatness of a thing. If a thing comes to have more wisdom than it did before (given that its other characteristics remain the same), then that thing has become a greater, better, more worthy thing than it was. Wisdom, Anselm is saying, is a great-making quality. But the mere fact that something increases in size (physical greatness) does not make that thing a better thing than it was before. So size, unlike wisdom, is not a great-making quality. By *greater than* Anselm means *better than, superior to,* or *more worthy than,* and he believes that some characteristics, like wisdom and moral goodness, are great-making characteristics in that anything which has them is a *better thing* than it would be (other characteristics of it remaining the same) were it to lack them.

We come now to what we may call the *key idea* in Anselm's Ontological Argument. Anselm believes that existence *in reality is a great-making quality.* How are we to understand this idea? Does Anselm mean that anything that exists is a greater thing than anything that doesn't? Although he doesn't ask or answer this question, it is perhaps reasonable to believe that Anselm did not mean this. For when he discusses wisdom as a great-making quality he is careful not to say that any wise thing is better than any unwise thing—for he recognizes that a just but unwise person might be a better being than a wise but unjust person.[5] I suggest that what Anselm means is that anything that doesn't exist but might have existed (is on the right side of our line but might have been on the left) would have been a greater thing than it is if it had existed (if it had been on the left side of our line). He is not comparing two different things (one existing and one not existing) and saying that the first is therefore greater than the second. Rather he is talking about one and the same thing and pointing out that if it does not exist but might have existed then *it* would have been a

greater thing if it had existed. Using Anselm's distinction between existence in the understanding and existence in reality, we may express the key idea in Anselm's reasoning as follows: If something exists only in the understanding, but might have existed in reality, then it might have been greater than it is. Since the Fountain of Youth, for example, exists only in the understanding but, unlike the round square, might have existed in reality, it follows by Anselm's principle that the Fountain of Youth might have been a greater thing than it is.

DEVELOPING ANSELM'S ONTOLOGICAL ARGUMENT

Having looked at some of the important ideas at work in Anselm's Ontological Argument, we can now consider its step-by-step development. In presenting Anselm's argument I shall use the term *God* in place of the longer phrase "the being than which none greater is possible"—wherever the term *God* appears we are to think of it as simply an abbreviation of the longer phrase.

1. God exists in the understanding.

As we've noted, anyone who hears of the being than which none greater is possible is, in Anselm's view, committed to premise 1.

2. God might have existed in reality (God is a possible being).

Anselm, I think, assumes the truth of premise 2 without making it explicit in his reasoning. By asserting 2, I don't mean to imply that God does not exist in reality. All that is meant is that, unlike the round square, God is a possible being.

3. If something exists only in the understanding and might have existed in reality, then it might have been greater than it is.

As we noted earlier this is the key idea in Anselm's Ontological Argument. It is intended as a general principle true of anything.

Steps 1–3 constitute the basic premises of Anselm's Ontological Argument. From these three items it follows, so Anselm believes, that God exists in reality. But how does Anselm propose to convince us that if we accept 1–3 we are committed by the rules of logic to accept his conclusion that God exists in reality? Anselm's procedure is to offer what is called a *reductio ad absurdum* proof of his conclusion. Instead of showing directly that the existence of God follows from 1–3, Anselm invites us to *suppose* that God does not exist (that is, that the conclusion he wants to establish is false) and then shows how this supposition when conjoined with 1–3 leads to an absurd result, a result that couldn't possibly be true because it is contradictory. In short, with the help of 1–3 Anselm shows that the supposition that God does not exist reduces to an absurdity. Since the supposition that God does not exist leads to an absurdity, that supposition must be rejected in favor of the conclusion that God does exist.

Does Anselm succeed in reducing the fool's belief that God does not exist to an absurdity? The best way to answer this question is to follow the steps of his argument.

4. Suppose God exists only in the understanding.

This supposition, as we saw earlier, is Anselm's way of expressing the fool's belief that God does not exist.

5. God might have been greater than he is. (2, 4, and 3)[6]

Step 5 follows from steps 2, 4, and 3. Since 3, if true, is true of anything it will be true of God. Step 3, therefore, implies that if God exists only in the understanding and might have existed in reality, then God might have been greater than he is. If so, then given 2 and 4, 5 must be true. For what 3 says when applied to God is that given 2 and 4 it follows that 5.

6. God is a being than which a greater is possible. (5)

Surely if God is such that he logically might have been greater, then he is such than which a greater is possible.

We're now in a position to appreciate Anselm's *reductio* argument. He has shown us that if we accept 1–4 we must accept 6. But 6 is unacceptable; it is the absurdity Anselm was after. For replacing *God* in step 6 with the longer phrase it abbreviates, we see that 6 amounts to the absurd assertion:

7. The being than which none greater is possible is a being than which a greater is possible.

Now since 1–4 have led us to an obviously false conclusion, if we accept Anselm's basic premises 1–3 as true, 4, the supposition that God exists only in the understanding, must be rejected as false. Thus we have shown that

8. It is false that God exists only in the understanding.

But since premise 1 tells us that God does exist in the understanding, and 8 tells us that God does not exist only there, we may infer that

9. God exists in reality as well as in the understanding. (1, 8)

What are we to say of this argument? Most of the philosophers who have considered the argument have rejected it because of a basic conviction that from the logical analysis of a certain idea or concept we can never determine that there exists in reality anything answering to that idea or concept. We may examine and analyze, for example, the idea of an elephant or the idea of a unicorn, but it is only by our experience of the world that we can determine that there exist things answering to our first idea and not to the second. Anselm, however, believes that the concept of God is utterly unique—from an analysis of this concept he believes that it can be determined that there exists in reality a being which answers to it. Moreover, he presents us with an argument to show that it can be done in the case of the idea of God. We can, of course, simply reject his argument on the grounds that it violates the basic conviction noted above. Many critics, however, have sought to prove more directly that Anselm's argument is a bad argument and to point out the particular step in his argument that is mistaken. In what follows we shall examine the three major objections that have been advanced by the argument's critics.

Gaunilo's Criticism

The first major criticism was advanced by a contemporary of Anselm's, a monk named Gaunilo, who wrote a response entitled "On Behalf of the Fool."[7] Gaunilo sought to prove that Anselm's reasoning is mistaken by applying it to things other than God, things which we know don't exist. He took as his example the island than which none greater is possible. No such island really exists. But, argues Gaunilo, if Anselm's reasoning were correct we could show that such an island really does exist. For since it is greater to exist than not to exist, if the island than which none greater is possible doesn't exist then it is an island than which a greater is possible. But it is impossible for the island than which none greater is possible to be an island than which a greater is possible. Therefore, the island than which none greater is possible must exist. About this argument Gaunilo remarks:

> If a man should try to prove to me by such reasoning that this island truly exists, and that its existence should no longer be doubted, either I should believe that he was jesting, or I know not which I ought to regard as the greater fool: myself, supposing I should allow this proof; or him, if he should suppose that he had established with any certainty the existence of this island.[8]

Gaunilo's strategy is clear. By using the very same reasoning Anselm employs in his argument, we can prove the existence of things we know don't exist. Therefore, Anselm's reasoning in his proof of the existence of God must be mistaken. In his reply to Gaunilo, Anselm insisted that his reasoning applies only to God and cannot be used to establish the existence of things other

than God. Unfortunately, Anselm did not explain just why his reasoning cannot be applied to things like Gaunilo's island.

In defense of Anselm against Gaunilo's objection, we should note that the objection supposes that Gaunilo's island is a possible thing. But this requires us to believe that some finite, limited thing (an island) might have unlimited perfections. And it is not at all clear that this is possible. Try to think, for example, of a hockey player than which none greater is possible. How fast would he have to skate? How many goals would such a player have to score in a game? How fast would he have to shoot the puck? Could this player ever fall down, be checked, or receive a penalty? Although the phrase "The hockey player than which none greater is possible" seems meaningful, as soon as we try to get a clear idea of what such a being would be like, we discover that we can't form a coherent idea of it at all. For we are being invited to think of some limited, finite thing—a hockey player or an island—and then to think of it as exhibiting unlimited, infinite perfections. Perhaps, then, since Anselm's reasoning applies only to possible things, Anselm can reject its application to Gaunilo's island on the grounds that the island than which none greater is possible is, like the round square, an impossible thing.

Kant's Criticism

By far the most famous objection to the Ontological Argument was set forth by Immanuel Kant in the eighteenth century. According to this objection, the mistake in the argument is its claim, implicit in premise 3, that existence is a quality or predicate that adds to the greatness of a thing. There are two parts to this claim: (1) existence is a quality or predicate, and (2) existence, like wisdom and unlike physical size, is a great-making quality or predicate. Someone might accept (1) but object to (2). The objection made famous by Kant, however, is directed at (1). According to this objection, existence is not a predicate at all. Therefore, since in its third premise Anselm's argument implies that existence is a predicate, the argument must be rejected.

What is meant by the philosophical doctrine that existence is not a predicate? The central point in this doctrine concerns what we do when we ascribe a certain quality or predicate to something, as, for example, when we say of a woman next door that she is intelligent, six feet tall, or thin. In each case we seem to assert or presuppose that there *exists* a woman next door and then go on to ascribe to her a certain predicate — "intelligent," "six feet tall," or "thin." And what is claimed by many proponents of the doctrine that existence is not a predicate is that this is a *general feature* of predication. They hold that when we ascribe a quality or predicate to anything, we assert or presuppose that the thing exists and then ascribe the predicate to it. Now, if this is so, then it's clear that existence cannot be a predicate which we may ascribe to or deny of something. For if it were predicate, then when we assert of some thing that it exists we would be asserting or presupposing that it exists and then going on to predicate existence of it. For example, if existence were a predicate, then in asserting "Tigers exist" we would be asserting or presupposing that tigers exist and then going on to predicate existence of them. Furthermore, in asserting "Dragons do not exist" we would be asserting or presupposing, if existence were a predicate, that dragons do exist and then going on to deny that existence attaches to them. In short, if existence were a predicate, the affirmative existential statement "Tigers exist" would be a redundancy, and the negative existential statement "Dragons do not exist" would be contradictory. But clearly "Tigers exist" is not a redundancy and "Dragons do not exist" is true and, therefore, not contradictory. What this shows, according to the proponents of Kant's objection, is that existence is not a genuine predicate.

According to the proponents of the above objection, what we are asserting when we assert that tigers exist and that dragons do not is not that certain things (tigers) have and certain other things (dragons) do not have a peculiar predicate, *existence,* rather, we are saying something about the *concept* of a tiger and the *concept* of a dragon. In the first case we are saying that the concept of a tiger applies to something in the world; in the second case we are saying that the concept of a dragon does not apply to anything in the world.

Although this objection to the Ontological Argument has been widely accepted, it is doubtful that it provides us with a conclusive refutation of the argument. It may be true that existence is not a predicate, that in asserting the existence of something we are not ascribing a certain predicate or attribute to that thing. But the arguments presented for this view seem to rest on mistaken or incomplete claims about the nature of predication. For example, the argument which we stated earlier rests on the claim that when we ascribe a predicate to anything we assert or presuppose that that thing exists. But this claim appears to be mistaken. In asserting that Dr. Doolittle is an animal lover I seem to be ascribing the predicate *animal lover* to Dr. Doolittle, but in doing so I certainly am not asserting or presupposing that Dr. Doolittle actually exists. Dr. Doolittle doesn't exist but it is, nevertheless, true that he is an animal lover. The plain fact is that we can talk about and ascribe predicates to many things which do not and never did exist. Merlin, for example, no less than Houdini, was a magician, although Houdini existed but Merlin did not. If, as these examples suggest, the claim that whenever we ascribe a predicate to something we assert or presuppose that the thing exists is a false claim, then we will need a better argument for the doctrine that existence is not a predicate. There is some question, however, whether anyone has succeeded in giving a really conclusive argument for the view that existence is not a predicate.[9]

A Third Criticism

A third objection against the Ontological Argument calls into question the premise that God might have existed in reality (God is a possible being). As we saw, this premise claims that "the being than which none greater is possible" is not an impossible object. But is this true? Consider the series of positive integers—1, 2, 3, 4 and so on. We know that any integer in this series, no matter how large, is such that a larger than it is possible. Therefore, "the positive integer than which none larger is possible" is an impossible object. Perhaps this is also true of "the being than which none greater is possible." That is, perhaps no matter how great a being may be, it is possible for there to be a being greater than it. If this were so, then, like "the integer than which none larger is possible," Anselm's God would not be a possible object. The mere fact that there are degrees of greatness, however, does not entitle us to conclude that Anselm's God is like "the integer than which none larger is possible." There are, for example, degrees of size in angles—one angle is larger than another—but it is not true that no matter how large an angle is it is possible for there to be an angle larger than it. It is logically impossible for an angle to exceed four right angles. The notion of an angle, unlike the notion of a positive integer, implies a degree of size beyond which it is impossible to go. Is Anselm's God like a largest integer, and therefore impossible, or like a largest angle, and therefore possible? Some philosophers have argued that Anselm's God is impossible.[10] But the arguments for this conclusion are not very compelling. Perhaps, then, this objection is best construed not as proving that Anselm's God is impossible, but as raising the question whether any of us is in a position to know that "the being than which none greater is possible" is a possible object. For Anselm's argument cannot be a successful proof of the existence of God unless its premises are not just true, but are really *known* to be true. Therefore, if we don't know that Anselm's God is a possible object, then his argument cannot prove the existence of God to us, cannot enable us to know that God exists.

A Final Critique

We've had a look at both Anselm's argument, and the three major objections philosophers have

raised against it. In this final section I want to present a somewhat different critique of the argument, a critique suggested by the basic conviction noted earlier: namely, that from the mere logical analysis of a certain idea or concept, we can never determine that there exists in reality anything answering to that idea or concept.

Suppose someone comes to us and says:

> I propose to define the term *God* as *an existing, wholly perfect being*. Now since it can't be true that an existing, wholly perfect being does not exist, it can't be true that God, as I've defined him, does not exist. Therefore, God must exist.

This argument appears to be a very simple Ontological Argument. It begins with a particular idea or concept of God and ends by concluding that God, so conceived, must exist. What can we say in response? We might start by objecting to this definition of *God*, claiming (1) that only predicates can be used to define a term, and (2) that existence is not a predicate. But suppose our friend is not impressed by this response—either because he thinks no one has fully explained what a predicate is or proved that existence isn't one, or because he thinks that anyone can define a word in whatever way he pleases. Can we allow our friend to define the word *God* in any way he pleases and still hope to show that it will not follow from that definition that there actually exists something to which this concept of God applies? I think we can. Let's first invite him, however, to consider some concepts other than this peculiar concept of God.

Earlier we noted that the term *magician* may be applied both to Houdini and Merlin, even though the former existed whereas the latter did not. Noting that our friend has used *existing* as part of this definition of *God*, suppose we agree with him that we can define a word in any way we please, and, accordingly, introduce the following words with the following definitions:

> A *magican* is defined as an *existing magician*.
> A *magico* is defined as a *nonexisting magician*.

Here we have introduced two words and used *existing* or *nonexisting* in their definitions. Now something of interest follows from the fact that *existing* is part of our definition of a magican. For while it's true that Merlin was a *magician* it isn't true that Merlin was a *magican*. And something of interest follows from our including *nonexisting* in the definition of a magico. For while it's true that Houdini was a *magician* it isn't true that Houdini was a *magico*. Houdini was a *magician* and a *magican*, but not a *magico*, whereas Merlin was a *magician* and a *magico*, but not a *magican*.

What we have just seen is that introducing *existing* or *nonexisting* into the definition of a concept has a very important implication. If we introduce *existing* into the definition of a concept, it follows that no nonexisting thing can exemplify that concept. And if we introduce *nonexisting* into the definition of a concept, it follows that no existing thing can exemplify that concept. No nonexisting thing can be a *magican* and no existing thing can be a *magico*.

But must some existing thing exemplify the concept *magican*? No! From the fact that *existing* is included in the definition of *magican* it does not follow that some existing thing is a *magican*—all that follows is that no nonexisting thing is a *magican*. If there were no magicians in existence there would be nothing to which the term *magican* would apply. This being so, it clearly does not follow merely from our definition of *magican* that some existing thing is a *magican*. Only if magicians exist will it be true that some existing thing is a *magican*.

We are now in a position to help our friend see that, from the mere fact that *God* is defined as an existing, wholly perfect being, it will not follow that some existing being is God. Something of interest does follow from his definition: namely, that no nonexisting being can be God. But whether some existing thing is God will depend entirely on whether some existing thing is a wholly perfect being. If no wholly perfect being exists there will be nothing to which this concept of God can apply. This being so, it clearly does not follow merely from this definition of *God* that some existing thing is God. Only if a wholly per-

fect being exists will it be true that God, as our friend conceives of him, exists.

Implications for Anselm's Argument

The implications of these considerations for Anselm's ingenious argument can now be traced. Anselm conceives of God as a being than which none greater is possible. He then claims that existence is a great-making quality, something that has it is greater than it would have been had it lacked existence. Clearly then, no nonexisting thing can exemplify Anselm's concept of God. For if we suppose that some nonexisting thing exemplifies Anselm's concept of God and also suppose that that nonexisting thing might have existed in reality (is a possible thing), then we are supposing that that nonexisting thing (1) might have been a greater thing, and (2) is, nevertheless, a thing than which a greater is not possible. Thus far Anselm's reasoning is, I believe, impeccable. But what follows from it? All that follows from it is that no nonexisting thing can be God (as Anselm conceives of God). All that follows is that given Anselm's concept of God, the proposition "Some nonexisting thing is God" cannot be true. But, as we saw earlier, this is also the case with the proposition "Some nonexisting thing is a magican." What remains to be shown is that some existing thing exemplifies Anselm's concept of God. What really does follow from his reasoning is that the only thing that logically could exemplify his concept of God is something which actually exists. And this conclusion is not without interest. But from the mere fact that nothing but an existing thing could exemplify Anselm's concept of God, it does not follow that some existing thing actually does exemplify his concept of God—no more than it follows from the mere fact that no nonexisting thing can be a magican that some existing thing is a magican.[11]

There is, however, one major difficulty in this critique of Anselm's argument. This difficulty arises when we take into account Anselm's implicit claim that God is a possible thing. To see just what this difficulty is, let's return to the idea of a possible thing. A possible thing, we determined, is any thing that either is on the left side of our imaginary line or logically might have been on the left side of the line. Possible things, then, will be all those things that, unlike the round square, are not impossible things. Suppose we concede to Anselm that God, as he conceives of him, is a possible thing. Now, of course, the mere knowledge that something is a possible thing doesn't enable us to conclude that that thing is an existing thing. For many possible things, like the Fountain of Youth, do not exist. But if something is a possible thing, then it is either an existing thing or a nonexisting thing. The set of possible things can be exhaustively divided into those possible things which actually exist and those possible things which do not exist. Therefore, if Anselm's God is a possible thing, it is either an existing thing or a nonexisting thing. We have concluded, however, that no nonexisting thing can be Anselm's God; therefore, it seems we must conclude with Anselm that some actually existing thing does exemplify his concept of God.

To see the solution to this major difficulty we need to return to an earlier example. Let's consider again the idea of a magican, an existing magician. It so happens that some magicians have existed—Houdini, The Great Blackstone, and others. But, of course, it might have been otherwise. Suppose, for the moment, that no magicians have ever existed. The concept "magician" would still have application, for it would still be true that Merlin was a magician. But what about the concept of a "magican?" Would any possible object be picked out by that concept? No! For no nonexisting thing could exemplify the concept "magican." And on the supposition that no magicians ever existed, no existing thing would exemplify the concept "magican."[12] We then would have a coherent concept "magican" which would not be exemplified by any possible object at all. For if all the possible objects which are magicians are nonexisting things, none of them would be a magican and, since no possible objects which exist are magicians, none of them would be a magican. We then would have a coherent, consistent con-

cept "magican," which in fact is not exemplified by any possible object at all. Put in this way, our result seems paradoxical. For we are inclined to think that only contradictory concepts like "the round square" are not exemplified by any possible things. The truth is, however, that when *existing* is included in or implied by a certain concept, it may be the case that no possible object does in fact exemplify that concept. For no possible object that doesn't exist will exemplify a concept like "magican" in which *existing* is included; and if there are no existing things which exemplify the other features included in the concept—for example, "being a magician" in the case of the concept "magican"—then no possible object that exists will exemplify the concept. Put in its simplest terms, if we ask whether any possible thing is a magican, the answer will depend entirely on whether any existing thing is a magican. If no existing things are magicians, then no possible things are magicans. Some possible object is a magican just in case some actually existing thing is a magician.[13]

Applying these considerations to Anselm's argument we can find the solution to our major difficulty. Given Anselm's concept of God and his principle that existence is a great-making quality, it really does follow that the only thing that logically could exemplify his concept of God is something which actually exists. But, we argued, it doesn't follow from these considerations alone that God actually exists, that some existing thing exemplifies Anselm's concept of God. The difficulty we fell into, however, is that when we add the premise that God is a possible thing, that some possible object exemplifies his concept of God, it really does follow that God actually exists, that some actually existing thing exemplifies Anselm's concept of God. For if some possible object exemplifies his concept of God, that object is either an existing thing or a nonexisting thing. But since no nonexisting thing could exemplify Anselm's concept of God, it follows that the possible object which exemplifies his concept of God must be a possible object that actually exists. Therefore, given (1) Anselm's concept of God,

(2) his principle that existence is a great-making quality, and (3) the premise that God, as conceived by Anselm, is a possible thing, it really does follow that Anselm's God actually exists.

A Too Generous Grant

I think we now can see that in granting Anselm the premise that God is a possible thing we have granted far more than we intended to grant. All we thought we were granting is that Anselm's concept of God, unlike the concept of a round square, is not contradictory or incoherent. But without realizing it we were in fact granting much more than this, as became apparent when we considered the idea of a "magican." There is nothing contradictory in the idea of a magican, an existing magician. But in asserting that a magican is a possible thing, we are, as we saw, directly implying that some existing thing is a magican. For if no existing thing is a magican, the concept of a magican will apply to no possible object whatever. The same point holds with respect to Anselm's God. Since Anselm's concept of God logically cannot apply to some nonexisting thing, the only possible objects to which it could apply are possible objects which actually exist. Therefore, in granting that Anselm's God is a possible thing, we are granting far more than that his idea of God isn't incoherent or contradictory. Suppose, for example, that every existing being has some defect which it might not have had. Without realizing it, we were denying this when we granted that Anselm's God is a possible being. For if every existing being has a defect it might not have had, then every existing being might have been greater. But if every existing being might have been greater, then Anselm's concept of God will apply to no possible object whatever. Therefore, if we allow Anselm his concept of God and his principle that existence is a great-making quality, then in granting that God, as Anselm conceives of him, is a possible being, we will be granting much more than that his concept of God is not contradictory. We will be granting, for example, that some existing thing is as perfect as it can be. For the plain fact is that Anselm's God is a possible thing only if some *existing* thing is as perfect as it can be.

Our final critique of Anselm's argument is simply this. In granting that Anselm's God is a possible thing, we are in fact granting that Anselm's God actually exists. But since the purpose of the argument is to prove to us that Anselm's God exists, we cannot be asked to grant as a premise a statement which is virtually equivalent to the conclusion that is to be proved. Anselm's concept of God may be coherent and his principle that existence is a great-making quality may be true. But all that follows from this is that no nonexisting thing can be Anselm's God. If we add to all of this the premise that God is a possible thing it will follow that God actually exists. But the additional premise claims more than that Anselm's concept of God isn't incoherent or contradictory. It amounts to the assertion that some existing being is supremely great. And since this is, in part, the point the argument endeavors to prove, the argument begs the question: it assumes the point it is supposed to prove.

If the above critique is correct, Anselm's argument fails as a proof of the existence of God. This is not to say, however, that the argument isn't a work of genius. Perhaps no other argument in the history of thought has raised so many basic philosophical questions and stimulated so much hard thought. Even if it fails as a proof of the existence of God, it will remain as one of the high achievements of the human intellect.

NOTES

1. Some philosophers believe that Anselm sets forth a different and more cogent argument in Chapter Three of his *Proslogium*. For this viewpoint see Charles Hartshorne, *Anselm's Discovery* (La Salle, Illinois: Open Court Publishing Co., 1965), and Norman Malcolm, "Anselm's Ontological Arguments," *The Philosophical Review*, LXIX, No. 1 (1960), pp. 41–62. For an illuminating account both of Anselm's intensions in *Proslogium*, II and III and of recent interpretations of Anselm, see Arthur C. McGill's essay "Recent Discussions of Anselm's Argument" in

The Many-faced Argument, ed. John Hick and Arthur C. McGill (New York: The Macmillan Co., 1967), pp. 33–110.

2. Anselm does allow that someone may assert the sentence "God does not exist" without having in his understanding the object or idea for which the word *God* stands (See *Proslogium,* IV in *Saint Anselm: Basic Writings,* tr. Sidney N. Deane). But when a person does understand the object for which a word stands, then when he uses that word in a sentence denying the existence of that object, he must have that object in his understanding. It is doubtful, however, that Anselm thought that incoherent or contradictory expressions like *round square* stand for objects which may exist in the understanding.

3. Anselm speaks of *a being* rather than *the being* than which none greater can be conceived. His argument is easier to present if we express his idea of God in terms of *the being.* Secondly, to avoid the psychological connotations of *can be conceived* I have substituted *possible.*

4. St. Anselm, *Monologium,* II in *Saint Anselm, Basic Writings,* tr. Sidney N. Deane.

5. See *Monologium,* XV in *Saint Anselm, Basic Writings,* tr. Sidney N. Deane.

6. The numbers in parentheses refer to the earlier steps in the argument from which the present step is derived.

7. Gaunilo's brief essay, Anselm's reply, and several of Anselm's major works, as translated by S. N. Deane, are collected together in *Saint Anselm: Basic Writings* (La Salle, Illinois: Open Court Publishing Co., 1962).

8. Deane, *Saint Anselm: Basic Writings,* p. 151.

9. Perhaps the most sophisticated presentation of the objection that existence is not a predicate is William P. Alston's "The Ontological Argument Revisited" in *The Philosophical Review,* LXIX (1960), pp. 452–74.

10. See, for example, C. D. Broad's discussion of the Ontological Argument in *Religion, Philosophy, and Psychical Research* (New York: Harcourt, Brace & Co., 1953).

11. An argument along the lines just presented may be found in J. Shaffer's illuminating essay, "Existence, Predication and the Ontological Argument," *Mind* LXXI (1962), pp. 307–25.

12. I am indebted to Professor William Wainwright for bringing this point to my attention.

13. In the language of possible worlds, we can say that some object x is a *magican* in a possible world w, provided (i) x is a magician in w, and (ii) x is a magician in whatever world happens to be actual. For more on this matter, as well as a critical discussion of some other versions of the Ontological Argument, see my essay "Modal Versions of the Ontological Argument" in *Philosophy of Religion,* ed. Louis Pojman (Belmont, CA: Wadsworth, 1987), pp. 69–73.

For Further Reflection

1. Discuss the concepts *possible being, impossible being, contingent being,* and *necessary being* and show how they function in the ontological argument.

2. What is Anselm's distinction between *existence in the understanding* and *existence in reality?*

3. Discuss Rowe's criticisms of the ontological argument. Are they convincing? Overall, do you think the ontological argument has merit?

II.B Why Is There Evil?

Is he willing to prevent evil, but not able? then he is impotent. Is he able, but not willing? then he is malevolent. Is he both able and willing? whence then is evil? (Epicurus 341–270 B.C.)

We have been looking at arguments in favor of God's existence. The agnostic and atheist usually base their case on the *absence* of evidence for God's existence. But they have one arrow in their own quiver, the **argument from evil**. With it the "atheologian" (one who argues against the existence of God) hopes either to neutralize any positive evidence for God's existence based on whatever in the traditional arguments survives their criticism or to demonstrate that it is unreasonable to believe in God.

The problem of evil arises because of the paradox of an omnibenevolent, omnipotent deity allowing the existence of evil. The Judeo-Christian tradition has affirmed these three propositions:

1. God is all-powerful (including omniscience).
2. God is perfectly good.
3. Evil exists.

But if God is perfectly good, why does he allow evil to exist? Why didn't he create a better world, if not with no evil, at least with substantially less evil than in this world? Many have contended that this paradox, first schematized by Epicurus, is worse than a paradox. It is an implicit contradiction for it contains premises that are inconsistent with one another. These philosophers argue something like the following:

4. If God (an all-powerful, omniscient, omnibenevolent being) exists, there would be no (or no unnecessary) evil in the world.
5. There is evil (or unnecessary evil) in the world.
6. Therefore, God does not exist.

You should examine each of these premises carefully. A few words are in order. Generally, Western thought has distinguished between two types of evil: moral and natural. "Moral evil" covers all those bad things for which humans are morally responsible. "Natural evil" or "surd evil" stands for all those terrible events that nature does of her own accord, for example, hurricanes, tornadoes, earthquakes, volcano eruptions, natural diseases, which bring on suffering to humans and animals. However, some defenses of theism affirm that all evil is essentially moral evil. Here the devil is brought in as the cause of natural evil.

The main defense of theism in the light of evil is the *free-will defense,* going back as far as St. Augustine (354–430) and receiving modern treatment in the work of John Hick, Alvin Plantinga, and Richard Swinburne. The free-will defense adds a fourth premise to Epicurus' paradox to show that premises 1–3 are consistent and not contradictory. This premise is

7. It is logically impossible for God to create free creatures and guarantee that they will never do evil.

The proponent of the free-will defense claims that all moral evil derives from creature freedom of the will. But what about natural evil? How does the theist account for it? There are two different ways. The first one, suggested by Alvin Plantinga (see also bibliography), is to attribute natural evil to the work of the devil and his angels. Disease and tornadoes are caused by the devil and his minions. The second way, favored by Hick and Swinburne, argues that natural evil is part and parcel of the nature of things: a result of the combination of deterministic physical laws that are necessary for consistent action and the responsibility given to humans to exercise their freedom.

One further distinction is necessary to work through this problem. Some theists attempt to answer the charge of inconsistency by simply showing that there is no formal contradiction between propositions 1 through 3, so that the nontheist hasn't proved his point. But others want to go beyond this negative function and offer a plausible account of evil. These latter are called "theodicists," for they attempt to justify the ways of God before humankind. They endeavor to show that God allows the temporary evil to bring out greater good. In our readings, John Hick represents the theodicist position.

II.12   Why Is There Evil?

FYODOR DOSTOEVSKY

Fyodor Dostoevsky (1822–1881) was one of the greatest Russian novelists. He was born in Moscow. His revolutionary sympathies and a penchant for gambling managed to keep him in constant danger. Among his famous writings are *Crime and Punishment* (1866), *The Idiot* (1868), and *The Brothers Karamazov* (1880), from which our reading is taken.

In this scene from Dostoevsky's most famous work, Ivan Karamazov is explaining to his pious brother, Alyosha, a Christian monk, why he cannot accept God.

Study Questions

1. Does Ivan believe that God exists? What does he think of the hypothesis that humanity invented the notion of God?
2. Does Ivan think that we can understand God? Why or why not?
3. What is Ivan's creed? Has he stated his position very clearly or consistently? How can he speak of God as holy and yet admit that God is the cause of children's suffering?
4. What does Ivan mean in saying that there can be solidarity with the suffering and guilt of humanity (or other adults) but not with children?
5. What is Ivan's response to the proposal that the solution of the problem of evil is to be found in an eternal harmony?
6. What does he mean when he says, "I most respectfully return Him the ticket"?

From *Fyodor Dostoevsky,* The Brothers Karamazov, *trans. by Constance Garnett (London: Heinemann, 1912).*

"WELL, TELL ME WHERE TO BEGIN, give your orders. The existence of God, eh?"

"Begin where you like. You declared yesterday at father's that there was no God." Alyosha looked searchingly at his brother.

"I said that yesterday at dinner on purpose to tease you and I saw your eyes glow. But now I've no objection to discussing with you, and I say so very seriously. I want to be friends with you, Alyosha, for I have no friends and want to try it. Well, only fancy, perhaps I too accept God," laughed Ivan, "that's a surprise for you, isn't it?"

"Yes of course, if you are not joking now."

"Joking? I was told at the elder's yesterday that I was joking. You know, dear boy, there was an old sinner in the eighteenth century who declared that, if there were no God, he would have to be invented. . . . And man has actually invented God. And what's strange, what would be marvelous, is not that God should really exist; the marvel is that such an idea, the idea of the necessity of God, could enter the head of such a savage, vicious beast as man. So holy it is, so touching, so wise and so great a credit it does to man. As for me, I've long resolved not to think whether man created God or God man. . . . For what are we aiming at now? I am trying to explain as quickly as possible my essential nature, that is what manner of man I am, what I believe in, and for what I hope, that's it, isn't it? And therefore I tell you that I accept God simply. But you must note this: if God exists and if He really did create the world, then, as we all know, He created it according to the geometry of Euclid and the human mind with the conception of only three dimensions in space. Yet there have been and still are geometricians and philosophers, and even some of the most distinguished, who doubt whether the whole universe, or to speak more widely the whole of being, was only created in Euclid's geometry; they even dare to dream that two parallel lines, which according to Euclid can never meet on earth, may meet somewhere in infinity. I have come to the conclusion that, since I can't understand even that, I can't expect to understand about God. I acknowledge humbly that I have no faculty for settling such questions. I have a

Euclidian earthly mind, and how could I solve problems that are not of this world? And I advise you never to think about it either, my dear Alyosha, especially about God, whether He exists or not. All such questions are utterly inappropriate for a mind created with an idea of only three dimensions. And so I accept God and am glad to, and what's more I accept His wisdom, His purpose—which are utterly beyond our ken; I believe in the underlying order and the meaning of life; I believe in the eternal harmony in which they say we shall one day be blended. I believe in the Word to Which the universe is striving, and Which Itself was 'with God,' and Which Itself is God and so on, and so on, to infinity. There are all sorts of phrases for it. I seem to be on the right path, don't I? Yet would you believe it, in the final result I don't accept this world of God's, and, although I know it exists, I don't accept it at all. It's not that I don't accept God, you must understand, it's the world created by Him I don't and cannot accept. Let me make it plain. I believe like a child that suffering will be healed and made up for, that all the humiliating absurdity of human contradictions will vanish like a pitiful mirage, like the despicable fabrication of the impotent and infinitely small Euclidian mind of man, that in the world's finale, at the moment of eternal harmony, something so precious will come to pass that it will suffice for all hearts, for the comforting of all resentments, for the atonement of all the crimes of humanity, of all the blood they've shed; that it will make it not only possible to forgive but to justify all that has happened with men—but though all that may come to pass, I don't accept it. I won't accept it. Even if parallel lines do meet and I see it myself, I shall see it and say that they've met, but still I won't accept it. That's what's at the root of me, Alyosha; that's my creed.

". . . Do you understand why this infamy must be and is permitted? Without it, I am told, man could not have known good and evil. Why should he know that diabolical good and evil when it costs so much? Why, the whole world of knowledge is not worth that child's prayer to 'dear, Kind God'! I say nothing of the sufferings of grown-up people, they have eaten the apple, damn them, and the devil take them all! But these little ones! I am making you suffer, Alyosha, you are not yourself. I'll leave off if you like."

"Never mind. I want to suffer too," muttered Alyosha.

"One picture, only one more, because it's so curious, so characteristic, and I have only just read it in some collection of Russian antiquities. I've forgotten the name. I must look it up. It was in the darkest days of serfdom at the beginning of the century, and long live the Liberator of the People! There was in those days a general of aristocratic connections, the owner of great estates, one of these men—somewhat exceptional, I believe, even then—who, retiring from the service into a life of leisure, are convinced that they've earned absolute power over the lives of their subjects. There were such men then. So our general, settled on his property of two thousand souls, lives in pomp and domineers over his poor neighbors as though they were dependents and buffoons. He has kennels of hundreds of hounds and nearly a hundred dog-boys—all mounted, and in uniform. One day a serf boy, a little child of eight, threw a stone in play and hurt the paw of the general's favorite hound. 'Why is my favorite dog lame?' He is told that the boy threw a stone that hurt the dog's paw. 'So you did it.' The general looked the child up and down. 'Take him.' He was taken—taken from his mother and kept shut up all night. Early that morning the general comes out on horseback, with the hounds, his dependents, dog-boys, and huntsmen, all mounted around him in full hunting parade. The servants are summoned for their edification, and in front of them all stands the mother of the child. The child is brought from the lockup. It's a gloomy, cold, foggy autumn day, a capital day for hunting. The general orders the child to be undressed; the child is stripped naked. He shivers, numb with terror not daring to cry. . . . 'Make him run,' commands the general. 'Run! run!' shout the dog-boys. The boy runs. . . . 'At him!' yells the general, and he sets the whole pack of hounds on the child. The hounds catch him, and tear him to pieces before his mother's eyes! . . . I believe the general was after-

wards declared incapable of administering his estates. Well—what did he deserve? To be shot? to be shot for the satisfaction of our moral feelings? Speak, Alyosha!"

"To be shot," murmured Alyosha, lifting his eyes to Ivan with a pale twisted smile.

"Bravo!" cried Ivan delighted. "If even you say so . . . You're a pretty monk! So there is a little devil sitting in your heart, Alyosha Karamazov!"

"What I said was absurd, but—"

"That's just the point that 'but'!" cried Ivan. "Let me tell you, novice, that the absurd is only too necessary on earth. The world stands on absurdities, and perhaps nothing would have come to pass in it without them. We know what we know!"

"What do you know?"

"I understand nothing," Ivan went on, as though in delirium. "I don't want to understand anything now. I want to stick to the fact. I made up my mind long ago not to understand. If I try to understand anything, I shall be false to the fact and I have determined to stick to the fact."

"Why are you trying me?" Alyosha cried, with sudden distress. "Will you say what you mean at last?"

"Of course, I will; that's what I've been leading up to. You are dear to me, I don't want to let you go, and I won't give you up to your Zossima."

Ivan for a minute was silent, his face became all at once very sad.

"Listen! I took the case of the children only to make my case clearer. Of the other tears of humanity with which the earth is soaked from its crust to its center, I will say nothing. I have narrowed my subject on purpose. I am a bug, and I recognize in all humility that I cannot understand why the world is arranged as it is. Men are themselves to blame, I suppose; they were given paradise, they wanted freedom, and stole fire from heaven, though they knew they would become unhappy, so there is no need to pity them. With my pitiful, earthly, Euclidian understanding, all I know is that there is suffering and that there are none guilty; that cause follows effect, simply and directly; that everything flows and finds its level—but that's only Euclidian nonsense, I know that, and I can't consent to live by it! What comfort is it to me that there are none guilty and that cause follows effect simply and directly, and that I know it—I must have justice, or I will destroy myself. And not justice in some remote infinite time and space, but here on earth, and that I could see myself. I have believed in it. I want to see it, and if I am dead by then, let me rise again, for if it all happens without me, it will be too unfair. Surely I haven't suffered, simply that I, my crimes and my sufferings, may manure the soil of the future harmony for somebody else. I want to see with my own eyes the hind lie down with the lion and the victim rise up and embrace his murderer. I want to be there when everyone suddenly understands what it has all been for. All the religions of the world are built on this longing, and I am a believer. But then there are the children, and what am I to do about them? That's a question I can't answer. For the hundredth time I repeat, there are numbers of questions, but I've only taken the children, because in their case what I mean is so unanswerably clear. Listen! If all must suffer to pay for the eternal harmony, what have children to do with it, tell me, please? It's beyond all comprehension why they should suffer, and why they should pay for the harmony. Why should they, too, furnish material to enrich the soil for the harmony of the future? I understand solidarity in sin among men. I understand solidarity in retribution, too; but there can be no such solidarity with children. And if it is really true that they must share responsibility for all their fathers' crimes, such a truth is not of this world and is beyond my comprehension. Some jester will say, perhaps, that the child would have grown up and have sinned, but you see he didn't grow up, he was torn to pieces by the dogs, at eight years old. Oh, Alyosha, I am not blaspheming! I understand, of course, what an upheaval of the universe it will be, when everything in heaven and earth blends in one hymn of praise and everything that lives and has lived cries aloud: 'Thou art just, O Lord, for Thy ways are revealed,' when the mother embraces the fiend who threw her child to the dogs, and all three cry aloud with tears, 'Thou are just, O Lord!' then, of course, the crown of knowledge will be reached and all will be made clear. But what pulls me up here is that I can't accept that harmony. And while I am on earth, I make haste to take my own measures. You see, Alyosha, perhaps it really may happen that if I live to that moment, or rise again to see it, I, too, perhaps, may cry aloud with the rest, looking at the mother embracing the child's torturer, 'Thou art just, O Lord!' but I don't want to cry aloud then. While there is still time, I hasten to protect myself and so I renounce the higher harmony altogether. It's not worth the tears of that one tortured child who beat itself on the breast with its little fist and prayed in its stinking outhouse, with its unexpiated tears to 'dear, kind God'! It's not worth it, because those tears are unatoned for. They must be atoned for, or there can be no harmony. But how? How are you going to atone for them? Is it possible? By their being avenged? But what do I care for avenging them? What do I care for a hell for oppressors? What good can hell do, since those children have already been tortured? And what becomes of harmony, if there is hell? I want to forgive. I want to embrace. I don't want more suffering. And if the sufferings of children go to swell the sum of sufferings which was necessary to pay for truth, then I protest that the truth is not worth such a price. I don't want the mother to embrace the oppressor who threw her son to the dogs! She dare not forgive him! Let her forgive him for herself, if she will, let her forgive the torturer for the immeasurable suffering of her mother's heart. But the sufferings of her tortured child she has no right to forgive; she dare not forgive the torturer, even if the child were to forgive him! And if that is so, if they dare not forgive, what becomes of harmony? Is there in the whole world a being who would have the right to forgive and could forgive? I don't want harmony. From love for humanity I don't want it. I would rather be left with the unavenged suffering. I would rather remain with my unavenged suffering and unsatisfied indignation, *even if I were wrong*. Besides, too high a price is asked for harmony; it's beyond our means to pay so much to enter on it. And so I hasten to give back my entrance ticket, and if I am an honest man I am bound to give it back as soon as possible. And that I am doing. It's not God that I don't accept, Alyosha, only I most respectfully return Him the ticket."

"That's rebellion," murmured Alyosha, looking down.

"Rebellion? I am sorry you call it that," said Ivan earnestly. "One can hardly live in rebellion, and I want to live. Tell me yourself, I challenge you—answer. Imagine that you are creating a fabric of human destiny with the object of making men happy in the end, giving them peace and rest at last, but that it was essential and inevitable to torture to death only one tiny creature—that baby beating its breast with its fist, for instance—and to found that edifice on its unavenged tears, would you consent to be the architect on those conditions? Tell me, and tell the truth."

"No, I wouldn't consent," said Alyosha softly.

For Further Reflection

1. There are three propositions involved in the traditional formulation of the problem of evil: a. God is all-powerful (including omniscience); b. God is perfectly good; and c. Evil exists. How would Ivan deal with them?

2. Do you think that the fact of evil counts against the proposition that God exists? Explain why or why not.

3. Some people believe that we are completely causally determined, a subject that will be discussed in Part V. What will they make of the free-will defense?

II.13   Why Doesn't God Intervene to Prevent Evil?

B. C. JOHNSON

B. C. Johnson is a pen name for the author, who wishes to remain anonymous. In this essay, Johnson compares God's behavior with that of a morally good person. If you know that a six-month-old baby is in a burning building and you have the opportunity to save it without undue risk to your life, you would no doubt save it. Of course, if you couldn't save it, you would be excused. The question is "Why doesn't God intervene to save not just babies who are caught in fires but people everywhere who are suffering and in great need of help?" Johnson considers various "excuses" the theist might claim for God and argues that they all fail. His conclusion is that if there is a God, he or she is probably either evil or both good and evil.

Study Questions

1. What, according to Johnson, are some of the bad explanations for God not intervening to prevent evil?

2. How is God like a bystander who, though he didn't start the fire, refuses to help save the baby, even when he could easily do so.

3. How does Johnson respond to the suggestion that it is best for us to face disaster without assistance?
4. What does Johnson say to the objection that God's intervention would destroy a considerable amount of moral urgency?
5. What does Johnson say about the claim that evil is a necessary by-product of the laws of nature, so that it would be irrational for God to interfere every time a disaster happens?
6. What do people mean when they say that God has a "higher morality" than we have, so that we cannot apply our standards to him? What is Johnson's response to this defense of theism?
7. What are the three possibilities concerning God's moral character? Which does Johnson argue for? Do you agree?

HERE IS A COMMON SITUATION: A house catches on fire and a six-month-old baby is painfully burned to death. Could we possibly describe as "good" any person who had the power to save this child and yet refused to do so? God undoubtedly has this power and yet in many cases of this sort he has refused to help. Can we call God "good"? Are there adequate excuses for his behavior?

First, it will not do to claim that the baby will go to heaven. It was either necessary for the baby to suffer or it was not. If it was not, then it was wrong to allow it. The child's ascent to heaven does not change this fact. If it was necessary, the fact that the baby will go to heaven does not explain why it was necessary, and we are still left without an excuse for God's inaction.

It is not enough to say that the baby's painful death would in the long run have good results and therefore should have happened, otherwise God would not have permitted it. For if we know this to be true, then we know—just as God knows—that every action successfully performed must in the end be good and therefore the right thing to do, otherwise God would not have allowed it to happen. We could deliberately set houses ablaze to kill innocent people and if successful we would then know we had a duty to do it. A defense of God's goodness which takes as its foundation duties known only after the fact would result in a morality unworthy of the name. Furthermore, this argument does not explain why God allowed the child to burn to death. It merely claims that there is some reason discoverable in the long run. But the belief that such a reason is within our grasp must rest upon the additional belief that God is good. This is just to counter evidence against such a belief by assuming the belief to be true. It is not unlike a lawyer defending his client by claiming that the client is innocent and therefore the evidence against him must be misleading—that proof vindicating the defendant will be found in the long run. No jury of reasonable men and women would accept such a defense and the theist cannot expect a more favorable outcome.

The theist often claims that man has been given free will so that if he accidentally or purposefully causes fires, killing small children, it is his fault alone. Consider a bystander who had nothing to do with starting the fire but who refused to help even though he could have saved the child with no harm to himself. Could such a bystander be called good? Certainly not. If we would not consider a mortal human being good under these circumstances, what grounds could we possibly have for continuing to assert the goodness of an all-powerful God?

From B. C. Johnson, The Atheist Debater's Handbook. *(Amherst, NY: Prometheus Books, 1983),*
pp. 99–108. Copyright © 1981 by B. C. Johnson. Reprinted by permission of the publisher.

The suggestion is sometimes made that it is best for us to face disasters without assistance, otherwise we would become dependent on an outside power for aid. Should we then abolish modern medical care or do away with efficient fire departments? Are we not dependent on their help? Is it not the case that their presence transforms us into soft, dependent creatures? The vast majority are not physicians or firemen. These people help in their capacity as professional outside sources of aid in much the same way that we would expect God to be helpful. Theists refer to aid from firemen and physicians as cases of man helping himself. In reality, it is a tiny minority of men helping a great many. We can become just as dependent on them as we can on God. Now the existence of this kind of outside help is either wrong or right. If it is right, then God should assist those areas of the world which do not have this kind of help. In fact, throughout history, such help has not been available. If aid ought to have been provided, then God should have provided it. On the other hand, if it is wrong to provide this kind of assistance, then we should abolish the aid altogether. But we obviously do not believe it is wrong.

Similar considerations apply to the claim that if God interferes in disasters, he would destroy a considerable amount of moral urgency to make things right. Once again, note that such institutions as modern medicine and fire departments are relatively recent. They function irrespective of whether we as individuals feel any moral urgency to support them. To the extent that they help others, opportunities to feel moral urgency are destroyed because they reduce the number of cases which appeal to us for help. Since we have not always had such institutions, there must have been a time when there was greater moral urgency than there is now. If such a situation is morally desirable, then we should abolish modem medical care and fire departments. If the situation is not morally desirable, then God should have remedied it.

Besides this point, we should note that God is represented as one who tolerates disasters, such as infants burning to death, in order to create moral urgency. It follows that God approves of these disasters as a means to encourage the creation of moral urgency. Furthermore, if there were no such disasters occurring, God would have to see to it that they occur. If it so happened that we lived in a world in which babies never perished in burning houses, God would be morally obliged to take an active hand in setting fire to houses with infants in them. In fact, if the frequency of infant mortality due to fire should happen to fall below a level necessary for the creation of maximum moral urgency in our real world, God would be justified in setting a few fires of his own. This may well be happening right now, for there is no guarantee that the maximum number of infant deaths necessary for moral urgency are occurring.

All of this is of course absurd. If I see an opportunity to create otherwise nonexistent opportunities for moral urgency by burning an infant or two, then I should *not* do so. But if it is good to maximize moral urgency, then I *should* do so. Therefore, it is not good to maximize moral urgency. Plainly we do not in general believe that it is a good thing to maximize moral urgency. The fact that we approve of modern medical care and applaud medical advances is proof enough of this.

The theist may point out that in a world without suffering there would be no occasion for the production of such virtues as courage, sympathy, and the like. This may be true, but the atheist need not demand a world without suffering. He need only claim that there is suffering which is in excess of that needed for the production of various virtues. For example, God's active attempts to save six-month-old infants from fires would not in itself create a world without suffering. But no one could sincerely doubt that it would improve the world.

The two arguments against the previous theistic excuse apply here also. "Moral urgency" and "building virtue" are susceptible to the same criticisms. It is worthwhile to emphasize, however, that we encourage efforts to eliminate evils; we approve of efforts to promote peace, prevent famine, and wipe out disease. In other words, we do value a world with fewer or (if possible) no opportunities for the development of virtue (when "virtue" is understood to mean the reduction of suffering). If we produce such a world for succeeding generations, how will they develop virtues? Without war, disease, and famine, they will not be virtuous. Should we then cease our attempts to wipe out war, disease, and famine? If we do not believe that it is right to cease attempts at improving the world, then by implication we admit that virtue-building is not an excuse for God to permit disasters. For we admit that the development of virtue is no excuse for permitting disasters.

It might be said that God allows innocent people to suffer in order to deflate man's ego so that the latter will not be proud of his apparently deserved good fortune. But this excuse succumbs to the arguments used against the preceding excuses and we need discuss them no further.

Theists may claim that evil is a necessary by-product of the laws of nature and therefore it is irrational for God to interfere every time a disaster happens. Such a state of affairs would alter the whole causal order and we would then find it impossible to predict anything. But the death of a child caused by an electrical fire could have been prevented by a miracle and no one would ever have known. Only a minor alteration in electrical equipment would have been necessary. A very large disaster could have been avoided simply by producing in Hitler a miraculous heart attack— and no one would have known it was a miracle. To argue that continued miraculous intervention by God would be wrong is like insisting that one should never use salt because ingesting five pounds of it would be fatal. No one is requesting that God interfere all of the time. He should, however, intervene to prevent especially horrible disasters. Of course, the question arises: where does one draw the line? Well, certainly the line should be drawn somewhere this side of infants burning to death. To argue that we do not know where the line should be drawn is no excuse for

failing to interfere in those instances that would be called clear cases of evil.

It will not do to claim that evil exists as a necessary contrast to good so that we might know what good is. A very small amount of evil, such as a toothache, would allow that. It is not necessary to destroy innocent human beings.

The claim could be made that God has a "higher morality" by which his actions are to be judged. But it is a strange "higher morality" which claims that what we call "bad" is good and what we call "good" is bad. Such a morality can have no meaning to us. It would be like calling black "white" and white "black." In reply the theist may say that God is the wise Father and we are ignorant children. How can we judge God any more than a child is able to judge his parent? It is true that a child may be puzzled by his parents' conduct, but his basis for deciding that their conduct is nevertheless good would be the many instances of good behavior he has observed. Even so, this could be misleading. Hitler, by all accounts, loved animals and children of the proper race; but if Hitler had had a child, this offspring would hardly have been justified in arguing that his father was a good man. At any rate, God's "higher morality," being the opposite of ours, cannot offer any grounds for deciding that he is somehow good.

Perhaps the main problem with the solutions to the problem of evil we have thus far considered is that no matter how convincing they may be in the abstract, they are implausible in certain particular cases. Picture an infant dying in a burning house and then imagine God simply observing from afar. Perhaps God is reciting excuses in his own behalf. As the child succumbs to the smoke and flames, God may be pictured as saying: "Sorry, but if I helped you I would have considerable trouble deflating the ego of your parents. And don't forget I have to keep those laws of nature consistent. And anyway if you weren't dying in that fire, a lot of moral urgency would just go down the drain. Besides, I didn't start this fire, so you can't blame *me*."

It does no good to assert that God may not be all-powerful and thus not able to prevent evil. He can create a universe and yet is conveniently unable to do what the fire department can do—rescue a baby from a burning building. God should at least be as powerful as a man. A man, if he had been at the right place and time, could have killed Hitler. Was this beyond God's abilities? If God knew in 1910 how to produce polio vaccine and if he was able to communicate with somebody, he should have communicated this knowledge. He must be incredibly limited if he could not have managed this modest accomplishment. Such a God if not dead, is the next thing to it. And a person who believes in such a ghost of a God is practically an atheist. To call such a thing a god would be to strain the meaning of the word.

The theist, as usual, may retreat to faith. He may say that he has faith in God's goodness and therefore the Christian Deity's existence has not been disproved. "Faith" is here understood as being much like confidence in a friend's innocence despite the evidence against him. Now in order to have confidence in a friend one must know him well enough to justify faith in his goodness. We cannot have justifiable faith in the supreme goodness of strangers. Moreover, such confidence must come not just from a speaking acquaintance. The friend may continually assure us with his words that he is good but if he does not act like a good person, we would have no reason to trust him. A person who says he has faith in God's goodness is speaking as if he had known God for a long time and during that time had never seen Him do any serious evil. But we know that throughout history God has allowed numerous atrocities to occur. No one can have justifiable faith in the goodness of such a God.

This faith would have to be based on a close friendship wherein God was never found to do anything wrong. But a person would have to be blind and deaf to have had such a relationship with God. Suppose a friend of yours had always claimed to be good yet refused to help people when he was in a position to render aid. Could you have justifiable faith in his goodness?

You can of course say that you trust God anyway—that no arguments can undermine your faith. But this is just a statement describing how stubborn you are; it has no bearing whatsoever on the question of God's goodness.

The various excuses theists offer for why God has allowed evil to exist have been demonstrated to be inadequate. However, the conclusive objection to these excuses does not depend on their inadequacy.

First, we should note that every possible excuse making the actual world consistent with the existence of a good God could be used in reverse to make that same world consistent with an evil God. For example, we could say that God is evil and that he allows free will so that we can freely do evil things, which would make us more truly evil than we would be if forced to perform evil acts. Or we could say that natural disasters occur in order to make people more selfish and bitter, for most people tend to have a "me-first" attitude in a disaster (note, for example, stampedes to leave burning buildings). Even though some people achieve virtue from disasters, this outcome is necessary if persons are to react freely to disaster—necessary if the development of moral degeneracy is to continue freely. But, enough; the point is made. Every excuse we could provide to make the world consistent with a good God can be paralleled by an excuse to make the world consistent with an evil God. This is so because the world is a mixture of both good and bad.

Now there are only three possibilities concerning God's moral character. Considering the world as it actually is, we may believe: (*a*) that God is more likely to be all evil than he is to be all good; (*b*) that God is less likely to be all evil than he is to be all good; or (*c*) that God is equally as likely to be all evil as he is to be good. In case (*a*) it would be admitted that God is unlikely to be all good. Case (*b*) cannot be true at all, since—as we have seen—the belief that God is all evil can be justified to precisely the same extent as the belief that God is all good. Case (*c*) leaves us with no reasonable excuses for a good God to permit evil. The reason is as follows: if an excuse is to be a reasonable excuse, the circumstances it identifies as excusing conditions must be actual. For example, if I run over a pedestrian and my excuse is that the brakes failed because someone tampered with them, then the facts had better bear this out. Otherwise the excuse will not hold. Now if case (*c*) is correct and, given the facts of the actual world, God is as likely to be all evil as he is to be all good, then these facts do not support the excuses which could be made for a good God permitting evil. Consider an analogous example. If my excuse for running over the pedestrian is that my brakes were tampered with, and if the actual facts lead us to believe that it is no more likely that they were tampered with than that they were not, the excuse is no longer reasonable. To make good my excuse, I must

show that it is a fact or at least highly probable that my brakes were tampered with—not that it is just a possibility. The same point holds for God. His excuse must not be a possible excuse, but an actual one. But case (*c*), in maintaining that it is just as likely that God is all evil as that he is all good, rules this out. For if case (*c*) is true, then the facts of the actual world do not make it any more likely that God is all good than that he is all evil. Therefore, they do not make it any more likely that his excuses are good than that they are not. But, as we have seen, good excuses have a higher probability of being true.

Cases (*a*) and (*c*) conclude that it is unlikely that God is all good, and case (*b*) cannot be true. Since these are the only possible cases, there is no escape from the conclusion that it is unlikely that God is all good. Thus the problem of evil triumphs over traditional theism.

For Further Reflection

1. Do you find Johnson's arguments cogent? How might a theist reply to them?

2. Some theologians have argued that the biblical picture of God is not the same as the philosopher's. The philosopher pictures God as being all-powerful, while the Bible sees God as very powerful but still limited: He cannot prevent all evils. Would this revision of theism be an acceptable way to get around the problem of evil? Why or why not?

3. Suppose someone objects to the way the problem of evil is set forth, arguing that the problem is unjustifiably anthropomorphic. As someone said, "Who put human beings at the center of the definition of evil?" Should we take a more global view of evil, considering the harm done to animals and the environment? Is it a self-serving bias (sometimes called *speciesism*) that makes humanity the ultimate object of concern here?

There Is a Reason Why God Allows Evil   II.14

JOHN HICK

John Hick (1922–) was for many years professor of theology at the University of Birmingham in England. He is now emeritus professor of philosophy at Claremont Graduate School. His book *Evil and the God of Love* (1966) is considered one of the most thorough treatises on the problem of evil. Our reading is a shorter version of some of the ideas presented there. Hick presents a *theodicy,* a justification of God's creation in the face of evil. Theodicies can be of two types, depending on how they justify the ways of God. The Augustinian position is that God created humans without sin and set them in a sinless, paradisical world. However, humanity fell into sin through misuse of its free will. God's grace will save some of us, but others will perish everlastingly. The second type of theodicy stems from the thinking of Irenaeus (120–202), of the Greek church. The Irenaean tradition views Adam not as a free agent rebelling against God, but as a child. The fall is humanity's first faulty step in the direction of freedom. God is still working with humanity to bring it from undeveloped life (*bios:* biological life) to a state of self-realization in divine love, spiritual life (*zoe*). This life is a vale of soul-making.

Hick accepts the soul-making view of life in this defense of God's ways in the face of evil.

Study Questions

1. Why is the problem of evil a dilemma?
2. Which solutions to the problem does Hick rule out as unacceptable?
3. Does the Hebrew-Christian view of the world judge matter to be evil?
4. What is a *negative* theodicy?
5. What does Hick mean by *moral* versus *non-moral* evil?
6. Why couldn't God create people who were both free and totally good?
7. What does Hick say about non-moral evil? Why is it here, and what is its function in human development?
8. According to Hick what is the purpose of our creation?
9. Why does Hick reject a world without suffering and harm?

TO MANY, THE MOST powerful objection to belief in God is the fact of evil. Probably for most agnostics it is the appalling depth and extent of human suffering, more than anything else, that makes the idea of a loving Creator seem too implausible and disposes them toward one or another of the various naturalistic theories of religion.

As a challenge to theism, the problem of evil has traditionally been posed in the form of a dilemma: If God is perfectly loving, he must wish to abolish evil, and if he is all-powerful, he must be able to abolish evil. But evil exists; therefore God cannot be both omnipotent and perfectly loving.

Certain solutions, which at once suggest themselves, have to be ruled out so far as the Judaic-Christian faith is concerned.

To say, for example (with contemporary Christian Science), that evil is an illusion of the human mind, is impossible within a religion based upon the stark realism of the Bible. Its pages faithfully reflect the characteristic mixture of good and evil in human experience. They record every kind of sorrow and suffering, every mode of man's inhumanity to man and of his painfully insecure existence in the world. There is no attempt to regard evil as anything but dark, menacingly ugly, heartrending, and crushing. In the Christian scriptures, the

From John Hick, Philosophy of Religion, *3rd. ed., © 1963, pp. 40–46. Reprinted by permission of Prentice Hall, Inc., Englewood Cliffs, NJ.*

climax of this history of evil is the crucifixion of Jesus, which is presented not only as a case of utterly unjust suffering, but as the violent and murderous rejection of God's Messiah. There can be no doubt, then, that for biblical faith, evil is unambiguously evil, and stands in direct opposition to God's will.

Again, to solve the problem of evil by means of the theory (sponsored for example, by the Boston "Personalist" School) of a finite deity who does the best he can with a material, intractable and coeternal with himself, is to have abandoned the basic premise of Hebrew-Christian monotheism; for the theory amounts to rejecting belief in the infinity and sovereignty of God.

Indeed, any theory which would avoid the problem of the origin of evil by depicting it as an ultimate constituent of the universe, coordinate with good, has been repudiated in advance by the classic Christian teaching, first developed by Augustine, that evil represents the going wrong of something which in itself is good. Augustine holds firmly to the Hebrew-Christian conviction that the universe is *good*—that is to say, it is the creation of a good God for a good purpose. He completely rejects the ancient prejudice, widespread in his day, that matter is evil. There are, according to Augustine, higher and lower, greater and lesser goods in immense abundance and variety, but everything which has being is good in its own way and degree, except insofar as it may have become spoiled or corrupted. Evil—whether it be an evil will, an instance of pain, or some disorder or decay in nature—has not been set there by God, but represents the distortion of something that is inherently valuable. Whatever exists is, as such, and in its proper place, good: Evil is essentially parasitic upon good, being disorder and perversion in a fundamentally good creation. This understanding of evil as something negative means that it is not willed and created by God, but it does not mean (as some have supposed) that evil is unreal and can be disregarded. On the contrary, the first effect of this doctrine is to accentuate even more the question of the origin of evil.

Theodicy,[1] as many modern Christian thinkers see it, is a modest enterprise, negative rather than positive in its conclusions. It does not claim to explain, nor to explain away, every instance of evil in human experience, but only to point to certain considerations which prevent the fact of evil (largely incomprehensible though it remains) from constituting a final and insuperable bar to rational belief in God.

In indicating these considerations it will be useful to follow the traditional division of the subject. There is the problem of *moral evil* or wickedness: why does an all-good and all-powerful God permit this? And there is the problem of the *non-moral evil* of suffering and pain, both physical and mental: Why has an all-good and all-powerful God created a world in which this occurs?

Christian thought has always considered moral evil in its relation to human freedom and responsibility. To be a person is to be a finite center of freedom, a (relatively) free and self-directing agent responsible for one's own decisions. This involves being free to act wrongly as well as to act rightly. The idea of a person who can be infallibly guaranteed always to act rightly is self-contradictory. There can be no guarantee in advance that a genuinely free moral agent will never choose amiss. Consequently, the possibility of wrongdoing or sin is logically inseparable from the creation of finite persons, and to say that God should not have created beings who might sin amounts to saying he should not have created people.

This thesis has been challenged in some recent philosophical discussions of the problem of evil, in which it is claimed that no contradiction is involved in saying that God might have made people who would be genuinely free and who could yet be guaranteed always to act rightly. A quote from one of these discussions follows:

> If there is no logical impossibility in a man's freely choosing the good on one, or on several occasions, there cannot be a logical impossibility in his freely choosing the good on every occasion. God was not, then, faced with a choice

between making innocent automata and making beings who, in acting freely, would sometimes go wrong: there was open to him the obviously better possibility of making beings who would act freely but always go right. Clearly, his failure to avail himself of this possibility is inconsistent with his being both omnipotent and wholly good.[2]

A reply to this argument is suggested in another recent contribution to the discussion.[3] If by a free action we mean an action which is not externally compelled but which flows from the nature of the agent as he reacts to the circumstances in which he finds himself, there is, indeed, no contradiction between our being free and our actions being "caused" (by our own nature) and therefore being in principle predictable. There is a contradiction, however, in saying that God is the cause of our acting as we do but that we are free beings in relation to God. There is, in other words, a contradiction in saying that God has made us so that we shall of necessity act in a certain way, and that we are genuinely independent persons in relation to him. If all our thoughts and actions are divinely predestined, however free and morally responsible we may seem to be to ourselves, we cannot be free and morally responsible in the sight of God, but must instead be his helpless puppets. Such "freedom" is like that of a patient acting out a series of post-hypnotic suggestions: he appears, even to himself, to be free, but his volitions have actually been pre-determined by another will, that of the hypnotist, in relation to whom the patient is not a free agent.

A different objector might raise the question of whether or not we deny God's omnipotence if we admit that he is unable to create persons who are free from the risks inherent in personal freedom. The answer that has always been given is that to create such beings is logically impossible. It is no limitation upon God's power that he cannot accomplish the logically impossible, since there is nothing here to accomplish, but only a meaningless conjunction of words—in this case "person who is not a person." God is able to cre-

ate beings of any and every conceivable kind, but creatures who lack moral freedom, however superior they might be to human beings in other respects, would not be what we mean by persons. They would constitute a different form of life which God might have brought into existence instead of persons. When we ask why God did not create such beings in place of persons, the traditional answer is that only persons could, in any meaningful sense, become "children of God," capable of entering into a personal relationship with their Creator by a free and uncompelled response to his love.

When we turn from the possibility of moral evil as a correlate of man's personal freedom to its actuality, we face something which must remain inexplicable even when it can be seen to be possible. For we can never provide a complete causal explanation of a free act; if we could, it would not be a free act. The origin of moral evil lies forever concealed within the mystery of human freedom.

The necessary connection between moral freedom and the possibility, now actualized, of sin throws light upon a great deal of the suffering which afflicts mankind. For an enormous amount of human pain arises either from the inhumanity or the culpable incompetence of mankind. This includes such major scourges as poverty, oppression and persecution, war, and all the injustice, indignity, and inequity which occur even in the most advanced societies. These evils are manifestations of human sin. Even disease is fostered to an extent, the limits of which have not yet been determined by psychosomatic medicine, by moral and emotional factors seated both in the individual and in his social environment. To the extent that all of these evils stem from human failures and wrong decisions, their possibility is inherent in the creation of free persons inhabiting a world which presents them with real choices which are followed by real consequences.

We may now turn more directly to the problem of suffering. Even though the major bulk of actual human pain is traceable to man's misused freedom as a sole or part cause, there remain other sources of pain which are entirely independent of the human will, for example, earthquake, hurricane, storm, flood, drought, and blight. In practice it is often impossible to trace a boundary between the suffering which results from human wickedness and folly and that which falls upon mankind from without. Both kinds of suffering are inextricably mingled together in human experience. For our present purpose, however, it is important to note that the latter category does exist and that it seems to be built into the very structure of our world. In response to it, theodicy, if it is wisely conducted, follows a negative path. It is not possible to show positively that each item of human pain serves the divine purpose of good, but, on the other hand, it does seem possible to show that the divine purpose as it is understood in Judaism and Christianity could not be forwarded in a world which was designed as a permanent hedonistic paradise.

An essential premise of this argument concerns the divine purpose in creating the world. The skeptic's assumption is that man is to be viewed as a completed creation and that God's purpose in making the world was to provide a suitable dwelling-place for this fully-formed creature. Since God is good and loving, the environment which he has created for human life to inhabit is naturally as pleasant and comfortable as possible. The problem is essentially similar to that of a man who builds a cage for some pet animal. Since our world, in fact, contains sources of hardship, inconvenience, and danger of innumerable kinds, the conclusion follows that this world cannot have been created by a perfectly benevolent and all-powerful deity.

Christianity, however, has never supposed that God's purpose in the creation of the world was to construct a paradise whose inhabitants would experience a maximum of pleasure and a minimum of pain. The world is seen, instead, as a place of "soul-making" in which free beings, grappling with the tasks and challenges of their existence in a common environment, may become "children of God" and "heirs of eternal life." A way of thinking theologically of God's continuing creative purpose for man was suggested by some of the early Hellenistic Fathers of the Christian Church, especially Irenaeus. Following hints from St. Paul, Irenaeus taught that man has been made as a person in the image of God but has not yet been brought as a free and responsible agent into the finite likeness of God, which is revealed in Christ. Our world, with all its rough edges, is the sphere in which this second and harder stage of the creative process is taking place.

This conception of the world (whether or not set in Irenaeus' theological framework) can be supported by the method of negative theodicy. Suppose, contrary to fact, that his world were a paradise from which all possibility of pain and suffering were excluded. The consequences would be very far-reaching. For example, no one could ever injure anyone else; the murderer's knife would turn to paper or his bullets to thin air; the bank safe, robbed of a million dollars, would miraculously become filled with another million dollars (without this device, on however large a scale, proving inflationary); fraud, deceit, conspiracy, and treason would somehow always leave the fabric of society undamaged. Again, no one would ever be injured by accident: the mountain-climber, steeplejack, or playing child falling from a height would float unharmed to the ground; the reckless driver would never meet with disaster. There would be no need to work, since no harm could result from avoiding work; there would be no call to be concerned for others in time of need or danger, for in such a world there could be no real needs or dangers.

To make possible this continual series of individual adjustments, nature would have to work by "special providences" instead of running according to general laws which men must learn to respect on penalty of pain or death. The laws of nature would have to be extremely flexible: sometimes gravity would operate, sometimes not; sometimes an object would be hard and solid, sometimes soft. There could be no sciences, for there would be no enduring world structure to investigate. In eliminating the problems and hardships of an objective environment, with its own laws, life would become like a dream in which, delightfully but aimlessly, we would float and drift at ease.

One can at least begin to imagine such a world. It is evident that our present ethical concepts would have no meaning in it. If, for example, the notion of harming someone is an essential element in the concept of a wrong action, in our hedonistic paradise there could be no wrong actions—nor any right actions in distinction from wrong. Courage and fortitude would have no point in an environment in which there is, by definition, no danger of difficulty. Generosity, kindness, the *agape* aspect of love, prudence, unselfishness, and all other ethical notions which presuppose life in a stable environment, could not even be formed. Consequently, such a world, however well it might promote pleasure, would be very ill adapted for the development of the moral qualities of human personality. In relation to this purpose it would be the worst of all possible worlds.

It would seem, then, that an environment intended to make possible the growth in free beings of the finest characteristics of personal life, must have a good deal in common with our present world. It must operate according to general and dependable laws, and it must involve real dangers, difficulties, problems, obstacles, and possibilities of pain, failure, sorrow, frustration, and defeat. If it did not contain the particular trials and perils which—subtracting man's own very considerable contribution—our world contains, it would have to contain others instead.

To realize this is not, by any means, to be in possession of a detailed theodicy. It is to understand that this world, with all its "heartaches and the thousand natural shocks that flesh is heir to," an environment so manifestly not designed for the maximization of human pleasure and the minimization of human pain, may be rather well adapted to the quite different purpose of "soul-making."

NOTES

1. The word "theodicy," from the Greek *theos* (God) and *dike* (righteous), means the justification of God's goodness in the face of the fact of evil.

2. J. L. Mackie, "Evil and Omnipotence." *Mind* (April 1955), 209.

3. Flew, in *New Essays in Philosophical Theology.* [See Reading II.18.]

For Further Reflection

1. How convincing is Hick's argument? Does it explain natural evil (what Hick calls *nonmoral evil*; that is, disease, earthquakes, famines, and floods)?

2. What would Hick say to the problem of animal suffering? How does that work toward soul-making?

3. Some have said that it is not just the existence of evil but the sheer quantity of evil in the world that makes it hard to believe that a good God exists. Why doesn't God intervene at crucial moments to prevent a holocaust or, to take Dostoevsky's example, to prevent a child from being torn to death by ferocious dogs?

II.C   Is Faith Compatible with Reason?

One of the most important areas of philosophy of religion is that of the relationship of faith to reason. Is religious belief rational? Or is faith essentially irrational? If we cannot prove the claims of religious belief, is it nevertheless reasonable to believe these claims? For example, even if we do not have a deductive proof for the existence of God, is it nevertheless reasonable to believe that God exists? In the debate over faith and reason, two opposing positions have dominated the field. The first position asserts that faith and reason are compatible (that is, it is rational to believe in God).

The second position denies this assertion. Those holding to the first position differ among themselves as to the extent of the compatibility between faith and reason; most adherents follow Thomas Aquinas in relegating the compatibility to the "preambles of faith" (for example, the existence of God and his nature) over against the "articles of faith" (for example, the doctrine of the incarnation). Few have gone as far as Immanuel Kant, who maintained complete harmony between reason and faith, that is, a religious belief within the realm of reason alone. The second position divides into two subpositions: (1) that which asserts that faith is opposed to reason (which includes such unlikely bedfellows as David Hume and Søren Kierkegaard), placing faith in the area of irrationality; and (2) that which asserts that faith is higher than reason, transcends reason. John Calvin and Karl Barth assert that a natural theology is inappropriate because it seeks to meet unbelief on its own ground (ordinary, finite reason). Revelation, however, is "self-authenticating," "carrying with it its own evidence." We may call this position the *transrational* view of faith. Faith is not against reason but above it and beyond its proper domain.

The irrationalist and transrationalist positions are sometimes hard to separate in the incompatibilist's argument. At least, it seems that faith gets such a high value that reason looks not simply inadequate but culpable. To use reason where faith claims the field is not only inappropriate but irreverent and faithless.

In the following readings, each of these positions is represented.

Yes, Faith Is a Logical Bet   II.15

BLAISE PASCAL

Blaise Pascal (1623–1662) was a French scientist, philosopher, and mathematician. He founded probability theory and made important contributions to science through his studies of barometric pressure. His conversion to a radical form of Catholicism in 1653 caused him to turn all his attention to religious matters. In this famous section from his *Pensées* (Thoughts), Pascal argues that if we do a cost-benefit analysis of the matter, it turns out that it is eminently reasonable to get ourselves to believe that God exists, regardless of whether we have good evidence for that belief. The argument goes something like this: Regarding the proposition "God exists," reason is neutral. It can neither prove nor disprove it. But we must make a choice on this matter, for not to choose for God is in effect to choose against him and lose the possible benefits that belief would bring. Since these benefits of faith promise to be infinite and the loss equally infinite, we must take a gamble on faith.

Study Questions

1. What is the relationship between our finitude and infinity? What is the infinite?
2. Why can we not know the existence or nature of God?
3. What does Pascal say regarding those who blame Christians for not producing evidence or proofs for the existence of God? Can God's existence be proved? Why or why not?
4. What is the wager Pascal advocates, and how does he calculate the cost-benefit ratio?

INFINITE — NOTHING. — Our soul is cast into a body, where it finds number, time, dimension. Thereupon it reasons, and calls this nature, necessity, and can believe nothing else.

Unity joined to infinity adds nothing to it, no more than one foot to an infinite measure. The finite is annihilated in the presence of the infinite, and becomes a pure nothing. So our spirit before God, so our justice before divine justice. There is not so great disproportion between our justice and that of God, as between unity and infinity.

The justice of God must be vast like His compassion. Now, justice to the outcast is less vast, and ought less to offend our feelings than mercy towards the elect.

We know that there is an infinite, and are ignorant of its nature. As we know it to be false that numbers are finite, it is therefore true that there is an infinity in number. But we do not know what it is. It is false that it is even, it is false that it is odd; for the addition of a unit can make no change in its nature. Yet it is a number, and every number is odd or even (this is certainly true of every finite number). So we may well know that there is a God without knowing what He is. Is there not one substantial truth, seeing there are so many things which are not the truth itself?

We know then the existence and nature of the finite, because we also are finite and have extension. We know the existence of the infinite, and are ignorant of its nature, because it has extension like us, but not limits like us. But we know neither the existence nor the nature of God, because He has neither extension nor limits.

But by faith we know His existence; in glory we shall know His nature. Now, I have already shown that we may well know the existence of a thing, without knowing its nature.

Let us now speak according to natural lights.

If there is a God, He is infinitely incomprehensible, since, having neither parts nor limits, He has no affinity to us. We are then incapable of knowing either what He is or if He is. This being so, who will dare to undertake the decision of the question? Not we, who have no affinity to Him.

Who then will blame Christians for not being able to give a reason for their belief, since they profess a religion for which they cannot give a reason? They declare, in expounding it to the world, that it is a foolishness, *stultitiam;* and then you complain that they do not prove it! If they proved it, they would not keep their words; it is in lacking proofs, that they are not lacking in sense. "Yes, but although this excuses those who offer it as such, and takes away from them the blame of putting it forward without reason, it does not excuse those who receive it." Let us then examine this point, and say, "God is, or He is not." But to which side shall we incline? Reason can decide nothing here. There is an infinite chaos which separates us. A game is being played at the extremity of this infinite distance where heads or tails will turn up. What will you wager?

Reprinted from Blaise Pascal, Thoughts, *translated by W. F. Trotter (New York: Collier & Son, 1910).*

According to reason, you can do neither the one thing nor the other; according to reason, you can defend neither of the propositions.

Do not then reprove for error those who have made a choice; for you know nothing about it. "No, but I blame them for having made, not this choice, but a choice; for again both he who chooses heads and he who chooses tails are equally at fault, they are both in the wrong. The true course is not to wager at all."

—Yes; but you must wager. It is not optional. You are embarked. Which will you choose then; Let us see. Since you must choose, let us see which interests you least. You have two things to lose, the true and the good; and two things to stake, your reason and your will, your knowledge and your happiness; and your nature has two things to shun, error and misery. Your reason is no more shocked in choosing one rather than the other, since you must of necessity choose. This is one point settled. But your happiness? Let us weigh the gain and the loss in wagering that God is. Let us estimate these two chances. If you gain, you gain all; if you lose, you lose nothing. Wager then without hesitation that He is.—"That is very fine. Yes, I must wager, but I may perhaps wager too much."—Let us see. Since there is an equal risk of gain and of loss, if you had only to gain two lives, instead of one, you might still wager. But if there were three lives to gain, you would have to play (since you are under the necessity of playing), and you would be imprudent, when you are forced to play, not to chance your life to gain three at a game where there is an equal risk of loss and gain. But there is an eternity of life and happiness. And this being so, if there were an infinity of chances, of which one only would be for you, you would still be right in wagering one to win two, and you would act stupidly, being obliged to play, by refusing to stake one life against three at a game in which you had an infinity of an infinitely happy life to gain. But there is here an infinity of an infinitely happy life to gain, a chance of gain against a finite number of chances of loss, and what you stake is finite. It is all divided; wherever the infinite is and there is

not an infinity of chances of loss against that of gain, there is no time to hesitate, you must give all. And thus, when one is forced to play, he must renounce reason to preserve his life, rather than risk it for infinite gain, as likely to happen as the loss of nothingness.

For it is no use to say it is uncertain if we will gain, and it is certain that we risk, and that the infinite distance between the *certainty* of what is staked and the *uncertainty* of what will be gained, equals the finite good which is certainly staked against the uncertain infinite. It is not so, as every player stakes a certainty to gain an uncertainty, and yet he stakes a finite certainty to gain a finite uncertainty, without transgressing against reason. There is not an infinite distance between the certainty staked and the uncertainty of the gain; that is untrue. In truth, there is an infinity between the certainty of gain and the certainty of loss. But the uncertainty of the gain is proportioned to the certainty of the stake according to the proportion of the chances of gain and loss. Hence it comes that, if there are as many risks on one side as on the other, the course is to play even, and then the certainty of the stake is equal to the uncertainty of the gain, so far is it from the fact that there is an infinite distance between them. And so our proposition is of infinite force, when there is the finite to stake in a game where there are equal risks of gain and of loss, and the infinite to gain. This is demonstrable, and if men are capable of any truths, this is one.

"I confess it, I admit it. But still is there no means of seeing the faces of the cards?"—Yes, Scripture and the rest, &c.—"Yes, but I have my hands tied and my mouth closed; I am forced to wager, and am not free. I am not released, and am so made that I cannot believe. What then would you have me do?"

True. But at least learn your inability to believe, since reason brings you to this, and yet you cannot believe. Endeavour then to convince yourself, not by increase of proofs of God, but by the abatement of your passions. You would like to attain faith, and do not know the way; you would like to cure yourself of unbelief, and ask the remedy for it. Learn of those who have been bound like you, and who now stake all their possessions. These are people who know the way which you would follow, and who are cured of an ill of which you would be cured. Follow the way by which they began; by acting as if they believe, taking the holy water, having masses said, &c. Even this will naturally make you believe, and deaden your acuteness.—"But this is what I am afraid of."—And why? What have you to lose?

But to show you that this leads you there, it is this which will lessen the passions, which are your stumbling-blocks.

The end of this discourse.—Now what harm will befall you in taking this side? You will be faithful, honest, humble, grateful, generous, a sincere friend, truthful. Certainly you will not have those poisonous pleasures, glory and luxury, but will you not have others? I will tell you that you will thereby gain in this life, and that, at each step you take on this road, you will see so great certainty of gain, so much nothingness in what you risk, that you will at last recognize that you have wagered for something certain and infinite, for which you have given nothing.

"Ah! This discourse transports me, charms me," &c.

If this discourse pleases you and seems impressive, know that it is made by a man who has knelt, both before and after it, in prayer to that Being, infinite and without parts, before whom he lays all he has, for you also to lay before Him all you have for your own good and for His glory, so that strength may be given to lowliness.

For Further Reflection

1. Do you agree with Pascal that by a cost-benefit analysis it is good common sense to wager on God?

2. Is there anything problematic with Pascal's argument? Can other religions make similar or even more striking claims and use Pascal's argument to urge us to give up our religion and join theirs?

3. Could it be that God, if there be one, disdains making faith in him an outcome of a wager and not an honest estimation of the evidence?

II.16   The Ethics of Belief

W. K. CLIFFORD

In this essay the British philosopher W. K. Clifford (1845–1879) argues against Pascalian Wagers and against all pragmatic justification for religious belief. He contends that believing involves ethical principles, so we violate our moral duty if we obtain beliefs where the evidence is insufficient. Such acquisitions of beliefs are tantamount to theft. Clifford begins this essay by relating the story of a shipowner who sends a ship full of emigrants out to sea, knowing that the ship is old and not well-built. He stifles doubts and launches it anyway, sincerely trusting Providence to care for it. When it sinks and all passengers are drowned, he collects his insurance money without a trace of guilt. Clifford argues that sincerity in no way excuses the shipowner, because "he had no right to believe on such evidence as was before him." The rest of the essay is a discussion of the ethics of acquiring beliefs on insufficient evidence.

Study Questions

1. What, according to Clifford, did the shipowner do wrong and why was it wrong?
2. What did the accusers of the religious people on the island (the second illustration) do wrong?
3. What do these two illustrations have in common? What is the lesson Clifford seeks to bring out in discussing them?
4. What is the *Ethics of Belief*? How do moral duties apply to beliefs?
5. What is the danger to a society of becoming credulous?
6. How does Clifford set forth his principle of acquiring beliefs?
7. Does Clifford admit any exceptions to his principle?

A SHIPOWNER WAS ABOUT TO SEND to sea an emigrant ship. He knew that she was old, and not over-well built at the first; that she had seen many seas and climes, and often had needed repairs. Doubts had been suggested to him that possibly she was not seaworthy. These doubts preyed upon his mind and made him unhappy; he thought that perhaps he ought to have her thoroughly overhauled and refitted, even though this should put him to great expense. Before the ship sailed, however, he succeeded in overcoming these melancholy reflections. He said to himself that she had gone safely through so many voyages and weathered so many storms that it was idle to suppose she would not come safely home from this trip also. He would put his trust in Providence, which could hardly fail to protect all these unhappy families that were leaving their fatherland to seek for better times elsewhere. He would dismiss from his mind all ungenerous suspicions about the honesty of builders and contractors. In such ways he acquired a sincere and comfortable conviction that his vessel was thoroughly safe and seaworthy; he watched her departure with a light heart, and benevolent wishes for the success of the exiles in their strange new home that was to be; and he got his insurance money when she went down in midocean and told no tales.

What shall we say of him? Surely this, that he was verily guilty of the death of those men. It is admitted that he did sincerely believe in the soundness of his ship; but the sincerity of his conviction can in no wise help him, because *he had no right to believe on such evidence as was before him.* He had acquired his belief not by honestly earning it in patient investigation, but by stifling his doubts. And although in the end he may have felt so sure about it that he could not think otherwise, yet inasmuch as he had knowingly and willingly worked himself into that frame of mind, he must be held responsible for it.

Let us alter the case a little, and suppose that the ship was not unsound after all; that she made her voyage safely, and many others after it. Will that diminish the guilt of her owner? Not one jot. When an action is once done, it is right or wrong forever; no accidental failure of its good or evil fruits can possibly alter that. The man would not have been innocent, he would only have been not found out. The question of right or wrong has to do with the origin of his belief,

Reprinted from W. K. Clifford's Lectures and Essays *(London: Macmillan, 1879).*

not the matter of it; not what it was, but how he got it; not whether it turned out to be true or false, but whether he had a right to believe on such evidence as was before him.

There was once an island in which some of the inhabitants professed a religion teaching neither the doctrine of original sin nor that of eternal punishment. A suspicion got abroad that the professors of this religion had made use of unfair means to get their doctrines taught to children. They were accused of wresting the laws of their country in such a way as to remove children from the care of their natural and legal guardians; and even of stealing them away and keeping them concealed from their friends and relations. A certain number of men formed themselves into a society for the purpose of agitating the public about this matter. They published grave accusations against individual citizens of the highest position and character, and did all in their power to injure those citizens in the exercise of their professions. So great was the noise they made, that a Commission was appointed to investigate the facts, but after the Commission had carefully inquired into all the evidence that could be got, it appeared that the accused were innocent. Not only had they been accused on insufficient evidence, but the evidence of their innocence was such as the agitators might easily have obtained, if they had attempted a fair inquiry. After these disclosures the inhabitants of that country looked upon the members of the agitating society not only as persons whose judgment was to be distrusted, but also as no longer to be counted honorable men. For although they had sincerely and conscientiously believed in the charges they had made, *yet they had no right to believe on such evidence as was before them.* Their sincere convictions, instead of being honestly earned by patient inquiring, were stolen by listening to the voice of prejudice and passion.

Let us vary this case also, and suppose, other things remaining as before, that a still more accurate investigation proved the accused to have been really guilty. Would this make any difference in the guilt of the accusers? Clearly not; the question is not whether their belief was true or false, but whether they entertained it on wrong grounds. They would no doubt say, "Now you see that we were right after all; next time perhaps you will believe us." And they might be believed, but they would not thereby become honorable men. They would not be innocent, they would only be not found out. Every one of them, if he chose to examine himself *in foro conscientiae,* would know that he had acquired and nourished a belief, when he had no right to believe on such evidence as was before him; and therein he would know that he had done a wrong thing.

It may be said, however, that in both of these supposed cases it is not the belief which is judged to be wrong, but the action following upon it. The shipowner might say, "I am perfectly certain that my ship is sound, but still I feel it my duty to have her examined, before trusting the lives of so many people to her." And it might be said to the agitator, "However convinced you were of the justice of your cause and the truth of your convictions, you ought not to have made public attack upon any man's character until you had examined the evidence on both sides with the utmost patience and care."

In the first place, let us admit that, so far as it goes, this view of the case is right and necessary; right, because even when a man's belief is so fixed that he cannot think otherwise, he still has a choice in regard to the action suggested by it, and so cannot escape the duty of investigating on the ground of the strength of his convictions; and necessary, because those who are not yet capable of controlling their feelings and thoughts must have a plain rule dealing with overt acts.

But this being premised as necessary, it becomes clear that it is not sufficient, and that our previous judgment is required to supplement it. For it is not possible so to sever the belief from the action it suggests as to condemn the one without condemning the other. No man holding a strong belief on one side of a question, or even wishing to hold a belief on one side, can investigate it with such fairness and completeness as if he were really in doubt and unbiased; so that the existence of a belief not founded on fair inquiry unfits a man for the performance of this necessary duty.

Nor is that truly a belief at all which has not some influence upon the actions of him who holds it. He who truly believes that which prompts him to an action has looked upon the action to lust after it, he has committed it already in his heart. If a belief is not realized immediately in open deeds, it is stored up for the guidance of the future. It goes to make a part of that aggregate of beliefs which is the link between sensation and action at every moment of all our lives, and which is so organized and compacted together that no part of it can be isolated from the rest, but every new addition modifies the structure of the whole. No real belief, however trifling and fragmentary it may seem, is ever truly insignificant; it prepares us to receive more of its like, confirms those which resembled it before, and weakens others; and so gradually it lays a stealthy train in our inmost thoughts, which may some day explode into overt action, and leave its stamp upon our character forever.

And no one man's belief is in any case a private matter which concerns himself alone. Our lives are guided by that general conception of the course of things which has been created by society for social purposes. Our words, our phrases, our forms and processes and modes of thought are common property, fashioned and perfected from age to age; an heirloom which every succeeding generation inherits as a precious deposit and a sacred trust to be handed on to the next one, not unchanged but enlarged and purified, with some clear marks of its proper handiwork. Into this, for good or ill, is woven every belief of every man who has speech of his fellows. An awful privilege, and an awful responsibility, that we should help to create the world in which posterity will live.

In the two supposed cases which have been considered, it has been judged wrong to believe on insufficient evidence, or to nourish belief by suppressing doubts and avoiding investigation.

The reason of this judgment is not far to seek; it is that in both these cases the belief held by one man was of great importance to other men. But for as much as no belief held by one man, however seemingly trivial the belief, and however obscure the believer, is ever actually insignificant or without its effect on the fate of mankind, we have no choice but to extend our judgment to all cases of belief whatever. Belief, that sacred faculty which prompts the decisions of our will, and knits into harmonious working all the compacted energies of our being, is ours not for ourselves but for humanity. It is rightly used on truths which have been established by long experience and waiting toil, and which have stood in the fierce light of free and fearless questioning. Then it helps to bind men together, and to strengthen and direct their common action. It is desecrated when given to unproved and unquestioned statements, for the solace and private pleasure of the believer; to add a tinsel splendor to the plain straight road of our life and display a bright mirage beyond it; or even to drown the common sorrows of our kind by a self-deception which allows them not only to cast down, but also to degrade us. Whoso would deserve well of his fellows in this matter will guard the purity of his belief with a very fanaticism of jealous care, lest at any time it should rest on an unworthy object, and catch a stain which can never be wiped away.

It is not only the leader of men, statesman, philosopher, or poet, that owes this bounden duty to mankind. Every rustic who delivers in the village alehouse his slow, infrequent sentences, may help to kill or keep alive the fatal superstitions which clog his race. Every hard-worked wife of an artisan may transmit to her children beliefs which shall knit society together, or rend it in pieces. No simplicity of mind, no obscurity of station, can escape the universal duty of questioning all that we believe.

It is true that this duty is a hard one, and the doubt which comes out of it is often a very bitter thing. It leaves us bare and powerless where we thought that we were safe and strong. To know all about anything is to know how to deal with it under all circumstances. We feel much happier and more secure when we think we know precisely what to do, no matter what happens, than when we have lost our way and do not know where to turn. And if we have supposed ourselves to know all about anything, and to be capable of doing what is fit in regard to it, we naturally do not like to find that we are really ignorant and powerless, that we have to begin again at the beginning, and try to learn what the thing is and how it is to be dealt with—if indeed anything can be learned about it. It is the sense of power attached to a sense of knowledge that makes men desirous of believing, and afraid of doubting.

This sense of power is the highest and best of pleasures when the belief on which it is founded is true belief, and has been fairly earned by investigation. For then we may justly feel that it is common property, and holds good for others as well as for ourselves. Then we may be glad, not that *I* have learned secrets by which I am safer and stronger, but that *we men* have got mastery over more of the world; and we shall be strong, not for ourselves, but in the name of Man and in his strength. But if the belief has been accepted on insufficient evidence, the pleasure is a stolen one. Not only does it deceive ourselves by giving us a sense of power which we do not really possess, but it is sinful, because it is stolen in defiance of our duty to mankind. That duty is to guard ourselves from such beliefs as from a pestilence, which may shortly master our own body and then spread to the rest of the town. What would be thought of one who, for the sake of a sweet fruit, should deliberately run the risk of bringing a plague upon his family and his neighbors?

And, as in other such cases, it is not the risk only which has to be considered; for a bad action is always bad at the time when it is done, no matter what happens afterwards. Every time we let ourselves believe for unworthy reasons, we weaken our powers of self-control, of doubting, of judicially and fairly weighing evidence. We all suffer severely enough from the maintenance and support of false beliefs and the fatally wrong actions which they lead to, and the evil born when one such belief is entertained is great and wide. But a greater and wider evil arises when the credulous character is maintained and supported, when a habit of believing for unworthy reasons is fostered and made permanent. If I steal money from any person, there may be no harm done by the mere transfer of possession; he may not feel the loss, or it may prevent him from using the money badly. But I cannot help doing this great wrong towards Man, that I make myself dishonest. What hurts society is not that it should lose its property, but that it should become a den of thieves; for then it must cease to be society. This is why we ought not to do evil that good may come; for at any rate this great evil has come, that we have done evil and are made wicked thereby. In like manner, if I let myself believe anything on insufficient evidence, there may be no great harm done by the mere belief; it may be true after all, or I may never have occasion to exhibit it in outward acts. But I cannot help doing this great wrong toward Man, that I make myself credulous. The danger to society is not merely that it should believe wrong things, though that is great enough; but that it should become credulous, and lose the habit of testing things and inquiring into them; for then it must sink back into savagery.

The harm which is done by credulity in a man is not confined to the fostering of a credulous character in others, and consequent support of false beliefs. Habitual want of care about what I believe leads to habitual want of care in others about the truth of what is told to me. Men speak the truth to one another when each reveres the truth in his own mind and in the other's mind; but how shall my friend revere the truth in my mind when I myself am careless about it, when I believe things because I want to believe them, and because they are comforting and pleasant? Will he not learn to cry, "Peace," to me, when there is no peace? By such a course I shall surround myself with a thick atmosphere of falsehood and fraud, and in that I must live. It may matter little to me, in my cloud-castle of sweet illusions and darling lies; but it matters much to Man that I have made my neighbors ready to deceive. The credulous man is father to the liar and the cheat; he lives in the bosom of this his family, and it is no marvel if he should become even as they are. So closely are our duties knit together, that whoso shall keep the whole law, and yet offend in one point, he is guilty of all.

To sum up; it is wrong always, everywhere, and for anyone, to believe anything upon insufficient evidence.

If a man, holding a belief which he was taught in childhood or persuaded of afterwards, keeps down and pushes away any doubts which arise about it in his mind, purposely avoids the reading of books and the company of men that call in question or discuss it, and regards as impious those questions which cannot easily be asked without disturbing it—the life of that man is one long sin against mankind.

If this judgment seems harsh when applied to those simple souls who have never known better, who have been brought up from the cradle with a horror of doubt, and taught that their eternal welfare depends on what they believe, then it leads to the very serious question. Who hath made Israel to sin?

Inquiry into the evidence of a doctrine is not to be made once for all, and then taken as finally settled. It is never lawful to stifle a doubt; for either it can be honestly answered by means of the inquiry already made, or else it proves that the inquiry was not complete.

"But," says one, "I am a busy man; I have no time for the long course of study which would be necessary to make me in any degree a competent judge of certain questions, or even able to understand the nature of the arguments." Then he would have no time to believe. . . .

For Further Reflection

1. Describe Clifford's ethics of belief. Does Clifford exaggerate our duty to believe exactly according to the evidence? Does he falsely suppose that we can measure the evidence? Explain your position.

2. Is Clifford's shipowner example relevant to religious belief, or are there significant dissimilarities? (If so, describe them.)

3. Is it sometimes permissible to believe some proposition without strong evidence? Consider the following situation: There is evidence that your best friend has committed a crime, but something deep inside of you tells you that he is innocent and you find yourself believing against the evidence. If it turned out that you were right, would this justify you in your confidence in your friend? Would this serve as a counterexample to Clifford's rationalism? Or can Clifford give a plausible account of this sort of situation? Explain.

The Will to Believe   II.17

WILLIAM JAMES

William James (1842–1910), an American philosopher and psychologist, was born in New York City and educated at Harvard. He was the brother of Henry James the novelist. William James struggled through much of his life with ill health. He was assailed by doubts over freedom of the will and the existence of God, and he developed the philosophy of pragmatism in part as a response to these difficulties. Pragmatism originated with James' friend Charles Peirce but underwent crucial changes and popularization in the hands of James. His principal works are *The Principles of Psychology* (1890), *The Will to Believe* (1897), *The Varieties of Religious Experience* (1902), and *Pragmatism, A New Name for Some Old Ways of Thinking* (1907).

The classic response to Clifford's ethics of belief is William James' "The Will to Believe" (1896), in which James argues that life would be greatly impoverished if we confined our beliefs to such a Scrooge-like epistemology as Clifford proposes. In everyday life, where the evidence for important propositions is often unclear, we must live by faith or cease to act at all. Although we may not make leaps of faith just anywhere, sometimes practical considerations force us to make decisions regarding propositions that do not have their truth value written on their faces. "Belief" is defined as a live, momentous optional hypothesis on which we cannot avoid a decision, for not to choose is in effect to choose against the hypothesis. James claims that religion can be such an optional hypothesis for many people, and in this case one has the right to believe the better story rather than the worse. To do so, one must will to believe what the evidence alone is inadequate to support.

Study Questions

1. What does James mean by *live* or *dead* hypotheses?
2. What does he mean by a *genuine option*?
3. What does he think about the validity of Pascal's Wager?
4. Does James think Clifford's *Ethics of Belief* is valid? What does he think of Clifford's views?
5. How does James think our passional nature functions with regard to acquiring beliefs?
6. How does James reply to Clifford's fear of being duped, that is, by having false beliefs?
7. What are the two ways of looking at our duty in matters of opinion? That is, regarding acquiring beliefs?
8. How can faith change reality?
9. What two things does religion say? What does James mean by these two things?
10. Does James think we ought to withhold belief regarding religion if we lack sufficient evidence?

LET US GIVE THE NAME of hypothesis to anything that may be proposed to our belief; and just as the electricians speak of live and dead wires, let us speak of any hypothesis as either *live* or *dead*. A live hypothesis is one which appeals as a real possibility to him to whom it is proposed. If I ask you to believe in the Mahdi [1844–1885, a Sudanese leader who led a successful revolt against Egypt in 1885], the notion makes no electric connection with your nature—it refuses to scintillate with any credibility at all. As an hypothesis it is completely dead. To an Arab, however (even if he be not one of the Mahdi's followers), the hypothesis is among the mind's possibilities: It is alive. This shows that deadness and liveness in an hypothesis are not intrinsic properties, but relations to the individual thinker. They are measured by his willingness to act. The maximum of liveness in an hypothesis means willingness to act irrevocably. Practically, that means belief; but there is some believing tendency wherever there is willingness to act at all.

Next, let us call the decision between two hypotheses an *option*. Options may be of several kinds. They may be first, *living* or *dead;* secondly, *forced* or *avoidable;* thirdly, *momentous* or *trivial;* and for our purposes we may call an option a genuine option when it is of a forced, living, and momentous kind.

1. A living option is one in which both hypotheses are live ones. If I say to you: "Be a theosophist or be a Mohammedan," it is probably a dead option, because for you neither hypothesis is likely to be alive. But if I say: "Be an agnostic or be a Christian," it is otherwise: trained as you are, each hypothesis makes some appeal, however small, to your belief.

2. Next, if I say to you: "Choose between going out with your umbrella or without it," I do not offer you a genuine option, for it is not forced. You can easily avoid it by not going out at all. Similarly, if I say, "Either love me or hate me," "Either call my theory true or call it false," your option is avoidable. You may remain indifferent to me, neither loving nor hating, and you may decline to offer any judgment as to my theory. But if I say, "Either accept this truth or go without it," I put on you a forced option, for there is no standing place outside of the alternative. Every dilemma based on a complete logical disjunction, with no possibility of not choosing, is an option of this forced kind.

3. Finally, if I were Dr. Nansen and proposed to you to join my North Pole expedition, your option would be momentous; for this would probably be your similar opportunity, and your choice now would either exclude you from the North Pole sort of immortality altogether or put at

least the chance of it into your hands. He who refuses to embrace a unique opportunity loses the prize as surely as if he tried and failed. *Per contra,* the option is trivial when the opportunity is not unique, when the stake is insignificant, or when the decision is reversible if it later prove unwise. Such trivial options abound in the scientific life. A chemist finds an hypothesis live enough to spend a year in its verification: he believes in it to that extent. But if his experiments prove inconclusive either way, he is quit for his loss of time, no vital harm being done.

It will facilitate our discussion if we keep all these distinctions well in mind.

The next matter to consider is the actual psychology of human opinion. When we look at certain facts, it seems as if our passional and volitional nature lay at the root of all our convictions. When we look at others, it seems as if they could do nothing when the intellect had once said its say. Let us take the latter facts up first.

Does it not seem preposterous on the very face of it to talk of our opinions being modifiable at will? Can our will either help or hinder our intellect in its perceptions of truth? Can we, by just willing it, believe that Abraham Lincoln's existence is a myth, and that the portraits of him in *McClure's Magazine* are all of some one else? Can we, by any effort of our will, or by any strength of wish that it were true, believe ourselves well and about when we are roaring with rheumatism in bed, or feel certain that the sum of the two one-dollar bills in our pocket must be a hundred dollars? We can say any of these things, but we are absolutely impotent to believe them; and of just such things is the whole fabric of the truths that we do believe in made up—matters of fact, immediate or remote, as Hume said, and relations between ideas, which are either there or not there for us if we see them so,

Reprinted from William James, The Will to Believe (*New York: Longmans, Gree & Co., 1897*).

and which if not there cannot be put there by any action of our own.

In Pascal's *Thoughts* there is a celebrated passage known in literature as Pascal's wager. In it he tries to force us into Christianity by reasoning as if our concern with truth resembled our concern with the stakes in a game of chance. Translated freely his words are these: You must either believe or not believe that God is—which will you do? Your human reason cannot say. A game is going on between you and the nature of things which at the day of judgment will bring out either heads or tails. Weigh what your gains and your losses would be if you should stake all you have on heads, or God's existence: if you win in such case, you gain eternal beatitude; if you lose, you lose nothing at all. If there were an infinity of chances, and only one for God in this wager, still you ought to stake your all on God; for though you surely risk a finite loss by this procedure, any finite loss is reasonable, even a certain one is reasonable, if there is but the possibility of infinite gain. Go, then, and take holy water, and have masses said; belief will come and stupefy your scruples. Why should you not? At bottom, what have you to lose?

You probably feel that when religious faith expresses itself thus, in the language of the gaming-table, it is put to its last trumps. Surely Pascal's own personal belief in masses and holy water had far other springs; and this celebrated page of his is but an argument for others, a last desperate snatch at a weapon against the hardness of the unbelieving heart. We feel that a faith in masses and holy water adopted wilfully after such a mechanical calculation would lack the inner soul of faith's reality; and if we were ourselves in the place of the Deity, we should probably take particular pleasure in cutting off believers of this pattern from their infinite reward. It is evident that unless there be some preexisting tendency to believe in masses and holy water, the option offered to the will by Pascal is not a living option. Certainly no Turk ever took to masses and holy water on its account; and even to us Protestants these means of salvation seem such foregone impossibilities that Pascal's logic, invoked for them specifically, leaves us unmoved. As well might the Mahdi write to us, saying, "I am the Expected One whom God has created in his effulgence. You shall be infinitely happy if you confess me; otherwise you shall be cut off from the light of the sun. Weigh, then, your infinite gain if I am genuine against your finite sacrifice if I am not!" His logic would be that of Pascal; but he would vainly use it on us, for the hypothesis he offers us is dead. No tendency to act on it exists in us to any degree.

The talk of believing by our volition seems, then, from one point of view, simply silly. From another point of view it is worse than silly, it is vile. When one turns to the magnificent edifice of the physical sciences, and sees how it was reared; what thousands of disinterested moral lives of men lie buried in its mere foundations; what patience and postponement, what choking down of preference, what submission to the icy laws of outer fact are wrought into its very stones and mortar; how absolutely impersonal it stands in its vast augustness—then how besotted and contemptible seems every little sentimentalist who comes blowing his voluntary smoke-wreaths, and pretending to decide things from out of his private dream! Can we wonder if those bred in the rugged and manly school of science should feel like spewing such subjectivism out of their mouths? The whole system of loyalties which grow up in the schools of science go dead against its toleration; so that it is only natural that those who have caught the scientific fever should pass over to the opposite extreme, and write sometimes as if the incorruptibly truthful intellect ought positively to prefer bitterness and unacceptableness to the heart in its cup.

> It fortifies my soul to know
> That though I perish, Truth is so.

sings Clough, while Huxley exclaims: "My only consolation lies in the reflection that, however bad our posterity may become, so far as they hold by the plain rule of not pretending to believe what they have no reason to believe, because it may be to their advantage so to pretend [the word 'pretend' is surely here redundant], they will not have reached the lowest depth of immorality." And that delicious *enfant terrible* Clifford writes: "Belief is desecrated when given to unproved and unquestioned statements for the solace and private pleasure of the believer. . . . Whoso would deserve well of his fellows in this matter will guard the purity of his belief with a very fanaticism of jealous care, lest at any time it should rest on an unworthy object, and catch a stain which can never be wiped away. . . . If [a] belief has been accepted on insufficient evidence [even though the belief be true, as Clifford on the same page explains] the pleasure is a stolen one. . . . It is sinful because it is stolen in defiance of our duty to mankind. That duty is to guard ourselves from such beliefs as from a pestilence which may shortly master our own body and then spread to the rest of the town. . . . It is wrong always, everywhere, and for every one, to believe anything upon insufficient evidence."

All this strikes one as healthy, even when expressed, as by Clifford, with somewhat too much of robustious pathos in the voice. Free will and simple wishing do seem, in the matter of our credences, to be only fifth wheels to the coach. Yet if any one should thereupon assume that intellectual insight is what remains after wish and will and sentimental preference have taken wing, or that pure reason is what then settles our opinions, he would fly quite as directly in the teeth of the facts.

It is only our already dead hypotheses that our willing nature is unable to bring to life again. But what has made them dead for us is for the most part a previous action of our willing nature of an antagonistic kind. When I say "willing nature," I do not mean only such deliberate volitions as may have set up habits of belief that we cannot now escape from—I mean all such factors of belief as fear and hope, prejudice and passion, imitation and partisanship, the circumpressure of our caste and set. As a matter of fact we find our-

selves believing, we hardly know how or why. Mr. Balfour gives the name of "authority" to all those influences, born of the intellectual climate, that make hypotheses possible or impossible for us, alive or dead. Here in this room, we all of us believe in molecules and the conservation of energy, in democracy and necessary progress, in Protestant Christianity and the duty of fighting for "the doctrine of the immortal Monroe," all for no reasons worthy of the name. We see into these matters with no more inner clearness, and probably with much less, than any disbeliever in them might possess. His unconventionality would probably have some grounds to show for its conclusions; but for us, not insight, but the *prestige* of the opinions, is what makes the spark shoot from them and light up our sleeping magazines of faith. Our reason is quite satisfied, in nine hundred and ninety-nine cases out of every thousand of us, if it can find a few arguments that will do to recite in case our credulity is criticized by some one else. Our faith is faith in some one else's faith, and in the greatest matters this is the most the case. . . .

Evidently, then, our non-intellectual nature does influence our convictions. There are passional tendencies and volitions which run before and others which come after belief, and it is only the latter that are too late for the fair; and they are not too late when the previous passional work has been already in their own direction. Pascal's argument, instead of being powerless, then seems a regular clincher, and is the last stroke needed to make our faith in masses and holy water complete. The state of things is evidently far from simple; and pure insight and logic, whatever they might do ideally, are not the only things that really do produce our creeds.

Our next duty, having recognized this mixed-up state of affairs, is to ask whether it be simply reprehensible and pathological, or whether, on the contrary, we must treat it as a normal element in making up our minds. The thesis I defend is, briefly stated, this: *Our passional nature not only lawfully may, but must, decide an option between propositions, whenever it is a genuine option that cannot by its nature be decided on intellectual grounds; for to say, under such circumstances, "Do not decide, but leave the question open," is itself a passional decision—just like deciding yes or no— and is attended with the same risk of losing the truth. . . .*

One more point, small but important, and our preliminaries are done. There are two ways of looking at our duty in the matter of opinion— ways entirely different, and yet ways about whose difference the theory of knowledge seems hitherto to have shown very little concern. *We must know the truth;* and *we must avoid error*—these are our first and great commandments as would- be knowers; but they are not two ways of stating an identical commandment, they are two separa- ble laws. Although it may indeed happen that when we believe the truth A, we escape as an inci- dental consequence from believing the falsehood B, it hardly ever happens that by merely disbe- lieving B we necessarily believe A. We may in escaping B fall into believing other falsehoods, C or D, just as bad as B; or we may escape B by not believing anything at all, not even A.

Believe truth! Shun error!—these, we see, are two materially different laws; and by choosing between them we may end by coloring differently our whole intellectual life. We may regard the chase for truth as paramount, and the avoidance of error as secondary; or we may, on the other hand, treat the avoidance of error as more imper- ative, and let truth take its chance. Clifford, in the instructive passage which I have quoted, exhorts us to the latter course. Believe nothing, he tells us, keep your mind in suspense forever, rather than by closing it on insufficient evidence incur the awful risk of believing lies. You, on the other hand, may think that the risk of being in error is a very small matter when compared with the bless- ings of real knowledge, and be ready to be duped many times in your investigation rather than postpone indefinitely the chance of guessing true. I myself find it impossible to go with Clifford. We must remember that these feelings of our duty

about either truth or error are in any case only expressions of our passional life. Biologically con- sidered, our minds are as ready to grind out false- hood as veracity, and he who says, "Better go without belief forever than believe a lie!" merely shows his own preponderant private horror of becoming a dupe. He may be critical of many of his desires and fears, but this fear he slavishly obeys. He cannot imagine any one questioning its binding force. For my own part, I have also a hor- ror of being duped; but I can believe that worse things than being duped may happen to a man in this world: so Clifford's exhortation has to my ears a thoroughly fantastic sound. It is like a gen- eral informing his soldiers that it is better to keep out of battle forever than to risk a single wound. Not so are victories either over enemies or over nature gained. Our errors are surely not such awfully solemn things. In a world where we are so certain to incur them in spite of all our caution, a certain lightness of heart seems healthier than this excessive nervousness on their behalf. At any rate, it seems the fittest thing for the empiricist philosopher.

And now, after all this introduction, let us go straight at our question. I have said, and now repeat it, that not only as a matter of fact do we find our passional nature influencing us in our opinions, but that there are some options between opinions in which this influence must be regarded both as an inevitable and as a lawful determinant of our choice.

I fear here that some of you my hearers will begin to scent danger, and lend an inhospitable ear. Two first steps of passion you have indeed had to admit as necessary—we must think so as to avoid dupery, and we must think so as to gain truth; but the surest path to those ideal consum- mations, you will probably consider, is from now onwards to take no further passional step.

Well, of course, I agree as far as the facts will allow. Wherever the option between losing truth and gaining it is not momentous, we can throw the chance of *gaining truth* away, and at any rate save ourselves from any chance of *believing falsehood,* by not making up our minds at all till objective evidence has come. In scientific questions, this is almost always the case; and even in human affairs in general, the need of acting is seldom so urgent that a false belief to act on is better than no belief at all. Law courts, indeed, have to decide on the best evidence attainable for the moment, because a judge's duty is to make law as well as to ascertain it, and (as a learned judge once said to me) few cases are worth spending much time over: the great thing is to have them decided on *any* acceptable principle, and got out of the way. But in our dealings with objective nature we obviously are recorders, not makers, of the truth; and decisions for the mere sake of deciding promptly and getting on to the next business would be wholly out of place. Throughout the breadth of physical nature facts are what they are quite independently of us, and seldom is there any such hurry about them that the risks of being duped by believing a premature theory need be faced. The questions here are always trivial options, the hypotheses are hardly living (at any rate not living for us spectators), the choice between believing truth or falsehood is seldom forced. The attitude of sceptical balance is therefore the absolutely wise one if we would escape mistakes. What difference, indeed, does it make to most of us whether we have or have not a theory of the Röntgen rays, whether we believe or not in mind-stuff, or have a conviction about the causality of conscious states? It makes no difference. Such options are not forced on us. On every account it is better not to make them, but still keep weighing reasons *pro et contra* with an indifferent hand.

I speak, of course, here of the purely judging mind. For purposes of discovery such indifference is to be less highly recommended, and science would be far less advanced than she is if the passionate desires of individuals to get their own faiths confirmed had been kept out of the game. See for example the sagacity which Spencer and Weismann now display. On the other hand, if you want an absolute duffer in an investigation, you must, after all, take the man who has no interest whatever in its results: he is the warranted incapable, the positive fool. The most useful investigator, because the most sensitive observer, is always he whose eager interest in one side of the question is balanced by an equally keen nervousness lest he become deceived. Science has organized this nervousness into a regular *technique,* her so-called method of verification; and she has fallen so deeply in love with the method that one may even say she has ceased to care for truth by itself at all. It is only truth as technically verified that interests her. The truth of truths might come in merely affirmative form, and she would decline to touch it. Such truth as that, she might repeat with Clifford, would be stolen in defiance of her duty to mankind. Human passions, however, are stronger than technical rules. *"Le coeur a ses raisons,"* as Pascal says, *"que la raison ne connait pas"**; and however indifferent to all but the bare rules of the game the umpire, the abstract intellect, may be, the concrete players who furnish him the materials to judge of are usually, each one of them, in love with some pet "live hypothesis" of his own. Let us agree, however, that wherever there is no forced option, the dispassionately judicial intellect with no pet hypothesis, saving us, as it does, from dupery at any rate, ought to be our ideal.

The question next arises: Are there not somewhere forced options in our speculative questions, and can we (as men who may be interested at least as much in positively gaining truth as in merely escaping dupery) always wait with impunity till the coercive evidence shall have arrived? It seems *a priori* improbable that the truth should be so nicely adjusted to our needs and powers as that. In the great boarding-house of nature, the cakes and the butter and the syrup seldom come out so even and leave the plates so clean. Indeed, we should view them with scientific suspicion if they did.

Moral questions immediately present themselves as questions whose solution cannot wait for

---

* "The heart has its reasons which reason does not know."

sensible proof. A moral question is a question not of what sensibly exists, but of what is good, or would be good if it did exist. Science can tell us what exists; but to compare the worths, both of what exists and of what does not exist, we must consult not science, but what Pascal calls our heart. . . .

Turn now from these wide questions of good to a certain class of questions of fact, questions concerning personal relations, states of mind between one man and another. *Do you like me or not?*—for example. Whether you do or not depends, in countless instances, on whether I meet you halfway, am willing to assume that you must like me, and show you trust and expectation. The previous faith on my part in your liking's existence is in such cases what makes your liking come. But if I stand aloof, and refuse to budge an inch until I have objective evidence, until you shall have done something apt, as the absolutists say, *ad extorquendum assensum meum,* ten to one your liking never comes. How many women's hearts are vanquished by the mere sanguine insistence of some man that they *must* love him! He will not consent to the hypothesis that they cannot. The desire for a certain kind of truth here brings about that special truth's existence; and so it is in innumerable cases of other sorts. . . . *And where faith in a fact can help create the fact,* that would be an insane logic which should say that faith running ahead of scientific evidence is the "lowest kind of immorality" into which a thinking being can fall. Yet such is the logic by which our scientific absolutists pretend to regulate our lives!

In truths dependent on our personal action, then, faith based on desire is certainly a lawful and possibly an indispensable thing.

But now, it will be said, these are all childish human cases, and have nothing to do with great cosmical matters, like the question of religious faith. Let us then pass on to that. Religions differ so much in their accidents that in discussing the religious question we must make it very generic and broad. What then do we now mean by the religious hypothesis? Science says things are; morality says some things are better than other things; and religion says essentially two things.

First, she says that the best things are the more eternal things, the overlapping things, the things in the universe that throw the last stone, so to speak, and say the final word. "Perfection is eternal"—this phrase of Charles Secrétan seems a good way of putting this first affirmation of religion, an affirmation which obviously cannot yet be verified scientifically at all.

The second affirmation of religion is that we are better off even now if we believe her first affirmation to be true.

Now, let us consider what the logical elements of this situation are *in case the religious hypothesis in both its branches be really true.* (Of course, we must admit that possibility at the outset. If we are to discuss the question at all, it must involve a living option. If for any of you religion be a hypothesis that cannot, by any living possibility, be true, then you need go no farther. I speak to the "saving remnant" alone.) So proceeding, we see, first, that religion offers itself as a momentous option. We are supposed to gain, even now, by our belief, and to lose by our non-belief, a certain vital good. Secondly, religion is a *forced* option, so far as that good goes. We cannot escape the issue by remaining sceptical and waiting for more light, because, although we do avoid error in that way *if religion be untrue,* we lose the good, *if it be true,* just as certainly as if we positively chose to disbelieve. It is as if a man should hesitate indefinitely to ask a certain woman to marry him because he was not perfectly sure that she would prove an angel after he brought her home. Would he not cut himself off from that particular angel-possibility as decisively as if he went and married some one else? Scepticism, then, is not avoidance of option; it is option of a certain particular kind of risk. *Better risk loss of truth than chance of error*—that is your faith-vetoer's exact position. He is actively playing his stake as much as the believer is; he is backing the field against the religious hypothesis, just as the believer is backing the religious hypothesis against the field. To preach scepticism to us as a duty until "sufficient evidence" for religion be found, is tantamount therefore to telling us, when in presence of the religious hypothesis, that to yield to our fear of its being error is wiser and better than to yield to our hope that it may be true. It is not intellect against all passions, then; it is only intellect with one passion laying down its law. And by what, forsooth, is the supreme wisdom of this passion warranted? Dupery for dupery, what proof is there that dupery through hope is so much worse than dupery through fear? I, for one, can see no proof; and I simply refuse obedience to the scientist's command to imitate his kind of option, in a case where my own stake is important enough to give me the right to choose my own form of risk. If religion be true and the evidence for it be still insufficient, I do not wish, by putting your extinguisher upon my nature (which feels to me as if it had after all some business in this matter), to forfeit my sole chance in life of getting upon the winning side—that chance depending, of course, on my willingness to run the risk of acting as if my passional need of taking the world religiously might be prophetic and right.

All this is on the supposition that it really may be prophetic and right, and that, even to us who are discussing the matter, religion is a live hypothesis which may be true. Now, to most of us religion comes in a still further way that makes a veto on our active faith even more illogical. The more perfect and more eternal aspect of the universe is represented in our religions as having personal form. The universe is no longer a mere *It* to us, but a *Thou,* if we are religious; and any relation that may be possible from person to person might be possible here. For instance, although in one sense we are passive portions of the universe, in another we show a curious autonomy, as if we were small active centers on our own account. We feel, too, as if the appeal of religion to us were made to our own active goodwill, as if evidence might be forever withheld from us unless we met the hypothesis halfway to take a trivial illustration: just as a man who in a company of gentlemen made no advances, asked a warrant for every concession, and believed no one's word without

proof, would cut himself off by such churlishness from all the social rewards that a more trusting spirit would earn—so here, one who should shut himself up in snarling logicality and try to make the gods extort his recognition willy-nilly, or not get it at all, might cut himself off forever from his only opportunity of making the gods' acquaintance. This feeling, forced on us we know not whence that by obstinately believing that there are gods (although not to do so would be so easy both for our logic and our life) we are doing the universe the deepest service we can, seems part of the living essence of the religious hypothesis. If the hypothesis were true in all its parts, including this one, then pure intellectualism, with its veto on our making willing advances, would be an absurdity; and some participation of our sympathetic nature would be logically required. I, therefore, for one, cannot see my way to accepting the agnostic rules for truth-seeking, or wilfully agree to keep my willing nature out of the game. I cannot do so for this plain reason, that *a rule of thinking which would absolutely prevent me from acknowledging certain kinds of truth if those kinds of truth were really there, would be an irrational rule.* That for me is the long and short of the formal logic of the situation, no matter what the kinds of truth might materially be.

I confess I do not see how this logic can be escaped. But sad experience makes me fear that some of you may still shrink from radically saying with me, *in abstracto,* that we have the right to believe at our own risk any hypothesis that is live enough to tempt our will. I suspect, however, that if this is so, it is because you have got away from the abstract logical point of view altogether, and are thinking (perhaps without realizing it) of some particular religious hypothesis which for you is dead. The freedom to 'believe what we will' you apply to the case of some patent superstition; and the faith you think of is the faith defined by the schoolboy when he said, "Faith is when you believe something that you know ain't true." I can only repeat that this is misapprehension. *In concreto,* the freedom to believe can only cover living options which the intellect of the individual cannot by itself resolve; and living options never seem absurdities to him who has them to consider. When I look at the religious question as it really puts itself to concrete men, and when I think of all the possibilities which both practically and theoretically it involves, then this command that we shall put a stopper on our heart, instincts, and courage, and *wait*—acting of course meanwhile more or less as if religion were *not* true—till doomsday, or till such time as our intellect and senses working together may have raked in evidence enough,—this command, I say, seems to me the queerest idol ever manufactured in the philosophic cave. Were we scholastic absolutists, there might be more excuse. If we had an infallible intellect with its objective certitudes, we might feel ourselves disloyal to such a perfect organ of knowledge in not trusting to it exclusively, in not waiting

for its releasing word. But if we are empiricists, if we believe that no bell in us tolls to let us know for certain when truth is in our grasp, then it seems a piece of idle fantasticality to preach so solemnly our duty of waiting for the bell. Indeed we *may* wait if we will—I hope you do not think that I am denying that—but if we do so, we do so at our peril as much as if we believed. In either case we *act*, taking our life in our hands. No one of us ought to issue vetoes to the other, nor should we bandy words of abuse. We ought, on the contrary, delicately and profoundly to respect one another's mental freedom: then only shall we bring about the intellectual republic: then only shall we have that spirit of inner tolerance without which all our Outer tolerance is soulless, and which is empiricism's glory; then only shall we live and let live, in speculative as well as in practical things. . . .

For Further Reflection

1. Explain what James means by a "genuine" option. Is he correct in calling religious belief a genuine option? Why or why not?

2. Has James successfully met Clifford's objections to religious belief, or has he confused self-creating beliefs with wishful thinking? That is, by getting myself into the state where I believe I am capable of winning a race (although there's not enough evidence to decide the likelihood of the matter), I might actually increase my chances of winning the race; but my *believing* that God exists doesn't increase the probability that God does exist because God either exists, or does not exist, independently of my beliefs. How would James or one of his followers respond to this objection?

3. Can we obtain beliefs simply by *willing* to have them, or is this an exercise in futility? Explain your answer.

II.18   A Debate on the Rationality of Religious Belief

ANTONY FLEW, R. M. HARE, AND BASIL MITCHELL

Antony Flew was for many years professor of philosophy at the University of Reading in England. R. M. Hare and Basil Mitchell were professors of philosophy at Oxford University. All three were educated at Oxford University, where they all began their teaching careers. In this 1948 Oxford University symposium, Flew challenges theists to state the conditions under which they would give up their faith, for, he contends, unless one can state what would falsify one's belief, one does not have a meaningful belief. If nothing could count against the belief, it does not make a serious assertion, for serious truth claims must be ready to undergo rational scrutiny. Hare responds by arguing that this is the wrong way to describe faith, for religious faith consists of a set of profoundly unfalsifiable assumptions, which he calls "bliks," which govern all of a person's other beliefs. There are insane and sane bliks, but we cannot escape having them. Even the scientist has such fundamental assumptions. Hence religion should not be subject to the kind of rational scrutiny Flew urges. Mitchell opts for a compromise position. Rational considerations enter into the debate on faith, but no one can say exactly when a gradual accumulation of evidence is sufficient to overthrow religious belief. Although rational considerations count against faith, the believer will not let them count decisively against it.

Study Questions

1. What is the significance of the parable of the garden? How does Flew interpret it? Do you agree with him?
2. What does Flew mean by his statement that a brash hypothesis can be "killed by inches, the death by a thousand qualifications"?
3. What is Hare's strategy in telling the story of the paranoid student who believes that all dons (teachers) intend to harm him?
4. What is a "blik"? Describe it.
5. How does Hare disagree with Flew?
6. What is the one thing that Mitchell allows to count against his faith in God? How much should it count against one's faith?
7. How does Mitchell illustrate his thesis? How does his story throw light on the relationship of faith to reason?

ANTONY FLEW

LET US BEGIN WITH A PARABLE. It is a parable developed from a tale told by John Wisdom in his haunting and revelatory article "Gods."[1] Once upon a time two explorers came upon a clearing in the jungle. In the clearing were growing many flowers and many weeds. One explorer says, "Some gardener must tend this plot." The other disagrees, "There is no gardener." So they pitch their tents and set a watch. No gardener is ever seen. "But perhaps he is an invisible gardener." So they set up a barbed-wire fence. They electrify it. They patrol with bloodhounds. (For they remember how H. G. Wells's *The Invisible Man* could be both smelt and touched though he could not be seen.) But no shrieks ever suggest that some intruder has received a shock. No movements of the wire ever betray an invisible climber. The bloodhounds never give cry. Yet still the Believer is not convinced. "But there is a gardener, invisible, intangible, insensible to electric shocks, a gardener who has no scent and makes no sound, a gardener who comes secretly to look after the garden which he loves." At last the Sceptic despairs. "But what remains of your original assertion? Just how does what you call an invisible, intangible, eternally elusive gardener differ from an imaginary gardener or even from no gardener at all?"

In this parable we can see how what starts as an assertion, that something exists or that there is some analogy between certain complexes of phenomena, may be reduced step by step to an altogether different status, to an expression perhaps of a "picture preference." The Sceptic says there is no gardener. The Believer says there is a gardener (but invisible, etc.). One man talks about sexual behaviour. Another man prefers to talk of Aphrodite (but knows that there is not really a superhuman person additional to, and somehow responsible for, all sexual phenomena). The process of qualification may be checked at any point before the original assertion is completely withdrawn and something of that first assertion will remain (Tautology). Mr. Wells's invisible man could not, admittedly, be seen, but in all other respects he was a man like the rest of us. But though the process of qualification may be, and of course usually is, checked in time, it is not always judiciously so halted. Someone may dissipate his assertion completely without noticing that he has done so. A fine brash hypothesis may thus be killed by inches, the death by a thousand qualifications.

And in this, it seems to me, lies the peculiar danger, the endemic evil, of theological utterance. Take such utterances as "God has a plan," "God created the world," "God loves us as a father loves his children." They look at first sight very much like assertions, vast cosmological assertions. Of course, this is no sure sign that they either are, or are intended to be, assertions. But let us confine ourselves to the cases where those who utter such sentences intend them to express assertions. (Merely remarking parenthetically that those who intend or interpret such utterances as crypto-commands, expressions of wishes, disguised ejaculations, concealed ethics, or as anything else but assertions, are unlikely to succeed in making them either properly orthodox or practically effective.)

Now to assert that such and such is the case is necessarily equivalent to denying that such and such is not the case. Suppose then that we are in doubt as to what someone who gives vent to an utterance is asserting, or suppose that, more radically, we are sceptical as to whether he is really asserting anything at all, one way of trying to understand (or perhaps it will be to expose) his utterance is to attempt to find what he would regard as counting against, or as being incompatible with, its truth. For if the utterance is indeed an assertion, it will necessarily be equivalent to a denial of the negation of that assertion. And anything which would count against the assertion, or which would induce the speaker to withdraw it and to admit that it had been mistaken, must be part of (or the whole of) the meaning of the negation of that assertion. And to know the meaning of the negation of an assertion, is as near as makes no matter, to know the meaning of that assertion. And if there is nothing which a putative assertion denies then there is nothing which it asserts either: and so it is not really an assertion. When the Sceptic in the parable asked the Believer, "Just how does what you call an invisible, intangible, eternally elusive gardener differ from an imaginary gardener or even from no gardener at all?" he was suggesting that the Believer's earlier statement had been eroded by qualification so that it was no longer an assertion at all.

Now it often seems to people who are not religious as if there was no conceivable event or series of events the occurrence of which would be admitted by sophisticated religious people to be a sufficient reason for conceding "There wasn't a God after all" or "God does not really love us then." Someone tells us that God loves us as a father loves his children. We are reassured. But then we see a child dying of inoperable cancer of the throat. His earthly father is driven frantic in his efforts to help, but his Heavenly Father reveals no obvious sign of concern. Some qualification is made—God's love is "not a merely human love" or it is "an inscrutable love," perhaps—and we realize that such sufferings are quite compatible with the truth of the assertion that "God loves us as a father (but, of course, . . .)." We are reassured again. But then perhaps we ask: What is this assurance of God's (appropriately qualified) love worth, what is this apparent guarantee really a guarantee against? Just what would have to happen not merely (morally and wrongly) to tempt but also (logically and rightly) to entitle us to say "God does not love us" or even "God does not exist"? I therefore put to the succeeding symposiasts the simple central questions, "What would have to occur or to have occurred to constitute for you a disproof of the love of, or of the existence of, God?"

R. M. HARE

I WISH TO MAKE IT CLEAR that I shall not try to defend Christianity in particular, but religion in general—not because I do not believe in Christianity, but because you cannot understand what Christianity is, until you have understood what religion is.

I must begin by confessing that, on the ground marked out by Flew, he seems to me to be completely victorious. I therefore shift my ground by relating another parable. A certain lunatic is convinced that all dons want to murder him. His friends introduce him to all the mildest and most respectable dons that they can find, and after each of them has retired, they say, "You see, he doesn't really want to murder you; he spoke to you in a most cordial manner; surely you are convinced now?" But the lunatic replies "Yes, but that was only his diabolical cunning; he's really plotting against me the whole time, like the rest of them; I know it, I tell you." However many kindly dons are produced, the reaction is still the same.

Now we say that such a person is deluded. But what is he deluded about? About the truth or falsity of an assertion? Let us apply Flew's test to him. There is no behaviour of dons that can be enacted which he will accept as counting against his theory, and therefore his theory, on this test, asserts nothing. But it does not follow that there is no difference between what he thinks about dons and what most of us think about them— otherwise we should not call him a lunatic and ourselves sane, and dons would have no reason to feel uneasy about his presence in Oxford.

Let us call that in which we differ from this lunatic, our respective *bliks*. He has an insane *blik* about dons; we have a sane one. It is important to realize that we have a sane one, not no *blik* at all; for there must be two sides to any argument—if he has a wrong *blik*, then those who are right about dons must have a right one. Flew has shown that a *blik* does not consist in an assertion or system of them, but nevertheless it is very important to have the right *blik*.

Let us try to imagine what it would be like to have different *bliks* about other things than dons. When I am driving my car, it sometimes occurs to me to wonder whether my movements of the steering-wheel will always continue to be followed by corresponding alterations in the direction of the car. I have never had a steering failure, though I have had skids, which must be similar. Moreover, I know enough about how the steering of my car is made, to know the sort of thing that would have to go wrong for the steering to fail—steel joints would have to part, or steel rods break, or something—but how do I know that this won't happen? The truth is, I don't know; I just have a *blik* about steel and its properties, so that normally I trust the steering of my car; but I find it not at all difficult to imagine what it would be like to lose this *blik* and acquire the opposite one. People would say I was silly about steel, but there would be no mistaking the reality of the difference between our respective *bliks*—for example, I should never go in a motor-car. Yet I should hesitate to say that the difference between us was the difference between contradictory assertions. No amount of safe arrivals or bench-tests will remove my *blik* and restore the normal one: for my *blik* is compatible with any finite number of such tests.

It was Hume who taught us that our whole commerce with the world depends upon our *blik* about the world, and that differences between *bliks* about the world cannot be settled by observation of what happens in the world. That was why, having performed the interesting experiment of doubting the ordinary man's *blik* about the world, and showing that no proof could be given to make us adopt one *blik* rather than another, he turned to backgammon to take his mind off the problem. It seems, indeed, to be impossible even to formulate as an assertion the normal *blik* about the world which makes me put my confidence in the future reliability of steel joints, in the continued ability of the road to support my car, and not gape beneath it revealing nothing below; in the general non-homicidal tendencies of dons; in my own continued well-being (in some sense of that word that I may not now fully understand) if I continued to do what is right according to my lights; in the general likelihood of people like Hitler coming to a bad end. But perhaps a formulation less inadequate than most is to be found in the Psalms: "The earth is weak and all the inhabiters thereof: I bear up the pillars of it."

The mistake of the position which Flew selects for attack is to regard this kind of talk as some sort of *explanation*, as scientists are accustomed to use the word. As such, it would obviously be ludicrous. We no longer believe in God as an Atlas—*nous n'avons pas besoin de cette hypothèse*. But it is nevertheless true to say that, as Hume saw, without a *blik* there can be no explanation; for it is by our *bliks* that we decide what is and what is not an explanation. Suppose we believed that everything that happened, happened by pure chance. This would not of course be an assertion; for it is compatible with anything happening or not happening, and so, incidentally, is its contradictory. But if we had this belief, we should not be able to explain or predict or plan anything. Thus, although we should not be *asserting* anything different from those of a more normal belief, there

would be a great difference between us; and this is the sort of difference that there is between those who really believe in God and those who really disbelieve in him.

The word "really" is important, and may excite suspicion. I put it in, because when people have had a good Christian upbringing, as have most of those who now profess not to believe in any sort of religion, it is very hard to discover what they really believe. The reason why they find it so easy to think that they are not religious, is that they have never got into the frame of mind of one who suffers from the doubts to which religion is the answer. Not for them the terrors of the primitive jungle. Having abandoned some of the more picturesque fringes of religion, they think that they have abandoned the whole thing—whereas in fact they still have got, and could not live without, a religion of a comfortably substantial, albeit highly sophisticated, kind, which differs from that of many "religious people" in little more than this, that "religious people" like to sing Psalms about theirs—a very natural and proper thing to do. But nevertheless there may be a big difference lying behind—the difference between two people who, though side by side, are walking in different directions. I do not know in what direction Flew is walking; perhaps he does not know either. But we have had some examples recently of various ways in which one can walk away from Christianity, and there are any number of possibilities. After all, man has not changed biologically since primitive times; it is his religion that has changed, and it can easily change again. And if you do not think that such changes make a difference, get acquainted with some Sikhs and some Mussulmans of the same Punjabi stock; you will find them quite different sorts of people.

There is an important difference between Flew's parable and my own which we have not yet noticed. The explorers do not *mind* about their garden; they discuss it with interest, but not with concern. But my lunatic, poor fellow, minds about dons, and I mind about the steering of my car; it often has people in it that I care for. It is because I mind very much about what goes on in the garden in which I find myself, that I am unable to share the explorers' detachment.

BASIL MITCHELL

FLEW'S ARTICLE IS SEARCHING and perceptive, but there is, I think, something odd about his conduct of the theologian's case. The theologian surely would not deny that the fact of pain counts against the assertion that God loves men. This very incompatibility generates the most intractable of theological problems—the problem of evil. So the theologian *does* recognize the fact of pain as counting against Christian doctrine. But it is true that he will not allow it—or anything—to count decisively against it; for he is committed by his faith to trust in God. His attitude is not that of the detached observer, but of the believer.

Perhaps this can be brought out by yet another parable. In time of war in an occupied country, a member of the resistance meets one night a stranger who deeply impresses him. They spend that night together in conversation. The Stranger tells the partisan that he himself is on the side of the resistance—indeed that he is in command of it, and urges the partisan to have faith in him no matter what happens. The partisan is utterly convinced at that meeting of the Stranger's sincerity and constancy and undertakes to trust him.

They never meet in conditions of intimacy again. But sometimes the Stranger is seen helping members of the resistance, and the partisan is grateful and says to his friends, "He is on our side."

Sometimes he is seen in the uniform of the police handing over patriots to the occupying power. On these occasions his friends murmur against him, but the partisan still says, "He is on our side." He still believes that, in spite of appearances, the Stranger did not deceive him. Sometimes he asks the Stranger for help and receives it. He is then thankful. Sometimes he asks and does not receive it. Then he says, "The Stranger knows best." Sometimes his friends, in exasperation, say

"Well, what *would* he have to do for you to admit that you were wrong and that he is not on our side?" But the partisan refuses to answer. He will not consent to put the Stranger to the test. And sometimes his friends complain, "Well, if *that's* what you mean by his being on our side, the sooner he goes over to the other side the better."

The partisan of the parable does not allow anything to count decisively against the proposition "The Stranger is on our side." This is because he has committed himself to trust the Stranger. But he of course recognizes that the Stranger's ambiguous behaviour *does* count against what he believes about him. It is precisely this situation which constitutes the trial of his faith.

When the partisan asks for help and doesn't get it, what can he do? He can (*a*) conclude that the stranger is not on our side, or (*b*) maintain that he is on our side, but that he has reasons for withholding help.

The first he will refuse to do. How long can he uphold the second position without its becoming just silly?

I don't think one can say in advance. It will depend on the nature of the impression created by the Stranger in the first place. It will depend, too, on the manner in which he takes the Stranger's behaviour. If he blandly dismisses it as of no consequence, as having no bearing upon his belief, it will be assumed that he is thoughtless or insane. And it quite obviously won't do for him to say easily, "Oh, when used of the Stranger the phrase 'is on our side' *means* ambiguous behavior of this sort." In that case he would be like the religious man who says blandly of a terrible disaster "It is God's will." No, he will only be regarded as sane and reasonable in his belief, if he experiences in himself the full force of the conflict.

It is here that my parable differs from Hare's. The partisan admits that many things may and do count against his belief: whereas Hare's lunatic who has a *blik* about dons doesn't admit that anything counts against his *blik*. Nothing *can* count against *bliks*. Also the partisan has a reason for having in the first instance committed himself, viz. the character of the Stranger; whereas the lunatic has no reason for his *blik* about dons—because, of course, you can't have reasons for *bliks*.

This means that I agree with Flew that theological utterances must be assertions. The partisan is making an assertion when he says, "The Stranger is on our side."

Do I want to say that the partisan's belief about the Stranger is, in any sense, an explanation? I think I do. It explains and makes sense of the Stranger's behaviour: It helps to explain also the resistance movement in the context of which he appears. In each case it differs from the interpretation which the others put upon the same facts.

"God loves men" resembles "the Stranger is on our side" (and many other significant statements, e.g., historical ones) in not being conclusively falsifiable. They can both be treated in at least three different ways: (1) As provisional hypotheses to be discarded if experience tells against them; (2) As significant articles of faith; (3) As vacuous formulae (expressing, perhaps, a desire for reassurance) to which experience makes no difference and which make no difference to life.

The Christian, once he has committed himself, is precluded by his faith from taking up the first attitude: "Thou shalt not tempt the Lord thy God." He is in constant danger, as Flew has observed, of slipping into the third. But he need not, and, if he does, it is a failure in faith as well as in logic.

NOTE

1. *P.A.S.*, 1944–1945, reprinted as Chapter X of *Logic and Language*, Vol. I (Blackwell, 1951), and in his *Philosophy and Psychoanalysis* (Blackwell, 1953).

For Further Reflection

1. Analyze the different strategies in our three philosophers' statements. Who has made the best case?

2. Should the believer follow Flew's advice and give an account of what would count against his or her faith? Should one's faith be open to revision or rejection on the basis of arguments?

3. Does the believer need to be able to cite evidence before he or she can affirm that it is rational to believe in God?

II.19   Religious Belief Without Evidence

ALVIN PLANTINGA

Alvin Plantinga (1932–) is a professor of philosophy at the University of Notre Dame and has written widely in metaphysics and philosophy of religion, including *The Nature of Necessity* (1974) and *God, Freedom and Evil* (1974). In the following essay, he argues that it is rational to believe in God despite the lack of evidence for such belief. Those (like W. K. Clifford) who insist that we must have evidence for all our beliefs simply fail to make their case, because the evidentialists have not set forth clear criteria that would account for all the clear cases of justified beliefs and that would exclude the belief in God. Plantinga outlines the position of the foundationalist-evidentialist as claiming that all justified beliefs must either (1) be "properly basic" by fulfilling certain criteria, or (2) be based on other beliefs that eventually result in a treelike construction with properly basic beliefs at the bottom, or foundation. Plantinga shows that many beliefs we seem to be justified in holding do not fit into the foundationalist framework; such beliefs as memory beliefs (for example, that I ate breakfast this morning), belief in an external world, and belief in other minds. These beliefs do not depend on other beliefs, yet neither are they self-evident, incorrigible (impossible not to believe), or evident to the senses.

Having shown the looseness of what we can accept as "properly basic," Plantinga next shows that the Protestant reformers saw belief in God as "properly basic." He asks us to consider this belief as a legitimate option and examines possible objections to it.

Study Questions

1. What is the main objection many philosophers have raised against belief in God?
2. What does W. K. Clifford say about the correct or ethical way to believe?
3. How does Antony Flew think the debate between theism and atheism should begin? Where should the burden of proof lie? Does Plantinga agree with Flew?
4. What are the two premises of the evidentialist's objection to belief in God?
5. Do Reformed thinkers and theologians accept natural theology (the attempt to establish God's existence through human reason)? Why (or why not)?
6. How do Reformed theologians view belief in God?
7. What is the difference between *prima facie* obligations and *all-things-considered* obligations?
8. Plantinga links evidentialism with classical foundationalism. What is classical foundationalism?
9. What does Plantinga say is wrong with classical foundationalism?
10. What is the Great Pumpkin objection?

THE EVIDENTIALIST OBJECTION TO THEISTIC BELIEF

MANY PHILOSOPHERS—Clifford, Blanshard, Russell, Scriven, and Flew, to name a few—have argued that belief in God is irrational, or unreasonable, or not rationally acceptable, or intellectually irresponsible, or somehow noetically below par because, as they say, there is *insufficient evidence* for it.[1] Bertrand Russell was once asked what he would say if, after dying, he were brought into the presence of God and asked why he hadn't been a believer. Russell's reply: "I'd say, 'Not enough evidence, God! Not enough evidence!'"[2] I don't know just how such a response would be received, but Russell, like many others, held that theistic belief is unreasonable because there is insufficient evidence for it. We all remember W. K. Clifford, that delicious *enfant terrible*, as William James called him, and his insistence that it is immoral, wicked, and monstrous, and maybe even impolite to accept a belief for which you don't have sufficient evidence:

Who so would deserve well of his fellows in this matter will guard the purity of his belief with a very fanaticism of jealous care, lest at

Reprinted with permission from Religious Experience and Religious Belief: Essays in the Epistemology of Religion, *eds. Joseph Runzo and Craig Ihara (New York: University Press of America, 1986).*

any time it should rest on an unworthy object, and catch a stain which can never be wiped away.

He adds that if a

> belief has been accepted on insufficient evidence, the pleasure is a stolen one. Not only does it deceive ourselves by giving us a sense of power which we do not really possess, but it is sinful, because it is stolen in defiance of our duty to mankind. That duty is to guard ourselves from such beliefs as from a pestilence which may shortly master our body and spread to the rest of the town.

and finally:

> To sum up: it is wrong always, everywhere, and for anyone to believe anything upon insufficient evidence.

(It is not hard to detect, in these quotations, the "tone of robustious pathos" with which James credits him.) Clifford, of course, held that one who accepts belief in God *does* accept that belief on insufficient evidence, and has indeed defied his duty to mankind. More recently, Bertrand Russell has endorsed the evidentialist injunction "Give to any hypothesis which is worth your while to consider, just that degree or credence which the evidence warrants."

More recently, Antony Flew[3] has commended what he calls Clifford's "luminous and compulsive essay" (perhaps "compulsive" here is a misprint for "compelling"), and Flew goes on to claim that there is, in his words a "presumption of atheism." What is a presumption of atheism, and why should we think there is one? Flew puts it as follows:

> The debate about the existence of God should properly begin from the presumption of atheism . . . the onus of proof must lie upon the theist. The word "atheism," however, has in this contention to be construed unusually. Whereas nowadays the usual meaning of "atheist" in English is "someone who asserts there is no such being as God," I want the word to be understood not positively but negatively. I want the original Greek prefix "a" to be read in the same way in "atheist" as it is customarily read in

such other Greco-English words as "amoral," "atypical," and "asymmetrical." In this interpretation an atheist becomes not someone who positively asserts the non-existence of God, but someone who is simply not a theist.

What the protagonist of my presumption of atheism wants to show is that the debate about the existence of God ought to be conducted in a particular way, and that the issue should be seen in a certain perspective. His thesis about the onus of proof involves that it is up to the theist: first to introduce and to defend his proposed concept of God, and second, to provide sufficient reason for believing that this concept of his does in fact have an application.

How shall we understand this? What does it mean, for example, to say that the debate "should properly begin from the presumption of atheism"? What sorts of things do debates begin from, and what is it for one to begin from such a thing? Perhaps Flew means something like this: to speak of where a debate should begin is to speak of the sorts of premises to which the affirmative and negative sides can properly appeal in arguing their cases. Suppose you and I are debating the question whether, say, the United States has a right to seize Mideast oil fields if the OPEC countries refuse to sell us oil at what we think is a fair price. I take the affirmative, and produce for my conclusion an argument one premise of which is the proposition that the United States has indeed a right to seize these oil fields under those conditions. Doubtless that maneuver would earn me very few points. Similarly, a debate about the existence of God cannot sensibly start from the assumption that God does indeed exist. That is to say, the affirmative can't properly appeal, in its arguments, to such premises as that there is such a person as God; if it could, it'd have much too easy a time of it. So in this sense of "start," Flew is quite right: the debate can't start from the assumption that God exists.

Of course, it is also true that the debate can't start from the assumption that God does *not* exist; using "atheism" in its ordinary sense, there is equally a presumption of aatheism (which, by a familiar principle of logic, reduces to theism). So it looks as if there is in Flew's sense a presumption of atheism, all right, but in that same sense an equal presumption of aatheism. If this is what Flew means, then what he says is entirely correct, if something of a truism.

In another passage, however, Flew seems to understand the presumption of atheism in quite another different fashion:

> It is by reference to this inescapable demand for grounds that the presumption of atheism is justified. If it is to be established that there is a God, then we have to have good grounds for believing that this is indeed so. Until or unless some such grounds are produced we have literally no reason at all for believing; and in that situation the only reasonable posture must be that of either the negative atheist or the agnostic.

Here we have the much more substantial suggestion that it is unreasonable or irrational to accept theistic belief in the absence of sufficient grounds or reasons. And of course Flew, along with Russell, Clifford, and many others, holds that in fact there aren't sufficient grounds or evidence for belief in God. The evidentialist objection, therefore, appeals to the following two premises:

(A) It is irrational or unreasonable to accept theistic belief in the absence of sufficient evidence or reasons.

and

(B) There is no evidence, or at any rate not sufficient evidence, for the proposition that God exists.

(B), I think, is at best dubious. At present, however, I'm interested in the objector's other premise—the claim that it is irrational or unreasonable to accept theistic belief in the absence of evidence or reasons. Why suppose *that's* true? Why suppose a theist must have evidence or reason to think there *is* evidence for this belief, if he is not to be irrational? This isn't just *obvious*, after all.

Now many Reformed thinkers and theologians[4] have rejected *natural theology* (thought of as the attempt to provide proofs or arguments for the existence of God). They have held not merely that the proffered arguments are unsuccessful, but that the whole enterprise is in some way radically misguided. I have argued (1980) that the Reformed rejection of natural theology is best construed as an inchoate and unfocused rejection of (A). What these Reformed thinkers really mean to hold, I think, is that belief in God is properly basic: it need not be based on argument or evidence from other propositions at all. They mean to hold that the believer is entirely within his intellectual right in believing as he does, even if he doesn't know of any good theistic argument (deductive or inductive), even if he doesn't believe that there is any such argument, and even if in fact no such argument exists. They hold that it is perfectly rational to accept belief in God without accepting it on the basis of any other beliefs or propositions at all. Why suppose that the believer must have evidence if he is not to be irrational? Why should anyone accept (A)? What is to be said in its favor?

Suppose we begin by asking what the objector means by describing a belief as *irrational*. What is the force of his claim that the theistic belief is irrational and how is it to be understood? The first thing to see is that this claim is rooted in a *normative* contention. It lays down conditions that must be met by anyone whose system of beliefs is *rational;* and here "rational" is to be taken as a normative or evaluative term. According to the objector, there is a right way and a wrong way with respect to belief. People have responsibilities, duties and obligations with respect to their believings just as they do with respect to their actions—or if we think believings are a kind of action, their *other* actions. Professor Brand Blanshard puts this clearly:

> everywhere and always belief has an ethical aspect. There is such a thing as a general ethics of the intellect. The main principle of that ethic I hold to be the same inside and outside religion. This principle is simple and sweeping: Equate your assent to the evidence. (*Reason and Belief,* p. 401)

and according to Michael Scriven:

> Now even belief in something for which there is no evidence, i.e., a belief which goes beyond the evidence, although a lesser sin than a belief in something which is contrary to well-established laws, is plainly irrational in that it simply amounts to attaching belief where it is not justified. So the proper alternative, when there is no evidence, is not mere suspension of belief, e.g., about Santa Claus, it is disbelief. It most certainly is not faith. (*Primary Philosophy*, p. 103)

Perhaps this sort of obligation is really a special case of a more general moral obligation; or perhaps, on the other hand, it is *sui generis*. In any event, says the objector, there are such obligations: to conform to them is to be rational and to go against them is to be irrational.

Now here the objector seems right; there are duties and obligations with respect to beliefs. One's own welfare and that of others sometimes depends on what one believes. If we're descending the Grand Teton and I'm setting the anchor for the 120-foot rappel into the Upper Saddle, I have an obligation to form such beliefs as *this anchor point is solid* only on the basis of careful scrutiny and testing. One commissioned to gather intelligence—the spies Joshua sent into Canaan, for example—has an obligation to get it right. I have an obligation with respect to the belief that Justin Martyr was a Latin apologist—an obligation arising from the fact that I teach medieval philosophy, must make a declaration on this issue, and am obliged not to mislead my students here. The precise *form* of these obligations may be hard to specify: Am I obliged to believe that J. M. was a Latin apologist if and only if J. M. *was* a Latin apologist? Or to form a belief on this topic only after the appropriate amount of checking and investigating? Or maybe just to tell the students the truth about it, whatever I myself believe in the privacy of my own study? Or to tell them what's generally thought by those who should know? In the rappel case: Do I have a duty to believe that the anchor point is solid if and only if it is? Or just to check carefully before forming the belief? Or perhaps there's no obligation to believe at all, but only to *act on* a certain belief only after appropriate investigation. In any event, it seems plausible to hold that there are obligations and norms with respect to belief, and I do not intend to contest this assumption.

The objector begins, therefore, from the plausible contention that there are duties or obligations with respect to belief: call them *intellectual duties*. These duties can be understood in several ways. First, we could construe them teleologically; we could adopt an intellectual utilitarianism. Here the rough idea is that our intellectual obligations arise out of a connection between our beliefs and what is intrinsically good and intrinsically bad, and our intellectual obligations are just a special case of the general obligation so to act to maximize good and minimize evil. Perhaps this is how W. K. Clifford thinks of the matter. If people accepted such propositions as *this DC-10 is airworthy* when the evidence is insufficient, the consequences could be disastrous; so perhaps some of us, at any rate, have an obligation to believe that proposition only in the presence of adequate evidence. The intellectual utilitarian could be an ideal utilitarian; he could hold that certain epistemic states are intrinsically valuable—knowledge, perhaps, or believing the truth, or a skeptical and judicial temper that is not blown about by every wind of doctrine. Among our duties, then, is a duty to try to bring about these valuable states of affairs. Perhaps this is how Professor Roderick Chisholm is to be understood when he says

> Let us consider the concept of what might be called an "intellectual requirement." We may assume that every person is subject to a purely intellectual requirement: that of trying his best to bring it about that, for every proposition that he considers, he accepts it if and only if it is true. (*Theory of Knowledge*, 2nd ed., p. 9)

Secondly, we could construe intellectual obligations *aretetically*; we could adopt what Professor Frankena calls a "mixed ethics of virtue" with respect to the intellect. There are valuable noetic or intellectual states (whether intrinsically or extrinsically valuable); there are also the corresponding intellectual virtues, the habits of acting so as to produce or promote or enhance those valuable states. One's intellectual obligations, then, are to try to produce and enhance these intellectual virtues in oneself and others.

Thirdly, we could construe intellectual obligations *deontologically*; we could adopt a *pure* ethics of obligation with respect to the intellect. Perhaps there are intellectual obligations that do not arise from any connection with good or evil, but attach to us just by virtue of our having the sorts of noetic powers human beings do in fact display. The quotation from Chisholm could also be understood along these lines.

Intellectual obligations, therefore, can be understood teleologically or aretetically or deontologically. And perhaps there are purely intellectual obligations of the following sorts. Perhaps I have a duty not to take as basic a proposition whose denial seems self-evident. Perhaps I have a duty to take as basic the proposition *I seem to see a tree* under certain conditions. With respect to certain kinds of propositions, perhaps I have a duty to believe them only if I have evidence for them, and a duty to proportion the strength of my belief to the strength of my evidence.

Of course, these would be *prima facie* obligations. One presumably has an obligation not to take bread from the grocery store without permission and another to tell the truth. Both can be overridden, in specific circumstances, by other obligations—in the first case, perhaps, an obligation to feed my starving children and in the second, an obligation to protect a human life. So we must distinguish *prima facie* duties or obligations from *all-things-considered* or *on-balance (ultima facie?)* obligations. I have a *prima facie* obligation to tell the truth; in a given situation, however, that obligation may be overridden by others, so that my duty, all things considered, is to tell a lie. This is the grain of truth contained in situation ethics and the ill-named "new morality."

And *prima facie* intellectual obligations can conflict, just as obligations of other sorts. Perhaps I have a *prima facie* obligation to believe what

seems to me self-evident, and what seems to me to follow self-evidently from what seems to me self-evident. But what if, as in the Russell paradoxes, something that seems self-evidently false apparently follows, self-evidently, from what seems self-evidently true? Here *prima facie* intellectual obligations conflict, and no matter what I do I will violate a *prima facie* obligation. Another example: in reporting the Grand Teton rappel, I neglected to mention the violent electrical storm coming in from the southwest; to escape it we must get off in a hurry, so that I have a *prima facie* obligation to inspect the anchor point carefully, but anchor to set up the rappel rapidly, which means I can't spend a lot of time inspecting the anchor point.

Thus lightly armed, suppose we return to the evidential objector. Does he mean to hold that the theist without evidence is violating some intellectual obligation? If so, which one? Does he claim, for example, that the theist is violating his *ultima facie* intellectual obligation in thus believing? Perhaps he thinks anyone who believes in God without evidence is violating his all-things-considered intellectual duty. This, however, seems unduly harsh. What about the fourteen-year-old theist brought up to believe in God in a community where everyone believes? This fourteen-year-old theist, we may suppose, doesn't believe on the basis of evidence. He doesn't argue thus: everyone around here says God loves us and cares for us; most of what everyone around here says is true; so probably *that's* true. Instead, he simply believes what he's taught. Is he violating an all-things-considered intellectual duty? Surely not. And what about the mature theist—Thomas Aquinas, let's say—who thinks he *does* have adequate evidence? Let's suppose he's wrong; let's suppose all of his arguments are failures. Nevertheless, he has reflected long, hard, and conscientiously on the matter and thinks he *does* have adequate evidence. Shall we suppose he's violating an all-things-considered intellectual duty here? I should think not. So construed, the objector's contention is totally implausible.

Perhaps, then, he is to be understood as claiming that there is a *prima facie* intellectual duty not to believe in God without evidence. This duty can be overridden by circumstances, of course, but there is a *prima facie* obligation to believe propositions of this sort only on the basis of evidence. But here too there are problems. The suggestion is that I now have the *prima facie* obligation to believe propositions of this sort only on the basis of evidence. I have a *prima facie* duty to comply with the following command: either have evidence or don't believe. But this may be a command I can't comply with. The objector thinks there *isn't* adequate evidence for this belief, so presumably I can't *have* adequate evidence for it, unless we suppose I could create some. And it is also not within my power to refrain from believing this proposition. My beliefs aren't for the most part directly within my control. If you order me now, for example, to cease believing that the earth is very old, there's no way I can comply with your order. But in the same way it isn't within my power to cease believing in God now. So this alleged *prima facie* duty is one it isn't within my power to comply with. But how can I have a *prima facie* duty to do what isn't within my power to do?

Presumably, then, the objector means to be understood in still another fashion. Although it is not within my power now to cease believing now, there may be a series of actions now, such that I can now take the first, and after taking the first, will be able to take the second, and so on, and after taking the whole series of actions, I will no longer believe in God. Perhaps the objector thinks it is my *prima facie* duty to undertake whatever sort of regimen will at some time in the future result in my not believing without evidence. Perhaps I should attend a Universalist Unitarian Church, for example, and consort with members of the Rationalist Society of America. Perhaps I should read a lot of Voltaire and Bertrand Russell. Even if I can't now stop believing without evidence, perhaps there are other actions I can now take, such that if I do take them, then at some time in the future I won't be in this deplorable condition.

There is still another option available to the objector. He need not hold that the theist without evidence is violating some duty, *prima facie, ultima facie* or otherwise. Consider someone who believes that Venus is smaller than Mercury, not because he has evidence, but because he finds it amusing to believe what everyone disbelieves—or consider someone who holds this belief on the basis of an outrageously bad argument. Perhaps there is no obligation he has failed to meet; nevertheless his intellectual condition is defective in some way; or perhaps alternatively there is a commonly achieved excellence he fails to display. Perhaps he is like someone who is easily gulled, or walks with a limp, or has a serious astigmatism, or is unduly clumsy. And perhaps the evidentialist objection is to be understood, not as the claim that the theist without evidence has failed to meet some obligation, but that he suffers from a certain sort of intellectual deficiency. If this is the objector's view, then his proper attitude towards the theist would be one of sympathy rather than censure.

These are some of the ways, then, in which the evidentialist objection could be developed, and of course there are still other possibilities. For ease of exposition, let us take the claim deontologically; what I shall say will apply *mutatis mutandis* if we take it one of the other ways. The evidentialist objector, then, holds that it is irrational to believe in God without evidence. He doesn't typically hold, however, that the same goes for *every* proposition; for given certain plausible conditions on the evidence relation it would follow that if we believe anything, then we are under obligation to believe infinitely many propositions. Let's say that proposition *p* is *basic* for a person *S* if *S* believes *p* but does not have evidence for *p*; and let's say that *p* is *properly basic* for *S* if *S* is within his epistemic rights in taking *p* as basic. The evidentialist objection, therefore, presupposes some view about what sorts of propositions are correctly or rightly or justifiably taken as basic; it presupposes a view about what is properly basic. And the minimally relevant claim for the evidentialist objector is that belief in God is *not* properly basic. Typically this objection has been rooted in some form of *classical foundationalism,* an enormously popular picture or total way of looking at faith, knowledge, justified belief, rationality and allied topics. This picture has been widely accepted ever since the days of Plato and Aristotle; its near relatives, perhaps, remain the dominant ways of thinking about these topics. According to the classical foundationalist, some propositions are *properly* or *rightly* basic for a person and some are not. Those that are not are rationally accepted only on the basis of *evidence* where the evidence must trace back, ultimately, to what is properly basic. Now there are two varieties of classical foundationalism. According to the ancient and medieval variety, a proposition is properly basic for a person *S* if and only if it is either self-evident to *S* or "evident to the senses," to use Aquinas' term, for *S*; according to the modern variety, a proposition is properly basic for *S* if and only if it is either self- evident to *S* or incorrigible for him. For ease of exposition, let's say that classical foundationalism is the disjunction of ancient and medieval with modern foundationalism; according to the classical foundationalist, then, a proposition is properly basic for a person *S* if and only if it is either self-evident to *S* or incorrigible for *S* or evident to the senses for *S*.

Now I said that the evidentialist objection to theistic belief is typically rooted in classical foundationalism. Insofar as it is so rooted, it is *poorly* rooted. For classical foundationalism is self-referentially incoherent. Consider the main tenet of classical foundationalism:

(C)   *p* is properly basic for *S* if and only if *p* is self-evident, incorrigible, or evident to the senses for *S*.

Now of course the classical foundationalist accepts (C) and proposes that we do so as well. And either he takes (C) as basic or he doesn't. If he doesn't, then if he is rational in accepting it, he must by his own claims have an argument for it from propositions that are properly basic, by argument forms whose corresponding conditionals are properly basic. Classical foundationalists do not, so far as I know, offer such arguments for (C). I suspect the reason is that they don't know of any arguments of that sort for (C). It is certainly hard to see what such an argument would be. Accordingly, classical foundationalists probably take (C) as basic. But then according to (C) itself, if (C) is properly taken as basic, it must be either self-evident, incorrigible, or evident to the senses for the foundationalist, and clearly it isn't any of those. If the foundationalist takes (C) as basic, therefore, he is self-referentially inconsistent. We must conclude, I think, that the classical foundationalist is in self-referential hot water—his own acceptance of the central tenet of his view is irrational by his own standards.

OBJECTIONS TO TAKING BELIEF IN GOD AS BASIC

Insofar as the evidentialist objection is rooted in classical foundationalism, it is poorly rooted indeed; and so far as I know, no one has developed and articulated any other reason for supporting that belief in God is not properly basic. Of course it doesn't follow that it *is* properly basic; perhaps the class of properly basic propositions is broader than classical foundationalists think, but still not broad enough to admit belief in God. But why think so? What might be the objections to the Reformed view that belief in God is properly basic?

I've heard it argued that if I have no evidence for the existence of God, then if I accept that proposition, my belief will be *groundless,* or *gratuitous,* or *arbitrary.* I think this is an error; let me explain.

Suppose we consider perceptual beliefs, memory beliefs, and beliefs ascribing mental states to other persons; such beliefs as

(1)   I see a tree.

(2)   I had breakfast this morning.

(3)   That person is angry.

Although beliefs of this sort are typically and properly taken as basic, it would be a mistake to describe them as *groundless*. Upon having experience of a certain sort, I believe that I am perceiving a tree. In the typical case I do not hold this belief on the basis of other beliefs; it is nonetheless not groundless. My having that characteristic sort of experience—to use Professor Chisholm's language, my being appeared treely to—plays a crucial role in the formation and justification of that belief. We might say this experience, together, perhaps, with other circumstances, is what *justifies* me in holding it; this is the *ground* of my justification, and, by extension, the ground of the belief itself.

If I see someone displaying typical pain behavior, I take it that he or she is in pain. Again, I don't take the displayed behavior as *evidence* for that belief; I don't infer that belief from others I hold; I don't accept it on the basis of other beliefs. Still, my perceiving the pain behavior plays a unique role in the formation and justification of that belief; as in the previous case, it forms the ground of my justification for the belief in question. The same holds for memory beliefs. I seem to remember having breakfast this morning; that is, I have an inclination to believe the proposition that I had breakfast, along with a certain past-tinged experience that is familiar to all but hard to describe. Perhaps we should say that I am appeared to pastly, but perhaps that insufficiently distinguishes the experience in question from that accompanying beliefs about the past not grounded in my own memory. The phenomenology of memory is a rich and unexplored realm; here I have no time to explore it. In this case as in the others, however, there is a justifying circumstance present, a condition that forms the ground of my justification for accepting the memory belief in question.

In each of these cases, a belief is taken as basic, and in each case properly taken as basic. In each case there is some circumstance or condition that confers justification; there is a circumstance that serves as the *ground* of justification.

So in each case there will be some true proposition of the sort:

(4) In condition *C, S* is justified in taking *p* as basic. Of course *C* will vary with *p*.

For a perceptual judgment such as

(5) I see a rose-colored wall before me,

C will include my being appeared to in a certain fashion. No doubt *C* will include more. If I'm appeared to in the familiar fashion but know that I am wearing rose-colored glasses, or that I am suffering from a disease that causes me to be thus appeared to, no matter what the color of the nearby objects, then I am not justified in taking (5) as basic. Similarly for memory. Suppose I know that my memory is unreliable; it often plays me tricks. In particular, when I seem to remember having breakfast, then, more often than not, I *haven't* had breakfast. Under these conditions I am not justified in taking it as basic that I had breakfast, even though I seem to remember that I did.

So being appropriately appeared to, in the perceptual case, is not sufficient for justification; some further condition—a condition hard to state in detail—is clearly necessary. The central point, here, however, is that a belief is properly basic only in certain conditions; these conditions are, we might say, the ground of its justification and, by extension, the ground of the belief itself. In this sense, basic beliefs are not, or are not necessarily, *groundless* beliefs.

Now similar things may be said about belief in God. When the Reformers claim that this belief is properly basic, they do not mean to say, of course, that there are no justifying circumstances for it, or that it is in that sense groundless or gratuitous. Quite the contrary. Calvin holds that God "reveals and daily discloses himself in the whole workmanship of the universe," and the divine art "reveals itself in the innumerable and yet distinct and well-ordered variety of the heavenly host." God has so created us that we have a tendency or disposition to see his hand in the world about us. More precisely, there is in us a disposition to believe propositions of the sort *this flower was created by God* or *this vast and intricate universe was created by God* when we contemplate the flower or behold the starry heavens or think about the vast reaches of the universe.

Calvin recognizes, at least implicitly, that other sorts of conditions may trigger this disposition. Upon reading the Bible, one may be impressed with a deep sense that God is speaking to one. Upon having done what I know is cheap, or wrong, or wicked, I may feel guilty in God's sight and form the belief *God disapproves of what I've done*. Upon confession and repentance, I may feel forgiven, forming the belief *God forgives me for what I've done*. A person in grave danger may turn to God, asking for His protection and help, and of course he or she then forms the belief that God is indeed able to hear and help if He sees fit. When life is sweet and satisfying, a spontaneous sense of gratitude may well up within the soul; someone in this condition may thank and praise the Lord for His goodness, and will of course form the accompanying belief that indeed the Lord is to be thanked and praised.

There are therefore many conditions and circumstances that call forth belief in God: guilt, gratitude, danger, a sense of God's presence, a sense that He speaks, perception of various parts of the universe. A complete job would explore the phenomenology of all these conditions and of more besides. This is a large and important topic, but here I can only point to the existence of these conditions.

Of course, none of the beliefs I mentioned a moment ago is the simple belief that God exists. What we have instead are such beliefs as

(6) God is speaking to me.

(7) God has created all this.

(8) God disapproves of what I have done.

(9) God forgives me.

(10) God is to be thanked and praised.

These propositions are properly basic in the right circumstances. But it is quite consistent with this to suppose that the proposition *there is such a person as God* is neither properly basic nor taken as basic by those who believe in God. Perhaps what they take as basic are such propositions as (6)–(10), believing in the existence of God on the basis of such propositions. From this point of view, it isn't exactly right to say that belief in God is properly basic; more exactly, what are properly basic are such propositions (6)–(10), each of which self-evidently entails that God exists. It isn't the relatively high level and general proposition *God exists* that is properly basic, but instead propositions detailing some of His attributes or actions.

Suppose we return to the analogy between belief in God and belief in the existence of perceptual objects, other persons, and the past. Here too it is relatively specific and concrete propositions rather than their more general and abstract colleagues that are properly basic. Perhaps such items as

(11) There are trees.

(12) There are other persons.

(13) The world has existed for more than 5 minutes

are not properly basic; it is instead such propositions as

(14) I see a tree.

(15) That person is pleased.

(16) I had breakfast more than an hour ago

that deserve the accolade. Of course, propositions of the latter sort immediately and self-evidently entail propositions of the former sort, and perhaps there is thus no harm in speaking of the former as properly basic, even though so to speak is to speak a bit loosely.

The same must be said about belief in God. We may say, speaking loosely, that belief in God is properly basic; strictly speaking, however, it is probably not that proposition but such propositions as (6)–(10) that enjoy that status. But the main point, here, is this: belief in God or (6)–(10) are properly basic; to say so, however, is not to deny that there are justifying conditions for these beliefs, or conditions that confer justification on one who accepts them as basic. They are therefore not groundless or gratuitous.

A second objection I've often heard: If belief in God is properly basic, why can't *just any* belief be properly basic? What about voodoo or astrology? What about the belief that the Great Pumpkin returns every Halloween? Could I properly take *that* as basic? And if I can't, why can I properly take belief in God as basic? Suppose I believe that if I flap my arms with sufficient vigor, I can take off and fly about the room; could I defend myself against the charge of irrationality by claiming this belief is basic? If we say that belief in God is properly basic, won't we be committed to holding that just anything, or nearly anything, can properly be taken as basic, thus throwing wide the gates to irrationalism and superstition?

Certainly not. What might lead one to think the Reformed epistemologist is in this kind of trouble? The fact that he rejects the criteria for proper basicality purveyed by classical foundationalism? But why should *that* be thought to commit him to such tolerance or irrationality? Consider an analogy. In the palmy days of positivism, the positivists went about confidently wielding their verifiability criterion and declaring meaningless much that was obviously meaningful. Now suppose someone rejected a formulation of that criterion—the one to be found in the second edition of A. J. Ayer's *Language, Truth and Logic,* for example. Would that mean she was committed to holding that

(17) 'Twas brillig; and the slithy toves did gyre and gimble in the wabe

contrary to appearances, makes good sense? Of course not. But then the same goes for the Reformed epistemologist; the fact that he rejects the Classical Foundationalist's criterion of proper basicality does not mean that he is committed to supposing just anything is properly basic.

But what then is the problem? Is it that the Reformed epistemologist not only rejects those criteria for proper basicality, but seems in no hurry to produce what he takes to be a better

substitute? If he has no such criterion, how can he fairly reject belief in the Great Pumpkin as properly basic?

This objection betrays an important misconception. How do we rightly arrive at or develop criteria for meaningfulness, or justified belief, or proper basicality? Where do they come from? Must one have such a criterion before one can sensibly make any judgments—positive or negative—about proper basicality? Surely not. Suppose I don't know of a satisfactory substitute for the criteria proposed by Classical Foundationalism; I am nevertheless entirely within my rights in holding that certain propositions are not properly basic in certain conditions. Some propositions seem self-evident when in fact they are not; that is the lesson of some of the Russell paradoxes. Nevertheless it would be irrational to take as basic the denial of a proposition that seems self-evident to you. Similarly, suppose it seems to you that you see a tree; you would then be irrational in taking as basic the proposition that you don't see a tree, or that there aren't any trees. In the same way, even if I don't know of some illuminating criterion of meaning, I can quite properly declare (17) meaningless.

And this raises an important question—one Roderick Chisholm has taught us to ask. What is the status of the criteria for knowledge, or proper basicality, or justified belief? Typically, these are universal statements. The modern foundationalist's criterion for proper basicality, for example, is doubly universal:

(18) For any proposition *A* and person *S, A* is properly basic for *S* if and only if *A* is incorrigible for *S* or self-evident to *S.*

But how could one know a thing like that? What are its credentials? Clearly enough, (18) isn't self-evident or just obviously true. But if it isn't, how does one arrive at it? What sorts of arguments would be appropriate? Of course, a foundationalist might find (18) so appealing, he simply takes it to be true, neither offering argument for it, nor accepting it on the basis of other things he believes. If he does so, however, his noetic structure will be self-referentially incoherent. (18) itself is neither self-evident nor incorrigible; hence in accepting (18) as basic, the modern foundationalist violates the condition of proper basicality he himself lays down in accepting it. On the other hand, perhaps the foundationalist will try to produce some argument for it from premises that are self-evident or incorrigible: it is exceedingly hard to see, however, what such an argument might be like. And until he has produced such arguments, what shall the rest of us do—we who do not find (18) at all obvious or compelling? How could he use (18) to show us that belief in God, for example, is not properly basic? Why should we believe (18), or pay it any attention?

The fact is, I think, that neither (18) nor any other revealing necessary and sufficient condition for proper basicality follows from clearly self-evident premises by clearly acceptable arguments. And hence the proper way to arrive at such a criterion is, broadly speaking, *inductive*. We must assemble examples of beliefs and conditions such that the former are obviously properly basic in the latter, and examples of beliefs and conditions such that the former are obviously *not* properly basic in the latter. We must then frame hypotheses on the necessary and sufficient conditions of proper basicality and test these hypotheses by reference to those examples. Under the right conditions, for example, it is clearly rational to believe that you see a human person before you: a being who has thoughts and feelings, who knows and believes things, who makes decisions and acts. It is clear, furthermore, that you are under no obligation to reason to this belief from others you hold; under those conditions that belief is properly basic for you. But then (18) must be mistaken; the belief in question, under those circumstances, is properly basic, though neither self-evident nor incorrigible for you. Similarly, you may seem to remember that you had breakfast this morning, and perhaps you know of no reason to suppose your memory is playing you tricks. If so, you are entirely justified in taking that belief as basic. Of course it isn't properly basic on the criteria offered by classical foundationalists,

but that fact counts not against you but against those criteria.

Accordingly, criteria for proper basicality must be reached from below rather than above; they should not be presented as *obiter dicta,* but argued to and tested by a relevant set of examples. But there is no reason to assume, in advance, that everyone will agree on the examples. The Christian will of course suppose that belief in God is entirely proper and rational; if he doesn't accept this belief on the basis of other propositions, he will conclude that it is basic for him and quite properly so. Followers of Bertrand Russell and Madelyn Murray O'Hare may disagree, but how is that relevant? Must my criteria, or those of the Christian community, conform to their examples? Surely not. The Christian community is responsible to *its* set of examples, not to theirs.

Accordingly, the Reformed epistemologist can properly hold that belief in the Great Pumpkin is not properly basic, even though he holds that belief in God *is* properly basic and even if he has no full-fledged criterion of proper basicality. Of course he is committed to supposing that there is a relevant *difference* between belief in God and belief in the Great Pumpkin, if he holds that the former, but not the latter, is properly basic. But this should prove no great embarrassment; there are plenty of candidates. These candidates are to be found in the neighborhood of the conditions I mentioned in the last section that justify and ground belief in God. Thus, for example, the Reformed epistemologist may concur with Calvin in holding that God has implanted in us a natural tendency to see his hand in the world around us; the same cannot be said for the Great Pumpkin, there being no Great Pumpkin and no natural tendency to accept beliefs about the Great Pumpkin.

By way of conclusion, then: being self-evident, or incorrigible, or evident to the senses is not a necessary condition of proper basicality. Furthermore, one who holds that belief in God *is* properly basic is not thereby committed to the idea that belief in God is groundless or gratuitous or without justifying circumstances. And even if he lacks a general criterion of proper basicality, he is not obliged to suppose that just any, or nearly any, belief—belief in the Great Pumpkin, for example—is properly basic. Like everyone should, he begins with examples, and he may take belief in the Great Pumpkin, in certain circumstances, as a paradigm of irrational basic belief.

NOTES

1. See, for example, Blanshard, *Reason and Belief,* pp. 400ff; Clifford, "The Ethics of Belief," pp. 345ff;

Flew, *The Presumption of Atheism,* p. 22; Russell, "Why I Am Not a Christian," pp. 3ff; and Scriven, *Primary Philosophy,* pp. 87ff. In Plantinga, "Is Belief in God Rational?"

2. W. Salmon, "Religion and Science: A New Look at Hume's Dialogues," *Philosophical Studies* 33 (1978), p. 176.

3. A. G. N. Flew, *The Presumption of Atheism* (London: Pemberton Publishing Co., 1976).

4. A Reformed thinker or theologian is one whose intellectual sympathies lie with the Protestant tradition going back to John Calvin (not someone who was formerly a theologian and has since seen the light).

For Further Reflection

1. Has Plantinga successfully defended the view that one has no rational obligation to support one's belief in God with evidence? Explain. Compare Plantinga's view with the argument that anyone who claims that something exists must be able to give good reasons for its existence.

2. Is there a relevant difference between believing in the Great Pumpkin and believing in God? Could a worshiper of a devil use Plantinga's argument to claim that there is a natural human tendency to believe in a Creator Devil?

II.20   Faith and Truth

SØREN KIERKEGAARD

Danish philosopher and theologian Søren Aabye Kierkegaard (1813–1855) is the acknowledged father of modern existentialism and the champion of a radical form of fideism. Like many philosophers, he arrived at his views via a tortuous path. He was born into a family of pious Lutherans, but after entering the University of Copenhagen, he rejected the church as well as the system-building philosophy of Hegel that was in vogue at the time. After years of dissolute living at the university, he experienced a resurgence of religious sentiments and once again embraced Christianity. For most of the rest of his years, he lived the life of a reclusive, suffering scholar, penning several influential books, including *Either-Or* (1843) and *Concluding Unscientific Postscript* (1846), from which our reading is taken. In it, Kierkegaard declares that faith is the highest virtue, far superior to reason. The latter can render belief in God only a barren probability, a dry uncertainty or approximation, but the former gives you a deeply fulfilling subjective certainty. This risky "leap of faith" requires an utmost act of will—an extreme passion—to believe what cannot otherwise be believed, to believe what is absurd. Great absurdities (such as Christianity's central story, says Kierkegaard) require great, passionate faith, and such faith is "the highest truth there is for an existing human being."

Study Questions

1. What is Kierkegaard's definition of truth?
2. What is the highest virtue a human can reach?
3. What does Kierkegaard mean by "Without risk there is no faith"?
4. Can a person achieve faith through objective inquiries into the existence of God? Why or why not?
5. What is faith's object?

When a person objectively inquires about the problem of immortality and another person embraces it as an uncertainty with infinite passion, where is there most truth, and who really has the greater certainty? The one has entered into an inexhaustible approximation, for certainty of immortality lies precisely in the subjectivity of the individual. The other is immortal and fights against his uncertainty.

Let us consider Socrates. Today everyone is playing with some proof or other. Some have many, some fewer. But Socrates! He put the question objectively in a hypothetical manner: "*if* there is immortality." Compared to the modern philosopher with three proofs for immortality, should we consider Socrates a doubter? Not at all. On this little *if* he risks his entire life, he dares to face death, and he has directed his life with infinite passion so that the *if* is confirmed—*if* there is immortality. Is there any better proof for life after death? But those who have the three proofs do not at all pattern their lives in conformity with the idea. If there is an immortality, it must feel disgust over their lackadaisical manner of life. Can any better refutation be given of the three proofs? These crumbs of uncertainty helped Socrates because they hastened the process along, inciting the passions. The three proofs that others have are of no help at all

because they are dead to the spirit, and the fact that they need three proofs proves that they are spiritually dead. The Socratic ignorance that Socrates held fast with the entire passion of his inwardness was an expression of the idea that eternal truth is related to an existing individual, and that this will be in the form of a paradox as long as he exists; and yet it is just possible that there is more truth in Socratic ignorance than is contained in the "objective truth" of the philosophical systems, which flirts with the spirit of the times and cuddles up to associate professors.

The objective accent falls on *what* is said; the subjective accent falls on *how* it is said. This distinction is valid even for aesthetics and shows itself in the notion that what may be objectively true may in the mouth of certain people become false. This distinction is illustrated by the saying that the difference between the older days and our day is that in the old days only a few knew the truth while in ours all know it, except that the inwardness towards it is in inverse proportion to the scope of its possession. Aesthetically the contradiction that the truth becomes error in certain mouths is best understood comically. In the ethical-religious domain the accent is again on the *how*. But this is not to be understood as referring to decorum, modulation, delivery, and so on, but to the individual's relationship to the

From Concluding Unscientific Postscript *by Søren Kierkegaard, 1835, translated from the Danish by Louis P. Pojman. Previously published in* Classics of Philosophy Volume II: Modern and Contemporary, *Louis P. Pojman (Oxford University Press, 1996). By permission of Trudy Pojman.*

proposition, the way he relates himself to it. Objectively it is a question simply about the content of the proposition, but subjectively it is a question of inwardness. At its maximum this inward *how* is the passion of infinity and the passion of the infinite is itself the truth. But since the passion of the infinite is exactly subjectivity, subjectivity is the truth. Objectively there is no infinite decision or commitment, and so it is objectively correct to annul the difference between good and evil as well as the law of non-contradiction and the difference between truth and untruth. Only in subjectivity is there decision and commitment, so that to seek this in objectivity is to be in error. It is the passion of infinity that brings forth decisiveness, not its content, for its content is precisely itself. In this manner the subjective *how* and subjectivity are the truth.

But the *how* that is subjectively emphasized because the subject is an existing individual is also subject to a temporal dialectic. In passion's decisive moment, where the road swings off from the way to objective knowledge, it appears that the infinite decision is ready to be made. But in that moment the existing individual finds himself in time, and the subjective *how* becomes transformed into a striving, a striving that is motivated by and is repeatedly experienced in the decisive passion of the infinite. But this is still a striving.

When subjectivity is truth, subjectivity's definition must include an expression for an opposition to objectivity, a reminder of the fork in the road, and this expression must also convey the tension of inwardness. Here is such a definition of truth: *the objective uncertainty, held fast in an appropriation process of the most passionate inwardness is the truth,* the highest truth available for an existing person. There where the way swings off (and where that is cannot be discovered objectively but only subjectively), at that place objective knowledge is annulled. Objectively speaking he has only uncertainty, but precisely there the infinite passion of inwardness is intensified, and truth is precisely the adventure

to choose objective uncertainty with the passion of inwardness.

When I consider nature in order to discover God, I do indeed see his omnipotence and wisdom, but I see much more that disturbs me. The result of all this is objective uncertainty, but precisely here is the place for inwardness because inwardness apprehends the objective uncertainty with the entire passion of infinity. In the case of mathematical statements objectivity is already given, but because of the nature of mathematics, this truth is existentially indifferent.

Now the above definition of truth is an equivalent description of faith. Without risk there is no faith. Faith is precisely the contradiction between the infinite passion of inwardness and objective uncertainty. If I can grasp God objectively, I do not believe, but because I cannot know God objectively, I must have faith, and if I will preserve myself in faith, I must constantly be determined to hold fast to the objective uncertainty, so as to remain out upon the ocean's deep, over seventy thousand fathoms of water, and still believe.

In the sentence "subjectivity, inwardness is truth," we see the essence of Socratic wisdom, whose immortal service is exactly to have recognized the essential meaning of existence, that the knower is an *existing* subject, and for this reason in his ignorance Socrates enjoyed the highest relationship to truth within paganism. This is a truth that speculative philosophy unhappily again and again forgets: that the knower is an existing subject. It is difficult enough to recognize this fact in our objective age, long after the genius of Socrates.

When subjectivity, inwardness, is the truth, the truth becomes objectively determined as a paradox, and that it is paradoxical is made clear by the fact that subjectivity is truth, for it repels objectivity, and the expression for the objective repulsion is the intensity and measure of inwardness. The paradox is the objective uncertainty, which is the expression for the passion of inwardness, which is precisely the truth. This is the Socratic principle. The eternal, essential truth, that is, that which relates itself essentially to the individual because it concerns his existence (all other knowledge is, Socratically speaking, accidental, its degree and scope being indifferent), is a paradox. Nevertheless, the eternal truth is not essentially in itself paradoxical, but it becomes so by relating itself to an existing individual. Socratic ignorance is the expression of this objective uncertainty, the inwardness of the existential subject is the truth. To anticipate what I will develop later, Socratic ignorance is an analogy to the category of the absurd, only that there is still less objective certainty in the absurd, and therefore infinitely greater tension in its inwardness. The Socratic inwardness that involves existence is an analogy to faith, except that this inwardness is repulsed not by ignorance but by the absurd, which is infinitely deeper. Socratically the eternal, essential truth is by no means paradoxical in itself, but only by virtue of its relation to an existing individual.

Subjectivity, inwardness, is the truth. Is there a still more inward expression for this? Yes, there is. If subjectivity is seen as the truth, we may posit the opposite principle: that subjectivity is untruth, error. Socratically speaking, subjectivity is untruth if it fails to understand that subjectivity is truth and desires to understand itself objectively. But now we are presupposing that subjectivity in becoming the truth has a difficulty to overcome in as much as it is in untruth. So we must work backwards, back to inwardness. Socratically, the way back to the truth takes place through recollection, supposing that we have memories of that truth deep within us.

Let us call this untruth of the individual "sin." Seen from eternity the individual cannot be in sin, nor can he be eternally presupposed as having been in sin. So it must be that he becomes a sinner by coming into existence (for the beginning point is that subjectivity is untruth). He is not born as a sinner in the sense that he is sinful before he is born, but he is born in sin and as a sinner. We shall call this state *original sin*. But if existence has acquired such power over him, he is impotent to make his way back to eternity

through the use of his memory (supposing that there is truth in the Platonic idea that we may discover truth through recollection). If it was already paradoxical that the eternal truth related itself to an existing individual, now it is absolutely paradoxical that it relates itself to such an individual. But the more difficult it is for him through memory to transcend existence, the more inwardness must increase in intense passion, and when it is made impossible for him, when he is held so fast in existence that the back door of recollection is forever closed to him through sin, then his inwardness will be the deepest possible.

Subjectivity is truth. Through this relationship between the eternal truth and the existing individual the paradox comes into existence. Let us now go further and suppose that the eternal truth is essentially a paradox. How does this paradox come into existence? By juxtaposing the eternal, essential truth with temporal existence. When we set them together within the truth itself, the truth becomes paradoxical. The eternal truth has come into time. This is the paradox. If the subject is hindered by sin from making his way back to eternity by looking inward through recollection, he need not trouble himself about this, for now the eternal essential truth is no longer behind him, but it is in front of him, through its being in existence or having existed, so that if the individual does not *existentially* get hold of the truth, he will never get hold of it.

It is impossible to accentuate existence more than this. When the eternal truth is related to an existing individual, truth becomes a paradox. The paradox repels the individual because of the objective uncertainty and ignorance towards inwardness. But since this paradox in itself is not paradoxical, it does not push the spirit far enough. For without risk there is no faith, and the greater the risk the greater the faith, and the more objective reliability, the less inwardness (for inwardness is precisely subjectivity). Indeed, the less objective reliability, the deeper becomes the possible inwardness. When the paradox is in itself paradoxical, it repels the individual by the power of the absurd, and the corresponding passion, which is produced in the process, is faith. But subjectivity, inwardness, is truth, for otherwise we have forgotten the Socratic contribution; but there is no more striking expression for inwardness than when the retreat from existence through recollection back to eternity is made impossible; and when the truth as paradox encounters the individual who is caught in the vice-grip of sin's anxiety and suffering, but who is also aware of the tremendous risk involved in faith—when he nevertheless makes the leap of faith—this is subjectivity at its height.

When Socrates believed in the existence of God, he held fast to an objective uncertainty in passionate inwardness, and in that contradiction, in that risk faith came into being. Now it is different. Instead of the objective uncertainty, there is objective certainty about the object—certainty that it is absurd, and it is, again, faith that holds fast to that object in passionate inwardness. Compared with the gravity of the absurd, Socratic ignorance is a joke, and compared with the strenuosity of faith in believing the paradox, Socratic existential inwardness is a Greek life of leisure.

What is the absurd? The absurd is that the eternal truth has entered time, that God has entered existence, has been born, has grown, and so on, has become precisely like any other human being, quite indistinguishable from other humans. The absurd is precisely by its objective repulsion the measure of the inwardness of faith. Suppose there is a man who desires to have faith. Let the comedy begin. He desires to obtain faith with the help of objective investigation and what the approximation process of evidential inquiry yields. What happens? With the help of the increment of evidence the absurd is transformed to something else; it becomes probable, it becomes more probable still, it becomes perhaps highly and overwhelmingly probable. Now that there is respectable evidence for the content of his faith, he is ready to believe it, and he prides himself that his faith is not like that of the shoemaker,

the tailor, and the simple folk, but comes after a long investigation. Now he prepares himself to believe it. Any proposition that is almost probable, reasonably probable, highly and overwhelmingly probable, is something that is almost known and as good as known, highly and overwhelmingly known—but it is not believed, not through faith; for the absurd is precisely faith's object and the only positive attitude possible in relation to it is faith and not knowledge.

Christianity has declared itself to be the eternal that has entered time, that has proclaimed itself as the *paradox* and demands faith's inwardness in relation to that which is a scandal to the Jews and folly to the Greeks—and as absurd to the understanding. It is impossible to say this more strongly than by saying: subjectivity is truth, and objectivity is repelled by it—by virtue of the absurd.

Subjectivity culminates in passion. Christianity is the paradox; paradox and passion belong together as a perfect match, and the paradox is perfectly suited to one whose situation is to be in the extremity of existence. Indeed, there never has been found in all the world two lovers more suited to each other than passion and paradox, and the strife between them is a lover's quarrel, when they argue about which one first aroused the other's passion. And so it is here. The existing individual by means of the paradox has come to the extremity of existence. And what is more wonderful for lovers than to be granted a long time together with each other without anything disturbing their relationship except that which makes it more inwardly passionate? And this is what is granted to the unspeculative understanding between the passion and paradox, for they will dwell harmoniously together in time and be changed first in eternity.

But the speculative philosopher views things altogether differently. He believes but only to a certain degree. He puts his hand to the plow but quickly looks about for something to know. From a Christian perspective it is hard to see how he could reach the highest good in this manner.

For Further Reflection

    1. Kierkegaard believes that in the search for religious truth, extremely passionate belief is a good thing. What would a scientist say about this view? What would you say? Is there a risk in holding a view passionately? Explain.

    2. Kierkegaard thinks that rational argument and objective evidence about religious matters are impediments to true belief and spirituality. Do you agree? Why or why not?

    3. Some interpret Kierkegaard as saying that if you believe something with extreme passion, it is not only subjectively true, it becomes objectively true. Is this a plausible view of truth? Can you make something true by believing it to be true? What if someone believes passionately in a religious doctrine, and someone else believes equally passionately in a contradictory religious doctrine. Would both doctrines be objectively true? Neither?

Holy Spirit Epistemology

II.21

MICHAEL MARTIN

Michael Martin is professor emeritus of philosophy at Boston University and the author of numerous books in the philosophy of religion, including *The Impossibility of God* (2003), *Atheism, Morality, and Meaning* (2002), and *Atheism: A Philosophical Justification* (1990). In this reading he critiques William Lane Craig's claim that someone can know that Christianity is true through an indubitable and self-authenticating interaction with the Holy Spirit. He argues that Craig does not explain what he means by "the experience of the Holy Spirit" and provides no justification for his assertion that the experience is universal, veridical, and unmistakable. Craig maintains that in light of the Holy Spirit's universal ministrations, nonbelievers have no excuse for not believing. He seems to assume that they experience the Holy Spirit but choose not to believe anyway. Martin argues that this view is unfounded because it is based on the dubious supposition that what a person believes is always a matter of choice.

Study Questions

1. What is the view that Martin is evaluating?
2. According to Martin, what role does Craig's thesis play in his defense of Christianity?
3. According to Craig, what are the main characteristics of the experience of the Holy Spirit?
4. Martin does not accept Craig's claim that the experience of the Holy Spirit is universal, veridical, and unmistakable. What reasons does he give for this judgment?
5. What is strong doxastic voluntarism? What is Martin's view on this doctrine?

In *Reasonable Faith,* William Lane Craig makes a sharp distinction between knowing that God exists and being able to show this. He maintains that one *knows* that Christianity is true "by the self-authenticating witness of God's Holy Spirit."[1] One can *show* that God exists, that Jesus is his Son, and that other alleged Christian theological doctrines are true only by argument. In this paper I will not be concerned whether this distinction is a viable one or whether Craig has shown that Christian theological doctrines are true by argument.[2] Rather I will concentrate on the epistemological problems connected with Craig's claim that one can know that Christianity is true by the self-authenticating witness of God's Holy Spirit.

I will argue that Craig fails to make clear what an experience of the Holy Spirit is and does not justify his thesis that this experience is universal, veridical, and unmistakable. I will further maintain that, even if one grants his position, his claim that nonbelievers are without excuse for nonbelieving must be rejected unless one assumes that all beliefs are actions, and that he gives no reason to accept this assumption.

A. CRAIG'S THEORY EXPLAINED

Craig's appeal to a direct knowledge of the Holy Spirit by all human beings plays an important role in his defense of Christianity. Combined with his assumption that belief is an action under voluntary control, it enables him to blame atheists for not believing in God even when they are faced by unsound theistic arguments and are in possession of persuasive arguments for the nonexistence of God. If a skeptic objects to theistic arguments, Craig can always claim that she is just being obstinate and that she knows in her heart that God exists. The assumption of human perversity also enables Craig to defend against objections to his own arguments. It allows him to claim without argument that humans know in

their hearts that God exists, but stubbornly refuse to admit it. In addition, it permits Craig to claim that human perversity induces them to reject his arguments for the existence of God. Obviously, Craig's strategy can have great rhetorical force. The question is whether it has any logical or philosophical merit.

By a self-authenticating experience of the Holy Spirit, Craig means an experience that is veridical and unmistakable for "him who has it" (p. 32) although it is "not necessarily irresistible or indubitable" (pp. 31–32). Such an experience does not function, he says, as a premise in an argument from religious experience to the existence of God. Although arguments and evidence may be used to support a believer's faith, they are never the basis of that faith. Rather, the basis is the immediate experience of God himself. Craig maintains, however, that "in certain contexts" this experience of the Holy Spirit will imply the apprehension of basic truths of the Christian religion such as "Christ lives in me" and "I am condemned by God."

Although Craig does not say so explicitly, he assumes that the experience of the Holy Spirit is universal. This assumption becomes clear in his view that although unbelievers have experienced the Holy Spirit, they have rejected it. According to Craig, the Holy Spirit "convicts the unbeliever of his own sin, of God's righteousness, and of his own condemnation before God. The unbeliever so convicted can therefore be said to know such truths, as 'God exists,' 'I am guilty before God,' and so forth" (p. 35). Craig believes that natural man left to himself would not come to God, for although God draws human beings to him, some people ignore and reject him. However, nonbelievers who are given bad arguments for the existence of God and reject God because of these arguments have no excuse for not believing:

> Suppose someone had been told to believe in
> God because of an invalid argument. Could he

From Michael Martin, "Craig's Holy Spirit Epistemology," The Secular Web, *www.infidels.org, 2007. Reprinted with permission.*

stand before God on judgment day and say, "God, those Christians only gave me lousy arguments for believing in you. That is why I didn't believe"? Of course not! The Bible says all men are without excuse. Even those who are given no good reason to believe and many persuasive reasons to disbelieve have no excuse, because the ultimate reason they do not believe is that they have deliberately rejected God's Holy Spirit. (p. 37)

Craig maintains that although nonbelievers have rejected the Holy Spirit, Christians should use evidence and argument to convince them and holds that sometimes they can be converted. However, he adds, "we can never argue anyone into the kingdom of God. Conversion is exclusively the role of the Holy Spirit. But the Holy Spirit may use our arguments to draw people to himself" (p. 47). If an apologist is unsuccessful in converting people by argument, this is not God's fault. It means that the apologist is a bad apologist or that the nonbeliever perversely refuses to accept a premise of the apologist's argument. Indeed, nonbelievers may adopt some "outlandish hypothesis," for example, that the Universe came into being uncaused out of nothing rather than accept an argument that proves that God exists (p. 45)

B. CRAIG'S THEORY EVALUATED

In what follows I will show that Craig fails to make clear what an experience of the Holy Spirit is and does not justify his thesis that this experience is universal, veridical, and unmistakable. In addition, in order to make his case he must assume that all beliefs are actions. However, Craig gives us no reason to suppose that all beliefs are actions. Moreover, the supposition that nonbelievers' beliefs are under their control generates deep mysteries that indicate its implausibility: the action of nonbelievers is inexplicably irrational and the reasons for the geographical and temporal distribution of Christian belief is an enigma.

1. The Unspecified Nature of the Experience

In order to evaluate Craig's view it is important to know precisely what he means by "the experience of the Holy Spirit." Unfortunately, however, he offers no clear explanation of this phrase. Is it a mystical experience in which ordinary consciousness is replaced by special consciousness of oneness with God? Is it rather a vision perhaps similar to that of angels or Jesus, that could be described as perceptual? Is it merely the feeling of being in the presence of a particular holy being? Could it be one or the other of these experiences depending on the circumstances? Craig does not answer these questions. Since, however, having an experience of the Holy Spirit would presumably differ in content from the religious experiences of nontheists such as Buddhists and even from those of non-Christian theists such as Jews and Moslems, not just any religious experience would be considered an experience of the Holy Spirit.

2. The Alleged Universal Nature of the Experience

Whatever its exact nature, Craig assumes that all human beings have the experience of the Holy Spirit. This sweeping assumption presumably includes all nontheists down through the ages. Whether it is also meant to include infants who die shortly after birth and severely retarded people who cannot think or reason is not clear. But even if Craig's thesis does not include such people, it is dubious.

There is absolutely no reason whatsoever to suppose that everyone exclusive of infants and mentally retarded people have had an experience of the Holy Spirit. Granted, people in various religious traditions have reported having had religious experiences. Whether or not any of these experiences are veridical is itself a difficult question.[3] But, whether veridical or not, there is no reason to think that even all professed Christians have experienced the Holy Spirit, let alone that all non-Christians have done so.

To accept Craig's thesis one must believe an outrageous and outlandish hypothesis: namely, that billions of people now and in the past were not telling the truth when they claimed that they never had such an experience. Craig complains that atheists are reduced to assuming the outlandish hypothesis that the Universe came into being uncaused out of nothing in order to avoid the conclusion of the Cosmological Argument. However, atheists can at least use various cosmological theories and arguments to support their controversial theory.[4] Craig can point to nothing except some questionable passages in Scripture to support his thesis that all human beings have experienced the Holy Spirit.[5]

3. The Alleged Veridical and Unmistakable Nature of the Experience

Craig gives us no reasons for supposing that people's experiences of the Holy Spirit are veridical.[6] To be sure, they may *seem* veridical to those who have them. However, seeming veridical says nothing about the actual veridical nature of the experience. Indeed, to say that such experiences are self-authenticating simply begs the question. Since people have all sorts of experiences that seem true to them and are not, it behooves Craig to explain why the experience of the Holy Spirit is any different. He fails to do this.

The same can be said about the allegedly unmistakable nature of the experience of the Holy Spirit. Craig provides no reasons why one cannot be mistaken. After all, one can be mistaken about ordinary experiences. Why should this one be any different? If one can misdescribe the experience of something red and mistakenly call it blue, why could one not misdescribe the experience of the Holy Spirit? Imagine an African woman living in the 10th century who has no knowledge of Christianity but actually has had an experience of the Holy Spirit. Given her conceptual and linguistic repertoires it would be impossible for her to describe her experience in Christian terms and concepts. She

would naturally describe her experience in terms familiar to her and, by hypothesis, she would be wrong.

Moreover, because of inattention or lack of focus or the complexity of the experience, one can have a mistaken belief about what one is experiencing. Thus, for example, a person who has an experience of a 31 sided figure may wrongly believe that she is experiencing a 32 sided figure. In a similar way a Buddhist monk possessing the linguistic and conceptual apparatus to give a correct description may mistake his experience of the Holy Spirit for the experience of the Nirvana if these two experiences were very similar in content.

Now Craig says that the experience of the Holy Spirit is not necessarily indubitable but he does not explain the difference between being "unmistakable" and being "indubitable." Since in one obvious sense they mean the same thing, without further clarification Craig's thesis is *prima facie* incoherent. *Prima facie* he cannot claim that the experience of the Holy Spirit is unmistakable and yet not indubitable.

4. The Unsupported Assumption of Strong Doxastic Voluntarism

Let us now assume for the sake of argument that the experience of the Holy Spirit is in fact universal and veridical and unmistakable. Craig's major thesis, namely, that nonbelievers have no excuse for their nonbelieving, is not thereby justified. After all, some people, for example, because of a psychological block, are able to believe that something is true even if confronted with unmistakable evidence. Perhaps, however, Craig assumes that what a person believes is a matter of choice; in other words, that belief is an action rather than something beyond one's control. Thus, he may suppose that when confronted with the experience of the Holy Spirit, those who do not believe it, have chosen not to. This supposition would allow him to argue that no one has an excuse for not believing in that they could believe if they decided to.

I will call the position that belief is always a matter of choice strong doxastic voluntarism.[7] Now there is no reason to suppose that strong doxastic voluntarism is true, but it is not necessary to go to the opposite extreme and adopt strong doxastic involuntarism – the position that belief is never a matter of choice. A more moderate position is possible, namely, that whether belief is a matter of choice or not is relative to the belief and the person.[8] Indeed, there seems to be good evidence based on self-reports that many people are incapable of believing something by an act of will. Craig has to reject this evidence and base his thesis on dogma.

5. The Inexplicable Irrational Nature and Distribution of Belief

When strong doxastic voluntarism is combined with Craig's thesis that everyone has had an experience of the Holy Spirit, two mysteries are generated. The first is that billions of human beings have been and continue to be inexplicably irrational. For Craig assumes that non-Christians perversely reject, not only what is manifest and obvious, but what is to their eternal advantage to accept. In other words, he assumes not only that disbelief in Christianity is an action rather than something beyond our control, but that it involves the actor knowingly and irrationally rejecting what will bring about his or her ultimate salvation.[9] It is conceivable that a few human beings would be so irrational, but Craig must assume much more. Since he assumes that everyone has an experience of the Holy Spirit, he must assume that there have been and continue to be billions of human beings who knowingly bring about their eternal damnation. If such mass irrationalism really existed, the reason for its existence would be a deep mystery which Craig makes no attempt to explain.

The second mystery is the temporal and geographical distribution of Christian belief. Before the rise of Christianity no person accepted the Christian God, although, according to Craig, everyone had an experience of the Holy Spirit.

But then, one has to assume that before the rise of Christianity everyone was inexplicably irrational in that they had an experience of the Christian God but irrationally decided not to believe. Moreover, since the rise of Christianity, Christianity has been concentrated in certain geographical regions. Yet if Craig is correct, everyone has had an experience of the Holy Spirit. One has to assume, then, that people in certain geographical regions are more irrational than people in other regions. However, it is difficult to understand why this should be the case and Craig does not even attempt to explain why this should be.

CONCLUSION

In presenting an epistemology based on the Holy Spirit Craig makes no effort to answer the most elementary criticisms of his position. Although he assumes that every human being has had an experience of the Holy Spirit that is veridical and unmistakable, he provides neither a clarification of the content of this experience nor any reason to suppose that his claims are true. Furthermore, even if these claims were true, his view that nonbelievers have no excuse for not believing is unsupported without the assumption of strong doxastic voluntarism. But Craig gives no reason to accept this assumption and he leaves unexplained why billions of nonbelievers could be so irrational as to reject God.

Notes

1. William Lane Craig, *Reasonable Faith* (Wheaton. Ill: Crossway Books, 1994), pp. 31. Subsequent references to this book will be placed in the body of the text.

2. Serious questions can be raised about whether Craig's views are coherent. For example, as Jeffery Jay Lowder has pointed out in correspondence, Craig's Holy Spirit Epistemology seems inconsistent with his evidentialism. Although Craig, as an evidential

apologist, must disagree fundamentally with presuppositionalism, his position seems closer to that of the presuppositionalist. Consider Craig's position on the role of argument and evidence:

> The magisterial use of reason occurs when reason stands over and above the gospel like a magistrate and judges it on the basis of argument and evidence. The ministerial use of reason occurs when reason submits to and serves the gospel. Only the ministerial use of reason can be allowed. . . . Should a conflict arise between the witness of the Holy Spirit to the fundamental truth of the Christian faith and beliefs based on argument and evidence, then it is the former which must take precedence over the latter, not vice versa." (p. 36)

Craig concludes that "the Holy Spirit teaches us directly which teaching is really from God" (p. 37). In this sense, Craig sounds like a presuppositionalist, for as R.C. Sproul, et al., explain, "The testimony of the Holy Spirit is the heart of the heart of presuppositionalism. The Holy Spirit is the one who convinces inwardly of the truth of the self-attesting God." See R.C. Sproul, John Gerstner, and Arthur Lindsley, *Classical Apologetics: A Rational Defense of the Christian Faith and a Critique of Presuppositional Apologetics* (Grand Rapids: Zondervan, 1984), p. 296.

The upshot is that many of the same criticisms which evidential apologists level against presuppositionalists on their doctrine on the internal testimony of the Holy Spirit can be leveled against Craig's Holy Spirit Epistemology. For example, Craig asserts that "the Holy Spirit teaches us directly which teaching [e.g., the Bible, the Koran, or the Baghavad-Gita] is really from God" (p. 37). What prevents a non-Christian from saying, "I understand. *My* holy book is correct because God has told *me* so?" If Craig replies that the non-Christian is mistaken and that God has really revealed that the Bible is His word, how can Craig reply to the non-Christian who says that it is *Craig* who is mistaken and that God has revealed some other

book as the Word of God? If Craig *then* gives arguments and evidence in favor of his position, how can Craig reply to the non-Christian who says that, "Should a conflict arise between the witness of *my god* to the fundamental truth of *my religion,* and beliefs based on argument and evidence, then it is the former which must take precedence over the latter, not vice versa"?

3. Michael Martin, *Atheism: A Philosophical Justification* (Philadelphia, PA: Temple University Press, 1990), Chapter 6.

4. See William Lane Craig and Quentin Smith, *Theism, Atheism and Big Bang Cosmology,* (Oxford: Clarendon Press, 1995).

5. At times even Craig does not seem to believe in the universal nature of the experience of the Holy Spirit. For example, on p. 32 he says an experience of the Holy Spirit is veridical and unmistakable for "him who has it." This seems to suggest that some people have such experiences and some people do not.

6. The completely subjective nature of Craig's claim is discussed by Robert M. Price in "By This Time He Stinketh (<*URL:http://www.infidels.org/library/modern/ robert_price/stinketh.html*>.1997).

7. In what follows I am indebted to the discussion of Ted Drange in *Nonbelief and Evil: Two Atheological Arguments* (Unpublished, 1996), Appendix C.

8. This is the position taken by Drange.

9. As Mark Vuletic has pointed out in correspondence, there may be another mystery connected with Craig's theory. Although Craig does not say so explicitly, the experience of the Holy Spirit presumably allows one to directly comprehend that God is perfectly and absolutely good, thus providing the moral standard for all human conduct. Since, according to Craig, everyone has had such an experience, all unbelievers must knowingly and willingly reject this standard, which they know to be the absolute good. However, unbelievers are as obsessed as anyone else with doing what they believe to be good. How could they want to do what is good yet reject what they know to be the standard of good?

For Further Reflection

1. Is Martin's argument against Craig's Holy Spirit theory successful? Explain.

2. Suppose Craig is correct about the universal nature of the Holy Spirit experience. Would it follow that the experience is veridical and unmistakable?

3. Does anthropological and psychological evidence support Craig's assertion that everyone has an experience of the Holy Spirit? If millions of people say they have never experienced the Holy Spirit, should that be taken as evidence that they have had no such experience? Why or why not?

4. If people think they are having experiences of the Holy Spirit, could they *know* that the experiences are true Holy Spirit encounters and not, say, experiences of the devil or wishful thinking? If so, *how* would they know this?

Can Religion Cure Our Troubles?   II.22

BERTRAND RUSSELL

Bertrand Russell (1872–1970), the great twentieth-century British philosopher and Nobel laureate, was a renowned agnostic and unflinching critic of religion. In the preface to his *Why I Am Not a Christian* (1957), from which our reading is taken, he declares, "I am as firmly convinced that religions do harm as I am that they are untrue." In this essay he argues against the idea that adherence to religious dogma is mankind's best hope for alleviating the world's evils. Uncritical acceptance of faith-based morality is dangerous and noxious because it leads to coercion by authorities who wish to preserve orthodoxy, to intolerance of opposing views, and to discouragement of honest inquiry. Contrary to general opinion, he says, Christianity has historically not embodied better morality than rival worldviews have: "Christianity has been distinguished from other religions by its greater readiness for persecution." To those who believe that intelligence has caused our troubles, he says that "it is not unintelligence that will cure them. Only more and wiser intelligence can make a happier world."

(A biographical sketch of Bertrand Russell precedes Reading I.4.)

Study Questions

1. According to Russell, what usually happens when people begin to doubt received theology?
2. What "host of evils" result when a belief is thought to be important for some other reason than its being true?
3. How are Soviet Communism and Christianity similar?
4. What is Russell's response to the view that Christians of the past who did evil deeds (persecutions, pogroms, anti-Semitism, etc.) were not true Christians?
5. Why does Russell conclude that our troubles in the modern world have Christian origins?

I

Mankind is in mortal peril, and fear now, as in the past, is inclining men to seek refuge in God. Throughout the West there is a very general revival of religion. Nazis and Communists dismissed Christianity and did things which we deplore. It is easy to conclude that the repudiation of Christianity by Hitler and the Soviet Government is at least in part the cause of our troubles and that if the world returned to Christianity, our international problems would be solved. I believe this to be a complete delusion born of terror. And I think it is a dangerous delusion because it misleads men whose thinking might otherwise be fruitful and thus stands in the way of a valid solution.

The question involved is not concerned only with the present state of the world. It is a much more general question, and one which has been debated for many centuries. It is the question whether societies can practice a sufficient modicum of morality if they are not helped by dogmatic religion. I do not myself think that the dependence of morals upon religion is nearly as close as religious people believe it to be. I even think that some very important virtues are more likely to be found among those who reject religious dogmas than among those who accept them. I think this applies especially to the virtue of truthfulness or intellectual integrity. I mean by intellectual integrity the habit of deciding vexed questions in accordance with the evidence, or of leaving them undecided where the evidence is inconclusive. This virtue, though it is underestimated by almost all adherents of any system of dogma, is to my mind of the very greatest social importance and far more likely to benefit the world than Christianity or any other system of organized beliefs.

Let us consider for a moment how moral rules have come to be accepted. Moral rules are broadly of two kinds: there are those which have no basis except in a religious creed; and there are those which have an obvious basis in social utility. In the Greek Orthodox Church, two godparents of the same child must not marry. For this rule, clearly, there is only a theological basis; and, if you think the rule important, you will be quite right in saying that the decay of religion is to be deprecated because it will lead to the rule's being infringed. But it is not this kind of moral rule that is in question. The moral rules that are in question are those for which there is a social justification independently of theology.

Let us take theft, for example. A community in which everybody steals is inconvenient for everybody, and it is obvious that most people can get more of the sort of life they desire if they live in a community where theft is rare. But in the absence of laws and morals and religion a difficulty arises: for each individual, the ideal community would be one in which everybody else is honest and he alone is a thief. It follows that a social institution is necessary if the interest of the individual is to be reconciled with that of the community. This is effected more or less successfully by the criminal law and the police. But criminals are not always caught, and the police may be unduly lenient to the powerful. If people can be persuaded that there is a God who will punish theft, even when the police fail, it would seem likely that this belief would promote honesty. Given a population that already believes in God, it will readily believe that God has prohibited theft. The usefulness of religion in this respect is illustrated by the story of Naboth's vineyard, where the thief is the King, who is above earthly justice.

I will not deny that among semicivilized communities in the past such considerations may have helped to promote socially desirable conduct. But in the present day such good as may be done by imputing a theological origin to morals is inextricably bound up with such grave evils that the good becomes insignificant in comparison. As civilization progresses, the earthly sanctions become more secure and the divine sanctions less so. People see more and more reason to think that if they steal they will be caught and less and less reason to think that if they are not caught God will nevertheless punish them. Even highly religious people in the present day hardly expect to go to Hell for stealing. They reflect that they can repent in time, and that in any case Hell is neither so certain nor so hot as it used to be. Most people in civilized communities do not steal, and I think the usual motive is the great likelihood of punishment here on earth. This is borne out by the fact that in a mining camp during a gold rush, or in any such disorderly community, almost everybody steals.

But, you may say, although the theological prohibition of theft may no longer be very necessary, it at any rate does no harm, since we all wish people not to steal. The trouble is, however, that as soon as men incline to doubt received theology it comes to be supported by odious and harmful means. If a theology is thought necessary to virtue and if candid inquirers see no reason to think the *theology* true, the authorities will set to work to discourage candid inquiry. In former centuries they did so by burning the inquirers at the stake. In Russia they still have methods which are little better; but in Western countries the authorities have perfected somewhat milder forms of persuasion. Of these, schools are perhaps the most important: the young must be preserved from hearing the arguments in favor of the opinions which the authorities dislike, and those who nevertheless persist in showing an inquiring disposition will incur social displeasure and, if possible, be made to feel morally reprehensible. In this way, any system of morals which has a theological basis becomes one of the tools by which the holders of power preserve their authority and impair the intellectual vigor of the young.

I find among many people at the present day an indifference to truth which I cannot but think extremely dangerous. When people argue, for example, in defense of Christianity, they do not, like Thomas Aquinas, give reasons for supposing that there is a God and that He has expressed His will in the Scriptures. They argue instead that, if people think this, they will act better than if they do not.

We ought not therefore—so these people contend—to permit ourselves to speculate as to whether God exists. If, in an unguarded moment, doubt rears its head, we must suppress it vigorously. If candid thought is a cause of doubt, we must eschew candid thought. If the official exponents of orthodoxy tell you that it is wicked to marry your deceased wife's sister, you must believe them lest morals collapse. If they tell you that birth control is sin, you must accept their dictum, however obvious it may be to you that without birth control disaster is certain. As soon as it is held that any belief, no matter what, is important for some other reason than that it is true, a whole host of evils is ready to spring up. Discouragement of inquiry, which I spoke of before, is the first of these, but others are pretty sure to follow. Positions of authority will be open to the orthodox. Historical records must be falsified if they throw doubt on received opinions. Sooner or later unorthodoxy will come to be considered a crime to be dealt with by the stake, the purge, or the concentration camp. I can respect the men who argue that religion is true and therefore ought to be believed, but I can only feel profound moral reprobation for those who say that religion ought to be believed because it is useful, and that to ask whether it is true is a waste of time.

It is customary among Christian apologists to regard Communism as something very different from Christianity and to contrast its evils with the supposed blessings enjoyed by Christian nations. This seems to me a profound mistake. The evils of Communism are the same as those that existed in Christianity during the Ages of Faith. The Ogpu differs only quantitatively from the Inquisition. Its cruelties are of the same sort, and the damage that it does to the intellectual and moral life of Russians is of the same sort as that which was done by the Inquisitors wherever they prevailed. The Communists falsify history, and the church did the same until the Renaissance. If the church is not now as bad as the Soviet Government, that is due to the influence of those who attacked the church: from the Council of Trent to the present day, whatever improvements it has effected have been due to its enemies. There are many who object to the Soviet Government because they dislike the Communist economic doctrine, but this the Kremlin shares with the early Christians, the Franciscans, and the majority of medieval Christian heretics. Nor was the Communist doctrine confined to heretics: Sir Thomas More, an orthodox martyr, speaks of Christianity as communistic and says that this was the only aspect of the Christian religion which commended it to the Utopians. It is not Soviet doctrine in itself that can be justly regarded as a danger. It is the way in which the doctrine is held. It is held as sacred and inviolable truth, to doubt which is sin and deserving of the severest punishment. The Communist, like the Christian, believes that his doctrine is essential to salvation, and it is this belief which makes salvation possible for him. It is the similarities between Christianity and Communism that make them incompatible with each other. When two men of science disagree, they do not invoke the secular arm; they wait for further evidence to decide the issue, because, as men of science, they know that neither is infallible. But when two theologians differ, since there are no criteria to which either can appeal, there is nothing for it but mutual hatred and an open or covert appeal to force. Christianity, I will admit, does less harm than it used to do; but that is because it is less fervently believed. Perhaps, in time, the same change will come over Communism; and, if it does, that creed will lose much of what now makes it obnoxious.

But if in the West the view prevails that Christianity is essential to virtue and social stability, Christianity will once again acquire the vices which it had in the Middle Ages; and, in becoming more and more like Communism, will become more and more difficult to reconcile with it. It is not along this road that the world can be saved from disaster.

II

In my first article I was concerned with the evils resulting from any system of dogmas presented for acceptance, not on the ground of truth, but on the ground of social utility. What I had to say applies equally to Christianity, Communism, Islam, Buddhism, Hinduism, and all theological systems, except in so far as they rely upon grounds making a universal appeal of the sort that is made by men of science. There are, however, special arguments which are advanced in favor of Christianity on account of its supposed special merits. These have been set forth eloquently and with a show of erudition by Herbert Butterfield, Professor of Modern History at the University of Cambridge,* and I shall take him as spokesman of the large body of opinion to which he adheres.

Professor Butterfield seeks to secure certain controversial advantages by concessions that make him seem more open-minded than in fact he is. He admits that the Christian Church has relied upon persecution and that it is pressure from without that has led it to abandon this practice in so far as it has been abandoned. He admits that the present tension between Russia and the West is a result of Power Politics such as might have been expected even if the Government of Russia had continued to adhere to the Greek Orthodox Church. He admits that some of the virtues which he regards as distinctively Christian have been displayed by some freethinkers and have been absent in the behavior of many Christians. But, in spite of these concessions, he still holds that the evils from which the world is suffering are to be cured by adherence to Christian dogma, and he includes in the necessary minimum of Christian dogma not only belief in God and immortality but also belief in the Incarnation. He emphasizes the connection of Christianity with certain historical events, and he accepts these events as historical on evidence which would certainly not convince him if it were not connected with his religion. 1 do not think the evidence for the Virgin Birth is such as would convince any

* *Christianity and History* (London, 1950).

impartial inquirer if it were presented outside the circle of theological beliefs he was accustomed to. There are innumerable such stories in pagan mythology, but no one dreams of taking them seriously. Professor Butterfield, however, in spite of being a historian, appears to be quite uninterested in questions of historicity wherever the origins of Christianity are concerned. His argument, robbed of his urbanity and his deceptive air of broad-mindedness, may be stated crudely, but accurately, as follows: "It is not worth while to inquire whether Christ really was born of a Virgin and conceived of the Holy Ghost because, whether or not this was the case, the belief that it was the case offers the best hope of escape from the present troubles of the world." Nowhere in Professor Butterfield's work is there the faintest attempt to prove the truth of any Christian dogma. There is only the pragmatic argument that belief in Christian dogma is useful. There are many steps in Professor Butterfield's contention which are not stated with as much clarity and precision as one could desire, and I fear the reason is that clarity and precision make them implausible. I think the contention, stripped of inessentials, is as follows: It would be a good thing if people loved their neighbors, but they do not show much inclination to do so; Christ said they ought to, and if they believe that Christ was God, they are more likely to pay attention to his teachings on this point than if they do not; therefore, men who wish people to love their neighbors will try to persuade them that Christ was God.

The objections to this kind of argumentation are so many that it is difficult to know where to begin. In the first place, Professor Butterfield and all who think as he does are persuaded that it is a good thing to love your neighbor, and their reasons for holding this view are not derived from Christ's teaching. On the contrary, it is because they already hold this view that they regard Christ's teaching as evidence of his divinity. They have, that is to say, not an ethic based on theology but a theology based on their ethic. They apparently hold, however, that the nontheological grounds which make them think it a good thing to love your neighbor are not likely

to make a wide appeal, and they therefore proceed to invent other arguments which they hope will be more effective. This is a very dangerous procedure. Many Protestants used to think it as wicked to break the Sabbath as to commit murder. If you persuaded them it was not wicked to break the Sabbath, they might infer that it was not wicked to commit murder. Every theological ethic is in part such as can be defended rationally, and in part a mere embodiment of superstitious taboos. The part which can be defended rationally should be so defended, since otherwise those who discover the irrationality of the other part may rashly reject the whole.

But has Christianity, in fact, stood for a better morality than that of its rivals and opponents? I do not see how any honest student of history can maintain that this is the case. Christianity has been distinguished from other religions by its greater readiness for persecution. Buddhism has never been a persecuting religion. The Empire of the Caliphs was much kinder to Jews and Christians than Christian states were to Jews and Mohammedans. It left Jews and Christians unmolested, provided they paid tribute. Anti-Semitism was promoted by Christianity from the moment the Roman Empire became Christian. The religious fervor of the Crusades led to pogroms in western Europe. It was Christians who unjustly accused Dreyfus, and freethinkers who secured his final rehabilitation. Abominations have in modern times been defended by Christians not only when Jews were the victims but also in other connections. The abominations of King Leopold's government of the Congo were concealed or minimized by the church and were ended only by an agitation conducted mainly by freethinkers. The whole contention that Christianity has had an elevating moral influence can only be maintained by wholesale ignoring or falsification of the historical evidence.

The habitual answer is that the Christians who did things which we deplore were not *true* Christians in the sense that they did not follow the teachings of Christ. One might, of course, equally well argue that the Soviet Government does not consist of true Marxists, for Marx taught that Slavs are inferior to Germans, and this doctrine is not accepted in the Kremlin. The followers of a teacher always depart in some respects from the doctrine of the master. Those who aim at founding a church ought to remember this. Every church develops an instinct of self-preservation and minimizes those parts of the founder's doctrine which do not minister to that end. But in any case, what modern apologists call "true" Christianity is something depending upon a very selective process. It ignores much that is to be found in the Gospels: for example, the parable of the sheep and the goats, and the doctrine that the wicked will suffer eternal torment in hell-fire. It picks out certain parts of the Sermon on the Mount, though even these it often rejects in practice. It leaves the doctrine of nonresistance, for example, to be practiced only by non-Christians such as Gandhi. The precepts that it particularly favors are held to embody such a lofty morality that they must have had a divine origin. And yet Professor Butterfield must know that these precepts were all uttered by Jews before the time of Christ. They are to be found, for example, in the teaching of Hillel and in the Testaments of the Twelve Patriarchs, concerning which the Rev. Dr. R. H. Charles, a leading authority in this matter, says, "The Sermon on the Mount reflects in several instances the spirit and even reproduces the very phrases of our text: many passages in the Gospels exhibit traces of the same, and St. Paul seems to have used the book as a vade mecum." Dr. Charles is of the opinion that Christ must have been acquainted with this work. If, as we are sometimes told, the loftiness of the ethical teaching proves the divinity of its author, it is the unknown writer of these Testaments who must have been divine.

That the world is in a bad way is undeniable, but there is not the faintest reason in history to suppose that Christianity offers a way out. Our troubles have sprung, with the inexorability of Greek tragedy, from the First World War, of which the Communists and the Nazis were products. The First World War was wholly Christian in origin. The three emperors were devout, and so were the more warlike of the British Cabinet. Opposition to the war came, in Germany and Russia, from the Socialists, who were anti-Christian; in France, from Jaurès, whose assassin was applauded by earnest Christians; in England, from John Morley, a noted atheist. The most dangerous features of Communism are reminiscent of the medieval church. They consist of fanatical acceptance of doctrines embodied in a sacred book, unwillingness to examine these doctrines critically, and savage persecution of those who reject them. It is not to a revival of fanaticism and bigotry in the West that we must look for a happy issue. Such a revival, if it occurs, will only mean that the hateful features of the Communist regime have become universal. What the world needs is reasonableness, tolerance, and a realization of the interdependence of the parts of the human family. This interdependence has been enormously increased by modern inventions, and the purely mundane arguments for a kindly attitude to one's neighbor are very much stronger than they were at any earlier time. It is to such considerations that we must look, and not to a return to obscurantist myths. Intelligence, it might be said, has caused our troubles; but it is not unintelligence that will cure them. Only more and wiser intelligence can make a happier world.

For Further Reflection

1. Russell maintains that fear compels people to seek refuge in God. Is this a plausible explanation for belief in a deity? Why or why not? What are some alternative explanations? What credence do you give each of these?

2. Russell thinks that the virtue of truthfulness or intellectual integrity is more likely to be found among nonbelievers than believers. Do you agree? Explain.

3. Do you agree that when people doubt the preferred theology, authorities use harmful means to preserve it? In asserting this generalization, does Russell go beyond the evidence? Explain.

4. Do you believe that morality depends in some way on religion? If so, how? If not, why not?

Key Terms

a posteriori argument   *a priori* argument   cosmological argument

teleological argument   ontological argument   argument from evil

Suggestions for Further Reading

GENERAL

Davies, Brian. *An Introduction to the Philosophy of Religion.* Oxford: Oxford University Press, 1982. Readable, reliable, written from a distinctive theistic framework.

Harrison, Jonathan. *God, Freedom and Immortality.* London: Aylesbury, 1999.

Hick, John. *Arguments for the Existence of God.* London: Macmillan, 1971. A clearly written, insightful examination.

Mackie, J. L. *The Miracle of Theism.* Oxford: Oxford University Press, 1982. A lively discussion of the proofs by one of the ablest atheist philosophers of our time, but uneven.

Martin, Michael. *Atheism: A Philosphical Justification.* Philadelphia: Temple University Press, 1990.

Matson, Wallace. *The Existence of God.* Ithaca, NY: Cornell University Press, 1965. A cogent attack on the traditional arguments.

Moreland, J. P., and Kay Nielsen. *Does God Exist? The Great Debate.* Buffalo, NY: Prometheus, 1995.

Pojman, Louis. *Philosophy of Religion: An Anthology,* 3rd ed. Belmont, CA: Wadsworth, 1998.

Rowe, William. *Philosophy of Religion: An Introduction.* Belmont, CA: Dickenson, 1978. A very readable and reliable introduction for beginners.

Swinburne, Richard. *The Existence of God.* Oxford: Clarendon, 1979. Perhaps the most sustained, if not the overall best, defense of the traditional arguments since the Middle Ages.

Yandell, Keith. *Christianity and Philosophy.* Grand Rapids, MI: Eerdmans, 1984. A rigorously analytic approach, crammed full of outlines of arguments without as much discussion as one might like.

THE COSMOLOGICAL ARGUMENT

Craig, William. *The Cosmological Argument from Plato to Leibniz.* New York: Barnes & Noble, 1980. A good survey of the history of the argument.

Gale, Richard M. *On the Nature and Existence of God.* Cambridge: Cambridge University Press, 1991.

Rowe, William. *The Cosmological Argument.* Princeton, NJ: Princeton University Press, 1975. A very thorough and penetrating study of the classic formulations (especially Aquinas, Scotus, and Clark).

THE TELEOLOGICAL ARGUMENT

McPherson, Thomas. *The Argument from Design.* London: Macmillan, 1972. A good introduction to the various forms of the argument.

Salmon, Wesley. "Religion and Science: A New Look at Hume's Dialogue." *Philosophical Studies* 33 (1978), 145.

Swinburne, Richard. "The Argument from Design—A Defence." *Religious Studies* 8 (1972), 193–205.

Swinburne, Richard. "The Argument from Design." *Philosophy* 43 (1968). A detailed response to Hume.

Tennant, R. R. *Philosophical Theology.* Cambridge, England: Cambridge University Press, 1928–30. A classic post-Humean version of the teleological argument.

THE ONTOLOGICAL ARGUMENT

Barnes, Jonathan. *The Ontological Argument.* London: Macmillan, 1972. A good general discussion of the argument.

Gale, Richard M. *On the Nature and Existence of God.* Cambridge: Cambridge University Press, 1991.

Plantinga, Alvin, ed. *The Ontological Argument from St. Anselm to Contemporary Philosophers.* Garden City, NY: Doubleday, 1965.

THE PROBLEM OF EVIL

Lewis, C. S. *The Problem of Pain*. London: Geoffrey Bles, 1940. Clear and cogent.

Mackie, J. L. "Evil and Omnipotence." *Mind* 64 (1955), 200–212. One of the earlier contemporary attacks on the existence of God from the argument from evil, used in many anthologies.

Mackie, J. L. *The Miracle of Theism*. Oxford: Oxford University Press, 1982. Chapter 9 is insightful and well-argued from an atheist's point of view.

McCloskey, H. J. "God and Evil." *The Philosophical Quarterly* 10 (1960). A sharp attack on theism, arguing that given the problem of evil, theism is indefensible.

Pike, Nelson. "Hume on Evil." *The Philosophical Review* LXXII (1963), 180–97. A trenchant criticism of Hume's position.

Plantinga, Alvin. *The Nature of Necessity*. Oxford: Clarendon, 1974. Chapter 9 is an excellent article developing in detail a version of the free-will defense. A more accessible version of his argument is found in Plantinga's *God, Freedom and Evil* (New York: Harper & Row, 1974).

Rowe, William. "The Problem of Evil and Some Varieties of Atheism." *APQ* 16 (1970), 335–41.

Swinburne, Richard. *The Existence of God*. Oxford: Oxford University Press, 1978. Chapter 11 contains a fuller defense than is in the article included in this volume.

Wainwright, William J. "God and the Necessity of Physical Evils." *Sophia* 11 (1972), 16–19.

FAITH AND REASON

Delaney, C. F., ed. *Rationality and Religious Belief*. Notre Dame, IN: University of Notre Dame Press, 1978. A good collection of essays on faith and reason.

Flew, Antony. *The Presumption of Atheism*. New York: Harper & Row, 1976. Part I, Chapters 1, 2, and 5 are relevant to the discussion.

Mackie, J. L. *The Miracle of Theism: Arguments for and against the Existence of God*. Oxford: Clarendon, 1982. Probably the best defense of atheism in recent years, taking into consideration every major argument in the field.

Mavrodes, George. *Belief in God*. New York: Random House, 1970. A clear presentation of religious epistemology.

Mitchell, Basil. *The Justification of Religious Belief*. London: Macmillan, 1973. A good discussion of the cumulative case for theism.

Phillips, D. Z. *Religion Without Explanation*. Oxford: Basil Blackwell, 1976. A valuable study by one of the foremost Wittgensteinian philosophers.

Plantinga, Alvin. *Warranted Christian Belief*. New York: Oxford University Press, 2000.

Plantinga, Alvin, and Nicholas Wolterstorff, eds. *Faith and Rationality*. Notre Dame, IN: University of Notre Dame Press, 1983.

Pojman, Louis. *Religious Belief and the Will*. London: Routledge & Kegan Paul, 1986.

Swinburne, Richard. *Faith and Reason*. Oxford: Clarendon, 1981. One of the best studies of the subject in recent years.

Part III

Knowledge

I am the wisest man alive, for I know one thing, and that is that I know nothing.

SOCRATES in Plato's *Apology*

III.A What Can We Know?
Classical Theories of Knowledge

What do we really know? How can we be certain that we have the truth?

Epistemology is the philosophical study of knowledge. It is the branch of philosophy that systematically investigates whether, how, and to what extent we know things. We claim to know much, we assume a particular understanding of what that involves, and we continually use what we think we know to try to make our way through life. But philosophy asks us to take a closer look at knowledge, to ask (1) whether we really know what we think we know, and (2), assuming we know, how we know. For well over two thousand years, philosophers have been asking such things because, contrary to what most people believe, the answers are not obvious, and both the asking and the answering can be valuable beyond measure. Whatever the answers we ourselves give, if we take them seriously they surely will affect how we see the world and what we do in it.

We can classify knowledge by kinds of things known. We might claim to know what influenza feels like, or how to throw a ball, or that an elm tree grows in the quad. The latter claim is an example of **propositional knowledge**—knowledge of a proposition, or *knowing that* something is the case. A proposition is a statement that is either true or false, an assertion that something is or is not a fact. This kind of knowledge has been the main focus of philosophers and will be our primary concern in this chapter.

What exactly does propositional knowledge require? Philosophers going back as far as Plato have said that propositional knowledge has three necessary and sufficient conditions: to know a proposition, (1) we must *believe* it, (2) it must be *true*, and (3) we must have good *reasons* for—be justified in—believing it true. On this traditional account, merely believing something is not enough; what we believe must *be* true. A belief does not count as knowledge unless it is true. But a mere true belief is not knowledge because it seems that we can have a true belief and yet not genuinely know. Let's say that you believe for no reason that five crows are now perched on a tree in the quad, and suppose your belief is true—there really are five crows perched on a tree in the quad. Does your true belief count as knowledge? According to the traditional view, no—because you have no reason to think five crows are now perched on a tree in the quad. You have only a true belief by accident, a lucky guess, and that's not knowledge. To have knowledge, our belief must be true, and we must have good reasons to believe it true. Knowledge, then, is true belief that is justified. Philosophers disagree about the exact nature of the required justification, but most accept that knowledge is true belief that is in some sense backed by good reasons.

Knowledge, say epistemologists, is of two types: that derived from reason and that based on sense experience. The former is called *a priori;* it is acquired independently of or prior to sense experience. The latter is known as *a posteriori;* it depends entirely on sense experience. Examples of *a priori* knowledge are such propositions as 2 + 2 = 4, the sum of the interior angles of a triangle is 180 degrees, all bachelors are unmarried, and something either is a cat or is not a cat. The denial of an *a priori* truth is logically self-contradictory. In contrast, *a posteriori* knowledge includes propositions like four ducks are on the pond, Mary drew a triangle, John claims to be a bachelor, and the cat is on the mat.

For centuries philosophers have been at odds over whether our knowledge of the world is fundamentally *a priori* or *a posteriori,* and the debates continue today in many forms in both philosophy and science. **Rationalists** believe that through unaided reason we can come to know what the world is like. They maintain that some or all knowledge of the empirical world is *a priori,* discoverable simply through the workings of our minds. **Empiricists** contend that our knowledge of the empirical world comes solely from sense experience. It is entirely *a posteriori.* We may come to know logical and mathematical truths through reason, but we can know nothing of empirical reality except through our senses.

Among the greatest of the rationalist philosophers is René Descartes (1596–1650), inventor of analytic geometry and founder of modern philosophy. [Others include Plato, Benedict Spinoza (1632–1677), and Gottfried Leibniz (1646–1716)]. As Descartes suggests in our first reading, he sees sense experience as an unreliable source of knowledge, but he wants to give all our knowledge a foundation as firm as that which supports unshakeable mathematical truths. His method is first to doubt everything that he cannot be certain of, a process that leaves him knowing hardly anything. But through reason he soon uncovers what he considers to be self-evident, certain truths from which he derives other indubitable propositions. In this way he tries to build an edifice of knowledge that, like an inverted pyramid, rests on one or two rock-solid foundation stones that support all the others.

Descartes assumes at the outset that knowledge requires certainty. When he concludes at one point that through sense experience he cannot know anything for certain, he sinks into **skepticism,** the view that we cannot or do not have knowledge. He reasons that our senses are unreliable because, for all we know, we may be dreaming that we are having sensory experiences. We cannot be certain that we are not dreaming, so we cannot trust our senses—and therefore we do not have knowledge. In a similar vein, he supposes that for all we know an evil genius may be manipulating our minds so that all our sensory experiences are delusions. Since we cannot be certain that this possibility is not actual, our sense experience is suspect—and again we do not have knowledge. These two scenarios are among the most famous in philosophy, and they have launched a raft of discussion and argument about the plausibility of skepticism.

Descartes eventually finds a way out of his skeptical darkness. Though it seems that he must doubt everything, he finds it impossible to doubt that he exists. He sees that even when he is doubting, he is thinking, and if he knows that he is thinking, he knows with certainty that he exists. He sums up this insight in his famous maxim, "I think, therefore I am." From this starting point, he derives a method that he believes will allow him reliably to discover truths about the world.

The empiricist approach to knowledge is represented in our next three readings by British empiricists John Locke (1632–1704), George Berkeley (1685–1753), and David Hume (1711–1776). Among these, Hume probably has been most influential, arguing for an uncompromising empiricism that leads to skepticism—a far-reaching skepticism that not all empiricists have shared. He holds that all our knowledge (aside from purely logical truths) is derived from sense perceptions or ideas about those perceptions. Like other empiricists, he believes that the mind is empty—a blank slate—until experience gives it content. We can have knowledge of something only if it can be sensed, and any proposition that does not refer to what can be sensed is meaningless. Guided by this latter empiricist principle, Hume is driven to skepticism about many things that others have taken for granted, including the existence of the external world, causation, a continuing self, religious doctrines, and inductive reasoning. Provoked by Hume's radical skepticism, philosophers have expended a great deal of energy trying to show that his views are partly or wholly unfounded.

As a card-carrying empiricist, Berkeley also might be expected to arrive at some skeptical conclusions, but he thinks his brand of empiricism can actually defeat the skeptic. Empiricists agree that all we are directly aware of are sense data (the content of our experience), but they differ on how sense data relate to the external world. Locke, for example, argues that our sensory experience is caused by material objects and that some sense data resemble material objects, giving us knowledge of them. Berkeley accepts the empiricist notion of our being aware only of sense data (what he calls ideas) but rejects Locke's belief in the existence of material objects. He argues that not only do we know just our own ideas, but also that there is no reason to suppose that they resemble or are caused by material objects. Locke, like most people, presumes that material objects exist independently of our sense experience, that they exist even when we do not perceive them. But Berkeley denies this, insisting that it is logically impossible for physical objects to exist, for we cannot "conceive them existing unconceived." All that exist, he says, are minds and their ideas, a view known as subjective idealism. Nothing exists except what is perceived in some mind—or, in his famous phrase, "to be is to be perceived." What we usually call physical objects, then, are simply compilations of sense data. They are "real" and exist even when we are not sensing them because they are ideas in the mind of God, who perceives them continually. On Berkeley's view, skepticism is defeated because there is no hard-to-bridge gap between our sense experience and reality, as empiricists believe. We know reality intimately because reality is our sense experience.

Our final reading is John Hospers' rebuttal of skepticism.

III.23   Cartesian Doubt and the Search for Foundational Knowledge

RENÉ DESCARTES

René Descartes (1596–1650) was born in France and educated by the Jesuits at the College of La Fleche. After a three-year career as a professional soldier, he traveled through Europe, trying to complete his education by reading the "great book of the world." Finally, he settled in Holland and began to write philosophical treatises. These were radically innovative because instead of starting with the accumulated authority of the medieval tradition, Descartes began with his own experience and philosophized from there. The self becomes the center of authority instead of the tradition. His two major works are *Discourse on Method* (1637) and *Meditations on First Philosophy* (1641), from which our present selection is taken.

Descartes writes philosophy in the first person singular. He desires to know the truth, and he realizes that this will be an arduous enterprise because he has discovered by painful experience that much of what he has been taught and has taken for granted is false. He must destroy his tottering house of "knowledge" and lay a new foundation on which to construct an indestructible edifice. The method consists of doubting everything that can be doubted, and then, on the pure remainder of certain truth, beginning the process of constructing an indubitable system of knowledge. The result is a type of rationalism in which the only certainties are discovered by the mind through self-evident insight or reason.

Study Questions

1. What caused Descartes to begin the process of doubting everything?
2. Why does he not examine all of his beliefs separately?
3. Why does he doubt his senses?
4. Why does he posit the idea of an evil genius who always deceives him?
5. What is the first thing that Descartes comes to know with certainty?

MEDITATION ONE: CONCERNING THOSE THINGS THAT CAN BE CALLED INTO DOUBT

SEVERAL YEARS HAVE NOW PASSED since I first realized how many were the false opinions that in my youth I took to be true, and thus how doubtful were all the things that I subsequently built upon these opinions. From the time I became aware of this, I realized that for once I had to raze everything in my life, down to the very bottom, so as to begin again from the first foundations, if I wanted to establish anything firm and lasting in the sciences. But the task seemed so enormous that I waited for a point in my life that was so ripe that no more suitable a time for laying hold of these disciplines would come to pass. For this reason, I have delayed so long that I would be at fault were I to waste on deliberation the time that is left for action. Therefore, now that I have liberated my mind from all cares, and I have secured for myself some leisurely and carefree time, I withdraw in solitude. I will, in short, apply myself earnestly and openly to the general destruction of my former opinions.

Yet to this end it will not be necessary that I show that all my opinions are false, which perhaps I could never accomplish anyway. But because reason now persuades me that I should withhold my assent no less carefully from things which are not plainly certain and indubitable than I would to what is patently false, it will be sufficient justification for rejecting them all, if I find a reason for doubting even the least of them. Nor therefore need one survey each opinion one after the other, a task of endless proportion. Rather—because undermining the foundations will cause whatever has been built upon them to fall down of its own accord—I will at once attack those principles which supported everything that I once believed.

Whatever I had admitted until now as most true I took in either from the senses or through the senses; however, I noticed that they sometimes deceived me. And it is a mark of prudence never to trust wholly in those things which have once deceived us.

But perhaps, although the senses sometimes deceive us when it is a question of very small and distant things, still there are many other matters which one certainly cannot doubt, although they are derived from the very same senses: that I am sitting here before the fireplace wearing my dressing gown, that I feel this sheet of paper in my hands, and so on. But how could one deny that these hands and that my whole body exist? Unless perhaps I should compare myself to insane people whose brains are so impaired by a stubborn vapor from a black bile that they continually insist that they are kings when they are in utter poverty, or that they are wearing purple robes when they are naked, or that they have a head made of clay, or that they are gourds, or that they are made of glass. But they are all demented, and I would appear no less demented if I were to take their conduct as a model for myself.

All of this would be well and good, were I not a man who is accustomed to sleeping at night, and to undergoing in my sleep the very same things—or now and then even less likely ones— as do these insane people when they are awake. How often has my evening slumber persuaded me of such customary things as these: that I am here, clothed in my dressing gown, seated at the fireplace, when in fact I am lying undressed between the blankets! But right now I certainly am gazing upon this piece of paper with eyes wide awake. This head which I am moving is not heavy with sleep. I extend this hand consciously and deliberately and I feel it. These things would not be so distinct for one who is asleep. But this all seems as if I do not recall having been deceived by similar thoughts on other occasions in my dreams. As I consider these cases more intently, I see so plainly that there are no definite signs to distinguish being awake from being asleep that I am quite astonished, and this astonishment almost convinces me that I am sleeping.

Let us say, then, for the sake of argument, that we are sleeping and that such particulars as these are not true: that we open our eyes, move our heads, extend our hands. Perhaps we do not even have these hands, or any such body at all. Nevertheless, it really must be admitted that things seen in sleep are, as it were, like painted images, which could have been produced only in the likeness of true things. Therefore at least these general things (eyes, head, hands, the whole body) are not imaginary things, but are true and exist. For indeed when painters wish to represent sirens and satyrs by means of bizarre and unusual forms, they surely cannot ascribe utterly new natures to these creatures. Rather, they simply intermingle the members of various animals. And even if they concoct something so utterly novel that its likes have never been seen before (being utterly fictitious and false), certainly at the very minimum the colors from which the painters compose the thing ought to be true. And for the same reason, although even these general things (eyes, head, hands, and the like) can be imaginary, still one must necessarily admit that at least other things that are even more simple and universal are true, from which, as from true colors, all these things—be they true or false—which in our thought are images of things, are constructed.

To this class seems to belong corporeal nature in general, together with its extension; likewise the shape of extended things, their quantity or size, their number; as well as the place where they exist, the time of their duration, and other such things.

Hence perhaps we do not conclude improperly that physics, astronomy, medicine, and all the other disciplines that are dependent upon the consideration of composite things are all doubtful. But arithmetic, geometry, and other such disciplines—which treat of nothing but the simplest and most general things and which are indifferent as to whether these composite things do or do not exist—contain something certain and indubitable. For whether I be awake or asleep, two plus three makes five, and a square does not have more than four sides; nor does it seem possible that such obvious truths can fall under the suspicion of falsity.

All the same, a certain opinion of long standing has been fixed in my mind, namely that there exists a God who is able to do anything and by whom I, such as I am, have been created. How do I know that he did not bring it about that there be no earth at all, no heavens, no extended thing, no figure, no size, no place, and yet all these things should seem to me to exist precisely as they appear to do now? Moreover—for I judge that others sometimes make mistakes in matters that they believe they know most perfectly—how do I know that I am not deceived every time I add two and three or count the sides of a square or perform an even simpler operation, if such can be imagined? But perhaps God has not willed that I be thus deceived, for it is said that he is good in the highest degree. Nonetheless, if it were repugnant to his goodness that he should have created me such that I be deceived all the time, it would seem, from this same consideration, to be foreign to him to permit me to be deceived occasionally. But we cannot make this last assertion.

Perhaps there are some who would rather deny such a powerful God, than believe that all other matters are uncertain. Let us not put these people off just yet; rather, let us grant that everything said here about God is fictitious. Now they suppose that I came to be what I am either by fate or by chance or by a continuous series of events or by some other way. But because being deceived and being mistaken seem to be imperfections, the less powerful they take the author of my being to be, the more probable it will be that I would be so imperfect as to be deceived perpetually. I have nothing to say in response to these arguments. At length I am forced to admit that there is nothing, among the things I once believed to be true, which it is not permissible to doubt—not for reasons of frivolity or a lack of forethought, but because of valid and considered arguments. Thus I must carefully withhold assent no less from these things than from the patently false, if I wish to find anything certain.

But it is not enough simply to have made a note of this; I must take care to keep it before my mind. For long-standing opinions keep coming back again and again, almost against my will; they seize upon my credulity, as if it were bound over to them by long use and the claims of intimacy. Nor will I get out of the habit of assenting to them and believing in them, so long as I take them to be exactly what they are, namely, in some respects doubtful as by now is obvious, but nevertheless highly probable, so that it is much more consonant with reason to believe them than to deny them. Hence, it seems to me, I would do well to turn my will in the opposite direction, to deceive myself and pretend for a considerable period that they are wholly false and imaginary, until finally, as if with equal weight of prejudice* on both sides, no bad habit should turn my judgment from the correct perception of things. For indeed I know that no danger or error will follow and that it is impossible for me to indulge in too much distrust, since I now am concentrating only on knowledge, not on action.

Thus I will suppose not a supremely good God, the source of truth, but rather an evil genius, as clever and deceitful as he is powerful, who has directed his entire effort to misleading me. I will regard the heavens, the air, the earth, colors, shapes, sounds, and all external things as nothing but the deceptive games of my dreams, with which

---

*A "prejudice" is a prejudgement, that is, an adjudication of an issue without having first reviewed the appropriate evidence.

he lays snares for my credulity. I will regard myself as having no hands, no eyes, no flesh, no blood, no senses, but as nevertheless falsely believing that I possess all these things. I will remain resolutely fixed in this meditation, and, even if it be out of my power to know anything true, certainly it is within my power to take care resolutely to withhold my assent to what is false, lest this deceiver, powerful and clever as he is, have an effect on me. But this undertaking is arduous, and laziness brings me back to my customary way of living. I am not unlike a prisoner who might enjoy an imaginary freedom in his sleep. When he later begins to suspect that he is sleeping, he fears being awakened and conspires slowly with these pleasant illusions. In just this way, I spontaneously fall back into my old beliefs, and dread being awakened, lest the toilsome wakefulness which follows upon a peaceful rest, have to be spent thenceforward not in the light but among the inextricable shadows of the difficulties now brought forward.

MEDITATION TWO: CONCERNING THE NATURE OF THE HUMAN MIND: THAT THE MIND IS MORE KNOWN THAN THE BODY

Yesterday's meditation filled my mind with so many doubts that I can no longer forget about them—nor yet do I see how they are to be resolved. But, as if I had suddenly fallen into a deep whirlpool, I am so disturbed that I can neither touch my foot to the bottom, nor swim up to the top. Nevertheless I will work my way up, and I will follow the same path I took yesterday, putting aside everything which admits of the least doubt, as if I had discovered it to be absolutely false. I will go forward until I know something certain—or, if nothing else, until I at least know for certain that nothing is certain. Archimedes sought only a firm and immovable point in order to move the entire earth from one place to another. Surely great things are to be hoped for if I am lucky enough to find at least one thing that is certain and indubitable.

Therefore I will suppose that all I see is false. I will believe that none of those things that my deceitful memory brings before my eyes ever existed. I thus have no senses: body, shape, extension, movement, and place are all figments of my imagination. What then will count as true? Perhaps only this one thing: that nothing is certain.

But on what grounds do I know that there is nothing over and above all those which I have just reviewed, concerning which there is not even the least cause for doubt? Is there not a God (or whatever name I might call him) who instills these thoughts in me? But why should I think that, since perhaps I myself could be the author of these things? Therefore am I not at least something? But I have already denied that I have any senses and any body. Still, I hesitate; for what follows from that? Am I so tied to the body and to the senses that I cannot exist without them? But I have persuaded myself that there is nothing at all in the world: no heaven, no earth, no minds, no bodies. Is it not then true that I do not exist? But certainly I should exist, if I were to persuade myself of something. But there is a deceiver (I know not who he is) powerful and sly in the highest degree, who is always purposely deceiving me. Then there is no doubt that I exist, if he deceives me. And deceive me as he will, he can never bring it about that I am nothing so long as I shall think that I am something. Thus it must be granted that, after weighing carefully and sufficiently everything, one must come to the considered judgment that the statement "I am, I exist" is necessarily true every time it is uttered by me or conceived in my mind.

But I do not yet understand well enough who I am—I, who now necessarily exist. And from this point on, I must take care lest I imprudently substitute something else in place of myself; and thus be mistaken even in that knowledge which I claim to be the most certain and evident of all. To this end, I shall meditate once more on what I once believed myself to be before having embarked upon these deliberations. For this reason, then, I will set aside whatever can be refuted even to a slight degree by the arguments brought forward, so that at length there shall remain precisely nothing but what is certain and unshaken.

What therefore did I formerly think I was? A man, of course. But what is a man? Might I not say a rational animal? No, because then one would have to inquire what an "animal" is and what "rational" means. And then from only one question we slide into many more difficult ones. Nor do I now have enough free time that I want to waste it on subtleties of this sort. But rather here I pay attention to what spontaneously and by my own nature came into my thought beforehand whenever I pondered what I was. Namely, it occurred to me first that I have a face, hands, arms, and this entire mechanism of bodily members, the very same as are discerned in a corpse—which I referred to by the name "body." It also occurred to me that I eat, walk, feel and think; these actions I used to assign to the soul as their cause. But what this soul was I either did not think about or I imagined it was something terribly insubstantial—after the fashion of a wind, fire, or ether—which has been poured into my coarser parts. I truly was not in doubt regarding the body; rather I believed that I distinctly knew its nature, which, were I perhaps tempted to describe it such as I mentally conceived it, I would explain it thus: by "body," I understand all that is suitable for being bounded by some shape, for being enclosed in some place, and thus for filling up space, so that it excludes every other body from that space; for being perceived by touch, sight, hearing, taste, or smell; for being moved in several ways, not surely by itself, but by whatever else that touches it. For I judged that the power of self-motion, and likewise of sensing or of thinking, in no way pertains to the nature of the body. Nonetheless, I used to marvel especially that such faculties were found in certain bodies.

But now what am I, when I suppose that some deceiver—omnipotent and, if I may be allowed to say it, malicious—takes all the pains he can in order to deceive me? Can I not affirm that I possess at least a small measure of all those traits which I already have said pertain to the nature of the body? I pay attention, I think, I deliberate—but nothing happens. I am wearied of repeating this in vain. But which of these am I to ascribe to the soul? How about eating or walking? These are surely nothing but illusions, because I do not have a body. How about sensing? Again, this also does not happen without a body, and I judge that I really did not sense those many things I seemed to have sensed in my dreams. How about thinking? Here I discover that thought is an attribute that really does belong to me. This alone cannot be detached from me. I am; I exist; this is certain. But for how long? For as long as I think. Because perhaps it could also come to pass that if I should cease from all thinking I would then utterly cease to exist. I now admit nothing that is not necessarily true. I am therefore precisely only a thing that thinks; that is, a mind, or soul, or intellect, or reason—words the meaning of which I was ignorant before. Now, I am a true thing, and truly existing, but what kind of thing? I have said it already: a thing that thinks.

What then? I will set my imagination going to see if I am not something more. I am not that connection of members which is called the human body. Neither am I some subtle air infused into these members, not a wind, not a fire, not a vapor, not a breath—nothing that I imagine to myself, for I have supposed all these to be nothing. The assertion stands: the fact still remains that I am something. But perhaps it is the case that nevertheless, these very things which I take to be nothing (because I am ignorant of them) in reality do not differ from that self which I know. This I do not know. I shall not quarrel about it right now; I can make a judgment only regarding things which are known to me. I know that I exist; I ask now who is this "I" whom I know. Most certainly the knowledge of this matter, thus precisely understood, does not depend upon things that I do not yet know to exist. Therefore, it is not dependent upon any of those things that I feign in my imagination. But this word "feign" warns me of my error. For I would be feigning if I should "imagine" that I am something, because imagining is merely the contemplation of the shape or image of a corporeal thing. But I know now with certainty that I am, and at the same time it could happen that all these images—and, generally, everything that pertains to the nature of the body—are nothing but dreams. When these things are taken into account, I would speak no less foolishly were I to say: "I will imagine so that I might recognize more distinctly who I am," than were I to say: "Now I surely am awake, and I see something true, but because I do not yet see it with sufficient evidence, I will take the trouble of going to sleep so that my dreams might show this to me more truly and more evidently." Thus I know that none of what I can comprehend by means of the imagination pertains to this understanding that I have of myself. Moreover, I know that I must be most diligent about withdrawing my mind from these things so that it can perceive its nature as distinctly as possible.

But what then am I? A thing that thinks. What is that? A thing that doubts, understands, affirms, denies, wills, refuses, and which also imagines and knows.

For Further Reflection

1. Are you convinced by Descartes' argument? Is the self the most certain of objects?

2. Is Descartes' argument against trusting the senses a valid one? Why should we always distrust the senses? Discuss this issue and compare it with what Locke says when you get to the next reading. Descartes is a *rationalist,* believing that unaided reason can discover all truth, whereas Locke and Hume are *empiricists,* believing that sense perception is the only way to knowledge. Keep this in mind as you continue in this section.

3. Does Descartes convince you that the mind is more certain than matter?

III.24   The Empiricist Theory of Knowledge

JOHN LOCKE

Locke's work in the theory of knowledge, *An Essay Concerning Human Understanding* (1689), is the first systematic assault on Cartesian rationalism, the view that reason alone guarantees knowledge. Locke argues that if our claims to knowledge make any sense, they must be derived from the world. He rejects the rationalist notion that we have innate ideas (actual knowledge of metaphysical truths, such as mathematical truths, universals, and the laws of nature) because (1) there is no good deductive argument establishing the existence of such entities, (2) children and idiots do not seem to possess them, and (3) an empirical way of knowing, which seems far more reasonable, has no place for such entities. Locke does believe that we have intuitive knowledge of our own existence and that the existence of God can be demonstrated by reason (see Book IV, Chapter XI in this selection). Scholars are puzzled at this apparent inconsistency, but Locke would respond that it is no inconsistency. We know that we exist on immediate reflection because of the nature of consciousness, not because of any poor knowledge hidden within us. Nor do we have innate knowledge of God. It is simply that we can reason from empirical truths about the world to the existence of God (using such arguments as the cosmological and teleological arguments we discussed in Part II).

According to Locke, the mind at birth is a *tabula rasa*, a blank slate. It is like white paper, devoid of characteristics until it receives sense perceptions. All knowledge begins with sensory experience on which the powers of the mind operate, developing complex ideas, abstractions, and the like. In place of the absolute certainty that the rationalists sought to find, Locke says that apart from the knowledge of the self, most of what we know we know in degrees of certainty derived from inductive generalizations. For example, we see the sun rise every morning and infer that it is highly probable that it will rise tomorrow, but we cannot be absolutely certain.

(A biographical sketch of John Locke [1632–1704] precedes Reading I.3.)

Study Questions

1. Why is it important to inquire into the structure of human understanding?
2. Describe Locke's design of purpose. Which ideas does he plan to treat and which to omit?
3. What is his method?
4. What does he mean by the word "idea"?
5. What are so-called "innate principles" (or "ideas")? What is Locke's view of them?
6. What does Locke argue is the origin of our ideas?
7. What is the difference between primary and secondary qualities?
8. Describe Locke's view of the degrees of knowledge. What are the highest degrees of knowledge and what do we know to lesser degrees?
9. What is Locke's view of probability?

INTRODUCTION

1. AN INQUIRY INTO THE UNDERSTANDING *pleasant and useful.*—Since it is the *understanding* that sets man above the rest of sensible beings, and gives him all the advantage and dominion which he has over them; it is certainly a subject, even for its nobleness, worth our labour to inquire into. The understanding, like the eye, whilst it makes us see and perceive all other things, takes no notice of itself; and it requires art and pains to set it at a distance and make it its own object. But whatever be the difficulties that lie in the way of this inquiry; whatever it be that keeps us so much in the dark to ourselves; sure I am that all the light we can let in upon our minds, all the acquaintance we can make with our own understandings, will not only be very pleasant, but bring us great advantage, in directing our thoughts in the search of other things.

2. *Design.*—This, therefore, being my purpose—to inquire into the origin, certainty, and extent of *human knowledge,* together with the grounds and degrees of *belief, opinion,* and *assent*—I shall not at present meddle with the physical consideration of the mind, or trouble myself to examine wherein its essence consists; or by what motions of our spirits or alterations of our bodies we come to have any *sensation* by our organs, or any *ideas* in our understandings, and whether those ideas do in their formation, any or

From An Essay Concerning Human Understanding *(London: E. Holt, 1689).*

all of them, depend on matter or not. These are speculations which, however curious and entertaining, I shall decline, as lying out of my way in the design I am now upon. It shall suffice to my present purpose, to consider the discerning faculties of a man, as they are employed about the objects which they have to do with. And I shall imagine I have not wholly misemployed myself in the thoughts I shall have on this occasion, if, in this historical, plain method, I can give any account of the ways whereby our understandings come to attain those notions of things we have; and can set down any measures of the certainty of our knowledge; or the grounds of those persuasions which are to be found amongst men, so various, different, and wholly contradictory; and yet asserted somewhere or other with such assurance and confidence, that he that shall take a view of the opinions of mankind, observe their opposition, and at the same time consider the fondness and devotion wherewith they are embraced, the resolution and eagerness wherewith they are maintained, may perhaps have reason to suspect, that either there is no such thing as truth at all, or that mankind hath no sufficient means to attain a certain knowledge of it.

3. *Method.*—It is therefore worth while to search out the bounds between opinion and knowledge, and examine by what measures, in things whereof we have no certain knowledge, we ought to regulate our assent and moderate our persuasion. In order whereunto I shall pursue this following method:

First, I shall inquire into the original of those *ideas,* notions, or whatever else you please to call them, which a man observes, and is conscious to himself he has in his mind, and the ways whereby the understanding comes to be furnished with them.

Secondly, I shall endeavour to show what *knowledge* the understanding hath by those ideas; and the certainty, evidence, and extent of it. Thirdly, I shall make some inquiry into the nature and grounds of *faith* or *opinion:* whereby I mean that assent which we give to any proposition as true, of whose truth yet we have no certain knowledge. And here we shall have occasion to examine the reasons and degrees of *assent.*

BOOK I

Chapter I

1. It is an established opinion amongst some men, that there are in the understanding certain *innate principles,* some primary notions, κοιναὶ ἔννοιαι, characters, as it were stamped upon the mind of man, which the soul receives in its very first being, and brings into the world with it. It would be sufficient to convince unprejudiced readers of the falseness of this supposition, if I should only show (as I hope I shall in the following parts of this Discourse) how men, barely by the use of their natural faculties, may attain to all the knowledge they have, without the help of any innate impressions, and may arrive at certainty, without any such original notions or principles. For I imagine any one will easily grant that it would be impertinent to suppose the ideas of colours innate in a creature to whom god hath given sight, and a power to receive them by the eyes from external objects: and no less unreasonable would it be to attribute several truths to the impressions of nature, and innate characters, when we may observe in ourselves faculties fit to attain as easy and certain knowledge of them as if they were originally imprinted on the mind.

But because a man is not permitted without censure to follow his own thoughts in the search of truth, when they lead him ever so little out of the common road, I shall set down the reasons that made me doubt of the truth of that opinion, as an excuse for my mistake, if I be in one, which I leave to be considered by those who, with me, dispose themselves to embrace truth wherever they find it.

2. There is nothing more commonly taken for granted than that there are certain *principles,* both *speculative* and *practical* (for they speak of both), universally agreed upon by all mankind, which therefore, they argue, must needs be the constant impressions which the souls of men

receive in their first beings, and which they bring into the world with them, as necessarily and really as they do any of their inherent faculties.

3. This argument, drawn from universal consent, has this misfortune in it, that if it were true in matter of fact, that there were certain truths wherein all mankind agreed, it would not prove them innate, if there can be any other way shown how men may come to that universal agreement, in the things they do consent in, which I presume may be done.

4. But, which is worse, this argument of universal consent, which is made use of to prove innate principles, seems to me a demonstration that there are none such because there are none to which all mankind give an universal assent. I shall begin with the speculative, and instance in those magnified principles of demonstration, "Whatsoever is, is," and "It is impossible for the same thing to be and not to be," which, of all others, I think have the most allowed title to innate. These have so settled a reputation of maxims universally received, that it will no doubt be thought strange if any one should seem to question it. But yet I take liberty to say, that these propositions are so far from having an universal assent, that there are a great part of mankind to whom they are not so much as known.

5. For, first, it is evident, that all children and idiots have not the least apprehension or thought of them. And the want of that is enough to destroy that universal assent which must needs be the necessary concomitant of all innate truths: it seeming to me near a contradiction to say, that there are truths imprinted on the soul, which it perceives or understands not: imprinting, if it signify anything, being nothing else but the making certain truths to be perceived. For to imprint anything on the mind without the mind's perceiving it, seems to me hardly intelligible. If therefore children and idiots have souls, have minds, with those impressions upon them, *they* must unavoidably perceive them, and necessarily know and assent to these truths; which since they do not, it is evident that there are no such impressions. For if they are not notions naturally imprinted, how can they be innate? and if they are notions imprinted, how can they be unknown? To say a notion is imprinted on the mind, and yet at the same time to say that the mind is ignorant of it, and never yet took notice of it, is to make this impression nothing. No proposition can be said to be in the mind which it never yet knew, which it was never yet conscious of. For if any one may, then, by the same reason, all propositions that are true, and the mind is capable ever of assenting to, may be said to be in the mind, and to be imprinted: since, if any one can be said to be in the mind, which it never yet knew, it must be only because it is capable of knowing it, and so the mind is of all truths it ever shall know. Nay, thus truths may be imprinted on the mind which it never did, nor ever shall know; for a man may live long, and die at last in ignorance of many truths which his mind was capable of knowing, and that with certainty. So that if the capacity of knowing be the natural impression contended for, all the truths a man ever comes to know will, by this account, be every one of them innate; and this great point will amount to no more, but only to a very improper way of speaking; which, whilst it pretends to assert the contrary, says nothing different from those who deny innate principles. For nobody, I think, ever denied that the mind was capable of knowing several truths. The capacity, they say, is innate; the knowledge acquired. But then to what end such contest for certain innate maxims? If truths can be imprinted on the understanding without being perceived, I can see no difference there can be between any truths the mind is *capable* of knowing in respect of their original: they must all be innate or all adventitious: in vain shall a man go about to distinguish them. He therefore that talks of innate notions in the understanding, cannot (if he intend thereby any distinct sort of truths) mean such truths to be in the understanding as it never perceived, and is yet wholly ignorant of. For if these words "to be in the understanding" have any propriety, they signify to be understood. So that to be in the understanding, and not to be understood; to be in the mind and never to be perceived, is all one

as to say anything is and is not in the mind or understanding. If therefore these two propositions, "Whatsoever is, is," and "It is impossible for the same thing to be and not to be," are by nature imprinted, children cannot be ignorant of them: infants, and all that have souls, must necessarily have them in their understandings, know the truth of them, and assent to it. . . .

BOOK II

Chapter I

1. Every man being conscious to himself that he thinks and that which his mind is applied about whilst thinking being the *ideas* that are there, it is past doubt that men have in their minds several ideas—such as are those expressed by the words *whiteness, hardness, sweetness, thinking, motion, man, elephant, army, drunkenness,* and others; it is in the first place then to be inquired, *How he comes by them?*

I know it is a received doctrine, that men have native ideas, and original characters, stamped upon their minds in their very first being. This opinion I have at large examined already; and, I suppose what I have said in the foregoing Book will be much more easily admitted, when I have shown whence the understanding may get all the ideas it has; and by what ways and degrees they may come into the mind—for which I shall appeal to every one's own observation and experience.

2. Let us then suppose the mind to be, as we say, white paper, void of all characters, without any ideas:—How comes it to be furnished? Whence comes it by that vast store which the busy and boundless fancy of man has painted on it with an almost endless variety? Whence has it all the *materials* of reason and knowledge? To this I answer, in one word, from EXPERIENCE. In that all our knowledge is founded, and from that it ultimately derives itself. Our observation employed either, about external sensible objects, or about the internal operations of our minds perceived and reflected on by ourselves, is that which supplies our understandings with all the

materials of thinking. These two are the fountains of knowledge, from whence all the ideas we have, or can naturally have, do spring.

3. First, our Senses, conversant about particular sensible objects, do convey into the mind several distinct perceptions of things, according to those various ways wherein those objects do affect them. And thus we come by those *ideas* we have of *yellow, white, heat, cold, soft, hard, bitter, sweet,* and all those which we call sensible qualities, which when I say the senses convey into the mind, I mean, they from external objects convey into the mind what produces there those perceptions. This great source of most of the ideas we have, depending wholly upon our senses, and derived by them to the understanding, I call SENSATION.

4. Secondly, the other fountain from which experience furnisheth the understanding with ideas is—the perception of the operations of our own mind within us, as it is employed about the ideas it has got—which operations, when the soul comes to reflect on and consider, do furnish the understanding with another set of ideas, which could not be had from things without. And such are *perception, thinking, doubting, believing, reasoning, knowing, willing,* and all the different actings of our own minds, which we being conscious of, and observing in ourselves, do from these receive into our understandings as distinct ideas as we do from bodies affecting our senses. This source of ideas every man has wholly in himself, and though it be not sense, as having nothing to do with external objects, yet it is very like it, and might properly enough be called *internal sense.* But as I call the other Sensation, so I call this REFLECTION, the ideas it affords being such only as the mind gets by reflecting on its own operations within itself. By reflection then, in the following part of this discourse, I would be understood to mean, that notice which the mind takes of its own operations, and the manner of them, by reason whereof there come to be ideas of these operations in the understanding. These two, I say, viz. external material things, as the objects of SENSATION, and the operations of our

own minds within, as the objects of REFLECTION, are to me the only originals from whence all our ideas take their beginnings. The term *operations* here I use in a large sense, as comprehending not barely the actions of the mind about its ideas, but some sort of passions arising sometimes from them, such as is the satisfaction or uneasiness arising from any thought.

5. The understanding seems to me not to have the least glimmering of any ideas which it doth not receive from one of these two. *External objects* furnish the mind with the ideas of sensible qualities, which are all those different perceptions they produce in us, and *the mind* furnishes the understanding with ideas of its own operations.

These, when we have taken a full survey of them, and their several modes, combinations, and relations, we shall find to contain all our whole stock of ideas, and that we have nothing in our minds which did not come in one of these two ways. Let any one examine his own thoughts, and thoroughly search into his understanding, and then let him tell me, whether all the original ideas he has there, are any other than of the objects of his senses, or of the operations of his mind, considered as objects of his reflection. And how great a mass of knowledge soever he imagines to be lodged there, he will, upon taking a strict view, see that he has not any idea in his mind but what one of these two have imprinted—though perhaps, with infinite variety compounded and enlarged by the understanding, as we shall see hereafter.

6. He that attentively considers the state of a child, at his first coming into the world, will have little reason to think him stored with plenty of ideas, that are to be the matter of his future knowledge. It is *by degrees* he comes to be furnished with them. And though the ideas of obvious and familiar qualities imprint themselves before the memory begins to keep a register of time or order, yet it is often so late before some unusual qualities come in the way, that there are few men that cannot recollect the beginning of their acquaintance with them. And if it were worth

while, no doubt a child might be so ordered as to have but a very few, even of the ordinary ideas, till he were grown up to a man. But all that are born into the world, being surrounded with bodies that perpetually and diversely affect them, variety of ideas, whether care be taken of it or not, are imprinted on the minds of children. Light and colours are busy at hand everywhere, when the eye is but open; sounds and some tangible qualities fail not to solicit their proper senses, and force an entrance to the mind—but yet, I think, it will be granted easily, that if a child were kept in a place where he never saw any other but black and white till he were a man, he would have no more ideas of scarlet or green, than he that from his childhood never tasted an oyster, or a pineapple, has of those particular relishes. . . .

Chapter VIII

8. Whatsoever the mind perceives *in itself,* or is the immediate object of perception, thought, or understanding, that I call *idea,* and the power to produce any idea in our mind, I call *quality* of the subject wherein that power is. Thus a snowball having the power to produce in us the ideas of white, cold, and round,—the power to produce those ideas in us, as they are in the snowball, I call qualities, and as they are sensations or perceptions in our understandings, I call them ideas, which *ideas,* if I speak of sometimes as in the things themselves, I would be understood to mean those qualities in the objects which produce them in us.

9. Qualities thus considered in bodies are, *First,* such as are utterly inseparable from the body, in what state soever it be, and such as in all the alterations and changes it suffers, all the force can be used upon it, it constantly keeps; and such as sense constantly finds in every particle of matter which has bulk enough to be perceived; and the mind finds inseparable from every particle of matter, though less than to make itself singly be perceived by our senses: v.g. Take a grain of wheat, divide it into two parts; each part has still solidity, extension, figure, and mobility. Divide it again, and it retains still the same qualities, and so

divide it on, till the parts become insensible; they must retain still each of them all those qualities. For division (which is all that a mill, or pestle, or any other body, does upon another, in reducing it to insensible parts) can never take away either solidity, extension, figure, or mobility from any body, but only makes two or more distinct separate masses of matter, of that which was but one before; all which distinct masses, reckoned as so many distinct bodies, after division, make a certain number.

These I call *original* or *primary qualities* of body, which I think we may observe to produce simple ideas in us, viz. solidity, extension, figure, motion or rest, and number.

10. *Secondly,* such qualities which in truth are nothing in the objects themselves but powers to produce various sensations in us by their primary qualities, i.e., by the bulk, figure, texture, and motion of their insensible parts, as colours, sounds, tastes, etc. These I call *secondary qualities.* To these might be added a *third* sort, which are allowed to be barely powers; though they are as much real qualities in the subject as those which I, to comply with the common way of speaking, call qualities, but for distinction, secondary qualities. For the power in fire to produce a new colour, or consistency, in *wax* or *clay,*—by its primary qualities, is as much a quality in fire, as the power it has to produce in *me* a new idea or sensation of warmth or burning, which I felt not before—by the same primary qualities, viz. the bulk, texture, and motion of its insensible parts. . . .

13. . . . let us suppose at present that the different motions and figures, bulk and number, of such particles, affecting the several organs of our senses, produce in us those different sensations which we have from the colours and smells of bodies; v.g. that a violet, by the impulse of such insensible particles of matter, of peculiar figures and bulks, and in different degrees and modifications of their motions, causes the ideas of the blue colour, and sweet scent of that flower to be produced in our minds. It being no more impossible to conceive that God should annex such ideas to such motions, with which they have no simili-

tude, than that he should annex the idea of pain to the motion of a piece of steel dividing our flesh, with which that idea hath no resemblance.

14. What I have said concerning colours and smells may be understood also of tastes and sounds, and other the like sensible qualities, which, whatever reality we by mistake attribute to them, are in truth nothing in the objects themselves, but powers to produce various sensations in us; and depend on those primary qualities, viz. bulk, figure, texture, and motion of parts as I have said.

15. From whence I think it easy to draw this observation—that the ideas of primary qualities of bodies are resemblances of them, and their patterns do really exist in the bodies themselves, but the ideas produced in us by these secondary qualities have no resemblance of them at all. There is nothing like our ideas, existing in the bodies themselves. They are, in the bodies we denominate from them, only a power to produce those sensations in us, and what is sweet, blue, or warm in idea, is but the certain bulk, figure, and motion of the insensible parts, in the bodies themselves, which we call so.

16. Flame is denominated hot and light; snow, white and cold; and manna, white and sweet, from the ideas they produce in us. Which qualities are commonly thought to be the same in those bodies that those ideas are in us, the one the perfect resemblance of the other, as they are in a mirror, and it would by most men be judged very extravagant if one should say otherwise. And yet he that will consider that the same fire that, at one distance produces in us the sensation of warmth, does, at a nearer approach, produce in us the far different sensation of pain, ought to bethink himself what reason he has to say—that this idea of warmth, which was produced in him by the fire, is *actually in the fire,* and his idea of pain, which the same fire produced in him the same way, is *not* in the fire. Why are whiteness and coldness in snow, and pain not, when it produces the one and the other idea in us, and can do neither, but by the bulk, figure, number, and motion of its solid parts? . . .

21. Ideas being thus distinguished and understood, we may be able to give an account how the same water, at the same time, may produce the idea of cold by one hand and of heat by the other; whereas it is impossible that the same water, if those ideas were really in it, should at the same time be both hot and cold. For, if we imagine *warmth,* as it is in our hands, to be nothing but a certain sort and degree of motion in the minute particles of our nerves or animal spirits, we may understand how it is possible that the same water may, at the same time, produce the sensations of heat in one hand and cold in the other, which yet *figure* never does, that never producing the idea of a square by one hand which has produced the idea of a globe by another. But if the sensation of heat and cold be nothing but the increase or diminution of the motion of the minute parts of our bodies, caused by the corpuscles of any other body, it is easy to be understood, that if that motion be greater in one hand than in the other; if a body be applied to the two hands, which has in its minute particles a greater motion than in those of one of the hands, and a less than in those of the other, it will increase the motion of the one hand and lessen it in the other, and so cause the different sensations of heat and cold that depend thereon. . . .

When children have, by repeated sensations, got ideas fixed in their memories, they begin by degrees to learn the use of signs. And when they have got the skill to apply the organs of speech to the framing of articulate sounds, they begin to make use of words, to signify their ideas to others. These verbal signs they sometimes borrow from others, and sometimes make themselves, as one may observe among the new and unusual names children often give to things in the first use of language.

The use of words then being to stand as outward marks of our internal ideas, and those ideas being taken from particular things, if every particular idea that we take in should have a distinct name, names must be endless. To prevent this, the mind makes the particular ideas received from particular objects to become general, which is done by considering them as they are in the mind such appearances—separate from all other existences, and the circumstances of real existence, as time, place, or any other concomitant ideas. This is called ABSTRACTION, whereby ideas taken from particular beings become general representatives of all of the same kind; and their names general names, applicable to whatever exists conformable to such abstract ideas. Such precise, naked appearances in the mind, without considering how, whence, or with what others they came there, the understanding lays up (with names commonly annexed to them) as the standards to rank real existences into sorts, as they agree with these patterns, and to denominate them accordingly. Thus the same colour being observed today in chalk or snow, which the mind yesterday received from milk, it considers that appearance alone, makes it a representative of all of that kind; and having given it the name *whiteness,* it by that sound signifies the same quality wheresoever to be imagined or met with; and thus universals, whether ideas or terms, are made. . . .

BOOK IV

Chapter II

1. All our knowledge consisting, as I have said, in the view the mind has of its own ideas, which is the utmost light and greatest certainty we, with our faculties, and in our way of knowledge, are capable of, it may not be amiss to consider a little the degrees of its evidence. The different clearness of our knowledge seems to me to lie in the different way of perception the mind has of the agreement or disagreement of any of its ideas. For if we will reflect on our own ways of thinking, we will find, that sometimes the mind perceives the agreement or disagreement of two ideas *immediately by themselves,* without the intervention of any other: and this I think we may call *intuitive knowledge.* For in this the mind is at no pains of proving or examining, but perceives the truth as the eye doth light, only by being directed towards it. Thus the mind perceives that *white* is

not *black,* that a *circle* is not a *triangle,* that *three* are more than *two* and equal to *one and two.* Such kinds of truths the mind perceives at the first sight of the ideas together, by bare intuition, without the intervention of any other idea; and this kind of knowledge is the clearest and most certain that human frailty is capable of. This part of knowledge is irresistible, and, like bright sunshine, forces itself immediately to be perceived, as soon as ever the mind turns its view that way, and leaves no room for hesitation, doubt, or examination, but the mind is presently filled with the clear light of it. *It is on this intuition that depends all the certainty and evidence of all our knowledge;* which certainty every one finds to be so great, that he cannot imagine, and therefore not require a greater: for a man cannot conceive himself capable of a greater certainty than to know that any idea in his mind is such as he perceives it to be, and that two ideas, wherein he perceives a difference, are different and not precisely the same. He that demands a greater certainty than this, demands he knows not what, and shows only that he has a mind to be a sceptic, without being able to be so. Certainty depends so wholly on this intuition, that, in the next degree of knowledge which I call demonstrative, this intuition is necessary in all the connexions of the intermediate ideas, without which we cannot attain knowledge and certainty.

2. The next degree of knowledge is, where the mind perceives the agreement or disagreement of any ideas, but not immediately. Though wherever the mind perceives the agreement or disagreement of any of its ideas, there be certain knowledge; yet it does not always happen, that the mind sees that agreement or disagreement, which there is between them, even where it is discoverable; and in that case remains in ignorance, and at most gets no further than a probable conjecture. The reason why the mind cannot always perceive presently the agreement or disagreement of two ideas, is, because those ideas, concerning whose agreement or disagreement the inquiry is made, cannot by the mind be so put together as to show it. In this case then, when the mind cannot so bring its ideas together as by their immediate comparison, and as it were juxtaposition or application one to another, to perceive their agreement or disagreement, it is fain, *by the intervention of other ideas* (one or more, as it happens) to discover the agreement or disagreement which it searches; and this is that which we call *reasoning.* Thus, the mind being willing to know the agreement or disagreement in bigness between the three angles of a triangle and two right ones, cannot by an immediate view and comparing them do it: because the three angles of a triangle cannot be brought at once, and be compared with any other one, or two, angles; and so of this the mind has no immediate, no intuitive knowledge. In this case the mind is fain to find out some other angles, to which the three angles of a triangle have an equality; and, finding those equal to two right ones, comes to know their equality to two right ones.

3. Those intervening ideas, which serve to show the agreement of any two others, are called *proofs;* and where the agreement and disagreement is by this means plainly and clearly perceived, it is called *demonstration;* it being *shown* to the understanding, and the mind made to see that it is so. A quickness in the mind to find out these intermediate ideas (that shall discover the agreement or disagreement of any other), and to apply them right, is, I suppose, that which is called *sagacity.*

4. This knowledge, by intervening proofs, though it be certain, yet the evidence of it is not altogether so clear and bright, nor the assent so ready, as in intuitive knowledge. For, though in demonstration the mind does at last perceive the agreement or disagreement of the ideas it considers; yet it is not without pains and attention: There must be more than one transient view to find it. A steady application and pursuit are required to this discovery, and there must be a progression by steps and degrees, before the mind can in this way arrive at certainty, and come to perceive the agreement or repugnancy between two ideas that need proofs and the use of reason to show it.

5. Another difference between intuitive and demonstrative knowledge is, that, though in the latter all doubt be removed when, by the intervention of the intermediate ideas, the agreement or disagreement is perceived, yet before the demonstration there was a doubt; which in intuitive knowledge cannot happen to the mind that has its faculty of perception left to a degree capable of distinct ideas; no more than it can be a doubt to the eye (that can distinctly see white and black), whether this ink and this paper be all of a colour. If there be sight in the eyes, it will, at first glimpse, without hesitation, perceive the words printed on this paper different from the colour of the paper, and so if the mind have the faculty of distinct perception, it will perceive the agreement or disagreement of those ideas that produce intuitive knowledge. If the eyes have lost the faculty of seeing, or the mind of perceiving, we in vain inquire after the quickness of sight in one, or clearness of perception in the other. . . .

14. These two, viz. intuition and demonstration, are the degrees of our *knowledge;* whatever comes short of one of these, with what assurance soever embraced, is but *faith* or *opinion,* but not knowledge, at least in all general truths. There is, indeed, another perception of the mind, employed about *the particular existence of finite beings without us,* which, going beyond bare probability, and yet not reaching perfectly to either of the foregoing degrees of certainty, passes under the name of *knowledge.* There can be nothing more certain than that the idea we receive from an external object is in our minds: this is intuitive knowledge. But whether there be anything more than barely that idea in our minds; whether we can thence certainly infer the existence of anything without us, which corresponds to that idea, is that whereof some men think there may be a question made; because men may have such ideas in their minds, when no such thing exists, no such object affects their senses. But yet here I think we are provided with an evidence that puts us past doubting. For I ask any one, Whether he be not invincibly conscious to himself of a different perception, when he looks on the sun by day, and thinks on it

by night; when he actually tastes wormwood, or smells a rose, or only thinks on that savour or odour? We as plainly find the difference there is between any idea revived in our minds by our own memory, and actually coming into our minds by our senses, as we do between any two distinct ideas. If any one says, a dream may do the same thing, and all these ideas may be produced in us without any external objects, he may please to dream that I make him this answer: 1. That it is no great matter, whether I remove his scruple or no; where all is but dream, reasoning and arguments are of no use, truth and knowledge nothing. 2. That I believe he will allow a very manifest difference between dreaming of being in the fire, and being actually in it. But yet if he be resolved to appear so sceptical as to maintain, that what I call being actually in the fire is nothing but a dream; and that we cannot thereby certainly know, that any such thing as fire actually exists without us: I answer, That we certainly finding that pleasure or pain follows upon the application of certain objects to us, whose existence we perceive, or dream that we perceive, by our senses; this certainty is as great as our happiness or misery, beyond which we have no concernment to know or to be. So that, I think, we may add to the two former sorts of knowledge this also, of the existence of particular external objects, by that perception and consciousness we have of the actual entrance of ideas from them, and allow these three degrees of knowledge, viz. *intuitive, demonstrative,* and *sensitive:* in each of which there are different degrees and ways of evidence and certainty. . . .

Chapter XI   Of Our Knowledge of the Existence of Other Things

1. The knowledge of our own being we have by intuition. The existence of a God, reason clearly makes known to us, as has been shown.

The knowledge of the existence of *any other thing* we can have only by *sensation:* for there being no necessary connexion of real existence with any *idea* a man hath in his memory; nor of any other existence but that of God with the existence of any particular man: no particular man can know the existence of any other being, but only when, by actual operating upon him, it makes itself perceived by him. For, the having the idea of anything in our mind, no more proves the existence of that thing, than the picture of a man evidences his being in the world, or the visions of a dream make thereby a true history.

2. It is therefore the *actual receiving* of ideas from without that gives us notice of the existence of other things, and makes us know, that something doth exist at that time without us, which causes that idea in us; though perhaps we neither know nor consider how it docs it. For it takes not from the certainty of our senses, and the ideas we receive by them, that we know not the manner wherein they are produced: v.g. whilst I write this, I have, by the paper affecting my eyes, that idea produced in my mind, which, whatever object causes, I call *white;* by which I know that that quality or accident (i.e., whose appearance before my eyes always causes that idea) doth really exist, and hath a being without me. And of this, the greatest assurance I can possibly have, and to which my faculties can attain, is the testimony of my eyes, which are the proper and sole judges of this thing; whose testimony I have reason to rely on as so certain, that I can no more doubt, whilst I write this, that I see white and black, and that something really exists that causes that sensation in me, than that I write or move my hand; which is a certainty as great as human nature is capable of, concerning the existence of anything, but a man's self alone, and of God.

3. The notice we have by our senses of the existing of things without us, though it be not altogether so certain as our intuitive knowledge, or the deductions of our reason employed about the clear abstract ideas of our own minds; yet it is an assurance that deserves the name of *knowledge.* If we persuade ourselves that our faculties act and inform us right concerning the existence of those objects that affect them, it cannot pass for an ill-grounded confidence; for I think nobody can, in earnest, be so sceptical as to be uncertain of the existence of those things which he sees and feels. At least, he that can doubt so far (whatever he may have with his own thoughts), will never have any controversy with me; since he can never be sure I say anything contrary to his own opinion. As to myself, I think God has given me assurance enough of the existence of things without me: Since, by their different application, I can produce in myself both pleasure and pain, which is one great concernment of my present state. This is certain: The confidence that our faculties do not herein deceive us, is the greatest assurance we are capable of concerning the existence of material beings. For we cannot act anything but by our faculties; nor talk of knowledge itself, but by the help of those faculties which are fitted to apprehend even what knowledge is. But besides the assurance we have from our senses themselves, that they do not err in the information they give us of the existence of things without us, when they are affected by them, we are further confirmed in this assurance by other concurrent reasons:

4. I. It is plain those perceptions are produced in us by exterior causes affecting our senses: because those that want the *organs* of any sense, never can have the ideas belonging to that sense produced in their minds. This is too evident to be doubted, and therefore we cannot but be assured that they come in by the organs of that sense, and no other way. The organs themselves, it is plain, do not produce them: for then the eyes of a man in the dark would produce colours, and his nose smell roses in the winter. But we see nobody gets the relish of a pineapple, till he goes to the Indies, where it is, and tastes it.

5. II. Because sometimes I find that *I cannot avoid the having those ideas produced in my mind.* For though, when my eyes are shut, or windows fast, I can at pleasure recall to my mind the ideas of light, or the sun, which former sensations had lodged in my memory; so I can at pleasure lay by *that* idea, and take into my view that of the smell of a rose, or taste of sugar. But, if I turn my eyes at noon towards the sun, I cannot avoid the ideas which the light or sun then produces in me. So that there is a manifest difference between the ideas laid up in my memory (over which, if they

were there only, I should have constantly the same power to dispose of them, and lay them by at pleasure), and those which force themselves upon me, and I cannot avoid having. And therefore it must needs be some exterior cause, and the brisk acting of some objects without me, whose efficacy I cannot resist, that produces those ideas in my mind, whether I will or no. Besides, there is nobody who doth not perceive the difference in himself between contemplating the sun, as he hath the idea of it in his memory, and actually looking upon it, of which two, his perception is so distinct, that few of his ideas are more distinguishable one from another. And therefore he hath certain knowledge that they are not *both* memory, or the actions of his mind, and fancies only within him, but that actual seeing hath a cause without. . . .

Chapter XV   Of Probability

1. As *demonstration* is the showing the agreement or disagreement of two ideas, by the intervention of one or more proofs, which have a constant, immutable, and visible connexion one with another, so *probability* is nothing but the appearance of such an agreement or disagreement, by the intervention of proofs, whose connexion is not constant and immutable, or at least is not perceived to be so, but is, or appears for the most part to be so, and is enough to induce the mind to judge the proposition to be true or false, rather than the contrary. For example: in the demonstration of it a man perceives the certain, immutable connexion there is of equality between the three angles of a triangle, and those intermediate ones which are made use of to show their equality to two right ones; and so, by an intuitive knowledge of the agreement or disagreement of the intermediate ideas in each step of the progress, the whole series is continued with an evidence, which clearly shows the agreement or disagreement of those three angles in equality to two right ones, and thus he has certain knowledge that it is so. But another man, who never took the pains to observe the demonstration, hearing a mathematician, a man of credit, affirm the three

angles of a triangle to be equal to two right ones, assents to it, i.e., receives it for true, in which case the foundation of his assent is the probability of the thing; the proof being such as for the most part carries truth with it: The man on whose testimony he receives it, not being wont to affirm anything contrary to or besides his knowledge, especially in matters of this kind, so that that which causes his assent to this proposition, that the three angles of a triangle are equal to two right ones, that which makes him take these ideas to agree, without knowing them to do so, is the wonted veracity of the speaker in other cases, or his supposed veracity in this.

2. Our knowledge, as has been shown, being very narrow, and we not happy enough to find certain truth in everything which we have occasion to consider; most of the propositions we think, reason, discourse—nay, act upon, are such as we cannot have undoubted knowledge of their truth, yet some of them border so near upon certainty, that we make no doubt at all about them, but assent to them as firmly, and act, according to that assent, as resolutely as if they were infallibly demonstrated, and that our knowledge of them was perfect and certain. But there being degrees herein, from the very neighbourhood of certainty and demonstration, quite down to improbability and unlikeness, even to the confines of impossibility; and also degrees of assent from full assurance and confidence, quite down to conjecture, doubt, and distrust. I shall come now (having, as I think, found out *the bounds of human knowledge and certainty*), in the next place, to consider *the several degrees and grounds of probability, and assent or faith.* . . .

5. Probability wanting that intuitive evidence which infallibly determines the understanding and produces certain knowledge, the mind, if it *will proceed rationally*, ought to examine all the grounds of probability, and see how they make more or less for or against any proposition, before it assents to or dissents from it; and, upon a due balancing the whole, reject or receive it, with a more or less firm assent, proportionably to the preponderancy of the greater grounds of probability on one side or the other.

For Further Reflection

1. Has Locke successfully refuted the theory of innate ideas? How does he account for our intuitive certainty of the laws of logic or the reality of the self, two items which the rationalists consider innate knowledge?

2. Is Lockean empiricism plausible? Are our minds like empty paper until experience writes its message upon them? Note: Locke is not denying that the mind has capabilities and that some humans have greater capabilities to learn than others.

3. How does Locke deal with the problem of skepticism about sensory experience, which is so prominent in Descartes? Is he successful? Hume will disagree with him, as you will see in a later reading.

III.25   An Idealist Theory of Knowledge

GEORGE BERKELEY

George Berkeley (1685–1753), an Irish philosopher and Anglican bishop, was educated at Trinity College, Dublin, where he subsequently taught. A deeply committed Christian, he sought to reconcile science with his faith by proving that although matter does not exist, the laws of physics, being God's laws, govern a universe made up of ideas. To exist is to be perceived, and God is that being who, perceiving all, causes them to exist as ideas in his mind. This position is called *philosophical idealism*. Berkeley's principal works are *A Treatise on the Principles of Knowledge* (1710) and *Three Dialogues Between Hylas and Philonous* (1713), from which the present selection is taken.

In this dialogue, Berkeley defends his idealism, that is, his belief that only ideas exist. "To be is to be perceived"—to be is to be an idea in a mind—and hence matter existing apart from the mind does not exist. In this dialogue Hylas (from the Greek word for "matter") debates with Philonous (from the Greek "love of mind"). The unique thing about Berkeley's idealism is that unlike traditional idealism (for example, Plato's), it is not rationalistic. Berkeley does not propose that ideas exist independently, but rather assumes an empirical foundation. He agrees with Locke that all ideas originate in sense experience, and proceeds to show that all we ever experience is ideas. The only reality that exists to be known is perceivers and perceptions. To hold all of this ideal reality together one must posit a Divine mind who perceives us and hence causes our existence as ideas in his mind.

Study Questions

1. What is the most "extravagant opinion that ever entered into the mind of man"?
2. What is Philonous' response to Hylas' surprise at his views? How does he attempt to rebut the charge of skepticism?
3. What are sensible things according to Hylas and Philonous?

4. How does Philonous convince Hylas that heat and pain are ideas in the mind? Go through the argument step by step.
5. What is the point Philonous makes with the experiment of putting a cold and a warm hand into the same vessel of water?
6. What does Hylas mean by "to exist is one thing and to be perceived is another"?
7. Why does Philonous reject the notion of a material substratum, that is, matter that exists independently of our perceptions?
8. What conclusion does Philonous eventually force Hylas to accept regarding perceptions?
9. Why does the world continue to exist when we are not perceiving it, for example, when we are asleep?

HYLAS: YOU WERE REPRESENTED in last night's conversation as one who maintained the most extravagant opinion that ever entered into the mind of man, to wit, that there is no such thing as "material substance" in the world.

PHILONOUS: That there is no such thing as what philosophers call "material substance," I am seriously persuaded, but if I were made to see anything absurd or skeptical in this, I should then have the same reason to renounce this that I imagine I have now to reject the contrary opinion.

HYL.: What! Can anything be more fantastical, more repugnant to common sense or a more manifest piece of skepticism than to believe there is no such thing as matter?

PHIL.: Softly, good Hylas. What if it should prove that you, who hold there is, are, by virtue of that opinion, a greater skeptic and maintain more paradoxes and repugnances to common sense than I who believe no such thing? . . .

How comes it to pass then, Hylas, that you pronounce me a skeptic because I deny what you affirm, to wit, the existence of matter? Since, for aught you can tell, I am as peremptory in my denial as you in your affirmation.

HYL.: Hold, Philonous, I have been a little out in my definition; but every false step a man makes in discourse is not to be insisted on. I said indeed that a "skeptic" was one who doubted of everything, but I should have added: or who denies the reality and truth of things.

PHIL.: What things? Do you mean the principles and theorems of sciences? But these you know are universal intellectual notions, and consequently independent of matter; the denial therefore of this does not imply the denying them.

HYL.: I grant it. But are there no other things? What think you of distrusting the senses, of denying the real existence of sensible things, or pretending to know nothing of them. Is not this sufficient to denominate a man a skeptic?

PHIL.: Shall we therefore examine which of us it is that denies the reality of sensible things or professes the greatest ignorance of them, since, if I take you rightly, he is to be esteemed the greatest skeptic?

HYL.: That is what I desire.

PHIL.: What mean you by "sensible things"?

HYL.: Those things which are perceived by the senses. Can you imagine that I mean anything else?

PHIL.: Pardon me, Hylas, if I am desirous clearly to apprehend your notions, since this may much shorten our inquiry. Suffer me then to ask you this further question. Are those things only perceived by the senses which are perceived immediately? Or may those things properly be said to be "sensible" which are perceived immediately, or not without the intervention of others?

HYL.: I do not sufficiently understand you.

PHIL.: In reading a book, what I immediately perceive are the letters, but mediately, or by means of these, are suggested to my mind the

From George Berkeley, Three Dialogues Between Hylas and Philonous, *1713.*

notions of God, virtue, truth, etc. Now, that the letters are truly sensible things, or perceived by sense, there is no doubt; but I would know whether you take the things suggested by them to be so too.

HYL.: No, certainly; it were absurd to think God or virtue sensible things, though they may be signified and suggested to the mind by sensible marks with which they have an arbitrary connection.

PHIL.: It seems, then, that by "sensible things" you mean those only which can be perceived immediately by sense.

HYL.: Right.

PHIL.: Does it not follow from this that, though I see one part of the sky red, and another blue, and that my reason does thence evidently conclude there must be some cause of that diversity of colors, yet that cause cannot be said to be a sensible thing or perceived by the sense of seeing?

HYL.: It does.

PHIL.: In like manner, though I hear variety of sounds, yet I cannot be said to hear the causes of those sounds.

HYL.: You cannot.

PHIL.: And when by my touch I perceive a thing to be hot and heavy, I cannot say, with any truth or propriety, that I feel the cause of its heat or weight.

HYL.: To prevent any more questions of this kind, I tell you once for all that by "sensible things" I mean those only which are perceived by sense, and that in truth the senses perceive nothing which they do not perceive immediately, for they make no inferences. The deducing therefore of causes or occasions from effects and appearances, which alone are perceived by sense, entirely relates to reason.

PHIL.: This point then is agreed between us—that *sensible things are those only which are immediately perceived by sense.* You will further inform me whether we immediately perceive by sight anything besides light and colors and figures; or by hearing, anything but sounds; by the palate, anything besides tastes; by the smell, besides odors; or by the touch, more than tangible qualities.

HYL.: We do not.

PHIL.: It seems, therefore, that if you take away all sensible qualities, there remains nothing sensible?

HYL.: I grant it.

PHIL.: Sensible things therefore are nothing else but so many sensible qualities or combinations of sensible qualities?

HYL.: Nothing else.

PHIL.: Heat is then a sensible thing?

HYL.: Certainly.

PHIL.: Does the reality of sensible things consist in being perceived, or is it something distinct from their being perceived, and that bears no relation to the mind?

HYL.: To *exist* is one thing, and to be *perceived* is another.

PHIL.: I speak with regard to sensible things only; and of these I ask, whether by their real existence you mean a subsistence exterior to the mind and distinct from their being perceived?

HYL.: I mean a real absolute being, distinct from and without any relation to their being perceived.

PHIL.: Heat therefore, if it be allowed a real being, must exist without the mind?

HYL.: It must.

PHIL.: Tell me, Hylas, is this real existence equally compatible to all degrees of heat, which we perceive, or is there any reason why we should attribute it to some and deny it to others? And if there be, pray, let me know that reason.

HYL.: Whatever degree of heat we perceive by sense, we may be sure the same exists in the object that occasions it.

PHIL.: What! the greatest as well as the least?

HYL.: I tell you, the reason is plainly the same in respect of both: They are both perceived by sense; nay, the greater degree of heat is more sensibly perceived; and consequently, if there is any difference, we are more certain of its real existence than we can be of the reality of a lesser degree.

PHIL.: But is not the most vehement and intense degree of heat a very great pain?

HYL.: No one can deny it.

PHIL.: And is any unperceiving thing capable of pain or pleasure?

HYL.: No, certainly.

PHIL.: Is your material substance a senseless being or a being endowed with sense and perception?

HYL.: It is senseless, without doubt.

PHIL.: It cannot, therefore, be the subject of pain?

HYL.: By no means.

PHIL.: Nor, consequently, of the greatest heat perceived by sense, since you acknowledge this to be no small pain?

HYL.: I grant it.

PHIL.: What shall we say then of your external object: is it a material substance, or no?

HYL.: It is a material substance with the sensible qualities inhering in it.

PHIL.: How then can a great heat exist in it, since you own it cannot in a material substance? I desire you would clear this point.

HYL.: Hold, Philonous, I fear I was out in yielding intense heat to be a pain. It should seem rather that pain is something distinct from heat, and the consequence or effect of it.

PHIL.: Upon putting your hand near the fire, do you perceive one simple uniform sensation or two distinct sensations?

HYL.: But one simple sensation.

PHIL.: Is not the heat immediately perceived?

HYL.: It is.

PHIL.: And the pain?

HYL.: True.

PHIL.: Seeing therefore they are both immediately perceived at the same time, and the fire affects you only with one simple or uncompounded idea, it follows that this same simple idea is both the intense heat immediately perceived and the pain; and, consequently, that the intense heat immediately perceived is nothing distinct from a particular sort of pain.

HYL.: It seems so.

PHIL.: Again, try in your thoughts, Hylas, if you can conceive a vehement sensation to be without pain or pleasure.

HYL.: I cannot.

PHIL.: Or can you frame to yourself an idea of sensible pain or pleasure, in general, abstracted from every particular idea of heat, cold, tastes, smells, etc.?

HYL.: I do not find that I can.

PHIL.: Does it not therefore follow that sensible pain is nothing distinct from those sensations or ideas—in an intense degree?

HYL.: It is undeniable; and, to speak the truth, I begin to suspect a very great heat cannot exist but in a mind perceiving it.

PHIL.: What! Are you then in that *skeptical* state of suspense, between affirming and denying?

HYL.: I think I may be positive in the point. A very violent and painful heat cannot exist without the mind.

PHIL.: It has not therefore, according to you, any real being?

HYL.: I own it.

PHIL.: Is it therefore certain that there is no body in nature really hot?

HYL.: I have not denied there is any real heat in bodies. I only say there is no such thing as an intense real heat.

PHIL.: But did you not say before that all degrees of heat were equally real, or, if there was any difference, that the greater were more undoubtedly real than the lesser?

HYL.: True, but it was because I did not then consider the ground there is for distinguishing between them, which I now plainly see. And it is this: because intense heat is nothing else but a particular kind of painful sensation, and pain cannot exist but in a perceiving being, it follows that no intense heat can really exist in an unperceiving corporeal substance. But this is no reason why we should deny heat in an inferior degree to exist in such a substance.

PHIL.: But how shall we be able to discern those degrees of heat which exist only in the mind from those which exist without it?

HYL.: That is no difficult matter. You know the least pain cannot exist unperceived; whatever, therefore, degree of heat is a pain exists only in the mind. But as for all other degrees of heat nothing obliges us to think the same of them.

PHIL.: I think you granted before that no unperceiving being was capable of pleasure any more than of pain.

HYL.: I did.

PHIL.: And is not warmth, or a more gentle degree of heat than what causes uneasiness, a pleasure?

HYL.: What then?

PHIL.: Consequently, it cannot exist without the mind in an unperceiving substance, or body.

HYL.: So it seems.

PHIL.: Since, therefore, as well those degrees of heat that are not painful, as those that are, can exist only in a thinking substance, may we not conclude that external bodies are absolutely incapable of any degree of heat whatsoever?

HYL.: On second thoughts, I do not think it is so evident that warmth is a pleasure as that a great degree of heat is pain.

PHIL.: I do not pretend that warmth is as great a pleasure as heat is a pain. But if you grant it to be even a small pleasure, it serves to make good my conclusion.

HYL.: I could rather call it an "indolence." It seems to be nothing more than a privation of both pain and pleasure. And that such a quality or state as this may agree to an unthinking substance, I hope you will not deny.

PHIL.: If you are resolved to maintain that warmth, or a gentle degree of heat, is no pleasure, I know not how to convince you otherwise than by appealing to your own sense. But what think you of cold?

HYL.: The same that I do of heat. An intense degree of cold is a pain; for to feel a very great cold is to perceive a great uneasiness; it cannot therefore exist without the mind, but a lesser degree of cold may, as well as a lesser degree of heat.

PHIL.: Those bodies, therefore, upon whose application to our own we perceive a moderate degree of heat must be concluded to have a moderate degree of heat or warmth in them; and those upon whose application we feel a like degree of cold must be thought to have cold in them.

HYL.: They must.

PHIL.: Can any doctrine be true that necessarily leads a man into an absurdity?

HYL.: Without doubt it cannot.

PHIL.: Is it not an absurdity to think that the same thing should be at the same time both cold and warm?

HYL.: It is.

PHIL.: Suppose now one of your hands is hot, and the other cold, and that they are both at once put into the same vessel of water, in an intermediate state, will not the water seem cold to one hand, and warm to the other?

HYL.: It will.

PHIL.: Ought we not therefore, by your principles, to conclude it is really both cold and warm at the same time, that is, according to your own concession, to believe an absurdity?

HYL.: I confess it seems so.

PHIL.: Consequently, the principles themselves are false, since you have granted that no true principle leads to an absurdity.

HYL.: But, after all, can anything be more absurd than to say, *there is no heat in the fire?*

PHIL.: To make the point still clearer; tell me whether, in two cases exactly alike, we ought not to make the same judgment?

HYL.: We ought.

PHIL.: When a pin pricks your finger, does it not rend and divide the fibres of your flesh?

HYL.: It does.

PHIL.: And when a coal burns your finger, does it any more?

HYL.: It does not.

PHIL.: Since, therefore, you neither judge the sensation itself occasioned by the pin, nor anything like it to be in the pin, you should not, conformably to what you have now granted, judge the sensation occasioned by the fire, or anything like it, to be in the fire.

HYL.: Well, since it must be so, I am content to yield this point and acknowledge that heat and cold are only sensations existing in our minds. But there still remain qualities enough to secure the reality of external things.

PHIL.: But what will you say, Hylas, if it shall appear that the case is the same with regard to all other sensible qualities, and that they can no more be supposed to exist without the mind than heat and cold?

HYL.: Then, indeed, you will have done something to the purpose; but this is what I despair of seeing proved.

PHIL.: Let us examine them in order. What think you of tastes—do they exist without the mind, or no?

HYL.: Can any man in his senses doubt whether sugar is sweet or wormwood bitter?

PHIL.: Inform me, Hylas. Is a sweet taste a particular kind of pleasure or pleasant sensation, or is it not?

HYL.: It is.

PHIL.: And is not bitterness some kind of uneasiness or pain?

HYL.: I grant it.

PHIL.: If therefore sugar and wormwood are unthinking corporeal substances existing without the mind, how can sweetness and bitterness, that is, pleasure and pain, agree to them? . . .

HYL.: I see it is to no purpose to hold out, so I give up the cause as to those mentioned qualities, though I profess it sounds oddly to say that sugar is not sweet.

PHIL.: But, for your further satisfaction, take this along with you: that which at other times seems sweet shall, to a distempered palate, appear bitter, and nothing can be plainer than that divers persons perceive different tastes in the same food, since that which one man delights in, another abhors. And how could this be if the taste was something really inherent in the food?

HYL.: I acknowledge I know not how.

PHIL.: In the next place, odors are to be considered. And with regard to these I would fain know whether what has been said of tastes does not exactly agree to them? Are they not so many pleasing or displeasing sensations?

HYL.: They are.

PHIL.: Can you then conceive it possible that they should exist in an unperceiving thing?

HYL.: I cannot.

PHIL.: Or can you imagine that filth and ordure affect those brute animals that feed on

them out of choice with the same smells which we perceive in them?

HYL.: By no means.

PHIL.: May we not therefore conclude of smells, as of the other forementioned qualities, that they cannot exist in any but a perceiving substance or mind?

HYL.: I think so.

PHIL.: Then as to sounds, what must we think of them, are they accidents really inherent in external bodies or not?

HYL.: That they inhere not in the sonorous bodies is plain from hence; because a bell struck in the exhausted receiver of an air-pump sends forth no sound. The air, therefore, must be thought the subject of sound.

PHIL.: What reason is there for that, Hylas?

HYL.: Because, when any motion is raised in the air, we perceive a sound greater or less, in proportion to the air's motion; but without some motion in the air we never hear any sound at all.

PHIL.: And granting that we never hear a sound but when some motion is produced in the air, yet I do not see how you can infer from thence that the sound itself is in the air.

HYL.: It is this very motion in the external air that produces in the mind the sensation of sound. For, striking on the drum of the ear, it causes a vibration which by the auditory nerves being communicated to the brain, the soul is thereupon affected with the sensation called "sound."

PHIL.: What! is sound then a sensation?

HYL.: I tell you, as perceived by us, it is a particular sensation in the mind.

PHIL.: And can any sensation exist without the mind?

HYL.: No, certainly.

PHIL.: How then can sound, being a sensation, exist in the air if by the "air" you mean a senseless substance existing without the mind?

HYL.: You must distinguish, Philonous, between sound as it is perceived by us, and as it is in itself; or (which is the same thing) between the sound we immediately perceive and that which exists without us. The former, indeed, is a particular kind of sensation, but the latter is merely a vibrative or undulatory motion in the air.

PHIL.: I thought I had already obviated that distinction by the answer I gave when you were applying it in a like case before. But, to say no more of that, are you sure then that sound is really nothing but motion?

HYL.: I am.

PHIL.: Whatever, therefore, agrees to real sound may with truth be attributed to motion?

HYL.: It may.

PHIL.: It is then good sense to speak of "motion" as of a thing that is *loud, sweet, acute,* or *grave.*

HYL.: I see you are resolved not to understand me. Is it not evident those accidents or modes belong only to sensible sound, or sound in the common acceptation of the word, but not to sound in the real and philosophic sense, which, as I just now told you, is nothing but a certain motion of the air?

PHIL.: It seems then there are two sorts of sound—the one vulgar, or that which is heard, the other philosophical and real?

HYL.: Even so.

PHIL.: And the latter consists in motion?

HYL.: I told you so before.

PHIL.: Tell me, Hylas, to which of the senses, think you, the idea of motion belongs? To the hearing?

HYL.: No, certainly, but to the sight and touch.

PHIL.: It should follow then that, according to you, real sounds may possibly be *seen* or *felt,* but never *heard.*

HYL.: Look you, Philonous, you may, if you please, make a jest of my opinion, but that will not alter the truth of things. I own, indeed, the inferences you draw me into sound something oddly, but common language, you know, is framed by, and for the use of, the vulgar. We must not therefore wonder if expressions adapted to exact philosophic notions seem uncouth and out of the way.

PHIL.: Is it come to that? I assure you I imagine myself to have gained no small point since you make so light of departing from common phrases and opinions, it being a main part of our inquiry to examine whose notions are widest of the common road and most repugnant to the general sense of the world. But can you think it no more than a philosophical paradox to say that "real sounds are never heard," and that the idea of them is obtained by some other sense? And is there nothing in this contrary to nature and the truth of things?

HYL.: To deal ingenuously, I do not like it. And, after the concessions already made, I had as well grant that sounds, too, have no real being without the mind. . . .

I frankly own, Philonous, that it is in vain to stand out any longer. Colors, sounds, tastes, in a word, all those termed "secondary qualities," have certainly no existence without the mind. But by this acknowledgment I must not be supposed to derogate anything from the reality of matter or external objects; seeing it is no more than several philosophers maintain, who nevertheless are the farthest imaginable from denying matter. For the clearer understanding of this you must know sensible qualities are by philosophers divided into "primary" and "secondary." The former are extension, figure, solidity, gravity, motion, and rest. And these they hold exist really in bodies. The latter are those above enumerated, or, briefly, all sensible qualities besides the primary, which they assert are only so many sensations or ideas existing nowhere but in the mind. But all this, I doubt not, you are already apprised of. For my part I have been a long time sensible there was such an opinion current among philosophers, but was never thoroughly convinced of its truth till now.

PHIL.: You are still then of opinion that *extension* and *figures* are inherent in external unthinking substances?

HYL.: I am.

PHIL.: But what if the same arguments which are brought against secondary qualities will hold good against these also?

HYL.: Why then I shall be obliged to think they too exist only in the mind. . . .

I acknowledge, Philonous, that, upon a fair observation of what passes in my mind, I can discover nothing else but that I am a thinking being affected with variety of sensations; neither is it possible to conceive how a sensation should exist in an unperceiving substance. But then, on the other hand, when I look on sensible things in a different view, considering them as so many modes and qualities, I find it necessary to suppose a material *substratum,* without which they cannot be conceived to exist.

PHIL.: "Material substratum" call you it? Pray, by which of your senses came you acquainted with that being?

HYL.: It is not itself sensible; its modes and qualities only being perceived by the senses.

PHIL.: I presume then it was by reflection and reason you obtained the idea of it?

HYL.: I do not pretend to any proper positive idea of it. However, I conclude it exists because qualities cannot be conceived to exist without a support.

PHIL.: It seems then you have only a relative notion of it, or that you conceive it not otherwise than by conceiving the relation it bears to sensible qualities? . . .

HYL.: Right.

PHIL.: Be pleased, therefore, to let me know wherein that relation consists.

HYL.: Is it not sufficiently expressed in the term "substratum" or "substance"?

PHIL.: If so, the word "substratum" should import that it is spread under the sensible qualities or accidents?

HYL.: True.

PHIL.: And consequently under extension?

HYL.: I own it.

PHIL.: It is therefore somewhat in its own nature distinct from extension?

HYL.: I tell you extension is only a mode, and matter is something that supports modes. And is it not evident the thing supported is different from the thing supporting?

PHIL.: So that something distinct from, and exclusive of, extension is supposed to be the *substratum* of extension?

HYL.: Just so.

PHIL.: Answer me, Hylas, can a thing be spread without extension, or is not the idea of extension necessarily included in *spreading*?

HYL.: It is.

PHIL.: Whatsoever therefore you suppose spread under anything must have in itself an extension distinct from the extension of that thing under which it is spread?

HYL.: It must.

PHIL.: Consequently, every corporeal substance being the *substratum* of extension must have in itself another extension by which it is qualified to be a *substratum,* and so on to infinity? And I ask whether this be not absurd in itself and repugnant to what you granted just now, to wit, that the *substratum* was something distinct from and exclusive of extension?

HYL.: Aye, but, Philonous, you take me wrong. I do not mean that matter is *spread* in a gross literal sense under extension. The word "substratum" is used only to express in general the same thing with "substance."

PHIL.: Well then, let us examine the relation implied in the term "substance." Is it not that it stands under accidents?

HYL.: The very same.

PHIL.: But that one thing may stand under or support another, must it not be extended?

HYL.: It must.

PHIL.: Is not therefore this supposition liable to the same absurdity with the former?

HYL.: You still take things in a strict literal sense; that is not fair, Philonous.

PHIL.: I am not for imposing any sense on your words; you are at liberty to explain them as you please. Only, I beseech you, make me understand something by them. You tell me matter supports or stands under accidents. How! Is it as your legs support your body?

HYL.: No, that is the literal sense.

PHIL.: Pray let me know any sense, literal or not literal, that you understand it in—How long must I wait for an answer, Hylas?

HYL.: I declare I know not what to say. I once thought I understood well enough what was meant by matter's supporting accidents. But now, the more I think on it, the less can I comprehend it; in short, I find that I know nothing of it.

PHIL.: It seems then you have no idea at all, neither relative nor positive, of matter? You know neither what it is in itself nor what relation it bears to accidents?

HYL.: I acknowledge it . . .

Other men may think as they please, but for your part you have nothing to reproach me with. My comfort is you are as much a skeptic as I am.

PHIL.: There, Hylas, I must beg leave to differ from you.

HYL.: What! Have you all along agreed to the premises, and do you now deny the conclusion and leave me to maintain those paradoxes by myself which you led me into? This surely is not fair.

PHIL.: I deny that I agreed with you in those notions that led to skepticism. You indeed said the *reality* of sensible things consisted in an *absolute existence* out of the minds of spirits, or distinct from their being perceived. And, pursuant to this notion of reality, you are obliged to deny sensible things any real existence; that is, according to your own definition, you profess yourself a skeptic. But I neither said nor thought the reality of sensible things was to be defined after that manner. To me it is evident, for the reasons you allow of, that sensible things cannot exist otherwise than in a mind or spirit. Whence I conclude, not that they have no real existence, but that, seeing they depend not on my thought and have an existence distinct from being perceived by me, *there must be some other mind wherein they exist.* As sure, therefore, as the sensible world really exists, so sure is there an infinite omnipresent Spirit, who contains and supports it.

HYL.: What! this is no more than I and all Christians hold; nay, and all others, too, who believe there is a God and that He knows and comprehends all things.

PHIL.: Aye, but here lies the difference. Men commonly believe that all things are known or perceived by God, because they believe the being of a God; whereas I, on the other side, immediately and necessarily conclude the being of a God, because all sensible things must be perceived by him.

HYL.: But so long as we all believe the same thing, what matter is it how we come by that belief?

PHIL.: But neither do we agree in the same opinion. For philosophers, though they acknowledge all corporeal beings to be perceived by God, yet they attribute to them an absolute subsistence distinct from their being perceived by any mind whatever, which I do not. Besides, is there no difference between saying, *there is a God, therefore He perceives all things,* and saying, *sensible things do really exist; and if they really exist, they are necessarily perceived by an infinite mind: therefore there is an infinite mind, or God?* This furnishes you with a direct and immediate demonstration, from a most evident principle, of the *being of a God.* Divines and philosophers had proved beyond all controversy, from the beauty and usefulness of the several parts of the creation, that it was the workmanship of God. But that—setting aside all help of astronomy and natural philosophy, all contemplation of the contrivance, order and adjustment of things—an infinite mind should be necessarily inferred from the bare *existence* of the sensible world is an advantage peculiar to them only who have made this easy reflection, that the sensible world is that which we perceive by our several senses; and that nothing is perceived by the senses besides ideas; and that no idea or archetype of an idea can exist otherwise than in a mind.

For Further Reflection

1. Do you agree with Berkeley that only ideas exist? Does it seem obvious to you that matter really does exist? If you disagree with Berkeley, can you show where he has made an error in his argument?

2. According to Berkeley there is no sound independent of our hearing it and no reality but our experiencing it. Does this mean that when we leave our rooms, they disappear? There is an old Oxford limerick on this point:

> There was a young man who said, "God
> Must think it exceedingly odd
> If he finds that this tree
> Continues to be,
> When there's no one about in the quad."

> Dear Sir, your astonishment's odd
> I'm always about in the quad,
> And that's why the tree
> Continues to be,
> Since observed by,
>
> > Yours faithfully,
> >
> > > God

The question is, In whose mind does God exist? Does the notion of God fit into Berkeley's system?

The Origin of Our Ideas III.26

DAVID HUME

In this selection from *An Enquiry Concerning Human Understanding* (1748), we see an extension of the empiricism begun with Locke. We also get a glimpse of the source of Hume's expansive skepticism. He argues that all of the contents of the mind are derived from sense experience. Every idea we have comes from the data of our senses, what he calls *perceptions*. So he declares that we can have no knowledge unless we can trace its origin back to perceptions. If a philosophical concept is not in some way derived from the senses, it is absolutely meaningless.

(A biographical note on Hume precedes Reading II.9.)

Study Questions

1. What is the origin of our ideas? How does Hume distinguish ideas from impressions?
2. What does Hume say about the reputed "unbounded liberty" of thought? How free is it?
3. What are the practical implications of Hume's empiricism? What effect would it have on metaphysical speculation?

OF THE ORIGIN OF IDEAS

EVERY ONE WILL READILY ALLOW, that there is a considerable difference between the perceptions of the mind, when a man feels the pain of excessive heat, or the pleasure of moderate warmth, and when he afterwards recalls to his memory this sensation, or anticipates it by his imagination. These faculties may mimic or copy the perceptions of the senses; but they never can entirely reach the force and vivacity of the original sentiment. The utmost we say of them, even when they operate with greatest vigor, is, that they represent their object in so lively a manner, that we could *almost* say we feel or see it: But, except the mind be disordered by disease or madness, they never can arrive at such a pitch of vivacity, as to render these perceptions altogether undistinguishable. All the colors of poetry, however splendid, can never paint natural objects in such a manner as to make the description be taken for a real landscape. The most lively thought is still inferior to the dullest sensation.

We may observe a like distinction to run through all the other perceptions of the mind. A man in a fit of anger, is actuated in a very different manner from one who only thinks of that emotion. If you tell me, that any person is in love, I easily understand your meaning, and form a just conception of his situation, but never can mistake that conception for the real disorders and agitations of the passion. When we reflect on our past sentiments and affections, our thought is a faithful mirror, and copies its objects truly; but the colors which it employs are faint and dull, in comparison of those in which our original perceptions were clothed. It requires no nice discernment or metaphysical head to mark the distinction between them.

Here therefore we may divide all the perceptions of the mind into two classes or species, which are distinguished by their different degrees of force and vivacity. The less forcible and lively are commonly denominated *Thoughts* or *Ideas.* The other species want a name in our language, and in most others; I suppose, because it was not requisite for any, but philosophical purposes, to rank them under a general term or appellation. Let us, therefore, use a little freedom, and call them *Impressions;* employing that word in a sense somewhat different from the usual. By the term *impression,* then, I mean all our more lively perceptions, when we hear, or see, or feel, or love, or hate, or desire, or will. And impressions are distinguished from ideas, which are the less lively perceptions, of which we are conscious, when we reflect on any of those sensations or movements above mentioned.

Nothing, at first view, may seem more unbounded than the thought of man, which not only escapes all human power and authority, but is not even restrained within the limits of nature and reality. To form monsters, and join incongruous shapes and appearances, costs the imagination no more trouble than to conceive the most natural and familiar objects. And

---

Reprinted from David Hume, An Enquiry Concerning Human Understanding *(Oxford: Clarendon Press, 1748).*

while the body is confined to one planet, along which it creeps with pain and difficulty, the thought can in an instant transport us into the most distant regions of the universe, or even beyond the universe, into the unbounded chaos, where nature is supposed to lie in total confusion. What never was seen, or heard of, may yet be conceived; nor is any thing beyond the power of thought, except what implies an absolute contradiction.

But though our thought seems to possess this unbounded liberty, we shall find, upon a nearer examination, that it is really confined within very narrow limits, and that all this creative power of the mind amounts to no more than the faculty of compounding, transposing, augmenting, or diminishing the materials afforded us by the senses and experience. When we think of a golden mountain, we only join two consistent ideas, *gold,* and *mountain,* with which we were formerly acquainted. A virtuous horse we can conceive; because, from our own feeling, we can conceive virtue; and this we may unite to the figure and shape of a horse, which is an animal familiar to us. In short, all the materials of thinking are derived either from our outward or inward sentiment: The mixture and composition of these belongs alone to the mind and will. Or, to express myself in philosophical language, all our ideas or more feeble perceptions are copies of our impressions or more lively ones.

To prove this, the two following arguments will, I hope, be sufficient. First, when we analyze our thoughts or ideas, however compounded or sublime, we always find that they resolve themselves into such simple ideas as were copied from a precedent feeling or sentiment. Even those ideas, which, at first view, seem the most wide of this origin, are found, upon a nearer scrutiny, to be derived from it. The idea of God, as meaning an infinitely intelligent, wise, and good Being, arises from reflecting on the operations of our own mind, and augmenting, without limit, those qualities of goodness and wisdom. We may prosecute this enquiry to what length we please,

where we shall always find that every idea which we examine is copied from a similar impression. Those who would assert that this position is not universally true nor without exception, have only one, and that an easy method of refuting it; by producing that idea, which, in their opinion, is not derived from this source. It will then be incumbent on us, if we would maintain our doctrine, to produce the impression, or lively perception, which corresponds to it.

Secondly. If it happen, from a defect of the organ, that a man is not susceptible of any species of sensation, we always find that he is as little susceptible of the correspondent ideas. A blind man can form no notion of colors; a deaf man of sounds. Restore either of them that sense in which he is deficient; by opening this new inlet for his sensations, you also open an inlet for the ideas; and he finds no difficulty in conceiving these objects. . . .

Here, therefore, is a proposition, which not only seems, in itself, simple and intelligible, but, if a proper use were made of it, might render every dispute equally intelligible, and banish all that jargon, which has so long taken possession of metaphysical reasonings, and drawn disgrace upon them. All ideas, especially abstract ones, are naturally faint and obscure: the mind has but a slender hold of them: they are apt to be confounded with other resembling ideas; and when we have often employed any term, though without a distinct meaning, we are apt to imagine it has a determinate idea annexed to it. On the contrary, all impressions, that is, all sensations, either outward or inward, are strong and determined, nor is it easy to fall into any error or mistake with regard to them. When we entertain, therefore, any suspicion that a philosophical term is employed without any meaning or idea (as is but too frequent), we need but enquire, *from what impression is that supposed idea derived?* And if it be impossible to assign any, this will serve to confirm our suspicion. By bringing ideas into so clear a light we may reasonably hope to remove all dispute, which may arise, concerning their nature and reality.

For Further Reflection

1. Hume's empiricism is more radical than Locke's because it leads to skepticism over metaphysical issues which Locke thought safe (for example, the nature of the self, causality, the existence of God). Hume closes the book from which our selection comes with these words: "By way of conclusion to these reflections on diverse questions: When we run over libraries, persuaded of the principles here expounded, what havoc must we make? If we take in hand any volume, of divinity or metaphysics, for instance, let us ask: Does it contain any reasoning concerning quantity or number? No. Does it contain any experimental (probable) reasoning concerning matter of fact? No. Commit it then to the flames: for it can contain nothing but sophistry and illusion." Are you convinced by Hume's reasoning? If not, how would you go about arguing against him?

2. How might a rationalist try to refute Hume?

III.27   An Argument Against Skepticism

JOHN HOSPERS

John Hospers is professor emeritus of philosophy at the University of Southern California and editor of the *Pacific Journal of Philosophy*. He is the founder of the Libertarian Party and was that party's candidate for president of the United States in 1972. He is the author of several textbooks as well as *Libertarianism: A Political Philosophy for Tomorrow* (1971). In this essay, Hospers first analyzes the different uses of the word "know" and then sets forth the conditions of descriptive knowledge. After that he distinguishes a weak sense of knowledge from a strong sense and uses this distinction to argue against the claims of skepticism.

Study Questions

1. What are the three senses of "know" that Hospers describes? Which is the most important philosophically?
2. What are the three conditions for propositional knowledge?
3. Why is it important to have good evidence before one can rightly be said to know?
4. What are the weak and strong senses of knowledge?
5. How does this distinction bear on the claims of skepticism?

I. REQUIREMENTS FOR KNOWING

THE WORD "KNOW" IS SLIPPERY. It is not always used in the same way. Here are some of its principal uses:

[*Senses of "know"*] 1. Sometimes when we talk about knowing, we are referring to *acquaintance* of some kind. For example, "Do you know Richard Smith?" means approximately the same

From John Hospers, An Introduction to Philosophical Analysis, *2nd ed. © 1967, pp. 143–145, 148–155. Reprinted by permission of Pearson Education, Inc., Upper Saddle River, NJ.*

as "Are you acquainted with Richard Smith? (have you met him? etc.) . . ."

2. Sometimes we speak of knowing *how:* Do you know how to ride a horse, do you know how to use a soldering iron? We even use a colloquial noun, "know-how," in talking about this. Knowing how is an *ability*—we know how to ride a horse if we have the ability to ride a horse, and the test of whether we have the ability is whether in the appropriate situation we can perform the activity in question. . . .

3. But by far the most frequent use of the word "know"—and the one with which we shall be primarily concerned—is the *propositional* sense: "I know that . . ." where the word "that" is followed by a proposition: "I know that I am now reading a book," "I know that I am an American citizen," and so on. There is some relation between this last sense of "know" and the earlier ones. We cannot be acquainted with Smith without knowing some things about him (without knowing *that* certain propositions about him are true), and it is difficult to see how one can know *how* to swim without knowing some true propositions about swimming, concerning what you must do with your arms and legs when in the water. (But the dog knows how to swim, though presumably he knows no propositions about swimming.) . . .

[*Conditions for knowing that*] Now, what is required for us to know in this third and most important sense? Taking the letter p to stand for any proposition, what requirements must be met in order for one to assert truly that he knows p? There are, after all, many people who claim to know something when they don't; so how can one separate the rightful claims to know from the mistaken ones?

a. *p must be true.* The moment you have some reason to believe that a proposition is not true, this immediately negates a person's claim to know it: You can't know p if p isn't true. If I say, "I know p, but p is not true," my statement is self-contradictory, for part of what is involved in knowing p is that p is true. Similarly, if I say, "He knows p, but p is not true," this too is self-contradictory. It may be that I *thought* I knew p;

but if p is false, I didn't really know it. I only thought I did. If I nevertheless claim to know p, while admitting that p is false, my hearers may rightly conclude that I have not yet learned how to use the word "know." This is already implicit in our previous discussion, for what is it that you know about p when you know p? You know *that p is true,* of course; the very formulation gives away the case: Knowing p is knowing that p is true. . . .

But the truth-requirement, though necessary, is not sufficient. There are plenty of true propositions, for example in nuclear physics, that you and I do not know to be true unless we happen to be specialists in that area. But the fact that they are true does not imply that we know them to be true. . . .

b. *Not only must p be true: We must believe that p is true.* This may be called the "subjective requirement": We must have a certain attitude toward p—not merely that of wondering or speculating about p, but positively *believing* that p is true. "I know that p is true, but I don't believe that it is" would not only be a very peculiar thing to say, it would entitle our hearers to conclude that we had not learned in what circumstances to use the word "know." There may be numerous statements that you believe but do not know to be true, but there can be none which you know to be true but don't believe, since believing is a part (a defining characteristic) of knowing.

"I know p" implies "I believe p," and "He knows p" implies "He believes p," for believing is a defining characteristic of knowing. But believing p is *not* a defining characteristic of p's being true: p can be true even though neither he nor I nor anyone else believes it. (The earth was round even before anyone believed that it was.) There is no contradiction whatever in saying, "He believed p (that is, believed it to be true), but p is not true." Indeed, we say things of this kind all the time: "He believes that people are persecuting him, but of course it isn't true." . . .

We have now discussed two requirements for knowing, an "objective" one (p must be true) and a "subjective" one (one must believe p). Are these sufficient? Can you be said to know something if you believe it and if what you believe is true? If so, we can simply define knowledge as true belief, and that will be the end of the matter.

Unfortunately, however, the situation is not so simple. True belief is not yet knowledge. A proposition may be true, and you may believe it to be true, and yet you may not *know* it to be true. Suppose you believe that there are sentient beings on Mars, and suppose that in the course of time, after space-travelers from the earth have landed there, your belief turns out to be true. The statement was true at the time you uttered it, and you also believed it at the time you uttered it—but did you *know* it to be true at the time you uttered it? Certainly not, we would be inclined to say; you were not in a position to know. It was a lucky guess. Even if you had *some* evidence that it was true, you didn't *know* that it was true at the time you said it. Some further condition, therefore, is required to prevent a lucky guess from passing as knowledge. . . .

c. *You must have evidence for p (reason to believe p).* When you guessed which tosses of the coin would be heads, you had no reason to believe that your guesses would be correct, so you did not *know.* But after you watched all the tosses and carefully observed which way the coin tossed each time, then you knew. You had the evidence of your senses—as well as of people around you, and photographs if you wished to take them—that this throw was heads, that one tails, and so on. Similarly, when you predict on the basis of tonight's red sunset that tomorrow's weather will be fair, you don't yet *know* that your prediction will be borne out by the facts; you have some reason (perhaps) to believe it, but you cannot be sure. But tomorrow when you go outdoors and see for yourself what the weather is like, you do know for sure; when tomorrow comes you have the full evidence before you, which you do not yet have tonight. Tomorrow "the evidence is in"; tonight, it is not knowledge but only an "educated guess."

[*Problem*] This, then, is our third requirement—evidence. But at this point our troubles begin.

How much evidence must there be? "Some evidence" won't suffice as an answer: there may be *some* evidence that tomorrow will be sunny, but you don't yet know it. How about "all the evidence that is available"? But this won't do either; all the evidence that is now available may not be enough. All the evidence that is now available is far from sufficient to enable us to know whether there are conscious beings on other planets. We just don't know, even after we have examined all the evidence at our disposal.

How about "enough evidence to give us *good reason* to believe it"? But how much evidence is this? I may have known someone for years and found him to be scrupulously honest during all that time; by virtually any criterion, this would constitute good evidence that he will be honest the next time—and yet he may not be; suppose that the next time he steals someone's wallet. I had good reason to believe that he would remain honest, but nevertheless I didn't *know* that he would remain honest, for it was not true. We are all familiar with cases in which someone had good reason to believe a proposition that nevertheless turned out to be false.

What then *is* sufficient? We are now tempted to say, "Complete evidence—all the evidence there could ever be—the works, everything." But if we say this, let us notice at once that there are very few propositions whose truth we can claim to know. Most of those propositions that in daily life we claim to know without the slightest hesitation we would *not* know according to this criterion. For example, we say, "I know that if I were to let go of this pencil, it would fall," and we don't have the slightest hesitation about it; but although we may have excellent evidence (pencils and other objects have always fallen when let go), we don't have *complete* evidence, for we have not yet observed the outcome of letting go of it *this* time. To take an even more obvious case, we say, "I know that there is a book before me now," but we have not engaged in every possible observation that would be relevant to determining the truth of this statement: We have not examined the object (the one we take to be a book) from *all* angles (and since there are an infinite number of angles, who could?), and even if we have looked at it steadily for half an hour, we have not done so for a hundred hours, or a million; and yet it would *seem* (though some have disputed this, as we shall see) that if one observation provides evidence, a thousand observations should provide more evidence—and when could the accumulation of evidence end? . . .

We might, nevertheless, stick to our definition and say that we really do *not* know most of the propositions that in daily life we claim to know: Perhaps I don't *know* that this is a book before me, that I am now indoors and not outdoors, that I am now reading sentences written in the English language, or that there are any other people in the world. But this is a rather astounding claim and needs to be justified. We are all convinced that we know these things: We act on them every day of our lives, and if we were asked outside a philosophy classroom whether we knew them, we would say "yes" without hesitation. Surely we cannot accept a definition of "know" that would practically define knowledge out of existence? But if not, what alternative have we?

"Perhaps we don't have to go so far as to say 'all the evidence,' 'complete evidence,' and so on. All we have to say is that we must have "*adequate* evidence." But when is the evidence adequate? Is anything less than "all the evidence there could ever be" adequate? "Well, adequate for enabling us to know." But this little addition to our definition lands us in a circle. We are trying to define "know," and we cannot in doing so employ the convenient phrase "enough to enable us to know"—for the last word in this definition is the very one we are trying to define. But once we have dropped the phrase "to know," we are left with our problem once more: How much evidence is adequate evidence? Is it adequate when anything less than *all* the evidence is in? If not all the evidence is in, but only 99.99 percent of it, couldn't that .01 percent go contrary to the rest of it and require us to conclude that the proposition might not be true after all, and that therefore we didn't know it? Surely it has happened often enough

that a statement that we thought we knew, perhaps even would have staked our lives on, turned out in the end to be false, or just doubtful. But in that case we didn't really *know* it after all: The evidence was good, even overwhelming, but yet not good enough, not really adequate, for it was not enough to guarantee the truth of the proposition. Can we know *p* with anything less than *all* the evidence there ever could be for *p*?

II. STRONG AND WEAK SENSES OF "KNOW"

[*Disputes About Knowing*] In daily life we say we know—not just believe or surmise, but *know*—that heavier-than-air objects fall, that snow is white, that we can read and write, and countless other things. If someone denies this, and no fact cited by the one disputant suffices to convince the other, we may well suspect that there is a verbal issue involved: In this case, that they are operating on two different meanings of "know," because they construe the third requirement—the evidence requirement—differently.

[*Case 1*] Suppose I say, "There is a bookcase in my office," and someone challenges this assertion. I reply, "I *know* that there is a bookcase in my office. I put it there myself, and I've seen it there for years. In fact, I saw it there just two minutes ago when I took a book out of it and left the office to go into the classroom." Now suppose we both go to my office, take a look, and there is the bookcase, exactly as before. "See, I *knew* it was here," I say. "Oh no," he replies, "you *believed with good reason* that it was still there, because you had seen it there often before and you didn't see or hear anyone removing it. But you didn't *know* it was there when you said it, for at that moment you were in the classroom and not in your office."

At this point, I may reply, "But I did know it was there, even when I said it. I knew it because *(1) I believed it, (2) I had good grounds on which to base the belief, and (3) the belief was true*. And I would call it knowledge whenever these three conditions are fulfilled. This is the way we use the word 'know' every day of our lives. One knows those true propositions that one believes with good reason. And when I said the bookcase was still in my office, I was uttering one of those propositions."

But now my opponent may reply, "But you still didn't know it. You had good reason to say it, I admit, for you had not seen or heard anyone removing it. You had good reason, but not *sufficient* reason. The evidence you gave was still compatible with your statement being false—and if it was false, you of course did not *know* that it was true. [*Case 2*] Suppose that you had made your claim to knowledge, and I had denied your claim, and we had both gone into your office, and to your great surprise (and mine too) the bookcase was no longer there. Could you *then* have claimed to know that it was still there?"

"Of course not. The falsity of a statement always invalidates the claim to know it. If the bookcase had not been there, I would not have been entitled to say that I knew it was there; my claim would have been mistaken."

"Right—it would have been mistaken. But now please note that the only difference between the two cases is that in the first case the bookcase was there and in the second case it wasn't. *The evidence in the two cases was exactly the same.* You had exactly the same reason for saying that the bookcase was still there in the *second* case (when we found it missing) that you did in the *first* case (when we found it still there). And since you—as you yourself admit—didn't know it in the second case, you couldn't have known it in the first case either. You believed it with good reason, but you didn't *know* it."

[*Solution*] Here my opponent may have scored an important point; he may have convinced me that since I admittedly didn't know in the second case I couldn't have known in the first case either. But here I may make an important point in return: "My belief was the same in the two cases; the evidence was the same in the two cases (I had seen the bookcase two minutes before, had heard or seen no one removing it). The only difference

was that in the first case the bookcase was there and in the second case it wasn't (*p* was true in the first case, false in the second). But *this doesn't show that I didn't know* in the first case. What it does show is that *although I might have been mistaken, I wasn't mistaken.* Had the bookcase not been there, I couldn't have claimed to know that it was; but since the bookcase in fact *was* still there, I *did* know, although (on the basis of the evidence I had) I *might* have been mistaken."

"Yes, it turned out to be true—you were lucky. But as we both agree, a lucky guess isn't the same as knowledge."

"But this wasn't just a lucky guess. I had excellent reasons for believing that the bookcase was still there. So the evidence requirement was fulfilled."

"No, it wasn't. You had good reason, excellent reason, but not *sufficient* reason—both times—for believing that the bookcase was still there. But in the second case it wasn't there, so you didn't know; therefore, in the first case where your evidence was *exactly the same,* you didn't know either; you just believed it with good reason, but that wasn't enough: Your reason wasn't sufficient, and so you didn't *know*."

Now the difference in the criterion of knowing between the two disputants begins to emerge. According to me, I did know *p* in the first case because my belief was based on excellent evidence and was also true. According to my opponent, I did not know *p* in the first case because my evidence was still less than complete—I wasn't in the room seeing or touching the bookcase when I made the statement. It seems, then, that I am operating with a less demanding definition of "know" than he is. I am using "know" in the *weak* sense, in which I know a proposition when I believe it, have good reason for believing it, and it is true. But he is using "know" in a more demanding sense: He is using it in the *strong* sense, which requires that in order to know a proposition, it must be true, I must believe it, and I must have absolutely *conclusive* evidence in favor of it.

[*Examples*] Let us contrast these two cases: Suppose that after a routine medical examination the excited doctor reports to me that the X-ray photographs show that I have no heart. I should tell him to get a new machine. I should be inclined to say that the fact that I have a heart is one of the few things that I can count on as absolutely certain. I can feel it beat. I know it's there. Furthermore, how could my blood circulate if I didn't have one? Suppose that later on I suffer a chest injury and undergo a surgical operation. Afterwards the astonished surgeons solemnly declare that they searched my chest cavity and found no heart, and that they made incisions and looked about in other likely places but found it not. They are convinced that I am without a heart. They are unable to understand how circulation can occur or what accounts for the thumping in my chest. But they are in agreement and obviously sincere, and they have clear photographs of my interior spaces. What would be my attitude? Would it be to insist that they were all mistaken? I think not. I believe that I should eventually accept their testimony and the evidence of the photographs. I should consider to be false what I now regard as an absolute certainty. [When I say I know I have a heart, I know it in the weak sense.]

Suppose that as I write this paper someone in the next room were to call out to me, "I can't find an ink-bottle; is there one in the house?" I should reply, "Here is an ink-bottle." If he said in a doubtful tone, "Are you sure? I looked there before," I should reply, "Yes, I know there is; come and get it."

Now could it turn out to be false that there is an ink-bottle directly in front of me on this desk? Many philosophers have thought so. They would say that many things could happen of such a nature that if they did happen it would be proved that I am deceived. I agree that many extraordinary things could happen, in the sense that there is no logical absurdity in the supposition. It could happen that when I next reach for this ink-bottle my hand should seem to pass *through* it and I should not feel the contact of any object. It could happen that in the next moment the ink-bottle will suddenly vanish from sight; or that I should find myself under a tree in the garden with no ink-bottle about; or that one or more persons should enter this room and declare with apparent sincerity that they see no ink-bottle on this desk; or that a photograph taken now of the top of the desk should clearly show all of the objects on it except the ink-bottle. Having admitted that these things *could happen,* am I compelled to admit that if they did happen, then it would be proved that there is no ink-bottle here *now?* Not at all. I could say that when my hand seemed to pass through the ink-bottle I should *then* be suffering from hallucination; that if the ink-bottle suddenly vanished, it would have miraculously ceased to exist; that the other persons were conspiring to drive me mad, or were themselves victims of remarkable concurrent hallucinations; that the camera possessed some strange flaw or that there was trickery in developing the negative: . . . Not only do I not *have* to admit that those extraordinary occurrences would be evidence that there is no ink-bottle here; the fact is that I *do not* admit it. There is nothing whatever that could happen in the next moment or the next year that would by me be called *evidence* that there is not an ink-bottle here now. No future experience or investigation could prove to me that I am mistaken. Therefore, if I were to say, "I know that there is an ink-bottle here," I should be using "know" in the strong sense.[1]

It is in the weak sense that we use the word "know" in daily life, as when I say I know that I have a heart, that if I let go of this piece of chalk it will fall, that the sun will rise tomorrow, and so on. I have excellent reason (evidence) to believe all these things, evidence so strong that (so we say) it amounts to certainty. And yet there are events that could conceivably occur which, if they did occur, would cast doubt on the beliefs or even show them to be false. . . .

III. ARGUMENT AGAINST SKEPTICISM

[*Skepticism*] But the philosopher is apt to be more concerned with "know" in the strong sense. He wants to inquire whether there are any propositions that we can know without the shadow of a doubt will never be proved false, or even rendered dubious to the smallest degree. "You can say," he will argue, "and I admit that it would be good English usage to say, that you know that you have a heart and that the sun is more than 90 million miles from the earth. But you don't know it until you have absolutely conclusive evidence, and you must admit that the evidence you have, while very strong, is not conclusive. So I shall say, using 'know' in the strong sense, that you do not know these propositions. I want then to ask what propositions can be known in the strong sense, the sense that puts the proposition forever past the possibility of doubt."

And on this point many philosophers have been quite skeptical; they have granted few if any propositions whose truth we could know in the strong sense. . . . Such a person is a *skeptic*. We claim (he says) to know many things about the world, but in fact none of these propositions can be known for certain. What are we to say of the skeptic's position?

[*Criticism*] Let us first note that in the phrase "know for certain" the "for certain" is redundant—how can we know except for certain? If it is less than certain, how can it be knowledge? We do, however, use the word "certain" ambiguously: (1) Sometimes we say "I am certain," which just means that I have a feeling of certainty about it—"I feel certain that I locked the door of the apartment"—and of course the feeling of certainty is no guarantee that the statement is true. People have very strong feelings of certainty about many propositions that they have no evidence for at all, particularly if they want to believe them or are consoled by believing them. The phrase "feeling certain," then, refers simply to a psychological state, whose existence in no way guarantees that what the person feels certain about is true. But (2) sometimes when we say "I am certain" we mean that it *is* certain—in other words, that we *do* know the proposition in question to be true. This, of course, is the sense of "certain" that is of interest to philosophers (the

first sense is of more interest to psychiatrists in dealing with patients). Thus we could reformulate our question, "Is anything certain?" or "Are any propositions certain?"

"I can well understand," one might argue, "how you could question some statements, even most statements. But if you carry on this merry game until you have covered *all* statements, you are simply mistaken, and I think I can show you why. You may see someone in a fog or in a bad light and not know (not be certain) whether he has a right hand. But don't you know that *you* have a right hand? There it is! Suppose I now raise my hand and say, 'Here is a hand.' Now you say to me, 'I doubt that there's a hand.' But what evidence do you want? What does your doubt consist of? You don't believe your eyes, perhaps? Very well, then come up and touch the hand. You still aren't satisfied? Then keep on looking at it steadily and touching it, photograph it, call in other people for testimony if you like. If after all this you still say it isn't certain, what more do you want? Under what conditions would you admit that it *is* certain, that you *do* know it? I can understand your doubt when there is some condition left unfulfilled, some test left uncompleted. At the beginning, perhaps you doubted that *if* you tried to touch my hand you would find anything there to touch; but then you did touch, and so you resolved *that* doubt. You resolved further doubts by calling in other people and so on. You performed all the relevant tests, and they turned out favorably. So now, at the end of the process, what is it that you doubt? Oh, I know what you *say:* 'I still doubt that that's a hand.' But isn't this saying 'I doubt' now an empty formula? I can no longer attach any content to that so-called doubt, for there is nothing left to doubt; you yourself *cannot specify any further test that, if performed, would resolve your doubt.* 'Doubt' now becomes an empty word. You're not doubting now that *if* you raised your hand to touch mine, you would touch it, or that *if* Smith and others were brought in, they would also testify that this is a hand—we've already gone through all that. So what is it specifically that you doubt? What possible test is there the negative result of which you fear? I submit that there isn't any. You are confusing a situation in which doubt is understandable (*before* you made the tests) with the later situation in which it isn't, for it has all been dispelled. . . .

"But your so-called doubt becomes meaningless when there is nothing left to doubt—when the tests have been carried out and their results are all favorable. Suppose a physician examines a patient and says, 'It's probable that you have an inflamed appendix.' Here one can still doubt, for the signs may be misleading. So the physician operates on the patient, finds an inflamed appendix and removes it, and the patient recovers. *Now* what would be the sense of the physician's saying, 'It's *probable* that he had an inflamed appendix'? If seeing it and removing it made it only *probable,* what would make it certain? Or you are driving along and you hear a rapid regular thumping sound and you say, 'It's probable that I have a flat tire.' So far you're right; it's only probable—the thumping might be caused by something else. So you go out and have a look, and there is the tire, flat. You find a nail embedded in it, change the tire, and then resume your ride with no more thumping. Are you *now* going to say, 'It's merely *probable* that the car had a flat tire'? But if given all those conditions it would be merely probable, what in the world would make it certain? Can you describe to me the circumstances in which you would say it's certain? If you can't, then the phrase 'being certain' has no meaning as you are using it. You are simply using it in such a special way that it has no application at all, and there is no reason at all why anyone else should follow your usage. In daily life we have a very convenient and useful distinction between the application of the words 'probable' and 'certain.' We say appendicitis is probable *before* the operation, but when the physician has the patient's appendix visible before him on the operating table, now it's certain—that's just the kind of situation in which we apply the word 'certain,' as opposed to 'probable.' Now you, for some reason, are so fond of the word 'probable' that you want to use it for everything—you use it to describe *both* the preoperative and postoperative situations, and the word 'certain' is left without any application at all. But this is nothing but a *verbal manipulation* on your part. You have changed nothing; you have only taken, as it were, two bottles with different contents, and instead of labeling them differently ('probable' and 'certain'), as the rest of us do, you put the same label ('probable') on both of them! What possible advantage is there in this? It's just verbal contrariness. And since you have preempted the word 'probable' to cover *both* the situations, we now have to devise a *different* pair of words to mark the perfectly obvious distinction between the situation *before* the surgery and the situation *during* the surgery—the same difference we previously marked by the words 'probable' and 'certain' until you used the word 'probable' to apply to both of them. What gain is there in this *verbal manipulation* of yours?" . . .

NOTE

1. Norman Malcolm, "Knowledge and Belief," in *Knowledge and Certainty,* pp. 66–68.

For Further Reflection

1. Do you think that Hospers' conditions for knowing are adequate? Do you see how they differ from Descartes', who would only allow absolute certainty to count as knowledge? Who is right?

2. Is Hospers correct in saying that the skeptic holds up an unrealistic standard (too strong a sense) of knowledge?

3. In Hospers' sense of knowledge can we ever "know that we know"? Or can we be justified only in believing that we know? If this is so, then should the focus of discussion be on the adequacy of justified belief?

III.B   Truth, Rationality, and Cognitive Relativism

To say that what is, is not, or that what is not is, is false; but to say that what is, is, and what is not, is not, is true. (Aristotle 384–322 B.C.)

Man is the measure of all things,
Both of things that are,
Man is the measure that they are,
And of the things that are not,
Man is the measure that they are not.
(Protagoras the Sophist, 5th century B.C.)

Recently a professor, call him D, from the English department at a major university gave a talk on political biases in university curriculum, arguing that curricula was oppressive to women and minorities. After the speech, a philosopher came up to D and pointed out that he, D, had contradicted himself in his speech. The English professor responded, saying, "So, what's wrong with that? Look young man, I'm sure you know more logic than I do, but I know more about logic than you do! I know that it's a phallologocentric instrument for the oppression of minorities."

Two diametrically opposed views on truth exist in contemporary culture, especially among intellectuals in academia. One position, call it **cognitive realism**, accepts one or another version of the correspondence theory of truth and holds the classical view that some things exist independently of whether anyone thinks about them. Some propositions are true whether or not anyone believes them. There are mind-independent facts, and they exist whether or not anyone believes them. Examples of this are the propositions "2 + 2 = 4," "the solar system has more than one planet," and "pigs can't fly."

The other position, which is called **cognitive relativism** or "anti-realism," holds that there are no mind-independent facts or truths. Cognitive relativists generally combine anti-realism with a pragmatic notion of truth. A pragmatic theory of truth defines truth in terms of usefulness or workability. The proposition "2 + 2 = 4" is part of a human mathematical invention, and the proposition that "the solar system has more than one planet" can be analyzed into specific concepts, which are human inventions: the idea of a "planet," a "sun," a "system," and "more." Similarly, "pigs can't fly" depends on the way we divide up reality. A culture might not have a concept of "pig" or "fly," or it might have several "pig-concepts" or "fly-concepts." We invent reality via our conceptual-linguistic systems. Many cognitive relativists would not go as far as our English professor (D) who believes even the laws of logic are inventions, for they might agree that there are formal constraints on what can be intelligibly said to be within a system of thought and that contradictions are formal criteria of exclusion. But other intellectuals would bite the bullet, as it were, and deny that contradictions need be false. The classic expression of the pragmatic theory of truth is given by William James in our second reading.

The realists trace their lineage back to Plato, who distinguished reality from appearance, and Aristotle, who (see the earlier quotation) defined truth as a *correspondence* between statements and facts. In our readings, Bertrand Russell (III.28) explains and defends the correspondence theory of truth.

The new cognitive relativists can trace their roots back to Protagoras, who said "Man is the measure of all things"—that is, what we think is true is so. Their beliefs are also reminiscent of Berkeley's idealism (see Reading III.25), with the important difference that they reject idealism, as well as Berkeley's God. They agree with Berkeley against Locke that we cannot build a bridge from our conceptual schemes to the world itself, but they reject a God's-eye perspective wherein reality is unified ideally. Instead, we have many worlds, many realities, many perspectives. In the words of Nietzsche, who is quoted approvingly:

> Truth is a mobile army of metaphors, metonyms, and anthropomorphisms—in short a sum of human relations, which have been enhanced, transposed, and embellished poetically and rhetorically and which after long use seem firm, canonical, and obligatory to a people.

In our third reading, Richard Rorty identifies his version of this anti-realism with the pragmatism of the American philosophers William James (1842–1910)—our second reading—and John Dewey (1859–1952). Rorty characterizes it as a civilized ethnocentrism, one which chooses social solidarity over objectivity and rejects the notion that truth is the correspondence between our ideas and an independent reality. There is no privileged perspective and no unifying reality, so there is no absolute knowledge, no Truth (with a capital "T"). These ideas must be deconstructed. What is left is our ways of justifying our beliefs, "warranted assertibility," as Dewey would say. So the division between truth and opinion collapses and truth becomes what our peers will let us get away with. For a fuller defense of his epistemological pragmatism you should see his *Philosophy and the Mirror of Nature* (1979), where he develops his thesis that truth, rather than being a correspondence between our ideas and the world, is what we agree on, what it is better to believe. In the present selection, "Dismantling Truth: Solidarity versus Objectivity," Rorty applies his thesis to the idea that science seeks to secure objectivity, arguing that science, objectivity, and truth need to be replaced or reinterpreted by more pragmatic, ethnocentric notions.

In our fourth reading Daniel Dennett begins with the analogy of researchers introducing a deadly virus into a developing country. He goes on to apply the analogy to postmodernists like Richard Rorty, whose irrational cognitive relativism undermines intellectual well-being.

In our fifth reading Harvey Siegel lays out what many philosophers believe is the most fundamental criticism of cognitive relativism (or epistemological relativism, as he calls it): the doctrine is "self-referentially incoherent."

The Correspondence Theory of Truth III.28

BERTRAND RUSSELL

In this selection, Russell first distinguishes between knowledge by acquaintance (for example, knowledge by appearances, such as "I seem to see a red book" or "I am in pain" or "I think therefore I am") and knowledge by description (knowledge of truths, such as your knowing that you are really seeing a red book or that your pain is caused by having twisted your ankle). Knowledge by acquaintance is infallible, for believing it makes the proposition true. But the same is not the case for descriptive knowledge claims, for your beliefs could be false. Thus, descriptive knowledge is dualistic—it has the properties of truth and falsity as opposites—whereas knowledge by acquaintance is monistic and does not admit such opposites.

Russell goes on to specify the conditions for an adequate theory of truth and shows how the correspondence theory meets these conditions, whereas the coherence theory does not.

(A biographical sketch of Russell precedes Reading I.4.)

Study Questions

1. How is knowledge of truths unlike knowledge of things?
2. What are the three conditions a theory of truth must meet?
3. What are the two major difficulties with the coherence theory of truth?
4. What is the proper role for coherence in a theory of truth?
5. What is Russell's theory of belief as relational? How does this fit into his theory of truth?
6. What does Russell mean by saying, "Minds do not create truth or falsehood"?

OUR KNOWLEDGE OF TRUTHS, unlike our knowledge of things, has an opposite, namely *error*. So far as things are concerned, we may know them or not know them, but there is no positive state of mind which can be described as erroneous knowledge of things, so long, at any rate, as we confine ourselves to knowledge by acquaintance. Whatever we are acquainted with must be something: We may draw wrong inference from our acquaintance, but the acquaintance itself cannot be deceptive. Thus there is no dualism as regards acquaintance. But as regards knowledge of truths, there is a dualism. We may believe what is false as well as what is true. We know that on very many subjects different people hold different and incompatible opinions: Hence some beliefs must be erroneous. Since erroneous beliefs are often held just as strongly as true beliefs, it becomes a difficult question how they are to be distinguished from true beliefs. How are we to know, in a given case, that our belief is not erroneous? That is a

question of the very greatest difficulty, to which no completely satisfactory answer is possible. There is, however, a preliminary question which is rather less difficult, and that is: What do we *mean* by truth and falsehood? It is this preliminary question which is to be considered in this chapter. . . .

. . . We are not asking how we can know whether a belief is true or false: We are asking what is meant by the question whether a belief is true or false. It is to be hoped that a clear answer to this question may help us to obtain an answer to the question what beliefs are true, but for the present we ask only "What is truth?" and "What is falsehood?" not "What beliefs are true?" and "What beliefs are false?" It is very important to keep these different questions entirely separate, since any confusion between them is sure to produce an answer which is not really applicable to either.

There are three points to observe in the attempt to discover the nature of truth, three requisites which any theory must fulfill.

From *Bertrand Russell*, The Problems of Philosophy *(Oxford: Oxford University Press, 1912).*
Reprinted by permission of Oxford University Press.

(1) Our theory of truth must be such as to admit of its opposite, falsehood. A good many philosophers have failed adequately to satisfy this condition: they have constructed theories according to which all our thinking ought to have been true and have then had the greatest difficulty in finding a place for falsehood. In this respect our theory of belief must differ from our theory of acquaintance, since in the case of acquaintance it was not necessary to take account of any opposite.

(2) It seems fairly evident that if there were no beliefs there could be no falsehood, and no truth either, in the sense in which truth is correlative to falsehood. If we imagine a world of mere matter, there would be no room for falsehood in such a world, and although it would contain what may be called "facts," it would not contain any truths, in the sense in which truths are things of the same kind as falsehoods. In fact, truth and falsehood are properties of beliefs and statements: hence a world of mere matter, since it would contain no beliefs or statements, would also contain no truth or falsehood.

(3) But, as against what we have just said, it is to be observed that the truth or falsehood of a belief always depends upon something which lies outside the belief itself. If I believe that Charles I died on the scaffold, I believe truly, not because of any intrinsic quality of my belief, which could be discovered by merely examining the belief, but because of an historical event which happened two and a half centuries ago. If I believe that Charles I died in his bed, I believe falsely: no degree of vividness in my belief, or of care in arriving at it, prevents it from being false, again because of what happened long ago, and not because of any intrinsic property of my belief. Hence, although truth and falsehood are properties of beliefs, they are properties dependent upon the relations of the beliefs to other things, not upon any internal quality of the beliefs.

The third of the above requisites leads us to adopt the view—which has on the whole been commonest among philosophers—that truth consists in some form of correspondence between belief and fact. It is, however, by no means an easy matter to discover a form of correspondence to which there are no irrefutable objections. By this partly—and partly by the feeling that, if truth consists in a correspondence of thought with something outside thought, thought can never know when truth has been attained—many philosophers have been led to try to find some definition of truth which shall not consist in relation to something wholly outside belief. The most important attempt at a definition of this sort is the theory that truth consists in *coherence*. It is said that the mark of falsehood is failure to cohere in the body of our beliefs, and that it is the essence of a truth to form part of the completely rounded system which is The Truth.

There is, however, a great difficulty in this view, or rather two great difficulties. The first is that there is no reason to suppose that only *one* coherent body of beliefs is possible. It may be that, with sufficient imagination, a novelist might invent a past for the world that would perfectly fit on to what we know, and yet be quite different from the real past. In more scientific matters, it is certain that there are often two or more hypotheses which account for all the known facts on some subject, and although, in such cases, men of science endeavor to find facts which will rule out all the hypotheses except one, there is no reason why they should always succeed.

In philosophy, again, it seems not uncommon for two rival hypotheses to be both able to account for all the facts. Thus, for example, it is possible that life is one long dream, and that the outer world has only that degree of reality that the objects of dreams have; but although such a view does not seem inconsistent with known facts, there is no reason to prefer it to the commonsense view, according to which other people and things do really exist. Thus coherence as the definition of truth fails because there is no proof that there can be only one coherent system.

The other objection to this definition of truth is that it assumes the meaning of "coherence" known, whereas, in fact, "coherence" presupposes the truth of the laws of logic. Two propositions are coherent when both may be true and are incoherent when one at least must be false. Now in order to know whether two propositions can both be true, we must know such truths as the law of contradiction. For example, the two propositions "this tree is a beech" and "this tree is not a beech," are not coherent, because of the law of contradiction. But if the law of contradiction itself were subjected to the test of coherence, we should find that, if we choose to suppose it false, nothing will any longer be incoherent with anything else. Thus the laws of logic supply the skeleton or framework within which the test of coherence applies, and they themselves cannot be established by this test.

For the above two reasons, coherence cannot be accepted as giving the *meaning* of truth, though it is often a most important *test* of truth after a certain amount of truth has become known.

Hence we are driven back to *correspondence with fact* as constituting the nature of truth. It remains to define precisely what we mean by "fact," and what is the nature of the correspondence which must subsist between belief and fact, in order that belief may be true.

In accordance with our three requisites, we have to seek a theory of truth which (1) allows truth to have an opposite, namely falsehood, (2) makes truth a property of beliefs, but (3) makes it a property wholly dependent upon the relation of the beliefs to outside things.

The necessity of allowing for falsehood makes it impossible to regard belief as a relation of the mind to a single object, which could be said to be what is believed. If belief were so regarded, we should find that, like acquaintance, it would not admit of the opposition of truth and falsehood, but would have to be always true. This may be made clear by examples. Othello believes falsely that Desdemona loves Cassio. We cannot say that this belief consists in a relation to a single object, "Desdemona's love for Cassio," for if there were

such an object, the belief would be true. There is in fact no such object, and therefore Othello cannot have any relation to such an object. Hence his belief cannot possibly consist in a relation to this object.

It might be said that his belief is a relation to a different object, namely "that Desdemona loves Cassio"; but it is almost as difficult to suppose that there is such an object as this, when Desdemona does not love Cassio, as it was to suppose that there is "Desdemona's love for Cassio." Hence it will be better to seek for a theory of belief which does not make it consist in a relation of the mind to a single object.

It is common to think of relations as though they always held between *two* terms, but in fact this is not always the case. Some relations demand three terms, some four, and so on. Take, for instance, the relation "between." So long as only two terms come in, the relation "between" is impossible: three terms are the smallest number that render it possible. York is between London and Edinburgh; but if London and Edinburgh were the only places in the world, there could be nothing which was between one place and another. Similarly *jealousy* requires three people: there can be no such relation that does not involve three at least. Such a position as "A wishes B to promote C's marriage with D" involves a relation of four terms; that is to say, A and B and C and D all come in, and the relation involved cannot be expressed otherwise than in a form involving all four. Instances might be multiplied indefinitely, but enough has been said to show that there are relations which require more than two terms before they can occur.

The relation involved in *judging* or *believing* must, if falsehood is to be duly allowed for, be taken to be a relation between several terms, not between two. When Othello believes that Desdemona loves Cassio, he must not have before his mind a single object, "Desdemona's love for Cassio," or "that Desdemona loves Cassio," for that would require that there should be objective falsehoods, which subsist independently of any minds; and this, though not logically refutable, is a theory to be avoided if possible. Thus it is easier to account for falsehood if we take judgment to be a relation in which the mind and the various objects concerned all occur severally; that is to say, Desdemona and loving and Cassio must all be terms in the relation which subsists when Othello believes that Desdemona loves Cassio. This relation, therefore, is a relation of four terms, since Othello also is one of the terms of the relation. When we say that it is a relation of four terms, we do not mean that Othello has a certain relation to Desdemona, and has the same relation to loving and also to Cassio. This may be true of some other relation than believing; but believing, plainly, is not a relation which Othello has to *each* of the three terms concerned, but to *all* of them together: there is only one example of the relation of believing involved, but this one example knits together four terms. Thus the actual occurrence, at the moment when Othello is entertaining his belief, is that the relation called "believing" is knitting together into one complex whole the four terms Othello, Desdemona, loving, and Cassio. What is called belief or judgment is nothing but this relation of believing or judging, which relates a mind to several things other than itself. An *act* of belief or of judgment is the occurrence between certain terms at some particular time, of the relation of believing or judging.

We are now in a position to understand what it is that distinguishes a true judgment from a false one. For this purpose we will adopt certain definitions. In every act of judgment there is a mind which judges, and there are terms concerning which it judges. We will call the mind the *subject* in the judgment, and the remaining terms the *objects*. Thus, when Othello judges that Desdemona loves Cassio, Othello is the subject, while the objects are Desdemona and loving and Cassio. The subject and the objects together are called the *constituents* of the judgment. It will be observed that the relation of judging has what is called a "sense" or "direction." We may say, metaphorically, that it puts its objects in a certain

order, which we may indicate by means of the order of the words in the sentence. (In an inflected language, the same thing will be indicated by inflections, e.g., by the difference between nominative and accusative.) Othello's judgment that Cassio loves Desdemona differs from his judgment that Desdemona loves Cassio, in spite of the fact that it consists of the same constituents, because the relation of judging places the constituents in a different order in the two cases. Similarly, if Cassio judges that Desdemona loves Othello, the constituents of the judgment are still the same, but their order is different. This property of having a "sense" or "direction" is one which the relation of judging shares with all other relations. The "sense" of relations is the ultimate source of order and series and a host of mathematical concepts; but we need not concern ourselves further with this aspect.

We spoke of the relation called "judging" or "believing" as knitting together into one complex whole the subject and the objects. In this respect, judging is exactly like every other relation. Whenever a relation holds between two or more terms, it unites the terms into a complex whole. If Othello loves Desdemona, there is such a complex whole as "Othello's love for Desdemona." The terms united by the relation may be themselves complex, or may be simple, but the whole which results from their being united must be complex. Wherever there is a relation which relates certain terms, there is a complex object formed of the union of those terms; and conversely, wherever there is a complex object, there is a relation which relates its constituents. When an act of believing occurs, there is a complex, in which "believing" is the uniting relation, and subject and objects are arranged in a certain order by the "sense" of the relation of believing. Among the objects, as we saw in considering "Othello believes that Desdemona loves Cassio," one must be a relation—in this instance, the relation "loving." But this relation, as it occurs in the act of believing, is not the relation which creates the unity of the complex whole consisting of the subject and the objects.

The relation "loving," as it occurs in the act of believing, is one of the objects—it is a brick in the structure, not the cement. The cement is the relation "believing." When the belief is *true,* there is another complex unity, in which the relation which was one of the objects of the belief relates the other objects. Thus, e.g., if Othello believes *truly* that Desdemona loves Cassio, then there is a complex unity, "Desdemona's love for Cassio," which is composed exclusively of the *objects* of the belief, in the same order as they had in the belief, with the relation which was one of the objects occurring now as the cement that binds together the other objects of the belief. On the other hand, when a belief is *false,* there is no such complex unity composed only of the objects of the belief. If Othello believes *falsely* that Desdemona loves Cassio, then there is no such complex unity as "Desdemona's love for Cassio."

Thus a belief is *true* when it *corresponds* to a certain associated complex, and *false* when it does not. Assuming, for the sake of definiteness, that the objects of the belief are two terms and a relation, the terms being put in a certain order by the "sense" of the believing, then if the two terms in that order are united by the relation into a complex, the belief is true; if not, it is false. This constitutes the definition of truth and falsehood that we were in search of. Judging or believing is a certain complex unity of which a mind is a constituent; if the remaining constituents, taken in the order which they have in the belief, form a complex unity, then the belief is true; if not, it is false.

Thus although truth and falsehood are properties of beliefs, yet they are in a sense extrinsic properties, for the condition of the truth of a belief is something not involving beliefs, or (in general) any mind at all, but only the *objects* of the belief. A mind, which believes, believes truly when there is a *corresponding* complex not involving the mind, but only its objects. This correspondence ensures truth, and its absence entails falsehood. Hence we account simultaneously for the two facts that beliefs (*a*) depend on mind for their *existence,* (*b*) do not depend on minds for their *truth*.

We may restate our theory as follows: If we take such a belief as "Othello believes that Desdemona loves Cassio," we will call Desdemona and Cassio the *object-terms,* and loving the *object-relation.* If there is a complex unity "Desdemona's love for Cassio," consisting of the object-terms related by the object-relation in the same order as they have in the belief, then this complex unity is called the *fact corresponding to the belief.* Thus a belief is true when there is a corresponding fact and is false when there is no corresponding fact. . . .

. . . Minds do not *create* truth or falsehood. They create beliefs, but when once the beliefs are created, the mind cannot make them true or false, except in the special case where they concern future things which are within the power of the person believing, such as catching trains. What makes a belief true is a *fact,* and this fact does not (except in exceptional cases) in any way involve the mind of the person who has the belief.

For Further Reflection

1. Is the correspondence theory of truth plausible? Do you think that it adequately conveys what we mean by "truth," or is something missing?

2. Some opponents of the correspondence theory say it has a certain usefulness for trivial statements like "the cat is on the mat," where correspondence between words and things is plausible, but it loses its appeal when applied to more complex matters such as "there is no such thing as natural motion" or "the universe is infinite" (examples of Richard Rorty). How would a defender of the correspondence theory respond to this criticism?

The Pragmatic Theory of Truth   III.29

WILLIAM JAMES

After a brief introduction to pragmatism by way of a fascinating example of resolving a dispute about the correct characterization of a squirrel's behavior, James sets forth his view of truth. He holds that truth is dynamic rather than static and is to be defined in terms of beliefs that are useful or satisfying. Unlike the "intellectualists" (James' characterization of the traditional static approaches to the question of truth, viz., the correspondence theorists) truth is in process—still becoming and changing. Yesterday's truth is today's falsehood, and today's truth is tomorrow's half-truth. What really matters is what you can *do* with an idea, what difference it makes to your life, its (in James' term) "cash-value."

(A biographical note on William James precedes Reading II.17.)

Study Questions

1. What is the dispute regarding the squirrel's behavior?
2. How does James' solution illustrate the meaning of pragmatism?
3. What is the problem with the dictionary definition of truth?
4. What is James' argument against the "intellectualists" (that is, e.g., philosophers who believe in the correspondence theory)?
5. How does James define true and false ideas?
6. What does he mean by "Truth lives . . . for the most part on a credit system"? Does this make truth relative to the beholder?
7. How does James interpret the idea that truth is an agreement with reality?
8. What does James mean by, "'The true' . . . is only the expedient in the way of our thinking, just as 'the right' is only the expedient in the way of our behaving" (by "expedient" James means prudent or suitable to achieve success)? What is the significance of the phrase that it is expedient "in the long run and on the whole"?
9. How does an idea become retrospectively true?
10. What is the relationship between the good and the true?

WHAT PRAGMATISM MEANS

SOME YEARS AGO, being with a camping party in the mountains, I returned from a solitary ramble to find every one engaged in a ferocious metaphysical dispute. The *corpus* of the dispute was a squirrel— a live squirrel supposed to be clinging to one side of a tree-trunk; while over against the tree's opposite side a human being was imagined to stand.

This human witness tries to get sight of the squirrel by moving rapidly round the tree, but no matter how fast he goes, the squirrel moves as fast in the same direction, and always keeps the tree between himself and the man, so that never a glimpse of him is caught. The resultant metaphysical problem now is this: *Does the man go round the squirrel or not?* He goes round the tree, sure enough, and the squirrel is on the tree; but does he

From *William James*, Pragmatism, A New Name for Some Old Ways of Thinking (*Lectures II and VI*), New York, 1907.

go round the squirrel? In the unlimited leisure of the wilderness, discussion had been worn threadbare. Every one had taken sides, and was obstinate; and the numbers on both sides were even. Each side, when I appeared, therefore appealed to me to make it a majority. Mindful of the scholastic adage that whenever you meet a contradiction you must make a distinction, I immediately sought and found one, as follows: "Which party is right," I said, "depends on what you *practically mean* by 'going round' the squirrel. If you mean passing from the north of him to the east, then to the south, then to the west, and then to the north of him again, obviously the man does go round him, for he occupies these successive positions. But if on the contrary you mean being first in front of him, then on the right of him, then behind him, then on his left, and finally in front again, it is quite as obvious that the man fails to go round him, for by the compensating movements the squirrel makes, he keeps his belly turned towards the man all the time, and his back turned away. Make the distinction, and there is no occasion for any further dispute. You are both right and both wrong according as you conceive the verb 'to go round' in one practical fashion or the other."

Although one or two of the hotter disputants called my speech a shuffling evasion, saying they wanted no quibbling or scholastic hair-splitting, but meant just plain honest English "round," the majority seemed to think that the distinction had assuaged the dispute.

I tell this trivial anecdote because it is a peculiarly simple example of what I wish now to speak of as *the pragmatic method*. The pragmatic method is primarily a method of settling metaphysical disputes that otherwise might be interminable. Is the world one or many?—fated or free?—material or spiritual?—here are notions either of which may or may not hold good of the world; and disputes over such notions are unending. The pragmatic method in such cases is to try to interpret each notion by tracing its respective practical consequences. What difference would it practically make to any one if this notion rather than that notion were true? If no practical difference whatever can be traced, then

the alternatives mean practically the same thing, and all dispute is idle. Whenever a dispute is serious, we ought to be able to show some practical difference that must follow from one side or the other's being right.

A glance at the history of the idea will show you still better what pragmatism means. The term is derived from the same Greek word pragma, meaning action, from which our words "practice" and "practical" come. It was first introduced into philosophy by Mr. Charles Peirce in 1878. In an article entitled "How to Make Our Ideas Clear," in the *Popular Science Monthly* for January of that year. Mr. Peirce, after pointing out that our beliefs are really rules for action, said that, to develop a thought's meaning, we need only determine what conduct it is fitted to produce: that conduct is for us its sole significance. And the tangible fact at the root of all our thought-distinctions, however subtle, is that there is no one of them so fine as to consist in anything but a possible difference of practice. To attain perfect clearness in our thoughts of an object, then, we need only consider what conceivable effects of a practical kind the object may involve—what sensations we are to expect from it, and what reactions we must prepare. Our conception of these effects, whether immediate or remote, is then for us the whole of our conception of the object, so far as that conception has positive significance at all. . . .

[Next James turns to the pragmatist theory of truth.]

PRAGMATISM'S CONCEPTION OF TRUTH

I fully expect to see the pragmatist view of truth run through the classic stages of a theory's career. First, you know, a new theory is attacked as absurd; then it is admitted to be true, but obvious and insignificant; finally it is seen to be so important that its adversaries claim that they themselves discovered it. Our doctrine of truth is at present in the first of these three stages, with symptoms of the second stage having begun in certain quarters. I wish that this lecture might help it beyond the first stage in the eyes of many of you.

Truth, as any dictionary will tell you, is a property of certain of our ideas. It means their "agreement," as falsity means their "disagreement," with "reality." Pragmatists and intellectualists both accept this definition as a matter of course. They begin to quarrel only after the question is raised as to what may precisely be meant by the term "agreement," and what by the term "reality," when reality is taken as something for our ideas to agree with.

In answering these questions the pragmatists are more analytic and painstaking, the intellectualists more offhand and irreflective. The popular notion is that a true idea must copy its reality. Like other popular views, this one follows the analogy of the most usual experience. Our true ideas of sensible things do indeed copy them. Shut your eyes and think of yonder clock on the wall, and you get just such a true picture or copy of its dial. But your idea of its "works" (unless you are a clockmaker) is much less of a copy, yet it passes muster, for it in no way clashes with the reality. Even though it should shrink to the mere word "works," that word still serves you truly; and when you speak of the "time-keeping function" of the clock, or of its spring's "elasticity," it is hard to see exactly what your ideas can copy.

You perceive that there is a problem here. Where our ideas cannot copy definitely their object, what does agreement with that object mean? Some idealists seem to say that they are true whenever they are what God means that we ought to think about that subject. Others hold the copy-view all through, and speak as if our ideas possessed truth just in proportion as they approach to being copies of the Absolute's eternal way of thinking.

These views, you see, invite pragmatistic discussion. But the great assumption of the intellectualists is that truth means essentially an inert static relation. When you've got your true idea of anything, there's an end of the matter.

You're in possession; you *know;* you have fulfilled your thinking destiny. You are where you ought to be mentally; you have obeyed your categorical imperative; and nothing more need follow on that climax of your rational destiny. Epistemologically you are in stable equilibrium.

Pragmatism, on the other hand, asks its usual question. "Grant an idea or belief to be true," it says, "what concrete difference will its being true make in any one's actual life? How will the truth be realized? What experiences will be different from those which would obtain if the belief were false? What, in short, is the truth's cash-value in experiential terms?"

The moment pragmatism asks this question, it sees the answer: *True ideas are those that we can assimilate, validate, corroborate and verify. False ideas are those that we cannot.* That is the practical difference it makes to us to have true ideas; that, therefore, is the meaning of truth, for it is all that truth is known-as.

This thesis is what I have to defend. The truth of an idea is not a stagnant property inherent in it. Truth *happens* to an idea. It *becomes* true, is *made* true by events. Its verity *is* in fact an event, a process: the process namely of its verifying itself, its veri-*fication.* Its validity is the process of its valid-*ation.*

But what do the words verification and validation themselves pragmatically mean? They again signify certain practical consequences of the verified and validated idea. It is hard to find any one phrase that characterizes these consequences better than the ordinary agreement-formula—just such consequences being what we have in mind whenever we say that our ideas "agree" with reality. They lead us, namely, through the acts and other ideas which they instigate, into or up to, or towards, other parts of experience with which we feel all the while—such feeling being among our potentialities—that the original ideas remain in agreement. The connexions and transitions come to us from point to point as being progressive, harmonious, satisfactory. This function of agreeable leading is what we mean by an idea's verification. . . .

. . . The possession of true thoughts means everywhere the possession of invaluable instruments of action; and that our duty to gain truth, so far from being a blank command from out of the blue, or a "stunt" self-imposed by our intellect, can account for itself by excellent practical reasons.

The importance to human life of having true beliefs about matters of fact is a thing too notorious. We live in a world of realities that can be infinitely useful or infinitely harmful. Ideas that tell us which of them to expect count as the true ideas in all this primary sphere of verification, and the pursuit of such ideas is a primary human duty. The possession of truth, so far from being here an end in itself, is only a preliminary means towards other vital satisfactions. If I am lost in the woods and starved, and find what looks like a cow-path, it is of the utmost importance that I should think of a human habitation at the end of it, for if I do so and follow it, I save myself. The true thought is useful here because the house which is its object is useful. The practical value of true ideas is thus primarily derived from the practical importance of their objects to us. Their objects are, indeed, not important at all times. I may on another occasion have no use for the house; and then my idea of it, however verifiable, will be practically irrelevant, and had better remain latent. Yet since almost any object may some day become temporarily important, the advantage of having a general stock of *extra* truths, of ideas that shall be true of merely possible situations, is obvious. We store such extra truths away in our memories, and with the overflow we fill our books of reference. Whenever such an extra truth becomes practically relevant to one of our emergencies, it passes from cold-storage to do work in the world and our belief in it grows active. You can say of it then either that "it is useful because it is true" or that "it is true because it is useful." Both these phrases mean exactly the same thing, namely that here is an idea that gets fulfilled and can be verified. True is the name for whatever idea starts the verification-process, useful is the name for its completed function in experience. True ideas would never

have been singled out as such, would never have acquired a class-name, least of all a name suggesting value, unless they had been useful from the outset in this way.

From this simple cue pragmatism gets her general notion of truth as something essentially bound up with the way in which one moment in our experience may lead us towards other moments which it will be worth while to have been led to. Primarily, and on the common-sense level, the truth of a state of mind means this function of *a leading that is worth while.* When a moment in our experience, of any kind whatever, inspires us with a thought that is true, that means that sooner or later we dip by that thought's guidance into the particulars of experience again and make advantageous connexion with them. This is a vague enough statement, but I beg you to retain it, for it is essential.

Our experience meanwhile is all shot through with regularities. One bit of it can warn us to get ready for another bit, can "intend" or be "significant of" that remoter object. The object's advent is the significance's verification. Truth, in these cases, meaning nothing but eventual verification, is manifestly incompatible with waywardness on our part. Woe to him whose beliefs play fast and loose with the order which realities follow in his experience; they will lead him nowhere or else make false connexions.

By "realities" or "objects" here, we mean either things of common sense, sensibly present, or else common-sense relations, such as dates, places, distances, kinds, activities. Following our mental image of a house along the cow-path, we actually come to see the house; we get the image's full verification. *Such simply and fully verified leadings are certainly the originals and prototypes of the truth-process.* Experience offers indeed other forms of truth-process, but they are all conceivable as being primary verifications arrested, multiplied or substituted one for another.

Take, for instance, yonder object on the wall. You and I consider it to be a "clock," altho no one of us has seen the hidden works that make it one. We let our notion pass for true without attempting to verify. If truths mean verification-process essentially, ought we then to call such unverified truths as this abortive? No, for they form the overwhelmingly large number of the truths we live by. Indirect as well as direct verifications pass muster. Where circumstantial evidence is sufficient, we can go without eye-witnessing. Just as we here assume Japan to exist without ever having been there, because it *works* to do so, everything we know conspiring with the belief, and nothing interfering, so we assume that thing to be a clock. We *use* it as a clock, regulating the length of our lecture by it. The verification of the assumption here means its leading to no frustration or contradiction. Verif*ability* of wheels and weights and pendulum is as good as verification. For one truth-process completed there are a million in our lives that function in this state of nascency. They turn us *towards* direct verification; lead us into the *surroundings* of the objects they envisage; and then, if everything runs on harmoniously, we are so sure that verification is possible that we omit it, and are usually justified by all that happens.

Truth lives, in fact, for the most part on a credit system. Our thoughts and beliefs "pass," so long as nothing challenges them, just as bank-notes pass so long as nobody refuses them. But this all points to direct face-to-face verifications somewhere, without which the fabric of truth collapses like a financial system with no cash-basis whatever. You accept my verification of one thing, I yours of another. We trade on each other's truth. But beliefs verified concretely by *somebody* are the posts of the whole superstructure.

Another great reason—beside economy of time—for waiving complete verification in the usual business of life is that all things exist in kinds and not singly. Our world is found once for all to have that peculiarity. So that when we have once directly verified our ideas about one specimen of a kind, we consider ourselves free to apply them to other specimens without verification. A mind that habitually discerns the kind of thing before it, and acts by the law of the kind immediately, without pausing to verify, will be a "true"

mind in ninety-nine out of a hundred emergencies, proved so by its conduct fitting everything it meets, and getting no refutation.

Indirectly or only potentially verifying processes may thus be true as well as full verification-processes. They work as true processes would work, give us the same advantages, and claim our recognition for the same reasons. . . .

[James returns to the notion that truth is an agreement with reality.]

Here it is that pragmatism and intellectualism begin to part company. Primarily, no doubt, to agree means to copy, but we saw that the mere word "clock" would do instead of a mental picture of its works, and that of many realities our ideas can only be symbols and not copies. "Past time," "power," "spontaneity"—how can our mind copy such realities?

To "agree" in the widest sense with a reality *can only mean to be guided either straight up to it or into its surroundings, or to be put into such working touch with it as to handle either it or something connected with it better than if we disagreed.* Better either intellectually or practically! And often agreement will only mean the negative fact that nothing contradictory from the quarter of that reality comes to interfere with the way in which our ideas guide us elsewhere. To copy a reality is, indeed, one very important way of agreeing with it, but it is far from being essential. The essential thing is the process of being guided. Any idea that helps us to *deal,* whether practically or intellectually, with either the reality or its belongings, that doesn't entangle our progress in frustrations, that *fits,* in fact, and adapts our life to the reality's whole setting, will agree sufficiently to meet the requirement. It will hold true of that reality.

Thus, *names* are just as "true" or "false" as definite mental pictures are. They set up similar verification-processes, and lead to fully equivalent practical results.

All human thinking gets discursified; we exchange ideas; we lend and borrow verifications, get them from one another by means of social intercourse. All truth thus gets verbally built out, stored up, and made available for every one. Hence, we must *talk* consistently just as we must *think* consistently: for both in talk and thought we deal with kinds. Names are arbitrary, but once understood they must be kept to. We mustn't now call Abel "Cain" or Cain "Abel." If we do, we ungear ourselves from the whole book of Genesis, and from all its connexions with the universe of speech and fact down to the present time. We throw ourselves out of whatever truth that entire system of speech and fact may embody.

The overwhelming majority of our true ideas admit of no direct or face-to-face verification—those of past history, for example, as of Cain and Abel. The stream of time can be remounted only verbally, or verified directly by the present prolongations or effects of what the past harbored. Yet if they agree with these verbalities and effects, we can know that our ideas of the past are true. *As true as past time itself was,* so true was Julius Caesar, so true were antediluvian monsters all in their proper dates and settings. That past time itself was, is guaranteed by its coherence with everything that's present. True as the present *is,* the past *was* also.

Agreement thus turns out to be essentially an affair of leading—leading that is useful because it is into quarters that contain objects that are important. True ideas lead us into useful verbal and conceptual quarters as well as directly up to useful sensible termini. They lead to consistency, stability and flowing human intercourse. They lead away from excentricity and isolation, from foiled and barren thinking. The untrammelled flowing of the leading-process, its general freedom from clash and contradiction, passes for its indirect verification; but all roads lead to Rome, and in the end and eventually, all true processes must lead to the face of directly verifying sensible experiences *somewhere,* which somebody's ideas have copied.

Such is the large loose way in which the pragmatist interprets the word agreement. He treats it altogether practically. He lets it cover any process of conduction from a present idea to a future terminus, provided only it run prosperously. It is only thus that "scientific" ideas, flying as they do beyond common sense, can be said to agree with their realities. It is, as I have already said, *as if* reality were made of ether, atoms or electrons, but we mustn't think so literally. The term "energy" doesn't even pretend to stand for anything "objective." It is only a way of measuring the surface of phenomena so as to string their changes on a simple formula.

Yet in the choice of these man-made formulas we cannot be capricious with impunity any more than we can be capricious on the common-sense practical level. We must find a theory that will *work;* and that means something extremely difficult; for our theory must mediate between all previous truths and certain new experiences. It must derange common sense and previous belief as little as possible, and it must lead to some sensible terminus or other that can be verified exactly. To "work" means both these things; and the squeeze is so tight that there is little loose play for any hypothesis. Our theories are wedged and controlled as nothing else is. Yet sometimes alternative theoretic formulas are equally compatible with all the truths we know, and then we choose between them for subjective reasons. We choose the kind of theory to which we are already partial; we follow "elegance" or "economy." Clerk-Maxwell somewhere says it would be "poor scientific taste" to choose the more complicated of two equally well-evidenced conceptions; and you will all agree with him. Truth in science is what gives us the maximum possible sum of satisfactions, taste included, but consistency both with previous truth and with novel fact is always the most imperious claimant. . . .

Our account of truth is an account of truths in the plural, of processes of leading, realized *in rebus,** and having only this quality in common, that they *pay.* They pay by guiding us into or towards some part of a system that dips at numerous points into sense-percepts, which we may copy mentally or not, but with which at any

*[in things]

rate we are now in the kind of commerce vaguely designated as verification. Truth for us is simply a collective name for verification-processes, just as health, wealth, strength, etc., are names for other processes connected with life, and also pursued because it pays to pursue them. Truth is *made,* just as health, wealth and strength are made, in the course of experience.

Here rationalism is instantaneously up in arms against us. I can imagine a rationalist to talk as follows:

"Truth is not made," he will say; "it absolutely obtains, being a unique relation that does not wait upon any process, but shoots straight over the head of experience, and hits its reality every time. Our belief that yon thing on the wall is a clock is true already, altho no one in the whole history of the world should verify it. The bare quality of standing in that transcendent relation is what makes any thought true that possesses it, whether or not there be verification. You pragmatists put the cart before the horse in making truth's being reside in verification-processes. These are merely signs of its being, merely our lame ways of ascertaining after the fact, which of our ideas already has possessed the wondrous quality. The quality itself is timeless, like all essences and natures. Thoughts partake of it directly, as they partake of falsity or of irrelevancy. It can't be analyzed away into pragmatic consequences."

The whole plausibility of this rationalist tirade is due to the fact to which we have already paid so much attention. In our world, namely, abounding as it does in things of similar kinds and similarly associated, one verification serves for others of its kind, and one great use of knowing things is to be led not so much to them as to their associates, especially to human talk about them. The quality of truth, obtaining *ante rem,** pragmatically means, then, the fact that in such a world innumerable ideas work better by their indirect or possible than by their direct and actual verification. Truth *ante rem* means only verifiability, then; or else it is a case of the stock

*[before the thing]

rationalist trick of treating the *name* of a concrete phenomenal reality as an independent prior entity, and placing it behind the reality as its explanation. . . .

In the case of "wealth" we all see the fallacy. We know that wealth is but a name for concrete processes that certain men's lives play a part in, and not a natural excellence found in Messrs. Rockefeller and Carnegie, but not in the rest of us.

Like wealth, "health" also lives *in rebus.* It is a name for processes, as digestion, circulation, sleep, etc., that go on happily, tho in this instance we are more inclined to think of it as a principle and to say the man digests and sleeps so well *because* he is so healthy.

With "strength" we are, I think, more rationalistic still, and decidedly inclined to treat it as an excellence preexisting in the man and explanatory of the herculean performances of his muscles.

With "truth" most people go over the border entirely, and treat the rationalistic account as self-evident. But really all these words in *th* are exactly similar. Truth exists *ante rem* just as much and as little as the other things do.

The scholastics, following Aristotle, made much of the distinction between habit and act. Health *in actu* means, among other things, good sleeping and digesting. But a healthy man need not always be sleeping, or always digesting, any more than a wealthy man need be always handling money, or a strong man always lifting weights. All such qualities sink to the status of "habits" between their times of exercise; and similarly truth becomes a habit of certain of our ideas and beliefs in their intervals of rest from their verifying activities. But those activities are the root of the whole matter, and the condition of there being any habit to exist in the intervals.

"The true," to put it very briefly, is only the expedient in the way of our thinking, just as "the right" is only the expedient in the way of our behaving. Expedient in almost any fashion; and expedient in the long run and on the whole of course; for what meets expediently all the experience in sight won't necessarily meet all further experiences equally satisfactorily. Experience, as we

know, has ways of *boiling over,* and making us correct our present formulas.

The "absolutely" true, meaning what no further experience will ever alter, is that ideal vanishing-point towards which we imagine that all our temporary truths will some day converge. It runs on all fours with the perfectly wise man, and with the absolutely complete experience; and, if these ideals are ever realized, they will all be realized together. Meanwhile we have to live today by what truth we can get today, and be ready tomorrow to call it falsehood. Ptolemaic astronomy, Euclidean space, Aristotelian logic, Scholastic metaphysics, were expedient for centuries, but human experience has boiled over those limits, and we now call these things only relatively true, or true within those borders of experience. "Absolutely" they are false; for we know that those limits were casual, and might have been transcended by past theorists just as they are by present thinkers.

When new experiences lead to retrospective judgments, using the past tense, what these judgments utter *was* true, even tho no past thinker had been led there. We live forwards, a Danish thinker [Kierkegaard] has said, but we understand backwards. The present sheds a backward light on the world's previous processes. They may have been truth-processes for the actors in them. They are not so for one who knows the latter revelations of the story.

This regulative notion of a potential better truth to be established later, possibly to be established some day absolutely, and having powers of retroactive legislation, turns its face, like all pragmatist notions, towards concreteness of fact, and towards the future. Like the half-truths, the absolute truth will have to be *made,* made as a relation incidental to the growth of a mass of verification-experience, to which the half-true ideas are all along contributing their quota.

I have already insisted on the fact that truth is made largely out of previous truths. Men's beliefs at any time are so much experience *funded.* But the beliefs are themselves parts of the sum total of the world's experience, and become matter, therefore, for the next day's funding operations. So far as reality means experienceable reality, both it and

the truths men gain about it are everlastingly in process of mutation—mutation towards a definite goal, it may be—but still mutation.

Mathematicians can solve problems with two variables. On the Newtonian theory, for instance, acceleration varies with distance, but distance also varies with acceleration. In the realm of truth-processes facts come independently and determine our beliefs provisionally. But these beliefs make us act, and as fast as they do so, they bring into sight or into existence new facts which redetermine the beliefs accordingly. So the whole coil and ball of truth, as it rolls up, is the product of a double influence. Truths emerge from facts; but they dip forward into facts again and add to them; which facts again create or reveal new truth (the word is indifferent) and so on indefinitely. The "facts" themselves meanwhile are not *true.* They simply *are.* Truth is the function of the beliefs that start and terminate among them. . . .

The case is like a snowball's growth, due as it is to the distribution of the snow on the one hand, and to the successive pushes of the boys on the other, with these factors co-determining each other incessantly. . . .

I am well aware how odd it must seem to some of you to hear me say that an idea is "true" so long as to believe it is profitable to our lives. That it is *good,* for as much as it profits, you will gladly admit. If what we do by its aid is good, you will allow the idea itself to be good in so far forth, for we are the better for possessing it. But is it not a strange misuse of the word "truth," you will say, to call ideas also "true" for this reason? . . .

. . . Let me now say only this, that truth is *one species of good,* and not, as is usually supposed, a category distinct from good, and co-ordinate with it. *The true is the name of whatever proves itself to be good in the way of belief, and good, too, for definite, assignable reasons.* Surely you must admit this, that if there were *no* good for life in true ideas, or if the knowledge of them were positively disadvantageous and false ideas the only useful ones, then the current notion that truth is divine and precious, and its pursuit a duty, could never have grown up or become a dogma. In a world like that, our duty would be to *shun* truth, rather. But in this world, just as certain foods are not only agreeable to our taste, but good for our teeth, our stomach, and our tissues; so certain ideas are not only agreeable to think about, or agreeable as supporting other ideas that we are fond of, but they are also helpful in life's practical struggles. If there be any life that it is really better we should lead, and if there be any idea which, if believed in, would help us to lead that life, then it would be really *better for us* to believe in that idea, *unless, indeed, belief in it incidentally clashed with other greater vital benefits.*

"What would be better for us to believe!" This sounds very like a definition of truth. It comes very near to saying "what we *ought* to believe"; and in *that* definition none of you would find any oddity. Ought we ever not to believe what it is *better for us* to believe? And can we then keep the notion of what is better for us, and what is true for us, permanently apart?

Pragmatism says no, and I fully agree with her. Probably you also agree, so far as the abstract state-ment goes, but with a suspicion that if we practically did believe everything that made for good in our own personal lives, we should be found indulging all kinds of fancies about this world's affairs, and all kinds of sentimental superstitions about a world hereafter. Your suspicion here is undoubtedly well founded, and it is evident that something happens when you pass from the abstract to the concrete that complicates the situation.

I said just now that what is better for us to believe is true *unless the belief incidentally clashes with some other vital benefit.* Now in real life what vital benefits is any particular belief of ours most liable to clash with? What indeed except the vital benefits yielded by *other beliefs* when these prove incompatible with the first ones? In other words, the greatest enemy of any one of our truths may be the rest of our truths. Truths have once for all this desperate instinct of self-preservation and of desire to extinguish whatever contradicts them.

For Further Reflection

1. Does James' dynamic idea of truth appeal to you? What are its strengths?

2. Is James' criterion of truth as the success of an idea in practice clear? What problems, if any, do you see with it? Suppose that the Nazis had been successful in winning the Second World War; would their theories be "true"? Is success or usefulness the correct criterion of the true?

3. James elsewhere applied his ideas to religion and maintained that since religious beliefs were inspiring, we ought to believe them and make them true for ourselves. Do you agree with this? What if it turned out that the truth was bad news, not a gospel (literally, "good news") but a badspel (or "bad news"). Would you still rather know it than believe a falsehood that was expedient or inspiring? Is truth in the neutral, nonpragmatic sense good in itself?

Dismantling Truth: Solidarity Versus Objectivity   III.30

RICHARD RORTY

Richard Rorty (1931–2007) was professor of comparative literature at Stanford University and the author of several works, including *Philosophy and the Mirror of Nature* (1979).

In this selection, Rorty attacks the distinction between objectivity and subjectivity as well as the correspondence theory of truth. He sides with Thomas Kuhn in arguing that we can have no theory-independent notion of reality and proposes to erase the essential difference between science and the humanities and arts. Embracing the title of "the new fuzzies," Rorty proposes that a notion of social solidarity replace the enlightenment notion of objective truth.

Study Questions

1. What is the present relationship in our culture between science and the humanities? Which receives greater respect and why?
2. What are the two meanings of "rational" which Rorty discusses? Which does he think superior to the other?
3. What are the criteria of scientific rationality? How do the humanities measure up to those criteria?
4. What does Rorty think should be done about the idea of objective truth?
5. What is Rorty's criticism of the correspondence theory of truth?
6. What role does Thomas Kuhn's work play in the debate between science and the humanities? Why does Rorty congratulate Kuhn?
7. What is the central idea of Rorty's "pragmatism"? Why is it called by its critics "the new fuzziness"?
8. What would be a pragmatist's paradise? What was the charge against John Dewey in proposing such a paradise?

IN OUR CULTURE, the notions of "science," "rationality," "objectivity" and "truth" are bound up with one another. Science is thought of as offering "hard," "objective" truth—truth as correspondence to reality, the only sort of truth worthy of the name. Humanists—philosophers, theologians, historians, literary critics—have to worry about whether they are being "scientific"—whether they are entitled to think of their conclusions, no matter how carefully argued, as worthy of the term "true." We tend to identify seeking "objective truth" with "using reason," and so we think of the natural sciences as paradigms of rationality. We also think of rationality as a matter of following procedures laid down in advance, of being "methodical." So we tend to use "methodical," "rational," "scientific" and "objective" as synonyms.

Worries about "cognitive status" and "objectivity" are characteristic of a secularized culture in which the scientist replaces the priest. The scientist is now seen as the person who keeps humanity in touch with something beyond itself. As the universe was depersonalized, beauty (and, in time, even moral goodness) came to be thought of as "subjective." So truth is now thought of as the only point at which human beings are responsible to something non-human. A commitment to "rationality" and to "method" is thought to be a recognition of this responsibility. The scientist becomes a moral exemplar, one who selflessly exposes himself again and again to the hardness of facts.

One result of this way of thinking is that any academic discipline which wants a place at the trough, but is unable to offer the predictions and

From Richard Rorty, "Science and Solidarity," in Rhetoric of the Human Sciences: Language and Arguments in Scholarship and Public Affairs, edited by Nelson et al. (Madison: University of Wisconsin Press, 1987). Reprinted with permission of the University of Wisconsin Press.

the technology provided by the natural sciences, must either pretend to imitate science or find some way of obtaining "cognitive status" without the necessity of discovering facts. Practitioners of these disciplines must either affiliate themselves with this quasi-priestly order by using terms like "behavioral sciences" or else find something other than "fact" to be concerned with. People in the humanities typically choose the latter strategy. They describe themselves either as concerned with "values" as opposed to facts, or as developing and inculcating habits of "critical reflection."

Neither sort of rhetoric is very satisfactory. No matter how much humanists talk about "objective values," the phrase always sounds vaguely confused. It gives with one hand what it takes back with the other. The distinction between the objective and the subjective was designed to parallel that between fact and value, so an objective value sounds vaguely mythological as a winged horse. Talk about the humanists' special skill at critical reflection fares no better. Nobody really believes that philosophers or literary critics are better at critical thinking, or at taking big broad views of things, than theoretical physicists or microbiologists. So society tends to ignore both these kinds of rhetoric. It treats humanities as on a par with the arts, and thinks of both as providing pleasure rather than truth. Both are, to be sure, thought of as providing "high" rather than "low" pleasure. But an elevated and spiritual sort of pleasure is still a long way from the grasp of a truth.

These distinctions between hard facts and soft values, truth and pleasure, and objectivity and subjectivity are awkward and clumsy instruments. They are not suited to divide up culture; they create more difficulties than they resolve. It would be best to find another vocabulary, to start afresh. But in order to do so we first have to find a new way of describing the natural sciences. It is not a question of debunking or downgrading the natural sciences, but simply of ceasing to see them on the model of the priest. We need to stop thinking of science as the place where the human mind confronts the world. We need a way of explaining why scientists are, and deserve to be, moral exemplars which does not depend on a distinction between objective fact and something softer, squishier and more dubious.

To get to such a way of thinking we can start by distinguishing two senses of the term "rationality." In one sense, the one I have already discussed, to be rational is to be methodical: that is, to have criteria for success laid down in advance. We think of poets and painters as using some other faculty than "reason" in their work because, by their own confession, they are not sure of what they want to do before they have done it. They make up new standards of achievement as they go along. By contrast, we think of judges as knowing in advance what criteria a brief will have to satisfy in order to invoke a favorable decision, and of businessmen as setting well-defined goals and being judged by their success in achieving them. Law and business are good examples of rationality, but the scientist, knowing in advance what would count as disconfirming his hypothesis and prepared to abandon that hypothesis as a result of the unfavorable outcome of a single experiment, seems a truly heroic example. Further, we seem to have a clear criterion of the success of a scientific theory—namely, its ability to predict, and thereby to enable us to control some portion of the world. If to be rational means to be able to lay down criteria in advance, then it is plausible to take natural science as the paradigm of rationality.

The trouble is that in this sense of "rational" the humanities are never going to qualify as rational activities. If the humanities are concerned with ends rather than means, then there is no way to evaluate their success in terms of antecedently specified criteria. If we already knew what criteria we wanted to satisfy, we would not worry about whether we were pursuing the right ends. If we thought we knew the goals of culture and society in advance, we would have no use for the humanities—as totalitarian societies in fact do not. It is characteristic of democracies and pluralistic societies to redefine their goals continually. But if to be rational means to satisfy criteria, then this process of redefinition will be bound to be non-rational. So if the humanities are to be viewed as rational activities, rationality will have to be thought of as something other than the satisfaction of criteria which are statable in advance.

[The second] meaning of "rational" is, in fact, available. In this sense, the word means something like "sane" or "reasonable" rather than "methodical." It names a set of moral virtues: tolerance, respect for the opinion of those around one, willingness to listen, reliance on persuasion rather than force. These are the virtues which members of a civilized society must possess if the society is to endure. In this sense of "rational," the word means something more like "civilized" than like "methodical." When so construed, the distinction between the rational and the irrational has nothing in particular to do with the difference between the arts and the sciences. On this construction, to be rational is simply to discuss any topic—religious, literary, or scientific—in a way which eschews dogmatism, defensiveness, and righteous indignation.

There is no problem about whether, in this latter, weaker sense the humanities are "rational disciplines." Usually humanists display the moral virtues in question. Sometimes they do not, but then sometimes scientists don't either. Yet these moral virtues are felt to be not enough. Both humanists and the public hanker after rationality in the first, stronger sense of the term: a sense which is associated with objective truth, correspondence to reality, method and criteria.

We should not try to satisfy this hankering, but rather try to eradicate it. No matter what one's opinion of the secularization of culture, it was a mistake to try to make the natural scientist into a new sort of priest, a link between the human and the non-human. So was the idea that some sorts of truths are "objective" whereas others are merely "subjective" or "relative"—the attempt to divide up the set of true sentences into "genuine knowledge" and "mere opinion," or into the "factual" and the "judgmental." So was the idea that the scientist has a special method which, if only the humanists would

apply it to ultimate values, would give us the same kind of self-confidence about moral ends as we now have about technological means. I think that we should content ourselves with the second, "weaker" conception of rationality and avoid the first, "stronger" conception. We should avoid the idea that there is some special virtue in knowing in advance what criteria you are going to satisfy, in having standards by which to measure progress.

[IS SCIENCE RATIONAL?]

One can make these issues somewhat more concrete by taking up the current controversy among philosophers about the "rationality of science." For some twenty years, ever since the publication of Thomas Kuhn's book, *The Structure of Scientific Revolutions* philosophers have been debating the question of "whether science is rational." Attacks on Kuhn for being "irrational" are now as frequent and urgent as, in the 1930s and 1940s, were attacks on the logical positivists for saying that moral judgments were "meaningless." We are constantly being warned of the danger of "relativism" which will beset us if we give up our attachment to objectivity and to the idea of rationality as obedience to criteria.

Whereas Kuhn's enemies routinely accuse him of reducing science to "mob psychology," and pride themselves on having (by a new theory of meaning or reference or verisimilitude) vindicated the "rationality of science," his pragmatic friends (such as myself) routinely congratulate him on having softened the distinction between science and non-science. . . . [H]e has said that "there is no theory-independent way to reconstruct phrases like 'really there.'" He has asked whether it really helps "to imagine that there is some one full, objective, true account of nature and that the proper measure of scientific achievement is the extent to which it brings us closer to the ultimate goal." We pragmatists quote these passages incessantly in the course of our effort to enlist Kuhn in our campaign to drop the objective-subjective distinction altogether.

What I am calling "pragmatism" might also be called "left-wing Kuhnianism." It has also been rather endearingly called (by one of its critics, Clark Glymour) "the new fuzziness," because it is an attempt to blur just those distinctions between the objective and the subjective and between fact and value which the criterial conception of rationality has developed. We fuzzies would like to substitute the idea of "unforced agreement" for that of "objectivity." We should like to put all culture on an epistemological level (or get rid of the idea of "epistemological level"). . . . On our view, "truth" is a univocal term. It applies equally to the judgments of lawyers, anthropologists, physicists, philologists and literary critics. There is point in assigning degrees of "objectivity" or "hardness" to such disciplines. For the presence of unforced agreement in all of them gives us everything in the way of "objective truth" which one could possibly want: namely, intersubjective agreement.

As soon as one says that all there is to objectivity is intersubjectivity, one is likely to be accused of being a relativist. That is the epithet traditionally applied to pragmatists. But this epithet is ambiguous. It can name any of three different views:

1. The silly and self-refuting view that every belief is as good as every other.

2. The wrong-headed view that "true" is an equivocal term, having as many meanings as there are contexts of justification.

3. The ethnocentric view that there is nothing to be said about either truth or rationality apart from descriptions of the familiar procedures of justification which a given society—*ours*—uses in one or another area of inquiry.

The pragmatist does hold this third, ethnocentric view. But he does not hold the first or the second view of relativism.

But "relativism" is not an appropriate term to describe this sort of ethnocentrism. For we pragmatists are not holding a positive theory which says that something is relative to something else. Instead, we are making the purely *negative* point that we would be better off without the traditional distinctions between knowledge and opinion, construed as the distinction between truth as correspondence to reality and truth as a commendatory term for well-justified beliefs. Our opponents call this negative claim "relativistic" because they cannot imagine that anybody would seriously deny that truth has an intrinsic nature. So when we say that there is nothing to be said about truth save that each of us will commend as true those beliefs which he or she finds good to believe, the realist is inclined to interpret this as one more positive theory about the nature of truth: a theory according to which truth is simply the contemporary opinion of a chosen individual or group. Such a theory would, of course, be self-refuting. But we pragmatists do not have a theory of truth, much less a relativistic one. As partisans of solidarity, our account of the value of cooperative human enquiry has only an ethical base, not an epistemological or metaphysical one.

To say that we must be ethnocentric may sound suspicious, but this will only happen if we identify ethnocentrism with pigheaded refusal to talk to representatives of other communities. In my sense of ethnocentrism, to be ethnocentric is simply to work by our own lights. The defense of ethnocentrism is simply that there are no other lights to work by. Beliefs suggested by another individual or another culture must be tested by trying to weave them together with beliefs which we already have. . . .

This way of thinking runs counter to the attempts, familiar since the eighteenth century, to think of political liberalism as based on a conception of the nature of man. To most thinkers of the Enlightenment, it seemed clear that the access to Nature which physical science had provided should now be followed by the establishment of social, political and economic institutions which were "in accordance with Nature." Ever since, liberal social thought has centered around social reform as made possible by objective knowledge of what human beings are like—not knowledge of what Greeks or

Frenchmen or Chinese are like, but of humanity as such. This tradition dreams of a universal human community which will exhibit a non-parochial solidarity because it is the expression of an ahistorical human nature.

Philosophers who belong to this tradition, who wish to ground solidarity in objectivity, have to construe truth as correspondence to reality. So they must construct an epistemology which has room for a kind of justification which is not merely social but natural, springing from human nature itself, and made possible by a link between that part of nature and the rest of nature. By contrast we pragmatists, who wish to reduce objectivity to solidarity, do not require either a metaphysics or an epistemology. . . . We see the gap between truth and justification not as something to be bridged by isolating a natural and transcultural sort of rationality which can be used to criticize certain cultures and praise others, but simply as the gap between the actual good and the possible better. From a pragmatist point of view, to say that what is rational for us now to believe may not be *true*, is simply to say that somebody may come up with a better idea. . . .

Another reason for describing us as "relativistic" is that we pragmatists drop the idea that enquiry is destined to converge to a single point—that Truth is "out there" waiting for human beings to arrive at it. This idea seems to us an unfortunate attempt to carry a religious conception over into a secular culture. All that is worth preserving of the claim that rational inquiry will converge to a single point is the claim that we must be able to explain why past false views were held in the past, and thus explain how we go about re-educating our benighted ancestors. To say that we think we're heading in the right direction is just to say, with Kuhn, that we can, by hindsight, tell the story of the past as a story of progress.

But the fact that we can trace such a direction and tell such a story does not mean that we have come closer to a goal which is out there waiting for us. We cannot, I think, imagine a moment at which the human race could settle back and say, "Well, now that we've finally arrived at the Truth we can relax." Paul Feyerabend is right in suggesting that we should discard the metaphor of inquiry, and human activity generally, as converging rather than proliferating, becoming more unified rather than more diverse. On the contrary, we should *relish* that thought that the sciences as well as the arts will *always* provide a spectacle of fierce competition between alternative theories, movements and schools. The end of human activity is not rest, but rather richer and better human activity. We should think of human progress as making it possible for human beings to do more interesting things and be more interesting people, not as heading toward a place which has somehow been prepared for us in advance. To drop the criterial conception of rationality in favor of the pragmatist conception would be to give up the idea of Truth as something to which we were responsible. Instead we should think of "true" as a word which applies to those beliefs upon which we are able to agree, as roughly synonymous with "justified." . . .

. . . Pragmatists would like to replace the desire for objectivity—the desire to be in touch with a reality which is more than some community with which we identify ourselves—with the desire for solidarity with that community. They think that the habits of relying on persuasion rather than force, of respect for opinions of colleagues, of curiosity and eagerness for new data and ideas, are the *only* virtues which scientists have. They do not think that there is an intellectual virtue called "rationality" over and above these moral virtues. . . .

Pragmatists interpret the goal of inquiry (in any sphere of culture) as the attainment of an appropriate mixture of unforced agreement with tolerant disagreement (where what counts as appropriate is determined, within that sphere, by trial and error). Such a reinterpretation of our sense of responsibility would, if carried through, gradually make unintelligible the subject-object model of enquiry, the child-parent model of moral obligation, and the correspondence theory of truth. A world in which those models, and that theory, no longer had any intuitive appeal would be a pragmatist's paradise.

When Dewey urged that we try to create such a paradise he was said to be irresponsible. For, it was said, he left us bereft of weapons to use against our enemies; he gave us nothing with which to "answer the Nazis." When we new fuzzies try to revive Dewey's repudiation of criteriology we are said to be "relativistic." We must, people say, believe that every coherent view is as good as every other, since we have no "outside" touchstone for choice among such views. We are said to leave the general public defenseless against the witch doctor, the defender of creationism, or anyone else who is clever and patient enough to deduce a consistent and wide-ranging set of theorems from his "alternative first principles."

Nobody is convinced when we fuzzies say that we can be just as morally indignant as the next philosopher. We are suspected of being contritely fallibilist when righteous fury is called for. Even when we actually display appropriate emotions we get nowhere, for we are told that we have no *right* to these emotions. When we suggest that one of the few things we know (or need to know) about truth is that it is what wins in a free and open encounter, we are told that we have defined "true" as "satisfies the standards of our community." But we pragmatists do not hold this relativist view. We do not infer from "There is no way to step outside communities to a neutral standpoint" to "There is no rational way to justify liberal communities over totalitarian communities." For that inference involves just the notion of "rationality" as a set of ahistorical principles which pragmatists abjure. What we in fact infer is that there is no way to beat totalitarians in argument by appealing to shared common premises, and no point in pretending that a common

human nature makes the totalitarians unconsciously hold such premises.

The claim that we fuzzies have no right to be furious at moral evil, no right to commend our views as true unless we simultaneously refute ourselves by claiming that there are objects out there which *make* those views true, begs all the theoretical questions. But it gets to the practical and moral heart of the matter. This is the question of whether notions like "unforced agreement" and "free and open encounter"—descriptions of social situations—can take the place in our moral lives of notions like "the world," "the will of God," "the moral law," "what our beliefs are trying to represent accurately" and "what makes our beliefs true." All the philosophical presuppositions which make Hume's fork seem inevitable are ways of suggesting that human communities must justify their existence by striving to attain a non-human goal. To suggest that we can forget about Hume's fork [the radical separation of facts from values], forget about being responsible to what is "out there," is to suggest that human communities can justify their existence only by comparisons with other actual and possible human communities. . . .

Imagine . . . that a few years from now you open your copy of the *New York Times* and read that the philosophers, in convention assembled, have unanimously agreed that values are objective, science rational, truth a matter of correspondence to reality, etc. Recent breakthroughs in semantics and meta-ethics, the report goes on, have caused the last remaining non-cognitivists in ethics to recant. Similarly breakthroughs in the philosophy of science have led Kuhn formally to abjure his claim that there is no theory-independent way to reconstruct statements about what is "really there." All the new fuzzies have repudiated all their former views. By way of making amends for the intellectual confusion which the philosophical profession has recently caused, the philosophers have adopted a short, crisp set of standards of rationality and morality. Next year the convention is expected to adopt the report of the committee charged with formulating a standard of aesthetic taste.

Surely the public reaction to this would not be "Saved!" but rather "Who on earth do these philosophers think they *are?*" It is one of the best things about the form of intellectual life we Western liberals lead that this *would* be our reaction. No matter how much we moan about the disorder and confusion of the current philosophical scene, about the treason of the clerks, we do not really want things any other way. What prevents us from relaxing and enjoying the new fuzziness is perhaps no more than cultural lag, the fact that the rhetoric of the Enlightenment praised the emerging natural sciences in a vocabulary which was left over from a less liberal and tolerant era. This rhetoric enshrined all the old philosophical opposition between mind and world, appearance and reality, subject and object, truth and pleasure. Dewey thought that it was the continued prevalence of such opposition which prevented us from seeing that modern science was a new and promising invention, a way of life which had not existed before and which ought to be encouraged and imitated, something which required a new rhetoric rather than justification by an old one.

Suppose that Dewey were right about this, and that eventually we learn to find the fuzziness which results from breaking down such opposition spiritually comforting rather than morally offensive. What would the rhetoric of the culture, and in particular of the humanities, sound like? Presumably it would be more Kuhnian, in the sense that it would mention particular concrete achievements —paradigms—more, and "method" less. There would be less talk about rigor and more about originality. The image of the great scientist would not be of somebody who got it right but of somebody who made it new. The new rhetoric would draw more on the vocabulary of Romantic poetry and socialist politics, and less on that of Greek metaphysics, religious morality or Enlightenment scientism. A scientist would rely on a sense of solidarity with the rest of her profession, rather than a picture of herself as battling through the veils of illusion, guided by the light of reason.

If all this happened, the term "science," and thus the opposition between the humanities, the arts and the sciences might gradually fade away. Once "science" was deprived of an honorific sense, we might not need it for taxonomy. . . . The people now called "scientists" would no longer think of themselves as members of a quasi-priestly order, nor would the public think of themselves as in the care of such an order.

In this situation, the "humanities" would no longer think of themselves as such, nor would they share a common rhetoric. Each of the disciplines which now fall under that rubric would worry as little about its method, cognitive status or "philosophical foundations" as do mathematics, civil engineering or sculpture. For terms which denoted disciplines would not be thought to divide "subject matter," chunks of the world which had "interfaces" with each other. Rather, they would be thought to denote communities whose boundaries were as fluid as the interests of their members. In this heyday of the fuzzies, there would be as little reason to be self-conscious about the nature and status of one's discipline as, in the ideal democratic community, about the nature and status of one's race or sex. For one's ultimate loyalty would be to the larger community which permitted and encouraged this kind of freedom and insouciance. This community would serve no higher end than its own preservation and self-improvement, the preservation and enhancement of civilization. It would identify rationality with that effort, rather than with the desire for objectivity. So it would feel no need for a foundation more solid than reciprocal loyalty.

For Further Reflection

1. What are the major motivations of Rorty in rejecting the correspondence theory of truth and the object-subject distinction? Why does he think that the notion of intersubjective agreement (or unforced agreement) is a better idea? What are the strengths and weaknesses of Rorty's proposal?

2. Rorty distinguishes three types of relativism. What are they and which does he choose? Do you agree with his argument here? Explain your answer.

3. What does Rorty mean by saying that pragmatic truth has only an ethical base, not an epistemological or metaphysical one? What is his argument for this? Is it sound?

4. Has Rorty successfully eliminated metaphysical and epistemological notions? Has he argued successfully against the distinction between the ideas of objectivity and subjectivity and against the correspondence theory of truth? Critique his argument.

5. Do you detect any hidden assumptions in this article? Who is in the community with which Rorty identifies? What are its values? Does it include religious people? conservatives? socialists? Explain your answer.

6. Elsewhere, in *Philosophy and the Mirror of Nature* (p. 176), Rorty describes "truth" as "what you can defend against all comers, . . . what our peers will *ceteris paribus* let us get away with saying." Analyze this characterization of truth.

Postmodernism and Truth   III.31

DANIEL DENNETT

Daniel Dennett is Distinguished Arts and Science Professor at Tufts University and the author of several works in philosophy of mind, including *Conscious Explained* (1991) and *Darwin's Dangerous Idea* (1995). In this essay Dennett argues that postmodernist ideas, such as Rorty's, fail to understand the importance of truth. They either reject the concept in favor of an irrational cognitive relativism or undervalue truth, giving it minor importance.

Study Questions

1. What were the consequences of the virus that the American researchers inadvertently introduced into the third world?
2. Who were these researchers?
3. What is a *meme*?
4. Are multiculturalists responsible people?
5. What is the significance of Dennett's encounter with the colleague from the Comparative Literature Department? What was Dennett's reaction to his question?
6. On what point does Dennett disagree with Richard Rorty?
7. What is vegetarian truth?
8. According to Dennett, how do postmodernists treat the concept of truth?

HERE IS A STORY you probably haven't heard, about how a team of American researchers inadvertently introduced a virus into a third-world country they were studying.[1] They were experts in their field, and they had the best intentions; they thought they were helping the people they were studying, but in fact they had never really seriously considered whether what they were doing might have ill effects. It had not occurred to them that a side-effect of their research might be damaging to the fragile ecology of the country they were studying. The virus they introduced had some dire effects indeed: it raised infant mortality rates, led to a general decline in the health and well-being of women and children, and, perhaps worst of all, indirectly undermined the only effective political force for democracy in the country, strengthening the hand of the traditional despot who ruled the nation. These American researchers had something to answer for, surely, but when confronted with the devastation they had wrought, their response was frustrating, to say the least: they still thought that what they were doing was, all things considered, in the interests of the people, and declared that the standards by which this so-called devastation was being measured were simply not appropriate. Their critics, they contended, were trying to impose "Western" standards in a cultural environment that had no use for such standards. In this strange defense they were warmly supported by the country's leaders—not surprisingly—and little was heard—not surprisingly—from those who *might* have been said, by Western standards, to have suffered as a result of their activities.

These researchers were not biologists intent on introducing new strains of rice, nor were they agri-business chemists testing new pesticides, or doctors trying out vaccines that couldn't legally be tested in the U.S.A. They were postmodernist science critics and other multiculturalists who were arguing, in the course of their professional researches on the culture and traditional "science" of this country, that Western science was just one among many equally valid narratives, not to be "privileged" in its competition with native traditions which other researchers—biologists, chemists, doctors and others—were eager to supplant. The virus they introduced was not a macromolecule but a meme (a replicating idea): the idea that science was a "colonial" imposition, not a worthy substitute for the practices and beliefs that had carried the third-world country to its current condition. And the reason you have not heard of this particular incident is that I made it up, to dramatize the issue and to try to unsettle what seems to be current orthodoxy among the *literati* about such matters. But it is inspired by real incidents—that is to say, true reports. Events of just this sort have occurred in India and elsewhere, reported, movingly, by a number of writers, among them:

Meera Nanda, "The Epistemic Charity of the Social Constructivist Critics of Science and Why the Third World Should Refuse the Offer," in N. Koertge, ed., *A House Built on Sand: Exposing Postmodernist Myths about Science*, Oxford University Press, 1998, pp. 286–311.

Reza Afshari, "An Essay on Islamic Cultural Relativism in the Discourse of Human Rights," in *Human Rights Quarterly*, 16, 1994, pp. 235–76.

Susan Okin, "Is Multiculturalism Bad for Women?" *Boston Review*, October/November 1997, pp. 25–28.

Pervez Hoodbhoy, *Islam and Science: Religious Orthodoxy and the Battle for Rationality*, London and New Jersey: Zed Books Ltd., 1991.

My little fable is also inspired by a wonderful remark of E. O. Wilson, in *Atlantic Monthly* a few months ago: "Scientists, being held responsible for what they say, have not found postmodernism

This is the final draft of a paper given at the 1998 World Congress of Philosophy. It appears here by permission of the author, Daniel Dennett.

useful." Actually, of course, we are all held responsible for what we say. The laws of libel and slander, for instance, exempt none of us, but most of us—including scientists in many or even most fields—do not typically make assertions that, independently of libel and slander considerations, might bring harm to others, even indirectly. A handy measure of this fact is the evident ridiculousness we discover in the idea of malpractice insurance for . . . literary critics, philosophers, mathematicians, historians, cosmologists. What on earth could a mathematician or literary critic do, in the course of executing her professional duties, that might need the security blanket of malpractice insurance? She might inadvertently trip a student in the corridor, or drop a book on somebody's head, but aside from such *outré* side-effects, our activities are paradigmatically innocuous. One would think. But in those fields where the stakes are higher— and more direct—there is a longstanding tradition of being especially cautious, and of taking particular responsibility for ensuring that no harm results (as explicitly honored in the Hippocratic Oath). Engineers, knowing that thousands of people's safety may depend on the bridge they design, engage in focussed exercises with specified constraints designed to determine that, according to all current knowledge, their designs are safe and sound. Even economists—often derided for the risks they take with *other* people's livelihoods—when they find themselves in positions to endorse specific economic measures considered by government bodies or by their private clients, are known to attempt to put a salutary strain on their underlying assumptions, just to be safe. They are used to asking themselves, and to being expected to ask themselves: "What if I'm wrong?" We others seldom ask ourselves this question, since we have spent our student and professional lives working on topics that are, according both to tradition and common sense, incapable of affecting any lives in ways worth worrying about. If my topic is whether or not Vlastos had the best interpretation of Plato's *Parmenides* or how the wool trade affected imagery in Tudor poetry, or what the best version of string theory

says about time, or how to recast proofs in topology in some new formalism, if I am wrong, dead wrong, in what I say, the only damage I am likely to do is to my own scholarly reputation. But when we aspire to have a greater impact on the "real" (as opposed to "academic") world—and many philosophers do aspire to this today—we need to adopt the attitudes and habits of these more applied disciplines. We need to hold ourselves responsible for what we say, recognizing that our words, if believed, can have profound effects for good or ill.

When I was a young untenured professor of philosophy, I once received a visit from a colleague from the Comparative Literature Department, an eminent and fashionable literary theorist, who wanted some help from me. I was flattered to be asked, and did my best to oblige, but the drift of his questions about various philosophical topics was strangely perplexing to me. For quite a while we were getting nowhere, until finally he managed to make clear to me what he had come for. He wanted "an epistemology," he said. *An* epistemology. Every self-respecting literary theorist had to sport an epistemology that season, it seems, and without one he felt naked, so he had come to me for an epistemology to wear—it was the very next fashion, he was sure, and he wanted the *dernier cri* in epistemologies. It didn't matter to him that it be sound, or defensible, or (as one might as well say) *true;* it just had to be new and different and stylish. Accessorize, my good fellow, or be overlooked at the party.

At that moment I perceived a gulf between us that I had only dimly seen before. It struck me at first as simply the gulf between being serious and being frivolous. But that initial surge of self-righteousness on my part was, in fact, a naive reaction. My sense of outrage, my sense that my time had been wasted by this man's bizarre project, was in its own way as unsophisticated as the reaction of the first-time theater-goer who leaps on the stage to protect the heroine from the villain. "Don't you understand?" we ask incredulously. "It's *make believe*. It's *art*. It isn't *supposed* to be taken literally!" Put in that context, perhaps this man's quest was not so disreputable after all. I would not have been offended, would I, if a colleague in the Drama Department had come by and asked if he could borrow a few yards of my books to put on the shelves of the set for his production of Tom Stoppard's play, *Jumpers*. What if anything would be wrong in outfitting this fellow with a snazzy set of outrageous epistemological doctrines with which he could titillate or confound his colleagues?

What would be wrong would be that since this man didn't acknowledge the gulf, didn't even recognize that it existed, my acquiescence in his shopping spree would have contributed to the debasement of a precious commodity, the erosion of a valuable distinction. Many people, including both onlookers and participants, don't see this gulf, or actively deny its existence, and therein lies the problem. The sad fact is that in some intellectual circles, inhabited by some of our more advanced thinkers in the arts and humanities, this attitude passes as a sophisticated appreciation of the futility of proof and the relativity of all knowledge claims. In fact this opinion, far from being sophisticated, is the height of sheltered naiveté, made possible only by flat-footed ignorance of the proven methods of scientific truth-seeking and their power. Like many another naif, these thinkers, reflecting on the manifest inability of *their* methods of truth-seeking to achieve stable and valuable results, innocently generalize from their own cases and conclude that nobody *else* knows how to discover the truth either.

Among those who contribute to this problem, I am sorry to say, is my good friend Dick Rorty. Richard Rorty and I have been constructively disagreeing with each other for over a quarter of a century now. Each of us has taught the other a great deal, I believe, in the reciprocal process of chipping away at our residual points of disagreement. I can't name a living philosopher from whom I have learned more. Rorty has opened up the horizons of contemporary philosophy, shrewdly showing us philosophers many things about how our own projects have grown out of the philosophical projects of the distant and recent past, while boldly describing and prescribing future paths for us to take. But there is one point over which he and I do not agree at all—not yet—and that concerns his attempt over the years to show that philosophers' debates about Truth and Reality really do erase the gulf, really do license a slide into some form of relativism. In the end, Rorty tells us, it is all just "conversations," and there are only political or historical or aesthetic grounds for taking one role or another in an ongoing conversation.

Rorty has often tried to enlist me in his campaign, declaring that he could find in my own work one explosive insight or another that would help him with his project of destroying the illusory edifice of objectivity. One of his favorite passages is the one with which I ended my book *Consciousness Explained* (1991):

> It's just a war of metaphors, you say—but metaphors are not "just" metaphors; metaphors are the tools of thought. No one can think about consciousness without them, so it is important to equip yourself with the best set of tools available. Look what we have built with our tools. Could you have imagined it without them? [p. 455]

"I wish," Rorty says, "he had taken one step further, and had added that such tools are all that inquiry can ever provide, because inquiry is never 'pure' in the sense of [Bernard] Williams' 'project of pure inquiry.' It is always a matter of getting us something we want" ("Holism, Intrinsicality, Transcendence," in Dahlbom, ed., *Dennett and His Critics,* 1993). But I would never take that step, for although metaphors are indeed irreplaceable tools of thought, they are not the only such tools. Microscopes and mathematics and MRI scanners are among the others. Yes, any inquiry is a matter of getting us something we want: the truth about something that matters to us, if all goes as it should.

When philosophers argue about truth, they are arguing about how not to inflate the truth about truth into the Truth about Truth, some absolutistic doctrine that makes indefensible demands on our systems of thought. It is in this regard similar to debates about, say, the reality of time, or the reality of the past. There are some deep, sophisticated, worthy philosophical investigations into whether, properly speaking, the past is real. Opinion is divided, but you entirely misunderstand the point of these disagreements if you suppose that they undercut claims such as the following:

> Life first emerged on this planet more than three thousand million years ago.
>
> The Holocaust happened during World War II.
>
> Jack Ruby shot and killed Lee Harvey Oswald at 11:21 am, Dallas time, November 24, 1963.

These are truths about events that really happened. Their denials are falsehoods. No sane philosopher has ever thought otherwise, though in the heat of battle, they have sometimes made claims that could be so interpreted.

Richard Rorty deserves his large and enthralled readership in the arts and humanities, and in the "humanistic" social sciences, but when his readers enthusiastically interpret him as encouraging their postmodernist skepticism about truth, they trundle down paths he himself has refrained from traveling. When I press him on these points, he concedes that there is indeed a useful concept of truth that survives intact after all the corrosive philosophical objections have been duly entered. This serviceable, modest concept of truth, Rorty acknowledges, has its uses: when we want to compare two maps of the countryside for reliability, for instance, or when the issue is whether the accused did or did not commit the crime as charged.

Even Richard Rorty, then, acknowledges the gap, and the importance of the gap, between appearance and reality, between those theatrical exercises that may entertain us without pretence of truth-telling, and those that aim for, and often hit, the truth. He calls it a "vegetarian" concept of truth. Very well, then, let's all be vegetarians about the truth. Scientists never wanted to go the whole hog anyway.

So now, let's ask about the sources or foundations of this mild, uncontroversial, vegetarian concept of truth.

Right now, as I speak, billions of organisms on this planet are engaged in a game of hide and seek. It is not just a game for them. It is a matter of life and death. *Getting it right,* not making mistakes, has been of paramount importance to every living thing on this planet for more than three billion years, and so these organisms have evolved thousands of different ways of finding out about the world they live in, discriminating friends from foes, meals from mates, and ignoring the rest for the most part. It matters to them that they not be misinformed about these matters—indeed nothing matters more—but they don't, as a rule, appreciate this. They are the beneficiaries of equipment exquisitely designed to get what matters right but when their equipment malfunctions and gets matters wrong, they have no resources, as a rule, for noticing this, let alone deploring it. They soldier on, unwittingly. The difference between how things seem and how things really are is just as fatal a gap for them as it can be for us, but they are largely oblivious to it. The *recognition* of the difference between appearance and reality is a human discovery. A few other species—some primates, some cetaceans, maybe even some birds—show signs of appreciating the phenomenon of "false belief"—*getting it wrong.* They exhibit sensitivity to the errors of others, and perhaps even some sensitivity to their own errors as errors, but they lack the capacity for the reflection required to *dwell* on this possibility, and so they cannot use this sensitivity in the deliberate design of repairs or improvements of their own seeking gear or hiding gear. That sort of bridging of the gap between appearance and reality is a wrinkle that we human beings alone have mastered.

We are the species that discovered doubt. Is there enough food laid by for winter? Have I miscalculated? Is my mate cheating on me? Should we have moved south? Is it safe to enter this cave? Other creatures are often visibly agitated by their own uncertainties about just such questions, but because they cannot actually *ask themselves these questions,* they cannot articulate their predicaments for themselves or take steps to improve their grip on the truth. They are stuck in a world of appearances, making the best they can of how things seem and seldom if ever worrying about whether how things seem is how they truly are.

We alone can be wracked with doubt, and we alone have been provoked by that epistemic itch to seek a remedy: better truth-seeking methods. Wanting to keep better track of our food supplies, our territories, our families, our enemies, we discovered the benefits of talking it over with others, asking questions, passing on lore. We invented culture. Then we invented measuring, and arithmetic, and maps, and writing. These communicative and recording innovations come with a built-in ideal: truth. The point of asking questions is to find *true* answers; the point of measuring is to measure *accurately;* the point of making maps is to *find your way* to your destination. There may be an Island of the Color-blind (allowing Oliver Sacks his usual large dose of poetic license), but no Island of the People Who Do Not Recognize Their Own Children. The Land of the Liars could exist only in philosophers' puzzles; there are no traditions of False Calendar Systems for mis-recording the passage of time. In short, the goal of truth goes without saying, in every human culture.

We human beings use our communicative skills not just for truth-telling, but also for promise-making, threatening, bargaining, story-telling, entertaining, mystifying, inducing hypnotic trances, and just plain kidding around, but prince of these activities is truth-telling, and for this activity we have invented ever better tools. Alongside our tools for agriculture, building, warfare, and transportation, we have created a technology of truth: science. Try to draw a straight line, or a circle, "freehand." Unless you have considerable artistic talent, the result will not be impressive. With a straight edge and a compass,

on the other hand, you can practically eliminate the sources of human variability and get a nice, clean, objective result, the same every time.

Is the line really straight? How straight is it? In response to these questions, we develop ever finer tests, and then tests of the accuracy of those tests, and so forth, bootstrapping our way to ever greater accuracy and objectivity. Scientists are just as vulnerable to wishful thinking, just as likely to be tempted by base motives, just as venal and gullible and forgetful as the rest of humankind. Scientists don't consider themselves to be saints; they don't even pretend to be priests (who according to tradition are supposed to do a better job than the rest of us at fighting off human temptation and frailty). Scientists take themselves to be just as weak and fallible as anybody else, but recognizing those very sources of error in themselves and in the groups to which they belong, they have devised elaborate systems to tie their own hands, forcibly preventing their frailties and prejudices from infecting their results.

It is not just the implements, the physical tools of the trade, that are designed to be resistant to human error. The organization of methods is also under severe selection pressure for improved reliability and objectivity. The classic example is the double blind experiment, in which, for instance, neither the human subjects nor the experimenters themselves are permitted to know which subjects get the test drug and which the placebo, so that nobody's subliminal hankerings and hunches can influence the perception of the results. The statistical design of both individual experiments and suites of experiments is then embedded in the larger practice of routine attempts at replication by independent investigators, which is further embedded in a tradition—flawed, but recognized—of publication of both positive and negative results.

What inspires faith in arithmetic is the fact that hundreds of scribblers, working independently on the same problem, will all arrive at the same answer (except for those negligible few whose errors can be found and identified to the mutual satisfaction of all). This unrivalled objectivity is also found in geometry and the other branches of mathematics, which since antiquity have been the very model of certain knowledge set against the world of flux and controversy. In Plato's early dialogue, the *Meno,* Socrates and the slave boy work out together a special case of the Pythagorean theorem. Plato's example expresses the frank recognition of a standard of truth to be aspired to by all truth-seekers, a standard that has not only never been seriously challenged, but that has been tacitly accepted— indeed heavily relied upon, even in matters of life and death—by the most vigorous opponents of science. (Or do you know a church that keeps track of its flock, and their donations, without benefit of arithmetic?)

Yes, but science almost never looks as uncontroversial, as cut-and-dried, as arithmetic. Indeed rival scientific factions often engage in propaganda battles as ferocious as anything to be found in politics, or even in religious conflict. The fury with which the defenders of scientific orthodoxy often defend their doctrines against the heretics is probably unmatched in other arenas of human rhetorical combat. These competitions for allegiance   and, of course, funding— are designed to capture attention, and being well-designed, they typically succeed. This has the side effect that the warfare on the cutting edge of any science draws attention away from the huge uncontested background, the dull metal heft of the axe that gives the cutting edge its power. What goes without saying, during these heated disagreements, is an organized, encyclopedic collection of agreed-upon, humdrum, scientific fact.

Robert Proctor usefully draws our attention to a distinction between neutrality and objectivity.[2] Geologists, he notes, know a lot more about oil-bearing shales than about other rocks—for the obvious economic and political reasons—but they do *know* objectively about oil-bearing shales. And much of what they learn about oil-bearing shales can be generalized to other, less favored rocks. We want science to be objective; we should not want science to be neutral. Biologists

know a lot more about the fruit fly, *Drosophila,* than they do about other insects—not because you can get rich off fruit flies, but because you can get knowledge out of fruit flies easier than you can get it out of most other species. Biologists also know a lot more about mosquitoes than about other insects, and here it is because mosquitoes are more harmful to people than other species that might be much easier to study. Many are the reasons for concentrating attention in science, and they all conspire to making the paths of investigation far from neutral; they do not, in general, make those paths any less objective. Sometimes, to be sure, one bias or another leads to a violation of the canons of scientific method. Studying the pattern of a disease in men, for instance, while neglecting to gather the data on the same disease in women is not just not neutral; it is bad science, as indefensible in scientific terms as it is in political terms.

It is true that past scientific orthodoxies have themselves inspired policies that hindsight reveals to be seriously flawed. One can sympathize, for instance, with Ashis Nandy, editor of the passionately anti-scientific anthology *Science, Hegemony and Violence: A Requiem for Modernity,* Delhi: Oxford Univ. Press, 1988. Having lived through Atoms for Peace and the Green Revolution, to name two of the most ballyhooed scientific juggernauts that have seriously disrupted third-world societies, he sees how "the adaptation in India of decades-old western technologies are advertised and purchased as great leaps forward in science, even when such adaptations turn entire disciplines or areas of knowledge into mere intellectual machines for the adaptation, replication and testing of shop-worn western models which have often been given up in the west itself as too dangerous or as ecologically non-viable" (p. 8). But we should recognize this as a political misuse of science, not as a fundamental flaw in science itself.

The methods of science aren't foolproof, but they are indefinitely perfectible. Just as important: there is a tradition of criticism that enforces improvement whenever and wherever flaws are discovered. The methods of science, like everything else under the sun, are themselves objects of scientific scrutiny, as *method* becomes *methodology*, the analysis of methods. Methodology in turn falls under the gaze of *epistemology*, the investigation of investigation itself—nothing is off limits to scientific questioning. The irony is that these fruits of scientific reflection, showing us the ineliminable smudges of imperfection, are sometimes used by those who are suspicious of science as their grounds for denying it a privileged status in the truth-seeking department—as if the institutions and practices they see competing with it were no worse off in these regards. But where are the examples of religious orthodoxy being simply abandoned in the face of irresistible evidence? Again and again in science, yesterday's heresies have become today's new orthodoxies. No religion exhibits that pattern in its history.

NOTES

1. Portions of this paper are derived from "Faith in the Truth," my Amnesty Lecture, Oxford, February 17, 1997.

2. *Value-Free Science?*, Harvard Univ. Press, 1991.

For Further Reflection

1. Examine Dennett's parable of the American researchers introducing a virus into a third-world country. What is the significance of this story?

2. Evaluate Dennett's rejection of cognitive relativism, the idea that there is no objective truth, but that truth is relative to each person or culture. How does he argue against this position? Is he correct?

3. According to Dennett, what is the role of science in the pursuit of truth? Is science neutral with regard to truth? Explain.

4. Compare Dennett's essay with the previous one by Richard Rorty. Discuss their comparative merits.

5. Is there something self-referentially incoherent in the postmodernist claim that *there is no objective truth*? Are they claiming that that statement is objectively true?

III.32   Relativism

HARVEY SIEGEL

Harvey Siegel is a professor of philosophy at the University of Miami and the author of several books, including *Relativism Refuted: A Critique of Contemporary Epistemological Relativism* (1987). He reviews the strongest charge against relativism—namely, that it incoherently implies that "if it is right, the very notion of rightness is undermined, in which case relativism itself cannot be right."

Study Questions

1. What does it mean for a doctrine to be "self-referentially incoherent"?
2. Can relativism be coherently asserted and defended? Why or why not?
3. Can the notion of "relative truth" provide support to cognitive relativism? Explain.

EPISTEMOLOGICAL RELATIVISM MAY BE defined as the view that knowledge (and/or truth) is relative—to time, to place, to society, to culture, to historical epoch, to conceptual scheme or framework, or to personal training or conviction—so that what counts as knowledge depends upon the value of one or more of these variables. If knowledge and truth are relative in this way, this will be because different cultures, societies, etc. accept different sets of background principles and standards of evaluation for knowledge-claims, and there is no neutral way of choosing between these alternative sets of standards. So the relativist's basic claim is that the truth and rational justifiability of knowledge-claims are relative to the standards used in evaluating such claims.

The doctrine of relativism is usually traced to Protagoras, who is portrayed in Plato's *Theaetetus* as holding that "man is the measure of all things" ("homo mensura"), and that any given thing "is to me such as it appears to me, and is to you such as it appears to you" (152a). Plato's Socrates characterizes Protagorean relativism as consisting in the view that "what seems true to anyone is true for him to whom it seems so" (*Theaetetus* 170a). This view is a form of relativism in our sense, since for Protagoras there is no standard higher than the individual with reference to which claims to truth and knowledge can be adjudicated. But relativism as defined above is more general than Protagorean relativism, for it places the source of relativism at the level of standards rather than at the level of personal opinion or perception, and as such aptly characterizes more recent versions of relativism.

Opponents of relativism have made many criticisms of the doctrine; by far the most fundamental is the charge that relativism is *self-referentially incoherent*, in that defending the doctrine requires one to give it up. There are several versions of the incoherence charge. The most powerful is that relativism precludes the possibility of determining the truth, warrant or epistemic merit of contentious claims and doctrines—including itself—since according to relativism no claim or doctrine can fail any test of epistemic adequacy or be judged unjustified, false or unwarranted. Take Protagorean relativism as an example. If "what seems true [or warranted] to anyone *is* true [or warranted] for him to whom it seems so," then no sincere claim can fail any test of epistemic adequacy or be judged unjustified or false. But if there is no possibility that a claim or doctrine can fail a test of epistemic adequacy or rightness, then the distinction between adequacy and inadequacy, rightness and wrongness is given up. If so, then the very notions of rightness, truth and warrantedness are undermined. But if this is so, then relativism itself cannot be right. In short, relativism is incoherent because, if it is right the very notion of rightness is undermined, in which case relativism itself cannot be right. The assertion *and defence* of relativism requires one to presuppose neutral standards in accordance with which contentious claims and doctrines can be assessed; but relativism denies the possibility of evaluation in accordance with such neutral standards. Thus the doctrine of relativism cannot be coherently defended—it can be defended only by being given up. Relativism is thus impotent to defend itself, and falls to this fundamental reflexive difficulty.

A further difficulty worth noting is that concerning the notion of *relative truth*. Many versions of relativism rely on such a notion, but it is very difficult to make sense of it. An assertion that a proposition is "true for me" (or "true for members of my culture") is more readily understood as a claim about what I (or members of my culture) *believe* than it is as a claim ascribing to that proposition some peculiar form of truth. Moreover, even if this notion could be made sense of, it would still fall to the incoherence argument above.

From Harvey Siegel "Relativism" in A Companion to Epistemology, *ed. Jonathan Dancy and Ernest Sosa (Malden, MA: Blackwell, 1992), 428–429.*

For Further Reflection

1. The view that truth is relative to societies—that truth depends on society's beliefs—is known as social relativism. On this view, a claim can be true for Christians but false for Jews, true for Americans but false for Iraqis, true for college students but false for U.S. senators. Does this form of relativism then imply that societies are infallible, that a society cannot be mistaken if it believes something to be true? Does it imply that no one can legitimately criticize another society for doing something wrong (because if the society believes an action to be right, it is right)? Explain.

2. If truth were relative to individuals (a view known as subjective relativism), truth would be whatever a person believes it to be. In that case, wouldn't disagreement between two people on an issue be pointless? Wouldn't disagreements on any issue be like disagreements about the taste of pizza, in which no sincere view could be wrong? Why or why not?

3. Suppose a relativist declares, "All truth is relative (that is, there is no objective truth)." Explain how this claim would be, as Siegel says, "self-referentially incoherent."

III.C   Induction

When we reason inductively, we assume that events that followed one another in the past will do the same in the future, that the future will be like the past. We presuppose, in other words, the *principle of induction*. Because of previous experience, we expect night to follow day, fire to burn, bread to nourish, and dogs to bark. Likewise the whole scientific enterprise runs on this principle, with scientists making inferences from empirical regularities to predictions about events to come. At first glance, it might seem that no one would seriously question the legitimacy of inductive reasoning. But Hume does.

He asks, Do we have any grounds whatsoever for believing the principle of induction? What justifies our assumption that the future will be like the past? He argues that the principle cannot be an *a priori* truth, and it cannot be an *a posteriori* fact. It cannot be the former because the denial of an *a priori* truth (such as "All bachelors are unmarried") is self-contradictory, and the denial of the principle of induction is not like that. It cannot be the latter because no amount of empirical evidence can show it to be true. Why? As Hume observes, to maintain that the principle of induction is an *a posteriori* fact is to say that it can be established by experience (that is, inductively). That is equivalent to saying that the principle of induction can be proved by the principle of induction—which is to beg the question. Arguing in a circle like this offers no support to the principle at all.

Wesley Salmon, speaking of the scientific method, puts the point like this:

We can all agree that science has, up to now, a very impressive record of success in predicting the future. The question we are asking, however, is this: should we predict that science will continue to have the kind of success it has had in the past? It is quite natural to assume that its record will continue, but this is just a case of applying the scientific method to itself. . . . But using the scientific method to judge the scientific method is circular reasoning.*

*Wesley C. Salmon, "An Encounter with David Hume," in ed. Joel Feinberg and Russ Shafer-Landau, *Reason and Responsibility* (Belmont, CA: Wadsworth, 2008), 257–258.

This difficulty of justifying the assumption that the future will be like the past is known as the *problem of induction*, and it has incited generations of thinkers to try to solve it. They have explored whether there are grounds for believing that the inductive principle—so indispensible in science and daily life—is true. All the while we use the principle to make all kinds of inferences and predictions, which usually serve us well.

Skeptical Doubts Concerning the Operations of the Understanding

III.33

DAVID HUME

Regarding the principle of induction, Hume asserts, "It is impossible…that any arguments from experience can prove this resemblance of the past to the future; since all these arguments are founded on the supposition of that resemblance."* He holds that we rely on the principle of induction not because it is an established truth but because it is a habit of mind. Because of our long experience of seeing one event repeatedly follow another, we develop a feeling of expectation that they will always follow one another.

Study Questions

1. Why does Hume think that the principle of induction cannot be justified? Why does he insist that trying to support the principle by empirical evidence is circular reasoning?
2. Why can't the principle of induction be justified *a priori*? Why can't it be justified *a posteriori*?
3. According to Hume, why do we trust that the future will in fact resemble the past? That is, why do we rely so heavily on the principle of induction if it cannot be logically justified?

SECTION 4   SCEPTICAL DOUBTS CONCERNING THE OPERATIONS OF THE UNDERSTANDING

Part 1

1 All the objects of human reason or enquiry may naturally be divided into two kinds, to wit, *Relations of Ideas* and *Matters of Fact*. Of the first kind are the sciences of Geometry, Algebra, and Arithmetic; and in short, every affirmation, which is either intuitively or demonstratively certain. *That the square of the hypothenuse is equal to the square of the two sides*, is a proposition, which expresses a relation between these figures. *That three times five is equal to the half of thirty*, expresses a relation between these numbers. Propositions of this kind are discoverable by the mere operation of thought, without dependence

---

*David Hume, *Enquiries Concerning the Human Understanding and Concerning the Principles of Morals*, sec. II, para. 20, ed. L. A. Selby-Bigge (Oxford: Clarendon Press, 1972), 38.

on what is any where existent in the universe. Though there never were a circle or triangle in nature, the truths, demonstrated by Euclid, would for ever retain their certainty and evidence.

2   Matters of fact, which are the second objects of human reason, are not ascertained in the same manner; nor is our evidence of their truth, however great, of a like nature with the foregoing. The contrary of every matter of fact is still possible; because it can never imply a contradiction, and is conceived by the mind with the same facility and distinctness, as if ever so conformable to reality. *That the sun will not rise to-morrow* is no less intelligible a proposition, and implies no more contradiction, than the affirmation, *that it will rise*. We should in vain, therefore, attempt to demonstrate its falsehood. Were it demonstratively false, it would imply a contradiction, and could never be distinctly conceived by the mind.

3   It may, therefore, be a subject worthy of curiosity, to enquire what is the nature of that evidence, which assures us of any real existence and matter of fact, beyond the present testimony of our senses, or the records of our memory. This part of philosophy, it is observable, has been little cultivated, either by the ancients or moderns; and therefore our doubts and errors, in the prosecution of so important an enquiry, may be the more excusable; while we march through such difficult paths, without any guide or direction. They may even prove useful, by exciting curiosity, and destroying that implicit faith and security, which is the bane of all reasoning and free enquiry. The discovery of defects in the common philosophy, if any such there be, will not, I presume, be a discouragement, but rather an incitement, as is usual, to attempt something more full and satisfactory, than has yet been proposed to the public.

4   All reasonings concerning matter of fact seem to be founded on the relation of *Cause and Effect*. By means of that relation alone we can go beyond the evidence of our memory and senses. If you were to ask a man, why he believes any matter of fact, which is absent; for instance, that his friend is in the country, or in France; he would give you a reason; and this reason would be some other fact; as a letter received from him, or the knowledge of his former resolutions and promises. A man, finding a watch or any other machine in a desert island, would conclude, that there had once been men in that island. All our reasonings concerning fact are of the same nature. And here it is constantly supposed, that there is a connexion between the present fact and that which is inferred from it. Were there nothing to bind them together, the inference would be entirely precarious. The hearing of an articulate voice and rational discourse in the dark assures us of the presence of some person: Why? Because these are the effects of the human make and fabric, and closely connected with it. If we anatomize all the other reasonings of this nature, we shall find, that they are founded on the relation of cause and effect, and that this relation is either near or remote, direct or collateral. Heat and light are collateral effects of fire, and the one effect may justly be inferred from the other.

5   If we would satisfy ourselves, therefore, concerning the nature of that evidence, which assures us of matters of fact, we must enquire how we arrive at the knowledge of cause and effect.

6   I shall venture to affirm, as a general proposition, which admits of no exception, that the knowledge of this relation is not, in any instance, attained by reasonings *a priori*; but arises entirely from experience, when we find, that any particular objects are constantly conjoined with each other. Let an object be presented to a man of ever so strong natural reason and abilities; if that object be entirely new to him, he will not be able, by the most accurate examination of its sensible qualities, to discover any of its causes or effects. Adam, though his rational faculties be

From David Hume, An Enquiry Concerning Human Understanding, *Sections II, IV, and V, in* An Enquiry Concerning Human Understanding, *ed. Tom L. Beauchamp (2000), pp. 24–39. By permission of Oxford University Press, Inc.*

supposed, at the very first, entirely perfect, could not have inferred from the fluidity and transparency of water, that it would suffocate him, or from the light and warmth of fire, that it would consume him. No object ever discovers, by the qualities which appear to the senses, either the causes, which produced it, or the effects, which will arise from it; nor can our reason, unassisted by experience, ever draw any inference concerning real existence and matter of fact.

7   This proposition, *that causes and effects are discoverable, not by reason, but by experience*, will readily be admitted with regard to such objects, as we remember to have once been altogether unknown to us; since we must be conscious of the utter inability, which we then lay under, of foretelling, what would arise from them. Present two smooth pieces of marble to a man, who has no tincture of natural philosophy; he will never discover, that they will adhere together, in such a manner as to require great force to separate them in a direct line, while they make so small a resistance to a lateral pressure. Such events, as bear little analogy to the common course of nature, are also readily confessed to be known only by experience; nor does any man imagine that the explosion of gunpowder, or the attraction of a loadstone, could ever be discovered by arguments *a priori*. In like manner, when an effect is supposed to depend upon an intricate machinery or secret structure of parts, we make no difficulty in attributing all our knowledge of it to experience. Who will assert, that he can give the ultimate reason, why milk or bread is proper nourishment for a man, not for a lion or a tyger?

8   But the same truth may not appear, at first sight, to have the same evidence with regard to events, which have become familiar to us from our first appearance in the world, which bear a close analogy to the whole course of nature, and which are supposed to depend on the simple qualities of objects, without any secret structure of parts. We are apt to imagine, that we could discover these effects by the mere operation of our reason, without experience. We fancy, that were we brought, on a sudden, into this world,

we could at first have inferred, that one billiard-ball would communicate motion to another upon impulse; and that we needed not to have waited for the event, in order to pronounce with certainty concerning it. Such is the influence of custom, that, where it is strongest, it not only covers our natural ignorance, but even conceals itself, and seems not to take place, merely because it is found in the highest degree.

   But to convince us, that all the laws of nature, 9 and all the operations of bodies without exception, are known only by experience, the following reflections may, perhaps, suffice. Were any object presented to us, and were we required to pronounce concerning the effect, which will result from it, without consulting past observation; after what manner, I beseech you, must the mind proceed in this operation? It must invent or imagine some event, which it ascribes to the object as its effect; and it is plain that this invention must be entirely arbitrary. The mind can never possibly find the effect in the supposed cause, by the most accurate scrutiny and examination. For the effect is totally different from the cause, and consequently can never be discovered in it. Motion in the second billiard-ball is a quite distinct event from motion in the first; nor is there any thing in the one to suggest the smallest hint of the other. A stone or piece of metal raised into the air, and left without any support, immediately falls: But to consider the matter *a priori*, is there any thing we discover in this situation, which can beget the idea of a downward, rather than an upward, or any other motion, in the stone or metal?

   And as the first imagination or invention of a 10 particular effect, in all natural operations, is arbitrary, where we consult not experience; so must we also esteem the supposed tye or connexion between the cause and effect, which binds them together, and renders it impossible, that any other effect could result from the operation of that cause. When I see, for instance, a billiard-ball moving in a straight line towards another; even suppose motion in the second ball should by accident be suggested to me, as the result of their contact or impulse; may I not conceive, that a hundred different events might as well follow from that cause? May not both these balls remain at absolute rest? May not the first ball return in a straight line, or leap off from the second in any line or direction? All these suppositions are consistent and conceivable. Why then should we give the preference to one, which is no more consistent or conceivable than the rest? All our reasonings *a priori* will never be able to show us any foundation for this preference.

11   In a word, then, every effect is a distinct event from its cause. It could not, therefore, be discovered in the cause, and the first invention or conception of it, *a priori*, must be entirely arbitrary. And even after it is suggested, the conjunction of it with the cause must appear equally arbitrary; since there are always many other effects, which, to reason, must seem fully as consistent and natural. In vain, therefore, should we pretend to determine any single event, or infer any cause or effect, without the assistance of observation and experience.

12   Hence we may discover the reason, why no philosopher, who is rational and modest, has ever pretended to assign the ultimate cause of any natural operation, or to show distinctly the action of that power, which produces any single effect in the universe. It is confessed, that the utmost effort of human reason is, to reduce the principles, productive of natural phænomena, to a greater simplicity, and to resolve the many particular effects into a few general causes, by means of reasonings from analogy, experience, and observation. But as to the causes of these general causes, we should in vain attempt their discovery; nor shall we ever be able to satisfy ourselves, by any particular explication of them. These ultimate springs and principles are totally shut up from human curiosity and enquiry. Elasticity, gravity, cohesion of parts, communication of motion by impulse; these are probably the ultimate causes and principles which we shall ever discover in nature; and we may esteem ourselves sufficiently happy, if, by accurate enquiry and reasoning, we can trace up the particular phænom-

ena to, or near to, these general principles. The most perfect philosophy of the natural kind only staves off our ignorance a little longer: As perhaps the most perfect philosophy of the moral or metaphysical kind serves only to discover larger portions of our ignorance. Thus the observation of human blindness and weakness is the result of all philosophy, and meets us, at every turn, in spite of our endeavours to elude or avoid it.

Nor is geometry, when taken into the assis- 13
tance of natural philosophy, ever able to remedy this defect, or lead us into the knowledge of ultimate causes, by all that accuracy of reasoning, for which it is so justly celebrated. Every part of mixed mathematics proceeds upon the supposition, that certain laws are established by nature in her operations; and abstract reasonings are employed, either to assist experience in the discovery of these laws, or to determine their influence in particular instances, where it depends upon any precise degree of distance and quantity. Thus, it is a law of motion, discovered by experience, that the moment or force of any body in motion is in the compound ratio or proportion of its solid contents and its velocity; and consequently, that a small force may remove the greatest obstacle or raise the greatest weight, if, by any contrivance or machinery, we can encrease the velocity of that force, so as to make it an overmatch for its antagonist. Geometry assists us in the application of this law, by giving us the just dimensions of all the parts and figures, which can enter into any species of machine; but still the discovery of the law itself is owing merely to experience, and all the abstract reasonings in the world could never lead us one step towards the knowledge of it. When we reason *a priori*, and consider merely any object or cause, as it appears to the mind, independent of all observation, it never could suggest to us the notion of any distinct object, such as its effect; much less, show us the inseparable and inviolable connexion between them. A man must be very sagacious, who could discover by reasoning, that crystal is the effect of heat, and ice of cold, without being previously acquainted with the operations of these qualities.

Part 2

14 But we have not, as yet, attained any tolerable satisfaction with regard to the question first proposed. Each solution still gives rise to a new question as difficult as the foregoing, and leads us on to farther enquiries. When it is asked, *What is the nature of all our reasonings concerning matter of fact?* the proper answer seems to be, that they are founded on the relation of cause and effect. When again it is asked, *What is the foundation of all our reasonings and conclusions concerning that relation?* it may be replied in one word, EXPERIENCE. But if we still carry on our sifting humour, and ask, *What is the foundation of all conclusions from experience?* this implies a new question, which may be of more difficult solution and explication. Philosophers, that give themselves airs of superior wisdom and sufficiency, have a hard task, when they encounter persons of inquisitive dispositions, who push them from every corner, to which they retreat, and who are sure at last to bring them to some dangerous dilemma. The best expedient to prevent this confusion, is to be modest in our pretensions; and even to discover the difficulty ourselves before it is objected to us. By this means, we may make a kind of merit of our very ignorance.

15   I shall content myself, in this section, with an easy task, and shall pretend only to give a negative answer to the question here proposed. I say then, that, even after we have experience of the operations of cause and effect, our conclusions from that experience are *not* founded on reasoning, or any process of the understanding. This answer we must endeavour, both to explain and to defend.

16   It must certainly be allowed, that nature has kept us at a great distance from all her secrets, and has afforded us only the knowledge of a few superficial qualities of objects; while she conceals from us those powers and principles, on which the influence of these objects entirely depends. Our senses inform us of the colour, weight, and consistence of bread; but neither sense nor reason can ever inform us of those qualities, which fit it for the nourishment and support of a human body. Sight or feeling conveys an idea of the actual motion of bodies; but as to that wonderful force or power, which would carry on a moving body for ever in a continued change of place, and which bodies never lose but by communicating it to others; of this we cannot form the most distant conception. But notwithstanding this ignorance of natural powers[1] and principles, we always presume, when we see like sensible qualities, that they have like secret powers, and expect, that effects, similar to those, which we have experienced, will follow from them. If a body of like colour and consistence with that bread, which we have formerly eat, be presented to us, we make no scruple of repeating the experiment, and foresee, with certainty, like nourishment and support. Now this is a process of the mind or thought, of which I would willingly know the foundation. It is allowed on all hands, that there is no known connexion between the sensible qualities and the secret powers; and consequently, that the mind is not led to form such a conclusion concerning their constant and regular conjunction, by any thing which it knows of their nature. As to past *Experience*, it can be allowed to give *direct* and *certain* information of those precise objects only, and that precise period of time, which fell under its cognizance: But why this experience should be extended to future times, and to other objects, which, for aught we know, may be only in appearance similar; this is the main question on which I would insist. The bread, which I formerly eat, nourished me; that is, a body of such sensible qualities, was, at that time, endowed with such secret powers: But does it follow, that other bread must also nourish me at another time, and that like sensible qualities must always be attended with like secret powers? The consequence seems nowise necessary. At least, it must be acknowledged, that there is here a consequence drawn by the mind; that there is a certain step taken; a process of thought, and an inference, which wants to be explained. These two propositions are far from being the same, *I have found that*

such an object has always been attended with such an effect, and *I foresee, that other objects, which are, in appearance, similar, will be attended with similar effects.* I shall allow, if you please, that the one proposition may justly be inferred from the other: I know in fact, that it always is inferred. But if you insist, that the inference is made by a chain of reasoning, I desire you to produce that reasoning. The connexion between these propositions is not intuitive. There is required a medium, which may enable the mind to draw such an inference, if indeed it be drawn by reasoning and argument. What that medium is, I must confess, passes my comprehension; and it is incumbent on those to produce it, who assert, that it really exists, and is the origin of all our conclusions concerning matter of fact.

17   This negative argument must certainly, in process of time, become altogether convincing, if many penetrating and able philosophers shall turn their enquiries this way; and no one be ever able to discover any connecting proposition or intermediate step, which supports the understanding in this conclusion. But as the question is yet new, every reader may not trust so far to his own penetration, as to conclude, because an argument escapes his enquiry, that therefore it does not really exist. For this reason it may be requisite to venture upon a more difficult task; and enumerating all the branches of human knowledge, endeavour to show, that none of them can afford such an argument.

18   All reasonings may be divided into two kinds, namely, demonstrative reasoning, or that concerning relations of ideas, and moral reasoning, or that concerning matter of fact and existence. That there are no demonstrative arguments in the case, seems evident; since it implies no contradiction, that the course of nature may change, and that an object, seemingly like those which we have experienced, may be attended with different or contrary effects. May I not clearly and distinctly conceive, that a body, falling from the clouds, and which, in all other respects, resembles snow, has yet the taste of salt or feeling of fire? Is there any more intelligible proposition than to affirm, that all the trees will flourish in December and January, and decay in May and June? Now whatever is intelligible, and can be distinctly conceived, implies no contradiction, and can never be proved false by any demonstrative argument or abstract reasoning *a priori*.

19   If we be, therefore, engaged by arguments to put trust in past experience, and make it the standard of our future judgment, these arguments must be probable only, or such as regard matter of fact and real existence, according to the division above-mentioned. But that there is no argument of this kind, must appear, if our explication of that species of reasoning be admitted as solid and satisfactory. We have said, that all arguments concerning existence are founded on the relation of cause and effect; that our knowledge of that relation is derived entirely from experience; and that all our experimental conclusions proceed upon the supposition, that the future will be conformable to the past. To endeavour, therefore, the proof of this last supposition by probable arguments, or arguments regarding existence, must be evidently going in a circle, and taking that for granted, which is the very point in question.

20   In reality, all arguments from experience are founded on the similarity, which we discover among natural objects, and by which we are induced to expect effects similar to those, which we have found to follow from such objects. And though none but a fool or madman will ever pretend to dispute the authority of experience, or to reject that great guide of human life; it may surely be allowed a philosopher to have so much curiosity at least, as to examine the principle of human nature, which gives this mighty authority to experience, and makes us draw advantage from that similarity, which nature has placed among different objects. From causes, which appear *similar*, we expect similar effects. This is the sum of all our experimental conclusions. Now it seems evident, that, if this conclusion were formed by reason, it would be as perfect at first, and upon one instance, as after ever so long a course of experience. But the case is far other-

wise. Nothing so like as eggs; yet no one, on account of this appearing similarity, expects the same taste and relish in all of them. It is only after a long course of uniform experiments in any kind, that we attain a firm reliance and security with regard to a particular event. Now where is that process of reasoning, which, from one instance, draws a conclusion, so different from that which it infers from a hundred instances, that are nowise different from that single one? This question I propose as much for the sake of information, as with an intention of raising difficulties. I cannot find, I cannot imagine any such reasoning. But I keep my mind still open to instruction, if any one will vouchsafe to bestow it on me.

21   Should it be said, that, from a number of uniform experiments, we *infer* a connexion between the sensible qualities and the secret powers; this, I must confess, seems the same difficulty, couched in different terms. The question still recurs, On what process of argument this *inference* is founded? Where is the medium, the interposing ideas, which join propositions so very wide of each other? It is confessed, that the colour, consistence, and other sensible qualities of bread appear not, of themselves, to have any connexion with the secret powers of nourishment and support. For otherwise we could infer these secret powers from the first appearance of these sensible qualities, without the aid of experience; contrary to the sentiment of all philosophers, and contrary to plain matter of fact. Here then is our natural state of ignorance with regard to the powers and influence of all objects. How is this remedied by experience? It only shows us a number of uniform effects, resulting from certain objects, and teaches us, that those particular objects, at that particular time, were endowed with such powers and forces. When a new object, endowed with similar sensible qualities, is produced, we expect similar powers and forces, and look for a like effect. From a body of like colour and consistence with bread, we expect like nourishment and support. But this surely is a step or progress of the mind, which wants to be explained. When a man says, *I have found, in all past instances, such sensible qualities conjoined with such secret powers*: And when he says, *similar sensible qualities will always be conjoined with similar secret powers*, he is not guilty of a tautology, nor are these propositions in any respect the same. You say that the one proposition is an inference from the other. But you must confess, that the inference is not intuitive; neither is it demonstrative: Of what nature is it then? To say it is experimental, is begging the question. For all inferences from experience suppose, as their foundation, that the future will resemble the past, and that similar powers will be conjoined with similar sensible qualities. If there be any suspicion, that the course of nature may change, and that the past may be no rule for the future, all experience becomes useless, and can give rise to no inference or conclusion. It is impossible, therefore, that any arguments from experience can prove this resemblance of the past to the future; since all these arguments are founded on the supposition of that resemblance. Let the course of things be allowed hitherto ever so regular; that alone, without some new argument or inference, proves not, that, for the future, it will continue so. In vain do you pretend to have learned the nature of bodies from your past experience. Their secret nature, and consequently, all their effects and influence, may change, without any change in their sensible qualities. This happens sometimes, and with regard to some objects: Why may it not happen always, and with regard to all objects? What logic, what process of argument secures you against this supposition? My practice, you say, refutes my doubts. But you mistake the purport of my question. As an agent, I am quite satisfied in the point; but as a philosopher, who has some share of curiosity, I will not say scepticism, I want to learn the foundation of this inference. No reading, no enquiry has yet been able to remove my difficulty, or give me satisfaction in a matter of such importance. Can I do better than propose the difficulty to the public, even though, perhaps, I have small hopes of obtaining

a solution? We shall at least, by this means, be sensible of our ignorance, if we do not augment our knowledge.

22   I must confess, that a man is guilty of unpardonable arrogance, who concludes, because an argument has escaped his own investigation, that therefore it does not really exist. I must also confess, that, though all the learned, for several ages, should have employed themselves in fruitless search upon any subject, it may still, perhaps, be rash to conclude positively, that the subject must, therefore, pass all human comprehension. Even though we examine all the sources of our knowledge, and conclude them unfit for such a subject, there may still remain a suspicion, that the enumeration is not compleat, or the examination not accurate. But with regard to the present subject, there are some considerations, which seem to remove all this accusation of arrogance or suspicion of mistake.

23   It is certain, that the most ignorant and stupid peasants, nay infants, nay even brute beasts, improve by experience, and learn the qualities of natural objects, by observing the effects, which result from them. When a child has felt the sensation of pain from touching the flame of a candle, he will be careful not to put his hand near any candle; but will expect a similar effect from a cause, which is similar in its sensible qualities and appearance. If you assert, therefore, that the understanding of the child is led into this conclusion by any process of argument or ratiocination, I may justly require you to produce that argument; nor have you any pretence to refuse so equitable a demand. You cannot say, that the argument is abstruse, and may possibly escape your enquiry; since you confess, that it is obvious to the capacity of a mere infant. If you hesitate, therefore, a moment, or if, after reflection, you produce any intricate or profound argument, you, in a manner, give up the question, and confess, that it is not reasoning which engages us to suppose the past resembling the future, and to expect similar effects from causes, which are, to appearance, similar. This is the

proposition which I intended to enforce in the present section. If I be right, I pretend not to have made any mighty discovery. And if I be wrong, I must acknowledge myself to be indeed a very backward scholar; since I cannot now discover an argument, which, it seems, was perfectly familiar to me, long before I was out of my cradle.

SECTION 5   SCEPTICAL SOLUTION OF THESE DOUBTS

Part 1

1   The passion for philosophy, like that for religion, seems liable to this inconvenience, that, though it aims at the correction of our manners, and extirpation of our vices, it may only serve, by imprudent management, to foster a predominant inclination, and push the mind, with more determined resolution, towards that side, which already *draws* too much, by the biass and propensity of the natural temper. It is certain, that, while we aspire to the magnanimous firmness of the philosophic sage, and endeavour to confine our pleasures altogether within our own minds, we may, at last, render our philosophy like that of Epictetus, and other Stoics, only a more refined system of selfishness, and reason ourselves out of all virtue, as well as social enjoyment. While we study with attention the vanity of human life, and turn all our thoughts towards the empty and transitory nature of riches and honours, we are, perhaps, all the while, flattering our natural indolence, which, hating the bustle of the world, and drudgery of business, seeks a pretence of reason, to give itself a full and uncontrouled indulgence. There is, however, one species of philosophy, which seems little liable to this inconvenience, and that because it strikes in with no disorderly passion of the human mind, nor can mingle itself with any natural affection or propensity; and that is the Academic or Sceptical philosophy. The Academics always talk of doubt and suspense of judgment,

of danger in hasty determinations, of confining to very narrow bounds the enquiries of the understanding, and of renouncing all speculations which lie not within the limits of common life and practice. Nothing, therefore, can be more contrary than such a philosophy to the supine indolence of the mind, its rash arrogance, its lofty pretensions, and its superstitious credulity. Every passion is mortified by it, except the love of truth; and that passion never is, nor can be carried to too high a degree. It is surprizing, therefore, that this philosophy, which, in almost every instance, must be harmless and innocent, should be the subject of so much groundless reproach and obloquy. But, perhaps, the very circumstance, which renders it so innocent, is what chiefly exposes it to the public hatred and resentment. By flattering no irregular passion, it gains few partizans: By opposing so many vices and follies, it raises to itself abundance of enemies, who stigmatize it as libertine, profane, and irreligious.

2 Nor need we fear, that this philosophy, while it endeavours to limit our enquiries to common life, should ever undermine the reasonings of common life, and carry its doubts so far as to destroy all action, as well as speculation. Nature will always maintain her rights, and prevail in the end over any abstract reasoning whatsoever. Though we should conclude, for instance, as in the foregoing section, that, in all reasonings from experience, there is a step taken by the mind, which is not supported by any argument or process of the understanding; there is no danger, that these reasonings, on which almost all knowledge depends, will ever be affected by such a discovery. If the mind be not engaged by argument to make this step, it must be induced by some other principle of equal weight and authority; and that principle will preserve its influence as long as human nature remains the same. What that principle is, may well be worth the pains of enquiry.

3 Suppose a person, though endowed with the strongest faculties of reason and reflection, to be brought on a sudden into this world; he would, indeed, immediately observe a continual succession of objects, and one event following another; but he would not be able to discover any thing farther. He would not, at first, by any reasoning, be able to reach the idea of cause and effect; since the particular powers, by which all natural operations are performed, never appear to the senses; nor is it reasonable to conclude, merely because one event, in one instance, precedes another, that therefore the one is the cause, the other the effect. Their conjunction may be arbitrary and casual. There may be no reason to infer the existence of one from the appearance of the other. And in a word, such a person, without more experience, could never employ his conjecture or reasoning concerning any matter of fact, or be assured of any thing beyond what was immediately present to his memory and senses.

4 Suppose again, that he has acquired more experience, and has lived so long in the world as to have observed similar objects or events to be constantly conjoined together; what is the consequence of this experience? He immediately infers the existence of one object from the appearance of the other. Yet he has not, by all his experience, acquired any idea or knowledge of the secret power, by which the one object produces the other; nor is it, by any process of reasoning, he is engaged to draw this inference. But still he finds himself determined to draw it: And though he should be convinced, that his understanding has no part in the operation, he would nevertheless continue in the same course of thinking. There is some other principle, which determines him to form such a conclusion.

5 This principle is Custom or Habit. For wherever the repetition of any particular act or operation produces a propensity to renew the same act or operation, without being impelled by any reasoning or process of the understanding; we always say, that this propensity is the effect of *Custom*. By employing that word, we pretend not to have given the ultimate reason of such a propensity. We only point out a principle of

human nature, which is universally acknowl-edged, and which is well known by its effects. Perhaps, we can push our enquiries no farther, or pretend to give the cause of this cause; but must rest contented with it as the ultimate principle, which we can assign, of all our conclusions from experience. It is sufficient satisfaction, that we can go so far; without repining at the narrowness of our faculties, because they will carry us no far-ther. And it is certain we here advance a very intelligible proposition at least, if not a true one, when we assert, that, after the constant conjunc-tion of two objects, heat and flame, for instance, weight and solidity, we are determined by cus-tom alone to expect the one from the appearance of the other. This hypothesis seems even the only one, which explains the difficulty, why we draw, from a thousand instances, an inference, which we are not able to draw from one instance, that is, in no respect, different from them. Reason is incapable of any such variation. The conclusions, which it draws from considering one circle, are the same which it would form upon surveying all the circles in the universe. But no man, having seen only one body move after being impelled by another, could infer, that every other body will move after a like impulse. All inferences from experience, therefore, are effects of custom, not of reasoning.[2]

6   Custom, then, is the great guide of human life. It is that principle alone, which renders our experience useful to us, and makes us expect, for the future, a similar train of events with those which have appeared in the past. Without the influence of custom, we should be entirely igno-rant of every matter of fact, beyond what is immediately present to the memory and senses. We should never know how to adjust means to ends, or to employ our natural powers in the production of any effect. There would be an end at once of all action, as well as of the chief part of speculation.

7   But here it may be proper to remark, that though our conclusions from experience carry us beyond our memory and senses, and assure us of matters of fact, which happened in the most dis-tant places and most remote ages; yet some fact must always be present to the senses or memory, from which we may first proceed in drawing these conclusions. A man, who should find in a desert country the remains of pompous build-ings, would conclude, that the country had, in ancient times, been cultivated by civilized inhab-itants; but did nothing of this nature occur to him, he could never form such an inference. We learn the events of former ages from history; but then we must peruse the volumes, in which this instruction is contained, and thence carry up our inferences from one testimony to another, till we arrive at the eyewitnesses and spectators of these distant events. In a word, if we proceed not upon some fact, present to the memory or senses, our reasonings would be merely hypothetical; and however the particular links might be connected with each other, the whole chain of inferences would have nothing to support it, nor could we ever, by its means, arrive at the knowledge of any real existence. If I ask, why you believe any par-ticular matter of fact, which you relate, you must tell me some reason; and this reason will be some other fact, connected with it. But as you cannot proceed after this manner, *in infinitum*, you must at last terminate in some fact, which is pres-ent to your memory or senses; or must allow that your belief is entirely without foundation.

8   What then is the conclusion of the whole mat-ter? A simple one; though, it must be confessed, pretty remote from the common theories of phi-losophy. All belief of matter of fact or real exis-tence is derived merely from some object, pres-ent to the memory or senses, and a customary conjunction between that and some other object. Or in other words; having found, in many instances, that any two kinds of objects, flame and heat, snow and cold, have always been conjoined together; if flame or snow be pre-sented anew to the senses, the mind is carried by custom to expect heat or cold, and to *believe*, that such a quality does exist, and will discover itself upon a nearer approach. This belief is the

necessary result of placing the mind in such circumstances. It is an operation of the soul, when we are so situated, as unavoidable as to feel the passion of love, when we receive benefits; or hatred, when we meet with injuries. All these operations are a species of natural instincts, which no reasoning or process of the thought and understanding is able, either to produce, or to prevent.

9 At this point, it would be very allowable for us to stop our philosophical researches. In most questions, we can never make a single step farther; and in all questions, we must terminate here at last, after our most restless and curious enquiries. But still our curiosity will be pardonable, perhaps commendable, if it carry us on to still farther researches, and make us examine more accurately the nature of this *belief*, and of the *customary conjunction*, whence it is derived. By this means we may meet with some explications and analogies, that will give satisfaction; at least to such as love the abstract sciences, and can be entertained with speculations, which, however accurate, may still retain a degree of doubt and uncertainty. As to readers of a different taste; the remaining part of this section is not calculated for them, and the following enquiries may well be understood, though it be neglected.

NOTES

1. The word, *power*, is here used in a loose and popular sense. The more accurate explication of it would give additional evidence to this argument.

2. Nothing is more usual than for writers, even on *moral, political,* or *physical* subjects, to distinguish between *reason* and *experience*, and to suppose, that these species of argumentation are entirely different from each other. The former are taken for the mere result of our intellectual faculties, which, by considering *a priori* the nature of things, and examining the effects, that must follow from their operation, establish particular principles of science and philosophy. The latter are supposed to be derived entirely from sense and observation, by which we learn what has actually resulted from the operation of particular objects, and are thence able to infer, what will, for the future, result from them. Thus, for instance, the limitations and restraints of civil government, and a legal constitution, may be defended, either from *reason*, which, reflecting on the great frailty and corruption of human nature, teaches, that no man can safely be trusted with unlimited authority; or from *experience* and history, which inform us of the enormous abuses, that ambition, in every age and country, has been found to make of so imprudent a confidence.

The same distinction between reason and experience is maintained in all our deliberations concerning the conduct of life; while the experienced statesman, general, physician, or merchant is trusted and followed; and the unpractised novice, with whatever natural talents endowed, neglected, and despised. Though it be allowed, that reason may form very plausible conjectures with regard to the consequences of such a particular conduct in such particular circumstances; it is still supposed imperfect, without the assistance of experience, which is alone able to give stability and certainty to the maxims, derived from study and reflection.

But notwithstanding that this distinction be thus universally received, both in the active and speculative scenes of life, I shall not scruple to pronounce, that it is, at bottom, erroneous, or at least, superficial.

If we examine those arguments, which, in any of the sciences above-mentioned, are supposed to be the mere effects of reasoning and reflection, they will be found to terminate, at last, in some general principle or conclusion, for which we can assign no reason but observation and experience. The only difference between them and those maxims, which are vulgarly esteemed the result of pure experience, is, that the former cannot be established without some process of thought, and some reflection on what we have observed, in order to distinguish its circumstances, and trace its consequences: Whereas in the latter, the experienced event is exactly and fully similar to that which we infer as the result of any particular situation. The history of a Tiberius or a Nero makes us dread a like tyranny, were our monarchs freed from the restraints of laws and senates: But the observation of any fraud or cruelty in private life is sufficient, with the aid of a little thought, to give us the same apprehension; while it serves as an instance of the general corruption of human nature, and shows us the danger which we must incur by reposing an entire confidence in mankind. In both cases, it is experience which is ultimately the foundation of our inference and conclusion.

There is no man so young and unexperienced, as not to have formed, from observation, many general and just maxims concerning human affairs and the conduct of life; but it must be confessed, that, when a man comes to put these in practice, he will be extremely liable to error, till time and farther experience both enlarge these maxims, and teach him their proper use and application. In every situation or incident, there are many particular and seemingly minute circumstances, which the man of greatest talents is, at first, apt to overlook, though on them the justness of his conclusions, and consequently the prudence of his conduct, entirely depend. Not to mention, that, to a young beginner, the general observations and maxims occur not always on the proper occasions, nor can be immediately applied with due calmness and distinction. The truth is, an unexperienced reasoner could be no reasoner at all, were he absolutely unexperienced; and when we assign that character to any one, we mean it only in a comparative sense, and suppose him possessed of experience, in a smaller and more imperfect degree.

For Further Reflection

1. If the principle of induction cannot be proven, does that imply that science is based on faith? Why or why not?

2. If we cannot prove that the future will resemble the past, does that mean we cannot rely on our inductive reasoning? Explain.

3. Does Hume's argument show that the predictive success of science is a matter of chance? How plausible is chance as an explanation for science's success?

III.34   The Problem of Induction

WESLEY C. SALMON

Wesley Salmon (1925–2001) was a philosopher of science who taught at Indiana University and the University of Pittsburgh. In this reading, he explains the problem of induction raised by Hume and examines several answers to it, including inductive, probabilistic, and pragmatic solutions.

Study Questions

1. What is the problem of induction?
2. Why can't induction be justified inductively? Why not deductively?
3. What is a demonstrative inference? A nondemonstrative inference?
4. What is the "pragmatic" justification of induction?

I. THE PROBLEM OF INDUCTION

We all believe that we have knowledge of facts extending far beyond those we directly perceive. The scope of our senses is severely limited in space and time; our immediate perceptual knowledge does not reach to events that happened before we were born to events that are happening now in certain other places or to any future events. We believe, nevertheless, that we have some kind of indirect knowledge of such facts. We know that a glacier once covered a large part of North America, that the sun continues to exist at night, and that the tides will rise and fall tomorrow. Science and common sense have at least this one thing in common: Each embodies knowledge of matters of fact that are not open to our direct inspection. Indeed, science purports to establish general laws or theories that apply to all parts of space and time without restriction. A "science" that consisted of no more than a mere summary of the results of direct observation would not deserve the name.

Hume's profound critique of induction begins with a simple and apparently innocent question: How do we acquire knowledge of the unobserved? This question, as posed, may seem to call for an empirical answer. We observe that human beings utilize what may be roughly characterized as inductive or scientific methods of extending knowledge from the observed to the unobserved. The sciences, in fact, embody the most powerful and highly developed methods known, and we may make an empirical investigation of scientific methods much as we might for any other sort of human behavior. We may consider the historical development of science. We may study the psychological, sociological, and political factors relevant to the pursuit of science. We may try to give an exact characterization of the behavior of scientists. In doing all these things, however, important and interesting as they are, we will have ignored the *philosophical* aspect of the problem Hume raised. Putting the matter very simply, these

empirical investigations may enable us to describe the ways in which people arrive at *beliefs* about unobserved facts, but they leave open the question of whether beliefs arrived at in this way actually constitute *knowledge*. It is one thing to describe how people go about seeking to extend their knowledge; it is quite another to claim that the methods employed actually do yield knowledge.

One of the basic differences between knowledge and belief is that knowledge must be founded upon evidence—i.e., it must be belief founded upon some rational justification. To say that certain methods yield knowledge of the unobserved is to make a cognitive claim for them. Hume called into question the justification of such cognitive claims. The answer cannot be found entirely within an empirical study of human behavior, for a *logical* problem has been raised. It is the problem of understanding the logical relationship between evidence and conclusion in logically correct inferences. It is the problem of determining whether the inferences by which we attempt to make the transition from knowledge of the observed to knowledge of the unobserved are logically correct. The fact that people do or do not use a certain type of inference is irrelevant to its justifiability. Whether people have confidence in the correctness of a certain type of inference has nothing to do with whether such confidence is justified. If we should adopt a logically incorrect method for inferring one fact from others, these facts would not actually constitute evidence for the conclusion we have drawn. The problem of induction is the problem of explicating the very concept of *inductive evidence*.

There is another possibly misleading feature of the question as I have formulated it. When we ask how we can *acquire* knowledge of the unobserved, it sounds very much as if we are asking for a method for the *discovery* of new knowledge. This is, of course, a vital problem, but it is not the fundamental problem Hume raised. Whether there is or can be any sort of inductive logic of discovery is a controversial question I shall discuss in detail in

Excerpts from The Foundations of Scientific Inference, *by Wesley C. Salmon, © 1967. Reprinted by permission of the University of Pittsburgh Press.*

a later section. Leaving this question aside for now, there remains the problem of *justification* of conclusions concerning unobserved matters of fact. Given some conclusion, however arrived at, regarding unobserved facts, and given some alleged evidence to support that conclusion, the question remains whether that conclusion is, indeed, supported by the evidence offered in support of it.

Consider a simple and highly artificial situation. Suppose a number of balls have been drawn from an urn, and that all of the black ones that have been drawn are licorice-flavored. I am not now concerned with such psychological questions as what makes the observer note the color of these balls, what leads him to taste the black ones, what makes him take note of the fact that licorice flavor is associated with black color in his sample, or what makes him suppose that the black balls not yet drawn will also be licorice-flavored. The problem—Hume's basic *philosophical* problem—is this: Given that all of the observed black balls have been licorice-flavored, and given that somehow the conclusion has been entertained that the unobserved black balls in the urn are also licorice-flavored, do the observed facts constitute sound *evidence* for that conclusion? Would we be *justified* in accepting that conclusion on the basis of the facts alleged to be evidence for it?

As a first answer to this question we may point out that the inference does conform to an accepted inductive principle, a principle saying roughly that observed instances conforming to a generalization constitute evidence for it. It is, however, a very small step to the next question: What grounds have we for accepting this or any other inductive principle? Is there any reason or justification for placing confidence in the conclusions of inferences of this type? Given that the premises of this inference are true, and given that the inference conforms to a certain rule, can we provide any rational justification for accepting its conclusion rather than, for instance, the conclusion that black balls yet to be drawn will taste like quinine?

It is well known that Hume's answer to this problem was essentially skeptical. It was his great

merit to have shown that a justification of induction, if possible at all, is by no means easy to provide. In order to appreciate the force of his argument it is first necessary to clarify some terminological points. This is particularly important because the word *induction* has been used in a wide variety of ways.

For purposes of systematic discussion one distinction is fundamental, namely, the distinction between demonstrative and nondemonstrative inference. A *demonstrative* inference is one whose premises necessitate its conclusion; the conclusion cannot be false if the premises are true. All valid deductions are demonstrative inferences. A *nondemonstrative* inference is simply one that fails to be demonstrative. Its conclusion is not necessitated by its premises; the conclusion could be false even if the premises are true. A demonstrative inference is *necessarily truth-preserving*; a nondemonstrative inference is not.

The category of nondemonstrative inferences, as I have characterized it, contains, among other things perhaps, all kinds of fallacious inferences. If, however, there is any kind of inference whose premises, although not necessitating the conclusion, do lend it weight, support it, or make it probable, then such inferences possess a certain kind of logical rectitude. It is not deductive validity, but it is important anyway. Inferences possessing it are *correct inductive inferences*.

Since demonstrative inferences have been characterized in terms of their basic property of necessary truth preservation, it is natural to ask how they achieve this very desirable trait. For a large group of demonstrative inferences, including those discussed under "valid deduction" in most logic texts, the answer is rather easy. Inferences of this type purchase necessary truth preservation by sacrificing any extension of content. The conclusion of such an inference says no more than do the premises—often less. The conclusion cannot be false if the premises are true *because* the conclusion says nothing that was not already stated in the premises. The conclusion is a mere reformulation of all or part of the content of the premises. In some cases the reformulation is unanticipated and therefore psychologically surprising, but the conclusion cannot augment the content of the premises. Such inferences are *nonampliative;* an ampliative inference, then, has a conclusion with content not present either explicitly or implicitly in the premises.

While it is easy to understand why nonampliative inferences are necessarily truth-preserving, the further question arises whether there are any necessarily truth-preserving inferences that are also ampliative. Is there any type of inference whose conclusion must, of necessity, be true if the premises are true, but whose conclusion says something not stated by the premises? Hume believed that the answer is negative and so do I, but it is not easy to produce an adequate defense of this answer. . . .

II. ATTEMPTED SOLUTIONS

It hardly needs remarking that philosophers have attempted to meet Hume's intriguing challenge in a wide variety of ways. There have been direct attacks upon some of Hume's arguments. Attempts to provide inductive arguments to support induction and attempts to supply a synthetic a priori principle of uniformity of nature belong in this category. Some authors have claimed that the whole problem arises out of linguistic confusion, and that careful analysis shows it to be a pseudoproblem. Some have even denied that inductive inference is needed, either in science or in everyday affairs. In this section I shall survey what seem to me to be the most important efforts to deal with the problem.

1. Inductive Justification. If Hume's arguments had never been propounded and we were asked why we accept the methods of science, the most natural answer would be, I think, that these methods have proved themselves by their results. We can point to astonishing technological advances, to vastly increased comprehension, and to impressive predictions. Science has provided us with foresight, control, and understanding. No other method can claim a comparable record of successful accomplishment. If methods are to be judged by their fruits, there is no doubt that the scientific method will come out on top.

Unfortunately, Hume examined this argument and showed that it is viciously circular. It is an example of an attempt to justify inductive methods inductively. From the premise that science has had considerable predictive success in the past, we conclude that it will continue to have substantial predictive success in the future. Observed cases of the application of scientific method have yielded successful prediction; therefore, as yet unobserved cases of the application of scientific method will yield successful predictions. This argument has the same structure as our black-balls-in-the-urn example; it is precisely the sort of ampliative inference from the observed to the unobserved whose justifiability is in question.

Consider the parallel case for a radically different sort of method. A crystal gazer claims that his method is the appropriate method for making predictions. When we question his claim he says, "Wait a moment; I will find out whether the method of crystal gazing is the best method for making predictions." He looks into his crystal ball and announces that future cases of crystal gazing will yield predictive success. If we should protest that his method has not been especially successful in the past, he might well make certain remarks about parity of reasoning. "Since you have used your method to justify your method, why shouldn't I use my method to justify my method? If you insist upon judging my method by using your method, why shouldn't I use my method to evaluate your method? By the way, I note by gazing into my crystal ball that the scientific method is now in for a very bad run of luck."

The trouble with circular arguments is obvious: with an appropriate circular argument you can prove anything. In recent years, nevertheless, there have been several notable attempts to show how inductive rules can be supported inductively.

The authors of such attempts try to show, of course, that their arguments are not circular. Although they argue persuasively, it seems to me that they do not succeed in escaping circularity. . . .

7. A Probabilistic Approach. It may seem strange in the extreme that this discussion of the problem of induction has proceeded at such great length without seriously bringing in the concept of probability. It is very tempting to react immediately to Hume's argument with the admission that we do not have *knowledge* of the unobserved. Scientific results are not established with absolute certainty. At best we can make probabilistic statements about unobserved matters of fact, and at best we can claim that scientific generalizations and theories are highly confirmed. We who live in an age of scientific empiricism can accept with perfect equanimity the fact that the quest for certainty is futile; indeed, our thanks go to Hume for helping to destroy false hopes for certainty in science.

Hume's search for a justification of induction, it might be continued, was fundamentally misconceived. He tried to find a way of proving that inductive inferences with true premises would have *true* conclusions. He properly failed to find any such justification precisely because it is the function of *deduction* to prove the truth of conclusions, given true premises. Induction has a different function. An inductive inference with true premises establishes its conclusions as *probable*. No wonder Hume failed to find a justification of induction. He was trying to make induction into deduction, and he succeeded only in proving the platitude that induction is not deduction. If we want to justify induction, we must show that inductive inferences establish their conclusions as probable, not as true.

The foregoing sort of criticism of Hume's arguments is extremely appealing, and it has given rise to the most popular sort of attempt, currently, to deal with the problem. In order to examine this approach, we must consider, at least superficially, the meaning of the concept of probability. Two basic meanings must be taken into account at present.

One leading probability concept identifies probability with frequency—roughly, the probable is that which happens often, and the improbable is that which happens seldom. Let us see what becomes of Hume's argument under this interpretation of probability. If we were to claim that inductive conclusions are probable in this sense, we would be claiming that inductive inferences with true premises often have true conclusions, although not always. Hume's argument shows, unhappily, that this claim cannot be substantiated. It was recognized long before Hume that inductive inferences cannot be expected always to lead to the truth. Hume's argument shows, not only that we cannot justify the claim that *every* inductive inference with true premises will have a true conclusion, but also, that we cannot justify the claim that *any* inductive inference with true premises will have a true conclusion. Hume's argument shows that, for all we can know, every inductive inference made from now on might have a false conclusion despite true premises. Thus, Hume has proved, we can show neither that inductive inferences establish their conclusions as true nor that they establish their conclusions as probable in the frequency sense. The introduction of the frequency concept of probability gives no help whatever in circumventing the problem of induction, but this is no surprise, for we should not have expected it to be suitable for this purpose.

A more promising probability concept identifies probability with degree of rational belief. To say that a statement is probable in this sense means that one would be rationally justified in believing it; the degree of probability is the degree of assent a person would be rationally justified in giving. We are not, of course, referring to the degree to which anyone *actually* believes in the statement, but rather to the degree to which one could *rationally* believe it. Degree of actual belief is a purely psychological concept, but degree of rational belief is determined objectively by the evidence. To say that a statement is probable in this sense means that it is supported by evidence. But, so the argument goes, if a statement is the conclusion of an inductive inference with true premises, it *is* supported by evidence—by inductive evidence—this is part of what it *means* to be supported by evidence. The very concept of evidence depends upon the nature of induction, and it becomes incoherent if we try to divorce the two. Trivially, then, the conclusion of an inductive inference is probable under this concept of probability. To ask, with Hume, if we should accept inductive conclusions is tantamount to asking if we should fashion our beliefs in terms of the evidence, and this, in turn, is tantamount to asking whether we should be rational. In this way we arrive at an "ordinary language dissolution" of the problem of induction. Once we understand clearly the meanings of such key terms as "rational," "probable," and "evidence," we see that the problem arose out of linguistic confusion and evaporates into the question of whether it is rational to be rational. Such tautological questions, if meaningful at all, demand affirmative answers.

Unfortunately, the dissolution is not satisfactory. Its inadequacy can be exhibited by focusing upon the concept of inductive evidence and seeing how it figures in the foregoing argument. The fundamental difficulty arises from the fact that the very notion of inductive evidence is determined by the rules of inductive inference. If a conclusion is to be supported by inductive evidence, it must be the conclusion of a correct inductive inference with true premises. Whether the inductive inference is correct depends upon whether the rule governing that inference is correct. The relation of inductive evidential support is, therefore, inseparably bound to the correctness of rules of inductive inference. In order to be able to say whether a given statement is supported by inductive evidence we must be able to say which inductive rules are correct. . . .

8. *Pragmatic Justification.* Of all the solutions and dissolution proposed to deal with Hume's problem of induction, Hans Reichenbach's attempt to provide a pragmatic justification seems to me the most fruitful and promising. This approach accepts Hume's arguments up to the point of agreeing that it is impossible to establish, either deductively or inductively, that any inductive inferences will ever again have true conclusions. Nevertheless, Reichenbach claims, the standard method of inductive generalization can be justified. Although its *success* as a method of prediction cannot be established in advance, it can be shown to be superior to any alternative method of prediction.

The argument can be put rather simply. Nature may be sufficiently uniform in suitable respects for us to make successful inductive inferences from the observed to the unobserved. On the other hand, for all we know, she may not. Hume has shown that we cannot prove in advance which case holds. All we can say is that nature may or may not be uniform—if she is, induction works; if she is not, induction fails. Even in the face of our ignorance about the uniformity of nature, we can ask what would happen if we adopted some radically different method of inference. Consider, for instance, the method of the crystal gazer. Since we do not know whether nature is uniform or not, we must consider both possibilities. If nature is uniform, the method of crystal gazing might work successfully, or it might fail. We cannot prove a priori that it will not work. At the same time, we cannot prove a priori that it will work, even if nature exhibits a high degree of uniformity. Thus, in case nature is reasonably uniform, the standard inductive method *must* work while the alternative method of crystal gazing *may or may not* work. In this case, the superiority of the standard inductive method is evident. Now, suppose nature lacks uniformity to such a degree that the standard inductive method is a complete failure. In this case, Reichenbach argues, the alternative method must likewise fail. Suppose it did not fail—suppose, for instance, that the method of crystal gazing worked consistently. This would constitute an important relevant uniformity that could be exploited inductively. If a crystal gazer had consistently predicted future occurrences, we could infer inductively that he has a method of prediction that will enjoy continued success. The inductive method would, in this way, share the success of the method of crystal gazing, and would therefore be, contrary to hypothesis, successful. Hence, Reichenbach concludes, the standard inductive method will be successful *if any other method could succeed*. As a result, we have everything to gain and nothing to lose by adopting the inductive method. If any method works, induction works. If we adopt the inductive method and it fails, we have lost nothing, for any other method we might have adopted would likewise have failed. Reichenbach does not claim to prove that nature is uniform, or that the standard inductive method will be successful. He does not postulate the uniformity of nature. He tries to show that the inductive method is the best method for ampliative inference, whether it turns out to be successful or not.

This ingenious argument, although extremely suggestive, is ultimately unsatisfactory. As I have just presented it, it is impossibly vague. I have not specified the nature of the standard inductive method. I have not stated with any exactness what constitutes success for the inductive method or any other. Moreover, the uniformity of nature is not an all-or-none affair. Nature appears to be uniform to some extent and also to be lacking in uniformity to some degree. As we have already seen, it is not easy to state a principle of uniformity that is strong enough to assure the success of inductive inference and weak enough to be plausible. The vagueness of the foregoing argument is not, however, its fundamental drawback. It can be made precise, and I shall do so below in connection with the discussion of the frequency interpretation of probability. When it is made precise, as we shall see, it suffers the serious defect of equally justifying too wide a variety of rules for ampliative inference.

I have presented Reichenbach's argument rather loosely in order to make intuitively clear its basic strategy. The sense in which it is a pragmatic justification should be clear. Unlike many authors who have sought a justification of induction,

Reichenbach does not try to prove the truth of any synthetic proposition. He recognizes that the problem concerns the justification of a rule, and rules are neither true nor false. Hence, he tries to show that the adoption of a standard inductive rule is practically useful in the attempt to learn about and deal with the unobserved. He maintains that this can be shown even though we cannot prove the truth of the assertion that inductive methods will lead to predictive success. This pragmatic aspect is, it seems to me, the source of the fertility of Reichenbach's approach. Even though his argument does not constitute an adequate justification of induction, it seems to me to provide a valid core from which we may attempt to develop a more satisfactory justification.

III. SIGNIFICANCE OF THE PROBLEM

Hume's problem of induction evokes, understandably, a wide variety of reactions. It is not difficult to appreciate the response of the man engaged in active scientific research or practical affairs who says, in effect, "Don't bother me with these silly puzzles; I'm too busy doing science, building bridges, or managing affairs of state." No one, including Hume, seriously suggests any suspension of scientific investigation or practical decision pending a solution of the problem of induction. The problem concerns the *foundations* of science. As Hume eloquently remarks in *Enquiry Concerning Human Understanding:*

Let the course of things be allowed hitherto ever so regular; that alone, without some new argument or inference, proves not that, for the future, it will continue so. In vain do you pretend to have learned the nature of bodies from your past experience. Their secret nature, and consequently all their effects and influence, may change, without any change in their sensible qualities. This happens sometimes, and with regard to some objects: Why may it not happen always, and with regard to all objects? What logic, what process of argument secures you against this supposition? My practice, you say, refutes my doubts. But you mistake the purport of my question. As an agent, I am quite satisfied in the point; but as a philosopher, who has some share of curiosity, I will not say scepticism, I want to learn the foundation of this inference.

We should know by now that the foundations of a subject are usually established long after the subject has been well developed, not before. To suppose otherwise would be a glaring example of "naïve first-things-firstism."

Nevertheless, there is something intellectually disquieting about a serious gap in the foundations of a discipline, and it is especially disquieting when the discipline in question is so broad as to include the whole of empirical science, all of its applications, and indeed, all of common sense. As human beings we pride ourselves on rationality—so much so that for centuries rationality was enshrined as the very essence of humanity and the characteristic that distinguishes man from the lower brutes. Questionable as such pride may be, our intellectual consciences should be troubled by a gaping lacuna in the structure of our knowledge and the foundations of scientific inference. I do not mean to suggest that the structure of empirical science is teetering because of foundational difficulties; the architectural metaphor is really quite inappropriate. I do suggest that intellectual integrity requires that foundational problems not be ignored.

Each of two opposing attitudes has its own immediate appeal. One of these claims that the scientific method is so obviously the correct method that there is no need to waste our time trying to show that this is so. There are two difficulties. First, we have enough painful experience to know that the appeal to obviousness is dangerously likely to be an appeal to prejudice and superstition. What is obvious to one age or culture may well turn out, on closer examination, to be just plain false. Second, if the method of science is so obviously superior to other methods we might adopt, then I should think we ought to be able to point to those characteristics of the method by which it gains its obvious superiority.

The second tempting attitude is one of pessimism. In the face of Hume's arguments and the failure of many attempts to solve the problem, it is easy to conclude that the problem is hopeless. Whether motivated by Hume's arguments or, as is probably more often the case, by simple impatience with foundational problems, this attitude seems quite widespread. It is often expressed by the formula that science is, at bottom, a matter of faith. While it is no part of my purpose to launch a wholesale attack on faith as such, this attitude toward the foundations of scientific inference is unsatisfactory. The crucial fact is that science makes a *cognitive claim*, and this cognitive claim is a fundamental part of the rationale for doing science at all. Hume has presented us with a serious challenge to that cognitive claim. If we cannot legitimize the cognitive claim, it is difficult to see what reason remains for doing science. Why not turn to voodoo, which would be simpler, cheaper, less time consuming, and more fun?

If science is basically a matter of faith, then the scientific faith exists on a par with other faiths. Although we may be culturally conditioned to accept this faith, others are not. Science has no ground on which to maintain its *cognitive* superiority to any form of irrationalism, however repugnant. This situation is, it seems to me, intellectually and socially undesirable. We have had enough experience with various forms of irrationalism to recognize the importance of being able to distinguish them logically from genuine science. I find it intolerable to suppose that a theory of biological evolution, supported as it is by extensive scientific evidence, has no more rational foundation than has its rejection by ignorant fundamentalists. I, too, have faith that the scientific method is especially well suited for establishing knowledge of the unobserved, but I believe this faith should be justified. It seems to me extremely important that some people should earnestly seek a solution to this problem concerning the foundations of scientific inference.

One cannot say in advance what consequences will follow from a solution to a foundational problem. It would seem to depend largely upon the nature of the solution. But a discipline with well-laid foundations is surely far more satisfactory than one whose foundations are in doubt. We have only to compare the foundationally insecure calculus of the seventeenth and eighteenth centuries with the calculus of the late nineteenth century to appreciate the gains in elegance, simplicity, and rigor. Furthermore, the foundations of calculus provided a basis for a number of other developments, interesting in their own right and *greatly extending the power and fertility of the original theory*. Whether similar extensions will occur as a result of a satisfactory resolution of Hume's problem is a point on which it would be rash to hazard any prediction, but we know from experience that important consequences result from the most unexpected sources. The subsequent discussion of the foundations of probability will indicate directions in which some significant consequences may be found, but for the moment it will suffice to note that a serious concern for the solution of Hume's problem cannot fail to deepen our understanding of the nature of scientific inference. This, after all, is the ultimate goal of the whole enterprise.

For Further Reflection

1. Salmon argues that the inductive solution to the problem of induction is inadequate. Why does he say this? Do you agree that the solution fails? Why or why not?

2. What does Salmon conclude about the pragmatic solution? Do you agree with him? When you make inferences about the future, do you take a pragmatic attitude toward your inductive reasoning?

3. Of the three solutions that Salmon reviews, which do you think is most plausible? Why?

Key Terms

epistemology	propositional knowledge	*a priori* knowledge
a posteriori knowledge	rationalism	empiricism
skepticism	cognitive realism	cognitive relativism

Suggestions for Further Reading

Audi, Robert. *Belief, Justification and Knowledge.* Belmont, CA: Wadsworth, 1988. The best short introduction to the subject.
Audi, Robert. *Epistemology.* Routledge, 1998.
Blanshard, Brand. *The Nature of Thought.* 2 vols. London: George Allen & Unwin, 1940.
BonJour, Laurence. *In Defense of Pure Reason.* Cambridge University Press, 1998.
Chisholm, R. M. *Theory of Knowledge*, 2nd. ed. Englewood Cliffs, NJ: Prentice Hall, 1977.
    A rich outline of a foundational approach to epistemology.
Dancy, Jonathan. *Introduction to Contemporary Epistemology.* Oxford: Blackwell, 1985.
    A penetrating analysis of contemporary problems, though not always clear.
Horwich, Paul. *Truth.* Oxford: Basil Blackwell, 1990.
James, William. *Pragmatism.* London: Longman's, Green & Co., 1907.
Johnson, Lawrence E. *Focusing on Truth.* London: Routledge, 1992.
Landsman, Charles. *An Introduction to Epistemology.* Oxford, Eng.: Blackwell's 1997.
Lawson, Hilary, and Lisa Applignanesi, eds. *Dismantling Truth.* London: Weidenfeld and Nicolson, 1989.

Lehrer, Keith. *Theory of Knowledge*. Boulder, CO: Westview Press, 1990.

Moser, Paul, and Arnold Vander Nat, eds. *Human Knowledge*. Oxford: Oxford University Press, 1987. A recent comprehensive anthology.

Pojman, Louis, ed. *The Theory of Knowledge*. Belmont, CA: Wadsworth, 1999.

Pojman, Louis. *What Can We Know?* 2nd ed., Belmont, CA: Wadsworth, 2001.

Pollock, John. *Knowledge and Justification*. Totowa, NJ: Rowman and Littlefield, 1986. Innovative and well argued.

Quine, W. V., and Joseph Ullian. *The Web of Belief*, 2nd ed. New York: Random House, 1978. A very useful book for beginners.

Rorty, Richard. *Philosophy and the Mirror of Nature*. Princeton, NJ: Princeton University Press, 1979.

Russell, Bertrand. *The Problems of Philosophy*. Oxford University Press, 1912.

Woozley, A. D. *Theory of Knowledge*. London: George Allen & Unwin, 1949.

Part IV

~

Philosophy of Mind: The Mind-Body Problem

The curiosity of Man, and the cunning of his Reason, have revealed much of what Nature held hidden. The structure of space-time, the constitution of matter, the many forms of energy, the nature of life itself; all of these mysteries have become open books to us. To be sure, deep questions remain unanswered and revolutions await us still, but it is difficult to exaggerate the explosion in scientific understanding we humans have fashioned over the past 500 years. Despite this general advance, a central mystery remains largely a mystery: the nature of conscious intelligence.

PAUL CHURCHLAND, *Matter and Consciousness*

For MILLENNIA, from biblical times until very recently, human beings thought of themselves as standing midway between the ape and the angel. The Psalmist praised God for our essential dignity:

> When I consider Thy heavens, the work of Thy fingers, the moon and the stars, which Thou hast ordained; What is man, that Thou art mindful of him? and the son of man, that Thou hast visitest him? For Thou hast made him a little lower than the angels, and hast crowned him with glory and honor. Thou madest him to have dominion over the works of Thy hands; Thou hast put all things under his feet. (Ps. 8 : 3–6)

Today there is a tendency to see humans as standing somewhere between the ape and the computer. It was never seriously denied that we were animals or had an animal aspect in behaving like animals in eating, excreting, procreating, breathing, sleeping, and dying. But there was something more. We were esteemed as rational, spiritual, deliberative beings, made in the image of God, a little lower than the angels. The biblical image of humanity is noble and inspiring. The contemporary model of homo-computer is less inspiring. Being mechanistic, we are seen as lacking a free will, hence as lacking responsibility and intrinsic value altogether. Indeed, all that marks us off from a moderately reliable computer is the animal in us, the nonrational elements of sensation, emotions, and consciousness. If the latter model is closer to the truth, we will have to make the best of it. But the question of our essential nature is worth asking and pursuing: Is there something special about us, a soul or mind which perdures through change and survives our death, something that constitutes our true identity and is the locus of eternal value? Or is the mind simply the body, in particular, the brain? The theory that there is a mind (or soul) separate from the body is called **dualism**. The theory that the mind (or soul) is physical or can be reduced to the physical is called **materialism** (or **physicalism**). In this part of our book we will examine arguments for and against these two theses.

IV.A   What Am I? A Mind or a Body?

Intuitively, there seem to be two different types of reality: mind and body, that is, mental and physical (material).

Bodies are solid, material entities, extended in three-dimensional space, publicly observable, measurable, capable of causing things to happen in accordance with invariant laws of mechanics.

A mind, on the other hand, has none of these properties. Consciousness is not solid or material, is not extended in three-dimensional space, does not occupy space at all, is directly observable only by the person who owns it, cannot be measured, and seems incapable of causing things to happen in accordance with invariant laws of mechanics. Only the person him- or herself can think his thoughts, feel his emotions, and suffer his pain. Although neurosurgeons can open your skull and observe your brain, they cannot observe your mind or your beliefs, sensations, emotions, or desires.

Unlike physical bodies, mental entities have no shape, weight, length, width, height, color, mass, velocity, or temperature. It would sound odd, indeed, to speak of a belief weighing 16 ounces like a cut of beef, or a feeling of love measuring $4'' \times 4'' \times 10'$ like a piece of lumber, or a pain being as heavy as a cement bag, or a desire that was green and had a temperature of 102 degrees.

Yet common sense tells us that these two entities somehow interact. We step on a nail, and it pierces our skin, sending a message through our nervous system which results in something altogether different from the shape or size of the nail or skin, something that does not possess size or shape and which cannot be seen, smelt, tasted, or heard—a feeling of distress or pain. Whereas the nail is public, the pain is private.

On the other hand, our mind informs us that it would be a good thing to get a bandage to put over the cut that has resulted (maybe a tetanus shot, too)—so the mind causes us to move our body. Our legs carry us to the medicine cabinet, where we stop, raise our arms, and with our hands take hold of the cabinet door, open it, take the bandage out, then apply it dexterously to the wound.

Here we have an instance where the body affects the mind and the mind, in turn, affects the body. So common sense shows that there is an interaction between the two radically different entities. But how exactly does this transaction occur? And where does it occur? Or could it be that the mind is really simply a function of the body, not a separate substance at all? Or that the body is really an illusion and that there is only one substance, the mind alone? The following schema may help you through the readings in this section.

Theory	Dualism	Idealism	Materialism
Nature of Substance	Mental and physical	Mental	Physical
Philosophers	Plato	Berkeley	Hume
	Descartes	Hinduism	Russell
	Locke	Christian Science	Taylor
	Moreland		Churchland

Idealism was represented in the last part (III.25) by George Berkeley. Traditional dualism is represented by Descartes and J. P. Moreland in this part (Readings IV.35 and IV.37, respectively). Gilbert Ryle, in Reading IV.36, attacks all versions of dualism. Some common forms of materialism are discussed in Reading IV.38 by Paul Churchland.

There are different kinds of dualism and materialism, each with its proponents and detractors. The most influential form of dualism is known as **substance dualism,** the notion that mind and body consist of two fundamentally different kinds of stuff, or substances—the mind being of nonphysical stuff and the body of physical stuff. The mind's mental states—desires, sensations, emotions, and thoughts—are states of nonphysical stuff. The body's physical states—electrochemical and biomechanical—are states of physical stuff. The most famous champion of this type of dualism is René Descartes (1596–1650). He argues that the mind (soul) and body are completely independent of one another and interact causally—a view that underpins belief in an immortal soul that lives on after death.

Although Descartes argues brilliantly for his brand of dualism, most contemporary philosophers reject it. Their primary concern is that it is mysterious how a nonphysical thing could interact with a physical thing. Many thinkers go further and insist that the idea of such interaction is simply nonsensical, and Descartes does not provide a convincing explanation of how the physical and nonphysical relate causally. He tries to explain the connection by claiming that the two realms intermingle in a small appendage of the brain known as the pineal gland, but many find this incredible. Whatever the gland's function (which was unknown in Descartes' day), it still is a physical thing, and positing it does not banish the mystery of how the material can affect the immaterial.

One prominent materialist approach is the **identity theory,** the view that mental states are identical to physical brain states. As some identity theorists would say, the mental state of pain is identical to the physical state of C-fibers firing in the brain. The mind and body (brain) are not distinct substances as Descartes holds; the mind is the brain.

The identity theory has drawn criticism from several directions. One major argument against it goes like this: If the identity theory is true, then we can know all about a person's mental states by knowing all about her brain states (because brain states are identical to mental states). But it is impossible to know all about mental states just by knowing all about brain states. Mental states have a subjective qualitative content that cannot be known through objective empirical investigation. Therefore, mental states are not identical to brain states, and so the identity theory is false.

Some have rejected the identity theory on the grounds that it seems to leave something out of account—namely, the subjective qualitative content of mental states. It ignores the character, or feel, of conscious experience. (This criticism applies to all materialist positions, not just to the identity theory.) Thomas Nagel (Reading IV.39) argues along these lines using a provocative thought experiment about bats.

The identity theory maintains that since the mind is identical to the brain, no being can have a mind unless it has a brain. To some critics, this conclusion is implausible. It seems possible, they argue, that some beings (alien life forms, for example) could possess minds (have desires, emotions, sensations, etc.) without having brains. (Think: the fictional alien E.T. or *Star Trek*'s android Mr. Data.) It is conceivable that such creatures could have minds but be made of an entirely different kind of stuff than we are. If so, the identity theory seems to have dubious implications.

Materialists eventually devised a theory that did not identify the mind with the brain: **functionalism**. This theory asserts that the mind is the functions that the brain performs. A mental state is defined by its causal role—by the stimuli that generate it, its interactions with other mental states, and the behavior that it produces. A mental state, then, is just a characteristic set of inputs and outputs. For example, pain is what is caused by some kind of unpleasant stimuli (such as a burn to Rosa's hand), causes other mental states (such as Rosa's believing that she should put ice on the burn), and causes external behavior (as when she reaches for ice in the refrigerator). Pain is whatever manifests such typical functional roles in a physical system, and anything that exhibits these kinds of functions is a mind. In Reading IV.40. Jerry Fodor makes a case for functionalism, and in Reading IV.43. Ned Block critiques the theory.

Taking a cue from functionalism, some philosophers see the mind as a sophisticated computer that's running some sort of software. Functionalism holds that the mind is the performance of functions, the processing of inputs and outputs—which is what any computer does. A computer runs software that determines what and how the inputs and outputs are processed. So some functionalists claim that to have a mind is just to run the appropriate type of software. The brain is hardware; the mind, software. If so, it is possible for computers to have minds as long as they process inputs and outputs in the right way.

But many theorists claim that functionalism does not do justice to the subjective, qualitative nature of our experience. They argue that it is possible to be in a mental state that does not correspond at all with a specific functional state. Mental states such as pain seem to have a certain qualitative feel that is not equivalent to any particular functional situation.

The view known as **property dualism** (or nonreductive materialism) is a significant departure from these other theories. It says that mental properties are not functional, physical, or spiritual. They are something above and beyond physical properties and are not reducible to them, emerging from the physical processes and structures of the brain. David Chalmers advocates this view in his reading.

Finally, we turn to a problem of whether computers can think. If materialists are correct, mental states are really physical states. If so, then why can't we say that sophisticated computers or highly developed robots think? In our final reading in this section, John Searle argues that computers can't think because they can't have intentional states. Through an ingenious thought experiment, he argues that strong AI (artificial intelligence) is misguided because computers lack the requisite conditions for understanding.

Let us turn to our readings.

Substance Dualism   IV.35

RENÉ DESCARTES

According to René Descartes there are three kinds of objects or substances in the universe: (1) the eternal substance, God; (2) his creation in terms of mind; (3) his creation in terms of matter: "We may thus easily have two clear and distinct notions or ideas, the one of created substance which thinks, and the other of corporeal substances, provided we carefully separate all the attributes of thought from those of extension."

We are thinking substances or embodied minds, "for I am not only lodged in my body as a pilot in a ship, but I am very closely united to it, and so to speak so intermingled with it that I seem to compose with it one whole. For if that were not the case, when my body hurt, I, who am merely a thinking thing, should perceive this wound by the understanding only, just as the sailor perceives by sight when something is damaged in his vessel."

The two kinds of substances which make us each a person intermingle in such a way that they causally act upon each other. Although it might be that a mind interacts with each part of its body separately, Descartes' view is that mind interacts only with the brain. The material event that causally stimulates one of our five senses (for example, light hitting the retina of the eye) results in a chain of physical causation that leads to a certain brain process from which a certain sensation results. Then, in turn, being affected by the brain, the mind through mental events acts on the brain, which in turn affects the body.

With this introduction we turn to our reading. We pick up the discussion where we left off toward the end of the second meditation (Reading III.23), where Descartes has discovered his self as the only indubitable piece of knowledge and begins to realize that all knowledge is a mental experience.

(A biographical sketch of Descartes precedes Reading III.23.)

Study Questions

1. How does Descartes characterize the self? What characteristics does it have? Can you recall the argument that led him to his conclusion about the nature of the self?
2. Why is Descartes tempted to regard the material as more certain than the mental? What is his explanation of this phenomenon?
3. How does the illustration of the piece of wax illustrate his thesis about the priority of the mental over the material?
4. What reason does Descartes give for believing that he has a body?
5. Why does he believe that there are other bodies besides his own?
6. What is the difference between the body and the mind?
7. What is the relationship of the body to the mind?
8. Where do the body and mind interact?

I SHALL EXERCISE MY IMAGINATION [in order to see if I am not something more]. I am not a collection of members which we call the human body: I am not a subtle air distributed through these members, I am not a wind, a fire, a vapour, a breath, nor anything at all which I can imagine or conceive; because I have assumed that all these were nothing. Without changing that supposition I find that I only leave myself certain of the fact that I am somewhat. But perhaps it is true that these same things which I supposed were non-existent because they are unknown to me, are really not different from the self which I know. I am not sure about this, I shall not dispute about it now; I can

Reprinted from the Philosophical Works of Descartes, *trans. Elizabeth Haldane and G. Ross, vol. I (Cambridge University Press, 1931).*

only give judgment on things that are known to me. I know that I exist, and I inquire what I am, I whom I know to exist. But it is very certain that the knowledge of my existence taken in its precise significance does not depend on things whose existence is not yet known to me; consequently it does not depend on those which I can feign in imagination. And indeed the very term *feign* in imagination proves to me my error, for I really do this if I image myself a something, since to imagine is nothing else than to contemplate the figure or image of a corporeal thing. But I already know for certain that I am, and that it may be that all these images, and, speaking generally, all things that relate to the nature of body are nothing but dreams [and chimeras]. For this reason I see clearly that I have as little reason to say, "I shall stimulate my imagination in order to know more distinctly what I am," than if I were to say, "I am now awake, and I perceive somewhat that is real and true: but because I do not yet perceive it distinctly enough, I shall go to sleep of express purpose, so that my dreams may represent the perception with greatest truth and evidence." And, thus, I know for certain that nothing of all that I can understand by means of my imagination belongs to this knowledge which I have of myself, and that it is necessary to recall the mind from this mode of thought with the utmost diligence in order that it may be able to know its own nature with perfect distinctness.

But what then am I? A thing which thinks. What is a thing which thinks? It is a thing which doubts, understands, [conceives], affirms, denies, wills, refuses, which also imagines and feels.

Certainly it is no small matter if all these things pertain to my nature. But why should they not so pertain? Am I not that being who now doubts nearly everything, who nevertheless understands certain things, who affirms that one only is true, who denies all the others, who desires to know more, is averse from being deceived, who imagines many things, sometimes indeed despite his will, and who perceives many likewise, as by the intervention of the bodily organs? Is there nothing in all this which is as true as it is certain that I exist, even though I should always sleep and though he who has given me being employed all his ingenuity in deceiving me? Is there likewise any one of these attributes which can be distinguished from my thought, or which might be said to be separated from myself? For it is so evident of itself that it is I who doubts, who understands, and who desires, that there is no reason here to add anything to explain it. And I have certainly the power of imagining likewise; for although it may happen (as I formerly supposed) that none of the things which I imagine are true, nevertheless this power of imagining does not cease to be really in use, and it forms part of my thought. Finally, I am the same who feels, that is to say, who perceives certain things, as by the organs of sense, since in truth I see light, I hear noise, I feel heat. But it will be said that these phenomena are false and that I am dreaming. Let it be so; still it is at least quite certain that it seems to me that I see light, that I hear noise and that I feel heat. That cannot be false; properly speaking it is what is in me called feeling, and used in this precise sense that is no other thing than thinking.

From this time I begin to know what I am with a little more clearness and distinction than before; but nevertheless it still seems to me, and I cannot prevent myself from thinking, that corporeal things, whose images are framed by thought, which are tested by the senses, are much more distinctly known than that obscure part of me which does not come under the imagination. Although really it is very strange to say that I know and understand more distinctly these things whose existence seems to me dubious, which are unknown to me, and which do not belong to me, than others of the truth of which I am convinced, which are known to me and which pertain to my real nature, in a word, than myself. But I see clearly how the case stands: My mind loves to wander, and cannot yet suffer itself to be retained within the just limits of truth. Very good, let us once more give it the freest rein, so that, when afterwards we seize the proper occasion for pulling up, it may the more easily be regulated and controlled.

Let us begin by considering the commonest matters, those which we believe to be the most distinctly comprehended, to wit, the bodies which we touch and see; not indeed bodies in general, for these general ideas are usually a little more confused, but let us consider one body in particular. Let us take, for example, this piece of wax: It has been taken quite freshly from the hive, and it has not yet lost the sweetness of the honey which it contains; it still retains somewhat of the odour of the flowers from which it has been culled; its colour, its figure, its size are apparent; it is hard, cold, easily handled, and if you strike it with the finger, it will emit a sound. Finally all the things which are requisite to cause us distinctly to recognise a body, are met with in it. But notice that while I speak and approach the fire what remained of the taste is exhaled, the smell evaporates, the colour alters, the figure is destroyed, the size increases, it becomes liquid, it heats, scarcely can one handle it, and when one strikes it, no sound is emitted. Does the same wax remain after this change? We must confess that it remains; none would judge otherwise. What then did I know so distinctly in this piece of wax? It could certainly be nothing of all that the senses brought to my notice, since all these things which fall under taste, smell, sight, touch, and hearing, are found to be changed, and yet the same wax remains.

Perhaps it was what I now think, viz. that this wax was not that sweetness of honey, nor that agreeable scent of flowers, nor that particular whiteness, nor that figure, nor that sound, but simply a body which a little while before appeared to me as perceptible under these forms, and which is now perceptible under others. But what, precisely, is it that I imagine when I form such conceptions? Let us attentively consider this, and, abstracting from all that does not belong to the wax, let us see what remains. Certainly nothing remains excepting a certain extended thing which is flexible and movable. But what is the meaning of flexible and movable? Is it not that I imagine that this piece of wax being round is capable of becom-

ing square and of passing from a square to a triangular figure? No, certainly it is not that, since I imagine it admits of an infinitude of similar changes, and I nevertheless do not know how to compass the infinitude by my imagination, and consequently this conception which I have of the wax is not brought about by the faculty of imagination. What now is this extension? Is it not also unknown? For it becomes greater when the wax is melted, greater when it is boiled, and greater still when the heat increases; and I should not conceive [clearly] according to truth what wax is, if I did not think that even this piece that we are considering is capable of receiving more variations in extension than I have ever imagined. We must then grant that I could not even understand through the imagination what this piece of wax is, and that it is my mind alone which perceives it. I say this piece of wax in particular, for as to wax in general it is yet clearer. But what is this piece of wax which cannot be understood excepting by the [understanding or] mind? It is certainly the same that I see, touch, imagine, and finally it is the same which I have always believed it to be from the beginning. But what must particularly be observed is that its perception is neither an act of vision, nor of touch, nor of imagination, and has never been such, although it may have appeared formerly to be so, but only an intuition of the mind, which may be imperfect and confused as it was formerly, or clear and distinct as it is at present, according as my attention is more or less directed to the elements which are found in it, and of which it is composed.

Yet in the meantime I am greatly astonished when I consider [the great feebleness of mind] and its proneness to fall [insensibly] into error; for although without giving expression to my thoughts I consider all this in my own mind, words often impede me and I am almost deceived by the terms of ordinary language. For we say that we see the same wax, if it is present, and not that we simply judge that it is the same from its having the same colour and figure. From this I should conclude that I knew the wax by means of vision and not simply by the intuition of the mind; unless by chance I remember that, when looking from a window and saying I see men who pass in the street, I really do not see them, but infer that what I see is men, just as I say that I see wax. And yet what do I see from the window but hats and coats which may cover automatic machines? Yet I judge these to be men. And similarly solely by the faculty of judgment which rests in my mind, I comprehend that which I believed I saw with my eyes.

A man who makes it his aim to raise his knowledge above the common should be ashamed to derive the occasion for doubting from the forms of speech invented by the vulgar; I prefer to pass on and consider whether I had a more evident and perfect conception of what the wax was when I first perceived it, and when I believed I knew it by means of the external senses or at least by the common sense as it is called, that is to say by the imaginative faculty, or whether my present conception is clearer now that I have most carefully examined what it is, and in what way it can be known. It would certainly be absurd to doubt as to this. For what was there in this first perception which was distinct? What was there which might not as well have been perceived by any of the animals? But when I distinguish the wax from its external forms, and when, just as if I had taken from it its vestments, I consider it quite naked, it is certain that although some error may still be found in my judgment, I can nevertheless not perceive it thus without a human mind.

But finally what shall I say of this mind, that is, of myself, for up to this point I do not admit in myself anything but mind? What then, I who seem to perceive this piece of wax so distinctly, do I not know myself, not only with much more truth and certainty, but also with much more distinctness and clearness? For if I judge that the wax is or exists from the fact that I see it, it certainly follows much more clearly that I am or that I exist myself from the fact that I see it. For it may be that what I see is not really wax, it may also be that I do not possess eyes with which to see anything; but it cannot be that when I see, or (for I no longer take account of the distinction) when I think I see, that I myself who think am nought. So if I judge that the wax exists from the fact that I touch it, the same thing will follow, to wit, that I am; and if I judge that my imagination, or some other cause, whatever it is, persuades me that the wax exists, I shall still conclude the same. And what I have here remarked of wax may be applied to all other things which are external to me [and which are met with outside of me]. And further, if the [notion or] perception of wax has seemed to me clearer and more distinct, not only after the sight or the touch, but also after many other causes have rendered it quite manifest to me, with how much more [evidence] and distinctness must it be said that I now know myself, since all the reasons which contribute to the knowledge of wax, or any other body whatever, are yet better proofs of the nature of my mind! And there are so many other things in the mind itself which may contribute to the elucidation of its nature, that those which depend on body such as these just mentioned, hardly merit being taken into account.

But finally here I am, having insensibly reverted to the point I desired, for, since it is now manifest to me that even bodies are not properly speaking known by the senses or by the faculty of imagination, but by the understanding only, and since they are not known from the fact that they are seen or touched, but only because they are understood, I see clearly that there is nothing which is easier for me to know than my mind. But because it is difficult to rid oneself so promptly of an opinion to which one was accustomed for so long, it will be well that I should halt a little at this point, so that by the length of my meditation I may more deeply imprint on my memory this new knowledge.

MEDITATION III:
OF GOD: THAT HE EXISTS

I shall now close my eyes, I shall stop my ears, I shall call away all my senses, I shall efface even from my thoughts all the images of corporeal things, or at least (for that is hardly possible) I shall esteem them as vain and false; and thus holding converse only with myself and considering my own nature, I shall try little by little to reach a better knowledge of and a more familiar acquaintanceship with myself. I am a thing that thinks, that is to say, that doubts, affirms, denies, that knows a few things, that is ignorant of many [that loves, that hates], that wills, that desires, that also imagines and perceives; for as I remarked before, although the things which I perceive and imagine are perhaps nothing at all apart from me and in themselves, I am nevertheless assured that these modes of thought that I call perceptions and imaginations, inasmuch only as they are modes of thought, certainly reside [and are met with] in me. . . .

ON THE SEPARATION OF THE MIND FROM THE BODY

But now that I begin to know myself better, and to discover more clearly the author of my being, I do not in truth think that I should rashly admit all the matters which the senses seem to teach us, but, on the other hand, I do not think that I should doubt them all universally.

And first of all, because I know that all things which I apprehend clearly and distinctly can be created by God as I apprehend them, it suffices that I am able to apprehend one thing apart from another clearly and distinctly in order to be certain that the one is different from the other, since they may be made to exist in separation at least by the omnipotence of God; and it does not signify by what power this separation is made in order to compel me to judge them to be different: and, therefore, just because I know certainly that I exist, and that meanwhile I do not notice that any other thing necessarily pertains to my nature or essence, excepting that I am a thinking thing, I rightly conclude that my essence consists solely in the fact that I am a thinking thing [or a

substance whose whole essence or nature is to think]. And although possibly (or rather certainly, as I shall say in a moment) I possess a body with which I am very intimately conjoined, yet because, on the one side, I have a clear and distinct idea of myself inasmuch as I am only a thinking and unextended thing, and as, on the other, I possess a distinct idea of body, inasmuch as it is only an extended and unthinking thing, it is certain that this I [that is to say, my soul by which I am what I am], is entirely and absolutely distinct from my body, and can exist without it.

I further find in myself faculties employing modes of thinking peculiar to themselves, to wit, the faculties of imagination and feeling, without which I can easily conceive myself clearly and distinctly as a complete being; while, on the other hand, they cannot be so conceived apart from me, that is without an intelligent substance in which they reside, for [in the notion we have of these faculties, or, to use the language of the Schools] in their formal concept, some kind of intellection is comprised, from which I infer that they are distinct from me as its modes are from a thing. I observe also in me some other faculties such as that of change of position, the assumption of different figures and such like, which cannot be conceived, any more than can the preceding, apart from some substance to which they are attached, and consequently cannot exist without it; but it is very clear that these faculties, if it be true that they exist, must be attached to some corporeal or extended substance, and not to an intelligent substance, since in the clear and distinct conception of these there is some sort of extension found to be present, but no intellection at all. There is certainly further in me a certain passive faculty of perception, that is, of receiving and recognising the ideas of sensible things, but this would be useless to me [and I could in no way avail myself of it], if there were not either in me or in some other thing another active faculty capable of forming and producing these ideas. But this active faculty cannot exist in me [inasmuch as I am a thing that thinks] seeing that it does not presuppose thought, and also that those ideas are often produced in me without my contributing in any way to the same, and often even against my will; it is thus necessarily the case that the faculty resides in some substance different from me in which all the reality which is objectively in the ideas that are produced by this faculty is formally or eminently contained, as I remarked before. And this substance is either a body, that is, a corporeal nature in which there is contained formally [and really] all that which is objectively [and by representation] in those ideas, or it is God Himself, or some other creature more noble than body in which that same is contained eminently. But, since God is no deceiver, it is very manifest that He does not communicate to me these ideas immediately and by Himself, nor yet by the intervention of some creature in which their reality is not formally, but only eminently, contained. For since He has given me no faculty to recognise that this is the case, but, on the other hand, a very great inclination to believe [that they are sent to me or] that they are conveyed to me by corporeal objects, I do not see how He could be defended from the accusation of deceit if these ideas were produced by causes other than corporeal objects. Hence we must allow that corporeal things exist. However, they are perhaps not exactly what we perceive by the senses, since this comprehension by the senses is in many instances very obscure and confused; but we must at least admit that all things which I conceive in them clearly and distinctly, that is to say, all things which, speaking generally, are comprehended in the object of pure mathematics, are truly to be recognised as external objects.

As to other things, however, which are either particular only, as, for example, that the sun is of such and such a figure, etc., or which are less clearly and distinctly conceived, such as light, sound, pain and the like, it is certain that although they are very dubious and uncertain, yet on the sole ground that God is not a deceiver, and that consequently He has not permitted any falsity to exist in my opinion which He has not likewise given me the faculty of correcting, I may assuredly hope to conclude that I have within me the means of arriving at the truth even here. And first of all there is no doubt that in all things which nature teaches me there is some truth contained; for by nature, considered in general, I now understand no other thing than either God Himself or else the order and disposition which God has established in created things; and by my nature in particular I understand no other thing than the complexus of all the things which God has given me.

But there is nothing which this nature teaches me more expressly [nor more sensibly] than that I have a body which is adversely affected when I feel pain, which has need of food or drink when I experience the feelings of hunger and thirst, and so on; nor can I doubt there being some truth in all this.

Nature also teaches me by these sensations of pain, hunger, thirst, etc., that I am not only lodged in my body as a pilot in a vessel, but that I am very closely united to it, and so to speak so intermingled with it that I seem to compose with it one whole. For if that were not the case, when my body is hurt, I, who am merely a thinking thing, should not feel pain, for I should perceive this wound by the understanding only, just as the sailor perceives by sight when something is damaged in his vessel; and when my body has need of drink or food, I should clearly understand the fact without being warned of it by confused feelings of hunger and thirst. For all these sensations of hunger, thirst, pain, etc. are in truth none other than certain confused modes of thought which are produced by the union and apparent intermingling of mind and body. . . .

. . . It still remains to inquire how the goodness of God does not prevent the nature of man so regarded from being fallacious.

In order to begin this examination, then, I here say, in the first place, that there is a great difference between mind and body, inasmuch as body is by nature always divisible, and the mind is entirely indivisible. For, as a matter of fact, when I consider the mind, that is to say, myself inasmuch as I am only a thinking thing, I cannot distinguish in myself any parts, but apprehend myself to be clearly one and entire; and although the whole mind seems to be united to the whole body, yet if a foot, or an arm, or some other part, is separated from my body, I am aware that nothing has been taken away from my mind. And the faculties of willing, feeling, conceiving, etc. cannot be properly speaking said to be its parts, for it is one and the same mind which employs itself in willing and in feeling and understanding. But it is quite otherwise with corporeal or extended objects, for there is not one of these imaginable by me which my mind cannot easily divide into parts, and which consequently I do not recognise as being divisible; this would be sufficient to teach me that the mind or soul of man is entirely different from the body, if I had not already learned it from other sources.

I further notice that the mind does not receive the impressions from all parts of the body immediately, but only from the brain, or perhaps even from one of its smallest parts, to wit, from that in which the common sense is said to reside, which, whenever it is disposed in the same particular way, conveys the same thing to the mind, although meanwhile the other portions of the body may be differently disposed, as is testified by innumerable experiments which it is unnecessary here to recount. . . .

[From *The Passions of the Souls*]

The small gland which is the main seat of the souls is so suspended between the cavities which contain the spirits that it can be moved by them in as many ways as there are sensible diversities in the object, but that it may also be moved in diverse ways by the soul, whose nature is such that it receives in itself as many diverse impressions, that is to say, that it possesses as many diverse perceptions, as there are diverse movements in this gland. Reciprocally, likewise, the machine of the body is so formed that from the simple fact that this gland is diversely moved by the soul, or by such other cause, whatever it is, it thrusts the spirits which surround it towards the pores of the brain, which conducts them by the nerves into the muscles, by which means it causes them to move the limbs.

For Further Reflection

Here is a summary of Descartes' argument. Examine it and see whether you agree with his premises and his reasoning.

1. We can know the mind better than anything else (except possibly God's existence).

2. We can know the mind as distinct from the body (waking up in the morning, I do not need to open my eyes to see that I exist in order to know that I do).

3. It makes more sense to suppose that the mind and the body interact and face the difficulties of interactionist dualism than to say that they are one and struggle to explain the phenomena of consciousness.

4. The mind is in the pineal gland within the brain. At least it is clear that consciousness must reside in the brain since (a) sleep and disease which affect only the brain interrupt the operations of the senses; (b) if the nerves between external sense organs and the brain are cut, no sensations occur; and (c) it is possible to have sensations when the apparent place of sensation no longer exists (e.g., the phantom limb syndrome wherein an amputee imagines pain in his arm—even though he has none).

Exorcising Descartes' "Ghost in the Machine"   IV.36

GILBERT RYLE

Gilbert Ryle (1900–1976), an English philosopher, was educated at Oxford University, where he taught and greatly influenced a generation of students until his death in 1976. He was the editor of *Mind*, one of the most important philosophy journals, from 1948–1971. His principal works are *The Concept of Mind*, from which the present selection is taken, and *Dilemmas* (1954).

In this selection Ryle criticizes Cartesian dualism, which he labels "the Ghost in the Machine," as involving a category mistake. A category mistake is a confusion one slips into when something that belongs to one category or context is mistakenly taken to belong to another. Jokes intentionally thrive on this. For example, "The average woman in the United States has 2.5 children" would be an example of such a mistake if one went looking for the .5 child, treating a functional term "average woman" as a proper noun.

Ryle attempts to show that Descartes' dualism commits a similar category confusion. That is, just because we speak of bodily functions and mental functions as different in no way entails that they are two entirely separate entities. Ryle believes that this functional language can be reduced to observation language.

Study Questions

1. What is the official doctrine? Describe it.
2. What are the person's private and public histories? What does Ryle say about them?
3. What is Ryle's estimation of the official doctrine?
4. What is a category mistake? How does Ryle illustrate this concept?
5. What is the origin of the Cartesian category mistake?

THE ABSURDITY OF THE OFFICIAL DOCTRINE OF "THE GHOST IN THE MACHINE"

The Official Doctrine

THERE IS A DOCTRINE about the nature and place of minds which is so prevalent among theorists and even among laymen that it deserves to be described as the official theory. Most philosophers, psychologists and religious teachers subscribe, with minor reservations, to its main articles and, although they admit certain theoretical difficulties in it, they tend to assume that these can be overcome without serious modifications being made to the architecture of the theory. It will be argued here that the central principles of the doctrine are unsound and conflict with the whole body of what we know about minds when we are not speculating about them.

The official doctrine, which hails chiefly from Descartes, is something like this. With the doubtful exceptions of idiots and infants in arms, every human being has both a body and a mind. Some would prefer to say that every human being is both

Reprinted from Gilbert Ryle, The Concept of Mind, *1949.*

a body and a mind. His body and his mind are ordinarily harnessed together, but after the death of the body, his mind may continue to exist and function.

Human bodies are in space and are subject to the mechanical laws which govern all other bodies in space. Bodily processes and states can be inspected by external observers. So a man's bodily life is as much a public affair as are the lives of animals and reptiles and even as the careers of trees, crystals and planets.

But minds are not in space, nor are their operations subject to mechanical laws. The workings of one mind are not witnessable by other observers; its career is private. Only I can take direct cognisance of the states and processes of my own mind. A person therefore lives through two collateral histories, one consisting of what happens in and to his body, the other consisting of what happens in and to his mind. The first is public, the second private. The events in the first history are events in the physical world, those in the second are events in the mental world.

It has been disputed whether a person does or can directly monitor all or only some of the episodes of his own private history, but, according to the official doctrine, of at least some of these episodes he has direct and unchallengeable cognisance. In consciousness, self-consciousness and introspection he is directly and authentically apprised of the present states and operations of his mind. He may have great or small uncertainties about concurrent and adjacent episodes in the physical world, but he can have none about at least part of what is momentarily occupying his mind.

It is customary to express this bifurcation of his two lives and of his two worlds by saying that the things and events which belong to the physical world, including his own body, are external, while the workings of his own mind are internal. This antithesis of outer and inner is of course meant to be construed as a metaphor, since minds, not being in space, could not be described as being spatially inside anything else, or as having things going on spatially inside themselves. But relapses from this good intention are common and theorists are found speculating how stimuli, the physical sources of which are yards or miles outside a person's skin, can generate mental responses inside his skull, or how decisions framed inside his cranium can set going movements of his extremities.

Even when "inner" and "outer" are construed as metaphors, the problem of how a person's mind and body influence one another is notoriously charged with theoretical difficulties. What the mind wills, the legs, arms and the tongue execute; what affects the ear and the eye has something to do with what the mind perceives; grimaces and smiles betray the mind's moods and bodily castigations lead, it is hoped, to moral improvement. But the actual transactions between the episodes of the private history and those of the public history remain mysterious, since by definition they can belong to neither series. They could not be reported among the happenings described in a person's autobiography of his inner life, nor could they be reported among those described in some one else's biography of that person's overt career. They can be inspected neither by introspection nor by laboratory experiment. They are theoretical shuttlecocks which are forever being bandied from the physiologist back to the psychologist and from the psychologist back to the physiologist.

Underlying this partly metaphorical representation of the bifurcation of a person's two lives there is a seemingly more profound and philosophical assumption. It is assumed that there are two different kinds of existence or status. What exists or happens may have the status of physical existence, or it may have the status of mental existence. Somewhat as the faces of coins are either heads or tails, or somewhat as living creatures are either male or female, so, it is supposed, some existing is physical existing, other existing is mental existing. It is a necessary feature of what has physical existence that it is in space and time; it is a necessary feature of what has mental existence that it is in time but not in space. What has physical existence is composed of matter, or else is a function of matter; what has mental existence consists of consciousness, or else is a function of consciousness.

There is thus a polar opposition between mind and matter, an opposition which is often brought out as follows. Material objects are situated in a common field, known as "space," and what happens to one body in one part of space is mechanically connected with what happens to other bodies in other parts of space. But mental happenings occur in insulated fields, known as "minds," and there is, apart maybe from telepathy, no direct causal connection between what happens in one mind and what happens in another. Only through the medium of the public physical world can the mind of one person make a difference to the mind of another. The mind is its own place and in his inner life each of us lives the life of a ghostly Robinson Crusoe. People can see, hear and jolt one another's bodies, but they are irremediably blind and deaf to the workings of one another's minds and inoperative upon them.

What sort of knowledge can be secured of the workings of a mind? On the one side, according to the official theory, a person has direct knowledge of the best imaginable kind of the workings of his own mind. Mental states and processes are (or are normally) conscious states and processes, and the consciousness which irradiates them can engender no illusions and leaves the door open for no doubts. A person's present thinkings, feelings and willings, his perceivings, rememberings and imaginings are intrinsically "phosphorescent"; their existence and their nature are inevitably betrayed to their owner. The inner life is a stream of consciousness of such a sort that it would be absurd to suggest that the mind whose life is that stream might be unaware of what is passing down it.

True, the evidence adduced recently by Freud seems to show that there exist channels tributary to this stream, which run hidden from their owner. People are actuated by impulses the existence of which they vigorously disavow; some of their thoughts differ from the thoughts which they acknowledge; and some of the actions which they think they will to perform they do not really will. They are thoroughly gulled by some of their own hypocrisies, and they successfully ignore facts about their mental lives, which, on the official theory, ought to be patent to them. Holders of the official theory tend, however, to maintain that anyhow in normal circumstances a person must be directly and authentically seized of the present state and workings of his own mind.

Besides being currently supplied with these alleged immediate data of consciousness, a person is also generally supposed to be able to exercise from time to time a special kind of perception, namely inner perception, or introspection. He can take a (non-optical) "look" at what is passing in his mind. Not only can he view and scrutinize a flower through his sense of sight and listen to and discriminate the notes of a bell through his sense of hearing; he can also reflectively or introspectively watch, without any bodily organ of sense, the current episodes of his inner life. This self-observation is also commonly supposed to be immune from illusion, confusion or doubt. A mind's reports of its own affairs have a certainty superior to the best that is possessed by its reports of matters in the physical world. Sense-perceptions can, but consciousness and introspection cannot, be mistaken or confused.

On the other side, one person has no direct access of any sort to the events of the inner life of another. He cannot do better than make problematic inferences from the observed behaviour of the other person's body to the states of mind which, by analogy from his own conduct, he supposes to be signalised by that behaviour. Direct access to the workings of a mind is the privilege of that mind itself; in default of such privileged access, the workings of one mind are inevitably occult to everyone else. For the supposed arguments from bodily movements similar to their own, to mental workings similar to their own, would lack any possibility of observational corroboration. Not unnaturally, therefore, an adherent of the official theory finds it difficult to resist this consequence of his premises, that he has no good reason to believe that there do exist minds other than his own. Even if he prefers to believe that to other human bodies there are harnessed minds not unlike his own, he cannot claim to be able to discover their individual characteristics, or the particular things that they undergo and do. Absolute solitude is on this showing the ineluctable destiny of the soul. Only our bodies can meet.

As a necessary corollary of this general scheme there is implicitly prescribed a special way of construing our ordinary concepts of mental powers and operations. The verbs, nouns and adjectives, with which in ordinary life we describe the wits, characters and higher-grade performances of the people with whom we have to do, are required to be construed as signifying special episodes in their secret histories, or else as signifying tendencies for such episodes to occur. When someone is described as knowing, believing or guessing something, as hoping, dreading, intending or shirking something, as designing this or being amused at that, these verbs are supposed to denote the occurrence of specific modifications in his (to us) occult stream of consciousness. Only his own privileged access to this stream in direct awareness and introspection could provide authentic testimony that these mental-conduct verbs were correctly or incorrectly applied. The onlooker, be he teacher, critic, biographer or friend, can never assure himself that his comments have any vestige of truth. Yet it was just because we do in fact all know how to make such comments, make them with general correctness and correct them when they turn out to be confused or mistaken, that philosophers found it necessary to construct their theories of the nature and place of minds. Finding mental-conduct concepts being regularly and effectively used, they properly sought to fix their logical geography. But the logical geography officially recommended would entail that there could be no regular or effective use of these mental-conduct concepts in our descriptions of, and prescriptions for, other people's minds.

The Absurdity of the Official Doctrine

Such in outline is the official theory. I shall often speak of it, with deliberate abusiveness, as "the dogma of the Ghost in the Machine." I hope to prove that it is entirely false, and false not in detail but in principle. It is not merely an assemblage of particular mistakes. It is one big mistake and a mistake of a special kind. It is, namely, a category-mistake. It represents the facts of mental life as if they belonged to one logical type or category (or range of types or categories), when they actually belong to another. The dogma is therefore a philosopher's myth. In attempting to explode the myth I shall probably be taken to be denying well-known facts about the mental life of human beings, and my plea that I aim at doing nothing more than rectify the logic of mental-conduct concepts will probably be disallowed as mere subterfuge.

I must first indicate what is meant by the phrase "Category-mistake." This I do in a series of illustrations.

A foreigner visiting Oxford or Cambridge for the first time is shown a number of colleges, libraries, playing fields, museums, scientific departments and administrative offices. He then asks "But where is the University? I have seen where the members of the Colleges live, where the Registrar works, where the scientists experiment and the rest. But I have not yet seen the University in which reside and work the members of your University." It has then to be explained to him that the University is not another collateral institution, some ulterior counterpart to the colleges, laboratories and offices which he has seen. The university is just the way in which all that he has already seen is organized. When they are seen and when their co-ordination is understood, the University has been seen. His mistake lay in his innocent assumption that it was correct to speak of Christ Church, the Bodleian Library, the Ashmolean Museum *and* the University, to speak, that is, as if "the University" stood for an extra member of the class of which these other units are members. He was mistakenly allocating the

University to the same category as that to which the other institutions belong.

The same mistake would be made by a child witnessing the march-past of a division who, having had pointed out to him such and such battalions, batteries, squadrons, etc., asked when the division was going to appear. He would be supposing that a division was a counterpart to the units already seen, partly similar to them and partly unlike them. He would be shown his mistake by being told that in watching the battalions, batteries and squadrons marching past he had been watching the division marching past. The march-past was not a parade of battalions, batteries, squadrons *and* a division; it was a parade of the battalions, batteries and squadrons *of* a division.

One more illustration. A foreigner watching his first game of cricket learns what are the functions of the bowlers, the batsmen, the fielders, the umpires and the scorers. He then says, "But there is no one left on the field to contribute the famous element of team-spirit. I see who does the bowling, the batting and the wicket-keeping, but I do not see whose role it is to exercise *esprit de corps*." Once more, it would have to be explained that he was looking for the wrong type of thing. Team-spirit is not another cricketing-operation supplementary to all of the other special tasks. It is, roughly, the keenness with which each of the special tasks is performed, and performing a task keenly is not performing two tasks. Certainly exhibiting team-spirit is not the same thing as bowling or catching, but nor is it a third thing such that we can say that the bowler first bowls *and* then exhibits team-spirit or that a fielder is at a given moment *either* catching *or* displaying *esprit de corps*.

These illustrations of category-mistakes have a common feature which must be noticed. The mistakes were made by people who did not know how to wield the concepts *University, division* and *team-spirit*. Their puzzles arose from inability to use certain items in the English vocabulary.

The theoretically interesting category-mistakes are those made by people who are perfectly competent to apply concepts, at least in the situations with which they are familiar, but are still liable in their abstract thinking to allocate those concepts to logical types to which they do not belong. An instance of a mistake of this sort would be the following story. A student of politics has learned the main differences between the British, the French and the American Constitutions, and has learned also the differences and connections between the Cabinet, Parliament, the various Ministries, the Judicature and the Church of England. But he still becomes embarrassed when asked questions about the connections between the Church of England, the Home Office and the British Constitution. For while the Church and the Home Office are institutions, the British Constitution is not another institution in the same sense of that noun. So inter-institutional relations which can be asserted or denied to hold between the Church and the Home Office cannot be asserted or denied to hold between either of them and the British Constitution. "The British Constitution" is not a term of the same logical type as "the Home Office" and "the Church of England." In a partially similar way, John Doe may be a relative, a friend, an enemy or a stranger to Richard Roe; but he cannot be any of these things to the Average Taxpayer. He knows how to talk sense in certain sorts of discussions about the Average Taxpayer, but he is baffled to say why he could not come across him in the street as he can come across Richard Roe.

It is pertinent to our main subject to notice that, so long as the student of politics continues to think of the British Constitution as a counterpart to the other institutions, he will tend to describe it as a mysteriously occult institution; and so long as John Doe continues to think of the Average Taxpayer as a fellow-citizen, he will tend to think of him as an elusive insubstantial man, a ghost who is everywhere yet nowhere.

My destructive purpose is to show that a family of radical category-mistakes is the source of the double-life theory. The representation of a person as a ghost mysteriously ensconced in a machine derives from this argument. Because, as is true, a person's thinking, feeling and purposive doing cannot be described solely in the idioms of physics, chemistry and physiology, therefore they must be described in counterpart idioms. As the human body is a complex organised unit, so the human mind must be another complex organised unit, though one made of a different sort of stuff and with a different sort of structure. Or, again, as the human body, like any other parcel of matter, is a field of causes and effects, so the mind must be another field of causes and effects, though not (Heaven be praised) mechanical causes and effects.

The Origin of the Category-Mistake

One of the chief intellectual origins of what I have yet to prove to be the Cartesian category-mistake seems to be this. When Galileo showed that his methods of scientific discovery were competent to provide a mechanical theory which should cover every occupant of space, Descartes found in himself two conflicting motives. As a man of scientific genius he could not but endorse the claims of mechanics, yet as a religious and moral man he could not accept, as Hobbes accepted, the discouraging rider to those claims, namely that human nature differs only in degree of complexity from clockwork. The mental could not be just a variety of the mechanical.

[Descartes] and subsequent philosophers naturally but erroneously availed themselves of the following escape-route. Since mental-conduct words are not to be construed as signifying the occurrence of mechanical processes, they must be construed as signifying the occurrence of non-mechanical processes; since mechanical laws explain movements in space as the effects of other movements in space, other laws must explain some of the non-spatial workings of minds as the effects of other non-spatial workings of minds.

The difference between the human behaviours which we describe as intelligent and those which we describe as unintelligent must be a difference in their causation; so, while some movements of human tongues and limbs are the effects of mechanical causes, others must be the effects of non-mechanical causes, i.e., some issue from movements of particles of matter, others from workings of the mind. The differences between the physical and the mental were thus represented as differences inside the common framework of the categories of "thing," "stuff," "attribute," "state," "process," "change," "cause" and "effect." Minds are things, but different sorts of things from bodies; mental processes are causes and effects, but different sorts of causes and effects from bodily movements. And so on. Somewhat as the foreigner expected the University to be an extra edifice, rather like a college but also considerably different, so the repudiators of mechanism represented minds as extra centres of causal processes, rather like machines but also considerably different from them. Their theory was a para-mechanical hypothesis. . . .

If my argument is successful, there will follow some interesting consequences. First, the hallowed contrast between mind and matter will be dissipated, but dissipated not by either of the equally hallowed absorptions of mind by matter or of matter by mind, but in quite a different way. For the seeming contrast of the two will be shown to be as illegitimate as would be the contrast of "she came home in a flood of tears" and "she came home in a sedan-chair." The belief that there is a polar opposition between mind and matter is the belief that they are terms of the same logical type.

For Further Reflection

1. What is the value of Ryle's essay? Does it severely undermine Cartesian dualism? Does it argue directly against dualism or does it try to suggest another way of looking at the problem?

2. Do you think that Descartes has committed a category mistake as Ryle charges? Is there something missing, unaccounted for, in Ryle's portrayal of dualism? Can a functional monism successfully escape the problems of the mind-body controversy?

A Contemporary Defense of Dualism   IV.37

J. P. MORELAND

J. P. Moreland (1948–) teaches philosophy at Talbot School of Theology at Biola University in California. He is the author of *Scaling the Secular City* and *Christianity and the Nature of Science*. In this selection, Moreland defends dualist interactionism, arguing that the mind is distinct from the brain. He compares physicalism, the view that the only thing that exists in the universe is matter, with substance dualism, the view that mind is separate from matter. He gives several reasons for rejecting physicalism and accepting dualism. Moreland claims that the idea of dualism is best understood from within a wider metaphysic, such as theism.

Study Questions

1. What are the two primary issues involved in the mind-body dispute?
2. What is the name for the view that holds that matter is the only thing that exists?
3. Identify the two varieties of dualism. Which has been the historic Christian view?
4. What are some problems with physicalism?
5. Moreland contends that the physicalist must show that mental and brain phenomena are not only inseparable (like the redness and roundness of an apple) but also that they are _____ [fill in blank].
6. What are examples of mental events?
7. What are some of Moreland's reasons for believing in the distinction between physical and mental events?
8. How does Moreland describe *intentionality*? How does it support a dualist view?
9. How do dualists and physicalists differ regarding personal identity?
10. What is Quine's view on personal identity?
11. What is the emergent property view (EPV)?
12. Why does Moreland reject the EPV?

ARGUMENTS FOR DUALISM: DUALISM DEFINED

THE MIND-BODY PROBLEM focuses on two main issues. First, is a human being composed of just one ultimate component or two? Second, if the answer is two, how do these two relate to one another? Physicalism is one solution to the problem. As a general worldview, physicalism holds that the only thing which exists is matter (where matter is defined by an ideal, completed form of physics). Applied to the mind body problem, physicalism asserts that a human being is just a physical system. There is no mind or soul, just a brain and central nervous system. Dualism is the opponent of physicalism, and it asserts that in addition to the body, a human being also has a nonphysical component called a soul, mind, or

From J. P. Moreland, Scaling the Secular City *(Baker Books, 1987). Reprinted by permission of* Baker Academic, a division of Baker Publishing Group, and the author.

self (words which will be used interchangeably for our purposes).

There are two main varieties of dualism—property dualism and substance dualism. In order to understand the difference, we must first spell out the distinction between a property and a substance. A property is an entity: redness, hardness, wisdom, triangularity, or painfulness. A property has at least four characteristics which distinguish it from a substance. First, a property is a universal, not a particular. It can be in more than one thing or at more than one place at the same time. Redness can be in my coat and your flag at the same time. Second, a property is immutable and does not contain opposites (hot and cold, red and green) within it. When a leaf goes from green to red, the *leaf* changes. Greenness does not become redness. Greenness leaves the leaf and redness replaces it. Greenness and redness remain the same. Third, properties can be had by something else. They can be in another thing which has them. Redness is in the apple. The apple *has* the redness. Fourth, properties do not have causal powers. They do not act as efficient causes. Properties are not agents which act on other agents in the world.

A substance is an entity like an apple, my dog Fido, a carbon atom, a leaf, or an angel. Substances contrast with properties in the four characteristics listed. First, substances are particulars. For example, my dog Fido cannot be in more than one place at the same time. Second, a substance can change and have opposites. A leaf can go from green to red or hot to cold by gaining or losing properties. During the process of change, the substance gains and loses properties, but it is still the same substance. The same leaf which was green is now red. Third, substances are basic, fundamental existents. They are not *in* other things or *had by* other things. Fido is not a property of some more basic entity. Rather, Fido *has* properties. Fido is a unity of properties (dogness, brownness, shape), parts (paws, teeth, ears), and dispositions or capacities (law-like tendencies to realize certain properties in the process of growth if certain con-

ditions obtain; for instance, the capacity to grow teeth if the fetus is nourished). They are all united into the substance Fido and possessed by him. Finally, a substance has causal powers. It can act as a causal agent in the world. A carbon atom can act on another atom. A dog can bark or pick up a bone. A leaf can hit the ground.

Property dualists hold that the mind is a property of the body. As Richard Taylor puts it, "A person is a living physical body having mind, the mind consisting, however, of nothing but a more or less continuous series of conscious or unconscious states and events . . . which are the effects but never the causes of bodily activity." This view is called *epiphenomenalism*. The mind is to the body as smoke is to fire. Smoke is different from fire, but smoke does not cause anything. Smoke is a byproduct of fire. Similarly, mind is a byproduct of the body which does not cause anything. It just "rides" on top of the events in the body. Body events cause mind as a byproduct. The mind is a property of the body which ceases to exist when the body ceases to function. Though some theists have denied it recently, the historic Christian view has been substance dualism. The mind, distinct from the body, is a real substance which can cause things to happen by acting and which can exist when the body ceases to function.

DUALISM DEFENDED

Problems with Physicalism as a General Worldview

Physicalism as a worldview holds that everything that exists is nothing but a single spatio-temporal system which can be completely described in terms of some ideal form of physics. Matter/energy is all that exists. God, souls, and nonphysical abstract entities do not exist. If physicalism is true at the worldview level, then obviously, mind-body physicalism would follow. But is physicalism adequate as a worldview? Several factors indicate that it is not.

First, if theism is true, then physicalism as a worldview is false. God is not a physical being. Second, a number of people have argued that numbers exist and that they are abstract, non-physical entities (e.g., sets, substances, or properties). Several arguments can be offered for the existence of numbers, but two appear frequently. For one thing, mathematics claims to give us knowledge. But if this is so, there must be something that mathematics is about. Just as the biologist *discovers* biological truths about biological objects (organisms), so the mathematician often *discovers* mathematical truths (he does not invent them all the time) and these truths are about mathematical objects. If one denies the existence of numbers, then it is hard to rescue mathematics as a field which conveys knowledge about something. Without numbers, mathematics becomes merely an internally consistent game which is invented.

A second argument is often given for holding to the existence of numbers. Scientific laws and theories seem to assert their existence. For example, a calcium ion has a positive charge of two which is expressed in the formula Ca^{+2}. The number two here seems to be more than a mere formula for calculating relative amounts of compounds in laboratory reactions. Two expresses a property of the calcium ion itself. The property of twoness is just as much a real property of the charge of the calcium as the property of positiveness. If one denies that numbers exist, it is hard to continue to maintain that science gives us a real description of the world rather than a set of operations that work in the laboratory. In sum, without numbers, mathematical and scientific knowledge is hard to maintain. But if numbers exist, physicalism as a worldview is false because numbers are not physical entities.

Some have argued that values, in addition to God and numbers, exist and are not physical. Certain objects (persons, animals) and certain events (helping a stranger, for example) have a nonphysical property of worth or goodness. Furthermore, moral laws are often held to be absolute, objective realities (e.g., one should not torture babies). But if certain objects possess goodness, and if certain moral laws are objective realities, then physicalism must be false, because the property of goodness and the nature of moral laws are not physical. For example, it makes no sense to ask how much goodness weighs, or to ask where a moral law exists. Such realities are not physical.

Fourth, if physicalism is true, it is hard to see what one should make of the existence and nature of theories, meanings, concepts, propositions, the laws of logic, and truth itself. It would seem that theories themselves exist and can be discovered. The laws of logic seem to be real laws that govern the relationships between propositions. Propositions seem to exist and be the content of thoughts which become associated with the physical scratchings of a given language called sentences. Sentences may be made of black ink, be on a page, and be four inches long. But it is hard to see how the *content* of the sentence (i.e., the proposition or thought expressed by the sentence) could be on the page. Such entities seem to be nonphysical entities which can be in the mind. Truth appears to be a relation of correspondence between a thought and the world. If a thought really describes the world accurately, it is true. It stands to the world in a relation of correspondence. But whatever else one wants to say about the relation of correspondence, it does not seem to be a physical relation like cause and effect.

Finally, universals seem to exist and they are not material. A universal is an entity that can be in more than one place at the same time. Some universals are properties (redness, hardness, triangularity); others are relations (larger than, to the left of). Whatever else one may use to characterize the nature of matter, it is clear that a clump of matter is a particular. A piece of matter cannot be in more than one place at the same time. Physicalists deny the existence of universals at the level of general worldview, because universals are not physical entities.

The entities listed have caused a lot of difficulty for physicalists. They have spent a good deal of time trying to do away with numbers, values, propositions, laws of logic, and universals by reducing them to notions compatible with physicalism. But these reductionist attempts have failed and physicalism as a worldview cannot adequately handle the existence of these entities. Theism can embrace them, however, by holding that God created these nonphysical entities and sustains them in existence. The falsity of physicalism as a worldview does not refute mind-body physicalism. One could hold to the existence of numbers and values but deny the existence of the soul. But much of the motivation for mind-body physicalism has been the desire to argue for physicalism at the worldview level. If physicalism at that level is false, then part of the reason for holding to mind-body physicalism is removed. For example, just because one cannot see the soul, weigh it, or say where it is, it does not follow that the soul does not exist. One cannot see, weigh, or locate numbers or values, but they still exist.

Problems with Mind-Body Physicalism

In order to facilitate an understanding of some of the arguments against mind-body physicalism, we must first examine the nature of identity. Suppose you know that someone named J. P. Moreland exists and that the author of this book exists. Assume further that you do not know that J. P. Moreland wrote this book. If someone asked you whether J. P. Moreland is identical to the author of this book, how would you decide? How would you determine that the "two" individuals are identical instead of being two different people? If you could find something true of J. P. Moreland which is not true of the author of this book or vice versa, then they would be different people. They could not be identical. For example, if J. P. Moreland is married to Hope Moreland but the author of this book is not, they would be different people. On the other hand, if everything true of one is true of the other, "they" would be one person. In general, if "two" things are identical, then whatever is true of the one is true of the other, since in reality only one thing is being discussed. However, if something is true of the one which is not true of the other, then they are two things and not one. This is sometimes called the indiscernibility of identicals and is expressed as follows:

$$(x)(y)[(x = y) \rightarrow (P)(Px \leftrightarrow Py)]$$

For any entities x and y, if x and y are really the same thing, then for any property P, P is true of x if and only if P is true of y.[1] If x is the mind or one of its states and y is a body or part or state of the body (e.g., the brain), then if physicalism is true, x must be identical to y. On the other hand, if something is true of the mind which is not true of the body, then the mind is not identical to the body and physicalism is false. This would be true even if the mind and body are inseparable. The roundness of an apple cannot be separated from its redness. One does not find redness sitting on a table by itself and roundness sitting next to it. But the redness of an apple is not identical to the roundness of the apple. One is a color and one is a shape.

Every time something happens in the mind (someone has a thought of an ice cream cone), some event may be going on in the brain which could be described by a neurophysiologist. In general, brain events may always have mental events that correlate with them and vice versa. They may be inseparable in that one does not occur without the other in an embodied person. But this does not mean that the mental thought is identical to the brain event. The redness and roundness of an apple, though inseparable, are not identical. The property of having three sides (trilaterality) and the property of having three angles (triangularity) always go together. They are inseparable. But they are not identical. Physicalists must not only show that mental and brain phenomena are inseparable to make their case. They must also show that they are identical. With this in mind let us turn to some arguments for dualism.

The Distinctiveness of Mental and Physical Properties. Mental events include episodes of thoughts, feelings of pain, the experience of being a person, or episodes of having sensory experience, e.g., a picture of a ball in my mind. Physical events are events in the brain or central nervous system which can be described exhaustively using terms of chemistry, physics, and (for now) biology. The difficulty for physicalism is that mental events do not seem to have properties that hold for physical events. My thought of Kansas City is not ten centimeters long, it does not weigh anything, it is not located anywhere (it is not two inches from my left ear). Nor is it identical to any behavior or tendency to behave in a certain way (shouting "Kansas City" when I hear the name *George Brett*). But the brain event associated with having this thought may be located inside my head, it may have a certain chemical composition and electrical current, and so forth. My afterimage of a ball (the impression of the ball present to my consciousness when I close my eyes after seeing the ball) may be pink, but nothing in my brain is pink.[2] Mental events and properties have different attributes and therefore they are not identical.[3]

Private Access and Incorrigibility. Mental events are self-presenting. I seem to be in a position to know my own thoughts and mental processes in a way not available to anyone else. I am in a privileged position with regard to my own mental life. I have private access to my own thoughts in a way not open to anyone else. Furthermore, my mental states seem to be incorrigible, at least some of the time. That is, I cannot be mistaken about them. Suppose I am experiencing what I take to be a green rug. It is possible that the rug is not there or that the light is poor and the rug is really gray. I could be mistaken about the rug itself. But it does not seem to be possible for me to be mistaken that I am experiencing what I take to be a green rug right now. That is, my mental state is directly present to me and I know my own mental states immediately.

It would be possible for a brain surgeon to know more about my brain than I do. He may be looking into my brain, seeing it better than I,

and knowing its operations better than I. But he does not—indeed, he cannot—know my mental life as well as I. I have private, privileged access to that. Further, it seems that one could always be wrong about his knowledge of some physical state of affairs in the world. The brain surgeon could be wrong about what is happening in my brain. But I cannot be wrong about what is currently happening in my mind. It would seem then that I have privileged, private access to my mental states which is sometimes incorrigible. But neither I nor anyone else has private access to my brain states, and whatever access someone has is irreducibly third-person access (described from a standpoint outside of me) and is not incorrigible.[4]

The Experience of First-Person Subjectivity. The subjective character of experience is hard to capture in physicalist terms. The simple fact of consciousness is a serious difficulty for physicalism. To see this, consider the following. Suppose a deaf scientist became the world's leading expert on the neurology of hearing. It would be possible for him to know and describe everything there is to the physical processes involved in hearing. However, something would still be left out of such a description—the experience of what it is like to be a human who hears. As Howard Robinson puts it:

> The notion of *having something as an object of experience* is not, *prima facie*, a physical notion; it does not figure in any physical science. *Having something as an object of experience* is the same as the subjective feel or the *what it is like* of experience (*Matter and Sense*, p. 7).

Subjective states of experiences exist. My experience of what it is like to be me, to hear a bird or see a tree, exists, and I have a first-person awareness of it. Such first-person experiences of my own self or "I" which has experiences cannot be reduced to a third-person "he" or "it," because the latter do not describe the experience itself or its first-person standpoint. A physicalist, scientific description of the world leaves out this character of subjective awareness. Such a description characterizes the world in impersonal, third-person terms (e.g., "there exists an object with such and such properties and states") and leaves out the first-person, subjective experience itself (e.g., "I feel sad and food tastes sour to me").

Speaking of the character of subjective awareness, Thomas Nagel has this to say:

> If physicalism is to be defended, the phenomenological features [the sounds, colors, smells, tastes of experience that make the experience what it is] must themselves be given a physical account. But when we examine their subjective character it seems that such a result is impossible. The reason is that every subjective phenomenon is essentially connected with a single point of view, and it seems inevitable that an objective, physical theory will abandon that point of view (*Mortal Questions*, p. 167).

Secondary Qualities.   Secondary qualities are qualities such as colors, tastes, sounds, smells, and textures. Physicalism seems to imply that such qualities do not exist in the external world. But we do sense such qualities, so where are they, if they are not in the external world? They must exist as sense data (mental objects or images) in the mind. Frank Jackson has put the point this way:

> It is a commonplace that there is an apparent clash between the picture Science gives of the world around us and the picture our senses give us. We *sense* the world as made up of coloured, materially continuous, macroscopic, stable objects; Science and, in particular, Physics, tells us that the material world is constituted of clouds of minute, colourless, highly-mobile particles. . . . Science forces us to acknowledge that physical or material things are not coloured. . . . This will enable us to conclude that sense-data are all mental, for they are coloured (*Perception*, p. 121).

In other words, science does away with secondary qualities, but since we know they do exist—we see them—they must exist in our minds as sense data. This shows that there must

be minds, and sense data must be little images or pictures which exist as mental objects in minds.

I do not accept this understanding of secondary qualities, because it implies that I do not see the world when I use my senses. Rather, it implies that I see my sense images of the world. But if this view is correct, then it would seem that some form of dualism is correct. If, on the other hand, one holds (as I do) that secondary qualities are real properties of objects in the world, physicalism as a worldview may still be in trouble. If macroscopic objects (regular-sized tables, apples, dogs) do have properties of color, odor, stability, continuous surfaces, and the like, then there must be more to them than what physics tells us. Physics tends to reduce objects to mere heaps of colorless, odorless, rapid-moving packets of matter/ energy. But if objects have macroproperties which escape description in these terms, then these properties, call them metaphysical properties, are not physical. That does not mean that they are mental. But it does show that a full treatment of objects must appeal to metaphysical properties which deal with the objects as wholes. If physicalism reduces objects to the mere heaps of microphysics, then physicalism is incomplete as a worldview. On the other hand, if secondary qualities are in fact mental sense data, then physicalism is inadequate as a mind-body theory. Either way, physicalism as a general theory is in trouble.

Intentionality.   Some have argued that the mark of the mental is intentionality. Intentionality is the mind's aboutness or ofness. Mental states point beyond themselves to other objects even if those objects do not exist. I have a thought *about* my wife, I hope *for* a new car, I dream *of* a unicorn. The mind has the ability to transcend itself and be of or about something else. This aboutness is not a property of anything physical. Some physicalists have tried to reduce intentionality to the mere ability to receive input, give output, and advance to some other internal state. A computer receives input from a keyboard, gives output on a printer, and advances to a new internal state where it is ready to receive new input. But the computer still has no awareness of or about anything. It seems, then, that physical states do not have intentionality and thus the fact of intentionality is evidence that the self is not physical but mental.

Personal Identity.　Imagine a wooden table which had all its parts removed one by one and replaced by metal parts. When the top and all the legs were replaced would it still be the same table? The answer would seem to be no. In fact, it would be possible to take all the original wooden parts and rearrange them into the original table. Even when the table had just one leg replaced, it would not literally be the same table. It would be a table similar to the original.

Losing old parts and gaining new ones changes the identity of the object in question. But now a question arises regarding persons. Am I literally the same self that I was a moment ago? Are my baby pictures really pictures of *me* or are they pictures of an ancestor of me who resembles me? I am constantly losing physical parts. I lose hair and fingernails; atoms are constantly being replaced, and every seven years my cells are almost entirely replaced. Do I maintain literal, absolute identity through change or not?

Substance dualists argue that persons do maintain absolute identity through change, because they have, in addition to their bodies, a soul that remains constant through change, and personal identity is constituted by sameness of soul, not sameness of body.

Physicalists have no alternative but to hold that personal identity is not absolute. Usually they argue that persons are really ancestral chains of successive "selves" which are connected with one another in some way. At each moment a new self exists (since the self or physical organism is constantly in flux, losing and gaining parts) and this self resembles the self prior to and after it. The relation of resemblance between selves plus the fact that later selves have the same memories as earlier selves and the body of each self traces a continuous path through space when the whole

chain of selves is put together, constitute a relative sense of personal identity.

So substance dualists hold to a literal, absolute sense of personal identity and physicalists hold to a loose, relative sense of personal identity which amounts to a stream of successive selves held together into "one" person by resemblance between each self (also called a person stage), similarity of memory, and spatial continuity. For the physicalist, a person becomes a space-time worm (i.e., a path traced through space and time). The person is the entire path marked off at the time and place of his birth and death. At any given moment and location where "I" happen to be, "I" am not a person, just a person stage. The person is the whole path. So there is no literal sameness through change.

But now certain problems arise for physicalism. First, why should "I" ever fear the future? When it gets here, "I" will not be present; rather, another self who looks like me will be there but "I" will have ceased to exist. Second, why should anyone be punished? The self who did the crime in the past is not literally the same self who is present at the time of punishment. Physicalism seems to require a radical readjustment of our common-sense notions of future expectations and past actions because both presuppose a literal identity of the same self present in past, present, and future.

Third, physicalists not only have difficulty handling the unity of the self through time, but also cannot explain the unity of the self at a given time. As Harvard philosopher W. V. O. Quine puts it, according to physicalism, the self becomes a sum or heap of scattered physical parts. The unity of the self is like the unity of an assembly of building blocks. If I have a pain in my foot while I am thinking about baseball, each is a distinct experience involving different physical parts. There is no self which *has* each experience. The self is merely a bundle or heap of parts and experiences. It has no real unity. The dualist says that the soul is diffused throughout the body and it is present before each experience. The soul has each experience. The unity of consciousness is due to the fact that the same soul is the possessor of each and every experience of consciousness. But the physicalist must say that each experience is possessed by different parts of the body and there is no real unity. However, my own experience of the unity of my consciousness shows this unity to be genuine and not arbitrary. *I* have my experiences. They are all *mine*. Physicalism does not adequately explain this fact.

THE ORIGIN OF MIND: THE EMERGENT PROPERTY VIEW

We have seen that there are good reasons for holding that strict physicalism is false. But most physicalists are recalcitrant. If they embrace dualism at all, they embrace epiphenomenalism because, as I will show later, it is more compatible with physicalism than is substance dualism. Mind is not matter, but it comes from matter through evolution when matter reaches a suitable structural arrangement for mind to emerge. . . . There are serious difficulties with epiphenomenalism. To see these we must first clarify what epiphenomenalism involves. The view is also called holism, and when mind is seen to emerge through the coming together of matter in a certain way (for instance, through the evolution of the central nervous system and brain) the position is called the emergent property view (EPV). Here are four main features of the EPV.

Wholes and Parts.   In nature, wholes are often greater than the sum of their parts. Nature exhibits a hierarchy of systems—subatomic particles, atoms, molecules, cells, organs, whole organisms. Each level has properties of the wholes at that level which are not properties of their constituent parts. For example, water has the property of being wet, but this property is not true of either hydrogen or oxygen. Similarly, the mind is a property of the brain.

Levels of Explanation and Complementarity. Each level in a hierarchy can be explained by using concepts appropriate at that level. Further, all the levels are complementary. For example, an explanation of a person's behavior could be given at a psychological level which used the concepts *beliefs, desires,* or *fears*. The same behavior could be given an explanation at the neurophysiological level using the concepts *neurons, synapses,* and so forth. These two levels of explanation are not in competition; they complement one another by offering descriptions of the same behavior at different levels.

Causation Between Levels.   Lower levels in the hierarchy cause things to happen at higher levels but not vice versa. When it comes to persons, events at the physical level can be characterized in terms of physical laws which make no reference to the causal efficaciousness of future events (e.g., the purposes of the agent) or higher levels of organization. The events at the physical level obey deterministic physical laws and mental events are mere byproducts.

Resultant View of the Self.   The self is not some mental substance added to the brain from the "outside" when the brain reaches a certain level of complexity. It is an emergent property which supervenes upon the brain. The self becomes a discontinuous series of mental events when mental properties are instanced in different brain events. The self is a series of events which "ride" on top of the brain. Consider the following diagram:

$$M_1 \quad M_2 \quad M_3 \quad M_4$$
$$\nearrow \quad \nearrow \quad \nearrow \quad \nearrow$$
$$B_1 \rightarrow B_2 \rightarrow B_3 \rightarrow B_4$$

Suppose M_1 is the mental state of seeing an apple from a distance of five feet. It is a *mental* state since it involves the conscious awareness of seeing the apple, and conscious awareness is something true of minds and not matter. Now suppose M_2 is the mental state of seeing the apple from one foot, M_3 the state of feeling a pain on the toe, and M_4 the state of hearing a plane fly overhead. B_1 through B_4 are brain states which are associated with each mental state.

Three things stand out immediately. First, B_1 through B_4 stand in rigid physical, causal relations with one another. B_1 causes B_2 and so on. There is no room for a rational agent to intervene in this causal sequence. Mental agents do not act here. The physical level determines all the action. Mental states are mere byproducts of their physical states as smoke is a byproduct of fire.

Second, there is no unified, enduring self at the mental level. According to substance dualism, the self is not identical to its states; it *has* its states. The mind *has* its thoughts and experiences, and the same mind can have two experiences at the same time (hearing a plane and seeing an apple) or it can have one experience followed by another. The *self* is present at both experiences and underlies the change of experiences.

When a leaf goes from green to red, green does not become red. Rather, green leaves and is replaced by red *in* the leaf. The leaf is the same substance present at both ends of the process. When a substance gains or loses properties, *it* remains the same while the properties come and go. They are replaced. Red replaces green. The EPV says that M_1 through M_4 are properties of the body. There is no enduring mental substance which has them. There is just one mental property at one time which leaves and is replaced by another mental property at another time. The "self" is a series of mental events where mental properties are had by physical states.

Third, it is hard to see what sense can be given to intentionality. How is it that M_1 is of or about an apple? M_1 is just a dummy, a free rider on B_1. At best, B_1 would just be a state caused by light waves from the apple but it is hard to see how this would cause M_1 to be really a state *about* that apple. Even if it were, what difference would it make? Any further body states (the act of touching the apple or eating it) would be caused totally by brain states and make no reference to mental states at all.

It should now be clear why epiphenomenalism was ruled out as an inadequate account of the necessary features of rationality. It cannot account for the existence of intentionality, it leaves no room for genuine rational agency to freely choose mental beliefs, and there is no enduring "I" to be present through the process of thought.

But let us waive these problems for the moment. Where would the mind as an emergent property come from? How can mind, the capacity to know truth, and so forth, emerge from mindless, nonrational matter? Remember, mind here is not identical to the brain's structure. If it were, then the view would be some form of crude materialism or, perhaps, some unclear intermediate view between dualism and physicalism. But in either case, the position would be worse than epiphenomenalism, for it would suffer from the same deficiencies as the latter, as well as those raised earlier against physicalism in its pure form.

The EPV holds that mind is a genuine mental property (or series of properties) which supervenes on top of matter. Consider water again. Wetness emerges when hydrogen and oxygen come together into a structure known as H_2O. Wetness is not identical to that structure. Wetness is a simple quality; the structure is a set of relationships which can be quantified (spatial relations, relations of force, which can be given numerical values). So the structure is not the same thing as the wetness. Similarly, the mind is not the same thing as the brain's structure; it supervenes over that structure in the EPV view. So it is a genuinely new entity which must come into being somehow or other.

It does not seem that it could come into being from nothing. For one thing, that would violate a generally accepted principle that something does not come from nothing. Some have disputed this principle, but it still seems reasonable, especially at the macroscopic level and not the level of the microparticles of physics (though I believe it to hold at that level as well). And it is the macroscopic level that is involved when mind emerges, since it emerges over an object the size of a structured brain.

One could respond that the mind is not itself a macroscopic entity—perhaps by saying that the macro/micro distinction does not hold for minds. But if the EPV view means that mind emerges over a structured brain out of nothing and that this fact is not anchored to the nature of that brain, then it is hard to see why mind emerges time and again over just this type of structured matter and not over a nickel or a bowling pin. The defender of the EPV cannot appeal to the causal efficacy of the mind itself and argue that the mind of a child comes from the mind of its parents, for this allows minds to cause something, and this is not allowed according to the EPV.

At the level of normal-sized macroscopic objects (objects visible to normal sight) things just do not pop in and out of existence. Even if mind is not such an object, its emergence seems to be tied to the brain. And the brain is such an object. So it is not very promising to account for the emergence of mind by saying it comes from nothing.

There is, however, a more promising view. Aristotle taught us long ago that when something new emerges, it does not come from nothing but from potentiality. When a leaf turns from green to red, the red does not simply come into existence; it was already in the leaf potentially. When an apple seed produces apples, the apples were in the seed potentially. In general, when a property emerges in a substance, it comes to actuality from potentiality, not from pure non-being. The property was in the substance potentially and when it emerges, it becomes actual.

Mind must somehow be in matter potentially such that when matter reaches a certain stage of development, mind becomes actual. This is a more plausible version of the EPV, but it still has serious difficulties.

First, it is hard to see how this is compatible with the doctrines and motives of physicalism. Physicalism is embraced in part out of a desire to promote science as the ultimate, perhaps only, kind of knowledge. So physicalists often assert that the world is a network of physical causes wherein only

physical causality does anything. Further, the world for a physicalist is in principle describable in strictly physical laws. But if mind is potential in matter, then physicalism seems to become some form of panpsychism, the view that mind is ultimate. Matter no longer is describable in terms of familiar physical properties and laws alone. Now it contains elusive mental potentialities.

After wrestling with this problem, Nobel Prize–winning scientist Max Delbruck argued that "our ideas about the objective character of the physical world, and hence of the nature of truth have been revised. In other words, mind looks less psychic and matter looks less materialistic. . . ." So if one admits that mind is potential in matter, then one can no longer hold that reality is exhausted by the spatiotemporal physical universe.

Second, this emergent property view could not rule out the future existence of God. If mind can emerge from matter when a high-level system reaches a certain point of complexity, why is it not possible for a large-scale Mind to emerge at a later period in evolutionary development? In other words, the EPV cannot rule out Hegelianism, the view that mind emerges from matter all the way up to the emergence of God himself. This may sound far-fetched. But the point is that the EPV cannot rule it out, for the emergence of mind over brains is a startling fact which could hardly have been predicted from the properties of matter alone. So why should one think the process of emergence should stop with finite, human minds? Why could not some form of deity emerge, since mind is in some sense a basic constituent of the universe? Christian philosopher Richard Purtill has called this the God-not-yet view. And it should come as no comfort to an atheist, who is trying to save some form of minimal physicalism, to be told that his view seems to imply some form of emergent theism. At the very least, emergent theism cannot be ruled out.

Finally, Clark points out that it is hard to specify just what these potential mental properties are. Are these potential properties conscious? If so, then why do we have no memory from them when they emerge to form our own minds? Does it really make sense to say that my mind is composed of several particles of mind dust (i.e., little selves which came together to form my own mental life)? If these potential properties are not conscious, how are they still mental? These questions may have an answer, but they are certainly puzzling, and the EPV seems to commit one to the existence of rather odd potential mental properties, odd at least from the standpoint of one who wants to maintain some form of respectable physicalism.

The simple fact is that the existence of mind has always been a problem for the physicalist. As physicalist Paul M. Churchland argues,

> The important point about the standard evolutionary story is that the human species and all of its features are the wholly physical outcome of a purely physical process. . . . If this is the correct account of our origins, then there seems neither need, nor room, to fit any nonphysical substances or properties into our theoretical account of ourselves. We are creatures of matter (*Matter and Consciousness,* p. 21).

Physicalism is false because it fails to adequately handle several general arguments raised against it. And it is self-refuting, for it undercuts the very prerequisites of rational thought itself. Once one grants the existence of mind, then the question arises as to where it came from. The emergent property view is one answer to this question. But it fails as an adequate theory of mind itself, and it postulates either the origin of mind from nothing or its emergence from potentiality in matter. Both options are problematic. Mind appears to be a basic feature of the cosmos, and its origin at a finite level of persons is best explained by postulating a fundamental Mind who gave finite minds being and design. As Calvin put it, the endowments which we possess cannot possibly be from ourselves. They point to the ultimate Mind and ground of rationality himself.

NOTES

1. The identity relation is necessary. That is, for all *x* and all *y*, if *x* is identical to *y*, then, *necessarily,* *x* is identical to *y*. There is no possible world where one obtains without the other.

2. Again, pains are natural kinds whose essential nature is a conscious feeling, but a conscious feeling is not an essential part of anything physical.

3. An individual pain or type of pain could exist without the presence of any individual physical state existing. Indeed, it is logically possible for a person to exist and have a pain in a completely disembodied state. Thus, persons and their states are not identical to bodies and their states, given that the identity relation is necessary.

4. Private access and incorrigibility are two pieces of evidence for the claim that mental entities are self-presenting. But no physical entity is self presenting.

For Further Reflection

1. Do you accept Moreland's analysis of the mind-body problem? Can you find weaknesses in his rejection of physicalism or acceptance of dualism? Can you think of other alternatives? What do you make of the *panpsychism* hinted at by the view of the physicist Max Delbruck, mentioned in the article? Could matter itself already contain mind?

2. He lists two issues: (1) "Is a human being composed of just one ultimate component or two?" and (2) "If the answer is two, how do these two relate to one another?" Has Moreland given a clear explanation of how dualism solves the second problem? Is physicalism more plausible on this problem?

3. Is Moreland's argument for mathematical entities relevant to the mind-body problem? Explain.

IV.38   On Functionalism and Materialism

PAUL CHURCHLAND

Paul Churchland is a professor of philosophy at the University of California at San Diego. He has written a number of books and articles in philosophy of mind, including *Scientific Realism and the Plasticity of Mind* (1979) and *Matter and Consciousness* (1984), from which this selection is taken. His work has won him a reputation for clarity, fairness, and insight.

In this selection Churchland examines functionalism and the two prominent versions of materialism in philosophy of mind. Reductivism claims that there is an identity of mental states with brain states. Functionalism rejects any one-to-one correlation between mental types and physical types, and concentrates on the relationship between inputs and outputs. For example, the mental event of pain could be similar in two beings that have altogether different types of bodies and brains. Most functionalists are materialists but someone could be a functionalist *and* be a nonmaterialist. Eliminative materialism is more radical than either of these other theories and seeks to eliminate "folk psychology"—talk of beliefs, feelings, and perceptions—in favor of more scientific descriptions of what is going on in the brain. Churchland concludes that the truth may be a combination of the two materialist theories, although the evidence points more in the direction of eliminativism.

Study Questions

1. Why is reductive materialism referred to as the "identity theory"?
2. What is intertheoretic reduction?
3. What are the four arguments for the identity theory?
4. What are the arguments against the identity theory?
5. What is Leibniz's law? Is it always valid?
6. Explain functionalism.
7. What are the main arguments against functionalism?
8. What is eliminative materialism?
9. What does Churchland say are the historical parallels to it?
10. What are the main arguments for eliminativism?
11. What are the main arguments against eliminativism?

I. REDUCTIVE MATERIALISM (THE IDENTITY THEORY)

REDUCTIVE MATERIALISM, more commonly known as *the identity theory*, is the most straightforward of the several materialist theories of mind. Its central claim is simplicity itself: Mental states *are* physical states of the brain. That is, each type of mental state or process is *numerically identical with* (is one and the very same

Reprinted from Paul Churchland, Matter and Consciousness *pp. 26–34, © 1984, Massachusetts Institute of Technology, by permission of the MIT Press and the author.*

thing as) some type of physical state or process within the brain or central nervous system. At present we do not know enough about the intricate functionings of the brain actually to state the relevant identities, but the identity theory is committed to the idea that brain research will eventually reveal them. . . .

Historical Parallels

As the identity theorist sees it, the result here predicted has familiar parallels elsewhere in our scientific history. Consider sound. We now know that sound is just a train of compression waves traveling through the air, and that the property of being high pitched is identical with the property of having a high oscillatory frequency. We have learned that light is just electromagnetic waves, and our best current theory says that the color of an object is identical with a triplet of reflectance efficiencies the object has, rather like a musical chord that it strikes, though the "notes" are struck in electromagnetic waves instead of in sound waves. We now appreciate that the warmth or coolness of a body is just the energy of motion of the molecules that make it up: Warmth is identical with high average molecular kinetic energy, and coolness is identical with low average molecular kinetic energy. We know that lightning is identical with a sudden large-scale discharge of electrons between clouds, or between the atmosphere and the ground. What we now think of as "mental states," argues the identity theorist, are identical with brain states in exactly the same way.

Intertheoretic Reduction

These illustrative parallels are all cases of successful *intertheoretic reduction*. That is, they are all cases where a new and very powerful theory turns out to entail a set of propositions and principles that mirror perfectly (or almost perfectly) the propositions and principles of some older theory or conceptual framework. The relevant principles entailed by the new theory have the same structure as the corresponding principles of the old

framework, and they apply in exactly the same cases. The only difference is that where the old principles contained (for example) the notions of "heat," "is hot," and "is cold," the new principles contain instead the notions of "total molecular kinetic energy," "has a high mean molecular kinetic energy," and "has a low mean molecular kinetic energy."

If the new framework is far better than the old at explaining and predicting phenomena, then we have excellent reason for believing that the theoretical terms of the *new* framework are the terms that describe reality correctly. But if the old framework worked adequately, so far as it went, and if it parallels a portion of the new theory in the systematic way described, then we may properly conclude that the old terms and the new terms refer to the very same things, or express the very same properties. We conclude that we have apprehended the very same reality that is incompletely described by the old framework, but with a new and more penetrating conceptual framework. And we announce what philosophers of science call "intertheoretic identities": light *is* electromagnetic waves, temperature *is* mean molecular kinetic energy, and so forth.

The examples of the preceding two paragraphs share one more important feature in common. They are all cases where the things or properties on the receiving end of the reduction are *observable* things and properties within our *common-sense* conceptual framework. They show that intertheoretic reduction occurs not only between conceptual frameworks in the theoretical stratosphere: common-sense observables can also be reduced. There would therefore be nothing particularly surprising about a reduction of our familiar introspectible mental states to physical states of the brain. All that would be required would be that an explanatorily successful neuro-science develop to the point where it entails a suitable "mirror image" of the assumptions and principles that constitute our common-sense conceptual framework for mental states, an image where brain-state terms occupy the positions held by mental-state terms in the assumptions and principles of common sense. If this (rather demanding) condition were indeed met, then, as in the historical cases cited, we would be justified in announcing a reduction, and in asserting the identity of mental states with brain states.

Arguments for the Identity Theory

What reasons does the identity theorist have for believing that neuroscience will eventually achieve the strong conditions necessary for the reduction of our "folk" psychology? There are at least four reasons, all directed at the conclusion that the correct account of human-behavior-and-its-causes must reside in the physical neurosciences.

We can point first to the purely physical origins and ostensibly physical constitution of each individual human. One begins as a genetically programmed monocellular organization of molecules (a fertilized ovum), and one develops from there by the accretion of further molecules whose structure and integration is controlled by the information coded in the DNA molecules of the cell nucleus. The result of such a process would be a purely physical system whose behavior arises from its internal operations and its interactions with the rest of the physical world. And those behavior-controlling internal operations are precisely what the neurosciences are about.

This argument coheres with a second argument. The origins of each *type* of animal also appear exhaustively physical in nature. The argument from evolutionary history discussed earlier . . . lends further support to the identity theorist's claim, since evolutionary theory provides the only serious explanation we have for the behavior-controlling capacities of the brain and central nervous system. Those systems were selected for because of the many advantages (ultimately, the reproductive advantage) held by creatures whose behavior was thus controlled. Again our behavior appears to have its basic causes in neural activity.

The identity theorist finds further support in the argument, discussed earlier, from the neural dependence of all known mental phenomena. . . . This is precisely what one should expect, if the identity theory is true. Of course, systematic neural dependence is also a consequence of property dualism, but here the identity theorist will appeal to considerations of simplicity. Why admit two radically different classes of properties and operations if the explanatory job can be done by one?

A final argument derives from the growing success of the neurosciences in unraveling the nervous systems of many creatures and in explaining their behavioral capacities and deficits in terms of the structures discovered. The preceding arguments all suggest that neuroscience should be successful in this endeavor, and the fact is that the continuing history of neuroscience bears them out. Especially in the case of very simple creatures (as one would expect), progress has been rapid. And progress has also been made with humans, though for obvious moral reasons exploration must be more cautious and circumspect. In sum, the neurosciences have a long way to go, but progress to date provides substantial encouragement to the identity theorist.

Even so, these arguments are far from decisive in favor of the identity theory. No doubt they do provide an overwhelming case for the idea that the causes of human and animal behavior are essentially physical in nature, but the identity theory claims more than just this. It claims that neuroscience will discover a taxonomy of neural states that stand in a one-to-one correspondence with the mental states of our common-sense taxonomy. Claims for intertheoretic identity will be justified only if such a match-up can be found. But nothing in the preceding arguments guarantees that the old and new frameworks will match up in this way, even if the new framework is a roaring success at explaining and predicting our behavior. Furthermore, there are arguments from other positions within the materialist camp to the effect that such convenient match-ups are rather unlikely. Before exploring those, however, let us look at some more traditional objections to the identity theory.

Arguments Against the Identity Theory

We may begin with the argument from introspection discussed. Introspection reveals a domain of thoughts, sensations, and emotions, not a domain of electrochemical impulses in a neural network. Mental states and properties, as revealed in introspection, appear radically different from any neurophysiological states and properties. How could they possibly be the very same things?

The answer, as we have already seen, is, "Easily." In discriminating red from blue, sweet from sour, and hot from cold, our external senses are actually discriminating between subtle differences in intricate electromagnetic, stereochemical, and micromechanical properties of physical objects. But our senses are not sufficiently penetrating to reveal on their own the detailed nature of those intricate properties. That requires theoretical research and experimental exploration with specially designed instruments. The same is presumably true of our "inner" sense: introspection. It may discriminate efficiently between a great variety of neural states, without being able to reveal on its own the detailed nature of the states being discriminated. Indeed, it would be faintly miraculous if it did reveal them, just as miraculous as if unaided sight were to reveal the existence of interacting electric and magnetic fields whizzing by with an oscillatory frequency of a million billion hertz and a wavelength of less than a millionth of a meter. For despite "appearances," that is what light is. The argument from introspection, therefore, is quite without force.

The next objection argues that the identification of mental states with brain states would commit us to statements that are literally unintelligible, to what philosophers have called "category errors," and that the identification is therefore a case of sheer conceptual confusion. We may begin the discussion by noting a most important law concerning numerical identity. Leibniz's Law states that two items are numerically identical just in case any property had by either one of them is also had by the other: in logical notation,

$$(x)(y)[(x = y) \equiv (F)(Fx \equiv Fy)]$$

This law suggests a way of refuting the identity theory: find some property that is true of brain states, but not of mental states (or vice versa), and the theory would be exploded.

Spatial properties were often cited to this end. Brain states and processes must of course have some specific spatial location: in the brain as a whole, or in some part of it. And if mental states are identical with brain states, then they must have the very same spatial location. But it is literally meaningless, runs the argument, to say that my feeling-of-pain is located in my ventral thalamus, or that my belief-that-the-sun-is-a-star is located in the temporal lobe of my left cerebral hemisphere. Such claims are as meaningless as the claim that the number 5 is green, or that love weighs twenty grams.

Trying the same move from the other direction, some have argued that it is senseless to ascribe the various *semantic* properties to brain states. Our thoughts and beliefs, for example, have a meaning, a specific propositional content; they are either true or false; and they can enjoy relations such as consistency and entailment. If thoughts and beliefs were brain states, then all these semantic properties would have to be true of brain states. But it is senseless, runs the argument, to say that some resonance in my association cortex is true, or logically entails some other resonance close by, or has the meaning that *P*.

Neither of these moves has the same bite it did twenty years ago, since familiarity with the identity theory and growing awareness of the brain's role have tended to reduce the feelings of semantic oddity produced by the claims at issue. But even if they still struck all of us as semantically confused, this would carry little weight. The claim that sound has a wavelength, or that light has a frequency, must have seemed equally unintelligible in advance of the conviction that both sound and light are wave phenomena. (See, for example,

Bishop Berkeley's eighteenth-century dismissal of the idea that sound is a vibratory motion of the air, in Dialogue I of his *Three Dialogues*. The objections are voiced by Philonous.)* The claim that warmth is measured in kilogram • meters^2/seconds^2 would have seemed semantically perverse before we understood that temperature is mean molecular kinetic energy. And Copernicus' sixteenth-century claim that the earth *moves* also struck people as absurd to the point of perversity. It is not difficult to appreciate why. Consider the following argument.

> Copernicus' claim that the earth moves is sheer conceptual confusion. For consider what it *means* to say that something moves: "*x* moves" means "*x* changes position relative to the earth." Thus, to say that the earth moves is to say that the earth changes position relative to itself! Which is absurd. Copernicus' position is therefore an abuse of language.

The *meaning analysis* here invoked might well have been correct, but all that would have meant is that the speaker should have set about changing his meanings. The fact is, any language involves a rich network of assumptions about the structure of the world, and if a sentence *S* provokes intuitions of semantic oddness, that is usually because *S* violates one or more of those background assumptions. But one cannot always reject *S* for that reason alone, since the overthrow of those background assumptions may be precisely what the facts require. The "abuse" of accepted modes of speech is often an essential feature of real scientific progress! Perhaps we shall just have to get used to the idea that mental states have anatomical locations and brain states have semantic properties.

While the charge of sheer senselessness can be put aside, the identity theorist does owe us some account of exactly how physical brain states can have semantic properties. The account currently being explored can be outlined as follows. Let us begin by asking how it is that a particular *sentence* (= utterance type) has the specific proposi-

*Part of this dialogue is reprinted in Reading III.25.

tional content it has: the sentence "La pomme est rouge," for example. Note first that a sentence is always an integrated part of an entire system of sentences: a language. Any given sentence enjoys many relations with countless other sentences: it entails many sentences, is entailed by many others, is consistent with some, is inconsistent with others, provides confirming evidence for yet others, and so forth. And speakers who use that sentence within that language draw inferences in accordance with those relations. Evidently, each sentence (or each set of equivalent sentences) enjoys a unique pattern of such entailment relations: It plays a distinct inferential role in a complex linguistic economy. Accordingly, we say that the sentence "La pomme est rouge" has the propositional content, *the apple is red*, because the sentence "La pomme est rouge" plays *the same role* in French that the sentence "The apple is red" plays in English. To have the relevant propositional content is just to play the relevant inferential role in a cognitive economy.

Returning now to types of brain states, there is no problem in principle in assuming that one's brain is the seat of a complex inferential economy in which types of brain states are the role-playing elements. According to the theory of meaning just sketched, such states would then have propositional content, since having content is not a matter of whether the contentful item is a pattern of sound, a pattern of letters on paper, a set of raised Braille bumps, or a pattern of neural activity. What matters is the inferential role the item plays. Propositional content, therefore, seems within the reach of brain states after all. We began this subsection with an argument against materialism that appealed to the qualitative *nature* of our mental states, as revealed in introspection. The next argument appeals to the simple fact that they are introspectible at all.

1. My mental states are introspectively known by me as states of my conscious self.

2. My brain states are *not* introspectively known by me as states of my conscious self.

Therefore, by Leibniz's Law (that numerically identical things must have exactly the same properties),

3. My mental states are not identical with my brain states.

This, in my experience, is the most beguiling form of the argument from introspection, seductive of freshmen and faculty alike. But it is a straightforward instance of a well-known fallacy, which is clearly illustrated in the following parallel arguments:

1. Muhammad Ali is widely known as a heavyweight champion.
2. Cassius Clay is *not* widely known as a heavyweight champion.

Therefore, by Leibniz's Law,

3. Muhammad Ali is not identical with Cassius Clay.

or,

1. Aspirin is recognized by John to be a pain reliever.
2. Acetylsalicylic acid is *not* recognized by John to be a pain reliever.

Therefore, by Leibniz's Law,

3. Aspirin is not identical with acetylsalicylic acid.

Despite the truth of the relevant premises, both conclusions are false: the identities are wholly genuine. Which means that both arguments are invalid. The problem is that the "property" ascribed in premise (1), and withheld in premise (2), consists only in the subject item's being *recognized, perceived*, or *known* as something-or-other. But such apprehension is not a genuine property of the item itself, fit for divining identities, since one and the same subject may be successfully recognized under one name or description, and yet fail to be recognized under another (accurate, coreferential) description. Bluntly, Leibniz's Law is not valid for these

bogus "properties." The attempt to use them as above commits what logicians call an *intensional* fallacy. The premises may reflect, not the failure of certain objective identities, but only our continuing failure to appreciate them.

A different version of the preceding argument must also be considered, since it may be urged that one's brain states are more than merely not (yet) known by introspection: they are not know *able* by introspection under any circumstances. Thus,

1. My mental states are knowable by introspection.
2. My brain states are *not* knowable by introspection.

Therefore, by Leibniz's Law,

3. My mental states are not identical with my brain states.

Here the critic will insist that being know *able* by introspection *is* a genuine property of a thing, and that this modified version of the argument is free of the "intensional fallacy" discussed above.

And so it is. But now the materialist is in a position to insist that the argument contains a false premise—premise (2) For if mental states are indeed brain states, then it is really brain states we have been introspecting all along, though without fully appreciating what they are. And if we can learn to think of and recognize those states under mentalistic descriptions, as we all have, then we can certainly learn to think of and recognize them under their more penetrating neurophysiological descriptions. At the very least, premise (2) simply begs the question against the identity theorist. The mistake is amply illustrated in the following parallel argument:

1. Temperature is knowable by feeling.
2. Mean molecular kinetic energy is *not* knowable by feeling.

Therefore, by Leibniz's Law,

3. Temperature is not identical with mean molecular kinetic energy.

This identity, at least, is long established, and this argument is certainly unsound: premise (2) is false. Just as one can learn to feel that the summer air is about 70° F, or 21° C, so one can learn to feel that the mean KE of its molecules is about 6.2 × 10^{-21} joules, for whether we realize it or not, that is what our discriminatory mechanisms are keyed to. Perhaps our brain states are similarly accessible. . . .

Consider now a final argument, again based on the introspectible qualities of our sensations. Imagine a future neuroscientist who comes to know everything there is to know about the physical structure and activity of the brain and its visual system, of its actual and possible states. If for some reason she has never actually *had* a sensation-of-red (because of color blindness, say, or an unusual environment), then there will remain something she does *not* know about certain sensations: *what it is like to have a sensation-of-red*. Therefore, complete knowledge of the physical facts of visual perception and its related brain activity still leaves something out. Accordingly, materialism cannot give an adequate account of all mental phenomena, and the identity theory must be false.

The identity theorist can reply that this argument exploits an unwitting equivocation on the term "know." Concerning our neuroscientist's utopian knowledge of the brain, "knows" means something like "has mastered the relevant set of neuroscientific propositions." Concerning her (missing) knowledge of what it is like to have a sensation-of-red, "knows" means something like "has a prelinguistic representation of redness in her mechanisms for noninferential discrimination." It is true that one might have the former without the latter, but the materialist is not committed to the idea that having knowledge in the former sense automatically constitutes having knowledge in the second sense. The identity theorist can admit a duality, or even a plurality, of different *types of knowledge* without thereby committing himself to a duality in *types of things known*. The difference between a person who knows all about the visual cortex but has never enjoyed the sensation-of-red, and a person who knows no

neuroscience but knows well the sensation-of-red, may reside not in *what* is respectively known by each (brain states by the former, nonphysical *qualia* by the latter), but rather in the different *type,* or *medium,* or *level* of representation each has of exactly the same thing: brain states.

In sum, there are pretty clearly more ways of "having knowledge" than just having mastered a set of sentences, and the materialist can freely admit that one has "knowledge" of one's sensations in a way that is independent of the neuroscience one may have learned. Animals, including humans, presumably have a prelinguistic mode of sensory representation. This does not mean that sensations are beyond the reach of physical science. *It just means that the brain uses more modes and media of representation than the mere storage of sentences.* All the identity theorist needs to claim is that those other modes of representation will also yield to neuroscientific explanation.

The identity theory has proved to be very resilient in the face of these predominantly antimaterialist objections. But further objections, rooted in competing forms of materialism, constitute a much more serious threat, as the following sections will show.

II. FUNCTIONALISM

According to *functionalism,* the essential or defining feature of any type of mental state is the set of causal relations it bears to (1) environmental effects on the body, (2) other types of mental states, and (3) bodily behavior. Pain, for example, characteristically results from some bodily damage or trauma; it causes distress, annoyance, and practical reasoning aimed at relief; and it causes wincing, blanching, and nursing of the traumatized area. Any state that plays exactly that functional role is a pain, according to functionalism. Similarly, other types of mental states (sensations, fears, beliefs, and so on) are also defined by their unique causal roles in a complex economy of internal states mediating sensory inputs and behavioral outputs.

This view may remind the reader of behaviorism, and indeed it is the heir to behaviorism, but there is one fundamental difference between the two theories. Where the behaviorist hoped to define each type of mental state solely in terms of environmental input and behavioral output, the functionalist denies that this is possible. As he sees it, the adequate characterization of almost any mental state involves an ineliminable reference to a variety of other mental states with which it is causally connected, and so a reductive definition solely in terms of publicly observable inputs and outputs is quite impossible. Functionalism is therefore immune to one of the main objections against behaviorism.

Thus the difference between functionalism and behaviorism. The difference between functionalism and the identity theory will emerge from the following argument raised against the identity theory.

Imagine a being from another planet, says the functionalist, a being with an alien physiological constitution, a constitution based on the chemical element silicon, for example, instead of on the element carbon, as ours is. The chemistry and even the physical structure of the alien's brain would have to be systematically different from ours. But even so, that alien brain could well sustain a functional economy of internal states whose mutual *relations* parallel perfectly the mutual relations that define our own mental states. The alien may have an internal state that meets all the conditions for being a pain state, as outlined earlier. That state, considered from a purely physical point of view, would have a very different makeup from a human pain state, but it could nevertheless be identical to a human pain state from a purely functional point of view. And so for all of his functional states.

If the alien's functional economy of internal states were indeed *functionally isomorphic* with our own internal economy—if those states were causally connected to inputs, to one another, and to behavior in ways that parallel our own internal connections—then the alien would have pains, and desires, and hopes, and fears just as fully as

we, despite the differences in the physical system that sustains or realizes those functional states. What is important for mentality is not the matter of which the creature is made, but the structure of the internal activities which that matter sustains.

If we can think of one alien constitution, we can think of many, and the point just made can also be made with an artificial system. Were we to create an electronic system—a computer of some kind—whose internal economy were functionally isomorphic with our own in all the relevant ways, then it too would be the subject of mental states.

What this illustrates is that there are almost certainly many more ways than one for nature, and perhaps even for man, to put together a thinking, feeling, perceiving creature. And this raises a problem for the identity theory, for it seems that there is no single type of physical state to which a given type of mental state must always correspond. Ironically, there are *too many* different kinds of physical systems that can realize the functional economy characteristic of conscious intelligence. If we consider the universe at large, therefore, and the future as well as the present, it seems quite unlikely that the identity theorist is going to find the one-to-one match-ups between the concepts of our common-sense mental taxonomy and the concepts of an overarching theory that encompasses all of the relevant physical systems. But that is what intertheoretic reduction is standardly said to require. The prospects for universal identities, between types of mental states and types of brain states, are therefore slim.

If the functionalists reject the traditional "mental-type = physical type" identity theory, virtually all of them remain committed to a weaker "mental token = physical token" identity theory, for they still maintain that each *instance* of a given type of mental state is numerically identical with some specific physical state in some physical system or other. It is only universal (type/type) identities that are rejected. Even so, this rejection is typically taken to support the claim that the science of psychology is or should be *methodologically autonomous* from the various physical sciences such as physics, biology, and even neurophysiology. Psychology, it is claimed, has its own irreducible laws and its own abstract subject matter.

As this book is written, functionalism is probably the most widely held theory of mind among philosophers, cognitive psychologists, and artificial intelligence researchers. Some of the reasons are apparent from the preceding discussion, and there are further reasons as well. In characterizing mental states as essentially functional states, functionalism places the concerns of psychology at a level that abstracts from the teeming detail of a brain's neurophysiological (or crystallographic, or microelectronic) structure. The science of psychology, it is occasionally said, is methodologically autonomous from those other sciences (biology, neuroscience, circuit theory) whose concerns are with what amount to engineering details. This provides a rationale for a great deal of work in cognitive psychology and artificial intelligence, where researchers postulate a system of abstract functional states and then test the postulated system, often by way of its computer simulation, against human behavior in similar circumstances. The aim of such work is to discover in detail the functional organization that makes us what we are.

Arguments Against Functionalism

Current popularity aside, functionalism also faces difficulties. The most commonly posed objection cites an old friend: sensory qualia. Functionalism may escape one of behaviorism's fatal flaws, it is said, but it still falls prey to the other. By attempting to make its *relational* properties the definitive feature of any mental state, functionalism ignores the "inner" or qualitative nature of our mental states. But their qualitative nature is the essential feature of a great many types of mental state (pain, sensations of color, of temperature, of pitch, and so on), runs the objection, and functionalism is therefore false.

The standard illustration of this apparent failing is called "the inverted spectrum thought-experiment." It is entirely conceivable, runs the story, that the range of color sensations that I

enjoy upon viewing standard objects is simply inverted relative to the color sensations that you enjoy. When viewing a tomato, I may have what is really a sensation-of-green where you have the normal sensation-of-red; when viewing a banana, I may have what is really sensation-of-blue where you have the normal sensation-of-yellow; and so forth. But since we have no way of comparing our inner qualia, and since I shall make all the same observational discriminations among objects that you will, there is no way to tell whether my spectrum is inverted relative to yours.

The problem for functionalism arises as follows. Even if my spectrum is inverted relative to yours, we remain functionally isomorphic with one another. My visual sensation upon viewing a tomato is *functionally* identical with your visual sensation upon viewing a tomato. According to functionalism, therefore, they are the very same type of state, and it does not even make sense to suppose that my sensation is "really" a sensation-of-green. If it meets the functional conditions for being a sensation-of-red, then by definition it is a sensation-of-red. According to functionalism, apparently, a spectrum inversion of the kind described is ruled out by definition. But such inversions are entirely conceivable, concludes the objection, and if functionalism entails that they are not conceivable, then functionalism is false.

Another qualia-related worry for functionalism is the so-called "absent qualia problem." The functional organization characteristic of conscious intelligence can be instantiated (= realized or instanced) in a considerable variety of physical systems, some of them radically different from a normal human. For example, a giant electronic computer might instantiate it, and there are more radical possibilities still. One writer asks us to imagine the people of China—all 10^9 of them—organized into an intricate game of mutual interactions so that collectively they constitute a giant brain which exchanges inputs and outputs with a single robot body. That system of the robot-plus-10^9-unit-brain could presumably instantiate the relevant functional organization (though no doubt it would be much slower in its activities than a human or a computer), and would therefore be the subject of mental states, according to functionalism. But surely, it is urged, the complex states that there play the functional roles of pain, pleasure, and sensations-of-color would not have intrinsic qualia as ours do, and would therefore fail to be genuine mental states. Again, functionalism seems at best an incomplete account of the nature of mental states.

It has recently been argued that both the inverted-qualia and the absent-qualia objections can be met, without violence to functionalism and without significant violence to our common-sense intuitions about qualia. Consider the inversion problem first. I think the functionalist is right to insist that the type-identity of our visual sensations be reckoned according to their functional role. But the objector is also right in insisting that a relative inversion of two people's qualia, without functional inversion, is entirely conceivable. The apparent inconsistency between these positions can be dissolved by insisting that (1) our functional states (or rather, their physical realizations) do indeed have an intrinsic nature on which our introspective identification of those states depends, while also insisting that (2) such intrinsic natures are nevertheless not essential to the type-identity of a given mental state, and may indeed *vary* from instance to instance of the same type of mental state.

What this means is that the qualitative character of your sensation-of-red might be different from the qualitative character of my sensation-of-red, slightly or substantially, and a third person's sensation-of-red might be different again. But so long as all three states are standardly caused by red objects and standardly cause all three of us to believe that something is red, then all three states are sensations-of-red, whatever their intrinsic qualitative character. Such intrinsic qualia merely serve as salient features that permit the quick introspective identification of sensations, as black-on-orange stripes serve as a salient feature for the quick visual identification of tigers. But specific qualia are not essential to the type-identity of mental states, any more than black-on-orange stripes are essential to the type-identity of tigers.

Plainly, this solution requires the functionalist to admit the *reality* of qualia, and we may wonder how there can be room for qualia in his materialist world-picture. Perhaps they can be fit in as follows: *identify* them with physical properties of whatever physical states instantiate the mental (functional) states that display them. For example, identify the qualitative nature of your sensations-of-red with that physical feature (of the brain state that instantiates it) to which your mechanisms of introspective discrimination are in fact responding when you judge that you have a sensation-of-red. If materialism is true, then there must *be* some internal physical feature or other to which your discrimination of sensations-of-red is keyed: *that* is the quale of your sensations-of-red. If the pitch of a sound can turn out to be the frequency of an oscillation in air pressure, there is no reason why the quale of a sensation cannot turn out to be, say, a spiking frequency in a certain neural pathway. ("Spikes" are the tiny electrochemical pulses by which our brain cells communicate.)

This entails that creatures with a constitution different from ours may have qualia different from ours, despite being psychologically isomorphic with us. It does not entail that they *must* have different qualia, however. If the qualitative character of my sensation-of-red is really a spiking frequency of 90 hertz in a certain neural pathway, it is possible that an electromechanical robot might enjoy the very same qualitative character if, in reporting sensations-of-red, the robot were responding to a spiking frequency of 90 hertz in a corresponding *copper* pathway. It might be the spiking frequency that matters to our respective mechanisms of discrimination, not the nature of the medium that carries it. This proposal also suggests a solution to the absent qualia problem. So long as the physical system at issue is functionally isomorphic with us, to the last detail, then it will be equally capable of subtle introspective discriminations among its sensations. Those discriminations must be made on some systematic physical basis, that is, on some characteristic physical features of the states being discriminated. Those features at the objective focus of the system's discriminatory mechanisms, *those* are its sensory qualia—though the alien system is no more likely to appreciate their true physical nature than we appreciate the true physical nature of our own qualia. Sensory qualia are therefore an inevitable concomitant of any system with the kind of functional organization at issue. It may be difficult or impossible to "see" the qualia in an alien system, but it is equally difficult to "see" them even when looking into a human brain.

I leave it to the reader to judge the adequacy of these responses. If they are adequate, then, given its other virtues, functionalism must be conceded a very strong position among the competing contemporary theories of mind. It is interesting, however, that the defense offered in the last paragraph found it necessary to take a leaf from the identity theorist's book (types of quale are reduced to or identified with types of physical state), since the final objection we shall consider also tends to blur the distinction between functionalism and reductive materialism.

Consider the property of *temperature,* runs the objection. Here we have a paradigm of a physical property, one that has also been cited as the paradigm of a successfully *reduced* property, as expressed in the intertheoretic identity

"temperature = mean kinetic energy of constituent molecules."

Strictly speaking, however, this identity is true only for the temperature of a gas, where simple particles are free to move in ballistic fashion. In a *solid,* temperature is realized differently, since the interconnected molecules are confined to a variety of vibrational motions. In a *plasma,* temperature is something else again, since a plasma has no constituent molecules; they, and their constituent atoms, have been ripped to pieces. And even a *vacuum* has a so-called "blackbody" temperature—in the distribution of electromagnetic waves coursing through it. Here temperature has nothing to do with the kinetic energy of particles.

It is plain that the physical property of temperature enjoys "multiple instantiations" no less than do psychological properties. Does this

mean that thermodynamics (the theory of heat and temperature) is an "autonomous science," separable from the rest of physics, with its own irreducible laws and its own abstract nonphysical subject matter?

Presumably not. What it means, concludes the objection, is that *reductions are domain-specific:*

temperature-in-a-gas
= mean kinetic energy of
the gas's molecules,

whereas

temperature-in-a-vacuum
= blackbody distribution of the vacuum's
transient radiation.

Similarly, perhaps

joy-in-a-human = resonances in the lateral
hypothalamus,

whereas

joy-in-a-Martian = something else entirely.

This means that we may expect some type/type reductions of mental states to physical states after all, though they will be much narrower than was first suggested. Furthermore, it means that functionalist claims concerning the radical autonomy of psychology cannot be sustained. And last, it suggests that functionalism is not so profoundly different from the identity theory as was first made out.

As with the defense of functionalism outlined earlier, I leave the evaluation of this criticism to the reader. We shall have occasion for further discussion of functionalism in later chapters. At this point, let us turn to the final materialist theory of mind, for functionalism is not the only major reaction against the identity theory.

III. ELIMINATIVE MATERIALISM

The identity theory was called into doubt not because the prospects for a materialist account of our mental capacities were thought to be poor, but because it seemed unlikely that the arrival of an adequate materialist theory would bring with it the nice one-to-one match-ups, between the concepts of folk psychology and the concepts of theoretical neuroscience, that intertheoretic reduction requires. The reason for that doubt was the great variety of quite different physical systems that could instantiate the required functional organization. *Eliminative materialism* also doubts that the correct neuroscientific account of human capacities will produce a neat reduction of our commonsense framework, but here the doubts arise from a quite different source.

As the eliminative materialists see it, the one-to-one match-ups will not be found, and our common-sense psychological framework will not enjoy an intertheoretic reduction, *because our common-sense psychological framework is a false and radically misleading conception of the causes of human behavior and the nature of cognitive activity.* On this view, folk psychology is not just an incomplete representation of our inner natures; it is an outright *mis*representation of our internal states and activities. Consequently, we cannot expect a truly adequate neuroscientific account of our inner lives to provide theoretical categories that match up nicely with the categories of our common-sense framework. Accordingly, we must expect that the older framework will simply be eliminated, rather than be reduced, by a matured neuroscience.

Historical Parallels

As the identity theorist can point to historical cases of successful intertheoretic reduction, so the eliminative materialist can point to historical cases of the outright elimination of the ontology of an older theory in favor of the ontology of a new and superior theory. For most of the eighteenth and nineteenth centuries, learned people believed that heat was a subtle *fluid* held in bodies, much in the way water is held in a sponge. A fair body of moderately successful theory described the way this fluid substance—called "caloric"—flowed within a body, or from one body to another, and how it produced thermal expansion, melting,

boiling, and so forth. But by the end of the last century it had become abundantly clear that heat was not a substance at all, but just the energy of motion of the trillions of jostling molecules that make up the heated body itself. The new theory—the "corpuscular/ kinetic theory of matter and heat"—was much more successful than the old in explaining and predicting the thermal behavior of bodies. And since we were unable to *identify* caloric fluid with kinetic energy (according to the old theory, caloric is a material *substance;* according to the new theory, kinetic energy is a form of *motion*), it was finally agreed that there is *no such thing* as caloric. Caloric was simply eliminated from our accepted ontology.

A second example. It used to be thought that when a piece of wood burns, or a piece of metal rusts, a spiritlike substance called "phlogiston" was being released: briskly, in the former case, slowly in the latter. Once gone, that "noble" substance left only a base pile of ash or rust. It later came to be appreciated that both processes involve, not the loss of something, but the *gaining* of a substance taken from the atmosphere: oxygen. Phlogiston emerged, not as an incomplete description of what was going on, but as a radical misdescription. Phlogiston was therefore not suitable for reduction to or identification with some notion from within the new oxygen chemistry, and it was simply eliminated from science. Admittedly, both of these examples concern the elimination of something nonobservable, but our history also includes the elimination of certain widely accepted "observables." Before Copernicus' views became available, almost any human who ventured out at night could look up at *the starry sphere of the heavens,* and if he stayed for more than a few minutes he could also see that it *turned,* around an axis through Polaris. What the sphere was made of (crystal?) and what made it turn (the gods?) were theoretical questions that exercised us for over two millennia. But hardly anyone doubted the existence of what everyone could observe with their own eyes. In the end, however, we learned to reinterpret our visual experience of the night sky within a very different conceptual framework, and the turning sphere evaporated.

Witches provide another example. Psychosis is a fairly common affliction among humans, and in earlier centuries its victims were standardly seen as cases of demonic possession, as instances of Satan's spirit itself, glaring malevolently out at us from behind the victims' eyes. That witches exist was not a matter of any controversy. One would occasionally see them, in any city or hamlet, engaged in incoherent, paranoid, or even murderous behavior. But observable or not, we eventually decided that witches simply do not exist. We concluded that the concept of a witch is an element in a conceptual framework that misrepresents so badly the phenomena to which it was standardly applied that literal application of the notion should be permanently withdrawn. Modern theories of mental dysfunction led to the elimination of witches from our serious ontology.

The concepts of folk psychology—belief, desire, fear, sensation, pain, joy, and so on—await a similar fate, according to the view at issue. And when neuroscience has matured to the point where the poverty of our current conceptions is apparent to everyone, and the superiority of the new framework is established, we shall then be able to set about *re*conceiving our internal states and activities, within a truly adequate conceptual framework at last. Our explanations of one another's behavior will appeal to such things as our neuropharmacological states, the neural activity in specialized anatomical areas, and whatever other states are deemed relevant by the new theory. Our private introspection will also be transformed, and may be profoundly enhanced by reason of the more accurate and penetrating framework it will have to work with—just as the astronomer's perception of the night sky is much enhanced by the detailed knowledge of modern astronomical theory that he or she possesses.

The magnitude of the conceptual revolution here suggested should not be minimized: it would be enormous. And the benefits to humanity might be equally great. If each of us possessed an accurate neuroscientific understanding of (what we now conceive dimly as) the varieties and causes of mental illness, the factors involved in learning, the neural basis of emotions, intelligence, and socialization, then the sum total of human misery might be much reduced. The simple increase in mutual understanding that the new framework made possible could contribute substantially toward a more peaceful and humane society. Of course, there would be dangers as well: increased knowledge means increased power, and power can always be misused.

Arguments for Eliminative Materialism

The arguments for eliminative materialism are diffuse and less than decisive, but they are stronger than is widely supposed. The distinguishing feature of this position is its denial that a smooth intertheoretic reduction is to be expected—even a species-specific reduction—of the framework of folk psychology to the framework of a matured neuroscience. The reason for this denial is the eliminative materialist's conviction that folk psychology is a hopelessly primitive and deeply confused conception of our internal activities. But why this low opinion of our commonsense conceptions?

There are at least three reasons. First, the eliminative materialist will point to the widespread explanatory, predictive, and manipulative failures of folk psychology. So much of what is central and familiar to us remains a complete mystery from within folk psychology. We do not know what *sleep* is, or why we have to have it, despite spending a full third of our lives in that condition. (The answer, "For rest," is mistaken. Even if people are allowed to rest continuously, their need for sleep is undiminished. Apparently, sleep serves some deeper functions, but we do not yet know what they are.) We do not understand how *learning* transforms each of us from a gaping infant to a cunning adult, or how differences in *intelligence* are grounded. We have not the slightest idea how *memory* works, or how we manage to retrieve relevant bits of information instantly from the awesome mass we have stored. We do not know what *mental illness* is, nor how to cure it.

In sum, the most central things about us remain almost entirely mysterious from within folk psychology. And the defects noted cannot be blamed on inadequate time allowed for their correction, for folk psychology has enjoyed no significant changes or advances in well over 2,000 years, despite its manifest failures. Truly successful theories may be expected to reduce, but significantly unsuccessful theories merit no such expectation.

This argument from explanatory poverty has a further aspect. So long as one sticks to normal brains, the poverty of folk psychology is perhaps not strikingly evident. But as soon as one examines the many perplexing behavioral and cognitive deficits suffered by people with *damaged* brains, one's descriptive and explanatory resources start to claw the air. . . . As with other humble theories asked to operate successfully in unexplored extensions of their old domain (for example, Newtonian mechanics in the domain of velocities close to the velocity of light, and the classical gas law in the domain of high pressures or temperatures), the descriptive and explanatory inadequacies of folk psychology become starkly evident.

The second argument tries to draw an inductive lesson from our conceptual history. Our early folk theories of motion were profoundly confused, and were eventually displaced entirely by more sophisticated theories. Our early folk theories of the structure and activity of the heavens were wildly off the mark, and survive only as historical lessons in how wrong we can be. Our folk theories of the nature of fire, and the nature of life, were similarly cockeyed. And one could go on, since the vast majority of our past folk conceptions have been similarly exploded. All except folk psychology, which survives to this day and has only recently begun to feel pressure. But the phenomenon of conscious intelligence is surely a more complex and difficult phenomenon than any of those just listed. So far as accurate understanding is concerned, it would be a *miracle* if we had got *that* one right the very first time, when we fell down so badly on all the others. Folk psychology has survived for so very long, presumably, not because it is basically correct in its representations, but because the phenomena addressed are so surpassingly difficult that any useful handle on them, no matter how feeble, is unlikely to be displaced in a hurry.

A third argument attempts to find an a priori advantage for eliminative materialism over the identity theory and functionalism. It attempts to counter the common intuition that eliminative materialism is distantly possible, perhaps, but is much less probable than either the identity theory or functionalism. The focus again is on whether the concepts of folk psychology will find vindicating match-ups in a matured neuroscience. The eliminativist bets no; the other two bet yes. (Even the functionalist bets yes, but expects the match-ups to be only species-specific, or only person-specific. Functionalism, recall, denies the existence of *universal* type/type identities.)

The eliminativist will point out that the requirements on a reduction are rather demanding. The new theory must entail a set of principles and embedded concepts that mirrors very closely the specific conceptual structure to be reduced. And the fact is, there are vastly many more ways of being an explanatorily successful neuroscience while *not* mirroring the structure of folk psychology, than there are ways of being an explanatorily successful neuroscience while also *mirroring* the very specific structure of folk psychology. Accordingly, the a priori probability of eliminative materialism is not lower, but substantially *higher* than that of either of its competitors. One's initial intuitions here are simply mistaken.

Granted, this initial a priori advantage could be reduced if there were a very strong presumption in favor of the truth of folk psychology—true theories are better bets to win reduction. But according to the first two arguments, the presumptions on this point should run in precisely the opposite direction.

Arguments Against Eliminative Materialism

The initial plausibility of this rather radical view is low for almost everyone, since it denies deeply entrenched assumptions. That is at best a question-begging complaint, of course, since those assumptions are precisely what is at issue. But the following line of thought does attempt to mount a real argument.

Eliminative materialism is false, runs the argument, because one's introspection reveals directly the existence of pains, beliefs, desires, fears, and so forth. Their existence is as obvious as anything could be.

The eliminative materialist will reply that this argument makes the same mistake that an ancient or medieval person would be making if he insisted that he could just see with his own eyes that the heavens form a turning sphere, or that witches exist. The fact is, all observation occurs within some system of concepts, and our observation judgments are only as good as the conceptual framework in which they are expressed. In all three cases—the starry sphere, witches, and the familiar mental states—precisely what is challenged is the integrity of the background conceptual frameworks in which the observation judgments are expressed. To insist on the validity of one's experiences, *traditionally interpreted,* is therefore to beg the very question at issue. For in all three cases, the question is whether we should *re*conceive the nature of some familiar observational domain.

A second criticism attempts to find an incoherence in the eliminative materialist's position. The bald statement of eliminative materialism is that the familiar mental states do not really exist. But that statement is meaningful, runs the argument, only if it is the expression of a certain *belief,* and an *intention* to communicate, and a *knowledge* of the language, and so forth. But if the statement is true, then no such mental states exist, and the statement is therefore a meaningless string of marks or noises, and cannot be true. Evidently, the assumption that eliminative materialism is true entails that it cannot be true.

The hole in this argument is the premise concerning the conditions necessary for a statement to be meaningful. It begs the question. If eliminative materialism is true, then meaningfulness must have some different source. To insist on the "old" source is to insist on the validity of the very framework at issue. Again, an historical parallel may be helpful here. Consider the medieval theory that being biologically *alive* is a matter of being ensouled by an immaterial *vital spirit.* And consider the following response to someone who has expressed disbelief in that theory.

> My learned friend has stated that there is no such thing as vital spirit. But this statement is incoherent. For if it is true, then my friend does not have vital spirit, and must therefore be *dead.* But if he is dead, then his statement is just a string of noises, devoid of meaning or truth. Evidently, the assumption that antivitalism is true entails that it cannot be true! Q.E.D.

This second argument is now a joke, but the first argument begs the question in exactly the same way.

A final criticism draws a much weaker conclusion, but makes a rather stronger case. Eliminative materialism, it has been said, is making mountains out of molehills. It exaggerates the defects in folk psychology, and underplays its real successes. Perhaps the arrival of a matured neuroscience will require the elimination of the occasional folk-psychological concept, continues the criticism, and a minor adjustment in certain folk-psychological principles may have to be endured. But the large-scale elimination forecast by the eliminative materialist is just an alarmist worry or a romantic enthusiasm.

Perhaps this complaint is correct. And perhaps it is merely complacent. Whichever, it does bring out the important point that we do not confront two simple and mutually exclusive possibilities here: pure reduction versus pure elimination. Rather, these are the end points of a smooth spectrum of possible outcomes, between which there are mixed cases of partial elimination and partial reduction. Only empirical research . . . can tell us where on that spectrum our own case will fall. Perhaps we should speak here, more liberally, of "revisionary materialism," instead of concentrating on the more radical possibility of an across-the-board elimination. Perhaps we should. But it has been my aim in this section to make it at least intelligible to you that our collective conceptual destiny lies substantially toward the revolutionary end of the spectrum.

For Further Reflection

1. Evaluate the arguments for and against reductive and eliminative materialism. Do you agree with Churchland's assessment? Explain.

2. Try to imagine how we would describe our beliefs, perceptions, feelings, and desires within an eliminative framework. Describe two people talking to each other who have just fallen in love. Eliminative materialism does sound revolutionary, but the question is, is it true?

3. Evaluate functionalism. Why is it attractive to many philosophers of mind?

4. Compare the three theories discussed in this article with dualism. What are the strengths and weaknesses of each?

What Is It Like to Be a Bat?   IV.39

THOMAS NAGEL

Thomas Nagel is professor of philosophy at New York University and the author of several works in ethics and philosophy of mind, including *The View from Nowhere* (1986). Much of Nagel's work involves showing the incongruities between objective and subjective perspectives, especially between the scientific explanation of humanness and our subjective experience of it. Something vital is lost in the reduction of mental states to brain states.

In this article Nagel argues against the view that the objective perspective is the correct one. He contends that the peculiarity of the subjective character of experience is that increased objectivity actually takes us further from its real nature.

Study Questions

1. What is Nagel's main concern in this article?
2. What is the "subjective character of experience," according to Nagel?
3. How does the bat serve as an example of Nagel's thesis? Why does he choose a bat to illustrate his thesis?
4. Does Nagel think we can be aware of facts without being able to express or comprehend them? Give some examples.
5. What is Nagel's speculative proposal regarding bridging the gap between the subjective and the objective?

CONSCIOUSNESS IS WHAT MAKES the mind-body problem really intractable. Perhaps that is why current discussions of the problem give it little attention or get it obviously wrong. The recent wave of reductionist euphoria has produced several analyses of mental phenomena and mental concepts designed to explain the possibility of some variety of materialism, psychophysical identification, or reduction. But the problems dealt with are those common to this type of reduction and other types, and what makes the mind-body problem unique, and unlike the water–H_2O problem or the Turing machine–IBM machine problem or the lightning–electrical discharge problem or the gene-DNA problem or the oak tree–hydrocarbon problem, is ignored. Every reductionist has his favorite analogy from modern science. It is most unlikely that any of these unrelated examples of successful reduction will shed light on the relation of mind to brain. But philosophers share the general human weakness for explanations of what is incomprehensible in terms suited for what is familiar and well understood, though entirely different. This has led to the acceptance of implausible accounts of the mental largely because they would permit familiar kinds of reduction. I shall try to explain why the usual examples do not help us to understand the relation between mind and body—why, indeed, we have at present no conception of what an explanation of the physical nature of a mental phenomenon would be. Without consciousness the mind-body problem would be much less interesting. With consciousness it seems hopeless. The most important and characteristic feature of conscious mental phenomena is very poorly understood. Most reductionist theories do not even try to explain it. And careful examination will show that no currently available concept of reduction is applicable to it. Perhaps a new theoretical form can be devised for the purpose, but such a solution, if it exists, lies in the distant intellectual future.

Conscious experience is a widespread phenomenon. It occurs at many levels of animal life, though we cannot be sure of its presence in the simpler organisms, and it is very difficult to say in general what provides evidence of it. (Some extremists have been prepared to deny it even of mammals other than man.) No doubt it occurs in countless forms totally unimaginable to us, on other planets in other solar systems throughout the universe. But no matter how the form may vary, the fact that an organism has conscious experience *at all* means, basically, that there is something it is like to *be* that organism. There may be further implications about the form of the experience; there may even (though I doubt it) be implications about the behavior of the organism. But fundamentally an organism has conscious mental states if and only if there is something that it is like to *be* that organism—something it is like *for* the organism.

We may call this the subjective character of experience. It is not captured by any of the familiar, recently devised reductive analyses of the mental, for all of them are logically compatible with its absence. It is not analyzable in terms of any explanatory system of functional states, or intentional states, since these could be ascribed to robots or automata that behaved like people though they experienced nothing. It is not analyzable in terms of the causal role of experiences in relation to typical human behavior—for similar reasons. I do not deny that conscious mental states and events cause behavior, nor that they may be given functional characterizations. I deny only that this kind of thing exhausts their analysis. Any reductionist program has to be based on an analysis of what is to be reduced. If the analysis leaves something out, the problem will be falsely posed. It is useless to base the defense of materialism on any analysis of mental phenomena that fails to deal explicitly with their subjective character.

For there is no reason to suppose that a reduction which seems plausible when no attempt is made to account for consciousness can be extended to include consciousness. Without some idea, therefore, of what the subjective character of experience is, we cannot know what is required of physicalist theory.

While an account of the physical basis of mind must explain many things, this appears to be the most difficult. It is impossible to exclude the phenomenological features of experience from a reduction in the same way that one excludes the phenomenal features of an ordinary substance from a physical or chemical reduction of it— namely, by explaining them as effects on the minds of human observers. If physicalism is to be defended, the phenomenological features must themselves be given a physical account. But when we examine their subjective character it seems that such a result is impossible. The reason is that every subjective phenomenon is essentially connected with a single point of view, and it seems inevitable that an objective, physical theory will abandon that point of view.

Let me first try to state the issue somewhat more fully than by referring to the relation between the subjective and the objective. This is far from easy. Facts about what it is like to be an X are very peculiar, so peculiar that some may be inclined to doubt their reality, or the significance of claims about them. To illustrate the connexion between subjectivity and a point of view, and to make evident the importance of subjective features, it will help to explore the matter in relation to an example that brings out clearly the divergence between the two types of conception, subjective and objective.

I assume we all believe that bats have experience. After all, they are mammals, and there is no more doubt that they have experience than that mice or pigeons or whales have experience. I have chosen bats instead of wasps or flounders because if one travels too far down the phylogenetic tree, people gradually shed their faith that there is experience there at all. Bats, although more closely related to us than those other species, nevertheless present a range of activity and a sensory apparatus so different from ours that the problem I want to pose is exceptionally vivid (though it certainly could be raised with other species). Even without the benefit of philosophical reflection, anyone who has spent some time in an enclosed space with an excited bat knows what it is to encounter a fundamentally *alien* form of life.

I have said that the essence of the belief that bats have experience is that there is something that it is like to be a bat. Now we know that most bats (the microchiroptera, to be precise) perceive the external world primarily by sonar, or echolocation, detecting the reflections, from objects within range, of their own rapid, subtly modulated, high-frequency shrieks. Their brains are designed to correlate the outgoing impulses with the subsequent echoes, and the information thus acquired enables bats to make precise discrimination of distance, size, shape, motion, and texture comparable to those we make by vision. But bat sonar, though clearly a form of perception, is not similar in its operation to any sense that we possess, and there is no reason to suppose that it is subjectively like anything we can experience or imagine. This appears to create difficulties for the notion of what it is like to be a bat. We must consider whether any method will permit us to extrapolate to the inner life of the bat from our own case,[1] and if not, what alternative methods there may be for understanding the notion.

Our own experience provides the basic material for our imagination, whose range is therefore limited. It will not help to try to imagine that one has webbing on one's arms, which enables one to fly around at dusk and dawn catching insects in one's mouth; that one has very poor vision, and perceives the surrounding world by a system of reflected high-frequency sound signals; and that one spends the day hanging upside down by one's feet in an attic. Insofar as I can imagine this (which is not very far), it tells me only what it would be like for *me* to behave as a bat behaves. But that is not the question. I want to know what it is like for a *bat* to be a bat. Yet if I try to imagine this, I am restricted to the resources of my own mind, and those resources are inadequate to the task. I cannot perform it either by imagining additions to my present experience, or by imagining segments gradually subtracted from it, or by imagining some combination of additions, subtractions, and modifications.

To the extent that I could look and behave like a wasp or a bat without changing my fundamental structure, my experiences would not be anything like the experiences of those animals. On the other hand, it is doubtful that any meaning can be attached to the supposition that I should possess the internal neurophysiological constitution of a bat. Even if I could by gradual degrees be transformed into a bat, nothing in my present constitution enables me to imagine what the experiences of such a future stage of myself thus metamorphosed would be like. The best evidence would come from the experiences of bats, if we only knew what they were like.

So if extrapolation from our own case is involved in the idea of what it is like to be a bat, the extrapolation must be incompletable. We cannot form more than a schematic conception of what it *is* like. For example, we may ascribe general *types* of experience on the basis of the animal's structure and behavior. Thus we describe bat sonar as a form of three-dimensional forward perception; we believe that bats feel some versions of pain, fear, hunger, and lust, and that they have other, more familiar types of perception besides sonar. But we believe that these experiences also have in each case a specific subjective character, which it is beyond our ability to conceive. And if there is conscious life elsewhere in the universe, it is likely that some of it will not be describable even in the most general experiential terms available to us.[2] (The problem is not confined to exotic cases, however, for it exists between one person and another. The subjective character of the experience of a person deaf and blind from birth is not accessible to me, for example, nor presumably is mine to him. This does not prevent us each from believing that the other's experience has such a subjective character.)

If anyone is inclined to deny that we can believe in the existence of facts like this whose exact nature we cannot possibly conceive, he should reflect that in contemplating the bats we are in much the same position that intelligent bats or Martians[3] would occupy if they tried to form a conception of what it was like to be us. The structure of their own minds might make it impossible for them to succeed, but we know they would be wrong to conclude that there is not anything precise that it is like to be us: that only certain general types of mental state could be ascribed to us (perhaps perception and appetite would be concepts common to us both; perhaps not). We know they would be wrong to draw such a skeptical conclusion because we know what it is like to be us. And we know that while it includes an enormous amount of variation and complexity, and while we do not possess the vocabulary to describe it adequately, its subjective character is highly specific, and in some respects describable in terms that can be understood only by creatures like us. The fact that we cannot expect ever to accommodate in our language a detailed description of Martian or bat phenomenology should not lead us to dismiss as meaningless the claim that bats and Martians have experiences fully comparable in richness of detail to our own. It would be fine if someone were to develop concepts and a theory that enabled us to think about those things, but such an understanding may be permanently denied to us by the limits of our nature. And to deny the reality or logical significance of what we can never describe or understand is the crudest form of cognitive dissonance.

This brings us to the edge of a topic that requires much more discussion than I can give it here: namely, the relation between facts on the one hand and conceptual schemes or systems of representation on the other. My realism about the subjective domain in all its forms implies a belief in the existence of facts beyond the reach of human concepts. Certainly it is possible for a human being to believe that there are facts which humans never *will* possess the requisite concepts to represent or comprehend. Indeed, it would be foolish to doubt this, given the finiteness of humanity's expectations. After all, there would have been transfinite numbers even if everyone had been wiped out by the Black Death before Cantor discovered them. But one might also believe that there are facts which *could* not ever be represented or comprehended by human beings, even if the species lasted for ever—simply because our structure does not permit us to operate with concepts of the requisite type. This impossibility might even be observed by other beings, but it is not clear that the existence of such beings, or the possibility of their existence, is a precondition of the significance of the hypothesis that there are humanly inaccessible facts. (After all, the nature of beings with access to humanly inaccessible facts is presumably itself a humanly inaccessible fact.) Reflection on what it is like to be a bat seems to lead us, therefore, to the conclusion that there are facts that do not consist in the truth of propositions expressible in a human language. We can be compelled to recognize the existence of such facts without being able to state or comprehend them.

I shall not pursue this subject, however. Its bearing on the topic before us (namely, the mind-body problem) is that it enables us to make a general observation about the subjective character of experience. Whatever may be the status of facts about what it is like to be a human being, or a bat, or a Martian, these appear to be facts that embody a particular point of view.

I am not adverting here to the alleged privacy of experience to its possessor. The point of view in question is not one accessible only to a single individual. Rather it is a *type*. It is often possible to take up a point of view other than one's own, so the comprehension of such facts is not limited to one's own case. There is a sense in which phenomenological facts are perfectly objective: One person can know or say of another what the quality of the other's experience is. They are subjective, however, in the sense that even this objective ascription of experience is possible only for someone sufficiently similar to the object of ascription

to be able to adopt his point of view—to understand the ascription in the first person as well as in the third, so to speak. The more different from oneself the other experiencer is, the less success one can expect with this enterprise. In our own case we occupy the relevant point of view, but we will have as much difficulty understanding our own experience properly if we approach it from another point of view as we would if we tried to understand the experience of another species without taking up *its* point of view.

This bears directly on the mind-body problem. For if the facts of experience—facts about what it is like *for* the experiencing organism—are accessible only from one point of view, then it is a mystery how the true character of experiences could be revealed in the physical operation of that organism. The latter is a domain of objective facts *par excellence*—the kind that can be observed and understood from many points of view and by individuals with differing perceptual systems. There are no comparable imaginative obstacles to the acquisition of knowledge about bat neurophysiology by human scientists, and intelligent bats or Martians might learn more about the human brain than we ever will.

This is not by itself an argument against reduction. A Martian scientist with no understanding of visual perception could understand the rainbow, or lightning, or clouds as physical phenomena, though he would never be able to understand the human concepts of rainbow, lightning, or cloud, or the place these things occupy in our phenomenal world. The objective nature of the things picked out by these concepts could be apprehended by him because, although the concepts themselves are connected with a particular point of view and a particular visual phenomenology, the things apprehended from that point of view are not: They are observable from the point of view but external to it; hence they can be comprehended from other points of view also, either by the same organisms or by others. Lightning has an objective character that is not exhausted by its visual appearance, and this can be investigated by a Martian without vision. To be precise, it has a *more* objective character than is revealed in its visual appearance. In speaking of the move from subjective characterization, I wish to remain non-committal about the existence of an end point, the completely objective intrinsic nature of the thing, which one might or might not be able to reach. It may be more accurate to think of objectivity as a direction in which the understanding can travel. And in understanding a phenomenon like lightning, it is legitimate to go as far away as one can from a strictly human viewpoint.

In the case of experience, on the other hand, the connexion with a particular point of view seems much closer. It is difficult to understand what could be meant by the *objective* character of an experience, apart from the particular point of view from which its subject apprehends it. After all, what would be left of what it was like to be a bat if one removed the viewpoint of the bat? But if experience does not have, in addition to its subjective character, an objective nature that can be apprehended from many different points of view, then how can it be supposed that a Martian investigating my brain might be observing physical processes which were my mental processes (as he might observe physical processes which were bolts of lightning), only from a different point of view? How, for that matter, could a human physiologist observe them from another point of view?[4]

We appear to be faced with a general difficulty about psychophysical reduction. In other areas the process of reduction is a move in the direction of greater objectivity, toward a more accurate view of the real nature of things. This is accomplished by reducing our dependence on individual or species-specific points of view toward the object of investigation. We describe it not in terms of the impressions it makes on our senses, but in terms of its more general effects and of properties detectable by means other than the human senses. The less it depends on a specifically human viewpoint, the more objective is our description. It is possible to follow this path because although the

concepts and ideas we employ in thinking about the external world are initially applied from a point of view that involves our perceptual apparatus, they are used by us to refer to things beyond themselves—toward which we *have* the phenomenal point of view. Therefore we can abandon it in favor of another, and still be thinking about the same things.

Experience itself, however, does not seem to fit the pattern. The idea of moving from appearance to reality seems to make no sense here. What is the analogue in this case to pursuing a more objective understanding of the same phenomena by abandoning the initial subjective viewpoint toward them in favour of another that is more objective but concerns the same thing? Certainly it *appears* unlikely that we will get closer to the real nature of human experience by leaving behind the particularity of our human point of view and striving for a description in terms accessible to beings that could not imagine what it was like to be us. If the subjective character of experience is fully comprehensible only from one point of view, then any shift to greater objectivity—that is, less attachment to a specific viewpoint—does not take us nearer to the real nature of the phenomenon: It takes us farther away from it.

In a sense, the seeds of this objection to the reducibility of experience are already detectable in successful cases of reduction; for in discovering sound to be, in reality, a wave phenomenon in air or other media, we leave behind one viewpoint to take up another, and the auditory, human or animal viewpoint that we leave behind remains unreduced. Members of radically different species may both understand the same physical events in objective terms, and this does not require that they understand the phenomenal forms in which those events appear to the senses of members of the other species. Thus it is a condition of their referring to a common reality that their more particular viewpoints are not part of the common reality that they both apprehend. The reduction can succeed only if the species-specific viewpoint is omitted from what is to be reduced.

But while we are right to leave this point of view aside in seeking a fuller understanding of the external world, we cannot ignore it permanently, since it is the essence of the internal world, and not merely a point of view on it. Most of the neobehaviorism of recent philosophical psychology results from the effort to substitute an objective concept of mind for the real thing, in order to have nothing left over which cannot be reduced. If we acknowledge that a physical theory of mind must account for the subjective character of experience, we must admit that no presently available conception gives us a clue how this could be done. The problem is unique. If mental processes are indeed physical processes, then there is something it is like, intrinsically, to undergo certain physical processes. What it is for such a thing to be the case remains a mystery.

What moral should be drawn from these reflections, and what should be done next? It would be a mistake to conclude that physicalism must be false. Nothing is proved by the inadequacy of physicalist hypotheses that assume a faulty objective analysis of mind. It would be truer to say that physicalism is a position we cannot understand because we do not at present have any conception of how it might be true. Perhaps it will be thought unreasonable to require such a conception as a condition of understanding. After all, it might be said, the meaning of physicalism is clear enough: Mental states are states of the body; mental events are physical events. We do not know *which* physical states and events they are, but that should not prevent us from understanding the hypothesis. What could be clearer than the words "is" and "are"?

But I believe it is precisely this apparent clarity of the word "is" that is deceptive. Usually, when we are told that X is Y we know *how* it is supposed to be true, but that depends on a conceptual or theoretical background and is not conveyed by the "is" alone. We know how both "X" and "Y" refer, and the kinds of things to which they refer, and we have a rough idea how the two referential paths might converge on a single thing, be it an object, a person, a process, an event or whatever. But when the two terms of the identification are very disparate it may not be so clear how it could be true. We may not have even a rough idea of how the two referential paths could converge, or what kind of things they might converge on, and a theoretical framework may have to be supplied to enable us to understand this. Without the framework, an air of mysticism surrounds the identification.

This explains the magical flavor of popular presentations of fundamental scientific discoveries, given out as propositions to which one must subscribe without really understanding them. For example, people are now told at an early age that all matter is really energy. But despite the fact that they know what "is" means, most of them never form a conception of what makes this claim true, because they lack the theoretical background.

At the present time the status of physicalism is similar to that which the hypothesis that matter is energy would have had if uttered by a pre-Socratic philosopher. We do not have the beginnings of a conception of how it might be true. In order to understand the hypothesis that a mental event is a physical event, we require more than an understanding of the word "is." The idea of how a mental and a physical term might refer to the same thing is lacking, and the usual analogies with theoretical identification in other fields fail to supply it. They fail because if we construe the reference of mental terms to physical events on the usual model, we either get a reappearance of separate subjective events as the effects through which mental reference to physical events is secured, or else we get a false account of how mental terms refer (for example, a causal behaviorist one).

Strangely enough, we may have evidence for the truth of something we cannot really understand. Suppose a caterpillar is locked in a sterile safe by someone unfamiliar with insect metamorphosis, and weeks later the safe is reopened, revealing a butterfly. If the person knows that the safe has been shut the whole time, he has reason to believe that the butterfly is or was once the caterpillar, without having any idea in what sense this might be so. (One possibility is that the caterpillar contained a tiny winged parasite that devoured it and grew into the butterfly.) It is conceivable that we are in such a position with regard to physicalism. Donald Davidson has argued that if mental events have physical causes and effects, they must have physical descriptions. He holds that we have reason to believe this even though we do not—and in fact *could* not—have a general psychophysical theory. His argument applies to intentional mental events, but I think we also have some reason to believe that sensations are physical processes, without being in a position to understand how. Davidson's position is that certain physical events have irreducibly mental properties, and perhaps some view describable in this way is correct. But nothing of which we can now form a conception corresponds to it; nor have we any idea what a theory would be like that enabled us to conceive of it. Very little work has been done on the basic question (from which mention of the brain can be entirely omitted) whether any sense can be made of experiences' having an objective character at all. Does it make sense, in other words, to ask what my experiences are *really* like, as opposed to how they appear to me? We cannot genuinely understand the hypothesis that their nature is captured in a physical description unless we understand the more fundamental idea that they *have* an objective nature (or that objective processes can have a subjective nature).

I should like to close with a speculative proposal. It may be possible to approach the gap between subjective and objective from another direction. Setting aside temporarily the relation between the mind and the brain, we can pursue a more objective understanding of the mental in its own right. At present we are completely unequipped to think about the subjective character of experience without relying on the imagination—without taking up the point of view of the experiential subject. This should be regarded as a challenge to form new concepts and devise a new method—an objective phenomenology not dependent on empathy or the imagination. Though presumably it would not capture everything, its goal would be to describe, at least in part, the subjective character of experiences in a form comprehensible to beings incapable of having those experiences.

We would have to develop such a phenomenology to describe the sonar experiences of bats; but it would also be possible to begin with humans. One might try, for example, to develop concepts that could be used to explain to a person blind from birth what it was like to see. One would reach a blank wall eventually, but it should be possible to devise a method of expressing in objective terms much more than we can at present, and with much greater precision. The loose intermodal analogies—for example, 'Red is like the sound of a trumpet'—which crop up in discussions of this subject are of little use. That should be clear to anyone who has both heard a trumpet and seen red. But structural features of perception might be more accessible to objective description, even though something would be left out. And concepts alternative to those we learn in the first person may enable us to arrive at a kind of understanding even of our own experience which is denied us by the very ease of description and lack of distance that subjective concepts afford.

Apart from its own interest, a phenomenology that is in this sense objective may permit questions about the physical basis of experience to assume a more intelligible form. Aspects of subjective experience that admitted this kind of objective description might be better candidates for objective explanations of a more familiar sort. But whether or not this guess is correct, it seems unlikely that any physical theory of mind can be contemplated until more thought has been given to the general problem of subjective and objective. Otherwise we cannot even pose the mind-body problem without sidestepping it.

NOTES

1. By "our own case," I do not mean just "my own case," but rather the mentalistic ideas that we apply unproblematically to ourselves and other human beings.

2. Therefore the analogical form of the English expression "what it is *like*" is misleading. It does not mean "what (in our experience) it *resembles*," but rather "how it is for the subject himself."

3. Any intelligent extraterrestrial beings totally different from us.

4. The problem is not just that when I look at the *Mona Lisa*, my visual experience has a certain quality, no trace of which is to be found by someone looking into my brain. For even if he did observe there a tiny image of the *Mona Lisa*, he would have no reason to identify it with the experience.

For Further Reflection

1. Explain Nagel's case against reductionism. How strong is it? What would Churchland be likely to say in response to Nagel's arguments?

2. In another place Nagel states his thesis this way:

> There are things about the world and life and ourselves that cannot be adequately understood from a maximally objective standpoint, however much it may extend our understanding beyond the point from which we started. A great deal is essentially connected to a particular point of view, and the attempt to give a complete account of the world in objective terms detached from these perspectives inevitably leads to false reductions or to outright denials that certain patently real phenomena exist at all. To the extent that such no-nonsense theories have an effect, they merely threaten to impoverish the intellectual landscape for a while by inhibiting the serious expression of certain questions. In the name of liberation, these movements have offered us intellectual repression. (*A View from Nowhere* [Oxford: Oxford University Press, 1986], pp. 7, 11)

Do you agree with Nagel? Or is the objective perspective really the true perspective? Or is the objective compatible with the subjective? Explain your answer.

The Mind-Body Problem   IV.40

JERRY A. FODOR

Jerry A. Fodor is a professor of philosophy at Rutgers University and an influential thinker in the philosophy of mind. His books include *The Language of Thought (1975), The Modularity of Mind* (1983), and *The Mind Doesn't Work That Way* (2000). In this essay he criticizes traditional mind-body theories and argues for functionalism, a distinctive departure from both dualism and identity theory. "In the functionalist view," he says, "the psychology of a system depends not on the stuff it is made of (living cells, mental or spiritual energy) but on how the stuff is put together." Mental states are functional states—systems of causal relationships—typically realized in, or supported by, the brain. But these relationships need not occur only in neurons; any suitable material will do. The mind is like computer software (a system of functional or logical relationships), which can be realized in, or run on, any suitable hardware.

Study Questions

1. Why does Fodor think that dualism is an untenable theory?
2. What is "radical behaviorism"? What does Fodor think about it?
3. What is the central-state identity theory? What are its advantages and disadvantages?
4. Why does Fodor favor functionalism over its rivals?

Modern philosophy of science has been devoted largely to the formal and systematic description of the successful practices of working scientists. The philosopher does not try to dictate how scientific inquiry and argument ought to be conducted. Instead he tries to enumerate the principles and practices that have contributed to good science. The philosopher has devoted the most attention to analyzing the methodological peculiarities of the physical sciences. The analysis has helped to clarify the nature of confirmation, the logical structure of scientific theories, the formal properties of statements that express laws and the question of whether theoretical entities actually exist.

It is only rather recently that philosophers have become seriously interested in the methodological tenets of psychology. Psychological explanations of behavior refer liberally to the mind and to states, operations and processes of the mind. The philosophical difficulty comes in stating in unambiguous language what such references imply.

Traditional philosophies of mind can be divided into two broad categories: dualist theories and materialist theories. In the dualist approach the mind is a nonphysical substance. In materialist theories the mental is not distinct from the physical; indeed, all mental states, properties, processes and operations are in principle identical with physical states, properties, processes and operations. Some materialists, known as behaviorists, maintain that all talk of mental causes can be eliminated from the language of psychology in favor of talk of environmental stimuli and behavioral responses. Other materialists, the identity theorists, contend that there are mental causes and that they are identical with neurophysiological events in the brain.

In the past fifteen years a philosophy of mind called functionalism that is neither dualist nor materialist has emerged from philosophical reflection on developments in artificial intelligence, computational theory, linguistics, cybernetics and psychology. All these fields, which are collectively known as the cognitive sciences, have in common a certain level of abstraction and a concern with systems that process information. Functionalism, which seeks to provide a philosophical account of this level of abstraction, recognizes the possibility that systems as diverse as human beings, calculating machines and disembodied spirits could all have mental states. In the functionalist view the psychology of a system depends not on the stuff it is made of (living cells, mental or spiritual energy) but on how the stuff is put together. Functionalism is a difficult concept, and one way of coming to grips with it is to

From Jerry A. Fodor, "The Mind-Body Problem," Scientific American, 244 (January 1981).

review the deficiencies of the dualist and materialist philosophies of mind it aims to displace.

The chief drawback of dualism is its failure to account adequately for mental causation. If the mind is nonphysical, it has no position in physical space. How, then, can a mental cause give rise to a behavioral effect that has a position in space? To put it another way, how can the nonphysical give rise to the physical without violating the laws of the conservation of mass, of energy and of momentum?

The dualist might respond that the problem of how an immaterial substance can cause physical events is not much obscurer than the problem of how one physical event can cause another. Yet there is an important difference: there are many clear cases of physical causation but not one clear case of nonphysical causation. Physical interaction is something philosophers, like all other people, have to live with. Nonphysical interaction, however, may be no more than an artifact of the immaterialist construal of the mental. Most philosophers now agree that no argument has successfully demonstrated why mind-body causation should not be regarded as a species of physical causation.

Dualism is also incompatible with the practices of working psychologists. The psychologist frequently applies the experimental methods of the physical sciences to the study of the mind. If mental processes were different in kind from physical processes, there would be no reason to expect these methods to work in the realm of the mental. In order to justify their experimental methods many psychologists urgently sought an alternative to dualism.

In the 1920s John B. Watson of Johns Hopkins University made the radical suggestion that behavior does not have mental causes. He regarded the behavior of an organism as its observable responses to stimuli, which he took to be the causes of its behavior. Over the next thirty years psychologists such as B. F. Skinner of Harvard University developed Watson's ideas into an elaborate world view in which the role of psychology was to catalogue the laws that determine causal relations between stimuli and responses. In this "radical behaviorist" view the problem of explaining the nature of the mind-body interaction vanishes; there is no such interaction.

Radical behaviorism has always worn an air of paradox. For better or worse, the idea of mental causation is deeply ingrained in our everyday language and in our ways of understanding our fellow men and ourselves. For example, people commonly attribute behavior to beliefs, to knowledge and to expectations. Brown puts gas in his tank because he believes the car will not run without it. Jones writes not "acheive" but "achieve" because he knows the rule about putting *i* before *e*. Even when a behavioral response is closely tied to an environmental stimulus, mental processes often intervene. Smith carries an umbrella because the sky is cloudy, but the weather is only part of the story. There are apparently also mental links in the causal chain: observation and expectation. The clouds affect Smith's behavior only because he observes them and because they induce in him an expectation of rain.

The radical behaviorist is unmoved by appeals to such cases. He is prepared to dismiss references to mental causes, however plausible they may seem, as the residue of outworn creeds. The radical behaviorist predicts that as psychologists come to understand more about the relations between stimuli and responses they will find it increasingly possible to explain behavior without postulating mental causes.

The strongest argument against behaviorism is that psychology has not turned out this way; the opposite has happened. As psychology has matured, the framework of mental states and processes that is apparently needed to account for experimental observations has grown all the more elaborate. Particularly in the case of human behavior psychological theories satisfying the methodological tenets of radical behaviorism have proved largely sterile, as would be expected if the postulated mental processes are real and causally effective.

Nevertheless, many philosophers were initially drawn to radical behaviorism because, paradoxes and all, it seemed better than dualism. Since a psychology committed to immaterial substances was unacceptable, philosophers turned to radical behaviorism because it seemed to be the only alternative materialist philosophy of mind. The choice, as they saw it, was between radical behaviorism and ghosts.

By the early 1960s philosophers began to have doubts that dualism and radical behaviorism exhausted the possible approaches to the philosophy of mind. Since the two theories seemed unattractive, the right strategy might be to develop a materialist philosophy of mind that nonetheless allowed for mental causes. Two such philosophies emerged, one called logical behaviorism and the other called the central-state identity theory.

Logical behaviorism is a semantic theory about what mental terms mean. The basic idea is that attributing a mental state (say thirst) to an organism is the same as saying that the organism is disposed to behave in a particular way (for example to drink if there is water available). On this view every mental ascription is equivalent in meaning to an if-then statement (called a behavioral hypothetical) that expresses a behavioral disposition. For example, "Smith is thirsty" might be taken to be equivalent to the dispositional statement "If there were water available, then Smith would drink some." By definition a behavioral hypothetical includes no mental terms. The if-clause of the hypothetical speaks only of stimuli and the then-clause speaks only of behavioral responses. Since stimuli and responses are physical events, logical behaviorism is a species of materialism.

The strength of logical behaviorism is that by translating mental language into the language of stimuli and responses it provides an interpretation of psychological explanations in which behavioral effects are attributed to mental causes. Mental causation is simply the manifestation of a behavioral disposition. More precisely, mental causation is what happens when an organism has a behavioral disposition and the if-clause of the behavioral hypothetical expressing the disposition happens to be true. For example, the causal statement "Smith drank some water because he was thirsty" might be taken to mean "If there were water available, then Smith would drink some, and there was water available."

I have somewhat oversimplified logical behaviorism by assuming that each mental ascription can be translated by a unique behavioral hypothetical. Actually the logical behaviorist often maintains that it takes an open-ended set (perhaps an infinite set) of behavioral hypotheticals to spell out the behavioral disposition expressed by a mental term. The mental ascription "Smith is thirsty" might also be satisfied by the hypothetical "If there were orange juice available, then Smith would drink some" and by a host of other hypotheticals. In any event the logical behaviorist does not usually maintain he can actually enumerate all the hypotheticals that correspond to a behavioral disposition expressing a given mental term. He only insists that in principle the meaning of any mental term can be conveyed by behavioral hypotheticals.

The way the logical behaviorist has interpreted a mental term such as thirsty is modeled after the way many philosophers have interpreted a physical disposition such as fragility. The physical disposition "The glass is fragile" is often taken to mean something like "If the glass were struck, then it would break." By the same token the logical behaviorist's analysis of mental causation is similar to the received analysis of one kind of physical causation. The causal statement "The glass broke because it was fragile" is taken to mean something like "If the glass were struck, then it would break, and the glass was struck."

By equating mental terms with behavioral dispositions the logical behaviorist has put mental terms on a par with the nonbehavioral dispositions of the physical sciences. That is a promising move, because the analysis of nonbehavioral dispositions is on relatively solid philosophical ground. An explanation attributing the breaking of a glass to its fragility is surely something even the staunchest materialist can accept. By arguing that mental terms are synonymous with dispositional terms, the logical behaviorist has provided something the radical behaviorist could not: a materialist account of mental causation.

Nevertheless, the analogy between mental causation as construed by the logical behaviorist and physical causation goes only so far. The logical behaviorist treats the manifestation of a disposition as the sole form of mental causation whereas the physical sciences recognize additional kinds of causation. There is the kind of causation where one physical event causes another, as when the breaking of a glass is attributed to its having been struck. In fact, explanations that involve event-event causation are presumably more basic than dispositional explanations, because the manifestation of a disposition (the breaking of a fragile glass) always involves event-event causation and not vice versa. In the realm of the mental many examples of event-event causation involve one mental state's causing another, and for this kind of causation logical behaviorism provides no analysis. As a result the logical behaviorist is committed to the tacit and implausible assumption that psychology requires a less robust notion of causation than the physical sciences require.

Event-event causation actually seems to be quite common in the realm of the mental. Mental causes typically give rise to behavioral effects by virtue of their interaction with other mental causes. For example, having a headache causes a disposition to take aspirin only if one also has the desire to get rid of the headache, the belief that aspirin exists, the belief that taking aspirin reduces headaches and so on. Since mental states interact in generating behavior, it will be necessary to find a construal of psychological explanations that posits mental processes: causal sequences of mental events. It is this construal that logical behaviorism fails to provide.

Such considerations bring out a fundamental way in which logical behaviorism is quite similar to radical behaviorism. It is true that the logical behaviorist, unlike the radical behaviorist, acknowledges the existence of mental states. Yet since the underlying tenet of logical behaviorism is that references to mental states can be translated out of psychological explanations by employing behavioral hypotheticals, all talk of mental states and processes is in a sense heuristic. The only facts to which the behaviorist is actually committed are facts about relations between stimuli and responses. In this respect logical behaviorism is just radical behaviorism in a semantic form. Although the former theory offers a construal of mental causation, the construal is Pickwickian. What does not really exist cannot cause anything, and the logical behaviorist, like the radical behaviorist, believes deep down that mental causes do not exist.

An alternative materialist theory of the mind to logical behaviorism is the central-state identity theory. According to this theory, mental events, states and processes are identical with neurophysiological events in the brain, and the property of being in a certain mental state (such as having a headache or believing it will rain) is identical with the property of being in a certain neurophysiological state. On this basis it is easy to make sense of the idea that a behavioral effect might sometimes have a chain of mental causes; that will be the case whenever a behavioral effect is contingent on the appropriate sequence of neurophysiological events.

The central-state identity theory acknowledges that it is possible for mental causes to interact causally without ever giving rise to any behavioral effect, as when a person thinks for a while about what he ought to do and then decides to do nothing. If mental processes are neurophysiological, they must have the causal properties of neurophysiological processes. Since neurophysiological processes are presumably physical processes, the central-state identity theory ensures that the concept of mental causation is as rich as the concept of physical causation.

The central-state identity theory provides a satisfactory account of what the mental terms in psychological explanations refer to, and so it is favored by psychologists who are dissatisfied with behaviorism. The behaviorist maintains that mental terms refer to nothing or that they refer to the parameters of stimulus-response relations. Either way the existence of mental entities is only illusory. The identity theorist, on the other hand, argues that mental terms refer to neurophysiological states. Thus he can take seriously the project of explaining behavior by appealing to its mental causes.

The chief advantage of the identity theory is that it takes the explanatory constructs of psychology at face value, which is surely something a philosophy of mind ought to do if it can. The identity theory shows how the mentalistic explanations of psychology could be not mere heuristics but literal accounts of the causal history of behavior. Moreover, since the identity theory is not a semantic thesis, it is immune to many arguments that cast in doubt logical behaviorism. A drawback of logical behaviorism is that the observation "John has a headache" does not seem to mean the same thing as a statement of the form "John is disposed to behave in such and such a way." The identity theorist, however, can live with the fact that "John has a headache" and "John is in such and such a brain state" are not synonymous. The assertion of the identity theorist is not that these sentences mean the same thing but only that they are rendered true (or false) by the same neurophysiological phenomena.

The identity theory can be held either as a doctrine about mental particulars (John's current pain or Bill's fear of animals) or as a doctrine about mental universals, or properties (having a pain or being afraid of animals). The two doctrines, called respectively token physicalism and type physicalism, differ in strength and plausibility. Token physicalism maintains only that all the mental particulars that happen to exist are neurophysiological, whereas type physicalism makes the more sweeping assertion that all the mental particulars there could possibly be are neurophysiological. Token physicalism does not rule out the logical possibility of machines and disembodied

spirits having mental properties. Type physicalism dismisses this possibility because neither machines nor disembodied spirits have neurons.

Type physicalism is not a plausible doctrine about mental properties even if token physicalism is right about mental particulars. The problem with type physicalism is that the psychological constitution of a system seems to depend not on its hardware, or physical composition, but on its software, or program. Why should the philosopher dismiss the possibility that silicon-based Martians have pains, assuming that the silicon is properly organized? And why should the philosopher rule out the possibility of machines having beliefs, assuming that the machines are correctly programmed? If it is logically possible that Martians and machines could have mental properties, then mental properties and neurophysiological processes cannot be identical, however much they may prove to be coextensive.

What it all comes down to is that there seems to be a level of abstraction at which the generalizations of psychology are most naturally pitched. This level of abstraction cuts across differences in the physical composition of the systems to which psychological generalizations apply. In the cognitive sciences, at least, the natural domain for psychological theorizing seems to be all systems that process information. The problem with type physicalism is that there are possible information-processing systems with the same psychological constitution as human beings but not the same physical organization. In principle all kinds of physically different things could have human software.

This situation calls for a relational account of mental properties that abstracts them from the physical structure of their bearers. In spite of the objections to logical behaviorism that I presented above, logical behaviorism was at least on the right track in offering a relational interpretation of mental properties: to have a headache is to be disposed to exhibit a certain pattern of relations between the stimuli one encounters and the responses one exhibits. If that is what having a headache is, however, there is no reason in principle why only heads that are physically similar to ours can ache. Indeed, according to logical behaviorism, it is a necessary truth that any system that has our stimulus-response contingencies also has our headaches.

All of this emerged ten or fifteen years ago as a nasty dilemma for the materialist program in the philosophy of mind. On the one hand the identity theorist (and not the logical behaviorist) had got right the causal character of the interactions of mind and body. On the other the logical behaviorist (and not the identity theorist) had got right the relational character of mental properties. Functionalism has apparently been able to resolve the dilemma. By stressing the distinction computer science draws between hardware and software the functionalist can make sense of both the causal and the relational character of the mental.

The intuition underlying functionalism is that what determines the psychological type to which a mental particular belongs is the causal role of the particular in the mental life of the organism. Functional individuation is differentiation with respect to causal role. A headache, for example, is identified with the type of mental state that among other things causes a disposition for taking aspirin in people who believe aspirin relieves a headache, causes a desire to rid oneself of the pain one is feeling, often causes someone who speaks English to say such things as "I have a headache" and is brought on by overwork, eyestrain and tension. This list is presumably not complete. More will be known about the nature of a headache as psychological and physiological research discovers more about its causal role.

Functionalism construes the concept of causal role in such a way that a mental state can be defined by its causal relations to other mental states. In this respect functionalism is completely different from logical behaviorism. Another major difference is that functionalism is not a reductionist thesis. It does not foresee, even in principle, the elimination of mentalistic concepts from the explanatory apparatus of psychological theories.

The difference between functionalism and logical behaviorism is brought out by the fact that functionalism is fully compatible with token physicalism. The functionalist would not be disturbed if brain events turn out to be the only things with the functional properties that define mental states. Indeed, most functionalists fully expect it will turn out that way.

Since functionalism recognizes that mental particulars may be physical, it is compatible with the idea that mental causation is a species of physical causation. In other words, functionalism tolerates the materialist solution to the mind-body problem provided by the central-state identity theory. It is possible for the functionalist to assert both that mental properties are typically defined in terms of their relations and that interactions of mind and body are typically causal in however robust a notion of causality is required by psychological explanations. The logical behaviorist can endorse only the first assertion and the type physicalist only the second. As a result functionalism seems to capture the best features of the materialist alternatives to dualism. It is no wonder that functionalism has become increasingly popular.

Machines provide good examples of two concepts that are central to functionalism: the concept that mental states are interdefined and the concept that they can be realized by many systems. The illustration ... contrasts a behavioristic Coke machine with a mentalistic one. Both machines dispense a Coke for 10 cents. (The price has not been affected by inflation.) The states of the machines are defined by reference to their causal roles, but only one machine would satisfy the behaviorist. Its single state (*SO*) is completely specified in terms of stimuli and responses. *SO* is the state a machine is in if, and only if, given a dime as the input, it dispenses a Coke as the output.

The machine in the illustration has interdefined states (S1 and S2), which are characteristic of functionalism. $S1$ is the state a machine is in if, and only if, (1) given a nickel, it dispenses nothing and proceeds to $S2$, and (2) given a dime, it dispenses a Coke and stays in $S1$. $S2$ is the state a machine is in if, and only if, (1) given a nickel, it dispenses a Coke and proceeds to $S1$, and (2) given a dime, it dispenses a Coke and a nickel and proceeds to $S1$. What $S1$ and $S2$ jointly amount to is the machine's dispensing a Coke if it is given a dime, dispensing a Coke and a nickel if it is given a dime and a nickel and waiting to be given a second nickel if it has been given a first one.

Since $S1$ and $S2$ are each defined by hypothetical statements, they can be viewed as dispositions. Nevertheless, they are not behavioral dispositions because the consequences an input has for a machine in $S1$ or $S2$ are not specified solely in terms of the output of the machine. Rather, the consequences also involve the machine's internal states.

Nothing about the way I have described the behavioristic and mentalistic Coke machines puts constraints on what they could be made of. Any system whose states bore the proper relations to inputs, outputs and other states could be one of these machines. No doubt it is reasonable to expect such a system to be constructed out of such things as wheels, levers and diodes (token physicalism for Coke machines). Similarly, it is reasonable to expect that our minds may prove to be neurophysiological (token physicalism for human beings).

Nevertheless, the software description of a Coke machine does not logically require wheels, levers and diodes for its concrete realization. By the same token, the software description of the mind does not logically require neurons. As far as functionalism is concerned a Coke machine with states $S1$ and $S2$ could be made of ectoplasm, if there is such stuff and if its states have the right causal properties. Functionalism allows for the possibility of disembodied Coke machines in exactly the same way and to the same extent that it allows for the possibility of disembodied minds.

To say that $S1$ and $S2$ are interdefined and realizable by different kinds of hardware is not, of course, to say that a Coke machine has a mind. Although interdefinition and functional specification are typical features of mental states, they are clearly not sufficient for mentality. . . .

An obvious objection to functionalism as a theory of the mind is that the functionalist definition is not limited to mental states and processes. Catalysts, Coke machines, valve openers, pencil sharpeners, mousetraps and ministers of finance are all in one way or another concepts that are functionally defined, but none is a mental concept such as pain, belief and desire. What, then, characterizes the mental? And can it be captured in a functionalist framework?

The traditional view in the philosophy of mind has it that mental states are distinguished by their having what are called either qualitative content or intentional content. I shall discuss qualitative content first.

It is not easy to say what qualitative content is; indeed, according to some theories, it is not even possible to say what it is because it can be known not by description but only by direct experience. I shall nonetheless attempt to describe it. Try to imagine looking at a blank wall through a red filter. Now change the filter to a green one and leave everything else exactly the way it was. Something about the character of your experience changes when the filter does, and it is this kind of thing that philosophers call qualitative content. I am not entirely comfortable about introducing qualitative content in this way, but it is a subject with which many philosophers are not comfortable.

The reason qualitative content is a problem for functionalism is straightforward. Functionalism is committed to defining mental states in terms of their causes and effects. It seems, however, as if two mental states could have all the same causal relations and yet could differ in their qualitative content. Let me illustrate this with the classic puzzle of the inverted spectrum.

It seems possible to imagine two observers who are alike in all relevant psychological respects except that experiences having the qualitative content of red for one observer would have the qualitative content of green for the other. Nothing about their behavior need reveal the difference because both of them see ripe tomatoes and flaming sunsets as being similar in color and both of them call that color "red." Moreover, the causal connection between their (qualitatively distinct) experiences and their other mental states could also be identical. Perhaps they both think of Little Red Riding Hood when they see ripe tomatoes, feel depressed when they see the color green and so on. It seems as if anything that could be packed into the notion of the causal role of their experiences could be shared by them, and yet the qualitative content of the experiences could be as different as you like. If this is possible, then the functionalist account does not work for mental states that have qualitative content. If one person is having a green experience while another person is having a red one, then surely they must be in different mental states.

The example of the inverted spectrum is more than a verbal puzzle. Having qualitative content is supposed to be a chief factor in what makes a mental state conscious. Many psychologists who are inclined to accept the functionalist framework are nonetheless worried about the failure of functionalism to reveal much about the nature of consciousness. Functionalists have made a few ingenious attempts to talk themselves and their colleagues out of this worry, but they have not, in my view, done so with much success. (For example, perhaps one is wrong in thinking one can imagine what an inverted spectrum would be like.) As matters stand, the problem of qualitative content poses a serious threat to the assertion that functionalism can provide a general theory of the mental.

Functionalism has fared much better with the intentional content of mental states. Indeed, it is here that the major achievements of recent cognitive science are found. To say that a mental state has intentional content is to say that it has certain semantic properties. For example, for

Enrico to believe Galileo was Italian apparently involves a three-way relation between Enrico, a belief and a proposition that is the content of the belief (namely the proposition that Galileo was Italian). In particular it is an essential property of Enrico's belief that it is about Galileo (and not about, say, Newton) and that it is true if, and only if, Galileo was indeed Italian. Philosophers are divided on how these considerations fit together, but it is widely agreed that beliefs involve semantic properties such as expressing a proposition, being true or false and being about one thing rather than another.

It is important to understand the semantic properties of beliefs because theories in the cognitive sciences are largely about the beliefs organisms have. Theories of learning and perception, for example, are chiefly accounts of how the host of beliefs an organism has are determined by the character of its experiences and its genetic endowment. The functionalist account of mental states does not by itself provide the required insights. Mousetraps are functionally defined, yet mousetraps do not express propositions and they are not true or false.

There is at least one kind of thing other than a mental state that has intentional content: a symbol. Like thoughts, symbols seem to be about things. If someone says "Galileo was Italian," his utterance, like Enrico's belief, expresses a proposition about Galileo that is true or false depending on Galileo's homeland. This parallel between the symbolic and the mental underlies the traditional quest for a unified treatment of language and mind. Cognitive science is now trying to provide such a treatment.

The basic concept is simple but striking. Assume that there are such things as mental symbols (mental representations) and that mental symbols have semantic properties. On this view having a belief involves being related to a mental symbol, and the belief inherits its semantic properties from the mental symbol that figures in the relation. Mental processes (thinking, perceiving, learning and so on) involve causal interactions among relational states such as having a belief.

The semantic properties of the words and sentences we utter are in turn inherited from the semantic properties of the mental states that language expresses.

Associating the semantic properties of mental states with those of mental symbols is fully compatible with the computer metaphor, because it is natural to think of the computer as a mechanism that manipulates symbols. A computation is a causal chain of computer states and the links in the chain are operations on semantically interpreted formulas in a machine code. To think of a system (such as the nervous system) as a computer is to raise questions about the nature of the code in which it computes and the semantic properties of the symbols in the code. In fact, the analogy between minds and computers actually implies the postulation of mental symbols. There is no computation without representation.

The representational account of the mind, however, predates considerably the invention of the computing machine. It is a throwback to classical epistemology, which is a tradition that includes philosophers as diverse as John Locke, David Hume, George Berkeley, René Descartes, Immanuel Kant, John Stuart Mill and William James.

Hume, for one, developed a representational theory of the mind that included five points. First, there exist "Ideas," which are a species of mental symbol. Second, having a belief involves entertaining an Idea. Third, mental processes are causal associations of Ideas. Fourth, Ideas are like pictures. And fifth, Ideas have their semantic properties by virtue of what they resemble: the Idea of John is about John because it looks like him.

Contemporary cognitive psychologists do not accept the details of Hume's theory, although they endorse much of its spirit. Theories of computation provide a far richer account of mental processes than the mere association of Ideas. And only a few psychologists still think that imagery is the chief vehicle of mental representation. Nevertheless, the most significant break

with Hume's theory lies in the abandoning of resemblance as an explanation of the semantic properties of mental representations.

Many philosophers, starting with Berkeley, have argued that there is something seriously wrong with the suggestion that the semantic relation between a thought and what the thought is about could be one of resemblance. Consider the thought that John is tall. Clearly the thought is true only of the state of affairs consisting of John's being tall. A theory of the semantic properties of a thought should therefore explain how this particular thought is related to this particular state of affairs. According to the resemblance theory, entertaining the thought involves having a mental image that shows John to be tall. To put it another way, the relation between the thought that John is tall and his being tall is like the relation between a tall man and his portrait.

The difficulty with the resemblance theory is that any portrait showing John to be tall must also show him to be many other things: clothed or naked, lying, standing or sitting, having a head or not having one, and so on. A portrait of a tall man who is sitting down resembles a man's being seated as much as it resembles a man's being tall. On the resemblance theory it is not clear what distinguishes thoughts about John's height from thoughts about his posture.

The resemblance theory turns out to encounter paradoxes at every turn. The possibility of construing beliefs as involving relations to semantically interpreted mental representations clearly depends on having an acceptable account of where the semantic properties of the mental representations come from. If resemblance will not provide this account, what will?

The current idea is that the semantic properties of a mental representation are determined by aspects of its functional role. In other words, a sufficient condition for having semantic properties can be specified in causal terms. This is the connection between functionalism and the representational theory of the mind. Modern cognitive psychology rests largely on the hope that these two doctrines can be made to support each other.

No philosopher is now prepared to say exactly how the functional role of a mental representation determines its semantic properties. Nevertheless, the functionalist recognizes three types of causal relation among psychological states involving mental representations, and they might serve to fix the semantic properties of mental representations. The three types are causal relations among mental states and stimuli, mental states and responses and some mental states and other ones.

Consider the belief that John is tall. Presumably the following facts, which correspond respectively to the three types of causal relation, are relevant to determining the semantic properties of the mental representation involved in the belief. First, the belief is a normal effect of certain stimulations, such as seeing John in circumstances that reveal his height. Second, the belief is the normal cause of certain behavioral effects, such as uttering "John is tall." Third, the belief is a normal cause of certain other beliefs and a normal effect of certain other beliefs. For example, anyone who believes John is tall is very likely also to believe someone is tall. Having the first belief is normally causally sufficient for having the second belief. And anyone who believes everyone in the room is tall and also believes John is in the room will very likely believe John is tall. The third belief is a normal effect of the first two. In short, the functionalist maintains that the proposition expressed by a given mental representation depends on the causal properties of the mental states in which that mental representation figures.

The concept that the semantic properties of mental representations are determined by aspects of their functional role is at the center of current work in the cognitive sciences. Nevertheless, the concept may not be true. Many philosophers who are unsympathetic to the cognitive turn in modern psychology doubt its truth, and many psychologists would probably reject it in the bald and unelaborated way that I have sketched it. Yet even in its skeletal form, there is this much to be said in its favor: It legitimizes the notion of mental representation, which has become increasingly important to theorizing in every branch of the cognitive sciences. Recent advances in formulating and testing hypotheses about the character of mental representations in fields ranging from phonetics to computer vision suggest that the concept of mental representation is fundamental to empirical theories of the mind.

The behaviorist has rejected the appeal to mental representation because it runs counter to his view of the explanatory mechanisms that can figure in psychological theories. Nevertheless, the science of mental representation is now flourishing. The history of science reveals that when a successful theory comes into conflict with a methodological scruple, it is generally the scruple that gives way. Accordingly the functionalist has relaxed the behaviorist constraints on psychological explanations. There is probably no better way to decide what is methodologically permissible in science than by investigating what successful science requires.

For Further Reflection

1. If Fodor's view is correct, would it be logically possible for minds like ours to be realized in, say, a cat? a space alien? metal? Why or why not?

2. Which theory of mind do you think is more plausible—dualism or functionalism? Explain.

3. Could two people be in the same functional state yet have different mental states? For example, could both of them be in the same functional state for seeing color yet have completely different visual experiences? If so, would this possibility be a counterexample to functionalism? Explain.

IV.41   Property Dualism

DAVID CHALMERS

At the Australian National University, David Chalmers is a professor of philosophy and director of the Centre for Consciousness. He is a leading scholar in the philosophy of mind and consciousness and the author of *The Conscious Mind: In Search of a Fundamental Theory* (1996). He is a proponent of the theory of mind known as *property dualism* (also nonreductive materialism and naturalistic dualism). On this view, mental states, or properties, are distinct from physical properties, arising from the physical properties without being reducible to, or identical to, them (and without being some kind of Cartesian substance). Philosophers like to say that this relationship between the mental and physical is one of *supervenience*—that is, mental properties supervene on the physical ones. This means that something possesses a mental property in virtue of having a physical property. The mental property depends on the physical one, arises from it, but is not identical to it. If true, reductive materialism must be false. "This failure of materialism," says Chalmers, "leads to a kind of *dualism:* there are both physical and nonphysical features of the world." Mental properties are features of the world that are "over and above the physical features of the world."

Study Questions

1. What is property (or naturalistic) dualism?
2. What is Chalmers' view of substance dualism?
3. According to Chalmers, does property dualism conflict with science?
4. If this theory is true, what happens to the mind when the brain dies?

THERE APPEARS TO BE A systematic dependence of conscious experience on physical structure in the cases with which we are familiar, and nothing in the arguments of the last chapter suggests otherwise. It remains as plausible as ever, for example, that if my physical structure were to be replicated by some creature in the actual world, my conscious experience would be replicated, too. So it remains plausible that consciousness supervenes *naturally* on the physical. . . .

The arguments do not lead us to a dualism such as that of Descartes, with a separate realm of mental substance that exerts its own influence on physical processes. The best evidence of contemporary science tells us that the physical world is more or less causally closed: for every physical event, there is a physical sufficient cause. If so, there is no room for a mental "ghost in the machine" to do any extra causal work. A small loophole may be opened by the existence of quantum indeterminacy, but I argue later that this probably cannot be exploited to yield a causal role for a nonphysical mind. In any case . . . it remains plausible that *physical* events can be explained in physical terms, so a move to a

Reprinted from David Chalmers, The Conscious Mind *(New York: Oxford University Press, 1996), 124–126, 128, by permission of the publisher.*

Cartesian dualism would be a stronger reaction than is warranted.

The dualism implied here is instead a kind of *property* dualism: conscious experience involves properties of an individual that are not entailed by the physical properties of that individual, although they may depend lawfully on those properties. Consciousness is a *feature* of the world over and above the physical features of the world. This is not to say it is a separate "substance"; the issue of what it would take to constitute a dualism of substances seems quite unclear to me. All we know is that there are properties of individuals in this world—the phenomenal properties—that are ontologically independent of physical properties.

There is a weaker sort of property dualism with which this view should not be confused. It is sometimes said that property dualism applies to any domain in which the properties are not themselves properties invoked by physics, or directly reducible to such properties. In this sense, even biological fitness is not a physical property. But this sort of "dualism" is a very weak variety. There is nothing *fundamentally* ontologically new about properties such as fitness, as they are still logically supervenient on microphysical properties. Property dualism of this variety is entirely compatible with materialism. By contrast, the property dualism that I advocate involves fundamentally new features of the world. Because these properties are not even logically supervenient on microphysical properties, they are nonphysical in a much stronger sense. When I speak of property dualism and nonphysical properties, it is this stronger view and the stronger sense of nonphysicality that I have in mind.

It remains plausible, however, that consciousness *arises* from a physical basis, even though it is not *entailed* by that basis. The position we are left with is that consciousness arises from a physical substrate in virtue of certain contingent laws of nature, which are not themselves implied by physical laws. This position is implicitly held by many people who think of themselves as materialists. It is common to hear, "Of course I'm a materialist; the mind certainly arises from the brain." The very presence of the word "arises" should be a tip-off here. One tends not to say "learning arises from the brain," for instance—and if one did, it would be in a temporal sense of "arises." Rather, one would more naturally say that learning *is* a process in the brain. The very fact that the mind needs to *arise* from the brain indicates that there is something further going on, over and above the physical facts.

Some people will think that the view should count as a version of materialism rather than dualism, because it posits such a strong lawful dependence of the phenomenal facts on the physical facts, and because the physical domain remains autonomous. Of course there is little point arguing over a name, but it seems to me that the existence of further contingent facts over and above the physical facts is a significant enough modification to the received materialist world view to deserve a different label. Certainly, if all that is required for materialism is that all facts be lawfully connected to the physical facts, then materialism becomes a weak doctrine indeed. . . .

To capture the spirit of the view I advocate, I call it *naturalistic dualism*. It is naturalistic because it posits that everything is a consequence of a network of basic properties and laws, and because it is compatible with all the results of contemporary science. And as with naturalistic theories in other domains, this view allows that we can *explain* consciousness in terms of basic natural laws. There need be nothing especially transcendental about consciousness; it is just another natural phenomenon. All that has happened is that our picture of nature has expanded. Sometimes "naturalism" is taken to be synonymous with "materialism," but it seems to me that a commitment to a naturalistic understanding of the world can survive the failure of materialism. (If a reader doubts this, I point to the rest of this work as evidence.) Some might find a certain irony in the name of the view, but what is most important is that it conveys the central message: to embrace dualism is not necessarily to embrace mystery.

In some ways, those who hold this sort of dualism may be temperamentally closer to materialists than to dualists of other varieties. This is partly because of its avoidance of any transcendental element and its commitment to natural explanation, and partly because of its commitment to the physical causation of behavior. Conversely, by avoiding any commitment to a ghost in the machine, this view avoids the worst implausibilities of the traditional dualist views. One often hears that the successes of cognitive science and neuroscience make dualism implausible, but not all varieties of dualism are affected equally. These successes are all grounded in physical explanations of behavior and of other physical phenomena, and so do not distinguish between the materialist and the naturalistic dualist view.

For Further Reflection

1. Is property dualism more plausible than substance dualism? Explain.
2. Do you believe that consciousness arises from the brain, as Chalmers says? If so, what are your reasons? If not, why not?
3. Chalmers argues that mental properties are not reducible to physical properties, that the former are further facts about the world that are over and above the physical facts. To show this, he asks us to consider a world of zombies—a world physically identical to ours, populated by individuals that are physically and behaviorally identical to the people in our world but where no one has any conscious experiences (because they're all zombies). If such a world is logically possible, then consciousness must be an *extra* fact about our world, something over and above the physical facts. If so, consciousness (mind) cannot be reduced to or identified with physical properties, and reductive materialism is false. Do you think this is a good argument? Explain.

IV.42   Minds, Brains, and Computers

JOHN SEARLE

John Searle is professor of philosophy at the University of California, Berkeley, and the author of several works in the philosophy of language and the philosophy of mind, including *Intentionality* (1983) and *The Rediscovery of the Mind* (1992). In this essay, Searle argues that although weak AI (artificial intelligence), which states that the mind functions somewhat like a computer, might be correct, strong AI, which states the appropriately programmed computer *is* mind and has intentions, is false.

Study Questions

1. What is the difference between weak and strong AI?
2. What two claims do partisans of strong AI make?
3. What does the example of correlating sets of Chinese symbols illustrate?
4. How does Searle address the two claims of strong AI?
5. Does Searle believe that a man-made machine could be made to think?

WHAT PSYCHOLOGICAL AND PHILOSOPHICAL significance should we attach to recent efforts at computer simulations of human cognitive capacities? In answering this question, I find it useful to distinguish what I will call "strong" AI from "weak" or "cautious" AI (artificial intelligence). According to weak AI, the principal value of the computer in the study of the mind is that it gives us a very powerful tool. For example, it enables us to formulate and test hypotheses in a more rigorous and precise fashion. But according to strong AI, the computer is not merely a tool in the study of the mind; rather, the appropriately programmed computer really *is* a mind, in the sense that computers given the right programs can be literally said to *understand* and have other cognitive states. In strong AI, because the programmed computer has cognitive states, the programs are not mere tools that enable us to test psychological explanations; rather, the programs are themselves the explanations.

I have no objection to the claims of weak AI, at least as far as this article is concerned. My discussion here will be directed at the claims I have defined as those of strong AI, specifically the claim that the appropriately programmed computer literally has cognitive states and that the programs thereby explain human cognition. When I hereafter refer to AI, I have in mind the strong version, as expressed by these two claims.

I will consider the work of Roger Schank and his colleagues at Yale (Schank and Abelson 1977), because I am more familiar with it than I am with any other similar claims, and because it provides a very clear example of the sort of work I wish to examine. But nothing that follows depends upon the details of Schank's programs. The same arguments would apply to Winograd's SHRDLU (Winograd 1973), Weizenbaum's ELIZA (Weizenbaum 1965), and indeed any Turing machine simulation of human mental phenomena. . . .

Very briefly, and leaving out the various details, one can describe Schank's program as fol-

lows: The aim of the program is to simulate the human ability to understand stories. It is characteristic of human beings' story-understanding capacity that they can answer questions about the story even though the information that they give was never explicitly stated in the story. Thus, for example, suppose you are given the following story: "A man went into a restaurant and ordered a hamburger. When the hamburger arrived it was burned to a crisp, and the man stormed out of the restaurant angrily, without paying for the hamburger or leaving a tip." Now, if you are asked "Did the man eat the hamburger?" you will presumably answer, "No, he did not." Similarly, if you are given the following story: "A man went into a restaurant and ordered a hamburger; when the hamburger came he was very pleased with it; and as he left the restaurant he gave the waitress a large tip before paying his bill," and you are asked the question, "Did the man eat the hamburger?" you will presumably answer, "Yes, he ate the hamburger." Now Schank's machines can similarly answer questions about restaurants in this fashion. To do this, they have a "representation" of the sort of information that human beings have about restaurants, which enables them to answer such questions as those above, given these sorts of stories. When the machine is given the story and then asked the question, the machine will print out answers of the sort that we would expect human beings to give if told similar stories. Partisans of strong AI claim that in this question and answer sequence the machine is not only simulating a human ability but also (1) that the machine can literally be said to *understand* the story and provide the answers to questions, and (2) that what the machine and its programs do *explains* the human ability to understand the story and answer questions about it.

Both claims seem to me to be totally unsupported by Schank's work, as I will attempt to show in what follows. I am not, of course, saying that

---

From John R. Searle, "Minds, Brains, and Programs," in The Behavioral and Brain Sciences, *Vol. 3. Copyright © 1980 Cambridge University Press. Reprinted by permission of Cambridge University Press and the author. Footnotes edited.*

Schank himself is committed to these claims. One way to test any theory of the mind is to ask oneself what it would be like if my mind actually worked on the principles that the theory says all minds work on. Let us apply this test to the Schank program with the following thought experiment. Suppose that I'm locked in a room and given a large batch of Chinese writing. Suppose furthermore (as is indeed the case) that I know no Chinese, either written or spoken, and that I'm not even confident that I could recognize Chinese writing as Chinese writing distinct from, say, Japanese writing or meaningless squiggles. To me, Chinese writing is just so many meaningless squiggles. Now suppose further that after this first batch of Chinese writing I am given a second batch of Chinese script together with a set of rules for correlating the second batch with the first batch. The rules are in English, and I understand these rules as well as any other native speaker of English. They enable me to correlate one set of formal symbols with another set of formal symbols, and all that "formal" means here is that I can identify the symbols entirely by their shapes. Now suppose also that I am given a third batch of Chinese symbols together with some instructions, again in English, that enable me to correlate elements of this third batch with the first two batches, and these rules instruct me how to give back certain Chinese symbols with certain sorts of shapes in response to certain sorts of shapes given me in the third batch. Unknown to me, the people who are giving me all of these symbols call the first batch a "script," they call the second batch a "story," and they call the third batch "questions." Furthermore, they call the symbols I give them back in response to the third batch "answers to the questions," and the set of rules in English that they gave me, they call the "program." Now just to complicate the story a little, imagine that these people also give me stories in English, which I understand, and they then ask me questions in English about these stories, and I give them back answers in English. Suppose also that after a while I get so good at following the instructions for manipulating the Chinese symbols and the programmers get so good at writing the programs that from the external point of view—that is, from the point of view of somebody outside the room in which I am locked—my answers to the questions are absolutely indistinguishable from those of native Chinese speakers. Nobody just looking at my answers can tell that I don't speak a word of Chinese. Let us also suppose that my answers to the English questions are, as they no doubt would be, indistinguishable from those of other native English speakers, for the simple reason that I am a native English speaker. From the external point of view—from the point of view of someone reading my "answers"—the answers to the Chinese questions and the English questions are equally good. But in the Chinese case, unlike the English case, I produce the answers by manipulating uninterpreted formal symbols. As far as the Chinese is concerned, I simply behave like a computer; I perform computational operations on formally specified elements. For the purposes of the Chinese, I am simply an instantiation of the computer program.

Now the claims made by strong AI are that the programmed computer understands the stories and that the program in some sense explains human understanding. But we are now in a position to examine these claims in light of our thought experiment.

1. As regards the first claim, it seems to me quite obvious in the example that I do not understand a word of the Chinese stories. I have in-puts and out-puts that are indistinguishable from those of the native Chinese speaker, and I can have any formal program you like, but I still understand nothing. For the same reasons, Schank's computer understands nothing of any stories, whether in Chinese, English, or whatever, since in the Chinese case the computer is me, and in cases where the computer is not me, the computer has nothing more than I have in the case where I understand nothing.

2. As regards the second claim, that the program explains human understanding, we can see that the computer and its program do not provide sufficient conditions of understanding since

the computer and the program are functioning, and there is no understanding. But does it even provide a necessary condition or a significant contribution to understanding? One of the claims made by the supporters of strong AI is that when I understand a story in English, what I am doing is exactly the same—or perhaps more of the same—as what I was doing in manipulating the Chinese symbols. It is simply more formal symbol manipulation that distinguishes the case in English, where I do understand, from the case in Chinese, where I don't. I have not demonstrated that this claim is false, but it would certainly appear an incredible claim in the example. Such plausibility as the claim has derives from the supposition that we can construct a program that will have the same inputs and outputs as native speakers, and in addition we assume that speakers have some level of description where they are also instantiations of a program. On the basis of these two assumptions we assume that even if Schank's program isn't the whole story about understanding, it may be part of the story. Well, I suppose that is an empirical possibility, but not the slightest reason has so far been given to believe that it is true, since what is suggested—though certainly not demonstrated—by the example is that the computer program is simply irrelevant to my understanding of the story. In the Chinese case I have everything that artificial intelligence can put into me by way of a program, and I understand nothing; in the English case I understand everything, and there is so far no reason at all to suppose that my understanding has anything to do with computer programs, that is, with computational operations on purely formally specified elements. As long as the program is defined in terms of computational operations on purely formally defined elements, what the example suggests is that these by themselves have no interesting connection with understanding. They are certainly not sufficient conditions, and not the slightest reason has been given to suppose that they are necessary conditions or even that they make a significant contribution to understanding. No-

tice that the force of the argument is not simply that different machines can have the same input and output while operating on different formal principles—that is not the point at all. Rather, whatever purely formal principles you put into the computer, they will not be sufficient for understanding, since a human will be able to follow the formal principles without understanding anything. No reason whatever has been offered to suppose that such principles are necessary or even contributory, since no reason has been given to suppose that when I understand English I am operating with any formal program at all.

Well, then, what is it that I have in the case of the English sentences that I do not have in the case of the Chinese sentences? The obvious answer is that I know what the former mean, while I haven't the faintest idea what the latter mean. But in what does this consist and why couldn't we give it to a machine, whatever it is? . . .

I have had the occasions to present this example to several workers in artificial intelligence, and, interestingly, they do not seem to agree on what the proper reply to it is. . . .

. . . I want to block some common misunderstandings about "understanding": In many of these discussions one finds a lot of fancy footwork about the word "understanding." My critics point out that there are many different degrees of understanding; that "understanding" is not a simple two-place predicate; that there are even different kinds and levels of understanding, and often the law of excluded middle doesn't even apply in a straightforward way to statements of the form "x understands y"; that in many cases it is a matter for decision and not a simple matter of fact whether x understands y; and so on. To all of these points I want to say: of course, of course. But they have nothing to do with the points at issue. There are clear cases in which "understanding" literally applies and clear cases in which it does not apply; and these two sorts of cases are all I need for this argument. I understand stories in English; to a lesser degree I can understand stories in French; to a still lesser degree, stories in German; and in

Chinese, not at all. My car and my adding machine, on the other hand, understand nothing: they are not in that line of business.* We often attribute "understanding" and other cognitive predicates by metaphor and analogy to cars, adding machines, and other artifacts, but nothing is proved by such attributions. We say, "The door *knows* when to open because of its photoelectric cell," "The adding machine *knows how* (*understands how*, is *able*) to do addition and subtraction but not division," and "The thermostat *perceives* changes in the temperature." The reason we make these attributions is quite interesting, and it has to do with the fact that in artifacts we extend our own intentionality;† our tools are extensions of our purposes, and so we find it natural to make metaphorical attributions of intentionality to them; but I take it no philosophical ice is cut by such examples. The sense in which an automatic door "understands instructions" from its photoelectric cell is not at all the sense in which I understand English. If the sense in which Schank's programmed computers understand stories is supposed to be the metaphorical sense in which the door understands, and not the sense in which I understand English, the issue would not be worth discussing. But Newell and Simon (1963) write that the kind of cognition they claim for computers is exactly the same as for human beings. I like the straightforwardness of this claim, and it is the sort of claim I will be considering. I will argue that in the literal sense the programmed computer understands what the car and the adding machine understand, namely, exactly nothing. The computer's understanding is not just (like my understanding of German) partial or incomplete; it is zero. . . .

*Also, "understanding" implies both the possession of mental (intentional) states and the truth (validity, success) of these states. For the purposes of this discussion we are concerned only with the possession of the states.

†Intentionality is by definition that feature of certain mental states by which they are directed at or about objects and states of affairs in the world. Thus, beliefs, desires, and intentions are intentional states; undirected forms of anxiety and depression are not.

By way of concluding I want to try to state some of the general philosophical points implicit in the argument. For clarity I will try to do it in a question-and-answer fashion, and begin with that old chestnut of a question:

"Could a machine think?"

The answer is, obviously, yes. We are precisely such machines.

"Yes, but could an artificial, a man-made machine, think?"

Assuming it is possible to produce artificially a machine with a nervous system, neurons, with axons and dendrites, and all the rest of it, sufficiently like ours, again the answer to the question seems to be obviously, yes. If you can exactly duplicate the causes, you could duplicate the effects. And indeed it might be possible to produce consciousness, intentionality, and all the rest of it using some other sorts of chemical principles than those that human beings use. It is, as I said, an empirical question.

"OK, but could a digital computer think?"

If by "digital computer" we mean anything at all that has a level of description where it can correctly be described as the instantiation of a computer program, then again the answer is, of course, yes, since we are the instantiations of any number of computer programs, and we can think.

"But could something think, understand, and so on *solely* by virtue of being a computer with the right sort of program? Could instantiating a program, the right program of course, by itself be a sufficient condition of understanding?" This I think is the right question to ask, though it is usually confused with one or more of the earlier questions, and the answer to it is no.

"Why not?"

Because the formal symbol manipulations by themselves don't have any intentionality; they are quite meaningless; they aren't even *symbol* manipulations, since the symbols don't symbolize anything. In the linguistic jargon, they have only a syntax but no semantics. Such intentionality as computers appear to have is solely in the minds of those who program them and those who use them, those who send in the input and those who interpret the output.

The aim of the Chinese room example was to try to show this by showing that as soon as we put something into the system that really does have intentionality (a man), and we program him with the formal program, you can see that the formal program carries no additional intentionality. It adds nothing, for example, to a man's ability to understand Chinese.

Precisely that feature of AI that seemed so appealing—the distinction between the program and the realization—proves fatal to the claim that simulation could be duplication. The distinction between the program and its realization in the hardware seems to be parallel to the distinction between the level of mental operations and the level of brain operations. And if we could describe the level of mental operations as a formal program, then it seems we could describe what was essential about the mind without doing either introspective psychology or neurophysiology of the brain. But the equation "mind is to brain as program is to hardware" breaks down at several points, among them the following three:

First, the distinction between program and realization has the consequence that the same program could have all sorts of crazy realizations that had no form of intentionality. Weizenbaum (1976, Ch. 2), for example, shows in detail how to construct a computer using a roll of toilet paper and a pile of small stones. Similarly, the Chinese story understanding program can be programmed into a sequence of water pipes, a set of wind machines, or a monolingual English speaker, none of which thereby acquires an understanding of Chinese. Stones, toilet paper, wind, and water pipes are the wrong kind of stuff to have intentionality in the first place—only something that has the same causal powers as brains can have intentionality—and though the English speaker has the right kind of stuff for intentionality you can easily see that he doesn't get any extra intentionality by memorizing the program, since memorizing it won't teach him Chinese.

Second, the program is purely formal, but the intentional states are not in that way formal. They are defined in terms of their content, not their form. The belief that it is raining, for example, is not defined as a certain formal shape, but as a certain mental content with conditions of satisfaction, a direction of fit (see Searle 1979), and the like. Indeed the belief as such hasn't even got a formal shape in this syntactic sense, since one and the same belief can be given an indefinite number of different syntactic expressions in different linguistic systems.

Third, as I mentioned before, mental states and events are literally a product of the operation of the brain, but the program is not in that way a product of the computer.

"Well if programs are in no way constitutive of mental processes, why have so many people believed the converse? That at least needs some explanation."

I don't really know the answer to that one. The idea that computer simulations could be the real thing ought to have seemed suspicious in the first place because the computer isn't confined to simulating mental operations, by any means. No one supposes that computer simulations of a five-alarm fire will burn the neighborhood down or that a computer simulation of a rainstorm will leave us all drenched. Why on earth would anyone suppose that a computer simulation of understanding actually understood anything? It is sometimes said that it would be frightfully hard to get computers to feel pain or fall in love, but love and pain are neither harder nor easier than cognition or anything else. For simulation, all you need is the right input and output and a program in the middle that transforms the former into the latter. That is all the computer has for anything it does. To confuse simulation with duplication is the same mistake, whether it is pain, love, cognition, fires, or rainstorms.

Still, there are several reasons why AI must have seemed—and to many people perhaps still does seem—in some way to reproduce and thereby explain mental phenomena, and I believe we will not succeed in removing these illusions until we have fully exposed the reasons that give rise to them.

First, and perhaps most important, is a confusion about the notion of "information processing": Many people in cognitive science believe that the human brain, with its mind, does something called "information processing," and analogously the computer with its program does information processing; but fires and rainstorms, on the other hand, don't do information processing at all. Thus, though the computer can simulate the formal features of any process whatever, it stands in a special relation to the mind and brain because when the computer is properly programmed, ideally with the same program as the brain, the information processing is identical in the two cases, and this information processing is really the essence of the mental. But the trouble with this argument is that it rests on an ambiguity in the notion of "information." In the sense in which people "process information" when they reflect, say, on problems in arithmetic or when they read and answer questions about stories, the programmed computer does not do "information processing." Rather, what it does is manipulate formal symbols. The fact that the programmer and the interpreter of the computer output use the symbols to stand for objects in the world is totally beyond the scope of the computer. The computer, to repeat, has a syntax but no semantics. Thus, if you type into the computer "2 plus 2 equals?" it will type out "4." But it has no idea that "4" means 4 or that it means anything at all. And the point is not that it lacks some second-order information about the interpretation of its first-order symbols, but rather that its first-order symbols don't have any interpretations as far as the computer is concerned. All the computer has is more symbols. The introduction of the notion of "information processing" therefore produces a dilemma: Either we construe the notion of "information processing" in such a way that it implies intentionality as part of the process or we don't. If the former, then the programmed computer does not do information

processing: it only manipulates formal symbols. If the latter, then, though the computer does information processing, it is only doing so in the sense in which adding machines, typewriters, stomachs, thermostats, rainstorms, and hurricanes do information processing; namely, they have a level of description at which we can describe them as taking information in at one end, transforming it, and producing information as output. But in this case it is up to outside observers to interpret the input and output as information in the ordinary sense. And no similarity is established between the computer and the brain in terms of any similarity of information processing.

Second, in much of AI there is a residual behaviorism or operationalism. Since appropriately programmed computers can have input-output patterns similar to those of human beings, we are tempted to postulate mental states in the computer similar to human mental states. But once we see that it is both conceptually and empirically possible for a system to have human capacities in some realm without having any intentionality at all, we should be able to overcome this impulse. My desk adding machine has calculating capacities, but no intentionality, and in this paper I have tried to show that a system could have input and output capabilities that duplicated those of a native Chinese speaker and still not understand Chinese, regardless of how it was programmed. The Turing test is typical of the tradition in being unashamedly behavioristic and operationalistic, and I believe that if AI workers totally repudiated behaviorism and operationalism much of the confusion between simulation and duplication would be eliminated.

Third, this residual operationalism is joined to a residual form of dualism; indeed strong AI only makes sense given the dualistic assumption that, where the mind is concerned, the brain doesn't matter. In strong AI (and in functionalism, as well) what matters are programs, and programs are independent of their realization in machines; indeed, as far as AI is concerned, the same program could be realized by an electronic machine, a Cartesian mental substance, or a Hegelian world spirit. The single most surprising discovery that I have made in discussing these issues is that many AI workers are quite shocked by my idea that actual human mental phenomena might be dependent on actual physical-chemical properties of actual human brains. But if you think about it a minute you can see that I should not have been surprised; for unless you accept some form of dualism, the strong AI project hasn't got a chance. The project is to reproduce and explain the mental by designing programs, but unless the mind is not only conceptually but empirically independent of the brain you couldn't carry out the project, for the program is completely independent of any realization. Unless you believe that the mind is separable from the brain both conceptually and empirically—dualism in a strong form—you cannot hope to reproduce the mental by writing and running programs since programs must be independent of brains or any other particular forms of instantiation. If mental operations consist in computational operations on formal symbols, then it follows that they have no interesting connection with the brain; the only connection would be that the brain just happens to be one of the indefinitely many types of machines capable of instantiating the program. This form of dualism is not the traditional Cartesian variety that claims there are two sorts of *substances,* but it is Cartesian in the sense that it insists that what is specifically mental about the mind has no intrinsic connection with the actual properties of the brain. This underlying dualism is masked from us by the fact that AI literature contains frequent fulminations against "dualism"; what the authors seem to be unaware of is that their position presupposes a strong version of dualism.

"Could a machine think?" My own view is that *only* a machine could think, and indeed only very special kinds of machines, namely brains and machines that had the same causal powers as brains. And that is the main reason strong AI has had little to tell us about thinking, since it has nothing to tell us about machines. By its own definition, it is about programs, and programs are not machines. Whatever else intentionality is, it is a biological phenomenon, and it is as likely to be as causally dependent on the specific biochemistry of its origins as lactation, photosynthesis, or any other biological phenomena. No one would suppose that we could produce milk and sugar by running a computer simulation of the formal sequences in lactation and photosynthesis, but where the mind is concerned many people are willing to believe in such a miracle because of a deep and abiding dualism: The mind they suppose is a matter of formal processes and is independent of quite specific material causes in the way that milk and sugar are not.

In defense of this dualism the hope is often expressed that the brain is a digital computer (early computers, by the way, were often called "electronic brains"). But that is no help. Of course the brain is a digital computer. Since everything is a digital computer, brains are too. The point is that the brain's causal capacity to produce intentionality cannot consist in its instantiating a computer program, since for any program you like it is possible for something to instantiate that program and still not have any mental states. Whatever it is that the brain does to produce intentionality, it cannot consist in instantiating a program since no program, by itself, is sufficient for intentionality.

For Further Reflection

1. Evaluate Searle's argument against strong AI. Can you see any weaknesses in it? How might a proponent of strong AI defend his or her position?

2. Suppose we could devise a robot with a television camera inside enabling it to see and a voice machine to utter meaningful sentences in response to its environmental input. Would this be an advance on the Schank program that would meet Searle's objections?

3. Here is one reply of an AI proponent discussed in Searle's original essay:

Your whole argument presupposes that AI is only about analog and digital computers. But that just happens to be the present state of technology. Whatever these causal processes are that you say are essential for intentionality, eventually we will be able to build devices that have these causal processes, and that will be artificial intelligence. So your arguments are in no way directed at the ability of artificial intelligence to produce and explain cognition. (*The Many Mansions Reply* [Berkeley])

Evaluate this response. Does it show that artificial intelligence could eventually become conscious, have intentional states, and understand language?

IV.43   Troubles with Functionalism

NED BLOCK

Ned Block is professor of philosophy, psychology, and neural science at New York University, specializing in philosophy of mind, neuroscience, and cognitive science. In this essay, he critiques functionalism, the view that the mind is the functions that the brain performs, and finds it implausible because it fails to account for conscious experience such as being in pain or seeing colors. Block puts forth what is known as an *absent qualia argument*. The gist is that it is possible to introduce a functional organization into some system so that, if functionalism is correct, a mind would be brought into existence. But it seems intuitively obvious that no mind at all is constituted. So functionalism is false. He makes his case using his famous "Chinese nation" or "Chinese brain" thought experiment.

Study Questions

1. *Qualia* are the qualitative feel of conscious experience. Why is Block's criticism of functionalism called an absent qualia argument?
2. What is the "Chinese nation" thought experiment?
3. How is Block's thought experiment supposed to show that functionalism is false?
4. What does Block mean by his remark that "physicalism is a *chauvinist* theory"?
5. According to Block, how are all versions of functionalism guilty of "liberalism"?

One characterization of functionalism that is probably vague enough to be accepted by most functionalists is: each type of mental state is a state consisting of a disposition to act in certain ways *and to have certain mental states*, given certain sensory inputs and certain mental states. So put, functionalism can be seen as a new incarnation of behaviorism. Behaviorism identifies mental states with dispositions to act in certain ways in certain input situations. But as critics have pointed out (Chisholm, 1957; Putnam, 1963), desire for goal G cannot be identified with, say, the disposition to do A in input circumstances in which A leads to G, since, after all, the agent might not *know* A leads to G and thus might not be disposed to do A. Functionalism replaces behaviorism's "sensory inputs" with "sensory inputs and mental states"; and functionalism replaces behaviorism's "disposition to act" with "disposition to act and have certain mental states." Functionalists want to individuate mental states causally, and since mental states have mental causes and effects as well as sensory causes and behavioral effects, functionalists individuate mental states partly in terms of causal relations to other mental states. One consequence of this difference between functionalism and behaviorism is that there are organisms that according to behaviorism, have mental states but, according to functionalism, do not have mental states.

So, necessary conditions for mentality that are postulated by functionalism are in one respect stronger than those postulated by behaviorism. According to behaviorism, it is necessary and sufficient for desiring that G that a system be characterized by a certain set (perhaps infinite) of input-output relations; that is, according to behaviorism, a system desires that G just in case a certain set of conditionals of the form 'It will emit O given I' are true of it. According to functionalism, however, a system might have these input-output relations, yet not desire that G; for according to functionalism, whether a system desires that G depends on whether it has internal states which have certain causal relations to other internal states (and to inputs and outputs). Since behaviorism makes no such "internal state" requirement, there are possible systems of which behaviorism affirms and functionalism denies that they have mental states.[1] One way of stating this is that, according to functionalism, behaviorism is guilty of *liberalism*—ascribing mental properties to things that do not in fact have them. . . .

By 'physicalism,' I mean the doctrine that pain, for example, is identical to a physical (or physiological) state.[2] As many philosophers have argued (notably Fodor, 1965, and Putnam, 1966; see also Block & Fodor, 1972), if functionalism is true, physicalism is false. The point is at its clearest with regard to Turing-machine versions of functionalism. Any given abstract Turing machine can be realized by a wide variety of physical devices; indeed, it is plausible that, given any putative correspondence between a Turing-machine state and a configurational physical (or physiological) state, there will be a possible realization of the Turing machine that will provide a counterexample to that correspondence. (See Kalke, 1969; Gendron, 1971; Mucciolo, 1974, for unconvincing arguments to the contrary; see also Kim, 1972.) Therefore, if pain is a functional state, it cannot, for example, be a brain state, because creatures without brains can realize the same Turing machine as creatures with brains. . . .

One way of expressing this point is that, according to functionalism, physicalism is a *chauvinist* theory: it withholds mental properties from systems that in fact have them. In saying mental states are brain states, for example, physicalists unfairly exclude those poor brainless creatures who nonetheless have minds. . . .

From Ned Block, "Troubles with Functionalism," in Perception and Cognition: Issues in Foundations of Psychology, *Minnesota Studies in the Philosophy of Science, vol. 9, ed. C.W. Savage (University of Minnesota Press, 1978), pp. 261–325.*

One can also categorize functionalists in terms of whether they regard functional identities as part of a priori psychology or empirical psychology. (Since this distinction crosscuts the machine/nonmachine distinction, I shall be able to illustrate nonmachine versions of functionalism in what follows.) The a priori functionalists (e.g., Smart, Armstrong, Lewis, Shoemaker) are the heirs of the logical behaviorists. They tend to regard functional analyses as analyses of the meanings of mental terms, whereas the empirical functionalists (e.g., Fodor, Putnam, Harman) regard functional analyses as substantive scientific hypotheses. In what follows, I shall refer to the former view as 'Functionalism' and the latter as 'Psychofunctionalism.' (I shall use 'functionalism' with a lowercase 'f' as neutral between Functionalism and Psychofunctionalism. When distinguishing between Functionalism and Psychofunctionalism, I shall always use capitals.)

Functionalism and Psychofunctionalism and the difference between them can be made clearer in terms of the notion of the Ramsey sentence of a psychological theory. Mental-state terms that appear in a psychological theory can be defined in various ways by means of the Ramsey sentence of the theory (see. p. 269). All functional-state identity theories (and functional-property identity theories) can be understood as defining a set of functional states (or functional properties) by means of the Ramsey sentence of a psychological theory—with one functional state corresponding to each mental state (or one functional property corresponding to each mental property). The functional state corresponding to pain will be called the 'Ramsey functional correlate' of pain, with respect to the psychological theory. In terms of the notion of a Ramsey functional correlate with respect to a theory, the distinction between Functionalism and Psychofunctionalism can be defined as follows: Functionalism identifies mental state S with S's Ramsey functional correlate with respect to a *common-sense* psychological theory; Psychofunctionalism identifies S with S's Ramsey functional correlate with respect to a *scientific* psychological theory. . . .

1.2 HOMUNCULI-HEADED ROBOTS

In this section I shall describe a class of devices that embarrass all versions of functionalism in that they indicate functionalism is guilty of liberalism—classifying systems that lack mentality as having mentality.

Consider the simple version of machine functionalism already described. It says that each system having mental states is described by at least one Turing-machine table of a certain kind, and each mental state of the system is identical to one of the machine-table states specified by the machine table. I shall consider inputs and outputs to be specified by descriptions of neural impulses in sense organs and motor-output neurons. This assumption should not be regarded as restricting what will be said to Psychofunctionalism rather than Functionalism. As already mentioned, every version of functionalism assumes *some* specification of inputs and outputs. A Functionalist specification would do as well for the purposes of what follows.

Imagine a body externally like a human body, say yours, but internally quite different. The neurons from sensory organs are connected to a bank of lights in a hollow cavity in the head. A set of buttons connects to the motor-output neurons. Inside the cavity resides a group of little men. Each has a very simple task: to implement a "square" of a reasonably adequate machine table that describes you. On one wall is a bulletin board on which is posted a state card, i.e., a card that bears a symbol designating one of the states specified in the machine table. Here is what the little men do: Suppose the posted card has a 'G' on it. This alerts the little men who implement G squares—'G-men' they call themselves. Suppose the light representing input I_{17} goes on. One of the G-men has the following as his sole task: when the card reads 'G' and the I_{17} light goes on, he presses output button O_{191} and changes the state card to 'M'. This G-man is called upon to exercise his task only rarely. In spite of the low level of intelligence required of each little man, the system as a whole manages to simulate you because the functional organization they have been trained to realize is yours. A Turing machine can be represented as a finite set of quadruples (or quintuples, if the output is divided into two parts)—current state, current input; next state, next output. Each little man has the task corresponding to a single quadruple. Through the efforts of the little men, the system realizes the same (reasonably adequate) machine table as you do and is thus functionally equivalent to you.

I shall describe a version of the homunculi-headed simulation, which is more clearly nomologically possible. How many homunculi are required? Perhaps a billion are enough; after all, there are only about a billion neurons in the brain.

Suppose we convert the government of China to functionalism, and we convince its officials that it would enormously enhance their international prestige to realize a human mind for an hour. We provide each of the billion people in China (I chose China because it has a billion inhabitants.) with a specially designed two-way radio that connects them in the appropriate way to other persons and to the artificial body mentioned in the previous example. We replace the little men with a radio transmitter and receiver connected to the input and output neurons. Instead of a bulletin board, we arrange to have letters displayed on a series of satellites placed so that they can be seen from anywhere in China. Surely such a system is not physically impossible. It could be functionally equivalent to you for a short time, say an hour.

"But," you may object, "how could something be functionally equivalent to me for *an hour?* Doesn't my functional organization determine, say, how I would react to doing nothing for a week but reading *Reader's Digest?*" Remember that a machine table specifies a set of conditionals of the form: if the machine is in S_i and receives input I_j, it emits output O_k and goes into S_1. Any system that has a set of inputs, outputs, and states related in the way described realizes that machine table, even if it exists for only

an instant. For the hour the Chinese system is "on," it *does* have a set of inputs, outputs, and states of which such conditionals are true. Whatever the initial state, the system will respond in whatever way the machine table directs. This is how *any* computer realizes the machine table it realizes.

Of course, there are signals the system would respond to that you would not respond to, e.g., massive radio interference or a flood of the Yangtze River. Such events might cause a malfunction, scotching the simulation, just as a bomb in a computer can make it fail to realize the machine table it was built to realize. But just as the computer *without* the bomb *can* realize the machine table, the system consisting of the people and artificial body can realize the machine table so long as there are no catastrophic interferences, e.g., floods, etc.

"But," someone may object, "there is a difference between a bomb in a computer and a bomb in the Chinese system, for in the case of the latter (unlike the former), inputs as specified in the machine table can be the cause of the malfunction. Unusual neural activity in the sense organs of residents of Chungking Province caused by a bomb or by a flood of the Yangtze can cause the system to go haywire."

Reply: the person who says what system he or she is talking about gets to say what counts as inputs and outputs. I count as inputs and outputs only neural activity in the artificial body connected by radio to the people of China. Neural signals in the people of Chungking count no more as inputs to this system than input tape jammed by a saboteur between the relay contacts in the innards of a computer counts as an input to the computer.

Of course, the object consisting of the people of China + the artificial body has *other* Turing machine descriptions under which neural signals in the inhabitants of Chungking *would* count as inputs. Such a new system (i.e., the object under such a new Turing-machine description) would not be functionally equivalent to you. Likewise, any commercial computer can be redescribed in a way that allows tape jammed into its innards to count as inputs. In describing an object as a Turing machine, one draws a line between the inside and the outside. (If we count only neural impulses as inputs and outputs, we draw that line inside the body; if we count only peripheral stimulations as inputs and only bodily movements as outputs, we draw that line at the skin.) In describing the Chinese system as a Turing machine, I have drawn the line in such a way that it satisfies a certain type of functional description—one that you *also* satisfy, and one that, according to functionalism, justifies attributions of mentality. Functionalism does not claim that every mental system has a machine table of a sort that justifies attributions of mentality with respect to *every* specification of inputs and outputs, but rather, only with respect to *some* specification.

Objection: The Chinese system would work too slowly. The kind of events and processes with which we normally have contact would pass by far too quickly for the system to detect them. Thus, we would be unable to converse with it, play bridge with it, etc.[3]

Reply: It is hard to see why the system's time scale should matter. What reason is there to believe that *your* mental operations could not be very much slowed down, yet remain mental operations? Is it really contradictory or nonsensical to suppose we could meet a race of intelligent beings with whom we could communicate only by devices such as time-lapse photography. When we observe these creatures, they seem almost inanimate. But when we view the time-lapse movies, we see them conversing with one another. Indeed, we find they are saying that the only way they can make any sense of us is by viewing movies greatly slowed down. To take time scale as all important seems crudely behavioristic. Further, even if the timescale objection is right, I can elude it by retreating to the point that a homunculus-head that works in normal time is *metaphysically* possible, even if not nomologically possible. Metaphysical possibility is all my argument requires.[4]

What makes the homunculi-headed system (count the two systems as variants of a single system) just described a prima facie counterexample to (machine) functionalism is that there is prima facie doubt whether it has any mental states at all—especially whether it has what philosophers have variously called "qualitative states," "raw feels," or "immediate phenomenological qualities." (You ask: What is it that philosophers have called qualitative states? I answer, only half in jest: As Louis Armstrong said when asked what jazz is, "If you got to ask, you ain't never gonna get to know.") In Nagel's terms (1974), there is a prima facie doubt whether there is anything which it is like to be the homunculi-headed system.

The force of the prima facie counterexample can be made clearer as follows: Machine functionalism says that each mental state is identical to a machine-table state. For example, a particular qualitative state, Q, is identical to a machine-table state, S_q. But if there is nothing it is like to be the homunculi-headed system, it cannot be in Q even when it is in S_q. Thus, if there is prima facie doubt about the homunculi-headed system's mentality, there is prima facie doubt that Q = S_q, i.e., doubt that the kind of functionalism under consideration is true.[5] Call this argument the Absent Qualia Argument.

NOTES

1. The converse is also true.

2. State type, not state token. Throughout the chapter, I shall mean by 'physicalism' the doctrine that says each distinct type of mental state is identical to a distinct type of physical state; for example, pain (the universal) is a physical state. Token physicalism, on the other hand, is the (weaker) doctrine that each particular datable pain is a state of some physical type or other. Functionalism shows that type physicalism is false, but it does not show that token physicalism is false.

By 'physicalism,' I mean *first order* physicalism, the doctrine that, e.g., the property of being in pain is a first-order (in the Russell-Whitehead sense) physical property. (A first-order property is one whose definition does not require quantification over properties; a second-order property is one whose definition requires quantification over first-order properties.) The claim that being in pain is a second-order physical property is actually a (physicalist) form of functionalism. See Putnam, 1970.

'Physical property' could be defined for the purposes of this chapter as a property expressed by a predicate of some true physical theory or, more broadly, by a predicate of some true theory of physiology, biology, chemistry, or physics. Of course, such a definition is unsatisfactory without characterizations of these branches of science. See Hempel, 1970 for further discussion of this problem.

3. This point has been raised with me by persons too numerous to mention.

4. One potential difficulty for Functionalism is provided by the possibility that one person may have two radically different Functional descriptions of the sort that justify attribution of mentality. In such a case, Functionalists might have to ascribe two radically different systems of belief, desire, etc., to the same person, or suppose that there is no fact of the matter about what the person's propositional attitudes are. Undoubtedly, Functionalists differ greatly on what they make of this possibility, and the differences reflect positions on such issues as indeterminacy of translation.

5. Shoemaker, 1975, argues (in reply to Block & Fodor, 1972) that absent qualia are logically impossible, that is, that it is logically impossible that two systems be in the same functional state yet one's state have and the other's state lack qualitative content. If Shoemaker is right, it is wrong to doubt whether the homunculi-headed system has qualia. I attempt to show Shoemaker's argument to be fallacious in Block, forthcoming.

REFERENCES

Block, N. Are absent qualia impossible? forthcoming.

Block, N. & Fodor, J. What psychological states are not. *Philosophical Review*, 1972, 81, 159–81.

Chisholm, Roderick. *Perceiving.* Ithaca: Cornell University Press, 1957.

Fodor, J. Explanations in psychology. In M. Black (Ed.), *Philosophy in America.* London: Routledge & Kegan Paul, 1965.

Gendron, B. On the relation of neurological and psychological theories: A critique of the hardware thesis. In R. C. Buck and R. S. Cohen (Eds.), *Boston studies in the philosophy of Science VIII.* Dordrecht: Reidel, 1971.

Hempel, C. Reduction: Ontological and linguistic facets. In S. Morgenbesser, P. Suppes & M. White (Eds.), *Essays in honor of Ernest Nagel.* New York: St. Martin's Press, 1970.

Kalke, W. What is wrong with Fodor and Putnam's functionalism? *Nous*, 1969, 3, 83–93.

Kim, J. Phenomenal properties, psychophysical laws, and the identity theory. *The Monist*, 1972, 56(2), 177–92.

Mucciolo, L. F. The identity thesis and neuropsychology. *Nous*, 1974, 8, 327–42.

Nagel, T. What is it like to be a bat? *Philosophical Review*, 1974, 83, 435–50.

Putnam, H. Brains and behavior. 1963. Reprinted as are all Putnam's articles referred to here (except "On properties") in *Mind, language and reality; philosophical papers*, Vol. 2. London: Cambridge University Press, 1975.

Putnam, H. The mental life of some machines. 1966.

Putnam, H. On properties. In *Mathematics, matter and method; philosophical papers*, Vol. 1. London: Cambridge University Press, 1970.

Shoemaker, S. Functionalism and qualia. *Philosophical studies*, 1975, 27, 271–315.

For Further Reflection

1. Do you think Block's "Chinese nation" argument disproves functionalism? Why or why not?

2. What might a functionalist say in reply to Block?

3. If Block is correct, can a computer ever be built that is conscious (capable of having experiences)?

IV.B   Who Am I? Do We Have Personal Identity?

Suppose you wake up tomorrow in a strange room. There are pictures of unfamiliar people on the light blue walls. The furniture in the room is very odd. You wonder how you got here. You remember being in the hospital where you were dying of cancer. Your body was wasting away, and your death was thought to be a few days away. Dr. Thomas had kindly given you an extra dose of morphine to kill the pain. That's all you can remember. You notice a calendar on the wall in front of you. The date is April 1, 1992. "This can't be," you think, "for yesterday was December 2nd, 1991. Where have I been all this time?" Suddenly, you see a mirror. In horror you reel back, for it's not your body that you spy in the glass, but a large woman's body. You have more than doubled your previous weight and look 20 years older. You feel tired and confused and frightened and start to cry. Soon a strange man, about 45 years of age, comes into your room. "I was wondering when you would waken, Maria. The doctor said that I should let you sleep as long as possible, but I didn't think that you would be asleep two whole days. Anyway, the operation was a success. We had feared that the accident had ended your life. The children and I are so grateful. Juanita and Caesar will be home in an hour and will be so happy to see you awake. How do you feel?"

"Can this be a bad joke?" you wonder. "Who is this strange man and who am I?" Unbeknownst to you, your doctor, Dr. Thomas, needed a living brain to implant in the head of Mrs. Maria Garcia, mother of four children. She had been in a car accident and arrived at the hospital on a ventilator but brain dead. Your brain was in excellent shape but lacked a healthy body. Maria Garcia's body was intact but needed a brain. Being an enterprising brain surgeon, Dr. Thomas saw his chance of performing the first successful brain transplant. Frightened and confused, you wonder if this fate is worse than death. The fact that the operation was a success was of little comfort to you, for you're not sure whether you are *you*!

The problem of personal identity is one of the most fascinating in the history of philosophy. It is especially complicated because it involves not one but three, and possibly four, philosophical questions: (1) What is it to be a person? (2) What is identity? (3) What is personal identity? and (4) How is survival possible given the problems of personal identity? Let us look briefly at the first three questions with reference to the readings in this section of our book. We will discuss the fourth question in the next section of this part.

1. What is it to be a person?
In our first reading, John Locke (1632–1704) says that a person is defined by having a soul, and the criterion of having a soul is the ability to reflect and reason. That is, our ability to introspect and survey our memories and intentions sets us apart from the animals as being of greater value. The view might be challenged by the materialist who says that it is really our brain (or our brain and our body) that defines our personhood; it is the fact that we have a more developed brain that sets us apart from other animals. Of

course, we are conscious beings. Although we do not understand how consciousness works, the physicalist believes that consciousness is a function of the brain.

In our second reading, David Hume (1711–1776) argues that the notion of a self or soul is very likely a fiction. "I" am merely a bundle of perceptions. There is consciousness of a continuing succession of experiences, but not of a continuing experiencer. This view is compatible with the physicalist view of personhood.

The bundle theory of self or soul that Hume embraces was long ago anticipated by Buddhism, which teaches that the notion of a continuing self is an illusion that is responsible for all the evils of the world. There is no unified self that has experiences; there is only awareness of a fleeting succession of perceptions and feelings (Reading IV.45).

2. What is identity?

This sounds like an absurdly simple question. Identity is the fact that everything is itself and not another. In logic, the Law of Identity (A = A) formally states the definition of identity. But we are not interested in a formal definition of mere identity but identity *over time,* or *reidentification* (sometimes this is referred to as "numerical identity"). What is it to be the *same* thing over time? Suppose that you go to an automobile dealership to buy a new car. You see several blue Fords parked side by side. They resemble each other so much that you cannot tell them apart. They are the same type of car and are exactly similar to each other. Suppose you pick one out at random and buy it. Your car is a different car than the other blue Fords even though you couldn't tell the difference between them. A year passes and your blue Ford now has 20,000 miles on it and a few scratches. Is it the same car that you originally bought? Most of us would probably agree that it is. The changes have altered it but not destroyed its identity as the blue car that you bought and have driven 20,000 miles.

What does your blue Ford have that causes it to be the same car over the period of one year? A common history, continuity over time. The car is linked by a succession of spatial-temporal events from its origins in Detroit to its present place in your parking lot. This distinguishes it from all the other Fords that were ever built, no matter how similar they appear. So we might conclude that *continuity over time* is the criterion of identity.

But immediately we find problems with this criterion. The Rio Grande dries up in places in New Mexico every summer, only to reappear as a running river in the early spring. Is the Rio Grande the same river this year as it was the last? There isn't any continuity over time of water flowing over the riverbed. Perhaps we can escape the problem by saying that by "river" we really mean the riverbed, which must hold running water sometimes but need not always convey it. Does this solve the problem?

Consider another counterexample: The Chicago White Sox are playing the New York Yankees in Yankee Stadium in late April. The game is called in the fifth inning with the Yankees leading 3–2. Shortly afterwards there is a baseball strike and all the players take to the picket lines while a new set of players come up from the minor leagues to fill their positions. The "game" is continued in Chicago in August with a whole new set of players on both sides. The White Sox win, and the game decides who wins the division. Suppose a Yankee player who has studied some philosophy argues that this latter game was not part of the original game played in April. There was no *continuity* between them. He demands that a new game be played from the start since it is impossible to play the same game as was played four months ago or even four days ago. Would he have a point? Should the commissioner of baseball call for a make-up game?

The most perplexing problem regarding the notion of "sameness" or identity over time is illustrated by the ancient tale of Theseus' ship. Suppose you have a small ship that is in need of some repairs. You begin (at time t) to replace the old planks and material with new planks and material until after one year (time t_1) the ship is completely composed of different material. Do you have the same ship at t_1 as you had at t? If so, at what point did it (call it *Theseus 2*) become a different ship?

People disagree whether Theseus' ship has changed its identity. Suppose that you argue that it has not changed its identity, for it had a continuous history over time and therefore is the same ship. But now suppose that your friend takes the material discarded from the original *Theseus* and reconstructs "that" ship (call it *Theseus 3*). Which ship is now Theseus' ship? There is continuity of the ship between *Theseus 1* and *2* but continuity of material between *Theseus 1* and *3*. If it worries you that there was a time when the material of *Theseus 1* was not functioning as a ship, we could alter the example and suppose that as the planks were taken from *Theseus 1*, they were transformed to another ship, *Argos,* where they replaced the *Argos'* planks, ending up with a ship that contained every board and nail from the original *Theseus* (call this transformed *Argos, Theseus 4*). Which is now the original *Theseus*?

Does there seem something peculiar about the notion of identity?

3. What is personal identity?

What is it to be the same person over time? Are you the same person that you were when you were one year old or even sixteen years old? We recall Locke's idea of personhood. The mental characteristics (ability to reflect or introspect) constituted personhood. Personal identity was indicated by the successive memories that the person had, the continuity over time of a set of experiences which were remembered. We can call this the *psychological states criterion of personal identity*. The main competitor of this view is the *brain criterion*, though some philosophers hold to a *body criterion*. Let us examine each of these briefly.

The psychological states criterion holds that our memories constitute our identity over time. You are the same person you were at ten years of age because you have a continuous set of memories that contains all those that you had at ten plus others that continued after that year. There are several problems with this view. In the first place, our memories are not continuous in our consciousness. When we sleep, we cease to have memories at all. In partial amnesia, do we cease to be who we were? Thomas Reid suggests a problem of transitivity in memories. Suppose there is a gallant officer who at age twenty-five is a hero in a battle and who remembers getting a flogging in his childhood. Later, at age sixty-five, he recalls the heroic deed done at twenty-five but cannot recall the flogging. Since he cannot remember the earlier deed, is he the same person he was when he did remember it? Can Locke answer Reid?

What about the phenomenon of split personalities and multiple personalities—the most famous of which is Sybil, who allegedly expressed sixteen different personalities with sixteen different sets of memories? On a psychological states account, would we have to say that one body contains sixteen persons? Are there different persons inside each of us, expressed by different "sides" of our personalities?

Sometimes a person expresses apparent memories of events that occurred in distant times and to different "persons." Is the body of the contemporary being possessed by another person? If your friend suddenly starts reminiscing about the Battle of Waterloo and the beautiful Empress Josephine, has Napoleon suddenly come alive in your friend's body? This would truly be a case of reincarnation. But what if two of your friends came to you with the same "foreign" memories? And what is to prohibit complete soul flow, a different person inside you each day? How do you know that the soul that is remembering today is the same soul that remembered yesterday? You might object that this couldn't be the case because you have the same body, but that objection won't work since the body has nothing to do with the psychological states criterion. If you think that the body is important, this might be an indication that the memory criterion is inadequate on its own and depends on a physical body for continuity.

The body criterion has difficulties, one of which is the fact that the body can undergo radical changes and we would still want to call the person the same person. Almost all of the cells of our body change every seven years. Do we become a new person every seven years? Or think of the story at the beginning of this section in which Dr. Thomas transplants your brain into Maria Garcia's body. Wouldn't you still be you?

This suggests the third criterion, the brain criterion of personal identity. Our memories are contained within our brains, so we might want to say that having the same brain constitutes the same person. But this has difficulties. It is well known that if the corpus callosum, the great band of fibers that unites the two hemispheres of the brain, is cut, two different centers of consciousness can be created. When either side of the brain's cerebral cortex is destroyed, the person can live on as a conscious being. It is also possible in principle to transplant brains. Suppose that your body is destroyed and neurologists transplant each half of your brain into a different body. Dr. Thomas transplants one half of your brain into Maria Garcia and the other half into the head of Kareem Abdul Jabbar's look-alike. "You" wake up with two personalities. Do you survive the operation? There seem to be just three possible answers: (1) you do not survive; (2) you survive as one of the two; and (3) you survive as two people.

All these options seem unsatisfactory. It seems absurd to say (1) that you don't survive, for there is continuity of consciousness (in the Lockean sense) as though you had gone to sleep and awakened. If you had experienced the destruction of one half of your brain, we would still say you survived with half a brain, so why not say so now when each half is autonomous? The logic of this thesis would seem to say that double life equals death.

But (2) seems arbitrary. Why say that you only survive as one of the two, and which one is it? And (3) that you survive as both is not satisfactory either since it gives up the notion of identity. You cannot be numerically one with two centers of consciousness and two spatial-temporal bodies. Otherwise we might say when we wreck our new

Ford that the other one left in the automobile dealer's parking lot (the blue Ford which was exactly like yours) was indeed yours.

If this is an accurate analysis of the personal identity problem, what sense can we make of the concept? Some say we should speak of survival of the person, not the identity of the person. Persons, as psychological states, survive and gradually merge (like Theseus' rebuilt ship) into descendent persons. Your memories and personality gradually emerged from the sixteen-year-old who gradually developed from the ten-year-old who bore your name. These were your ancestor selves. But you too will merge with future or descendent selves as you have different experiences, take on new memories, and forget old ones. Suppose every year neurologists could transplant half of your brain into another body, in which a new half would duplicate the present state of the transferred half. In this way a tree-like operation would continue to spread successors of yourself as though by psychological parthenogenesis. You would survive in a sense, but it would make no sense to speak of personal identity. We could also imagine a neurological game of musical hemispheres as half of your brain was merged with half of someone else's brain in a third person's head. You could continue the hemisphere-moving game every six months so that you might even get re-merged with your own other half at some future time—kind of like meeting your spouse again after other adventures. You'd have a lot to talk about through the medium of the corpus callosum!

If identity is relative, then we might be less interested in our long-term future than our immediate future. After all, that person ten years down the line is less like us than the person we'll be tomorrow. This might encourage a sort of general utilitarianism—since our distant interests really are not as pressing, we would be free to work for the total greater good. On the other hand, it could have the opposite effect of making us indifferent to the future of society. This notion of proximate identity also raises the question of whether we should be concerned about our distant death fifty years down the line that one of our successor selves will have to face. This view might also cause us to prohibit long-term prison sentences for criminal actions, for why punish a descendent for what one of his or her ancestors did? Finally, it could be used to argue against exorbitant awards in malpractice litigation. Often a jury is asked to award a sum of money (as high as $12 million) to a severely retarded child whose damage has been incurred through medical malpractice. The justification for the large sum is the expectation that the child could have become, for example, a physician or lawyer and made an enormous sum of money in his or her lifetime. But if we were to take the notion of proximate identity seriously, we could only sue the physician for the damages done to the immediate person, not to his or her descendent selves.

What is the truth about personal identity? Are you the same person that you were at sixteen? And will you be still the same person at sixty?

Our Psychological Properties Define the Self   IV.44

JOHN LOCKE

In this selection Locke sets forth his psychological state theory of personal identity, locating the criterion of personal identity in terms of consciousness, especially memory. The soul or essence of the person, defined as a reflective being, could take on different bodily forms and still preserve the same identity.

(A biographical sketch of Locke precedes Reading I.3.)

Study Questions

1. What is Locke's definition of a person?
2. In what does personal identity consist?
3. Is it necessary that consciousness be the same identical substance?
4. Can we be the same persons though we have different bodies?
5. How is Locke's view relevant to the question of life after death?
6. What is the lesson of the story of the prince and the cobbler?

. . . IF THE IDENTITY OF *soul alone* makes the same *man*, and there be nothing in the nature of matter why the same individual spirit may not be united to different bodies, it will be possible that those men, living in distant ages, and of different tempers, may have been the same man: which way of speaking must be from a very strange use of the word man, applied to an idea out of which body and shape are excluded. . . .

An animal is a living organized body; and consequently the same animal, as we have observed, is the same continued *life* communicated to different particles of matter, as they happen successively to be united to that organized living body. And whatever is talked of other definitions, ingenious observation puts it past doubt, that the idea in our minds, of which the sound "man" in our mouths is the sign, is nothing else but of an animal of such a certain form. . . .

I presume it is not the idea of a thinking or rational being alone that makes the *idea of a man* in most people's sense: but of a body, so and so shaped, joined to it; and if that be the idea of a man, the same successive body not shifted all at once, must, as well as the same immaterial spirit, go to the making of the same man.

This being premised, to find wherein personal identity consists, we must consider what *person* stands for—which, I think, is a thinking intelligent being, that has reason and reflection, and can consider itself as itself, the same thinking thing, in different times and places; which it does only by that consciousness which is inseparable from thinking, and, as it seems to me, essential to it: it being impossible for any one to perceive without

From *John Locke*, An Essay Concerning Human Understanding, *Book II, Chapter 27, "Of Ideas of Identity and Diversity." First published in 1690.*

perceiving that he does perceive. When we see, hear, smell, taste, feel, meditate, or will anything, we know that we do so. Thus it is always as to our present sensations and perceptions: and by this every one is to himself that which he calls self—it not being considered, in this case, whether the same self be continued in the same or divers substances. For, since consciousness always accompanies thinking, and it is that which makes every one to be what he calls self, and thereby distinguishes himself from all other thinking things, in this alone consists personal identity, i.e., the sameness of a rational being: and as far as this consciousness can be extended backwards to any past action or thought, so far reaches the identity of that person; it is the same self now it was then; and it is by the same self with this present one that now reflects on it, that that action was done.

But it is further inquired, whether it be the same identical substance. This few would think they had reason to doubt of, if these perceptions, with their consciousness, always remained present in the mind, whereby the same thinking thing would be always consciously present, and, as would be thought, evidently the same to itself. But that which seems to make the difficulty is this, that this consciousness being interrupted always by forgetfulness, there being no moment of our lives wherein we have the whole train of all our past actions before our eyes in one view, but even the best memories losing the sight of one part whilst they are viewing another; and we sometimes, and that the greatest part of our lives, not reflecting on our past selves, being intent on our present thoughts, and in sound sleep having no thoughts at all, or at least none with that consciousness which remarks our waking thoughts— I say, in all these cases, our consciousness being interrupted, and we losing the sight of our past selves, doubts are raised whether we are the same thinking thing, i.e., the same *substance* or no. Which, however reasonable or unreasonable, concerns not *personal* identity at all. The question being what makes the same person; and not whether it be the same identical substance, which always thinks in the same person, which, in this case, matters not at all: different substances, by the same consciousness (where they do partake in it) being united into one person, as well as different bodies by the same life are united into one animal, whose identity is perceived in that change of substances by the unity of one continued life. For, it being the same consciousness that makes a man be himself to himself, personal identity depends on that only, whether it be annexed solely to one individual substance, or can be continued in a succession of several substances. For as far as any intelligent being *can* repeat the idea of any past action with the same consciousness it had of it at first, and with the same consciousness it has of any present action; so far it is the same personal self. For it is by the consciousness it has of its present thoughts and actions, that it is *self to itself* now, and so will be the same self, as far as the same consciousness can extend to actions past or to come; and would be by distance of time, or change of substance, no more two persons, than a man be two men by wearing other clothes today than he did yesterday, with a long or a short sleep between: the same consciousness uniting those distant actions in the same person, whatever substances contributed to their production.

That this is so, we have some kind of evidence in our very bodies, all whose particles, whilst vitally united to this same thinking conscious self, so that *we feel* when they are touched, and are affected by, and conscious of good or harm that happens to them, are a part of ourselves; i.e., of our thinking conscious self. Thus, the limbs of his body are to every one a part of himself; he sympathizes and is concerned for them. Cut off a hand, and thereby separate it from that consciousness he had of its heat, cold, and other affections, and it is then no longer a part of that which is himself, any more than the remotest part of matter. Thus, we see the *substance* whereof personal self consisted at one time may be varied at another, without the change of personal identity; there being no question about the same person, though the limbs which but now were a part of it, be cut off. . . .

And thus may we be able, without any difficulty, to conceive the same person at the resurrection, though in a body not exactly in make or parts the same which he had here,—the same consciousness going along with the soul that inhabits it. But yet the soul alone, in the change of bodies, would scarce to any one but to him that makes the soul the man, be enough to make the same man. For should the soul of a prince, carrying with it the consciousness of the prince's past life, enter and inform the body of a cobbler, as soon as deserted by his own soul, every one sees he would be the same *person* with the prince, accountable only for the prince's actions: but who would say it was the same *man*? The body too goes to the making the man, and would, I guess, to everybody determine the man in this case, wherein the soul, with all its princely thoughts about it, would not make another man: but he would be the same cobbler to every one besides himself. I know that, in the ordinary way of speaking, the same person, and the same man, stand for one and the same thing. And indeed every one will always have a liberty to speak as he pleases, and to apply what articulate sounds to what ideas he thinks fit, and change them as often as he pleases. But yet, when we will inquire what makes the same *spirit, man,* or *person,* we must fix the ideas of spirit, man, or person in our minds; and having resolved with ourselves what we mean by them, it will not be hard to determine in either of them, or the like, when it is the same, and when not.

But though the immaterial substance or soul does not alone, wherever it be, and in whatsoever state, make the same *man;* yet it is plain, consciousness, as far as ever it can be extended—should it be to ages past—unites existences and actions very remote in time into the same *person,* as well as it does the existences and actions of the immediately preceding moment: so that whatever has the consciousness of present and past actions, is the same person to whom they both

belong. Had I the same consciousness that I saw the ark and Noah's flood, as that I saw an overflowing of the Thames last winter, or as that I write now, I could no more doubt that I who write this now, that saw the Thames overflowed last winter, and that viewed the flood at the general deluge, was the same *self*—place that self in what *substance* you please—than that I who write this am the same *myself* now whilst I write (whether I consist of all the same substance, material or immaterial, or no) that I was yesterday. For as to this point of being the same self, it matters not whether this present self be made up of the same or other substances—I being as much concerned, and as justly accountable for any action that was done a thousand years since, appropriated to me now by this self-consciousness, as I am for what I did the last moment. . . .

But yet possibly it will still be objected—Suppose I wholly lose the memory of some parts of my life, beyond a possibility of retrieving them, so that perhaps I shall never be conscious of them again; yet am I not the same person that did those actions, had those thoughts that I once was conscious of, though I have now forgot them? To which I answer, that we must here take notice what the word *I* is applied to; which, in this case, is the *man* only. And the same man being presumed to be the same person, *I* is easily here supposed to stand also for the same person. But if it be possible for the same man to have distinct incommunicable consciousness at different times, it is past doubt the same man would at different times make different persons; which, we see, is the sense of mankind in the solemnest declaration of their opinions, human laws not punishing the mad man for the sober man's actions, nor the sober man for what the mad man did,—thereby making them two persons: which is somewhat explained by our way of speaking in English when we say such an one is "not himself," or is "beside himself"; in which phrases it is insinuated, as if those who now, or at least first used them, thought that self was changed; the selfsame person was no longer in that man.

But yet it is hard to conceive that Socrates, the same individual man, should be two persons. To help us a little in this, we must consider what is meant by Socrates, or the same individual *man*.

First, it must be either the same individual, immaterial, thinking substance; in short, the same numerical soul, and nothing else.

Secondly, or the same animal, without any regard to the immaterial soul.

Thirdly, or the same immaterial spirit united to the same animal.

Now, take which of these suppositions you please, it is impossible to make personal identity to consist in anything but consciousness; or reach any further than that does.

For Further Reflection

1. How would Locke respond to the objection that memories are not continuous in our consciousness? When we sleep, we cease to have memories at all. In partial amnesia do we cease to be who we were? Recall Thomas Reid's suggestion in the introduction to IV.B, of the problem of transitivity in memories. Suppose there is a gallant officer who at age twenty-five is a hero in a battle and who remembers getting a flogging in his childhood. Later, at age sixty-five, he recalls the heroic deed done at twenty-five but cannot recall the flogging. Since he cannot remember the earlier deed, is he the same person he was when he did remember it? Can Locke answer Reid?

2. What about the phenomenon of split personalities and multiple personalities, also discussed in the introduction to this section, the most famous of which is Sybil, who allegedly expressed sixteen different personalities with sixteen different sets of memories? On a psychological states account, would we have to say that one body contains sixteen persons? Are there different persons inside each of us, expressed by different "sides" of our personalities?

We Have No Substantial Self with Which We Are Identical

IV.45

DAVID HUME

Hume does not believe that we have a self. For Hume, you might recall from Reading III.26, all learning comes from sensory impressions. There does not seem to be a separate impression of the self which we experience, so there is no reason to believe that we have a self. The most we can identify ourselves with is our consciousness and that constantly changes. There is no separate, permanent self which endures over time. Hence, personal identity is a fiction.

(A biographical sketch of Hume precedes Reading II.9.)

Study Questions

1. What does Hume mean by saying that the self is not any one impression, and what significance does this have for him?
2. What does Hume say of people who differ with him?
3. What is the "self"?
4. What does Hume say about the problem of identity?

THERE ARE SOME PHILOSOPHERS, who imagine we are every moment intimately conscious of what we call our Self; that we feel its existence and its continuance in existence; and are certain, beyond the evidence of a demonstration, both of its perfect identity and simplicity. . . .

Unluckily all these positive assertions are contrary to that very experience, which is pleaded for them, nor have we any idea of *self,* after the manner it is here explained. For from what impression could this idea be derived? This question 'tis impossible to answer without a manifest contradiction and absurdity; and yet 'tis a question, which must necessarily be answered, if we would have the idea of self pass for clear and intelligible. It must be some one impression, that gives rise to every real idea. But self or person is not any one

impression, but that to which our several impressions and ideas are supposed to have a reference. If any impression gives rise to the idea of self, that impression must continue invariably the same, through the whole course of our lives; since self is supposed to exist after that manner. But there is no impression constant and invariable. Pain and pleasure, grief and joy, passions and sensations succeed each other, and never all exist at the same time. It cannot, therefore, be from any of these impressions, or from any other, that the idea of self is derived; and consequently there is no such idea.

But farther, what must become of all our particular perceptions upon this hypothesis? All these are different, and distinguishable, and separable from each other, and may be separately

From *David Hume,* A Treatise of Human Nature. *First published in England in 1738.*

considered, and may exist separately, and have no need of any thing to support their existence. After what manner, therefore, do they belong to self; and how are they connected with it? For my part, when I enter most intimately into what I call *myself*, I always stumble on some particular perception or other, of heat or cold, light or shade, love or hatred, pain or pleasure. I never can catch *myself* at any time without a perception, and never can observe any thing but the perception. When my perceptions are removed for any time, as by sound sleep; so long am I insensible of *myself*, and may truly be said not to exist. And were all my perceptions removed by death, and could I neither think, nor feel, nor see, nor love, nor hate after the dissolution of my body, I should be entirely annihilated, nor do I conceive what is farther requisite to make me a perfect nonentity. If any one upon serious and unprejudiced reflection, thinks he has a different notion of *himself*, I must confess I can reason no longer with him. All I can allow him is, that he may be in the right as well as I, and that we are essentially different in this particular. He may, perhaps, perceive something simple and continued, which he calls *himself*; though I am certain there is no such principle in me.

But setting aside some metaphysicians of this kind, I may venture to affirm of the rest of mankind, that they are nothing but a bundle or collection of different perceptions, which succeed each other with an inconceivable rapidity, and are in a perpetual flux and movement. Our eyes cannot turn in their sockets without varying our perceptions. Our thought is still more variable than our sight; and all our other senses and faculties contribute to this change; nor is there any single power of the soul, which remains unalterably the same, perhaps for one moment. The mind is a kind of theatre, where several perceptions successively make their appearance; pass, re-pass, glide away, and mingle in an infinite variety of postures and situations. There is properly no *simplicity* in it at one time, nor *identity* in different; whatever natural propension we may have to imagine that

simplicity and identity. The comparison of the theatre must not mislead us. They are the successive perceptions only, that constitute the mind; nor have we the most distant notion of the place, where these scenes are represented, or of the materials, of which it is composed.

What then gives us so great a propension to ascribe an identity to these successive perceptions, and to suppose ourselves possessed of an invariable and uninterrupted existence through the whole course of our lives? . . .

We have a distinct idea of an object, that remains invariable and uninterrupted through a supposed variation of time; and this idea we call that of *identity* or *sameness*. We have also a distinct idea of several different objects existing in succession, and connected together by a close relation; and this to an accurate view affords as perfect a notion of *diversity*, as if there was no manner of relation among the objects. But though these two ideas of identity, and a succession of related objects be in themselves perfectly distinct, and even contrary, yet 'tis certain, that in our common way of thinking they are generally confounded with each other. That action of the imagination, by which we consider the uninterrupted and invariable object, and that by which we reflect on the succession of related objects, are almost the same to the feeling, nor is there much more effort of thought required in the latter case than in the former. The relation facilitates the transition of the mind from one object to another, and renders its passage as smooth as if it contemplated one continued object. This resemblance is the cause of the confusion and mistake, and makes us substitute the notion of identity, instead of that of related objects. . . .

Thus we feign the continued existence of the perceptions of our senses, to remove the interruption; and run into the notion of a *soul*, and *self*, and *substance*, to disguise the variation. But we may farther observe, that where we do not give rise to such a fiction, our propension to confound identity with relation is so great, that we are apt to imagine something unknown and mysterious, connecting the parts, beside their relation; and this I take to be the case with regard to the identity we ascribe to plants and vegetables. And even when this does not take place, we still feel a propensity to confound these ideas, though we are not able fully to satisfy ourselves in that particular, nor find any thing invariable and uninterrupted to justify our notion of identity.

Thus the controversy concerning identity is not merely a dispute of words. For when we attribute identity, in an improper sense, to variable or interrupted objects, our mistake is not confined to the expression, but is commonly attended with a fiction, either of something invariable and uninterrupted, or of something mysterious and inexplicable, or at least with a propensity to such fictions. What will suffice to prove this hypothesis to the satisfaction of every fair enquirer, is to show from daily experience and observation, that the objects, which are variable or interrupted, and yet are supposed to continue the same, are such only as consist of a succession of parts, connected together by resemblance, contiguity, or causation. . . .

A ship, of which a considerable part has been changed by frequent reparations, is still considered as the same; nor does the difference of the materials hinder us from ascribing an identity to it. The common end, in which the parts conspire, is the same under all their variations, and affords an easy transition of the imagination from one situation of the body to another. . . .

Though every one must allow, that in a very few years both vegetables and animals endure a *total* change, yet we still attribute identity to them, while their form, size, and substance are entirely altered. An oak, that grows from a small plant to a large tree, is still the same oak; though there be not one particle of matter, or figure of its parts the same. An infant becomes a man, and is sometimes fat, sometimes lean, without any change in his identity. . . . A man, who hears a noise, that is frequently interrupted and renewed, says, it is still the same noise; though 'tis evident the sounds have only a specific identity or resemblance, and there is nothing numerically the same, but the cause, which produced them. In like manner it may be said without breach of the propriety of language, that such a church, which was formerly of brick, fell to ruin, and that the parish rebuilt the same church of free-stone, and according to modern architecture. Here neither the form nor materials are the same, nor is there any thing common to the two objects, but their relation to the inhabitants of the parish; and yet this alone is sufficient to make us denominate them the same. . . .

From thence it evidently follows, that identity is nothing really belonging to these different perceptions, and uniting them together; but is merely a quality, which we attribute to them, because of the union of their ideas in the imagination, when we reflect upon them. . . .

The only question, therefore, which remains, is, by what relations this uninterrupted progress of our thought is produced, when we consider the successive existence of a mind or thinking person. And here 'tis evident we must confine ourselves to resemblance and causation. . . . Also, as memory alone acquaints us with the continuance and extent of this succession of perceptions, 'tis to be considered, upon that account chiefly, as the source of personal identity. Had we no memory, we never should have any notion of causation, nor consequently of that chain of causes and effects, which constitute our self or person.

For Further Reflection

Kant criticized Hume for reducing the mind to a stream of consciousness. The fact to be explained, says Kant, is not the succession of awarenesses, but an awareness of succession. If that which is aware passed with the awareness, there would be no awareness of succession, but it *doesn't* pass with it. This suggests that there is a transcendent self beyond the stream of consciousness of which Hume speaks. What do you make of this as an objection to Hume?

IV.46   Questions to King Milinda

BUDDHIST SCRIPTURE

The bundle theory of the self is central to Buddhism; it is the doctrine of no soul, or *anatman*. In this reading from Buddhist writings, King Milinda (160–135 B.C.) is discussing with the Buddhist monk Nāgasena the properties of the self and of physical objects. The central point is that the apparent unity of the self, or ego, is an illusion devised by the mind, just as the apparent stability of objects is a trick of consciousness.

Study Questions

1. How does Nāgasena argue that the soul or ego is an illusion?
2. How does Nāgasena apply the metaphor of the chariot to the case of the soul?
3. Does Nāgasena believe in life after death—that is, a unified consciousness that persists before and after the death of the body?

§ 15. THERE IS NO EGO

Then drew near Milinda the king to where the venerable Nāgasena was; and having drawn near, he greeted the venerable Nāgasena; and having passed the compliments of friendship and civility, he sat down respectfully at one side. And the venerable Nāgasena returned the greeting; by which, verily, he won the heart of king Milinda.

And Milinda the king spoke to the venerable Nāgasena as follows:—

"How is your reverence called? Bhante, what is your name?"

"Your majesty, I am called Nāgasena; my fellow-priests, your majesty, address me as Nāgasena: but whether parents give one the name Nāgasena, or Sūrasena, or Vīrasena, or Sīhasena, it is, nevertheless, your majesty, but a way of counting, a term, an appellation, a convenient designation, a mere name, this Nāgasena; for there is no Ego here to be found."

Then said Milinda the king,—

"Listen to me, my lords, ye five hundred Yonakas, and ye eighty thousand priests! Nāgasena here says thus: 'There is no Ego here to be found.' Is it possible, pray, for me to assent to what he says?"

And Milinda the king spoke to the venerable Nāgasena as follows:—

"Bhante Nāgasena, if there is no Ego to be found, who is it then furnishes you priests with the priestly requisites,—robes, food, bedding, and medicine, the reliance of the sick? who is it makes use of the same? who is it keeps the precepts? who is it applies himself to meditation? who is it realizes the Paths, the Fruits, and Nirvana? who is it destroys life? who is it takes what is not given him? who is it commits immorality? who is it tells lies? who is it drinks intoxicating liquor? who is it commits the five crimes that constitute 'proximate karma'?[1] In that case, there is no merit; there is no demerit; there is no one who does or causes to be done meritorious or demeritorious deeds; neither good nor evil deeds can have any fruit or result. Bhante Nāgasena, neither is he a murderer who kills a priest, nor can you priests, bhante Nāgasena, have any teacher, preceptor, or ordination. When you say, 'My fellow-priests, your majesty, address me as Nāgasena,' what then is this Nāgasena? Pray, bhante, is the hair of the head Nāgasena?"

"Nay, verily, your majesty."

"Is the hair of the body Nāgasena?"

"Nay, verily, your majesty."

"Are nails . . . teeth . . . skin . . . flesh . . . sinews . . . bones . . . marrow of the bones . . . kidneys . . . heart . . . liver . . . pleura . . . spleen . . . lungs . . . intestines . . . mesentery . . . stomach . . . faeces . . . bile . . . phlegm . . . pus . . . blood . . . sweat . . . fat . . . tears . . . lymph . . . saliva . . . snot . . . synovial fluid . . . urine . . . brain of the head Nāgasena?"

"Nay, verily, your majesty."

"Is now, bhante, form Nāgasena?"

"Nay, verily, your majesty."

"Is sensation Nāgasena?"

"Nay, verily, your majesty."

"Is perception Nāgasena?"

"Nay, verily, your majesty."

"Are the predispositions Nāgasena?"

"Nay, verily, your majesty."

"Is consciousness Nāgasena?"

"Nay, verily, your majesty."

"Are, then, bhante, form, sensation, perception, the predispositions, and consciousness unitedly Nāgasena?"

"Nay, verily, your majesty."

"Is it, then, bhante, something besides form, sensation, perception, the predispositions, and consciousness, which is Nāgasena?"

"Nay, verily, your majesty."

"Bhante, although I question you very closely, I fail to discover any Nāgasena. Verily, now, bhante, Nāgasena is a mere empty sound. What Nāgasena is there here? Bhante, you speak a falsehood, a lie: there is no Nāgasena."

Then the venerable Nāgasena spoke to Milinda the king as follows:—

"Your majesty, you are a delicate prince, an exceedingly delicate prince; and if, your majesty, you walk in the middle of the day on hot sandy ground, and you tread on rough grit, gravel, and sand, your feet become sore, your body tired, the mind is oppressed, and the body-consciousness suffers. Pray, did you come afoot, or riding?"

"Bhante, I do not go afoot: I came in a chariot."

"Your majesty, if you came in a chariot, declare to me the chariot. Pray, your majesty, is the pole the chariot?"

"Nay, verily, bhante."

"Is the axle the chariot?"

"Nay, verily, bhante."

"Are the wheels the chariot?"

"Nay, verily, bhante."

"Is the chariot-body the chariot?"

"Nay, verily, bhante."

"Is the banner-staff the chariot?"

"Nay, verily, bhante."

"Is the yoke the chariot?"

"Nay, verily, bhante."

"Are the reins the chariot?"

"Nay, verily, bhante."

"Is the goading-stick the chariot?"

"Nay, verily, bhante."

"Pray, your majesty, are pole, axle, wheels, chariot-body, banner-staff, yoke, reins, and goad unitedly the chariot?"

"Nay, verily, bhante."

"Is it, then, your majesty, something else besides pole, axle, wheels, chariot-body, banner-staff, yoke, reins, and goad which is the chariot?"

"Nay, verily, bhante."

"Your majesty, although I question you very closely, I fail to discover any chariot. Verily now, your majesty, the word chariot is a mere empty sound. What chariot is there here? Your majesty, you speak a falsehood, a lie: there is no chariot. Your majesty, you are the chief king in all the continent of India; of whom are you afraid that you speak a lie? Listen to me, my lords, ye five hundred Yonakas, and ye eighty thousand priests! Milinda the king here says thus: 'I came in a chariot;' and being requested, 'Your majesty, if you came in a chariot, declare to me the chariot,' he fails to produce any chariot. Is it possible, pray, for me to assent to what he says?"

When he had thus spoken, the five hundred Yonakas applauded the venerable Nāgasena and spoke to Milinda the king as follows:—

"Now, your majesty, answer, if you can."

Then Milinda the king spoke to the venerable Nāgasena as follows:—

"Bhante Nāgasena, I speak no lie: the word 'chariot' is but a way of counting, term, appellation, convenient designation, and name for pole, axle, wheels, chariot-body, and banner-staff."

"Thoroughly well, your majesty, do you understand a chariot. In exactly the same way, your majesty, in respect of me, Nāgasena is but a way of counting, term, appellation, convenient designation, mere name for the hair of my head, hair of my body...brain of the head, form, sensation, perception, the predispositions, and consciousness. But in the absolute sense there is no Ego here to be found. And the priestess Vajirā, your majesty, said as follows in the presence of The Blessed One:—

" 'Even as the word of "chariot" means
That members join to frame a whole;
So when the Groups appear to view,
We use the phrase, "A living being.2" ' "

"It is wonderful, bhante Nāgasena! It is marvellous, bhante Nāgasena! Brilliant and prompt is the wit of your replies. If The Buddha were alive, he would applaud. Well done, well done, Nāgasena! Brilliant and prompt is the wit of your replies."

§ 15b.—Translated from the Visuddhi-Magga (chap. xviii.)

Just as the word "chariot" is but a mode of expression for axle, wheels, chariot-body, pole,

and other constituent members, placed in a certain relation to each other, but when we come to examine the members one by one, we discover that in the absolute sense there is no chariot; and just as the word "house" is but a mode of expression for wood and other constituents of a house, surrounding space in a certain relation, but in the absolute sense there is no house; and just as the word "fist" is but a mode of expression for the fingers, the thumb, etc., in a certain relation; and the word "lute" for the body of the lute, strings, etc.; "army" for elephants, horses, etc.; "city" for fortifications, houses, gates, etc.; "tree" for trunk, branches, foliage, etc., in a certain relation, but when we come to examine the parts one by one, we discover that in the absolute sense there is no tree; in exactly the same way the words "living entity" and "Ego" are but a mode of expression for the presence of the five attachment groups, but when we come to examine the elements of being one by one, we discover that in the absolute sense there is no living entity there to form a basis for such figments as "I am," or "I"; in other words, that in the absolute sense there is only name and form. The insight of him who perceives this is called knowledge of the truth.

NOTES

1. Translated from the Sārasaṅgaha, as quoted in Trenckner's note to this passage: "By proximate karma is meant karma that ripens in the next existence. To show what this is, I [the author of the Sārasaṅgaha] give the following passage from the Atthānasutta of the first book of the Aṅguttara-Nikāya:—'It is an impossibility, O priests, the case can never occur, that an individual imbued with the correct doctrine should deprive his mother of life, should deprive his father of life, should deprive a saint of life, should in a revengeful spirit cause a bloody wound to a Tathāgata, should cause a schism in the church. This is an impossibility.' "

2. That is, "a living entity."

For Further Reflection

  1. How do Hume and Nāgasena differ in how they argue for the bundle theory of self?
  2. Do you accept the bundle theory? Why or why not?
  3. How does the bundle theory differ from Descartes' view of the mind or soul as a continuing substance? Which theory do you think is correct? Why?

IV.C   Is There Life After Death? Am I Immortal?

Suppose the ingenious neurologist Dr. Thomas were to design a brain just like yours in his laboratory, and suppose he were to design a body like yours but virtually indestructible (well, a nuclear bomb could destroy it, but failing that it would be impervious to alteration). The brain is now dormant, but at your death, Dr. Thomas will activate it and bring it to life within the prosthetic body. Now Thomas tells you that he needs to kill you to allow your alter ego to exist. You complain, but Thomas assures you that one exactly similar to you will live again with all your memories (or copies of them, but Alter Ego won't know the difference). Would you be comforted by that news? Would you take comfort in the fact that you will live again?

Where does all of this leave us with regard to survival after death? If there is no continuity of consciousness, is it the same person who would be resurrected or reconstituted by God at some future time? Or is the reconstituted person like Thomas' replica of you? A different token of the same generic type? Could God make several tokens of your type—say, five of you—that could be reconstituted and go on to live a new and eternal life? Quintuple resurrection!

Are the disembodied memories of a person enough to constitute survival? The question is perplexing. On the one hand, it seems that our identity is somehow tied to our psychological states (for example, memories and personality traits), which don't seem to depend on a body. But, then, if this is so, would our survival occur if a computer stored much of the information about our personalities and memory states?

We do seem to need a body and brain to instantiate our consciousness and personalities. It is hard to imagine any learning or experiencing or communication with others without a recognizable body. And the brain seems to be the locus of conscious experience. But our bodies and brains die and disintegrate. What happens to our consciousness and our personal identity? Is the gap between the present conscious life and the next simply like a long sleep during which God prepares a new and glorified body for our personality? Or does the fact that there will have to be a new creation rule out the possibility of personal survival altogether? Or can it be that there is an intrinsically spiritual character to our selves that both survives the death of the body and perdures in a life beyond this one?

The issue is as difficult as it is important to us. In this section, our first reading from Plato's *Phaedo* sets forth a view of the soul that is separate and of infinitely higher value than the body. The soul is good and the body evil. The body is really an encumbrance of the soul, which longs to be liberated from it. Death releases the soul from the body so that it can attain a wholly spiritual existence devoid of evil. In our second reading, Paul Edwards challenges the notion of survival after death and argues that it is essentially incoherent. In our third reading, John Hick responds to those who say that personal immortality is impossible. He sets forth conditions for justifying our belief in survival and shows that those conditions could be met. According to Hick, there is nothing incoherent about the notion of immortality.

IV.47   Arguments for the Immortality of the Soul

PLATO

Plato (427–347 B.C.) believed that human beings were composed of two substances, a body and a soul. Of these, the true self is the soul, which lives on after the death of the body. All Plato's writings are in the form of dialogues. In the first dialogue (from *Alcibiades I*) Socrates argues with Alcibiades about the true self. The second dialogue (from *Phaedo*) takes place in prison, where Socrates has been condemned to die. He is offered a way of escape but rejects it, arguing that it would be immoral to flee such a fate at this time and that he is certain of a better life after death. He is speaking with Simmias and Cebes.

Study Questions

1. How does Socrates argue in *Alcibiades I* for the reality of the soul?
2. In the *Phaedo*, what is the role of the body with regard to attaining knowledge? What should the philosopher do about the body?
3. What is the significance in the argument of ideas such as absolute justice and beauty?
4. What is the attitude of the true philosopher toward death, and why?
5. How does Plato describe the process that leads to the attainment of wisdom?
6. How does the soul resemble the divine?

FROM ALCIBIADES I

Socrates: And is self-knowledge an easy thing, and was he to be lightly esteemed who inscribed the text on the temple at Delphi? ["Know Thyself"] Or is self-knowledge a difficult thing, which few are able to attain?

Alcibiades: At times, I fancy, Socrates, that anybody can know himself; at other times, the task appears to be very difficult.

From Plato, Alcibiades I *and the* Phaedo, *translated by William Jowett (New York: Charles Scribner's Sons, 1889).*

Soc.: But whether easy or difficult, Alcibiades, still there is no other way; knowing what we are, we shall know how to take care of ourselves, and if we are ignorant we shall not know.

Al.: That is true.

Soc.: Well, then, let us see in what way the self-existent can be discovered by us; that will give us a chance to discover our own existence, which without that we can never know.

Al.: You say truly.

Soc.: Come, now, I beseech you, tell me with whom you are conversing?—with whom but with me?

Al.: Yes.

Soc.: As I am with you?

Al.: Yes.

Soc.: That is to say, I, Socrates, am talking?

Al.: Yes.

Soc.: And I in talking use words?

Al.: Certainly.

Soc.: And talking and using words are, as you would say, the same?

Al.: Very true.

Soc.: And the user is not the same as the thing which he uses?

Al.: What do you mean?

Soc.: I will explain: the shoemaker, for example, uses a square tool, and a circular tool, and other tools for cutting?

Al.: Yes.

Soc.: But the tool is not the same as the cutter and user of the tool?

Al.: Of course not.

Soc.: And in the same way the instrument of the harper is to be distinguished from the harper himself?

Al.: He is.

Soc.: Now the question which I asked was whether you conceive the user to be always different from that which he uses?

Al.: I do.

Soc.: Then what shall we say of the shoemaker? Does he cut with his tools only or with his hands?

Al.: With his hands as well.

Soc.: He uses his hands too?

Al.: Yes.

Soc.: And does he use his eyes in cutting leather?

Al.: He does.

Soc.: And we admit that the user is not the same with the things which he uses?

Al.: Yes.

Soc.: Then the shoemaker and the harper are to be distinguished from the hands and feet which they use?

Al.: That is clear.

Soc.: And does not a man use the whole body?

Al.: Certainly.

Soc.: And that which uses is different from that which is used?

Al.: True.

Soc.: Then a man is not the same as his own body?

Al.: That is the inference.

Soc.: What is he, then?

Al.: I cannot say.

Soc.: Nay, you can say that he is the user of the body.

Al.: Yes.

Soc.: And the user of the body is the soul?

Al.: Yes, the soul.

Soc.: And the soul rules?

Al.: Yes.

Soc.: Let me make an assertion which will, I think, be universally admitted.

Al.: What is that?

Soc.: That man is one of three things.

Al.: What are they?

Soc.: Soul, body, or the union of the two.

Al.: Certainly.

Soc.: But did we not say that the actual ruling principle of the body is man?

Al.: Yes, we did.

Soc.: And does the body rule over itself?

Al.: Certainly not.

Soc.: It is subject, as we were saying?

Al.: Yes.

Soc.: Then that is not what we are seeking?

Al.: It would seem not.

Soc.: But may we say that the union of the two rules over the body, and consequently that this is man?

Al.: Very likely.

Soc.: The most unlikely of all things: for if one of the members is subject, the two united cannot possibly rule.

Al.: True.

Soc.: But since neither the body, nor the union of the two, is man, either man has no real existence, or the soul is man?

Al.: Just so.

Soc.: Would you have a more precise proof that the soul is man?

Al.: No; I think that the proof is sufficient.

Soc.: If the proof, although not quite precise, is fair, that is enough for us; more precise proof will be supplied when we have discovered that which we were led to omit, from a fear that the inquiry would be too much protracted.

Al.: What was that?

Soc.: What I meant, when I said that absolute existence must be first considered; but now, instead of absolute existence, we have been considering the nature of individual existence, and that may be sufficient; for surely there is nothing belonging to us which has more absolute existence than the soul?

Al.: There is nothing.

Soc.: Then we may truly conceive that you and I are conversing with one another, soul to soul?

Al.: Very true.

Soc.: And that is just what I was saying—that I, Socrates, am not arguing or talking with the face of Alcibiades, but with the real Alcibiades; and that is with his soul.

Al.: True. . . .

FROM PHAEDO

Socrates: What again shall we say of the actual acquirement of knowledge?—is the body, if invited to share in the inquiry, a hinderer or a helper? I mean to say, have sight and hearing any truth in them? Are they not, as the poets are always telling us, inaccurate witnesses? and yet, if even they are inaccurate and indistinct, what is to be said of the other senses?—for you will allow that they are the best of them?

Certainly, he [Simmias] replied.

Then when does the soul attain truth?—for in attempting to consider anything in company with the body she is obviously deceived.

Yes, that is true.

Then must not existence be revealed to her in thought, if at all?

Yes.

And thought is best when the mind is gathered into herself and none of these things trouble her—neither sounds nor sights nor pain nor any pleasure,—when she has as little as possible to do with the body, and has no bodily sense of feeling, but is aspiring after being?

That is true.

And in this the philosopher dishonors the body; his soul runs away from the body and desires to be alone and by herself?

That is true.

Well, but there is another thing, Simmias: Is there or is there not an absolute justice?

Assuredly there is.

And an absolute beauty and absolute good?

Of course.

But did you ever behold any of them with your eyes?

Certainly not.

Or did you ever reach them with any other bodily sense? (and I speak not of these alone, but of absolute greatness, and health, and strength, and of the essence of true nature of everything). Has the reality of them ever been perceived by you through the bodily organs? or rather, is not the nearest approach to the knowledge of their several natures made by him who so orders his intellectual vision as to have the most exact conception of the essence of that which he considers?

Certainly.

And he attains to the knowledge of them in their highest purity who goes to each of them with the mind alone, not allowing when in the act of thought the intrusion or introduction of sight or any other sense in the company of reason, but with the very light of the mind in her clearness penetrates into the very light of truth in each; he has got rid, as far as he can, of eyes and ears and of the whole body, which he conceives of only as a disturbing element, hindering the soul from the acquisition of knowledge when in company with her—is not this the sort of man who, if ever man did, is likely to attain the knowledge of existence?

There is admirable truth in that, Socrates, replied Simmias.

And when they consider all this, must not true philosophers make a reflection, of which they will speak to one another in such words as these: We have found, they will say, a path of speculation which seems to bring us and the argument to the conclusion, that while we are in the body, and while the soul is mingled with this mass of evil, our desire will not be satisfied, and our desire is of the truth. For the body is a source of endless trouble to us by reason of the mere requirement of food; and also is liable to diseases which overtake and impede us in the search after truth: and by filling us so full of loves, and lusts, and fears, and fancies, and idols, and every sort of folly, prevents our ever having, as people say, so much as a thought. From whence come wars, and fightings, and factions? whence but from the body and the lusts of the body? For wars are occasioned by the love of money, and money has to be acquired for the sake and in the service of the body; and in consequence of all these things the time which ought to be given to philosophy is lost. Moreover, if there is time and an inclination toward philosophy, yet the body introduces a turmoil and confusion and fear into the course of speculation, and hinders us from seeing the truth, and all experience shows that if we would have pure knowledge of anything we must be quit of the body, and the soul in herself must behold all things in themselves: then I suppose that we shall attain that which we desire, and of which we say that we are lovers, and that is wisdom; not while

we live, but after death, as the argument shows; for if while in company with the body, the soul cannot have pure knowledge, one of two things seems to follow—either knowledge is not to be attained at all, or, if at all, after death. For then, and not till then, the soul will be in herself alone and without the body. In this present life, I reckon that we make the nearest approach to knowledge when we have the least possible concern or interest in the body, and are not saturated with the bodily nature, but remain pure until the hour when God himself is pleased to release us. And then the foolishness of the body will be cleared away and we shall be pure and hold converse with other pure souls, and know of ourselves the clear light everywhere; and this is surely the light of truth. For no impure thing is allowed to approach the pure. These are the sort of words, Simmias, which the true lovers of wisdom cannot help saying to one another, and thinking. You will agree with me in that?

Certainly, Socrates.

But if this is true, O my friend, then there is great hope that, going whither I go, I shall there be satisfied with that which has been the chief concern of you and me in our past lives. And now that the hour of departure is appointed to me, this is the hope with which I depart, and not I only, but every man who believes that he has his mind purified.

Certainly, replied Simmias.

And what is purification but the separation of the soul from the body, as I was saying before; the habit of the soul gathering and collecting herself into herself, out of all the courses of the body; the dwelling in her own place alone, as in another life, so also in this, as far as she can; the release of the soul from the chains of the body?

Very true, he said.

And what is that which is termed death, but this very separation and release of the soul from the body?

To be sure, he said.

And the true philosophers, and they only, study and are eager to release the soul. Is not the separation and release of the soul from the body their especial study?

That is true.

And as I was saying at first, there would be a ridiculous contradiction in men studying to live as nearly as they can in a state of death, and yet repining when death comes.

Certainly.

Then Simmias, as the true philosophers are ever studying death, to them, of all men, death is the least terrible. Look at the matter in this way: how inconsistent of them to have been always enemies of the body, and wanting to have the soul alone, and when this is granted to them, to be trembling and repining; instead of rejoicing at their departing to that place where, when they arrive, they hope to gain that which in life they loved (and this was wisdom), and at the same time to be rid of the company of their enemy. Many a man has been willing to go to the world below in the hope of seeing there an earthly love, or wife, or son, and conversing with them. And will he who is a true lover of wisdom, and is persuaded in like manner that only in the world below he can worthily enjoy her, still repine at death? Will he not depart with joy? Surely, he will, my friend, if he be a true philosopher. For he will have a firm conviction that there only, and nowhere else, he can find wisdom in her purity. And if this be true, he would be very absurd, as I was saying, if he were to fear death. . . .

Socrates: And were we not saying long ago that the soul when using the body as an instrument of perception, that is to say, when using the sense of sight or hearing or some other sense (for the meaning of perceiving through the body is perceiving through the senses)—were we not saying that the soul too is then dragged by the body into the region of the changeable, and wanders and is confused; the world spins round her, and she is like a drunkard when under their influence?

Very true.

But when returning into herself she reflects; then she passes into the realm of purity, and eternity, and immortality, and unchangeableness,

which are her kindred, and with them she ever lives, when she is by herself and is not let or hindered; then she ceases from her erring ways, and being in communion with the unchanging, is unchanging. And this state of the soul is called wisdom?

That is well and truly said, Socrates, he replied.

And to which class is the soul more nearly alike and akin, as far as may be inferred from this argument, as well as from the preceding one?

I think, Socrates, that, in the opinion of every one who follows the argument, the soul will be infinitely more like the unchangeable—even the most stupid person will not deny that.

And the body is more like the changing?

Yes.

Yet once more consider the matter in this light: When the soul and the body are united, then nature orders the soul to rule and govern, and the body to obey and serve. Now which of these two functions is akin to the divine? and which to the mortal? Does not the divine appear to you to be that which naturally orders and rules, and the mortal that which is subject and servant?

True.

And which does the soul resemble?

The soul resembles the divine, and the body the mortal—there can be no doubt of that, Socrates.

Then reflect, Cebes: is not the conclusion of the whole matter this—that the soul is in the very likeness of the divine, and immortal, and intelligible, and uniform, and indissoluble, and unchangeable; and the body is in the very likeness of the human, and mortal, and unintelligible, and multiform, and dissoluble, and changeable. Can this, my dear Cebes, be denied?

No indeed.

But if this is true, then is not the body liable to speedy dissolution? and is not the soul almost or altogether indissoluble?

Certainly.

And do you further observe, that after a man is dead, the body, which is the visible part of man, and has a visible framework, which is called a corpse, and which would naturally be dissolved and decomposed and dissipated, is not dissolved or decomposed at once, but may remain for a good while, if the constitution be sound at the time of death, and the season of the year favorable? For the body when shrunk and embalmed, as is the custom in Egypt, may remain almost entire through infinite ages; and even in decay, still there are some portions, such as the bones and ligaments, which are practically indestructible. You allow that?

Yes.

And are we to suppose that the soul, which is invisible, in passing to the true Hades, which like her is invisible, and pure, and noble, and on her way to the good and wise God, whither, if God will, my soul is also soon to go—that the soul, I repeat, if this be her nature and origin, is blown away and perishes immediately on quitting the body, as the many say? That can never be, my dear Simmias and Cebes. The truth rather is, that the soul which is pure at departing draws after her no bodily taint, having never voluntarily had connection with the body, which she is ever avoiding, herself gathered into herself (for such abstraction has been the study of her life). And what does this mean but that she has been a true disciple of philosophy, and has practiced how to die easily? And is not philosophy the practice of death?

Certainly.

That soul, I say, herself invisible, departs to the invisible world—to the divine and immortal and rational: thither arriving, she lives in bliss and is released from the error and folly of men, their fears and wild passions and all other human ills, and forever dwells, as they say of the initiated, in company with the gods? Is not this true, Cebes?

Yes, said Cebes, beyond a doubt.

For Further Reflection

1. Are Plato's arguments in these two dialogues persuasive? Do the arguments depend overly much on his theory of the forms, which gives ideas separate existence?

2. Is Plato correct in thinking that the body always hinders pure thought? How might a contemporary materialist respond to Plato?

An Argument Against Survival: The Dependence of Consciousness on the Brain IV.48

PAUL EDWARDS

In this essay Edwards argues that a powerful case against survival after death can be made from what we know about the dependence of consciousness on the brain. Edwards grants his opponent dualist assumptions, that is, that the mind cannot be identified with the brain and that corporealism (the doctrine that we are wholly material beings) is false. He argues that, even with these generous concessions, the case against survival is overwhelming.

(A biographical sketch of Paul Edwards precedes Reading II.7.)

Study Questions

1. What is Hume's argument against immortality?
2. How does J. J. C. Smart differ from Hume?
3. To which versions of survival does Edwards' argument apply? What is the "literal resurrection" view?
4. How does Edwards use the nature of Alzheimer's Disease in his argument?
5. What does Edwards say about the view that the body is an instrument of the mind?
6. How does Stevenson argue for reincarnation against Cohen and Taylor?
7. What is Mill's argument for complete agnosticism over survival?
8. At the end of his essay Edwards offers two final objections to the idea that our self or soul is a spiritual substance. What are they?

IN THIS ARTICLE I will discuss the case against survival after death based on what is known about the dependence of consciousness on the brain. This may be called the body-mind dependence argument. I shall try to bring out what a formidable argument it is. Among other things I shall try to show that the various replies to it by philosophers and theologians are unsound.

I will make two assumptions which are favorable to the case for survival. By this I mean that without them one of the major forms of survival-belief would be ruled out from the start. I will assume, first, that some form of dualism is true, i.e., that a person is a body and a mind in a sense in which the mind cannot be identified with any bodily processes or behavior. I will also assume that when we talk about personal identity, bodily continuity is not an essential ingredient in what we mean. The view that bodily continuity is an essential ingredient in personal identity has sometimes been referred to as "corporealism" and I will here assume that corporealism is false.

THE SCOPE OF THE ARGUMENT

In a rudimentary form the argument can already be found in Lucretius and Pomponazzi and, since Bishop Butler expressly argued against it in the first chapter of his *Analogy of Religion* we may infer that it was current among English free-thinkers in the early years of the eighteenth century. However, the first full statement with which I am familiar occurs in Hume's posthumous essay on immortality:

> Where any two objects are so closely connected that all alterations which we have ever seen in the one are attended with proportionable alterations in the other, we ought to conclude, by all rules of analogy, that, when there are still greater alterations produced in the former, and it is totally dissolved, there follows a total dissolution of the latter. . . . The weakness of the body and that of the mind in infancy are exactly proportioned; their vigour in manhood, their sympathetic disorder in sickness; their common gradual decay in old age. The step further seems unavoidable; their common dissolution in death. The last symptoms which the mind discovers, are disorder, weakness, insensibility, and stupidity; the forerunners of its annihilation. The further progress of the same causes increasing, the same effects totally extinguish it.

Some of Hume's detailed observations are of course quite indefensible. There is surely no "exact" proportionality between physical and mental development or between bodily and mental "decay." Nor is it true that all human beings are "insensible" and "stupid" immediately before their death. Hume was also handicapped by the undeveloped state of brain physiology in the eighteenth century. Nevertheless his statement conveys very vividly the basic idea of the argument.

More recent defenders have placed heavy emphasis on information about the relation between the brain and our mental states and processes. Unlike Hume Professor J. J. C. Smart rejects dualism. As a materialist he maintains that mental states are identical with brain states, but he nevertheless endorses the body-mind dependence argument as valid within a dualistic framework:

> Even if some form of philosophical dualism is accepted and the mind is thought of as something over and above the body, the empirical evidence in favor of an invariable correlation between mental states and brain states is extremely strong: that is, the mind may be thought of as in some sense distinct from the body but also as fundamentally dependent upon physical states. Without oxygen or under the influence of anesthetics or soporific drugs, we rapidly lose consciousness. Moreover, the quality of our consciousness can be influenced in spectacular ways by appropriate drugs or by mechanical stimulation of different areas of the brain. In the face of all the evidence that is being accumulated by modern research in neurology, it is hard to believe that after the dissolution of the brain there could be any thought or conscious experience whatever.

I will add one other recent formulation which states the argument simply and forcefully and is based on the most recent evidence from neurology. "What we call 'the mind,'" writes Colin McGinn,

> is in fact made up of a great number of subcapacities, and each of these depends upon the functioning of the brain.

Now, the facts of neurology

> compellingly demonstrate . . . that everything about the mind, from the sensory-motor periphery to the inner sense of self, is minutely controlled by the brain: if your brain lacks certain chemicals or gets locally damaged, your mind is apt to fall apart at the seams. . . . If parts of the mind depend for their existence upon parts of the brain, then the whole of the mind must so depend too. Hence the soul dies with the brain, which is to say it is mortal.[1]

It should be emphasized that the argument does *not* start from the premise that after a person is dead he never again acts in the world. A correspondent in the *London Review* replied to McGinn by observing that we do not need his or the neuropathologist's "assistance to learn that all behavior stops at death." Similarly, John Stuart Mill in his chapter on "Immortality" in *Three Essays on Religion* thought the argument inconclusive on the ground that the absence of any acts by an individual after his death is as consistent with the view that he will "recommence" his existence "elsewhere" as it is with the assumption that he has been extinguished forever. Such remarks are due to a misunderstanding. The absence of any actions by the dead is certainly not irrelevant, but the argument is primarily based on the observed dependence of our mental states and processes on what goes on in the brain.

At first sight it may seem that, if valid, the argument merely rules out the survival of the disembodied mind and leaves other forms of survival untouched. In fact, however, it equally rules out reincarnation and the more sophisticated or replica-version of resurrectionism. This is so because the conclusion of the argument is that my mind depends on *my* brain. It does not merely support the less specific conclusion that my mind needs *some* brain as its foundation. If my mind is finished when my brain dies, then it cannot transmigrate to any other body. Similarly, if God created a duplicate of my body containing a duplicate of my brain, *my* mind would not be able to make use of it since it stopped existing with the death of my original body. The argument does not refute belief in the literal resurrection of the body. For on this view God will reconstitute our *original* bodies and hence also our original brains on the Day of Judgment. There are indeed vast numbers of fundamentalists and also a few pious philosophers who believe or say that they believe in resurrection in this literal sense, but to the great majority of scientists and philosophers and of educated persons generally it seems totally incredible. However, if anybody does believe in survival in *this* sense our argument has no bearing on his view.

ALZHEIMER'S DISEASE AND COMAS

The literature on survival contains a number of standard rejoinders to the body-mind dependence argument. Before turning to them, I will consider two concrete instances of body-mind dependence which will help to bring out the full force of the argument. The first is Alzheimer's disease, a dreadful affliction that ruins the last years of a sizable percentage of the world's population. Almost everybody above the age of thirty has known some elderly relative or friend afflicted with this illness. I can therefore be brief in my description of what happens to Alzheimer patients. In the early stages the person misses appointments, he constantly loses and mislays objects, and he frequently cannot recall events in the recent past. As the illness progresses he can no longer read or write and his speech tends to be incoherent. In nursing homes Alzheimer patients commonly watch television, but there is no evidence that they understand what is happening on the screen. The decline in intellectual function is generally accompanied by severe emotional symptoms, such as extreme irritability and violent reactions to persons in the environment, as well as hallucinations and paranoid fears. In the final stages the patient is totally confused, frequently incontinent, and quite unable to recognize anybody, including the closest relatives and friends. At present Alzheimer's is incurable and, unlike in the case of Parkinson's disease, there are no known means of slowing down the deterioration. It is also as yet a mystery why Alzheimer's strikes certain individuals while sparing the majority of old people. However, a great deal is known about what goes on in the brains of Alzheimer patients. Alois Alzheimer,

the neurologist after whom the disease is named, found in 1906 that the cerebral cortex and the hippocampus of his patients contained twisted tangles and filaments as well as abnormal neurites known as "neuritic" or "senile plaques." It has since been determined that the density of these abnormal components is directly proportional to the severity of the disorder. Autopsies have shown that Alzheimer victims have a vastly reduced level of an enzyme called "choline acetyltransferase," which is needed for producing the neurotransmitter acetylcholine. Although the reduced level of the enzyme and the neurotransmitter appear in the cortex, the origin of the trouble lies in another region of the brain, the nucleus basalis, which is situated just above the place where the optic nerves meet and cross. Autopsies have revealed a dramatic loss of neurons from the nucleus basalis in Alzheimer victims, and this explains why so little of the enzyme is manufactured in their brains.

The information just summarized has been culled from articles about Alzheimer's that have appeared in magazines and popular science monthlies in recent years. The authors of these articles are evidently not concerned with the question of survival after death, but they invariably use such phrases as "destruction of the mind" in describing what happens to the victims. In an article in *Science 84* entitled "The Clouded Mind," the author, Michael Shodell, speaks of Alzheimer's as "an illness that destroys the mind, leaving the body behind as a grim reminder of the person who once was there." Similarly, the cover story in *Newsweek* of December 3, 1984, which contained many heart-rending illustrations and listed some of the famous men and women who are suffering from Alzheimer's, was entitled "A Slow Death of the Mind." I think that these descriptions are entirely appropriate: A person who can no longer read or write, whose memory has largely disappeared, whose speech is incoherent, and who is totally indifferent to his environment has in effect lost all or most of what we normally call his mind. The relevance of this to our discussion is obvious. While still alive, an Alzheimer patient's brain is severely damaged and most of his mind has disappeared. After his death his brain is not merely damaged but completely destroyed. It is surely logical to conclude that now his mind is also gone. It seems preposterous to assert that, when the brain is completely destroyed, the mind suddenly returns intact, with its emotional and intellectual capacities, including its memory, restored. How does the *complete* destruction of the brain bring about a cure that has so far totally eluded medical science?

The same obviously applies to people in irreversible comas. Karen Ann Quinlan lay in a coma for over ten years before she finally died. The damage to her brain had made her, in the phrase used by the newspapers, nothing more than a "vegetable." Her E.E.G. was flat; she was unable to speak or write; visits by her foster parents did not register the slightest response. A more recent widely publicized case was that of the great American tenor Jan Peerce. Peerce had amazed the musical public by singing right into his seventies with only a slight decline in his vocal powers. In the end, however, he was felled by two severe strokes, and he spent the last year of his life in an irreversible coma. Relatives and friends could get no response of any kind. Peerce died in December 1984, and Karen Ann Quinlan in June 1985. Did the total destruction of the bodies of these individuals suddenly bring back their emotional and intellectual capacities? If so, where were these during the intervening periods?

THE BODY AS THE INSTRUMENT OF THE MIND

The first of the rejoinders I will consider does not dispute the manifold dependence of mental functions on brain processes. It is claimed, however, that these facts are not inconsistent with survival. They are indeed compatible with the view that the mind is annihilated at death, but they are also compatible with the very different position that the mind continues to exist but has lost its "instrument" for acting in the world, and more specifically, for communicating with people who are still alive. An excellent illustration of what the supporters of this rejoinder have in mind is supplied by Father John A. O'Brien in his pamphlet: *The Soul—What Is It?* In order to carve a statue, Father O'Brien writes, a sculptor needs his tools, his hammer and chisel. If the tools are seriously damaged, the quality of his work will be correspondingly impaired, but this does not mean that the sculptor cannot exist if the tools are completely destroyed.

Variants of this argument are found in numerous Protestant theologians, in Catholic philosophers who have frequently relied on the distinction between what they call "extrinsic" and "intrinsic" dependence, and in several secular philosophers, including Descartes, Kant, James, Schiller and McTaggart. "I do not agree with you," writes Descartes to Gassendi in his "Reply to the Fifth Objection" to his *Meditations,*

> that the mind waxes and wanes with the body; for from the fact that it does not work equally well in the body of a child and in that of a grown man, and that its actions are often impeded by wine and other bodily things, it follows merely that while it is united to the body it uses the body as an instrument in its normal operations.

Have we any reason, asks McTaggart, to suppose that "a body is essential to a self"? Not at all. The facts support the very different proposition that "while a self has a body, that body is essentially connected with the self's mental life." A self needs "sufficient data" for its mental activity. In this life the material is given in the form of sensations, and these can only be obtained by means of a body. It does not follow, however, that "it would be impossible for a self without a body to get data in some other way." McTaggart then offers an analogy which has frequently been quoted by believers in survival:

> If a man is shut up in a house, the transparency of the windows is an essential condition of his seeing the sky. But it would not be prudent to infer that, if he walked out of the house, he

could not see the sky because there was no longer any glass through which he might see it.

McTaggart is totally unimpressed by the evidence from brain physiology which, it is safe to say, he did not study in detail and which was very extensive even in 1906 when his book was published. He does not dispute that "diseases or mutilations of the brain affect the course of thought," but "the fact that an abnormal state of the brain may affect our thought does not prove that the normal states of the brain are necessary for thought."

It may be instructive at this stage to consider some of the exchanges between Professor Ian Stevenson, the well-known champion of reincarnation, and two of his skeptical interrogators in the course of a BBC program that took place in the spring of 1976. The program dealt with the claims of Edward Ryall, an elderly Englishman who in May 1970 had written a letter to the *Daily Express* in which he mentioned his clear and extensive memories of a life in the seventeenth century as a West Country farmer by the name of John Fletcher. Stevenson corresponded with Ryall and became convinced of the authenticity of his recollections. He encouraged Ryall to write a book about his previous life. *Second Time Around* appeared in 1974, with an introduction and supplementary notes by Stevenson. Besides Stevenson and Ryall, the participants in the BBC program were John Taylor, professor of mathematics at London University, and John Cohen, professor of psychology at Manchester. Here are some of the exchanges that are relevant to our discussion.

> Cohen: . . . memories are tied to a particular brain tissue. If you take away the brain, there is no memory.
> Stevenson: I think that's an assumption. Memories may exist in the brain and exist elsewhere also.
> Cohen: But we have not the slightest evidence, even a single case, of a memory existing without a brain. We have plenty of slight damage to a brain which destroys memory, but not the other way around.

> Stevenson: I feel that's one of the issues here—whether memories can, in fact, survive the destruction of the brain.
> Taylor: Professor Stevenson, do you have any evidence, other than these reincarnation cases, that memories can survive the destruction of physical tissue?
> Stevenson: No. I think the best evidence comes from the reincarnation cases.

Taylor then brought up the well-known case of people who lose all or most of their memories as a result of brain injuries. Stevenson was not fazed.[2]

> Stevenson: Well, it's possible that what is affected is his ability to express memories that he may still have.
> Taylor: But are you suggesting, in fact, that memories themselves are in some way nonphysically bound up, and can be stored in a nonphysical manner?
> Stevenson: Yes, I'm suggesting that there might be a nonphysical process of storage.
> Taylor: What does that mean? Nonphysical storage of what?
> Stevenson: The potentiality for the reproduction of an image memory.
> Taylor: But information itself involves energy. Is there such a thing as nonphysical energy?
> Stevenson: I think there may be, yes.
> Taylor: How can you define it? Nonphysical energy, to me, is a complete contradiction in terms. I can't conceive how on earth you could ever conceive of such a quantity.
> Stevenson: Well, it might be in some dimension of which we are just beginning to form crude ideas, through the study of what we parapsychologists call paranormal phenomena. We are making an assumption of some kind of process that is not, and maybe cannot be, understood in terms of current physical concepts. That is a jump, a gap, I freely admit.

These exchanges bring out very clearly what is at issue between those who accept the body-mind dependence argument and the supporters of the instrument theory.

It has on occasion been suggested that we have no way of deciding between these two rival explanations of the relevant facts. I see no reason to accept such an agnostic conclusion. It seems to me that by retrodictive extrapolation to cases like Alzheimer patients or people in comas we can see that the alternative to annihilation proposed by the instrument theory is absurd. Let us consider the behavior of Alzheimer patients in the later stages of their affliction. The more specific the case, the clearer the implications of the rival views will appear. The mother of a close friend of mine, Mrs. D., recently died from Alzheimer's after suffering from the disease for about eight years. Mrs. D. was a prosperous lady from Virginia, the widow of a banker. In her pre-Alzheimer days she was a courteous and well-behaved person, and she had of course no difficulty recognizing her daughter or any of her other relatives or friends. I do not know what her feelings were about paralyzed people, but my guess is that she pitied them and certainly had no wish to beat them up. As her illness progressed she was put into a nursing home run by nuns who were renowned for their gentle and compassionate ways. She shared a room with an older lady who was paralyzed. For the first year or so Mrs. D. did not become violent. Then she started hitting the nurses. At about the time when she could no longer recognize her daughter, she beat up the paralyzed lady on two or three occasions. From then on she had to be confined to the "seventh floor," which was reserved for violent and exceptionally difficult patients.

Let us now see what the survival theorists would have to say about Mrs. D.'s behavior. It should be remembered that on this view Mrs. D., after her death, will exist with her mind intact and will only lack the means of communicating with people on earth. This view implies that throughout her affliction with Alzheimer's Mrs. D.'s mind *was* intact. She recognized her daughter but had lost her ability to express this recognition. She had no wish to beat up an inoffensive paralyzed old woman. On the contrary, "inside" she was the same considerate person as before the onset of the illness. It is simply that her brain disease prevented her from acting in accordance with her true emotions. I must insist that these *are* the implications

of the theory that the mind survives the death of the brain and that the brain is only an instrument for communication. Surely these consequences are absurd: The facts are that Mrs. D. no longer recognized her daughter and that she no longer had any compassionate feelings about paralyzed old women. At any rate, we have the same grounds for saying this as we do in any number of undisputed cases in which people do not suffer from Alzheimer's and fail to recognize other human beings or fail to feel compassion.

The guards in Argentine dungeons who tortured and killed liberals had no compassion for their victims, and neither of course did the Nazis who rounded up and then shot Jews in Poland and elsewhere. We have exactly the same kind of evidence for concluding that Mrs. D., who probably did feel compassion for paralyzed people before she suffered from Alzheimer's, no longer felt compassion when beating up her paralyzed roommate. As for memories, all of us sometimes cannot place a familiar tune or remember the name of a person we know well; and in such cases it makes good sense to say that the memories are still there. Even when the name never comes back there is a suspicion that the memory may not have been lost: it is entirely possible that one could bring it back under hypnosis. However, the memory loss in Alzheimer's is totally different, and the same of course applies to people in irreversible comas. It is surely fantastic to maintain that during his last months Jan Peerce did recognize his wife and children and simply could not express his recognition. If anybody makes such a claim it can only be for ulterior metaphysical reasons and not because it is supported by the slightest evidence.

MILL, BUTLER, EWING— THE ABSENSE OF DIRECT NEGATIVE EVIDENCE

Mill's posthumously published essay on "Theism" contains a chapter on immortality in which he surveys and evaluates all the major arguments on both sides that were known to him. Mill finds all of them defective and concludes on a note of complete agnosticism. We have here, he writes, "one of those very rare cases in which there is really a total absence of evidence on either side" and "in which the absence of evidence for the affirmative does not, as in so many other cases, create a strong presumption in favor of the negative."[3]

Mill discusses in some detail the evidence from brain physiology. It supplies us with "sufficient evidence that cerebral action is, if not the cause, at least, in our present state of existence, a condition *sine qua non* of mental operations." We are entitled to conclude that the death of the brain would put a stop to all mental function and "remand it [the mind] to unconsciousness unless and until some other set of conditions supervenes, capable of recalling it into activity." The facts of brain physiology most emphatically do not prove that the mind cannot exist after death. "The same thoughts, emotions, volitions, and even sensations which we have here" may, for all we can tell, "persist or recommence somewhere else under other conditions." This is no less possible than that "other thoughts and sensations may exist under other conditions in other parts of the universe." What Mill evidently seems to require in order to establish the negative case is that we observe the nonexistence of the thoughts, volitions, and sensations of the dead person; and this the body-mind dependence argument does not give us.

Independently of this argument, Bishop Butler insists on the same requirement and regards its nonfulfillment as a fatal flaw in the unbeliever's position. Not only do we never directly observe the nonexistence of human minds, but the same is also true of animals. We never "find anything throughout the whole analogy of nature" that could afford us "even the slightest presumption, that animals ever lose their living powers." This is so because we have "no faculties wherewith to trace any beyond or through death to see what becomes of them." In the case of human beings and animals alike death only destroys "the sensible proof which we had before their death of their being possessed of living powers," but it does not "afford the least reason" for supposing that death causes the extinction of their minds.

A much more recent philosopher, the late A. C. Ewing, used the same kind of reasoning to rebut the unbeliever's argument. Ewing first observes that there is no logically necessary connection between bodily and mental events, something that all dualists would endorse. This means that no deductive argument is available to the unbeliever. At the same time he is also unable to mount an inductive argument. He cannot do this because "we have never observed a mind being annihilated at death." The only one who could do this is the person himself. "No one could observe this," Ewing writes, "but the mind in question itself, and even that could not because it was annihilated, so, if a phenomenon, it is certainly an unobservable one." Ewing is happy to note that once we have disposed of the argument from the connection between body and mind the field is left open "for any empirical evidence drawn from psychical research and any arguments for survival there may be based on ethics and religion."

Butler deserves credit for realizing that his reasoning applies to animals and not only to human beings. It is not clear that either Mill or Ewing saw this. However, not even Butler carried the argument far enough. What reason do we have for denying that purely inanimate objects have an "inner" psychic life? What evidence do I have that the chocolate cream puff I am about to eat does not bitterly resent this murderous activity on my part and how do I know that a tennis ball I am about to serve does not acutely suffer as a result of being hit? For that matter how do I know that the tennis ball does not enjoy the experience of being hit? Since we have no access to the inner life of tennis balls, if they have any, we cannot know either that the tennis ball does or does not like being hit. Not only cannot we know that tennis balls do not have an inner life. We also cannot know that they, or any other inanimate objects, do not continue to have an inner, psychical life after the death of their bodies, whether as disembodied minds or in conjunction with replicas that will be produced in a resurrection world. It is true that we have no evidence that such an inner life will continue after the death of their bodies, but we equally have none that it will not. A complete suspense of judgment is the only defensible attitude.

All who regard *panpsychism* as either false or meaningless will surely regard the fact that the rejoinder here under discussion can be extended to inanimate objects as its *reductio ad absurdum*. Others will go further and treat the entire rejoinder as a *reductio ad absurdum* of dualism. For clearly we do know that tennis balls and cream puffs do not have an inner life and we can and do know that human beings and animals have certain feelings or sensations. However, we have agreed to accept dualism throughout this article, and it can be shown that the rejoinder is invalid even within a dualistic framework. After all, dualists allow that although we cannot inspect the minds of others we can frequently know that they have certain experiences. We can know that another person is in pain or that he is angry, and we can at least have strong evidence that he has certain thoughts. Now, the same *kind* of evidence is available to us that other people do *not* have these experiences. We can know that somebody has ceased to be in pain, that his anger is gone, or that he no longer thinks about a certain subject. I do not have to *be* the other person to know that he is no longer in pain or angry. By the same token I do not have to be Mrs. D., the Alzheimer patient herself, to know that her memory is gone and I equally do not have to be Jan Peerce in his coma to know that he no longer recognizes his family. In such cases we surely have the right to assert more than that the memories and thoughts have been "remanded to unconsciousness." This description fits a person under general anesthesia or during dreamless sleep who may very well return to full consciousness, but it is highly misleading about people in a coma or with advanced Alzheimer's. The only description that is fitting in such cases is that the thoughts and memories have been destroyed; and if they have been destroyed then they cannot be "recalled into activity" when a "different set of conditions supervenes."

THE MIND AND THE SOUL

The last rejoinder to be considered involves a distinction between the mind, which is identical with the phenomenal or empirical self whose existence is not disputed by Hume and other empiricists, and another nonphysical entity to which various labels have been applied. It is the immaterial or spiritual substance of Clarke, Butler, and Reid and numerous other philosophers, past and present, it is the Atman of the Hindu version of reincarnation, the noumenal self of Kant, and the soul (in one of its senses) of the Christian and Jewish traditions. It is argued that, although the mind may indeed so closely depend on the body that it must cease with the body's death, the same is not true of the soul. The soul is the "I" that "owns" both the body and the mind. I am five feet seven inches tall, I weigh one hundred and fifty pounds, I have blue eyes and brown hair; but I also have certain sensations and feelings and thoughts. I have various physical skills and I also possess certain emotional and intellectual dispositions. It is this underlying "I"—the subject of both the body and the mind—that has not been shown to require a body for its existence.

There are two objections to this rejoinder, each of them fatal. In the first place, although the way we speak in certain contexts suggests an underlying subject of both body and mind, there is no reason to suppose that it exists. Hume's theory that human beings are nothing but "bundles of impressions and ideas" is seriously inadequate. Each of us, at least while he is sane, has a sense of himself, more specifically, a sense of himself as continuing the same person from moment to moment. However, what this consists in is not the totally unchanging meta-physical entity that Hume rightly rebelled against. It is a sense of continuity in certain bodily sensations (especially of our limbs and certain muscle groups) and of our various tastes, opinions, and habits—more generally of our emotional and intellectual dispositions. These, together with our bodies, make us the kinds of persons we are. Although our emotional and intellectual dispositions are subject to change, unlike our moods and sensations, they are rela-tively stable. If this is what is meant by "soul," there is no reason to deny that we have a soul; but the soul in this sense is just as dependent on the body and the brain as any particular sensa-tions, feelings, and thoughts.

The second objection to this rejoinder is that if there were such a thing as the spiritual substance or the metaphysical soul, it would not be what anybody means by "I." Human beings who are afraid of death dread the anni-hilation of their *empirical* selves and it is these empirical selves which they would like to sur-vive. This is true of Western and Eastern believers alike. The great seventeenth-century philosopher Pierre Gassendi, who was both a Catholic priest and an atomistic materialist, professed belief in the metaphysical soul. He also believed that insanity was a brain disease. Since the soul or reason (Gassendi preferred the latter word) did not depend on the body, he concluded quite consistently that the soul or reason remained sane even when the indi-vidual had become insane. Gassendi's consis-tency led to a *reductio ad absurdum* of his position. If I go mad and if at the same time my soul remains sane then I and my soul are not the same thing.

NOTES

1. *London Review of Books,* January 23, 1986, pp. 24–25.

2. *The Listener,* June 3, 1976, p. 698.

3. *Three Essays on Religion* (London: Longman's Green, Reader and Dyer, 1876), p. 203.

For Further Reflection

1. Outline Edwards' argument against survival. How successful is he in defending his con-clusion that we don't survive death?

2. Examine Edwards' criticism of Mill's agnosticism. How strong is his objection to Mill?

IV.49   In Defense of Immortality

JOHN HICK

John Hick, a British philosopher who retired from Claremont Graduate School in California, examines the Platonic notion of the immortality of the soul and argues that it is filled with problems. In its place, he argues for the New Testament view of the re-creation of the psychophysical person, a holistic person who is body-soul in one. He then offers a thought experiment of "John Smith" reappearances to show that re-creation is conceivable and worthy of rational belief. In the last part of this essay, Hick considers whether parapsychology can provide evidence for our survival after death.

(A biographical sketch of John Hick precedes Reading II.14.)

Study Questions

1. How old is the idea of a soul separate from the body?
2. How, according to Hick, is the biblical view of human nature different from the Greek view?
3. What is the significance of the story of John Smith?
4. What does Hick take to be the significance of data obtained through parapsychology?

THE IMMORTALITY OF THE SOUL

SOME KIND OF DISTINCTION between physical body and immaterial or semimaterial soul seems to be as old as human culture; the existence of such a distinction has been indicated by the manner of burial of the earliest human skeletons yet discovered. Anthropologists offer various conjectures about the origin of the distinction: perhaps it was first suggested by memories of dead persons; by dreams of them; by the sight of reflections of oneself in water and on other bright surfaces; or by meditation upon the significance of religious rites which grew up spontaneously in face of the fact of death.

It was Plato (428–348 B.C.), the philosopher who has most deeply and lastingly influenced Western culture, who systematically developed the body-mind dichotomy and first attempted to prove the immortality of the soul.[1]

Plato argues that although the body belongs to the sensible world,[2] and shares its changing and impermanent nature, the intellect is related to the unchanging realities of which we are aware when we think not of particular good things but of Goodness itself, not of specific just acts but of Justice itself, and of the other "universals" or eternal Ideas in virtue of which physical things and events have their own specific characteristics. Being related to this higher and abiding realm, rather than to the evanescent world of sense, reason or the soul is immortal. Hence, one who devotes his life to the contemplation of eternal realities rather than to the gratification of the fleeting desires of the body will find at death that whereas his body turns to dust, his soul gravitates to the realm of the unchanging, there to live forever. Plato painted an awe-inspiring picture, of haunting beauty and persuasiveness, which has moved and elevated the minds of men in many different centuries and lands. Nevertheless, it is not today (as it was during the first centuries of the Christian era) the common philosophy of the West; and a demonstration of immortality which presupposes Plato's metaphysical system cannot claim to constitute a proof for the twentieth-century disbeliever.

Plato used the further argument that the only things that can suffer destruction are those that are composite, since to destroy something means to disintegrate it into its constituent parts. All material bodies are composite; the soul, however, is simple and therefore imperishable. This argument was adopted by Aquinas and has become standard in Roman Catholic theology, as in the following passage from the modern Catholic philosopher, Jacques Maritain:

A spiritual soul cannot be corrupted, since it possesses no matter; it cannot be disintegrated,

From John H. Hick, Philosophy of Religion, *4th ed., copyright © 1990, pp. 122–132. Reprinted by permission of Pearson Education, Inc., Upper Saddle River, NJ. Footnotes edited.*

since it has no substantial parts; it cannot lose its individual unity, since it is self-subsisting, nor its internal energy, since it contains within itself all the sources of its energies. The human soul cannot die. Once it exists, it cannot disappear; it will necessarily exist for ever, endure without end. Thus, philosophic reason, put to work by a great metaphysician like Thomas Aquinas, is able to prove the immortality of the human soul in a demonstrative manner.[3]

This type of reasoning has been criticized on several grounds. Kant pointed out that although it is true that a simple substance cannot disintegrate, consciousness may nevertheless cease to exist through the diminution of its intensity to zero.[4] Modern psychology has also questioned the basic premise that the mind is a simple entity. It seems instead to be a structure of only relative unity, normally fairly stable and tightly integrated but capable under stress of various degrees of division and dissolution. This comment from psychology makes it clear that the assumption that the soul is a simple substance is not an empirical observation but a metaphysical theory. As such, it cannot provide the basis for a general proof of immortality.

The body-soul distinction, first formulated as a philosophical doctrine in ancient Greece, was baptized into Christianity, ran through the medieval period, and entered the modern world with the public status of a self-evident truth when it was redefined in the seventeenth century by Descartes. Since World War II, however, the Cartesian mind-matter dualism, having been taken for granted for many centuries, has been strongly criticized by philosophers of the contemporary analytical school.[5] It is argued that the words that describe mental characteristics and operations—such as "intelligent," "thoughtful," "carefree," "happy," "calculating" and the like—apply in practice to types of human behavior and to behavioral dispositions. They refer to the empirical individual, the observable human being who is born and grows and acts and feels and dies, and not to the shadowy proceedings of a mysterious "ghost in the machine." Man is thus very much what he appears to be—a creature of flesh and blood, who behaves and is capable of behaving in a characteristic range of ways—rather than a nonphysical soul incomprehensibly interacting with a physical body.

As a result of this development much mid-twentieth-century philosophy has come to see man in the way he is seen in the biblical writings, not as an eternal soul temporarily attached to a mortal body, but as a form of finite, mortal, psychophysical life. Thus, the Old Testament scholar, J. Pedersen, says of the Hebrews that for them ". . . the body is the soul in its outward form."[6] This way of thinking has led to quite a different conception of death from that found in Plato and the neo-Platonic strand of European thought.

THE RE-CREATION OF THE PSYCHOPHYSICAL PERSON

Only toward the end of the Old Testament period did after-life beliefs come to have any real importance in Judaism. Previously, Hebrew religious insight had focused so fully upon God's covenant with the nation, as an organism that continued through the centuries while successive generations lived and died, that the thought of a divine purpose for the individual, a purpose that transcended this present life, developed only when the breakdown of the nation as a political entity threw into prominence the individual and the problem of his personal destiny.

When a positive conviction arose of God's purpose holding the individual in being beyond the crisis of death, this conviction took the non-Platonic form of belief in the resurrection of the body. By the turn of the eras, this had become an article of faith for one Jewish sect, the Pharisees, although it was still rejected as an innovation by the more conservative Sadducees.

The religious difference between the Platonic belief in the immortality of the soul, and the Judaic-Christian belief in the resurrection of the body is that the latter postulates a special divine act of re-creation. This produces a sense of utter dependence upon God in the hour of death, a feeling that is in accordance with the biblical understanding of man as having been formed out of "the dust of the earth,"[7] a product (as we say today) of the slow evolution of life from its lowly beginnings in the primeval slime. Hence, in the Jewish and Christian conception, death is something real and fearful. It is not thought to be like walking from one room to another, or taking off an old coat and putting on a new one. It means sheer unqualified extinction—passing out from the lighted circle of life into "death's dateless night." Only through the sovereign creative love of God can there be a new existence beyond the grave.

What does "the resurrection of the dead" mean? Saint Paul's discussion provides the basic Christian answer to this question.[8] His conception of the general resurrection (distinguished from the unique resurrection of Jesus) has nothing to do with the resuscitation of corpses in a cemetery. It concerns God's re-creation or reconstitution of the human psychophysical individual, not as the organism that has died but as a *soma pneumatikon,* a "spiritual body," inhabiting a spiritual world as the physical body inhabits our present physical world.

A major problem confronting any such doctrine is that of providing criteria of personal identity to link the earthly life and the resurrection life. Paul does not specifically consider this question, but one may, perhaps, develop his thought along lines such as the following.[9]

Suppose, first, that someone—John Smith—living in the USA were suddenly and inexplicably to disappear from before the eyes of his friends, and that at the same moment an exact replica of him were inexplicably to appear in India. The person who appears in India is exactly similar in both physical and mental characteristics to the person who disappeared in America. There is continuity of memory, complete similarity of bodily features including fingerprints, hair and eye coloration, and stomach contents, and also of beliefs, habits, emotions, and mental dispositions. Further, the "John Smith" replica thinks of himself as being the John Smith who disappeared in the USA. After all possible tests have been made and have proved positive, the factors leading his friends to

accept "John Smith" as John Smith would surely prevail and would cause them to overlook even his mysterious transference from one continent to another, rather than treat "John Smith," with all John Smith's memories and other characteristics, as someone other than John Smith.

Suppose, second, that our John Smith, instead of inexplicably disappearing, dies, but that at the moment of his death a "John Smith" replica, again complete with memories and all other characteristics, appears in India. Even with the corpse on our hands we would, I think, still have to accept this "John Smith" as the John Smith who died. We would have to say that he had been miraculously re-created in another place.

Now suppose, third, that on John Smith's death the "John Smith" replica appears, not in India, but as a resurrection replica in a different world altogether, a resurrection world inhabited only by resurrected persons. This world occupies its own space distinct from that with which we are now familiar. That is to say, an object in the resurrection world is not situated at any distance or in any direction from the objects in our present world, although each object in either world is spatially related to every other object in the same world.

This supposition provides a model by which one may conceive of the divine re-creation of the embodied human personality. In this model, the element of the strange and the mysterious has been reduced to a minimum by following the view of some of the early Church Fathers that the resurrection body has the same shape as the physical body,[10] and ignoring Paul's own hint that it may be as unlike the physical body as a full grain of wheat differs from the wheat seed.[11]

What is the basis for this Judaic-Christian belief in the divine re-creation or reconstitution of the human personality after death? There is, of course, an argument from authority, in that life after death is taught throughout the New Testament (although very rarely in the Old Testament). But, more basically, belief in the resurrection arises as a corollary of faith in the sovereign purpose of God, which is not restricted by death and which holds man in being beyond his natural mortality. In the words of Martin Luther, "Anyone with whom God speaks, whether in wrath or in mercy, the same is certainly immortal. The Person of God who speaks, and the Word, show that we are creatures with whom God wills to speak, right into eternity, and in an immortal manner."[12] In a similar vein it is argued that if it be God's plan to create finite persons to exist in fellowship with himself, then it contradicts both his own intention and his love for the creatures made in his image if he allows men to pass out of existence when his purpose for them remains largely unfulfilled.

It is this promised fulfillment of God's purpose for man, in which the full possibilities of human nature will be realized, that constitutes the "heaven" symbolized in the New Testament as a joyous banquet in which all and sundry rejoice together. As we saw when discussing the problem of evil, no theodicy can succeed without drawing into itself this eschatological[13] faith in an eternal, and therefore infinite, good which thus outweighs all the pains and sorrows that have been endured on the way to it.

Balancing the idea of heaven in Christian tradition is the idea of *hell*. This, too, is relevant to the problem of theodicy. For just as the reconciling of God's goodness and power with the fact of evil requires that out of the travail of history there shall come in the end an eternal good for man, so likewise it would seem to preclude man's eternal misery. The only kind of evil that is finally incompatible with God's unlimited power and love would be utterly pointless and wasted suffering, pain which is never redeemed and worked into the fulfilling of God's good purpose. Unending torment would constitute precisely such suffering; for being eternal, it could never lead to a good end beyond itself. Thus, hell as conceived by its enthusiasts, such as Augustine or Calvin, is a major part of the problem of evil! If hell is construed as eternal torment, the theological motive behind the idea is directly at variance with the urge to seek a theodicy. However, it is by no

means clear that the doctrine of eternal punishment can claim a secure New Testament basis.[14] If, on the other hand, "hell" means a continuation of the purgatorial suffering often experienced in this life, and leading eventually to the high good of heaven, it no longer stands in conflict with the needs of theodicy. Again, the idea of hell may be deliteralized and valued as a *mythos,* as a powerful and pregnant symbol of the grave responsibility inherent in man's freedom in relation to his Maker.

DOES PARAPSYCHOLOGY HELP?

The spiritualist movement claims that life after death has been proved by well-attested cases of communication between the living and the "dead." During the closing quarter of the nineteenth century and the decades of the present century this claim has been made the subject of careful and prolonged study by a number of responsible and competent persons.[15] This work, which may be approximately dated from the founding in London of the Society for Psychical Research in 1882, is known either by the name adopted by that society or in the United States by the name parapsychology.

Approaching the subject from the standpoint of our interest in this chapter, we may initially divide the phenomena studied by the parapsychologist into two groups. There are those phenomena that involve no reference to the idea of a life after death, chief among these being psychokinesis and extrasensory perception (ESP) in its various forms (such as telepathy, clairvoyance, and precognition). And there are those phenomena that raise the question of personal survival after death, such as the apparitions and other sensory manifestations of dead persons and the "spirit messages" received through mediums. This division is, however, only of preliminary use, for ESP has emerged as a clue to the understanding of much that occurs in the second group. We shall begin with a brief outline of the reasons that have induced the majority of workers in this field to be willing to postulate so strange an occurrence as telepathy.

Telepathy is a name for the mysterious fact that sometimes a thought in the mind of one person apparently causes a similar thought to occur to someone else when there are no normal means of communication between them, and under circumstances such that mere coincidence seems to be excluded.

For example, one person may draw a series of pictures or diagrams on paper and somehow transmit an impression of these to someone else in another room who then draws recognizable reproductions of them. This might well be a coincidence in the case of a single successful reproduction; but can a series consist entirely of coincidences?

Experiments have been devised to measure the probability of chance coincidence in supposed cases of telepathy. In the simplest of these, cards printed in turn with five different symbols are used. A pack of fifty, consisting of ten bearing each symbol, is then thoroughly shuffled, and the sender concentrates on the cards one at a time while the receiver (who of course can see neither sender nor cards) tries to write down the correct order of symbols. This procedure is repeated, with constant reshuffling, hundreds or thousands of times. Since there are only five different symbols, a random guess would stand one chance in five of being correct. Consequently, on the assumption that only "chance" is operating, the receiver should be right in about 20 per cent of his tries, and wrong in about 80 per cent; and the longer the series, the closer should be the approach to this proportion. However, good telepathic subjects are right in a far larger number of cases than can be reconciled with random guessing. The deviation from chance expectation can be converted mathematically into "odds against chance" (increasing as the proportion of hits is maintained over a longer and longer series of tries). In this way, odds of over a million to one have been recorded. J. B. Rhine (Duke University) has reported results showing "antichance" values ranging from seven (which equals odds against

chance of 100,000 to one) to eighty-two (which converts the odds against chance to billions).[16] S. G. Soal (London University) has reported positive results for precognitive telepathy with odds against chance of $10^{35} \times 5$, or of billions to one.[17] Other researchers have also recorded confirming results. In the light of these reports, it is difficult to deny that some positive factor, and not merely "chance," is operating. "Telepathy" is simply a name for this unknown positive factor.

How does telepathy operate? Only negative conclusions seem to be justified to date. It can, for example, be said with reasonable certainty that telepathy does not consist in any kind of physical radiation, analogous to radio waves. For, first, telepathy is not delayed or weakened in proportion to distance, as are all known forms of radiation; and, second, there is no organ in the brain or elsewhere that can plausibly be regarded as its sending or receiving center. Telepathy appears to be a purely mental occurrence.

It is not, however, a matter of transferring or transporting a thought out of one mind into another—if, indeed, such an idea makes sense at all. The telepathized thought does not leave the sender's consciousness in order to enter that of the receiver. What happens would be better described by saying that the sender's thought gives rise to a mental "echo" in the mind of the receiver. This "echo" occurs at the unconscious level, and consequently the version of it that rises into the receiver's consciousness may be only fragmentary and may be distorted or symbolized in various ways, as in dreams.

According to one theory that has been tentatively suggested to explain telepathy, our minds are separate and mutually insulated only at the conscious (and preconscious) level. But at the deepest level of the unconscious, we are constantly influencing one another, and it is at this level that telepathy takes place.

How is a telepathized thought directed to one particular receiver among so many? Apparently the thoughts are directed by some link of emotion or common interest. For example, two friends are sometimes telepathically aware of any grave crisis or shock experienced by the other, even though they are at opposite ends of the earth.

We shall turn now to the other branch of parapsychology, which has more obvious bearing upon our subject. The *Proceedings of the Society for Psychical Research* contains a large number of carefully recorded and satisfactorily attested cases of the appearance of the figure of someone who has recently died to living people (in rare instances to more than one at a time) who were, in many cases, at a distance and unaware of the death. The S.P.R. reports also establish beyond reasonable doubt that the minds that operate in the mediumistic trance, purporting to be spirits of the departed, sometimes give personal information the medium could not have acquired by normal means and at times even give information, later verified, which had not been known to any living person.

On the other hand, physical happenings, such as the "materializations" of spirit forms in a visible and tangible form, are much more doubtful. But even if we discount the entire range of physical phenomena, it remains true that the best cases of trance utterance are impressive and puzzling, and taken at face value are indicative of survival and communication after death. If, through a medium, one talks with an intelligence that gives a coherent impression of being an intimately known friend who has died and establishes identity by a wealth of private information and indefinable personal characteristics—as has occasionally happened—then we cannot dismiss without careful trial the theory that what is taking place is the return of a consciousness from the spirit world.

However, the advance of knowledge in the other branch of parapsychology, centering upon the study of extrasensory perception, has thrown unexpected light upon this apparent commerce with the departed. For it suggests that unconscious telepathic contact between the medium and his or her client is an important and possibly a sufficient explanatory factor. This was vividly illustrated by the experience of two women who

decided to test the spirits by taking into their minds, over a period of weeks, the personality and atmosphere of an entirely imaginary character in an unpublished novel written by one of the women. After thus filling their minds with the characteristics of this fictitious person, they went to a reputable medium, who proceeded to describe accurately their imaginary friend as a visitant from beyond the grave and to deliver appropriate messages from him.

An even more striking case is that of the "direct voice" medium (i.e., a medium in whose séances the voice of the communicating "spirit" is heard apparently speaking out of the air) who produced the spirit of one "Gordon Davis" who spoke in his own recognizable voice, displayed considerable knowledge about Gordon Davis, and remembered his death. This was extremely impressive until it was discovered that Gordon Davis was still alive; he was, of all ghostly occupations, a real-estate agent, and had been trying to sell a house at the time when the séance took place!

Such cases suggest that genuine mediums are simply persons of exceptional telepathic sensitiveness who unconsciously derive the "spirits" from their clients' minds.

In connection with "ghosts," in the sense of apparitions of the dead, it has been established that there can be "meaningful hallucinations," the source of which is almost certainly telepathic. To quote a classic and somewhat dramatic example: a woman sitting by a lake sees the figure of a man running toward the lake and throwing himself in. A few days later a man commits suicide by throwing himself into this same lake. Presumably, the explanation of the vision is that the man's thought while he was contemplating suicide had been telepathically projected onto the scene via the woman's mind.

In many of the cases recorded there is delayed action. The telepathically projected thought lingers in the recipient's unconscious mind until a suitable state of inattention to the outside world enables it to appear to his conscious mind in a dramatized form—for example, by a hallucinatory voice or vision—by means of the same mechanism that operates in dreams.

If phantoms of the living can be created by previously experienced thoughts and emotions of the person whom they represent, the parallel possibility arises that phantoms of the dead are caused by thoughts and emotions that were experienced by the person represented when he was alive. In other words, ghosts may be "psychic footprints," a kind of mental trace left behind by the dead, but not involving the presence or even the continued existence of those whom they represent.

These considerations tend away from the hopeful view that parapsychology will open a window onto another world. However, it is too early for a final verdict; and in the meantime one should be careful not to confuse absence of knowledge with knowledge of absence.

NOTES

1. *Phaedo.*
2. The world known to us through our physical senses.
3. Jacques Maritain, *The Range of Reason* (London: Geoffrey Bles Ltd. and New York: Charles Scribner's Sons, 1953), p. 60.
4. Kant, *Critique of Pure Reason, Transcendental Dialectic,* "Refutation of Mendelssohn's Proof of the Permanence of the Soul."
5. Gilbert Ryle's *The Concept of Mind* (London: Hutchinson & Co., Ltd., 1949) is a classic statement of this critique.

6. *Israel* (London: Oxford University Press, 1926), I, 170.
7. Genesis, 2 : 7; Psalm 103 : 14.
8. I Corinthians 15.
9. The following paragraphs are adapted, with permission, from a section of my article, "Theology and Verification," published in *Theology Today* (April, 1960) and reprinted in *The Existence of God* (New York: The Macmillan Company, 1964).
10. For example, Irenaeus, *Against Heresies,* Book II, Chap. 34, para. 1.
11. 1 Corinthians 15 : 37.
12. Quoted by Emil Brunner, *Dogmatics,* II, 69.
13. From the Greek *eschaton,* end.
14. The Greek word *aionios,* which is used in the New Testament and which is usually translated as "eternal" or "everlasting," can bear either this meaning or the more limited meaning of "for the aeon, or age."
15. The list of past presidents of the Society for Psychical Research includes the philosophers Henri Bergson, William James, Hans Driesch, Henry Sidgwick, F. C. S. Schiller, C. D. Broad, and H. H. Price; the psychologists William McDougall, Gardner Murphy, Franklin Prince, and R. H. Thouless; the physicists Sir William Crookes, Sir Oliver Lodge, Sir William Barrett, and Lord Rayleigh; and the classicist Gilbert Murray.
16. J. B. Rhine, *Extrasensory Perception* (Boston: Society for Psychical Research, 1935), Table XLIII, p. 162. See also Rhine, *New Frontiers of the Mind* (New York: Farrar and Rinehart, Inc., 1937), pp. 69 f.
17. S. G. Soal, *Proceedings of the Society for Psychical Research,* XLVI, 152–98 and XLVII, 21–150. See also S. G. Soal's *The Experimental Situation in Psychical Research* (London: The Society for Psychical Research, 1947).

For Further Reflection

1. Has Hick successfully shown the plausibility of survival after death? Has he made the Judeo-Christian view intelligible in the light of modern psychology?

Key Terms

dualism	materialism	substance dualism
identity theory	functionalism	property dualism

Suggestions for Further Reading

Borst, C. V., ed. *The Mind/Brain Identity Theory*. New York: St. Martin's, 1970. Contains the best overall collection on the identity theory.

Campbell, Keith. *Body and Mind*. New York: Doubleday, 1970.

Chalmers, David J. *Philosophy of Mind: Classical and Contemporary Readings*. New York: Oxford University Press, 2002.

Churchland, Paul. *Matter and Consciousness*. Cambridge, MA: MIT Press, 1984.

Cornman, James, and Keith Lehrer. *Philosophical Problems and Arguments*. New York: Macmillan, 1982. Chapter 4, "The Mind-Body Problem," is excellent and accessible to lower-division college students.

Dennett, Daniel. *Brainstorms*. Cambridge, MA: MIT Press, 1978.

Ducasse, Curt J. *A Critical Examination of the Belief in Life after Death*. Thomas, 1961.

Flew, Antony, ed. *Body, Mind and Death*. New York: Macmillan, 1974. Contains the classic readings.

Hofstadter, Douglas, and Daniel Dennett, eds. *The Mind's I*. New York: Bantam, 1982. A scintillating set of articles on the idea of the self.

McGinn, Colin. *The Character of Mind*. Oxford: Oxford University Press, 1982. A good, concise introduction to the subject.

Penelhum, Terrence. *Survival and Disembodied Existence*. London: Routledge and Kegan Paul, 1970.

Perry, John. *Personal Identity*. Berkeley: University of California, 1975. A very fine set of articles.

Quinton, Anthony. "The Soul." *Journal of Philosophy*, 1962.

Ryle, Gilbert. *The Concept of Mind*. New York: Barnes and Noble, 1949. A classic in logical behaviorism.

Searle, John R. *Mind: A Brief Introduction*. New York: Oxford University Press, 2004.

Shaffer, Jerome. *Philosophy of Mind*. Englewood Cliffs, NJ: Prentice Hall, 1963. Almost a classic summary of the problems.

Swinburne, Richard. *The Evolution of the Soul*. Oxford: Clarendon Press, 1986. This contains Swinburne's 1983–1984 Gifford's Lectures. It treats the subject from a theistic perspective.

Part V

‿

Freedom of the Will and Determinism

If I were capable of correct reasoning, and if, at the same time, I had a complete knowledge both of his disposition and of all the events by which he was surrounded, I should be able to foresee the line of conduct which, in consequence of those events, [any person] would adopt.

H. T. BUCKLE, *History of Civilization in England*, 1857

T HE PROBLEM OF FREEDOM OF THE WILL and determinism is one of the most intriguing and difficult in the whole of philosophy. It constitutes a paradox. If we look at ourselves, at our ability to deliberate and make choices, it seems obvious that we are free. On the other hand, if we look at what we believe about causality (that is, that every event and thing must have a cause), then it appears that we do not have free wills but are determined. So we seem to have inconsistent beliefs.

Let us look closer at the two theses involved in order to see how they work and what support there is for each of them.

1. **Determinism:** The theory that everything in the universe (or at least the macroscopic universe) is entirely determined by causal laws, so that whatever happens at any given moment is the effect of some antecedent cause.
2. **Libertarianism:** The theory that there are some actions in which the individual is the sole (or decisive) cause.

There is a third position which tries to combine the best of the two positions. Called **compatibilism** or soft determinism, it admits that while everything is determined, we can still be free insofar as we can still act voluntarily.

Hard Determinism

Determinism is the theory that everything in the universe is governed by causal laws. That is, everything in the universe is entirely determined so that whatever happens at any given moment is the effect of some antecedent cause. If we were omniscient, we could predict exactly everything that would happen for the rest of this hour, for the rest of our lifetime, for the rest of time itself, simply because we know how everything hitherto is causally related. This theory, which, it is claimed, is the basic presupposition of science, implies that there is no such thing as an uncaused event (sometimes this is modified to include only the macrocosmic world, leaving the microcosmic world in doubt).

Many have inferred from the notion of determinism that no actions are free, that there is no free will—a view known as **hard determinism**. They reason that if everything has a cause, then human actions have causes; if human actions have causes, they are determined and therefore cannot be free. Actions are simply the result of a long chain of causes over which people have no control.

Although the hypothesis of universal causality cannot be proved, it is something we all assume—either because of considerable inductive evidence or as an *a priori* truth which seems to make sense of the world. We cannot easily imagine an uncaused event taking place in ordinary life. For example, imagine how you would feel if, on visiting your dentist for relief of a toothache, he were to conclude his oral examination with the remark, "I certainly can see that you are in great pain because of your toothache, but I'm afraid that I can't help you, for there is no cause of this toothache." Perhaps he calls his partner over to confirm his judgment. "Sure enough," she says, "this is one of those interesting noncausal cases. Sorry, there's nothing we can do for you. Even medicine and pain-relievers won't help these noncausal types."

Why do we believe that everything has a cause? Most philosophers have echoed John Stuart Mill's answer that the doctrine of universal causality is a conclusion of inductive reasoning. We have had an enormous range of experience wherein we have found causal explanations to individual events, which in turn seem to participate in a further causal chain. The problem with this answer, however, is that we have only experienced a very small part of the universe, not enough of it to warrant the conclusion that every event must have a cause.

David Hume (see also Reading III.26) pointed out that the idea of causality was not a logical truth (like the notion that all triangles have three sides). The hypothesis that every event has a cause arises from the observation of regular conjunctions. "When many uniform instances appear, and the same object is always followed by the same event; we then begin to entertain the notion of cause and connexion" (*Enquiry*, p. 78). So after a number of successful tries at putting water over a fire and seeing it disappear, we conclude that heat (or fire) causes water to disappear (or vaporize). But we cannot prove causality. We never see it. All we see are two events in constant spatio-temporal order and infer from this constant conjunction a binding relation between them. For example, we see one billiard ball (a) hit another (b), and we see (b) move away from (a), and we conclude that (a's) hitting (b) at a certain velocity is the cause of (b's) moving away as it did. However, we cannot prove that it is the sufficient cause of the movement.

Immanuel Kant first suggested that the principle of universal causality is a synthetic *a priori*—that is, an assumption that we cannot prove by experience but simply cannot conceive not to be the case. Our mental construction demands that we read all experience in the light of universal causation. We have no knowledge of what the world is in itself, or whether there really is universal causation, but we cannot understand experience except by means of causal explanation. The necessary idea of causality is part and parcel of our noetic structure. We are programmed to read our experience in the causal script.

Kant saw that there was a powerful incentive to believe in hard determinism, but he also thought that the notion of morality provided a powerful incentive to believe in freedom of the will. Hence, Kant's dilemma.

The man who used the idea of hard determinism more effectively for practical purposes than anyone before him was the great American criminal lawyer Clarence Darrow. In the 1920s, two teenage geniuses from the University of Chicago, Leopold and Loeb, committed what they regarded as the perfect murder. They grotesquely dismembered a child and buried the parts in a prairie. Caught, they faced an outraged public who demanded the death penalty. The defense attorney was Clarence Darrow, champion of lost causes. He conceded that the boys committed the deed, but argued that they were, nevertheless, "innocent." His argument was based on the theory of determinism. It is worth reading part of the plea:

> We are all helpless. . . . This weary world goes on, begetting, with birth and with living and with death; and all of it is blind from the beginning to the end. I do not know what it was that made these boys do this mad act, but I do know there is a reason for it. I know they did not beget themselves. I know that any one of an infinite number of causes reaching back to the beginning might be working out in these boys' minds, whom you are asked to hang in malice and in hatred and injustice. . . .
>
> Nature is strong and she is pitiless. She works in her own mysterious way, and we are her victims.
>
> We have not much to do with it ourselves. Nature takes this job in hand, and we play our part. In the words of old Omar Khayam, we are:
>
> *But helpless pieces in the game He plays*
> *Upon the chess board of nights and days;*
> *Hither and thither moves, and checks and slays,*
> *And one by one back in the closet lays.*
>
> What had this boy to do with it? He was not his own father, he was not his own mother; he was not his own grandparents. All of this was handed to him. He did not surround himself with governesses and wealth. He did not make himself. And yet he is to be compelled to pay. (Clarence Darrow, *Attorney for the Damned* [New York: Simon and Schuster, 1957])

This was sufficient to convince the jury to go against public opinion and recommend a life sentence in lieu of the death penalty. If Leopold and Loeb were determined by antecedent causes to do the deed, we cannot blame them for what they did, any more than we can blame a cow for not being able to fly.

Hard determinism has received new attention and respect because of modern neurological studies that suggest the hypothesis that there is a one-to-one correlation between mental states and brain states, so that every conscious action can be traced back to a causally sufficient brain state. In other words, the laws of physics deterministically produce mental states.

Libertarianism

Libertarianism is the theory that we do have free wills. It contends that given the same antecedent conditions at time t_1, an agent S could do either act A1 or A2. That is, it is up to S what the world will look like after t_1, and that his act is causally underdetermined, the self making the unexplained difference. As Roderick Chisholm would have it (Reading V.53), the agent causes the act. Peter van Inwagen (Reading V.52) concurs while insisting that in no way are determinism and free will compatible. Libertarians do not contend that all our actions are free, only some of them. They offer two main arguments for their position: the argument from deliberation and the argument from moral responsibility.

The Argument from Deliberation

The position is nicely summed up in the words of Corliss Lamont: "[There] is the unmistakable intuition of virtually every human being that he is free to make the choices he does and that the deliberations leading to those choices are also free flowing. The normal man feels too, after he has made a decision, that he could have decided differently. That is why regret or remorse for a past choice can be so disturbing."

There is a difference between a knee jerk and purposefully kicking a football. In the first case, the behavior is involuntary, a reflex action. In the second case, we deliberate, notice that we have an alternative (namely, not kicking the ball), consciously choose to kick the ball, and, if successful, we find our body moving in the requisite manner, so that the ball is kicked.

Deliberation can take a short or long time, be foolish or wise, but the process is a conscious one wherein we believe that we really can do either of the actions (or any of many possible actions). That is, in deliberating we assume we are free to choose between alternatives and that we are not determined to do simply one action. Otherwise, why deliberate?

Furthermore, there seems to be something psychologically lethal about accepting determinism in human relations; it tends to curtail deliberation and paralyze actions. If people really believe themselves totally determined, the tendency is for them to excuse their behavior. Human effort seems pointless. As Arthur Eddington put it, "What significance is there to my mental struggle tonight whether I shall or shall not give up smoking, if the laws which govern the matter of the physical universe already preordain for the morrow a configuration of matter consisting of pipe, tobacco, and smoke connected to my lips?" The determinist has an objection to this argument, which you will encounter in d'Holbach's essays. But in Reading V.51, William James argues that determinism is a superstition.

The Argument from Moral Responsibility

Determinism seems to conflict with the thesis that we have moral responsibilities, for responsibility implies that we could have done otherwise than we did. We do not hold a dog responsible for chewing up our philosophy book or a one-month-old baby responsible for crying, because they could not help it, but we do hold a twenty-year-old student responsible for her cheating because (we believe) she could have done otherwise. Blackbacked sea gulls will tear apart a stray baby herring gull without the slightest suspicion that their act may be immoral, but if humans lack this sense, we judge them as pathological, as substandard.

Moral responsibility is something that we take very seriously. We believe that we do have duties, oughts, over which we feel rational guilt at failure to perform. But there can be no such things as duties, oughts, praise, blame, or rational guilt if we are not essentially free. The argument form is the following:

1. If determinism is true and our actions are merely the product of the laws of nature and antecedent states of affairs, then it is not up to us to choose what we do.

2. But if it is not up to us to choose what we do, we cannot be said to be responsible for what we do.

3. So if determinism is true, we are not responsible for what we do.

4. But our belief in moral responsibility is self-evident, at least as strong as our belief in universal causality.

5. So, if we believe that we have moral responsibilities, determinism cannot be accepted.

We must reject the notion of determinism even if we cannot give a full explanatory account of how agents choose.

Here the determinist usually bites the bullet and admits that we do not have moral responsibilities, and that it is just an illusion that we do. But we are determined to have such an illusion, so there is nothing we can do about it. We cannot consciously live as determinists, but why should we think that we can? We are finite and fallible creatures, driven by causal laws, but with self-consciousness that makes us aware of part (but only a part) of the process that governs our behavior.

Compatibilism

However, there is another response to the problem of free will and determinism, one similar to Kant but perhaps more subtle. It can be called reconciling determinism or soft determinism or compatibilism. It argues that although we are determined, we still have moral responsibilities, that the distinction is between *voluntary* and *involuntary* behavior.

The language of freedom and the language of determinism are but two different ways of talking about certain human or rational events, both necessary for mankind (one is necessary for science and the other is necessary for morality and personal relationships). The compatibilist argues that the fact that we are determined does not affect our interpersonal relations. We will still have feelings that we must deal with, using internalist insights. We will still feel resentment when someone hurts us "on purpose." We will still feel grateful for services rendered and hold people responsible for their actions. Only we will still acknowledge that from the external perspective the determinist's account of all of this is valid. A classic statement of compatibilism is given by Hume in Reading V.56.

Along these lines, Walter T. Stace (Reading V.54) argues that the problem of freedom and determinism is really only a semantic one, a dispute about the meanings of words. Freedom has to do with acts done voluntarily and determinism with the causal processes that underlie all behavior and events. These need not be incompatible. Gandhi's fasting because he wanted to free India was a voluntary or free act, whereas a man starving in the desert is not doing so voluntarily or as a free act. A thief purposefully and voluntarily steals, whereas a kleptomaniac cannot help stealing. In both cases each act or event has causal antecedents, but the former in each set are free, whereas the latter are unfree. According to Stace, "Acts freely done are those whose immediate causes are psychological states in the agent. Acts not freely done are those whose immediate causes are states of affairs external to the agent." In our readings compatibilism is attacked by James, who calls it a "quagmire of evasion."

Harry Frankfurt (Reading V.55) counters with a sophisticated defense of compatibilism, linking it to personhood and motivational states.

In our final reading Richard Taylor, using the story of Osmo, illustrates the plausibility of fatalist determinism, the thesis that our whole life is determined, so that nothing we can do can falsify the predetermined trajectory.

We Are Completely Determined   V.50

BARON D'HOLBACH

Baron Paul Henri d'Holbach (1723–1789), born in Edesheim, Germany, and growing up in France, was one of the leading philosophers of the French Enlightenment. He was a materialist who believed that nature is one grand machine, and humans are particular machines within this grand machine—a machine which needs no machinist. He was a significant contributor to the *Encyclopedie* and a friend of Diderot, Hume, and Rousseau. His principal writings are *Christianity Unveiled* (1767), *The System of Nature* (1770), from which the present selection is taken, and *Common Sense, or Natural Ideas Opposed to Supernatural Ideas* (1772).

d'Holbach is one of the first philosophers to provide a sustained systematic critique of the doctrine of free will. According to him, if we accept science, which he equates with a system of material particles operating according to fixed laws of motion, then we will see that free will is an illusion. There is no such entity as a soul, but we are simply material objects in motion, having very complicated brains that lead the unreflective to believe that they are free.

Study Questions

1. What is the result of dualism, which separates soul from body?
2. What does d'Holbach believe has been proved about the relation of the soul to body?
3. How does he characterize human life?
4. What is the role that the doctrine of free will plays in religion and our system of punishment?
5. Deliberation between alternative courses of action has often been used by libertarians as evidence of free will. What does d'Holbach say about this psychological activity?
6. What are the causes of our belief in free will?

THOSE WHO HAVE AFFIRMED that the *soul* is distinguished from the body, is immaterial, draws its ideas from its own peculiar source, acts by its own energies, without the aid of any exterior object, have, by a consequence of their own system, enfranchised [liberated] it from those physical laws according to which all beings of which we have a knowledge are obliged to act. They have believed that the soul is mistress of its own conduct, is able to regulate its own peculiar operations, has the faculty to determine its will by its own natural energy; in a word, they have pretended that man is a *free agent*.

It has been already sufficiently proved that the soul is nothing more than the body considered relatively to some of its functions more concealed than others: it has been shown that this soul, even when it shall be supposed immaterial, is continually modified conjointly with the body, is submitted to all its motion, and that without this it would remain inert and dead; that, consequently, it is subjected to the influence of those material and physical causes which give impulse to the body; of which the mode of existence, whether habitual or transitory, depends upon the material elements by which it is surrounded, that form its texture, constitute its temperament, enter into it by means of the aliments, and penetrate it by their subtility. The faculties which are called *intellectual,* and those qualities which are styled *moral,* have been explained in a manner purely physical and natural. In the last place it has been demonstrated that all the ideas, all the systems, all the affections, all the opinions, whether true or false, which man forms to himself, are to be attributed to his physical and material senses. Thus man is a being purely physical; in whatever manner he is considered, he is connected to universal nature, and submitted to the necessary and immutable laws that she imposes on all the beings she contains, according to their peculiar essences or to the respective properties with which, without consulting them, she endows each particular

species. Man's life is a line that nature commands him to describe upon the surface of the earth, without his ever being able to swerve from it, even for an instant. He is born without his own consent; his organization does in nowise depend upon himself; his ideas come to him involuntarily; his habits are in the power of those who cause him to contract them; he is unceasingly modified by causes, whether visible or concealed, over which he has no control, which necessarily regulate his mode of existence, give the hue to his way of thinking, and determine his manner of acting. He is good or bad, happy or miserable, wise or foolish, reasonable or irrational, without his will being for any thing in these various states. Nevertheless, in despite of the shackles by which he is bound, it is pretended he is a free agent, or that independent of the causes by which he is moved, he determines his own will, and regulates his own condition.

However slender the foundation of this opinion, of which every thing ought to point out to him the error, it is current at this day and passes for an incontestable truth with a great number of people, otherwise extremely enlightened; it is the basis of religion, which, supposing relations between man and the unknown being she has placed above nature, has been incapable of imagining how man could either merit reward or deserve punishment from this being, if he was not a free agent. Society has been believed interested in this system; because an idea has gone abroad, that if all the actions of man were to be contemplated as necessary, the right of punishing those who injure their associates would no longer exist. At length human vanity accommodated itself to a hypothesis which, unquestionably, appears to distinguish man from all other physical beings, by assigning to him the special privilege of a total independence of all other causes, but of which a very little reflection would have shown him the impossibility. . . .

From Chapter XI, "Of the System of Man's Free Agency," of The System of Nature *(1770). The translation is by H. D. Robinson.*

The will . . . is a modification of the brain, by which it is disposed to action, or prepared to give play to the organs. This will is necessarily determined by the qualities, good or bad, agreeable or painful, of the object or the motive that acts upon his senses, or of which the idea remains with him, and is resuscitated by his memory. In consequence, he acts necessarily, his action is the result of the impulse he receives either from the motive, from the object, or from the idea which has modified his brain, or disposed his will. When he does not act according to this impulse, it is because there comes some new cause, some new motive, some new idea, which modifies his brain in a different manner, gives him a new impulse, determines his will in another way, by which the action of the former impulse is suspended: thus, the sight of an agreeable object, or its idea, determines his will to set him in action to procure it; but if a new object or a new idea more powerfully attracts him, it gives a new direction to his will, annihilates the effect of the former, and prevents the action by which it was to be procured. This is the mode in which reflection, experience, reason, necessarily arrests or suspends the action of man's will: without this he would of necessity have followed the anterior impulse which carried him towards a then desirable object. In all this he always acts according to necessary laws, from which he has no means of emancipating himself.

If when tormented with violent thirst, he figures to himself in idea, or really perceives a fountain, whose limpid streams might cool his feverish want, is he sufficient master of himself to desire or not to desire the object competent to satisfy so lively a want? It will no doubt be conceded, that it is impossible he should not be desirous to satisfy it; but it will be said—if at this moment it is announced to him that the water he so ardently desires is poisoned, he will, notwithstanding his vehement thirst, abstain from drinking it: and it has, therefore, been falsely concluded that he is a free agent. The fact, however, is, that the motive in either case is exactly the same: his own conservation. The same necessity that determined him to drink before he knew the water was deleteri-

ous, upon this new discovery equally determines him not to drink; the desire of conserving himself either annihilates or suspends the former impulse; the second motive becomes stronger than the preceding, that is, the fear of death, or the desire of preserving himself, necessarily prevails over the painful sensation caused by his eagerness to drink; but, it will be said, if the thirst is very parching, an inconsiderate man without regarding the danger will risk swallowing the water. Nothing is gained by this remark: in this case the anterior impulse only regains the ascendency; he is persuaded that life may possibly be longer preserved, or that he shall derive a greater good by drinking the poisoned water than by enduring the torment, which, to his mind, threatens instant dissolution: thus the first becomes the strongest and necessarily urges him on to action. Nevertheless, in either case, whether he partakes of the water, or whether he does not, the two actions will be equally necessary; they will be the effect of that motive which finds itself most puissant; which consequently acts in the most coercive manner upon his will.

This example will serve to explain the whole phenomena of the human will. This will, or rather the brain, finds itself in the same situation as a ball, which, although it has received an impulse that drives it forward in a straight line, is deranged in its course whenever a force superior to the first obliges it to change its direction. The man who drinks the poisoned water appears a madman; but the actions of fools are as necessary as those of the most prudent individuals. The motives that determine the voluptuary and the debauchee to risk their health, are as powerful, and their actions are as necessary, as those which decide the wise man to manage his. But, it will be insisted, the debauchee may be prevailed on to change his conduct: this does not imply that he is a free agent; but that motives may be found sufficiently powerful to annihilate the effect of those that previously acted upon him; then these new motives determine his will to the new mode of conduct he may adopt as necessarily as the former did to the old mode.

Man is said to *deliberate,* when the action of the will is suspended; this happens when two opposite motives act alternately upon him. *To deliberate,* is to hate and to love in succession; it is to be alternately attracted and repelled; it is to be moved, sometimes by one motive, sometimes by another. Man only deliberates when he does not distinctly understand the quality of the objects from which he receives impulse, or when experience has not sufficiently apprised him of the effects, more or less remote, which his actions will produce. He would take the air, but the weather is uncertain; he deliberates in consequence; he weighs the various motives that urge his will to go out or to stay at home; he is at length determined by that motive which is most probable; this removes his indecision, which necessarily settles his will, either to remain within or to go abroad: his motive is always either the immediate or ultimate advantage he finds, or thinks he finds, in the action to which he is persuaded.

Man's will frequently fluctuates between two objects, of which either the presence or the ideas move him alternately: he waits until he has contemplated the objects, or the ideas they have left in his brain which solicit him to different actions; he then compares these objects or ideas; but even in the time of deliberation, during the comparison, pending these alternatives of love and hatred which succeed each other, sometimes with the utmost rapidity, he is not a free agent for a single instant; the good or the evil which he believes he finds successively in the objects, are the necessary motives of these momentary wills; of the rapid motion of desire or fear, that he experiences as long as his uncertainty continues. From this it will be obvious that deliberation is necessary; that uncertainty is necessary; that whatever part he takes, in consequence of this deliberation, it will always necessarily be that which he has judged, whether well or ill, is most probable to turn to his advantage.

When the soul is assailed by two motives that act alternately upon it, or modify it successively, it deliberates; the brain is in a sort of equilibrium, accompanied with perpetual oscillations, sometimes towards one object, sometimes towards the other, until the most forcible carries the point, and thereby extricates it from this state of suspense, in which consists the indecision of his will. But when the brain is simultaneously assailed by causes equally strong that move it in opposite directions, agreeable to the general law of all bodies when they are struck equally by contrary powers, it stops . . . it is neither capable to will nor to act; it waits until one of the two causes has obtained sufficient force to overpower the other; to determine its will; to attract it in such a manner that it may prevail over the efforts of the other cause.

This mechanism, so simple, so natural, suffices to demonstrate why uncertainty is painful, and why suspense is always a violent state for man. The brain, an organ so delicate and so mobile, experiences such rapid modifications that it is fatigued; or when it is urged in contrary directions, by causes equally powerful, it suffers a kind of compression, that prevents the activity which is suitable to the preservation of the whole, and which is necessary to procure what is advantageous to its existence. This mechanism will also explain the irregularity, the indecision, the inconstancy of man, and account for that conduct which frequently appears an inexplicable mystery, and which is, indeed, the effect of the received systems. In consulting experience, it will be found that the soul is submitted to precisely the same physical laws as the material body. If the will of each individual, during a given time, was only moved by a single cause or passion, nothing would be more easy than to foresee his actions; but his heart is frequently assailed by contrary powers, by adverse motives, which either act on him simultaneously or in succession; then his brain, attracted in opposite directions, is either fatigued, or else tormented by a state of compression, which deprives it of activity. Sometimes it is in a state of incommodious inaction; sometimes it is the sport of the alternate shocks it undergoes. Such, no doubt, is the state in which man finds himself when a lively passion solicits him to the commission of crime, whilst fear points out to him the danger by which it is attended; such, also, is the condition of him whom remorse, by the continued labour of his distracted soul, prevents from enjoying the objects he has criminally obtained.

Choice by no means proves the free agency of man: he only deliberates when he does not yet know which to choose of the many objects that move him; he is then in an embarrassment, which does not terminate until his will is decided by the greater advantage he believes he shall find in the object he chooses, or the action he undertakes. From whence it may be seen, that choice is necessary, because he would not determine for an object, or for an action, if he did not believe that he should find in it some direct advantage. That man should have free agency it were needful that he should be able to will or choose without motive, or that he could prevent motives coercing his will. Action always being the effect of his will once determined, and as his will cannot be determined but by a motive which is not in his own power, it follows that he is never the master of the determination of his own peculiar will; that consequently he never acts as a free agent. It has been believed that man was a free agent because he had a will with the power of choosing; but attention has not been paid to the fact that even his will is moved by causes independent of himself; is owing to that which is inherent in his own organization, or which belongs to the nature of the beings acting on him. Is he the master of willing not to withdraw his hand from the fire when he fears it will be burnt? Or has he the power to take away from fire the property which makes him fear it? Is he the master of not choosing a dish of meat, which he knows to be agreeable or analogous to his palate; of not preferring it to that which he knows to be disagreeable or dangerous? It is always according to his sensations, to his own peculiar experience, or to his suppositions, that he judges of things, either well or ill; but whatever may be his judgment, it depends necessarily on his mode of feeling, whether habitual or accidental,

and the qualities he finds in the causes that move him, which exist in despite of himself. . . .

When it is said, that man is not a free agent, it is not pretended to compare him to a body moved by a simple impulsive cause: he contains within himself causes inherent to his existence; he is moved by an interior organ, which has its own peculiar laws, and is itself necessarily determined in consequence of ideas formed from perceptions resulting from sensations which it receives from exterior objects. As the mechanism of these sensations, of these perceptions, and the manner they engrave ideas on the brain of man, are not known to him; because he is unable to unravel all these motions; because he cannot perceive the chain of operations in his soul, or the motive principle that acts within him, he supposes himself a free agent; which, literally translated, signifies, that he moves himself by himself; that he determines himself without cause: when he rather ought to say, that he is ignorant how or for why he acts in the manner he does. It is true the soul enjoys an activity peculiar to itself; but it is equally certain that this activity would never be displayed, if some motive or some cause did not put it in a condition to exercise itself: at least it will not be pretended that the soul is able either to love or to hate without being moved, without knowing the objects, without having some idea of their qualities. Gunpowder has unquestionably a particular activity, but this activity will never display itself, unless fire be applied to it; this, however, immediately sets it in motion.

It is the great complication of motion in man, it is the variety of his action, it is the multiplicity of causes that move him, whether simultaneously or in continual succession, that persuades him he is a free agent: if all his motions were simple, if the causes that move him did not confound themselves with each other, if they were distinct, if his machine were less complicated, he would perceive that all his actions were necessary, because he would be enabled to recur instantly to the cause that made him act. A man who should be always obliged to go towards the west, would always go on that side; but he would feel that, in so going, he was not a free agent: if he had another sense, as his actions or his motion, augmented by a sixth, would be still more varied and much more complicated, he would believe himself still more a free agent than he does with his five senses.

It is, then, for want of recurring to the causes that move him; for want of being able to analyze, from not being competent to decompose the complicated motion of his machine, that man believes himself a free agent; it is only upon his own ignorance that he founds the profound yet deceitful notion he has of his free agency; that he builds those opinions which he brings forward as a striking proof of his pretended freedom of action. If, for a short time, each man was willing to examine his own peculiar actions, search out their true motives to discover their concatenation, he would remain convinced that the sentiment he has of his natural free agency, is a chimera that must speedily be destroyed by experience.

Nevertheless it must be acknowledged that the multiplicity and diversity of the causes which continually act upon man, frequently without even his knowledge, render it impossible, or at least extremely difficult for him to recur to the true principles of his own peculiar actions, much less the actions of others: they frequently depend upon causes so fugitive, so remote from their effects, and which, superficially examined, appear to have so little analogy, so slender a relation with them, that it requires singular sagacity to bring them into light. This is what renders the study of the moral man a task of such difficulty; this is the reason why his heart is an abyss, of which it is frequently impossible for him to fathom the depth. He is then obliged to content himself with a knowledge of the general and necessary laws by which the human heart is regulated: for the individuals of his own species these laws are pretty nearly the same; they vary only in consequence of the organization that is peculiar to each, and of the modification it undergoes: This, however, cannot be rigorously the same in any two. It suffices to know, that by his essence, man tends to conserve himself, and to render his existence happy: this granted, whatever may be his actions, if he recur back to this first principle, to this general, this necessary tendency of his will, he never can be deceived with regard to his motives.

For Further Reflection

1. Has d'Holbach proved that we do not have free will? Is his argument that science precludes such a notion convincing?

2. d'Holbach points out that without the doctrine of free will, the notion of just punishment crumbles: that religion could not justify God's sending people to hell for their sins, and the Law could not justify its system of punishments without the doctrine. Do you agree with d'Holbach?

3. Could we go even further and say that we would not have any place for moral praise or blame without a notion of free will? What would d'Holbach make of moral responsibility?

4. J. B. S. Haldane has written, "If my mental processes are determined wholly by the motion of atoms in my brain, I have no reason to suppose that my beliefs are true . . . and hence I have no reason for supposing my brain to be composed of atoms." Does this show that determinism is self-refuting?

The Dilemma of Determinism   V.51

WILLIAM JAMES

In this essay, James argues that although neither the doctrine of freedom of the will nor the doctrine of determinism can be proved, there are good reasons to choose the doctrine of free will. First, it makes better sense of the universe in terms of satisfying our deepest intellectual and emotional needs. Second, it makes sense of the notions of regret, especially moral regret that things are not better. Essentially, the choice between the two doctrines is not intellectual but is based on different personality types: "possibility men" and "anti-possibility men."

(A biographical note on William James precedes Reading II.17.)

Study Questions

1. What is James' purpose in this essay?
2. What are the two suppositions set forth at the outset?
3. How does James characterize the principle of causality?
4. What are the two types of determinism, and why is one type a "quagmire of evasion"?
5. How is determinism described with regard to the idea of possibilities?
6. How is indeterminism described with regard to the notion of possibilities?
7. How does James think that people choose between these two ways of looking at the world?
8. How is the notion of chance described?
9. What are the limits put on the idea of free will?
10. Formulate James' argument that the notion of regret involves the determinist in a dilemma.
11. What is James' conclusion to the problem of free will versus determinism?

A COMMON OPINION PREVAILS that the juice has ages ago been pressed out of the free-will controversy, and that no new champion can do more than warm up stale arguments which everyone has heard. This is a radical mistake. I know of no subject less worn out, or in which inventive genius has a better chance of breaking open new ground— not, perhaps, of forcing a conclusion or of coercing assent, but of deepening our sense of what the issue between the two parties really is, and of what the ideas of fate and of free will imply. At our very side almost, in the past few years, we have seen falling in rapid succession from the press works that present the alternative in entirely novel lights. Not to speak of the English disciples of Hegel, such as Green and Bradley; not to speak of Hinton and Hodgson, nor of Hazard here—we see in the writings of Renouvier, Fouillée, and Delboeuf how completely changed and refreshed is the form of the old disputes. I cannot pretend to vie in originality with any of the masters I have named, and my ambition limits itself to just one little

Reprinted from William James, The Will to Believe *(1897).*

point. If I can make two of the necessarily implied corollaries of determinism clearer to you than they have been made before, I shall have made it possible for you to decide before or against that doctrine with a better understanding of what you are about. And if you prefer not to decide at all, but to remain doubters, you will at least see more plainly what the subject of your hesitation is. I thus declaim openly on the threshold all pretension to prove to you that the freedom of the will is true. The most I hope is to induce some of you to follow my own example in assuming it true, and acting as if it were true. If it be true, it seems to me that this is involved in the strict logic of the case. Its truth ought not to be forced willy-nilly down our indifferent throats. It ought to be freely espoused by men who can equally well turn their backs upon it. In other words, our first act of freedom, if we are free, ought in all inward propriety to be to affirm that we are free. This should exclude, it seems to me, from the free-will side of the question all hope of a coercive demonstration—a demonstration which I, for one, am perfectly contented to go without.

With thus much understood at the outset, we can advance. But, not without one more point understood as well. The arguments I am about to urge all proceed on two suppositions: first, when we make theories about the world and discuss them with one another, we do so in order to attain a conception of things which shall give us subjective satisfaction; and, second, if there be two conceptions, and the one seems to us, on the whole, more rational than the other, we are entitled to suppose that the more rational one is truer of the two. I hope that you are all willing to make these suppositions with me; for I am afraid that if there be any of you here who are not, they will find little edification in the rest of what I have to say. I cannot stop to argue the point; but I myself believe that all the magnificent achievements of mathematical and physical science—our doctrines of evolution, of uniformity of law, and the rest—proceed from our indomitable desire to cast the world into a more rational shape in our minds than the shape into which it is thrown

there by the crude order of our experience. The world has shown itself, to a great extent, plastic to this demand of ours for rationality. How much farther it will show itself plastic no one can say. Our only means of finding out is to try; and I, for one, feel as free to try conceptions of moral as of mechanical or of logical rationality. If a certain formula for expressing the nature of the world violates my moral demand, I shall feel free to throw it overboard, or at least to doubt it, as if it disappointed my demand for uniformity of sequence, for example; the one demand being, so far as I can see, quite as subjective and emotional as the other is. The principle of causality, for example—what is it but a postulate, an empty name covering simply a demand that the sequence of events shall some day manifest a deeper kind of belonging of one thing with another than the mere juxtaposition which now phenomenally appears? It is as much an altar to an unknown god as the one that Saint Paul found at Athens. All our scientific and philosophic ideals are altars to unknown gods. Uniformity is as much so as is free will. If this be admitted, we can debate on even terms. But if any one pretends that while freedom and variety are, in the first instance, subjective demands, necessity and uniformity are something altogether different, I do not see how we can debate at all.

To begin, then, I must suppose you are acquainted with all the usual arguments on the subject. I cannot stop to take up the old proofs from causation, from statistics, from the certainty with which we can foretell one another's conduct, from the fixity of character, and all the rest. But there are two *words* which usually encumber these classical arguments, and which we must immediately dispose of if we are to make any progress. One is the eulogistic word *freedom*, and the other is the opprobrious word *chance*. The word "chance" I wish to keep, but I wish to get rid of the word "freedom." Its eulogistic associations have so far overshadowed all the rest of its meaning that both parties claim the sole right to use it, and determinists today insist that they alone are freedom's champions.

Old-fashioned determinism was what we may call *hard* determinism. It did not shrink from such words as fatality, bondage of the will, necessitation, and the like. Nowadays, we have a *soft* determinism which abhors harsh words, and, repudiating fatality, necessity, and even predetermination, says that its real name is freedom; for freedom is only necessity understood, and bondage to the highest is identical with true freedom. Even a writer as little used to making capital out of soft words as Mr. Hodgson hesitates not to call himself a "free-will determinist."

Now, all this is a quagmire of evasion under which the real issue of fact has been entirely smothered. Freedom in all these senses presents simply no problem at all. No matter what the soft determinist mean by it—whether he mean the acting without external constraint; whether he mean the acting rightly, or whether he mean the acquiescing in the law of the whole—who cannot answer him that sometimes we are free and sometimes we are not? But there *is* a problem, an issue of fact and not of words, an issue of the most momentous importance, which is often decided without discussion in one sentence—nay, in one clause of a sentence—by those very writers who spin out whole chapters in their efforts to show what "true" freedom is; and that is the question of determinism, about which we are to talk tonight.

POSSIBILITIES AND ACTUALITIES

Fortunately, no ambiguities hang about this word or about its opposite, indeterminism. Both designate an outward way in which things may happen, and their cold and mathematical sound has no sentimental associations that can bribe our partiality either way in advance. Now, evidence of an external kind to decide between determinism and indeterminism is, as I intimated a while back, strictly impossible to find. Let us look at the difference between them and see for ourselves. What does determinism profess?

It professes that those parts of the universe already laid down absolutely appoint and decree what the other parts shall be. The future has no ambiguous possibilities hidden in its womb: the part we call the present is compatible with only one totality. Any other future complement than the one fixed from eternity is impossible. The whole is in each and every part, and welds it with the rest into an absolute unity, an iron block, in which there can be no equivocation or shadow of turning.

> With earth's first clay they did the last man
>   knead,
> And there of the last harvest sowed the seed.
> And the first morning of creation wrote
> What the last dawn of reckoning shall read.

Indeterminism, on the contrary, says that the parts have a certain amount of loose play on one another, so that the laying down of one of them does not necessarily determine what the others shall be. It admits that possibilities may be in excess of actualities, and that things not yet revealed to our knowledge may really in themselves be ambiguous. Of two alternative futures which we conceive, both may now be really possible; and the one become impossible only at the very moment when the other excludes it by becoming real itself. Indeterminism thus denies the world to be one unbending unit of fact. It says there is a certain ultimate pluralism in it; and, so saying, it corroborates our ordinary unsophisticated view of things. To that view, actualities seem to float in a wider sea of possibilities from out of which they are chosen; and, somewhere, indeterminism says, such possibilities exist, and form a part of truth.

Determinism, on the contrary, says they exist *nowhere,* and that necessity on the one hand and impossibility on the other are the sole categories of the real. Possibilities that fail to get realized are, for determinism, pure illusions: they never were possibilities at all. There is nothing inchoate, it says, about this universe of ours, all that was or is or shall be actual in it having been from eternity virtually there. The cloud of alternatives our minds escort this mass of actuality withal is a cloud of sheer deceptions, to which "impossibilities" is the only name which rightfully belongs.

The issue, it will be seen, is a perfectly sharp one, which no eulogistic terminology can smear over or wipe out. The truth *must* lie with one side or the other, and its lying with one side makes the other false.

The question relates solely to the existence of possibilities, in the strict sense of the term, as things that may, but need not, be. Both sides admit that a volition, for instance, has occurred. The indeterminists say another volition might have occurred in its place: the determinists swear that nothing could possibly have occurred in its place. Now, can science be called in to tell us which of these two point-blank contradicters of each other is right? Science professes to draw no conclusions but such as are based on matters of fact, things that have actually happened; but how can any amount of assurance that something actually happened give us the least grain of information as to whether another thing might or might not have happened in its place? Only facts can be proved by other facts. With things that are possibilities and not facts, facts have no concern. If we have no other evidence than the evidence of existing facts, the possibility-question must remain a mystery never to be cleared up.

And the truth is that facts practically have hardly anything to do with making us either determinists or indeterminists. Sure enough, we make a flourish of quoting facts this way or that; and if we are determinists, we talk about the infallibility with which we can predict one another's conduct; while if we are indeterminists, we lay great stress on the fact that it is just because we cannot foretell one another's conduct, either in war or statecraft or in any of the great and small intrigues and businesses of men, that life is so intensely anxious and hazardous a game. But who does not see the wretched insufficiency of this so-called objective testimony on both sides? What fills up the gaps in our minds is something not objective, not external. What divides us into *possibility* men and *anti-possibility* men is different faiths or postulates—postulates of rationality. To this man the world seems more rational with possibilities in it—to that man more rational with possibilities excluded; and talk as we will about having to yield to evidence, what makes us monists or pluralists, determinists or indeterminists, is at bottom always some sentiment like this.

THE IDEA OF CHANCE

The stronghold of the deterministic sentiment is the antipathy to the idea of chance. As soon as we begin to talk indeterminism to our friends, we find a number of them shaking their heads. This notion of alternative possibility, they say, this admission that any one of several things may come to pass, is, after all, only a round-about name for chance; and chance is something the notion of which no sane mind can for an instant tolerate in the world. What is it, they ask, but barefaced crazy unreason, the negation of intelligibility and law? And if the slightest particle of it exists anywhere, what is to prevent the whole fabric from falling together, the stars from going out, and chaos from recommencing her topsy-turvy reign?

Remarks of this sort about chance will put an end to discussion as quickly as anything one can find. I have already told you that "chance" was a word I wished to keep and use. Let us then examine exactly what it means, and see whether it ought to be such a terrible bugbear to us. I fancy that squeezing the thistle boldly will rob it of its sting.

The sting of the word "chance" seems to lie in the assumption that it means something positive, and that if anything happens by chance, it must needs be something of an intrinsically irrational and preposterous sort. Now, chance means nothing of the kind. It is a purely negative and relative term, giving us no information about that of which it is predicated, except that it happens to be disconnected with something else—not controlled, secured, or necessitated by other things in advance of its own actual presence. As this point is the most subtle one of the whole lecture, and at the same time the point on which all the rest hinges, I beg you to pay particular attention to it. What I say is that it tells us nothing about what a thing may be in itself to call it "chance." It may be a bad thing, it may be a good thing. It may be lucidity, transparency, fitness incarnate, matching the whole system of other things, when it has once befallen, in an unimaginably perfect way. All you mean by calling it "chance" is that this is not guaranteed, that it may also fall out otherwise. For the system of other things has no positive hold on the chance-thing. Its origin is in a certain fashion negative: it escapes, and says, "Hands off!" coming, when it comes, as a free gift, or not at all.

This negativeness, however, and this opacity of the chance-thing when thus considered *ab extra,* or from the point of view of previous things or distant things, do not preclude its having any amount of positiveness and luminosity from within, and at its own place and moment. All that its chance-character asserts about it is that there is something in it really of its own, something that is not the unconditional property of the whole. If the whole wants this property, the whole must wait till it can get it, if it be a matter of chance. That the universe may actually be a sort of joint-stock society of this sort, in which the sharers have both limited liabilities and limited powers, is of course a simple and conceivable notion.

Nevertheless, many persons talk as if the minutest dose of disconnectedness of one part with another, the smallest modicum of independence, the faintest tremor of ambiguity about the future, for example, would ruin everything, and turn this goodly universe into a sort of insane sand-heap or nulliverse—no universe at all. Since future human volitions are, as a matter of fact, the only ambiguous things we are tempted to believe in, let us stop for a moment to make ourselves sure whether their independent and accidental character need be fraught with such direful consequences to the universe as these.

What is meant by saying that my choice of which way to walk home after the lecture is ambiguous and a matter of chance as far as the present moment is concerned? It means that both

Divinity Avenue and Oxford Street are called; but that only one, and that one *either* one shall be chosen. Now, I ask you seriously to suppose that this ambiguity of my choice is real; and then to make the impossible hypothesis that the choice is made twice over, and each time falls on a different street. In other words, imagine that I first walk through Divinity Avenue, and then imagine that the powers governing the universe annihilate ten minutes of time with all that it contained, and set me back at the door of this hall just as I was before the choice was made. Imagine then that, everything else being the same, I now make a different choice and traverse Oxford Street. You, as passive spectators, look on and see the two alternative universes—one of them with me walking through Divinity Avenue in it, the other with the same me walking through Oxford Street. Now, if you are determinists you believe one of these universes to have been from eternity impossible: you believe it to have been impossible because of the intrinsic irrationality or accidentality somewhere involved in it. But looking outwardly at these universes, can you say which is the impossible and accidental one, and which the rational and necessary one? I doubt if the most iron-clad determinist among you could have the slightest glimmer of light at this point. In other words, either universe *after the fact* and once there would, to our means of observation and understanding, appear just as rational as the other. There would be absolutely no criterion by which we might judge one necessary and the other matter of chance. Suppose now we relieve the gods of their hypothetical task and assume my choice, once made, to be made forever. I go through Divinity Avenue for good and all. If, as good determinists, you now begin to affirm, what all good determinists punctually do affirm, that in the nature of things I couldn't have gone through Oxford Street—had I done so it would have been chance, irrationality, insanity, a horrid gap in nature—I simply call your attention to this, that your affirmation is what the Germans call a *Machtspruch,* a mere conception fulminated as a dogma and based on no insight into details. Before my choice, either street seemed as natural to you as to me. Had I happened to take Oxford Street, Divinity Avenue would have figured in your philosophy as the gap in nature; and you would have so proclaimed it with the best deterministic conscience in the world.

But what a hollow outcry, then, is this against a chance which, if it were present to us, we could by no character whatever distinguish from a rational necessity! I have taken the most trivial of examples, but no possible example could lead to any different result. For what are the alternatives which, in point of fact, offer themselves to human volition? What are those futures that now seem matters of chance? Are they not one and all like the Divinity Avenue and Oxford Street of our example? Are they not all of them *kinds* of things already here and based in the existing frame of nature? Is any one ever tempted to produce an *absolute* accident, something utterly irrelevant to the rest of the world? Do not all the motives that assail us, all the futures that offer themselves to our choice, spring equally from the soil of the past; and would not either one of them, whether realized through chance or through necessity, the moment it was realized, seem to us to fit that past, and in the completest and most continuous manner to interdigitate with the phenomena already there?

A favorite argument against free will is that if it be true, a man's murderer may as probably be his best friend as his worst enemy, a mother be as likely to strangle as to suckle her first-born, and all of us be as ready to jump from fourth-story windows as to go out of front doors, etc. Users of this argument should probably be excluded from debate till they learn what the real question is. "Free-will" does not say that everything that is physically conceivable is also morally possible. It merely says that of alternatives that really *tempt* our will more than one is really possible. Of course, the alternatives that do thus tempt our will are vastly fewer than the physical possibilities we can coldly fancy. Persons really tempted often do murder their best friends, mothers do strangle their first-born, people do jump out of fourth stories, etc.

The more one thinks of the matter, the more one wonders that so empty and gratuitous a hubbub as this outcry against chance should have found so great an echo in the hearts of men. It is a word which tells us absolutely nothing about what chances, or about the *modus operandi* of the chancing; and the use of it as a war-cry shows only a temper of intellectual absolutism, a demand that the world shall be a solid block, subject to one control—which temper, which demand, the world may not be bound to gratify at all. In every outwardly verifiable and practical respect, a world in which the alternatives that now actually distract *your* choice were decided by pure chance would be by *me* absolutely undistinguished from the world in which I now live. I am, therefore, entirely willing to call it, so far as your choices go, a world of chance for me. To *yourselves,* it is true, those very acts of choice, which to me are so blind, opaque, and external, are the opposites of this, for you are within them and effect them. To you they appear as decisions; and decisions, for him who makes them, are altogether peculiar psychic facts. Self-luminous and self-justifying at the living moment in which they occur, they appeal to no outside moment to put its stamp upon them or make them continuous with the rest of nature. Themselves it is rather who seem to make nature continuous; and in their strange and intense function of granting consent to one possibility and withholding it from another, to transform an equivocal and double future into an inalterable and simple past.

But with the psychology of the matter we have no concern this evening. The quarrel which determinism has with chance fortunately has nothing to do with this or that psychological detail. It is a quarrel altogether metaphysical. Determinism denies the ambiguity of future volitions, because it affirms that nothing future can be ambiguous. But we have said enough to meet the issue. Indeterminate future volitions *do* mean chance. Let us not fear to shout it from the house-tops if need be; for we now know that the idea of chance is, at bottom, exactly the same thing as the idea of gift—the one simply being a disparaging, and the other a eulogistic, name for anything on which we have no effective *claim*. And whether the world be the better or the worse for having either chances or gifts in it will depend altogether on *what* these uncertain and unclaimable things turn out to be.

THE MORAL IMPLICATIONS OF DETERMINISM

And this at last brings us within sight of our subject. We have seen what determinism means: we have seen that indeterminism is rightly described as meaning chance; and we have seen that chance, the very name of which we are urged to shrink from as from a metaphysical pestilence, means only the negative fact that no part of the world, however big, can claim to control absolutely the destinies of the whole. But although, in discussing the word "chance," I may at moments have seemed to be arguing for its real existence, I have not meant to do so yet. We have not yet ascertained whether this be a world of chance or no; at most, we have agreed that it seems so. And I now repeat what I said at the outset, that, from any strict theoretical point of view, the question is insoluble. To deepen our theoretic sense of the *difference* between a world with chances in it and a deterministic world is the most I can hope to do; and this I may now at last begin upon, after all our tedious clearing of the way.

I wish first of all to show you just what the notion that this is a deterministic world implies. The implications I call your attention to are all bound up with the fact that it is a world in which we constantly have to make what I shall, with your permission, call judgments of regret. Hardly an hour passes in which we do not wish that something might be otherwise; and happy indeed are those of us whose hearts have never echoed the wish of Omar Khayyam—

> That we might clasp, ere closed, the book of fate,
> And make the writer on a fairer leaf
> Inscribe our names, or quite obliterate.

> Ah! Love, could you and I with fate conspire
> To mend this sorry scheme of things entire,
> Would we not shatter it to bits, and then
> Remould it nearer to the heart's desire?

Now, it is undeniable that most of these regrets are foolish, and quite on a par in point of philosophic value with the criticisms on the universe of that friend of our infancy, the hero of the fable, "The Atheist and the Acorn"—

> Fool! had that bough a pumpkin bore,
> Thy whimsies would have worked no more,
> etc.

Even from the point of view of our own ends, we should probably make a botch of remodelling the universe. How much more then from the point of view of ends we cannot see! Wise men therefore regret as little as they can. But still some regrets are pretty obstinate and hard to stifle—regrets for acts of wanton cruelty or treachery, for example, whether performed by others or by ourselves. Hardly any one can remain *entirely* optimistic after reading the confession of the murderer at Brockton the other day: how, to get rid of the wife whose continued existence bored him, he inveigled her into a deserted spot, shot her four times, and then, as she lay on the ground and said to him, "You didn't do it on purpose, did you, dear?" replied, "No, I didn't do it on purpose," as he raised a rock and smashed her skull. Such an occurrence, with the mild sentence and self-satisfaction of the prisoner, is a field for a crop of regrets, which one need not take up in detail. We feel that, although a perfect mechanical fit to the rest of the universe, it is a bad moral fit, and that something else would really have been better in its place.

But for the deterministic philosophy the murder, the sentence, and the prisoner's optimism were all necessary from eternity; and nothing else for a moment had a ghost of a chance of being put in their place. To admit such a chance, the determinists tell us, would be to make a suicide of reason; so we must steel our hearts against the thought. And here our plot thickens, for we see the first of those difficult implications of determinism and monism which it is my purpose to make you feel. If this Brockton murder was called for by the rest of the universe, if it had come at its preappointed hour, and if nothing else would have been consistent with the sense of the whole, what are we to think of the universe? Are we stubbornly to stick to our judgment of regret, and say, though it *couldn't* be, yet it *would* have been a better universe with something different from this Brockton murder in it? That, of course, seems the natural and spontaneous thing for us to do; and yet it is nothing short of deliberately espousing a kind of pessimism. The judgment of regret calls the murder bad. Calling a thing bad means, if it means anything at all, that the thing ought not be, that something else ought to be in its stead. Determinism, in denying that anything else can be in its stead, virtually defines the universe as a place in which what ought to be is impossible—in other words, as an organism whose constitution is afflicted with an incurable taint, and irremediable flaw. The pessimism of a Schopenhauer says no more than this—that the murder is a symptom; and that it is a vicious symptom because it belongs to a vicious whole, which can express its nature no otherwise than by bringing forth just such a symptom as that at this particular spot. Regret for the murder must transform itself, if we are determinists and wise, into a larger regret. It is absurd to regret the murder alone. Other things being what they are, *it* could not be different. What we should regret is that whole frame of things of which the murder is one member. I see no escape whatever from this pessimistic conclusion if, being determinists, our judgment of regret is to be allowed to stand at all.

The only deterministic escape from pessimism is everywhere to abandon the judgment of regret. That this can be done, history shows to be not impossible. The devil, *quoad existentiam,* may be good. That is, although he be a *principle* of evil, yet the universe, with such a principle in it, may practically be a better universe than it could have been without. On every hand, in a small way, we find that a certain amount of evil is a condition by which a higher form of good is brought. There is nothing to prevent anybody from generalizing this view, and trusting that if we could but see things in the largest of all ways, even such matters as this Brockton murder would appear to be paid for by the uses which follow in their train. An optimism *quand même,* a systematic and infatuated optimism like that ridiculed by Voltaire in his *Candide,* is one of the possible ideal ways in which a man may train himself to look upon life. Bereft of dogmatic hardness and lit up with the expression of a tender and pathetic hope, such an optimism has been the grace of some of the most religious characters that ever lived.

> Throb thine with Nature's throbbing breast,
> And all is clear from east to west.

Even cruelty and treachery may be among the absolutely blessed fruits of time, and to quarrel with any of their details may be blasphemy. The only real blasphemy, in short, may be that pessimistic temper of the soul which lets it give way to such things as regrets, remorse, and grief. Thus, our deterministic pessimism may become a deterministic optimism at the price of extinguishing our judgments of regret.

But does not this immediately bring us into a curious logical predicament? Our determinism leads us to call our judgments of regret wrong, because they are pessimistic in implying that what is impossible yet ought to be. But how then about the judgments of regret themselves? If they are wrong, other judgments, judgments of approval presumably, ought to be in their place. But as they are necessitated, nothing else *can* be in their place; and the universe is just what it was before—namely, a place in which what ought to be appears impossible. We have got one foot out of the pessimistic bog, but the other one sinks all the deeper. We have rescued our actions from the bonds of evil, but our judgments are now held fast. When murders and treacheries cease to be sins, regrets are theoretic absurdities and errors. The theoretic and the active life thus play a kind of see-saw with each other on the ground of evil. The rise of either sends the other down. Murder and treachery cannot be good without regret being bad:

regret cannot be good without treachery and murder being bad. Both, however, are supposed to have been foredoomed; so something must be fatally unreasonable, absurd, and wrong in the world. It must be a place of which either sin or error forms a necessary part. From this dilemma there seems at first sight no escape. Are we then so soon to fall back into the pessimism from which we thought we had emerged? And is there no possible way by which we may, with good intellectual consciences, call the cruelties and the treacheries, the reluctances and the regrets, *all* good together?

Certainly there is such a way, and you are probably most of you ready to formulate it yourselves. But, before doing so, remark how inevitably the question of determinism and indeterminism slides us into the question of optimism and pessimism, or, as our fathers called it, "The question of evil." The theological form of all these disputes is simplest and the deepest, the form from which there is the least escape—not because, as some have sarcastically said, remorse and regret are clung to with a morbid fondness by the theologians as spiritual luxuries, but because they are existing facts in the world, and as such must be taken into account in the deterministic interpretation of all that is fated to be. If they are fated to be error, does not the bat's wing of irrationality cast its shadow over the world? . . .

MORALITY AND INDETERMINISM

The only consistent way of representing a pluralism and a world whose parts may affect one another through their conduct being either good or bad is the indeterministic way. What interest, zest, or excitement can there be in achieving the right way, unless we are enabled to feel that the wrong way is also a possible and a natural way—nay, more, a menacing and an imminent way? And what sense can there be in condemning ourselves for taking the wrong way, unless we need have done nothing of the sort, unless the right way was open to us as well? I cannot understand the willingness to act, no matter how we feel, without the belief that acts are really good and bad. I cannot understand the belief that an act is bad, without regret at its happening. I cannot understand regret without the admission of real, genuine possibilities in the world. Only then is it other than a mockery to feel, after we have failed to do our best, that an irreparable opportunity is gone from the universe, the loss of which it must forever after mourn.

If you insist that this is all superstition, that possibility is in the eye of science and reason impossibility, and that if I act badly 'tis that the universe was foredoomed to suffer this defect, you fall right back into the dilemma, the labyrinth, of pessimism and subjectivism, from out of whose toils we have just wound our way.

Now, we are of course free to fall back, if we please. For my own part, though, whatever difficulties may beset the philosophy of objective right and wrong, and the indeterminism it seems to imply, determinism, with its alternative pessimism or romanticism, contains difficulties that are greater still. But you will remember that I expressly repudiated awhile ago the pretension to offer any arguments which could be coercive in a so-called scientific fashion in this matter. And I consequently find myself, at the end of this long talk, obliged to state my conclusions in an altogether personal way. This personal method of appeal seems to be among the very conditions of the problem; and the most any one can do is to confess as candidly as he can the grounds for the faith that is in him, and leave his example to work on others as it may.

Let me, then, without circumlocution say just this. The world is enigmatical enough in all conscience, whatever theory we may take up toward it. The indeterminism I defend, the free-will theory of popular sense based on the judgment of regret, represents that world as vulnerable, and liable to be injured by certain of its parts if they act wrong. And it represents their acting wrong as a matter of possibility or accident, neither inevitable nor yet to be infallibly warded off. In all this, it is a theory devoid either of transparency or of stability. It gives us a pluralistic, restless universe, in which no single point of view can ever take in the whole scene; and to a mind possessed of the love of unity at any cost, it will, no doubt, remain forever inacceptable. A friend with such a mind once told me that the thought of my universe made him sick, like the sight of the horrible motion of a mass of maggots in their carrion bed.

But while I freely admit that the pluralism and the restlessness are repugnant and irrational in a certain way, I find that every alternative to them is irrational in a deeper way. The indeterminism with its maggots, if you please to speak so about it, offends only the native absolutism of my intellect—an absolutism which, after all, perhaps, deserves to be snubbed and kept in check. But the determinism with its necessary carrion, to continue the figure of speech, and with no possible maggots to eat the latter up, violates my sense of moral reality through and through. When, for example, I imagine such carrion as the Brockton murder, I cannot conceive it as an act by which the universe, as a whole, logically and necessarily expresses its nature without shrinking from complicity with such a whole. And I deliberately refuse to keep on terms of loyalty with the universe by saying blankly that the murder, since it does flow from the nature of the whole, is not carrion. There are *some* instinctive reactions which I, for one, will not tamper with. The only remaining alternative, the attitude of gnostical romanticism, wrenches my personal instincts in quite as violent a way. It falsifies the simple objectivity of their deliverance. It makes the goose-flesh the murder excites in me a sufficient reason for the perpetration of the crime. It transforms life from a tragic reality into an insincere melodramatic exhibition, as foul or as tawdry as any one's diseased curiosity pleases to carry it out. And with its consecration of the *roman naturaliste* state of mind, and its enthronement of the baser crew of Parisian *littérateurs* among the eternally indispensable organs by which the infinite spirit of things attains to that subjective illumination which is the task of its life, it leaves me in presence of a sort of subjective carrion considerably more noisome than the objective carrion I called it in to take away.

No! better a thousand times, than such systematic corruption of our moral sanity, the plainest pessimism, so that it be straightforward; but better far than that, the world of chance. Make as great an uproar about chance as you please, I know that chance means pluralism and nothing more. If some of the members of the pluralism are bad, the philosophy of pluralism, whatever broad views it may deny me, permits me, at least, to turn to the other members with a clean breast of affection and an unsophisticated moral sense. And if I still wish to think of the world as a totality, it lets me feel that a world with a chance in it of being altogether good, even if the chance never comes to pass, is better than a world with no such chance at all. That "chance" whose very notion I am exhorted and conjured to banish from my view of the future as the suicide of reason concerning it, that "chance" is—what? Just this—the chance that in moral respects the future may be other and better than the past has been. This is the only chance we have any motive for supposing to exist. Shame, rather, on its repudiation and its denial! For its presence is the vital air which lets the world live, the salt which keeps it sweet.

For Further Reflection

1. Do you agree with James that the question of free will versus determinism is unprovable and largely a matter of sentiment based on personality type? In that case, are we determined to choose one view or the other?

2. Is James correct to reject the high status of the principle of causality (the idea that every event or state of affairs must have an antecedent cause), characterizing it as an "altar to an unknown god"?

The Powers of Rational Beings: Freedom of the Will   V.52

PETER VAN INWAGEN

Peter van Inwagen is professor of philosophy at the University of Notre Dame and the author of several books, including *An Essay on Free Will, Material Beings,* and *God, Knowledge, and Mystery.* In this selection, he argues that free will, determinism, and indeterminism are profound mysteries. It is a mystery how free will and determinism could both be true, or how we could reasonably accept the one and reject the other. He concludes that "there is no position one can take concerning free will that does not confront its adherent with mystery." He prefers what he considers the least mysterious of the options: "I believe that the outcome of our deliberations about what to do is undetermined and that it is nevertheless—in some way I have no shadow of an understanding of—sometimes up to us what the outcome of these deliberations will be."

Study Questions

1. What are the distinctions that van Inwagen clarifies with the "garden of forking paths" diagrams?
2. According to van Inwagen, what is determinism? compatibilism? incompatibilism?
3. Why does van Inwagen say that determinism and free will present us with profound mysteries? What is the mystery of compatibilism and incompatibilism?

We now turn to another mystery, a mystery about the *powers* of rational beings; that is, a mystery about what human beings are able to do. This mystery is the mystery of free will and determinism. The best way to get an intuitive grip on the concepts of free will and determinism and the relations between them is to think of time as a "garden of forking paths." That is, to think of the alternatives one considers when one is deciding what to do as being parts of various "alternative futures" and to think of these alternative futures diagrammatically, in the way sug-gested by a path or a river or a road that literally forks:

Let us first consider the concept of free will. If Jane is trying to decide whether to tell all or to continue her life of deception, she is in a situation

From Peter van Inwagen, "The Powers of Rational Beings: Freedom of the Will," in Metaphysics *(Westview Press, 2002).*

strongly analogous to that of someone who is hesitating between forks in a road. That is why this sort of diagram is so helpful to someone who is thinking about decisions and the future. To say that one has free will is to say that when one decides among forks in the road of time (or, more prosaically, when one decides what to do), one is at least sometimes able to take more than one of the forks. Thus, Jane, who is deciding between a fork that leads to telling all and a fork that leads to a life of continued deception, has free will (on this particular occasion) if she is able to tell all and is also able to continue living a life of deception. One has free will if sometimes more than one of the forks in the road of time is "open" to one. One lacks free will if, on every occasion on which one must make a decision, only one of the forks before one—of course it will be the fork one in fact takes—is open to one. If John is locked in a room and doesn't know the door is locked, and if he is in the process of deliberating about whether to leave, one of the alternative futures he is contemplating—leaving—is, in point of fact, not open to him, and he thus lacks free will in the matter of staying or leaving.[1]

It is a common opinion that free will is required by morality. Let us examine this common opinion from the perspective provided our picture of time as a garden of forking paths. Although it is obviously false—for about six independent reasons—that the whole of morality consists in making judgments of the form 'You should not have done X,' we can at least illustrate certain important features of the relation between free will and morality by examining the relation between the concept of free will and the content of such judgments. The judgment that you shouldn't have done X implies that you should have done something else instead; that you should have done something else instead implies that there was something else for you to do; that there was something else for you to do implies that you were *able* to do something else; that you were able to do something else implies that you have free will. To make a negative moral judgment about one of your acts is to evaluate

your taking one of the forks in the road of time, to characterize that fork as a worse choice than at least one of the other forks open to you. (Note that if you have made a choice by taking one of the forks in what is literally a road, no one could say you should have taken one of the other forks if all the other forks were blocked.) A negative moral evaluation of what someone has done requires two or more alternative possibilities of action for that person just as surely as a contest requires two or more contestants.

Let us now turn from the concept of free will to the concept of determinism. We shall see how thinking of time as a garden of forking paths can help us to understand this concept. Determinism is the thesis that it is true at every moment that the way things then are determines a unique future, that only *one* of the alternative futures that may exist relative to a given moment is a physically possible continuation of the state of things at that moment. Or, if you like, we may say that determinism is the thesis that only one continuation of the state of things at a given moment is consistent with the laws of nature. (For it is the laws of nature that determine what is physically possible. It is, for example, now physically possible for you to be in Chicago at noon tomorrow if and only if your being in Chicago at noon tomorrow is consistent with both the present state of things and the laws of nature.) Thus, according to determinism, although it may often seem to us that we confront a sheaf of possible futures (like this)

what we really confront is something like this

This figure is almost shaped like a road that splits into four roads, but not quite: three of the four "branches" leading away from the "fork" are not connected with the original road, although they come very close to it.[2] (Thus they are not really branches in the road, and the place at which they almost touch the road is not really a fork.) If we were to view this figure from a distance—from across the room, say—it would seem to us to have the shape of a road that forks. We have to look at it closely to see that what appeared from a distance to be three "branches" are not connected with the long line or with one another. In the figure, the point at which the three unconnected lines *almost* touch the long line represents the present. The unconnected lines represent possible futures that are not *physically* possible futures—because they are not physically possible continuations of the present. The part of the long line to the right of the "present" represents a future that is a physically possible continuation of the present. The gaps between the long line and the unconnected lines represent causal discontinuities, violations of the laws of nature—in a word, miracles. The reason these futures are not physically possible continuations of the present is that "getting into" any of them from the present would require a miracle. The fact that the part of the long line that lies to the right of the "present" actually proceeds from that point represents the fact that this line-segment corresponds to a physically possible future.

This figure, then, represents four futures, three of which are physically impossible and exactly one of which is physically possible. If these four futures are *all* the futures that "follow" the present, the figure represents the way each moment of time must be if the universe is deterministic: each moment must be followed by *exactly one* physically possible future.

The earlier diagram, however, represents an indeterministic situation. The road really does fork. The present is followed by four possible futures. Any one of them could, consistently with the laws of nature, evolve out of the present. Any one of them could, consistently with

the laws of nature, turn out to be the actual future. It is only if the universe is indeterministic, therefore, that time *really is* a "garden of forking paths." But even in a deterministic universe, time could *look like* a garden of forking paths. Remember that the second figure, when viewed from across the room, *looked* as if it had the shape of a road that forked. We cannot see all, or even very many, of the causes operating in any situation. It might therefore be that the universe is deterministic, despite the fact that it sometimes seems to us human beings that there is more than one possible future. It may seem to Jane that she faces two possible futures, in one of which she tells all and in the other of which she continues her life of deception. But it may well be that the possibility of one or the other of these contemplated futures is mere appearance—an illusion, in fact. It may be that, in reality, causes now at work in her brain and central nervous system and immediate environment have already "ruled out" one or the other of these futures: it may be that one or the other of them is such that it could not come to pass unless a physically impossible event, a miracle, were to happen in her brain or central nervous system or environment.

Ask yourself this question. What would happen if some supernatural agency—God, say—were to "roll history back" to some point in the past and then "let things go forward again"? Suppose the agency were to cause things to be once more just as they were at high noon, Greenwich mean solar time, on 11 March 1893 and were thereafter to let things go on of their own accord. Would history literally repeat itself? Would there be two world wars, each the same in every detail as the wars that occurred the "first time around"? Would a president of the United States called 'John F. Kennedy' be assassinated in Dallas on the date that in the new reckoning is called '22 November 1963'? Would you, or at least someone exactly like you, exist? If the answer to any of these questions is No, determinism is false. Equivalently, if determinism is true, the answer to all these questions is Yes. If determinism is true, then, if the universe were "rolled back" to a previous state by a miracle (and there were no further miracles), the history of the world would repeat itself. If the universe were rolled back to a previous state thousands of times, exactly the same events would follow each of these thousands of "reversions." If there are no forks in the road of time—if all the apparent forks are merely apparent, illusions due to our limited knowledge of the causes of things—, restoring the universe to some earlier condition is like moving a traveler on a road without forks back to an earlier point on that road. If there are no forks in the road, the traveler must traverse the same path a second time.

It has seemed obvious to most people who have not been exposed (perhaps 'subjected' would be a better word) to philosophy that free will and determinism are incompatible. It is almost impossible to get beginning students of philosophy to take seriously the idea that there could be such a thing as free will in a deterministic universe. Indeed, people who have not been exposed to philosophy usually understand the word 'determinism' (if they know the word at all) to stand for the thesis that there is no free will. And you might think that the incompatibility of free will and determinism deserves to seem obvious—because it *is* obvious. To say that we have free will is to say that more than one future is sometimes open to us. To affirm determinism is to say that every future but the actual future is physically impossible. And, surely, a physically impossible future can't be open to anyone, can it? If we know that a "Star Trek" sort of future is physically impossible (because, say, the "warp drives" and "transporter beams" that figure essentially in such futures are physically impossible), we know that a "Star Trek" future is not open to us or to our descendants.

People who are convinced by this sort of reasoning are called *incompatibilists*: they hold that free will and determinism are incompatible. As I have hinted, however, many philosophers are *compatibilists*: they hold that free will and determinism are compatible. Compatibilism has an illustrious history among English-speaking philosophers, a history embracing such figures as the seventeenth-century English philosopher Thomas Hobbes, the eighteenth-century Scottish philosopher David Hume, and the nineteenth-century English philosopher John Stuart Mill. And the majority of English-speaking philosophers in the twentieth century were compatibilists. (But compatibilism has not had many adherents on the continent of Europe. Kant, for example, called it a "wretched subterfuge.")

A modern compatibilist can be expected to reply to the line of reasoning I have just presented in some such way as follows:

> Yes, a future, in order to be open to one, does need to be physically possible—*in one sense*. I agree that a future can't be open to one if it contains faster-than-light travel and faster-than-light travel is physically impossible. But we must distinguish between a future's being "internally" physically possible and its *having a physically possible connection with the present*. A future is internally physically possible if everything that happens in it is permitted by the laws of nature. A future has a physically possible connection with the present if it could be "joined" to the present without any violation of the laws of nature. A physically possible future that does not have a physically possible connection with the present is one that, given the present state of things, would have to be "inaugurated" by a miracle (an event that violated the laws of nature) but in which, thereafter, events proceeded in accordance with the laws. Determinism indeed says that, of all the internally physically possible futures, one and only one has a physically possible connection with the present—one and only one could be joined to the present without a violation of the laws of nature. My position is that some futures that could not be joined to the present without a violation of the laws of nature are, nevertheless, open to some people. Fortunately, this does not commit me to the thesis that some of the futures open to some people are not internally physically possible—"fortunately" because *that* thesis is obviously false.

Two philosophical problems face the defenders of compatibilism. The easier is to provide a clear statement of *which* futures that do not have a physically possible connection with the present are "open" to us. The more difficult is to make it seem at least plausible that futures that are in this sense open to an agent really deserve to be so described.

An example of a solution to these problems may make the nature of the problems clearer. The solution I shall briefly describe would almost certainly be regarded by all present-day compatibilists as defective, although it has a respectable history. I choose it not to suggest that compatibilists can't do better but simply because it can be described in fairly simple terms.

According to this solution, a future is open to an agent, if, given that the agent chose that future, chose that path leading away from (what seemed to be) a fork in the road of time, it would come to pass. Thus it is open to me to stop writing this book and do a little dance because, if I so chose, that's what I'd do. But if Alice is locked in a prison cell, it is not open to her to leave: if she chose to leave, her choice would be ineffective because she would come up against a locked prison door. Now consider the future I said was open to me—to stop writing and do a little dance— and suppose determinism is true. Although a choice on my part to behave in that remarkable fashion would (no doubt) be effective if it occurred, it is as a matter of fact *not* going to occur, and, therefore, given determinism, it is determined by the present state of things and the laws of nature that such a choice is not going to occur. It is in fact determined that *nothing* is going to occur that would have the consequence that I stop writing and do a little dance. There- fore, none of the futures in which I act in that bizarre way is a future that has a physically possi- ble connection with the present: such a future could come to pass only if it were inaugurated by an event of a sort ruled out by the present state of things and the laws of nature. And yet, as we have seen, many of these futures are "open" to

me in the sense of 'open' the compatibilist has proposed.

Is this a reasonable sense to give to this word? (We now take up the second problem con- fronting the compatibilist.) This is a very large question. The core of the compatibilist's answer is an attempt to show that the reason we are interested in open or accessible futures is that we are interested in modifying the way people behave. One important way in which we modify behavior is by rewarding behavior we like and punishing behavior we dislike. We tell people that we will put them in jail if they steal and that they will get a tax break if they invest their money in such-and-such a way. But there is no point in trying to get people to act in a certain way if that way is not in some sense open to them. There is no point in telling Alfred that he will go to jail if he steals unless it is somehow open to him not to steal.

And what is the relevant sense of "open"? Just the one I have proposed, says the compatibilist. One modifies behavior by modifying the choices people make. That procedure is effective just insofar as choices are effective in producing behavior. If Alfred chooses not to steal (and remains constant in that choice), then he won't steal. But if Alfred chooses not to be subject to the force of gravity, he will nevertheless be sub- ject to the force of gravity. Although it would no doubt be socially useful if there were some peo- ple who were not subject to the force of gravity, there is no point in threatening people with grave consequences if they do not break the bonds of gravity, for even if you managed to induce some people to choose not to be subject to the force of gravity, their choice would not be effective. Therefore (the compatibilist con- cludes), it is entirely appropriate to speak of a future as "open" if it is a future that would be brought about by a choice—even if it were a choice that was determined not to occur. And if Alfred protests when you punish him for not choosing a future that was in this sense open to him, on the ground that it was determined by events that occurred before his birth that he not make the choice that would have inaugurated that future—if he protests that only a *miracle* could have inaugurated such a future—you can tell him his punishment will not be less effective in modifying his behavior (and the behavior of those who witness his punishment) on *that* account.

When things are put that way, compatibilism can look like nothing more than robust common sense. Why, then, do people have so much trouble believing it? Why does it arouse so much resistance? In my view, it arouses resistance because compatibilists make their doctrine look like robust common sense by sweeping a mystery under the carpet (and, despite their best efforts, the bulge shows). People are aware that something is amiss with compatibilism even when they are unable to articulate their misgivings. I believe it is possible to lift the carpet and display the hidden mystery.

There are certain facts that no human being can do anything about—and that no human being in history could *ever* have done anything about. Among these are the fact that the earth is round, the fact that magnets attract iron, the fact that there were once dinosaurs, and the fact that 317 is a prime number. Although no one would deny this, it must be conceded that the concept expressed by the words "*x* can't do anything about *y* (and never could have)" is not entirely unproblematic. Consider this case. I ask you whether you can do anything about the fact that the document we need is locked in the safe. You reply, "No, I can't. I don't know the combination." Or this case. Your number was not drawn in the lottery, and I ask you whether you were ever able to do anything about that (that is, whether you were ever able so to arrange matters that your number be drawn). You reply, "No, my number wasn't drawn, and I wasn't able in any way to influence what number was drawn." Your replies certainly have a point. They would (assuming they are true statements) be excellent excuses if someone said it *wrong* of you not to open the safe, or maintained that you should be *punished* for failing to have a winning lottery ticket. But these facts differ in an important way from the facts in the above list of examples (the roundness of the earth and so on). You would have been able to open the safe if you had had knowledge you didn't have—or if you had made a guess about the combination and had guessed right. It could have happened that you won the lottery—*if* a different series of numbered balls had been drawn. But no knowledge, and no fantastic stroke of luck, would render you able to do anything about the shape of the earth, the physical properties of iron, the distant past, or the arithmetical properties of a number. Let us understand '*x* can't do anything about *y* (and never could have)' in the following very strong sense: '*x* can't do anything about *y* (and never could have), no matter what knowledge *x* might have had and no matter how lucky *x* might have been.' Even in this very strong sense of the words, it remains true that there are facts that no human being can do anything about—and that no human being in history could *ever* have done anything about: the four facts I have cited, and, of course, an enormous number of others. Let us call these facts "untouchable" facts. This term is a mere label. It has no meaning beyond the meaning of the longer phrase it abbreviates. I introduce it simply to avoid having to write phrases of the form '*x* can't do anything about *y* (and never could have), no matter what knowledge *x* might have had and no matter how lucky *x* might have been' over and over again.

The notion of an untouchable fact has a certain logic to it. One of the principles of this logic is, or so it seems, embodied in the following thesis, which I shall refer to simply as the Principle:

> Suppose it's an untouchable fact that *p*. And suppose also that the following conditional (if-then) statement expresses an untouchable fact: if *p*, then *q*.[3] It follows from these two suppositions that it's an untouchable fact that *q*.

To endorse the Principle is to endorse the following thesis: Replace the symbols '*p*' and '*q*' in the Principle with any declarative sentences you like (the same sentence must replace '*p*' at each place it occurs, and likewise with '*q*'); the result will be true. Here is an example that will illustrate what this thesis implies. We replace '*p*' with 'The last dinosaur died long before I was born' and '*q*' with 'I have never seen a living dinosaur'; the result is:

> Suppose it's an untouchable fact that the last dinosaur died long before I was born. And suppose also that the following conditional statement expresses an untouchable fact: if the last dinosaur died long before I was born, then I have never seen a living dinosaur. It follows from these two suppositions that it's an untouchable fact that I have never seen a living dinosaur.

And this statement or series of statements (the Principle tells us) is true. Is the Principle correct? It is hard to see how anyone could deny it. How could anyone be able to do anything about something that is an inevitable consequence of something no one can do anything about? And yet, as we shall see, the compatibilist must deny the Principle. To see why this is so, let us suppose that determinism is true and that the Principle is correct. Now let us consider some fact we should normally suppose was not an untouchable fact. Let us consider the fact that I am writing this book. Most people—at least most people who knew I was writing a book—would assume that this fact was not an untouchable fact because, if for no other reason, they would assume that *I* was (or once had been) in a position to "do something about it." They would assume that it was open to me to have undertaken some other project or no project at all. But we are supposing the truth of determinism, and that means that ten million years ago (say) there was only one physically possible future (only one physically possible continuation of the way things then were), a future that included my being engaged in writing this book at the present date (since that is what I am in fact doing): given the way things were ten million years ago and given the laws of nature, it had to come to pass that at the present time I should be

engaged in writing this book. But consider these two statements of fact

- Things were thus-and-so ten million years ago.
- If things were thus-and-so ten million years ago, then I am now writing this book.

(Here 'thus-and-so' is a sort of gesture at a complete description or specification of the way things were ten million years ago.) The facts expressed by these two statements are both untouchable facts. No human being is able, or ever has been able, to do anything about the way the world was ten million years ago. And no human being is able, or ever has been able, to do anything about the fact expressed by the second statement, for this statement is a consequence of the laws of nature, and no human being can do anything about what the laws of nature are or what their consequences are. If we imagine a possible world in which (as in the actual world) things were thus-and-so ten million years ago, but in which I decided to learn to sail instead of writing this book, we are imagining a world in which the laws of nature are different; for the *actual* laws dictate that if at some point in time things are thus-and-so, then, ten million years later I (or at any rate someone just like me) shall be writing and not sailing. (Remember: we are assuming that determinism is true.)

Recall, now, the Principle. If both the above statements are statements of untouchable fact, it follows, by the Principle, that the fact that I am now writing this book is an untouchable fact. And, obviously, the content of the particular example—my writing a book—played no role in the derivation of this conclusion: if determinism is true and if the Principle is correct, *all* facts are untouchable facts. It follows, given the Principle, that determinism implies that there is no free will. For if anyone on any occasion has ever been able to act otherwise, then someone has been able to cause certain things to be different from the way they in fact are. And if anyone has ever had *that* ability, then some facts are not untouchable facts. This is why the compatibilist must reject the Principle. This is the hidden mystery that, I contend, lies behind the facade of bluff common sense compatibilism presents to the world: the compatibilist must reject the Principle, and the Principle seems to be true beyond all possibility of dispute. (The compatibilist who does not reject the Principle must hold that facts about what went on in the world before there were any human beings are not untouchable facts—or that facts about what the laws of nature are are not untouchable facts. And these alternatives look even more implausible than a rejection of the Principle.) If the Principle were false, that would be a great mystery indeed.

We must not forget, however, that mysteries really do exist. There are principles that are commonly held, and with good reason, to be false and whose falsity seems to be just as great a mystery as the falsity of the Principle would be. Consider, for example the principle usually called the "Galilean Law of the Addition of Velocities." This principle is a generalization of cases like the following. Suppose an airplane is flying at a speed of 800 kilometers per hour relative to the ground; suppose that inside the aircraft a housefly is buzzing along at a speed of 30 kilometers per hour relative to the airplane in the direction of the airplane's travel; then the fly's speed relative to the ground is the sum of these two speeds: 830 kilometers per hour. According to the Special Theory of Relativity, an immensely useful and well-confirmed theory, the Galilean Law of the Addition of Velocities is not true (although what it tells us when it is applied to velocities of the magnitudes we usually consider in everyday life comes very, very close to the truth). And yet when one considers this principle in the abstract—in isolation from the considerations that guided Einstein in his development of Special Relativity—it seems to force itself upon the mind as true, to be true beyond all possibility of doubt. It seems, therefore, that the kind of "inner conviction" that sometimes moves one to say things like, "I can just *see* that that proposition *has* to be true" is not infallible. (This is not an isolated example. Consider the case of Euclid-

ean geometry, which seems to force itself upon the mind as the real geometry of the physical world. The physicists tell us, however, that Euclidean geometry is at best *approximately* true of the physical world.)

Nevertheless, a mystery is a mystery. Since compatibilism hides a mystery, should we not therefore be incompatibilists? Unfortunately, incompatibilism also hides a mystery.

Behold, I show you a mystery.

If we are incompatibilists, we must reject either free will or determinism (or both). What happens if we reject determinism? It is a bit easier now to reject determinism than it was in the nineteenth century, when it was commonly believed, and with reason, that determinism was underwritten by physics. But the quantum-mechanical world of current physics is irreversibly indeterministic (at least this is the usual view among physicists), and physics has therefore got out of the business of underwriting determinism. Nevertheless, the physical world is filled with objects and systems that seem to be deterministic "for all practical purposes"—digital computers, for example—and many philosophers and scientists believe that a human organism is deterministic for all practical purposes. But let us not debate this question. Let us suppose for the sake of argument that human organisms display a considerable degree of indeterminism. Let us suppose in fact that each human organism is such that when the human person associated with that organism (we leave aside the question whether the person and the organism are identical) is trying to decide whether to do A or to do B, there is a physically possible future in which the organism behaves in a way appropriate to a decision to do A and that there is also a physically possible future in which the organism behaves in a way appropriate to a decision to do B. We shall see that this supposition leads to a mystery. We shall see that the indeterminism that seems to be required by free will seems also to destroy free will.

Let us look carefully at the consequences of supposing human behavior to be undetermined.

Suppose Jane is in an agony of indecision; if her deliberations go one way, she will in a moment speak the words, "John, I lied to you about Alice," and if her deliberations go the other way, she will bite her tongue and remain silent. We have supposed there to be physically possible continuations of the present in which each of these things happens. Given the whole state of the physical world at the present moment, and given the laws of nature, both these things are possible; either might equally well happen.

Each contemplated action will, of course, have antecedents in Jane's cerebral cortex, for it is in that part of Jane (or of her body) that control over her vocal apparatus resides. Let us make a fanciful assumption about these antecedents, since it will make no real difference to our argument what they are. (It will help us to focus our thoughts if we have some sort of mental picture of what goes on inside Jane at the moment of decision.) Let us suppose that a certain current-pulse is proceeding along one of the neural pathways in Jane's brain and that it is about to come to a fork. And let us suppose that if it goes to the left, she will make her confession, and that if it goes to the right, she will remain silent. And let us suppose that it is undetermined which way the pulse will go when it comes to the fork: even an omniscient being with a complete knowledge of the state of Jane's brain and a complete knowledge of the laws of physics and unlimited powers of calculation could say no more than, "The laws and the present state of her brain would allow the pulse to go either way; consequently, no prediction of what the pulse will do when it comes to the fork is possible; it might go to the left, and it might go to the right, and that's all there is to be said."

Now let us ask: Is it *up to Jane* whether the pulse goes to the left or to the right?[4] If we think about this question for a moment, we shall see that it is very hard to see how this could be up to her. Nothing in the way things are at the instant before the pulse makes its "decision" to go one way or the other makes it happen that the pulse goes one way or goes the other. If it goes to the left, that *just happens*. If it goes to the right, *that* just happens. There is no way for Jane to *influence* the pulse. There is no way for her to make it go one way rather than the other. Or, at least, there is no way for her to make it go one way rather than the other and leave the "choice" it makes an undetermined event. If Jane did something to *make* the pulse go to the left, then, obviously, its going to the left would *not* be an undetermined event. It is a plausible idea that it is up to an agent what the outcome of a process will be only if the agent is able to arrange things in a way that would make the occurrence of *this* outcome inevitable or in a way that would make the occurrence of *that* outcome inevitable. If this plausible idea is right, there would seem to be no possibility of its being up to Jane (or to anyone else) what the outcome of an *indeterministic* process would be. And it seems to follow that if, when one is trying to decide what to do, it is truly undetermined what the outcome of one's deliberations will be, it cannot be up to one what the outcome of one's deliberations will be. It is, therefore, far from clear whether incompatibilism is a tenable position. The incompatibilist who believes in free will must say this: it is possible, despite the above argument, for it to be up to an agent what the outcome of an indeterministic process will be. But how is the argument to be met?

Some incompatibilists attempt to meet this argument by means of an appeal to a special sort of causation. Metaphysicians have disagreed about what kinds of things stand in the cause-and-effect relation. This is the orthodox, or "Humean" position: Although our idioms may sometimes suggest otherwise, causes and effects are always events. We may *say* that "Stalin caused" the deaths of millions of people, but when we talk in this way, we are not, in the strictest sense, saying that an *individual thing* (Stalin) was the cause of certain events. It was, strictly speaking, certain *events* (certain actions of Stalin) that were the cause of certain other events (the millions of deaths). It has been suggested, however, that, although events do indeed cause other events, in some cases, *persons* or *agents*, individual things, cause events. According to this suggestion, it might very well be that an event in Jane's brain—a current-pulse taking the left-hand branch of a neural fork, say—had Jane as its cause. And not some event or change involving Jane, not something taking place inside Jane, not something Jane *did*, but Jane herself, the person Jane, the agent Jane, the individual thing Jane.

This "type" of causation is usually labeled 'agent-causation,' and it is contrasted with 'event-causation,' the other "type" of causation, the kind of causation that occurs when one event causes another event. An event is a change in the intrinsic properties of an individual or a change in the ways certain individuals are related to one another. Event-causation occurs when a change that occurs at a certain time is due to a change that occurred at some earlier time. If there is such a thing as agent-causation, however, some changes are not due to earlier changes but simply to agents: to agents *full stop*; to agents *period*.

Let us now return to the question confronting the incompatibilist who believes in free will: How is it possible for it to be up to an agent what the outcome of an indeterministic process will be? Those incompatibilists who appeal to agent-causation answer this question as follows: "A process's having one outcome rather than one of the other outcomes it might have had is an event. For it to be up to an agent what the outcome of a process will be is for the agent to be able to cause each of the outcomes that process could have. Suppose, for example, that Jane's deciding what to do was an indeterministic process and that this process terminated in her deciding to speak, although, since it was indeterministic, the laws of nature and the way things were when the process was initiated were consistent with its terminating in her remaining silent. But suppose that Jane *caused* the process to terminate in her speaking and that she *once was able* to cause it to terminate in her being silent. Then it was up to her what the outcome was. That is what it is for it to have been up to an agent whether a process would terminate in A or

B: to have caused it to terminate in one of these two ways, and to have been *able* to cause it to terminate in the other."

There are two "standard" objections to this sort of answer. They take the form of questions. The first question is, "But what does one add to the assertion that Jane decided to speak when one says she was the agent-cause of her decision to speak?" The second is, "But what about the event *Jane's becoming the agent-cause of her decision to speak*? According to your position, this event occurred and it was undetermined—for if it were determined by some earlier state of things and the laws of nature, then her decision to speak would have been determined by these same factors. Even if there is such a thing as agent-causation and this event occurred, how could it have been *up to Jane* whether it occurred? And if Jane was the agent-cause of her decision to speak and it was not up to her whether she was the agent-cause of her decision to speak, then it was not up to her whether she would speak or remain silent."

These two standard objections have standard replies. The first reply is, "I don't know how to answer your question. But that is because causation is a mystery, and not because there is any *special* mystery about *agent*-causation. How would *you* answer the corresponding question about event-causation: What does one add to the assertion that two events occurred in succession when one says the earlier was the *cause* of the later?" The second reply is, "But it *was* up to Jane which of the two events *Jane's becoming the agent-cause of her decision to speak* and *Jane's becoming the agent-cause of her decision to remain silent* would occur. This is because she was the agent-cause of the former and was able to have been the agent-cause of the latter. In any case in which Jane is the agent-cause of an event, she is also the agent-cause of her being the agent-cause of that event, and the agent-cause of her being the agent-cause of her being the agent-cause of that event, and so on 'forever.' Of course, she is no doubt not *aware* of being the agent-cause of all these events, but the doctrine of agent-causation does not entail that agents are aware of all the events of which they are agent-causes."

Perhaps these replies are effective and perhaps not. I reproduce them because they are, as I have said, standard replies to standard objections. I have no clear sense of what is going on in this debate because I do not understand agent-causation. At least I don't think I understand it. To me, the suggestion that an individual thing, as opposed to a *change* in an individual thing, could be the cause of a change is a mystery. I do not intend this as an argument against the *existence* of agent-causation—of some relation between individual things and events that, when it is finally comprehended, will be seen to satisfy the descriptions of "agent-causation" that have been advanced by those who claim to grasp this concept. The world is full of mysteries. And there are many phrases that seem to some to be nonsense but which are in fact not nonsense at all. ("Curved space! What nonsense! Space is what things that are curved are curved *in*. Space itself can't be curved." And no doubt the phrase 'curved space' *wouldn't* mean anything in particular if it had been made up by, say, a science-fiction writer and had no actual use in science. But the general theory of relativity does imply that it is possible for space to have a feature for which, as it turns out, those who understand the theory all regard 'curved' as an appropriate label.) I am saying only that agent-causation is a mystery and that to explain, by an appeal to agent-causation, how it could be up to someone what the outcome of an indeterministic process would be, is to explain a mystery by a mystery.

But now a disquieting possibility suggests itself. Perhaps the explanation of the fact that both compatibilism and incompatibilism seem to lead to mysteries is simply that the concept of free will is self-contradictory. Perhaps free will is, as the incompatibilists say, incompatible with determinism. But perhaps it is also incompatible with *in*determinism, owing to the impossibility of its being up to an agent what the outcome of an indeterministic process will be. If free will is incompatible with both determinism and inde-

terminism, then, since either determinism or indeterminism has to be true, free will is impossible. And, of course, what is impossible does not exist. Can we avoid mystery by accepting the non-existence of free will? If we are willing to say that free will does not exist, then we need not reject the Principle—*and* we need not suppose it is possible for it to be up to an agent what the outcome of an indeterministic process will be.

But consider. Suppose you are trying to decide what to do. And suppose the choice that confronts you is not a trivial one. Let us not suppose you are trying to decide which of two movies to see or which flavor of ice cream to order. Let us suppose the matter to be one of great importance—of great importance to *you*, at any rate. You are, perhaps, trying to decide whether to marry a certain person or whether to risk losing your job by reporting unethical conduct on the part of a superior or whether to sign a "do not resuscitate" order on behalf of a beloved relative who is critically ill. Pick one of these situations and imagine you are in it. (If you are in fact faced with a non-trivial choice, you have no need to imagine anything. Think of your own situation.) Consider the two contemplated courses of action. Hold them before your mind's eye, and let your attention pass back and forth between them. Do you really think it isn't up to you which of these courses of action you will choose? Can you really believe that?

Many philosophers have said that although the choice between contemplated *future* courses of action always seems "open" to them at the time, when they look back on their *past* decisions, the particular decision they have made always or almost always seems inevitable from that perspective. Is this a plausible thesis? I can testify that I do not myself find any such thing when I examine my past decisions. And, even if I did, I should regard it as an open question whether "foresight" or "hindsight" was more to be trusted. (Why should we suppose that hindsight is trustworthy? Maybe there is within us some psychological mechanism that produces the illusion of the inevitability of our past decisions in order to enable us more effectively to put these decisions behind us and to spare us endless retrospective agonizing over them. Maybe we have a natural tendency to interpret our past decisions in a way that presents them in the best possible light. One can think of lots of not implausible hypotheses that imply that our present impression that our past decisions were the only possible ones—if we indeed have this impression—is untrustworthy.)

When I myself look at contemplated future courses of action in the way I have described above, I discover an irresistible tendency to believe that each of them is "open" to me. This tendency may be a vehicle of illusion. It may be that free will belongs to appearance, not to reality. If the concept of free choice were self-contradictory, a belief in this self-contradictory thing might nevertheless be indispensable to human action. Let us ask ourselves: "What would it be like to believe, really to *believe*, that only one course of action is ever open to me?"

It can plausibly be argued that it would be impossible under such circumstances ever to try to decide what to do. Suppose, for example, that you are in a certain room, a room with a single door, and that this door is the only possible way out of the room. Suppose that, as you are thinking about whether to leave the room, you hear a click that may or may not have been the sound of the door's being locked. You are now in a state of uncertainty about whether the door is locked and are therefore in a state of uncertainty about whether it is possible for you to leave the room. Can you continue to try to decide whether to leave the room? It would seem not. (Try the experiment of imagining yourself in this situation and seeing whether you can imagine yourself continuing to try to decide whether to leave.) You cannot because you no longer believe it's possible for you to leave the room. (It's not that you believe it's *im*possible for you to leave the room. You don't believe that either, for you are in a state of uncertainty about whether it is possible for you to leave.) You can, of course, try to decide whether to get up and try the door. But that *is*—at least you probably

believe this—possible for you. And you can try to decide, "conditionally," whether to leave the room *if* the door should prove to be unlocked. But that is not the same thing as trying to decide whether to leave the room.

This thought-experiment convinces me that I cannot try to decide whether to do A or B unless I believe that doing A and doing B are both possible for me. And, therefore, I am convinced that I could not try to decide what to do unless I believed that more than one course of action was sometimes open to me. And if I never tried to decide what to do, if I never deliberated, I should not be a very effective human being. In the state of nature, I should no doubt starve. In a civilized society, I should probably have to be institutionalized. Belief in one's own free will is therefore something we can hardly do without. It would seem to be an evolutionary necessity that beings like ourselves should believe in their own free will. And evolutionary necessity has scant respect for such niceties as logical consistency. It is arguable, therefore, that we cannot trust our conviction that we have free will (if, indeed, we do have this conviction). If evolution has forced a certain belief on us (for the simple reason that we can't survive without that belief), the fact that we hold it provides no evidential support for the hypothesis that the belief is true; it does not even support the hypothesis that that belief is logically consistent. (*Aren't* there people who think that no one, themselves included, has free will? Well, there are certainly people who *say* they think this. I suspect they are not describing their own beliefs correctly. But even if there are people who think no one has free will, it does not follow that these people do not think they have free will, for people do have contradictory beliefs. It may be that "on one level"—the abstract and theoretical—certain people believe free will to be an illusion, while on another level—the concrete and everyday—they believe themselves to have free will.)

Nevertheless, when all is said and done, I find myself with the belief that sometimes more than one course of action is open to me, and I cannot give it up. (As Dr. Johnson said, "Sir, we know our will is free, and there's an end on't.") And I don't find the least plausibility in the hypothesis that this belief is illusory. It can sometimes seem attractive to think of free will as an illusion. To think of free will as an illusion—or to toy with the idea in a theoretical sort of way—can be attractive to someone who has betrayed a friend or achieved success by spreading vicious rumors. If you had done something of that sort, wouldn't you want to believe that you couldn't have done otherwise, that no other course of action was really open to you? Wouldn't it be tempting to suppose that your actions were determined by your genes and your upbringing or by the way things were thousands or millions of years ago? (Jean-Paul Sartre once remarked that determinism was a bottomless well of excuses.) And it is immensely attractive to suppose oneself to be a member of an intellectual élite whose members have freed themselves from an illusion to which the mass of humanity is subject. The hypothesis has its unattractive aspects too, of course. For one thing, if it rules out blame, it presumably rules out praise on the same grounds. But, however attractive or unattractive it may be, it just seems to be false. If some unimpeachable source—God, say—were to tell me I didn't have free will, I'd have to regard that piece of information as proof that I didn't understand the World at all. It would be as if an unimpeachable source had told me that consciousness did not exist or that the physical world was an illusion or that self-contradictory statements could be true. I'd have to say, "Well, all right. You *are* an unimpeachable source. But I just don't see how what you're telling me could be true." In short: to propose that we believe that we do not have free will is to propose that we accept a mystery.

I conclude that there is no position one can take concerning free will that does not confront its adherents with mystery. I myself prefer the following mystery: I believe that the outcome of our deliberations about what to do is undetermined and that it is nevertheless—in some way I have no shadow of an understanding of—sometimes up to us what the outcome of these deliberations will be.

I believe that if Jane has freely decided to speak then the following must be true: if God were to create a thousand perfect duplicates of Jane as she was an instant before the decision to speak was made and were to place each one in circumstances that perfectly duplicated Jane's circumstances at that instant, some of the duplicates would choose to speak and some of them would choose to remain silent, and there would be no explanation whatever of the fact that any particular duplicate made whichever choice it was she made. And yet, I believe, Jane, the one actual Jane, was able to speak and able to remain silent.

I accept this mystery because it seems to me to be the smallest mystery available. If someone believes that human beings do not have free will, that person accepts a mystery—and, in my view, a greater, deeper mystery than the one I accept. Someone who denies the Principle, for example, accepts a mystery—and, in my view, a greater, deeper mystery than the one I accept. But others may judge the sizes of these mysteries differently.

It is important to be aware that we have not said everything there is to say about the size of the mysteries connected with the free-will problem. The most important of the topics we have not discussed in this connection is the relation between free will and morality. In our preliminary discussion of the concept of free will, we said it was a common opinion that free will was required by morality. If this common opinion is correct, then, in a world without free will, all moral judgments are false or in some other way out of place. If that were so, it would greatly aggravate the mystery confronting those who deny the existence of free will. Could it really be, for example, that racism or child abuse or genocide or serial murder are morally unobjectionable? If an unimpeachable source were to inform me that child abuse was morally unobjectionable, my dominant reaction would be one of horror. But I should also have a negative reaction to this revelation that was more intellectual, more theoretical. I should have to conclude that I didn't understand the World at all. I should have to say I simply didn't understand how it could *be* that there was nothing morally objectionable about child abuse.

It is, however, controversial whether a philosopher who rejects free will must concede that all moral judgments are false (or are all in some other way vehicles of illusion). The "common opinion" that morality requires free will is not so common as it used to be. When almost all English-speaking philosophers were compatibilists, this opinion was held by almost everyone in the English-speaking philosophical world. It was the common assumption of the compatibilists and the few incompatibilists there were. Now, however, compatibilists are less common than they used to be, owing principally to the fact that philosophers have come to realize that a compatibilist must reject the Principle. Many philosophers now reject compatibilism who might previously have been strongly attracted to this position. And because these philosophers, or many of them, reject the possibility of any sort of free will that requires indeterminism, they reject free will altogether. But most philosophers who reject free will are not willing to say that morality is an illusion. It has, therefore, become an increasingly popular position that morality does not require free will after all. For this reason, I have not included the thesis that morality is an illusion among the mysteries that must be accepted by those who reject free will. I myself continue to believe that morality is an illusion if there is no free will. (In fact, this conditional statement seems self-evident to me; if an unimpeachable source told me it was false, I'd regard its falsity as a great mystery.) But, since the issues involved in the debate about this thesis pertain to moral philosophy and not to metaphysics, I will not discuss them.

However one may judge the relative "sizes" of the mysteries that confront the adherents of the various positions one might take concerning free will, these mysteries exist. The metaphysician's task is to display these mysteries. Each of us must decide, with no further help from the metaphysician, how to respond to the array of mysteries that the metaphysician has placed before us.

NOTES

1. It should be evident from this discussion of "free will" that what we are calling by this name would be more appropriately called 'free choice.' 'Free will' is, however, the term that has traditionally been used to express this concept, and I use it out of respect for tradition.

2. This way of drawing the figure was suggested to me by David Lyons.

3. Conditional statements can be statements of fact. For example, the statement, 'If a crystal wine glass falls three meters to a stone floor, it will break' states a fact.

4. If a definition of 'it's up to Jane' is required, I offer the following: 'It's up to Jane whether p or q' means 'It must either be the case that p or be the case that q, and *both* (i) Jane is somehow able so to arrange matters that p, and (ii) Jane is somehow able so to arrange matters that q'.

For Further Reflection

1. Do you believe that determinism is true? Do you have free will? Are determinism and free will compatible? Give reasons for your answers.

2. Do you think it is impossible *not* to believe that we have free will? Why or why not?

3. Is morality possible without free will? Explain.

Human Freedom and the Self   V.53

RODERICK M. CHISHOLM

Roderick Chisholm (1916–1999) was professor emeritus of philosophy at Brown University and a distinguished author in epistemology and metaphysics, penning among other titles *Person and Object: A Metaphysical Study* (1976) and *Theory of Knowledge* (1989). In this essay, he argues that free actions are possible because they are caused, not by indefinitely long sequences of preceding events, but by an agent (or self). He calls the former kind of causation *event causation,* and the latter *agent causation.* In his view, when we act freely, we act like God—a prime mover that is itself unmoved, an uncaused cause of events.

Study Questions

1. What is Chisholm's argument against compatibilism?
2. How does he distinguish between event (or *transeunt)* causation and agent (or *immanent)* causation?
3. How does he attempt to settle the conflict between determinism and the notion of human beings as responsible agents?

"A staff moves a stone, and is moved by a hand, which is moved by a man."

ARISTOTLE, *Physics*, 256a.

1. The metaphysical problem of human freedom might be summarized in the following way: Human beings are responsible agents; but this fact appears to conflict with a deterministic view of human action (the view that every event that is involved in an act is caused by some other event); and it *also* appears to conflict with an indeterministic view of human action (the view that the act, or some event that is essential to the act, is not caused at all). To solve the problem, I believe, we must make somewhat far-reaching assumptions about the self or the agent—about the man who performs the act.

Perhaps it is needless to remark that, in all likelihood, it is impossible to say anything significant about this ancient problem that has not been said before.[1]

2. Let us consider some deed, or misdeed, that may be attributed to a responsible agent: one man, say, shot another. If the man *was* responsible for what he did, then, I would urge, what was to happen at the time of the shooting was something that was entirely up to the man himself. There was a moment at which it was true, both that he could have fired the shot and also that he could have refrained from firing it. And if this is so, then, even though he did fire it, he could have done something else instead. (He didn't find himself firing the shot "against his will," as we say.) I think we can say, more generally, then, that if a man is responsible for a certain event or a certain state of affairs (in our example, the shooting of another man), then that event or state of affairs was brought about by some act of his, and the act

From Roderick Chisholm, "Human Freedom and the Self," *originally published as "The Lindley Lecture," University of Kansas, 1964, pp. 3–15. Reprinted by permission.*

was something that was in his power either to perform or not to perform.

But now if the act which he *did* perform was an act that was also in his power *not* to perform, then it could not have been caused or determined by any event that was not itself within his power either to bring about or not to bring about. For example, if what we say he did was really something that was brought about by a second man, one who forced his hand upon the trigger, say, or who, by means of hypnosis, compelled him to perform the act, then since the act was caused by the *second* man it was nothing that was within the power of the *first* man to prevent. And precisely the same thing is true, I think, if instead of referring to a second man who compelled the first one, we speak instead of the *desires* and *beliefs* which the first man happens to have had. For if what we say he did was really something that was brought about by his own beliefs and desires, if these beliefs and desires in the particular situation in which he happened to have found himself caused him to do just what it was that we say he did do, then, since *they* caused it, *he* was unable to do anything other than just what it was that he did do. It makes no difference whether the cause of the deed was internal or external; if the cause was some state or event for which the man himself was not responsible, then he was not responsible for what we have been mistakenly calling his act. If a flood caused the poorly constructed dam to break, then, given the flood and the constitution of the dam, the break, we may say, *had* to occur and nothing could have happened in its place. And if the flood of desire caused the weak-willed man to give in, then he, too, had to do just what it was that he did do and he was no more responsible than was the dam for the results that followed. (It is true, of course, that if the man is responsible for the beliefs and desires that he happens to have, then he may also be responsible for the things they lead him to do. But the question now becomes: *is* he responsible for the beliefs and desires he happens to have? If he is, then there was a time when they were within his power either to acquire or not to acquire, and we are left, therefore, with our general point.)

One may object: But surely if there were such a thing as a man who is really *good,* then he would be responsible for things that he would do; yet, he would be unable to do anything other than just what it is that he does do, since, being good, he will always choose to do what is best. The answer, I think, is suggested by a comment that Thomas Reid makes upon an ancient author. The author had said of Cato, "He was good because he could not be otherwise," and Reid observes: "This saying, if understood literally and strictly, is not the praise of Cato, but of his constitution, which was no more the work of Cato than his existence."[2] If Cato was himself responsible for the good things that he did, then Cato, as Reid suggests, was such that, although he had the power to do what was not good, he exercised his power only for that which was good.

All of this, if it is true, may give a certain amount of comfort to those who are tender-minded. But we should remind them that it also conflicts with a familiar view about the nature of God—with the view that St. Thomas Aquinas expresses by saying that "every movement both of the will and of nature proceeds from God as the Prime Mover."[3] If the act of the sinner *did* proceed from God as the Prime Mover, then God was in the position of the second agent we just discussed—the man who forced the trigger finger, or the hypnotist—and the sinner, so-called, was *not* responsible for what he did. (This may be a bold assertion, in view of the history of western theology, but I must say that I have never encountered a single good reason for denying it.)

There is one standard objection to all of this and we should consider it briefly.

3. The objection takes the form of a stratagem—one designed to show that determinism (and divine providence) is consistent with human responsibility. The stratagem is one that was used by Jonathan Edwards and by many philosophers in the present century, most notably, G. E. Moore.[4]

One proceeds as follows: The expression

(a) He could have done otherwise,

it is argued, means no more nor less than

(b) If he had chosen to do otherwise, then he
  would have done otherwise.

(In place of "chosen," one might say "tried," "set out," "decided," "undertaken," or "willed.") The truth of statement (b), it is then pointed out, is consistent with determinism (and with divine providence); for even if all of the man's actions were causally determined, the man could still be such that, *if* he had chosen otherwise, then he would have done otherwise. What the murderer saw, let us suppose, along with his beliefs and desires, *caused* him to fire the shot; yet he was such that *if*, just then, he had chosen or decided *not* to fire the shot, then he would not have fired it. All of this is certainly possible. Similarly, we could say, of the dam, that the flood caused it to break and also that the dam was such that, *if* there had been no flood or any similar pressure, then the dam would have remained intact. And therefore, the argument proceeds, if (b) is consistent with determinism, and if (a) and (b) say the same thing, then (a) is also consistent with determinism; hence we can say that the agent *could* have done otherwise even though he was caused to do what he did do; and therefore determinism and moral responsibility are compatible.

Is the argument sound? The conclusion follows from the premises, but the catch, I think, lies in the first premise—the one saying that statement (a) tells us no more nor less than what statement (b) tells us. For (b), it would seem, could be true while (a) is false. That is to say, our man might be such that, if he had chosen to do otherwise, then he would have done otherwise, and yet *also* such that he could not have done otherwise. Suppose, after all, that our murderer could not have *chosen*, or could not have *decided*, to do otherwise. Then the fact that he happens also to be a man such that, if he had chosen not to shoot he would not have shot, would make no

difference. For if he could *not* have chosen *not* to shoot, then he could not have done anything other than just what it was that he did do. In a word: from our statement (b) above ("If he had chosen to do otherwise, then he would have done otherwise"), we cannot make an inference to (a) above ("He could have done otherwise") unless we can *also* assert:

(c) He could have chosen to do otherwise.

And therefore, if we must reject this third statement (c), then, even though we may be justified in asserting (b), we are not justified in asserting (a). If the man could not have chosen to do otherwise, then he would not have done otherwise—*even if* he was such that, if he *had* chosen to do otherwise, then he would have done otherwise.

The stratagem in question, then, seems to me not to work, and I would say, therefore, that the ascription of responsibility conflicts with a deterministic view of action.

4. Perhaps there is less need to argue that the ascription of responsibility also conflicts with an indeterministic view of action—with the view that the act, or some event that is essential to the act, is not caused at all. If the act—the firing of the shot—was not caused at all, if it was fortuitous or capricious, happening so to speak out of the blue, then, presumably, no one—and nothing—was responsible for the act. Our conception of action, therefore, should be neither deterministic nor indeterministic. Is there any other possibility?

5. We must not say that every event involved in the act is caused by some other event; and we must not say that the act is something that is not caused at all. The possibility that remains, therefore, is this: We should say that at least one of the events that are involved in the act is caused, not by any other events, but by something else instead. And this something else can only be the agent—the man. If there is an event that is caused, not by other events, but by the man, then there are some events involved in the act that are not caused by other events. But if the event in question is caused by the man then it *is*

caused and we are not committed to saying that there is something involved in the act that is not caused at all.

But this, of course, is a large consequence, implying something of considerable importance about the nature of the agent or the man.

6. If we consider only inanimate natural objects, we may say that causation, if it occurs, is a relation between *events* or *states of affairs*. The dam's breaking was an event that was caused by a set of other events—the dam being weak, the flood being strong, and so on. But if a man is responsible for a particular deed, then, if what I have said is true, there is some event, or set of events, that is caused, *not* by other events or states of affairs, but by the agent, whatever he may be.

I shall borrow a pair of medieval terms, using them, perhaps, in a way that is slightly different from that for which they were originally intended. I shall say that when one event or state of affairs (or set of events or states of affairs) causes some other event or state of affairs, then we have an instance of *transeunt* causation. And I shall say that when an *agent,* as distinguished from an event, causes an event or state of affairs, then we have an instance of *immanent* causation.

The nature of what is intended by the expression "immanent causation" may be illustrated by this sentence from Aristotle's *Physics:* "Thus, a staff moves a stone, and is moved by a hand, which is moved by a man." (VII, 5, 256a, 6–8) If the man was responsible, then we have in this illustration a number of instances of causation—most of them transeunt but at least one of them immanent. What the staff did to the stone was an instance of transeunt causation, and thus we may describe it as a relation between events: "the motion of the staff caused the motion of the stone." And similarly for what the hand did to the staff: "the motion of the hand caused the motion of the staff." And, as we know from physiology, there are still other events which caused the motion of the hand. Hence we need not introduce the agent at this particular point, as Aristotle does—we *need* not, though we *may.* We *may* say that the hand was moved by the man, but we may *also* say that the motion of the hand was caused by the motion of certain muscles; and we may say that the motion of the muscles was caused by certain events that took place within the brain. But some event, and presumably one of those that took place within the brain, was caused by the agent and not by any other events.

There are, of course, objections to this way of putting the matter, I shall consider the two that seem to me to be most important.

7. One may object, firstly: "If the *man* does anything, then, as Aristotle's remark suggests, what he does is to move the *hand.* But he certainly does not *do* anything to his brain—he may not even know that he *has* a brain. And if he doesn't do anything to the brain, and if the motion of the hand was caused by something that happened within the brain, then there is no point in appealing to 'immanent causation' as being something incompatible with 'transeunt causation'—for the whole thing, after all, is a matter of causal relations among events or states of affairs."

The answer to this objection, I think, is this: It is true that the agent does not *do* anything with his brain, or to his brain, in the sense in which he *does* something with his hand and does something to the staff. But from this it does not follow that the agent was not the immanent cause of something that happened within his brain.

We should note a useful distinction that has been proposed by Professor A. I. Melden—namely, the distinction between 'making something A happen' and "doing A."[5] If I reach for the staff and pick it up, then one of the things that I *do* is just that—reach for the staff and pick it up. And if it is something that I do, then there is a very clear sense in which it may be said to be something that I know that I do. If you ask me, "Are you doing something, or trying to do something, with the staff?" I will have no difficulty in finding an answer. But in doing something with the staff, I also make various things happen which are not in this same sense things that I do: I will make various air-particles move; I will free a number of blades of grass from the pressure that had been upon them; and I may cause a shadow to move from one place to another. If these are merely things that I make happen, as distinguished from things that I do, then I may know nothing whatever about them; I may not have the slightest idea that, in moving the staff, I am bringing about any such thing as the motion of air-particles, shadows, and blades of grass.

We may say, in answer to the first objection, therefore, that it is true that our agent does nothing to his brain or with his brain; but from this it does not follow that the agent is not the immanent cause of some event within his brain; for the brain event may be something which, like the motion of the air-particles, he made happen in picking up the staff. The only difference between the two cases is this: in each case, he made something happen when he picked up the staff; but in the one case—the motion of the air-particles or of the shadows—it was the motion of the staff that caused the event to happen; and in the other case—the event that took place in the brain—it was this event that caused the motion of the staff.

The point is, in a word, that whenever a man does something A, then (by "immanent causation") he makes a certain cerebral event happen, and this cerebral event (by 'transeunt causation') makes A happen.

8. The second objection is more difficult and concerns the very concept of "immanent causation," or causation by an agent, as this concept is to be interpreted here. The concept is subject to a difficulty which has long been associated with that of the prime mover unmoved. We have said that there must be some event A, presumably some cerebral event, which is caused not by any other event, but by the agent. Since A was not caused by any other event, then the agent himself cannot be said to have undergone any change or produced any other event (such as "an act of will" or the like) which brought A about. But if, when the agent made A happen, there was no event involved other than A itself, no event which could be described as *making* A happen, what did the agent's causation consist of? What, for example, is the difference between A's just happening, and the agent's *causing* A to happen? We cannot attribute the difference to any event that took place within the agent. And so far as the event A itself is concerned, there would seem to be no discernible difference. Thus Aristotle said that the activity of the prime mover is nothing in addition to the motion that it produces, and Suarez said that "the action is in reality nothing but the effect as it flows from the agent."[6] Must we conclude, then, that there is no more to the man's action in causing event A than there is to the event A's happening by itself? Here we would seem to have a distinction without a difference—in which case we have failed to find a *via media* between a deterministic and an indeterministic view of action.

The only answer, I think, can be this: that the difference between the man's causing A, on the one hand, and the event A just happening, on the other, lies in the fact that, in the first case but not the second, the event A *was* caused and was caused by the man. There was a brain event A; the agent did, in fact, cause the brain event; but there was nothing that he did to cause it.

This answer may not entirely satisfy and it will be likely to provoke the following question: "But what are you really *adding* to the assertion that A happened when you utter the words 'The agent *caused* A to happen'"? As soon as we have put the question this way, we see, I think, that whatever difficulty we may have encountered is one that may be traced to the concept of causation generally—whether "immanent" or "transeunt." The problem, in other words, is not a problem that is peculiar to our conception of human action. It is a problem that must be faced by anyone who makes use of the concept of causation at all; and therefore, I would say, it is a problem for everyone but the complete indeterminist.

For the problem, as we put it, referring just to "immanent causation," or causation by an agent, was this: "What is the difference between saying, of an event A, that A just happened and saying that someone caused A to happen?" The analogous problem, which holds for "transeunt causation," or causation by an event, is this: "What is the difference between saying, of two events A and B, that B happened and then A happened, and saying that B's happening was the *cause* of A's happening?" And the only answer that one can give is this—that in the one case the agent was the cause of A's happening and in the other case event B was the cause of A's happening. The nature of transeunt causation is no more clear than is that of immanent causation.

9. But we may plausibly say—and there is a respectable philosophical tradition to which we may appeal—that the notion of immanent causation, or causation by an agent, is in fact more clear than that of transeunt causation, or causation by an event, and that it is only by understanding our own causal efficacy, as agents, that we can grasp the concept of *cause* at all. Hume may be said to have shown that we do not derive the concept of *cause* from what we perceive of external things. How, then, do we derive it? The most plausible suggestion, it seems to me, is that of Reid, once again: namely that "the conception of an efficient cause may very probably be derived from the experience we have had . . . of our own power to produce certain effects."[7] If we did not understand the concept of immanent causation, we would not understand that of transeunt causation.

10. It may have been noted that I have avoided the term "free will" in all of this. For even if there is such a faculty as "the will," which somehow sets our acts agoing, the question of freedom, as John Locke said, is not the question *"whether the will be free"*; it is the question *"whether a man be free."*[8] For if there is a "will," as a moving faculty, the question is whether the man is free to will to do these things that he does will to do—and also whether he is free *not* to will any of those things that he does will to do, and again, whether he is free to will any of those things that he does not will to do. Jonathan Edwards tried to restrict himself to the question—"Is the man free to do what it is that

he wills?"—but the answer to this question will not tell us whether the man is responsible for what it is that he *does* will to do. Using still another pair of medieval terms, we may say that the metaphysical problem of freedom does not concern the *actus imperatus;* it does not concern the question whether we are free to accomplish whatever it is that we will or set out to do; it concerns the *actus elicitus,* the question whether we are free to will or to set out to do those things that we do will or set out to do.

11. If we are responsible, and if what 1 have been trying to say is true, then we have a prerogative which some would attribute only to God: each of us, when we act, is a prime mover unmoved. In doing what we do, we cause certain events to happen, and nothing—or no one—causes us to cause those events to happen.

12. If we are thus prime movers unmoved and if our actions, or those for which we are responsible, are not causally determined, then they are not causally determined by our *desires*. And this means that the relation between what we want or what we desire, on the one hand, and what it is that we do, on the other, is not as simple as most philosophers would have it.

We may distinguish between what we might call the "Hobbist approach" and what we might call the "Kantian approach" to this question. The Hobbist approach is the one that is generally accepted at the present time, but the Kantian approach, I believe, is the one that is true. According to Hobbism, if we *know,* of some man, what his beliefs and desires happen to be and how strong they are, if we know what he feels certain of, what he desires more than anything else, and if we know the state of his body and what stimuli he is being subjected to, then we may *deduce,* logically, just what it is that he will do—or, more accurately, just what it is that he will try, set out, or undertake to do. Thus Professor Melden has said that "the connection between wanting and doing is logical."[9] But according to the Kantian approach to our problem, and this is the one that I would take, there is no such logical connection between wanting and doing, nor need there even be a causal connection. No set of statements about a man's desires, beliefs, and stimulus situation at any time implies any statement telling us what the man will try, set out, or undertake to do at that time. As Reid put it, though we may "reason from men's motives to their actions and, in many cases, with great probability," we can never do so "with absolute certainty."[10]

This means that, in one very strict sense of the terms, there can be no science of man. If we think of science as a matter of finding out what laws happen to hold, and if the statement of a law tells us what kinds of events are caused by what other kinds of events, then there will be human actions which we cannot explain by subsuming them under any laws. We cannot say, "It is causally necessary that, given such and such desires and beliefs, and being subject to such and such stimuli, the agent will do so and so." For at times the agent, if he chooses, may rise above his desires and do something else instead.

But all of this is consistent with saying that, perhaps more often than not, our desires do exist under conditions such that those conditions necessitate us to act. And we may also say, with Leibniz, that at other times our desires may "incline without necessitating."

13. Leibniz's phrase presents us with our final philosophical problem. What does it mean to say that a desire, or a motive, might "incline without necessitating"? There is a temptation, certainly, to say that "to incline" means to cause and that "not to necessitate" means not to cause, but obviously we cannot have it both ways.

Nor will Leibniz's own solution do. In his letter to Coste, he puts the problem as follows: "When a choice is proposed, for example to go out or not to go out, it is a question whether, with all the circumstances, internal and external, motives, perceptions, dispositions, impressions, passions, inclinations taken together, I am still in a contingent state, or whether I am necessitated to make the choice, for example to go out; that is to say, whether this proposition true and deter-

mined in fact, *In all these circumstances taken together I shall choose to go out,* is contingent or necessary."[11] Leibniz's answer might be put as follows: in one sense of the terms "necessary" and "contingent," the proposition "In all these circumstances taken together I shall choose to go out," may be said to be contingent and not necessary, and in another sense of these terms, it may be said to be necessary and not contingent. But the sense in which the proposition may be said to be contingent, according to Leibniz, is only this: there is no logical contradiction involved in denying the proposition. And the sense in which it may be said to be necessary is this: since "nothing ever occurs without cause or determining reason," the proposition is causally necessary. "Whenever all the circumstances taken together are such that the balance of deliberation is heavier on one side than on the other, it is certain and infallible that that is the side that is going to win out." But if what we have been saying is true, the proposition "In all these circumstances taken together I shall choose to go out," may be causally as well as logically contingent. Hence we must find another interpretation for Leibniz's statement that our motives and desires may incline us, or influence us, to choose without thereby necessitating us to choose.

Let us consider a public official who has some moral scruples but who also, as one says, could be had. Because of the scruples that he does have, he would never take any positive steps to receive a bribe—he would not actively solicit one. But his morality has its limits and he is also such that, if we were to confront him with a fait accompli or to let him see what is about to happen ($10,000 in cash is being deposited behind the garage), then he would succumb and be unable to resist. The general situation is a familiar one and this is one reason that people pray to be delivered from temptation. (It also justifies Kant's remark: "And how many there are who may have led a long blameless life, who are only *fortunate* in having escaped so many temptations."[12] Our relation to the misdeed that we contemplate may not be a matter simply of being able to bring it about or not to bring it about. As St. Anselm noted, there are at least four possibilities. We may illustrate them by reference to our public official and the event which is his receiving the bribe, in the following way: (i) he may be able to bring the event about himself *(facere esse)*, in which case he would actively cause himself to receive the bribe; (ii) he may be able to refrain from bringing it about himself *(non facere esse)*, in which case he would not himself do anything to insure that he receive the bribe; (iii) he may be able to do something to prevent the event from occurring *(facere non esse)*, in which case he would make sure that the $10,000 was *not* left behind the garage; or (iv) he may be unable to do anything to prevent the event from occurring *(non facere non esse)*, in which case, though he may not solicit the bribe, he would allow himself to keep it.[13] We have envisaged our official as a man who can resist the temptation to (i) but cannot resist the temptation to (iv): he can refrain from bringing the event about himself, but he cannot bring himself to do anything to prevent it.

Let us think of "inclination without necessitation," then, in such terms as these. First we may contrast the two propositions:

(1) He can resist the temptation to do something in order to make A happen;

(2) He can resist the temptation to allow A to happen (i.e. to do nothing to prevent A from happening).

We may suppose that the man has some desire to have A happen and thus has a motive for making A happen. His motive for making A happen, I suggest, is one that *necessitates* provided that, because of the motive, (1) is false; he cannot resist the temptation to do something in order to make A happen. His motive for making A happen is one that *inclines* provided that, because of the motive, (2) is false; like our public official, he cannot bring himself to do anything to prevent A from happening. And therefore we can say that this motive

for making A happen is one that *inclines but does not necessitate* provided that, because of the motive, (1) is true and (2) is false; he can resist the temptation to make it happen but he cannot resist the temptation to allow it to happen.

NOTES

1. The general position to be presented here is suggested in the following writings, among others: Aristotle, *Eudemian Ethics*, bk. ii ch. 6; *Nicomachean Ethics*, bk. iii, ch. 1–5; Thomas Reid, *Essays on the Active Powers of Man;* C. A. Campbell, "Is 'Free Will' a Pseudo-Problem?" *Mind*, 1951, 441–65; Roderick M. Chisholm, "Responsibility and Avoidability," and Richard Taylor, "Determination and the Theory of Agency," in *Determinism and Freedom in the Age of Modern Science* ed. Sidney Hook (New York, 1958).

2. Thomas Reid, *Essays on the Active Powers of Man*, essay iv, ch. 4 *(Works*, 600).

3. *Summa Theologica*, First Part of the Second Part, qu. vi ("On the Voluntary and Involuntary").

4. Jonathan Edwards, *Freedom of the Will* (New Haven, 1957); G. E. Moore, *Ethics* (Home University Library, 1912), ch. 6.

5. A. I. Melden, *Free Action* (London, 1961), especially ch. 3. Mr. Melden's own views, however, are quite the contrary of those that are proposed here.

6. Aristotle, *Physics*, bk. iii, ch. 3; Suarez, *Disputationes Metaphysicae*, Disputation 18, s. 10.

7. Reid, *Works*. 524.

8. *Essay concerning Human Understanding*, bk. ii, ch. 21.

9. Melden, 166.

10. Reid, *Works*, 608, 612.

11. "Lettre à Mr. Coste de la Nécessité et de la Contingence" (1707) in *Opera Philosophica*, ed. Erdmann, 447–9.

12. In the Preface to the *Metaphysical Elements of Ethics*, in *Kant's Critique of Practical Reason and Other Works on the Theory of Ethics*, ed. T. K. Abbott (London, 1959). 303.

13. Cf. D. P. Henry, "Saint Anselm's *De 'Grammatico'*," *Philosophical Quarterly*, x (1960), 115–26. St. Anselm noted that (i) and (iii), respectively, may be thought of as forming the upper left and the upper right corners of a square of opposition, and (ii) and (iv) the lower left and the lower right.

For Further Reflection

1. Critics have thought Chisholm's notion of agent causation mysterious—a radically different kind of causation than what science recognizes—making free will equally mysterious. Chisholm later reformulated the idea, saying that what he "had called agent causation is a subspecies of event causation." How would this new conception make agent causation and free will less mysterious?

2. Do you find Chisholm's argument against compatibilism persuasive? Explain.

3. If actions were not caused by agents or selves (as libertarians claim), would free will still be possible? Why or why not?

Compatibilism   V.54

W. T. STACE

W. T. Stace (1886–1967) was born in Britain, educated at Trinity College, Dublin, and served in the British Civil Service in Ceylon. In 1932 he came to the United States to teach at Princeton University. One of his chief goals was to reconcile empiricism with mysticism. Among his works are *The Concept of Morals* (1952), *Time and Eternity* (1952), and *Mysticism and Philosophy* (1960).

Stace attempts to reconcile free will with causal determinism. He takes the position that William James labeled "soft determinism," what is sometimes called compatibilism. We must have free will to be held morally responsible, and yet it seems plausible that all our actions are caused. How can these two apparently inconsistent ideas be brought together? Stace argues that the problem is merely a verbal dispute, and that, rightly understood, there is no inconsistency in holding to both doctrines. Free actions are those we do voluntarily, whereas unfree actions are those that we do involuntarily.

Study Questions

1. Why is it important to discover whether we have free will? Explain Stace's argument.
2. In practice, by what doctrine do even determinists live?
3. How does Stace characterize the dispute between free will and determinism?
4. What is Stace's strategy in consulting common language usage to show that free will is compatible with determinism?
5. What is the difference between a free and an unfree act?
6. What is Stace's general conclusion?
7. How does moral responsibility actually require determinism, according to Stace?

I SHALL FIRST DISCUSS the problem of free will, for it is certain that if there is no free will there can be no morality. Morality is concerned with what men ought and ought not to do. But if a man has no freedom to choose what he will do, if whatever he does is done under compulsion, then it does not make sense to tell him that he ought not to have done what he did and that he ought to do something different. All moral precepts would in such case be meaningless. Also if he acts always under compulsion, how can he be held morally responsible for his actions? How can he, for example, be punished for what he could not help doing?

It is to be observed that those learned professors of philosophy or psychology who deny the existence of free will do so only in their professional moments and in their studies and lecture rooms. For when it comes to doing anything practical, even of the most trivial kind, they invariably behave as if they and others were free. They inquire from you at dinner whether you will choose this dish or that dish. They will ask a child why he told a lie, and will punish him for not having chosen the way of truthfulness. All of which is inconsistent with a disbelief in free will. This should cause us to suspect that the problem is not a real one; and this, I believe, is the case. The dispute is merely verbal, and is due to nothing but a confusion about the meanings of words. It is what is now fashionably called a semantic problem.

How does a verbal dispute arise? Let us consider a case which, although it is absurd in the sense that no one would ever make the mistake which is involved in it, yet illustrates the principle which we shall have to use in the solution of the problem. Suppose that someone believed that the word "man" means a certain sort of five-legged animal; in short that "five-legged animal" is the correct *definition* of man. He might then look around the world, and rightly observing that there are no five-legged animals in it, he might

proceed to deny the existence of men. This preposterous conclusion would have been reached because he was using an incorrect definition of "man." All you would have to do to show him his mistake would be to give him the correct definition; or at least show him that his definition was wrong. Both the problem and its solution would, of course, be entirely verbal. The problem of free will, and its solution, I shall maintain, is verbal in exactly the same way. The problem has been created by the fact that learned men, especially philosophers, have assumed an incorrect definition of free will, and then finding that there is nothing in the world which answers to their definition, have denied its existence. As far as logic is concerned, their conclusion is just as absurd as that of the man who denies the existence of men. The only difference is that the mistake in the latter case is obvious and crude, while the mistake which the deniers of free will have made is rather subtle and difficult to detect.

Throughout the modern period, until quite recently, it was assumed, both by the philosophers who denied free will and by those who defended it, that *determinism is inconsistent with free will.* If a man's actions were wholly determined by chains of causes stretching back into the remote past, so that they could be predicted beforehand by a mind which knew all the causes, it was assumed that they could not in that case be free. This implies that a certain definition of actions done from free will was assumed, namely that they are actions *not* wholly determined by causes or predictable beforehand. Let us shorten this by saying that free will was defined as meaning indeterminism. This is the incorrect definition which has led to the denial of free will. As soon as we see what the true definition is we shall find that the question whether the world is deterministic, as Newtonian science implied, or in a measure indeterministic, as current physics teaches, is wholly irrelevant to the problem.

Of course there is a sense in which one can define a word arbitrarily in any way one pleases. But a definition may nevertheless be called correct or incorrect. It is correct if it accords with a *common usage* of the word defined. It is incorrect if it does not. And if you give an incorrect definition, absurd and untrue results are likely to follow. For instance, there is nothing to prevent you from arbitrarily defining a man as a five-legged animal, but this is incorrect in the sense that it does not accord with the ordinary meaning of the word. Also it has the absurd result of leading to a denial of the existence of men. This shows that *common usage is the criterion for deciding whether a definition is correct or not.* And this is the principle which I shall apply to free will. I shall show that indeterminism is not what is meant by the phrase "free will" *as it is commonly used.* And I shall attempt to discover the correct definition by inquiring how the phrase is used in ordinary conversation.

Here are a few samples of how the phrase might be used in ordinary conversation. It will be noticed that they include cases in which the question whether a man acted with free will is asked in order to determine whether he was morally and legally responsible for his acts.

Jones: I once went without food for a week.
Smith: Did you do that of your own free will?
Jones: No. I did it because I was lost in a desert and could find no food.

But suppose that the man who had fasted was Mahatma Gandhi. The conversation might then have gone:

Gandhi: I once fasted for a week.
Smith: Did you do that of your own free will?
Gandhi: Yes. I did it because I wanted to compel the British Government to give India its independence.

Take another case. Suppose that I had stolen some bread, but that I was as truthful as George Washington. Then, if I were charged with the crime in court, some exchange of the following sort might take place:

Judge: Did you steal the bread of your own free will?
Stace: Yes. I stole it because I was hungry.

Or in different circumstances the conversation might run:

Judge: Did you steal of your own free will?
Stace: No. I stole because my employer threatened to beat me if I did not.

At a recent murder trial in Trenton some of the accused had signed confessions, but afterwards asserted that they had done so under police duress. The following exchange might have occurred:

Judge: Did you sign the confession of your own free will?
Prisoner: No. I signed it because the police beat me up.

Now suppose that a philosopher had been a member of the jury. We could imagine this conversation taking place in the jury room:

Foreman of the Jury: The prisoner says he signed the confession because he was beaten, and not of his own free will.
Philosopher: This is quite irrelevant to the case. There is no such thing as free will.
Foreman: Do you mean to say that it makes no difference whether he signed because his conscience made him want to tell the truth or because he was beaten?
Philosopher: None at all. Whether he was caused to sign by a beating or by some desire of his own—the desire to tell the truth, for example—in either case his signing was causally determined, and therefore in neither case did he act of his own free will. Since there is no such thing as free will, the question whether he signed of his own free will ought not to be discussed by us.

The foreman and the rest of the jury would rightly conclude that the philosopher must be making some mistake. What sort of a mistake could it be? There is only one possible answer. The philosopher must be using the phrase "free will" in some peculiar way of his own which is not the way in which men usually use it when they wish to determine a question of moral responsibility. That is, he must be using an incorrect definition of it as implying action not determined by causes.

Suppose a man left his office at noon, and were questioned about it. Then we might hear this:

Jones: Did you go out of your own free will?
Smith: Yes. I went out to get my lunch.

But we might hear:
Jones: Did you leave your office of your own free will?
Smith: No. I was forcibly removed by the police.

We have now collected a number of cases of actions which, in the ordinary usage of the English language, would be called cases in which people have acted of their own free will. We should also say in all these cases that they *chose* to act as they did. We should also say that they could have acted otherwise, if they had chosen. For instance, Mahatma Gandhi was not compelled to fast; he chose to do so. He could have eaten if he had wanted to. When Smith went out to get his lunch, he chose to do so. He could have stayed and done some work, if he had wanted to. We have also collected a number of cases of the opposite kind. They are cases in which men were not able to exercise their free will. They had no choice. They were compelled to do as they did. The man in the desert did not fast of his own free will. He had no choice in the matter. He was compelled to fast because there was nothing for him to eat. And so with the other cases. It ought to be quite easy, by an inspection of these cases, to tell what we ordinarily mean when we say that a man did or did not exercise free will. We ought therefore to be able to extract from them the proper definition of the term. Let us put the cases in a table:

Free Acts	*Unfree Acts*
Gandhi fasting because he wanted to free India.	The man fasting in the desert because there was no food.
Stealing bread because one is hungry.	Stealing because one's employer threatened to beat one.
Signing a confession because one wanted to tell the truth.	Signing because the police beat one.
Leaving the office because one wanted one's lunch.	Leaving because forcibly removed.

It is obvious that to find the correct definition of free acts we must discover what characteristic is common to all the acts in the left-hand column, and is, at the same time, absent from all the acts in the right-hand column. This characteristic which all free acts have, and which no unfree acts have, will be the defining characteristic of free will.

Is being uncaused, or not being determined by causes, the characteristic of which we are in search? It cannot be, because although it is true that all the acts in the right-hand column have causes, such as the beating by the police or the absence of food in the desert, so also do the acts in the left-hand column. Mr. Gandhi's fasting was caused by his desire to free India, the man leaving his office by his hunger, and so on. Moreover there is no reason to doubt that these causes of the free acts were in turn caused by prior conditions, and that these were again the results of causes, and so on back indefinitely into the past. Any physiologist can tell us the causes of hunger. What caused Mr. Gandhi's tremendously powerful desire to free India is no doubt more difficult to discover. But it must have had causes. Some of them may have lain in peculiarities of his glands or brain, others in his past experiences, others in his heredity, others in his education. Defenders of free will have usually tended to deny such facts. But to do so is plainly a case of special pleading, which is unsupported by any scrap of evidence. The only reasonable view is that all human actions, both those which are freely done and those which are not, are either wholly determined by causes, or at least as much determined as other events in nature. It may be true, as the physicists tell us, that nature is not as deterministic as was once thought. But whatever degree of determinism prevails in the world, human actions appear to be as much determined as anything else. And if this is so, it cannot be the case that what distinguishes actions freely chosen from those which are not free is that the latter are determined by causes while the former are not. Therefore, being uncaused or being undetermined by causes, must be an incorrect definition of free will.

What, then, is the difference between acts which are freely done and those which are not? What is the characteristic which is present to all the acts in the left-hand column and absent from all those in the right-hand column? Is it not obvious that, although both sets of actions have causes, the causes of those in the left-hand column are *of a different kind* from the causes of those in the right-hand column? The free acts are all caused by desires, or motives, or by some sort of internal psychological states of the agent's mind. The unfree acts, on the other hand, are all caused by physical forces or physical conditions, outside the agent. Police arrest means physical force exerted from the outside; the absence of food in the desert is a physical condition of the outside world. We may therefore frame the following rough definitions. *Acts freely done are those whose immediate causes are psychological states in the agent. Acts not freely done are those whose immediate causes are states of affairs external to the agent.*

It is plain that if we define free will in this way, then free will certainly exists, and the philosopher's denial of its existence is seen to be

what it is—nonsense. For it is obvious that all those actions of men which we should ordinarily attribute to the exercise of their free will, or of which we should say that they freely chose to do them, are in fact actions which have been caused by their own desires, wishes, thoughts, emotions, impulses, or other psychological states.

In applying our definition we shall find that it usually works well, but that there are some puzzling cases which it does not seem exactly to fit. These puzzles can always be solved by paying careful attention to the ways in which words are used, and remembering that they are not always used consistently. I have space for only one example. Suppose that a thug threatens to shoot you unless you give him your wallet, and suppose that you do so. Do you, in giving him your wallet, do so of your own free will or not? If we apply our definition, we find that you acted freely, since the immediate cause of the action was not an actual outside force but the fear of death, which is a psychological cause. Most people, however, would say that you did not act of your own free will but under compulsion. Does this show that our definition is wrong? I do not think so. Aristotle, who gave a solution of the problem of free will substantially the same as ours (though he did not use the term "free will") admitted that there are what he called "mixed" or borderline cases in which it is difficult to know whether we ought to call the acts free or compelled. In the case under discussion, though no actual force was used, the gun at your forehead so nearly approximated to actual force that we tend to say the case was one of compulsion. It is a borderline case.

Here is what may seem like another kind of puzzle. According to our view an action may be free though it could have been predicted beforehand with certainty. But suppose you told a lie, and it was certain beforehand that you would tell it. How could one then say, "You could have told the truth"? The answer is that it is perfectly true that you could have told the truth *if* you had wanted to. In fact you would have done so, for in that case the causes producing your action, namely your desires, would have been different, and would therefore have produced different effects. It is a delusion that predictability and free will are incompatible. This agrees with common sense. For if, knowing your character, I predict that you will act honorably, no one would say when you do act honorably, that this shows you did not do so of your own free will.

Since free will is a condition of moral responsibility, we must be sure that our theory of free will gives a sufficient basis for it. To be held morally responsible for one's actions means that one may be justly punished or rewarded, blamed or praised, for them. But it is not just to punish a man for what he cannot help doing. How can it be just to punish him for an action which it was certain beforehand that he would do? We have not attempted to decide whether, as a matter of fact, all events, including human actions, are completely determined. For that question is irrelevant to the problem of free will. But if we assume for the purposes of argument that complete determinism is true, but that we are nevertheless free, it may then be asked whether such a deterministic free will is compatible with moral responsibility. For it may seem unjust to punish a man for an action which it could have been predicted with certainty beforehand that he would do.

But that determinism is incompatible with moral responsibility is as much a delusion as that it is incompatible with free will. You do not excuse a man for doing a wrong act because, knowing his character, you felt certain beforehand that he would do it. Nor do you deprive a man of a reward or prize because, knowing his goodness or his capabilities, you felt certain beforehand that he would win it.

Volumes have been written on the justification of punishment. But so far as it affects the question of free will, the essential principles involved are quite simple. The punishment of a man for doing a wrong act is justified, either on the ground that it will correct his own character, or that it will deter other people from doing similar acts. The instrument of punishment has been in the past, and no doubt still is, often unwisely used; so that

it may often have done more harm than good. But that is not relevant to our present problem. Punishment, if and when it is justified, is justified only on one or both of the grounds just mentioned. The question then is how, if we assume determinism, punishment can correct character or deter people from evil actions.

Suppose that your child develops a habit of telling lies. You give him a mild beating. Why? Because you believe that his personality is such that the usual motives for telling the truth do not cause him to do so. You therefore supply the missing cause, or motive, in the shape of pain and the fear of future pain if he repeats his untrustful behavior. And you hope that a few treatments of this kind will condition him to the habit of truth-telling, so that he will come to tell the truth without the infliction of pain. You assume that his actions are determined by causes, but that the usual causes of truth-telling do not in him produce their usual effects. You therefore supply him with an artificially injected motive, pain and fear, which you think will in the future cause him to speak truthfully.

The principle is exactly the same where you hope, by punishing one man, to deter others from wrong actions. You believe that the fear of punishment will cause those who might otherwise do evil to do well.

We act on the same principle with non-human, and even with inanimate, things, if they do not behave in the way we think they ought to behave. The rose bushes in the garden produce only small and poor blooms, whereas we want large and rich ones. We supply a cause which will produce large blooms, namely fertilizer. Our automobile does not go properly. We supply a cause which will make it go better, namely oil in the works. The punishment for the man, the fertilizer for the plant, and the oil for the car, are all justified by the same principle and in the same way. The only difference is that different kinds of things require different kinds of causes to make them do what they should. Pain may be the appropriate remedy to apply, in certain cases, to human beings, and oil to the machine. It is, of course, of no use to inject motor oil into the boy or to beat the machine.

Thus we see that moral responsibility is not only consistent with determinism, but requires it. The assumption on which punishment is based is that human behavior is causally determined. If pain could not be a cause of truth-telling there would be no justification at all for punishing lies. If human actions and volitions were uncaused, it would be useless either to punish or reward, or indeed to do anything else to correct people's bad behavior. For nothing that you could do would in any way influence them. Thus moral responsibility would entirely disappear. If there were no determinism of human beings at all, their actions would be completely unpredictable and capricious, and therefore irresponsible. And this is in itself a strong argument against the common view of philosophers that free will means being undetermined by causes.

For Further Reflection

1. Has Stace successfully reconciled free will with determinism? Does his analysis of ordinary language settle the matter?

2. Do you think one can accept determinism and still hold people responsible for their voluntary actions? Can we really help holding people responsible for their purposive actions?

Freedom of the Will and the Concept of a Person   V.55

HARRY FRANKFURT

Harry Frankfurt (1929–   ) is an emeritus professor of philosophy at Princeton University who has made important contributions to the study of free will and to Descartes scholarship. Frankfurt, like Stace, is a compatibilist. But whereas Stace and most compatibilists defend their position by a controversial hypothetical interpretation of the formula "S is free just in case S *could have done otherwise*," Frankfurt offers a theory of the will in order to account for our notion of freedom. What distinguishes humans from other animals is our ability to deliberate and choose courses of actions. The strategy goes like this: Both animals and humans have straightforward, or *first-order,* desires—for example, desires to eat, to be comfortable, to sleep—but whereas animals act directly on their wants, humans can weigh them and accept or reject them. For example, Joan may have the first-order desire to smoke a cigarette, but she may also want to be healthy. She compares the two desires and forms a *second-order* desire, say, to refrain from smoking based on her desire to remain healthy. But since it is possible that she may have the second-order desire to refrain from smoking without wanting to act on it, there is one more step in the process. She must make her desire her will, her *volition,* and be committed to act on the desire not to smoke. The person must *identify* himself or herself with the second-order desire and thereby make it a second-order volition. As Frankfurt writes in another article, "To the extent that a person identifies himself with the springs of his actions, he takes a responsibility for those actions and acquires moral responsibility for them" ("Three Concepts of Free Action," in *Moral Responsibility,* ed. John Martin Fischer [Ithaca, NY: Cornell University Press, 1986], p. 120).

Study Questions

1. What is the relationship between the concepts of *person* and *human being*? Could some animals be persons and some humans nonpersons?
2. What do humans have that no animal appears to have?
3. Why is the verb "to want" "extraordinarily elusive"?
4. How does Frankfurt understand the statement "A wants to X"?
5. How does Frankfurt distinguish first-order from second-order desires? How does he illustrate this?
6. What is a wanton? How does Frankfurt illustrate this concept?
7. What according to Frankfurt is freedom of the will?
8. How does freedom of the will relate to our first-order desires?
9. What is the relationship between Frankfurt's conception of freedom of the will and determinism?

THERE IS A SENSE in which the word 'person'[1] is merely the singular form of 'people' and in which both terms connote no more than membership in a certain biological species. In those senses of the word which are of greater philosophical interest, however, the criteria for being a person do not serve primarily to distinguish the members of our own species from the members of other species. Rather, they are designed to capture those attributes which are the subject of our most humane concern with ourselves and the source of what we regard as most important and most problematical in our lives. Now these attributes would be of equal significance to us even if they were not in fact peculiar and common to the members of our own species. What interests us most in the human condition would not interest us less if it were also a feature of the condition of other creatures as well.

Our concept of ourselves as persons is not to be understood, therefore, as a concept of attributes that are necessarily species-specific. It is conceptually possible that members of novel or even of familiar non-human species should be persons; and it is also conceptually possible that some members of the human species are not persons. We do in fact assume, on the other hand, that no member of another species is a person. Accordingly, there is a presumption that what is essential to persons is a set of characteristics that we generally suppose—whether rightly or wrongly—to be uniquely human.

It is my view that one essential difference between persons and other creatures is to be found in the structure of a person's will. Human beings are not alone in having desires and motives, or in making choices. They share these things with the members of certain other species, some of whom even appear to engage in deliberation and to make decisions based upon prior thought. It seems to be peculiarly characteristic of humans, however, that they are able to form what I shall call 'second-order desires' or 'desires of the second order'.

Besides wanting and choosing and being moved *to do* this or that, men may also want to have (or not to have) certain desires and motives. They are capable of wanting to be different, in

From Harry Frankfurt, "Freedom of the Will and the Concept of a Person," Journal of Philosophy *LXVIII, 1 (Jan. 1971). Reprinted by permission.*

their preferences and purposes, from what they are. Many animals appear to have the capacity for what I shall call 'first-order desires' or 'desires of the first order', which are simply desires to do or not to do one thing or another. No animal other than man, however, appears to have the capacity for reflective self-evaluation that is manifested in the formation of second-order desires.

I

The concept designated by the verb 'to want' is extraordinarily elusive. A statement of the form '*A* wants to *X*'—taken by itself, apart from a context that serves to amplify or to specify its meaning—conveys remarkably little information. Such a statement may be consistent, for example, with each of the following statements: (a) the prospect of doing *X* elicits no sensation or introspectible emotional response in *A;* (b) *A* is unaware that he wants to *X;* (c) *A* believes that he does not want to *X;* (d) *A* wants to refrain from *X*-ing; (e) *A* wants to *Y* and believes that it is impossible for him both to *Y* and to *X;* (f) *A* does not 'really' want to *X;* (g) *A would rather die than X;* and so on. It is therefore hardly sufficient to formulate the distinction between first-order and second-order desires, as I have done, by suggesting merely that someone has a first-order desire when he wants to do or not to do such-and-such, and that he has a second-order desire when he wants to have or not to have a certain desire of the first order.

As I shall understand them, statements of the form '*A* wants to *X*' cover a rather broad range of possibilities. They may be true even when statements like (a) through (g) are true: when *A* is unaware of any feelings concerning *X*-ing, when he is unaware that he wants to *X,* when he deceives himself about what he wants and believes falsely that he does not want to *X,* when he also has other desires that conflict with his desire to *X,* or when he is ambivalent. The desires in question may be conscious or unconscious, they need not be univocal, and *A* may be mistaken about them. There is a further source of uncer-

tainty with regard to statements that identify someone's desires, however, and here it is important for my purposes to be less permissive.

Consider first those statements of the form '*A* wants to *X*' which identify first-order desires— that is, statements in which the term 'to *X*' refers to an action. A statement of this kind does not, by itself, indicate the relative strength of *A*'s desire to *X*. It does not make it clear whether this desire is at all likely to play a decisive role in what *A* actually does or tries to do. For it may correctly be said that *A* wants to *X* even when his desire to *X* is only one among his desires and when it is far from being paramount among them. Thus, it may be true that *A* wants to *X* when he strongly prefers to do something else instead; and it may be true that he wants to *X* despite the fact that, when he acts, it is not the desire to *X* that motivates him to do what he does. On the other hand, someone who states that *A* wants to *X* may mean to convey that it is this desire that is motivating or moving *A* to do what he is actually doing or that *A* will in fact be moved by this desire (unless he changes his mind) when he acts.

It is only when it is used in the second of these ways that, given the special usage of 'will' that I propose to adopt, the statement identifies *A*'s will. To identify an agent's will is either to identify the desire (or desires) by which he is motivated in some action he performs or to identify the desire (or desires) by which he will or would be motivated when or if he acts. An agent's will, then, is identical with one or more of his first-order desires. But the notion of the will, as I am employing it, is not coextensive with the notion of first-order desires. It is not the notion of something that merely inclines an agent in some degree to act in a certain way. Rather, it is the notion of an *effective* desire—one that moves (or will or would move) a person all the way to action. Thus the notion of the will is not coextensive with the notion of what an agent intends to do. For even though someone may have a settled intention to do *X,* he may none the less do something else instead of doing *X* because, despite his intention, his desire to do *X* proves to be weaker or less effective than some conflicting desire.

Now consider those statements of the form 'A wants to X' which identify second-order desires—that is, statements in which the term 'to X' refers to a desire of the first order. There are also two kinds of situation in which it may be true that A wants to want to X. In the first place, it might be true of A that he wants to have a desire to X despite the fact that he has a univocal desire, altogether free of conflict and ambivalence, to refrain from X-ing. Someone might want to have a certain desire, in other words, but univocally want that desire to be unsatisfied.

Suppose that a physician engaged in psychotherapy with narcotics addicts believes that his ability to help his patients would be enhanced if he understood better what it is like for them to desire the drug to which they are addicted. Suppose that he is led in this way to want to have a desire for the drug. If it is a genuine desire that he wants, then what he wants is not merely to feel the sensations that addicts characteristically feel when they are gripped by their desires for the drug. What the physician wants, in so far as he wants to have a desire, is to be inclined or moved to some extent to take the drug.

It is entirely possible, however, that, although he wants to be moved by a desire to take the drug, he does not want this desire to be effective. He may not want it to move him all the way to action. He need not be interested in finding out what it is like to take the drug. And in so far as he now wants only to *want* to take it, and not to *take* it, there is nothing in what he now wants that would be satisfied by the drug itself. He may now have, in fact, an altogether univocal desire *not* to take the drug; and he may prudently arrange to make it impossible for him to satisfy the desire he would have if his desire to want the drug should in time be satisfied.

It would thus be incorrect to infer, from the fact that the physician now wants to desire to take the drug, that he already does desire to take it. His second-order desire to be moved to take the drug does not entail that he has a first-order desire to take it. If the drug were now to be administered to him, this might satisfy no desire that is implicit in his desire to want to take it. While he wants to want to take the drug, he may have *no* desire to take it; it may be that *all* he wants is to taste the desire for it. That is, his desire to have a certain desire that he does not have may not be a desire that his will should be at all different than it is.

Someone who wants only in this truncated way to want to X stands at the margin of preciosity, and the fact that he wants to want to X is not pertinent to the identification of his will. There is, however, a second kind of situation that may be described by 'A wants to X'; and when the statement is used to describe a situation of this second kind, then it does pertain to what A wants his will to be. In such cases the statement means that A wants the desire to X to be the desire that moves him effectively to act. It is not merely that he wants the desire to X to be among the desires by which, to one degree or another, he is moved or inclined to act. He wants this desire to be effective—that is, to provide the motive in what he actually does. Now when the statement that A wants to want to X is used in this way, it does entail that A already has a desire to X. It could not be true both that A wants the desire to X to move him into action and that he does not want to X. It is only if he does want to X that he can coherently want the desire to X not merely to be one of his desires but, more decisively, to be his will.

Suppose a man wants to be motivated in what he does by the desire to concentrate on his work. It is necessarily true, if this supposition is correct, that he already wants to concentrate on his work. This desire is now among his desires. But the question of whether or not his second-order desire is fulfilled does not turn merely on whether the desire he wants is one of his desires. It turns on whether this desire is, as he wants it to be, his effective desire or will. If, when the chips are down, it is his desire to concentrate on his work that moves him to do what he does, then what he wants at that time is indeed (in the relevant sense) what he wants to want. If it is some other desire that actually moves him when he acts, on the other hand, then what he wants at that time is not (in the relevant sense) what he wants to want. This will be so despite the fact that the desire to concentrate on his work continues to be among his desires.

II

Someone has a desire of the second order either when he wants simply to have a certain desire or when he wants a certain desire to be his will. In situations of the latter kind, I shall call his second-order desires 'second-order volitions' or 'volitions of the second order'. Now it is having second-order volitions, and not having second-order desires generally, that I regard as essential to being a person. It is logically possible, however unlikely, that there should be an agent with second-order desires but with no volitions of the second order. Such a creature, in my view, would not be a person. I shall use the term 'wanton' to refer to agents who have first-order desires but who are not persons because, whether or not they have desires of the second order, they have no second-order volitions.

The essential characteristic of a wanton is that he does not care about his will. His desires move him to do certain things, without its being true of him either that he wants to be moved by those desires or that he prefers to be moved by other desires. The class of wantons includes all non-human animals that have desires and all very young children. Perhaps it also includes some adult human beings as well. In any case, adult humans may be more or less wanton; they may act wantonly, in response to first-order desires concerning which they have no volitions of the second order, more or less frequently.

The fact that a wanton has no second-order volitions does not mean that each of his first-order desires is translated heedlessly and at once into action. He may have no opportunity to act in accordance with some of his desires. Moreover, the translation of his desires into action may be delayed or precluded either by conflicting desires of the first order or by the intervention of deliber-

ation. For a wanton may possess and employ rational faculties of a high order. Nothing in the concept of a wanton implies that he cannot reason or that he cannot deliberate concerning how to do what he wants to do. What distinguishes the rational wanton from other rational agents is that he is not concerned with the desirability of his desires themselves. He ignores the question of what his will is to be. Not only does he pursue whatever course of action he is most strongly inclined to pursue, but he does not care which of his inclinations is the strongest.

Thus a rational creature, who reflects upon the suitability to his desires of one course of action or another, may none the less be a wanton. In maintaining that the essence of being a person lies not in reason but in will, I am far from suggesting that a creature without reason may be a person. For it is only in virtue of his rational capacities that a person is capable of becoming critically aware of his own will and of forming volitions of the second order. The structure of a person's will presupposes, accordingly, that he is a rational being.

The distinction between a person and a wanton may be illustrated by the difference between two narcotics addicts. Let us suppose that the physiological condition accounting for the addiction is the same in both men, and that both succumb inevitably to their periodic desires for the drug to which they are addicted. One of the addicts hates his addiction and always struggles desperately, although to no avail, against its thrust. He tries everything that he thinks might enable him to overcome his desires for the drug. But these desires are too powerful for him to withstand, and invariably, in the end, they conquer him. He is an unwilling addict, helplessly violated by his own desires.

The unwilling addict has conflicting first-order desires: he wants to take the drug, and he also wants to refrain from taking it. In addition to these first-order desires, however, he has a volition of the second order. He is not a neutral with regard to the conflict between his desire to take the drug and his desire to refrain from taking it. It is the latter desire, and not the former, that he wants to constitute his will; it is the latter desire, rather than the former, that he wants to be effective and to provide the purpose that he will seek to realize in what he actually does.

The other addict is a wanton. His actions reflect the economy of his first-order desires, without his being concerned whether the desires that move him to act are desires by which he wants to be moved to act. If he encounters problems in obtaining the drug or in administering it to himself, his responses to his urges to take it may involve deliberation. But it never occurs to him to consider whether he wants the relation among his desires to result in his having the will he has. The wanton addict may be an animal, and thus incapable of being concerned about his will. In any event he is, in respect of his wanton lack of concern, no different from an animal.

The second of these addicts may suffer a first-order conflict similar to the first-order conflict suffered by the first. Whether he is human or not, the wanton may (perhaps due to conditioning) both want to take the drug and want to refrain from taking it. Unlike the unwilling addict, however, he does not prefer that one of his conflicting desires should be paramount over the other; he does not prefer that one first-order desire rather than the other should constitute his will. It would be misleading to say that he is neutral as to the conflict between his desires, since this would suggest that he regards them as equally acceptable. Since he has no identity apart from his first-order desires, it is true neither that he prefers one to the other nor that he prefers not to take sides.

It makes a difference to the unwilling addict, who is a person, which of his conflicting first-order desires wins out. Both desires are his, to be sure; and whether he finally takes the drug or finally succeeds in refraining from taking it, he acts to satisfy what is in a literal sense his own desire. In either case he does something he himself wants to do, and he does it not because of some external influence whose aim happens to coincide with his own but because of his desire to do it. The unwilling addict identifies himself, however, through the formation of a second-order volition, with one rather than with the other of his conflicting first-order desires. He makes one of them more truly his own and, in so doing, he withdraws himself from the other. It is in virtue of this identification and withdrawal, accomplished through the formation of a second-order volition, that the unwilling addict may meaningfully make the analytically puzzling statements that the force moving him to take the drug is a force other than his own, and that it is not of his own free will but rather against his will that this force moves him to take it.

The wanton addict cannot or does not care which of his conflicting first-order desires wins out. His lack of concern is not due to his inability to find a convincing basis for preference. It is due either to his lack of capacity for reflection or to his mindless indifference to the enterprise of evaluating his own desires and motives. There is only one issue in the struggle to which his first-order conflict may lead: whether the one or the other of his conflicting desires is stronger. Since he is moved by both desires, he will not be altogether satisfied by what he does no matter which of them is effective. But it makes no difference *to him* whether his craving or his aversion gets the upper hand. He has no stake in the conflict between them and so, unlike the unwilling addict, he can neither win nor lose the struggle in which he is engaged. When a *person* acts, the desire by which he is moved is either the will he wants or a will he wants to be without. When a *wanton* acts, it is neither.

III

There is a very close relationship between the capacity for forming second-order volitions and another capacity that is essential to persons—one that has often been considered a distinguishing mark of the human condition. It is only because a person has volitions of the second order that he is capable both of enjoying and of lacking freedom of the will. The concept of a person is not only, then, the concept of a type of entity that has both first-order desires and volitions of the second order. It can also be construed as the concept of a type of entity for whom the freedom of its will may be a problem. This concept excludes all wantons, both infrahuman and human, since they fail to satisfy an essential condition for the enjoyment of freedom of the will. And it excludes those suprahuman beings, if any, whose wills are necessarily free.

Just what kind of freedom is the freedom of the will? This question calls for an identification of the special area of human experience to which the concept of freedom of the will, as distinct from the concepts of other sorts of freedom, is particularly germane. In dealing with it, my aim will be primarily to locate the problem with which a person is most immediately concerned when he is concerned with the freedom of his will.

According to one familiar philosophical tradition, being free is fundamentally a matter of doing what one wants to do. Now the notion of an agent who does what he wants to do is by no means an altogether clear one: both the doing and the wanting, and the appropriate relation between them as well, require elucidation. But although its focus needs to be sharpened and its formulation refined, I believe that this notion does capture at least part of what is implicit in the idea of an agent who *acts* freely. It misses entirely, however, the peculiar content of the quite different idea of an agent whose *will* is free.

We do not suppose that animals enjoy freedom of the will, although we recognize that an animal may be free to run in whatever direction it wants. Thus, having the freedom to do what one wants to do is not a sufficient condition of having a free will. It is not a necessary condition either. For to deprive someone of his freedom of action is not necessarily to undermine the freedom of his will. When an agent is aware that there are certain things he is not free to do, this doubtless affects his desires and limits the range of choices he can make. But suppose that someone, without being aware of it, has in fact lost or been deprived of his freedom of action. Even though he is no longer free to do what he wants to do, his will may remain as free as it was before. Despite the fact that he is not free to translate his desires into actions or to act according to the determinations

of his will, he may still form those desires and make those determinations as freely as if his freedom of action had not been impaired.

When we ask whether a person's will is free we are not asking whether he is in a position to translate his first-order desires into actions. That is the question of whether he is free to do as he pleases. The question of the freedom of his will does not concern the relation between what he does and what he wants to do. Rather, it concerns his desires themselves. But what question about them is it?

It seems to me both natural and useful to construe the question of whether a person's will is free in close analogy to the question of whether an agent enjoys freedom of action. Now freedom of action is (roughly, at least) the freedom to do what one wants to do. Analogously, then, the statement that a person enjoys freedom of the will means (also roughly) that he is free to want what he wants to want. More precisely, it means that he is free to will what he wants to will, or to have the will he wants. Just as the question about the freedom of an agent's action has to do with whether it is the action he wants to perform, so the question about the freedom of his will has to do with whether it is the will he wants to have.

It is in securing the conformity of his will to his second-order volitions, then, that a person exercises freedom of the will. And it is in the discrepancy between his will and his second-order volitions, or in his awareness that their coincidence is not his own doing but only a happy chance, that a person who does not have this freedom feels its lack. The unwilling addict's will is not free. This is shown by the fact that it is not the will he wants. It is also true, though in a different way, that the will of the wanton addict is not free. The wanton addict neither has the will he wants nor has a will that differs from the will he wants. Since he has no volitions of the second order, the freedom of his will cannot be a problem for him. He lacks it, so to speak, by default.

People are generally far more complicated than my sketchy account of the structure of a person's will may suggest. There is as much opportunity for ambivalence, conflict, and self-deception with regard to desires of the second order, for example, as there is with regard to first-order desires. If there is an unresolved conflict among someone's second-order desires, then he is in danger of having no second-order volition; for unless this conflict is resolved, he has no preference concerning which of his first-order desires is to be his will. This condition, if it is so severe that it prevents him from identifying himself in a sufficiently decisive way with *any* of his conflicting first-order desires, destroys him as a person. For it either tends to paralyse his will and to keep him from acting at all, or it tends to remove him from his will so that his will operates without his participation. In both cases he becomes, like the unwilling addict though in a different way, a helpless bystander to the forces that move him.

Another complexity is that a person may have, especially if his second-order desires are in conflict, desires and volitions of a higher order than the second. There is no theoretical limit to the length of the series of desires of higher and higher orders; nothing except common sense and, perhaps, a saving fatigue prevents an individual from obsessively refusing to identify himself with any of his desires until he forms a desire of the next higher order. The tendency to generate such a series of acts of forming desires, which would be a case of humanization run wild, also leads toward the destruction of a person.

It is possible, however, to terminate such a series of acts without cutting it off arbitrarily. When a person identifies himself *decisively* with one of his first-order desires, this commitment 'resounds' throughout the potentially endless array of higher orders. Consider a person who, without reservation or conflict, wants to be motivated by the desire to concentrate on his work. The fact that his second-order volition to be moved by this desire is a decisive one means that there is no room for questions concerning the pertinence of desires or volitions of higher orders. Suppose the person is asked whether he wants to want to concentrate on his work. He can properly insist that this question concerning a third-order desire does not arise. It would be a mistake to claim that, because he has not considered whether he wants the second-order volition he has formed, he is indifferent to the question of whether it is with this volition or with some other that he wants his will to accord. The decisiveness of the commitment he has made means that he has decided that no further question about his second-order volition, at any higher order, remains to be asked. It is relatively unimportant whether we explain this by saying that this commitment implicitly generates an endless series of confirming desires of higher orders, or by saying that the commitment is tantamount to a dissolution of the pointedness of all questions concerning higher orders of desire.

Examples such as the one concerning the unwilling addict may suggest that volitions of the second order, or of higher orders, must be formed deliberately and that a person characteristically struggles to ensure that they are satisfied. But the conformity of a person's will to his higher-order volitions may be far more thoughtless and spontaneous than this. Some people are naturally moved by kindness when they want to be kind, and by nastiness when they want to be nasty, without any explicit forethought and without any need for energetic self-control. Others are moved by nastiness when they want to be kind and by kindness when they intend to be nasty, equally without forethought and without active resistance to these violations of their higher-order desires. The enjoyment of freedom comes easily to some. Others must struggle to achieve it.

IV

My theory concerning the freedom of the will accounts easily for our disinclination to allow that this freedom is enjoyed by the members of any species inferior to our own. It also satisfies another condition that must be met by any such theory, by making it apparent why the freedom of the will should be regarded as desirable. The enjoyment of a free will means the satisfaction of certain desires—desires of the second or of higher orders—whereas its absence means their frustration. The satisfactions at stake are those which accrue to a person of whom it may be said that his will is his own. The corresponding frustrations are those suffered by a person of whom it may be said that he is estranged from himself, or that he finds himself a helpless or a passive bystander to the forces that move him.

A person who is free to do what he wants to do may yet not be in a position to have the will he wants. Suppose, however, that he enjoys both freedom of action and freedom of the will. Then he is not only free to do what he wants to do; he is also free to want what he wants to want. It seems to me that he has, in that case, all the freedom it is possible to desire or to conceive. There are other good things in life, and he may not possess some of them. But there is nothing in the way of freedom that he lacks.

It is far from clear that certain other theories of the freedom of the will meet these elementary but essential conditions: that it be understandable why we desire this freedom and why we refuse to ascribe it to animals. Consider, for example, Roderick Chisholm's quaint version of the doctrine that human freedom entails an absence of causal determination.[2] Whenever a person performs a free action, according to Chisholm, it's a miracle. The motion of a person's hand, when the person moves it, is the outcome of a series of physical causes; but some event in this series, "and presumably one of those that took place within the brain, was caused by the agent and not by any other events" (18). A free agent has, therefore, "a prerogative which some would attribute only to God: each of us, when we act, is a prime mover unmoved" (23).

This account fails to provide any basis for doubting that animals of subhuman species enjoy the freedom it defines. Chisholm says nothing that makes it seem less likely that a rabbit performs a miracle when it moves its leg than that a man does so when he moves his hand. But why, in any case, should anyone *care* whether he can interrupt the natural order of causes in the way Chisholm describes? Chisholm offers no reason for believing that there is a discernible difference between the experience of a man who miraculously initiates a series of causes when he

moves his hand and a man who moves his hand without any such breach of the normal causal sequence. There appears to be no concrete basis for preferring to be involved in the one state of affairs rather than in the other.

It is generally supposed that, in addition to satisfying the two conditions I have mentioned, a satisfactory theory of the freedom of the will necessarily provides an analysis of one of the conditions of moral responsibility. The most common recent approach to the problem of understanding the freedom of the will has been, indeed, to inquire what is entailed by the assumption that someone is morally responsible for what he has done. In my view, however, the relation between moral responsibility and the freedom of the will has been very widely misunderstood. It is not true that a person is morally responsible for what he has done only if his will was free when he did it. He may be morally responsible for having done it even though his will was not free at all.

A person's will is free only if he is free to have the will he wants. This means that, with regard to any of his first-order desires, he is free either to make that desire his will or to make some other first-order desire his will instead. Whatever his will, then, the will of the person whose will is free could have been otherwise; he could have done otherwise than to constitute his will as he did. It is a vexed question just how 'he could have done otherwise' is to be understood in contexts such as this one. But although this question is important to the theory of freedom, it has no bearing on the theory of moral responsibility. For the assumption that a person is morally responsible for what he has done does not entail that the person was in a position to have whatever will he wanted.

This assumption *does* entail that the person did what he did freely, or that he did it of his own free will. It is a mistake, however, to believe that someone acts freely only when he is free to do whatever he wants or that he acts of his own free will only if his will is free. Suppose that a person has done what he wanted to do, that he did it because he wanted to do it, and that the will by which he was moved when he did it was his will because it was the will he wanted. Then he did it freely and of his own free will. Even supposing that he could have done otherwise, he would not have done otherwise; and even supposing that he could have had a different will, he would not have wanted his will to differ from what it was. Moreover, since the will that moved him when he acted was his will because he wanted it to be, he cannot claim that his will was forced upon him or that he was a passive bystander to its constitution. Under these conditions, it is quite irrelevant to the evaluation of his moral responsibility to inquire whether the alternatives that he opted against were actually available to him.

In illustration, consider a third kind of addict. Suppose that his addiction has the same physiological basis and the same irresistible thrust as the addictions of the unwilling and wanton addicts, but that he is altogether delighted with his condition. He is a willing addict, who would not have things any other way. If the grip of his addiction should somehow weaken, he would do whatever he could to reinstate it; if his desire for the drug should begin to fade, he would take steps to renew its intensity.

The willing addict's will is not free, for his desire to take the drug will be effective regardless of whether or not he wants this desire to constitute his will. But when he takes the drug, he takes it freely and of his own free will. I am inclined to understand his situation as involving the overdetermination of his first-order desire to take the drug. This desire is his effective desire because he is physiologically addicted. But it is his effective desire also because he wants it to be. His will is outside his control, but, by his second-order desire that his desire for the drug should be effective, he has made this will his own. Given that it is therefore not only because of his addiction that his desire for the drug is effective, he may be morally responsible for taking the drug.

My conception of the freedom of the will appears to be neutral with regard to the problem of determinism. It seems conceivable that it should be causally determined that a person is free to want what he wants to want. If this is conceivable, then it might be causally determined that a person enjoys a free will. There is no more than an innocuous appearance of paradox in the proposition that it is determined, ineluctably and by forces beyond their control, that certain people have free wills and that others do not. There is no incoherence in the proposition that some agency other than a person's own is responsible (even *morally* responsible) for the fact that he enjoys or fails to enjoy freedom of the will. It is possible that a person should be morally responsible for what he does of his own free will and that some other person should also be morally responsible for his having done it.

On the other hand, it seems conceivable that it should come about by chance that a person is free to have the will he wants. If this is conceivable, then it might be a matter of chance that certain people enjoy freedom of the will and that certain others do not. Perhaps it is also conceivable, as a number of philosophers believe, for states of affairs to come about in a way other than by chance or as the outcome of a sequence of natural causes. If it is indeed conceivable for the relevant states of affairs to come about in some third way, then it is also possible that a person should in that third way come to enjoy the freedom of the will.

NOTES

1. P. F. Strawson, *Individuals* (London: Methuen, 1959), 101–2. Ayer's usage of "person" is similar: "it is characteristic of persons in this sense that besides having various physical properties they are also credited with various forms of consciousness" [A. J. Ayer, *The Concept of a Person* (New York: St. Martin's, 1963), 82]. What concerns Strawson and Ayer is the problem of understanding the relation between mind and body, rather than the quite different problem of understanding what it is to be a creature that not only has a mind and a body but is also a person.

2. "Freedom and Action," in *Freedom and Determinism,* ed. Keith Lehrer (New York: Random House, 1966), 11–44.

For Further Reflection

1. Compare Frankfurt's version of compatibilism with Stace's version. Is Frankfurt's analysis superior? Does it make compatibilism plausible? Can we be both free and determined? Explain your answers.

2. Philosopher Gary Watson (University of California at Irvine) criticized Frankfurt's theory as being too desire oriented. We not only weigh our conflicting desires in deciding what to do, but we make *evaluations* as to the appropriateness or moral status of our desires. These evaluations are not just other desires, but have a life of their own, so that although I may want to cheat very badly, I reject that desire on moral grounds. Is Watson correct in his analysis? Why or why not?

3. Is Frankfurt's equation of identification with freedom satisfactory? Consider this counterexample: John, who is tempted to cheat on his English test, deliberates on the matter and identifies with the second-order desire to cheat. However, unbeknownst to John, he has been hypnotized (to have a desire to cheat) by a clever psychologist, so that he cannot help willing as he does. Would you say that John acts freely? How would Frankfurt respond to such counterexamples?

4. Now that you have read through several essays on free will, determinism, and compatibilism, which arguments are the best and which position has the most evidence in its favor? Explain.

Liberty and Necessity   V.56

DAVID HUME

On the issue of free will, Hume is a compatibilist, persuaded that determinism (necessity) can be reconciled with free will (liberty). In this reading he maintains that reconciliation is possible if we define liberty as "a power of acting or not acting, according to the determinations of the will." The idea is that you act freely when your act is caused by your will (desires, motivations, etc.), even though your will is determined. If your will determines your actions, then they come from you, and you can therefore be held responsible for them. A will that is not itself caused is neither possible nor desirable.

(A biographical sketch of Hume precedes Reading II.9.)

Study Questions

1. Hume says that people generally agree that necessity belongs to the will of man. What does he mean by this?
2. Why does Hume believe that liberty (as he defines it) is essential to morality?
3. Suppose a man's desires are caused by forces beyond his control, and suppose he acts according to those desires and murders someone. Would Hume think that the man could be legitimately praised or blamed for what he did? Explain.

From David Hume, An Inquiry Concerning Human Understanding, *Sec.8. First Published in 1748.*

BUT TO PROCEED IN THIS reconciling project with regard to the question of liberty and necessity—the most contentious question of metaphysics, the most contentious science—it will not require many words to prove that all mankind have ever agreed in the doctrine of liberty as well as in that of necessity, and that the whole dispute, in this respect also, has been hitherto merely verbal. For what is meant by liberty when applied to voluntary actions? We cannot surely mean that actions have so little connection with motives, inclinations, and circumstances that one does not follow with a certain degree of uniformity from the other, and that one affords no inference by which we can conclude the existence of the other. For these are plain and acknowledged matters of fact. By liberty, then, we can only mean *a power of acting or not acting according to the determinations of the will;* that is, if we choose to remain at rest, we may; if we choose to move, we also may. Now this hypothetical liberty is universally allowed to belong to everyone who is not a prisoner and in chains. Here then is no subject of dispute.

Whatever definition we may give of liberty, we should be careful to observe two requisite circumstances: *first,* that it be consistent with plain matter of fact; *secondly,* that it be consistent with itself. If we observe these circumstances and render our definition intelligible, I am persuaded that all mankind will be found of one opinion with regard to it.

It is universally allowed that nothing exists without a cause of its existence, and that chance, when strictly examined, is a mere negative word and means not any real power which has anywhere a being in nature. But it is pretended that some causes are necessary, some not necessary. Here then is the advantage of definitions. Let anyone *define* a cause without comprehending, as a part of the definition, a *necessary connection* with its effect, and let him show distinctly the origin of the idea expressed by the definition, and I shall readily give up the whole controversy. But if the foregoing explication of the matter be received, this must be absolutely impracticable.

Had not objects a regular conjunction with each other, we should never have entertained any notion of cause and effect; and this regular conjunction produces that inference of the understanding which is the only connection that we can have any comprehension of. Whoever attempts a definition of cause exclusive of these circumstances will be obliged either to employ unintelligible terms or such as are synonymous to the term which he endeavors to define. And if the definition above mentioned be admitted, liberty, when opposed to necessity, not to constraint, is the same thing with chance, which is universally allowed to have no existence.

* * *

There is no method of reasoning more common, and yet none more blamable, than in philosophical disputes to endeavor the refutation of any hypothesis by a pretense of its dangerous consequences to religion and morality. When any opinion leads to absurdity, it is certainly false but it is not certain that an opinion is false because it is of dangerous consequence. Such topics, therefore, ought entirely to be forborne as serving nothing to the discovery of truth, but only to make the person of an antagonist odious. This I observe in general, without pretending to draw any advantage from it. I frankly submit to an examination of this kind, and shall venture to affirm that the doctrines both of necessity and liberty, as above explained, are not only consistent with morality, but are absolutely essential to its support.

Necessity may be defined two ways, conformably to the two definitions of *cause* of which it makes an essential part. It consists either in the constant conjunction of like objects or in the inference of the understanding from one object to another. Now necessity, in both these senses (which, indeed, are at bottom the same), has universally, though tacitly, in the schools, in the pulpit, and in common life been allowed to belong to the will of man, and no one has ever pretended to deny that we can draw inferences concerning human actions, and that those inferences are founded on the experienced union of like actions, with like motives, inclinations, and circumstances. The only particular in which anyone can differ is that either perhaps he will refuse to give the name of necessity to this property of human actions—but as long as the meaning is understood I hope the word can do no harm—or that he will maintain it possible to discover something further in the operations of matter. But this, it must be acknowledged, can be of no consequence to morality or religion, whatever it may be to natural philosophy or metaphysics. We may here be mistaken in asserting that there is no idea of any other necessity or connection in the actions of the body, but surely we ascribe nothing to the actions of the mind but what everyone does and must readily allow of. We change no circumstance in the received orthodox system with regard to the will, but only in that with regard to material objects and causes. Nothing, therefore, can be more innocent at least than this doctrine.

All laws being founded on rewards and punishments, it is supposed, as a fundamental principle, that these motives have a regular and uniform influence on the mind and both produce the good and prevent the evil actions. We may give to this influence what name we please; but as it is usually conjoined with the action, it must be esteemed a *cause* and be looked upon as an instance of that necessity which we would here establish.

The only proper object of hatred or vengeance is a person or creature endowed with thought and consciousness; and when any criminal or injurious actions excite that passion, it is only by their relation to the person, or connection with him. Actions are, by their very nature, temporary and perishing; and where they proceed not from some *cause* in the character and disposition of the person who performed them, they can neither redound to his honor if good, nor infamy if evil. The actions themselves may be blamable; they may be contrary to all the rules of morality and religion; but the person is not answerable for them and, as they proceeded

from nothing in him that is durable and constant and leave nothing of that nature behind them, it is impossible he can, upon their account, become the object of punishment or vengeance. According to the principle, therefore, which denies necessity and, consequently, causes, a man is as pure and untainted, after having committed the most horrid crime, as at the first moment of his birth, nor is his character anywise concerned in his actions, since they are not derived from it; and the wickedness of the one can never be used as a proof of the depravity of the other.

Men are not blamed for such actions as they perform ignorantly and casually, whatever may be the consequences. Why? But because the principles of these actions are only momentary and terminate in them alone. Men are less blamed for such actions as they perform hastily and unpremeditatedly than for such as proceed from deliberation. For what reason? But because a hasty temper, though a constant cause or principle in the mind, operates only by intervals and infects not the whole character. Again, repentance wipes off every crime if attended with a reformation of life and manners. How is this to be accounted for? But by asserting that actions render a person criminal merely as they are proofs of criminal principles in the mind; and when, by an alteration of these principles, they cease to be just proofs, they likewise cease to be criminal. But, except upon the doctrine of necessity, they never were just proofs, and consequently never were criminal.

It will be equally easy to prove, and from the same arguments, that *liberty,* according to that definition above mentioned, in which all men agree, is also essential to morality, and that no human actions, where it is wanting, are susceptible of any moral qualities or can be the objects of approbation or dislike. For as actions are objects of our moral sentiment so far only as they are indications of the internal character, passions, and affections, it is impossible that they can give rise either to praise or blame where they proceed not from these principles, but are derived altogether from external violence.

For Further Reflection

1. Imagine someone who always acts according to her desires—but the desires have been secretly created in her by a mad scientist using advanced technology. Can she really be said to act freely? Would Hume say that she acts freely? Explain.

2. Consider a college student who becomes addicted to crack cocaine and develops an overwhelming, irresistible desire for the drug. He becomes a slave to his habit and slides toward disaster. By Hume's lights, would the student be acting freely? Do you think he is acting freely? Why or why not?

V.57   Fate

RICHARD TAYLOR

Richard Taylor (1919–   ) was for many years a professor of philosophy at Brown University, Rochester University, and Union College. He is the author of several books, including *Metaphysics*, from which this selection is taken.

Taylor defines fatalism as the thesis that the future is unavoidable, that the course of our lives is fixed regardless of what we do. He illustrates his thesis with the story of Osmo, who discovers a book, *The Life of Osmo, as Given by God*, detailing his entire life, including his death, which Osmo cannot falsify, try as he might.

Study Questions

1. What is fatalism?
2. How is determinism related to fatalism?
3. What are the sources of fatalism?
4. What is the story of Osmo?
5. What are the four questions Taylor considers at the end of the story of Osmo?
6. What does Taylor say about the law of excluded middle?
7. What objections to his thesis does Taylor discuss at the end of the article?

WE ARE ALL, at certain moments of pain, threat, or bereavement, apt to entertain the idea of fatalism, the thought that what is happening at a particular moment is unavoidable, that we are powerless to prevent it. Sometimes we find ourselves in circumstances not of our own making, in which our very being and destinies are so thoroughly anchored that the thought of fatalism can be quite overwhelming, and sometimes consoling. One feels that whatever then happens, however good or ill, will be what those circumstances yield, and we are helpless. Soldiers, it is said, are sometimes possessed by such thoughts. Perhaps everyone would feel more inclined to them if they paused once in a while to think of how little they ever had to do with bringing themselves to wherever they have arrived in life, how much of their fortunes and destinies were decided for

From Richard Taylor, Metaphysics, *4th edition, copyright © 1992. Reprinted by permission of Pearson Education, Inc., Upper Saddle River, NJ.*

them by sheer circumstance, and how the entire course of their lives is often set, once and for all, by the most trivial incidents, which they did not produce and could not even have foreseen. If we are free to work on our destinies at all, which is doubtful, we have freedom that is at best exercised within exceedingly narrow paths. All the important things—when we are born, of what parents, into what culture, whether we are loved or rejected, whether we are male or female, our temperament, our intelligence or stupidity, indeed everything that makes for the bulk of our happiness and misery—all these are decided for us by the most casual and indifferent circumstances, by sheer coincidences, chance encounters, and seemingly insignificant fortuities. One can see this in retrospect if he searches, but few search. The fate that has given us our very being has given us also our pride and conceit, and has thereby formed us so that, being human, we congratulate ourselves on our blessings, which we call our achievements; blame the world for our blunders, which we call our misfortunes; and scarcely give a thought to that impersonal fate that arbitrarily dispenses both.

FATALISM AND DETERMINISM

Determinism, it will be recalled, is the theory that all events are rendered unavoidable by their causes. The attempt is sometimes made to distinguish this from fatalism by saying that, according to the fatalist, certain events are going to happen *no matter what,* or in other words, regardless of causes. But this is enormously contrived. It would be hard to find in the whole history of thought a single fatalist, on that conception of it.

Fatalism is the belief that whatever happens is unavoidable. That is the clearest expression of the doctrine, and it provides the basis of the attitude of calm acceptance that the fatalist is thought, quite correctly, to embody. One who endorses the claim of universal causation, then, and the theory of the causal determination of an human behavior, is a kind of fatalist—or at least he

should be, if he is consistent. For that theory, as we have seen, once it is clearly spelled out and not hedged about with unresolved "ifs," does entail that whatever happens is rendered inevitable by the causal conditions preceding it, and is therefore unavoidable. One can indeed think of verbal formulas for distinguishing the two theories, but if we think of a fatalist as one who has a certain attitude, we find it to be the attitude that a thoroughgoing determinist should, in consistency, assume. That some philosophical determinists are not fatalists does not so much illustrate a great difference between fatalism and determinism but rather the humiliation to one's pride that a fatalist position can deliver, and the comfort that can sometimes be found in evasion.

FATALISM WITH RESPECT TO THE FUTURE AND THE PAST

A fatalist, then, is someone who believes that whatever happens is and always was unavoidable. He thinks it is not up to him what will happen a thousand years hence, next year, tomorrow, or the very next moment. Of course he does not pretend always to *know* what is going to happen. Hence, he might try sometimes to read signs and portents, as meteorologists and astrologers do, or to contemplate the effects upon him of the various things that might, for all he knows, be fated to occur. But he does not suppose that whatever happens could ever have really been avoidable.

A fatalist thus thinks of the future in the way we all think of the past, for everyone is a fatalist as he looks *back* on things. To a large extent we know what has happened—some of it we can even remember—whereas the future is still obscure to us, and we are therefore tempted to imbue it, in our imagination, with all sorts of "possibilities." The fatalist resists this temptation, knowing that mere ignorance can hardly give rise to any genuine possibility in things. He thinks of both past and future "under the aspect of eternity," the way God is supposed to view them. We all think of the past this way, as something settled and fixed, to be taken for what it is. We are never in the least tempted to try to modify it. It is not in the least up to us what happened last year, yesterday, or even a moment ago, any more than are the motions of the heavens or the political developments in Tibet. If we are not fatalists, then we might think that past things once *were* up to us, to bring about or prevent, as long as they were still future, but this expresses our attitude toward the future, not the past.

Such is surely our conception of the whole past, whether near or remote. But the consistent fatalist thinks of the future in the same way. We say of past things that they are no longer within our power. The fatalist says they never were.

THE SOURCES OF FATALISM

A fatalistic way of thinking most often arises from theological ideas, or from what are generally thought to be certain presuppositions of science and logic. Thus, if God is really all-knowing and all-powerful, it is not hard to suppose that He has arranged for everything to happen just as it is going to happen, that He already knows every detail of the whole future course of the world, and there is nothing left for you and me to do except watch things unfold, in the here or the hereafter. But without bringing God into the picture, it is not hard to suppose, as we have seen, that everything that happens is wholly determined by what went before it, and hence that whatever happens at any future time is the only thing that can then happen, given what precedes it. Or even disregarding that, it seems natural to suppose that there is a body of truth concerning what the future holds, just as there is such truth concerning what is contained in the past, whether or not it is known to any person or even to God, and hence, that everything asserted in that body of truth will assuredly happen, in the fullness of time, precisely as it is described therein.

No one needs to be convinced that fatalism is the only proper way to view the past. That it is also the proper way to view the future is less obvious, due in part, perhaps, to our vastly greater ignorance of what the future holds. The consequences of holding such fatalism are obviously momentous. To say nothing of the consolation of fatalism, which enables a person to view all things as they arise with the same undisturbed mind with which he contemplates even the most revolting of history's horrors, the fatalist teaching also relieves one of all tendency towards both blame and approbation of others and of both guilt and conceit in himself. It promises that a perfect understanding is possible and removes the temptation to view things in terms of human wickedness and moral responsibility. This thought alone, once firmly grasped, yields a sublime acceptance of all that life and nature offer, whether to oneself or one's fellows; and although it thereby reduces one's pride, it simultaneously enhances the feelings, opens the heart, and expands the understanding.

DIVINE OMNISCIENCE

Suppose for the moment, just for the purpose of this discussion, that God exists and is omniscient. To say that God is omniscient means that He knows everything that is true. He cannot, of course, know that which is false. Concerning any falsehood, an omniscient being can know that it is false; but then it is a truth that is known, namely, the truth that the thing in question *is* a falsehood. So if it is false that the moon is a cube, then God can, like you or me, know that this is false; but He cannot know the falsehood itself, that the moon is a cube.

Thus, if God is omniscient He knows, as you probably do, the date of your birth. He also knows, as you may not, the hour of your birth. Furthermore, God knows, as you assuredly do not, the date of your conception—for there is such a truth, and we are supposing that God knows every truth. Moreover, He knows, as you surely do not, the date of your death, and the circumstances thereof—whether at that moment, known already to Him, you die as the result of accident, a fatal malady, suicide, murder, whatever. And, still assuming God exists and knows everything, He knows whether any ant walked across my desk last night, and if so, what ant it was, where it came from, how long it was on the desk, how it came to be there, and so on, to every truth about this insect that there is. Similarly, of course, He knows when some ant will again appear on my desk, if ever. He knows the number of hairs on my head, notes the fall of every sparrow, knows why it fell, and why it was going to fall. These are simply a few of the consequences of the omniscience that we are for the moment assuming. A more precise way of expressing all this is to say that God knows, concerning any statement whatever that anyone could formulate, that it is true, in case it is, and otherwise, that it is false. And let us suppose that God, at some time or other, or perhaps from time to time, vouchsafes some of his knowledge to people, or perhaps to certain chosen persons. Thus prophets arise, proclaiming the coming of certain events, and things do then happen as they have foretold. Of course it is not surprising that they should, on the supposition we are making; namely, that the foreknowledge of these things comes from God, who is omniscient.

THE STORY OF OSMO

Now, then, let us make one further supposition, which will get us squarely into the philosophical issue these ideas are intended to introduce. Let us suppose that God has revealed a particular set of facts to a chosen scribe who, believing (correctly) that they came from God, wrote them all down. The facts in question then turned out to be all the more or less significant episodes in the life of some perfectly ordinary man named Osmo. Osmo was entirely unknown to the scribe, and in fact to just about everyone, but there was no doubt concerning whom all these facts were about, for the very first thing received by the scribe from God, was: "He of whom I

speak is called Osmo." When the revelations reached a fairly voluminous bulk and appeared to be completed, the scribe arranged them in chronological order and assembled them into a book. He at first gave it the title *The Life of Osmo, as Given by God,* but thinking that people would take this to be some sort of joke, he dropped the reference to God.

The book was published but attracted no attention whatsoever, because it appeared to be nothing more than a record of the dull life of a very plain man named Osmo. The scribe wondered, in fact, why God had chosen to convey such a mass of seemingly pointless trivia.

The book eventually found its way into various libraries, where it gathered dust until one day a high school teacher in Indiana, who rejoiced under the name of Osmo, saw a copy on the shelf. The title caught his eye. Curiously picking it up and blowing the dust off, he was thunderstruck by the opening sentence: "Osmo is born in Mercy Hospital in Auburn, Indiana, on June 6, 1942, of Finnish parentage, and after nearly losing his life from an attack of pneumonia at the age of five, he is enrolled in the St. James school there." Osmo turned pale. The book nearly fell from his hands. He thumbed back in excitement to discover who had written it. Nothing was given of its authorship nor, for that matter, of its publisher. His questions of the librarian produced no further information, he being as ignorant as Osmo of how the book came to be there.

So Osmo, with the book pressed tightly under his arm, dashed across the street for some coffee, thinking to compose himself and then examine this book with care. Meanwhile he glanced at a few more of its opening remarks, at the things said there about his difficulties with his younger sister, how he was slow in learning to read, of the summer on Mackinac Island, and so on. His emotions now somewhat quieted, Osmo began a close reading. He noted that everything was expressed in the present tense, the way newspaper headlines are written. For example, the text read, "Osmo is born in Mercy Hospital," instead of saying he *was* born there, and is recorded that he quarrels with his sister, is a slow student, is fitted with dental braces at age eight, and so on, all in the journalistic present tense. But the text itself made quite clear approximately when all these various things happened, for everything was in chronological order, and in any case each year of its subject's life constituted a separate chapter and was so titled—"Osmo's Seventh Year," "Osmo's Eighth Year," and so on through the book.

Osmo became absolutely engrossed, to the extent that he forgot his original astonishment, bordering on panic, and for a while even lost his curiosity concerning authorship. He sat drinking coffee and reliving his childhood, much of which he had all but forgotten until the memories were revived by the book now before him. He had almost forgotten about the kitten, for example, and had entirely forgotten its name, until he read, in the chapter called "Osmo's Seventh Year," this observation: "Sobbing, Osmo takes Fluffy, now quite dead, to the garden, and buries her next to the rose bush." Ah yes! And then there was Louise, who sat next to him in the eighth grade—it was all right there. And how he got caught smoking one day. And how he felt when his father died. On and on. Osmo became so absorbed that he quite forgot the business of the day, until it occurred to him to turn to Chapter 26, to see what might be said there, he having just recently turned twenty-six. He had no sooner done so than his panic returned, for lo! what the book said was *true*! That it rains on his birthday for example, that his wife fails to give him the binoculars he had hinted he would like, that he receives a raise in salary shortly thereafter, and so on. Now how in God's name, Osmo pondered, could anyone know that apparently before it had happened? For these were quite recent events, and the book had dust on it. Quickly moving on, Osmo came to this: "Sitting and reading in the coffee shop across from the library, Osmo, perspiring copiously, entirely forgets, until it is too late, that he is supposed to collect his wife at the hairdresser's at four." Oh my god! He had forgotten all about that. Yank-

ing out his watch, Osmo discovered that it was nearly five o'clock—too late. She would be on her way home by now, and in a very sour mood.

Osmo's anguish at this discovery was nothing, though, compared with what the rest of the day held for him. He poured more coffee, and it now occurred to him to check the number of chapters in this amazing book: only twenty-nine! But surely, he thought, that doesn't mean anything. How anyone could have gotten all this stuff down so far was puzzling enough, to be sure, but no one on God's earth could possibly know in advance how long this or that person is going to live. (Only God could know that sort of thing, Osmo reflected.) So he read along; though not without considerable uneasiness and even depression, for the remaining three chapters were on the whole discouraging. He thought he had gotten that ulcer under control, for example. And he didn't see any reason to suppose his job was going to turn out that badly, or that he was really going to break a leg skiing; after all, he could just give up skiing. But then the book took on a terribly dismal note. It said: "And Osmo, having taken Northwest flight 569 from O'Hare, perishes when the aircraft crashes on the runway at Fort Wayne, with considerable loss of life, a tragedy rendered the far more calamitous by the fact that Osmo had neglected to renew his life insurance before the expiration of the grace period." And that was all. That was the end of the book.

So *that's* why it had only twenty-nine chapters. Some idiot thought he was going to get killed in a plane crash. But, Osmo thought, he just wouldn't get on that plane. And this would also remind him to keep his insurance in force.

(About three years later our hero, having boarded a flight for St. Paul, went berserk when the pilot announced they were going to land at Fort Wayne instead. According to one of the flight attendants, he tried to hijack the aircraft and divert it to another airfield. The Civil Aeronautics Board cited the resulting disruptions as contributing to the crash that followed as the plane tried to land.)

FOUR QUESTIONS

Osmo's extraordinary circumstances led him to embrace the doctrine of fatalism. Not quite completely, perhaps, for there he was, right up to the end, trying vainly to buck his fate—trying, in effect, to make a fool of God, though he did not know this, because he had no idea of the book's source. Still, he had the overwhelming evidence of his whole past life to make him think that everything was going to work out exactly as described in the book. It always had. It was, in fact, precisely this conviction that terrified him so.

But now let us ask these questions, in order to make Osmo's experiences more relevant to our own. First, why did he become, or nearly become, a fatalist? Second, just what did his fatalism amount to? Third, was his belief justified in terms of the evidence he had? And finally, is that belief justified in terms of the evidence *we* have—or in other words, should we be fatalists too?

This last, of course, is the important metaphysical question, but we have to approach it through the others.

Why did Osmo become a fatalist? Osmo became a fatalist because there existed a set of true statements about the details of his life, both past and future, and he came to know what some of these statements were and to believe them, including many concerning his future. That is the whole of it.

No theological ideas entered into his conviction, nor any presuppositions about causal determinism, the coercion of his actions by causes, or anything of this sort. The foundations of Osmo's fatalism were entirely in logic and epistemology, having to do only with truth and knowledge. Ideas about God did not enter in, for he never suspected that God was the ultimate source of those statements. And at no point did he think God was *making* him do what he did. All he was concerned about was that someone seemed somehow to *know* what he had done and was going to do.

What, then, did Osmo believe? He did not, it should be noted, believe that certain things were going to happen to him *no matter what*. That does not express a logically coherent belief. He did not think he was in danger of perishing in an airplane crash even in case he did not get into any airplane, for example, or that he was going to break his leg skiing, whether he went skiing or not. No one believes what he considers to be plainly impossible. If anyone believes that a given event is going to happen, he does not doubt that those things necessary for its occurrence are going to happen too. The expression "no matter what," by means of which some philosophers have sought an easy and even childish refutation of fatalism, is accordingly highly inappropriate in any description of the fatalist conviction.

Osmo's fatalism was simply the realization that the things described in the book were unavoidable.

Of course we are all fatalists in this sense about some things, and the metaphysical question is whether this familiar attitude should not be extended to everything. We know the sun will rise tomorrow, for example, and there is nothing we can do about it. Each of us knows he is sooner or later going to die, too, and there is nothing to be done about that either. We normally do not know just when, of course, but it is mercifully so! For otherwise we would sit simply checking off the days as they passed, with growing despair, like a man condemned to the gallows and knowing the hour set for his execution. The tides ebb and flow, and heavens revolve, the seasons follow in order, generations arise and pass, and no one speaks of taking preventive measures. With respect to those things each of us recognizes as beyond his control, we are of necessity fatalists.

The question of fatalism is simply: Of all the things that happen in the world, which, if any, are avoidable? And the philosophical fatalist replies: None of them. They never were. Some of them only seemed so.

Was Osmo's fatalism justified? Of course it was. When he could sit right there and read a true description of those parts of his life that had not yet been lived, it would be idle to suggest to him that his future might, nonetheless, contain alternative possibilities. The only doubts Osmo had were whether those statements could really be true. But here he had the proof of his own experience, as one by one they were tested. Whenever he tried to prevent what was set forth, he of course failed. Such failure, over and over, of even the most Herculean efforts, with never a single success, must surely suggest, sooner or later, that he was *destined* to fail. Even to the end, when Osmo tried so desperately to save himself from the destruction described in the book, his effort was totally in vain—as he should have realized it was going to be had he really known that what was said there was true. No power in heaven or earth can render false a statement that is true. It has never been done, and never will be.

Is the doctrine of fatalism, then, true? This amounts to asking whether our circumstances are significantly different from Osmo's. Of course we cannot read our own biographies the way he could. Only people who become famous ever have their lives recorded, and even so, it is always in retrospect. This is unfortunate. It is too bad that someone with sufficient knowledge—God, for example—cannot set down the lives of great men in advance, so that their achievements can be appreciated better by their contemporaries, and indeed, by their predecessors—their parents, for instance. But mortals do not have the requisite knowledge, and if there are any gods who do, they seem to keep it to themselves.

None of this matters, as far as our own fatalism is concerned. For the important thing to note is that, of the two considerations that explain Osmo's fatalism, only one of them was philosophically relevant, and that one applies to us no less than to him. The two considerations were: (1) there existed a set of true statements about his life, both past and future, and (2) he came to know what those statements were and to believe them. Now the second of these two considerations explains why, as a matter of psychological fact, Osmo became fatalistic, but it has nothing to do with the validity of that point of view. Its validity is assured by (1) alone. It was not the fact that the

statements happened to be written down that rendered the things they described unavoidable; that had nothing to do with it at all. Nor was it the fact that, because they had been written, Osmo could read them. His reading them and coming to believe them likewise had nothing to do with the inevitability of what they described. This was ensured simply by there being such a set of statements, whether written or not, whether read by anyone or not, and whether or not known to be true. All that is required is that they should *be* true.

Each of us has but one possible past, described by that totality of statements about us in the past tense, each of which happens to be true. No one ever thinks of rearranging things there; it is simply accepted as given. But so also, each of us has but one possible future, described by that totality of statements about oneself in the future tense, each of which happens to be true. The sum of these constitutes one's biography. Part of it has been lived. The main outlines of it can still be seen, in retrospect, though most of its details are obscure. The other part has not been lived, though it most assuredly is going to be, in exact accordance with that set of statements just referred to. Some of its outlines can already be seen, in prospect, but it is on the whole more obscure than the part belonging to the past. We have at best only premonitory glimpses of it. It is no doubt for this reason that not all of this part, the part that awaits us, is perceived as given, and people do sometimes speak absurdly of altering it—as though what the future holds, as identified by any true statement in the future tense, might after all *not* hold.

Osmo's biography was all expressed in the present tense because all that mattered was that the things referred to were real events, it did not matter to what part of time they belonged. His past consisted of those things that preceded his reading of the book, and he simply accepted it as given. He was not tempted to revise what was said there, for he was sure it was true. But it took the book to make him realize that his future was also something given. It was equally pointless for him to try to revise what was said there, for it, too, was true. As the past contains what has happened, the future contains what will happen, and neither contains, in addition to these things, various other things that did not and will not happen.

Of course we know relatively little of what the future contains. Some things we know. We know the sun will go on rising and setting, for example, that taxes will be levied and wars will rage, that people will continue to be callous and greedy, and that people will be murdered and robbed. It is only the details that remain to be discovered. But the same is true of the past; it is only a matter of degree. When I meet a total stranger, I do not know, and will probably never know, what his past has been, beyond certain obvious things—that he had a mother, and things of this sort. I know nothing of the particulars of that vast realm of fact that is unique to his past. And the same for his future, with only this difference—that *all* people are strangers to me as far as their futures are concerned, and here I am even a stranger to myself.

Yet there is one thing I know concerning any stranger's past and the past of everything under the sun; namely, that whatever it might hold, there is nothing anyone can do about it now. What has happened cannot be undone. The mere fact that it has happened guarantees this.

And so it is, by the same token, of the future of everything under the sun. Whatever the future might hold, there is nothing anyone can do about it now. What will happen cannot be altered. The mere fact that it is going to happen guarantees this.

THE LAW OF EXCLUDED MIDDLE

The presupposition of fatalism is therefore nothing but the commonest presupposition of all logic and inquiry; namely, that there is such a thing as truth, and that this has nothing at all to do with the passage of time. Nothing *becomes* true or *ceases* to be true; whatever is truth at all simply *is* true.

It comes to the same thing, and is perhaps more precise, to say that every meaningful statement, whether about oneself or anything else, is either true or else it is false; that is, its denial is true. There is no middle ground. The principle is thus appropriately called *the law of excluded middle*. It has nothing to do with what tense a statement happens to express, nor with the question for whether anyone, man or god, happens to know whether it is true or false.

Thus no one knows whether there was an ant on my desk last night, and no one ever will. But we do know that either this statement is true or else its denial is true—there is no third alternative. If we say it *might* be true, we mean only that we do not happen to know. Similarly, no one knows whether or not there is going to be an ant there tonight, but we know that either it will or else it will not be there.

In a similar way we can distinguish two mutually exclusive but exhaustive classes of statements about any person; namely, the class of all those that are true, and the class of all that are false. There are no others in addition to these. Included in each are statements never asserted or even considered by anyone, but such that, if anyone were to formulate one of them, it would either be a true statement or else a false one.

Consider, then, that class of statements about some particular person—you, let us suppose—each of which happens to be true. Their totality constitutes your biography. One combination of such statements describes the time, place, and circumstances of your birth. Another combination describes the time, place, and circumstances of your death. Others describe in detail the rises and falls of your fortunes, your achievements and failures, your joys and sorrows—absolutely everything that is true of you.

Some of these things you have already experienced, others await you. But the entire biography is there. It is not written, and probably never will be; but it is nevertheless there, all of it. If, like Osmo, you had some way of discovering those statements in advance, then like him you could hardly help becoming a fatalist. But foreknowledge of the truth would not create any truth, nor invest your philosophy with truth, nor add anything to the philosophical foundations of the fatalism that would then be so apparent to you. It would only serve to make it apparent.

OBJECTIONS

This thought, and the sense of its force, have tormented and frightened people from the beginning, and thinkers whose pride sometimes exceeds their acumen and their reverence for truth have attempted every means imaginable to demolish it. There are few articles of faith upon which virtually everyone can agree, but one of them is certainly the belief in their cherished free will. Any argument in opposition to the doctrine of fate, however feeble, is immediately and uncritically embraced, as though the refutation of fatalism required only the denial of it, supported by reasons that would hardly do credit to a child. It will be worthwhile, therefore, to look briefly at some of the arguments most commonly heard.

1. One can neither foresee the future nor prove that there is any god, or even if there is, that he could know in advance the free actions of men.

   The reply to this is that it is irrelevant. The thesis of fatalism rests on no theory of divination and on no theology. These ideas were introduced only illustratively.

2. True statements are not the causes of anything. Statements only entail; they do not cause, and hence threaten no man's freedom.

   But this, too, is irrelevant, for the claim here denied is not one that has been made,

3. The whole argument just conflates fact and necessity into one and the same thing, treating as unavoidable that which is merely true. The fact that a given thing is going to happen implies only that it is going to happen, not that it has to.

Someone might still be able to prevent it—though of course no one will. For example, President Kennedy was murdered. This means it was true that he was going to be murdered. But it does not mean his death at that time and place was unavoidable. Someone could have rendered that statement false; though of course no one did.

That is probably the commonest "refutation" of fatalism ever offered. But how strong is the claim that something can be done, when in fact it never has been done in the whole history of the universe, in spite, sometimes, of the most strenuous efforts? No one has ever rendered false a statement that was true, however hard some have tried. When an attempt, perhaps a heroic attempt, is made to avoid a given calamity, and the thing in question happens anyway, at just the moment and in just the way it was going to happen, we have reason to doubt that it could have been avoided. And in fact great effort was made to save President Kennedy, for example, from the destruction toward which he was heading on that fatal day, a whole legion of bodyguards having no other mission. And it failed. True, we can say that if more strenuous precautions had been taken, the event would not have happened. But to this we must add true, they were not taken, and hence true, they were not going to be taken—and we have on our hands again a true statement of the kind that no man has ever had the slightest degree of success in rendering false.

For Further Reflection

1. Describe and evaluate Taylor's argument for fatalism. How convincing is it?
2. How does the story of Osmo illustrate Taylor's thesis?
3. Discuss the four questions that Taylor raises at the end of the story of Osmo.
4. Examine the objections raised against fatalism at the end of the article.

Key Terms

determinism   libertarianism   compatibilism
hard determinism

Suggestions for Further Reading

Dennett, Daniel. *Elbow Room: Varieties of Free Will Worth Wanting.* Cambridge, MA: MIT Press, 1985. The best defense of compatibilism.

Feinberg, Joel, ed. *Reason and Responsibility.* Belmont, CA: Wadsworth, 1985. Part 4 contains a very good selection of readings, including four readings on the implications for justifying punishment.

Honderich, Ted, ed. *Essays on Freedom of Action.* London: Routledge & Kegan Paul, 1973. A good collection of essays.

Kane, Robert. *The Significance of Free Will.* New York: Oxford University Press, 1996.

Lehrer, Keith, and Cornman, James. *Philosophical Problems and Arguments,* 3rd ed. New York: Macmillan, 1982. Lehrer's essay (Chapter 3) is excellent.

MacKay, Donald M. *Freedom of Action in a Mechanistic Universe.* Cambridge: Cambridge University Press, 1967.

Morgenbesser, Sidney, and Walsh, James, eds. *Free Will.* Englewood Cliffs, NJ: Prentice Hall, 1962. This contains many of the classic readings.

O'Connor, Timothy, ed. *Agents, Causes, and Events.* Oxford: Oxford University Press, 1995.

Stace, Walter. *Religion and the Modern Mind.* New York: Lippincott, 1952.

Trusted, Jennifer. *Free Will and Responsibility.* Oxford: Oxford University Press, 1984. One of the clearest introductions to the subject. Accessible to beginners and reliable.

van Inwagen, Peter. *An Essay on Free Will.* Oxford: Oxford University Press, 1983. This is the best critique of compatibilism available.

Watson, Gary. *Free Will.* Oxford: Oxford University Press, 1982. This volume contains the best collections of recent articles on the subject, especially those of Frankfurt, van Inwagen, and Watson. It also contains two clear discussions of the problem of mechanism and freedom of the will: Norman Malcolm's "The Conceivability of Mechanism" and Daniel Dennett's "Mechanism and Responsibility."

Part VI

$\sim$

Ethics

We are discussing no small matter, but how we ought to live.

SOCRATES in Plato's *Republic*

SOME YEARS AGO THE NATION WAS STUNNED by a report from Kew Gardens, Queens, in New York City. A young woman, Kitty Genovese, was brutally stabbed in her neighborhood while thirty-eight respectable, law-abiding citizens watched a killer stalk and stab her in three separate attacks. Her neighbors looked on from their bedroom windows for some thirty-five minutes as the assailant beat her, stabbed her, left her, and returned to repeat the process two more times until she died. No one lifted a phone to call the police, no one shouted at the criminal, let alone went to the aid of Kitty. Finally, a 70-year-old woman called the police. It took them two minutes to arrive, but by that time Kitty was dead. Only one other woman came out to testify until the ambulance came an hour later. Then the whole neighborhood poured out. Asked why they didn't do anything, the responses ranged from "I don't know" and "I was tired" to "Frankly, we were afraid."

Who is my neighbor? What should these respectable citizens have done? What would you have done? What kinds of generalizations can we make from this episode about contemporary culture in America? Is it an anomaly or quite indicative of something deeply disturbing?

What is it to be a moral person in contemporary society? What is the nature of morality? Why should I be moral? What is the good and how shall I know it? Are moral principles absolute or simply relative to social group or culture? Is morality, like beauty, in the eye of the beholder? Is it in my interest to be moral or to be moral when it calls for personal sacrifice? How does one justify one's moral beliefs? What is the relationship between morality and religion? What is the basis of morality? Why do we need morality anyway?

These are some of the questions that we shall be looking at in this part of our work. We want to know how we should live.

What Is Ethics?

The terms "moral" and "ethics" come from Latin and Greek, respectively (*mores* and *ethos*), deriving their meaning from the idea of custom. I shall follow the custom of using "morality" and "ethics" synonymously to refer to actual or ideal moralities. Sometimes, however, we use the term **ethics** to refer to the philosophical analysis of morality, the systematic endeavor to understand moral concepts and justify moral principles and theories. It undertakes to analyze such concepts as "right," "wrong," "permissible," "ought," "good," and "evil" in their moral contexts. Moral philosophy seeks to establish principles of right behavior that can serve as action guides for individuals and groups. It investigates which values and virtues are paramount to the worthwhile life or society. It builds and scrutinizes arguments in ethical theories, and it seeks to discover valid principles (for example, "Never kill innocent human beings") and the relationship between those principles (for example, Does saving a life in some situations constitute a valid reason for breaking a promise?).

Ethics is concerned with values—not with what is, but what ought to be. How should I live my life? What is the right thing to do in this situation? Should I always tell the truth? Do I have a duty to report a coworker whom I have seen cheating our company? Should I tell my friend that his spouse is having an affair? Is premarital sex morally permissible? Ought a woman ever to have an abortion? Ethics has a distinct action-guiding aspect and, as such, belongs to the group of practical institutions that include religion, law, and etiquette.

Ethics can be closely allied to religion, but it need not be. There are both religious and secular ethical systems. Secular or purely philosophical ethics are grounded in reason and common human experience. To use a spatial metaphor, secular ethics are horizontal, lacking a vertical or transcendental dimension. Religious ethics has a vertical dimension, being grounded in revelation or divine authority. These two differing orientations will often generate different moral principles and standards of evaluation, but they need not. Some versions of religious ethics, which posit God's revelation of the moral law in nature or conscience, hold that reason can discover what is right or wrong even apart from divine revelation.

Ethics is also closely related to law, and in some societies (such as that depicted in the Hebrew Bible) the two are seen as the same—as a single reality. Many laws are instituted to promote well-being, resolve conflicts of interest, or promote social harmony, just as morality does, but ethics can judge that some laws are immoral without denying that they are valid laws: for example, laws permitting slavery or irrelevant discrimination against people on the basis of race or sex. A Catholic or anti-abortion advocate might believe that the laws permitting abortion are immoral.

In a 1989 PBS television series, *Ethics in America,* James Neal, a trial lawyer, was asked what he would do if he discovered that his client, some years back, had committed a murder for which another man had been convicted and was going to die in a few days. Mr. Neal said that he had a legal obligation to keep this information confidential and that if he divulged it he would be disbarred. Some would argue that he has a moral obligation that overrides his legal obligation and that demands that he take action to protect the innocent man from being executed.

Furthermore, there are some aspects of morality that are not covered by law. For example, although it is generally agreed that lying is usually immoral, there is no law against it. College newspapers publish advertisements for phony research papers, which students use in lieu of their own work. Publication of such ads is legal, but it is not moral. Likewise, Kitty Genovese's neighbors were not guilty of any legal wrongdoing, but they were very likely morally culpable for not calling the police or shouting at the assailant.

There is one other major difference between law and morality. In 1351 King Edward III of England promulgated a law against treason that made it a crime merely to think homicidal thoughts about the king. But, alas, the law could not be enforced, for no tribunal can search the heart and fathom the intentions of the mind. But there are other problems. If malicious intentions (called in law *mens rea*) were criminally illegal, would we not all deserve imprisonment? Even if it were possible to detect intentions, when should the punishment be administered? As soon as the subject has the intention? But how do we know that he will not change his mind? Furthermore, is there not a continuum between imagining some harm to X, wishing a harm to X, desiring a harm to X, and intending a harm to X?

Even though it is impractical to have laws against bad intentions, these intentions are still bad, still morally wrong. Suppose you buy a gun with the intention of killing Uncle Charlie to inherit his wealth, but never get a chance to fire it (for example, Uncle Charlie moves to Australia). Although you have not committed a crime, you have committed a moral wrong.

Finally, law differs from morality in that there are physical sanctions enforcing the law but only the sanctions of conscience and reputation enforcing morality. Etiquette also differs from morality in that it concerns form and style rather than the essence of social existence.

Etiquette determines what is polite behavior rather than what is *right* behavior in a deeper sense. Etiquette represents society's decision about how we are to dress, greet one another, eat, celebrate festivals, dispose of the dead, and carry out social transactions. Whether we greet each other with a handshake, a bow, a hug, or a kiss on the cheek will differ in different social systems, but none of these rituals has any moral superiority.

People in England hold their forks in their left hands when they eat (and sometimes look at Americans with wonder when they see us holding forks in our right hands), whereas people in other countries hold forks in their right hands or in whichever hand they feel like holding them, and people in India typically eat without a fork at all, using the fingers of the right hand to convey food from plate to mouth.

Although Americans pride themselves on tolerance and awareness of other cultures, custom and etiquette can be a bone of contention. A friend relates an incident that took place early in his marriage. John and his wife were hosting their first Thanksgiving meal. He had been used to small celebrations with his immediate family, whereas his wife had been used to grand celebrations. He writes, "I had been asked to carve, something I had never done before, but I was willing. I put on an apron, entered the kitchen, attacked the bird with as much artistry as I could muster. And what reward did I get? [My wife] burst into tears. In *her* family the turkey is brought to the *table,* laid before [the father], grace is said, and *then* he carves! 'So I fail patriarchy,' I hollered later. 'What do you expect?'"

Etiquette is a spice of life. Polite manners grace our social existence but they are not what social existence is about. They help social transactions to flow smoothly, but are not the substance of those transactions.

At the same time, it can be immoral to disregard or flout etiquette. A cultural crisis recently developed in India when Americans went to the beaches clad in bikini bathing suits. This was highly offensive to the Indians and an uproar erupted.

There is nothing intrinsically wrong with wearing skimpy bathing suits, or with wearing nothing at all, for that matter, but people get used to certain behavioral patterns and it's terribly insensitive to flout those customs—especially when you are a guest in someone else's home or country. Not the bathing suits themselves; the *insensitivity* is morally offensive.

Law, etiquette, and religion are all important institutions, but each has limitations. The limitation of the law is that you can't have a law against every social malady nor can you enforce every desirable rule. The limitation of etiquette is that it doesn't get to the heart of what is of vital importance for personal and social existence. Whether or not one eats with one's fingers pales in significance compared with being honest or trustworthy or just. Etiquette is a cultural invention, but morality claims to be a discovery.

The limitation of the religious injunction is that it rests on authority, and we are not always sure of or in agreement about the credentials of the authority, nor on how the authority would rule in ambiguous or new cases. Religion is founded not on reason but on revelation, so there is no way to convince someone who does not share your religious views that your view is the right one.

Ethics, as the analysis of morality, distinguishes itself from law and etiquette by going deeper into the essence of rational existence. Ethics distinguishes itself from religion in that it seeks reasons, rather than authority, to justify its principles. Its central purpose is to secure valid principles of conduct and values that can be instrumental in guiding human actions and producing good character. As such ethics is the most important activity known to humans, for it has to do with how we are to live.

We turn now to a discussion of one of the most pressing issues of our time, moral relativism.

VI.A   Are There Any Moral Absolutes or Is Morality Completely Relative?

Ethical relativism is the notion that there are no universally valid moral principles, but that all moral principles are valid relative to cultural or individual choice. Ethical relativism is to be distinguished from **moral skepticism**, the view that there are no valid moral principles at all (or at least none that we can be confident about). There are two forms of ethical relativism: (1) **subjectivism**, which views morality as a personal decision ("Morality is in the eye of the beholder"), and (2) **conventionalism**, which views moral validity by social acceptance. Opposed to ethical relativism are various theories of **ethical objectivism**. All forms of objectivism affirm the universal validity of some moral principles. The strongest form, **moral absolutism**, holds that there is exactly one right answer to every "What should I do in situation *X*?" question, whatever that situation be, and that a moral principle can never be overridden—even by another moral principle. A weaker form of objectivism sees moral principles as universally valid but not always applicable. That is, moral principle A could be overridden by moral principle B in a given situation, and in other situations, there might be no right answer.

We turn now to our readings. First we have a defense of ethical relativism, and after that an attack on moral relativism that defends moral objectivism.

VI.58   Morality Is Relative

RUTH BENEDICT

Ruth Benedict (1887–1948) was a foremost American anthropologist who taught at Columbia University and is best known for her book *Patterns of Culture* (1934). Benedict views social systems as communities with common beliefs and practices that have become more or less well-integrated patterns of ideas and practices. Like a work of art, the social system chooses which theme of its repertoire of basic tendencies to emphasize and then goes about producing a holistic grand design favoring those tendencies. The final systems differ from one another in striking ways, but there is no reason to say that one system is better than another. What is considered normal or abnormal behavior will depend on the choices of these social systems, or what Benedict calls the "idea-practice pattern of the culture."

Benedict views morality as dependent on the varying histories and environments of different cultures. In this essay, she assembles an impressive amount of data from her anthropological research of tribal behavior on an island in northwest Melanesia from which she draws her conclusion that moral relativism is the correct view of moral principles.

Study Questions

1. What does Benedict see as the purpose of modern social anthropology?
2. What is her thesis about normalcy and abnormalcy?
3. How does Benedict illustrate her thesis? Are the examples sufficient to make her case?
4. What is the point of her illustration of homosexual behavior? Do you find her point plausible?
5. How does Benedict characterize morality? With what phrase is the sentence "It is morally good" synonymous?
6. What is the significance of her final comments on the range of human behavioral tendencies? What does she mean by the phrase "the proportion in which behavior types stand to one another in different societies is not universal"?

MODERN SOCIAL ANTHROPOLOGY has become more and more a study of the varieties and common elements of cultural environment and the consequences of these in human behavior. For such a study of diverse social orders primitive peoples fortunately provide a laboratory not yet entirely vitiated by the spread of a standardized worldwide civilization. Dyaks and Hopis, Fijians and Yakuts are significant for psychological and sociological study because only among these

From "Anthropology and the Abnormal," by Ruth Benedict, in The Journal of General Psychology *10 (1934): 59–82. Reprinted with permission of the Helen Dwight Reid Educational Foundation. Published by Heldref Publications, 1319 Eighteenth St., NW, Washington, DC 20036-1802. Copyright © 1934.*

simpler peoples has there been sufficient isolation to give opportunity for the development of localized social forms. In the higher cultures the standardization of custom and belief over a couple of continents has given a false sense of the inevitability of the particular forms that have gained currency, and we need to turn to a wider survey in order to check the conclusions we hastily base upon this near-universality of familiar customs. Most of the simpler cultures did not gain the wide currency of the one which, out of our experience, we identify with human nature, but this was for various historical reasons, and certainly not for any that gives us as its carriers a monopoly of social good or of social sanity. Modern civilization, from this point of view, becomes not a necessary pinnacle of human achievement but one entry in a long series of possible adjustments.

These adjustments, whether they are in mannerisms like the ways of showing anger, or joy, or grief in any society, or in major human drives like those of sex, prove to be far more variable than experience in any one culture would suggest. In certain fields, such as that of religion or of formal marriage arrangements, these wide limits of variability are well known and can be fairly described. In others it is not yet possible to give a generalized account, but that does not absolve us of the task of indicating the significance of the work that has been done and of the problems that have arisen.

One of these problems relates to the customary modern normal-abnormal categories and our conclusions regarding them. In how far are such categories culturally determined, or in how far can we with assurance regard them as absolute? In how far can we regard inability to function socially as diagnostic of abnormality, or in how far is it necessary to regard this as a function of the culture?

As a matter of fact, one of the most striking facts that emerge from a study of widely varying cultures is the ease with which our abnormals function in other cultures. It does not matter what kind of "abnormality" we choose for illustration, those which indicate extreme instability, or those which are more in the nature of character traits like sadism or delusions of grandeur or of persecution, there are well-described cultures in which these abnormals function at ease and with honor, and apparently without danger or difficulty to the society. . . .

The most notorious of these is trance and catalepsy. Even a very mild mystic is aberrant in our culture. But most peoples have regarded even extreme psychic manifestations not only as normal and desirable, but even as characteristic of highly valued and gifted individuals. This was true even in our own cultural background in that period when Catholicism made the ecstatic experience the mark of sainthood. It is hard for us, born and brought up in a culture that makes no use of the experience, to realize how important a role it may play and how many individuals are capable of it, once it has been given an honorable place in any society. . . .

Cataleptic and trance phenomena are, of course, only one illustration of the fact that those whom we regard as abnormals may function adequately in other cultures. Many of our culturally discarded traits are selected for elaboration in different societies. Homosexuality is an excellent example, for in this case our attention is not constantly diverted, as in the consideration of trance, to the interruption of routine activity which it implies. Homosexuality poses the problem very simply. A tendency toward this trait in our culture exposes an individual to all the conflicts to which all aberrants are always exposed, and we tend to identify the consequences of this conflict with homosexuality. But these consequences are obviously local and cultural. Homosexuals in many societies are not incompetent, but they may be such if the culture asks adjustments of them that would strain any man's vitality. Wherever homosexuality has been given an honorable place in any society, those to whom it is congenial have filled adequately the honorable roles society assigns to them. Plato's *Republic* is, of course, the most convincing statement of such a reading of homosexuality. It is presented as one of the major means to the good life, and it was generally so regarded in Greece at that time.

The cultural attitude toward homosexuals has not always been on such a high ethical plane, but it has been very varied. Among many American Indian tribes there exists the institution of the berdache, as the French called them. These men-women were men who at puberty or thereafter took the dress and the occupations of women. Sometimes they married other men and lived with them. Sometimes they were men with no inversion, persons of weak sexual endowment who chose this role to avoid the jeers of the women. The berdaches were never regarded as of first-rate supernatural power, as similar men-women were in Siberia, but rather as leaders in women's occupations, good healers in certain diseases, or, among certain tribes, as the genial organizers of social affairs. In any case, they were socially placed. They were not left exposed to the conflicts that visit the deviant who is excluded from participation in the recognized patterns of his society.

The most spectacular illustrations of the extent to which normality may be culturally defined are those cultures where an abnormality of our culture is the cornerstone of their social structure. It is not possible to do justice to these possibilities in a short discussion. A recent study of an island of northwest Melanesia by Fortune describes a society built upon traits which we regard as beyond the border of paranoia. In this tribe the exogamic groups look upon each other as prime manipulators of black magic, so that one marries always into an enemy group which remains for life one's deadly and unappeasable foes. They look upon a good garden crop as a confession of theft, for everyone is engaged in making magic to induce into his garden the productiveness of his neighbors'; therefore no secrecy in the island is so rigidly insisted upon as the secrecy of a man's harvesting of his yams. Their polite phrase at the acceptance of a gift is, "And if you now poison me, how shall I repay you this present?" Their preoccupation with poisoning is constant; no woman ever leaves her cooking pot for a moment untended. Even the great affinal economic exchanges that are charac-

teristic of this Melanesian culture area are quite altered in Dobu since they are incompatible with this fear and distrust that pervades the culture. They go farther and people the whole world outside their own quarters with such malignant spirits that all-night feasts and ceremonials simply do not occur here. They have even rigorous religiously enforced customs that forbid the sharing of seed even in one family group. Anyone else's food is deadly poison to you, so that communality of stores is out of the question. For some months before harvest the whole society is on the verge of starvation, but if one falls to the temptation and eats up one's seed yams, one is an outcast and a beachcomber for life. There is no coming back. It involves, as a matter of course, divorce and the breaking of all social ties.

Now in this society where no one may work with another and no one may share with another, Fortune describes the individual who was regarded by all his fellows as crazy. He was not one of those who periodically ran amok and, beside himself and frothing at the mouth, fell with a knife upon anyone he could reach. Such behavior they did not regard as putting anyone outside the pale. They did not even put the individuals who were known to be liable to these attacks under any kind of control. They merely fled when they saw the attack coming on and kept out of the way. "He would be all right tomorrow." But there was one man of sunny, kindly disposition who liked work and liked to be helpful. The compulsion was too strong for him to repress it in favor of the opposite tendencies of his culture. Men and women never spoke of him without laughing; he was silly and simple and definitely crazy. Nevertheless, to the ethnologist used to a culture that has, in Christianity, made his type the model of all virtue, he seemed a pleasant fellow. . . .

. . . Among the Kwakiutl it did not matter whether a relative had died in bed of disease, or by the hand of an enemy; in either case death was an affront to be wiped out by the death of another person. The fact that one had been caused to mourn was proof that one had been put upon. A chief's sister and her daughter had gone up to

Victoria, and either because they drank bad whiskey or because their boat capsized they never came back. The chief called together his warriors, "Now I ask you, tribes, who shall wail? Shall I do it or shall another?" The spokesman answered, of course, "Not you, Chief. Let some other of the tribes." Immediately they set up the war pole to announce their intention of wiping out the injury, and gathered a war party. They set out, and found seven men and two children asleep and killed them. "Then they felt good when they arrived at Sebaa in the evening."

The point which is of interest to us is that in our society those who on that occasion would feel good when they arrived at Sebaa that evening would be the definitely abnormal. There would be some, even in our society, but it is not a recognized and approved mood under the circumstances. On the Northwest Coast those are favored and fortunate to whom that mood under those circumstances is congenial, and those to whom it is repugnant are unlucky. This latter minority can register in their own culture only by doing violence to their congenial responses and acquiring others that are difficult for them. The person, for instance, who, like a Plains Indian whose wife has been taken from him, is too proud to fight, can deal with the Northwest Coast civilization only by ignoring its strongest bents. If he cannot achieve it, he is the deviant in that culture, their instance of abnormality.

This head-hunting that takes place on the Northwest Coast after a death is no matter of blood revenge or of organized vengeance. There is no effort to tie up the subsequent killing with any responsibility on the part of the victim for the death of the person who is being mourned. A chief whose son has died goes visiting wherever his fancy dictates, and he says to his host, "My prince has died today, and you go with him." Then he kills him. In this, according to their interpretation, he acts nobly because he has not been downed. He has thrust back in return. The whole procedure is meaningless without the fundamental paranoid reading of bereavement. Death, like all the other untoward accidents of

existence, confounds man's pride and can only be handled in the category of insults.

Behavior honored upon the Northwest Coast is one which is recognized as abnormal in our civilization, and yet it is sufficiently close to the attitudes of our own culture to be intelligible to us and to have a definite vocabulary with which we may discuss it. The megalomaniac paranoid trend is a definite danger in our society. It is encouraged by some of our major preoccupations, and it confronts us with a choice of two possible attitudes. One is to brand it as abnormal and reprehensible, and is the attitude we have chosen in our civilization. The other is to make it an essential attribute of ideal man, and this is the solution in the culture of the Northwest Coast.

These illustrations, which it has been possible to indicate only in the briefest manner, force upon us the fact that normality is culturally defined. An adult shaped to the drives and standards of either of these cultures, if he were transported into our civilization, would fall into our categories of abnormality. He would be faced with the psychic dilemmas of the socially unavailable. In his own culture, however, he is the pillar of society, the end result of socially inculcated mores, and the problem of personal instability in his case simply does not arise.

No one civilization can possibly utilize in its mores the whole potential range of human behavior. Just as there are great numbers of possible phonetic articulations, and the possibility of language depends on a selection and standardization of a few of these in order that speech communication may be possible at all, so the possibility of organized behavior of every sort, from the fashions of local dress and houses to the dicta of a people's ethics and religion, depends upon a similar selection among the possible behavior traits. In the field of recognized economic obligations or sex taboos this selection is as nonrational and subconscious a process as it is in the field of phonetics. It is a process which goes on in the group for long periods of time and is historically conditioned by innumerable accidents of isolation or of contact of peoples. In any comprehensive study of psychology, the selection that different cultures have made in the course of history within the great circumference of potential behavior is of great significance.

Every society, beginning with some slight inclination in one direction or another, carries its preference farther and farther, integrating itself more and more completely upon its chosen basis, and discarding those types of behavior that are uncongenial. Most of those organizations of personality that seem to us most uncontrovertibly abnormal have been used by different civilizations in the very foundations of their institutional life. Conversely the most valued traits of our normal individuals have been looked on in differently organized cultures as aberrant. Normality, in short, within a very wide range, is culturally defined. It is primarily a term for the socially elaborated segment of human behavior in any culture; and abnormality, a term for the segment that that particular civilization does not use. The very eyes with which we see the problem are conditioned by the long traditional habits of our own society.

It is a point that has been made more often in relation to ethics than in relation to psychiatry. We do not any longer make the mistake of deriving the morality of our locality and decade directly from the inevitable constitution of human nature. We do not elevate it to the dignity of a first principle. We recognize that morality differs in every society, and is a convenient term for socially approved habits. Mankind has always preferred to say, "It is morally good," rather than "It is habitual," and the fact of this preference is matter enough for a critical science of ethics. But historically the two phrases are synonymous.

The concept of the normal is properly a variant of the concept of the good. It is that which society has approved. A normal action is one which falls well within the limits of expected behavior for a particular society. Its variability among different peoples is essentially a function of the variability of the behavior patterns that different societies have created for themselves, and can never be wholly divorced from a consideration of culturally institutionalized types of behavior.

Each culture is a more or less elaborate working-out of the potentialities of the segment it has chosen. In so far as a civilization is well integrated and consistent within itself, it will tend to carry farther and farther, according to its nature, its initial impulse toward a particular type of action, and from the point of view of any other culture those elaborations will include more and more extreme and aberrant traits.

Each of these traits, in proportion as it reinforces the chosen behavior patterns of that culture, is for that culture normal. Those individuals to whom it is congenial either congenitally, or as the result of childhood sets, are accorded prestige in that culture, and are not visited with the social contempt or disapproval which their traits would call down upon them in a society that was differently organized. On the other hand, those individuals whose characteristics are not congenial to the selected type of human behavior in that community are the deviants, no matter how valued their personality traits may be in a contrasted civilization.

The Dobuan who is not easily susceptible to fear of treachery, who enjoys work and likes to be helpful, is their neurotic and regarded as silly. On the Northwest Coast the person who finds it difficult to read life in terms of an insult contest will be the person upon whom fall all the difficulties of the culturally unprovided for. The person who does not find it easy to humiliate a neighbor, nor to see humiliation in his own experience, who is genial and loving, may, of course, find some unstandardized way of achieving satisfactions in his society, but not in the major patterned responses that his culture requires of him. If he is born to play an important role in a family with many hereditary privileges, he can succeed only by doing violence to his whole personality. If he does not succeed, he has betrayed his culture; that is, he is abnormal.

I have spoken of individuals as having sets toward certain types of behavior, and of these sets as running sometimes counter to the types of behavior which are institutionalized in the culture to which they belong. From all that we know of contrasting cultures it seems clear that differences of temperament occur in every society. The matter has never been made the subject of investigation, but from the available material it would appear that these temperament types are very likely of universal recurrence. That is, there is an ascertainable range of human behavior that is found wherever a sufficiently large series of individuals is observed. But the proportion in which behavior types stand to one another in different societies is not universal. The vast majority of individuals in any group are shaped to the fashion of that culture. In other words, most individuals are plastic to the moulding force of the society into which they are born. In a society that values trance, as in India, they will have supernormal experience. In a society that institutionalizes homosexuality, they will be homosexual. In a society that sets the gathering of possessions as the chief human objective, they will amass property. The deviants, whatever the type of behavior the culture has institutionalized, will remain few in number, and there seems no more difficulty in moulding the vast malleable majority to the "normality" of what we consider an aberrant trait, such as delusions of reference, than to the normality of such accepted behavior patterns as acquisitiveness. The small proportion of the number of the deviants in any culture is not a function of the sure instinct with which that society has built itself upon the fundamental sanities, but of the universal fact that, happily, the majority of mankind quite readily take any shape that is presented to them. . . .

For Further Reflection

1. Is Benedict correct in saying that our culture is "but one entry in a long series of possible adjustments"? What are the implications of this statement?

2. Can we separate the descriptive (or fact-stating) aspect of anthropological study from the prescriptive (evaluative) aspect of evaluating cultures? Are there some independent criteria by which we can say that some cultures are better than others? Can you think how this project might be begun?

3. What are the implications of Benedict's claim that morality is simply whatever a culture deems normal behavior? Is this a satisfactory equation? Can you apply it to the institution of slavery or the Nazi policy of anti-Semitism?

4. What is the significance of Benedict's statement, "The very eyes with which we see the problem are conditioned by the long traditional habits of our own society"? Can we apply the conceptual relativism embodied in this statement to her own position?

Morality Is Not Relative   VI.59

JAMES RACHELS

James Rachels (1941–2003) was a professor of philosophy at the University of Alabama. He wrote books and articles in the areas of philosophy of religion and ethics. Among his important works are his articles "Active and Passive Euthanasia" and "Can Ethics Provide Answers?" and his books *Moral Problems* (1971), *The Elements of Moral Philosophy* (1986), and *Created from Animals: The Moral Implications of Darwinism* (1990).

Rachels analyzes the structure of ethical relativism, which he calls "cultural relativism," to show that the claims made by its proponents go beyond what the facts or arguments can establish. He contends that the central argument, "the cultural difference argument," is invalid, for even if there is broad cultural disagreement over morality, it doesn't prove that there is no truth in the matter, any more than the fact that flat-earthers disagree with round-earthers proves that there is no independent truth of that matter. Rachels goes on to point out three unfavorable consequences of cultural relativism that make it implausible. Finally, he points out two virtues in the doctrine.

Study Questions

1. What is the significance of Herodotus' story of the Callatians and Greeks comparing funerary practices?
2. How do Eskimo practices seem to lend support to the thesis of cultural relativism? Note what Rachels says later about the reasons for these practices.
3. What is Graham Sumner's thesis about morality?
4. What is the basic idea behind the cultural difference argument? Is it a sound argument?
5. What are the three consequences for ethics of cultural relativism?
6. Why does the author believe that the ethical relativist is unable to offer moral criticism of cruel behavior in another culture?
7. Why, according to Rachels, is there really less moral disagreement than there seems at first sight?
8. What is the argument for universal shared values or an objective morality?
9. What does the author think are the two lessons of cultural relativism?

Morality differs in every society, and is a convenient term for socially approved habits.

RUTH BENEDICT, *Patterns of Culture*, 1934

1. HOW DIFFERENT CULTURES HAVE DIFFERENT MORAL CODES

DARIUS, A KING OF ANCIENT PERSIA, was intrigued by the variety of cultures he encountered in his travels. He had found, for example, that the Callatians (a tribe of Indians) customarily ate the bodies of their dead fathers. The Greeks, of course, did not do that—the Greeks practiced cremation and regarded the funeral pyre as the natural and fitting way to dispose of the dead. Darius

thought that a sophisticated understanding of the world must include an appreciation of such differences between cultures. One day, to teach this lesson, he summoned some Greeks who happened to be present at his court and asked them what they would take to eat the bodies of their dead fathers. They were shocked, as Darius knew they would be, and replied that no amount of money could persuade them to do such a thing. Then Darius called in some Callatians, and while the Greeks listened asked them what they would take to burn their dead fathers' bodies. The Callatians were horrified and told Darius not even to mention such a dreadful thing.

This story, recounted by Herodotus in his *History*, illustrates a recurring theme in the literature of social science: different cultures have different moral codes. What is thought right within one group may be utterly abhorrent to the members of another group, and vice versa. Should we eat the bodies of the dead or burn them? If you were a Greek, one answer would seem obviously correct; but if you were a Callatian, the opposite would seem equally certain.

It is easy to give additional examples of the same kind. Consider the Eskimos. They are a remote and inaccessible people. Numbering only about 25,000, they live in small, isolated settlements scattered mostly along the northern fringes of North America and Greenland. Until the beginning of this century, the outside world knew little about them. Then explorers began to bring back strange tales.

Eskimo customs turned out to be very different from our own. The men often had more than one wife, and they would share their wives with guests, lending them for the night as a sign of hospitality. Moreover, within a community, a dominant male might demand—and get—regular sexual access to other men's wives. The women, however, were free to break these arrangements simply by leaving their husbands and taking up with new partners—free, that is, so long as their former husbands chose not to make trouble. All in all, the Eskimo practice was a volatile scheme that bore little resemblance to what we call marriage.

But it was not only their marriage and sexual practices that were different. The Eskimos also seemed to have less regard for human life. Infanticide, for example, was common. Knud Rasmussen, one of the most famous early explorers, reported that he met one woman who had borne twenty children but had killed ten of them at birth. Female babies, he found, were especially liable to be destroyed, and this was permitted simply at the parents' discretion, with no social stigma attached to it. Old people also, when they became too feeble to contribute to the family, were left out in the snow to die. So there seemed to be, in this society, remarkably little respect for life.

To the general public, these were disturbing revelations. Our own way of living seems so natural and right that for many of us it is hard to conceive of others living so differently. And when we do hear of such things, we tend immediately to categorize those other peoples as "backward" or "primitive." But to anthropologists and sociologists, there was nothing particularly surprising about the Eskimos. Since the time of Herodotus, enlightened observers have been accustomed to the idea that conceptions of right and wrong differ from culture to culture. If we assume that *our* ideas of right and wrong will be shared by all peoples at all times, we are merely naive.

2. CULTURAL RELATIVISM

To many thinkers, this observation—"Different cultures have different moral codes"—has seemed to be the key to understanding morality. The idea of universal truth in ethics, they say, is a myth. The customs of different societies are all that exist. These customs cannot be said to be "correct" or "incorrect," for that implies we have an independent standard of right and wrong by which they may be judged. But there is no such independent standard; every standard is culture-bound. The great pioneering sociologist William Graham Sumner, writing in 1906, put the point like this:

> The "right" way is the way which the ancestors used and which has been handed down. The tradition is its own warrant. It is not held subject to verification by experience. The notion of right is in the folkways. It is not outside of them, of independent origin, and brought to test them. In the folkways, whatever is, is right. This is because they are traditional, and therefore contain in themselves the authority of the ancestral ghosts. When we come to the folkways we are at the end of our analysis.

This line of thought has probably persuaded more people to be skeptical about ethics than any other single thing. *Cultural Relativism,* as it has been called, challenges our ordinary belief in the objectivity and universality of moral truth. It says, in effect, that there is no such thing as universal truth in ethics; there are only the various cultural codes, and nothing more. Moreover, our own code has no special status; it is merely one among many. As we shall see, this basic idea is really a compound of several different thoughts. It is important to separate the various elements of the theory because, on analysis, some parts of the theory turn out to be correct, whereas others seem to be mistaken. As a beginning, we may distinguish the following claims, all of which have been made by cultural relativists:

1. Different societies have different moral codes.

2. There is no objective standard that can be used to judge one societal code better than another.

3. The moral code of our own society has no special status; it is merely one among many.

4. There is no "universal truth" in ethics—that is, there are no moral truths that hold for all peoples at all times.

5. The moral code of a society determines what is right within that society; that is, if the moral code of a society says that a certain action is right, then that action *is* right, at least within that society.

6. It is mere arrogance for us to try to judge the conduct of other peoples. We should adopt an attitude of tolerance toward the practices of other cultures.

Although it may seem that these six propositions go naturally together, they are independent of one another, in the sense that some of them might be true even if others are false. In what follows, we will try to identify what is correct in Cultural Relativism, but we will also be concerned to expose what is mistaken about it.

3. THE CULTURAL DIFFERENCES ARGUMENT

Cultural Relativism is a theory about the nature of morality. At first blush it seems quite plausible.

However, like all such theories, it may be evaluated by subjecting it to rational analysis; and when we analyze Cultural Relativism we find that it is not so plausible as it first appears to be.

The first thing we need to notice is that at the heart of Cultural Relativism there is a certain *form of argument*. The strategy used by cultural relativists is to argue from facts about the differences between cultural outlooks to a conclusion about the status of morality. Thus we are invited to accept this reasoning:

(1) The Greeks believed it was wrong to eat the dead, whereas the Callatians believed it was right to eat the dead.

(2) Therefore, eating the dead is neither objectively right nor objectively wrong. It is merely a matter of opinion, which varies from culture to culture.

Or, alternatively:

(1) The Eskimos see nothing wrong with infanticide, whereas Americans believe infanticide is immoral.

(2) Therefore, infanticide is neither objectively right nor objectively wrong. It is merely a matter of opinion, which varies from culture to culture.

Clearly, these arguments are variations of one fundamental idea. They are both special cases of a more general argument, which says:

(1) Different cultures have different moral codes.

(2) Therefore, there is no objective "truth" in morality. Right and wrong are only matters of opinion, and opinions vary from culture to culture.

We may call this the *Cultural Differences Argument*. To many people, it is very persuasive. But from a logical point of view, is it a *sound* argument?

It is not sound. The trouble is that the conclusion does not really follow from the premise—that is, even if the premise is true, the conclusion still might be false. The premise concerns what people *believe:* in some societies, people believe one thing; in other societies, people believe differently. The conclusion, however, concerns *what really is the case.* The trouble is that this sort of conclusion does not follow logically from this sort of premise.

Consider again the example of the Greeks and Callatians. The Greeks believed it was wrong to eat the dead; the Callatians believed it was right. Does it follow, *from the mere fact that they disagreed,* that there is no objective truth in the matter? No, it does not follow; for it *could* be that the practice was objectively right (or wrong) and that one or the other of them was simply mistaken.

To make the point clearer, consider a very different matter. In some societies, people believe the earth is flat. In other societies, such as our own, people believe the earth is (roughly) spherical. Does it follow, *from the mere fact that they disagree,* that there is no "objective truth" in geography? Of course not; we would never draw such a conclusion because we realize that, in their beliefs about the world, the members of some societies might simply be wrong. There is no reason to think that if the world is round everyone must know it. Similarly, there is no reason to think that if there is moral truth everyone must know it. The fundamental mistake in the Cultural Differences Argument is that it attempts to derive a substantive conclusion about a subject (morality) from the mere fact that people disagree about it.

It is important to understand the nature of the point that is being made here. We are *not* saying (not yet, anyway) that the conclusion of the argument is false. Insofar as anything being said here is concerned, it is still an open question whether the conclusion is true. We *are* making a purely logical point and saying that the conclusion does not *follow from* the premise. This is important, because in order to determine whether the conclusion is true, we need arguments in its support. Cultural Relativism proposes this argument, but unfortunately the argument turns out to be fallacious. So it proves nothing.

4. THE CONSEQUENCES OF TAKING CULTURAL RELATIVISM SERIOUSLY

Even if the Cultural Differences Argument is invalid, Cultural Relativism might still be true. What would it be like if it were true?

In the passage quoted above, William Graham Sumner summarizes the essence of Cultural Relativism. He says that there is no measure of right and wrong other than the standards of one's society: "The notion of right is in the folkways. It is not outside of them, of independent origin, and brought to test them. In the folkways, whatever is, is right."

Suppose we took this seriously. What would be some of the consequences?

1. *We could no longer say that the customs of other societies are morally inferior to our own.* This, of course, is one of the main points stressed by Cultural Relativism. We would have to stop condemning other societies merely because they are "different." So long as we concentrate on certain examples, such as the funerary practices of the Greeks and Callatians, this may seem to be a sophisticated, enlightened attitude.

However, we would also be stopped from criticizing other, less benign practices. Suppose a society waged war on its neighbors for the purpose of taking slaves. Or suppose a society was violently anti-Semitic and its leaders set out to destroy the Jews. Cultural Relativism would preclude us from saying that either of these practices was wrong. We would not even be able to say that a society tolerant of Jews is *better* than the anti-Semitic society, for that would imply some sort of transcultural standard of comparison. The failure to condemn *these* practices does not seem "enlightened"; on the contrary, slavery and anti-Semitism seem wrong *wherever* they occur. Nevertheless, if we took Cultural Relativism seriously, we would have to admit that these social practices also are immune from criticism.

2. *We could decide whether actions are right or wrong just by consulting the standards of our*

society. Cultural Relativism suggests a simple test for determining what is right and what is wrong: all one has to do is ask whether the action is in accordance with the code of one's society. Suppose a resident of South Africa is wondering whether his country's policy of *apartheid*—rigid racial segregation—is morally correct. All he has to do is ask whether this policy conforms to his society's moral code. If it does, there is nothing to worry about, at least from a moral point of view. This implication of Cultural Relativism is disturbing because few of us think that our society's code is perfect—we can think of ways it might be improved. Yet Cultural Relativism would not only forbid us from criticizing the codes of *other* societies; it would stop us from criticizing our *own*. After all, if right and wrong are relative to culture, this must be true for our own culture just as much as for others.

3. *The idea of moral progress is called into doubt.* Usually, we think that at least some changes in our society have been for the better. (Some, of course, may have been changes for the worse.) Consider this example: Throughout most of Western history the place of women in society was very narrowly circumscribed. They could not own property; they could not vote or hold political office; with a few exceptions, they were not permitted to have paying jobs; and generally they were under the almost absolute control of their husbands. Recently much of this has changed, and most people think of it as progress.

If Cultural Relativism is correct, can we legitimately think of this as progress? Progress means replacing a way of doing things with a *better* way. But by what standard do we judge the new ways as better? If the old ways were in accordance with the social standards of their time, then Cultural Relativism would say it is a mistake to judge them by the standards of a different time. Eighteenth-century society was, in effect, a different society from the one we have now. To say that we have made progress implies a judgment that present-day society is better, and that is just the sort of transcultural judgment that, according to Cultural Relativism, is impermissible.

Our idea of social *reform* will also have to be reconsidered. A reformer such as Martin Luther King, Jr., seeks to change his society for the better. Within the constraints imposed by Cultural Relativism, there is one way this might be done. If a society is not living up to its own ideals, the reformer may be regarded as acting for the best: the ideals of the society are the standard by which we judge his or her proposals as worthwhile. But the "reformer" may not challenge the ideals themselves, for those ideals are by definition correct. According to Cultural Relativism, then, the idea of social reform makes sense only in this very limited way.

These three consequences of Cultural Relativism have led many thinkers to reject it as implausible on its face. It does make sense, they say, to condemn some practices, such as slavery and anti-Semitism, wherever they occur. It makes sense to think that our own society has made some moral progress, while admitting that it is still imperfect and in need of reform. Because Cultural Relativism says that these judgments make no sense, the argument goes, it cannot be right.

5. WHY THERE IS LESS DISAGREEMENT THAN IT SEEMS

The original impetus for Cultural Relativism comes from the observation that cultures differ dramatically in their views of right and wrong. But just how much do they differ? It is true that there are differences. However, it is easy to overestimate the extent of those differences. Often, when we examine what *seems* to be a dramatic difference, we find that the cultures do not differ nearly as much as it appears.

Consider a culture in which people believe it is wrong to eat cows. This may even be a poor culture, in which there is not enough food; still, the cows are not to be touched. Such a society would *appear* to have values very different from our own. But does it? We have not yet asked why these people will not eat cows. Suppose it is because they believe that after death the souls of humans inhabit the bodies of animals, especially cows, so that a cow may be someone's grandmother. Now do we want to say that their values are different from ours? No; the difference lies elsewhere. The difference is in our belief systems, not in our values. We agree that we shouldn't eat Grandma; we simply disagree about whether the cow *is* (or could be) Grandma.

The general point is this. Many factors work together to produce the customs of a society. The society's values are only one of them. Other matters, such as the religious and factual beliefs held by its members and the physical circumstances in which they must live, are also important. We cannot conclude, then, merely because customs differ, that there is a disagreement about *values.* The difference in customs may be attributable to some other aspect of social life. Thus there may be less disagreement about values than there appears to be.

Consider the Eskimos again. They often kill perfectly normal infants, especially girls. We do not approve of this at all; a parent who did this in our society would be locked up. Thus there appears to be a great difference in the values of our two cultures. But suppose we ask *why* the Eskimos do this. The explanation is not that they have less affection for their children or less respect for human life. An Eskimo family will always protect its babies if conditions permit. But they live in a harsh environment, where food is often in short supply. A fundamental postulate of Eskimo thought is: "Life is hard, and the margin of safety small." A family may want to nourish its babies but be unable to do so.

As in many "primitive" societies, Eskimo mothers will nurse their infants over a much longer period of time than mothers in our culture. The child will take nourishment from its mother's breast for four years, perhaps even longer. So even in the best of times there are limits to the number of infants that one mother can sustain. Moreover, the Eskimos are a nomadic people—unable to farm, they must move about in search of food. Infants must be carried, and a mother can carry only one baby in her parka as she travels and goes about her outdoor work. Other family members can help, but this is not always possible.

Infant girls are more readily disposed of because, first, in this society the males are the primary food providers—they are the hunters, according to the traditional division of labor—and it is obviously important to maintain a sufficient number of food gatherers. But there is an important second reason as well. Because the hunters suffer a high casualty rate, the adult men who die prematurely far outnumber the women who die early. Thus if male and female infants survived in equal numbers, the female adult population would greatly outnumber the male adult population. Examining the available statistics, one writer concluded that "were it not for female infanticide . . . there would be approximately one-and-a-half times as many females in the average Eskimo local group as there are food-producing males."

So among the Eskimos, infanticide does not signal a fundamentally different attitude toward children. Instead, it is a recognition that drastic measures are sometimes needed to ensure the family's survival. Even then, however, killing the baby is not the first option considered. Adoption is common; childless couples are especially happy to take a more fertile couple's "surplus." Killing is only the last resort. I emphasize this in order to show that the raw data of the anthropologists can be misleading; it can make the differences in values between cultures appear greater than they are. The Eskimos' values are not all that different from our values. It is only that life forces upon them choices that we do not have to make.

6. HOW ALL CULTURES HAVE SOME VALUES IN COMMON

It should not be surprising that, despite appearances, the Eskimos are protective of their children. How could it be otherwise? How could a group survive that did *not* value its young? This suggests a certain argument, one which shows that all cultural groups must be protective of their infants:

(1) Human infants are helpless and cannot survive if they are not given extensive care for a period of years.

(2) Therefore, if a group did not care for its young, the young would not survive, and the older members of the group would not be replaced. After a while the group would die out.

(3) Therefore, any cultural group that continues to exist must care for its young. Infants that are not cared for must be the exception rather than the rule.

Similar reasoning shows that other values must be more or less universal. Imagine what it would be like for a society to place no value at all on truth telling. When one person spoke to another, there would be no presumption at all that he was telling the truth—for he could just as easily be speaking falsely. Within that society, there would be no reason to pay attention to what anyone says. (I ask you what time it is, and you say "Four o'clock." But there is no presumption that you are speaking truly; you could just as easily have said the first thing that came into your head. So I have no reason to pay attention to your answer—in fact, there was no point in my asking you in the first place!) Communication would then be extremely difficult, if not impossible. And because complex societies cannot exist without regular communication among their members, society would become impossible. It follows that in any complex society there *must* be a presumption in favor of truthfulness. There may of course be exceptions to this rule: there may be situations in which it is thought to be permissible to lie. Nevertheless, these will be exceptions to a rule that *is* in force in the society.

Let me give one further example of the same type. Could a society exist in which there was no

prohibition on murder? What would this be like? Suppose people were free to kill other people at will, and no one thought there was anything wrong with it. In such a "society," no one could feel secure. Everyone would have to be constantly on guard. People who wanted to survive would have to avoid other people as much as possible. This would inevitably result in individuals trying to become as self-sufficient as possible—after all, associating with others would be dangerous. Society on any large scale would collapse. Of course, people might band together in smaller groups with others that they *could* trust not to harm them. But notice what this means: they would be forming smaller societies that *did* acknowledge a rule against murder. The prohibition of murder, then, is a necessary feature of all societies.

There is a general theoretical point here, namely, that *there are some moral rules that all societies will have in common, because those rules are necessary for society to exist.* The rules against lying and murder are two examples. And in fact, we do find these rules in force in all viable cultures. Cultures may differ in what they regard as legitimate exceptions to the rules, but this disagreement exists against a background of agreement on the larger issues. Therefore, it is a mistake to overestimate the amount of difference between cultures. Not *every* moral rule can vary from society to society.

7. WHAT CAN BE LEARNED FROM CULTURAL RELATIVISM

At the outset, I said that we were going to identify both what is right and what is wrong in Cultural Relativism. Thus far I have mentioned only its mistakes: I have said that it rests on an invalid argument, that it has consequences that make it implausible on its face, and that the extent of cultural disagreement is far less than it implies. This all adds up to a pretty thorough repudiation of the theory. Nevertheless, it is still a very appealing idea, and the reader may have the feeling that all this is a little unfair. The theory *must* have something going for it, or else why has it been so influential? In fact, I think there *is* something right about Cultural Relativism, and now I want to say what that is. There are two lessons we should learn from the theory, even if we ultimately reject it.

1. Cultural Relativism warns us, quite rightly, about the danger of assuming that all our preferences are based on some absolute rational standard. They are not. Many (but not all) of our practices are merely peculiar to our society, and it is easy to lose sight of that fact. In reminding us of it, the theory does a service.

Funerary practices are one example. The Callatians, according to Herodotus, were "men who eat their fathers"—a shocking idea, to us at least. But eating the flesh of the dead could be understood as a sign of respect. It could be taken as a symbolic act that says: We wish this person's spirit to dwell within us. Perhaps this was the understanding of the Callatians. On such a way of thinking, burying the dead could be seen as an act of rejection, and burning the corpse as positively scornful. If this is hard to imagine, then we may need to have our imaginations stretched. Of course we may feel a visceral repugnance at the idea of eating human flesh in any circumstances. But what of it? This repugnance may be, as the relativists say, only a matter of what is customary in our particular society.

There are many other matters that we tend to think of in terms of objective right and wrong, but that are really nothing more than social conventions. Should women cover their breasts? A publicly exposed breast is scandalous in our society, whereas in other cultures it is unremarkable. Objectively speaking, it is neither right nor wrong—there is no objective reason why either custom is better. Cultural Relativism begins with the valuable insight that many of our practices are like this—they are only cultural products. Then it goes wrong by concluding that, because *some* practices are like this, *all* must be.

2. The second lesson has to do with keeping an open mind. In the course of growing up, each of us has acquired some strong feelings: we have learned to think of some types of conduct as acceptable, and others we have learned to regard as simply unacceptable. Occasionally, we may find those feelings challenged. We may encounter someone who claims that our feelings are mistaken. For example, we may have been taught that homosexuality is immoral, and we may feel quite uncomfortable around gay people and see them as alien and "different." Now someone suggests that this may be a mere prejudice; that there is nothing evil about homosexuality; that gay people are just people, like anyone else, who happen, through no choice of their own, to be attracted to others of the same sex. But because we feel so strongly about the matter, we may find it hard to take this seriously. Even after we listen to the arguments, we may still have the unshakable feeling that homosexuals *must*, somehow, be an unsavory lot.

Cultural Relativism, by stressing that our moral views can reflect the prejudices of our society, provides an antidote for this kind of dogmatism. When he tells the story of the Greeks and Callatians, Herodotus adds:

> For if anyone, no matter who, were given the opportunity of choosing from amongst all the nations of the world the set of beliefs which he thought best, he would inevitably, after careful consideration of their relative merits, choose that of his own country. Everyone without exception believes his own native customs, and the religion he was brought up in, to be the best.

Realizing this can result in our having more open minds. We can come to understand that our feelings are not necessarily perceptions of the truth—they may be nothing more than the result of cultural conditioning. Thus when we hear it suggested that some element of our social code is *not* really the best and we find ourselves instinctively resisting the suggestion, we might stop and remember this. Then we may be more open to discovering the truth, whatever that might be.

We can understand the appeal of Cultural Relativism, then, even though the theory has serious shortcomings. It is an attractive theory because it is based on a genuine insight—that many of the practices and attitudes we think so natural are really only cultural products. Moreover, keeping this insight firmly in view is important if we want to avoid arrogance and have open minds. These are important points, not to be taken lightly. But we can accept these points without going on to accept the whole theory.

For Further Reflection

1. On balance, which position is the stronger: some form of ethical relativism or some version of ethical objectivism? Could both theories be partly true? Explain.

2. Could Benedict respond to the objectivist that "the very eyes with which we see the problem are conditioned by the long traditional habits of our own society"? What are the implications of that view and does it rule out objectivism?

3. How would you go about building a suitable morality? What considerations are of most importance? Do you think that morality has a purpose? If so, what is it?

VI.B   Ethics and Egoism: Why Should We Be Moral?

Why should we be moral? That is, why should we do what morality requires even when it might not be in our best interest? Is it really in our best interest after all, even if we don't realize it? Or is morality only generally in our best interest, so that we should consider breaking its rules whenever they become too burdensome? Or is there some other answer?

In this section we look at various responses to this question. We begin with Glaucon's question to Socrates: Whether justice (what we would call morality) was really only a compromise relationship between the better but unattainable state of exploiting others with impunity (like the shepherd Gyges, who can become invisible) and the worst situation of being exploited by others. Socrates rejects this way of looking at the problem and argues that justice is intrinsically valuable and brings about a healthy soul, so that it is never in our interest to be immoral.

But many reject Socrates' way of viewing the matter. They accuse Socrates of supposing an objective world of values or a divine law which ensures that those who act selfishly will be punished. But take away the notion of a God or a transcendent moral order that affects us and the Socratic picture breaks down. Self-interest can involve exploiting others; treating them "unjustly."

In our second reading, Louis Pojman offers several arguments against **ethical egoism**, the doctrine that right actions are those that promote one's own best interests. He concludes that ethical egoism is unfounded.

Why Should I Be Moral?
Gyges' Ring and Socrates' Dilemma   VI.60

PLATO

Plato (427–347 B.C.) lived in Athens and is the earliest philosopher for whom extensive works still remain today. In a series of dialogues he immortalized his teacher, Socrates. Perhaps his greatest dialogue is the *Republic*, from which this present reading is taken. The *Republic* is a classic treatise on political philosophy, centering on the concept of justice or moral rightness. In this work, Plato, through his idealization of Socrates, argues there will only be justice when reason rules and the people are obedient to its commands. This Utopia is only possible in an aristocracy in which the rulers are philosophers—philosopher-kings. In our selection, Glaucon, who is Plato's older brother, asks Socrates whether justice is good in itself or only a necessary evil. Playing the devil's advocate, Glaucon puts forth the hypothesis that egotistic power-seeking in which we have complete freedom to indulge ourselves might be the ideal state of existence. However, the hypothesis continues, reason quickly shows us that others might seek to have the same power, which would interfere with our freedom and cause a state of chaos in which no one was likely to have any of one's desires fulfilled. So we compromise and limit our acquisitive instincts. Justice or a system of morality is simply the result of that compromise. It has no intrinsic value but is better than chaos but worse than undisturbed power. It is better to compromise and limit our acquisitive instincts.

To illustrate his point Glaucon tells the story of a shepherd named Gyges who comes upon a ring, which at his behest makes him invisible. He uses it to escape the external sanctions of society—its laws and censure—and to serve his greed to the fullest. Glaucon asks whether it is not plausible to suppose that we all would do likewise? Then he offers a thought experiment that compares the life of the seemingly just (but unjust) man who is incredibly successful with the life of the seemingly unjust (but just) man who is incredibly unsuccessful. Which would we choose?

We enter the dialogue in the second book of the *Republic*. Socrates has just shown that the type of egoism advocated by Thrasymachus is contradictory. Socrates is speaking.

Study Questions

1. Note the distinction between different kinds of goods: (1) things desirable in themselves, (2) things not desirable in themselves but instrumental to other goods, and (3) things both intrinsically and instrumentally good. Which kind of good is justice, according to Socrates, and why?
2. What is the popular view of justice, according to Glaucon?
3. What is the lesson to be drawn from the story of Gyges' ring? Do you agree with Glaucon's conclusion about human nature?
4. What is Glaucon's point in comparing the completely just-but-seemingly-unjust man with the completely unjust-but-seemingly-just man? Which would you choose?

GYGES' RING

WITH THESE WORDS I was thinking that I had made an end of the discussion; but the end, in truth, proved to be only a beginning. For Glaucon, who is always the most pugnacious of men, was dissatisfied at Thrasymachus' retirement; he wanted to have the battle out. So he said to me: Socrates, do you wish really to persuade us, or only to seem to have persuaded us, that to be just is always better than to be unjust?

I should wish really to persuade you, I replied, if I could.

Then you certainly have not succeeded. Let me ask you now:—How would you arrange goods— are there not some which we welcome for their own sakes, and independently of their consequences, as, for example, harmless pleasures and enjoyments, which delight us at the time, although nothing follows from them?

I agree in thinking that there is such a class, I replied.

Is there not also a second class of goods, such as knowledge, sight, health, which are desirable not only in themselves, but also for their results?

Certainly, I said.

And would you not recognize a third class, such as gymnastic, and the care of the sick, and the physician's art; also the various ways of money-making—these do us good but we regard them as disagreeable; and no one would choose them for their own sakes, but only for the sake of some reward or result which flows from them?

There is, I said, this third class also. But why do you ask?

Because I want to know in which of the three classes you would place justice?

In the highest class, I replied, among those goods which he who would be happy desires both for their own sake and for the sake of their results.

Then the many are of another mind; they think that justice is to be reckoned in the troublesome class, among goods which are to be pursued for the sake of rewards and of reputation, but in themselves are disagreeable and rather to be avoided.

I know, I said, that this is their manner of thinking, and that this was the thesis which Thrasymachus was maintaining just now, when he censured justice and praised injustice. But I am too stupid to be convinced by him.

I wish, he said, that you would hear me as well as him, and then I shall see whether you and I agree. For Thrasymachus seems to me, like a snake, to have been charmed by your voice sooner than he ought to have been; but to my mind the nature of justice and injustice have not yet been made clear. Setting aside their rewards and results, I want to know what they are in themselves, and how they inwardly work in the soul. If you please, then, I will revive the argument of Thrasymachus. And first I will speak of the nature and origin of justice according to the common view of them. Secondly, I will show that all men who practice justice do so against their will, of necessity, but not as a good. And thirdly, I will argue that there is reason in this view, for the life of the unjust is after all better far than the life of the just—if what they say is true, Socrates, since I myself am not of their opinion. But still I acknowledge that I am perplexed when I hear the voices of Thrasymachus and myriads of others dinning in my ears; and, on the other hand, I have never yet heard the superiority of justice to injustice maintained by any one in a satisfactory way. I want to hear justice praised in respect of itself; then I shall be satisfied, and you are the person from whom I think that I am most likely to hear this; and therefore I will praise the unjust life to the utmost of my power, and my manner of speaking will indicate the manner in which I desire to hear you too praising justice and censuring injustice. Will you say whether you approve of my proposal?

Indeed I do; nor can I imagine any theme about which a man of sense would oftener wish to converse.

Reprinted from The Dialogues of Plato, *translated by Benjamin Jowett (Charles Scribner's, 1889).*

I am delighted, he replied, to hear you say so, and shall begin by speaking, as I proposed, of the nature and origin of justice.

They say that to do injustice is, by nature, good; to suffer injustice, evil; but that the evil is greater than the good. And so when men have both done and suffered injustice and have had experience of both, not being able to avoid the one and obtain the other, they think that they had better agree among themselves to have neither; hence there arise laws and mutual covenants; and that which is ordained by law is termed by them lawful and just. This they affirm to be the origin and nature of justice:—it is a mean or compromise, between the best of all, which is to do injustice and not be punished, and the worst of all, which is to suffer injustice without the power of retaliation; and justice, being at a middle point between the two, is tolerated not as a good, but as the lesser evil, and honoured by reason of the inability of men to do injustice. For no man who is worthy to be called a man would ever submit to such an agreement if he were able to resist; he would be mad if he did. Such is the received account, Socrates, of the nature and origin of justice.

Now that those who practice justice do so involuntarily and because they have not the power to be unjust will best appear if we imagine something of this kind: having given both to the just and the unjust power to do what they will, let us watch and see whither desire will lead them; then we shall discover in the very act the just and unjust man to be proceeding along the same road, following their interest, which all natures deem to be their good, and are only diverted into the path of justice by the force of law. The liberty which we are supposing may be most completely given to them in the form of such a power as is said to have been possessed by Gyges the ancestor of Croesus the Lydian. According to the tradition, Gyges was a shepherd in the service of the king of Lydia; there was a great storm, and an earthquake made an opening in the earth at the place where he was feeding his flock. Amazed at the sight, he descended into the opening, where, among other marvels, he beheld a hollow brazen horse, having doors, at which he stooping and looking in saw a dead body of stature, as appeared to him, more than human, and having nothing on but a gold ring; this he took from the finger of the dead and reascended. Now the shepherds met together, according to custom, that they might send their monthly report about the flocks to the king; into their assembly he came having the ring on his finger, and as he was sitting among them he chanced to turn the collet of the ring inside his hand, when instantly he became invisible to the rest of the company and they began to speak of him as if he were no longer present. He was astonished at this, and again touching the ring he turned the collet outwards and reappeared; he made several trials of the ring, and always with the same result—when he turned the collet inwards he became invisible, when outwards he reappeared. Whereupon he contrived to be chosen one of the messengers who were sent to the court; where as soon as he arrived he seduced the queen, and with her help conspired against the king and slew him, and took the kingdom. Suppose now that there were two such magic rings, and the just put on one of them and the unjust the other; no man can be imagined to be of such an iron nature that he would stand fast in justice. No man would keep his hands off what was not his own when he could safely take what he liked out of the market, or go into houses and lie with any one at his pleasure, or kill or release from prison whom he would, and in all respects be like a God among men. Then the actions of the just would be as the actions of the unjust; they would both come at last to the same point. And this we may truly affirm to be a great proof that a man is just, not willingly or because he thinks that justice is any good to him individually, but of necessity, for wherever any one thinks that he can safely be unjust, there he is unjust. For all men believe in their hearts that injustice is far more profitable to the individual than justice, and he who argues as I have been supposing, will say that they are right. If you could imagine any one obtaining this power of becoming invisible, and never doing any wrong or touching what was another's, he would be thought by the lookers-on to be a most wretched idiot, although they would praise him to one another's faces, and keep up appearances with one another from a fear that they too might suffer injustice. Enough of this.

Now, if we are to form a real judgment of the life of the just and unjust, we must isolate them; there is no other way; and how is the isolation to be effected? I answer: Let the unjust man be entirely unjust, and the just man entirely just; nothing is to be taken away from either of them, and both are to be perfectly furnished for the work of their respective lives. First, let the unjust be like other distinguished masters of craft; like the skillful pilot or physician, who knows intuitively his own powers and keeps within their limits, and who, if he fails at any point, is able to recover himself. So let the unjust make his unjust attempts in the right way, and lie hidden if he means to be great in his injustice (he who is found out is nobody): for the highest reach of injustice is: to be deemed just when you are not. Therefore I say that in the perfectly unjust man we must assume the most perfect injustice; there is to be no deduction, but we must allow him, while doing the most unjust acts, to have acquired the greatest reputation for justice. If he have taken a false step he must be able to recover himself; he must be one who can speak with effect, if any of his deeds come to light, and who can force his way where force is required by his courage and strength, and command of money and friends. And at his side let us place the just man in his nobleness and simplicity, wishing, as Aeschylus says, to be and not to seem good. There must be no seeming, for if he seem to be just he will be honoured and rewarded, and then we shall not know whether he is just for the sake of justice or for the sake of honours and rewards; therefore, let him be clothed in justice only, and have no other covering; and he must be imagined in a state of life the opposite of the former. Let him be the best of men, and let him be thought the worst; then he will have been put to the proof; and we shall see whether he will be affected by the fear of infamy and its conse-

quences. And let him continue thus to the hour of death; being just and seeming to be unjust. When both have reached the uttermost extreme, the one of justice and the other of injustice, let judgment be given which of them is the happier of the two.

Heavens! my dear Glaucon, I said, how energetically you polish them up for the decision, first one and then the other, as if they were two statues.

I do my best, he said. And now that we know what they are like there is no difficulty in tracing out the sort of life which awaits either of them. This I will proceed to describe; but as you may think the description a little too coarse, I ask you to suppose, Socrates, that the words which follow are not mine.—Let me put them into the mouths of the eulogists of injustice: they will tell you that the just man who is thought unjust will be scourged, racked, bound—will have his eyes burnt out; and, at last, after suffering every kind of evil, he will be impaled: Then he will understand that he ought to seem only, and not to be, just; the words of Aeschylus may be more truly spoken of the unjust than of the just. For the unjust is pursuing a reality; he does not live with a view to appearances—he wants to be really unjust and not to seem only:—

> His mind has a soil deep and fertile.
> Out of which spring his prudent counsels.

In the first place, he is thought just, and therefore bears rule in the city; he can marry whom he will, and give in marriage to whom he will; also he can trade and deal where he likes, and always to his own advantage, because he has no misgivings about injustice; and at every contest, whether in public or private, he gets the better of his antagonists, and gains at their expense, and is rich, and out of his gains he can benefit his friends, and harm his enemies; moreover, he can offer sacrifices, and dedicate gifts to the gods abundantly and magnificently, and can honour the gods or any man whom he wants to honour in a far better style than the just, and therefore he is likely to be dearer than they are to the gods.

And thus, Socrates, gods and men are said to unite in making the life of the unjust better than the life of the just. . . .

[We pick up the discussion in Book 9.]

BOOK 9

"Now that we've gotten this far," I said, "let's go back to that statement made at the beginning, which brought us here: that it pays for a man to be perfectly unjust if he appears to be just. Isn't that what someone said?"

"Yes."

"Then since we've agreed what power justice and injustice each have, let's have a discussion with him."

"How?"

"By molding in words an image of the soul, so that the one who said that will realize what he was saying."

"What kind of image?"

"Oh, something like those natures the myths tell us were born in ancient times—the Chimaera, Scylla, Cerberus, and others in which many different shapes were supposed to have grown into one."

"So they tell us," he said.

"Then mold one figure of a colorful, many-headed beast with heads of wild and tame animals growing in a circle all around it; one that can change and grow all of them out of itself."

"That's a job for a skilled artist. Still, words mold easier than wax or clay, so consider it done."

"And another of a lion, and one of a man. Make the first by far the biggest, the second second largest."

"That's easier, and already done."

"Now join the three together so that they somehow grow."

"All right."

"Next mold the image of one, the man, around them all, so that to someone who can't see what's inside but looks only at the container it appears to be a single animal, man."

"I have."

"Then shall we inform the gentleman that when he says it pays for this man to be unjust, he's saying that it profits him to feast his multifarious beast and his lion and make them grow strong, but to starve and enfeeble the man in him so that he gets dragged wherever the animals lead him, and instead of making them friends and used to each other, to let them bite and fight and eat each other?"

"That's just what he's saying by praising injustice."

"The one who says justice pays, however, would be saying that he should practice and say whatever will give the most mastery to his inner man, who should care for the many-headed beast like a farmer, raising and domesticating its tame heads and preventing the wild ones from growing, making the lion's nature his partner and ally, and so raise them both to be friends to each other and to him."

"That's exactly what he means by praising justice."

"So in every way the commender of justice is telling the truth, the other a lie. Whether we examine pleasure, reputation, or profit, we find that the man who praises justice speaks truly, the one who disparages it disparages sickly and knows nothing of what he disparages."

"I don't think he does at all."

"Then let's gently persuade him—his error wasn't intended—by asking him a question: 'Shouldn't we say that the traditions of the beautiful and the ugly have come about like this: Beautiful things are those that make our bestial parts subservient to the human—or rather, perhaps, to the divine   part of our nature, while ugly ones are those that enslave the tame to the wild?' Won't he agree?"

"If he takes my advice."

"On this argument then, can it pay for a man to take money unjustly if that means making his best part a slave to the worst? If it wouldn't profit a man to sell his son or his daughter into slavery—to wild and evil men at that—even if he got a fortune for it, then if he has no pity on himself and enslaves the most godlike thing in him to the most godless and polluted, isn't he a wretch who gets bribed for gold into a destruction more horrible than Euriphyle's, who sold her husband's life for a necklace?"

"Much more horrible," said Glaucon.

". . . everyone is better off being ruled by the godlike and intelligent; preferably if he has it inside, but if not, it should be imposed on him from without so that we may all be friends and as nearly alike as possible, all steered by the same thing."

"Yes, and we're right," he said.

"Law, the ally of everyone in the city, clearly intends the same thing, as does the rule of children, which forbids us to let them be free until we've instituted a regime in them as in a city. We serve their best part with a similar part in us, install a like guardian and ruler in them, and only then set them free."

"Clearly."

"Then how, by what argument, Glaucon, can we say that it pays for a man to be unjust or self-indulgent or to do something shameful to get more money or power if by doing so he makes himself worse?"

"We can't," he said.

"And how can it pay to commit injustice without getting caught and being punished? Doesn't getting away with it make a man even worse? Whereas if a man gets caught and punished, his beastlike part is taken in and tamed, his tame part is set free, and his whole soul acquires justice and temperance and knowledge. Therefore his soul recovers its best nature and attains a state more honorable than the state the body attains when it acquires health and strength and beauty, by as much as the soul is more honorable than the body."

"Absolutely."

"Then won't a sensible man spend his life directing all his efforts to this end?"

For Further Reflection

1. Which would you choose to be, Glaucon's good but suffering person or his bad but successful person? Is there a third alternative?

2. Socrates' answer to Glaucon and Adeimantus is that, despite appearances, we should choose the life of the "unsuccessful" just person because it is to our advantage to be moral. Socrates' answer depends on a notion of mental health. He contends that immorality corrupts the inner person, so that one is happy or unhappy in exact proportion to one's moral integrity. Is this a plausible reply?

3. Is the good always good for you?

VI.61   Egoism and Altruism: A Critique of Ayn Rand

LOUIS P. POJMAN

Louis P. Pojman (1935–2005) was professor emeritus of philosophy at the United States Military Academy at West Point and the author and editor of several books in ethics, philosophy of religion, and epistemology, including this book. In this essay Pojman criticizes Ayn Rand's version of ethical egoism for creating a false dilemma between (1) a self-demeaning altruism and (2) a consummate egoism in which people always put themselves first. He argues that Rand conflates *selfishness* with *self-interest*, but the two concepts are only superficially similar. He then draws from evolutionary ethologists who describe animal behavior, illustrating a middle way between self-degrading sacrifice and selfish egoism.

Study Questions

1. What is Ayn Rand's attitude toward altruism?
2. What is Rand's argument for ethical egoism?
3. What is the publicity argument?
4. What is the paradox of egoism?
5. What is the argument from counterintuitive consequences?
6. What is Pojman's final conclusion about ethical egoism?

Universal ethical egoism is the theory that everyone ought always to serve his or her own self-interest. That is, everyone ought to do what will maximize one's own expected utility or bring about one's own greatest happiness, even if it requires harming others. Ethical egoism is utilitarianism reduced to the pinpoint of the single individual ego. Instead of advocating the greatest happiness for the greatest number, as utilitarianism does, it advocates the greatest happiness for myself, whoever I may be. It is a self-preoccupied prudence, urging one to postpone enjoyment today for long-term benefits. In its more sophisticated form, it compares life to a competitive game, perhaps a war-game, and urges each person to *try* to win in the game of life.

In her books *The Virtue of Selfishness* and *Atlas Shrugged*, Ayn Rand argues that selfishness is a virtue and altruism a vice, a totally destructive idea that leads to the undermining of individual worth. She defines *altruism* as the view that

> any action taken for the benefit of others is good, and any action taken for one's own benefit is evil. Thus, the beneficiary of an action is the only criterion of moral value—and so long as the beneficiary is anybody other than oneself, anything goes.[1]

As such, altruism is suicidal:

> If a man accepts the ethics of altruism, his first concern is not how to live his life, but how to sacrifice it. . . . Altruism erodes men's capacity to grasp the value of an individual life; it reveals a mind from which the reality of a human being has been wiped out.

Since finding happiness is the highest goal and good in life, altruism, which calls on us to sacrifice our happiness for the good of others, is contrary to our highest good.

Her argument seems to go like this:

1. The perfection of one's abilities in a state of happiness is the highest goal for humans. We have a moral duty to attempt to reach this goal.
2. The ethics of altruism prescribes that we sacrifice our interests and lives for the good of others.
3. Therefore, the ethics of altruism is incompatible with the goal of happiness.
4. Ethical egoism prescribes that we seek our own happiness exclusively, and as such it is consistent with the happiness goal.
5. Therefore ethical egoism is the correct moral theory.

Ayn Rand's argument for the virtue of selfishness is flawed by the fallacy of a false dilemma. It simplistically assumes that absolute altruism and absolute egoism are the only alternatives. But this is an extreme view of the matter. There are plenty of options between these two positions. Even a predominant egoist would admit that (analogous to the paradox of hedonism) sometimes the best way to reach self-fulfillment is for us to forget about ourselves and strive to live for goals, causes, or other persons. Even if altruism is not required (as a duty), it may be permissible in many cases. Furthermore, self-interest may not be incompatible with other-regarding motivation. Even the Second Great Commandment set forth by Moses and Jesus states not that you must always sacrifice yourself for the other person, but that you ought to love your neighbor *as* yourself (Lev. 19:19; Matt. 23). Self-interest and self-love are morally good things, but not at the expense of other people's legitimate interests. When there is moral conflict of interests, a fair process of adjudication needs to take place.

But Rand's version of egoism is only one of many. We need to go to the heart of ethical egoism: the thesis that our highest moral duty is always to promote our individual interests. Let us focus on the alleged problems of this thesis.

FOUR CRITICISMS OF ETHICAL EGOISM

The Inconsistent Outcomes Argument

Brian Medlin argues that ethical egoism cannot be true because it fails to meet a necessary condition of morality, that of being a guide to action. He claims that it will be like advising people to do inconsistent things based on incompatible desires.[2] His argument goes like this:

1. Moral principles must be universal and categorical.
2. I must universalize my egoist desire to come out on top over Tom, Dick, and Harry.

3. But I must also prescribe Tom's egoist desire to come out on top over Dick, Harry, and me (and so on).
4. Therefore I have prescribed incompatible outcomes and have not provided a way of adjudicating conflicts of desire. In effect, I have said nothing.

The proper response to this is that of Jesse Kalin, who argues that we can separate our beliefs about ethical situations from our desires.[3] He likens the situation to a competitive sports event, in which you believe that your opponent has a right to try to win as much as you, but you desire that you, not he, will in fact win. An even better example is that of the chess game in which you recognize that your opponent ought to move her bishop to prepare for checkmate, but you hope she won't see the move. Belief that A ought to do Y does not commit you to wanting A to do Y.

The Publicity Argument

On the one hand, in order for something to be a moral theory it seems necessary that its moral principles be publicized. Unless principles are put forth as universal prescriptions that are accessible to the public, they cannot serve as guides to action or as aids in resolving conflicts of interest. But on the other hand, it is not in the egoist's self-interest to publicize them. Egoists would rather that the rest of us be altruists. (Why did Nietzsche and Rand write books announcing their positions? Were the royalties taken in by announcing ethical egoism worth the price of letting the cat out of the bag?)

Thus it would be self-defeating for the egoist to argue for her position, and even worse that she should convince others of it. But it is perfectly possible to have a private morality that does not resolve conflicts of interest. So the egoist should publicly advocate standard principles of traditional morality—so that society doesn't break down—while adhering to a private, nonstandard, solely self-regarding morality. So, if you're willing to pay the price, you can accept the solipsistic-directed norms of egoism.

If the egoist is prepared to pay the price, egoism could be a consistent system that has some limitations. Although the egoist can cooperate with others in limited ways and perhaps even have friends—so long as their interests don't conflict with his—he has to be very careful about preserving his isolation. The egoist can't give advice or argue about his position—not sincerely at least. He must act alone, atomistically or solipsistically in moral isolation, for to announce his adherence to the principle of egoism would be dangerous to his project. He can't teach his children the true morality or justify himself to others or forgive others.

The Paradox of Egoism

The situation may be even worse than the sophisticated, self-conscious egoist supposes. Could the egoist have friends? And if limited friendship is possible, could he or she ever be in love or experience deep friendship? Suppose the egoist discovers that in the pursuit of the happiness goal, deep friendship is in his best interest. Can he become a friend? What is necessary to deep friendship? A true friend is one who is not always preoccupied about his own interest in the relationship but who forgets about himself altogether, at least sometimes, in order to serve or enhance the other person's interest. "Love seeketh not its own." It is an altruistic disposition, the very opposite of egoism. So the *paradox of egoism* is that in order to reach the goal of egoism one must give up egoism and become (to some extent) an altruist, the very antithesis of egoism.

The Argument from Counterintuitive Consequences

The final argument against ethical egoism is that it is an absolute ethics that not only permits egoistic behavior but demands it. Helping others at one's own expense is not only not required, it is morally wrong. Whenever I do not have good evidence that my helping you will end up to my advantage, I must refrain from helping you. If I can save the whole of Europe

and Africa from destruction by pressing a button, then so long as there is nothing for me to gain by it, it is wrong for me to press that button. The Good Samaritan was, by this logic, morally wrong in helping the injured victim and not collecting payment for his troubles. It is certainly hard to see why the egoist should be concerned about environmental matters if he or she is profiting from polluting the environment. (For example, if the egoist gains 40 hedons in producing P, which produces pollution that in turn causes others 1,000 dolors—units of suffering—but suffers only 10 of those dolors himself, then by an agent-maximizing calculus he is morally obligated to produce P.) There is certainly no obligation to preserve scarce natural resources for future generations. "Why should I do anything for posterity?" the egoist asks "What has posterity ever done for me?"

In conclusion, we see that ethical egoism has a number of serious problems. It cannot consistently publicize itself, nor often argue its case. It tends towards solipsism and the exclusion of many of the deepest human values, such as love and deep friendship. It violates the principle of fairness, and, most of all, it entails an absolute prohibition on altruistic behavior, which we intuitively sense as morally required (or, at least, permissible).

EVOLUTION AND ALTRUISM

If sheer unadulterated egoism is an inadequate moral theory, does that mean we ought to aim at complete altruism, total self-effacement for the sake of others? What is the role of self-love in morality? An interesting place to start answering these queries is with the new field of sociobiology, which theorizes that social structures and behavioral patterns, including morality, have a biological base, explained by evolutionary theory.

In the past, linking ethics to evolution meant justifying exploitation. Social Darwinism justified imperialism and the principle that "Might makes right" by saying that survival of the fittest is a law of nature. This philosophy lent itself to a promotion of ruthless egoism. This is nature's law, "nature red in tooth and claw." Against this view ethologists such as Robert Ardrey and Konrad Lorenz argued for a more benign view of the animal kingdom—one reminiscent of Rudyard Kipling's, in which the animal kingdom survives by cooperation, which is at least as important as competition. On Ardrey's and Lorenz's view it is the group or the species, not the individual, that is of primary importance.

With the development of sociobiology—in the work of E. O. Wilson but particularly the work of Robert Trivers, J. Maynard Smith, and Richard Dawkins—a theory has come to the fore that combines radical individualism with limited altruism. It is not the group or the species that is of evolutionary importance but the gene, or, more precisely, the gene type. Genes—the parts of the chromosomes that carry the blueprints for all our natural traits (e.g., height, hair color, skin color, intelligence)—copy themselves as they divide and multiply. At conception they combine with the genes of a member of the opposite sex to form a new individual.

In his fascinating sociobiological study, Richard Dawkins describes human behavior as determined evolutionarily by stable strategies set to replicate the gene.[4] This is not done consciously, of course, but by the invisible hand that drives consciousness. We are essentially gene machines.

Morality—that is, successful morality—can be seen as an evolutionary strategy for gene replication. Here's an example: Birds are afflicted with life-endangering parasites. Because they lack limbs to enable them to pick the parasites off their heads, they—like much of the animal kingdom—depend on the ritual of mutual grooming. It turns out that nature has evolved two basic types of birds in this regard: those who are disposed to groom anyone (the nonprejudiced type?), and those who refuse to groom anyone but who present themselves for grooming. The former type of bird Dawkins calls "Suckers" and the latter "Cheaters."

In a geographical area containing harmful parasites and where there are only Suckers or Cheaters, Suckers will do fairly well, but Cheaters will not survive, for want of cooperation. However, in a Sucker population in which a mutant Cheater arises, the Cheater will prosper, and the Cheater gene-type will multiply. As the Suckers are exploited, they will gradually die out. But if and when they become too few to groom the Cheaters, the Cheaters will start to die off too and eventually become extinct.

Why don't birds all die off, then? Well, somehow nature has come up with a third type, call them "Grudgers." Grudgers groom all and only those who reciprocate in grooming them. They groom each other and Suckers, but not Cheaters. In fact, once caught, a Cheater is marked forever. There is no forgiveness. It turns out then that unless there are a lot of Suckers around, Cheaters have a hard time of it—harder even than Suckers. However, it is the Grudgers that prosper. Unlike Suckers, they don't waste time messing with unappreciative Cheaters, so they are not exploited and have ample energy to gather food and build better nests for their loved ones.

J. L. Mackie argues that the real name for Suckers is "Christian," one who believes in complete altruism, even turning the other cheek to one's assailant and loving one's enemy. Cheaters are ruthless egoists who can survive only if there are enough naive altruists around. Whereas Grudgers are *reciprocal* altruists who have a rational morality based on cooperative self-interest, Suckers, such as Socrates and Jesus, advocate "turning the other cheek and repaying evil with good."[5] Instead of a Rule of Reciprocity, "I'll scratch your back if you'll scratch mine," the extreme altruist substitutes the Golden Rule, "If you want the other fellow to scratch your back, you scratch his—even if he won't reciprocate."

The moral of the story is this: Altruist morality (so interpreted) is only rational given the payoff of eternal life (with a scorekeeper as Woody Allen says). Take that away, and it looks like a Sucker system. What replaces the "Christian" vision of submission and saintliness is the reciprocal altruist with a tit-for-tat morality, someone who is willing to share with those willing to cooperate.

Mackie may caricature the position of the religious altruist, but he misses the subtleties of wisdom involved (Jesus said, "Be as wise as serpents but as harmless as doves"). Nevertheless, he does remind us that there is a difference between core morality and complete altruism. We have duties to cooperate and reciprocate, but no duty to serve those who manipulate us nor an obvious duty to sacrifice ourselves for people outside our domain of special responsibility. We have a special duty of high altruism toward those in the close circle of our concern, namely, our family and friends.

CONCLUSION

Martin Luther once said that humanity is like a man who, when mounting a horse, always falls off on the opposite side, especially when he tries to overcompensate for his previous exaggerations. So it is with ethical egoism. Trying to compensate for an irrational, guilt-ridden, Sucker altruism of the morality of self-effacement, it falls off the horse on the other side, embracing a Cheater's preoccupation with self-exaltation that robs the self of the deepest joys in life. Only the person who mounts properly, avoiding both extremes, is likely to ride the horse of happiness to its goal.

NOTES

1. Ayn Rand, *The Virtue of Selfishness* (New American Library, 1964), pp. vii and 27–32; 80ff.

2. Brian Medlin, "Ultimate Principles and Ethical Egoism," *Australasian Journal of Philosophy* (1957), pp. 111–118; reprinted in Louis Pojman, *Ethical Theory*, pp. 91–95.

3. See Jesse Kalin, "In Defense of Egoism," in *Ethical Theory*, 4th ed., ed. Louis Pojman (Wadsworth, 2002), p. 95f.

4. Richard Dawkins, *The Selfish Gene* (Oxford University Press, 1976), Ch.10

5. J. L. Mackie, "The Law of the Jungle: Moral Alternatives and Principles of Evolution," *Philosophy* 53 (1978).

For Further Reflection

1. Evaluate whether this statement, which I first encountered in a student paper, is true or false:

> "Everyone is an egoist, for everyone always tries to do what will bring them satisfaction."

2. Distinguish between individual and universal ethical egoism. Which theory appeals to you more? Does either constitute an adequate ethical theory? Explain your answer.

3. The introduction of this part of our book began with the story of the killing of Kitty Genovese. Review that story, and discuss how an ethical egoist would respond to the plight of Kitty Genovese. Would egoists admit that they had a duty to come to her aid?

4. Discuss the three arguments in favor of ethical egoism and the four against it. Which side has the best arguments? Why?

5. Does the egoist have a point in believing that most moral systems fail to recognize adequately that morality should be in our best interest? In this light, ethical egoism could be seen as an attempt to compensate for the inadequacies of other ethical views that emphasize doing duty for duty's sake or for the sake of others.

6. Some philosophers, beginning with Plato, have argued that ethical egoism is irrational, since it precludes psychological health. In an article entitled "Ethical Egoism and Psychological Dispositions" (*American Philosophical Quarterly* 17[1], 1980), Laurence Thomas sets forth the following argument:

> P1. A true friend could never, as a matter of course, be disposed to harm or to exploit anyone with whom he is a friend [definition of a friend].

P2. An egoist could never be a true friend to anyone [for the egoist must be ready to exploit others whenever it is in his or her interest].

P3. Only someone with an unhealthy personality could never be a true friend to anyone [definition of a healthy personality; that is, friendship is a necessary condition for a healthy personality].

P4. Ethical egoism requires that we have a kind of disposition which is incompatible with our having a healthy personality [from P1–P3].

Conclusion: Therefore, from the standpoint of our psychological makeup, ethical egoism is unacceptable as a moral theory.

Do you agree with Thomas? How might the ethical egoist respond?

7. What is the relationship between ethics and evolution? How does this relationship throw light on egoism? What is the significance of reciprocity for ethics?

VI.C   Which Is the Correct Ethical Theory?

There are three major types of moral theories in Western philosophy:

1. **Virtue ethics**, which says that the emphasis in ethics should be put not on rules, but on character—on the virtues and vices people exhibit in their lives. Ethical goodness is primarily a state of being, and only secondarily a doing.

2. **Deontological ethics**, which views moral value as inherent in certain acts or types of acts (for example, "killing innocents is just wrong [period]."). The main form of deontological ethics holds that we ought to follow principles of action, for these principles of action have inherent value. In every moral act we are acting in accordance with an appropriate principle. A second type of deontological ethics (set forth by Bishop Joseph Butler [1692–1752]) holds that the criterion of right and wrong is the voice of conscience.

3. **Teleological ethics**, which asserts that the rightness or wrongness of an act is determined by some nonmoral value. Teleological ethical systems can be subdivided into two major forms. *Ethical egoism* is the view that each person ought to do what will promote his or her own greatest good, and **utilitarianism** is the view that persons ought to do the act that will produce the greatest total (or average) good (for example, "The greatest happiness for the greatest number"—Francis Hutcheson [1694–1746]).

Our first four readings in this section represent these three types of theories. We begin with Aristotle's virtue theory, one of the oldest accounts of ethics in the history of philosophy, followed by Virginia Held's related essay on the **ethics of care**. Next we examine the most famous deontological theory, Kantian ethics, followed by a section from John Stuart Mill's classic *Utilitarianism*. These are followed by a type of ethics that defies systemization, yet is not in the virtue tradition, existentialist ethics, which leaves each decision to the individual in the moment. Jean-Paul Sartre's "Existentialist Ethics" represents this position. Finally, we inspect a common theme in religious ethics in "The Divine Command Theory" by James Rachels.

The Ethics of Virtue   VI.62

ARISTOTLE

Aristotle (384–322 B.C.), Greek physician, Plato's prize pupil, tutor to Alexander the Great, and one of the most important philosophers who ever lived, wrote importantly on every major subject in philosophy: metaphysics, philosophy of science, philosophical psychology, aesthetics, ethics, and politics. He is the father of formal logic. Although deeply indebted to his teacher, Plato, Aristotle broke with him over the idea of Forms (Plato thought that the Forms had independent existence whereas Aristotle thought that they were in things). Aristotle tended to be more empirical than Plato. The break with the master led to the formation of the second major school of philosophy in Athens, Aristotle's Lyceum.

In this selection from the *Nicomachean Ethics,* Aristotle first discusses the nature of ethics and its relationship to human existence. He next turns to the nature of virtue, which he characterizes as traits that enable individuals to live well in communities. To achieve a state of well being (*eudaimonia,* happiness), proper social institutions are necessary. Thus the moral person cannot really exist apart from a flourishing political setting that enables the individual to develop the requisite virtues for the good life. For this reason Aristotle considers ethics to be a branch of politics.

After locating ethics as a part of politics, Aristotle explains that the moral virtues are different from the intellectual ones. Although the intellectual virtues can be taught directly, the moral ones must be lived in order to be learned. By living well, we acquire the right habits. These habits are in fact the virtues. The virtues are to be sought as the best guarantee to the happy life. But, again, happiness requires that one be lucky enough to live in a flourishing state. The morally virtuous life consists in living in moderation, according to the "Golden Mean."

Study Questions

1. How does Aristotle define politics and ethics? What is the relationship between them?
2. What is the good at which political science and ethics aim?
3. What are the characteristics of the good?
4. What is the function of human beings? How does Aristotle build his case for our having a function and how does this relate to ethics?
5. What is the relationship between habit and ethics? What does Aristotle mean by the statement, "A just man becomes just by doing what is just"? How can one do just things if one isn't already just? How does Aristotle solve this problem?
6. Does every action and emotion have a proper mean (Book II.6)?

BOOK I

All Human Activities Aim at Some Good

Chapter 1. EVERY ART AND EVERY scientific inquiry, and similarly every action and purpose, may be said to aim at some good. Hence the good has been well defined as that at which all things aim. But it is clear that there is a difference in ends; for the ends are sometimes activities, and sometimes results beyond the mere activities. Where there are ends beyond the action, the results are naturally superior to the action.

As there are various actions, arts, and sciences, it follows that the ends are also various. Thus health is the end of the medical art, a ship of shipbuilding, victory of strategy, and wealth of economics. It often happens that a number of such arts or sciences combine for a single enterprise, as the art of making bridles and all such other arts as furnish the implements of horsemanship combine for horsemanship, and horsemanship and every military action for strategy; and in the same way, other arts or sciences combine for others. In all these cases, the ends of the master arts or sciences, whatever they may be, are more desirable than those of the subordinate arts or sciences, as it is for the sake of the former that the latter are pursued. It makes no difference to the argument whether the activities themselves are the ends of the action, or something beyond the activities, as in the above-mentioned sciences.

If it is true that in the sphere of action there is some end which we wish for its own sake, and for the sake of which we wish everything else, and if we do not desire everything for the sake of something else (for, if that is so, the process will go on *ad infinitum,* and our desire will be idle and futile), clearly this end will be good and the supreme good. Does it not follow then that the knowledge of this good is of great importance for the conduct of life? Like archers who have a mark at which to aim, shall we not have a better chance of attaining what we want? If this is so, we must endeavor to comprehend, at least in outline, what this good is, and what science or faculty makes it its object.

It would seem that this is the most authoritative science. Such a kind is evidently the political, for it is that which determines what sciences are necessary in states, and what kinds should be studied, and how far they should be studied by each class of inhabitant. We see too that even the faculties held in highest esteem, such as strategy, economics, and rhetoric, are subordinate to it. Then since politics makes use of the other sciences and also rules what people may do and what they may not do, it follows that its end will comprehend the ends of the other sciences, and will therefore be the good of mankind. For even if the good of an individual is identical with the good of a state, yet the good of the state is evidently greater and more perfect to attain or to preserve. For though the good of an individual by himself is something worth working for, to ensure the good of a nation or a state is nobler and more divine.

These then are the objects at which the present inquiry aims, and it is in a sense a political inquiry. . . .

The Science of the Good for Man Is Politics

Chapter 2. As every science and undertaking aims at some good, what is in our view the good at which political science aims, and what is the highest of all practical goods? As to its name there is, I may say, a general agreement. The masses and the cultured classes agree in calling it happiness, and conceive that "to live well" or "to do well" is the same thing as "to be happy." But as to what happiness is they do not agree, nor do the masses give the same account of it as the philosophers. The former take it to be something visible and palpable, such as pleasure, wealth, or honor; different people, however, give different definitions of it, and often even the same man gives different definitions at different times. When he is ill, it is health, when he is poor, it is wealth; if he is

Reprinted from Aristotle's Nicomachean Ethics, *translated by James E. C. Weldon (Macmillan, 1897).*

conscious of his own ignorance, he envies people who use grand language above his own comprehension. Some philosophers, on the other hand, have held that, besides these various goods, there is an absolute good which is the cause of goodness in them all.* It would perhaps be a waste of time to examine all these opinions; it will be enough to examine such as are most popular or as seem to be more or less reasonable.

Chapter 3. Men's conception of the good or of happiness may be read in the lives they lead. Ordinary or vulgar people conceive it to be a pleasure, and accordingly choose a life of enjoyment. For there are, we may say, three conspicuous types of life, the sensual, the political, and, thirdly, the life of thought. Now the mass of men present an absolutely slavish appearance, choosing the life of brute beasts, but they have ground for so doing because so many persons in authority share the tastes of Sardanapalus.† Cultivated and energetic people, on the other hand, identify happiness with honor, as honor is the general end of political life. But this seems too superficial an idea for our present purpose; for honor depends more upon the people who pay it than upon the person to whom it is paid, and the good we feel is something which is proper to a man himself and cannot be easily taken away from him. Men too appear to seek honor in order to be assured of their own goodness. Accordingly, they seek it at the hands of the sage and of those who know them well, and they seek it on the ground of their virtue; clearly then, in their judgment at any rate, virtue is better than honor. Perhaps then we might look on virtue rather than honor as the end of political life. Yet even this idea appears not quite complete; for a man may possess virtue and yet be asleep or inactive throughout life, and not only so, but he may experience the greatest calamities and misfortunes. Yet no one would call such a life a life of happiness, unless he were maintaining a paradox. But we need not dwell further on this subject, since it is sufficiently discussed in popular philo-

*Plato
†A half-legendary ruler whose name to the Greeks stood for extreme mental luxury and extravagance.

sophical treatises. The third life is the life of thought, which we will discuss later.

The life of money making is a life of constraint; and wealth is obviously not the good of which we are in quest; for it is useful merely as a means to something else. It would be more reasonable to take the things mentioned before—sensual pleasure, honor, and virtue—as ends than wealth, since they are things desired on their own account. Yet these too are evidently not ends, although much argument has been employed to show that they are. . . .

Characteristics of the Good

Chapter 5. But leaving this subject for the present, let us revert to the good of which we are in quest and consider what it may be. For it seems different in different activities or arts; it is one thing in medicine, another in strategy, and so on. What is the good in each of these instances? It is presumably that for the sake of which all else is done. In medicine this is health, in strategy victory, in architecture a house, and so on. In every activity and undertaking it is the end, since it is for the sake of the end that all people do whatever else they do. If then there is an end for all our activity, this will be the good to be accomplished; and if there are several such ends, it will be these.

Our argument has arrived by a different path at the same point as before; but we must endeavor to make it still plainer. Since there are more ends than one, and some of these ends—for example, wealth, flutes, and instruments generally—we desire as means to something else, it is evident that not all are final ends. But the highest good is clearly something final. Hence if there is only one final end, this will be the object of which we are in search; and if there are more than one, it will be the most final. We call that which is sought after for its own sake more final than that which is sought after as a means to something else; we call that which is never desired as a means to something else more final than things that are desired both for themselves and as means to something else. Therefore, we call absolutely final that which is always desired for itself and never as a means to something else. Now happiness more than any-thing else answers to this description. For happi-ness we always desire for its own sake and never as a means to something else, whereas honor, pleas-ure, intelligence, and every virtue we desire partly for their own sakes (for we should desire them independently of what might result from them), but partly also as means to happiness, because we suppose they will prove instruments of happiness. Happiness, on the other hand, nobody desires for the sake of these things, nor indeed as a means to anything else at all.

If we start from the point of view of self-suffi-ciency, we reach the same conclusion; for we assume that the final good is self-sufficient. By self-sufficiency we do not mean that a person leads a solitary life all by himself, but that he has parents, children, wife and friends and fellow cit-izens in general, as man is naturally a social being. Yet here it is necessary to set some limit; for if the circle must be extended to include ancestors, descendants, and friends' friends, it will go on indefinitely. Leaving this point, however, for future investigation, we call the self-sufficient that which, taken even by itself, makes life desir-able and wanting nothing at all; and this is what we mean by happiness.

Again, we think happiness the most desirable of all things, and that not merely as one good thing among others. If it were only that, the addition of the smallest more good would increase its desirableness; for the addition would make an increase of goods, and the greater of two goods is always the more desirable. Happi-ness is something final and self-sufficient and the end of all action.

Chapter 6. Perhaps, however, it seems a com-monplace to say that happiness is the supreme good; what is wanted is to define its nature a lit-tle more clearly. The best way of arriving at such a definition will probably be to ascertain the func-tion of man. For, as with a flute player, a sculptor, or any artist, or in fact anybody who has a special function or activity, his goodness and excellence seem to lie in his function, so it would seem to be with man, if indeed he has a special function. Can

it be said that, while a carpenter and a cobbler have special functions and activities, man, unlike them, is naturally functionless? Or, as the eye, the hand, the foot, and similarly each part of the body has a special function, so may man be regarded as having a special function apart from all these? What, then, can this function be? It is not life; for life is apparently something that man shares with plants; and we are looking for some-thing peculiar to him. We must exclude therefore the life of nutrition and growth. There is next what may be called the life of sensation. But this too, apparently, is shared by man with horses, cattle, and all other animals. There remains what I may call the active life of the rational part of man's being. Now this rational part is twofold; one part is rational in the sense of being obedient to reason, and the other in the sense of possess-ing and exercising reason and intelligence. The active life too may be conceived of in two ways, either as a state of character, or as an activity; but we mean by it the life of activity, as this seems to be the truer form of the conception.

The function of man then is activity of soul in accordance with reason, or not apart from rea-son. Now, the function of a man of a certain kind, and of a man who is good of that kind—for example, of a harpist and a good harpist—are in our view the same in kind. This is true of all peo-ple of all kinds without exception, the superior excellence being only an addition to the func-tion; for it is the function of a harpist to play the harp, and of a good harpist to play the harp well. This being so, if we define the function of man as a kind of life, and this life as an activity of the soul or a course of action in accordance with rea-son, and if the function of a good man is such activity of a good and noble kind, and if every-thing is well done when it is done in accordance with its proper excellence, it follows that the good of man is activity of soul in accordance with virtue, or, if there are more virtues than one, in accordance with the best and most complete virtue. But we must add the words "in a complete life." For as one swallow or one day does not make a spring, so one day or a short time does not make a man blessed or happy. . . .

Inasmuch as happiness is an activity of soul in accordance with perfect virtue, we must now consider virtue, as this will perhaps be the best way of studying happiness. . . . Clearly it is human virtue we have to consider; for the good of which we are in search is, as we said, human good, and the happiness, human happiness. By human virtue or excellence we mean not that of the body, but that of the soul, and by happiness we mean an activity of the soul. . . .

BOOK II

Moral virtues can best be acquired by practice and habit. They imply a right attitude toward pleasures and pains. A good man deliberately chooses to do what is noble and right for its own sake. What is right in matters of moral conduct is usually a mean between two extremes.

Chapter 1. Virtue then is twofold, partly intellectual and partly moral, and intellectual virtue is originated and fostered mainly by teaching; it demands therefore experience and time. Moral virtue on the other hand is the outcome of habit, and accordingly its name, *ethike,* is derived by a slight variation from *ethos,* habit. From this fact it is clear that moral virtue is not implanted in us by nature; for nothing that exists by nature can be transformed by habit. Thus a stone, that naturally tends to fall downwards, cannot be habituated or trained to rise upwards, even if we tried to train it by throwing it up ten thousand times. Nor again can fire be trained to sink downwards, nor anything else that follows one natural law be habituated or trained to follow another. It is neither by nature then nor in defiance of nature that virtues grow in us. Nature gives us the capacity to receive them, and that capacity is perfected by habit.

Again, if we take the various natural powers which belong to us, we first possess the proper faculties and afterwards display the activities. It is obviously so with the senses. Not by seeing frequently or hearing frequently do we acquire the sense of seeing or hearing; on the contrary, because we have the senses we make use of them; we do not get them by making use of them. But the virtues we get by first practicing them, as we do in the arts. For it is by doing what we ought to do when we study the arts that we learn the arts themselves; we become builders by building and harpists by playing the harp. Similarly, it is by doing just acts that we become just, by doing temperate acts that we become temperate, by doing brave acts that we become brave. The experience of states confirms this statement, for it is by training in good habits that lawmakers make the citizens good. This is the object all lawmakers have at heart; if they do not succeed in it, they fail of their purpose; and it makes the distinction between a good constitution and a bad one.

Again, the causes and means by which any virtue is produced and destroyed are the same; and equally so in any part. For it is by playing the harp that both good and bad harpists are produced; and the case of builders and others is similar, for it is by building well that they become good builders and by building badly that they become bad builders. If it were not so, there would be no need of anybody to teach them; they would all be born good or bad in their several crafts. The case of the virtues is the same. It is by our actions in dealings between man and man that we become either just or unjust. It is by our actions in the face of danger and by our training ourselves to fear or to courage that we become either cowardly or courageous. It is much the same with our appetites and angry passions. People become temperate and gentle, others licentious and passionate, by behaving in one or the other way in particular circumstances. In a word, moral states are the results of activities like the states themselves. It is our duty therefore to keep a certain character in our activities, since our moral states depend on the differences in our activities. So the difference between one and another training in habits in our childhood is not a light matter, but important, or rather, all-important.

Chapter 2. Our present study is not, like other studies, purely theoretical in intention; for the object of our inquiry is not to know what virtue is but how to become good, and that is the sole benefit of it. We must, therefore, consider the right way of performing actions, for it is acts, as we have said, that determine the character of the resulting moral states.

That we should act in accordance with right reason is a common general principle, which may here be taken for granted. The nature of right reason, and its relation to the virtues generally, will be discussed later. But first of all it must be admitted that all reasoning on matters of conduct must be like a sketch in outline; it cannot be scientifically exact. We began by laying down the principle that the kind of reasoning demanded in any subject must be such as the subject matter itself allows; and questions of conduct and expediency no more admit of hard and fast rules than questions of health.

If this is true of general reasoning on ethics, still more true is it that scientific exactitude is impossible in treating of particular ethical cases. They do not fall under any art or law, but the actors themselves have always to take account of circumstances, as much as in medicine or navigation. Still, although such is the nature of our present argument, we must try to make the best of it.

The first point to be observed is that in the matters we are now considering, deficiency and excess are both fatal. It is so, we see, in questions of health and strength. (We must judge of what we cannot see by the evidence of what we do see.) Too much or too little gymnastic exercise is fatal to strength. Similarly, too much or too little meat and drink is fatal to health, whereas a suitable amount produces, increases, and sustains it. It is the same with temperance, courage, and other moral virtues. A person who avoids and is afraid of everything and faces nothing becomes a coward; a person who is not afraid of anything but is ready to face everything becomes foolhardy. Similarly, he who enjoys every pleasure and abstains from none is licentious; he who refuses all pleasures, like a boor, is an insensible sort of person. For temperance and courage are destroyed by excess and deficiency but preserved by the mean.

Again, not only are the causes and agencies of production, increase, and destruction in moral states the same, but the field of their activity is the same also. It is so in other more obvious instances, as, for example, strength; for strength is produced by taking a great deal of food and undergoing a great deal of exertion, and it is the strong man who is able to take most food and undergo most exertion. So too with the virtues. By abstaining from pleasures we become temperate, and, when we have become temperate, we are best able to abstain from them. So again with courage; it is by training ourselves to despise and face terrifying things that we become brave, and when we have become brave, we shall be best able to face them.

The pleasure or pain which accompanies actions may be regarded as a test of a person's moral state. He who abstains from physical pleasures and feels pleasure in so doing is temperate; but he who feels pain at so doing is licentious. He who faces dangers with pleasure, or at least without pain, is brave; but he who feels pain at facing them is a coward. For moral virtue is concerned with pleasures and pains. It is pleasure which makes us do what is base, and pain which makes us abstain from doing what is noble. Hence the importance of having a certain training from very early days, as Plato says, so that we may feel pleasure and pain at the right objects; for this is true education. . . .

Chapter 3. But we may be asked what we mean by saying that people must become just by doing what is just and temperate by doing what is temperate. For, it will be said, if they do what is just and temperate they are already just and temperate themselves, in the same way as, if they practice grammar and music, they are grammarians and musicians.

But is this true even in the case of the arts? For a person may speak grammatically either by chance or at the suggestion of somebody else; hence he will not be a grammarian unless he not only speaks grammatically but does so in a grammatical manner, that is, because of the grammatical knowledge which he possesses.

There is a point of difference too between the arts and the virtues. The productions of art have their excellence in themselves. It is enough then that, when they are produced, they themselves should possess a certain character. But acts in accordance with virtue are not justly or temperately performed simply because they are in themselves just or temperate. The doer at the time of performing them must satisfy certain conditions; in the first place, he must know what he is doing; secondly, he must deliberately choose to do it and do it for his own sake; and thirdly, he must do it as part of his own firm and immutable character. If it be a question of art, these conditions, except only the condition of knowledge, are not raised; but if it be a question of virtue, mere knowledge is of little or no avail; it is the other conditions, which are the results of frequently performing just and temperate acts, that are not slightly but all-important. Accordingly, deeds are called just and temperate when they are such as a just and temperate person would do; and a just and temperate person is not merely one who does these deeds but one who does them in the spirit of the just and the temperate.

It may fairly be said that a just man becomes just by doing what is just, and a temperate man becomes temperate by doing what is temperate, and if a man did not so act, he would not have much chance of becoming good. But most people, instead of acting, take refuge in theorizing; they imagine that they are philosophers and that philosophy will make them virtuous; in fact, they behave like people who listen attentively to their doctors but never do anything that their doctors tell them. But a healthy state of the soul will no more be produced by this kind of philosophizing than a healthy state of the body by this kind of medical treatment.

Chapter 4. We have next to consider the nature of virtue. Now, as the properties of the soul are three, namely, emotions, faculties, and moral states, it follows that virtue must be one of the three. By emotions I mean desire, anger, fear, pride, envy, joy, love, hatred, regret, ambition, pity—in a word, whatever feeling is attended by pleasure or pain. I call those faculties through which we are said to be capable of experiencing these emotions, for instance, capable of getting angry or being pained or feeling pity. And I call those moral states through which we are well or ill disposed in our emotions, ill disposed, for instance, in anger, if our anger be too violent or too feeble, and well disposed, if it be rightly moderate; and similarly in our other emotions.

Now neither the virtues nor the vices are emotions; for we are not called good or bad for our emotions but for our virtues or vices. We are not praised or blamed simply for being angry, but only for being angry in a certain way; but we are praised or blamed for our virtues or vices. Again, whereas we are angry or afraid without deliberate purpose, the virtues are matters of deliberate purpose, or require deliberate purpose. Moreover, we are said to be moved by our emotions, but by our virtues or vices we are not said to be moved but to have a certain disposition.

For these reasons the virtues are not faculties. For we are not called either good or bad, nor are we praised or blamed for having simple capacity for emotion. Also while Nature gives us our faculties, it is not Nature that makes us good or bad; but this point we have already discussed. If then the virtues are neither emotions nor faculties, all that remains is that they must be moral states.

Chapter 5. The nature of virtue has been now described in kind. But it is not enough to say merely that virtue is a moral state; we must also describe the character of that moral state.

We may assert then that every virtue or excellence puts into good condition that of which it is a virtue or excellence, and enables it to perform its work well. Thus excellence in the eye makes the eye good and its function good, for by excellence in the eye we see well. Similarly, excellence of the horse makes a horse excellent himself and good at racing, at carrying its rider and at facing the enemy. If then this rule is universally true, the virtue or excellence of a man will be such a moral state as makes a man good and able to perform his proper function well. How this will be the case we have already explained, but another way of making it clear will be to study the nature or character of virtue.

Now of everything, whether it be continuous or divisible, it is possible to take a greater, a smaller, or an equal amount, and this either in terms of the thing itself or in relation to ourselves, the equal being a mean between too much and too little. By the mean in terms of the thing itself, I understand that which is equally distinct from both its extremes, which is one and the same for every man. By the mean relatively to ourselves, I understand that which is neither too much nor too little for us; but this is not one nor the same for everybody. Thus if 10 be too much and 2 too little, we take 6 as a mean in terms of the thing itself; for 6 is as much greater than 2 as it is less than 10, and this is a mean in arithmetical proportion. But the mean considered relatively to ourselves may not be ascertained in that way. It does not follow that if 10 pounds of meat is too much and 2 too little for a man to eat, the trainer will order him 6 pounds, since this also may be too much or too little for him who is to take it; it will be too little, for example, for Milo but too much for a beginner in gymnastics. The same with running and wrestling; the right amount will vary with the individual. This being so, the skillful in any art avoids alike excess and deficiency; he seeks and chooses the mean, not the absolute mean, but the mean considered relatively to himself.

Every art then does its work well, if it regards the mean and judges the works it produces by the mean. For this reason we often say of successful works of art that it is impossible to take anything from them or to add anything to them, which implies that excess or deficiency is fatal to excellence but that the mean state ensures it. Good artists too, as we say, have an eye to the mean in their works. Now virtue, like Nature herself, is more accurate and better than any art; virtue, therefore, will aim at the mean. I speak of moral virtue, since it is moral virtue which is concerned with emotions and actions, and it is in these we have excess and deficiency and the mean. Thus it is possible to go too far, or not far enough in fear, pride, desire, anger, pity, and pleasure and pain generally, and the excess and the deficiency are alike wrong; but to feel these emotions at the right times, for the right objects, towards the right persons, for the right motives, and in the right manner, is the mean or the best good, which signifies virtue. Similarly, there may be excess, deficiency, or the mean, in acts. Virtue is concerned with both emotions and actions, wherein excess is an error and deficiency a fault, while the mean is successful and praised, and success and praise are both characteristics of virtue.

It appears then that virtue is a kind of mean because it aims at the mean.

On the other hand, there are many different ways of going wrong; for evil is in its nature infinite, to use the Pythagorean phrase, but good is finite and there is only one possible way of going right. So the former is easy and the latter is difficult; it is easy to miss the mark but difficult to hit it. And so by our reasoning excess and deficiency are characteristics of vice and the mean is a characteristic of virtue.

"For good is simple, evil manifold."

Chapter 6. Virtue then is a state of deliberate moral purpose, consisting in a mean relative to ourselves, the mean being determined by reason, or as a prudent man would determine it. It is a mean, firstly, as lying between two vices, the vice of excess on the one hand, the vice of deficiency on the other, and, secondly, because, whereas the vices either fall short of or go beyond what is right in emotion and action, virtue discovers and chooses the mean. Accordingly, virtue, if regarded in its essence or theoretical definition, is a mean, though, if regarded from the point of view of what is best and most excellent, it is an extreme.

But not every action or every emotion admits of a mean. There are some whose very name implies wickedness, as, for example, malice, shamelessness, and envy among the emotions, and adultery, theft, and murder among the actions. All these and others like them are marked as intrinsically wicked, not merely the excesses or deficiencies of them. It is never possible then to be right in them; they are always sinful. Right or wrong in such acts as adultery does not depend on our committing it with the right woman, at the right time, or in the right manner; on the contrary, it is wrong to do it at all. It would be equally false to suppose that there can be a mean or an excess or deficiency in unjust, cowardly or licentious conduct; for, if that were so, it would be a mean of excess and deficiency, an excess of excess and a deficiency of deficiency. But as in temperance and courage there can be no excess or deficiency, because the mean there is in a sense an extreme, so too in these other cases there cannot be a mean or an excess or a deficiency, but however the acts are done, they are wrong. For in general an excess or deficiency does not have a mean, nor a mean an excess or deficiency. . . .

Chapter 8. There are then three dispositions, two being vices, namely, excess and deficiency, and one virtue, which is the mean between them; and they are all in a sense mutually opposed. The extremes are opposed both to the mean and to each other, and the mean is opposed to the extremes. For as the equal if compared with the less is greater, but if compared with the greater is less, so the mean state, whether in emotion or action, if compared with deficiency is excessive, but if compared with excess is deficient. Thus the brave man appears foolhardy compared with the coward, but cowardly compared with the foolhardy. Similarly, the temperate man appears licentious compared with the insensible man but insensible compared with the licentious; and the liberal man appears extravagant compared with the stingy man but stingy compared with the spendthrift. The result is that the extremes each denounce the mean as belonging to the other extreme; the coward calls the brave man foolhardy, and the foolhardy man calls him cowardly; and so on in other cases.

But while there is mutual opposition between the extremes and the mean, there is greater oppo-

sition between the two extremes than between extreme and the mean; for they are further removed from each other than from the mean, as the great is further from the small and the small from the great than either from the equal. Again, while some extremes show some likeness to the mean, as foolhardiness to courage and extravagance to liberality, there is the greatest possible dissimilarity between extremes. But things furthest removed from each other are called opposites; hence the further things are removed, the greater is the opposition between them.

In some cases it is deficiency and in others excess which is more opposed to the mean. Thus it is not foolhardiness, an excess, but cowardice, a deficiency, which is more opposed to courage, nor is it insensibility, a deficiency, but licentiousness, an excess, which is more opposed to temperance. There are two reasons why this should be so. One lies in the nature of the matter itself; for when one of two extremes is nearer and more like the mean, it is not this extreme but its opposite that we chiefly contrast with the mean. For instance, as foolhardiness seems more like and nearer to courage than cowardice, it is cowardice that we chiefly contrast with courage; for things further removed from the mean seem to be more opposite to it. This reason lies in the nature of the matter itself; there is a second which lies in our own nature. The things to which we ourselves are naturally more inclined we think more opposed to the mean. Thus we are ourselves naturally more inclined to pleasures than to their opposites, and are more prone therefore to self-indulgence than to moderation. Accordingly we speak of those things in which we are more likely to run to great lengths as more opposed to the mean. Hence licentiousness, which is an excess, seems more opposed to temperance than insensibility.

Chapter 9. We have now sufficiently shown that moral virtue is a mean, and in what sense it is so; that it is a mean as lying between two vices, a vice of excess on the one side and a vice of deficiency on the other, and as aiming at the mean in emotion and action.

That is why it is so hard to be good; for it is always hard to find the mean in anything; it is not everyone but only a man of science who can find the mean or center of a circle. So too anybody can get angry—that is easy—and anybody can give or spend money, but to give it to the right person, to give the right amount of it, at the right time, for the right cause and in the right way, this is not what anybody can do, nor is it easy. That is why goodness is rare and praise worthy and noble. One then who aims at a mean must begin by departing from the extreme that is more contrary to the mean; he must act in the spirit of Calypso's advice,

"Far from this spray and swell hold thou thy ship,"

for of the two extremes one is more wrong than the other. As it is difficult to hit the mean exactly, we should take the second best course, as the saying is, and choose the lesser of two evils. This we shall best do in the way described, that is, steering clear of the evil which is further from the mean. We must also note the weaknesses to which we are ourselves particularly prone, since different natures tend in different ways; and we may ascertain what our tendency is by observing our feelings of pleasure and pain. Then we must drag ourselves away towards the opposite extreme; for by pulling ourselves as far as possible from what is wrong we shall arrive at the mean, as we do when we pull a crooked stick straight.

In all cases we must especially be on our guard against the pleasant, or pleasure, for we are not impartial judges of pleasure. Hence our attitude towards pleasure must be like that of the elders of the people in the *Iliad* towards Helen, and we must constantly apply the words they use; for if we dismiss pleasure as they dismissed Helen, we shall be less likely to go wrong. By action of this kind, to put it summarily, we shall best succeed in hitting the mean.

Undoubtedly this is a difficult task, especially in individual cases. It is not easy to determine the right manner, objects, occasion and duration of anger. Sometimes we praise people who are deficient in anger, and call them gentle, and at other times we praise people who exhibit a fierce temper as high spirited. It is not however a man who deviates a little from goodness, but one who deviates a great deal, whether on the side of excess or of deficiency, that is blamed; for he is sure to call attention to himself. It is not easy to decide in theory how far and to what extent a man may go before he becomes blameworthy, but neither is it easy to define in theory anything else in the region of the senses; such things depend on circumstances, and our judgment of them depends on our perception.

So much then is plain, that the mean is everywhere praiseworthy, but that we ought to aim at one time towards an excess and at another towards a deficiency; for thus we shall most easily hit the mean, or in other words reach excellence.

For Further Reflection

1. Is Aristotle's concept of happiness clear? Is it a subjective or objective notion? That is, is it subjective, in the mind of the beholder, so one is just as happy as one feels oneself to be; or is it objective, defined by a state of being, and having certain characteristics regardless of how one feels? According to Aristotle, could a criminal be happy?

2. Is Aristotle's ethics sufficiently action guiding? Does it help us make decisions? If I ask what should I do in situation *X*, Aristotle would seem to say, "Do what the virtuous person would do." But if I ask how I am to recognize the virtuous person, he would seem to say, "He is one who acts justly." Is there something circular about this reasoning? Does virtue ethics need supplementation from other ethical systems or can it solve this problem?

The Ethics of Care   VI.63

VIRGINIA HELD

Virginia Held has taught philosophy at Hunter College and The Graduate Center of the City University of New York. In this reading, she explores the moral perspective known as the ethics of care, identifying its central themes, showing how it relates to an "ethic of justice," and distinguishing it from virtue ethics.

Study Questions

1. According to Held, what are the main features of the ethics of care?
2. What is the liberal individualist concept of a person? What is Held's critique of it?
3. What is the "ethic of justice"? How does Held think that the ethic of justice is related to the ethics of care?
4. As Held sees it, what are the main differences between the ethics of care and virtue ethics?

The ethics of care is only a few decades old. Some theorists do not like the term 'care' to designate this approach to moral issues and have tried substituting 'the ethic of love,' or 'relational ethics,' but the discourse keeps returning to 'care' as the so far more satisfactory of the terms considered, though dissatisfactions with it remain. The concept of care has the advantage of not losing sight of the work involved in caring for people and of not lending itself to the interpretation of morality as ideal but impractical to which advocates of the ethics of care often object. Care is both value and practice.

By now, the ethics of care has moved far beyond its original formulations, and any attempt to evaluate it should consider much more than the one or two early works so frequently cited. It has been developed as a moral theory relevant not only to the so-called private realms of family and friendship but to medical practice, law, political life, the organization of society, war, and international relations.

The ethics of care is sometimes seen as a potential moral theory to be substituted for such dominant moral theories as Kantian ethics, utilitarianism, or Aristotelian virtue ethics. It is sometimes seen as a form of virtue ethics. It is almost always developed as emphasizing neglected moral considerations of at least as much importance as the considerations central to moralities of justice and rights or of utility and preference satisfaction. And many who contribute to the understanding of the ethics of care seek to integrate the moral considerations, such as justice, which other moral theories have clarified, satisfactorily with those of care, though they often see the need to reconceptualize these considerations.

FEATURES OF THE ETHICS OF CARE

Some advocates of the ethics of care resist generalizing this approach into something that can be fitted into the form of a moral theory. They see it as a mosaic of insights and value the way it is sensitive to contextual nuance and particular narratives rather than making the abstract and

From Virginia Held, "The Ethics of Care," in The Ethics of Care: Personal, Political, and Global (2006), pp. 9–20. By permission of Oxford University Press, Inc.

universal claims of more familiar moral theories. Still, I think one can discern among various versions of the ethics of care a number of major features.

First, the central focus of the ethics of care is on the compelling moral salience of attending to and meeting the needs of the particular others for whom we take responsibility. Caring for one's child, for instance, may well and defensibly be at the forefront of a person's moral concerns. The ethics of care recognizes that human beings are dependent for many years of their lives, that the moral claim of those dependent on us for the care they need is pressing, and that there are highly important moral aspects in developing the relations of caring that enable human beings to live and progress. All persons need care for at least their early years. Prospects for human progress and flourishing hinge fundamentally on the care that those needing it receive, and the ethics of care stresses the moral force of the responsibility to respond to the needs of the dependent. Many persons will become ill and dependent for some periods of their later lives, including in frail old age, and some who are permanently disabled will need care the whole of their lives. Moralities built on the image of the independent, autonomous, rational individual largely overlook the reality of human dependence and the morality for which it calls. The ethics of care attends to this central concern of human life and delineates the moral values involved. It refuses to relegate care to a realm "outside morality." How caring for particular others should be reconciled with the claims of, for instance, universal justice is an issue that needs to be addressed. But the ethics of care starts with the moral claims of particular others, for instance, of one's child, whose claims can be compelling regardless of universal principles.

Second, in the epistemological process of trying to understand what morality would recommend and what it would be morally best for us to do and to be, the ethics of care values emotion rather than rejects it. Not all emotion is valued, of course, but in contrast with the dominant rationalist approaches, such emotions as sympathy, empathy, sensitivity, and responsiveness are seen as the kind of moral emotions that need to be cultivated not only to help in the implementation of the dictates of reason but to better ascertain what morality recommends. Even anger may be a component of the moral indignation that should be felt when people are treated unjustly or inhumanely, and it may contribute to (rather than interfere with) an appropriate interpretation of the moral wrong. This is not to say that raw emotion can be a guide to morality; feelings need to be reflected on and educated. But from the care perspective, moral inquiries that rely entirely on reason and rationalistic deductions or calculations are seen as deficient.

The emotions that are typically considered and rejected in rationalistic moral theories are the egoistic feelings that undermine universal moral norms, the favoritism that interferes with impartiality, and the aggressive and vengeful impulses for which morality is to provide restraints. The ethics of care, in contrast, typically appreciates the emotions and relational capabilities that enable morally concerned persons in actual interpersonal contexts to understand what would be best. Since even the helpful emotions can often become misguided or worse—as when excessive empathy with others leads to a wrongful degree of self-denial or when benevolent concern crosses over into controlling domination—we need an *ethics* of care, not just care itself. The various aspects and expressions of care and caring relations need to be subjected to moral scrutiny and *evaluated*, not just observed and described.

Third, the ethics of care rejects the view of the dominant moral theories that the more abstract the reasoning about a moral problem the better because the more likely to avoid bias and arbitrariness, the more nearly to achieve impartiality. The ethics of care respects rather than removes itself from the claims of particular others with whom we share actual relationships. It calls into question the universalistic and abstract rules of the dominant theories. When the latter consider such actual relations as between a parent and child, if they say anything about them at all, they may see them as permitted and cultivating them a preference that a person may have. Or they may recognize a universal obligation for all parents to care for their children. But they do not permit actual relations ever to take priority over the requirements of impartiality. As Brian Barry expresses this view, there can be universal rules permitting people to favor their friends in certain contexts, such as deciding to whom to give holiday gifts, but the latter partiality is morally acceptable only because universal rules have already so judged it. The ethics of care, in contrast, is skeptical of such abstraction and reliance on universal rules and questions the priority given to them. To most advocates of the ethics of care, the compelling moral claim of the particular other may be valid even when it conflicts with the requirement usually made by moral theories that moral judgments be universalizeable, and this is of fundamental moral importance. Hence the potential conflict between care and justice, friendship and impartiality, loyalty and universality. To others, however, there need be no conflict if universal judgments come to incorporate appropriately the norms of care previously disregarded.

Annette Baier considers how a feminist approach to morality differs from a Kantian one and Kant's claim that women are incapable of being fully moral because of their reliance on emotion rather than reason. She writes, "Where Kant concludes 'so much the worse for women,' we can conclude 'so much the worse for the male fixation on the special skill of drafting legislation, for the bureaucratic mentality of rule worship, and for the male exaggeration of the importance of independence over mutual interdependence.' "

Margaret Walker contrasts what she sees as feminist "moral understanding" with what has traditionally been thought of as moral "knowledge." She sees the moral understanding she advocates as involving "attention, contextual and narrative appreciation, and communication in the event of moral deliberation." This alternative moral epistemology holds that "the adequacy of moral understanding decreases as its form approaches generality through abstraction."

The ethics of care may seek to limit the applicability of universal rules to certain domains where they are more appropriate, like the domain of law, and resist their extension to other domains. Such rules may simply be inappropriate in, for instance, the contexts of family and friendship, yet relations in these domains should certainly be *evaluated*, not merely described, hence morality should not be limited to abstract rules. We should be able to give moral guidance concerning actual relations that are trusting, considerate, and caring and concerning those that are not.

Dominant moral theories tend to interpret moral problems as if they were conflicts between egoistic individual interests on the one hand, and universal moral principles on the other. The extremes of "selfish individual" and "humanity" are recognized, but what lies between these is often overlooked. The ethics of care, in contrast, focuses especially on the area between these extremes. Those who conscientiously care for others are not seeking primarily to further their own *individual* interests; their interests are intertwined with the persons they care for. Neither are they acting for the sake of *all others* or *humanity in general*; they seek instead to preserve or promote an actual human relation between themselves and *particular others*. Persons in caring relations are acting for self-and-other together. Their characteristic stance is neither egoistic nor altruistic; these are the options in a conflictual situation, but the well-being of a caring relation involves the cooperative well-being of those in the relation and the well-being of the relation itself.

In trying to overcome the attitudes and problems of tribalism and religious intolerance, dominant moralities have tended to assimilate the domains of family and friendship to the tribal, or to a source of the unfair favoring of one's own. Or they have seen the attachments people have in these areas as among the nonmoral private preferences people are permitted to pursue if restrained by impartial moral norms. The ethics of care recognizes the *moral* value and importance of relations of family and friendship and the need for *moral* guidance in these domains to understand how existing relations should often be changed and new ones developed. Having grasped the value of caring relations in such contexts as these more personal ones, the ethics of care then often examines social and political arrangements in the light of these values. In its more developed forms, the ethics of care as a feminist ethic offers suggestions for the radical transformation of society. It demands not just equality for women in existing structures of society but equal consideration for the experience that reveals the values, importance, and moral significance, of caring.

A fourth characteristic of the ethics of care is that like much feminist thought in many areas, it reconceptualizes traditional notions about the public and the private. The traditional view, built into the dominant moral theories, is that the household is a private sphere beyond politics into which government, based on consent, should not intrude. Feminists have shown how the greater social, political, economic, and cultural power of men has structured this "private" sphere to the disadvantage of women and children, rendering them vulnerable to domestic violence without outside interference, often leaving women economically dependent on men and subject to a highly inequitable division of labor in the family. The law has not hesitated to intervene into women's private decisions concerning reproduction but has been highly reluctant to intrude on men's exercise of coercive power within the "castles" of their homes.

Dominant moral theories have seen "public" life as relevant to morality while missing the moral significance of the "private" domains of family and friendship. Thus the dominant theories have assumed that morality should be sought for unrelated, independent, and mutually indifferent individuals assumed to be equal. They have posited an abstract, fully rational "agent as such" from which to construct morality, while missing the moral issues that arise between interconnected persons in the contexts of family, friendship, and social groups. In the context of the family, it is typical for relations to be between persons with highly unequal power who did not choose the ties and obligations in which they find themselves enmeshed. For instance, no child can choose her parents yet she may well have obligations to care for them. Relations of this kind are standardly noncontractual, and conceptualizing them as contractual would often undermine or at least obscure the trust on which their worth depends. The ethics of care addresses rather than neglects moral issues arising in relations among the unequal and dependent, relations that are often laden with emotion and involuntary, and then notices how often these attributes apply not only in the household but in the wider society as well. For instance, persons do not choose which gender, racial, class, ethnic, religious, national, or cultural groups to be brought up in, yet these sorts of ties may be important aspects of who they are and how their experience can contribute to moral understanding.

A fifth characteristic of the ethics of care is the conception of persons with which it begins. This will be dealt with in the next section.

THE CRITIQUE OF LIBERAL INDIVIDUALISM

The ethics of care usually works with a conception of persons as relational, rather than as the self-sufficient independent individuals of the dominant moral theories. The dominant theories can be interpreted as importing into moral theory a concept of the person developed primarily for liberal political and economic theory, seeing the person as a rational, autonomous agent, or a self-interested individual. On this view, society is made up of "independent, autonomous units who cooperate only when the terms of cooperation are such as to make it further the ends of each of the parties," in Brian Barry's words. Or, if they are Kantians, they refrain from actions that they could not will to be universal laws to which all fully rational and autonomous individual agents could agree. What such views hold, in Michael Sandel's critique of them, is that "what separates us is in some important sense prior to what connects us—epistemologically prior as well as morally prior. We are distinct individuals first and *then* we form relationships." In Martha Nussbaum's liberal feminist morality, "the flourishing of human beings taken one by one is both analytically and normatively prior to the flourishing" of any group.

The ethics of care, in contrast, characteristically sees persons as relational and interdependent, morally and epistemologically. Every person starts out as a child dependent on those providing us care, and we remain interdependent with others in thoroughly fundamental ways throughout our lives. That we can think and act as if we were independent depends on a network of social relations making it possible for us to do so. And our relations are part of what constitute our identity. This is not to say that we cannot become autonomous; feminists have done much interesting work developing an alternative conception of autonomy in place of the liberal individualist one. Feminists have much experience rejecting or reconstituting relational ties that are oppressive. But it means that from the perspective of an ethics of care, to construct morality *as if* we were Robinson Crusoes, or, to use Hobbes's image, mushrooms sprung from nowhere, is misleading. As Eva Kittay writes, this conception fosters the illusion that society is composed of free, equal, and independent individuals who can choose to associate with one another or not. It obscures the very real facts of dependency for everyone when they are young, for most people at various periods in their lives when they are ill or old and infirm, for some who are disabled, and for all those engaged in unpaid "dependency

work." And it obscures the innumerable ways persons and groups are interdependent in the modern world.

Not only does the liberal individualist conception of the person foster a false picture of society and the persons in it, it is, from the perspective of the ethics of care, impoverished also as an ideal. The ethics of care values the ties we have with particular other persons and the actual relationships that partly constitute our identity. Although persons often may and should reshape their relations with others—distancing themselves from some persons and groups and developing or strengthening ties with others—the autonomy sought within the ethics of care is a capacity to reshape and cultivate new relations, not to ever more closely resemble the unencumbered abstract rational self of liberal political and moral theories. Those motivated by the ethics of care would seek to become more admirable relational persons in better caring relations.

Even if the liberal ideal is meant only to instruct us on what would be rational in the terms of its ideal model, thinking of persons as the model presents them has effects that should not be welcomed. As Annette Baier writes, "Liberal morality, if unsupplemented, may *unfit* people to be anything other than what its justifying theories suppose them to be, ones who have no interest in each others' interests." There is strong empirical evidence of how adopting a theoretical model can lead to behavior that mirrors it. Various studies show that studying economics, with its "repeated and intensive exposure to a model whose unequivocal prediction" is that people will decide what to do on the basis of self-interest, leads economics students to be less cooperative and more inclined to free ride than other students.

The conception of the person adopted by the dominant moral theories provides moralities at best suitable for legal, political, and economic interactions between relative strangers, once adequate trust exists for them to form a political entity. The ethics of care is, instead, hospitable to the relatedness of persons. It sees many of our responsibilities as not freely entered into but presented to us by the accidents of our embeddedness in familial and social and historical contexts. It often calls on us to *take* responsibility, while liberal individualist morality focuses on how we should leave each other alone. The view of persons as embedded and encumbered seems fundamental to much feminist thinking about morality and especially to the ethics of care.

JUSTICE AND CARE

Some conceptions of the ethics of care see it as contrasting with an ethic of justice in ways that suggest one must choose between them. Carol Gilligan's suggestion of alternative perspectives in interpreting and organizing the elements of a moral problem lent itself to this implication; she herself used the metaphor of the ambiguous figure of the vase and the faces, from psychological research on perception, to illustrate how one could see a problem as either a problem of justice or a problem of care, but not as both simultaneously.

An ethic of justice focuses on questions of fairness, equality, individual rights, abstract principles, and the consistent application of them. An ethic of care focuses on attentiveness, trust, responsiveness to need, narrative nuance, and cultivating caring relations. Whereas an ethic of justice seeks a fair solution between competing individual interests and rights, an ethic of care sees the interests of carers and cared-for as importantly intertwined rather than as simply competing. Whereas justice protects equality and freedom, care fosters social bonds and cooperation.

These are very different emphases in what morality should consider. Yet both deal with what seems of great moral importance. This has led many to explore how they might be combined in a satisfactory morality. One can persuasively argue, for instance, that justice is needed in such contexts of care as the family, to protect

against violence and the unfair division of labor or treatment of children. One can also persuasively argue that care is needed in such contexts of justice as the streets and the courts, where persons should be treated humanely, and in the way education and health and welfare should be dealt with as social responsibilities. The implication may be that justice and care should not be separated into different "ethics," that, in Sara Ruddick's proposed approach, "justice is always seen in tandem with care."

Few would hold that considerations of justice have no place at all in care. One would not be caring well for two children, for instance, if one showed a persistent favoritism toward one of them that could not be justified on the basis of some such factor as greater need. The issues are rather what constellation of values have priority and which predominate in the practices of the ethics of care and the ethics of justice. It is quite possible to delineate significant differences between them. In the dominant moral theories of the ethics of justice, the values of equality, impartiality, fair distribution, and noninterference have priority; in practices of justice, individual rights are protected, impartial judgments are arrived at, punishments are deserved, and equal treatment is sought. In contrast, in the ethics of care, the values of trust, solidarity, mutual concern, and empathetic responsiveness have priority; in practices of care, relationships are cultivated, needs are responded to, and sensitivity is demonstrated.

An extended effort to integrate care and justice is offered by Diemut Bubeck. She makes clear that she "endorse[s] the ethic of care as a system of concepts, values, and ideas, arising from the practice of care as an organic part of this practice and responding to its material requirements, notably the meeting of needs." Yet her primary interest is in understanding the exploitation of women, which she sees as tied to the way women do most of the unpaid work of caring. She argues that such principles as equality in care and the minimization of harm are tacitly, if not explicitly, embedded in the practice of care, as carers whose capacities and time for engaging in caring labor are limited must decide how to respond to various others in need of being cared for. She writes that "far from being extraneous impositions…considerations of justice arise from within the practice of care itself and therefore are an important part of the ethic of care, properly understood." The ethics of care must thus also concern itself with the justice (or lack of it) of the ways the tasks of caring are distributed in society. Traditionally, women have been expected to do most of the caring work that needs to be done; the sexual division of labor exploits women by extracting unpaid care labor from them, making women less able than men to engage in paid work. "Femininity" constructs women as carers, contributing to the constraints by which women are pressed into accepting the sexual division of labor. An ethic of care that extols caring but that fails to be concerned with how the burdens of caring are distributed contributes to the exploitation of women, and of the minority groups whose members perform much of the paid but ill-paid work of caring in affluent households, in day care centers, hospitals, nursing homes, and the like.

The question remains, however, whether justice should be thought to be incorporated into any ethic of care that will be adequate or whether we should keep the notions of justice and care and their associated ethics conceptually distinct. There is much to be said for recognizing how the ethics of care values interrelatedness and responsiveness to the needs of particular others, how the ethics of justice values fairness and rights, and how these are different emphases. Too much integration will lose sight of these valid differences. I am more inclined to say that an adequate, comprehensive moral theory will have to include the insights of both the ethics of care and the ethics of justice, among other insights, rather than that either of these can be incorporated into the other in the sense of supposing that it can provide the grounds for the judgments characteristically found in the other.

Equitable caring is not necessarily better caring, it is fairer caring. And humane justice is not necessarily better justice, it is more caring justice.

Almost no advocates of the ethics of care are willing to see it as a moral outlook less valuable than the dominant ethics of justice. To imagine that the concerns of care can merely be added on to the dominant theories, as, for instance, Stephen Darwall suggests, is seen as unsatisfactory. Confining the ethics of care to the private sphere while holding it unsuitable for public life, as Nel Noddings did at first and as many accounts of it suggest, is also to be rejected. But how care and justice are to be meshed without losing sight of their differing priorities is a task still being worked on.

My own suggestions for integrating care and justice are to keep these concepts conceptually distinct and to delineate the domains in which they should have priority. In the realm of law, for instance, justice and the assurance of rights should have priority, although the humane considerations of care should not be absent. In the realm of the family and among friends, priority should be given to expansive care, though the basic requirements of justice surely should also be met. But these are the clearest cases; others will combine moral urgencies. Universal human rights (including the social and economic ones as well as the political and civil) should certainly be respected, but promoting care across continents may be a more promising way to achieve this than mere rational recognition. When needs are desperate, justice may be a lessened requirement on shared responsibility for meeting needs, although this rarely excuses violations of rights. At the level of what constitutes a society in the first place, a domain within which rights are to be assured and care provided, appeal must be made to something like the often weak but not negligible caring relations among persons that enable them to recognize each other as members of the same society. Such recognition must eventually be global; in the meantime, the civil society without which the liberal institutions of justice cannot function presumes a background of some degree of caring relations rather than of merely competing individuals. Furthermore, considerations of care provide a more fruitful basis than considerations of justice for deciding much about how society should be structured, for instance, how extensive or how restricted markets should be. And in the course of protecting the rights that ought to be recognized, such as those to basic necessities, policies that express the caring of the community for all its members will be better policies than those that grudgingly, though fairly, issue an allotment to those deemed unfit.

Care is probably the most deeply fundamental value. There can be care without justice: There has historically been little justice in the family, but care and life have gone on without it. There can be no justice without care, however, for without care no child would survive and there would be no persons to respect.

Care may thus provide the wider and deeper ethics within which justice should be sought, as when persons in caring relations may sometimes compete and in doing so should treat each other fairly, or, at the level of society, within caring relations of the thinner kind we can agree to treat each other for limited purposes as if we were the abstract individuals of liberal theory. But although care may be the more fundamental value, it may well be that the ethics of care does not itself provide adequate theoretical resources for dealing with issues of justice. Within its appropriate sphere and for its relevant questions, the ethics of justice may be best for what we seek. What should be resisted is the traditional inclination to expand the reach of justice in such a way that it is mistakenly imagined to be able to give us a comprehensive morality suitable for all moral questions.

IMPLICATIONS FOR SOCIETY

Many advocates of the ethics of care argue for its relevance in social and political and economic life. Sara Ruddick shows its implications for efforts to achieve peace. I argue that as we see the deficiencies of the contractual model of human relations within the household, we can see them also in the world beyond and begin to think about how society should be reorganized to be hospitable to care, rather than continuing to marginalize it. We can see how not only does every domain of society need transformation in light of the values of care but so would the relations between such domains if we took care seriously, as care would move to the center of our attention and become a primary concern of society. Instead of a society dominated by conflict restrained by law and preoccupied with economic gain, we might have a society that saw as its most important task the flourishing of children and the development of caring relations, not only in personal contexts but among citizens and using governmental institutions. We would see that instead of abandoning culture to the dictates of the marketplace, we should make it possible for culture to develop in ways best able to enlighten and enrich human life.

Joan Tronto argues for the political implications of the ethics of care, seeing care as a political as well as moral ideal advocating the meeting of needs for care as "the highest social goal." She shows how unacceptable are current arrangements for providing care: "Caring activities are devalued, underpaid, and disproportionately occupied by the relatively powerless in society." Bubeck, Kittay, and many others argue forcefully that care must be seen as a public concern, not relegated to the private responsibility of women, the inadequacy and arbitrariness of private charities, or the vagaries and distortions of the market. In her recent book *Starting at Home*, Noddings explores what a caring society would be like.

When we concern ourselves with caring relations between more distant others, this care should not be thought to reduce to the mere "caring about" that has little to do with the face-to-face interactions of caring labor and can easily become paternalistic or patronizing. The same characteristics of attentiveness, responsiveness to needs, and understanding situations from the points of view of others should characterize caring when the participants are more distant. This also requires the work of understanding and of expending varieties of effort.

Given how care is a value with the widest possible social implications, it is unfortunate that many who look at the ethics of care continue to suppose it is a "family ethics," confined to the "private" sphere. Although some of its earliest formulations suggested this, and some of its related values are to be seen most clearly in personal contexts, an adequate understanding of the ethics of care should recognize that it elaborates values as fundamental and as relevant to political institutions and to how society is organized, as those of justice. Perhaps its values are even more fundamental and more relevant to life in society than those traditionally relied on.

Instead of seeing the corporate sector, and military strength, and government and law as the most important segments of society deserving the highest levels of wealth and power, a caring society might see the tasks of bringing up children, educating its members, meeting the needs of all, achieving peace and treasuring the environment, and doing these in the best ways possible to be that to which the greatest social efforts of all should be devoted. One can recognize that something comparable to legal constraints and police enforcement, including at a global level, may always be necessary for special cases, but also that caring societies could greatly decrease the need for them. The social changes a focus on care would require would be as profound as can be imagined.

The ethics of care as it has developed is most certainly not limited to the sphere of family and personal relations. When its social and political implications are understood, it is a radical ethic calling for a profound restructuring of society. And it has the resources for dealing with power and violence.

THE ETHICS OF CARE AND VIRTUE ETHICS

Insofar as the ethics of care wishes to cultivate in persons the characteristics of a caring person and the skills of activities of caring, might an ethic of care be assimilated to virtue theory?

To some philosophers, the ethics of care is a form of virtue ethics. Several of the contributors to the volume *Feminists Doing Ethics* adopt this view. Leading virtue theorist Michael Slote argues extensively for the position that caring is the primary virtue and that a morality based on the motive of caring can offer a general account of right and wrong action and political justice.

Certainly there are some similarities between the ethics of care and virtue theory. Both examine practices and the moral values they embody. Both see more hope for moral development in reforming practices than in reasoning from abstract rules. Both understand that the practices of morality must be cultivated, nurtured, shaped.

Until recently, however, virtue theory has not paid adequate attention to the practices of caring in which women have been so heavily engaged. Although this might be corrected, virtue theory has characteristically seen the virtues as incorporated in various traditions or traditional communities. In contrast, the ethics of care as a feminist ethic is wary of existing traditions and traditional communities: Virtually all are patriarchal. The ethics of care envisions caring not as practiced under male domination, but as it should be practiced in postpatriarchal society, of which we do not yet have traditions or wide experience. Individual egalitarian families are still surrounded by inegalitarian social and cultural influences.

In my view, although there are similarities between them and although to be caring is no doubt a virtue, the ethics of care is not simply a kind of virtue ethics. Virtue ethics focuses especially on the states of character of individuals, whereas the ethics of care concerns itself especially with caring *relations*. Caring relations have primary value.

If virtue ethics is interpreted, as with Slote, as primarily a matter of motives, it may neglect unduly the labor and objective results of caring, as Bubeck's emphasis on actually meeting needs highlights. Caring is not only a question of motive or attitude or virtue. On the other hand, Bubeck's account is unduly close to a utilitarian interpretation of meeting needs, neglecting that care *also* has an aspect of motive and virtue. If virtue ethics is interpreted as less restricted to motives, and if it takes adequate account of the results of the virtuous person's activities for the persons cared for, it may better include the concerns of the ethics of care. It would still, however, focus on the dispositions of individuals, whereas the ethics of care focuses on social relations and the social practices and values that sustain them. The traditional Man of Virtue may be almost as haunted by his patriarchal past as the Man of Reason. The work of care has certainly not been among the virtuous activities to which he has adequately attended.

The ethics of care, in my view, is a distinctive ethical outlook, distinct even from virtue ethics. Certainly it has precursors, and such virtue theorists as Aristotle, Hume, and the moral sentimentalists contribute importantly to it. As a feminist ethic, the ethics of care is certainly not a mere description or generalization of women's attitudes and activities as developed under patriarchal conditions. To be acceptable, it must be a *feminist* ethic, open to both women and men to adopt. But in being feminist, it is different from the ethics of its precursors and different as well from virtue ethics.

The ethics of care is sometimes thought inadequate because of its inability to provide definite answers in cases of conflicting moral demands. Virtue theory has similarly been criticized for offering no more than what detractors call a "bag of virtues," with no clear indication of how to prioritize the virtues or apply their requirements, especially when they seem to conflict. Defenders of the ethics of care respond that the adequacy of the definite answers provided by, for instance, utilitarian and Kantian moral theories is illusory. Cost-benefit analysis is a good example of a form of utilitarian calculation that purports to provide clear answers to questions about what we ought to do, but from the point of view of moral understanding, its answers are notoriously dubious. So, too, often are casuistic reasonings about deontological rules. To advocates of the ethics of care, its alternative moral epistemology seems better. It stresses sensitivity to the multiple relevant considerations in particular contexts, cultivating the traits of character and of relationship that sustain caring, and promoting the dialogue that corrects and enriches the perspective of any one individual. The ethics of care is hospitable to the methods of discourse ethics, though with an emphasis on actual dialogue that empowers its participants to express themselves rather than on discourse so ideal that actual differences of viewpoint fall away.

For Further Reflection

1. Can an ethic of justice be plausibly combined with the ethics of care? Are they compatible at all? Explain.

2. Do you agree with the criticisms of the liberal individualist conception of a person? How does this conception compare with the ethics of care conception of a person? Is one better than the other—or does each capture a part of the truth?

3. Should the ethics of care be viewed as a type of virtue ethics? Why or why not?

The Moral Law   **VI.64**

IMMANUEL KANT

Immanuel Kant (1724–1804) was born into a deeply pietistic Lutheran family in Königsberg, Germany, lived in that town his entire life, and taught at the University of Königsberg. He lived a duty-bound, methodical life, so regular that citizens were said to have set their clocks by his walks. Kant is one of the premier philosophers in the Western tradition. In his monumental work *The Critique of Pure Reason* (1781) he inaugurated a Copernican-like revolution in the theory of knowledge.

Our reading is from Kant's classic work *The Foundations of the Metaphysic of Morals*, written in 1785, in which he outlines his ethical system. Kant rejects those ethical theories, such as the theory of moral sentiments set forth by the Scottish moralists Francis Hutcheson (1694) and David Hume (1711–1776), in which morality is contingent and hypothetical. The moral sentiment view is contingent in that it is based on human nature and, in particular, on our feelings or sentiments. Had we been created differently, we would have a different nature and, hence, different moral duties. Moral duties or imperatives are hypothetical in that they depend on our desires for their realization. For example, we should obey the law because we want a peaceful, orderly society.

Kant rejects this naturalistic account of ethics. Ethics is not contingent but absolute, he argues, and its duties or imperatives are not hypothetical but categorical (nonconditional). Ethics is based not on feeling but on reason. Because we are rational beings we are valuable and capable of discovering moral laws binding on all persons at all times. As such, our moral duties are not dependent on feelings but on reason. They are unconditional, universally valid, and necessary, regardless of the possible consequences or opposition to our inclinations.

Kant's first formulation of his *categorical imperative* is, "Act only on that maxim whereby thou canst at the same time will that it would become a universal law." This imperative is given as the criterion (or second-order principle) by which to judge all other principles. If we could consistently will that everyone would do some type of action, then there is an application of the categorical imperative enjoining that type of action. If we cannot consistently will that everyone would do some type of action, then that type of action is morally wrong. Kant argues, for example, that we cannot consistently will that everyone make lying promises, for the very institution of promising entails or depends on general adherence to keeping the promise or having an intention to do so.

Kant offers a second formulation of the categorical imperative: "So act as to treat humanity, whether in your own person or in that of any other, in every case as an end and never as merely a means only." Each person by virtue of his or her reason has dignity and profound worth, which entails that he or she must never be exploited or manipulated or merely used as a means to our idea of what is for the general good. Kant thought that this formulation was substantively identical with the first, but his view is controversial.

Study Questions

1. What is the aim of Kant's work? Why does he want to reject empirical (for example, socio-logical and anthropological) data in constructing a "pure moral philosophy"?
2. What is the only quality which is good without qualification? Analyze Kant's reasoning here. Is it cogent?
3. Why does Kant deprecate the role of reason in producing happiness? Is his view of the purposive function of a faculty (for example, our rational capacity, our will) in line with standard evolutionary theory?
4. What is the relationship between duty and inclination? Do acts done out of good inclina-tion have any moral worth?
5. What is the role of consequences in moral reasoning? According to Kant, should we ask ourselves what are the likely consequences before we decide what to do?
6. What is the categorical imperative?
7. What is the difference between a maxim and a principle of universal law?
8. How does Kant illustrate the moral law? Do you see any problems with his examples? Is it clear that none of them could be universalized?
9. What is Kant's second formulation of the moral law? Is it equivalent, as Kant thought, to the first formulation?

PREFACE

AS MY CONCERN HERE is with moral philoso-phy, I limit the question suggested to this: Whether it is not of the utmost necessity to construct a pure moral philosophy, perfectly cleared of everything which is only empirical, and which belongs to anthropology? for that such a philosophy must be possible is evident from the common idea of duty and of the moral laws. Everyone must admit that if a law is to have moral force, i.e. to be the basis of an obligation, it must carry with it absolute necessity; that, for example, the precept, "Thou shall not lie," is not valid for men alone, as if other rational beings had no need to observe it; and so with all the other moral laws properly so called; that, therefore, the basis of obligation must not be sought in the nature of man, or in the circumstances in the world in which he is placed, but *a priori* simply in the con-ception of pure reason; and although any other pre-cept which is founded on principles of mere experi-ence may be in certain respects universal, yet in as far as it rests even in the least degree on an empiri-cal basis, perhaps only as to a motive, such a pre-cept, while it may be a practical rule, can never be called a moral law. . . .

THE GOOD WILL

Nothing can possibly be conceived in the world, or even out of it, which can be called good, with-out qualification, except a Good Will. Intelligence, wit, judgment, and the other *talents* of the mind, however they may be named, or courage, resolu-tion, perseverance, as qualities of temperament, are undoubtedly good and desirable in many respects; but these gifts of nature may also become extremely bad and mischievous if the will which is to make use of them, and which, therefore, con-stitutes what is called *character*, is not good. It is the same with the *gifts of fortune*. Power, riches, honour, even health, and the general well-being and contentment with one's conditions which is

Reprinted from The Foundations of the Metaphysic of Morals, *translated by T. K. Abbott (this translation first published in 1873).*

called *happiness,* inspire pride, and often presumption, if there is not a good will to correct the influence of these on the mind, and with this also to rectify the whole principle of acting, and adapt it to its end. The sight of a being who is not adorned with a single feature of a pure and good will, enjoying unbroken prosperity, can never give pleasure to an impartial rational spectator. Thus a good will appears to constitute the indispensable condition even of being worthy of happiness.

There are even some qualities which are of service to this good will itself, and may facilitate its action, yet which have no intrinsic unconditional value, but always presuppose a good will, and this qualifies the esteem that we justly have for them, and does not permit us to regard them as absolutely good. Moderation in the affections and passions, self-control, and calm deliberation are not only good in many respects, but even seem to constitute part of the intrinsic worth of the person; but they are far from deserving to be called good without qualification, although they have been so unconditionally praised by the ancients. For without the principles of a good will, they may become extremely bad; and the coolness of a villain not only makes him far more dangerous, but also directly makes him more abominable in our eyes than he would have been without it.

A good will is good not because of what it performs or effects, not by its aptness for the attainment of some proposed end, but simply by virtue of the volition, that is, it is good in itself, and considered by itself to be esteemed much higher than all that can be brought about by it in favour of any inclination, nay, even of the sum-total of all inclinations. Even if it should happen that, owing to special disfavour of fortune, or the niggardly provision of a step-motherly nature, this will should wholly lack power to accomplish its purpose, if with its greatest efforts it should yet achieve nothing, and there should remain only the good will (not, to be sure, a mere wish, but the summoning of all means in our power), then, like a jewel, it would still shine by its own light, as a thing which has its whole value in itself. Its

usefulness or fruitlessness can neither add to nor take away anything from this value. It would be, as it were, only the setting to enable us to handle it the more conveniently in common commerce, or to attract to it the attention of those who are not yet connoisseurs, but not to recommend it to true connoisseurs, or to determine its value.

WHY REASON WAS MADE TO GUIDE THE WILL

There is, however, something so strange in this idea of the absolute value of the mere will, in which no account is taken of its utility, that notwithstanding the thorough assent of even common reason to the idea, yet a suspicion must arise that it may perhaps really be the product of mere high-blown fancy, and that we may have misunderstood the purpose of nature in assigning reason as the governor of our will. Therefore we will examine this idea from this point of view.

In the physical constitution of an organized being, that is, a being adapted suitably to the purposes of life, we assume it as a fundamental principle that no organ for any purpose will be found but what is also the fittest and best adapted for that purpose. Now in a being which has reason and a will, if the proper object of nature were its *conservatism,* its *welfare,* in a word, its *happiness,* then nature would have hit upon a very bad arrangement in selecting the reason of the creature to carry out this purpose. For all the actions which the creature has to perform with a view to this purpose, and the whole rule of its conduct, would be far more surely prescribed to it by instinct, and that end would have been attained thereby much more certainly than it ever can be by reason. Should reason have been communicated to this favoured creature over and above, it must only have served it to contemplate the happy constitution of its nature, to admire it, to congratulate itself thereon, and to feel thankful for it to the beneficent cause, but not that it should subject its desires to that weak and delusive guidance, and meddle bunglingly with the purpose of nature. In a word, nature would have taken care that reason should not break forth into *practical exercise*, nor have the presumption, with its weak insight, to think out for itself the plan of happiness, and of the means of attaining it. Nature would not only have taken on herself the choice of the ends, but also of the means, and with wise foresight would have entrusted both to instinct.

And, in fact, we find that the more a cultivated reason applies itself with deliberate purpose to the enjoyment of life and happiness, so much the more does the man fail of true satisfaction. And from this circumstance there arises in many, if they are candid enough to confess it, a certain degree of *misology*, that is, hatred of reason, especially in the case of those who are most experienced in the use of it, because after calculating all the advantages they derive, I do not say from the invention of all the arts of common luxury, but even from the sciences (which seem to them to be after all only a luxury of the understanding), they find that they have, in fact, only brought more trouble on their shoulders, rather than gained in happiness; and they end by envying, rather than despising, the more common stamp of men who keep closer to the guidance of mere instinct, and do not allow their reason much influence on their conduct. And this we must admit, that the judgment of those who would very much lower the lofty eulogies of the advantages which reason gives us in regard to the happiness and satisfaction of life, or who would even reduce them below zero, is by no means morose or ungrateful to the goodness with which the world is governed, but that there lies at the root of these judgments the idea that our existence has a different and far nobler end, for which, and not for happiness, reason is properly intended, and which must, therefore, be regarded as the supreme condition to which the private ends of man must, for the most part, be postponed.

For as reason is not competent to guide the will with certainty in regard to its objects and the satisfaction of all our wants (which it to some extent even multiplies), this being an end to which an implanted instinct would have led with much greater certainty; and since, nevertheless, reason is imparted to us as a practical faculty, i.e. as one which is to have influence on the *will,* therefore, admitting that nature generally in the distribution of her capacities has adapted the means to the end, its true destination must be to produce a *will,* not merely good as a *means* to something else, but *good in itself,* for which reason was absolutely necessary. This will then, though not indeed the sole and complete good, must be the supreme good and the condition of every other, even of the desire of happiness. Under these circumstances, there is nothing inconsistent with the wisdom of nature in the fact that the cultivation of the reason, which is requisite for the first and unconditional purpose, does in many ways interfere, at least in this life, with the attainment of the second, which is always conditional, namely, happiness. Nay, it may even reduce it to nothing, without nature thereby failing in her purpose. For reason recognizes the establishment of a good will as its highest practical destination, and in attaining this purpose is capable only of a satisfaction of its own proper kind, namely, that from the attainment of an end, which end again is determined by reason only, notwithstanding that this may involve many a disappointment to the ends of inclination.

THE FIRST PROPOSITION OF MORALITY

[An action must be done from a sense of duty, if it is to have moral worth]

We have then to develop the notion of a will which deserves to be highly esteemed for itself, and is good without a view to anything further, a notion which exists already in the sound natural understanding, requiring rather to be cleared up than to be taught, and which in estimating the value of our actions always takes the first place, and constitutes the condition of all the rest. In order to do this, we will take the notion of duty, which includes that of a good will, although implying certain subjective restrictions and hindrances. These, however, far from concealing it, or rendering it unrecognizable, rather bring it out by contrast, and make it shine forth so much the brighter.

I omit here all actions which are already recognized as inconsistent with duty although they may be useful for this or that purpose, for with these the question whether they are done *from duty* cannot arise at all, since they even conflict with it. I also set aside those actions which really conform to duty, but to which men have *no* direct *inclination,* performing them because they are impelled thereto by some other inclination. For in this case we can readily distinguish whether the action which agrees with duty is done *from duty,* or from a selfish view. It is much harder to make this distinction when the action accords with duty, and the subject has besides a *direct* inclination to it. For example, it is always a matter of duty that a dealer should not overcharge an inexperienced purchaser; and wherever there is much commerce the prudent tradesman does not overcharge, but keeps a fixed price for everyone, so that a child buys of him as well as any other. Men are thus *honestly* served; but this is not enough to make us believe that the tradesman has so acted from duty and from principles of honesty: his own advantage required it; it is out of the question in this case to suppose that he might besides have a direct inclination in favour of the buyers, so that, as it were, from love he should give no advantage to one over another. Accordingly the action was done neither from duty nor from direct inclination, but merely with a selfish view.

On the other hand, it is a duty to maintain one's life; and, in addition, everyone has also a direct inclination to do so. But on this account the often anxious care which most men take for it has no intrinsic worth, and their maxim has no moral import. They preserve their life *as duty requires,* no doubt, but not *because duty requires.* On the other hand, if adversity and hopeless sorrow have completely taken away the relish for life; if the unfortunate one, strong in mind, indignant at his fate rather than desponding or dejected, wishes for death, and yet preserves his life without loving it—not from inclination or fear, but from duty—then his maxim has a moral worth.

To be beneficent when we can is a duty; and besides this, there are many minds so sympathetically constituted that, without any other motive of vanity or self-interest, they find a pleasure in spreading joy around them, and can take delight in the satisfaction of others so far as it is their own work. But I maintain that in such a case an action of this kind, however proper, however amiable it may be, has nevertheless no true moral worth, but is on a level with other inclinations, e.g. the inclination to honour, which, if it is happily directed to that which is in fact of public utility and accordant with duty, and consequently honourable, deserves praise and encouragement, but not esteem. For the maxim lacks the moral import, namely, that such actions be done *from duty,* not from inclination. Put the case that the mind of that philanthropist was clouded by sorrow of his own, extinguishing all sympathy with the lot of others, and that while he still has the power to benefit others in distress, he is not touched by their trouble because he is absorbed with his own; and now suppose that he tears himself out of this dead insensibility, and performs the action without any inclination to it, but simply from duty, then first has his action its genuine moral worth. Further still; if nature has put little sympathy in the heart of this or that man; if he, supposed to be an upright man, is by temperament cold and indifferent to the sufferings of others, perhaps because in respect of his own he is provided with the special gift of patience and fortitude, and supposes, or even requires, that others should have the same—and such a man would certainly not be the meanest product of nature—but if nature had not specially framed him for a philanthropist, would he not still find in himself a source from whence to give himself a far higher worth than that of a good-natured temperament could be? Unquestionably. It is just in this that the moral worth of the character is brought out which is incomparably the highest of all, namely, that he is beneficent, not from inclination, but from duty.

To secure one's own happiness is a duty, at least indirectly; for discontent with one's condition, under a pressure of many anxieties and amidst unsatisfied wants, might easily become a great *temptation to transgression of duty*. But here again, without looking to duty, all men have already the strongest and most intimate inclination to happiness, because it is just in this idea that all inclinations are combined in one total. But the precept of happiness is often of such a sort that it greatly interferes with some inclinations, and yet a man cannot form any definite and certain conception of the sum of satisfaction of all of them which is called happiness. It is not then to be wondered at that a single inclination, definite both as to what it promises and as to the time within which it can be gratified, is often able to overcome such a fluctuating idea, and that a gouty patient, for instance, can choose to enjoy what he likes, and to suffer what he may, since, according to his calculation, on this occasion at least, he has [only] not sacrificed the enjoyment of the present moment to a possibly mistaken expectation of a happiness which is supposed to be found in health. But even in this case, if the general desire for happiness did not influence his will, and supposing that in his particular case health was not a necessary element in this calculation, there yet remains in this, as in all other cases, this law, namely, that he should promote his happiness not from inclination but from duty, and by this would his conduct first acquire true moral worth.

It is in this manner, undoubtedly, that we are to understand those passages of Scripture also in which we are commanded to love our neighbour, even our enemy. For love, as an affection, cannot be commanded, but beneficence for duty's sake may; even though we are not impelled to it by any inclination—nay, are even repelled by a natural and unconquerable aversion. This is *practical* love, and not *pathological**—a love which is seated in the will, and not in the propensions of sense—in principles of action and not of tender sympathy; and it is this love alone which can be commanded.

*passional or emotional

THE SECOND PROPOSITION OF MORALITY

The second proposition is: That an action done from duty derives its moral worth, *not from the purpose* which is to be attained by it, but from the maxim by which it is determined, and therefore does not depend on the realization of the object of the action, but merely on the *principle of volition* by which the action has taken place, without regard to any object of desire. It is clear from what precedes that the purposes which we may have in view in our actions, or their effects regarded as ends and springs of the will, cannot give to actions any unconditional or moral worth. In what, then, can their worth lie, if it is not to consist in the will and in reference to its expected effect? It cannot lie anywhere but in the *principle of the will* without regard to the ends which can be attained by the action. For the will stands between its *a priori principle*, which is formal, and its *a posteriori* spring, which is material, as between two roads, and as it must be determined by something, it follows that it must be determined by the formal principle of volition when an action is done from duty, in which case every material principle has been withdrawn from it.

THE THIRD PROPOSITION OF MORALITY

The third proposition, which is a consequence of the two preceding, I would express thus: *Duty is the necessity of acting from respect for the law.* I may have *inclination* for an object as the effect of my proposed action, but I cannot have *respect* for it, just for this reason, that it is an effect and not an energy of will. Similarly, I cannot have respect for inclination, whether my own or another's; I can at most, if my own, approve it; if another's, sometimes even love it; i.e. look on it as favourable to my own interest. It is only what is connected with my will as a principle, by no means as an effect— what does not subserve my inclination, but overpowers it, or at least in case of choice excludes it from its calculation—in other words, simply the law of itself, which can be an object of respect, and hence a command. Now an action done from duty must wholly exclude the influence of inclination, and with it every object of the will, so that nothing remains which can determine the will except objectively the *law,* and subjectively *pure respect* for this practical law, and consequently the maxim that I should follow this law even to the thwarting of all my inclinations. Thus the moral worth of an action does not lie in the effect expected from it, nor in any principle of action which requires to borrow its motive from this expected effect. For all these effects—agreeableness of one's condition, and even the promotion of the happiness of others—could have been also brought about by other causes, so that for this there would have been no need of the will of a rational being; whereas it is in this alone that the supreme and unconditional good can be found. The pre-eminent good which we call moral can therefore consist in nothing else than *the conception of law* in itself, *which certainly is only possible in a rational being,* in so far as this conception, and not the expected effect, determines the will. This is a good which is already present in the person who acts accordingly, and we have not to wait for it to appear first in the result.

THE SUPREME PRINCIPLE OF MORALITY: THE CATEGORICAL IMPERATIVE

But what sort of law can that be, the conception of which must determine the will, even without paying any regard to the effect expected from it, in order that this will may be called good absolutely and without qualification? As I have deprived the will of every impulse which could arise to it from obedience to any law, there remains nothing but the universal conformity of its actions to law in general, which alone is to serve the will as a principle, i.e. I am never to act otherwise than so *that I could also will that my maxim should become a universal law.* Here, now, it is the simple conformity to law in general,

without assuming any particular law applicable to certain actions, that serves the will as its principle, and must so serve it, if duty is not to be a vain delusion and a chimerical notion. The common reason of men in its practical judgments perfectly coincides with this, and always has in view the principle here suggested. Let the question be, for example: May I when in distress make a promise with the intention not to keep it? I readily distinguish here between the two significations which the question may have: Whether it is prudent, or whether it is right, to make a false promise? The former may undoubtedly often be the case. I see clearly indeed that it is not enough to extricate myself from a present difficulty by means of this subterfuge, but it must be well considered whether there may not hereafter spring from this lie much greater inconvenience than that from which I now free myself, and as, with all my supposed *cunning,* the consequences cannot be so easily foreseen but that credit once lost may be much more injurious to me than any mischief which I seek to avoid at present, it should be considered whether it would not be more *prudent* to act herein according to a universal maxim, and to make it a habit to promise nothing except with the intention of keeping it. But it is soon clear to me that such a maxim will still only be based on the fear of consequences. Now it is a wholly different thing to be truthful from duty, and to be so from apprehension of injurious consequences. In the first case, the very notion of the action already implies a law for me; in the second case, I must first look about elsewhere to see what results may be combined with it which would affect myself. For to deviate from the principle of duty is beyond all doubt wicked; but to be unfaithful to my maxim of prudence may often be very advantageous to me, although to abide by it is certainly safer. The shortest way, however, and an unerring one, to discover the answer to this question whether a lying promise is consistent with duty, is to ask myself, Should I be content that my maxim (to extricate myself from difficulty by a false promise) should hold good as a universal law, for myself as well as for others? and should I be able to say to myself,

"Every one may make a deceitful promise when he finds himself in a difficulty from which he cannot otherwise extricate himself"? Then I presently become aware that while I can will the lie, I can by no means will that lying should be a universal law. For with such a law there would be no promises at all, since it would be in vain to allege my intention in regard to my future actions to those who would not believe this allegation, or if they over-hastily did so, would pay me back in my own coin. Hence my maxim, as soon as it should be made a universal law, would necessarily destroy itself.

I do not, therefore, need any far-reaching penetration to discern what I have to do in order that my will may be morally good. Inexperienced in the course of the world, incapable of being prepared for all its contingencies, I only ask myself: Canst thou also will that thy maxim should be a universal law? If not, then it must be rejected, and that not because of a disadvantage accruing from myself or even to others, but because it cannot enter as a principle into a possible universal legislation, and reason extorts from me immediate respect for such legislation. I do not indeed as yet *discern* on what this respect is based (this the philosopher may inquire), but at least I understand this, that it is an estimation of the worth which far outweighs all worth of what is recommended by inclination, and that the necessity of acting from *pure* respect for the practical law is what constitutes duty, to which every other motive must give place, because it is the condition of a will being good *in itself,* and the worth of such a will is above everything.

Thus, then, without quitting the moral knowledge of common human reason, we have arrived at its principle. And although, no doubt, common men do not conceive it in such an abstract and universal form, yet they always have it really before their eyes, and use it as the standard of their decision. . . .

Nor could anything be more fatal to morality than that we should wish to derive it from examples. For every example of it that is set before me must be first itself tested by principles of morality, whether it is worthy to serve as an original example, i.e. as a pattern, but by no means can it authoritatively furnish the conception of morality. Even the Holy One of the Gospels must first be compared with our ideal of moral perfection before we can recognize Him as such; and so He says of Himself, "Why call ye Me [whom you see] good; none is good [the model of good] but God only [whom ye do not see]." But whence have we the conception of God as the supreme good? Simply from the *idea* of moral perfection, which reason frames *a priori,* and connects inseparably with the notion of a free will. Imitation finds no place at all in morality, and examples serve only for encouragement, i.e. they put beyond doubt the feasibility of what the law commands, they make visible that which the practical rule expresses more generally, but they can never authorize us to set aside the true original which lies in reason, and to guide ourselves by examples.

From what has been said, it is clear that all moral conceptions have their seat and origin completely *a priori* in the reason, and that, moreover, in the commonest reason just as truly as in that which is in the highest degree speculative; that they cannot be obtained by abstraction from any empirical, and therefore merely contingent knowledge; that it is just this purity of their origin that makes them worthy to serve as our supreme practical principle, and that just in proportion as we add anything empirical, we detract from their genuine influence, and from the absolute value of actions; that it is not only of the greatest necessity, in a purely speculative point of view, but is also of the greatest practical importance, to derive these notions and laws from pure reason, to present them pure and unmixed, and even to determine the compass of this practical or pure rational knowledge, i.e. to determine the whole faculty of pure practical reason; and, in doing so, we must not make its principles dependent on the particular nature of human reason, though in speculative philosophy this may be permitted, or may even at times be necessary; but since moral laws ought to hold good for every rational creature, we must derive them from the general concept of a rational being. In this way, although for its *application* to man morality has need of anthropology, yet, in the first instance, we must treat it independently as pure philosophy, i.e. as metaphysic, complete in itself (a thing which in such distinct branches of science is easily done); knowing well that unless we are in possession of this, it would not only be vain to determine the moral element of duty in right actions for purposes of speculative criticism, but it would be impossible to base morals on their genuine principles, even for common practical purposes, especially of moral instruction, so as to produce pure moral dispositions, and to engraft them on men's minds to the promotion of the greatest possible good in the world. . . .

THE RATIONAL GROUND OF THE CATEGORICAL IMPERATIVE

. . . the question, how the imperative of *morality* is possible, is undoubtedly one, the only one, demanding a solution, as this is not at all hypothetical, and the objective necessity which it presents cannot rest on any hypothesis, as is the case with the hypothetical imperatives. Only here we must never leave out of consideration that we *cannot* make out *by any example*, in other words empirically, whether there is such an imperative at all; but it is rather to be feared that all those which seem to be categorical may yet be at bottom hypothetical. For instance, when the precept is: Thou shalt not promise deceitfully; and it is assumed that the necessity of this is not a mere counsel to avoid some other evil, so that it should mean: Thou shalt not make a lying promise, lest if it become known thou shouldst destroy thy credit, but that an action of this kind must be regarded as evil in itself, so that the imperative of the prohibition is categorical; then we cannot show with certainty in any example that the will was determined merely by the law, without any other spring of action, although it may appear to be so. For it is always possible that fear of disgrace, perhaps also obscure dread of other dangers, may have a secret influence on the will. Who can prove by experience the nonexistence of a cause when all that experience tells us is that we do not perceive it? But in such a case the so-called moral imperative, which as such appears to be categorical and unconditional, would in reality be only a pragmatic precept, drawing our attention to our own interests, and merely teaching us to take these into consideration.

We shall therefore have to investigate *a priori* the possibility of a categorical imperative, as we have not in this case the advantage of its reality being given in experience, so that [the elucidation of] its possibility should be requisite only for its explanation, not for its establishment. In the meantime it may be discerned beforehand that the categorical imperative alone has the purport of a practical law: all the rest may indeed be called *principles* of the will but not laws, since whatever is only necessary for the attainment of some arbitrary purpose may be considered as in itself contingent, and we can at any time be free from the precept if we give up the purpose: on the contrary, the unconditional command leaves the will no liberty to choose the opposite; consequently it alone carries with it that necessity which we require in a law.

Secondly, in the case of this categorical imperative or law of morality, the difficulty (of discerning its possibility) is a very profound one. It is an *a priori* synthetical practical proposition; and as there is so much difficulty in discerning the possibility of speculative propositions of this kind, it may readily be supposed that the difficulty will be no less with the practical.

FIRST FORMULATION OF THE CATEGORICAL IMPERATIVE: UNIVERSAL LAW

In this problem we will first inquire whether the mere conception of a categorical imperative may not perhaps supply us also with the formula of it, containing the proposition which alone can be a categorical imperative; for even if we know the tenor of such an absolute command, yet how it is possible will require further special and laborious study, which we postpone to the last section. When I conceive a hypothetical imperative, in general I do not know beforehand what it will contain until I am given the condition. But when I conceive a categorical imperative, I know at once what it contains. For as the imperative contains besides the law only the necessity that the maxims shall conform to this law, while the law contain no conditions restricting it, there remains nothing but the general statement that the maxim of the action should conform to a universal law, and it is this conformity alone that the imperative properly represents as necessary.

There is therefore but one categorical imperative, namely, this: *Act only on that maxim whereby thou canst at the same time will that it should become a universal law.*

Now if all imperatives of duty can be deduced from this one imperative as from their principle, then, although it should remain undecided whether what is called duty is not merely a vain notion, yet at least we shall be able to show what we understand by it and what this notion means.

Since the universality of the law according to which effects are produced constitutes what is properly called *nature* in the most general sense (as to form), that is the existence of things so far as it is determined by general laws, the imperative of duty may be expressed thus: *Act as if the maxim of thy action were to become by thy will a universal law of nature.*

FOUR ILLUSTRATIONS

We will now enumerate a few duties, adopting the usual division of them into duties to ourselves and to others, and into perfect and imperfect duties.

1. A man reduced to despair by a series of misfortunes feels wearied of life, but is still so far in possession of his reason that he can ask himself whether it would not be contrary to his duty to himself to take his own life. Now he inquires whether the maxim of his action could become a universal law of nature. His maxim is: From self-love I adopt it as a principle to shorten my life when its longer duration is likely to bring more evil than satisfaction. It is asked then simply whether this principle founded on self-love can become a universal law of nature. Now we see at once that a system of nature of which it should be a law to destroy life by means of the very feeling whose special nature it is to impel to the improvement of life would contradict itself, and therefore could not exist as a system of nature; hence that maxim cannot possibly exist as a universal law of nature, and consequently would be wholly inconsistent with the supreme principle of all duty.

2. Another finds himself forced by necessity to borrow money. He knows that he will not be able to repay it, but sees also that nothing will be lent to him, unless he promises stoutly to repay it in a definite time. He desires to make this promise, but he has still so much conscience as to ask himself: Is it not unlawful and inconsistent with duty to get out of a difficulty in this way? Suppose, however, that he resolves to do so, then the maxim of his action would be expressed thus: When I think myself in want of money, I will borrow money and promise to repay it, although I know that I never can do so. Now this principle of self-love or of one's own advantage may perhaps be consistent with my whole future welfare; but the question is, Is it right? I change then the suggestion of self-love into a universal law, and state the question thus: How would it be if my maxim were a universal law? Then I see at once that it could never hold as a universal law of nature, but would necessarily contradict itself. For supposing it to be a universal law that everyone when he thinks himself in a difficulty should be able to promise whatever he pleases, with the purpose of not keeping his promise, the promise itself would become impossible, as well as the end that one might have in view in it, since no one would consider that anything was promised to him, but would ridicule all such statements as vain pretenses.

3. A third finds in himself a talent which with the help of some culture might make him a useful man in many respects. But he finds himself in comfortable circumstances, and prefers to indulge in pleasure rather than to take pains in enlarging and improving his happy natural capacities. He asks, however, whether his maxim of neglect of his natural gifts, besides agreeing with his inclination to indulgence, agrees also with what is called duty. He sees then that a system of nature could indeed subsist with such a universal law although men (like the South Sea islanders) should let their talents rest, and resolve to devote their lives merely to idleness, amusement, and propagation of their species—in a word, to enjoyment; but he cannot possibly *will* that this should be a universal law of nature, or be implanted in us as such by a natural instinct. For, as a rational being, he necessarily wills that his faculties be developed, since they serve him, and have been given him, for all sorts of possible purposes.

4. A fourth, who is in prosperity, while he sees that others have to contend with great wretchedness and that he could help them, thinks: What concern is it of mine? Let everyone be as happy as Heaven pleases, or as he can make himself; I will take nothing from him nor even envy him, only I do not wish to contribute anything to his welfare or to his assistance in distress! Now no doubt if such a mode of thinking were a universal law, the human race might very well subsist, and doubtless even better than in a state in which everyone talks of sympathy and good-will, or even takes care occasionally to put it into practice, but, on the other side, also cheats when he can, betrays the rights of men, or otherwise violates them. But although it is possible that a universal law of nature might exist in accordance with that maxim, it is impossible to *will* that such a principle should have the universal validity of a law of nature. For a will which resolved this would contradict itself, inasmuch as many cases might occur in which one would have need of the love and sympathy of others, and in which, by such a law of nature, sprung from his own will, he would deprive himself of all hope of the aid he desires.

These are a few of the many actual duties, or at least what we regard as such, which obviously fall into two classes on the one principle that we have laid down. We must be *able to will* that a maxim of our action should be a universal law. This is the canon of the moral appreciation of the action generally. Some actions are of such a character that their maxim cannot without contradiction be even *conceived* as a universal law of nature, far from it being possible that we should *will* that it *should* be so. In others this intrinsic impossibility is not found, but still it is impossible to *will* that their maxim should be raised to the universality of a law of nature, since such a will would contradict itself. It is easily seen that the former violate strict or rigorous (inflexible) duty; the latter only laxer (meritorious) duty. Thus it has been completely shown by these examples how all duties depend as regards the nature of the obligation (not the object of the action) on the same principle.

SECOND FORMULATION OF THE CATEGORICAL IMPERATIVE: HUMANITY AS AN END IN ITSELF

. . . Now I say: man and generally any rational being *exists* as an end in himself, *not merely as a means* to be arbitrarily used by this or that will, but in all his actions, whether they concern himself or other rational beings, must be always regarded at the same time as an end. All objects of the inclinations have only a conditional worth; for if the inclinations and the wants founded on them did not exist, then their object would be without value. But the inclinations themselves being sources of want are so far from having an absolute worth for which they should be desired, that, on the contrary, it must be the universal wish of every rational being to be wholly free from them. Thus the worth of any object which is *to be acquired* by our action is always conditional. Beings whose existence depends not on our will but on nature's, have nevertheless, if they are nonrational beings, only a relative value as means, and are therefore called *things;*

rational beings, on the contrary, are called *persons,* because their very nature points them out as ends in themselves, that is as something which must not be used merely as means, and so far therefore restricts freedom of action (and is an object of respect). These, therefore, are not merely subjective ends whose existence has a worth *for us* as an effect of our action, but *objective ends,* that is things whose existence is an end in itself: an end moreover for which no other can be substituted, which they should subserve *merely* as means, for otherwise nothing whatever would possess *absolute worth;* but if all worth were conditioned and therefore contingent, then there would be no supreme practical principle of reason whatever.

If then there is a supreme practical principle or, in respect of the human will, a categorical imperative, it must be one which, being drawn from the conception of that which is necessarily an end for everyone because it is *an end in itself,* constitutes an *objective* principle of will, and can therefore serve as a universal practical law. The foundation of this principle is: *rational nature exists as an end in itself.* Man necessarily conceives his own existence as being so: so far then this is a *subjective* principle of human actions. But every other rational being regards its existence similarly, just on the same rational principle that holds for me: so that it is at the same time an objective principle, from which as a supreme practical law all laws of the will must be capable of being deduced. Accordingly the practical imperative will be as follows: *So act as to treat humanity, whether in thine own person or in that of any other, in every case as an end withal, never as means only. . . .*

. . . Looking back now on all previous attempts to discover the principle of morality, we need not wonder why they all failed. It was seen that man was bound to laws by duty, but it was not observed that the laws to which he is subject are *only those of his own giving,* though at the same time they are *universal,* and that he is only bound to act in conformity with his own will; a will, however, which is designed by nature to give universal laws. For when one has conceived man only as subject to a law (no matter what),

then this law required some interest, either by way of attraction or constraint, since it did not originate as a law from *his own* will, but his will was according to a law obliged by *something else* to act in a certain manner. Now by this necessary consequence all the labour spent in finding a supreme principle of *duty* was irrevocably lost. For men never elicited duty, but only a necessity of acting from a certain interest. Whether this interest was private or otherwise, in any case the imperative must be conditional, and could not by any means be capable of being a moral command. I will therefore call this the principle of *Autonomy* of the will, in contrast with every other which I accordingly reckon as *Heteronomy.*

THE KINGDOM OF ENDS

The conception of every rational being as one which must consider itself as giving in all the maxims of its will universal laws, so as to judge itself and its actions from this point of view—this conception leads to another which depends on it and is very fruitful, that of a *kingdom of ends.*

By a *kingdom* I understand the union of different rational beings in a system by common laws. Now since it is by laws that ends are determined as regards their universal validity, hence, if we abstract from the personal differences of rational beings, and likewise from all the content of their private ends, we shall be able to conceive all ends combined in a systematic whole (including both rational beings as ends in themselves, and also the special ends which each may propose to himself), that is to say, we can conceive a kingdom of ends, which on the preceding principles is possible.

For all rational beings come under the *law* that each of them must treat itself and all others *never merely as means,* but in every case *at the same time as ends in themselves.* Hence results a systematic union of rational beings by common objective laws, i.e., a kingdom which may be called a kingdom of ends, since what these laws have in view is just the relation of these beings to one another as ends and means. . . .

For Further Reflection

1. Is Kant's philosophy merely a development of the Golden Rule: "Do unto others what you would have them do unto you"? If it is equivalent, does it make Kant's system more intuitively plausible? But does it also lead to problems with what Kant thought to be the implications of his system? For example, on the basis of the Golden Rule one might endorse certain instances of euthanasia, but Kant's discussion of suicide seems to rule this out.

2. Kant's ethics are called deontological (from the Greek word for "duty") because he believes that the value of an act is in the act itself rather than in its consequences (as teleologists hold). Deontological ethics have been criticized as being too rigid. Do you think that this is true? Should the notion of consequences be taken into consideration?

3. How would Kant deal with moral conflicts? When two universal principles conflict, how would Kant resolve the dilemma?

4. Kant's categorical imperative has also been criticized for being more wide open than he realized, for it doesn't limit what could be universalized. How would Kant respond to these counter-examples: (1) Everyone should tie his right shoe before his left shoe; (2) All retarded or senile people should be executed by the government (adding, if I should become retarded or senile, I should also undergo this fate)?

Utilitarianism   VI.65

JOHN STUART MILL

John Stuart Mill (1806–1873), one of the most important British philosophers of the nineteenth century, was born in London and educated by his father, learning Greek at the age of three and Latin at the age of eight. By the time he was fourteen he had received a thorough classical education at home. He began work as a clerk for the East India Company at the age of seventeen and eventually became director of the company. He was elected to Parliament in 1865. A man of liberal ideas and a penetrating mind, he made significant contributions to logic, philosophy of science, philosophy of religion, political theory, and ethics. His principal works are *A System of Logic* (1843), *Utilitarianism* (1863), *On Liberty* (1859), and *The Subjection of Women* (1869).

Mill defends utilitarianism, a form of teleological ethics, against more rule-bound deontological systems, the sort of system we considered in the last selection, Kant's categorical imperative. *Teleological* is from the Greek "telos," which means "end" or "goal." That is, the standard of right or wrong action for the teleologists is the comparative consequences of the available actions. That act is right that produces the best consequences. Whereas the deontologist is concerned only with the rightness of the act itself, the teleologist asserts that there is no such thing as an act having intrinsic worth. Although there is something intrinsically bad about lying for the deontologist, the only thing wrong with lying for the teleologist is the bad consequences it produces. If you can reasonably calculate that a lie will do even slightly more good than telling the truth, you have an obligation to lie.

The present selection was written against the background of a debate over Jeremy Bentham's hedonistic version of utilitarianism, which failed to differentiate between kinds and qualities of pleasure, and so received the name of "pig philosophy." Mill meets this charge by substituting a more complex theory of happiness for Bentham's undifferentiated pleasure.

Study Questions

1. How does Mill define utilitarianism?
2. How does Mill reply to the charge that utilitarianism is a pig philosophy?
3. What test is there to distinguish the higher pleasures from the lower?
4. What is meant by "Better to be Socrates dissatisfied than a pig satisfied"?
5. Why do some people prefer the lower pleasures?
6. How can utilitarianism attain its end?
7. Why do some critics say that utilitarianism sets too high a standard for humanity?
8. What is Mill's "proof" of the truth of utilitarianism? Is it a clear and cogent argument?

WHAT UTILITARIANISM IS

... THE CREED WHICH ACCEPTS as the foundation of morals, Utility, or the Greatest Happiness Principle, holds that actions are right in proportion as they tend to promote happiness, wrong as they tend to produce the reverse of happiness. By happiness is intended pleasure, and the absence of pain; by unhappiness, pain, and the privation of pleasure. To give a clear view of the moral standard set up by the theory, much more requires to be said; in particular, what things it includes in the ideas of pain and pleasure; and to what extent this is left an open question. But these supplementary explanations do not affect the theory of life on which this theory of morality is grounded—namely, that pleasure, and freedom from pain, are the only things desirable as ends; and that all desirable things (which are as numerous in the utilitarian as in any other scheme) are desirable either for the pleasure inherent in themselves, or as a means to the promotion of pleasure and the prevention of pain.

Now, such a theory of life excites in many minds, and among them in some of the most estimable in feeling and purpose, inveterate dislike. To suppose that life has (as they express it) no higher end than pleasure—no better and nobler object of desire and pursuit—they designate as utterly mean and grovelling; as a doctrine worthy only of swine, to whom the followers of Epicurus were, at a very early period, contemptuously likened; and modern holders of the doctrine are occasionally made the subject of equally polite comparisons by its German, French, and English assailants.

When thus attacked, the Epicureans have always answered, that it is not they, but their accusers, who represent human nature in a degrading light; since the accusation supposes human beings to be capable of no pleasures except those of which swine are capable. If this supposition were true, the charge could not be gainsaid, but would then be no longer an imputation; for if the sources of pleasure were precisely the same to human beings and to swine, the rule

---

From John Stuart Mill, Utilitarianism *(1861), Chapters 2 and 4.*

of life which is good enough for the one would be good enough for the other. The comparison of the Epicurean life to that of beasts is felt as degrading, precisely because a beast's pleasures do not satisfy a human being's conception of happiness. Human beings have faculties more elevated than the animal appetites, and when once made conscious of them, do not regard anything as happiness which does not include their gratification. I do not, indeed, consider the Epicureans to have been by any means faultless in drawing out their scheme of consequences from the utilitarian principle. To do this in any sufficient manner, many Stoic, as well as Christian elements require to be included. But there is no known Epicurean theory of life which does not assign to the pleasures of the intellect, of the feelings and imagination, and of the moral sentiments, a much higher value as pleasures than to those of mere sensation. It must be admitted, however, that utilitarian writers in general have placed the superiority of mental over bodily pleasures chiefly in the greater permanency, safety, uncostliness, etc., of the former— that is, in their circumstantial advantages rather than in their intrinsic nature. And on all these points utilitarians have fully proved their case; but they might have taken the other, and, as it may be called, higher ground, with entire consistency. It is quite compatible with the principle of utility to recognise the fact, that some *kinds* of pleasure are more desirable and more valuable than others. It would be absurd that while, in estimating all other things, quality is considered as well as quantity, the estimation of pleasures should be supposed to depend on quantity alone.

If I am asked, what I mean by difference of quality in pleasures, or what makes one pleasure more valuable than another, merely as a pleasure, except its being greater in amount, there is but one possible answer. Of two pleasures, if there be one which all or almost all who have experience of both give a decided preference, irrespective of any feeling of moral obligation to prefer it, that is the more desirable pleasure. If one of the two is, by those who are competently acquainted with both, placed so far above the other that

they prefer it, even though knowing it to be attended with a great amount of discontent, and would not resign it for any quantity of the other pleasure which their nature is capable of, we are justified in ascribing to the preferred enjoyment a superiority in quality, so far outweighing quantity as to render it, in comparison, of small account.

Now it is an unquestionable fact that those who are equally acquainted with, and equally capable of appreciating and enjoying, both, do give a most marked preference to the manner of existence which employs their higher faculties. Few human creatures would consent to be changed into any of the lower animals, for a promise of the fullest allowance of a beast's pleasures; no intelligent human being would consent to be a fool, no instructed person would be an ignoramus, no person of feeling and conscience would be selfish and base, even though they should be persuaded that the fool, the dunce, or the rascal is better satisfied with his lot than they are with theirs. They would not resign what they possess more than he for the most complete satisfaction of all the desires which they have in common with him. If they ever fancy they would, it is only in cases of unhappiness so extreme, that to escape from it they would exchange their lot for almost any other, however undesirable in their own eyes. A being of higher faculties requires more to make him happy, is capable probably of more acute suffering, and certainly accessible to it at more points, than one of an inferior type; but in spite of these liabilities, he can never really wish to sink into what he feels to be a lower grade of existence. We may give what explanation we please of this unwillingness; we may attribute it to pride, a name which is given indiscriminately to some of the most and to some of the least estimable feelings of which mankind are capable; we may refer it to the love of liberty and personal independence, an appeal to which was with the Stoics one of the most effective means for the inculcation of it; to the love of power, or to the love of excitement, both of which do really enter into and contribute to it:

but its most appropriate appellation is a sense of dignity, which all human beings possess in one form or another, and in some, though by no means in exact, proportion to their higher faculties, and which is so essential a part of the happiness of those in whom it is strong, that nothing which conflicts with it could be, otherwise than momentarily, an object of desire to them. Whoever supposes that this preference takes place at a sacrifice of happiness—that the superior being, in anything like equal circumstances, is not happier than the inferior—confounds the two very different ideas, of happiness, and content. It is indisputable that the being whose capacities of enjoyment are low, has the greatest chance of having them fully satisfied; and a highly endowed being will always feel that any happiness which he can look for, as the world is constituted, is imperfect. But he can learn to bear its imperfections, if they are at all bearable; and they will not make him envy the being who is indeed unconscious of the imperfections, but only because he feels not at all the good which those imperfections qualify. It is better to be a human being dissatisfied than a pig satisfied; better to be Socrates dissatisfied than a fool satisfied. And if the fool, or the pig, are of a different opinion, it is because they only know their own side of the question. The other party to the comparison knows both sides.

It may be objected, that many who are capable of the higher pleasures, occasionally, under the influence of temptation, postpone them to the lower. But this is quite compatible with a full appreciation of the intrinsic superiority of the higher. Men often, from infirmity of character, make their election for the nearer good, though they know it to be the less valuable; and this no less when the choice is between two bodily pleasures, than when it is between bodily and mental. They pursue sensual indulgences to the injury of health, though perfectly aware that health is the greater good. It may be further objected, that many who begin with youthful enthusiasm for everything noble, as they advance in years sink into indolence and selfishness. But I do not believe that those who undergo this very common change, voluntarily choose the lower description of pleasures in preference to the higher. I believe that before they devote themselves exclusively to the one, they have already become incapable of the other. Capacity for the nobler feelings is in most natures a very tender plant, easily killed, not only by hostile influences, but by mere want of sustenance; and in the majority of young persons it speedily dies away if the occupations to which their position in life has devoted them, and the society into which it has thrown them, are not favourable to keeping that higher capacity in exercise. Men lose their high aspirations as they lose their intellectual tastes, because they have not time or opportunity for indulging them; and they addict themselves to inferior pleasures, not because they deliberately prefer them, but because they are either the only ones to which they have access, or the only ones which they are any longer capable of enjoying. It may be questioned whether any one who has remained equally susceptible to both classes of pleasures, ever knowingly and calmly preferred the lower; though many, in all ages, have broken down in an ineffectual attempt to combine both.

From this verdict of the only competent judges, I apprehend there can be no appeal. On a question which is the best worth having of two pleasures, or which of two modes of existence is the most grateful to the feelings, apart from its moral attributes and from its consequences, the judgment of those who are qualified by knowledge of both, or, if they differ, that of the majority among them, must be admitted as final. And there needs to be the less hesitation to accept this judgment respecting the quality of pleasures, since there is no other tribunal to be referred to even on the question of quantity. What means are there of determining which is the acutest of two pains, or the intensest of two pleasurable sensations, except the general suffrage of those who are familiar with both? Neither pains nor pleasures are homogeneous, and pain is always heterogeneous with pleasure. What is there to decide whether a particular pleasure is worth purchasing at the cost of a particular pain, except the feelings and judgment of the experienced? When, therefore, those feelings and judgment declare the pleasures derived from the higher faculties to be preferable *in kind,* apart from the question of intensity, to those of which the animal nature, disjoined from the higher faculties, is susceptible, they are entitled on this subject to the same regard.

I have dwelt on this point, as being a necessary part of a perfectly just conception of Utility or Happiness, considered as the directive rule of human conduct. But it is by no means an indispensable condition to the acceptance of the utilitarian standard; for that standard is not the agent's own greatest happiness, but the greatest amount of happiness altogether; and if it may possibly be doubted whether a noble character is always the happier for its nobleness, there can be no doubt that it makes other people happier, and that the world in general is immensely a gainer by it. Utilitarianism, therefore, could only attain its end by the general cultivation of nobleness of character, even if each individual were only benefited by the nobleness of others, and his own, so far as happiness is concerned, were a sheer deduction from the benefit. But the bare enunciation of such an absurdity as this last, renders refutation superfluous.

According to the Greatest Happiness Principle, as above explained, the ultimate end, with reference to and for the sake of which all other things are desirable (whether we are considering our own good or that of other people), is an existence exempt as far as possible from pain, and as rich as possible in enjoyments, both in point of quantity and quality; the test of quality, and the rule for measuring it against quantity, being the preference felt by those who in their opportunities of experience, to which must be added their habits of self-consciousness and self-observation, are best furnished with the means of comparison. This, being, according to the utilitarian opinion, the end of human action, is necessarily also the standard of morality; which may accordingly be defined, the rules and precepts for human conduct, by the observance of which an existence such as has been described might be, to the greatest extent possible, secured to all mankind; and not to them only, but, so far as the nature of things admits, to the whole sentient creation. . . .

The objectors to utilitarianism cannot always be charged with representing it in a discreditable light. On the contrary, those among them who entertain anything like a just idea of its disinterested character, sometimes find fault with its standard as being too high for humanity. They say it is exacting too much to require that people shall always act from the inducement of promoting the general interests of society. But this is to mistake the very meaning of a standard of morals, and confound the rule of action with the motive of it. It is the business of ethics to tell us what are our duties, or by what test we may know them; but no system of ethics requires that the sole motive of all we do shall be a feeling of duty; on the contrary, ninety-nine hundredths of all our actions are done from other motives, and rightly so done, if the rule of duty does not condemn them. It is the more unjust to utilitarianism that this particular misapprehension should be made a ground of objection to it, inasmuch as utilitarian moralists have gone beyond almost all others in affirming that the motive has nothing to do with the morality of the action, though much with the worth of the agent. He who saves a fellow-creature from drowning does what is morally right, whether his motive be duty, or the hope of being paid for his trouble; he who betrays the friend that trusts him, is guilty of a crime, even if his object be to serve another friend to whom he is under greater obligation. But to speak only of actions done from the motive of duty, and in direct obedience to principle: it is a misapprehension of the utilitarian mode of thought, to conceive it as implying that people should fix their minds upon so wide a generality as the world, or society at large. The great majority of good actions are intended not for the benefit of the world, but for that of individuals, of which the good of the world is made up; and the thoughts of the most virtuous man need not on these occasions travel beyond the particular persons concerned, except so far as is necessary to assure himself that in benefiting them he is not violating the rights, that is, the legitimate and authorised expectations, of any one else. The multiplication of happiness is, according to the utilitarian ethics, the object of virtue: the occasions on which any person (except one in a thousand) has it in his power to do this on an extended scale, in other words to be a public benefactor, are but exceptional; and on these occasions alone is he called on to consider public utility; in every other case, private utility, the interest or happiness of some few persons, is all he has to attend to. Those alone the influence of whose actions extends to society in general, need concern themselves habitually about so large an object. In the case of abstinences indeed—of things which people forbear to do from moral considerations, though the consequences in the particular case might be beneficial—it would be unworthy of an intelligent agent not to be consciously aware that the action is of a class which, if practised generally, would be generally injurious, and that this is the ground of the obligation to abstain from it. The amount of regard for the public interest implied in this recognition, is no greater than is demanded by every system of morals, for they all enjoin to abstain from whatever is manifestly pernicious to society. . . .

CHAPTER IV OF WHAT SORT OF PROOF THE PRINCIPLE OF UTILITY IS SUSCEPTIBLE

It has already been remarked, that questions of ultimate ends do not admit of proof, in the ordinary acceptation of the term. To be incapable of proof by reasoning is common to all first principles; to the first premises of our knowledge, as well as to those of our conduct. But the former, being matters of fact, may be the subject of a direct appeal to the faculties which judge of fact—namely, our senses, and our internal consciousness. Can an appeal be made to the same faculties on questions of practical ends? Or by what other faculty is cognisance taken of them?

Questions about ends are, in other words, questions about what things are desirable. The utilitarian doctrine is, that happiness is desirable, and the only thing desirable, as an end; all other things being only desirable as means to that end. What ought to be required of this doctrine—what conditions is it requisite that the doctrine should fulfill—to make good its claim to be believed? The only proof capable of being given that an object is visible, is that people actually see it.

The only proof that a sound is audible, is that people hear it: and so of the other sources of our experience. In like manner, I apprehend, the sole evidence it is possible to produce that anything is desirable, is that people do actually desire it. If the end which the utilitarian doctrine proposes to itself were not, in theory and in practice, acknowledged to be an end, nothing could ever convince any person that it was so. No reason can be given why the general happiness is desirable, except that each person, so far as he believes it to be attainable, desires his own happiness. This, however, being a fact, we have not only all the proof which the case admits of, but all which it is possible to require, that happiness is a good: that each person's happiness is a good to that person, and the general happiness, therefore, a good to the aggregate of all persons. Happiness has made out its title as *one* of the ends of conduct, and consequently one of the criteria of morality.

But it has not, by this alone, proved itself to be the sole criterion. To do that, it would seem, by the same rule, necessary to show, not only that people desire happiness, but that they never desire anything else. . . .

We have now, then, an answer to the question, of what sort of proof the principle of utility is susceptible. If the opinion which I have now stated is psychologically true—if human nature is so constituted as to desire nothing which is not either a part of happiness or a means of happiness, we can have no other proof, and we require no other, that these are the only things desirable. If so, happiness is the sole end of human action, and the promotion of it the test by which to judge of all human conduct; from whence it necessarily follows that it must be the criterion of morality, since a part is included in the whole.

And now to decide whether this is really so; whether mankind does desire nothing for itself but that which is a pleasure to them, or of which the absence is a pain; we have evidently arrived at a question of fact and experience, dependent, like all similar questions, upon evidence. It can only be determined by practised self-consciousness and self-observation, assisted by observation of others. I believe that these sources of evidence, impartially consulted, will declare that desiring a thing and finding it pleasant, aversion to it and thinking of it as painful, are phenomena entirely inseparable, or rather two parts of the same phenomenon; in strictness of language, two different modes of naming the same psychological fact: that to think of an object as desirable (unless for the sake of its consequences), and to think of it as pleasant, are one and the same thing; and that to desire anything, except in proportion as the idea of it is pleasant, is a physical and metaphysical impossibility.

For Further Reflection

1. To better grasp the difference between utilitarianism and deontological ethics, consider this example. Suppose a raft is floating in the Pacific Ocean. On the raft are two men starving to death. One day they discover some food in an inner compartment of a box on the raft. They have reason to believe that the food will be sufficient to keep one of them alive until the raft reaches a certain island where help is available, but if they share the food, both will most likely die. Now, one of these men is a brilliant scientist who has in his mind the cure for cancer. The other man is undistinguished. Otherwise there is no relevant difference between the two. What is the morally right thing to do? Share the food and hope against the odds for a miracle? Flip a coin to see which man gets the food? Give the food to the scientist? If you voted to flip a coin or share the food, you sided with the deontologist, but if you voted to give the food to the scientist, you sided with the teleologist, the utilitarian, who would calculate that there would be greater good accomplished as a result of the scientist getting the food and living than in any of the other likely outcomes. It has often been admitted that utilitarianism could easily be misused. If people tried to "play God" and decide each case on the basis of what they thought would be the "best" consequences, chaos might result, so that some utilitarians have advocated keeping their doctrine a secret. What do you think of both the prediction of the anti-utilitarian consequences of widespread utilitarianism and the prescription of keeping the doctrine a secret?

2. John Rawls has argued that the fault of utilitarianism is that it makes a false inference from what one is allowed to do with one's own life to what one is allowed to do with other people's lives. We often have a right to forgo some present enjoyment for the sake of a future personal higher goal, but, he argues, we have not the same right to restrict some other person from a present enjoyment for what we deem to be his higher future goal. That is, utilitarianism is a paternalistic violator of human rights. It treats rights as expendable. Do you agree with this criticism?

3. What do you see as the overall merits and liabilities of deontological and utilitarian systems? Where do you stand at this juncture?

4. Nietzsche wrote, "If we possess our *why* of life we can put up with almost any *how*— Man does not strive after happiness; only the Englishman does that" (Friedrich Nietzsche, *Twilight of the Idols*). Do you agree or disagree with Nietzsche on the unimportance of the search for happiness?

VI.66   Existentialist Ethics

JEAN-PAUL SARTRE

Jean-Paul Sartre (1905–1980), born in Paris, was a teacher in a French high school. He served in the French army during World War II, was captured by the Germans, and spent his time in a prison camp reading German philosophers (especially Hegel, Husserl, and Heidegger). After the war, Sartre's plays, novels, and philosophical work, especially *Being and Nothingness* (1943), set him apart as Europe's premier existentialist. Later he combined existentialism with Marxism, though he never joined the Communist party.

Here is Paul Johnson's description of Sartre's impact, and the essay we are about to read, on French society:

> [On October 29, 1945, shortly after the end of the war], at the Club Maintenant, Jean-Paul Sartre delivered a lecture, "Existentialism is a Humanism." Here was the new Paris. This occasion . . . was packed. Men and women fainted, fought for chairs, smashing thirty of them, shouted and barracked. It coincided with the launching of Sartre's new review, *Les Temps Modernes,* in which he argued that literary culture, plus the haute couture of the fashion shops, were the only things France now had left—a symbol of Europe, really—and he produced Existentialism to give people a bit of dignity and to preserve their individuality in the midst of degradation and absurdity. The response was overwhelming. As his consort, Simone de Beauvoir, put it, "We were astounded by the furore we caused." Existentialism was remarkably un-Gallic; hence perhaps, its attractiveness. Sartre was half-Alsacian (Albert Schweitzer was his cousin) and he was brought up in the house of his grandfather, Karl Schweitzer. His culture was as much German as French. He was essentially a product of the Berlin school and especially Heidegger, from whom most of his ideas derived. . . . Thus Existentialism was a French cultural import, which Paris then re-exported to Germany, its country of origin, in a sophisticated and vastly more attractive guise. (Paul Johnson, *Modern Times,* Harper & Row, 1983, p. 575f)

In this essay Sartre sets forth the principles of atheistic existentialism: that we are completely free; that since there is no God to give us an essence, we must create our own essence; that we are completely responsible for our actions and are responsible for everyone else too; that because of the death of God and the human predicament, which leaves us totally free to create our values and our world, we must exist in anguish, forlornness, and despair. Yet there is a certain celebration and optimism in knowing that we are creators of our own values.

In this essay you will come across Sartre's notion that "existence precedes essence." This is a difficult idea, but he seems to mean something like the following. If you have an idea of something in your mind first and then create it, we would say that the idea (essence) of the thing preceded the actuality or existence of the thing. But if the thing existed before any idea of it, then its existence preceded its essence. If there were a God who created us, who had us in mind, we would have an essence (in terms of a function or purpose) and our existence would succeed our essence, but since, according to Sartre, there is no God to create us, we simply find ourselves existing and must create our own essence (that is, give ourselves a function or purpose). This is a start at getting at the meaning of this difficult phrase. Perhaps you can improve on this explanation.

Study Questions

1. What are the two meanings of "subjectivism" in this essay?
2. What does Sartre mean by saying that responsibility for our actions involves being responsible for everyone? How does he answer those who deny this thesis? Has Sartre begged the question against them?
3. Describe Sartre's notion of anguish. Why must we experience it? Is his argument cogent?
4. Describe Sartre's notion of forlornness. Why must we experience it? Is his argument clear and plausible?
5. What does Sartre mean by saying that we are "condemned to be free"?
6. Examine the case of the student who finds himself in a moral dilemma. Is Sartre correct, that there are no objective principles to help him make his decision, but he must make a leap of faith?

WHAT IS MEANT by the term *existentialism?*

Most people who use the word would be rather embarrassed if they had to explain it, since, now that the word is all the rage, even the work of a musician or painter is being called existentialist. . . . It seems that for want of an advance-guard doctrine analogous to surrealism, the kind of people who are eager for scandal and flurry turn to this philosophy which in other respects does not at all serve their purposes in this sphere.

Actually, it is the least scandalous, the most austere of doctrines. It is intended strictly for specialists and philosophers. Yet it can be defined easily. What complicates matters is that there are two kinds of existentialists; first, those who are Christian, among whom I would include Jaspers and Gabriel Marcel, both Catholic; and on the other hand, the atheistic existentialists, among whom I class Heidegger, and then the French existentialists and myself. What they have in common is that they think that existence precedes essence, or, if you prefer, that subjectivity must be the starting point.

Just what does that mean? Let us consider some object that is manufactured, for example, a book or a paper-cutter: here is an object which has been made by an artisan whose inspiration came from a concept. He referred to the concept of what a paper-cutter is and likewise to a known method of production, which is part of the concept, something which is, by and large, a routine. Thus, the paper-cutter is at once an object produced in a certain way and, on the other hand, one having a specific use; and one cannot postulate a man who produces a paper-cutter but does not know what it is used for. Therefore, let us say that, for the paper-cutter, essence—that is, the ensemble of both the production routines and the properties which enable it to be both produced and defined—precedes existence. Thus, the presence of the paper-cutter or book in front of me is determined. Therefore, we have here a technical view of the world whereby it can be said that production precedes existence.

When we conceive God as the Creator, He is generally thought of as a superior sort of artisan.

Jean-Paul Sartre, Existentialism, *trans. Bernard Frechtman (New York, 1947). Reprinted by permission of the Philosophical Library, Inc.*

Whatever doctrine we may be considering, whether one like that of Descartes or that of Leibnitz, we always grant that will more or less follows understanding or, at the very least, accompanies it, and that when God creates He knows exactly what He is creating. Thus, the concept of man in the mind of God is comparable to the concept of paper-cutter in the mind of the manufacturer, and, following certain techniques and a conception, God produces man, just as the artisan, following a definition and a technique, makes a paper-cutter. Thus, the individual man is the realization of a certain concept in the divine intelligence.

In the eighteenth century, the atheism of the *philosophes* discarded the idea of God, but not so much for the notion that essence precedes existence. To a certain extent, this idea is found everywhere; we find it in Diderot, in Voltaire, and even in Kant. Man has a human nature; this human nature, which is the concept of the human, is found in all men, which means that each man is a particular example of a universal concept, man. In Kant, the result of this universality is that the wild-man, the natural man, as well as the bourgeois, are circumscribed by the same definition and have the same basic qualities. Thus, here too the essence of man precedes the historical existence that we find in nature.

Atheistic existentialism, which I represent, is more coherent. It states that if God does not exist, there is at least one being in whom existence precedes essence, a being who exists before he can be defined by any concept, and that this being is man, or, as Heidegger says, human reality. What is meant here by saying that existence precedes essence? It means that, first of all, man exists, turns up, appears on the scene, and, only afterwards, defines himself. If man, as the existentialist conceives him, is indefinable, it is because at first he is nothing. Only afterward will he be something, and he himself will have made what he will be. Thus, there is no human nature, since there is no God to conceive it. Not only is man what he conceives himself to be, but he is also only what he wills himself to be after this thrust toward existence.

Man is nothing else but what he makes of himself. Such is the first principle of existentialism. It is also what is called subjectivity, the name we are labeled with when charges are brought against us. But what do we mean by this, if not that man has a greater dignity than a stone or table? For we mean that man first exists, that is, that man first of all is the being in the future. Man is at the start a plan which is aware of itself, rather than a patch of moss, a piece of garbage, or a cauliflower; nothing exists prior to this plan; there is nothing in heaven; man will be what he will have planned to be. Not what he will want to be. Because by the word "will" we generally mean a conscious decision, which is subsequent to what we have already made of ourselves. I may want to belong to a political party, write a book, get married; but all that is only a manifestation of an earlier, more spontaneous choice that is called "will." But if existence really does precede essence, man is responsible for what he is. Thus, existentialism's first move is to make every man aware of what he is and to make the full responsibility of his existence rest on him. And when we say that a man is responsible for himself, we do not only mean that he is responsible for his own individuality, but that he is responsible for all men.

The word subjectivism has two meanings, and our opponents play on the two. Subjectivism means, on the one hand, that an individual chooses and makes himself; and, on the other, that it is impossible for man to transcend human subjectivity. The second of these is the essential meaning of existentialism. When we say that man chooses his own self, we mean that every one of us does likewise; but we also mean by that that in making this choice he also chooses all men. In fact, in creating the man that we want to be, there is not a single one of our acts which does not at the same time create an image of man as we think he ought to be. To choose to be this or that is to affirm at the same time the value of what we choose, because we can never choose evil. We always choose the good, and nothing can be good for us without being good for all.

If, on the other hand, existence precedes essence, and if we grant that we exist and fashion our image at one and the same time, the image is valid for everybody and for our whole age. Thus, our responsibility is much greater than we might have supposed, because it involves all mankind. If I am a workingman and choose to join a Christian trade-union rather than be a communist, and if by being a member I want to show that the best thing for man is resignation, that the kingdom of man is not of this world, I am not only involving my own case—I want to be resigned for everyone. As a result, my action has involved all humanity. To take a more individual matter, if I want to marry, to have children; even if this marriage depends solely on my own circumstances or passion or wish, I am involving all humanity in monogamy and not merely myself. Therefore, I am responsible for myself and for everyone else. I am creating a certain image of man of my own choosing. In choosing myself, I choose man.

This helps us understand what the actual content is of such rather grandiloquent words as anguish, forlornness, despair. As you will see, it's all quite simple.

First, what is meant by anguish? The existentialists say at once that man is anguish. What that means is this: the man who involves himself and who realizes that he is not only the person he chooses to be, but also a law-maker who is, at the same time, choosing all mankind as well as himself, cannot help escape the feeling of his total and deep responsibility. Of course, there are many people who are not anxious; but we claim that they are hiding their anxiety, that they are fleeing from it. Certainly, many people believe that when they do something, they themselves are the only ones involved, and when someone says to them, "What if everyone acted that way?" they shrug their shoulders and answer, "Everyone doesn't act that way." But really, one should always ask himself, "What would happen if everybody looked at things that way?" There is no escaping this disturbing thought except by a kind of double-dealing. A man who lies and makes excuses for himself by saying "not everybody does that," is someone with an uneasy conscience, because the act of lying implies that a universal value is conferred upon the lie.

Anguish is evident even when it conceals itself. This is the anguish that Kierkegaard called the anguish of Abraham. You know the story: an angel has ordered Abraham to sacrifice his son; if it really were an angel who has come and said, "You are Abraham, you shall sacrifice your son," everything would be all right. But everyone might first wonder, "Is it really an angel, and am I really Abraham? What proof do I have?" . . .

Now, I'm not being singled out as an Abraham, and yet at every moment I'm obliged to perform exemplary acts. For every man, everything happens as if all mankind had its eyes fixed on him and were guiding itself by what he does. And every man ought to say to himself, "Am I really the kind of man who has the right to act in such a way that humanity might guide itself by my actions?" And if he does not say that to himself, he is masking his anguish.

There is no question here of the kind of anguish which would lead to quietism, to inaction. It is a matter of a simple sort of anguish that anybody who has had responsibilities is familiar with. For example, when a military officer takes the responsibility for an attack and sends a certain number of men to death, he chooses to do so, and in the main he alone makes the choice. Doubtless, orders come from above, but they are too broad; he interprets them, and on this interpretation depend the lives of ten or fourteen or twenty men. In making a decision he cannot help having a certain anguish. All leaders know this anguish. That doesn't keep them from acting; on the contrary, it is the very condition of their action. For it implies that they envisage a number of possibilities, and when they choose one, they realize that it has value only because it is chosen. We shall see that this kind of anguish, which is the kind that existentialism describes, is explained, in addition, by a direct responsibility to the other men whom it involves. It is not a curtain separating us from action, but is part of action itself.

When we speak of forlornness, a term Heidegger was fond of, we mean only that God does not exist and that we have to face all the consequences of this. The existentialist is strongly opposed to a certain kind of secular ethics which would like to abolish God with the least possible expense. About 1880, some French teachers tried to set up a secular ethics which went something like this: God is a useless and costly hypothesis; we are discarding it; but meanwhile, in order for there to be an ethics, a society, a civilization, it is essential that certain values be taken seriously and that they be considered as having an *a priori* existence. It must be obligatory, *a priori,* to be honest, not to lie, not to beat your wife, to have children, etc., etc. So we're going to try a little device which will make it possible to show that values exist all the same, inscribed in a heaven of ideas, though otherwise God does not exist. In other words—and this, I believe, is the tendency of everything called reformism in France—nothing will be changed if God does not exist. We shall find ourselves with the same norms of honesty, progress, and humanism, and we shall have made of God an outdated hypothesis which will peacefully die off by itself.

The existentialist, on the contrary, thinks it very distressing that God does not exist, because all possibility of finding values in a heaven of ideas disappears along with Him; there can be no longer an *a priori* Good, since there is no infinite and perfect consciousness to think it. Nowhere is it written that the Good exists, that we must be honest, that we must not lie; because the fact is we are on a plane where there are only men. Dostoievsky said, "If God didn't exist, everything would be possible." That is the very starting point of existentialism. Indeed, everything is permissible if God does not exist, and as a result man is forlorn, because neither within him nor without does he find anything to cling to. He can't start making excuses for himself.

If existence really does precede essence, there is no explaining things away by reference to a fixed and given human nature. In other words, there is no determinism, man is free, man is freedom. On the other hand, if God does not exist, we find no values or commands to turn to which legitimize our conduct. So, in the bright realm of values, we have no excuse behind us, no justification before us. We are alone, with no excuses.

That is the idea I shall try to convey when I say that man is condemned to be free. Condemned, because he did not create himself, yet, in other respects is free; because, once thrown into the world, he is responsible for everything he does.

The existentialist does not believe in the power of passion. He will never agree that a sweeping passion is a ravaging torrent which fatally leads a man to certain acts and is therefore an excuse. He thinks that man is responsible for his passion.

The existentialist does not think that man is going to help himself by finding in the world some omen by which to orient himself, because he thinks that man will interpret the omen to suit himself. Therefore, he thinks that man, with no support and no aid, is condemned every moment to invent man. Ponge, in a very fine article, has said, "Man is the future of man." That's exactly it. But if it is taken to mean that this future is recorded in heaven, that God sees it, then it is false, because it would really no longer be a future. If it is taken to mean that, whatever a man may be, there is a future to be forged, a virgin future before him, then this remark is sound. But then we are forlorn.

To give you an example which will enable you to understand forlornness better, I shall cite the case of one of my students who came to see me under the following circumstances: his father was on bad terms with his mother, and, moreover, was inclined to be a collaborationist; his older brother had been killed in the German offensive of 1940, and the young man, with somewhat immature but generous feelings, wanted to avenge him. His mother lived alone with him, very much upset by the half-treason of her husband and the death of her older son; the boy was her only consolation.

The boy was faced with the choice of leaving for England and joining the Free French Forces—that is, leaving his mother behind—or remaining with his mother and helping her to carry on. He was fully aware that the woman lived only for him and that his going-off—and perhaps his death—would plunge her into despair. He was also aware that every act that he did for his mother's sake was a sure thing, in the sense that it was helping her to carry on, whereas every effort he made toward going off and fighting was an uncertain move which might run aground and prove completely useless; for example, on his way to England he might, while passing through Spain, be detained indefinitely in a Spanish camp; he might reach England or Algiers and be stuck in an office at a desk job. As a result, he was faced with two very different kinds of action: one, concrete, immediate, but concerning only one individual; the other concerned an incomparably vaster group, a national collectivity, but for that very reason was dubious, and might be interrupted en route. And, at the same time, he was wavering between two kinds of ethics. On the one hand, an ethics of sympathy, of personal devotion; on the other, a broader ethics, but one whose efficacy was more dubious. He had to choose between the two.

Who could help him choose? Christian doctrine? No. Christian doctrine says, "Be charitable, love your neighbor, take the more rugged path, etc., etc." But which is the more rugged path? Whom should he love as a brother? The fighting man or his mother? Which does the greater good, the vague act of fighting in a group, or the concrete one of helping a particular human being to go on living? Who can decide *a priori*? Nobody. No book of ethics can tell him. The Kantian ethics says, "Never treat any person as a means, but as an end." Very well, if I stay with my mother, I'll treat her as an end and not as a means; but by virtue of this very fact, I'm running the risk of treating the people around me who are fighting, as means; and, conversely, if I go to join those who are fighting, I'll be treating them as an end, and, by doing that, I run the risk of treating my mother as a means.

If values are vague, and if they are always too broad for the concrete and specific case that we are considering, the only thing left for us is to trust our instincts. That's what this young man tried to do; and when I saw him, he said, "In the end, feeling is what counts. I ought to choose whichever pushes me in one direction. If I feel that I love my mother enough to sacrifice everything else for

her—my desire for vengeance, for action, for adventure—then I'll stay with her. If, on the contrary, I feel that my love for my mother isn't enough, I'll leave."

But how is the value of a feeling determined? What gives his feeling for his mother value? Precisely the fact that he remained with her. I may say that I like so-and-so well enough to sacrifice a certain amount of money for him, but I may say so only if I've done it. I may say, "I love my mother well enough to remain with her" if I have remained with her. The only way to determine the value of this affection is, precisely, to perform an act which confirms and defines it. But, since I require this affection to justify my act, I find myself caught in a vicious circle. . . .

As for despair, the term has a very simple meaning. It means that we shall confine ourselves to reckoning only with what depends upon our will, or on the ensemble of probabilities which make our action possible. When we want something, we always have to reckon with probabilities. I may be counting on the arrival of a friend. The friend is coming by rail or street-car; this supposes that the train will arrive on schedule, or that the street-car will not jump the track. I am left in the realm of possibility, but possibilities are to be reckoned with only to the point where my action comports with the ensemble of these possibilities, and no further. The moment the possibilities I am considering are not rigorously involved by my action, I ought to disengage myself from them, because no God, no scheme, can adapt the world and its possibilities to my will. When Descartes said, "Conquer yourself rather than the world," he meant essentially the same thing.

The Marxists to whom I have spoken reply, "You can rely on the support of others in your action, which obviously has certain limits because you're not going to live forever. That means: rely on both what others are doing elsewhere to help you, in China, in Russia, and what they will do later on, after your death, to carry on the action and lead it to its fulfillment, which will be the revolution. You even *have* to rely upon that, otherwise you're immortal." I reply at once that I will always rely on fellow fighters insofar as these comrades are involved with me in a common struggle, in the unity of a party or a group in which I can more or less make my weight felt; that is, one whose ranks I am in as a fighter and whose movements I am aware of at every moment. In such a situation, relying on the unity and will of the party is exactly like counting on the fact that the train will arrive on time or that the car won't jump the track. But, given that man is free and that there is no human nature for me to depend on, I cannot count on men whom I do not know by relying on human goodness or man's concern for the good of society. I don't know what will become of the Russian revolution; I may make an example of it to the extent that at the present time it is apparent that the proletariat plays a part in Russia that it plays in no other nation. But I can't swear that this will inevitably lead to a triumph of the proletariat. I've got to limit myself to what I see.

Given that men are free, and that tomorrow they will freely decide what man will be, I cannot be sure that, after my death, fellow fighters will carry on my work to bring it to its maximum perfection. Tomorrow, after my death, some men

may decide to set up Fascism, and the others may be cowardly and muddled enough to let them do it. Fascism will then be the human reality, so much the worse for us.

Actually, things will be as man will have decided they are to be. Does that mean that I should abandon myself to quietism? No. First, I should involve myself; then, act on the old saw, "Nothing ventured, nothing gained." Nor does it mean that I shouldn't belong to a party, but rather that I shall have no illusions and shall do what I can. For example, suppose I ask myself, "Will socialization, as such, ever come about?" I know nothing about it. All I know is that I'm going to do everything in my power to bring it about. Beyond that, I can't count on anything. Quietism is the attitude of people who say, "Let others do what I can't do." The doctrine I am presenting is the very opposite of quietism, since it declares, "There is no reality except in action." Moreover, it goes further, since it adds, "Man is nothing else than his plan; he exists only to the extent that he fulfills himself; he is, therefore, nothing else than the ensemble of his acts, nothing else than his life."

For Further Reflection

1. How are existentialist ethics different from other theories we have studied? What are its strengths and weaknesses?

2. Has Sartre gotten to the heart of the matter with his example of the student who must choose between his mother and the war effort? Could we object that he is making an exception to the norm? In normal situations we know perfectly well the right thing to do. For example, suppose that there was no war; then, wouldn't it be automatically right to take care of the mother? Does existentialism have a response to this criticism?

3. Sartre believes that it makes all the difference in the world whether God exists. If God does not exist, all things are morally permissible, there is no right or wrong, but thinking makes it so. Is this correct?

The Divine Command Theory   VI.67

JAMES RACHELS

Does morality depend on God for its legitimacy? Specifically, is an action right (or wrong) because God commands that it be so—or is it right (or wrong) independent of God's commands, so that God himself must answer to the moral law? The view that morality does depend on God is known as the divine command theory, and James Rachels critiques it in this reading. He argues that this conception of morality is false and that neither the theist nor nontheist should accept it.

(A biographical sketch of Rachels precedes Reading VI.59.)

Study Questions

1. Rachels says that if we accept the divine command theory, we are caught in a dilemma. Explain the dilemma.
2. According to Rachels, why shouldn't a religious person accept the divine command theory? What would be the implications of such acceptance?
3. What is the theory's arbitrariness problem?
4. What way out of the theory's problems does Rachels think is most reasonable?
5. Summarize Rachels' argument.

IN THE MAJOR THEISTIC TRADITIONS, including Judaism, Christianity, and Islam, God is conceived as a lawgiver who has laid down rules that we are to obey. He does not compel us to obey them. We were created as free agents, so we may choose to accept or to reject his commandments. But if we are to live as we should live, we must follow God's laws. This conception has been elaborated by some theologians into a theory about the nature of right and wrong known as the Divine Command Theory. Essentially, this theory says that "morally right" means "commanded by God" and "morally wrong" means "forbidden by God."

This theory has a number of attractive features. It immediately solves the old problem about the objectivity of ethics. Ethics is not merely a matter of personal feeling or social custom. Whether something is right or wrong is perfectly objective: It is right if God commands it, wrong if God forbids it. Moreover, the Divine Command Theory suggests an answer to the perennial question of why anyone should bother with morality. Why not forget about "ethics" and just look out for oneself? If immorality is the violation of God's commandments, there is an easy answer: On the day of final reckoning, you will be held accountable.

There are, however, serious problems for the theory. Of course, atheists would not accept it, because they do not believe that God exists. But there are difficulties even for believers. The main problem was first noted by Plato, the Greek philosopher who lived 400 years before the birth of Jesus.

Plato's writings were in the form of dialogues, usually between Socrates and one or more interlocutors. In one of these dialogues, the *Euthyphro,* there is a discussion concerning whether "right" can be defined as "that which the gods command." Socrates is skeptical and asks: Is conduct right because the gods command it, or do the gods command it because it is right? This is one of the most famous questions in the history of philosophy. The British philosopher Antony Flew suggests that "one good test of a person's aptitude for philosophy is to discover whether he can grasp its force and point."

The point is that if we accept the theological conception of right and wrong, we are caught in a dilemma. Socrates's question asks us to clarify what we mean. There are two things we might mean, and both lead to trouble.

1. First, we might mean that *right conduct is right because God commands it.* For example, according to Exodus 20:16, God commands us to be truthful. On this option, the reason we should be truthful is simply that God requires it. Apart from the divine command, truth telling is neither good nor bad. It is God's command that *makes* truthfulness right.

But this leads to trouble, for it represents God's commands as arbitrary. It means that God could have given different commands just as easily. He could have commanded us to be liars, and then lying, and not truthfulness, would be right. (You may be tempted to reply: "But God would never command us to lie." But why not? If he did endorse lying, God would not be commanding us to do wrong, because his command would make it right.) Remember that on this view, honesty was not right before God commanded it. Therefore, he could have had no more reason to command it than its opposite; and so, from a moral point of view, his command is arbitrary.

Another problem is that, on this view, the doctrine of the goodness of God is reduced to nonsense. It is important to religious believers that God is not only all-powerful and all-knowing, but that he is also good; yet if we accept the idea that good and bad are defined by reference to

God's will, this notion is deprived of any meaning. What could it mean to say that God's commands are good? If "X is good" means "X is commanded by God," then "God's commands are good" would mean only "God's commands are commanded by God," an empty truism. In 1686, Leibniz observed in his *Discourse on Metaphysics:*

> So in saying that things are not good by any rule of goodness, but sheerly by the will of God, it seems to me that one destroys, without realizing it, all the love of God and all his glory. For why praise him for what he has done if he would be equally praiseworthy in doing exactly the contrary?

Thus if we choose the first of Socrates's two options, we seem to be stuck with consequences that even the most religious people would find unacceptable.

2. There is a way to avoid these troublesome consequences. We can take the second of Socrates's options. We need not say that right conduct is right because God commands it. Instead, we may say that God commands us to do certain things *because they are right.* God, who is infinitely wise, realizes that truthfulness is better than deceitfulness, and so he commands us to be truthful; he sees that killing is wrong, and so he commands us not to kill; and so on for all the moral rules.

If we take this option, we avoid the troublesome consequences that spoiled the first alternative. God's commands are not arbitrary; they are the result of his wisdom in knowing what is best. And the doctrine of the goodness of God is preserved: To say that his commands are good means that he commands only what, in perfect wisdom, he sees to be best.

Unfortunately, however, this second option leads to a different problem, which is equally troublesome. In taking this option, we have abandoned the theological conception of right and wrong—when we say that God commands us to be truthful because truthfulness is right, we are acknowledging a standard of right and wrong that is independent of God's will. The rightness exists prior to and independent of God's command, and it is the reason for the command. Thus, if we want to know why we should be truthful, the reply "Because God commands it" does not really tell us, for we may still ask "But why does God command it?" and the answer to *that* question will provide the underlying reason why truthfulness is a good thing.

All this may be summarized in the following argument:

(1) Suppose God commands us to do what is right. Then either (a) the right actions are right because he commands them or (b) he commands them because they are right.

(2) If we take option (a), then God's commands are, from a moral point of view, arbitrary; moreover, the doctrine of the goodness of God is rendered meaningless.

(3) If we take option (b), then we will have acknowledged a standard of right and wrong that is independent of God's will. We will have, in effect, given up the theological conception of right and wrong.

(4) Therefore, we must either regard God's commands as arbitrary, and give up the doctrine of the goodness of God, or

admit that there is a standard of right and wrong that is independent of his will, and give up the theological conception of right and wrong.

(5) From a religious point of view, it is unacceptable to regard God's commands as arbitrary or to give up the doctrine of the goodness of God.

(6) Therefore, even from a religious point of view, a standard of right and wrong that is independent of God's will must be accepted.

Many religious people believe that they must accept a theological conception of right and wrong because it would be impious not to do so. They feel, somehow, that if they believe in God, they should say that right and wrong are to be defined in terms of his will. But this argument suggests otherwise: It suggests that, on the contrary, the Divine Command Theory itself leads to impious results, so that a devout person should not accept it. And in fact, some of the greatest theologians, such as St. Thomas Aquinas (1225–1274), rejected the theory for just this reason. Thinkers such as Aquinas connect morality with religion in a different way.

For Further Reflection

1. What would Rachels likely say to this objection to his argument: "The arbitrariness claim has no force because God would never command us to do wrong—to murder the innocent or to torture babies, for example—because God is all-good."

2. Why does Leibniz say that the divine command theory, if true, would destroy any reasons we might have for praising God?

3. Do you think Rachels' argument sound? Why or why not?

4. Would it be impious to reject the divine command theory? to accept it? Explain.

Key Terms

ethics	ethical relativism	moral skepticism
subjectivism	conventionalism	ethical objectivism
moral absolutism	ethical egoism	virtue ethics
deontological ethics	teleological ethics	utilitarianism
ethics of care		

Suggestions for Further Reading

GENERAL WORKS

Baier, Kurt. *The Moral Point of View*. Ithaca, NY: Cornell University Press, 1958.

Beauchamp, Tom L. *Philosophical Ethics*. New York: McGraw-Hill, 1982. A good blend of analysis with readings.

Brandt, Richard. *Ethical Theory*. Englewood Cliffs, NJ: Prentice Hall, 1959. A solid, comprehensive work on ethical theory.

Feldman, Fred. *Introductory Ethics*. Englewood Cliffs, NJ: Prentice Hall, 1978. An excellent expression of analytic method applied to ethical theory.

Harris, C. E. *Applying Moral Theories*. Belmont, CA: Wadsworth, 1986.

MacIntyre, A. *A Short History of Ethics*. New York: Macmillan, 1966.

Mackie, J. L. *Ethics: Inventing Right and Wrong*. New York: Penguin, 1977.

Pojman, Louis, ed. *Ethical Theory: Classic and Contemporary Readings*, 4th ed. Belmont, CA: Wadsworth, 2002.

Rachels, James. *The Elements of Moral Philosophy*. New York: Random House, 1986. An elementary, succinct introduction.

Singer, Peter, ed. *A Companion to Ethics*. Cambridge, MA: Blackwell, 1993.

Taylor, Paul. *Principles of Ethics*. Belmont, CA: Dickenson, 1975.

Vaughn, Lewis. *Doing Ethics: Moral Reasoning and Contemporary Issues*. New York: W. W.Norton, 2008.

ETHICAL RELATIVISM

Copp, David, and David Zimmerman, eds. *Morality, Reason and Truth: New Essays on the Foundations of Ethics*. Totowa, NJ: Rowman & Allanheld, 1984.

Gewirth, Alan. *Reason and Morality*. Chicago: University of Chicago Press, 1978.

Gillispie, Norman, ed. *Moral Realism (Southern Journal of Philosophy*, vol. XXIV, Supplement), 1986. This volume contains an excellent collection of essays on moral realism, including a bibliography on the subject by Geoffrey Sayre-McCord.

Ladd, John, ed. *Ethical Relativism*. Belmont, CA: Wadsworth, 1973.

Stace, W. T. *The Concept of Morals*. New York: Macmillan, 1937.

Wellman, Carl. "The Ethical Implications of Cultural Relativity." *Journal of Philosophy*, LX, 1963.

Werner, Richard. "Ethical Realism." *Ethics*, vol. 93, 1983.

Westermarck, Edward. *Ethical Relativity*. Humanities Press, 1960.

Williams, Bernard. *Morality*. Harper Torchbooks, 1972.

Wong, David. *Moral Relativity*. Berkeley: University of California Press, 1985.

MORALITY AND SELF-INTEREST

Gauthier, David, ed. *Morality and Rational Self-Interest*. Englewood Cliffs, NJ: Prentice Hall, 1970.

Gauthier, David. *Morality by Agreement*. Oxford: Clarendon Press, 1986.

MacIntyre, Alasdair. "Egoism and Altruism" in *The Encyclopedia of Philosophy*, ed. Paul Edwards. New York: Macmillan, 1967.

Sidgwick, Henry. *The Methods of Ethics*, 7th ed. Indianapolis: Hackett, 1981.

Slote, Michael. "An Empirical Basis for Psychological Egoism." *Journal of Philosophy*, vol. 61.

ETHICAL THEORIES

Aristotle. *Nicomachean Ethics,* trans. Terence Irwin. Indianapolis: Hackett, 1985.

Becker, Lawrence. *On Justifying Moral Arguments,* chap. 19. London: Routledge & Kegan Paul, 1973.

Cooper, John. *Reason and the Human Good in Aristotle.* Cambridge: Harvard University Press, 1975.

Donagan, Alan. *The Theory of Morality.* Chicago: University of Chicago Press, 1977.

Hare, Richard. *Reason and Freedom.* Oxford: Oxford University Press, 1961.

Kant, Immanuel. *Fundamental Principles of the Metaphysics of Morals,* trans. Lewis Beck. Indianapolis: Bobbs-Merrill, 1949.

Kruschwitz, Robert, and Robert Roberts, eds. *The Virtues.* Belmont, CA: Wadsworth, 1987. An excellent up-to-date anthology.

MacIntyre, Alasdair. *After Virtue.* Notre Dame, IN: University of Notre Dame Press, 1981.

Mill, John Stuart. *Utilitarianism.* Indianapolis: Bobbs-Merrill, 1957.

Singer, Peter. *The Expanding Circle.* Oxford: Oxford University Press, 1983. A nice job of integrating sociobiology with moral theory.

Smart, J. J. C., and Bernard Williams. *Utilitarianism: For and Against.* Cambridge: Cambridge University Press, 1973. A classic debate.

Sommers, Christina Hoff, ed. *Vice and Virtues in Everyday Life.* New York: Harcourt Brace Jovanovich, 1985.

Taylor, Richard. *Good and Evil.* New York: Macmillan, 1970.

Taylor, Richard. *Ethics, Faith and Reason.* Englewood Cliffs, NJ: Prentice Hall, 1985.

Warnock, G. J. *The Object of Morality.* London: Methuen, 1971.

Part VII

~

Political Philosophy

In heaven, there is laid up a pattern of the Ideal City, methinks, which he who desires may behold, and beholding, may set his own house in order. But whether such a one exists, or ever will exist in fact, is no matter: for he will live after the manner of that city, having nothing to do with any other.

PLATO, *Republic* IX, 592

YOU ARE FILLING OUT your yearly federal income tax forms and become irritated at the large sum of money that you are going to have to pay, $5,000. If that weren't bad enough, you don't believe in the programs for which most of the money will be spent. You ask yourself, what right does the government have to demand payment of me? But you don't like the likely consequences of not paying—a prison sentence—so you very reluctantly write out a check for $5,000, realizing that you will not be able to afford needed house repairs or a vacation this year.

So you put your forms with a check inside an envelope and go out to mail your income tax at the nearest mailbox. On your way home a man accosts you with a gun. "Your money or your life," he roughly demands. You open your wallet and hand him the $100 therein. You continue home, beaten in spirit, feeling twice robbed, and wondering which is the greater robber, the gunman or the government?

You ask yourself if that feeling is justified. Is the government, with its laws, only a gunman who observes reliable rituals and procedures and, unlike the robber, warns you in advance that it will take a percentage of your money at a certain time every year? You've always been a law-abiding citizen, but now you wonder, by what right does the government demand my obedience? Why should I obey the State? What is the justification of government?

Why Should I Obey the Government?
What Is the Justification of Political Authority?

Many answers have been given to these questions, some emphasizing the need for protection and orderly process as the justification of government, others emphasizing the promotion of the spiritual or cultural aspects of the people, and still others emphasizing economic well-being, which in turn is seen as the foundation for all other values. In our readings in this part of our book we find five different answers to these questions:

1. The **anarchist** answer: The State is not justified in imposing its wishes on you, for your autonomy is a fundamental moral requirement, and the State has no right to violate it. The State is without moral authority. We begin with Robert Paul Wolff's classic *In Defense of Anarchism*.

2. The **absolutist** (Hobbesian) answer: The state of nature without political security is so dangerous, barbarous, and impoverished that it is rational to give up significant freedom to the state to obtain peace and security. Hobbes argues for this in his *Leviathan*.

3. The **democratic** answer: John Locke agrees with Hobbes that we contract with the state to give up some freedom for security, but disagrees with Hobbes on the degree of the surrender. We do not give up our natural rights to life,

property, representation, and other goods—better a state of nature, which is not as bad as Hobbes makes out, than slavery to the state!

4. The **libertarian** answer: represented in our readings by John Stuart Mill. He goes further than Hobbes or Locke in honoring freedom, especially our right to own property, and in insisting that the only function of the State is to protect us from external and internal enemies—otherwise, the government that governs least, governs best.

5. The **liberal** answer: John Rawls sets forth a notion of a hypothetical contract in which parties in the original position choose a set of principles combining equal maximal liberty with social equality.

Political philosophy includes many related questions that are relevant to this part of our work and will be touched on in this section, as well as in other parts of this work, including: What is the best form of government? What are the limits of governmental authority in the light of the individual's right or need to be free? Is taxation legitimate? What exactly grounds the State's authority, making it legitimate? Do we have a general moral obligation to obey the law?

Political anarchism is the philosophy that the State is unjustified because it improperly infringes on human autonomy. Human freedom is treated as a paramount moral value that no amount of efficiency, utility, or stability may justly override. All forms of government are bad in that they restrict the free exercise of human reason that is necessary for the attainment of perfection. The French philosopher Pierre Joseph Proudhon (1809–1865) is regarded as the father of anarchism. He rejected all forms of authority from society in favor of complete individualism. One of his famous statements is "property is theft."*

We begin with Robert Wolff's anarchistic answer to the question of political authority.

In Defense of Anarchism   VII.68

ROBERT PAUL WOLFF

Robert Paul Wolff was for many years professor of philosophy at Columbia University and is presently professor of philosophy at the University of Massachusetts at Amherst. He is the author of many articles and books but is best known for his *In Defense of Anarchism,* from which the present selection is taken.

Wolff sets forth a version of anarchism, holding that all forms of government violate our overriding duty to act autonomously. Wolff's argument (and essay) can be divided into two parts. In the first, he describes the meaning of political authority, distinguishing it from mere power. In the second part, he defines autonomy and argues that it is incompatible with accepting authority. The selection has been edited with minor annotations to aid your study.

*P. J. Proudhon, *What Is Property?* (1840).

Study Questions

1. How does Wolff define political philosophy?
2. How does Wolff define the state?
3. How does he define authority?
4. What is the difference between *de facto* and *de jure* authority?
5. What is the basis of our responsibility?
6. How do authority and autonomy conflict? How does this conflict, according to Wolff, result in anarchism?
7. What is the relationship of the anarchist to his own country and government?

THE CONCEPT OF AUTHORITY

POLITICS IS THE EXERCISE of the power of the state, or the attempt to influence that exercise. Political philosophy is therefore, strictly speaking, the philosophy of the state. If we are to determine the content of political philosophy, and whether indeed it exists, we must begin with the concept of the state.

The state is a group of persons who have and exercise supreme authority within a given territory. Strictly, we should say that a state is a group of persons who have supreme authority within a given territory or *over a certain population*. A nomadic tribe may exhibit the authority structure of a state, so long as its subjects do not fall under the superior authority of a territorial state. The state may include all the persons who fall under its authority, as does the democratic state according to its theorists; it may also consist of a single individual to whom all the rest are subject. We may doubt whether the one-person state has ever actually existed, although Louis XIV evidently thought so when he announced, "L'etat c'est moi" [I am the State]. The distinctive characteristic of the state is supreme authority.

Authority is the right to command, and correlatively, the right to be obeyed. *It must be distinguished from power,* which is the ability to compel compliance, either through the use or threat of force. When I turn over my wallet to a thief who is holding me at gunpoint, I do so because the fate with which he threatens me is worse than the loss of money which I am made to suffer. I grant that he has power over me, but I would hardly suppose that he has *authority*, that is, that he has a right to demand my money and that I have an obligation to give it to him. When the government presents me with a bill for taxes, on the other hand, I pay it (normally) even though I do not wish to and even if I think I can get away with not paying. It is after all, the duly constituted government, and hence it has a *right* to tax me. It has *authority* over me. Sometimes, of course, I cheat the government, but even so, I acknowledge its authority, for who would speak of "cheating" a thief?

To claim authority is to claim the right to be obeyed. To *have* authority is then—what? It may mean to have that right, or it may mean to have one's claim acknowledged and accepted by those at whom it is directed. The term "authority" is ambiguous, having both a descriptive and a normative sense. Even the descriptive sense refers to norms or obligations, of course, but it does so by *describing* what men believe they ought to do rather than by *asserting* that they ought to do it. . . .

What is meant by *supreme* authority? Some political philosophers have held that the true state has ultimate authority over all matters whatsoever that occur within its venue. Jean

From Robert Paul Wolff, In Defense of Anarchism, *pages 446–448, by permission of the University of California Press.*

Jacques Rousseau, for example, asserted that the social contract by which a just political community is formed

> gives to the body absolute command over the members of which it is formed; and it is this power, when directed by the general will, that bears . . . the name of 'sovereign.'

John Locke, on the other hand, held that the supreme authority of the just state extends only to those matters which it is proper for a state to control. The state is, to be sure, the highest authority, but its right to command is less than absolute. One of the questions which political philosophy must answer is whether there is any limit to the range of affairs over which a just state has authority.

[Wolff next distinguishes an authoritative command from a persuasive argument. I may choose to do exactly as a sovereign commands because I see it as my moral duty, but the commanding or arguing party has no authority in himself. Ed.]

The person who issues the command functions merely as the *occasion* for my becoming aware of my duty, and his role might in other instances be filled by an admonishing friend, or even by my own conscience. But this is different from the notion that a government has a right to command and the correlative obligation to obey the person who gives the command: "Obedience is not a matter of doing what someone tells you to do. It is a matter of doing what he tells you to do *because he tells you to do it.*"

What can be inferred from the existence of de facto [actually existing] states is that men *believe* in the existence of legitimate authority, for of course a *de facto* state is simply a state whose subjects believe it to be legitimate (i.e., really to have the authority which it claims for itself). They may be wrong. Indeed, *all* beliefs in authority may be wrong—there may be not a single state in the history of mankind which has now or ever has had a right to be obeyed. It might even be impossible for such a state to exist; that is the question we must try to settle. But so long as

men believe in the authority of states, we can conclude that they possess the concept of *de jure* [legitimate] authority.

[Having clarified the concept of authority and left it an open question whether any state qualifies as a legitimate authority, Wolff turns to the second part of his argument, the concept of autonomy. Ed.]

THE CONCEPT OF AUTONOMY

The fundamental assumption of moral philosophy is that men are responsible for their actions. From this assumption it follows necessarily, as Kant pointed out, that men are metaphysically free, which is to say that in some sense they are capable of choosing how they shall act. Being able to choose how he acts makes a man responsible, but merely choosing is not in itself to constitute *taking* responsibility for one's actions. Taking responsibility involves attempting to determine what one ought to do, and that, as philosophers since Aristotle have recognized, lays upon one the additional burdens of gaining knowledge, reflecting on motives, predicting outcomes, criticizing principles, and so forth.

The obligation to take responsibility for one's actions does not derive from man's freedom of will alone, for more is required in taking responsibility than freedom of choice. Only because man has the capacity to reason about his choices can he be said to stand under a continuing obligation to take responsibility for them. It is quite appropriate that moral philosophers should group together children and madmen as being not fully responsible for their actions, for as madmen are thought to lack freedom of choice, so children do not yet possess the power of reason in a developed form. It is even just that we should assign a greater degree of responsibility to children, for madmen, by virtue of their lack of free will, are completely without responsibility, while children, insofar as they possess reason in a partially developed form, can be held responsible to a corresponding degree.

Every man who possesses both free will and reason has an obligation to take responsibility for his actions, even though he may not be actively engaged in a continuing process of reflection, investigation, and deliberation about how he ought to act. A man will sometimes announce his willingness to take responsibility for the consequences of his actions, even though he has not deliberated about them, or does not intend to do so in the future. Such a declaration is, of course, an advance over the refusal to take responsibility; it at least acknowledges the existence of the obligation. But it does not relieve the man of the duty to engage in the reflective process which he has thus far shunned.

The responsible man is not capricious or anarchic, for he does acknowledge himself bound by moral constraints. But he insists that he alone is the judge of those constraints. He may listen to the advice of others, but he makes it his own by determining for himself whether it is good advice. He may learn from others about his moral obligations, but only in the sense that a mathematician learns from other mathematicians—namely by hearing from them arguments whose validity he recognizes even though he did not think of them himself. He does not learn in the sense that one learns from an explorer, by accepting as true his account of things one cannot see for oneself.

Since the responsible man arrives at moral decisions which he expresses to himself in the form of imperatives, we may say that he gives laws to himself, or is self-legislating. In short, he is *autonomous*. As Kant argued, moral autonomy is a combination of freedom and responsibility; it is a submission to laws which one has made for oneself. The autonomous man, insofar as he is autonomous, is not subject to the will of another. He may do what another tells him, but not *because* he has been told to do it. He is therefore, in the political sense of the word, *free*.

[Wolff explains that we can neglect or forfeit our autonomy either by failing to take responsibility for our actions or by voluntarily putting ourselves in a position of servitude.

Finally, Wolff brings the conflict between authority and autonomy to full focus. Ed.]

The defining mark of the state is authority, the right to rule. The primary obligation of man is autonomy, the refusal to be ruled. It would seem, then, that there can be no resolution of the conflict between the autonomy of the individual and the putative authority of the state. Insofar as a man fulfills his obligation to make himself the author of his decisions, he will resist the state's claim to have authority over him. That is to say, he will deny that he has a duty to obey the laws of the state *simply because they are laws*. In that sense, it would seem that anarchism is the only political doctrine consistent with the virtue of autonomy.

Now, of course, an anarchist may grant the necessity of *complying* with the law under certain circumstances or for the time being. He may even doubt that there is any real prospect of eliminating the state as a human institution. But he will never view the commands of the state as *legitimate*, as having a binding moral force. In a sense, we might characterize the anarchist as a man without a country, for despite the ties which bind him to the land of his childhood, he stands in precisely the same moral relationship to "his" government as he does to the government of any other country in which he might happen to be staying for a time. When I take a vacation to Great Britain, I obey its laws, both because of prudential self-interest and because of the obvious moral considerations concerning the value of order, the general good consequences of preserving a system of property, and so forth. On my return to the United States, I have a sense of reentering *my* country, and if I think about the matter at all, I imagine myself to stand in a different and more intimate relation to American laws. They have been promulgated by *my* government, and I therefore have a special obligation to obey them. But the anarchist tells me that my feeling is purely sentimental and has no objective moral basis. All authority is equally illegitimate, although of course not therefore equally worthy or unworthy of support, and my obedience to American laws, if I am to be morally autonomous, must proceed from the same considerations which determine me abroad.

The dilemma which we have posed can be succinctly expressed in terms of the concept of a *de jure* state. If all men have a continuing obligation to achieve the highest degree of autonomy possible, then there would appear to be no state whose subjects have a moral obligation to obey its commands. Hence, the concept of a *de jure* legitimate state would appear to be vacuous, and philosophical anarchism would seem to be the only reasonable political belief for an enlightened man.

SUMMARY

Autonomy, for the anarchist, is the highest value and generates an absolute duty to act only from reasons the person regards as good. The state, on the other hand, claims authority over citizens, creating obligations for them even when they disagree with these obligations. Since moral autonomy is a higher obligation than obedience to the state, the state can have no moral authority over the individual. People may not forfeit or transfer their authority to the state. Hence, the state has no moral force. It is unjustified.

For Further Reflection

1. Go over the argument for anarchy. Do you see any problems with it? Is autonomy as high a value as the anarchist supposes?

2. Do you agree with Wolff regarding his anarchist argument? Is our obedience to the state unjustified and immoral? Can you find any weaknesses in Wolff's argument? Can political authority be justified?

3. Anarchism claims to offer hope for a sick world. Here is the definition of anarchism given by the Russian anarchist Peter Kropotkin:

> The name given to a principle or theory of life and conduct under which society is conceived without government—harmony in such a society being obtained, not by submission to law, or by obedience to any authority, but by free agreements concluded between various groups, territorial and professional, freely constituted for the sake of production and consumption, as also for the satisfaction of the infinite variety of needs and aspiration of civilized beings.

Evaluate this definition. How realistic is it?

The Absolutist Answer:
VII.69 The Justification of the State Is the Security It Affords

THOMAS HOBBES

Thomas Hobbes (1588–1679), the greatest English political philosopher, gave classic expression to the idea that morality and politics arise out of a social contract. He was born in the year of the Spanish Armada, was educated at Oxford University, and lived through an era of political revolutions as a scholar and tutor (he was tutor to Prince Charles, later King Charles II, of England). He was widely traveled and in communication with most of the intellectual luminaries of his day, both on the continent (Galileo, Gassendi, and Descartes) and in England (Francis Bacon, Ben Johnson, and William Harvey), and was regarded as a brilliant, if somewhat unorthodox and controversial, intellectual.

Hobbes is known today primarily for his masterpiece in political theory, *Leviathan* (1651), a book that was suppressed in his own day for its controversial ideas. In this book, from which our selection is taken, he develops a moral and political theory based on psychological egoism. Hobbes argues that people are all egoists who always act in their own self-interest, to obtain gratification and avoid harm. However, we cannot obtain any of the basic goods because of the inherent fear and insecurity in an unregulated "state of nature," in which life is "solitary, poor, nasty, brutish, and short." We cannot relax our guard, for everyone is constantly in fear of everyone else. In this state of anarchy the prudent person concludes that it really is in everyone's self-interest to make a contract to keep to a minimal morality of respecting human life, keeping covenants made, and obeying the society's laws. This minimal morality, which Hobbes refers to as "the laws of nature," is nothing more than a set of maxims of prudence. To ensure that we all obey this covenant Hobbes proposes a strong sovereign or "Leviathan" to impose severe penalties on those who disobey the laws, for "covenants without the sword are but words."

Study Questions

1. According to Hobbes, in what sense are all persons equal?
2. What is the natural relationship between people in the state of nature? Describe the state of nature. Are Hobbes' examples appropriate?
3. Does the notion of justice have any application in the state of nature? Why or why not?
4. What is necessary to establish morality and law?
5. What is the difference between the right of nature and the law of nature?
6. What is a contract, according to Hobbes?
7. How does Hobbes define good and evil?
8. What is the solution to the horrible state of nature?
9. What is the Leviathan? Why does Hobbes use this image?

OF THE NATURAL CONDITION OF MANKIND AS CONCERNING THEIR FELICITY, AND MISERY

NATURE HATH MADE men so equal, in the faculties of the body, and mind; as that though there be found one man sometimes manifestly stronger in body, or of quicker mind than another; yet when all is reckoned together, the difference between man, and man, is not so considerable, as that one man can thereupon claim to himself any benefit, to which another may not pretend, as well as he. For as to the strength of body, the weakest has strength enough to kill the strongest, either by secret machination, or by confederacy with others, that are in the same danger with himself.

And as to the faculties of the mind, setting aside the arts grounded upon words, and especially that skill of proceeding upon general, and infallible rules, called science; which very few have, and but in few things; as being not a native faculty, born with us; nor attained, as prudence, while we look after somewhat else, I find yet a greater equality amongst men, than that of strength. For prudence, is but experience; which equal time, equally bestows on all men, in those things they equally apply themselves unto. That which may perhaps make such equality incredible, is but a vain conceit of one's own wisdom, which almost all men think they have in a greater degree, than the vulgar; that is, than all men but themselves, and a few others, whom by fame, or for concurring with themselves, they approve. For such is the nature of men, that howsoever they may acknowledge many others to be more witty, or more eloquent, or more learned; yet they will hardly believe there be many so wise as themselves; for they see their own wit at hand, and other men's at a distance. But this proveth rather that men are in that point equal, than unequal. For there is not ordinarily a greater sign of the equal distribution of any thing, than that every man is contented with his share.

From this equality of ability, ariseth equality of hope in the attaining of our ends. And therefore if any two men desire the same thing, which nevertheless they cannot both enjoy, they become enemies; and in the way to their end, which is principally their own conservation, and sometimes their delectation only, endeavour to destroy, or subdue one another. And from hence it comes to pass, that where an invader hath no more to fear, than another man's single power; if one plant, sow, build, or possess a convenient seat, others may probably be expected to come prepared with forces united, to dispossess, and deprive him, not only of the fruit of his labour, but also of his life, or liberty. And the invader again is in the like danger of another.

And from this diffidence of one another, there is no way for any man to secure himself, so reasonable, as anticipation; that is, by force, or wiles, to master the persons of all men he can, so long, till he see no other power great enough to endanger him: and this is no more than his own conservation requireth, and is generally allowed. Also because there be some, that taking pleasure in contemplating their own power in the acts of conquest, which they pursue farther than their security requires; if others, that otherwise would be glad to be at ease within modest bounds, should not by invasion increase their power, they would not be able, long time, by standing only on their defence, to subsist. And by consequence, such augmentation of dominion over men being necessary to a man's conservation, it ought to be allowed him.

Again, men have no pleasure, but on the contrary a great deal of grief, in keeping company, where there is no power able to over-awe them

---

From Thomas Hobbes, Leviathan, *1651.*

all. For every man looketh that his companion should value him, at the same rate he sets upon himself: and upon all signs of contempt, or undervaluing, naturally endeavours, as far as he dares, (which amongst them that have no common power to keep them in quiet, is far enough to make them destroy each other), to extort a greater value from his contemners, by damage; and from others, by the example.

So that in the nature of man, we find three principal causes of quarrel. First, competition; secondly, diffidence; thirdly, glory.

The first, maketh men invade for gain; the second, for safety; and the third, for reputation. The first use violence, to make themselves masters of other men's persons, wives, children, and cattle; the second, defend them; the third, for trifles, as a word, a smile, a different option, and any other sign of undervalue, either direct in their persons, or by reflection in their kindred, their friends, their nation, their profession, or their name.

Hereby it is manifest, that during the time men live without a common power to keep them all in awe, they are in that condition which is called war; and such a war, as is of every man, against every man. For war, consisteth not in battle only, or the act of fighting; but in a tract of time, wherein the will to contend by battle is sufficiently known: and therefore the notion of *time,* is to be considered in the nature of war; as it is in the nature of weather. For as the nature of foul weather, lieth not in the shower or two of rain; but in an inclination thereto of many days together: so the nature of war, consisteth not in actual fighting; but in the known disposition thereto, during all the time there is no assurance to the contrary. All other time is PEACE.

Whatsoever therefore is consequent to a time of war, where every man is enemy to every man; the same is consequent to the time, wherein men live without other security, than what their own strength, and their own invention shall furnish them withal. In such condition, there is no place for industry; because the fruit thereof is uncertain: and consequently no culture of the earth;

no navigation, nor use of the commodities that may be imported by sea; no commodious building; no instruments of moving, and removing, such things as require much force; no knowledge of the face of the earth; no account of time; no arts; no letters; no society; and which is worst of all, continual fear, and danger of violent death; and the life of man, solitary, poor, nasty, brutish, and short.

It may seem strange to some man, that has not well weighed these things; that nature should thus dissociate, and render men apt to invade, and destroy one another: and he may therefore, not trusting to this inference, made from the passions, desire perhaps to have the same confirmed by experience. Let him therefore consider with himself, when taking a journey, he arms himself, and seeks to go well accompanied; when going to sleep, he locks his doors; when even in his house he locks his chests; and this when he knows there be laws, and public officers, armed, to revenge all injuries shall be done him; what opinion he has of his fellow-subjects, when he rides armed; of his fellow citizens, when he locks his doors; and of his children, and servants, when he locks his chests. Does he not there as much accuse mankind by his actions, as I do by my words? But neither of us accuse man's nature in it. The desires, and other passions of man, are in themselves no sin. No more are the actions, that proceed from those passions, till they know a law that forbids them: which till laws be made they cannot know: nor can any law be made, till they have agreed upon the person that shall make it.

It may peradventure be thought, there was never such a time, nor condition of war as this; and I believe it was never generally so, over all the world: but there are many places, where they live so now. For the savage people in many places of America, except the government of small families, the concord whereof dependeth on natural lust, have no government at all; and live at this day in that brutish manner, as I said before. Howsoever, it may be perceived what manner of life there would be, where there were no common power to fear, by the manner of life, which men that have formerly lived under a peaceful government, use to degenerate into, in a civil war.

But though there had never been any time, wherein particular men were in a condition of war one against another; yet in all times, kings, and persons of sovereign authority, because of their independency, are in continual jealousies, and in the state and posture of gladiators; having their weapons pointing, and their eyes fixed on one another; that is, their forts, garrisons, and guns upon the frontiers of their kingdoms; and continual spies upon their neighbours; which is a posture of war. But because they uphold thereby, the industry of their subjects; there does not follow from it, that misery, which accompanies the liberty of particular men.

To this war of every man, against every man, this also is consequent; that nothing can be unjust. The notions of right and wrong, justice and injustice have there no place. Where there is no common power, there is no law: where no law, no injustice. Force, and fraud, are in war the two cardinal virtues. Justice, and injustice are none of the faculties neither of the body, nor mind. If they were, they might be in a man that were alone in the world, as well as his senses, and passions. They are qualities, that relate to men in society, not in solitude. It is consequent also to the same condition, that there be no propriety, no dominion, no *mine* and *thine* distinct; but only that to be every man's, that he can get; and for so long, as he can keep it. And thus much for the ill condition, which man by mere nature is actually placed in; though with a possibility to come out of it, consisting partly in the passions, partly in his reason.

The passions that incline men to peace, are fear of death; desire of such things as are necessary to commodious living; and a hope by their industry to obtain them. And reason suggesteth convenient articles of peace, upon which men may be drawn to agreement. These articles, are they, which otherwise are called the Laws of Nature: whereof I shall speak more particularly, in the two following chapters.

OF THE FIRST AND SECOND NATURAL LAWS, AND OF CONTRACTS

The right of nature, which writers commonly call *jus naturale,* is the liberty each man hath, to use his own power, as he will himself, for the preservation of his own nature; that is to say, of his own life; and consequently, of doing any thing, which in his own judgment, and reason, he shall conceive to be the aptest means thereunto.

By LIBERTY, is understood, according to the proper signification of the word, the absence of external impediments: which impediments, may oft take away part of a man's power to do what he would; but cannot hinder him from using the power left him, according as his judgment, and reason shall dictate to him.

A LAW OF NATURE, *lex naturalis,* is a precept or general rule, found out by reason, by which a man is forbidden to do that, which is destructive of his life, or taketh away the means of preserving the same; and to omit that, by which he thinketh it may be best preserved. For though they that speak of this subject, use to confound *jus,* and *lex, right* and *law:* yet they ought to be distinguished; because RIGHT, consisteth in liberty to do, or to forbear; whereas LAW, determineth, and bindeth to one of them: so that law, and right, differ as much, as obligation, and liberty; which in one and the same matter are inconsistent.

And because the condition of man, as hath been declared in the precedent chapter, is a condition of war of every one against every one; in which case every one is governed by his own reason; and there is nothing he can make use of, that may not be a help unto him, in preserving his life against his enemies; it followeth, that in such a condition, every man has a right to every thing; even to one another's body. And therefore, as long as this natural right of every man to every thing endureth, there can be no security to any man, how strong or wise soever he be, of living out the time, which nature ordinarily alloweth men to live. And consequently it is a precept, or general rule of reason, *that every man, ought to endeavour peace, as far as he has hope of obtaining it; and when he cannot obtain it, that he may seek, and use, all helps, and advantages of war.* The first branch of which rule, containeth the first, and fundamental law of nature; which is, *to seek peace, and follow it.* The second, the sum of the right of nature; which is, *by all means we can, to defend ourselves.*

From this fundamental law of nature, by which men are commanded to endeavour peace, is derived this second law; *that a man be willing, when others are so too, as far-forth, as for peace, and defence of himself he shall think it necessary, to lay down this right to all things; and be contented with so much liberty against other men, as he would allow other men against himself.* For as long as every man holdeth this right, of doing any thing he liketh; so long are all men in the condition of war. But if other men will not lay down their right, as well as he; then there is no reason for any one, to divest himself of his: for that were to expose himself to prey, which no man is bound to, rather than to dispose himself to peace. This is that law of the Gospel; *whatsoever you require that others should do to you, that do ye to them.* And that law of all men, *quod tibi fieri non vis, alteri ne feceris.**

To *lay down* a man's *right* to any thing, is to *divest* himself of the *liberty,* of hindering another of the benefit of his own right to the same. For he that renounceth, or passeth away his right, giveth not to any other man a right which he had not before; because there is nothing to which every man had not right by nature: but only standeth out of his way, that he may enjoy his own original right, without hindrance from him; not without hindrance from another. So that the effect which redoundeth to one man, by another man's defect of right, is but so much diminution of impediments to the use of his own right original.

Right is laid aside, either by simply renouncing it; or by transferring it to another. By *simply* RENOUNCING; when he cares not to whom the benefit thereof redoundeth. By TRANSFERRING; when he intendeth the benefit thereof to some

certain person, or persons. And when a man hath in either manner abandoned, or granted away his right; then is he said to be OBLIGED, or BOUND, not to hinder those, to whom such right is granted, or abandoned, from the benefit of it: and that he *ought,* and it is his DUTY, not to make void that voluntary act of his own: and that such hindrance is INJUSTICE, and INJURY, as being *sine jure,*† the right being before renounced, or transferred. So that *injury,* or *injustice,* in the controversies of the world, is somewhat like to that, which in the disputations of scholars is called *absurdity.* For as it is there called an absurdity, to contradict what one maintained in the beginning: so in the world, it is called injustice, and injury, voluntarily to undo that, which from the beginning he had voluntarily done. The way by which a man either simply renounceth, or transferreth his right, is a declaration, or signification, by some voluntary and sufficient sign, or signs, that he doth so renounce, or transfer; or hath so renounced, or transferred the same, to him that accepteth it. And these signs are either words only, or actions only; or, as it happeneth most often, both words, and actions. And the same are the BONDS, by which men are bound, and obliged: bonds, that have their strength, not from their own nature, for nothing is more easily broken than a man's word, but from fear of some evil consequence upon the rupture.

Whensoever a man transferreth his right, or renounceth it; it is either in consideration of some right reciprocally transferred to himself; or for some other good he hopeth for thereby. For it is a voluntary act: and of the voluntary acts of every man, the object is some *good to himself.* And therefore there be some rights, which no man can be understood by any words, or other signs, to have abandoned, or transferred. At first a man cannot lay down the right of resisting them, that assault him by force, to take away his life; because he cannot be understood to aim thereby, at any good to himself. The same may be said of wounds, and chains, and imprisonment; both

---

*["What you do not want done to you, do not do to others."—ed. note]

†[That is, without right.—ed. note]

because there is no benefit consequent to such patience; as there is to the patience of suffering another to be wounded, or imprisoned: as also because a man cannot tell, when he seeth men proceed against him by violence, whether they intend his death or not. And lastly the motive, and end for which this renouncing, and transferring of right is introduced, is nothing else but the security of a man's person, in his life, and in the means of so preserving life, as not to be weary of it. And therefore if a man by words, or other signs, seem to despoil himself of the end, for which those signs were intended; he is not to be understood as if he meant it, or that it was his will; but that he was ignorant of how such words and actions were to be interpreted.

The mutual transferring of right, is that which men call CONTRACT.

There is a difference between transferring of right to the thing; and transferring, or tradition, that is delivery of the thing itself. For the thing may be delivered together with the translation of the right; as in buying and selling with ready-money; or exchange of goods, or lands: and it may be delivered some time after.

Again, one of the contractors, may deliver the thing contracted for on his part, and leave the other to perform his part at some determinate time after, and in the mean time be trusted; and then the contract on his part, is called PACT, or COVENANT: or both parts may contract now, to perform hereafter: in which cases, he that is to perform in time to come, being trusted, his performance is called *keeping of promise,* or faith; and the failing of performance, if it be voluntary, *violation of faith.*

When the transferring of right, is not mutual: but one of the parties transferreth, in hope to gain thereby friendship, or service from another, or from his friends; or in hope to gain the reputation of charity, or magnanimity; or to deliver his mind from the pain of compassion; or in hope of reward in heaven, this is not contract, but GIFT, FREE-GIFT, GRACE: which words signify one and the same thing.

Signs of contract, are either *express,* or *by inference.* Express, are words spoken with understanding of what they signify: and such words are either of the time *present,* or *past;* as, *I give, I grant, I have given, I have granted, I will that this be yours:* or of the future; as, *I will give, I will grant:* which words of the future are called PROMISE.

If a covenant be made, wherein neither of the parties perform presently, but trust one another; in the condition of mere nature, which is a condition of war of every man against every man, upon any reasonable suspicion, it is void: but if there be a common power set over them both, with right and force sufficient to compel performance, it is not void. For he that performeth first, has no assurance the other will perform after; because the bonds of words are too weak to bridle men's ambition, avarice, anger, and other passions, without the fear of some coercive power; which in the condition of mere nature, where all men are equal, and judges of the justness of their own fears, cannot possibly be supposed. And therefore he which performeth first, does but betray himself to his enemy; contrary to the right, he can never abandon, of defending his life, and means of living.

But in a civil estate, where there is a power set up to constrain those that would otherwise violate their faith, that fear is no more reasonable: and for that cause, he which by the covenant is to perform first, is obliged so to do.

The cause of fear, which maketh such a covenant invalid, must be always something arising after the covenant made; as some new fact, or other sign of the will not to perform: else it cannot make the covenant void. For that which could not hinder a man from promising, ought not to be admitted as a hindrance of performing.

OF OTHER LAWS OF NATURE

From that law of nature, by which we are obliged to transfer to another, such rights, as being retained, hinder the peace of mankind, there followeth a third; which is this, *that men perform their covenants made:* without which, covenants are in vain, and but empty words; and the right of all men to all things remaining, we are still in the condition of war.

And in this law of nature, consisteth the fountain and original of JUSTICE. For where no covenant hath preceded, there hath no right been transferred, and every man has right to every thing; and consequently, no action can be unjust. But when a covenant is made, then to break it is *unjust:* and the definition of INJUSTICE, is no other than *the not performance of covenant.* And whatsoever is not unjust, is *just.*

But because covenants of mutual trust, where there is a fear of no performance on either part, as hath been said in the former chapter, are invalid; though the original of justice be the making of covenants; yet injustice actually there can be none, till the cause of such fear be taken away; which while men are in the natural condition of war, cannot be done. Therefore before the names of just, and unjust can have place, there must be some coercive power, to compel men equally to the performance of their covenants, by the terror of some punishment, greater than the benefit they expect by the breach of their covenant; and to make good that propriety, which by mutual contract men acquire, in recompense of the universal right they abandon: and such power there is none before the erection of a commonwealth. And this is also to be gathered out of the ordinary definition of justice in the Schools: for they say, that *justice is the constant will of giving to every man his own,* and therefore where there is no *own,* that is, no propriety, there is no injustice; and where there is no coercive power erected, that is, where there is no commonwealth, there is no propriety; all men having right to all things: therefore where there is no commonwealth, there nothing is unjust. So that the nature of justice, consisteth in keeping of valid covenants: but the validity of covenants begins not but with the constitution of a civil power, sufficient to compel men to keep them: and then it is also that propriety begins. . . .

And because, though men be never so willing to observe these laws, there may nevertheless arise questions concerning a man's action; first, whether it were done, or not done; secondly, if done, whether against the law, or not against the law; the former whereof, is called a question *of fact;* the latter a question *of right,* therefore unless the parties to the question, covenant mutually to stand to the sentence of another, they are as far from peace as ever. This other to whose sentence they submit is called an ARBITRATOR. And therefore it is of the law of nature, *that they that are at controversy, submit their right to the judgment of an arbitrator.*

And seeing every man is presumed to do all things in order to his own benefit, no man is a fit arbitrator in his own cause; and if he were never so fit; yet equity allowing to each party equal benefit, if one be admitted to the judge, the other is to be admitted also; and so the controversy, that is, the cause of war, remains, against the law of nature.

For the same reason no man in any cause ought to be received for arbitrator, to whom greater profit, or honour, or pleasure apparently ariseth out of the victory of one party, than of the other: for he hath taken, though an unavoidable bribe, yet a bribe; and no man can be obliged to trust him. And thus also the controversy, and the condition of war remaineth, contrary to the law of nature.

And in a controversy of *fact,* the judge being to give no more credit to one, than to the other, if there be no other arguments, must give credit to a third; or to a third and fourth; or more: for else the question is undecided, and left to force, contrary to the law of nature.

These are the laws of nature, dictating peace, for a means of the conservation of men in multitudes; and which only concern the doctrine of civil society. There be other things tending to the destruction of particular men; as drunkenness, and all other parts of intemperance; which may therefore also be reckoned amongst those things which the law of nature hath forbidden;

but are not necessary to be mentioned, nor are pertinent enough to this place.

And though this may seem too subtle a deduction of the laws of nature, to be taken notice of by all men; whereof the most part are too busy in getting food, and the rest too negligent to understand; yet to leave all men inexcusable, they have been contracted into one easy sum, intelligible even to the meanest capacity; and that is, *Do not that to another, which thou wouldest not have done to thyself;* which sheweth him, that he has no more to do in learning the laws of nature, but, when weighing the actions of other men with his own, they seem too heavy, to put them into the other part of the balance, and his own into their place, that his own passions, and self-love, may add nothing to the weight; and then there is none of these laws of nature that will not appear unto him very reasonable.

The laws of nature oblige *in foro interno;** that is to say, they bind to a desire they should take place: but *in foro externo,†* that is, to the putting them in act, not always. For he that should be modest, and tractable, and perform all he promises, in such time, and place, where no man else should do so, should but make himself a prey to others, and procure his own certain ruin, contrary to the ground of all laws of nature, which tend to nature's preservation. And again, he that having sufficient security, that others shall observe the same laws towards him, observes them not himself, seeketh not peace, but war; and consequently the destruction of his nature by violence.

And whatsoever laws bind *in foro interno,* may be broken, not only by a fact contrary to the law, but also by a fact according to it, in case a man think it contrary. For though his action in this case, be according to the law; yet his purpose was against the law; which, where the obligation is *in foro interno,* is a breach.

The laws of nature are immutable and eternal; for injustice, ingratitude, arrogance, pride, iniquity, acception of persons, and the rest, can never be made lawful. For it can never be that war shall preserve life, and peace destroy it.

The same laws, because they oblige only to a desire, and endeavour, I mean an unfeigned and constant endeavour, are easy to be observed. For in that they require nothing but endeavour, he that endeavoureth their performance, fulfilleth them; and he that fulfilleth the law, is just.

And the science of them, is the true and only moral philosophy. For moral philosophy is nothing else but the science of what is *good,* and *evil,* in the conversation, and society of mankind. *Good,* and *evil,* are names that signify our appetites, and aversions; which in different tempers, customs, and doctrines of men, are different: and divers men, differ not only in their judgment, on the sense of what is pleasant, and unpleasant to the taste, smell, hearing, touch, and sight; but also of what is conformable, or disagreeable to reason, in the actions of common life. Nay, the same man, in divers times, differs from himself; and one time praiseth, that is, calleth good, what another time he dispraiseth, and called evil: from whence arise disputes, controversies, and at last war. And therefore so long as a man is in the condition of mere nature, which is a condition of war, as private appetite is the measure of good, and evil: and consequently all men agree on this, that peace is good, and therefore also the way, or means of peace, which, as I have shewed before, are *justice, gratitude, modesty, equity, mercy,* and the rest of the laws of nature, are good; that is to say; *moral virtues;* and their contrary *vices,* evil. Now the science of virtue and vice, is moral philosophy; and therefore the true doctrine of the laws of nature, is the true moral philosophy. But the writers of moral philosophy, though they acknowledge the same virtues and vices; yet not seeing wherein consisted their goodness; nor that they come to be praised, as the means of peaceable, sociable,

*[Literally, "in the internal forum"—that is, in a person's mind or conscience.—ed. note]
†[Literally, "in the external forum"—that is, in the public world of action.—ed. note]

and comfortable living, place them in a mediocrity of passions: as if not the cause, but the degree of daring, made fortitude; or not the cause, but the quantity of a gift, made liberality.

These dictates of reason, men used to call by the name of laws, but improperly: for they are but conclusions, of theorems concerning what conduceth to the conservation and defence of themselves; whereas law, properly, is the word of him, that by right hath command over others. But yet if we consider the same theorems, as delivered in the word of God, that by right commandeth all things; then are they properly called laws.

OF THE CAUSES, GENERATION, AND DEFINITION OF A COMMONWEALTH

The final cause, end, or design of men, who naturally love liberty, and dominion over others, in the introduction of that restraint upon themselves, in which we see them live in commonwealths, is the foresight of their own preservation, and of a more contented life thereby; that is to say, of getting themselves out from that miserable condition of war, which is necessarily consequent, as hath been shown in chapter XIII, to the natural passions of men, when there is no visible power to keep them in awe, and tie them by fear of punishment to the performance of their covenants, and observation of those laws of nature set down in the fourteenth and fifteenth chapters.

For the laws of nature, as *justice, equity, modesty, mercy,* and, in sum, *doing to others, as we would be done to,* of themselves, without the terror of some power, to cause them to be observed, are contrary to our natural passions, that carry us to partiality, pride, revenge, and the like. And covenants, without the sword, are but words, and of no strength to secure a man at all. Therefore notwithstanding the laws of nature, which every one hath then kept, when he has the will to keep them, when he can do it safely, if there be no power erected, or not great enough for our security; every man will, and may lawfully rely on his own strength and art, for cau-

tion against all other men. And in all places, where men have lived by small families, to rob and spoil one another, has been a trade, and so far from being reputed against the law of nature, that the greater spoils they gained, the greater was their honour; and men observed no other laws therein, but the laws of honour; that is, to abstain from cruelty, leaving to men their lives, and instruments of husbandry. And as small families did then; so now do cities and kingdoms which are but greater families, for their own security, enlarge their dominions, upon all pretences of danger, and fear of invasion, or assistance that may be given to invaders, and endeavour as much as they can, to subdue, or weaken their neighbours, by open force, and secret arts, for want of other caution, justly; and are remembered for it in after ages with honour.

It is true, that certain living creatures, as bees, and ants, live sociably one with another, which are therefore by Aristotle numbered amongst political creatures; and yet have no other direction, than their particular judgments and appetites; nor speech, whereby one of them can signify to another, what he thinks expedient for the common benefit: and therefore some man may perhaps desire to know, why mankind cannot do the same. To which I answer,

First, that men are continually in competition for honour and dignity, which these creatures are not; and consequently amongst men there ariseth on that ground, envy and hatred, and finally war; but amongst these not so.

Secondly, that amongst these creatures, the common good differeth not from the private; and being by nature inclined to their private, they procure thereby the common benefit. But man, whose joy consisteth in comparing himself with other men, can relish nothing but what is eminent.

Thirdly, that these creatures, having not, as man, the use of reason, do not see, nor think they see any fault, in the administration of their common business; whereas amongst men, there are very many, that think themselves wiser, and abler to govern the public, better than the rest; and these strive to reform and innovate, one this way, another that way; and thereby bring it into distraction and civil war.

Fourthly, that these creatures, though they have some use of voice, in making known to one another their desires, and other affections; yet they want that art of words, by which some men can represent to others, that which is good, in the likeness of evil; and evil, in the likeness of good; and augment, or diminish the apparent greatness of good and evil; discontenting men, and troubling their peace at their pleasure.

Fifthly, irrational creatures cannot distinguish between *injury,* and *damage;* and therefore as long as they be at ease, they are not offended with their fellows: whereas man is then most troublesome, when he is most at ease: for then it is that he loves to shew his wisdom, and control the actions of them that govern the commonwealth.

Lastly, the agreement of these creatures is natural; that of men, is by covenant only, which is artificial: and therefore it is no wonder if there be somewhat else required, besides covenant, to make their agreement constant and lasting; which is a common power, to keep them in awe, and to direct their actions to the common benefit.

The only way to erect such a common power, as may be able to defend them from the invasion of foreigners, and the injuries of one another, and thereby to secure them in such sort, as that by their own industry, and by the fruits of the earth, they may nourish themselves and live contentedly; is, to confer all their power and strength upon one man, or upon one assembly of men, that may reduce all their wills, by plurality of voices, unto one will: which is as much as to say, to appoint one man, or assembly of men, to bear their person; and every one to own, and acknowledge himself to be author of whatsoever he that so beareth their person, shall act, or cause to be acted, in those things which concern the common peace and safety; and therein to submit their wills, every one to his will, and their judgments, to his judgment. This is more than consent, or concord; it is a real unity of them all, in one and the same person, made by covenant of every man with every man, in such manner, as if every man should say to every man, *I authorize and give up my right of governing myself, to this man, or to this assembly of men, on this condition, that thou give up thy right to him, and authorize all his actions in like manner.* This done, the multitude so united in one person, is called a COMMONWEALTH, in Latin CIVITAS. This is the generation of that great LEVIATHAN, or rather, to speak more reverently, of that *mortal god,* to which we owe under the *immortal God,* our peace and defence. For by this authority, given him by every particular man in the commonwealth, he hath the use of so much power and strength conferred on him, that by terror thereof, he is enabled to perform the wills of them all, to peace at home, and mutual aid against their enemies abroad. And in him consisteth the essence of the commonwealth; which, to define it, is *one person, of whose acts a great multitude, by mutual covenants one with another, have made themselves every one the author, to the end he may use the strength and means of them all, as he shall think expedient, for their peace and common defence.*

And he that carrieth this person, is called SOVEREIGN, and said to have *sovereign* power; and every one besides, his SUBJECT.

For Further Reflection

1. Hobbes wrote, "The utility of morality and civil philosophy is to be estimated, not so much by the commodities we have by knowing these sciences, as by the calamities we receive from not knowing them." What does he mean by this, and does the selection illustrate it?

2. Is Hobbes' view of human nature accurate? Do we always act out of the motivations of fear and distrust? Are people entirely self-interested egoists? Is psychological egoism, the view that we always do what we perceive to be in our best interest, too bleak and one-sided?

3. Hobbes thought that only an absolute sovereign could establish or ensure peace and civil society. Is he correct? What would his estimation of democracy be? Could democratic society make use of his analysis? How would democrats modify Hobbes' theory?

4. David Hume criticized the idea that contract theories provide a justification of political authority. First, there is no evidence of an original contract ever being made and, secondly, even if our ancestors did sign an original contract, why should that give us any reason for obeying the laws of the state? Even as we are not bound by the marriage or business contracts of our ancestors, why should we be obligated by their political contracts? What do you think of Hume's criticisms?

VII.70 The Democratic Answer: The Justification of the State Is Its Promotion of Security and Natural Human Rights

JOHN LOCKE

With the Restoration of the Catholic royalty in 1660, after the English Civil War, Locke joined those who sought to limit the power of the King and give greater power to Parliament. After the Glorious Revolution of 1688, in which Locke's hopes were realized, he published two long essays on the justification of political authority. The second of these essays, the *Second Treatise of Civil Government*, is the most important single work on constitutional democracy and greatly influenced the formation of the United States Constitution.

Regarding human nature and the state of nature, Locke is not so pessimistic as Hobbes. Whereas Hobbes saw the state of nature as one in which life was "solitary, poor, nasty, brutish, and short," "a war of all against all," Locke sees it as an inferior state caused by lack of adequate cooperation and common laws, but still one in which our natural rights are enjoyed. Humans are not all as egoistic or innately cruel as Hobbes would make out. Government arises through a social contract in which individuals agree to be bound by the laws of a central authority that represents the will of the majority. The will of the majority and natural rights to life, liberty, and property limit the government. The government loses its legitimacy if it ceases to represent the will of the people and becomes tyrannical. In that case revolution is warranted.

There were those in Locke's day who rejected the contract theory of government (as set forth by Hobbes and others) on the basis that there was no record of an original social contract and that even if there were, it would not be binding on us. To this charge Locke responds that each of us upon reaching adulthood *implicitly* subscribes to the social contract by remaining in the country, living under its laws, and benefiting from its structure and security.

(A biographical note on Locke precedes Reading I.3.)

Study Questions

1. What is the natural state of human beings?
2. How does government come into existence?
3. How should decisions be made within the State?
4. How do we dissolve our relation to the State as individuals?
5. Why will people surrender some of their freedom to join the State? What do they gain thereby?
6. What two powers in the state of nature do we give up in joining the State?
7. When are we justified in dissolving the government? How do we dissolve the government?
8. What is the purpose of government?

OF THE BEGINNING OF POLITICAL SOCIETIES

MEN BEING BY NATURE ALL FREE, equal, and independent, no one can be put out of his estate and subjected to the political power of another without his own consent, which is done by agreeing with other men, to join and unite into a community for their comfortable, safe, and peaceful living, one amongst another, in a secure enjoyment of their properties, and a greater security against any that are not of it. This any number of men may do, because it injures not the freedom of the rest; they are left, as they were, in the liberty of the state of nature. When any number of men have so consented to make one community or government, they are thereby presently incorporated, and make one body politic, wherein the majority have a right to act and [include] the rest.

For, when any number of men have, by the consent of every individual, made a community, they have thereby made that community one body, with a power to act as one body, which is only by the will and determination of the majority. . . .

And thus every man, by consenting with others to make one body politic under one government, puts himself under an obligation to everyone of that society to submit to the determination of the majority, and to be [included] by it; or else this original compact, whereby he with others incorporates into one society, would signify nothing, and be no compact if he be left free and under no other ties than he was in before in the state of nature. For what appearance would there be of any compact? . . . For where the majority cannot include the rest, there they cannot act as one body, and consequently will be immediately dissolved again.

Whosoever therefore out of a state of nature unite into a community, must be understood to give up all the power necessary to the ends for

---

From John Locke, Second Treatise of Civil Government *(1690).*

which they unite society to the majority of the community, unless they expressly agreed in any number greater than the majority. And this is done by barely agreeing to unite into one political society, which is all the compact that is, or needs be, between the individuals that enter into or make up a commonwealth. And thus, that which begins and actually constitutes any political society is nothing but the consent of any number of freemen capable of a majority, to unite and incorporate into such a society. And this is that, and that only, which did or could give beginning to any lawful government in the world. . . .

Every man that hath any possession of enjoyment of any part of the dominions of any government doth thereby give his tacit consent, and is as far forth obliged to obedience to the laws of that government, during such enjoyment, as any one under it, whether this his possession be of land to him and his heirs for ever, or a lodging only for a week; or whether it be barely travelling freely on the highway; and, in effect, it reaches as far as the very being of anyone within the territories of that government.

To understand this better, it is fit to consider that every man when he at first incorporates himself into any commonwealth, he, by his uniting himself thereunto, annexes also, and submits to the community those possessions which he has, or shall acquire, that do not already belong to any other government. For it would be a direct contradiction for anyone to enter into society with others for the securing and regulating of property, and yet to suppose his land, whose property is to be regulated by the laws of the society, should be exempt from the jurisdiction of that government to which he himself, the proprietor of the land, is subject. By the same act, therefore, whereby anyone unites his person, which was before free, to any commonwealth, by the same he unites his possessions, which were before free, to it also; and they become, both of them, person and possession, subject to the government and dominion of that commonwealth as long as it hath a being. Whoever therefore from thenceforth, by inheritance, purchase, permission, or otherwise enjoys any part of the land so annexed to, and under the government of that commonwealth, must take it with the condition it is under; that is, of submitting to the government of the commonwealth, under whose jurisdiction it is, as far forth as any subject of it.

But since the government has a direct jurisdiction only over the land and reaches the possessor of it (before he has actually incorporated himself in the society) only as he dwells upon and enjoys that, the obligation anyone is under by virtue of such enjoyment to submit to the government begins and ends with the enjoyment; so that whenever the owner, who has given nothing but such a tacit consent to the government, will, by donation, sale or otherwise, quit the said possession, he is at liberty to go and incorporate himself into any other commonwealth, or agree with others to begin a new one in any part of the world they can find free and unpossessed; whereas he that has once, by actual agreement and any express declaration, given his consent to be of any commonwealth, is perpetually and indispensably obliged to be, and remain unalterably a subject to it, and can never be again in the liberty of the state of nature, unless by any calamity the government he was under comes to be dissolved; or else by some public act cuts him off from being any longer a member of it.

But submitting to the laws of any country, living quietly, and enjoying privileges and protection under them makes not a man a member of that society; this is only a local protection and homage due to and from all those who, not being in a state of war, come within the territories belonging to any government, to all parts whereof the force of its law extends. But this no more makes a man a member of that society than it would make a man a subject to another in whose family he found it convenient to abide for some time. . . . Nothing can make any man [a citizen] but his actually entering into it by positive engagement and express promise and compact.

OF THE ENDS OF POLITICAL SOCIETY AND GOVERNMENT

If man in the state of nature be so free as has been said; if he be absolute lord of his own person and possessions; equal to the greatest and subject to no body, why will he part with his freedom? Why will he give up this empire, and subject himself to the dominion and control of any other power? To which 'tis obvious to answer, that though in the state of nature he hath such a right, yet the enjoyment of it is very uncertain and constantly exposed to the invasion of others; for all being kings as much as he, every man his equal, and the greater part no strict observers of equity and justice, the enjoyment of the property he has in this state is very unsafe, very unsecure. This makes him willing to quit this condition which, however free, is full of fears and continual dangers; and 'tis not without reason that he seeks out and is willing to join in society with others who are already united, or have a mind to unite for the mutual preservation of their lives, liberties, and estates, which I call by the general name, property.

The great and chief end therefore, of men's uniting into commonwealths, and putting themselves under government, is the preservation of their property; to which in the state of nature there are many things wanting.

First, There wants an established, settled, known law, received and allowed by common consent to be the standard of right and wrong, and the common measure to decide all controversies between them. For though the law of nature be plain and intelligible to all rational creatures, yet men, being biased by their interest, as well as ignorant for want of study of it, are not apt to allow of it as a law binding to them in the application of it to their particular cases.

Secondly, In the state of nature there wants a known and indifferent judge, with authority to determine all differences according to the established law. For everyone in that state being both judge and executioner of the law of nature, men

being partial to themselves, passion and revenge is very apt to carry them too far, and with too much heat in their own cases, as well as negligence and unconcernedness, make them too remiss in other men's.

Thirdly, In the state of nature there often wants power to back and support the sentence when right, and to give it due execution. They who by any injustice offended, will seldom fail where they are able by force to make good their injustice. Such resistance many times makes the punishment dangerous, and frequently destructive to those who attempt it.

Thus mankind, notwithstanding all the privileges of the state of nature, being but in an ill condition while they remain in it, are quickly driven into society. Hence it comes to pass, that we seldom find any number of men live any time together in this state. The inconveniences that they are therein exposed to by the irregular and uncertain exercise of the power every man has of punishing the transgressions of others, make them take sanctuary under the established laws of government, and therein seek the preservation of their property. 'Tis this makes them so willingly give up every one his single power of punishing to be exercised by such alone as shall be appointed to it amongst them, and by such rules as the community, or those authorized by them to that purpose, shall agree on. And in this we have the original right and rise of both the legislative and executive power as well as of the governments and societies themselves.

For in the state of nature to omit the liberty he has of innocent delights, a man has two powers.

The first is to do whatsoever he thinks fit for the preservation of himself and others within the permission of the law of nature; by which law, common to them all, he and all the rest of mankind are one community, make up one society distinct from all other creatures and were it not for the corruption and viciousness of degenerate men, there would be no need of any other, no necessity that men should separate from this great and natural community, and associate into less combinations.

The other power a man has in the state of nature is the power to punish the crimes committed against that law. Both these he gives up when he joins in a private, if I may so call it, or particular political society, and incorporates into any commonwealth separate from the rest of mankind.

The first power, *viz.* of doing whatsoever he thought fit for the preservation of himself and the rest of mankind, he gives up to be regulated by laws made by the society, so far forth as the preservation of himself and the rest of that society shall require; which laws of the society in many things confine the liberty he had by the law of nature.

Secondly, the power of punishing he wholly gives up, and engages his natural force (which he might before employ in the execution of the law of nature, by his own single authority, as he thought fit) to assist the executive power of the society as the law thereof shall require. For being now in a new state, wherein he is to enjoy many conveniences from the labour, assistance, and society of others in the same community, as well as protection from its whole strength, he is to part also with as much of his natural liberty, in providing for himself, as the good, prosperity, and safety of the society shall require, which is not only necessary but just, since the other members of the society do the like.

But though men when they enter into society give up the equality, liberty, and executive power they had in the state of nature into the hands of the society, to be so far disposed of by the legislative as the good of the society shall require, yet it being only with an intention in everyone the better to preserve himself, his liberty and property (for no rational creature can be supposed to change his condition with an intention to be worse), the power of the society or legislative constituted by them can never be supposed to extend farther than the common good, but is obliged to secure everyone's property by providing against those three defects above-mentioned that made the state of nature so unsafe and uneasy. And so, whoever has the legislative or supreme power of any commonwealth, is bound to govern by established standing laws, promulgated and known to the people, and not by extemporary decrees, by indifferent and upright judges, who are to decide controversies by those laws; and to employ the force of the community at home only in the execution of such laws, or abroad to prevent or redress foreign injuries and secure the community from inroads and invasion. And all this to be directed to no other end but the peace, safety, and public good of the people. . . .

OF THE EXTENT OF THE LEGISLATIVE POWER

These are the bounds which the trust that is put in them by the society and the law of God and nature have set to the legislative power of every commonwealth, in all forms of government.

First, They are to govern by promulgated established laws, not to be varied in particular cases, but to have one rule for rich and poor, for the favourite at Court, and the countryman at plough.

Secondly, These laws also ought to be designed for no other end ultimately but the good of the people.

Thirdly, They must not raise taxes on the property of the people without the consent of the people given by themselves or their deputies. And this properly concerns only such governments where the legislative is always in being, or at least where the people have not reserved any part of the legislative to deputies, to be from time to time chosen by themselves.

Fourthly, The legislative neither must nor can transfer the power of making laws to anybody else, or place it anywhere but where the people have. . . .

THE LEGITIMACY OF REVOLUTION

The reason why men enter into society is the preservation of their property; and the end why they choose and authorize a legislative is that there may be laws made and rules set as guards and fences to the properties of all the members of the society to limit the power and moderate the dominion of every part and member of the society; for since it can never be supposed to be the will of the society that the legislative should have a power to destroy that which every one designs to secure by entering into society, and for which the people submitted themselves to legislators of their own making. Whenever the legislators endeavour to take away and destroy the property of the people, or to reduce them to slavery under arbitrary power, they put themselves into a state of war with the people who are thereupon absolved from any further obedience, and are left to the common refuge which God has provided for all men against force and violence. Whensoever, therefore, the legislative shall transgress this fundamental rule of society, and either by ambition, fear, folly, or corruption, endeavour to grasp themselves, or put into the hands of any other, an absolute power over the lives, liberties, and estates of the people, by this breach of trust they forfeit the power the people had put into their hands for quite contrary ends, and it devolves to the people, who have a right to resume their original liberty and, by the establishment of a new legislative, such as they shall think fit, provide for their own safety and security, which is the end for which they are in society. What I have said here concerning the legislative in general holds true also concerning the supreme executor, who having a double trust put in him—both to have a part in the legislative and the supreme execution of the law—acts against both when he goes about to set up his own arbitrary will as the law of the society. . . .

Here, it is like, the common question will be made: Who shall be judge whether the prince or legislative act contrary to their trust? This, perhaps, ill-affected and factious men may spread amongst the people, when the prince only makes use of his due prerogative. To this I reply: The people shall be judge; for who shall be judge whether his trustee or deputy acts well and according to the trust reposed in him but he who deputes him and must, by having deputed him, have still a power to discard him when he fails in his trust? If this be reasonable in particular cases of private men, why should it be otherwise in that of the greatest moment where the welfare of millions is concerned, and also where the evil, if not prevented, is greater and the redress very difficult, dear, and dangerous? . . .

To conclude, the power that every individual gave the society when he entered into it, can never revert to the individuals again as long as the society lasts, but will always remain in the community, because without this there can be no community, no commonwealth, which is contrary to the original agreement; so also when the society hath placed the legislative in any assembly of men to continue in them and their successors, with direction and authority for providing such successors, the legislative can never revert to the people whilst that government lasts, because having provided a legislative with power to continue for ever, they have given up their political power to the legislative and cannot resume it. But if they have set limits to the duration of their legislative, and made this supreme power in any person or assembly only temporary; or else when by the miscarriages of those in authority it is forfeited; upon the forfeiture, or at the determination of the time set, it reverts to the society, and the people have a right to act as supreme, and continue the legislative in themselves; or place it in a new form, or new hands as they think good.

For Further Reflection

1. Locke justifies his notion of obedience to the state as a social contract, saying that it is implicit and binding because we can leave the country if we don't like it. Is this a realistic solution?

2. Compare Hobbes' account of the social contract with Locke's account. Which do you think is more accurate?

3. What would Locke say about the rights of unpopular minorities? What if a majority of a community voted that pornography should not be allowed into the community, so that it was illegal for individuals to view certain forms of art in the privacy of their homes? Would Locke's theory permit the community to limit individual liberty in this way?

VII.71   A Classical Liberal Answer: Government Must Promote Freedom

JOHN STUART MILL

Although Mill (1806–1873) agrees with Locke in favoring representational democracy, he does not accept the notion of natural rights. Typically utilitarians such as Mill follow Jeremy Bentham in viewing the idea of natural rights as "nonsense on stilts." We should promote a democracy dedicated to individual liberty because that will maximize happiness. Furthermore, Mill disagrees with Locke's majoritarian emphasis and warns of a new form of tyranny, the "tyranny of the majority." Every educated adult must be free to do what he or she desires. The only grounds for interfering with individuals is to protect others from harm.

(A biographical sketch of John Stuart Mill precedes Reading VI.65.)

Study Questions

1. What is the subject of this essay?
2. How did the concern of the patriots to set limits to power arise in society?
3. In what two ways was this limiting of political power attempted in the past?
4. What is the main problem which popular government conceals from observation?
5. What sorts of tyrannies must the individual be protected against?
6. What is the sole justification of society's interfering in the lives of its members? What are some unjustified reasons?
7. Does the principle of liberty apply to all people everywhere? Explain.
8. Does Mill base his principle of liberty on a basic natural right to liberty? If so, why? If not, why not?
9. What are the areas of life covered by the principle of liberty?
10. What is the peculiar evil of silencing unpopular expressions of opinion?
11. What does Mill say about different lifestyles?

CHAPTER I. INTRODUCTORY

THE SUBJECT OF THIS ESSAY is not the so-called Liberty of the Will, so unfortunately opposed to the misnamed doctrine of Philosophical Necessity, but Civil, or Social Liberty: the nature and limits of the power which can be legitimately exercised by society over the individual. A question seldom stated, and hardly ever discussed, in general terms, but which profoundly influences the practical controversies of the age by its latent presence, and is likely soon to make itself recognised as the vital question of the future. It is so far from being new, that, in a certain sense, it has divided mankind, almost from the remotest ages; but in the stage of progress into which the more civilised portions of the species have now entered, it presents itself under new conditions, and requires a different and more fundamental treatment.

The struggle between Liberty and Authority is the most conspicuous feature in the portions of history with which we are earliest familiar, particularly in that of Greece, Rome, and England. But in old times this contest was between subjects, or some classes of subjects, and the Government. By liberty, was meant protection against the tyranny of the political rulers. The rulers were conceived (except in some of the popular governments of Greece) as in a necessarily antagonistic position to the people whom they ruled. They consisted of a governing One, or a governing tribe or caste, who derived their authority from inheritance or conquest, who, at all events, did not hold it at the pleasure of the governed, and whose supremacy men did not venture, perhaps did not desire, to contest, whatever precautions might be taken against its oppressive exercise. Their power was regarded as necessary, but also as highly dangerous; as a weapon which they would attempt to use against their subjects, no less than against external enemies. To prevent the weaker members of the community from being preyed upon by innumerable vultures, it was needful that there should be an animal of prey stronger than the rest, commissioned to keep them down. But as the king of the vultures would be no less bent upon preying on the flock than any of the minor harpies, it was indispensable to be in a perpetual attitude of defence against his beak and claws. The aim, therefore, of patriots was to set limits to the power which the ruler should be suffered to exercise over the community; and this limitation was what they meant by liberty. It was attempted in two ways. First, by obtaining a recognition of certain immunities, called political liberties or rights, which it was to be regarded as a breach of duty in the ruler to infringe, and which if he did infringe, specific resistance, or general rebellion, was held to be justifiable. A second, and generally a later expedient, was the establishment of constitutional checks, by which the consent of the community, or of a body of some sort, supposed to represent its interests, was made a necessary condition to some of the more important acts of the governing power. To the first of these modes of limitation, the ruling power, in most European countries, was compelled, more or less, to submit. It was not so with the second; and, to attain this, or when already in some degree possessed, to attain it more completely, became everywhere the principal object of the lovers of liberty. And so long as mankind were content to combat one enemy by another, and to be ruled by a master, on condition of being guaranteed more or less efficaciously against his tyranny, they did not carry their aspirations beyond this point.

A time, however, came, in the progress of human affairs, when men ceased to think it a necessity of nature that their governors should be an independent power, opposed in interest to themselves. It appeared to them much better that the various magistrates of the State should be their tenants or delegates, revocable at their pleasure.

From John Stuart Mill, On Liberty *(1859).*

In that way alone, it seemed, could they have complete security that the powers of government would never be abused to their disadvantage. By degrees this new demand for elective and temporary rulers became the prominent object of the exertions of the popular party, wherever any such party existed; and superseded, to a considerable extent, the previous efforts to limit the power of rulers. As the struggle proceeded for making the ruling power emanate from the periodical choice of the ruled, some persons began to think that too much importance had been attached to the limitation of the power itself. That (it might seem) was a resource against rulers whose interests were habitually opposed to those of the people. What was now wanted was, that the rulers should be identified with the people; that their interest and will should be the interest and will of the nation. The nation did not need to be protected against its own will. There was no fear of its tyrannising over itself. Let the rulers be effectually responsible to it, promptly removable by it, and it could afford to trust them with power of which it could itself dictate the use to be made. Their power was but the nation's own power, concentrated, and in a form convenient for exercise. This mode of thought, or rather perhaps of feeling, was common among the last generation of European liberalism, in the Continental section of which it still apparently predominates. Those who admit any limit to what a government may do, except in the case of such governments as they think ought not to exist, stand out as brilliant exceptions among the political thinkers of the Continent. A similar tone of sentiment might by this time have been prevalent in our own country, if the circumstances which for a time encouraged it, had continued unaltered.

But, in political and philosophical theories, as well as in persons, success discloses faults and infirmities which failure might have concealed from observation. The notion, that the people have no need to limit their power over themselves, might seem axiomatic, when popular government was a thing only dreamed about, or read of as having existed at some distant period of the past. Neither was that notion necessarily disturbed by such temporary aberrations as those of the French Revolution, the worst of which were the work of a usurping few, and which, in any case, belonged, not to the permanent working of popular institutions, but to a sudden and convulsive outbreak against monarchical and aristocratic despotism. In time, however, a democratic republic came to occupy a large portion of the earth's surface, and made itself felt as one of the most powerful members of the community of nations; and elective and responsible government became subject to the observations and criticisms which wait upon a great existing fact. It was now perceived that such phrases as 'self-government,' and 'the power of the people over themselves,' do not express the true state of the case. The 'people' who exercise the power are not always the same people with those over whom it is exercised; and the 'self-government' spoken of is not the government of each by himself, but of each by all the rest. The will of the people, moreover, practically means the will of the most numerous or the most active part of the people; the majority, or those who succeed in making themselves accepted as the majority; the people, consequently may desire to oppress a part of their number; and precautions are as much needed against this as against any other abuse of power. The limitation, therefore, of the power of government over individuals loses none of its importance when the holders of power are regularly accountable to the community, that is, to the strongest party therein. This view of things, recommending itself equally to the intelligence of thinkers and to the inclination of those important classes in European society to whose real or supposed interests democracy is adverse, has had no difficulty in establishing itself, and in political speculations 'the tyranny of the majority' is now generally included among the evils against which society requires to be on its guard.

Like other tyrannies, the tyranny of the majority was at first, and is still vulgarly, held in dread, chiefly as operating through the acts of the public authorities. But reflecting persons perceived that when society is itself the tyrant—society collectively over the separate individuals who compose it—its means of tyrannising are not restricted to the acts which it may do by the hands of its political functionaries. Society can and does execute its own mandates: and if it issues wrong mandates instead of right, or any mandates at all in things with which it ought not to meddle, it practises a social tyranny more formidable than many kinds of political oppression, since, though not usually upheld by such extreme penalties, it leaves fewer means of escape, penetrating much more deeply into the details of life, and enslaving the soul itself. Protection, therefore, against the tyranny of the magistrate is not enough: there needs protection also against the tyranny of the prevailing opinion and feeling; against the tendency of society to impose, by other means than civil penalties, its own ideas and practices as rules of conduct on those who dissent from them; to fetter the development, and, if possible, prevent the formation, of any individuality not in harmony with its ways, and compels all characters to fashion themselves upon the model of its own. There is a limit to the legitimate interference of collective opinion with individual independence: and to find that limit, and maintain it against encroachment, is as indispensable to a good condition of human affairs, as protection against political despotism. . . .

The object of this Essay is to assert one very simple principle, as entitled to govern absolutely the dealings of society with the individual in the way of compulsion and control, whether the means used be physical force in the form of legal penalties, or the moral coercion of public opinion. That principle is, that the sole end for which mankind are warranted, individually or collectively, in interfering with the liberty of action of any of their number, is self-protection. That the only purpose for which power can be rightfully exercised over any member of a civilised community, against his will, is to prevent harm to others. His own good, either physical or moral, is not a sufficient warrant. He cannot rightfully be compelled to do or forbear because it will be

better for him to do so, because it will make him happier, because, in the opinions of others, to do so would be wise, or even right. These are good reasons for remonstrating with him, or reasoning with him, or persuading him, or entreating him, but not for compelling him, or visiting him with any evil in case he do otherwise. To justify that, the conduct from which it is desired to deter him must be calculated to produce evil to some one else. The only part of the conduct of any one, for which he is amenable to society, is that which concerns others. In the part which merely concerns himself, his independence is, of right, absolute. Over himself, over his own body and mind, the individual is sovereign.

It is, perhaps, hardly necessary to say that this doctrine is meant to apply to human beings in the maturity of their faculties. We are not speaking of children, or of young persons below the age which the law may fix as that of manhood or womanhood. Those who are still in a state to require being taken care of by others, must be protected against their own actions as well as against external injury. For the same reason, we may leave out of consideration those backward states of society in which the race itself may be considered as in its nonage. The early difficulties in the way of spontaneous progress are so great, that there is seldom any choice of means for overcoming them; and a ruler full of the spirit of improvement is warranted in the use of any expedients that will attain an end, perhaps otherwise unattainable. Despotism is a legitimate mode of government in dealing with barbarians, provided the end be their improvement, and the means justified by actually effecting that end. Liberty, as a principle, has no application to any state of things anterior to the time when mankind became capable of being improved by free and equal discussion. Until then, there is nothing for them but implicit obedience to an Akbar or a Charlemagne, if they are so fortunate as to find one. But as soon as mankind have attained the capacity of being guided to their own improvement by conviction or persuasion (a period long since reached in all nations with whom we need here concern ourselves), compulsion, either in the direct form or in that of pains and penalties for noncompliance, is no longer admissible as a means to their own good, and justifiable only in the security of others.

It is proper to state that I forego any advantage which could be derived to my argument from the idea of abstract right as a thing independent of utility. I regard utility as the ultimate appeal on all ethical questions; but it must be utility in the largest sense, grounded on the permanent interests of man as a progressive being. Those interests, I contend, authorize the subjection of individual spontaneity to external control, only in respect to those actions of each, which concern the interest of other people. If any one does an act hurtful to others, there is a prima facie case for punishing him, by law, or, where legal penalties are not safely applicable, by general disapprobation. There are also many positive acts for the benefit of others, which he may rightfully be compelled to perform; such as, to give evidence in a court of justice; to bear his fair share in the common defense, or in any other joint work necessary to the interest of the society of which he enjoys the protection; and to perform certain acts of individual beneficence, such as saving a fellow-creature's life, or interposing to protect the defenseless against ill-usage, things which whenever it is obviously a man's duty to do, he may rightfully be made responsible to society for not doing. A person may cause evil to others not only by his actions but by his inaction, and in neither case he is justly accountable to them for the injury. The latter case, it is true, requires a much more cautious exercise of compulsion than the former. To make any one answerable for doing evil to others, is the rule; to make him answerable for not preventing evil, is, comparatively speaking, the exception. Yet there are many cases clear enough and grave enough to justify that exception. In all things which regard the external relations of the individual, he is *de jure* amenable to those whose interests are concerned, and if need be, to society as their protector. There are often good reasons for not holding him to the responsibility; but these reasons must arise from the special expediencies of the case: either because it is a kind of case in which he is on the whole likely to act better, when left to his own discretion, than when controlled in any way in which society have it in their power to control him; or because the attempt to exercise control would produce other evils, greater than those which it would prevent. When such reasons as these preclude the enforcement of responsibility, the conscience of the agent himself should step into the vacant judgment-seat, and protect those interests of others which have no external protection; judging himself all the more rigidly, because the case does not admit of his being made accountable to the judgment of his fellow creatures.

But there is a sphere of action in which society, as distinguished from the individual, has, if any, only an indirect interest; comprehending all that portion of a person's life and conduct which affects only himself, or, if it also affects others, only with their free, voluntary, and undeceived consent and participation. When I say only himself, I mean directly, and in the first instance: for whatever affects himself, may affect others through himself, and the objection which may be grounded on this contingency, will receive consideration in the sequel. This, then, is the appropriate region of human liberty. It comprises, first, the inward domain of consciousness; demanding liberty of conscience, in the most comprehensive sense; liberty of thought and feeling; absolute freedom of opinion and sentiment on all subjects, practical or speculative, scientific, moral, or theological. The liberty of expressing and publishing opinions may seem to fall under a different principle, since it belongs to that part of the conduct of an individual which concerns other people; but, being almost of as much importance as the liberty of thought itself, and resting in great part on the same reasons, is practically inseparable from it. Secondly, the principle requires liberty of tastes and pursuits; of framing the plan of our life to suit our own character; of doing as we like, subject to such consequences as may follow; without impediment from our fellow-creatures, so long as what we do does not harm them, even though they should think our conduct foolish, perverse, or wrong. Thirdly, from this liberty of each individual, follows the liberty, within the same limits, of combination among individuals; freedom to unite, for any purpose not involving harm to others: the persons combining being supposed to be of full age, and not forced or deceived.

No society in which these liberties are not, on the whole, respected, is free, whatever may be its form of government; and none is completely free in which they do not exist absolute and unqualified. The only freedom which deserves the name, is that of pursuing our own good in our own way, so long as we do not attempt to deprive others of theirs, or impede their efforts to obtain it. Each is the proper guardian of his own health, whether bodily, or mental and spiritual. Mankind are greater gainers by suffering each other to live as seems good to themselves, than by compelling each to live as seems good to the rest.

Though this doctrine is anything but new, and, to some persons, may have the air of a truism, there is no doctrine which stands more directly opposed to the general tendency of existing opinion and practice. Society has expended fully as much effort in the attempt (according to its lights) to compel people to conform to its notions of personal as of social excellence.

CHAPTER II. OF THE LIBERTY OF THOUGHT AND DISCUSSION

The time, it is to be hoped, is gone by, when any defence would be necessary of the 'liberty of the press' as one of the securities against corrupt or tyrannical government. No argument, we may suppose, can now be needed, against permitting a legislature or an executive, not identified in interest with the people, to prescribe opinions to them, and determine what doctrines or what arguments they shall be allowed to hear. This aspect of the question, besides, has been so often and so triumphantly enforced by preceding writers, that it needs not be specially insisted on

in this place. Though the law of England, on the subject of the press, is as servile to this day as it was in the time of the Tudors, there is little danger of its being actually put in force against political discussion, except during some temporary panic, when fear of insurrection drives ministers and judges from their propriety; and, speaking generally, it is not, in constitutional countries, to be apprehended, that the government, whether completely responsible to the people or not, will often attempt to control the expression of opinion, except when in doing so it makes itself the organ of the general intolerance of the public. Let us suppose, therefore, that the government is entirely at one with the people, and never thinks of exerting any power of coercion unless in agreement with what it conceives to be their voice. But I deny the right of the people to exercise such coercion, either by themselves or by their government. The power itself is illegitimate. The best government has no more title to it than the worst. It is as noxious, or more noxious, when exerted in accordance with public opinion, than when in opposition to it. If all mankind minus one were of one opinion, and only one person were of the contrary opinion, mankind would be no more justified in silencing that one person, than he, if he had the power, would be justified in silencing mankind. Were an opinion a personal possession of no value except to the owner; if to be obstructed in the enjoyment of it were simply a private injury, it would make some difference whether the injury was inflicted only on a few persons or on many. But the peculiar evil of silencing the expression of an opinion is, that it is robbing the human race; posterity as well as the existing generation; those who dissent from the opinion, still more than those who hold it. If the opinion is right, they are deprived of the opportunity of exchanging error for truth: If wrong, they lose, what is almost as great a benefit, the clearer perception and livelier impression of truth, produced by its collision with error.

As it is useful that while mankind are imperfect there should be different opinions, so is it that there should be different experiments of living; that free scope should be given to varieties of character, short of injury to others; and that the worth of different modes of life should be proved practically, when any one thinks fit to try them. It is desirable, in short, that in things which do not primarily concern others, individuality should assert itself. Where, not the person's own character, but the traditions or customs of other people are the rule of conduct, there is wanting one of the principal ingredients of human happiness, and quite the chief ingredient of individual and social progress.

In maintaining this principle, the greatest difficulty to be encountered does not lie in the appreciation of means towards an acknowledged end, but in the indifference of persons in general to the end itself. If it were felt that the free development of individuality is one of the leading essentials of well-being; that it is not only a coordinate element with all like that is designated by the terms civilization, instruction, education, culture, but is itself a necessary part and condition of all those things; there would be no danger that liberty should be undervalued, and the adjustment of the boundaries between it and social control would present no extraordinary difficulty. But the evil is, that individual spontaneity is hardly recognized by the common modes of thinking, as having any intrinsic worth, or deserving any regard on its own account.

He who lets the world, or his own portion of it, choose his plan of life for him, has no need of any other faculty than the ape-like one of imitation. He who chooses his plan for himself, employs all his faculties. He must use observation to see, reasoning and judgment to foresee activity to gather materials for decision, discrimination to decide, and when he has decided, firmness and self-control to hold to his deliberate decision. And these qualities he requires and exercises exactly in proportion as the part of his conduct which he determines according to his own judgment and feelings is a large one. It is possible that he might be guided in some good path, and kept out of harm's way, without any of these things. But what will be his comparative worth as a human being? It really is of importance, not only what men do, but also what manner of men they are that do it. Among the works of man, which human life is rightly employed in perfecting and beautifying, the first in importance surely is man himself. Supposing it were possible to get houses built, corn grown, battles fought, causes tried, and even churches erected and prayers said, by machinery—by automatons in human form—it would be a considerable loss to exchange for these automatons even the men and women who at present inhabit the more civilized parts of the world, and who assuredly are but starved specimens of what nature can and will produce. Human nature is not a machine to be built after a model, and set to do exactly the work prescribed for it, but a tree, which requires to grow and develop itself on all sides, according to the tendency of the inward forces which make it a living thing. . . .

For Further Reflection

1. Do you agree with Mill that the principle of liberty can be justified only by utilitarian considerations? Is he correct in rejecting the notion of natural rights?

2. Do you agree with Mill's formulation of the principle of liberty? Should we sometimes act paternalistically, even with educated adults? How would Mill's principle apply to someone using drugs? Should we intervene? Would Mill advocate legalizing drugs—and thereby taking the criminal and profit motive out of the drug abuse?

3. Mill wrote, "It is not useful, but hurtful, that the constitution of the country should declare ignorance to be entitled to as much political power as knowledge," and called for weighted voting rights in which the votes of higher intelligence would count for more than the uninformed and less intelligent. Do you agree with Mill?

The Contemporary Liberal Answer VII.72

JOHN RAWLS

John Rawls (1921–2002) was for many years professor of philosophy at Harvard University and is the author of several works in moral and political philosophy. No twentieth-century work in moral and political philosophy has had greater influence on our generation than John Rawls' *A Theory of Justice*. Robert Nisbett calls it the "long awaited successor to Rousseau's *Social Contract,* the Rock on which the Church of Equality can properly be founded in our time." In scope and power, this book rivals the classics of Hobbes, Locke, and Rousseau.

In *A Theory of Justice* Rawls sets forth a hypothetical contract theory in which the bargainers go behind a veil of ignorance in order to devise a set of fundamental agreements that will govern society. No one knows his or her place in society, class position or social status, fortune in the distribution of natural assets and abilities, or even intelligence.

> Nor, again, does anyone know his conception of the good, the particulars of his rational plan of life, or even the special features of his psychology such as his aversion to risk or liability to optimism or pessimism. More than this, I assume that the parties do not know the particular circumstances of their own society. That is, they do not know its economic or political situation, or the level of civilization and culture it has been able to achieve. The persons in the original position have no information as to which generation they belong, (p. 137)

Rawls calls this the original position. Each rational person, that is, one who is normally self-interested but who doesn't know his or her place in society, can judge impartially.

By denying individuals knowledge of their natural assets and social position, Rawls prevents them from exploiting their advantages, thus transforming a decision under risk (where probabilities of outcomes are known) to a decision under uncertainty (where probabilities are not known). To the question, "Why should the individual acknowledge the principles chosen in the original position as morally binding?" Rawls would answer, "We should abide by these principles because we all would choose them under fair conditions." That is, the rules and rights chosen by fair procedures are themselves fair, because these procedures take full account of our moral nature as equally capable of "doing justice." The two principles that would be chosen, Rawls argues, are

1. everyone will have an equal right to the most extensive basic liberties compatible with similar liberty for others;

2. social and economic inequalities must satisfy two conditions:

    (a) they are to the greatest benefit of the least advantaged ("the difference principle");

    (b) they are attached to positions open to all under conditions of fair equality of opportunity.

Study Questions

1. What does Rawls say about the relative importance of the individual versus the welfare of society?
2. What sort of people does Rawls envisage as parties to the original agreement of the social structure? Are they altruistic, egoists, selfish, or rationally self-interested?
3. Does Rawls believe that we should all get together to sign an actual social contract for our society?
4. What is the level of ignorance of the parties in the original position? How deep is their ignorance?
5. Why does Rawls choose the device of a veil of ignorance? What is its purpose?
6. How does Rawls deal with accidents and natural endowments of people?
7. What are the two principles that Rawls says we would choose behind the veil of ignorance?

EACH PERSON POSSESSES an inviolability founded on justice that even the welfare of society as a whole cannot override. For this reason justice denies that the loss of freedom for some is made right by a greater good shared by others. It does not allow that the sacrifices imposed on a few are outweighed by the larger sum of advantages enjoyed by the many. Therefore, in a just society the liberties of equal citizenship are taken as settled; the rights secured by justice are not subject to political bargaining or the calculus of social interests. . . .

My aim is to present a conception of justice which generalizes and carries to a higher level of abstraction the familiar theory of the social contract as found, say, in Locke, Rousseau, and Kant. In order to do this we are not to think of the original contract as one to enter a particular society or to set up a particular form of government. Rather, the guiding idea is that the principles of justice for the basic structure of society are the object of the original agreement. They are the principles that free and rational persons concerned to further their own interests would accept in an initial position of equality as defining the fundamental terms of their association. These principles are to regulate all further agreements; they specify the kinds of social cooperation that can be entered into and the forms of government that can be established. This way of regarding the principles of justice I shall call justice as fairness.

Thus we are to imagine that those who engage in social cooperation choose together, in one joint act, the principles which are to assign basic rights and duties and to determine the division of social benefits. Men are to decide in advance how they are to regulate their claims against one another and what is to be the foundation charter of their society. Just as each person must decide by rational reflection what constitutes his good, that is, the system of ends which it is rational for him to pursue, so a group of persons must decide once and for all what is to count among them as just and unjust. The choice which rational men would make in this hypothetical situation of equal liberty, assuming for the present that this choice problem has a solution, determines the principle of justice. In justice as fairness the original position of equality corresponds to the state of nature in the traditional theory of the social contract. This original position is not, of course, thought of as an actual historical state of affairs, much less as a primitive condition of culture. It is understood as a purely hypothetical situation characterized so as to lead to a certain conception of justice. Among the essential features of this situation is that no one knows his place in society, his class position or social status, nor does anyone know his fortune in the distribution of natural assets and abilities, his intelligence, strength, and the like. I shall even assume that the parties do not know their conceptions of the good or their special psychological propensities. The principles of justice are chosen behind the veil of ignorance. This ensures that no one is advantaged or disadvantaged in the choice of principles by the outcome of natural chance or the contingency of social circumstances. Since all are similarly situated and no one is able to design principles to favor his particular condition, the principles of justice are the result of a fair agreement or bargain. For given the circumstances of the original position, the symmetry of everyone's relations to each other, this initial situation is fair between individuals as moral persons, that is, as rational beings with their own ends and capable, I shall assume, of a sense of justice. The original position is, one might say, the appropriate initial status quo, and thus the fundamental agreements reached in it are fair. This explains the propriety of the name "justice as fairness": it conveys the idea that the principles of justice are agreed to in an initial situation that is fair. The name does not mean that the concepts of justice and fairness are the same, any more than the phrase "poetry as metaphor" means that the concepts of poetry and metaphor are the same.

Justice as fairness begins, as I have said, with one of the most general of all choices which persons might make together, namely, with the choice of the first principles of a conception of justice which is to regulate all subsequent criticism and reform of institutions. Then, having chosen a conception of justice, we can suppose that they are to choose a constitution and a legislature to enact laws, and so on, all in accordance with the principles of justice initially agreed upon. Our social situation is just if it is such that by this sequence of hypothetical agreements we would

have contracted into the general system of rules which defines it. Moreover, assuming that the original position does determine a set of principles (that is, that a particular conception of justice would be chosen), it will then be true that whenever social institutions satisfy these principles those engaged in them can say to one another that they are cooperating on terms to which they would agree if they were free and equal persons whose relations with respect to one another were fair. They could all view their arrangements in an initial situation that embodies widely accepted and reasonable constraints on the choice of principles. The general recognition of this fact would provide the basis for a public acceptance of the corresponding principles of justice. No society can, of course, be a scheme of cooperation which men enter voluntarily in a literal sense; each person finds himself placed at birth in some particular position in some particular society, and the nature of this position materially affects his life prospects. Yet a society satisfying the principles of justice as fairness comes as close as a society can to being a voluntary scheme, for it meets the principles which free and equal persons would assent to under circumstances that are fair. In this sense its members are autonomous and the obligations they recognize self-imposed. . . .

One feature of justice as fairness is to think of the parties in the initial situation as rational and mutually disinterested. This does not mean that the parties are egoists; that is, individuals with only certain kinds of interests, say in wealth, prestige, and domination. But they are conceived as not taking an interest in one another's interests. They are to presume that even their spiritual aims may be opposed, in the way that the aims of those of different religions may be opposed. Moreover, the concept of rationality must be interpreted as far as possible in the narrow sense, standard in economic theory, of taking the most effective means to given ends. I shall modify this concept to some extent . . . , but one must try to avoid introducing into it any controversial ethical elements. The initial situation must be characterized by stipulations that are widely accepted.

In working out the conception of justice as fairness one main task clearly is to determine which principles of justice would be chosen in the original position. To do this we must describe this situation in some detail and formulate with care the problem of choice which it presents. It may be observed, however, that once the principles of justice are thought of as arising from an original agreement in a situation of equality, it is an open question whether the principle of utility would be acknowledged. Offhand it hardly seems likely that persons who view themselves as equals, entitled to press their claims upon one another, would agree to a principle which may require lesser life prospects for some simply for the sake of a greater sum of advantages enjoyed by others. Since each desires to protect his interests, his capacity to advance his conception of the good, no one has a reason to acquiesce in an enduring loss for himself in order to bring about a greater net balance of satisfaction. In the absence of strong and lasting benevolent impulses, a rational man would not accept a basic structure merely because it maximized the algebraic sum of advantages irrespective of its permanent effects on his own basic rights and interests. Thus it seems that the principle of utility is incompatible with the conception of social cooperation among equals for mutual advantage. It appears to be inconsistent with the idea of reciprocity implicit in the notion of a well-ordered society. Or, at any rate, so I shall argue.

I shall maintain instead that the persons in the initial situation would choose two rather different principles: the first requires equality in the assignment of basic rights and duties, while the second holds that social and economic inequalities; for example, inequalities of wealth and authority; are just only if they result in compensating benefits for everyone, and in particular for the least advantaged members of society. These principles rule out justifying institutions on the grounds that the hardships of some are offset by a greater good in the aggregate. It may be expedient but it is not just

that some should have less in order that others may prosper. But there is no injustice in the greater benefits earned by a few provided that the situation of persons not so fortunate is thereby improved. The intuitive idea is that since everyone's well-being depends upon a scheme of cooperation without which no one could have a satisfactory life, the division of advantages should be such as to draw forth the willing cooperation of everyone taking part in it, including those less well situated. Yet this can be expected only if reasonable terms are proposed. The two principles mentioned seem to be a fair agreement on the basis of which those better endowed, or more fortunate in their social position, neither of which we can be said to deserve, could expect the willing cooperation of others when some workable scheme is a necessary condition of the welfare of all. Once we decide to look for a conception of justice that nullifies the accidents of natural endowment and the contingencies of social circumstance as counters in quest for political and economic advantage, we are led to these principles. They express the result of leaving aside those aspects of the social world that seem arbitrary from a moral point of view. . . .

No one deserves his greater natural capacity nor merits a more favorable starting place in society. But it does not follow that one should eliminate these distinctions. There is another way to deal with them. The basic structure can be arranged so that these contingencies work for the good of the least fortunate. . . .

It seems to be one of the fixed points of our considered judgments that no one deserves his place in the distribution of native endowments, any more than one deserves one's initial starting place in society. The assertion that a man deserves the superior character that enables him to make the effort to cultivate his abilities is equally problematic; for his character depends in large part upon fortunate family and social circumstances for which he can claim no credit. The notion of desert seems not to apply to these cases. Thus the more advantaged representative man cannot say that he deserves and therefore has a right to a scheme of cooperation in which he is permitted to acquire benefits in ways that do not contribute to the welfare of others. . . .

TWO PRINCIPLES OF JUSTICE

I shall now state in a provisional form the two principles of justice that I believe would be chosen in the original position. . . . This first formulation is tentative.

The first statement of the two principles reads as follows:

> First: each person is to have an equal right to the most extensive basic liberty compatible with a similar liberty for others.

> Second: social and economic inequalities are to be arranged so that they are both (a) reasonably expected to be to everyone's advantage, and (b) attached to positions and offices open to all.

There are two ambiguous phrases in the second principle, namely "everyone's advantage" and "open to all." Determining their sense more exactly will lead to a second formulation of the principle.

By way of general comment, these principles primarily apply, as I have said, to the basic structure of society. They are to govern the assignment of rights and duties and to regulate the distribution of social and economic advantages. As their formulation suggests, these principles presuppose that the social structure can be divided into two more or less distinct parts, the first principle applying to the one, the second to the other. They distinguish between those aspects of the social system that define and secure the equal liberties of citizenship and those that specify and establish social and economic inequalities. The basic liberties of citizenship are, roughly speaking, political liberty (the right to vote and to be eligible for public office) together with freedom of speech and assembly; liberty of conscience and freedom of thought; freedom of the person along with the right to hold (personal) property; and freedom from arbitrary arrest and seizure as defined by the concept of the rule of law. These liberties are all required to be equal by the first principle, since citizens of a just society are to have the same basic rights. The second principle applies, in the first approximation, to the distribution of income and wealth and to the design of organizations that make use of differences in authority and responsibility, or chains of command. While the distribution of wealth and income need not be equal, it must be to everyone's advantage, and at the same time, positions of authority and offices of command must be accessible to all. One applies the second principle by holding positions open, and then, subject to this constraint, arranges social and economic inequalities so that everyone benefits.

These principles are to be arranged in a serial order with the first principle prior to the second. This ordering means that a departure from the institutions of equal liberty required by the first principle cannot be justified by, or compensated for, by greater social and economic advantages. The distribution of wealth and income, and the hierarchies of authority, must be consistent with both the liberties of equal citizenship and equality of opportunity.

It is clear that these principles are rather specific in their content, and their acceptance rests on certain assumptions that I must eventually try to explain and justify. A theory of justice depends upon a theory of society in ways that will become evident as we proceed. For the present, it should be observed that the two principles (and this holds for all formulations) are a special case of a moral general conception of justice that can be expressed as follows:

> All social values—liberty and opportunity, income and wealth, and the bases of self-respect—are to be distributed equally unless an unequal distribution of any, or all, of these values is to everyone's advantage.

Injustice, then, is simply inequalities that are not to the benefit of all. Of course, this conception is extremely vague and requires interpretation.

As a first step, suppose that the basic structure of society distributes certain primary goods, that is, things that every rational man is presumed to want. These goods normally have a use whatever a person's rational plan of life. For simplicity, assume that the chief primary goods at the disposition of society are rights and liberties, powers and opportunities, income and wealth. (Later on . . . the primary good of self-respect has a central place.) These are the social primary goods. Other primary goods such as health and vigor, intelligence and imagination, are natural goods; although their possession is influenced by the basic structure, they are not so directly under its control. Imagine, then, a hypothetical initial arrangement in which all the social primary goods are equally distributed: everyone has similar rights and duties, and income and wealth are evenly shared. This state of affairs provides a benchmark for judging improvements. If certain inequalities of wealth and organizational powers would make everyone better off than in this hypothetical starting situation, then they accord with the general conception. Now it is possible, at least theoretically, that by giving up some of their fundamental liberties men are sufficiently compensated by the resulting social and economic gains. The general conception of justice imposes no restrictions on what sort of inequalities are permissible; it only requires that everyone's position be improved. We need not suppose anything so drastic as consenting to a condition of slavery. Imagine instead that men forgo certain political rights when the economic returns are significant and their capacity to influence the course of policy by the exercise of these rights would be marginal in any case. It is this kind of exchange which the two principles as stated rule out; being arranged in serial order they do not permit exchanges between basic liberties and economic and social gains. The serial ordering of principles expresses an underlying preference among primary social goods. When this preference is rational so likewise is the choice of these principles in this order.

THE REASONING LEADING TO THE TWO PRINCIPLES OF JUSTICE

It will be recalled that the general conception of justice as fairness requires that all primary social goods will be distributed equally unless an unequal distribution would be to everyone's advantage. No restrictions are placed on exchanges of these goods and therefore a lesser liberty can be compensated for by greater social and economic benefits. Now looking at the situation from the standpoint of one person selected arbitrarily, there is no way for him to win special advantages for himself. Nor, on the other hand, are there grounds for his acquiescing in special disadvantages. Since it is not reasonable for him to expect more than an equal share in the division of social goods, and since it is not rational for him to agree to less, the sensible thing for him to do is to acknowledge as the first principle of justice one requiring an equal distribution. Indeed, this principle is so obvious that we would expect it to occur to anyone immediately.

Thus, the parties start with a principle of establishing equal liberty for all, including equality of opportunity, as well as an equal distribution of income and wealth. But there is no reason why this acknowledgment should be final. If there are inequalities in the basic structure that work to make everyone better off in comparison with the benchmark of initial equality, why not permit them? The immediate gain which a greater equality might allow can be regarded as intelligently invested in view of its future return. If, for example, these inequalities set up various incentives which succeed in eliciting more productive efforts, a person in the original position may look upon them as necessary to cover the costs of training and to encourage effective performance. One might think that ideally individuals should want to serve one another. But since the parties are assumed not to take an interest in one another's interests, their acceptance of these inequalities is only the acceptance of the relations in which men stand in the circumstances of justice. They have no grounds for complaining of one another's motives. A person in the original position would, therefore, concede the justice of these inequalities. Indeed, it would be shortsighted of him not to do so. He would hesitate to agree to these regularities only if he would be dejected by the bare knowledge of perception that others were better situated; and I have assumed that the parties decide as if they are not moved by envy. In order to make the principle regulating inequalities determinate, one looks at the system from the standpoint of the least advantaged representative man. Inequalities are permissible when they maximize, or at least all contribute to, the long-term expectations of the least fortunate group in society.

Now this general conception imposes no constraints on what sorts of inequalities are allowed, whereas the special conception, by putting the two principles in serial order (with the necessary adjustments in meaning), forbids exchanges between basic liberties and economic and social benefits. I shall not try to justify this ordering here . . . But roughly, the idea underlying this ordering is that if the parties assume that their basic liberties can be effectively exercised, they will not exchange a lesser liberty for an improvement in economic well-being. It is only when social conditions do not allow the effective establishment of these rights that one can concede their limitation; and these restrictions can be granted only to the extent that they are necessary to prepare the way for a free society. The denial of equal liberty can be denied only if it is necessary to raise the level of civilization so that in due course these freedoms can be enjoyed. Thus in adopting a serial order we are in effect making a special assumption in the original position, namely, that the parties know that the conditions of their society, whatever they are, admit the effective realization of the equal liberties. The serial ordering of the two principles of justice eventually comes to be reasonable if the general conception is consistently followed. This lexical ranking is the long-run tendency of the general view. For the most part I shall assume that the requisite circumstances for the serial order obtain.

It seems clear from these remarks that the two principles are at least a plausible conception of justice. The question, though, is how one is to argue for them more systematically. Now there are several things to do. One can work out their consequences for institutions and note their implications for fundamental social policy. In this way they are tested by a comparison with our considered judgments of justice. . . . But one can also try to find arguments in their favor that are decisive from the standpoint of the original position. In order to see how this might be done, it is useful as a heuristic device to think of the two principles as the maximin solution to the problem of social justice. There is an analogy between the two principles and the maximin rule for choice under uncertainty. This is evident from the fact that the two principles are those a person would choose for the design of a society in which his enemy is to assign him his place. The maximin rule tells us to rank alternatives by their worst possible outcomes; we are to adopt the alternative the worst outcome of which is superior to the worst outcomes of the others. The persons in the original position do not, of course, assume that their initial place in society is decided by a malevolent opponent. As I note below, they should not reason from false premises. The veil of ignorance does not violate this idea, since an absence of information is not misinformation. But that the two principles of justice would be chosen if the parties were forced to protect themselves against such a contingency explains the sense in which this conception is the maximin solution. And this analogy suggests that if the original position has been described so that it is rational for the parties to adopt the conservative attitude expressed by this rule, a conclusive argument can indeed be constructed for these principles. Clearly the maximin rule is not, in general, a suitable guide for choices under uncertainty. But it is attractive in situations marked by certain special features. My aim, then, is to show that a good case can be made for the two principles based on the fact the original position manifests these features to the fullest possible degree, carrying them to the limit, so to speak.

Consider the gain-and-loss table below. It represents the gains and losses for a situation which is not a game of strategy. There is no one playing against the person making the decision; instead he is faced with several possible circumstances which may or may not obtain. Which circumstances happen to exist does not depend upon what the person choosing decides or whether he announces his moves in advance. The numbers in the table are monetary values (in hundreds of dollars) in comparison with some initial situation. The gain (g) depends upon the individual's decision (d) and the circumstances (c). Thus $g = f(d,c)$. Assuming that there are three possible decisions and three possible circumstances, we might have this gain-and-loss table.

	CIRCUMSTANCES		
	c_1	c_2	c_3
DECISIONS d_1	–7	8	12
d_2	–8	7	14
d_3	5	6	8

The maximin rule requires that we make the third decision. For in this case the worst that can happen is that one gains five hundred dollars, which is better than the worst for the other actions. If we adopt one of these we may lose either eight or seven hundred dollars. Thus, the choice of d_3 maximizes $f(d,c)$ for that value of c which for a given d, minimizes f. The term "maximin" means the *maximum minimorum;* and the rule directs our attention to the worst that can happen under any proposed course of action, and to decide in the light of that.

Now there appear to be three chief features of situations that give plausibility to this unusual rule. First, since the rule takes no account of the likelihoods of the possible circumstances, there must be some reason for sharply discounting estimates of these probabilities. Offhand, the most natural rule of choice would seem to be to compute the expectation of monetary gain for each decision and then to adopt the course of action with the highest prospect. (This expectation is defined as follows: let us suppose that g_{ij} represent the numbers in the gain-and-loss table, where i is the row index and j is the column index; and let p_j, j= 1, 2, 3, be the likelihoods of the circumstances, with $\Sigma p_j = 1$. Then the expectation for the *ith* decision is equal to $\Sigma p_j g_{ij}$.) Thus it must be, for example, that the situation is one in which a knowledge of likelihoods is impossible, or at best extremely insecure. In this case it is unreasonable not to be skeptical of probabilistic calculations unless there is no other way out, particularly if the decision is a fundamental one that needs to be justified to others.

The second feature that suggests the maximin rule is the following: the person choosing has a conception of the good such that he cares very little, if anything, for what he might gain above the minimum stipend that he can, in fact, be sure of by following the maximin rule. It is not worthwhile for him to take a chance for the sake of a further advantage, especially when it may turn out that he loses much that is important to him. This last provision brings in the third feature; namely, that the rejected alternatives have outcomes that one can hardly accept. The situation involves grave risks. Of course, these features work most effectively in combination. The paradigm situation for following the maximin rule is when all three features are realized to the highest degree. This rule does not, then, generally apply, nor of course is it self-evident. Rather, it is a maxim, a rule of thumb, that comes into its own in special circumstances. Its application depends upon the qualitative structure of the possible gains and losses in relation to one's conception of the good, all this against a background in which it is reasonable to discount conjectural estimates of likelihoods.

It should be noted, as the comments on the gain-and-loss table say, that the entries in the table represent monetary values and not utilities. This difference is significant since for one thing computing expectations on the basis of such objective values is not the same thing as computing expected utility and may lead to different results. The essential point, though, is that in justice as fairness the parties do not know their conception of the good and cannot estimate their utility in the ordinary sense. In any case, we want to go behind de facto preferences generated by given conditions. Therefore expectations are based upon an index of primary goods and the parties make their choice accordingly. The entries in the example are in terms of money and not utility to indicate this aspect of the contract doctrine.

Now, as I have suggested, the original position has been defined so that it is a situation in which the maximin rule applies. In order to see this, let us review briefly the nature of this situation with these three special features in mind. To begin with, the veil of ignorance excludes all but the vaguest knowledge of likelihoods. The parties have no basis for determining the probable nature of their society, or their place in it. Thus they have strong reasons for being wary of probability calculations if any other course is open to them. They must also take into account the fact that their choice of principles should seem reasonable to others, in particular their descendants, whose rights will be deeply affected by it. There are further grounds for discounting that I shall mention as we go along. For the present it suffices to note that these considerations are strengthened by the fact that the parties know very little about the gain-and-loss table. Not only are they unable to conjecture the likelihoods of the various possible circumstances, they cannot say much about what the possible circumstances are, much less enumerate them and foresee the outcome of each alternative available. Those deciding are much more in the dark than the illustration by a numerical table suggests. It is for this reason that I have spoken of an analogy with the maximin rule.

Several kinds of arguments for the two principles of justice illustrate the second feature. Thus, if we can maintain that these principles provide a workable theory of social justice, and that they are compatible with reasonable demands of efficiency, then this conception guarantees a satisfactory minimum. There may be, on reflection, little reason for trying to do better. Thus much of the argument . . . is to show, by their application to the main questions of social justice, that the two principles are a satisfactory conception. These details have a philosophical purpose. Moreover, this line of thought is practically decisive if we can establish the priority of liberty, the lexical ordering of the two principles. For this priority implies that the persons in the original position have no desire to try for greater gains at the expense of the equal liberties. The minimum assured by the two principles in lexical order is not one that the parties wish to jeopardize for the sake of greater economic and social advantages. . . .

Finally, the third feature holds if we can assume that other conceptions of justice may lead to institutions that the parties would find intolerable. For example, it has sometimes been held that under some conditions the utility principle (in either form) justifies, if not slavery or serfdom, at any rate serious infractions of liberty for the sake of greater social benefits. We need not consider here the truth of this claim, or the likelihood that the requisite conditions obtain. For the moment, this contention is only to illustrate the way in which conceptions of justice may allow for outcomes which the parties may not be able to accept. And having the ready alternative of the two principles of justice which secure a satisfactory minimum, it seems unwise, if not irrational, for them to take a chance that these outcomes are not realized.

So much, then, for a brief sketch of the features of situations in which the maximin rule comes into its own and of the way in which the arguments for the two principles of justice can be subsumed under them. . . .

General Conception: All social primary goods—liberty and opportunity, income and wealth, and the bases of self-respect—are to be distributed equally unless an unequal distribution of any or all of these goods is to the advantage of the least favored.

For Further Reflection

1. Why does Rawls choose the device of a veil of ignorance? What is its purpose? What is the level of ignorance of the parties in the original position? How deep is their ignorance?

2. Why does Rawls call his theory of justice "justice as fairness"? Wallace Matson ("What Rawls Calls Justice," *The Occasional Review,* Autumn, 1978, pp. 45–57) has argued that Rawls' theory really is not a theory of justice, since its main principle, equal liberty, is an independent notion from justice. In a monastery people could have justice, but not liberty, and in anarchy people would have liberty but not necessarily justice. Matson claims that Rawls is concerned about balancing claims and assigning rights, the work of judges, whereas justice is giving persons their due. Is Matson correct about this? Can you defend Rawls' theory as a theory of justice?

3. In the original position, behind the veil of ignorance, would you choose the principles that Rawls claims rational choosers would choose? Explain your answer.

4. Examine Rawls' two principles. Can you discover any problems with either of them? The controversial principle is 2.a, the difference principle: that "all social primary goods—liberty and opportunity, income and wealth, and the bases of self-respect—are to be distributed equally unless an unequal distribution . . . is to the advantage of the least favored" (*A Theory of Justice,* 304).

Rawls subsumes it under the ideal of fraternity, of "not wanting to have greater advantages unless this is to the benefit of others who are less well off" (*A Theory of Justice,* 105). He likens it to the relationship in a family where members do not wish to gain unless they do so in ways that advance the interests of the other members. Can you think of better ways to arrange society? What would a utilitarian or a libertarian say to Rawls' proposals?

5. Examine Rawls' view that we don't deserve our natural talents and abilities. What conclusions does Rawls draw from that premise? Examine the following passage.

> [N]one of the precepts of justice aims at rewarding virtue. The premiums earned by scarce natural talents, for example, are to cover the costs of training and to encourage the efforts of learning, as well as to direct ability to where it best furthers the common interest. The distributive shares that result do not correlate with moral worth, since the initial endowment of natural assets and the contingencies of their growth and nurture in early life are arbitrary from a moral point of view. The precept which seems intuitively to come closest to rewarding moral desert is that of distribution according to effort, or perhaps, conscientious effort. Once again, however, it seems clear that the effort a person is willing to make is influenced by his natural abilities and skills and the alternatives open to him. The better endowed are more likely, other things equal, to strive conscientiously, and there seems to be no way to discount for their greater good fortune. The idea of rewarding desert is impracticable. And certainly to the extent that the precept of need is emphasized, moral worth is ignored. . . . For a society to organize itself with the aim of rewarding moral desert as a first principle would be like having the institution of property in order to punish thieves. (*A Theory of Justice,* 312f)

Critically evaluate Rawls' views on rewarding desert.

6. What are the main strengths and weaknesses of Rawls' liberal theory of justice?

Key Terms

anarchism	absolutism, political	democracy
libertarianism, political	liberalism, political	

Suggestions for Further Reading

Barry, Brian. *Political Argument*. Routledge & Kegan Paul, 1965.

Bedau, Hugo, ed. *Justice and Equality*. Prentice Hall, 1971.

Benn, S. I., and R. S. Peters. *The Principles of Political Thought*. Free Press, 1995.

Benn, Stanley. "Justice," in *The Encyclopedia of Philosophy*. Macmillan, 1967.

Bowie, Norman, and Robert Simon. *The Individual and the Political Order*. Englewood Cliffs, NJ: Prentice Hall, 1977.

Daniels, Norman, ed. *Reading Rawls*. Basic Books, 1975.

Nagel, Thomas. *Equality and Partiality*. Oxford University Press, 1991.

Nielsen, Kai. "Radical Egalitarian Justice: Justice as Equality," *Social Theory and Practice*, vol. 5, no. 2, 1979.

Nozick, Robert. *Anarchy, State, and Utopia*. Basic Books, 1974.

Okin, Susan Moller. *Justice, Gender, and the Family*. Basic Books, 1989.

Pojman, Louis P. *Political Philosophy*. McGraw-Hill, 2003.

Rawls, John. *A Theory of Justice*. Harvard University Press, 1971.

Rawls, John. *Political Liberalism*. Columbia University Press, 1993.

Reiman, Jeffrey. *Justice and Modern Moral Philosophy*. Yale University Press, 1990.

Rescher, Nicholas. *Distributive Justice*. Bobbs-Merrill, 1966.

Sandel, Michael. *Liberalism and the Limits of Justice*. Cambridge University Press, 1988.

Sterba, James. *The Demands of Justice*. University of Notre Dame Press, 1980.

Sterba, James. *How to Make People Just*. Rowman and Littlefield, 1988.

Sterba, James P., ed. *Justice: Alternative Political Perspectives*. Wadsworth, 1992.

Sterba, James P. *Contemporary Social and Political Philosophy*. Wadsworth, 1995.

Taylor, Richard. *Freedom, Anarchy, and Law*, 2nd ed. Prometheus Books, 1982.

Veatch, Robert M. *The Foundations of Justice*. Oxford University Press, 1986.

Walzer, Michael. *Spheres of Justice*. Oxford University Press, 1983.

Wolgast, Elizabeth. *The Grammar of Justice*. Cornell University Press, 1987.

Part VIII

What Is the Meaning of Life?

To lose one's life is a little thing and I shall have the courage to do so if it is necessary; but to see the meaning of this life dissipated, to see our reason for existing disappear, that is what is unbearable. One cannot live without meaning.

ALBERT CAMUS

What is missing in my life is an understanding of what I must do, *not what I must know*—except, of course, that a certain amount of knowledge is presupposed in every action. I need to understand the purpose of my life, and this means that I must find a truth which is true for me, that I must discover *that Idea for which I can live and die. For what is truth but to live and die for an Idea?*

SØREN KIERKEGAARD as a twenty-two-year-old university student.
An entry in his journal August 1, 1835.

IN HIS AUTOBIOGRAPHY TOLSTOY tells the story of a traveler fleeing an infuriated animal. Attempting to save himself from the beast, the man runs towards a well and begins to climb down, when to his distress he spies a dragon at the bottom. The dragon is waiting for him with open jaws, ready to eat him. The poor fellow is caught in a dilemma. He dare not drop into the well for fear of the dragon, but he dare not climb out of the well for fear of the beast. So he clutches a branch of a bush growing in the cleft of the well and hangs onto it for dear life. His hands grow weak, and he feels that soon he shall have to give into his grim fate, but he still holds on desperately. As he grasps the branch for his salvation, he notices that two mice, one white and one black, are nibbling away at the main trunk of the branch onto which he is clinging. Soon they will dislodge the branch, and he will fall into the waiting jaws of the dragon.

The traveler knows that he will soon perish, but while clinging to the branch, he sees some drops of honey hanging on the leaves of the bush, and so sticks out his tongue and licks the leaves.

The traveler is you, and his plight is your plight, the danger of your demise on every hand. The white mouse represents your days and the black your nights. Together they are nibbling away at the three score years and ten which make up your branch of life. Inevitably all will be over, and what have you to show for it? Is your brief distraction of the taste of honey all you get out of life? Is this life all there is? Can this brief moment in the history of the universe have significance? What gives life importance?

The certainty of death heightens the question of the meaning of life. Like a prisoner sentenced to death or a patient with terminal illness, we know that, in a sense, we are all sentenced to death and are terminally ill, but we flee the thought in a thousand ways. What is the purpose of life?

Our readings represent some of the classic responses to this question. Epicurus advises moderate pleasure in a life that accepts mortality without tears. Epictetus distinguishes between those things in life that are up to us (intentions, desires, etc.) and those things that are not up to us (our bodies, property, reputation, etc.). If we keep these two things straight, he says, we will be free of burdens, harm, and grief. Camus argues that life is meaningless and, to illustrate his view, he tells the story of Sisyphus rolling a stone up a hill for eternity. Baggini criticizes the notion that life has meaning only when it is lived toward future goals and objectives. Pojman finds the essence of a purposeful life in religion. Nagel argues that our sense of the absurd is what contributes to our greatness as self-conscious beings. Russell argues that three things make life worth living: love, knowledge, and pity.

Moderate Hedonism　　　VIII.73

EPICURUS

Epicurus (341–271 B.C.) was a Greek philosopher who was born on the isle of Samos but lived much of his life in Athens, where he founded his very successful school of philosophy. He was influenced by the materialist Democritus (460–370 B.C.), who is the first philosopher known to believe that the world is made up of atoms. Only a few fragments of Epicurus' writings are extant.

Epicurus identified good with pleasure and evil with pain. This doctrine (repeated later in Bentham) is called *hedonism* (from the Greek word for pleasure). But contrary to popular opinion, Epicurus was not proposing what "Epicureanism" sometimes has been taken to mean: a sensuous, profligate life. He believed that the true life of pleasure consisted in an attitude of imperturbable emotional calm which needed only simple pleasures, a good diet, health, a prudent moral life, and good friends. Only good or bad sensations (pleasure or pain) should concern us, and death is not a sensation, so we should not fear death.

Study Questions

1. Does Epicurus believe in God? What sort of theology does he have?
2. What counsel does he give about death? What is his argument? Is it plausible?
3. What should the wise person seek? That is, what is the good?
4. What is the relationship between pleasure and pain? Describe his philosophy of life. What does he mean by the complete life?
5. What is his view of morality (justice)?

LETTER TO MENOECEUS

LET NO ONE WHEN YOUNG delay to study philosophy, nor when he is old grow weary of his study. For no one can come too early or too late to secure the health of his soul. And the man who says that the age for philosophy has either not yet come or has gone by is like the man who says that the age for happiness is not yet come to him, or has passed away. Wherefore both when young and old a man must study philosophy, that as he grows old he may be young in blessings through the grateful recollection of what has been, and that in youth he may be old as well, since he will know no fear of what is to come. We must then meditate on the things that make our happiness, seeing that when that is with us we have all, but when it is absent we do all to win it.

The things which I used unceasingly to commend to you, these do and practise, considering them to be the first principles of the good life. First of all believe that god is a being immortal and blessed, even as the common idea of a god is engraved on men's minds, and do not assign to

From Epicurus: The Extant Remains, *translated by Cyril Bailey, 1926. Reprinted by permission of* Oxford University Press.

him anything alien to his immortality or ill-suited to his blessedness: but believe about him everything that can uphold his blessedness and immortality. For gods there are, since the knowledge of them is by clear vision. But they are not such as the many believe them to be: for indeed they do not consistently represent them as they believe them to be. And the impious man is not he who denies the gods of the many, but he who attaches to the gods the beliefs of the many. For the statements of the many about the gods are not conceptions derived from sensation, but false suppositions, according to which the greatest misfortunes befall the wicked and the greatest blessings the good by the gift of the gods. For men being accustomed always to their own virtues welcome those like themselves, but regard all that is not of their nature as alien.

Become accustomed to the belief that death is nothing to us. For all good and evil consists in sensation, but death is deprivation of sensation. And therefore a right understanding that death is nothing to us makes the mortality of life enjoyable, not because it adds to it an infinite span of time, but because it takes away the craving for immortality. For there is nothing terrible in life for the man who has truly comprehended that there is nothing terrible in not living. So that the man speaks but idly who says that he fears death not because it will be painful when it comes, but because it is painful in anticipation. For that which gives no trouble when it comes, is but an empty pain in anticipation. So death, the most terrifying of ills, is nothing to us, since so long as we exist, death is not with us; but when death comes, then we do not exist. It does not then concern either the living or the dead, since for the former it is not, and the latter are no more.

But the many at one moment shun death as the greatest of evils, at another yearn for it as a respite from the evils in life. But the wise man neither seeks to escape life nor fears the cessation of life, for neither does life offend him nor does the absence of life seem to be any evil. And just as with food he does not seek simply the larger share and nothing else, but rather the most pleasant, so he seeks to enjoy not the longest period of time, but the most pleasant.

And he who counsels the young man to live well, but the old man to make a good end, is foolish, not merely because of the desirability of life, but also because it is the same training which teaches to live well and to die well. Yet much worse still is the man who says it is good not to be born, but

> once born make haste to pass the gates of Death.

For if he says this from conviction why does he not pass away out of life? For it is open to him to do so, if he had firmly made up his mind to this. But if he speaks in jest, his words are idle among men who cannot receive them.

We must then bear in mind that the future is neither ours, nor yet wholly not ours, so that we may not altogether expect it as sure to come, nor abandon hope of it, as if it will certainly not come.

We must consider that of desires some are natural, others vain, and of the natural some are necessary and others merely natural; and of the necessary some are necessary for happiness, others for the repose of the body, and others for very life. The right understanding of these facts enables us to refer all choice and avoidance to the health of the body and the soul's freedom from disturbance, since this is the aim of the life of blessedness. For it is to obtain this end that we always act, namely, to avoid pain and fear. And when this is once secured for us, all the tempest of the soul is dispersed, since the living creature has not to wander as though in search of something that is missing, and to look for some other thing by which he can fulfil the good of the soul and the good of the body. For it is then that we have need of pleasure, when we feel pain owing to the absence of pleasure; but when we do not feel pain, we no longer need pleasure. And for this cause we call pleasure the beginning and end of the blessed life. For we recognize pleasure as the first good innate in us, and from pleasure we begin every act of choice and avoidance, and to pleasure we return again, using the feeling as the standard by which we judge every good.

And since pleasure is the first good and natural to us, for this very reason we do not choose every pleasure, but sometimes we pass over many pleasures, when greater discomfort accrues to us as the result of them: and similarly we think many pains better than pleasures, since a greater pleasure comes to us when we have endured pains for a long time. Every pleasure then because of its natural kinship to us is good, yet not every pleasure is to be chosen: even as every pain also is an evil, yet not all are always of a nature to be avoided. Yet by a scale of comparison and by the consideration of advantages and disadvantages we must form our judgment on all these matters. For the good on certain occasions we treat as bad, and conversely the bad as good.

And again independence of desire we think a great good—not that we may at all times enjoy but a few things, but that, if we do not possess many, we may enjoy the few in the genuine persuasion that those have the sweetest pleasure in luxury who least need it, and that all that is natural is easy to be obtained, but that which is superfluous is hard. And so plain savours bring us pleasure equal to a luxurious diet, when all the pain due to want is removed; and bread and water produce the highest pleasure, when one who needs them puts them to his lips. To grow accustomed therefore to simple and not luxurious diet gives us health to the full, and makes a man alert for the needful employments of life, and when after long intervals we approach luxuries, disposes us better towards them, and fits us to be fearless of fortune.

When, therefore, we maintain that pleasure is the end, we do not mean the pleasures of profligates and those that consist in sensuality, as is supposed by some who are either ignorant or disagree with us or do not understand, but freedom from pain in the body and from trouble in the mind. For it is not continuous drinkings and revellings, nor the satisfaction of lusts, nor the enjoyment of fish and other luxuries of the wealthy table, which produce a pleasant life, but sober reasoning, searching out the motives for all choice and avoidance, and banishing mere opinions, to which are due the greatest disturbance of the spirit.

Of all this the beginning and the greatest good is prudence. Wherefore prudence is a more precious thing even than philosophy: for from prudence are sprung all the other virtues, and it teaches us that it is not possible to live pleasantly without living prudently and honourably and justly, nor, again, to live a life of prudence, honour, and justice without living pleasantly. For the virtues are by nature bound up with the pleasant life, and the pleasant life is inseparable from them. For indeed who, think you, is a better man than he who holds reverent opinions concerning the gods, and is at all times free from fear of death, and has reasoned out the end ordained by nature? He understands that the limit of good things is easy to fulfil and easy to attain, whereas the course of ills is either short in time or slight in pain: he laughs at destiny, whom some have introduced as the mistress of all things. He thinks that with us lies the chief power in determining events, some of which happen by necessity and some by chance, and some are within our control; for while necessity cannot be called to account, he sees that chance is inconstant, but that which is in our control is subject to no master, and to it are naturally attached praise and blame. For, indeed, it were better to follow the myths about the gods than to become a slave to the destiny of the natural philosophers: for the former suggests a hope of placating the gods by worship, whereas the latter involves a necessity which knows no placation. As to chance, he does not regard it as a god as most men do (for in a god's acts there is no disorder), nor as an uncertain cause of all things: for he does not believe that good and evil are given by chance to man for the framing of a blessed life, but that opportunities for great good and great evil are afforded by it. He therefore thinks it better to be unfortunate in reasonable action than to prosper in unreason. For it is better in a man's actions that what is well chosen should fail, rather than that what is ill chosen should be successful owing to chance.

Meditate therefore on these things and things akin to them night and day by yourself, and with a companion like to yourself, and never shall you be disturbed waking or asleep, but you shall live like a god among men. For a man who lives among immortal blessings is not like to a mortal being.

PRINCIPAL DOCTRINES

I. The blessed and immortal nature knows no trouble itself nor causes trouble to any other, so that it is never constrained by anger or favour. For all such things exist only in the weak.

II. Death is nothing to us: for that which is dissolved is without sensation; and that which lacks sensation is nothing to us.

III. The limit of quantity in pleasures is the removal of all that is painful. Wherever pleasure is present, as long as it is there, there is neither pain of body nor of mind, nor of both at once.

IV. Pain does not last continuously in the flesh, but the acutest pain is there for a very short time, and even that which just exceeds the pleasure in the flesh does not continue for many days at once. But chronic illnesses permit a predominance of pleasure over pain in the flesh.

V. It is not possible to live pleasantly without living prudently and honourably and justly, nor again to live a life of prudence, honour, and justice without living pleasantly. And the man who does not possess the pleasant life, is not living prudently and honourably and justly, and the man who does not possess the virtuous life, cannot possibly live pleasantly.

VI. To secure protection from men anything is a natural good, by which you may be able to attain this end.

VII. Some men wished to become famous and conspicuous, thinking that they would thus win for themselves safety from other men. Wherefore if the life of such men is safe, they have obtained the good which nature craves; but if it is not safe, they do not possess that for which they strove at first by the instinct of nature.

VIII. No pleasure is a bad thing in itself: but the means which produce some pleasures bring with them disturbances many times greater than the pleasures.

IX. If every pleasure could be intensified so that it lasted and influenced the whole organism or the most essential parts of our nature, pleasures would never differ from one another.

X. If the things that produce the pleasures of profligates could dispel the fears of the mind about the phenomena of the sky and death and its pains, and also teach the limits of desires and of pains, we should never have cause to blame them: for they would be filling themselves full with pleasures from every source and never have pain of body or mind, which is the evil of life.

XI. If we were not troubled by our suspicions of the phenomena of the sky and about death, fearing that it concerns us, and also by our failure to grasp the limits of pains and desires, we should have no need of natural science.

XII. A man cannot dispel his fear about the most important matters if he does not know what is the nature of the universe but suspects the truth of some mythical story. So that without natural science it is not possible to attain our pleasures unalloyed.

XIII. There is no profit in securing protection in relation to men, if things above and things beneath the earth and indeed all in the boundless universe remain matters of suspicion.

XIV. The most unalloyed source of protection from men, which is secured to some extent by a certain force of expulsion, is in fact the immunity which results from a quiet life and the retirement from the world.

XV. The wealth demanded by nature is both limited and easily procured; that demanded by idle imaginings stretches on to infinity.

XVI. In but few things chance hinders a wise man, but the greatest and most important matters reason has ordained and throughout the whole period of life does and will ordain.

XVII. The just man is most free from trouble, the unjust most full of trouble.

XVIII. The pleasure in the flesh is not increased, when once the pain due to want is removed, but is only varied: and the limit as regards pleasure in the mind is begotten by the reasoned understanding of these very pleasures and of the emotions akin to them, which used to cause the greatest fear to the mind.

XIX. Infinite time contains no greater pleasure than limited time, if one measures by reason the limits of pleasure.

XX. The flesh perceives the limits of pleasure as unlimited and unlimited time is required to supply it. But the mind, having attained a reasoned understanding of the ultimate good of the flesh and its limits and having dissipated the fears concerning the time to come, supplies us with the complete life, and we have no further need of infinite time: but neither does the mind shun pleasure, nor, when circumstances begin to bring about the departure from life, does it approach its end as though it fell short in any way of the best life.

XXI. He who has learned the limits of life knows that that which removes the pain due to want and makes the whole of life complete is easy to obtain; so that there is no need of actions which involve competition.

XXII. We must consider both the real purpose and all the evidence of direct perception, to which we always refer the conclusions of opinion; otherwise, all will be full of doubt and confusion.

XXIII. If you fight against all sensations, you will have no standard by which to judge even those of them which you say are false.

XXIV. If you reject any single sensation and fail to distinguish between the conclusion of opinion as to the appearance awaiting confirmation and that which is actually given by the sensation or feeling, or each intuitive apprehension of the mind, you will confound all other sensations as well with the same groundless opinion, so that you will reject every standard of judgment. And if among the mental images created by your opinion you affirm both that which awaits confirmation and that which does not, you will not escape error, since you will have preserved the whole cause of doubt in every judgment between what is right and what is wrong.

XXV. If on each occasion instead of referring your actions to the end of nature, you turn to some other nearer standard when you are making a choice or an avoidance, your actions will not be consistent with your principles.

XXVI. Of desires, all that do not lead to a sense of pain, if they are not satisfied, are not necessary, but involve a craving which is easily dispelled, when the object is hard to procure or they seem likely to produce harm.

XXVII. Of all the things which wisdom acquires to produce the blessedness of the complete life, far the greatest is the possession of friendship.

XXVIII. The same conviction which has given us confidence that there is nothing terrible that lasts for ever or even for long, has also seen the protection of friendship most fully completed in the limited evils of this life.

XXIX. Among desires some are natural and necessary, some natural but not necessary, and others neither natural nor necessary, but due to idle imagination.

XXX. Wherever in the case of desires which are physical, but do not lead to a sense of pain, if they are not fulfilled, the effort is intense, such pleasures are due to idle imagination, and it is not owing to their own nature that they fail to be dispelled, but owing to the empty imaginings of the man.

XXXI. The justice which arises from nature is a pledge of mutual advantage to restrain men from harming one another and save them from being harmed.

XXXII. For all living things which have not been able to make contracts not to harm one another or be harmed, nothing ever is either just or unjust; and likewise too for all tribes of men which have been unable or unwilling to make contracts not to harm or be harmed.

XXXIII. Justice never is anything in itself, but in the dealings of men with one another in any place whatever and at any time it is a kind of contract not to harm or be harmed.

XXXIV. Injustice is not an evil in itself, but only in consequence of the fear which attaches to the apprehension of being unable to escape those appointed to punish such actions.

XXXV. It is not possible for one who acts in secret contravention of the terms of the compact not to harm or be harmed, to be confident that he will escape detection, even if at present he escapes a thousand times. For up to the time of death it cannot be certain that he will indeed escape.

XXXVI. In its general aspect justice is the same for all, for it is a kind of mutual advantage in the dealings of men with one another: but with reference to the individual peculiarities of a country or any other circumstances the same thing does not turn out to be just for all.

XXXVII. Among actions which are sanctioned as just by law, that which is proved on examination to be of advantage in the requirements of men's dealings with one another, has the guarantee of justice, whether it is the same for all or not. But if a man makes a law and it does not turn out to lead to advantage in men's dealings with each other, then it no longer has the essential nature of justice. And even if the advantage in the matter of justice shifts from one side to the other, but for a while accords with the general concept, it is none the less just for that period in the eyes of those who do not confound themselves with empty sounds but look to the actual facts.

XXXVIII. Where, provided the circumstances have not been altered, actions which were considered just, have been shown not to accord with the general concept in actual practice, then they are not just. But where, when circumstances have changed, the same actions which were sanctioned as just no longer lead to advantage, there they were just at the time when they were of advantage for the dealings of fellow-citizens with one another; but subsequently they are no longer just, when no longer of advantage.

XXXIX. The man who has best ordered the element of disquiet arising from external circumstances has made those things that he could akin to himself and the rest at least not alien: but with all to which he could not do even this, he has refrained from mixing, and has expelled from his life all which it was of advantage to treat thus.

XL. As many as possess the power to procure complete immunity from their neighbours, these also live most pleasantly with one another, since they have the most certain pledge of security, and after they have enjoyed the fullest intimacy, they do not lament the previous departure of a dead friend, as though he were to be pitied.

For Further Reflection

1. Epicureanism is often thought of as a shallow, gluttonous, profligate life of undifferentiated pleasure, whose motto has been "Eat, drink, and be merry, for tomorrow we die" ("the pig philosophy"). Does one get this impression from Epicurus' writings?

2. Consider his view toward the fact of death: You ought not fear what never touches you. Death never touches you, for when you are, it is not; and when it is, you are not. Is this a reasonable argument against the fear of death? Why do we consider death an evil? What is the proper attitude toward death and why?

3. In the Hindu scripture *Bhagavad Gita*, Dharma, the personification of Duty, asks the young prince Yudhistira, "Of all the world's wonders, which is the most wonderful?" Yudhistira replies, "That no man, though he sees others dying all around him, believes that he himself will die." Is this applicable to Epicureanism? Is it a telling criticism?

4. How important is pleasure for the good life? What makes the "complete life" that Epicurus wrote about?

Stoicism: Enchiridion   VIII.74

EPICTETUS

Epictetus (c. 50–130 A.D.) was born a Greek slave in Asia Minor and was freed sometime after the death of Nero in 68 A.D. Epictetus was expelled from Rome by the Emperor Domitian in 90 A.D. and died in northern Greece about 130. He was known as a kindly man, humble and charitable, especially to children. He was crippled in slavery which might have influenced his motto: "Bear and forbear." He embraced Stoicism and taught that we should submit to our fate as God's sacred gift and design. Epictetus did not publish anything, but his pupil Flavius Arrianus has recorded his teachings, the most famous of which is the *Enchiridion* (a handbook).

Stoicism was a Greek school of philosophy founded in 108 B.C. in Athens by Zeno of Citium and developed into the dominant philosophy of the Roman Empire. The word "stoa" from which "Stoic" derives is the Greek word for porch. Apparently Zeno lectured from his porch. The Stoics believed that we should resign ourselves to our fate, do our duty faithfully, and thereby acquire tranquillity of mind. The world is transient and unstable. We cannot change very much, but we can master our souls so that we attain tranquillity amidst the chaos all around us. The Stoics were the first world citizens, "cosmopolitans," holding that a divine spark dwelt in every human being. Chrysippus (c. 280–206 B.C.), referred to in the text, was the third leader of the Stoics and credited with more than 700 treatises. The Stoics believed that all human beings were brothers and sisters under one Father, God.

The first short selection on Duty is from the Stoic Roman Emperor Marcus Aurelius (121–180 A.D.). The second short selection on Suicide is from the Stoic Seneca (3–65 A.D.). The third, long selection is from Epictetus's teachings.

Study Questions

1. What is Marcus Aurelius' attitude toward duty?
2. What is Seneca's attitude toward death and suicide?
3. According to Epictetus, which things are and are not up to us?
4. Why should we destroy desire altogether? Is Epictetus consistent on this point?
5. Should we be upset when our loved ones die? What should our attitude toward them be?
6. Should we seek for things to happen as we wish? How should we wish them?
7. What does illness impede? What does it not impede?
8. What does Epictetus mean when he says we ought to conduct ourselves as we would at a banquet?
9. Why shouldn't you be upset by the thought that you shall live without honor, a complete nobody?
10. Is there anything intrinsically evil?
11. What are Epictetus' views on laughter, oaths, luxury, and sex?
12. What role does Socrates play in Epictetus' philosophy?

1. MARCUS AURELIUS
DEDICATION TO DUTY

HOUR BY HOUR resolve to do the task of the hour carefully, with unaffected dignity, affectionately, freely and justly. You can avoid distractions that might interfere with such performance if every act is done as though it were the last act of your life. Free yourself from random aims and curb any tendency to let the passions of emotion, hypocrisy, self-love and dissatisfaction with your allotted share cause you to ignore the commands of reason.

2. SENECA *DEATH AND SUICIDE*

Life has carried some men with the greatest rapidity to the harbor, the harbor they were bound to reach if they tarried on the way, while others it has fretted and harassed. To such a life, as you are aware, one should not always cling. *For mere living is not a good, but living well.* Accordingly, the wise man will live as long as he ought, not as long as he can. He will mark in what place, with whom, and how he is to conduct his existence, and what he is about to do. He always reflects concerning the quality, and not the quantity of his life. As soon as there are many events in his life that give him trouble and disturb his peace of mind, he sets himself free. And this privilege is his, not only when the crisis is upon him, but as soon as Fortune seems to be playing him false; then he looks about carefully and sees whether he ought, or ought not, to end his life on that account . . . He does not regard death with fear, as if it were a great loss; for no man can lose very much when but a driblet remains. It is not a question of dying earlier or later, but of dying well or ill. And dying well means escape from the danger of living ill.

3. EPICTETUS *ENCHIRIDION*

1. Some things are up to us, some are not up to us. Up to us are perception, intention, desire, aversion, and in sum, whatever are our own doings; not up to us are body, property, reputation, political office and in sum, whatever are not our own doings. And the things that are up to us are naturally free, unforbidding, unimpeding, while those not up to us are weak, slavish, forbidding, alien. Remember, then, that if you think naturally slavish things are free and that alien things are your own, you will be impeded, grieved, troubled, you will blame gods and men; but if you think that what is yours is yours and what is alien is alien, as it really is, nobody will ever compel you, nobody will forbid you, you will not blame anyone, you will not complain about anything, you will not do a single thing unwillingly, you will have no enemy, no one will hurt you; for you will not suffer anything harmful.

If you are aiming for such great things, remember that you must not be moderate in exerting yourself to attain them: you must avoid some things altogether and postpone others for the time being. For if you want both to accomplish these aims, and also to achieve eminence and riches, it may come about that you will not get the latter because you were trying for the former, and certainly you will not get the former, which are the only things that produce freedom and well-being.

So take rigorous care to say to every menacing impression, "You are just an impression, not the real thing at all." Then test it and consider it according to your rules-first and foremost this: whether it belongs among the things that are up to us or to those not up to us. And if it is something not up to us, be ready to say "It is nothing to me."

2. Remember that the aim of desire is to get what arouses the desire, the aim of aversion is to

Epictetus, Enchiridion, *translation by Wallace I. Matson. Copyright © Wallace Matson 1996. Used by permission.*

avoid that to which you are averse; and he who fails to get what he desires is miserable, and so is he who gets what he is averse to. So then, if you are averse only to things contrary to nature that are up to you, you will not get anything to which you are averse; but if you are averse to sickness or death or poverty, you will be miserable. So take your aversion away from everything that is not up to you and transfer it to things contrary to nature that are up to you. But for the time being, destroy desire altogether; for if you desire something not up to you, necessarily you will be unfortunate; as for things that are up to us, and would be good to desire, none of them is yet within your grasp. But only make use of selection and rejection, and these lightly, discreetly, and tentatively.

3. As for every thing that delights your mind or is useful or beloved, remember to describe it as it really is, starting with the smallest thing. If you are fond of a pot, say "It is a pot that I am fond of." For then, if it breaks, you will not be upset. If you kiss your child or your wife, say that you are kissing a human being. Then if they die you will not be upset.

5. It is not things that upset people but rather ideas about things. For example, death is nothing terrible, else it would have seemed so even to Socrates; rather it is the idea that death is terrible that is terrible. So whenever we are frustrated or upset or grieved, let us not blame others, but ourselves-that is, our ideas. It is the act of a philosophically ignorant person to blame others for his own troubles. One who is beginning to learn blames himself. An educated person blames neither anyone else nor himself.

6. Do not pride yourself on superiority that is not your own. If a horse in its pride should say, "I am a fine horse," that could be tolerated. You however, when you boast "I have a fine horse," should realize that you are boasting about the excellence of a horse. What then is your own? The use of impressions. So, make use of your impressions in accord with nature, and then take pride; for your pride will be in a good thing that is your own.

8. Don't seek for things to happen as you wish, but wish for things to happen as they do, and you will get on well.

9. Illness is an impediment of the body, but not of the will, as long as the will itself does not so wish. Lameness is an impediment of the leg, not of the will. And say this to yourself of every accident that befalls you; for you will find it an impediment to something else, not to yourself.

10. Whatever occasion befalls you, remember to turn around and look into yourself to see what power you have to make use of it. If you see a handsome boy or a beautiful girl, you will find the relevant power to be self-control. If labor is heaped on you, endurance is what you need; if abuse, forbearance. And thus habituating yourself, you will not be carried away by impressions.

11. Never say about anything that you have "lost it," but that you have "given it back." Your child has died? It has been given back. Your wife has died? She has been given back. "I have been deprived of my estate." This too has been given back. "But the usurper is wicked." What concern is it of yours, through whom the gift was returned to the giver? For the time it is given to you, treat it as someone else's, as travellers do an inn.

12. If you want to make progress, shun these sorts of reasonings: "If I neglect my affairs, I shall have nothing to live on"; "if I don't punish my slave, he will be good for nothing." For it is better to attain freedom from sorrow and fear and then die of hunger than to live lavishly in vexation. It is better for your slave to be bad than for you to be unhappy. Begin with little things. A little oil has been spilled, a little wine has been swiped: say to yourself, "This is the price of peace, that of serenity." Nothing is gratis. When you call for your slave, consider that maybe he won't hear you, and even if he does he still won't do what you want him to do. But he is not so well off that your tranquillity should depend on him.

13. If you want to make progress, be content to appear stupid and foolish about externals, and don't wish to seem to know anything. And whenever you seem to be somebody to someone,

distrust yourself. For be aware that it is not easy both to have your will in accordance with nature and to be on your guard about externals also, if you are to take care of the one it is absolutely necessary to neglect the other.

14. If you want your children and your wife and friends to live forever, you are a fool; for you want what is not up to you to be up to you, and what is not yours to be yours. Thus also if you want your slave not to do anything wrong, you are stupid; for you want badness not to be badness but something else. But if what you want is not to fail in getting what you desire, that you can bring about. So practise what you are capable of. Every person's master is the one who controls whether that person shall get what he wants and avoid what he doesn't want. Thus whoever wishes to be free should neither seek nor avoid anything that is up to others; otherwise he will necessarily be a slave.

15. Remember that you ought to conduct yourself as you do at a banquet. When something passed around reaches you, extend your hand and take it politely. If it is passing you by, don't grab. If it has not yet reached you, don't crave for it, but wait until it gets to you. Thus toward children, thus toward women, thus toward jobs, thus toward riches; and in due time you will be worthy to dine with the gods. But if you do not take even the things set out for you, but despise them, then not only will you be a banquet companion of the gods, you will even be a co-ruler. By thus acting, Diogenes and Heraclitus and like men came to be called divine, and deservedly.

16. Whenever you see someone weeping in grief because his child is going away or he has lost his property, be careful not to be misled by the impression that he is in a bad way because of external things, but be ready to say at once "It is not the circumstances that distress him (for someone else would not be distressed), but the idea he has about them." Don't, of course, hesitate to condole with him in words, and, if there is occasion, even to groan with him; but take care not to groan inwardly.

17. Remember that you are an actor in a drama such as the playwright wishes it to be. If he wants it short, it will be short; if long, long. If he wants you to play a beggar, play even that capably; or a lame man, or a ruler, or a private person. For this is yours, to play the assigned role well. Casting is the business of another.

19. You can be unbeatable if you never enter a contest in which it is not up to you who wins. Beware lest ever, seeing someone else preferred in honor or having great power or otherwise esteemed, you get carried away by impressions and deem him blessed. For since the essence of the good lies in the things up to us, neither jealousy nor envy has a place; and you yourself will not wish to be a praetor* or a senator or a consul, but a free man. There is but one way to this: contempt for things not up to us.

20. Remember that it is not the man who curses you or the man who hits you that insults you, but the idea you have of them as insulting. So, whenever someone irritates you, realize that it is your own opinion that has irritated you. First of all, try not to be carried away by impressions; if you succeed just once in gaining time and avoiding hastiness, you will easily control yourself.

21. Let death and exile and all dreadful appearances be before your eyes every day, and most of all, death; and you will never deem anything trivial, nor desire anything excessively.

22. If you are eager for philosophy, be prepared from the beginning to be ridiculed and sneered at by the mob, who will say things like "All of a sudden he has come back to us a philosopher!" and "Where did he get that high brow?" But don't be a highbrow; hold fast to what seems best for you, as one who has been assigned to this territory by the god. And remember this: if you stay with it, the ones who ridicule you at first will admire you afterwards; but if they get the better of you, it will be your lot to be laughed at twice.

23. If ever it happens that you turn to externals because you want to please someone, realize

*Roman magistrate

that you have lost your bearings. It suffices to *be* a philosopher in all things; but if you also want to *appear* to be one, appear so to yourself and that will be enough.

24. Don't let reflections like this upset you: "I shall live without honor, a complete nobody." For suppose not being honored is an evil: you cannot be subjected to evil by another, any more than to shamefulness. Is it your business to acquire power or an invitation to a banquet? By no means. How then is this being without honor? How then will you be a complete nobody, when you ought to be somebody only with respect to those things that are up to you—the domain wherein it is given to you to be of the greatest worth? But your friends will get no help from you? What do you mean by help? They won't have a penny from you; nor will you make them Roman citizens. So who told you that these things are up to you, and not the business of others? Who can give to another things that he does not have himself? "Then get them," one says, "so that we can have them." If I can get them while preserving my self-respect and trustworthiness and high-mindedness, show me the way and I'll get them. But if you require me to be one who will lose my proper goods in order to produce worthless things for you, just look, how partial and unfair you are. Which do you want more? Money, or a faithful and upright friend? Then you had better help me to acquire the characteristics of one and not require me to do the things that would ruin them.

"But my country, as far as its fate is up to me," one says, "will be helpless." Again, what kind of help do you mean? She will not get arcades or baths from you. So what? Neither does she get shoes from smiths nor weapons from shoemakers. It is enough if everyone fulfills his own task. If you make someone else into a faithful and upright citizen, have you done something for the state? "Yes." Then you yourself are not unhelpful if you are that one. "Then what status," one asks, "will I have in the city?" Whatever you are capable of, while conserving your faithfulness and uprightness. If in wishing to aid her you throw

them away, what advantage will accrue to her when you have ended up shameless and faithless?

26. We can learn the will of nature by considering the matters about which we don't disagree with one another. For instance, when somebody else's miserable slave breaks a cup, you are ready right away to say "So it goes." But realize that when it is yours that gets broken, you ought to behave the same way you did when it was someone else's. Apply this to more important matters as well. Somebody else's child or wife has died; there is no one who would not say "That's life." But when his own child or wife dies, it is "Alas, woe is me!" We ought to remember what we feel when we hear the same thing about other people.

27. As a target is not set up for the purpose of being missed, so nothing in the world is intrinsically evil.

28. If someone were to hand over your body to just whomever happened along, you would be outraged. Why aren't you outraged at the fact that *you* turn over your own mind to whomever happens along—if he insults you and you let it upset and trouble you?

29. In every work examine the things that have to be done first and what is to follow, and only then get started on it. If you don't, you will go along eagerly at first, because you have given no consideration to what is coming next; later when difficulties appear the work will come to an ignoble halt. You want to win at Olympia? I do too, by the gods; for it is a fine thing. But look at what comes first, and what comes next, and then take on the work. You must keep discipline, diet, give up pastries, do the compulsory exercises at the set time in heat or in cold, never drink anything cold, take wine only with meals, completely submit yourself to your trainer as to your doctor, and then when the contest starts you have to wallow around in the mud, maybe dislocate your wrist or turn your ankle, swallow quantities of sand, perhaps sometimes be flogged, and after all this you still lose. Taking it all into consideration, go ahead and be an athlete, if you still want to. Otherwise you will be turning from one thing to another like children, who now play

wrestlers, now gladiators, now trumpeters, then tragic actors; you too would be now athlete, now gladiator, then orator, then philosopher, nothing with your whole soul; but like a monkey you mimic every sight that you see as one thing after another intrigues you. For you have never proceeded with something in accord with investigation, after looking at it from all sides; but just at random and out of frivolous enthusiasm.

Thus some people, when they have seen a philosopher and have heard someone speaking the way Euphrates speaks (but who can speak like him?), wish to philosophize themselves. Man, consider first what kind of business this is. And then learn what your own nature is; can you bear it? Do you want to be a pentathlete or a wrestler? Look at your arms, your thighs, learn about your hips. One man is naturally fitted for one thing, another for another. Do you suppose you can do these things and keep on eating and drinking and enthusing and sulking just as you do now? You will have to go without sleep, labor, leave home, be despised by a slave, have everyone laugh at you, get the worse in everything, in honors, in jobs, in lawsuits, in every trifle. Look these things over and decide whether you want to exchange them for tranquillity, freedom, and peace; if not, don't go ahead, don't be, like a child, now philosopher, afterwards tax collector, then orator, finally Caesar's procurator. These things do not go together. You ought to be one man, good or evil; you must cultivate either your own guiding principle or externals; that is, apply yourself either to the inner man or to outward things: assume either the role of philosopher or of layman.

30. What is proper for us to do is for the most part defined by our social relationships. He is your father: this means that it is for you to look after him, to defer to him in all things, to put up with his abuse and his beatings. "But he is a bad father." Did nature then assign you to a *good* father? No, just to a father. "My brother is wronging me." Then keep up your relationship toward him; don't look at what he may be doing, but at what you should do to keep your will in accord with nature. No other person will hurt you unless *you* will it; you will be hurt to the extent that you think you are hurt. Thus if you will make a habit of contemplating social relationships, you will discover what it is fitting to do as a neighbor, as a citizen, as a consul.

31. Concerning piety toward the gods, know that this is the main thing: have right beliefs about them-that they exist, that they run the world well and justly; and you have been appointed to obey them and to resign yourself to whatever happens and to follow willingly because you are led by the best judgment. Thus you will never blame the gods nor accuse them of unconcern. However, this can never come about unless you withdraw yourself from things not up to us and place good and evil exclusively in the class of things up to us. Thus, if you consider anything else to be good or evil, inevitably, when you fail to get what you want and stumble in to what you don't want, you will assign blame and hate those responsible. For it is natural for every creature to flee and avert itself from hurtful appearances and their causes, and on the other hand to go after and to admire the beneficial and their causes. So it is impossible for anyone who thinks he is being hurt to enjoy what he thinks is hurting him, just as enjoying harm itself is impossible. Consequently even a father is abused by his son, insofar as he does not give the child things that seem to be good; and Polyneices and Eteocles were made enemies of each other by the idea that having the tyranny would be a good thing. On this account also the farmer curses the gods, as do the sailor, the merchant, and those who have lost their wives and children. For wherever one's interest is, there also is one's piety. So, whoever concerns himself with desire and aversion as he ought, concerns himself in the same way with piety too. But libations and sacrifices and rites according to the traditions of the country are always appropriate, and they should be done with purity and not in a slovenly manner nor carelessly; neither stingily nor extravagantly.

33. Prescribe a certain character and type for yourself, and guard it both when you are by yourself and when you meet people. And be silent about most things, or chat only when necessary

and about few matters. On rare occasions, when the time is ripe and you are called on to talk, talk-but not about banal topics; not about gladiators, or athletes, or horse races, or food and drink, such as you hear everywhere; and above all, not about blaming or praising or comparing people. If you can, lead the conversation around to something proper. But if you happen to be alone with strange people, be silent.

Laugh seldom and about few things and with restraint.

Totally abstain from taking oaths, if you can; if not, then refuse whenever circumstances allow.

Avoid celebrations, both public and private; but if the occasion calls you, be alert not to lapse into vulgarity. For know that if a companion is defiled, necessarily also one who keeps company with him will be defiled, even if he himself happens to be pure.

Partake of things having to do with the body only as far as bare need goes: such things as food, drink, clothing, housing, slaves. Dispense altogether with whatever has to do with reputation or luxury.

As to sex, be as pure as you can before marriage; but if you are aroused, indulge only to the extent that is customary. However, don't by any means be troublesome to those who do indulge, or censorious; and don't keep mentioning that you yourself can get along without it.

If someone tells you that somebody else is saying awful things about you, don't defend yourself against the accusations, but reply, "He must not know about the other faults that I have, if these are the only ones he mentioned."

It isn't necessary to attend shows for the most part. But if there is a proper occasion, do not appear to be more enthusiastic for anyone else than for yourself, that is, wish only that those things should happen that do happen and that only the winner should win; that way you will not be frustrated. Abstain altogether from shouting and ridiculing anyone or getting emotionally involved. And after the performance don't talk much about what happened, if it does not tend toward your improvement. For it would be

evident from this that you were dazzled by the spectacle. . . .

Whenever you are going to meet someone, especially one reputed to be important, consider what Socrates or Zeno would have done in the circumstances, and you will not be puzzled about how to use the occasion properly. When you are going to visit a powerful personage, propose to yourself that you will not find him at home, that you will be shut out, that the gates will be slammed in your face, that he will not notice you. And if nevertheless it is your duty to go, when you arrive bear with what happens and by no means say to yourself "It wasn't worth it." For it is unphilosophical to be troubled by externals.

In conversation avoid overmuch talk about your own deeds and dangers. For although it is pleasant for you to recall your own adventures, it may not be so for others to hear about what happened to you.

Also avoid raising laughter; for this is a slippery slope to vulgarity and at the same time sufficient to cancel the respect that others have for you. It is also dangerous to get into dirty talk. Whenever anything of this sort begins, if you get the opportunity, you might rebuke the person who starts it; or if not, make it clear by being silent or blushing and scowling that you are displeased by the talk.

34. When you receive an impression of a certain pleasure, be on your guard, just as you are with other impressions, lest you get carried away by it. Take your time with the thing, wait a while. Next call to mind both times-the time when you will enjoy the pleasure, and the time when, after enjoying it, you will change your mind and scold yourself; and set against these the thought of how, if you abstain, you will rejoice and praise yourself. But if it still seems to you to be the proper occasion to indulge, consider, lest you be overcome by the gentleness and sweetness of it and its seductiveness; set against it, how much better it will be to be conscious of yourself as having won this victory.

35. When you do something because you have recognized that it ought to be done, never

go out of your way not to be seen doing it, not even if public opinion takes a different view of it. For if it isn't right for you to do, shun the deed itself; if it is right, why are you afraid of people who would be censuring you wrongly?

37. If you take on a role that is too much for you, you both disgrace yourself in it and neglect the one that you might have filled.

38. Just as in walking you pay attention not to step on a nail or to turn your ankle, pay attention not to hurt your ruling principle. And if we look out for this in all of our activities, we will take them on more securely.

40. Women, soon after they have reached the age of fourteen, are called "ladies" by men. Accordingly when they see how there is going to be nothing else for them but sleeping with men, they start in to adorn themselves and they put all their hopes in that. So it is worth thinking about: how they can be brought to sense that they are honored for no other reason than that they appear chaste and modest?

41. It is the sign of a weak mind to spend too much time on things having to do with the body, such as exercising a lot, eating a lot, drinking a lot, excreting, sex. Such things should be done incidentally; let all your attention be concentrated on your mind.

42. Whenever someone treats you badly or says bad things about you, remember that he does it or says it thinking that he is doing the right thing. Now it is not possible for him to adhere to *your* conception of the right, but only his own. Whence it follows that if he has a wrong view of things, he, being deceived, is the one who is hurt. For if someone believes that a true proposition is false, it is not the proposition that suffers but the deceived believer. If you consider these things you will deal gently with the slanderer. On each occasion just say, "So it seemed to him."

43. Every thing has two handles, one by which it may be borne, one by which it cannot be borne. If your brother has done wrong, don't grasp this by the "wrongdoing" handle-it can't

be borne by that one-but by the "brother," the "brought-up together" handle, and thereby you will be able to bear it.

44. These sorts of arguments are invalid: "I am richer than you are, therefore I am better than you"; "I am more eloquent than you are, therefore I am better than you." But these are valid: "I am richer than you are, therefore my possessions are better than yours"; "I am more eloquent than you are, therefore my speech is better than yours." *You*, however, are neither your possessions nor your speech.

46. Never refer to yourself as a philosopher or chatter much with laymen about philosophical principles, but do what the principles prescribe. For example, at a banquet do not talk about how one ought to eat, but eat as you ought. Remember that Socrates altogether eschewed ostentation. When people came to him who wanted him to introduce them to philosophers, he did so, being quite content to be over looked. And if an argument about some philosophical principle gets started among laymen, you should in most instances be silent; for there is great danger of straightway vomiting up what you have not digested. And if someone says to you that you know nothing, and you aren't hurt by the remark, you may then be sure that you are making a beginning at your task. Sheep brought to pasture don't show off to the shepherd how much they have eaten, but rather they digest their fodder internally and produce wool and milk on the outside. Likewise you should not show off your principles to laymen, but digest them and display the results.

48. Position and character of a vulgar person: he never expects help or harm from himself, but only from outside. Position and character of a philosopher: he expects all help and harm to come from himself.

Marks of one making progress: he blames nobody, he praises nobody, he complains about nobody, he accuses nobody, he never speaks of himself as if he were anybody or knew anything. If he is impeded or frustrated he blames himself.

And if someone praises him, he smiles to himself at the person giving the praise; but if he is blamed, he offers no defense. He comports himself as invalids do, taking care not to move a damaged limb before it has healed. He has purged himself of all desire; he has concentrated aversion solely on things that are against nature but up to us. He takes things as they come. If he appears stupid or ignorant, he doesn't care. In sum, he guards against himself as against an enemy lying in wait.

50. Whatever principles are set before you, follow them as laws, the dishonoring of which would be impious. But don't worry about what anyone says about you; for this is not at all up to you.

51. How much time will you take yet before you judge yourself worthy of the best, and never step over the bounds discriminated by reason? You have been apprised of the philosophical principles to which you ought to subscribe, and you have subscribed. So what sort of teacher are you still waiting for, that you put off your own reformation until he gets here? You are no longer a child, but a grown man. If now you take no care and loaf and always keep putting things off and set one day after another on which to start attending to your own affairs, you will lose yourself, making no progress but going on being a layman in life and in death. Right now, then, deem yourself worthy of living as an adult making progress. And let all that appears best to you be your inviolable law. And if some task is set for you, whether pleasant or glorious or inglorious, remember, that right now you are the contestant and here are the Olympic games, and there can't be any more delay, and that one day and one deed will determine whether progress is lost or saved. That is how Socrates became what he was: by attending in all things that he encountered to nothing other than reason. But you-even if you are not yet a Socrates, at least you ought to live as someone wishing to be like Socrates.

52. The primary and most essential topic in philosophy is that of the use of philosophical principles, for instance, not to lie. The secondary is that of proofs, for instance why one ought not to lie. Tertiary is of what gives certainty and consequence to the first two, for instance, why is this a proof? what indeed is a proof? implication? inconsistency? truth? falsity? The tertiary topic is required because of the secondary, the secondary because of the primary; but the one that is most necessary and that ought never to be neglected is the primary. But we turn them around: for we wrangle about the tertiary topics and bestow all our interest on them, while we altogether neglect the primary. And so we tell lies, and at the same time we are prepared to prove why lying is wrong.

53. On every occasion you ought to have the following ready for use:

> Lead thou me on O Zeus, and Destiny
> Wherever has been fixed by thy decree.
> I shall come willingly; though if I fall
> Into corruption, no less, come I shall.
>
> —CLEANTHES

> Whoever yields with grace to what must be,
> We deem him wise: he knows divinity.
>
> —EURIPIDES

> Well, Crito, if so it pleases the gods,
>   let it be so.
>   —SOCRATES

> Anytus and Meletus can kill me, but they
>   cannot harm me.
>   —SOCRATES

If the things are true which are said by the philosophers about the kinship between God and man, what else remains for men to do than what Socrates did? Never in reply to the question, to what country you belong, say that you are an Athenian or a Corinthian, but that you are a citizen of the world. . . . He then who has observed with intelligence the administration of the world, and has learned that the greatest and supreme and the most comprehensive community is that which is composed of men and God, and that from God have descended the seeds not only to my father and grandfather, but to all beings which are generated on the earth and are produced, and particularly to rational beings—for these only are by their nature formed to have communion with God, being by means of reason conjoined with him—why should not such a man call himself a citizen of the world, why not a son of God, and why should he be afraid of anything which happens among men? Is kinship with Caesar or with any other of the powerful in Rome sufficient to enable us to live in safety, and above contempt and without any fear at all? and to have God for your maker and father and guardian, shall not this release us from sorrows and fears? (*Discourses* Bk I, 9)

If the room is smoky, if only moderately, I will stay; if there is too much smoke, I will go. Remember this, keep firm hold on it, the door is always open.

For Further Reflection

1. Compare the Stoics with Epicurus' philosophy. How different are the two philosophies? In what ways, if any, do they differ? For example, compare what they say about death.

2. What are the main tenets of the Stoic philosophy? Is it really possible to live according to their principles? Which are the most plausible, and which the least plausible?

3. How strongly do Stoics value friendship and loyalty? Discuss and evaluate their views.

4. Consider the following questions: Is Stoicism an optimistic or pessimistic philosophy? What does it imply about human free will?

VIII.75   Life Is Absurd

ALBERT CAMUS

Albert Camus (1913–1960) was born in French colonial Algeria, into a poor working-class family. He was a French journalist, novelist, and philosopher who fought in the French underground during World War II and fought for courage and integrity in public life. He is most famous for his novels *The Stranger* (1942), *The Plague* (1947), and *The Fall* (1957), for which he received a Nobel Prize for literature. He was killed in a car crash in 1960. His rival existentialist, Jean-Paul Sartre, fittingly called it "an absurd death."

In this selection we see Camus' overall assessment that life is absurd, meaningless. The only important philosophical question is, why not commit suicide? Life is compared to the myth of Sisyphus, wherein that man is condemned by the gods to roll a huge stone up a mountain, watch it roll back down, and retrieve it, only to repeat the process again, endlessly.

Study Questions

1. What is the only important philosophical question and why is it important?
2. What is the "absurd"? What does it mean to say that life is absurd? How does this feeling arise?
3. What is the only important thing in life? Is Camus' notion of value clear?
4. What does Camus mean by living "without appeal"?
5. Why do the gods condemn Sisyphus to his awful fate?
6. What does Sisyphus symbolize?

ABSURDITY AND SUICIDE

THERE IS BUT ONE TRULY SERIOUS philosophical problem, and that is suicide. Judging whether life is or is not worth living amounts to answering the fundamental question of philosophy. All the rest—whether or not the world has three dimensions, whether the mind has nine or twelve categories—comes afterwards. These are games; one must first answer. And if it is true, as Nietzsche claims, that a philosopher, to deserve our respect, must preach by example, you can appreciate the importance of that reply, for it will precede the definitive act. These are facts the heart can feel; yet they call for careful study before they become clear to the intellect.

If I ask myself how to judge that this question is more urgent than that, I reply that one judges by the actions it entails. I have never seen anyone die for the ontological argument. Galileo, who held a scientific truth of great importance, abjured it with the greatest of ease as soon as it endangered his life. In a certain sense, he did right.* That truth was not worth the stake. Whether the earth or the sun revolves around the other is a matter of profound indifference. To tell the truth, it is a futile question. On the other hand, I see many people die because they judge that life is not worth living. I see others paradoxically getting

killed for the ideas or illusions that give them a reason for living (what is called a reason for living is also an excellent reason for dying). I therefore conclude that the meaning of life is the most urgent of questions. How to answer it? On all essential problems (I mean thereby those that run the risk of leading to death or those that intensify the passion of living) there are probably but two methods of thought: the method of La Palisse and the method of Don Quixote. Solely the balance between evidence and lyricism can allow us to achieve simultaneously emotion and lucidity. In a subject at once so humble and so heavy with emotion, the learned and classical dialectic must yield, one can see, to a more modest attitude of mind deriving at one and the same time from common sense and understanding.

Suicide has never been dealt with except as a social phenomenon. On the contrary, we are concerned here, at the outset, with the relationship between individual thought and suicide. An act like this is prepared within the silence of the heart, as is a great work of art. The man himself is ignorant of it. One evening he pulls the trigger or jumps. Of an apartment-building manager who had killed himself I was told that he had lost his daughter five years before, that he had changed greatly since, and that that experience had "undermined" him. A more exact word cannot be imagined. Beginning to think is beginning to be undermined. Society has

*From the point of view of the relative value of truth. On the other hand, from the point of view of virile behavior, this scholar's fragility may well make us smile.

but little connection with such beginnings. The worm is in man's heart. That is where it must be sought. One must follow and understand this fatal game that leads from lucidity in the face of existence to flight from light. . . .

But it is hard to fix the precise instant, the subtle step when the mind opted for death; it is easier to deduce from the act itself the consequences it implies. In a sense, and as in melodrama, killing yourself amounts to confessing. It is confessing that life is too much for you or that you do not understand it. Let's not go too far in such analogies, however, but rather return to everyday words. It is merely confessing that that "is not worth the trouble." Living, naturally, is never easy. You continue making the gestures commanded by existence for many reasons, the first of which is habit. Dying voluntarily implies that you have recognized, even instinctively, the ridiculous character of that habit, the absence of any profound reason for living, the insane character of that daily agitation, and the uselessness of suffering.

What, then, is that incalculable feeling that deprives the mind of the sleep necessary to life? A world that can be explained even with bad reasons is a familiar world. But, on the other hand, in a universe suddenly divested of illusions and lights, man feels an alien, a stranger. His exile is without remedy since he is deprived of the memory of a lost home or the hope of a promised land. This divorce between man and his life, the actor and his setting, is properly the feeling of absurdity. All healthy men having thought of their own suicide, it can be seen, without further explanation, that there is a direct connection between this feeling and the longing for death.

The subject of this essay is precisely this relationship between the absurd and suicide, the exact degree to which suicide is a solution to the absurd. The principle can be established that for a man who does not cheat, what he believes to be true must determine his action. Belief in the absurdity of existence must then dictate his conduct. It is legitimate to wonder, clearly and without false pathos, whether a conclusion of this importance requires forsaking as rapidly as possible an incomprehensible condition. I am speaking, of course, of men inclined to be in harmony with themselves. . . .

All great deeds and all great thoughts have a ridiculous beginning. Great works are often born on a street-corner or in a restaurant's revolving door. So it is with absurdity. The absurd world more than others derives its nobility from that abject birth. In certain situations, replying "nothing" when asked what one is thinking about may be pretense in a man. Those who are loved are well aware of this. But if that reply is sincere, if it symbolizes that odd state of soul in which the void becomes eloquent, in which the chain of daily gestures is broken, in which the heart vainly seeks the link that will connect it again, then it is as it were the first sign of absurdity.

It happens that the stage sets collapse. Rising, streetcar, four hours in the office or the factory, meal, streetcar, four hours of work, meal, sleep, and Monday Tuesday Wednesday Thursday Friday and Saturday according to the same rhythm—this path is easily followed most of the time. But one day the "why" arises and everything begins in that weariness tinged with amazement. "Begins"—this is important. Weariness comes at the end of the acts of a mechanical life, but at the same time it inaugurates the impulse of consciousness. It awakens consciousness and provokes what follows. What follows is the gradual return into the chain or it is the definitive awakening. At the end of the awakening comes, in time, the consequence: suicide or recovery. In itself weariness has something sickening about it. Here, I must conclude that it is good. For everything begins with consciousness and nothing is worth anything except through it. . . .

But what does life mean in such a universe? Nothing else for the moment but indifference to the future and a desire to use up everything that is given. Belief in the meaning of life always implies a scale of values, a choice, our preferences. Belief in the absurd, according to our definitions, teaches the contrary. But this is worth examining.

Knowing whether or not one can live *without appeal* is all that interests me. I do not want to get out of my depth. This aspect of life being given me, can I adapt myself to it? Now, faced with this particular concern, belief in the absurd is tantamount to substituting the quantity of experiences for the quality. If I convince myself that this life has no other aspect than that of the absurd, if I feel that its whole equilibrium depends on that perpetual opposition between my conscious revolt and the darkness in which it struggles, if I admit that my freedom has no meaning except in relation to its limited fate, then I must say that what counts is not the best of living but the most living. . . .

On the one hand the absurd teaches that all experiences are unimportant, and on the other it urges toward the greatest quantity of experiences. How, then, can one fail to do as so many of those men I was speaking of earlier—choose the form of life that brings us the most possible of that human matter, thereby introducing a scale of values that on the other hand one claims to reject?

But again it is the absurd and its contradictory life that teaches us. For the mistake is thinking that that quantity of experiences depends on the circumstances of our life when it depends solely on us. Here we have to be over-simple. To two men living the same number of years, the world always provides the same sum of experiences. It is up to us to be conscious of them. Being aware of one's life, one's revolt, one's freedom, and to the maximum, is living, and to the maximum. Where lucidity dominates, the scale of values becomes useless. . . .

THE MYTH OF SISYPHUS

The gods had condemned Sisyphus to ceaselessly rolling a rock to the top of a mountain, whence the stone would fall back of its own weight. They had thought with some reason that there is no more dreadful punishment than futile and hopeless labor.

If one believes Homer, Sisyphus was the wisest and most prudent of mortals. According to another tradition, however, he was disposed to practice the profession of highwayman. I see no contradiction in this. Opinions differ as to the reasons why he became the futile laborer of the underworld. To begin with, he is accused of a certain levity in regard to the gods. He stole their secrets. Ægina, the daughter of Æsopus, was carried off by Jupiter. The father was shocked by that disappearance and complained to Sisyphus. He, who knew of the abduction, offered to tell about it on condition that Æsopus would give water to the citadel of Corinth. To the celestial thunderbolts he preferred the benediction of water. He was punished for this in the underworld. Homer tells us also that Sisyphus had put Death in chains. Pluto could not endure the sight of his deserted, silent empire. He dispatched the god of war, who liberated Death from the hands of her conqueror.

It is said also that Sisyphus, being near to death, rashly wanted to test his wife's love. He ordered her to cast his unburied body into the middle of the public square. Sisyphus woke up in the underworld. And there, annoyed by an obedience so contrary to human love, he obtained from Pluto permission to return to earth in order to chastise his wife. But when he had seen again the face of this world, enjoyed water and sun, warm stones and the sea, he no longer wanted to go back to the infernal darkness. Recalls, signs of anger, warnings were of no avail. Many years more he lived facing the curve of the gulf, the sparkling sea, and the smiles of earth. A decree of the gods was necessary. Mercury came and seized the impudent man by the collar and, snatching him from his joys, led him forcibly back to the underworld, where his rock was ready for him.

You have already grasped that Sisyphus is the absurd hero. He *is*, as much through his passions as through his torture. His scorn of the gods, his hatred of death, and his passion for life won him that unspeakable penalty in which the whole being is exerted toward accomplishing nothing. This is the price that must be paid for the passions of this earth. Nothing is told us about Sisyphus in the underworld. Myths are made for the imagination to breathe life into them. As for this myth, one sees merely the whole effort of a body straining to raise the huge stone, to roll it and push it up a slope a hundred times over; one sees the face screwed up, the cheek tight against the stone, the shoulder bracing the clay-covered mass, the foot wedging it, the fresh start with arms outstretched, the wholly human security of two earth-clotted hands. At the very end of his long effort measured by skyless space and time without depth, the purpose is achieved. Then Sisyphus watches the stone rush down in a few moments toward that lower world whence he will have to push it up again toward the summit. He goes back down to the plain.

It is during that return, that pause, that Sisyphus interests me. A face that toils so close to stones is already stone itself ! I see that man going back down with a heavy yet measured step toward the torment of which he will never know the end. That hour like a breathing-space which returns as surely as his suffering, that is the hour of consciousness. At each of those moments when he leaves the heights and gradually sinks toward the lairs of the gods, he is superior to his fate. He is stronger than his rock.

If this myth is tragic, that is because its hero is conscious. Where would his torture be, indeed, if at every step the hope of succeeding upheld him? The workman of today works every day in his life at the same tasks, and this fate is no less absurd. But it is tragic only at the rare moments when it becomes conscious. Sisyphus, proletarian of the gods, powerless and rebellious, knows the whole extent of his wretched condition: it is what he thinks of during his descent. The lucidity that was to constitute his torture at the same time crowns his victory. There is no fate that cannot be surmounted by scorn.

If the descent is thus sometimes performed in sorrow, it can also take place in joy. This word is not too much. Again I fancy Sisyphus returning toward his rock, and the sorrow was in the beginning. When the images of earth cling too tightly to memory, when the call of happiness becomes too insistent, it happens that melancholy rises in man's heart: this is the rock's victory, this is the rock itself. The boundless grief is too heavy to bear. These are

our nights of Gethsemane. But crushing truths perish from being acknowledged. Thus, Œdipus at the outset obeys fate without knowing it. But from the moment he knows, his tragedy begins. Yet at the same moment, blind and desperate, he realizes that the only bond linking him to the world is the cool hand of a girl. Then a tremendous remark rings out: "Despite so many ordeals, my advanced age and the nobility of my soul make me conclude that all is well." Sophocles' Œdipus, like Dostoevsky's Kirilov, thus gives the recipe for the absurd victory. Ancient wisdom confirms modern heroism.

One does not discover the absurd without being tempted to write a manual of happiness. "What! by such narrow ways—?" There is but one world, however. Happiness and the absurd are two sons of the same earth. They are inseparable. It would be a mistake to say that happiness necessarily springs from the absurd discovery. It happens as well that the feeling of the absurd springs from happiness. "I conclude that all is well," says Œdipus, and that remark is sacred. It echoes in the wild and limited universe of man. It teaches that all is not, has not been, exhausted. It drives out of this world a god who had come into it with dissatisfaction and a preference for futile sufferings. It makes of fate a human matter, which must be settled among men.

All Sisyphus' silent joy is contained therein. His fate belongs to him. His rock is his thing. Likewise, the absurd man, when he contemplates his torment, silences all the idols. In the universe suddenly restored to its silence, the myriad wondering little voices of the earth rise up. Unconscious, secret calls, invitations from all the faces, they are the necessary reverse and price of victory. There is no sun without shadow, and it is essential to know the night. The absurd man says yes and his effort will henceforth be unceasing. If there is a personal fate, there is no higher destiny, or at least there is but one which he concludes is inevitable and despicable. For the rest, he knows himself to be the master of his days. At that subtle moment when man glances backward over his life, Sisyphus returning toward his rock, in that slight pivoting he contemplates that series of unrelated actions which becomes his fate, created by him, combined under his memory's eye and soon sealed by his death. Thus, convinced of the wholly human origin of all that is human, a blind man eager to see who knows that the night has no end, he is still on the go. The rock is still rolling.

I leave Sisyphus at the foot of the mountain! One always finds one's burden again. But Sisyphus teaches the higher fidelity that negates the gods and raises rocks. He too concludes that all is well. This universe henceforth without a master seems to him neither sterile nor futile. Each atom of that stone, each mineral flake of that night-filled mountain, in itself forms a world. The struggle itself toward the heights is enough to fill a man's heart. One must imagine Sisyphus happy.

For Further Reflection

1. Is life absurd, as Camus insists? Does Camus give good reasons for this claim? What leads him to this pessimistic conclusion?
2. Is Camus being irreverent in asking the question as "Why not commit suicide"?
3. Why does Camus say that Sisyphus must be imagined to be happy?
4. Compare Camus with Epicurus. In what ways are their views similar? In what ways different?

Living Life Forwards　　　　　　　　　　　　　　　VIII.76

JULIAN BAGGINI

Julian Baggini is the founding editor of *The Philosopher's Magazine* and the author of *The Pig That Wants to Be Eaten: 100 Experiments for the Armchair Philosopher* and *Atheism: A Very Short Introduction*. In this selection, he examines the "teleological" view of life, the notion that life has meaning only when it is lived toward future goals and objectives. He concludes that if life has meaning only because of some goal set in the future, "we would never be able to catch up with the purpose of life's existence and so purpose would permanently elude us, whether there is life after death or not. . . . we also need to find a way of living which is worthwhile in itself."

Study Questions

1. Does Baggini think that life's purpose can be understood by looking backward to its origins? by looking forward to some goal? Why or why not?
2. What are the problems that Baggini says arise when we see life's purpose as the achievement of future goals?
3. Does Baggini believe that life would have purpose if we were immortal? Explain.
4. What does Kierkegaard mean by "life must be lived forwards"?

Life can only be understood backwards, but it must be lived forwards.

SØREN KIERKEGAARD, *Journals*

ORDER IN THE CHAOS

The Wild West portrayed in the films of Sergio Leone is like the state of nature described by the seventeenth-century political philosopher Thomas Hobbes. With only weak sheriffs to uphold the law, there is a constant 'war of all against all' and so life is 'solitary, poor, nasty, brutish and short'. It is like the kind of amoral, anarchic world that many fear is an inevitable consequence of the death of God and the loss of absolute values that comes with it.

Yet there is the possibility of some kind of order and meaning even in this moral vacuum. In *For a Few Dollars More*, for example, the two main protagonists at first appear to be archetypes of amorality: bounty hunters. It transpires, however, that one of them, the Colonel (played by Lee Van Cleef), is driven by a greater purpose than simply wealth. He is on a lifelong mission to avenge the rape and murder of his sister by finding the man who did it and confronting him with the memory of his crime before killing him.

The same revenge theme is played out in *Once Upon a Time in the West*. This time a man with no name, played by Charles Bronson, seeks to avenge the murder of his brother and make the murderer know why he is about to die.

The objectives that drive the protagonists do not just give shape to the films' narratives. They show how a sense of purpose can give shape and meaning to lives even in a world filled with meaningless death and struggle. They reflect the desire we often feel for a clear future purpose that will make our own struggles meaningful and give our lives a clear direction.

A perceived lack of such a purpose is often at the root of much unease about the value of life. Many people believe that the world would not notice if they were gone, that nothing they do is of any significance. Life is taken up by earning money, eating, drinking and sleeping, punctuated by periods of rest and relaxation, all activities that have no further purpose other than keeping us alive and sane. It is tempting to think that if only our deeds could have a higher purpose or goal, then our lives would be meaningful.

What we seem to be looking for here is a 'teleological' account of human life: an explanation given in terms of future goals or objectives. The classic account of teleology and the human good is found in Aristotle's *Nicomachean Ethics*. Aristotle's great insight was that teleological explanations, in order to be complete, must terminate with something which is an end in itself. One can see why by simply considering how one responds to a curious and insistent child.

As many parents will know, most children go through a 'why phase' of varying length and intensity. They demand to know why they must do anything or why anything happens at all. It is for this reason that Isaiah Berlin reputedly described philosophers as adults who persist in asking childish questions. The problem for both parent and child is that the child does not know when to stop and the parent often does not know how to stop them.

Consider one such trying conversation:

- Why are there so many cars on the street?
- Because people have to get to work and take their children to school.
- Why do people have to go to work?
- Because they need to earn money.
- Why do they need to earn money?
- So they can afford to live in nice houses and eat well.

From Julian Baggini, *"Living Life Forwards,"* in What's It All About? *(2005), pp. 23–39. By permission of* Oxford University Press, Inc.

- Why can't they just live in huts and eat like they used to in the olden days?
- Because that isn't as nice as living in a comfortable house.
- Why not?
- *It just isn't!* Look! It's the ice-cream man!

The possibility of such a conversation being endless is inherent in its very structure. For any statement 'A' it is possible to ask 'Why A?' This will yield the answer 'because B'. But then, of course, it is always possible to ask 'Why B?' and so on, ad infinitum. The only way to end this potentially endless series is to draw the exchange to a halt arbitrarily, as the parent does, or come up with an answer, 'because X', for which the question 'Why X?' is unnecessary, misguided or nonsensical. We can often do this for activities where the context is understood and taken for granted.

For example, if you are playing chess and I ask you why you moved your rook, you might reply by saying that you are preparing to checkmate in three moves. In the context of chess it is clearly misguided for me to ask why you would want to do that. But if I am interested in why you are even bothering to live, the question becomes meaningful again. I might well wonder why you want to win your game, because I might want to know why you think playing chess forms part of a meaningful life.

The problem is that when it comes to life's overall purpose, such answers are hard to find. Can this difficulty be resolved?

TIME FOR JUSTIFICATIONS

A possible way out is provided by the logical structure of the dilemma. The 'why/because' series is essentially a sequence of justifications. It is easy to assume that this must correspond to a sequence in time. So, for example, when we considered the origins of life in the previous chapter we were essentially examining a 'why/because' series which stretched back from the present to the past. We asked why we were born, then why

our parents were born, back to why there are humans at all and ended up at the Big Bang or the myths of Genesis. That series terminated without revealing life's meaning.

In this chapter we have turned our attention to the future, and so it is tempting to think that the 'why/because' series will have to extend into the future until such time as we can stop it. However, a 'why/because' series need not be temporal. For example, consider everyone's role in a restaurant. If we ask why the waiters, cooks, dishwashers, maître d', diners and so on all do what they do, the explanations will not essentially be given in terms of future goals or past events. Rather everyone is fulfilling a mutually supportive role where the activities of one meet the needs of or supply purposes for the other. Our 'why' questions invite 'because' answers that explain things simultaneously, as well as with regard to past or future.

Even when a 'why/because' series has a temporal dimension, it need not follow one direction in time only. Consider this example:

- Why are you driving to Doncaster?
- Because I'm taking my uncle's ashes to where he wants them to be scattered. (Future)
- Why are you doing that?
- Because I promised him I would. (Past)
- But he's dead, so why do you feel the need to honour that promise? He'll never know.
- Because it's important to me that I'm the kind of person who keeps his word. (Present)
- Why?
- . . .

In this example, aspects of the past, present and future are all used as part of the 'why/because' series of justifications. This shows how it is far too limiting to see 'why/because' series as having to trail off either into the past or into the future.

This is an important point. I have rejected the view that life's purpose can be understood by looking backwards to its origins. But that doesn't mean the only alternative is looking forward to its ultimate end. Just as the restaurant staff are fulfilling their professional purposes in the present simply by doing their job, couldn't we fulfil life's purpose in the present simply by living our lives? I am going to argue that something like this must be true. But first we need to consider a little further the possibility that the future will provide us with meaning.

CAN I DIE NOW?

If we see life's purpose as the achievement of future goals, several problems arise. If we are mortal, the problem is simply that there will come a time when we have no future. Life would end with meaning unfulfilled, since death would eventually rob us of the future where the purposes for our actions lie.

For the same reason, even if we were immortal this would not provide life with a purpose. Indeed, it could make life seem even more futile. We would be condemned to live a life where the only answers to questions of why we do anything belong in the eternal future. We would be like donkeys wearing hats from which carrots are suspended two feet in front of our eyes, forever moving forward in time towards a forever unachievable future.

So if life is to be meaningful, the 'why/because' series cannot extend indefinitely into the future. At some point we have to reach an end point where a further 'why' question is unnecessary, misguided or nonsensical. Otherwise the purpose of life is forever beyond our reach.

These insights are reflected in Sergio Leone's Westerns. There is a completeness and closure at the end of the films because the goals of the protagonists have finally been achieved. Their objectives do not lie in the eternal future, but in a future which one day becomes the present, and in turn the past.

But this gives rise to a further problem. As the credits roll and the hero rides off into the desert, the question the films do not confront is what gives the gunslinger his purpose in life *now*.

When people fulfil a lifetime's ambition they often jokingly say, 'I can die happy.' But this invites the serious reply, 'Why not?' After all, if life is about the achievement of a goal, then once that goal is reached, what is there left to do? Once life's purpose has been fulfilled, it no longer guides our actions, apparently leaving us with nothing to live for.

This is not just intellectual sophistry. Many goal-orientated people do feel this way once they have achieved their ambitions. Initial elation provides a temporary glow, but soon they are left with a kind of emptiness as they realize that, now all they have been working for has been accomplished, they have nothing left to give purpose to their life.

A good example of this (originally from Alfie Kohn's *No Contest*) is cited by the contemporary Australian moral philosopher Peter Singer in his *How Are We to Live?* The coach of the Dallas Cowboys, Tom Landry, said, 'Even after you've just won the Super Bowl—*especially* after you've just won the Super Bowl—*there's always next year*. If "winning isn't everything. It's the only thing" then "the only thing" is nothing—emptiness, the nightmare of life without meaning.'

This illustrates how if the meaning of life is tied to goal-achievement, then achieving that goal can leave you with 'emptiness'—nothing left to provide meaning. The way many people try to get around this is simply to set another goal—'*there's always next year*'. But this simply avoids confronting the fundamental flaw in seeing life in this way. As the Danish existentialist Søren Kierkegaard said, life 'must be lived forwards', in a present that constantly transforms the future into the past. Moments in time cannot be kept hold of, yet achievements are of their essence tied to moments of success, which all too quickly drift into the past.

This reflects a tension in the human condition captured by Kierkegaard's distinction between what he called the aesthetic and ethical spheres of existence. Each sphere reflects an important aspect of human life, but neither by itself is sufficient to fully explain it. A neat illustration of this is provided by Patrice Leconte's film *L'Homme du train*. The two protagonists envy each other, and we can understand why by seeing how they have lived their lives too much on one side of Kierkegaard's aesthetic/ethical divide. The retired schoolteacher, Manesquier, has lived a quiet life, one which has been attached to things of 'eternal' value which belong to the ethical sphere: education, learning, art and poetry. Such a life does justice to our nature as beings that persist over time, with memories and plans as well as present sensations. It reflects the fact that we do not live just in the moment but over continuous and connected periods of time.

But there is more to life than the ethical, as Manesquier comes to realize. He yearns for some of the intense experiences that his new friend, Milan, a serial robber, has had. Milan has lived life in the aesthetic sphere, devoted to the present moment. 'Aesthetic' in this context is used not with its present-day associations with art and beauty, but with its original Greek meaning, as pertaining to sensory experience. We are aesthetic beings in that we experience the world through our senses, in the here and now. Milan's life recognizes this fact, but he is left weary and empty by his series of escapades, none of which has provided enduring satisfaction. He sees in Manesquier's life precisely what his life has been missing. This supports Kierkegaard's claim that a life which is lived only in the present is inherently unsatisfactory, for the very reason that the moment always eludes us. The present cannot be grasped: it always melts through our fingers and becomes the past.

Milan and Manesquier represent the duality of human life, its sometimes conflicting needs; and their contrasting dissatisfactions highlight the need to live with due respect to both the aesthetic and the ethical.

Kierkegaard thought that the ethical and the aesthetic could not be rationally reconciled. He ridiculed Hegel's view that opposites—thesis and antithesis—can always be resolved by the rational process of 'dialectic' into a harmonious 'synthesis'. Kierkegaard argued that only a leap of faith into the religious sphere could bring together these two conflicting aspects of human existence. In Christ, Kierkegaard saw the aesthetic and the ethical reconciled: finite man and infinite God coexisting in the figure of Jesus, not as something that can be rationally explained but as something that can only be embraced by going beyond rationality and into the realm of faith.

There are many reasons why Kierkegaard's analysis of the problem is more appealing than his solution. Kierkegaard's whole point is that there is no rational reason why one should make this leap of faith: the motivation to do so can only come from a prior commitment. Indeed, Kierkegaard himself saw his whole intellectual project as addressing the question of how he could become a true Christian. So unless we already have Christian faith, there is no good reason, even by Kierkegaard's own lights, to adopt that faith ourselves. For any inquiry that starts with no prior religious commitments, such as this one, embracing the contradiction of God made man has no great merits.

Nevertheless, Kierkegaard's analysis of the human condition can illuminate the problem of the goal-orientated life. The difficulty such a life faces is that it locates the purpose of life in the achievement of the goal, which is necessarily tied to a discrete moment in time. This reflects the aesthetic nature of human life. We are tied to the present and we must expect some of life's meaning to reflect that. But we also exist across time, and when our life's goals are fixed so narrowly on moments that are only briefly the present, we fail to do justice to the enduring aspect of human life.

LA DOLCE VITA

If the goal-orientated life is too rooted in the aesthetic, one obvious way to rectify the imbalance is to strive for desirable states of affairs as well as events. Consider the example of someone who thinks that once she has a large house in the south of France with a husband and children, then the 'why/because' series will have ended. This may sound shallow, but it is plausible. Consider this somewhat simplified version of how she might describe her life's goals.

- Why did you go to university?
- To get a degree so I could get a well-paid job.
- Why did you want a well-paid job?
- Because I wanted to earn lots of money.
- But that took hard work. Why was that more important than enjoying yourself?
- Well, it wasn't all hard work, and in any case, I was taking the longer view.
- Why?
- Because it enabled me to get where I am now: I have a huge house in the south of France with a swimming pool, a loving husband and wonderful children.
- Why would you want that?
- Are you nuts? Why wouldn't anyone want that?

The final 'why' question, although not nonsensical, could be seen as unnecessary or misguided. Hasn't the questioner just missed something if he thinks this idyllic life stands in need of some justification? We might question the morality of such a life in a world where so many go without basic necessities, but it does seem odd to question its desirability. After all, if this kind of life isn't worth living, which is?

The point here isn't to justify this particular lifestyle but to draw our attention to two important considerations. The first is that, as we have repeatedly seen, at some point we have to reach the stage where a 'why' question can be met with an answer along the lines of 'Are you nuts? Why wouldn't anyone want that?' If not, the 'why/because' series just extends into the indefinite future. And it does seem more satisfactory to end the series with a sustainable state of affairs than an event which then itself quickly passes into history.

The second point is even more telling. In justifying her life choices, this woman rests her case entirely on the final outcome: her wealth and

family in later life. So the life-plan this woman has followed is premised on the possibility that the purpose of human life can be, not a particular achievement, but a desirable and sustainable state of affairs or lifestyle.

Once we accept that this is true, it should be evident that the kind of lifestyle it takes years of hard work and the accumulation of wealth to enjoy is but one of the possible kinds of lifestyles which are desirable in themselves. Yet so many of us do look towards some idyllic future when we have 'made it' as providing purpose for what we do. This is a mistake and at its root is a failure to realize that if what is being worked towards is worthwhile in itself, then so are many other things that are within our grasp right now. After all, the difference between the luxury lifestyle described and a moderately affluent one is only a matter of degree. For most of us, life isn't improved that much because the music is being played on a better hi-fi, or because the car being driven is a Jaguar rather than a Ford.

The person who sacrifices too much enjoyment of life to serve the purpose of future wealth and security is thus making the mistake of overestimating the extent to which his future life will be better than the one he could have now. Being wealthy may make life a bit better but not so much better that it is worth sacrificing years of one's life to work for. This is even more important when it comes to personal relationships, which are consistently highlighted by psychologists as being important for personal happiness. Neglecting friendships for work is almost inevitably a poor trade-off in terms of life satisfaction, since they are precisely the kind of thing which cannot simply be bought once one has become sufficiently wealthy. How many marriages and partnerships have been put under strain or even ruined by one partner spending so much time at work that they neglect their relationship?

The risk is not only that the future won't be good enough to justify the past, but also that the future will never come. For one of the great risks of making life's purpose some future goal is that, as mortal creatures, we can never be sure we will live to see that day. Most of us can hope to live to seventy or more years. But to *assume* we will do so is to take for granted that which can only be hoped for.

Of course, when balancing considerations of future and present there is no simple either/or. Many entrepreneurs, for example, love the process of making money itself and are not simply driven by the thought of the lifestyle they will be able to enjoy in the future. Indeed, it is a feature of most entrepreneurs that they don't stop working hard, even when they have long ceased needing to earn more money.

Nevertheless, whether it is wealth or some other future achievement we seek, it is tempting to think that satisfaction in life depends on things that are yet to come. Just as soon as the kids have left home, the mortgage has been paid off, I've climbed the promotion ladder and won't have to work quite so hard. Then life will be good. Philip Larkin captures this brilliantly in his poem 'Next, Please':

> *Always too eager for the future, we*
> *Pick up bad habits of expectancy.*
> *Something is always approaching, every day*
> Till then *we say…*

This 'till then' way of thinking stands between us and getting the kind of satisfaction available from life right now.

Perhaps one reason why we fall prey to 'till then' thinking is a form of bad faith, whereby we refuse to accept that something lies within our own control and responsibility and think that it depends on external factors, such as our financial situation. But although it is true that financial strain has a negative impact on personal happiness, whether or not we feel under strain because of our finances depends, unless we are very poorly off, largely on how we perceive things. As the Roman Stoic philosopher and emperor Marcus Aurelius said, albeit with a dash of overstatement, 'If you are distressed by any external thing, it is not this thing which disturbs you, but your own judgement about it. And it is in your power to wipe out that judgement now.'

Modern psychology echoes this sentiment. As the psychologist Oliver James has repeatedly pointed out, we are more miserable if we compare our financial situation with those better off than ourselves, and yet people tend to do just that, ignoring all those people who are as well off as or worse off than themselves. Perceiving a comparative disadvantage, people then become less satisfied.

This kind of invidious comparison can go to ludicrous extremes and is satirized in Bret Easton Ellis's novel *American Psycho*. In the film adaptation, the protagonist, Patrick Bateman, is so infuriated that a Wall Street colleague has a better business card than his already excessively luxurious one that he becomes homicidal. The idea that someone is better off than him is just unbearable, even though he is obscenely well off in any case. The comparisons we tend to make are not usually as ridiculous as this, but if the content of the judgement is extraordinary, its form is most certainly not.

To acknowledge the central importance of our own responses, however, requires us to accept that it is within our own power to ease our dissatisfaction. Sartre claims that this kind of freedom is something we fear and try to deny. We don't like to think that it is all down to us, for if it is we have no one to blame if things go wrong. So we prefer instead to think, in bad faith, that it is not us but circumstances that are to blame.

Another reason why we might prefer to think we will be happy only when all the external factors are in place is that we find it hard to accept the imperfections of life. Sartre again has a word for this. He describes the need to accept the *facticity* of existence: the way the world is whether we like it or not.

This is very significant when it comes to what we desire and expect from life. What people in the affluent west typically want is a great partner who is both a terrific friend and a terrific lover; a good material standard of living; well-adjusted, happy children; a stimulating and fulfilling job; a varied social life with interesting, amusing and intelligent friends; and regular holidays abroad. Of course, one only needs to read the list to realize that very few people have all these things. Yet there is a widespread belief among the western middle classes, sometimes verging on the expectation, that all this can and should be achieved almost by right.

For example, author and journalist Hope Edelman would seem to have everything going for her: a good partner, a great job and a healthy child. But when her husband suggested they hired a nanny, she was horrified. 'Didn't he understand?' she explained. 'My plan hadn't been to hire someone to raise our child. My plan had been to do it together: two responsible parents with two fulfilling jobs, in an egalitarian marriage with a well-adjusted kid who was equally bonded to us both.' Such unrealistically high expectations are not uncommon.

With such absurdly high ideals setting the standards, when people look at their own lives at any given point they can only be disappointed by how they measure up. Your partner may well be great, but not the perfect lover or friend of your dreams. Your children may stubbornly refuse to grow up without problems. Work can be a grind. And those foreign holidays can be the source of as much stress as sun-drenched relaxation. And so, instead of accepting the facticity of the world, that such imperfections need to be dealt with, we imagine that we will have our ideal life sometime in the future.

In order to be honest and consistent we need to avoid these errors. If we think that a life without any difficulties and worries lies in the future we are mistaken. We need to recognize the fragility of good fortune and the impermanence of things. But do we have the courage and honesty to take life for what it is and make the most of it? Or do we fear that if we do so it will prove to be a disappointment?

LIFE'S COMPLICATIONS

At the heart of the arguments of this chapter has been a logical point about how 'why' questions and their 'because' answers generate a series of justifications, what I termed the 'why/because'

series. If we see this series as extending temporally into the future, then life becomes futile, since the answer to why we should be doing what we do is always some future 'because'. If this were true, we would never be able to catch up with the purpose of life's existence and so purpose would permanently elude us, whether there is life after death or not.

The 'why/because' series, then, must terminate in a 'because' answer for which a further 'why' question is unnecessary, misguided or nonsensical. If this final purpose is itself an achievement or moment in time, however, then it may only satisfy what Kierkegaard called the aesthetic part of our human nature. Moments slip away and so if life's purpose is tied to moments, life's purpose too must slip away. So although such moments can play a part, in order to find a purpose which is truly fulfilling, we also need to find a way of living which is worthwhile in itself. In doing this, however, we should resist the temptation to see this always as an aspiration for the perfect future when, having sorted out the external factors of money and so on, we will be able to sit back and enjoy life. We need to recognize instead both that life is rarely an undiluted pleasure and that our own attitudes are themselves important to our sense of well-being.

All of this, however, is premised on a very big 'if'. This 'if' is whether or not it is possible for there to be states of affairs or lifestyles which are worth living in themselves and which are sufficiently meaningful to give life a purpose. I haven't considered that possibility here but shall do so in the chapters to come.

There is one final consideration that needs examining. I have not assumed human mortality in this chapter, since what I say about the need to end the 'why/because' series applies whether we live seventy years or for ever. The feeling may remain, however, that not enough has been said about the possibility that the existence of a transcendental reality—a god or dimension beyond this earthly one—would completely transform our perception of what the meaning of life is. So it is to this possible other world that we must now turn.

For Further Reflection

　1. Are you, as Baggini says, living your life "forwards"? How would you characterize your quest for meaning or purpose?

　2. Is it possible to be goal-oriented and still "live life forwards"? Explain.

　3. If you lived your life for the purpose of one day reaching an eternal reward in heaven, would your life have meaning now? Why or why not?

Religion Gives Meaning to Life   VIII.77

LOUIS P. POJMAN

In this essay Louis Pojman argues that religion, specifically theistic religion, gives special meaning to life, unavailable in secular world views. Furthermore, the autonomy that secularists prize (sometimes value it beyond its worth) is not significantly diminished by religious faith.

Study Questions

　1. What are the two theses that the atheist holds, and how does Pojman argue against them?

　2. What are his definitions of "meaning" and "autonomy"?

　3. What is the relationship of meaning to freedom or autonomy?

　4. Which of Pojman's eight theses on the value of religious faith do you agree with and which do you disagree with?

SEVERAL YEARS AGO during a class break, I was discussing the significance of religion in our society with a few students in the college lounge. I, at that time an agnostic, was conceding to a devout Christian that it would be nice if theism were true, for then the world would not be simply a matter of chance and necessity, a sad tale with a sadder ending. Instead, "the world would be personal, a gift from our heavenly Father, who provides a basis for meaning and purpose." A mature woman from another class, whom I knew to be an atheist, overheard my remarks, charged through a group of coffee drinkers and angrily snapped at me, "That is the most disgusting thing I've ever heard!" I inquired why she thought this, and she replied, "Religion keeps humans from growing up. We don't need a big Daddy in the sky. We need to grow up and become our own parents."

I recalled Nietzsche's dictum that now that "God is dead," now that we have killed the Holy One, we must ourselves become gods to seem worthy of the deed. The atheist woman was prizing autonomy over meaning and claiming that religion did just the opposite.

This article first appeared in Philosophy: The Quest for Truth, *1st edition (Wadsworth Publishing co., 1989), Copyright © 2002 by Louis P. Pojman. Reprinted by permission of family. Originally published under the pseudonym Lois Hope Walker.*

In other words, she held two theses:

(1) It is more important to be free or autonomous than to have a grand meaning or purpose to life.

(2) Religion provides a grand meaning or purpose to life, but it does not allow humans to be free or autonomous.

I've thought a lot about that woman's response over the years. I think that she is wrong on both counts. In this essay I will defend religion against her two theses and try to show that meaning and autonomy are both necessary or important ingredients for an ideal existence and that they are compatible within a religious framework.

Let me begin with the first thesis, that it is more important to be free than that there be meaning in life. First let us define our terms. By "autonomy" I mean self-governing, the ability to make choices on the basis of good reasons rather than being coerced by threats or forces from without.

By "meaning" in life I mean that life has a purpose. There is some intrinsic rationale or plan to it. Now this purpose can be good, bad, or indifferent. An example of something with a bad purpose is the activity of poisoning a reservoir on which a community depends for its sustenance. An example of something with an indifferent purpose might be pacing back and forth to pass the time of day (it is arguable that this is bad or good depending on the options and context, and if you think that then either choose your own example or dismiss the category of indifferent purpose). An example of a good purpose is digging a well in order to provide water to a community in need of water.

Now it seems to be the case that, as a value, autonomy is superior to indifferent and bad purposes, since it has positive value while these other two categories do not. Autonomy may be more valuable to us than some good purposes, but it does not seem to be superior to *all* good purposes. While it may be more valuable to be free than to have this or that incidental purpose in life, freedom cannot really be understood apart from the notion of purposiveness. To be free is to be able to do some act A, when you want to, in order to reach some goal G. So the two ideas are related.

But the atheist woman meant more than this. She meant that if she had to choose whether to have free will or to live in a world that had a governing providential hand, she would choose the former. But this seems to make two mistakes. (1) It makes autonomy into an unjustified absolute and (2) it creates a false dilemma.

(1) Consider two situations: In situation A you are as free as you are now (say you have 100 units of autonomy—call these units "autonotoms") but are deeply miserable because you are locked in a large and interesting room which is being slowly filled with poisonous gas. You can do what ever you want for five more minutes but then you will be dead. In situation B, however, you have only 95 autonotoms (that is, there are a few things that you are unable to do in this world—say commit adultery or kill your neighbor) but the room is being filled with sunshine and fresh air. Which world would you choose? I would choose situation B, for autonomy, it seems to me, is not the only value in the universe, nor is it always the overriding value. I think most of us would be willing to give up a few autonotoms for an enormous increase in happiness. And I think that a world with a good purpose would be one in which we would be willing to give up a few bits of freedom. If we were told that we could eliminate poverty, crime, and great suffering in the world by each sacrificing one autonotom, wouldn't we do this? If so, then autonomy is not an absolute which always overrides every other value. It is one important value among others.

I turn to the atheist's second thesis, that religion always holds purpose, as superior to autonomy. I think that this is a misunderstanding of what the best types of religion try to do. As Jesus said in John 8 : 32, "Ye shall know the truth and the truth shall set you free." Rather than seeing freedom and meaning as opposites, theism sees them as inextricably bound together. Since it claims to offer us the truth about the world, and since having true beliefs is important in reaching one's goals, it follows that our autonomy is actually heightened in having the truth about the purpose of life. If we know why we are here and what the options in our destiny really are, we will be able to choose more intelligently than the blind who lead the blind in ignorance.

Indeed theistic religion (I have in mind Judaism, Christianity, and Islam, but this could apply to many forms of Hinduism and African religions as well) claims to place before us options of the greatest importance, so that if it is true the world is far better (infinitely better?) than if it is not.

Let me elaborate on this point. If theism is true and there is a benevolent supreme being governing the universe, the following eight theses are true:

1. We have a satisfying explanation of the origin and sustenance of the universe. We are the product not of chance and necessity or an impersonal Big Bang, but of a Heavenly Being who cares about us. As William James says, if religion is true, "the universe is no longer a mere *It* to us, but a *Thou* . . . and any relation that may be possible from person to person might be possible here." We can take comfort in knowing that the visible world is part of a more spiritual universe from which it draws its meaning and that there is, in spite of evil, an essential harmonious relationship between our world and the transcendent reality.

2. Good will win out over evil—we're not fighting alone, but God is on our side in the battle. So, you and I are not fighting in vain—we'll win eventually. This thought of the ultimate victory of Goodness gives us confidence to go on in the fight against injustice and cruelty when others calculate that the odds against righteousness are too great to fight against.

3. God loves and cares for us—His love compels us (II Corinthians 5 : 7), so that we have a deeper motive for morally good actions, including high altruism. We live deeply moral lives because of deep gratitude to One who loves us and whom we love. Secularism lacks this sense of cosmic love, and it is, therefore, no accident that it fails to produce moral saints like Jesus, St. Francis, Gandhi, Martin Luther King, and Mother Teresa. You need special love to leave a world of comfort in order to go to a desolate island to minister to lepers, as Father Damian did.

4. We have an answer to the problem why be moral—it's clearly in your interest. Secular ethics has a severe problem with the question, Why be moral when it is not in your best interest, when you can profitably advance yourself by an egoistic act? But such a dilemma does not arise in religious ethics, for Evil really is bad for you and the Good good for you.

5. Cosmic Justice reigns in the universe. The scales are perfectly balanced so that everyone will get what he or she deserves, according to their moral merit. There is no moral luck (unless you interpret the grace which will finally prevail as a type of "luck"), but each will be judged according to how one has used one's talents (Matthew, chapter 25).

6. All persons are of equal worth. Since we have all been created in the image of God and are His children, we are all brothers and sisters. We are family and ought to treat each other benevolently as we would family members of equal worth. Indeed, modern secular moral and political systems often assume this equal worth of the individual without justifying it. But without the Parenthood of God it makes no sense to say that all persons are innately of equal value. From a perspective of intelligence and utility, Aristotle and Nietzsche are right: there are enormous inequalities, and why shouldn't the superior persons use the baser types to their advantage? In this regard, secularism, in rejecting inegalitarianism, seems to be living off of the interest of a religious capital which it has relinquished.

7. Grace and forgiveness—a happy ending for all. All's well that ends well (the divine comedy). The moral guilt which we experience, even for the most heinous acts, can be removed, and we can be redeemed and given a new start. This is true moral liberation.

8. There is life after death. Death is not the end of the matter, but we shall live on, recognizing each other in a better world. We have eternity in our souls and are destined for a higher existence. (Of course, hell is a problem here—which vitiates the whole idea somewhat, but many variations of theism [e.g., varieties of theistic Hinduism and the Christian theologians Origen (in the second century), F. Maurice, and Karl Barth] hold to universal salvation in the end. Hell is only a temporary school in moral education—I think that this is a plausible view.) So if Hebraic-Christian theism is true, the world is a friendly home in which we are all related as siblings in one family, destined to live forever in cosmic bliss in a reality in which good defeats evil.

If theism is false and secularism is true, then there is no obvious basis for human equality, no reason to treat all people with equal respect, no simple and clear answer to the question, Why be moral even when it is not in my best interest? no sense of harmony and purpose in the universe, but "Whirl has replaced Zeus and is king" (Sophocles).

Add to this the fact that theism doesn't deprive us of any autonomy that we have in non-theistic systems. If we are equally free to choose the good or the evil whether or not God exists (assuming that the notions of good and evil make sense in a non-theistic universe)—then it seems clear that the world of the theist is far better and more satisfying to us than one in which God does not exist.

Of course, the problem is that we probably do not know if theism, let alone our particular religious version of it, is true. Here I must use a Pascalean argument to press my third point that we may have an obligation or, at least, it may be a good thing, to live *as if* theism is true. That is, unless you think that theism is so improbable that we should not even consider it as a candidate for truth, we should live in such a way as to allow the virtues of theism to inspire our lives and our culture. The theistic world view is so far superior to the secular that—even though we might be agnostics or weak atheists—it is in our interest to live as though it were true, to consider each person as a child of God, of high value, to work as though God is working with us in the battle of Good over evil, and to build a society based on these ideas. It is good then to gamble on God. Religion gives us a purpose to life and a basis for morality that is too valuable to dismiss lightly. It is a heritage that we may use to build a better civilization and one which we neglect at our own peril.

For Further Reflection

1. Does Pojman exaggerate the importance of religion for a meaningful life? How would a secularist respond?

2. Karl Marx said that religion was the opium of the people. Religion deludes people into thinking that all will be well with the world, leading to passive acceptance of evil and injustice. Is there some truth in Marx's dictum? How would Pojman respond to this?

The Absurd   VIII.78

THOMAS NAGEL

In this essay Nagel reflects on the sense of absurdity that most of us feel from time to time. He considers the experience from several perspectives and eventually concludes that it is a function of our advanced self-consciousness which marks us off from less reflective beings.

(A biographical sketch of Thomas Nagel precedes Reading IV.39.)

Study Questions

1. What are some reasons for feeling nothing matters?
2. What are some ordinary absurd situations in life and how do they relate to our sense of absurdity?
3. What two perspectives, by colliding, result in the sense that life is absurd?
4. What is the value of stepping back and viewing our lives *sub specie aeternitatis* [from the view of eternity]?
5. How does our perception of absurdity resemble epistemological skepticism?
6. What would we have to do to avoid the sense of absurdity?
7. What is the final escape from absurdity?

MOST PEOPLE FEEL ON OCCASION that life is absurd, and some feel it vividly and continually. Yet the reasons usually offered in defense of this conviction are patently inadequate: they *could* not really explain why life is absurd.Why then do they provide a natural expression for the sense that it is?

I

Consider some examples. It is often remarked that nothing we do now will matter in a million years. But if that is true, then by the same token, nothing that will be the case in a million years matters now. In particular, it does not matter now that in a million years nothing we do now will matter. Moreover, even if what we did now *were* going to matter in a million years, how could that keep our present concerns from being absurd? If their mattering now is not enough to accomplish that, how would it help if they mattered a million years from now?

Whether what we do now will matter in a million years could make the crucial difference only if its mattering in a million years depended on its mattering, period. But then to deny that whatever happens now will matter in a million years is to beg the question against its mattering, period; for in that sense one cannot know that it will not matter in a million years whether (for example) someone now is happy or miserable, without knowing that it does not matter, period.

What we say to convey the absurdity of our lives often has to do with space or time: we are tiny specks in the infinite vastness of the universe; our lives are mere instants even on a geological time scale, let alone a cosmic one; we will all be dead any minute. But of course none of these evident facts can be what *makes* life absurd, if it is absurd. For suppose we lived forever; would not a life that is absurd if it lasts seventy years be infinitely absurd if it lasted through eternity? And if our lives are absurd given our present size, why would they be any less absurd if we filled the universe (either because we were larger or because the universe was smaller)? Reflection on our minuteness and brevity appears to be intimately connected with the sense that life is meaningless; but it is not clear what the connection is.

Another inadequate argument is that because we are going to die, all chains of justification must leave off in mid-air: one studies and works to earn money to pay for clothing, housing, entertainment, food, to sustain oneself from year to year, perhaps to support a family and pursue a career—but to what final end? All of it is an elaborate journey leading nowhere. (One will also have some effect on other people's lives, but that simply reproduces the problem, for they will die too.)

There are several replies to this argument. First, life does not consist of a sequence of activities each of which has as its purpose some later member of the sequence. Chains of justification come repeatedly to an end within life, and whether the process as a whole can be justified has no bearing on the finality of these end-points. No further justification is needed to make it reasonable to take aspirin for a headache, attend an exhibition of the work of a painter one admires, or stop a child from putting his hand on a hot stove. No larger context or further purpose is needed to prevent these acts from being pointless.

Even if someone wished to supply a further justification for pursuing all the things in life that are commonly regarded as self-justifying, that justification would have to end somewhere too. If *nothing* can justify unless it is justified in terms of something outside itself, which is also justified, then an infinite regress results, and no chain of justification can be complete. Moreover, if a finite chain of reasons cannot justify anything, what could be accomplished by an infinite chain, each link of which must be justified by something outside itself?

Since justifications must come to an end somewhere, nothing is gained by denying that they end where they appear to, within life—or by trying to subsume the multiple, often trivial ordinary justifications of action under a single, controlling life scheme. We can be satisfied more easily than that. In fact, through its misrepresentation of the process of justification, the argument makes a vacuous demand. It insists that the reasons available within life are incomplete, but suggests thereby that all reasons that come to an end are incomplete. This makes it impossible to supply any reasons at all.

The standard arguments for absurdity appear therefore to fail as arguments. Yet I believe they attempt to express something that is difficult to state, but fundamentally correct.

II

In ordinary life a situation is absurd when it includes a conspicuous discrepancy between pretension or aspiration and reality: someone gives a complicated speech in support of a motion that has already been passed; a notorious criminal is made president of a major philanthropic foundation; you declare your love over the telephone to a recorded announcement; as you are being knighted, your pants fall down.

When a person finds himself in an absurd situation, he will usually attempt to change it, by modifying his aspirations, or by trying to bring reality into better accord with them, or by removing himself from the situation entirely. We are not always willing or able to extricate ourselves from a position whose absurdity has become clear to us. Nevertheless, it is usually possible to imagine some change that would remove the absurdity—whether or not we can or will implement it. The sense that life as a whole is absurd arises when we perceive, perhaps dimly, an inflated pretension or aspiration which is inseparable from the continuation of human life and which makes its absurdity inescapable, short of escape from life itself.

Many people's lives are absurd, temporarily or permanently, for conventional reasons having to do with their particular ambitions, circumstances, and personal relations. If there is a philosophical sense of absurdity, however, it must arise from the perception of something universal—some respect in which pretension and reality inevitably clash for us all. This condition is supplied, I shall argue, by the collison between the seriousness with which we take our lives and the perpetual possibility of regarding everything about which we are serious as arbitrary, or open to doubt.

We cannot live human lives without energy and attention, nor without making choices which show that we take some things more seriously than others. Yet we have always available a point of view outside the particular form of our lives, from which the seriousness appears gratuitous. These two inescapable viewpoints collide in us, and that is what makes life absurd. It is absurd because we ignore the doubts that we know cannot be settled, continuing to live with nearly undiminished seriousness in spite of them.

This analysis requires defense in two respects: first as regards the unavoidability of seriousness; second as regards the inescapability of doubt.

We take ourselves seriously whether we lead serious lives or not and whether we are concerned primarily with fame, pleasure, virtues, luxury, triumph, beauty, justice, knowledge, salvation, or mere survival. If we take other people seriously and devote ourselves to them, that only multiplies the problem. Human life is full of effort, plans, calculation, success and failure: we *pursue* our lives, with varying degrees of sloth and energy.

It would be different if we could not step back and reflect on the process, but were merely led from impulse to impulse without self-consciousness.

But human beings do not act solely on impulse. They are prudent, they reflect, they weigh consequences, they ask whether what they are doing is worthwhile. Not only are their lives full of particular choices that hang together in larger activities with temporal structure: they also decide in the broadest terms what to pursue and what to avoid, what the priorities among their various aims should be, and what kind of people they want to be or become. Some men are faced with such choices by the large decisions they make from time to time; some merely by reflection on the course their lives are taking as the product of countless small decisions. They decide whom to marry, what profession to follow, whether to join the Country Club, or the Resistance; or they may just wonder why they go on being salesmen or academics or taxi drivers, and then stop thinking about it after a certain period of inconclusive reflection.

Although they may be motivated from act to act by those immediate needs with which life presents them, they allow the process to continue by adhering to the general system of habits and the form of life in which such motives have their place—or perhaps only by clinging to life itself. They spend enormous quantities of energy, risk, and calculation on the details. Think of how an ordinary individual sweats over his appearance, his health, his sex life, his emotional honesty, his social utility, his self-knowledge, the quality of his ties with family, colleagues, and friends, how well he does his job, whether he understands the world and what is going on in it. Leading a human life is a full-time occupation, to which everyone devotes decades of intense concern.

This fact is so obvious that it is hard to find it extraordinary and important. Each of us lives his own life—lives with himself twenty-four hours a day. What else is he supposed to do—live someone else's life? Yet humans have the special capacity to step back and survey themselves, and the lives to which they are committed, with that detached amazement which comes from watching an ant struggle up a heap of sand. Without developing the illusion that they are able to escape from their highly specific and idiosyncratic position, they can view it *sub specie aeternitatis*—and the view is at once sobering and comical.

The crucial backward step is not taken by asking for still another justification in the chain, and failing to get it. The objections to that line of attack have already been stated; justifications come to an end. But this is precisely what provides universal doubt with its object. We step back to find that the whole system of justification and criticism, which controls our choices and supports our claims to rationality, rests on responses and habits that we never question, that we should not know how to defend without circularity, and to which we shall continue to adhere even after they are called into question.

The things we do or want without reasons, and without requiring reasons—the things that define what is a reason for us and what is not—are the starting points of our skepticism. We see ourselves from outside, and all the contingency and specificity of our aims and pursuits become clear. Yet when we take this view and recognize what we do as arbitrary, it does not disengage us from life, and there lies our absurdity: not in the fact that such an external view can be taken of us, but in the fact that we ourselves can take it, without ceasing to be the persons whose ultimate concerns are so coolly regarded.

III

One may try to escape the position by seeking broader ultimate concerns, from which it is impossible to step back—the idea being that absurdity results because what we take seriously is something small and insignificant and individual. Those seeking to supply their lives with meaning usually envision a role or function in something larger than themselves. They therefore seek fulfillment in service to society, the state, the revolution, the progress of history, the advance of science, or religion and the glory of God.

But a role in some larger enterprise cannot confer significance unless that enterprise is itself significant. And its significance must come back to what we can understand, or it will not even appear to give us what we are seeking. If we learned that we were being raised to provide food for other creatures fond of human flesh, who planned to turn us into cutlets before we got too stringy—even if we learned that the human race had been developed by animal breeders precisely for this purpose—that would still not give our lives meaning, for two reasons. First, we would still be in the dark as to the significance of the lives of those other beings; second, although we might acknowledge that this culinary role would make our lives meaningful to them, it is not clear how it would make them meaningful to us.

Admittedly, the usual form of service to a higher being is different from this. One is supposed to behold and partake of the glory of God, for example, in a way in which chickens do not share in the glory of coq au vin. The same is true of service to a state, a movement, or a revolution. People can come to feel, when they are part of something bigger, that it is part of them too. They worry less about what is peculiar to themselves, but identify enough with the larger enterprise to find their role in it fulfilling.

However, any such larger purpose can be put in doubt in the same way that the aims of an individual life can be, and for the same reasons. It is as legitimate to find ultimate justification there as to find it earlier, among the details of individual life. But this does not alter the fact that justifications come to an end when we are content to have them end—when we do not find it necessary to look any further. If we can step back from the purposes of individual life and doubt their point, we can step back also from the progress of human history, or of science, or the success of a society, or the kingdom, power, and glory of God, and put all these things into question in the same way. What seems to us to confer meaning, justification, significance, does so in virtue of the fact that we need no more reasons after a certain point.

What makes doubt inescapable with regard to the limited aims of individual life also makes it inescapable with regard to any larger purpose that encourages the sense that life is meaningful. Once the fundamental doubt has begun, it cannot be laid to rest.

Camus maintains in *The Myth of Sisyphus* that the absurd arises because the world fails to meet our demands for meaning. This suggests that the world might satisfy those demands if it were different. But now we can see that this is not the case. There does not appear to be any conceivable world (containing us) about which unsettleable doubts could not arise. Consequently the absurdity of our situation derives not from a collison between our expectations and the world, but from a collision within ourselves.

IV

It may be objected that the standpoint from which these doubts are supposed to be felt does not exist—that if we take the recommended backward step we will land on thin air, without any basis for judgement about the natural responses we are supposed to be surveying. If we retain our usual standards of what is important, then questions about the significance of what we are doing with our lives will be answerable in the usual way. But if we do not, then those questions can mean nothing to us, since there is no longer any content to the idea of what matters, and hence no content to the idea that nothing does.

But this objection misconceives the nature of the backward step. It is not supposed to give us an understanding of what is *really* important, so that we see by contrast that our lives are insignificant. We never, in the course of these reflections, abandon the ordinary standards that guide our lives. We merely observe them in operation, and recognize that if they are called into question we can justify them only by reference to themselves, uselessly. We adhere to them because of the way we are put together; what seems to us important or serious or valuable would not seem so if we were differently constituted.

In ordinary life, to be sure, we do not judge a situation absurd unless we have in mind some standards of seriousness, significance, or harmony with which the absurd can be contrasted. This contrast is not implied by the philosophical judgment of absurdity, and that might be thought to make the concept unsuitable for the expression of such judgments. This is not so, however, for the philosophical judgment depends on another contrast which makes it a natural extension from more ordinary cases. It departs from them only in contrasting the pretensions of life with a larger context in which *no* standards can be discovered, rather than with a context from which alternative, overriding standards may be applied.

V

In this respect, as in others, philosophical perception of the absurd resembles epistemological skepticism. In both cases the final, philosophical doubt is not contrasted with any unchallenged certainties, though it is arrived at by extrapolation from examples of doubt within the system of evidence or justification, where a contrast with other certainties *is* implied. In both cases our limitedness joins with a capacity to transcend those limitations in thought (thus seeing them as limitations, and as inescapable).

Skepticism begins when we include ourselves in the world about which we claim knowledge. We notice that certain types of evidence convince us, that we are content to allow justifications of belief to come to an end at certain points, that we feel we know many things even without knowing or having grounds for believing the denial of others which, if true, would make what we claim to know false.

For example, I know that I am looking at a piece of paper, although I have no adequate grounds for claiming I know that I am not dreaming; and if I am dreaming then I am not looking at a piece of paper. Here an ordinary conception of how appearance may diverge from reality is employed to show that we take our world largely for granted; the certainty that we are not dreaming cannot be justified except circularly, in terms of those very appearances which are being put in doubt. It is somewhat farfetched to suggest I may be dreaming; but the possibility is only illustrative. It reveals that our claims to knowledge depend on our not feeling it necessary to exclude certain incompatible alternatives, and the dreaming possibility or the total-hallucination possibility are just representatives for limitless possibilities most of which we cannot even conceive.[1]

Once we have taken the backward step to an abstract view of our whole system of beliefs, evidence, and justification, and seen that it works only, despite its pretensions, by taking the world largely for granted, we are *not* in a position to contrast all these appearances with an alternative reality. We cannot shed our ordinary responses, and if we could it would leave us with no means of conceiving a reality of any kind.

It is the same in the practical domain. We do not step outside our lives to a new vantage point from which we see what is really, objectively significant. We continue to take life largely for granted while seeing that all our decisions and certainties are possible only because there is a great deal we do not bother to rule out.

Both epistemological skepticism and a sense of the absurd can be reached via initial doubts posed within systems of evidence and justification that we accept, and can be stated without violence to our ordinary concepts. We can ask not only why we should believe there is a floor under us, but also why we should believe the evidence of our senses at all—and at some point the framable questions will have outlasted the answers. Similarly, we can ask not only why we should take aspirin, but why we should take trouble over our own comfort at all. The fact that we shall take the aspirin without waiting for an answer to this last question does not show that it is an unreal question. We shall also continue to believe there is a floor under us without waiting for an answer to the other question. In both cases it is this unsupported natural confidence that generates skeptical doubts; so it cannot be used to settle them.

Philosophical skepticism does not cause us to abandon our ordinary beliefs, but it lends them a peculiar flavor. After acknowledging that their truth is incompatible with possibilities that we have no grounds for believing do not obtain—apart from grounds in those very beliefs which we have called into question—we return to our familiar convictions with a certain irony and resignation. Unable to abandon the natural responses on which they depend, we take them back, like a spouse who has run off with someone else and then decided to return; but we regard them differently (not that the new attitude is necessarily inferior to the old, in either case).

The same situation obtains after we have put in question the seriousness with which we take our lives and human life in general and have looked at ourselves without presuppositions. We then return to our lives, as we must, but our seriousness is laced with irony. Not that irony enables us to escape the absurd. It is useless to mutter: "Life is meaningless; life is meaningless . . ." as an accompaniment to everything we do. In continuing to live and work and strive, we take ourselves seriously in action no matter what we say.

What sustains us, in belief as in action, is not reason for justification, but something more basic than these—for we go on in the same way even after we are convinced that the reasons have given out.[2] If we tried to rely entirely on reason, and pressed it hard, our lives and beliefs would collapse—a form of madness that may actually occur if the inertial force of taking the world and life for granted is somehow lost. If we lose our grip on that, reason will not give it back to us.

VI

In viewing ourselves from a perspective broader than we can occupy in the flesh, we become spectators of our own lives. We cannot do very much as pure spectators of our own lives, so we continue to lead them, and devote ourselves to what we are able at the same time to view as no more than a curiosity, like the ritual of an alien religion.

This explains why the sense of absurdity finds its natural expression in those bad arguments with which the discussion began. References to our small size and short lifespan and to the fact that all of mankind will eventually vanish without a trace are metaphors for the backward step which permits us to regard ourselves from without and to find the particular form of our lives curious and slightly surprising. By feigning a nebula's-eye view, we illustrate the capacity to see ourselves without presuppositions, as arbitrary, idiosyncratic, highly specific occupants of the world, one of countless possible forms of life.

Before turning to the question whether the absurdity of our lives is something to be regretted and if possible escaped, let me consider what would have to be given up in order to avoid it.

Why is the life of a mouse not absurd? The orbit of the moon is not absurd either, but that involves no strivings or aims at all. A mouse, however, has to work to stay alive. Yet he is not absurd, because he lacks the capacities for self-consciousness and self-transcendence that would enable him to see that he is only a mouse. If that *did* happen, his life would become absurd, since self-awareness would not make him cease to be a mouse and would not enable him to rise above his mousely strivings. Bringing his new-found self-consciousness with him, he would have to return to his meager yet frantic life, full of doubts that he was unable to answer, but also full of purposes that he was unable to abandon.

Given that the transcendental step is natural to us humans, can we avoid absurdity by refusing to take that step and remaining entirely within our sublunar lives? Well, we cannot refuse consciously, for to do that we would have to be aware of the viewpoint we were refusing to adopt. The only way to avoid the relevant self-consciousness would be either never to attain it or to forget it—neither of which can be achieved by the will.

On the other hand, it is possible to expend effort on an attempt to destroy the other component of the absurd—abandoning one's earthly, individual, human life in order to iden-tify as completely as possible with that universal viewpoint from which human life seems arbitrary and trivial. (This appears to be the ideal of certain Oriental religions.) If one succeeds, then one will not have to drag the superior awareness through a strenuous mundane life, and absurdity will be diminished.

However, insofar as this self-etiolation is the result of effort, will-power, aceticism, and so forth, it requires that one take oneself seriously as an individual—that one be willing to take considerable trouble to avoid being creaturely and absurd. Thus one may undermine the aim of unworldliness by pursuing it too vigorously. Still, if someone simply allowed his individual, animal nature to drift and respond to impulse, without making the pursuit of its needs a central conscious aim, then he might, at considerable dissociative cost, achieve a life that was less absurd than most. It would not be a meaningful life either, of course; but it would not involve the engagement of a transcendent awareness in the assiduous pursuit of mundane goals. And that is the main condition of absurdity—the dragooning of an unconvinced transcendent consciousness into the service of an immanent, limited enterprise like a human life.

The final escape is suicide; but before adopting any hasty solutions, it would be wise to consider carefully whether the absurdity of our existence truly presents us with *a problem*, to which some solution must be found—a way of dealing with prima facie disaster. That is certainly the attitude with which Camus approaches the issue, and it gains support from the fact that we are all eager to escape from absurd situations on a smaller scale.

Camus—not on uniformly good grounds—rejects suicide and the other solutions he regards as escapist. What he recommends is defiance or scorn. We can salvage our dignity, he appears to believe, by shaking a fist at the world which is deaf to our pleas, and continuing to live in spite of it. This will not make our lives un-absurd, but it will lend them a certain nobility.[3]

This seems to me romantic and slightly self-pitying. Our absurdity warrants neither that much distress nor that much defiance. At the risk of falling into romanticism by a different route, I would argue that absurdity is one of the most human things about us: a manifestation of our most advanced and interesting characteristics. Like skepticism in epistemology, it is possible only because we possess a certain kind of insight—the capacity to transcend ourselves in thought.

If a sense of the absurd is a way of perceiving our true situation (even though the situation is not absurd until the perception arises), then what reason can we have to resent or escape it? Like the capacity for epistemological skepticism, it results from the ability to understand our human limitations. It need not be a matter for agony unless we make it so. Nor need it evoke a defiant contempt of fate that allows us to feel brave or proud. Such dramatics, even if carried on in private, betray a failure to appreciate the cosmic unimportance of the situation. If *sub specie aeternitatis* there is no reason to believe that anything matters, then that does not matter either, and we can approach our absurd lives with irony instead of heroism or despair.

NOTES

1. I am aware that skepticism about the external world is widely thought to have been refuted, but I have remained convinced of its irrefutability since being exposed at Berkeley to Thompson Clarke's largely unpublished ideas on the subject.

2. As Hume says in a famous passage of the *Treatise:* 'Most fortunately it happens, that since reason is incapable of dispelling these clouds, nature herself suffices to that purpose, and cures me of this philosophical melancholy and delirium, either by relaxing this bent of mind, or by some avocation, and lively impression of my senses, which obliterate all these chimeras. I dine, I play a game of backgammon, I converse, and am merry with my friends; and when after three or four hours' amusement, I would return to these speculations, they appear so cold, and strain'd, and ridiculous, that I cannot find in my heart to enter into them any farther' (bk. 1, pt. iv, sect. 7; Selby-Bigge edition, p. 269).

3. "Sisyphus, proletarian of the gods, powerless and rebellious, knows the whole extent of his wretched condition: it is what he thinks of during his descent. The lucidity that was to constitute his torture at the same time crowns his victory. There is no fate that cannot be surmounted by scorn" (*The Myth of Sisyphus,* trans. Justin O'Brien [New York: Vintage, 1959], p. 90; first published, Paris: Gallimard, 1942).

For Further Reflection

1. Evaluate Nagel's claim that the sense of absurdity derives not from a collision between our expectations and the world, but from a collision within ourselves. Is he correct? Explain.

2. How, according to Nagel, can we escape the absurd? How can the universal viewpoint free us from the absurd?

3. How should we respond to our absurdity? Why is it something noble?

4. Do you agree that life is absurd? Explain.

Reflections on Suffering   VIII.79

BERTRAND RUSSELL

A philosopher whom we have studied at length in this work is Bertrand Russell, someone who thought deeply about the question of the meaning of life. Russell says in his
Autobiography that his youth was very unhappy and only the love of mathematics kept
him from committing suicide. Gradually, he learned to find happiness. In these two
short selections from his *Autobiography,* Russell first tells of an experience that greatly
affected his life and then goes on to summarize what gives him meaning in life.

(A biographical sketch of Russell precedes Reading I.4.)

Study Questions

1. Describe the situation in the first part of this essay.
2. What sort of feelings and thoughts did Russell experience in the face of the suffering he
   witnessed?
3. What are the three passions that have dominated Russell's life?

SPRING 1901

WHEN WE CAME HOME, we found Mrs. W
undergoing an unusually severe bout of pain.
She seemed cut off from everyone and everything by walls of agony, and the sense of the
solitude of each human soul suddenly over-
whelmed me. Ever since my marriage, my emotional life had been calm and superficial. I had
forgotten all the deeper issues, and had been
content with flippant cleverness. Suddenly the
ground seemed to give way beneath me, and I
found myself in quite another region. Within
five minutes I went thru some such reflections as
the following: the loneliness of the human soul
is unendurable; nothing can penetrate it except
the highest intensity of the sort of love that religious teachers have preached; whatever does not
spring from this motive is harmful, or at best
useless; it follows that war is wrong, that a public school education is abominable, that the use
of force is to be deprecated, and that in human
relations one should penetrate to the core of
loneliness in each person and speak to that. [The
writer then describes his sudden awareness of Mrs.
W's three year old son with whom he then and
there found an affinity.] . . . At the end of those
five minutes, I had become a completely different
person. For a time, a sort of mystic illumination
possessed me. I felt that I knew the inmost
thoughts of everybody that I met in the street, and
though this was, no doubt, a delusion, I did in

Reprinted from The Autobiography of Bertrand Russell, *vol. I, p. 146, 1951, by permission of Taylor &
Francis Books UK and The Bertrand Russell Peace Foundation.*

actual fact find myself in *far closer* touch than previously with all my friends, and many of my acquaintances. Having been an Imperialist, I became during those five minutes . . . a Pacificist. Having for years cared only for exactness and analysis, I found myself filled with semi-mystical feelings about beauty, and with an intense interest in children and with a desire almost as profound as that of the Buddha to find some philosophy which should make human life endurable. A strange excitement possessed me, containing intense pain but also some element of triumph through the fact that I could dominate pain, and make it, as I thought, a gateway to wisdom. The mystic insight which I then imagined myself to possess has largely faded, and the habit of analysis has reasserted itself. But something of what I thought I saw in that moment has remained always with me, *causing* my attitude during the first war, my interest in my children, my indifference to minor misfortunes and a certain emotional tone in all my human relations.

That man is the product of causes which had no prevision of the end they were achieving; that his origin, his growth, his hopes and fears, his loves and his beliefs are but the outcome of accidental colocations of atoms; that no fire, no heroism, no intensity of thought and feeling, can preserve an individual life beyond the grave; that all the labors of the ages, all the devotion, all the inspiration, all the noonday brightness of human genius, are destined to extinction in the vast death of the solar system, and that the whole temple of man's achievement must inevitably be buried beneath the debris of a universe in ruins—all these things, if not quite beyond dispute, are yet so nearly certain that no philosophy which rejects them can hope to stand. Only within the scaffolding of these truths, only on the firm foundation of unyielding despair, can the soul's habitation henceforth be safely built.

EPILOGUE

Love, Knowledge, and Pity

Three passions, simple but overwhelmingly strong, have governed my life: the longing for love, the search for knowledge, and unbearable pity for the suffering of mankind. These passions, like great winds, have blown me hither and thither, in a wayward course, over a deep ocean of anguish, reaching to the very verge of despair.

I have sought love, first, because it brings ecstasy—ecstasy so great that I would often have sacrificed all the rest of life for a few hours of this joy. I have sought it, next, because it relieves loneliness—that terrible loneliness in which one shivering consciousness looks over the rim of the world into the cold unfathomable lifeless abyss. I have sought it, finally, because in the union of love I have seen, in a mystic miniature, the prefiguring vision of the heaven that saints and poets have imagined. This is what I sought, and though it might seem too good for human life, this is what—at last—I have found.

With equal passion I have sought knowledge. I have wished to understand the hearts of men. I have wished to know why the stars shine. And I have tried to apprehend the Pythagorean power by which number holds sway above the flux. A little of this, but not much, I have achieved.

Love and knowledge, so far as they were possible, led upward toward the heavens. But always pity brought me back to earth. Echoes of cries of pain reverberate in my heart. Children in famine, victims tortured by oppressors, helpless old people a hated burden to their sons, and the whole world of loneliness, poverty, and pain make a mockery of what human life should be. I long to alleviate the evil, but I cannot, and I too suffer.

This has been my life. I have found it worth living, and would gladly live it again if the chance were offered me.

For Further Reflection

1. Compare the first selection with the second. Do you see any differences?

2. How does your set of values compare with Russell's? Do you think that Russell's philosophy of life is adequate for happiness and the good life? Compare it with the other readings in this part.

Suggestions for Further Reading

Baggini, Julian. *What's It All About?* New York: Oxford University Press, 2004.

Barrett, William. *Irrational Man.* New York: Doubleday, 1958.

Bretall, Robert, ed. *A Kierkegaard Anthology.* Princeton, NJ: Princeton University Press, 1946.

Camus, Albert. *The Myth of Sisyphus and Other Essays,* trans. J. O. O'Brien. New York: Random House, 1955.

Camus, Albert. *The Plague.* New York: Random House, 1948.

Frankl, Victor. *Man's Search for Meaning.* New York: Beacon Press, 1963.

Kaufmann, Walter. *Existentialism from Dostoevsky to Sartre.* New American Library, 1975.

Kaufmann, Walter, ed. and trans. *A Portable Nietzsche.* New York: Viking, 1954.

Kierkegaard, Søren. *Fear and Trembling,* trans. Walter Lowrie. Princeton, NJ: Princeton University Press, 1954.

Klemke, E. D. *The Meaning of Life.* Oxford: Oxford University Press, 1981.

Nietzsche, Friedrich. *The Will to Power.* New York: Random House, 1967.

Russell, Bertrand. *The Conquest of Happiness.* New American Library, 1930.

Sanders, Steven, and David Cheney, eds. *The Meaning of Life.* Englewood Cliffs, NJ: Prentice Hall, 1980.

Sartre, Jean Paul. *Existentialism and Human Emotions.* Philosophical Library, 1948.

Schopenhauer, Arthur. *The Will to Live. Selected Writings of Arthur Schopenhauer,* ed. Richard Taylor. Ungar, 1967.

Tolstoy, Leo. *My Confessions,* trans. Leo Wiener. Dent, 1905.

Part IX

Contemporary Moral Problems

What is the use of studying philosophy if all that it does for you is enable you to talk with some plausibility about some abstruse questions of logic, and so on and if it does not improve your thinking about the important questions of everyday life?

LUDWIG WITTGENSTEIN

S EVERAL MORAL ISSUES are tearing our society apart; among the most prominent are abortion, euthanasia, racism, the death penalty, the status of animals, and our obligations to the world's poor and hungry. Can philosophical analysis throw light on these issues? Can philosophy have practical implications?

Although this introduction to philosophy concentrates on the classical problems of philosophy, the topics covered in Parts I through VIII, this short section will provide examples of how philosophical reasoning can illuminate contemporary issues. We have chosen four that have special interest to students: abortion, capital punishment, animal rights, and world hunger and poverty.

IX.A   Is Abortion Morally Permissible?

Abortion during the first two or three months of gestation is morally equivalent to removal of a piece of tissue from the woman's body. (philosopher Thomas Szasz)

Every unborn child must be regarded as a human person with all the rights of a human person, from the moment of conception. (Ethical and Religious Directives for Catholic Hospitals)

One of the major social issues before us today, one that divides our nation as no other issue does, is that of the moral and legal status of the human fetus and the corresponding question of the moral permissibility of abortion. On the one hand, such organizations as the Roman Catholic Church and the Right to Life movement, appalled by the more than 1.5 million abortions that take place in this country each year, have exerted significant political pressure toward introducing a constitutional amendment that would grant full legal rights to fetuses. These movements have in some cases made the abortion issue the single issue in political campaigns. On the other hand, pro-choice groups such as the National Organization of Women (NOW), the National Abortion Rights Action League (NARAL), and feminist organizations have exerted enormous pressure on politicians to support pro-abortion legislation. The Republican and Democratic political platforms of the last few elections took diametrically opposite sides on this issue.

Why is abortion a moral issue? Take a fertilized egg, a zygote, a tiny diploid cell. By itself, it is hard to see what is so important about such an inconspicuous piece of matter. It is virtually indistinguishable from other clusters of cells, or the zygotes of other animals. On the other hand, take an adult human being, a class of beings that we all intuitively feel to be worthy of high respect, having rights, including the right to life. To kill an innocent human being is an act of murder and universally condemned. However, no obvious line of division separates that single-cell zygote from the adult it will become. Hence, the problem of abortion.

Don Marquis argues that what makes killing wrong is that it takes away someone's future, a life of experiences, activities, and pleasures—and abortion is wrong for this very reason. To the contrary, Mary Anne Warren contends that abortion is not wrong because it does not involve the killing of persons, for persons must have such characteristics as self-consciousness and rationality and fetuses do not have these. Judith Jarvis Thomson argues that even if a fetus is a person, abortion may be permissible in certain cases on grounds of a woman's right of self-defense. Finally, Jane English makes a case for a moderate position. Most early abortions are permissible, most late ones immoral.

Why Abortion Is Immoral   IX.80

DON MARQUIS

Don Marquis is a professor of philosophy at the University of Kansas. In this reading he examines the moral permissibility of abortion by first asking what makes killing someone wrong. His answer is that killing is wrong because it robs the victim of a future—all possible "experiences, activities, projects, and enjoyments." In the same way, abortion is (almost always) wrong because it deprives the fetus of an experienced future.

Study Questions

1. What are the premises and conclusion of Marquis' argument?
2. How does he support his contention that the wrongness of killing derives from the victim's loss of a future?
3. Does Marquis allow that in some cases abortion may be permissible? If so, what are these exceptions?

THE VIEW THAT ABORTION IS, with rare exceptions, seriously immoral has received little support in the recent philosophical literature. No doubt most philosophers affiliated with secular institutions of higher education believe that the anti-abortion position is either a symptom of irrational religious dogma or a conclusion generated by seriously confused philosophical argument. The purpose of this essay is to undermine this general belief. This essay sets out an argument that purports to show, as well as any argument in ethics can show, that abortion is, except possibly in rare cases, seriously immoral, that it is in the same moral category as killing an innocent adult human being.

The argument is based on a major assumption. Many of the most insightful and careful writers on the ethics of abortion—such as Joel Feinberg, Michael Tooley, Mary Anne Warren, H. Tristram Engelhardt, Jr., L. W. Sumner, John T. Noonan, Jr., and Philip Devine[1]—believe that whether

From Don Marquis, "Why Abortion Is Immoral," Journal of Philosophy, *LXXXVI, 4 (April 1989), pp. 183–202 by permission.*

or not abortion is morally permissible stands or falls on whether or not a fetus is the sort of being whose life it is seriously wrong to end. The argument of this essay will assume, but not argue, that they are correct.

Also, this essay will neglect issues of great importance to a complete ethics of abortion. Some anti-abortionists will allow that certain abortions, such as abortion before implantation or abortion when the life of a woman is threatened by a pregnancy or abortion after rape, may be morally permissible. This essay will not explore the casuistry of these hard cases. The purpose of this essay is to develop a general argument for the claim that the overwhelming majority of deliberate abortions are seriously immoral.

I

A sketch of standard anti-abortion and pro-choice arguments exhibits how those arguments possess certain symmetries that explain why partisans of those positions are so convinced of the correctness of their own positions, why they are not successful in convincing their opponents, and why, to others, this issue seems to be unresolvable. An analysis of the nature of this standoff suggests a strategy for surmounting it.

Consider the way a typical anti-abortionist argues. She will argue or assert that life is present from the moment of conception or that fetuses look like babies or that fetuses possess a characteristic such as a genetic code that is both necessary and sufficient for being human. Anti-abortionists seem to believe that (1) the truth of all of these claims is quite obvious, and (2) establishing any of these claims is sufficient to show that abortion is morally akin to murder.

A standard pro-choice strategy exhibits similarities. The pro-choicer will argue or assert that fetuses are not persons or that fetuses are not rational agents or that fetuses are not social beings. Pro-choicers seem to believe that (1) the truth of any of these claims is quite obvious, and

(2) establishing any of these claims is sufficient to show that an abortion is not a wrongful killing.

In fact, both the pro-choice and the anti-abortion claims do seem to be true, although the "it looks like a baby" claim is more difficult to establish the earlier the pregnancy. We seem to have a standoff. How can it be resolved?

As everyone who has taken a bit of logic knows, if any of these arguments concerning abortion is a good argument, it requires not only some claim characterizing fetuses, but also some general moral principle that ties a characteristic of fetuses to having or not having the right to life or to some other moral characteristic that will generate the obligation or the lack of obligation not to end the life of a fetus. Accordingly, the arguments of the anti-abortionist and the pro-choicer need a bit of filling in to be regarded as adequate.

Note what each partisan will say. The anti-abortionist will claim that her position is supported by such generally accepted moral principles as "It is always prima facie seriously wrong to take a human life" or "It is always prima facie seriously wrong to end the life of a baby." Since these are generally accepted moral principles, her position is certainly not obviously wrong. The pro-choicer will claim that her position is supported by such plausible moral principles as "Being a person is what gives an individual intrinsic moral worth" or "It is only seriously prima facie wrong to take the life of a member of the human community." Since these are generally accepted moral principles, the pro-choice position is certainly not obviously wrong. Unfortunately, we have again arrived at a standoff.

Now, how might one deal with this standoff? The standard approach is to try to show how the moral principles of one's opponent lose their plausibility under analysis. It is easy to see how this is possible. On the one hand, the anti-abortionist will defend a moral principle concerning the wrongness of killing which tends to be broad in scope in order that even fetuses at an early stage of pregnancy will fall under it. The problem with broad principles is that they often embrace too much. In this particular instance, the principle "It is always prima facie wrong to take a human life" seems to entail that it is wrong to end the existence of a living human cancer-cell culture, on the grounds that the culture is both living and human. Therefore, it seems that the anti-abortionist's favored principle is too broad.

On the other hand, the pro-choicer wants to find a moral principle concerning the wrongness of killing which tends to be narrow in scope in order that fetuses will *not* fall under it. The problem with narrow principles is that they often do not embrace enough. Hence, the needed principles such as "It is prima facie seriously wrong to kill only persons" or "It is prima facie wrong to kill only rational agents" do not explain why it is wrong to kill infants or young children or the severely retarded or even perhaps the severely mentally ill. Therefore, we seem again to have a stand off. The anti-abortionist charges, not unreasonably, that pro-choice principles concerning killing are too narrow to be acceptable; the pro-choicer charges, not unreasonably, that anti-abortionist principles concerning killing are too broad to be acceptable.

Attempts by both sides to patch up the difficulties in their positions run into further difficulties. The anti-abortionist will try to remove the problem in her position by reformulating her principle concerning killing in terms of human beings. Now we end up with: "It is always prima facie seriously wrong to end the life of a human being." This principle has the advantage of avoiding the problem of the human cancer-cell culture counterexample. But this advantage is purchased at a high price. For although it is clear that a fetus is both human and alive, it is not at all clear that a fetus is a human *being*. There is at least something to be said for the view that something becomes a human being only after a process of development, and that therefore first trimester fetuses and perhaps all fetuses are not yet human beings. Hence, the anti-abortionist, by this move, has merely exchanged one problem for another.[2]

The pro-choicer fares no better. She may attempt to find reasons why killing infants, young children, and the severely retarded is wrong which are independent of her major principle that is supposed to explain the wrongness of taking human life, but which will not also make abortion immoral. This is no easy task. Appeals to social utility will seem satisfactory only to those who resolve not to think of the enormous difficulties with a utilitarian account of the wrongness of killing and the significant social costs of preserving the lives of the unproductive.[3] A pro-choice strategy that extends the definition of "person" to infants or even to young children seems just as arbitrary as an anti-abortion strategy that extends the definition of "human being" to fetuses. Again, we find symmetries in the two positions and we arrive at a standoff.

There are even further problems that reflect symmetries in the two positions. In addition to counterexample problems, or the arbitrary application problems that can be exchanged for them, the standard anti-abortionist principle "It is prima facie seriously wrong to kill a human being," or one of its variants, can be objected to on the grounds of ambiguity. If "human being" is taken to be a *biological* category, then the anti-abortionist is left with the problem of explaining why a merely biological category should make a moral difference. Why, it is asked, is it any more reasonable to base a moral conclusion on the number of chromosomes in one's cells than on the color of one's skin?[4] If "human being," on the other hand, is taken to be a *moral* category, then the claim that a fetus is a human being cannot be taken to be a premise in the anti-abortion argument, for it is precisely what needs to be established. Hence, either the anti-abortionist's main category is a morally irrelevant, merely biological category, or it is of no use to the anti-abortionist in establishing (noncircularly, of course) that abortion is wrong.

Although this problem with the anti-abortionist position is often noticed, it is less often noticed that the pro-choice position suffers from an analogous problem. The principle "Only persons have the right to life" also suffers from an ambiguity. The term "person" is typically defined in terms of psychological characteristics, although there will certainly be disagreement concerning which characteristics are most important. Supposing that this matter can be settled, the pro-choicer is left with the problem of explaining why *psychological* characteristics should make a *moral* difference. If the pro-choicer should attempt to deal with this problem by claiming that an explanation is not necessary, that in fact we do treat such a cluster of psychological properties as having moral significance, the sharp-witted anti-abortionist should have a ready response. We do treat being both living and human as having moral significance. If it is legitimate for the pro-choicer to demand that the anti-abortionist provide an explanation of the connection between the biological character of being a human being and the wrongness of being killed (even though people accept this connection), then it is legitimate for the anti-abortionist to demand that the pro-choicer provide an explanation of the connection between psychological criteria for being a person and the wrongness of being killed (even though that connection is accepted).[5]

Feinberg has attempted to meet this objection (he calls psychological personhood "commonsense personhood"):

> The characteristics that confer commonsense personhood are not arbitrary bases for rights and duties, such as race, sex or species membership; rather they are traits that make sense out of rights and duties and without which those moral attributes would have no point or function. It is because people are conscious; have a sense of their personal identities; have plans, goals, and projects; experience emotions; are liable to pains, anxieties, and frustrations; can reason and bargain, and so on—it is because of these attributes that people have values and interests, desires and expectations of their own, including a stake in their own futures, and a personal well-being of a sort we cannot ascribe to

unconscious or nonrational beings. Because of their developed capacities they can assume duties and responsibilities and can have and make claims on one another. Only because of their sense of self, their life plans, their value hierarchies, and their stakes in their own futures can they be ascribed fundamental rights. There is nothing arbitrary about these linkages (*op. cit.*, p. 270).

The plausible aspects of this attempt should not be taken to obscure its implausible features. There is a great deal to be said for the view that being a psychological person under some description is a necessary condition for having duties. One cannot have a duty unless one is capable of behaving morally, and a being's capability of behaving morally will require having a certain psychology. It is far from obvious, however, that having rights entails consciousness or rationality, as Feinberg suggests. We speak of the rights of the severely retarded or the severely mentally ill, yet some of these persons are not rational. We speak of the rights of the temporarily unconscious. The New Jersey Supreme Court based their decision in the Quinlan case on Karen Ann Quinlan's right to privacy, and she was known to be permanently unconscious at that time. Hence, Feinberg's claim that having rights entails being conscious is, on its face, obviously false.

Of course, it might not make sense to attribute rights to a being that would never in its natural history have certain psychological traits. This modest connection between psychological personhood and moral personhood will create a place for Karen Ann Quinlan and the temporarily unconscious. But then it makes a place for fetuses also. Hence, it does not serve Feinberg's pro-choice purposes. Accordingly, it seems that the pro-choicer will have as much difficulty bridging the gap between psychological personhood and personhood in the moral sense as the anti-abortionist has bridging the gap between being a biological human being and being a human being in the moral sense.

Furthermore, the pro-choicer cannot any more escape her problem by making person a purely moral category than the anti-abortionist could escape by the analogous move. For if person is a moral category, then the pro-choicer is left without the resources for establishing (noncircularly, of course) the claim that a fetus is not a person, which is an essential premise in her argument. Again, we have both a symmetry and a standoff between pro-choice and anti-abortion views.

Passions in the abortion debate run high. There are both plausibilities and difficulties with the standard positions. Accordingly, it is hardly surprising that partisans of either side embrace with fervor the moral generalizations that support the conclusions they pre-analytically favor, and reject with disdain the moral generalizations of their opponents as being subject to inescapable difficulties. It is easy to believe that the counterexamples to one's own moral principles are merely temporary difficulties that will dissolve in the wake of further philosophical research, and that the counterexamples to the principles of one's opponents are as straightforward as the contradiction between *A* and *O* propositions in traditional logic. This might suggest to an impartial observer (if there are any) that the abortion issue is unresolvable.

There is a way out of this apparent dialectical quandary. The moral generalizations of both sides are not quite correct. The generalizations hold for the most part, for the usual cases. This suggests that they are all *accidental* generalizations, that the moral claims made by those on both sides of the dispute do not touch on the *essence* of the matter.

This use of the distinction between essence and accident is not meant to invoke obscure metaphysical categories. Rather, it is intended to reflect the rather atheoretical nature of the abortion discussion. If the generalization a partisan in the abortion dispute adopts were derived from the reason why ending the life of a human being is wrong, then there could not be exceptions to that generalization unless some special case obtains in which there are even more powerful countervailing reasons. Such generalizations would not be merely accidental generalizations; they would

point to, or be based upon, the essence of the wrongness of killing, what it is that makes killing wrong. All this suggests that a necessary condition of resolving the abortion controversy is a more theoretical account of the wrongness of killing. After all, if we merely believe, but do not understand, why killing adult human beings such as ourselves is wrong, how could we conceivably show that abortion is either immoral or permissible?

II

In order to develop such an account, we can start from the following unproblematic assumption concerning our own case: it is wrong to kill *us*. Why is it wrong? Some answers can be easily eliminated. It might be said that what makes killing us wrong is that a killing brutalizes the one who kills. But the brutalization consists of being inured to the performance of an act that is hideously immoral; hence, the brutalization does not explain the immorality. It might be said that what makes killing us wrong is the great loss others would experience due to our absence. Although such hubris is understandable, such an explanation does not account for the wrongness of killing hermits, or those whose lives are relatively independent and whose friends find it easy to make new friends.

A more obvious answer is better. What primarily makes killing wrong is neither its effect on the murderer nor its effect on the victim's friends and relatives, but its effect on the victim. The loss of one's life is one of the greatest losses one can suffer. The loss of one's life deprives one of all the experiences, activities, projects, and enjoyments that would otherwise have constituted one's future. Therefore, killing someone is wrong, primarily because the killing inflicts (one of) the greatest possible losses on the victim. To describe this as the loss of life can be misleading, however. The change in my biological state does not by itself make killing me wrong. The effect of the loss of my biological life is the loss to me of all those activities, projects, experiences, and

enjoyments which would otherwise have constituted my future personal life. These activities,
projects, experiences, and enjoyments are either
valuable for their own sakes or are means to
something else that is valuable for its own sake.
Some parts of my future are not valued by me
now, but will come to be valued by me as I grow
older and as my values and capacities change.
When I am killed, I am deprived both of what I
now value which would have been part of my
future personal life, but also what I would come
to value. Therefore, when I die, I am deprived of
all of the value of my future. Inflicting this loss
on me is ultimately what makes killing me
wrong. This being the case, it would seem that
what makes killing *any* adult human being prima
facie seriously wrong is the loss of his or her
future.[6]

How should this rudimentary theory of the
wrongness of killing be evaluated? It cannot be
faulted for deriving an "ought" from an "is,"
for it does not. The analysis assumes that killing
me (or you, reader) is prima facie seriously wrong.
The point of the analysis is to establish which
natural property ultimately explains the wrongness of the killing, given that it is wrong. A
natural property will ultimately explain the
wrongness of killing, only if (1) the explanation
fits with our intuitions about the matter and
(2) there is no other natural property that provides the basis for a better explanation of the
wrongness of killing. This analysis rests on the
intuition that what makes killing a particular
human or animal wrong is what it does to that
particular human or animal. What makes killing
wrong is some natural effect or other of the
killing. Some would deny this. For instance, a
divine-command theorist in ethics would deny
it. Surely this denial is, however, one of those
features of divine-command theory which renders it so implausible.

The claim that what makes killing wrong is
the loss of the victim's future is directly supported by two considerations. In the first place,
this theory explains why we regard killing as
one of the worst of crimes. Killing is especially

wrong, because it deprives the victim of more
than perhaps any other crime. In the second
place, people with AIDS or cancer who know
they are dying believe, of course, that dying is a
very bad thing for them. They believe that the
loss of a future to them that they would otherwise have experienced is what makes their premature death a very bad thing for them. A better
theory of the wrongness of killing would require
a different natural property associated with
killing which better fits with the attitudes of the
dying. What could it be?

The view that what makes killing wrong is the
loss to the victim of the value of the victim's
future gains additional support when some of its
implications are examined In the first place, it is
incompatible with the view that it is wrong to kill
only beings who are biologically human. It is
possible that there exists a different species from
another planet whose members have a future like
ours. Since having a future like that is what
makes killing someone wrong, this theory entails
that it would be wrong to kill members of such a
species. Hence, this theory is opposed to the
claim that only life that is biologically human
has great moral worth, a claim which many anti-
abortionists have seemed to adopt. This opposition, which this theory has in common with
personhood theories, seems to be a merit of the
theory.

In the second place, the claim that the loss of
one's future is the wrong-making feature of
one's being killed entails the possibility that the
futures of some actual nonhuman mammals on
our own planet are sufficiently like ours that it is
seriously wrong to kill them also. Whether some
animals do have the same right to life as human
beings depends on adding to the account of the
wrongness of killing some additional account of
just what it is about my future or the futures of
other adult human beings which makes it wrong
to kill us. No such additional account will be
offered in this essay. Undoubtedly, the provision
of such an account would be a very difficult
matter. Undoubtedly, any such account would
be quite controversial. Hence, it surely should

not reflect badly on this sketch of an elementary theory of the wrongness of killing that it is indeterminate with respect to some very difficult issues regarding animal rights.

In the third place, the claim that the loss of one's future is the wrong-making feature of one's being killed does not entail, as sanctity-of-human-life theories do, that active euthanasia is wrong. Persons who are severely and incurably ill, who face a future of pain and despair, and who wish to die will not have suffered a loss if they are killed. It is, strictly speaking, the value of a human's future which makes killing wrong in this theory. This being so, killing does not necessarily wrong some persons who are sick and dying. Of course, there may be other reasons for a prohibition of active euthanasia, but that is another matter. Sanctity-of-human-life theories seem to hold that active euthanasia is seriously wrong even in an individual case where there seems to be good reason for it independently of public policy considerations. This consequence is most implausible, and it is a plus for the claim that the loss of a future of value is what makes killing wrong that it does not share this consequence.

In the fourth place, the account of the wrongness of killing defended in this essay does straightforwardly entail that it is prima facie seriously wrong to kill children and infants, for we do presume that they have futures of value. Since we do believe that it is wrong to kill defenseless little babies, it is important that a theory of the wrongness of killing easily account for this. Personhood theories of the wrongness of killing, on the other hand, cannot straightforwardly account for the wrongness of killing infants and young children.[7] Hence, such theories must add special ad hoc accounts of the wrongness of killing the young. The plausibility of such ad hoc theories seems to be a function of how desperately one wants such theories to work. The claim that the primary wrong-making feature of a killing is the loss to the victim of the value of its future accounts for the wrongness of killing young children and infants directly; it makes the wrongness of such acts as

obvious as we actually think it is. This is a further merit of this theory. Accordingly, it seems that this value of a future-like-ours theory of the wrongness of killing shares strengths of both sanctity-of-life and personhood accounts while avoiding weaknesses of both. In addition, it meshes with a central intuition concerning what makes killing wrong.

The claim that the primary wrong-making feature of a killing is the loss to the victim of the value of its future has obvious consequences for the ethics of abortion. The future of a standard fetus includes a set of experiences, projects, activities, and such which are identical with the futures of adult human beings and are identical with the futures of young children. Since the reason that is sufficient to explain why it is wrong to kill human beings after the time of birth is a reason that also applies to fetuses, it follows that abortion is prima facie seriously morally wrong.

This argument does not rely on the invalid inference that, since it is wrong to kill persons, it is wrong to kill potential persons also. The category that is morally central to this analysis is the category of having a valuable future like ours; it is not the category of personhood. The argument to the conclusion that abortion is prima facie seriously morally wrong proceeded independently of the notion of person or potential person or any equivalent. Someone may wish to start with this analysis in terms of the value of a human future, conclude that abortion is, except perhaps in rare circumstances, seriously morally wrong, infer that fetuses have the right to life, and then call fetuses "persons" as a result of their having the right to life. Clearly, in this case, the category of person is being used to state the *conclusion* of the analysis rather than to generate the *argument* of the analysis.

The structure of this anti-abortion argument can be both illuminated and defended by comparing it to what appears to be the best argument for the wrongness of the wanton infliction of pain on animals. This latter argument is based on the assumption that it is prima facie wrong to inflict pain on me (or you, reader). What is the natural property associated with the infliction of pain which makes such infliction wrong? The obvious answer seems to be that the infliction of pain causes suffering and that suffering is a misfortune. The suffering caused by the infliction of pain is what makes the wanton infliction of pain on me wrong. The wanton infliction of pain on other adult humans causes suffering. The wanton infliction of pain on animals causes suffering. Since causing suffering is what makes the wanton infliction of pain wrong and since the wanton infliction of pain on animals causes suffering, it follows that the wanton infliction of pain on animals is wrong.

This argument for the wrongness of the wanton infliction of pain on animals shares a number of structural features with the argument for the serious prima facie wrongness of abortion. Both arguments start with an obvious assumption concerning what it is wrong to do to me (or you, reader). Both then look for the characteristic or the consequence of the wrong action which makes the action wrong. Both recognize that the wrong-making feature of these immoral actions is a property of actions sometimes directed at individuals other than postnatal human beings. If the structure of the argument for the wrongness of the wanton infliction of pain on animals is sound, then the structure of the argument for the prima facie serious wrongness of abortion is also sound, for the structure of the two arguments is the same. The structure common to both is the key to the explanation of how the wrongness of abortion can be demonstrated without recourse to the category of person. In neither argument is that category crucial.

This defense of an argument for the wrongness of abortion in terms of a structurally similar argument for the wrongness of the wanton infliction of pain on animals succeeds only if the account regarding animals is the correct account. Is it? In the first place, it seems plausible. In the second place, its major competition is Kant's account. Kant believed that we do not have direct duties to animals at all, because they are not persons. Hence, Kant had to explain and justify the wrongness of inflicting pain on animals on the grounds that "he who is hard in his dealings with animals becomes hard also in his dealing with men."[8] The problem with Kant's account is that there seems to be no reason for accepting this latter claim unless Kant's account is rejected. If the alternative to Kant's account is accepted, then it is easy to understand why someone who is indifferent to inflicting pain on animals is also indifferent to inflicting pain on humans, for one is indifferent to what makes inflicting pain wrong in both cases. But, if Kant's account is accepted, there is no intelligible reason why one who is hard in his dealings with animals (or crabgrass or stones) should also be hard in his dealings with men. After all, men are persons: animals are no more persons than crabgrass or stones. Persons are Kant's crucial moral category. Why, in short, should a Kantian accept the basic claim in Kant's argument?

Hence, Kant's argument for the wrongness of inflicting pain on animals rests on a claim that, in a world of Kantian moral agents, is demonstrably false. Therefore, the alternative analysis, being more plausible anyway, should be accepted. Since this alternative analysis has the same structure as the anti-abortion argument being defended here, we have further support for the argument for the immorality of abortion being defended in this essay.

Of course, this value of a future-like-ours argument, if sound, shows only that abortion is prima facie wrong, not that it is wrong in any and all circumstances. Since the loss of the future to a standard fetus, if killed, is, however, at least as great a loss as the loss of the future to a standard adult human being who is killed, abortion, like ordinary killing, could be justified only by the most compelling reasons. The loss of one's life is almost the greatest misfortune that can happen to one. Presumably abortion could be justified in some circumstances, only if the loss consequent on failing to abort would be at least as great. Accordingly, morally permissible abortions will be rare indeed unless, perhaps, they occur so early in pregnancy that a fetus is not yet definitely an individual. Hence, this argument should be taken as showing that abortion is presumptively very seriously wrong, where the presumption is very strong—as strong as the presumption that killing another adult human being is wrong.

III

How complete an account of the wrongness of killing does the value of a future-like-ours account have to be in order that the wrongness of abortion is a consequence? This account does not have to be an account of the necessary conditions for the wrongness of killing. Some persons in nursing homes may lack valuable human futures, yet it may be wrong to kill them for other reasons. Furthermore, this account does not obviously have to be the sole reason killing is wrong where the victim did have a valuable future. This analysis claims only that, for any killing where the victim did have a valuable future like ours, having that future by itself is sufficient to create the strong presumption that the killing is seriously wrong.

One way to overturn the value of a future-like-ours argument would be to find some account of the wrongness of killing which is at least as intelligible and which has different implications for the ethics of abortion. Two rival accounts possess at least some degree of plausibility. One account is based on the obvious fact that people value the experience of living and wish for that valuable experience to continue. Therefore, it might be said, what makes killing wrong is the discontinuation of that experience for the victim. Let us call this the *discontinuation account*.[9] Another rival account is based upon the obvious fact that people strongly desire to continue to live. This suggests that what makes killing us so wrong is that it interferes with the fulfillment of a strong and fundamental desire, the

fulfillment of which is necessary for the fulfillment of any other desires we might have. Let us call this the *desire account*.[10]

Consider first the desire account as a rival account of the ethics of killing which would provide the basis for rejecting the anti-abortion position. Such an account will have to be stronger than the value of a future-like-ours account of the wrongness of abortion if it is to do the job expected of it. To entail the wrongness of abortion, the value of a future-like-ours account has only to provide a sufficient, but not a necessary, condition for the wrongness of killing. The desire account, on the other hand, must provide us also with a necessary condition for the wrongness of killing in order to generate a pro-choice conclusion on abortion. The reason for this is that presumably the argument from the desire account moves from the claim that what makes killing wrong is interference with a very strong desire to the claim that abortion is not wrong because the fetus lacks a strong desire to live. Obviously, this inference fails if someone's having the desire to live is not a necessary condition of its being wrong to kill that individual.

One problem with the desire account is that we do regard it as seriously wrong to kill persons who have little desire to live or who have no desire to live or, indeed, have a desire not to live. We believe it is seriously wrong to kill the unconscious, the sleeping, those who are tired of life, and those who are suicidal. The value-of-a-human-future account renders standard morality intelligible in these cases; these cases appear to be incompatible with the desire account.

The desire account is subject to a deeper difficulty. We desire life, because we value the goods of this life. The goodness of life is not secondary to our desire for it. If this were not so, the pain of one's own premature death could be done away with merely by an appropriate alteration in the configuration of one's desires. This is absurd. Hence, it would seem that it is the loss of the goods of one's future, not the interference with the fulfillment of a strong desire to live, which accounts ultimately for the wrongness of killing.

It is worth noting that, if the desire account is modified so that it does not provide a necessary, but only a sufficient, condition for the wrongness of killing, the desire account is compatible with the value of a future-like-ours account. The combined accounts will yield an anti-abortion ethic. This suggests that one can retain what is intuitively plausible about the desire account without a challenge to the basic argument of this paper.

It is also worth noting that, if future desires have moral force in a modified desire account of the wrongness of killing, one can find support for an anti-abortion ethic even in the absence of a value of a future-like-ours account. If one decides that a morally relevant property, the possession of which is sufficient to make it wrong to kill some individual, is the desire at some future time to live—one might decide to justify one's refusal to kill suicidal teenagers on these grounds, for example—then, since typical fetuses will have the desire in the future to live, it is wrong to kill typical fetuses. Accordingly, it does not seem that a desire account of the wrongness of killing can provide a justification of a pro-choice ethic of abortion which is nearly as adequate as the value of a human-future justification of an anti-abortion ethic.

The discontinuation account looks more promising as an account of the wrongness of killing. It seems just as intelligible as the value of a future-like-ours account, but it does not justify an anti-abortion position. Obviously, if it is the continuation of one's activities, experiences, and projects, the loss of which makes killing wrong, then it is not wrong to kill fetuses for that reason, for fetuses do not have experiences, activities, and projects to be continued or discontinued. Accordingly, the discontinuation account does not have the anti-abortion consequences that the value of a future-like-ours account has. Yet, it seems as intelligible as the value of a future-like-ours account, for when we think of what would be wrong with our being killed, it does seem as if it

is the discontinuation of what makes our lives worthwhile which makes killing us wrong.

Is the discontinuation account just as good an account as the value of a future-like-ours account? The discontinuation account will not be adequate at all, if it does not refer to the *value* of the experience that may be discontinued. One does not want the discontinuation account to make it wrong to kill a patient who begs for death and who is in severe pain that cannot be relieved short of killing. (I leave open the question of whether it is wrong for other reasons.) Accordingly, the discontinuation account must be more than a bare discontinuation account. It must make some reference to the positive value of the patient's experiences. But, by the same token, the value of a future-like-ours account cannot be a bare future account either. Just having a future surely does not itself rule out killing the above patient This account must make some reference to the value of the patient's future experiences and projects also. Hence, both accounts involve the value of experiences, projects, and activities. So far we still have symmetry between the accounts.

The symmetry fades, however, when we focus on the time period of the value of the experiences, etc., which has moral consequences. Although both accounts leave open the possibility that the patient in our example may be killed, this possibility is left open only in virtue of the utterly bleak future for the patient. It makes no difference whether the patient's immediate past contains intolerable pain, or consists in being in a coma (which we can imagine is a situation of indifference), or consists in a life of value. If the patient's future is a future of value, we want our account to make it wrong to kill the patient. If the patient's future is intolerable, whatever his or her immediate past, we want our account to allow killing the patient. Obviously, then, it is the value of that patient's future which is doing the work in rendering the morality of killing the patient intelligible.

This being the case, it seems clear that whether one has immediate past experiences or not does no work in the explanation of what makes killing wrong. The addition the discontinuation account makes to the value of a human future account is otiose. Its addition to the value-of-a-future account plays no role at all in rendering intelligible the wrongness of killing. Therefore, it can be discarded with the discontinuation account of which it is a part.

IV

The analysis of the previous section suggests that alternative general accounts of the wrongness of killing are either inadequate or unsuccessful in getting around the anti-abortion consequences of the value of a future-like-ours argument. A different strategy for avoiding these anti-abortion consequences involves limiting the scope of the value of a future argument. More precisely, the strategy involves arguing that fetuses lack a property that is essential for the value-of-a-future argument (or for any anti-abortion argument) to apply to them.

One move of this sort is based upon the claim that a necessary condition of one's future being valuable is that one values it. Value implies a valuer. Given this one might argue that, since fetuses cannot value their futures, their futures are not valuable to them. Hence, it does not seriously wrong them deliberately to end their lives.

This move fails, however, because of some ambiguities. Let us assume that something cannot be of value unless it is valued by someone. This does not entail that my life is of no value unless it is valued by me. I may think, in a period of despair, that my future is of no worth whatsoever, but I may be wrong because others rightly see value—even great value—in it. Furthermore, my future can be valuable to me even if I do not value it. This is the case when a young person attempts suicide, but is rescued and goes on to significant human achievements. Such young people's futures are ultimately valuable to them, even though such futures do not seem to be valuable to them at the moment of attempted

suicide. A fetus's future can be valuable to it in the same way. Accordingly, this attempt to limit the anti-abortion argument fails.

Another similar attempt to reject the anti-abortion position is based on Tooley's claim that an entity cannot possess the right to life unless it has the capacity to desire its continued existence. It follows that, since fetuses lack the conceptual capacity to desire to continue to live, they lack the right to life. Accordingly, Tooley concludes that abortion cannot be seriously prima facie wrong *(op. cit.,* pp. 46/7).

What could be the evidence for Tooley's basic claim? Tooley once argued that individuals have a prima facie right to what they desire and that the lack of the capacity to desire something undercuts the basis of one's right to it *(op. cit.,* pp. 44/5). This argument plainly will not succeed in the context of the analysis of this essay, however, since the point here is to establish the fetus's right to life on other grounds. Tooley's argument assumes that the right to life cannot be established in general on some basis other than the desire for life. This position was considered and rejected in the preceding section of this paper.

One might attempt to defend Tooley's basic claim on the grounds that, because a fetus cannot apprehend continued life as a benefit, its continued life cannot be a benefit or cannot be something it has a right to or cannot be something that is in its interest. This might be defended in terms of the general proposition that, if an individual is literally incapable of caring about or taking an interest in some X, then one does not have a right to X or X is not a benefit or X is not something that is in one's interest.[11]

Each member of this family of claims seems to be open to objections. As John C. Stevens[12] has pointed out, one may have a right to be treated with a certain medical procedure (because of a health insurance policy one has purchased), even though one cannot conceive of the nature of the procedure. And, as Tooley himself has pointed out, persons who have been indoctrinated, or drugged, or rendered temporarily unconscious may be literally incapable of caring about or taking an interest in something that is in their interest or is something to which they have a right, or is something that benefits them. Hence, the Tooley claim that would restrict the scope of the value of a future-like-ours argument is undermined by counterexamples.[13]

Finally, Paul Bassen[14] has argued that, even though the prospects of an embryo might seem to be a basis for the wrongness of abortion, an embryo cannot be a victim and therefore cannot be wronged. An embryo cannot be a victim, he says, because it lacks sentience. His central argument for this seems to be that, even though plants and the permanently unconscious are alive, they clearly cannot be victims. What is the explanation of this? Bassen claims that the explanation is that their lives consist of mere metabolism and mere metabolism is not enough to ground victimizability. Mentation is required.

The problem with this attempt to establish the absence of victimizability is that both plants and the permanently unconscious clearly lack what Bassen calls "prospects" or what I have called "a future life like ours." Hence, it is surely open to one to argue that the real reason we believe plants and the permanently unconscious cannot be victims is that killing them cannot deprive them of a future life like ours; the real reason is not their absence of present mentation.

Bassen recognizes that his view is subject to this difficulty, and he recognizes that the case of children seems to support this difficulty, for "much of what we do for children is based on prospects." He argues, however, that, in the case of children and in other such cases, "potentiality comes into play only where victimizability has been secured on other grounds" (*ibid.*, p. 333).

Bassen's defense of his view is patently question-begging, since what is adequate to secure victimizability is exactly what is at issue. His examples do not support his own view against the thesis of this essay. Of course, embryos can be victims: when their lives are deliberately terminated, they are deprived of their futures of value, their prospects.

This makes them victims, for it directly wrongs them.

The seeming plausibility of Bassen's view stems from the fact that paradigmatic cases of imagining someone as a victim involve empathy, and empathy requires mentation of the victim. The victims of flood, famine, rape, or child abuse are all persons with whom we can empathize. That empathy seems to be part of seeing them as victims.[15]

In spite of the strength of these examples, the attractive intuition that a situation in which there is victimization requires the possibility of empathy is subject to counterexamples. Consider a case that Bassen himself offers: "Posthumous obliteration of an author's work constitutes a misfortune for him only if he had wished his work to endure" (*op cit.*, p. 318). The conditions Bassen wishes to impose upon the possibility of being victimized here seem far too strong. Perhaps this author, due to his unrealistic standards of excellence and his low self-esteem, regarded his work as unworthy of survival, even though it possessed genuine literary merit. Destruction of such work would surely victimize its author. In such a case, empathy with the victim concerning the loss is clearly impossible.

Of course, Bassen does not make the possibility of empathy a necessary condition of victimizability; he requires only mentation. Hence, on Bassen's actual view, this author, as I have described him, can be a victim. The problem is that the basic intuition that renders Bassen's view plausible is missing in the author's case. In order to attempt to avoid counterexamples, Bassen has made his thesis too weak to be supported by the intuitions that suggested it.

Even so, the mentation requirement on victimizability is still subject to counterexamples. Suppose a severe accident renders me totally unconscious for a month, after which I recover. Surely killing me while I am unconscious victimizes me, even though I am incapable of mentation during that time. It follows that Bassen's thesis fails. Apparently, attempts to restrict the value of a future-like-ours argument so that fetuses do not fall within its scope do not succeed.

V

In this essay, it has been argued that the correct ethic of the wrongness of killing can be extended to fetal life and used to show that there is a strong presumption that any abortion is morally impermissible. If the ethic of killing adopted here entails, however, that contraception is also seriously immoral, then there would appear to be a difficulty with the analysis of this essay.

But this analysis does not entail that contraception is wrong. Of course, contraception prevents the actualization of a possible future of value. Hence, it follows from the claim that futures of value should be maximized that contraception is prima facie immoral. This obligation to maximize does not exist, however; furthermore, nothing in the ethics of killing in this paper entails that it does. The ethics of killing in this essay would entail that contraception is wrong only if something were denied a human future of value by contraception. Nothing at all is denied such a future by contraception, however.

Candidates for a subject of harm by contraception fall into four categories: (1) some sperm or other, (2) some ovum or other, (3) a sperm and an ovum separately, and (4) a sperm and an ovum together. Assigning the harm to some sperm is utterly arbitrary, for no reason can be given for making a sperm the subject of harm rather than an ovum. Assigning the harm to some ovum is utterly arbitrary, for no reason can be given for making an ovum the subject of harm rather than a sperm. One might attempt to avoid these problems by insisting that contraception deprives both the sperm and the ovum separately of a valuable future like ours. On this alternative, too many futures are lost. Contraception was supposed to be wrong, because it deprived us of one future of value, not two. One might attempt to avoid this

problem by holding that contraception deprives the combination of sperm and ovum of a valuable future like ours. But here the definite article misleads. At the time of contraception, there are hundreds of millions of sperm, one (released) ovum and millions of possible combinations of all of these. There is no actual combination at all. Is the subject of the loss to be a merely possible combination? Which one? This alternative does not yield an actual subject of harm either. Accordingly, the immorality of contraception is not entailed by the loss of a future-like-ours argument simply because there is no nonarbitrarily identifiable subject of the loss in the case of contraception.

VI

The purpose of this essay has been to set out an argument for the serious presumptive wrongness of abortion subject to the assumption that the moral permissibility of abortion stands or falls on the moral status of the fetus. Since a fetus possesses a property, the possession of which in adult human beings is sufficient to make killing an adult human being wrong, abortion is wrong. This way of dealing with the problem of abortion seems superior to other approaches to the ethics of abortion, because it rests on an ethics of killing which is close to self-evident, because the crucial morally relevant property clearly applies to fetuses, and because the argument avoids the usual equivocations on "human life," "human being," or "person." The argument rests neither on religious claims nor on Papal dogma. It is not subject to the objection of "speciesism." Its soundness is compatible with the moral permissibility of euthanasia and contraception. It deals with our intuitions concerning young children.

Finally, this analysis can be viewed as resolving a standard problem—indeed, *the* standard problem—concerning the ethics of abortion. Clearly, it is wrong to kill adult human beings. Clearly, it is not wrong to end the life of some arbitrarily chosen single human cell. Fetuses seem to be like arbitrarily chosen human cells in some respects and like adult humans in other respects. The problem of the ethics of abortion is the problem of determining the fetal property that settles this moral controversy. The thesis of this essay is that the problem of the ethics of abortion, so understood, is solvable.

NOTES

1. Feinberg, "Abortion," in *Matters of Life and Death: New Introductory Essays in Moral Philosophy,* Tom Regan, ed. (New York: Random House, *1986),* pp. 256–293; Tooley, "Abortion and Infanticide," *Philosophy and Public Affairs,* II, 1 (1972):37–65, Tooley, *Abortion and Infanticide* (New York: Oxford, 1984); Warren, "On the Moral and Legal Status of Abortion," *The Monist,* LVII, 1 (1973):43–6l; Engelhardt, "The Ontology of Abortion," *Ethics,* LXXXIV, 3 (1974):217–234; Sumner, *Abortion and Moral Theory* (Princeton: University Press, 1981); Noonan, "An Almost Absolute Value in History," in *The Morality of Abortion: Legal and Historical Perspectives,* Noonan, ed. (Cambridge: Harvard, 1970); and Devine, *The Ethics of Homicide* (Ithaca: Cornell, 1978).

2. For interesting discussions of this issue, see Warren Quinn, "Abortion: Identity and Loss," *Philosophy and Public Affairs,* xiii, 1 (1984):24–25; and Lawrence C. Becker, "Human Being: The Boundaries of the Concept," *Philosophy and Public Affairs,* iv, 4 (1975):334–359.

3. For example, see my "Ethics and The Elderly: Some Problems," in Stuart Spicker, Kathleen Wood-

ward, and David Van Tassel, eds., *Aging and the Elderly: Humanistic Perspectives in Gerontology* (Atlantic Highlands, NJ: Humanities, 1978), pp. 341–355.

4. See Warren, *op. cit.,* and Tooley, "Abortion and Infanticide."

5. This seems to be the fatal flaw in Warren's treatment of this issue,

6. I have been most influenced on this matter by Jonathan Glover, *Causing Death and Saving Lives* (New York: Penguin, 1977), ch. 3; and Robert Young, "What Is So Wrong with Killing People?" *Philosophy,* LIV, 210 (l979): 515–528.

7. Felnberg, Tooley, Warren, and Engelhardt have all dealt with this problem.

8. "Duties to Animals and Spirits," in *Lectures on Ethics,* Louis Infeld, trans. (New York: Harper, 1963), p. 239.

9. I am indebted to Jack Bricke for raising this objection.

10. Presumably a preference utilitarian would press such an objection. Tooley once suggested that his account has such a theoretical underpinning. See his "Abortion and Infanticide," pp. 44/5.

11. Donald VanDeVeer seems to think this is self-evident. See his "Whither Baby Doe?" in *Matters of Life and Death,* p. 233.

12. "Must the Bearer of a Right Have the Concept of That to Which He Has a Right?" *Ethics,* xcv, 1 (1984):6–74.

13. See Tooley again in "Abortion and Infanticide," pp. 47–49.

14. "Present Sakes and Future Prospects: The Status of Early Abortion," *Philosophy and Public Affairs,* XL, 4 (1982):322–326.

15. Note carefully the reasons he gives on the bottom of p. 316.

For Further Reflection

1. Do you think Marquis' argument provides a good reason for believing that abortion is immoral? Why or why not?

2. Do you agree with Marquis' explanation of why killing someone is wrong? Explain.

3. Suppose someone argues that destroying human sperm or egg cells is wrong because doing so would deprive them of a future. What would you say in response?

4. In Marquis' terms, what would be the moral difference, if any, between killing an unfertilized human egg, an embryo, a baby, and an infant chimpanzee? Would each one be deprived of a morally significant future?

On the Moral and Legal Status of Abortion   IX.81

MARY ANNE WARREN

Mary Anne Warren teaches philosophy at San Francisco State University and has written in the area of feminism, including *The Nature of Woman: An Encyclopedia and Guide to the Literature* (1980). In this paper she defends the liberal view that abortion is always morally permissible. She attacks a conservative argument on the basis of an ambiguity in the use of the term *human being*, showing that the term has both a biological and moral sense. What is important is the moral sense, which presupposes certain characteristics, such as self-consciousness and rationality, which a fetus does not have. At the end of her article, she addresses the issue of infanticide.

Study Questions

1. What is the question which we must answer in order to solve the problem of whether abortion is morally permissible?
2. How is the term *human being* ambiguous?
3. How does this ambiguity undermine the conservative argument for the humanity of the fetus?
4. According to Warren, what characteristics make an entity a person? Which are the most important characteristics in this set?
5. Does potentiality for personhood grant a fetus a right to life? How does Warren illustrate her answer?
6. According to Warren, when does a woman have a right to an abortion?
7. What are Warren's views on infanticide?

THE QUESTION WHICH WE MUST answer in order to produce a satisfactory solution to the problem of the moral status of abortion is this: How are we to define the moral community, the set of beings with full and equal moral rights, such that we can decide whether a human fetus is a member of this community or not? What sort of entity, exactly, has the inalienable rights to life, liberty, and the pursuit of happiness? Jefferson attributed these rights to all *men,* and it may or may not be fair to suggest that he intended to attribute them *only* to men. Perhaps he ought to have attributed them to all human beings. If so, then we arrive, first, at Noonan's problem of defining what makes a being human, and, second,

at the equally vital question which Noonan does not consider, namely, What reason is there for identifying the moral community with the set of all human beings, in whatever way we have chosen to define that term?

1. ON THE DEFINITION OF "HUMAN"

One reason why this vital second question is so frequently overlooked in the debate over the moral status of abortion is that the term "human" has two distinct, but not often distinguished, senses. This fact results in a slide of meaning, which serves

Reprinted from The Monist: An International Quarterly Journal of General Philosophical Inquiry, *vol. 57, no. 1 (January 1973), with the permission of the author and the publisher. Endnotes deleted.*

to conceal the fallaciousness of the traditional argument that since (1) it is wrong to kill innocent human beings, and (2) fetuses are innocent human beings, then (3) it is wrong to kill fetuses. For if "human" is used in the same sense in both (1) and (2) then, whichever of the two senses is meant, one of these premises is question-begging. And if it is used in two different senses then of course the conclusion doesn't follow.

Thus, (1) is a self-evident moral truth, and avoids begging the question about abortion, only if "human being" is used to mean something like "a full-fledged member of the moral community." (It may or may not also be meant to refer exclusively to members of the species *Homo sapiens*.) We may call this the *moral* sense of "human." It is not to be confused with what we will call the *genetic* sense, i.e., the sense in which *any* member of the species is a human being, and no member of any other species could be. If (1) is acceptable only if the moral sense is intended, (2) is nonquestion-begging only if what is intended is the genetic sense.

In "Deciding Who Is Human," Noonan argues for the classification of fetuses with human beings by pointing to the presence of the full genetic code, and the potential capacity for rational thought. It is clear that what he needs to show, for his version of the traditional argument to be valid, is that fetuses are human in the moral sense, the sense in which it is analytically true that all human beings have full moral rights. But, in the absence of any argument showing that whatever is genetically human is also morally human, and he gives none, nothing more than genetic humanity can be demonstrated by the presence of the human genetic code. And, as we will see, the *potential* capacity for rational thought can at most show that an entity has the potential for *becoming* human in the moral sense.

2. DEFINING THE MORAL COMMUNITY

Can it be established that genetic humanity is sufficient for moral humanity? I think that there are very good reasons for not defining the moral community in this way. I would like to suggest an alternative way of defining the moral community, which I will argue for only to the extent of explaining why it is, or should be, self-evident. The suggestion is simply that the moral community consists of all and only *people*, rather than all and only human beings; and probably the best way of demonstrating its self-evidence is by considering the concept of personhood, to see what sorts of entity are and are not persons, and what the decision that a being is or is not a person implies about its moral rights.

What characteristics entitle an entity to be considered a person? This is obviously not the place to attempt a complete analysis of the concept of personhood, but we do not need such a fully adequate analysis just to determine whether and why a fetus is or isn't a person. All we need is a rough and approximate list of the most basic criteria of personhood, and some idea of which, or how many, of these an entity must satisfy in order to properly be considered a person.

In searching for such criteria, it is useful to look beyond the set of people with whom we are acquainted, and ask how we would decide whether a totally alien being was a person or not. (For we have no right to assume that genetic humanity is necessary for personhood.) Imagine a space traveler who lands on an unknown planet and encounters a race of beings utterly unlike any he has ever seen or heard of. If he wants to be sure of behaving morally toward these beings, he has to somehow decide whether they are people, and hence have full moral rights, or whether they are the sort of thing which he need not feel guilty about treating as, for example, a source of food.

How should he go about making this decision? If he has some anthropological background, he might look for such things as religion, art, and the manufacturing of tools, weapons, or shelters, since these factors have been used to distinguish our human from our prehuman ancestors, in what seems to be closer to the moral than the genetic sense of "human." And no doubt he would be right to consider the presence of such factors as good evidence that the alien beings were people, and morally human. It would, however, be overly anthropocentric of him to take the absence of these things as adequate evidence that they were not, since we can imagine people who have progressed beyond, or evolved without ever developing, these cultural characteristics.

I suggest that the traits which are most central to the concept of personhood, or humanity in the moral sense, are, very roughly, the following:

1. Consciousness (of objects and events external and/or internal to the being), and in particular the capacity to feel pain;

2. Reasoning (the *developed* capacity to solve new and relatively complex problems);

3. Self-motivated activity (activity which is relatively independent of either genetic or direct external control);

4. The capacity to communicate, by whatever means, messages of an indefinite variety of types, that is, not just with an indefinite number of possible contents, but on indefinitely many possible topics;

5. The presence of self-concepts, and self-awareness, either individual or racial, or both.

Admittedly, there are apt to be a great many problems involved in formulating precise definitions of these criteria, let alone in developing universally valid behavioral criteria for deciding when they apply. But I will assume that both we and our explorer know approximately what (1)–(5) mean, and that he is also able to determine whether or not they apply. How, then, should he use his findings to decide whether or not the alien beings are people? We needn't suppose that an entity must have *all* of these attributes to be properly considered a person; (1) and (2) alone may well be sufficient for personhood, and quite probably (1)–(3) are sufficient. Neither do we need to insist that any one of these criteria is *necessary* for personhood, although once again (1) and (2) look like fairly good candidates for necessary conditions, as does (3), if "activity" is construed so as to include the activity of reasoning.

All we need to claim, to demonstrate that a fetus is not a person, is that any being which satisfies *none* of (1)–(5) is certainly not a person. I consider this claim to be so obvious that I think anyone who denied it, and claimed that a being which satisfied none of (1)–(5) was a person all the same, would thereby demonstrate that he had no notion at all of what a person is—perhaps because he had confused the concept of a person with that of genetic humanity. If the opponents of abortion were to deny the appropriateness of these five criteria, I do not know what further arguments would convince them. We would probably have to admit that our conceptual schemes were indeed irreconcilably different, and that our dispute could not be settled objectively.

I do not expect this to happen, however, since I think that the concept of a person is one which is very nearly universal (to people), and that it is common to both proabortionists and antiabortionists, even though neither group has fully realized the relevance of this concept to the resolution of their dispute. Furthermore, I think that on reflection even the antiabortionists ought to agree not only that (1)–(5) are central to the concept of personhood, but also that it is a part of this concept that all and only people have full moral rights. The concept of a person is in part a moral concept; once we have admitted that *x* is a person we have recognized, even if we have not agreed to respect, *x*'s right to be treated as a member of the moral community. It is true that the claim that *x is a human being* is more commonly voiced as part of an appeal to treat *x* decently than is the claim that *x* is a person, but this is either because "human being" is here used in the sense which implies personhood, or because the genetic and moral senses of "human" have been confused.

Now if (1)–(5) are indeed the primary criteria of personhood, then it is clear that genetic humanity is neither necessary nor sufficient for establishing that an entity is a person. Some human beings are not people, and there may well be people who are not human beings. A man or woman whose consciousness has been permanently obliterated but who remains alive is a human being which is no longer a person;

defective human beings, with no appreciable mental capacity, are not and presumably never will be people; and a fetus is a human being which is not yet a person, and which therefore cannot coherently be said to have full moral rights. Citizens of the next century should be prepared to recognize highly advanced, self-aware robots or computers, should such be developed, and intelligent inhabitants of other worlds, should such be found, as people in the fullest sense, and to respect their moral rights. But to ascribe full moral rights to an entity which is not a person is as absurd as to ascribe moral obligations and responsibilities to such an entity.

3. FETAL DEVELOPMENT AND THE RIGHT TO LIFE

Two problems arise in the application of these suggestions for the definition of the moral community to the determination of the precise moral status of a human fetus. Given that the paradigm example of a person is a normal adult human being, then (1) How like this paradigm, in particular how far advanced since conception, does a human being need to be before it begins to have a right to life by virtue, not of being fully a person as of yet, but of being *like* a person? and (2) To what extent, if any, does the fact that a fetus has the *potential* for becoming a person endow it with some of the same rights? Each of these questions requires some comment.

In answering the first question, we need not attempt a detailed consideration of the moral rights of organisms which are not developed enough, aware enough, intelligent enough, etc., to be considered people, but which resemble people in some respects. It does seem reasonable to suggest that the more like a person, in the relevant respects, a being is, the stronger is the case for regarding it as having a right to life, and indeed the stronger its right to life is. Thus we ought to take seriously the suggestion that, insofar as "the human individual develops biologically in a continuous fashion . . . the rights of a human person might develop in the

same way." But we must keep in mind that the attributes which are relevant in determining whether or not an entity is enough like a person to be regarded as having some of the same moral rights are no different from those which are relevant to determining whether or not it is fully a person—i.e., are no different from (1)–(5)—and that being genetically human, or having recognizably human facial and other physical features, or detectable brain activity, or the capacity to survive outside the uterus, are simply not among these relevant attributes.

Thus it is clear that even though a seven- or eight-month fetus has features which make it apt to arouse in us almost the same powerful protective instinct as is commonly aroused by a small infant, nevertheless it is not significantly more personlike than is a very small embryo. It is *somewhat* more personlike; it can apparently feel and respond to pain, and it may even have a rudimentary form of consciousness, insofar as its brain is quite active. Nevertheless, it seems safe to say that it is not fully conscious, in the way that an infant of a few months is, and that it cannot reason, or communicate messages of indefinitely many sorts, does not engage in self-motivated activity, and has no self-awareness. Thus, in the *relevant* respects, a fetus, even a fully developed one, is considerably less personlike than is the average mature mammal, indeed the average fish. And I think that a rational person must conclude that if the right to life of a fetus is to be based upon its resemblance to a person, then it cannot be said to have any more right to life than, let us say, a newborn guppy (which also seems to be capable of feeling pain), and that a right of that magnitude could never override a woman's right to obtain an abortion, at any stage of her pregnancy.

There may, of course, be other arguments in favor of placing legal limits upon the stage of pregnancy in which an abortion may be performed. Given the relative safety of the new techniques of artificially inducing labor during the third trimester, the danger to the woman's life or health is no longer such an argument. Neither is the fact that people tend to respond to the thought of abortion in the later stages of pregnancy with emotional repulsion, since mere emotional responses cannot take the place of moral reasoning in determining what ought to be permitted. Nor, finally, is the frequently heard argument that legalizing abortion, especially late in the pregnancy, may erode the level of respect for human life, leading, perhaps, to an increase in unjustified euthanasia and other crimes. For this threat, if it is a threat, can be better met by educating people to the kinds of moral distinctions which we are making here than by limiting access to abortion (which limitation may, in its disregard for the rights of women, be just as damaging to the level of respect for human rights).

Thus, since the fact that even a fully developed fetus is not personlike enough to have any significant right to life on the basis of its personlikeness shows that no legal restrictions upon the stage of pregnancy in which an abortion may be performed can be justified on the grounds that we should protect the rights of the older fetus, and since there is no other apparent justification for such restrictions, we may conclude that they are entirely unjustified. Whether or not it would be *indecent* (whatever that means) for a woman in her seventh month to obtain an abortion just to avoid having to postpone a trip to Europe, it would not, in itself, be *immoral*, and therefore it ought to be permitted.

4. POTENTIAL PERSONHOOD AND THE RIGHT TO LIFE

We have seen that a fetus does not resemble a person in any way which can support the claim that it has even some of the same rights. But what about its *potential*, the fact that if nurtured and allowed to develop naturally it will very probably become a person? Doesn't that alone give it at least some right to life? It is hard to deny that the fact that an entity is a potential person is a strong prima facie reason for not destroying it; but we need not conclude from this that a potential person has a right to life, by virtue of that potential. It may be that our

feeling that it is better, other things being equal, not to destroy a potential person is better explained by the fact that potential people are still (felt to be) an invaluable resource, not to be lightly squandered. Surely, if every speck of dust were a potential person, we would be much less apt to conclude that every potential person has a right to become actual.

Still, we do not need to insist that a potential person has no right to life whatever. There may well be something immoral, and not just imprudent, about wantonly destroying potential people, when doing so isn't necessary to protect anyone's rights. But even if a potential person does have some *prima facie* right to life, such a right could not possibly outweigh the right of a woman to obtain an abortion, since the rights of any actual person invariably outweigh those of any potential person, whenever the two conflict. Since this may not be immediately obvious in the case of a human fetus, let us look at another case.

Suppose that our space explorer falls into the hands of an alien culture, whose scientists decide to create a few hundred thousand or more human beings, by breaking his body into its component cells, and using these to create fully developed human beings, with, of course, his genetic code. We may imagine that each of these newly created men will have all of the original man's abilities, skills, knowledge, and so on, and also have an individual self-concept, in short that each of them will be a bona fide (though hardly unique) person. Imagine that the whole project will take only seconds, and that its chances of success are extremely high, and that our explorer knows all of this, and also knows that these people will be treated fairly. I maintain that in such a situation he would have every right to escape if he could, and thus to deprive all of these potential people of their potential lives; for his right to life outweighs all of theirs together, in spite of the fact that they are all genetically human, all innocent, and all have a very high probability of becoming people very soon, if only he refrains from acting.

Indeed, I think he would have a right to escape even if it were not his life which the alien scientists planned to take, but only a year of his freedom, or, indeed, only a day. Nor would he be obligated to stay if he had gotten captured (thus bringing all these people-potentials into existence) because of his own carelessness, or even if he had done so deliberately, knowing the consequences. Regardless of how he got captured, he is not morally obligated to remain in captivity for *any* period of time for the sake of permitting any number of potential people to come into actuality, so great is the margin by which one actual person's right to liberty outweighs whatever right to life even a hundred thousand potential people have. And it seems reasonable to conclude that the rights of a woman will outweigh by a similar margin whatever right to life a fetus may have by virtue of its potential personhood.

Thus, neither a fetus's resemblance to a person, nor its potential for becoming a person provides any basis whatever for the claim that it has any significant right to life. Consequently, a woman's right to protect her health, happiness, freedom, and even her life, by terminating an unwanted pregnancy, will always override whatever right to life it may be appropriate to ascribe to a fetus, even a fully developed one. And thus, in the absence of any overwhelming social need for every possible child, the laws which restrict the right to obtain an abortion, or limit the period of pregnancy during which an abortion may be performed, are a wholly unjustified violation of a woman's most basic moral and constitutional rights.

POSTSCRIPT ON INFANTICIDE

Since the publication of this article, many people have written to point out that my argument appears to justify not only abortion, but infanticide as well, for a newborn infant is not significantly more personlike than an advanced fetus, and consequently it would seem that if the destruction of the latter is permissible so too must be that of the former. Inasmuch as most people, regardless of how they feel about the morality of abortion, consider infanticide a form of murder, this might appear to represent a serious flaw in my argument.

Now, if I am right in holding that it is only people who have a full-fledged right to life, and who can be murdered, and if the criteria of personhood are as I have described them, then it obviously follows that killing a newborn infant isn't murder. It does *not* follow, however, that infanticide is permissible, for two reasons. In the first place, it would be wrong, at least in this country and in this period of history, and other things being equal, to kill a newborn infant, because even if its parents do not want it and would not suffer from its destruction, there are other people who would like to have it, and would, in all probability, be deprived of a great deal of pleasure by its destruction. Thus, infanticide is wrong for reasons analogous to those which make it wrong to wantonly destroy natural resources, or great works of art.

Secondly, most people, at least in this country, value infants and would much prefer that they be preserved, even if foster parents are not immediately available. Most of us would rather be taxed to support orphanages than allow unwanted infants to be destroyed. So long as there are people who want an infant preserved, and who are willing and able to provide the means of caring for it, under reasonably humane conditions, it is *ceteris paribus*, wrong to destroy it.

But, it might be replied, if this argument shows that infanticide is wrong, at least at this time and in this country, doesn't it also show that abortion is wrong? After all, many people value fetuses, are disturbed by their destruction, and would much prefer that they be preserved, even at some cost to themselves. Furthermore, as a potential source of pleasure to some foster family, a fetus is just as valuable as an infant. There is, however, a crucial difference between the two cases: so long as the fetus is unborn, its preservation, contrary to the wishes of the pregnant woman, violates her rights to freedom, happiness, and self-determination. Her rights override the rights of those who would like the fetus preserved, just as if someone's life or limb is threatened by a wild animal, his right to protect himself by destroying the animal overrides the rights of those who would prefer that the animal not be harmed.

The minute the infant is born, however, its preservation no longer violates any of its mother's rights, even if she wants it destroyed, because she is free to put it up for adoption. Consequently, while the moment of birth does not mark any sharp discontinuity in the degree to which an infant possesses the right to life, it does mark the end of its mother's right to determine its fate. Indeed, if abortion could be performed without killing the fetus, she would never possess the right to have the fetus destroyed, for the same reasons that she has no right to have an infant destroyed.

On the other hand, it follows from my argument that when an unwanted or defective infant is born into a society which cannot afford and/or is not willing to care for it, then its destruction is permissible. This conclusion will, no doubt, strike many people as heartless and immoral; but remember that the very existence of people who feel this way, and who are willing and able to provide care for unwanted infants, is reason enough to conclude that they should be preserved.

For Further Reflection

1. Has Warren successfully refuted Noonan's argument against abortion? Explain.
2. Examine Warren's postscript on infanticide. Does Warren's analysis of the morality of abortion lead to the justification of infanticide? Does it lead to justification of killing the severely retarded, mentally ill, and senile?
3. Is there a middle ground between Noonan's conservatism and Warren's liberalism on abortion?

A Defense of Abortion   IX.82

JUDITH JARVIS THOMSON

Judith Jarvis Thomson is a professor of philosophy at Massachusetts Institute of Technology and the author of dozens of articles and several books including *Acts and Other Events* (1977), *The Realm of Rights* (1990), and *Goodness and Advice* (2001). In this famous essay, she argues that even if a fetus is a person at conception, abortion may still be morally permissible in a few instances. With the use of a striking analogy, she contends that a woman may sometimes be justified in having an abortion in self-defense—to prevent her body from being used against her will, a situation that arises if she becomes pregnant through no fault of her own (if she is a victim of rape, for example).

Study Questions

1. What is Thomson's violinist analogy? What point is she trying to make with it?
2. According to Thomson, in what kinds of cases might abortion be justified?
3. Does she think that abortion can be justified when a woman becomes pregnant due to contraceptive failure? Explain.
4. Does she believe that a right to an abortion entitles a woman to "secure the death of the unborn child"? Why or why not?

Most opposition to abortion relies on the premise that the fetus is a human being, a person, from the moment of conception. The premise is argued for, but, as I think, not well. Take, for example, the most common argument. We are asked to notice that the development of a human being from conception through birth into childhood is continuous; then it is said that to draw a line, to choose a point in this development and say "before this point the thing is not a person, after this point it is a person" is to make an arbitrary choice, a choice for which in the nature of things no good reason can be given. It is concluded that the fetus is, or anyway that we had better say it is, a person from the moment of conception. But this conclusion does not follow. Similar things might be said about the development of an acorn into an oak tree, and it does not follow that acorns are oak trees, or that we had better say they are. Arguments of this form are sometimes called "slippery slope arguments"—the phrase is perhaps self-explanatory—and it is dismaying that opponents of abortion rely on them so heavily and uncritically.

I am inclined to agree, however, that the prospects for "drawing a line" in the development of the fetus look dim. I am inclined to think also that we shall probably have to agree that the fetus has already become a human person well before birth. Indeed, it comes as a surprise when one first learns how early in its life it begins to acquire human characteristics. By the tenth week, for example, it already has a face, arms and legs, fingers and toes; it has internal organs, and brain activity is detectable.[1] On the other hand, I think that the premise is false, that the fetus is not a person from the moment of conception. A newly fertilized ovum, a newly implanted clump of cells, is no more a person than an acorn is an oak tree. But I shall not discuss any of this. For it seems to me to be of great interest to ask what happens if, for the sake of argument, we allow the premise. How, precisely, are we supposed to get from there to the conclusion that abortion is morally impermissible? Opponents of abortion commonly spend most of their time establishing that the fetus is a person, and hardly any time explaining the step from there to the impermissibility of abortion. Perhaps they think the step too simple and obvious to require much comment Or perhaps instead they are simply being economical in argument. Many of those who defend abortion rely on the premise that the fetus is not a person, but only a bit of tissue that will become a person at birth; and why pay out more arguments than you have to? Whatever the explanation, I suggest that the step they take is neither easy nor obvious, that it calls for closer examination than it is commonly given, and that when we do give it this closer examination we shall feel inclined to reject it.

I propose, then, that we grant that the fetus is a person from the moment of conception. How does the argument go from here? Something like this, I take it. Every person has a right to life. So the fetus has a right to life. No doubt the mother has a right to decide what shall happen in and to her body; everyone would grant that. But surely a person's right to life is stronger and more stringent than the mother's right to decide what happens in and to her body, and so outweighs it. So the fetus may not be killed; an abortion may not be performed.

It sounds plausible. But now let me ask you to imagine this. You wake up in the morning and find yourself back to back in bed with an unconscious violinist. A famous unconscious violinist. He has been found to have a fatal kidney ailment, and the Society of Music Lovers

I am very much indebted to James Thomson for discussion, criticism, and many helpful suggestions.
From Judith Jarvis Thomson, "A Defense of Abortion," Philosophy and Public Affairs, *vol. 1, no. 1 (Autumn 1971), pp. 47–66 (Blackwell Publishing, Oxford, UK). Reprinted with permission of the publisher. Footnotes renumbered.*

has canvassed all the available medical records and found that you alone have the right blood type to help. They have therefore kidnapped you, and last night the violinist's circulatory system was plugged into yours, so that your kidneys can be used to extract poisons from his blood as well as your own. The director of the hospital now tells you, "Look, we're sorry the Society of Music Lovers did this to you—we would never have permitted it if we had known. But still, they did it, and the violinist now is plugged into you. To unplug you would be to kill him. But never mind, it's only for nine months. By then he will have recovered from his ailment, and can safely be unplugged from you." Is it morally incumbent on you to accede to this situation? No doubt it would be very nice of you if you did, a great kindness. But do you *have* to accede to it? What if it were not nine months, but nine years? Or longer still? What if the director of the hospital says, "Tough luck, I agree, but you've now got to stay in bed, with the violinist plugged into you, for the rest of your life. Because remember this. All persons have a right to life, and violinists are persons. Granted you have a right to decide what happens in and to your body, but a person's right to life outweighs your right to decide what happens in and to your body. So you cannot ever be unplugged from him." I imagine you would regard this as outrageous, which suggests that something really is wrong with that plausible-sounding argument I mentioned a moment ago.

In this case, of course, you were kidnapped; you didn't volunteer for the operation that plugged the violinist into your kidneys. Can those who oppose abortion on the ground I mentioned make an exception for a pregnancy due to rape? Certainly. They can say that persons have a right to life only if they didn't come into existence because of rape; or they can say that all persons have a right to life, but that some have less of a right to life than others, in particular, that those who came into existence because of rape have less. But these statements have a rather unpleasant sound. Surely the question of whether you have a right to life at all, or how much of it you have, shouldn't turn on the question of whether or not you are the product of a rape. And in fact the people who oppose abortion on the ground I mentioned do not make this distinction, and hence do not make an exception in case of rape.

Nor do they make an exception for a case in which the mother has to spend the nine months of her pregnancy in bed. They would agree that would be a great pity, and hard on the mother; but all the same, all persons have a right to life, the fetus is a person, and so on. I suspect, in fact, that they would not make an exception for a case in which, miraculously enough, the pregnancy went on for nine years, or even the rest of the mother's life.

Some won't even make an exception for a case in which continuation of the pregnancy is likely to shorten the mother's life; they regard abortion as impermissible even to save the mother's life. Such cases are nowadays very rare, and many opponents of abortion do not accept this extreme view. All the same, it is a good place to begin: a number of points of interest come out in respect to it

1. Let us call the view that abortion is impermissible even to save the mother's life "the extreme view." I want to suggest first that it does not issue from the argument I mentioned earlier without the addition of some fairly powerful premises. Suppose a woman has become pregnant, and now learns that she has a cardiac condition such that she will die if she carries the baby to term. What may be done for her? The fetus, being a person, has a right to life, but as the mother is a person too, so has she a right to life. Presumably they have an equal right to life. How is it supposed to come out that an abortion may not be performed? If mother and child have an equal right to life, shouldn't we perhaps flip a coin? Or should we add to the mother's right to life her right to decide what happens in and to her body, which everybody seems to be ready to grant—the sum of her rights now outweighing the fetus' right to life?

The most familiar argument here is the following. We are told that performing the abortion would be directly killing[2] the child, whereas doing nothing would not be killing the mother, but only letting her die. Moreover, in killing the child, one would be killing an innocent person, for the child has committed no crime, and is not aiming at his mother's death. And then there are a variety of ways in which this might be continued. (1) But as directly killing an innocent person is always and absolutely impermissible, an abortion may not be performed. Or, (2) as directly killing an innocent person is murder, and murder is always and absolutely impermissible, an abortion may not be performed.[3] Or, (3) as one's duty to refrain from directly killing an innocent person is more stringent than one's duty to keep a person from dying, an abortion may not be performed. Or, (4) if one's only options are directly killing an innocent person or letting a person die, one must prefer letting the person die, and thus an abortion may not be performed.[4]

Some people seem to have thought that these are not further premises which must be added if the conclusion is to be reached, but that they follow from the very fact that an innocent person has a right to life.[5] But this seems to me to be a mistake, and perhaps the simplest way to show this is to bring out that while we must certainly grant that innocent persons have a right to life, the theses in (1) through (4) are all false. Take (2), for example. If directly killing an innocent person is murder, and thus is impermissible, then the mother's directly killing the innocent person inside her is murder, and thus is impermissible. But it cannot seriously be thought to be murder if the mother performs an abortion on herself to save her life. It cannot seriously be said that she *must* refrain, that she *must* sit passively by and wait for her death. Let us look again at the case of you and the violinist There you are, in bed with the violinist, and the director of the hospital says to you, "It's all most distressing, and I deeply sympathize, but you see this is putting an additional strain on your kidneys, and you'll be dead within the month. But you *have* to stay where you are all the same. Because unplugging you would be directly killing an innocent violinist, and that's murder, and that's impermissible." If anything in the world is true, it is that you do not commit murder, you do not do what is impermissible, if you reach around to your back and unplug yourself from that violinist to save your life.

The main focus of attention in writings on abortion has been on what a third party may or may not do in answer to a request from a woman for an abortion. This is in a way understandable. Things being as they are, there isn't much a woman can safely do to abort herself. So the question asked is what a third party may do, and what the mother may do, if it is mentioned at all, is deduced, almost as an after-thought, from what it is concluded that third parties may do. But it seems to me that to treat the matter in this way is to refuse to grant to the mother that very status of person which is so firmly insisted on for the fetus. For we cannot simply read off what a person may do from what a third party may do. Suppose you find yourself trapped in a tiny house with a growing child. I mean a very tiny house, and a rapidly growing child—you are already up against the wall of the house and in a few minutes you'll be crushed to death. The child on the other hand won't be crushed to death; if nothing is done to stop him from growing he'll be hurt, but in the end he'll simply burst open the house and walk out a free man. Now I could well understand it if a bystander were to say, "There's nothing we can do for you. We cannot choose between your life and his, we cannot be the ones to decide who is to live, we cannot intervene." But it cannot be concluded that you too can do nothing, that you cannot attack it to save your life. However innocent the child may be, you do not have to wait passively while it crushes you to death. Perhaps a pregnant woman is vaguely felt to have the status of house, to which we don't allow the right of self-defense. But if the woman houses the child, it should be remembered that she is a person who houses it.

I should perhaps stop to say explicitly that I am not claiming that people have a right to do anything whatever to save their lives. I think, rather, that there are drastic limits to the right of self-defense. If someone threatens you with death unless you torture someone else to death, I think you have not the right, even to save your life, to do so. But the case under consideration here is very different. In our case there are only two people involved, one whose life is threatened, and one who threatens it. Both are innocent: the one who is threatened is not threatened because of any fault, the one who threatens does not threaten because of any fault. For this reason we may feel that we bystanders cannot intervene. But the person threatened can.

In sum, a woman surely can defend her life against the threat to it posed by the unborn child, even if doing so involves its death. And this shows not merely that the theses in (1) through (4) are false; it shows also that the extreme view of abortion is false, and so we need not canvass any other possible ways of arriving at it from the argument I mentioned at the outset.

2. The extreme view could of course be weakened to say that while abortion is permissible to save the mother's life, it may not be performed by a third party, but only by the mother herself. But this cannot be right either. For what we have to keep in mind is that the mother and the unborn child are not like two tenants in a small house which has, by an unfortunate mistake, been rented to both; the mother *owns* the house. The fact that she does adds to the offensiveness of deducing that the mother can do nothing from the supposition that third parties can do nothing. But it does more than this: it casts a bright light on the supposition that third parties can do nothing. Certainly it lets us see that a third party who says "I cannot choose between you" is fooling himself if he thinks this is impartiality. If Jones has found and fastened on a certain coat, which he needs to keep him from freezing, but which Smith also needs to keep him from freezing, then it is not impartiality that says "I cannot choose between you" when Smith owns the coat. Women

have said again and again "This body is *my* body!" and they have reason to feel angry, reason to feel that it has been like shouting into the wind. Smith, after all, is hardly likely to bless us if we say to him, "Of course it's your coat, anybody would grant that it is. But no one may choose between you and Jones who is to have it."

We should really ask what it is that says "no one may choose" in the face of the fact that the body that houses the child is the mother's body. It may be simply a failure to appreciate this fact. But it may be something more interesting, namely the sense that one has a right to refuse to lay hands on people, even where it would be just and fair to do so, even where justice seems to require that somebody do so. Thus justice might call for somebody to get Smith's coat back from Jones, and yet you have a right to refuse to be the one to lay hands on Jones, a right to refuse to do physical violence to him. This, I think, must be granted. But then what should be said is not "no one may choose," but only "*I* cannot choose," and indeed not even this, but "*I* will not *act*," leaving it open that somebody else can or should, and in particular that anyone in a position of authority, with the job of securing people's rights, both can and should. So this is no difficulty. I have not been arguing that any given third party must accede to the mother's request that he perform an abortion to save her life, but only that he may.

I suppose that in some views of human life the mother's body is only on loan to her, the loan not being one which gives her any prior claim to it. One who held this view might well think it impartiality to say "I cannot choose." But I shall simply ignore this possibility. My own view is that if a human being has any just, prior claim to anything at all, he has a just, prior claim to his own body. And perhaps this needn't be argued for here anyway, since, as I mentioned, the arguments against abortion we are looking at do grant that the woman has a right to decide what happens in and to her body.

But although they do grant it, I have tried to show that they do not take seriously what is done in granting it. I suggest the same thing will reappear even more clearly when we turn away from cases in which the mother's life is at stake, and attend, as I propose we now do, to the vastly more common cases in which a woman wants an abortion for some less weighty reason than preserving her own life.

3. Where the mother's life is not at stake, the argument I mentioned at the outset seems to have a much stronger pull. "Everyone has a right to life, so the unborn person has a right to life." And isn't the child's right to life weightier than anything other than the mother's own right to life, which she might put forward as ground for an abortion?

This argument treats the right to life as if it were unproblematic. It is not, and this seems to me to be precisely the source of the mistake.

For we should now, at long last, ask what it comes to, to have a right to life. In some views having a right to life includes having a right to be given at least the bare minimum one needs for continued life. But suppose that what in fact *is* the bare minimum a man needs for continued life is something he has no right at all to be given? If I am sick unto death, and the only thing that will save my life is the touch of Henry Fonda's cool hand on my fevered brow, then all the same, I have no right to be given the touch of Henry Fonda's cool hand on my fevered brow. It would be frightfully nice of him to fly in from the West Coast to provide it. It would be less nice, though no doubt well meant, if my friends flew out to the West Coast and carried Henry Fonda back with them. But I have no right at all against anybody that he should do this for me. Or again, to return to the story I told earlier, the fact that for continued life that violinist needs the continued use of your kidneys does not establish that he has a right to be given the continued use of your kidneys. He certainly has no right against you that *you* should give him continued use of your kidneys. For nobody has any right to use your kidneys unless you give him such a right; and nobody has the right against you that you shall give him this right—if you do allow him to go on using your kidneys, this is a kindness on your part, and not something he can claim from you as his due. Nor has he any right against anybody else that *they* should give him continued use of your kidneys. Certainly he had no right against the Society of Music Lovers that they should plug him into you in the first place. And if you now start to unplug yourself, having learned that you will otherwise have to spend nine years in bed with him, there is nobody in the world who must try to prevent you, in order to see to it that he is given something he has a right to be given.

Some people are rather stricter about the right to life. In their view, it does not include the right to be given anything, but amounts to, and only to, the right not to be killed by anybody. But here a related difficulty arises. If everybody is to refrain from killing that violinist, then everybody must refrain from doing a great many different sorts of things. Everybody must refrain from slitting his throat, everybody must refrain from shooting him—and everybody must refrain from unplugging you from him. But does he have a right against everybody that they shall refrain from unplugging you from him? To refrain from doing this is to allow him to continue to use your kidneys. It could be argued that he has a right against us that *we* should allow him to continue to use your kidneys. That is, while he had no right against us that we should give him the use of your kidneys, it might be argued that he anyway has a right against us that we shall not now intervene and deprive him of the use of your kidneys. I shall come back to third-party interventions later. But certainly the violinist has no right against you that *you* shall allow him to continue to use your kidneys. As I said, if you do allow him to use them, it is a kindness on your part, and not something you owe him.

The difficulty I point to here is not peculiar to the right to life. It reappears in connection with all the other natural rights; and it is something which an adequate account of rights must deal with. For present purposes it is enough just to draw attention to it. But I would stress that I am not arguing that people do not have a right to life—quite to the contrary, it seems to me that the primary control we must place on the acceptability of an account of rights is that it should turn out in that account to be a truth that all persons have a right to life. I am arguing only that having a right to life does not guarantee having either a right to be given the use of or a right to be allowed continued use of another person's body— even if one needs it for life itself. So the right to life will not serve the opponents of abortion in the very simple and clear way in which they seem to have thought it would.

4. There is another way to bring out the difficulty. In the most ordinary sort of case, to deprive someone of what he has a right to is to treat him unjustly. Suppose a boy and his small brother are jointly given a box of chocolates for Christmas. If the older boy takes the box and refuses to give his brother any of the chocolates, he is unjust to him, for the brother has been given a right to half of them. But suppose that, having learned that otherwise it means nine years in bed with that violinist, you unplug yourself from him. You surely are not being unjust to him, for you gave him no right to use your kidneys, and no one else can have given him any such right. But we have to notice that in unplugging yourself, you are killing him; and violinists, like everybody else, have a right to life, and thus in the view we were considering just now, the right not to be killed. So here you do what he supposedly has a right you shall not do, but you do not act unjustly to him in doing it.

The emendation which may be made at this point is this: the right to life consists not in the right not to be killed, but rather in the right not to be killed unjustly. This runs a risk of circularity, but never mind: it would enable us to square the fact that the violinist has a right to life with the fact that you do not act unjustly toward him in unplugging yourself, thereby killing him. For if you do not kill him unjustly, you do not violate his right to life, and so it is no wonder you do him no injustice.

But if this emendation is accepted, the gap in the argument against abortion stares us plainly in the face: it is by no means enough to show that the fetus is a person, and to remind us that all persons have a right to life—we need to be shown also that killing the fetus violates its right to life, i.e., that abortion is unjust killing. And is it?

I suppose we may take it as a datum that in a case of pregnancy due to rape the mother has not given the unborn person a right to the use of her body for food and shelter. Indeed, in what pregnancy could it be supposed that the mother has given the unborn person such a right? It is not as if there were unborn persons drifting about the world, to whom a woman who wants a child says "I invite you in."

But it might be argued that there are other ways one can have acquired a right to the use of another person's body than by having been invited to use it by that person. Suppose a woman voluntarily indulges in intercourse, knowing of the chance it will issue in pregnancy, and then she does become pregnant; is she not in part responsible for the presence, in fact the very existence, of the unborn person inside her? No doubt she did not invite it in. But doesn't her partial responsibility for its being there itself give it a right to the use of her body?[6] If so, then her aborting it would be more like the boy's taking away the chocolates, and less like your unplugging yourself from the violinist—doing so would be depriving it of what it does have a right to, and thus would be doing it an injustice.

And then, too, it might be asked whether or not she can kill it even to save her own life: If she voluntarily called it into existence, how can she now kill it, even in self-defense?

The first thing to be said about this is that it is something new. Opponents of abortion have been so concerned to make out the independence of the fetus, in order to establish that it has a right to life, just as its mother does, that they have tended to overlook the possible support they might gain from making out that the fetus is *dependent* on the mother, in order to establish that she has a special kind of responsibility for it, a responsibility that gives it rights against her which are not possessed by any independent person—such as an ailing violinist who is a stranger to her.

On the other hand, this argument would give the unborn person a right to its mother's body only if her pregnancy resulted from a voluntary act, undertaken in full knowledge of the chance a pregnancy might result from it. It would leave out entirely the unborn person whose existence is due to rape. Pending the availability of some further argument, then, we would be left with the conclusion that unborn persons whose existence is due to rape have no right to the use of their mothers' bodies, and thus that aborting them is not depriving them of anything they have a right to and hence is not unjust killing.

And we should also notice that it is not at all plain that this argument really does go even as far as it purports to. For there are cases and cases, and the details make a difference. If the room is stuffy, and I therefore open a window to air it, and a burglar climbs in, it would be absurd to say, "Ah, now he can stay, she's given him a right to the use of her house—for she is partially responsible for his presence there, having voluntarily done what enabled him to get in, in full knowledge that there are such things as burglars, and that burglars burgle." It would be still more absurd to say this if I had had bars installed outside my windows, precisely to prevent burglars from getting in, and a burglar got in only because of a defect in the bars. It remains equally absurd if we imagine it is not a burglar who climbs in, but an innocent person who blunders or falls in. Again, suppose it were like this: people-seeds drift about in the air like pollen, and if you open your windows, one may drift in and take root in your carpets or upholstery. You don't want children, so you fix up your windows with fine mesh screens, the very best you can buy. As can happen, however, and on very, very rare occasions does happen, one of the screens is defective; and a seed drifts in and takes root. Does the person-plant who now develops have a right to the use of your house? Surely not— despite the fact that you voluntarily opened your windows, you knowingly kept carpets and upholstered furniture, and you knew that screens were sometimes defective. Someone may argue that you are responsible for its rooting, that it does have a right to your house, because after all you *could* have lived out your life with bare floors and furniture, or with sealed windows and doors. But this won't do— for by the same token anyone can avoid a pregnancy due to rape by having a hysterectomy, or anyway by never leaving home without a (reliable!) army.

It seems to me that the argument we are looking at can establish at most that there are *some* cases in which the unborn person has a right to the use of its mother's body, and therefore *some* cases in which abortion is unjust killing. There is room for much discussion and argument as to precisely which, if any. But I think we should sidestep this issue and leave it open, for at any rate the argument certainly does not establish that all abortion is unjust killing.

5. There is room for yet another argument here, however. We surely must all grant that there may be cases in which it would be morally indecent to detach a person from your body at the cost of his life. Suppose you learn that what the violinist needs is not nine years of your life, but only one hour: all you need do to save his life is to spend one hour in that bed with him. Suppose also that letting him use your kidneys for that one hour would not affect your health in the slightest. Admittedly you were kidnapped. Admittedly you did not give anyone permission to plug him into you. Nevertheless it seems to me plain you *ought* to allow him to use your kidneys for that hour—it would be indecent to refuse.

Again, suppose pregnancy lasted only an hour, and constituted no threat to life or health. And suppose that a woman becomes pregnant as a result of rape. Admittedly she did not voluntarily do anything to bring about the existence of a child. Admittedly she did nothing at all which would give the unborn person a right to the use of her body. All the same it might well be said, as in the newly emended violinist story, that she *ought* to allow it to remain for that hour—that it would be indecent in her to refuse.

Now some people are inclined to use the term "right" in such a way that it follows from the fact that you ought to allow a person to use your body for the hour he needs, that he has a right to use your body for the hour he needs, even though he has not been given that right by any person or act. They may say that it follows also that if you refuse, you act unjustly toward him. This use of the term is perhaps so common that it cannot be called wrong; nevertheless it seems to me to be an unfortunate loosening of what we would do better to keep a tight rein on. Suppose that box of chocolates I mentioned earlier had not been given to both boys jointly, but was given only to the older boy. There he sits, stolidly eating his way through the box, his small brother watching enviously. Here we are likely to say "You ought not to be so mean. You ought to give your brother some of those chocolates." My own view is that it just does not follow from the truth of this that the brother has any right to any of the chocolates. If the boy refuses to give his brother any, he is greedy, stingy, callous—but not unjust. I suppose that the people I have in mind will say it does follow that the brother has a right to some of the chocolates, and thus that the boy does act unjustly if he refuses to give his brother any. But the effect of saying this is to obscure what we should keep distinct, namely the difference between the boy's refusal in this case and the boy's refusal in the earlier case, in which the box was given to both boys jointly, and in which the small brother thus had what was from any point of view clear title to half.

A further objection to so using the term "right" that from the fact that A ought to do a thing for B, it follows that B has a right against A that A do it for him, is that it is going to make the question of whether or not a man has a right to a thing turn on how easy it is to provide him with it; and this seems not merely unfortunate, but morally unacceptable. Take the case of Henry Fonda again. I said earlier that I had no right to the touch of his cool hand on my fevered brow, even though I needed it to save my life. I said it would be frightfully nice of him to fly in

from the West Coast to provide me with it, but that I had no right against him that he should do so. But suppose he isn't on the West Coast. Suppose he has only to walk across the room, place a hand briefly on my brow—and lo, my life is saved. Then surely he ought to do it, it would be indecent to refuse. Is it to be said "Ah, well, it follows that in this case she has a right to the touch of his hand on her brow, and so it would be an injustice in him to refuse"? So that I have a right to it when it is easy for him to provide it, though no right when it's hard? It's rather a shocking idea that anyone's rights should fade away and disappear as it gets harder and harder to accord them to him.

So my own view is that even though you ought to let the violinist use your kidneys for the one hour he needs, we should not conclude that he has a right to do so—we should say that if you refuse, you are, like the boy who owns all the chocolates and will give none away, self-centered and callous, indecent in fact, but not unjust. And similarly, that even supposing a case in which a woman pregnant due to rape ought to allow the unborn person to use her body for the hour he needs, we should not conclude that he has a right to do so; we should conclude that she is self-centered, callous, indecent, but not unjust, if she refuses. The complaints are no less grave; they are just different. However, there is no need to insist on this point. If anyone does wish to deduce "he has a right" from "you ought," then all the same he must surely grant that there are cases in which it is not morally required of you that you allow that violinist to use your kidneys, and in which he does not have a right to use them, and in which you do not do him an injustice if you refuse. And so also for mother and unborn child. Except in such cases as the unborn person has a right to demand it—and we were leaving open the possibility that there may be such cases— nobody is morally *required* to make large sacrifices, of health, of all other interests and concerns, of all other duties and commitments, for nine years, or even for nine months, in order to keep another person alive.

6. We have in fact to distinguish between two kinds of Samaritan: the Good Samaritan and what we might call the Minimally Decent Samaritan. The story of the Good Samaritan, you will remember, goes like this:

> A certain man went down from Jerusalem to Jericho, and fell among thieves, which stripped him of his raiment, and wounded him, and departed, leaving him half dead.
>
> And by chance there came down a certain priest that way; and when he saw him, he passed by on the other side.
>
> And likewise a Levite, when he was at the place, came and looked on him, and passed by on the other side.
>
> But a certain Samaritan, as he journeyed, came where he was; and when he saw him he had compassion on him.
>
> And went to him, and bound up his wounds, pouring in oil and wine, and set him on his own beast, and brought him to an inn, and took care of him
>
> And on the morrow, when he departed, he took out two pence, and gave them to the host, and said unto him, "Take care of him; and whatsoever thou spendest more, when I come again, I will repay thee." (Luke 10:30–35)

The Good Samaritan went out of his way, at some cost to himself, to help one in need of it. We are not told what the options were, that is, whether or not the priest and the Levite could have helped by doing less than the Good Samaritan did, but assuming they could have, then the fact they did nothing at all shows they were not even Minimally Decent Samaritans, not because they were not Samaritans, but because they were not even minimally decent.

These things are a matter of degree, of course, but there is a difference, and it comes out perhaps most clearly in the story of Kitty Genovese, who, as you will remember, was murdered while thirty-eight people watched or listened, and did nothing at all to help her. A Good Samaritan would have rushed out to give direct assistance against the murderer. Or perhaps we had better allow that it would have been a Splendid Samaritan who did this, on the ground that it would have involved a risk of death for himself. But the thirty-eight not only did not do this, they did not even trouble to pick up a phone to call the police. Minimally Decent Samaritanism would call for doing at least that, and their not having done it was monstrous.

After telling the story of the Good Samaritan, Jesus said "Go, and do thou likewise." Perhaps he meant that we are morally required to act as the Good Samaritan did. Perhaps he was urging people to do more than is morally required of them. At all events it seems plain that it was not morally required of any of the thirty-eight that he rush out to give direct assistance at the risk of his own life, and that it is not morally required of anyone that he give long stretches of his life— nine years or nine months—to sustaining the life of a person who has no special right (we were leaving open the possibility of this) to demand it.

Indeed, with one rather striking class of exceptions, no one in any country in the world is *legally* required to do anywhere near as much as this for anyone else. The class of exceptions is obvious. My main concern here is not the state of the law in respect to abortion, but it is worth drawing attention to the fact that in no state in this country is any man compelled by law to be even a Minimally Decent Samaritan to any person; there is no law under which charges could be brought against the thirty-eight who stood by while Kitty Genovese died. By contrast, in most states in this country women are compelled by law to be not merely Minimally Decent Samaritans, but Good Samaritans to unborn persons inside them. This doesn't by itself settle anything one way or the other, because it may well be argued that there should be laws in this country— as there are in many European countries— compelling at least Minimally Decent Samaritanism.[7] But it does show that there is a gross injustice in the existing state of the law. And it shows also that the groups currently working against liberalization of abortion laws, in fact working toward having it declared unconstitutional for a state to permit abortion, had better start working for the adoption of Good Samaritan laws generally, or earn the charge that they are acting in bad faith.

I should think, myself, that Minimally Decent Samaritan laws would be one thing, Good Samaritan laws quite another, and in fact highly improper. But we are not here concerned with the law. What we should ask is not whether anybody should be compelled by law to be a Good Samaritan, but whether we must accede to a situation in which somebody is being compelled—by nature, perhaps—to be a Good Samaritan. We have, in other words, to look now at third-party interventions. I have been arguing that no person is morally required to make large sacrifices to sustain the life of another who has no right to demand them, and this even where the sacrifices do not include life itself; we are not morally required to be Good Samaritans or anyway Very Good Samaritans to one another. But what if a man cannot extricate himself from such a situation? What if he appeals to us to extricate him? It seems to me plain that there are cases in which we can, cases in which a Good Samaritan would extricate him. There you are, you were kidnapped, and nine years in bed with that violinist lie ahead of you. You have your own life to lead. You are sorry, but you simply cannot see giving up so much of your life to the sustaining of his. You cannot extricate yourself, and ask us to do so. I should have thought that—in light of his having no right to the use of your body—it was obvious that we do not have to accede to your being forced to give up so much. We can do what you ask. There is no injustice to the violinist in our doing so.

7. Following the lead of the opponents of abortion, I have throughout been speaking of the fetus merely as a person, and what I have been asking is whether or not the argument we began with, which proceeds only from the fetus' being a person, really does establish its conclusion. I have argued that it does not.

But of course there are arguments and arguments, and it may be said that I have simply fastened on the wrong one. It may be said that what is important is not merely the fact that the fetus is a person, but that it is a person for whom the woman has a special kind of responsibility issuing from the fact that she is its mother. And it might be argued that all my analogies are therefore irrelevant—for you do not have that special kind of responsibility for that violinist, Henry Fonda does not have that special kind of responsibility for me. And our attention might be drawn to the fact that men and women both *are* compelled by law to provide support for their children.

I have in effect dealt (briefly) with this argument in section 4 above; but a (still briefer) recapitulation now may be in order. Surely we do not have any such "special responsibility" for a person unless we have assumed it, explicitly or implicitly. If a set of parents do not try to prevent pregnancy, do not obtain an abortion, and then at the time of birth of the child do not put it out for adoption, but rather take it home with them, then they have assumed responsibility for it, they have given it rights, and they cannot *now* withdraw support from it at the cost of its life because they now find it difficult to go on providing for it. But if they have taken all reasonable precautions against having a child, they do not simply by virtue of their biological relationship to the child who comes into existence have a special responsibility for it. They may wish to assume responsibility for it, or they may not wish to. And I am suggesting that if assuming responsibility for it would require large sacrifices, then they may refuse. A Good Samaritan would not refuse— or anyway, a Splendid Samaritan, if the sacrifices that had to be made were enormous. But then so would a Good Samaritan assume responsibility for that violinist; so would Henry Fonda, if he is a Good Samaritan, fly in from the West Coast and assume responsibility for me.

8. My argument will be found unsatisfactory on two counts by many of those who want to regard abortion as morally permissible. First, while I do argue that abortion is not impermissible, I do not argue that it is always permissible. There may well be cases in which carrying the child to term requires only Minimally Decent

Samaritanism of the mother, and this is a standard we must not fall below. I am inclined to think it a merit of my account precisely that it does *not* give a general yes or a general no. It allows for and supports our sense that, for example, a sick and desperately frightened fourteen-year-old schoolgirl, pregnant due to rape, may *of course* choose abortion, and that any law which rules this out is an insane law. And it also allows for and supports our sense that in other cases resort to abortion is even positively indecent. It would be indecent in the woman to request an abortion, and indecent in a doctor to perform it, if she is in her seventh month, and wants the abortion just to avoid the nuisance of postponing a trip abroad. The very fact that the arguments I have been drawing attention to treat all cases of abortion, or even all cases of abortion in which the mother's life is not at stake, as morally on a par ought to have made them suspect at the outset

Secondly, while I am arguing for the permissibility of abortion in some cases, I am not arguing for the right to secure the death of the unborn child. It is easy to confuse these two things in that up to a certain point in the life of the fetus it is not able to survive outside the mother's body; hence removing it from her body guarantees its death. But they are importantly different. I have argued that you are not morally required to spend nine months in bed, sustaining the life of that violinist; but to say this is by no means to say that if, when you unplug yourself, there is a miracle and he survives, you then have a right to turn round and slit his throat. You may detach yourself even if this costs him his life; you have no right to be guaranteed his death, by some other means, if unplugging yourself does not kill him. There are some people who will feel dissatisfied by this feature of my argument. A woman may be utterly devastated by the thought of a child, a bit of herself, put out for adoption and never seen or heard of again. She may therefore want not merely that the child be detached from her, but more, that it die. Some opponents of abortion are inclined to regard this as beneath contempt—thereby showing insensitivity to what is surely a powerful source of despair. All the same, I agree that the desire for the child's death is not one which anybody may gratify, should it turn out to be possible to detach the child alive.

At this place, however, it should be remembered that we have only been pretending throughout that the fetus is a human being from the moment of conception. A very early abortion is surely not the killing of a person, and so is not dealt with by anything I have said here.

NOTES

1. Daniel Callahan, *Abortion: Law, Choice and Morality* (New York, 1970), p. 373. This book gives a fascinating survey of the available information on abortion. The Jewish tradition is surveyed in David M. Feldman, *Birth Control in Jewish Law* (New York, 1968), Part 5, the Catholic tradition in John T. Noonan, Jr., "An Almost Absolute Value in History," in *The Morality of Abortion,* ed. John T. Noonan, Jr. (Cambridge, Mass., 1970).

2. The term "direct" in the arguments I refer to is a technical one. Roughly, what is meant by "direct killing" is either killing as an end in itself, or killing as a means to some end, for example, the end of saving someone else's life. See note 5, below, for an example of its use.

3. Cf. *Encyclical Letter of Pope Pius XI on Christian Marriage*, St. Paul Editions (Boston, n.d), p. 32: "however much we may pity the mother whose health and even life is gravely imperiled in the performance of the duty allotted to her by nature, nevertheless what could ever be a sufficient reason for excusing in any way the direct murder of the innocent? This is precisely what we are dealing with here." Noonan *(The Morality of Abortion,* p. 43) reads this as follows: "What cause can ever avail to excuse in any way the direct killing of the innocent? For it is a question of that."

4. The thesis in (4) is in an interesting way weaker than those in (1), (2), and (3): they rule out abortion even in cases in which both mother *and* child will die if the abortion is not performed. By contrast, one who held the view expressed in (4) could consistently say that one needn't prefer letting two persons die to killing one.

5. Cf. the following passage from Pius XII, *Address to the Italian Catholic Society of Midwives:* "The baby in the maternal breast has the right to life immediately from God.—Hence there is no man, no human authority, no science, no medical, eugenic, social, economic or moral 'indication' which can establish or grant a valid juridical ground for a direct deliberate disposition of an innocent human life, that is a disposition which looks to its destruction either as an end or as a means to another end perhaps in itself not illicit.—The baby, still not born, is a man in the same degree and for the same reason as the mother" (quoted in Noonan, *The Morality of Abortion*, p. 45).

6. The need for a discussion of this argument was brought home to me by members of the Society for Ethical and Legal Philosophy, to whom this paper was originally presented.

7. For a discussion of the difficulties involved, and a survey of the European experience with such laws, see *The Good Samaritan and the Law*, ed. James M. Ratcliffe (New York, 1966).

For Further Reflection

1. State Thomson's argument for abortion. Is the argument a good one? Does the violinist analogy adequately support the conclusion? Why or why not?

2. Some opponents of Thomson's argument have maintained that a woman has no right of self-defense in cases where she becomes pregnant after voluntarily having sex. What is the rationale behind this claim? Do you agree with this criticism? Explain.

3. Suppose that during an abortion procedure the fetus is extracted from the uterus alive. Do you think that the mother has a right to demand that it be destroyed? Why or why not?

The Moderate Position: Beyond the Personhood Argument

IX.83

JANE ENGLISH

Jane English (1947–1978) taught philosophy at the University of North Carolina, Chapel Hill, and was the author of several essays in applied ethics, including the essay that is included here.

English argues that the issue, of whether a fetus is a person, cannot be resolved, and that the very concept of personhood is not clear or decisive enough to bear the weight of a solution to the abortion debate. Advancing a moderate position, similar to that of F. W. Sumner, English argues that regardless of whether a fetus is a person, the principle of self-defense permits a woman to have an abortion in some cases, especially in the early stages of pregnancy. On the other hand, even if the fetus is not a person, it is too much like a baby in the later stages of pregnancy to permit an abortion—except to avoid significant injury or death.

Study Questions

1. Why does English think that both the conservative and liberal positions on abortion are "clearly mistaken"?
2. What does English think is the key issue in the abortion debate?
3. What is English's conclusion regarding criteria for personhood? How does she describe personhood?
4. Does English think it is sometimes permissible to kill an innocent person? If so, under what conditions? If not, why not?
5. How are some cases of pregnancy like being attacked by an innocent (hypnotized) person?
6. Even if the fetus is a person, would it sometimes, according to English, be permissible to have an abortion? Under what conditions?
7. What is the anti-abortionist's strongest argument?
8. What is English's judgment on Tooley's argument?

THE ABORTION DEBATE rages on. Yet the two most popular positions seem to be clearly mistaken. Conservatives maintain that a human life begins at conception and that therefore abortion must be wrong because it is murder. But not all killings of humans are murders. Most notably, self defense may justify even the killing of an innocent person.

Liberals, on the other hand, are just as mistaken in their argument that since a fetus does not become a person until birth, a woman may do whatever she pleases in and to her own body. First, you cannot do as you please with your own body if it affects other people adversely. Second, if a fetus is not a person, that does not imply that you can do to it anything you wish. Animals, for example, are not persons, yet to kill or torture them for no reason at all is wrong.

At the center of the storm has been the issue of just when it is between ovulation and adulthood that a person appears on the scene. Conservatives draw the line at conception, liberals at birth. In this paper I first examine our concept of a person and conclude that no single criterion can capture the concept of a person and no sharp line can be drawn. Next I argue that if a fetus is a person, abortion is still justifiable in many cases; and if a fetus is not a person, killing it is still wrong in many cases. To a large extent, these two solutions are in agreement. I conclude that our concept of a person cannot and need not bear the weight that the abortion controversy has thrust upon it.

I

The several factions in the abortion argument have drawn battle lines around various proposed criteria for determining what is and what is not a person. For example, Mary Anne Warren lists five features (capacities for reasoning, self-awareness, complex communication, etc.) as her criteria for personhood and argues for the permissibility of abortion because a fetus falls outside this concept. Baruch Brody uses brain waves. Michael Tooley picks having-a-concept-of-self as his criterion and concludes that infanticide and abortion are justifiable, while the killing of adult animals is not. On the other side, Paul Ramsey claims a certain gene structure is the defining characteristic. John Noonan prefers conceived-of-humans and presents counterexamples to various other candidate criteria. For instance, he argues against viability as the

Reprinted from Jane English "Abortion and the Concept of a Person," Canadian Journal of Philosophy *vol. 5, 2 (October 1975) by permission. Footnotes deleted.*

criterion because the newborn and infirm would then be non-persons, since they cannot live without the aid of others. He rejects any criterion that calls upon the sorts of sentiments a being can evoke in adults on the grounds that this would allow us to exclude other races as nonpersons if we could just view them sufficiently unsentimentally.

These approaches are typical: Foes of abortion propose sufficient conditions for personhood which fetuses satisfy, while friends of abortion counter with necessary conditions for personhood which fetuses lack. But these both presuppose that the concept of a person can be captured in a strait jacket of necessary and/or sufficient conditions. Rather, "person" is a cluster of features, of which rationality, having a self concept and being conceived of humans are only part.

What is typical of persons? Within our concept of a person we include, first, certain biological factors: descended from humans, having a certain genetic makeup, having a head, hands, arms, eyes, capable of locomotion, breathing, eating, sleeping. There are psychological factors: sentience, perception, having a concept of self and of one's own interests and desires, the ability to use tools, the ability to use language or symbol systems, the ability to joke, to be angry, to doubt. There are rationality factors: the ability to reason and draw conclusions, the ability to generalize and to learn from past experience, the ability to sacrifice present interests for greater gains in the future. There are social factors: the ability to work in groups and respond to peer pressures, the ability to recognize and consider as valuable the interests of others, seeing oneself as one among "other minds," the ability to sympathize, encourage, love, the ability to evoke from others the responses of sympathy, encouragement, love, the ability to work with others for mutual advantage. Then there are legal factors: being subject to the law and protected by it, having the ability to sue and enter contracts, being counted in the census, having a name and citizenship, the ability to own property, inherit, and so forth.

Now the point is not that this list is incomplete, or that you can find counter-instances to

each of its points. People typically exhibit rationality, for instance, but someone who was irrational would not thereby fail to qualify as a person. On the other hand, something could exhibit the majority of these features and still fail to be a person, as an advanced robot might. There is no single core of necessary and sufficient features which we can draw upon with the assurance that they constitute what really makes a person: there are only features that are more or less typical.

This is not to say that no necessary or sufficient conditions can be given. Being alive is a necessary condition for being a person, and being a U.S. Senator is sufficient. But rather than falling inside a sufficient condition or outside a necessary one, a fetus lies in the penumbra region where our concept of a person is not so simple. For this reason I think a conclusive answer to the question whether a fetus is a person is unattainable.

Here we might note a family of simple fallacies that proceed by stating a necessary condition for personhood and showing that a fetus has that characteristic. This is a form of the fallacy of affirming the consequent. For example, some have mistakenly reasoned from the premise that a fetus is human (after all, it is a human fetus rather than, say, a canine fetus), to the conclusion that it is *a* human. Adding an equivocation on "being," we get the fallacious argument that since a fetus is something both living and human, it is a human being.

Nonetheless, it does seem clear that a fetus has very few of the above family of characteristics, whereas a newborn baby exhibits a much larger proportion of them—and a two-year-old has even more. Note that one traditional anti abortion argument has centered on pointing out the many ways in which a fetus resembles a baby. They emphasize its development ("It already has ten fingers . . .") without mentioning its dissimilarities to adults (it still has gills and a tail). They also try to evoke the sort of sympathy on our part that we only feel toward other persons ("Never to laugh . . . or feel the sunshine?") This all seems to be a relevant way to argue, since its purpose is to persuade us that a fetus satisfies so many of the important features on the list that it ought to be treated as a person. Also note that a fetus near the time of birth satisfies many more of these factors than a fetus in the early months of development. This could provide reason for making distinctions among the different stages of pregnancy, as the U.S. Supreme Court has done.

Historically, the time at which a person has been said to come into existence has varied widely. Muslims date personhood from fourteen days after conception. Some medievals followed Aristotle in placing ensoulment at forty days after conception for a male fetus and eighty days for a female fetus. In European common law since the Seventeenth Century, abortion was considered the killing of a person only after quickening, the time when a pregnant woman first feels the fetus move on its own. Nor is this variety of opinions surprising. Biologically, a human being develops gradually. We shouldn't expect there to be any specific time or sharp dividing point when a person appears on the scene.

For these reasons I believe our concept of a person is not sharp or decisive enough to bear the weight of a solution to the abortion controversy. To use it to solve that problem is to clarify *obscurum per obscurius*.

II

Next let us consider what follows if a fetus is a person after all. Judith Jarvis Thomson's landmark article, "A Defense of Abortion," correctly points out that some additional argumentation is needed at this point in the conservative argument to bridge the gap between the premise that a fetus is an innocent person and the conclusion that killing it is always wrong. To arrive at this conclusion, we would need the additional premise that killing an innocent person is always wrong. But killing an innocent person is sometimes permissible, most notably in self defense. Some examples may help draw out our intuitions or ordinary judgments about self defense.

Suppose a mad scientist, for instance, hypnotized innocent people to jump out of the bushes and attack innocent passers-by with knives. If you are so attacked, we agree you have a right to kill the attacker in self defense, if killing him is the only way to protect your life or to save yourself from serious injury. It does not seem to matter here that the attacker is not malicious but himself an innocent pawn, for your killing of him is not done in a spirit of retribution but only in self defense.

How severe an injury may you inflict in self defense? In part this depends upon the severity of the injury to be avoided: you may not shoot someone merely to avoid having your clothes torn. This might lead one to the mistaken conclusion that the defense may only equal the threatened injury in severity; that to avoid death you may kill, but to avoid a black eye you may only inflict a black eye or the equivalent. Rather, our laws and customs seem to say that you may create an injury somewhat, but not enormously, greater than the injury to be avoided. To fend off an attack whose outcome would be as serious as rape, a severe beating or the loss of a finger, you may shoot; to avoid having your clothes torn, you may blacken an eye.

Aside from this, the injury you may inflict should only be the minimum necessary to deter or incapacitate the attacker. Even if you know he intends to kill you, you are not justified in shooting him if you could equally well save yourself by the simple expedient of running away. Self defense is for the purpose of avoiding harms rather than equalizing harms.

Some cases of pregnancy present a parallel situation. Though the fetus is itself innocent, it may pose a threat to the pregnant woman's well-being, life prospects or health, mental or physical. If the pregnancy presents a slight threat to her interests, it seems self defense cannot justify abortion. But if the threat is on a par with a serious beating or the loss of a finger, she may kill the fetus that poses such a threat, even if it is an innocent person. If a lesser harm to the fetus could have the same defensive effect, killing it would not be justified. It is unfortunate that the only way to free the woman from the pregnancy entails the death of the fetus (except in very late stages of pregnancy). Thus a self defense model supports Thomson's point that the woman has a right only to be freed from fetus, not a right to demand its death.

The self defense model is most helpful when we take the pregnant woman's point of view. In the pre-Thomson literature, abortion is often framed as a question for a third party; do you, a doctor, have a right to choose between the life of the woman and that of the fetus? Some have claimed that if you were a passer-by who witnessed a struggle between the innocent hypnotized attacker and his equally innocent victim, you would have no reason to kill either in defense of the other. They have concluded that the self defense model implies that a woman may attempt to abort herself, but that a doctor should not assist her. I think the position of the third party is somewhat more complex. We do feel some inclination to intervene on behalf of the victim rather than the attacker, other things equal. But if both parties are innocent, other factors come into consideration. You would rush to the aid of your husband whether he was attacker or attackee. If a hypnotized famous violinist were attacking a skid row bum, we would try to save the individual who is of more value to society. These considerations would tend to support abortion in some cases.

But suppose you are a frail senior citizen who wishes to avoid being knifed by one of these innocent hypnotics, so you have hired a bodyguard to accompany you. If you are attacked, it is clear we believe that the bodyguard, acting as your agent, has a right to kill the attacker to save you from a serious beating. Your rights of self defense are transferred to your agent. I suggest that we should similarly view the doctor as the pregnant woman's agent in carrying out a defense she is physically incapable of accomplishing herself.

Thanks to modern technology, the cases are rare in which a pregnancy poses as clear a threat to a woman's bodily health as an attacker brandishing a switchblade. How does self defense

fare when more subtle, complex and long-range harms are involved?

To consider a somewhat fanciful example, suppose you are a highly trained surgeon when you are kidnapped by the hypnotic attacker. He says he does not intend to harm you but to take you back to the mad scientist who, it turns out, plans to hypnotize you to have a permanent mental block against all your knowledge of medicine. This would automatically destroy your career which would in turn have a serious adverse impact on your family, your personal relationships and your happiness. It seems to me that if the only way you can avoid this outcome is to shoot the innocent attacker, you are justified in so doing. You are defending yourself from a drastic injury to your life prospects. I think it is no exaggeration to claim that unwanted pregnancies (most obviously among teenagers) often have such adverse life-long consequences as the surgeon's loss of livelihood.

Several parallels arise between various views on abortion and the self defense model. Let's suppose further that these hypnotized attackers only operate at night, so that it is well known that they can be avoided completely by the considerable inconvenience of never leaving your house after dark. One view is that since you could stay home at night, therefore if you go out and are selected by one of these hypnotized people, you have no right to defend yourself. This parallels the view that abstinence is the only acceptable way to avoid pregnancy. Others might hold that you ought to take along some defense such as Mace which will deter the hypnotized person without killing him, but that if this defense fails, you are obliged to submit to the resulting injury, no matter how severe it is. This parallels the view that contraception is all right but abortion is always wrong, even in cases of contraceptive failure.

A third view is that you may kill the hypnotized person only if he will actually kill you, but not if he will only injure you. This is like the position that abortion is permissible only if it is required to save a woman's life. Finally, we have the view that it is all right to kill the attacker, even if only to avoid a very slight inconvenience to yourself and even if you knowingly walked down the very street where all these incidents have been taking place without taking along any Mace or protective escort. If we assume that a fetus is a person, this is the analogue of the view that abortion is always justifiable, "on demand."

The self defense model allows us to see an important difference that exists between abortion and infanticide, even if a fetus is a person from conception. Many have argued that the only way to justify abortion without justifying infanticide would be to find some characteristic of personhood that is acquired at birth. Michael Tooley, for one, claims infanticide is justifiable because the really significant characteristics of person are acquired some time after birth. But all such approaches look to characteristics of the developing human and ignore the relation between the fetus and the woman. What if, after birth, the presence of an infant or the need to support it posed a grave threat to the woman's sanity or life prospects? She could escape this threat by the simple expedient of running away. So a solution that does not entail the death of the infant is available. Before birth, such solutions are not available because of the biological dependence of the fetus on the woman. Birth is the crucial point not because of any characteristics the fetus gains, but because after birth the woman can defend herself by a means less drastic than killing the infant. Hence self defense can be used to justify abortion without necessarily thereby justifying infanticide.

III

On the other hand, supposing a fetus is not after all a person, would abortion always be morally permissible? Some opponents of abortion seem worried that if a fetus is not a full-fledged person, then we are justified in treating it in any way at all. However, this does not follow. Non-persons do get some consideration in our moral code, though of course they do not have the same rights as persons have (and in general they do not have moral responsibilities), and though their interests may be overridden by the interests of

persons. Still, we cannot just treat them in any way at all.

Treatment of animals is a case in point. It is wrong to torture dogs for fun or to kill wild birds for no reason at all. It is wrong Period, even though dogs and birds do not have the same rights persons do. However, few people think it is wrong to use dogs as experimental animals, causing them considerable suffering in some cases, provided that the resulting research will probably bring discoveries of great benefit to people. And most of us think it all right to kill birds for food or to protect our crops. People's rights are different from the consideration we give to animals, then, for it is wrong to experiment on people, even if others might later benefit a great deal as a result of their suffering. You might volunteer to be a subject, but this would be supererogatory; you certainly have a right to refuse to be a medical guinea pig.

But how do we decide what you may or may not do to non-persons? This is a difficult problem, one for which I believe no adequate account exists. You do not want to say, for instance, that torturing dogs is all right whenever the sum of its effects on people is good—when it doesn't warp the sensibilities of the torturer so much that he mistreats people. If that were the case, it would be all right to torture dogs if you did it in private, or if the torturer lived on a desert island or died soon afterward, so that his actions had no effect on people. This is an inadequate account, because whatever moral consideration animals get, it has to be indefeasible, too. It will have to be a general proscription of certain actions, not merely a weighing of the impact on people on a case-by-case basis.

Rather, we need to distinguish two levels on which consequences of actions can be taken into account in moral reasoning. The traditional objections to Utilitarianism focus on the fact that it operates solely on the first level, taking all the consequences into account in particular cases only. Thus Utilitarianism is open to "desert island" and "lifeboat" counterexamples because these cases are rigged to make the consequences of actions severely limited.

Rawls' theory could be described as a teleological sort of theory, but with teleology operating on a higher level. In choosing the principles to regulate society from the original position, his hypothetical choosers make their decision on the basis of the total consequences of various systems. Furthermore, they are constrained to choose a general set of rules which people can readily learn and apply. An ethical theory must operate by generating a set of sympathies and attitudes toward others which reinforces the functioning of that set of moral principles. Our prohibition against killing people operates by means of certain moral sentiments including sympathy, compassion and guilt. But if these attitudes are to form a coherent set, they carry us further: we tend to perform supererogatory actions, and we tend to feel similar compassion toward person-like non-persons.

It is crucial that psychological facts play a role here. Our psychological constitution makes it the case that for our ethical theory to work, it must prohibit certain treatment of non-persons which are significantly person-like. If our moral rules allowed people to treat some person-like non-persons in ways we do not want people to be treated, this would undermine the system of sympathies and attitudes that makes the ethical system work. For this reason, we would choose in the original position to make mistreatment of some sorts of animals wrong in general (not just wrong in the cases with public impact), even though animals are not themselves parties in the original position. Thus it makes sense that it is those animals whose appearance and behavior are most like those of people that get the most consideration in our moral scheme.

It is because of "coherence of attitudes," I think, that the similarity of a fetus to a baby is very significant. A fetus one week before birth is so much like a newborn baby in our psychological space that we cannot allow any cavalier treatment of the former while expecting full sympathy and nurturative support for the latter. Thus, I think that anti-abortion forces are indeed giving their strongest arguments when they point to the similarities between a fetus and a baby, and when they try to evoke our emotional attachment to and sympathy for the fetus. An

early horror story from New York about nurses who were expected to alternate between caring for six-week premature infants and disposing of viable 24-week aborted fetuses is just that—a horror story. These beings are so much alike that no one can be asked to draw a distinction and treat them so very differently.

Remember, however, that in the early weeks after conception, a fetus is very much unlike a person. It is hard to develop these feelings for a set of genes which doesn't yet have a head, hands, beating heart, response to touch or the ability to move by itself. Thus it seems to me that the alleged "slippery slope" between conception and birth is not so very slippery. In the early stages of pregnancy, abortion can hardly be compared to murder for psychological reasons, but in the latest stages it is psychologically akin to murder.

Another source of similarity is the bodily continuity between fetus and adult. Bodies play a surprisingly central role in our attitudes toward persons. One has only to think of the philosophical literature on how far physical identity suffices for personal identity or Wittgenstein's remark that the best picture of the human soul is the human body. Even after death, when all agree the body is no longer a person, we still observe elaborate customs of respect for the human body; like people who torture dogs, necrophiliacs are not to be trusted with people. So it is appropriate that we show respect to a fetus as the body continuous with the body of a person. This is a degree of resemblance to persons that animals cannot rival.

Michael Tooley also utilizes a parallel with animals. He claims that it is always permissible to drown newborn kittens and draws conclusions about infanticide. But it is only permissible to drown kittens when their survival would cause some hardship. Perhaps it would be a burden to feed and house six more cats or to find other homes for them. The alternative of letting them starve produces even more suffering than the drowning. Since the kittens get their rights second-hand, so to speak, *via* the need for coherence in our attitudes, their interests are often overridden by the interests of full-fledged persons. But if their survival would be no inconvenience to people at all, then it is wrong to drown them, *contra* Tooley.

Tooley's conclusions about abortion are wrong for the same reason. Even if a fetus is not a person, abortion is not always permissible, because of the resemblance of a fetus to a person. I agree with Thomson that it would be wrong for a woman who is seven months pregnant to have an abortion just to avoid having to postpone a trip to Europe. In the early months of pregnancy when the fetus hardly resembles a baby at all, then, abortion is permissible whenever it is in the interests of the pregnant woman or her family. The reasons would only need to outweigh the pain and inconvenience of the abortion itself. In the middle months, when the fetus comes to resemble a person, abortion would be justifiable only when the continuation of the pregnancy or the birth of the child would cause harms—physical, psychological, economic or social—to the woman. In the late months of pregnancy, even on our current assumption that a fetus is not a person, abortion seems to be wrong except to save a woman from significant injury or death.

The Supreme Court has recognized similar gradations in the alleged slippery slope stretching between conception and birth. To this point, the present paper has been a discussion of the moral status of abortion only, not its legal status. In view of the great physical, financial and sometimes psychological costs of abortion, perhaps the legal arrangements most compatible with the proposed moral solution would be the absence of restrictions, that is, so-called abortion "on demand."

So I conclude, first, that application of our concept of a person will not suffice to settle the abortion issue. After all, the biological development of a human being is gradual. Second, whether a fetus is a person or not, abortion is justifiable early in pregnancy to avoid modest harms and seldom justifiable late in pregnancy except to avoid significant injury or death.

For Further Reflection

1. Can we get beyond the personhood issue, as English proposes? Has she successfully shown that we don't need to resolve this issue in order to deal with the morality of abortion? Where do you agree or disagree with her?

2. English's view has been called moderate because she accepts most early stage abortions and rejects most later stage abortions. If so, how can this be reconciled with her proposal or, at least acceptance, of abortion "on demand"?

3. Does English's argument appeal too much to our emotions and too little to reason? For example, she says, "It is crucial that psychological facts play a role here. Our psychological constitution makes it the case that for our ethical theory to work, it must prohibit certain treatment of nonpersons which are significantly person-like." What does English mean? Is this an appeal to ignorance or to human irrationality or something else?

4. What is her "coherence of attitudes" argument? How much weight should such considerations be given in the abortion debate? Could my "coherence" structure be different from yours, and yours be different from other people's? Discuss the case of the New York nurses who were expected to alternate between caring for six-week premature infants and disposing of viable 24-week aborted fetuses. What bearing does this have on the question of the morality of abortion?

IX.B   Is the Death Penalty Morally Permissible?

What kind and what degree of punishment does public justice take as its principle and norm? None other than the principle of equality in the movement of the pointer of the scale of justice, the principle of not inclining to one side more than to the other. Thus any undeserved evil which you do to someone else among the people is an evil done to yourself. If you rob him, you rob yourself; if you slander him, you slander yourself; if you strike him, you strike yourself; and if you kill him, you kill yourself. (Immanuel Kant)

On August 15, 1990, Angel Diaz, age 19, was sentenced in the Bronx for the murder of an Israeli immigrant who had employed one of Diaz's friends. After strangling the man with a shoelace and stabbing him, Diaz and four friends donned Halloween masks to rob, beat, and gang-rape the man's wife and 16-year-old daughter. The women were then sexually tortured while the murdered man's 3-year-old daughter watched from her crib.

Angel Diaz already had been convicted of burglary four times before he was 16 years old. Diaz's lawyer, Paul Auerbach, said that Diaz was an honest boy forced by poverty to do bad things. Diaz was sentenced to prison for 38 and one-third years to life on 13 counts of murder, robbery, burglary, and conspiracy. His accomplice, Victor Sanchez, 21, who worked for the murdered man and planned the murder, had already been sentenced to 15 years to life.*

The National Center of Health Statistics has reported that the homicide rate for young men in the United States is 4 to 73 times the rate of other industrialized countries. In 1994, 23,330 murders were committed in the United States. Whereas killings per 100,000 by men 15 through 24 years old in 1987 was 0.3 in Austria and 0.5 in Japan, the figure was 21.9 in the United States and as high as 232 per 100,000 for blacks in some states. The nearest nation to the United States was Scotland, with a 5.0 homicide rate. In some central city areas the rate is 732 times that of men in Austria. In 1994, the rate was 37 per 100,000 men between the ages of 15 and 24.† In New York City there were more than 2,000 homicides in 1990. Black males in Harlem are said to have a lower life expectancy than males in Bangladesh. Escalating crime has caused an erosion in the quality of urban living. It is threatening the fabric of our social life.

What is to be done about crime? Improving social conditions, no doubt, is a large part of the answer. But people commit crimes even in good societies. So long as we hold people responsible for their actions, punishment will be a fitting response to crime, and among the modes of punishment to be considered is the death penalty for the most serious crimes.

We now turn to Burton Leiser's defense of the death penalty, and to Hugo Adam Bedau's rejection of the death penalty.

---

* "Jail for Crime That Shocked Even the Jaded," *New York Times* (August 16, 1990).

† Statistics are from the National Center of Health Statistics and are available from the Center for Disease Control. The National Center for Injury Prevention and Control reports that

in 1994 8,116 young people aged 15–24 were victims of homicide. This amounts to an average of 22 youth victims per day in the United States. This homicide rate is 10 times higher than Canada's, 15 times higher than Australia's, and 28 times higher than France's and Germany's. In 1994 in the United States 102,220 rapes and 618,950 robberies were reported.

IX.84   The Death Penalty Is Permissible

BURTON LEISER

Burton Leiser is professor emeritus of philosophy at Pace University and the author of several books and articles in the areas of law, morality, and religion, among them *Liberty, Justice and Morals,* from which this selection is taken.

Leiser rejects the idea that the death penalty constitutes a denial of the criminal's worth and dignity. On the contrary, argues Leiser, the death penalty, based on retributivism, actually affirms the offender's dignity and worth, for it treats him or her as a fully responsible person. In the last part of the essay Leiser discusses the limits of the death penalty.

Study Questions

1. How did the residents of a midwestern town take the law into their own hands regarding a ferocious bully?
2. How is this incident relevant to the death penalty?
3. Why, according to Leiser, isn't the death penalty "cruel and unusual"?
4. What does Leiser mean by *mens rea?*

RETRIBUTION

Vengeance and Vigilante Justice

IN HIS OPINION for the majority in *Gregg v. Georgia,* upholding the death penalty as constitutionally permissible, Justice Potter Stewart observed that capital punishment "is an expression of society's moral outrage at particularly offensive conduct," and that even though this function may be unappealing to many, "it is essential in an ordered society that asks its citizens to rely on legal processes rather than self-help to vindicate their wrongs." Without orderly means of imposing penalties upon offenders proportionate to what the aggrieved parties feel is deserved, society runs the risk of anarchy, vigilante justice, and lynch law. Even if retribution is not the dominant objective of the criminal law, he said, it is neither forbidden by the Constitution nor inconsistent with the dignity of men. Indeed, he went on, capital punishment "may be the appropriate sanction in extreme cases [as] an expression of the community's belief that certain crimes are themselves so grievous that the only adequate

Reprinted from Liberty, Justice and Morals, *3rd ed. (New York: Macmillan Publishing Company, 1986), by permission.*

response may be the penalty of death." As Lord Justice Denning told the British Royal Commission on Capital Punishment, "Some crimes are so outrageous that society insists on capital punishment, because the wrong-doer deserves it, irrespective of whether it is a deterrent or not."

In a report on "vicious youth gangs" in Detroit, the *New York Times* quoted a black resident as saying, "If I know who steals or breaks into my home, I'm going to get my gun. I'm going to hunt him. They can lock me up, but that's the only thing left. The police, they're not doing the job." Following another report on violent juvenile crime, a reader wrote to the *Times*, "Sudden death for a young man who does not want to surrender his wallet is cruel and unusual punishment. Why not let the punishment fit the crime, even if we have to amend the Constitution? The bleeding-heart mentality has caused too much bloodshed." And in a small town in the Midwest, after the residents concluded that the authorities would do nothing to relieve them of the violent behavior of a ferocious bully, a large group waylaid him and fatally shot him. Afterward, no one in the community could be found who was willing to cooperate with the authorities in their attempt to solve his murder. It is clear that their sense of justice was so outraged that they considered his death to be justifiable homicide, and not murder.

These sentiments are clearly consistent with those theories of government which declare that when people agree to lay down their rights to self-help, transferring their right to avenge themselves on those who harm them to their common sovereign (the government), the sovereign assumes the duty to see that justice is done. By conferring exclusive jurisdiction over criminal sanctions upon the government, the people prevent blood feuds from developing and bring order to the fixing of guilt and the exacting of retribution, which they would otherwise have done informally and summarily. As public frustration grows, as more and more innocent persons feel that they are direct or indirect victims of vicious criminals, and as more people become convinced that their demand for retribution will not be met by those into whose hands they placed the responsibility of exacting appropriate penalties from wrongdoers, the danger of vigilante justice grows. Thus, the move from orderly processes of exacting public retribution toward the arbitrary process of private vengeance gains greater momentum until it is finally translated into action, as it was in that Midwestern town.

Retribution and Human Dignity

In his dissent in *Gregg v. Georgia,* Justice Thurgood Marshall said that "it simply defies belief to suggest that the death penalty is necessary to prevent the American people from taking the law into their hands." He went on to assert that Lord Denning's contention that some crimes are so outrageous as to deserve the death penalty, regardless of its deterrent effects, is at odds with the Eighth Amendment. "The mere fact that the community demands the murderer's life for the evil he has done," he said, "cannot sustain the death penalty," for

> the Eighth Amendment demands more than that a challenged punishment be acceptable to contemporary society. To be sustained under the Eighth Amendment, the death penalty must [comport] with the basic concept of human dignity at the core of the Amendment; the objective in imposing it must be [consistent] with our respect for the dignity of [other] men. Under these standards, the taking of life "because the wrongdoer deserves it" surely must fail, for such a punishment has as its very basis the total denial of the wrongdoer's dignity and worth. The death penalty, unnecessary to promote the goal of deterrence or to further any legitimate notion of retribution, is an excessive penalty forbidden by the Eighth and Fourteenth Amendments.

Robert A. Pugsley has argued that the principle of retribution demands that the death penalty *not* be invoked. Capital punishment, he says, is symbolically the ultimate ostracization of an individual. It "emphatically transgresses the inviolability of the executed" and also "destroys those bonds of community which criminal punishment should strive to reaffirm." It is difficult, he says, to reconcile the "respect required for the individual's dignity and moral capacity," which he believes to be the essential point of retributivism, with the practice of execution. The executed criminal is not treated as a human being, but as an object to be discarded. Execution is dehumanizing. It is the "total negation of the moral worth of the person to be executed."

A more proper retributivist response, he says, may be derived from the following considerations:

> Even if [the convicted murderer] is sentenced to a life term without possibility of parole, he retains his membership in the community, and has had that status reaffirmed by the process of adjudication and punishment. His formal bond with the community *is* the punishment bond. It is that which signifies the community's recognition of him as a responsible moral agent and deserving of its respect, expressed of necessity through penalty and censure. He in turn accepts, if only tacitly, his punishment as justified; he acknowledges that he *ought* to feel guilty and suffer for his violative behavior. In the instance of the life term, particularly, there is this paradox: The community has "cared enough to give the very worst" punishment which, by abolishing the death penalty, it has permitted itself to impose.

As Justice Brennan put it in supporting the abolition of the death penalty, capital punishment treats members of the human race "as nonhumans, as objects to be toyed with and discarded." As such, it is inconsistent with the fundamental principle that "even the vilest criminal remains a human being possessed of common human dignity," whereas capital punishment is "uniquely degrading to human dignity." . . .

Retributive justice does not deny the wrongdoer's worth and dignity. It assumes it, and makes no sense at all unless the wrongdoer is regarded as a human being capable of making his own decisions, acting upon his own volition, and deserving moral praise or blame for what he does. The death penalty is the ultimate condemnation, morally and legally, of a person who has, through his actions, demonstrated his utter contempt for human worth and dignity and for the most fundamental

rules of human society. It is precisely because of a nation's belief in the dignity and worth of those who live under the protection of its laws and because of its adherence to the principle that human life is sacred that it may choose to employ the death penalty against those who have demonstated their disregard of those principles.

CRUEL AND UNUSUAL PUNISHMENT

The Eighth Amendment, which proscribed cruel and unusual punishments, was not intended to outlaw capital punishment as such. This is particularly evident if one considers that the Fifth Amendment, written and adopted at the same time, provides that "no person shall be held to answer for a capital . . . crime, unless on a presentment or indictment of a Grand Jury," and that no person "shall be deprived of life, liberty, or property, without due process of law." It is evident, then, that with a grand jury indictment, and with due process, a person may be deprived of his life, just as he may be deprived of his liberty or property. The cruel and unusual punishments that were banned by the Eighth Amendment were those that involved torture or a lingering death and those that were disproportionate to the offenses being punished. Later Courts have found, on the same basic principle, that *any* punishment for the mere status of being a drug addict is cruel and unusual, just as a single day in prison would be a cruel and unusual punishment for the "crime" of having a common cold.

The Court found that although the Eighth Amendment was dynamic, evolving over the years as public moral perceptions changed, capital punishment was not cruel and unusual as that term stands in the Constitution. As the liberal Chief Justice Earl Warren had once said, "the death penalty has been employed throughout our history, and, in a day when it is still widely accepted, it cannot be said to violate the constitutional concept of cruelty." Earlier Courts had found that that concept implied "something inhuman and barbarous, something more than the mere extinguishment of life," and that the suffering necessarily involved in any execution was not banned by the Eighth Amendment, though a cruel form of execution was. The Court noted that at least 35 state legislatures had enacted new statutes after *Furman,* providing for the death penalty, as had the Congress. It noted also that the people of California had amended their constitution, by referendum, so as to negate a decision by that state's highest court banning capital punishment. Juries, too, are a measure of public morality, and in March, 1976, more than 460 persons were subject to death sentences.

Arguing that the traditional justifications for capital punishment (deterrence and retribution) were sufficiently well founded, despite the reservations that some people have about them, to continue to play a role in penal policy, the Court concluded that the death penalty is not unreasonable, that it is consistent with contemporary moral standards, and that it is not a cruel and unusual punishment as that term is used in the Constitution. In view of the safeguards erected around defendants accused of capital offenses in Georgia and other states, the Court concluded that previous reservations about the death penalty being imposed in an arbitrary and capricious manner no longer applied and that it could therefore be imposed whenever similar safeguards existed.

THE LIMITS OF CAPITAL PUNISHMENT

The death penalty has historically been employed for such diverse offenses as murder, espionage, treason, kidnapping, rape, arson, robbery, burglary, and theft. Except for the most serious crimes, it is now agreed that lesser penalties are sufficient.

The distinction between first- and second-degree murder does not permit fine lines to be drawn between (for example) murder for hire and the killing of a husband by his jealous wife. Many murders committed in the United States are of a domestic nature—spouses or other close relatives

becoming involved in angry scenes that end in homicide. Such crimes, usually committed in the heat of a momentary passion, seem inappropriate for the supreme penalty. Although they are premeditated in the legal sense (for it takes no more than an instant for a person to form the intent that is necessary for the legal test to be satisfied), there seems to be a great difference between such crimes and those committed out of a desire for personal gain or for political motives, between a crime committed in an instant of overwrought emotion and one carefully charted and planned in advance. It is reasonable, therefore, to suggest that the vast majority of murders not be regarded as capital crimes, because the penalty may be disproportionate to the crime committed.

Only the most heinous offenses against the state and against individual persons seem to deserve the ultimate penalty. If the claim that life is sacred has any meaning at all, it must be that no man may deliberately cause another to lose his life without some compelling justification.

Such a justification appears to exist when individuals or groups employ wanton violence against others in order to achieve their ends, whatever those ends might be. However appealing the cause, however noble the motives, the deliberate, systematic destruction of innocent human beings is one of the gravest crimes any person can commit and may justify the imposition of the harshest available penalty, consistent with the principles of humanity, decency, and compassion. Some penalties, such as prolonged torture, may in fact be worse than death, and may be deemed such even by the intended victims. Civilized societies reject them as being too barbarous and too cruel to the victims, and too dehumanizing to those who must carry them out.

Perpetrators of such crimes as genocide (the deliberate extermination of entire peoples, racial, religious, or ethnic groups) deserve a penalty no less severe than death on purely retributive grounds. Those who perpetrate major war crimes, crimes against peace, or crimes against humanity, deliberately and without justification plunging nations into violent conflicts that entail widespread bloodshed or causing needless suffering on a vast scale, deserve no less.

Because of the reckless manner in which they endanger the lives of innocent citizens and their clear intention to take human lives on a massive scale in order to achieve their ends, terrorists should be subject to the death penalty, on retributive grounds, on the ground that it serves as the ultimate form of incapacitation—guaranteeing that terrorists who are executed will never again deprive an innocent person of his life, and on the ground that no other penalty can reasonably be expected to serve as a deterrent to persons whose colleagues are likely to engage in further acts of terrorism in order to achieve their release from prison.

Major crimes against the peace, security, and integrity of the state constitute particularly heinous offenses, for they shake the very foundations upon which civilization rests and endanger the lives, the liberties, and the fundamental rights of all the people who depend upon the state for protection. Treason, espionage, and sabotage, particularly during times of great danger (as in time of war), ought to be punishable by death.

Murder for personal gain and murder committed in the course of the commission of a felony that is being committed for personal gain or out of a reckless disregard for the lives or fundamental rights and interests of potential victims ought to be punishable by death.

Murder committed by a person who is serving a life sentence ought to be punishable by death, both because of the enormity of the crime itself and because no other penalty is likely to deter such crimes.

Needless to say, if a person is so deranged as to be legally insane, neither death nor any other punishment is appropriate. The very concept of punishment entails the assumption that the person being punished had the capacity, at the time he committed the act for which he is being punished, to act or refrain from acting, and of behaving at least in a minimally rational way. A person who commits a homicide while insane has not, strictly speaking, committed a murder or, for that matter, any crime at all; for no crime *can* (logically or legally) be committed without *mens rea,* the *intention* or *will* to carry it out.

The mere fact, however, that a person has carried out a homicide in a particularly vile, wanton, or malicious way is not sufficient to establish that that person is insane, for such a fact is consistent with many other explanations (e.g., that the perpetrator, making shrewd and calculated judgments as to what would most likely enable him to succeed without being caught, concluded that it would be in his own best interests if the crime *appeared* to be the act of an insane person who happened to be in the neighborhood).

Bearing these caveats in mind, we may conclude that any murder (as opposed to a mere homicide) committed in a particularly vile, wanton, or malicious way ought to be punishable by death.

One of the principal justifications for the state's existence is the protection it offers those who come under its jurisdiction against violations of their fundamental rights. Those who are entrusted with the responsibility for carrying out the duties of administering the state's functions, enforcing its laws, and seeing that justice is done carry an onerous burden and are particularly likely to become the targets of hostile, malicious, or rebellious individuals or groups. Their special vulnerability entitles them to special protection. Hence, any person guilty of murdering a policeman, a fireman, a judge, a governor, a president, a lawmaker, or any other person holding a comparable position while that person is carrying out his official duties or because of the office he holds has struck at the very heart of government and thus at the foundations upon which the state and civilized society depend. The gravity of such a crime warrants imposition of the death penalty.

From the fact that some persons who bring about the deaths of fellow humans do so under conditions that just and humane men would consider sufficient to justify either complete exculpation or penalties less than death, it does not follow that all of them do. If guilt is clearly established beyond a reasonable doubt under circumstances that guarantee a reasonable opportunity for the defendant to confront his accusers, to cross-examine witnesses, to present his case with the assistance of professional counsel, and in general to enjoy the benefits of due process of law; if in addition he has been given the protection of laws that prevent the use of torture to extract confessions and is provided immunity against self-incrimination; if those who are authorized to pass judgment find there were no excusing or mitigating circumstances; if he is found to have committed a wanton, brutal, callous murder or some other crime that is subversive of the very foundations of an ordered society; and if, finally, the representatives of the people, exercising the people's sovereign authority have prescribed death as the penalty for that crime; then the judge and jury are fully justified in imposing that penalty, and the proper authorities are justified in carrying it out.

For Further Reflection

1. How does Leiser respond to Marshall's point that the death penalty is a denial of the wrongdoer's dignity and worth? Is his response cogent? Explain.
2. What are the moral limits of the use of the death penalty?

No, the Death Penalty Is Not Morally Permissible   IX.85

HUGO ADAM BEDAU

Hugo Adam Bedau is professor emeritus of philosophy at Tufts University and past president of the American League to Abolish Capital Punishment. He has been a leading spokesman for the abolitionist movement and is the editor of *The Death Penalty in America* (1982) and the author of *The Courts, the Constitution and Capital Punishment* (1977).

In this selection Bedau first draws an analogy between self-defense and the death penalty. Just as in defending ourselves we are to use no more force than is necessary to prevent harm, so in punishing criminals we are to use no more violence than is necessary to adequately punish the criminal. Bedau then argues that neither the deterrence nor the retributive argument for capital punishment is a good argument. He thinks that the literal application of the *lex talionis* is barbaric and that long-term imprisonment is adequate punishment.

Study Questions

1. What is the analogy between self-defense and capital punishment?
2. When does the law impose "a duty to retreat"?
3. According to Bedau, how much violence can justifiably be used to ward off aggression?
4. How does Bedau apply this idea of resentment to the issue of punishment for crime?
5. Does Bedau think that the threat of the death penalty deters would-be murderers better than the threat of long-term prison sentences does?

6. Would Bedau oppose the death penalty if there was good evidence that it did deter would-be murderers?
7. What are the two principles of retributive justice relevant to the death penalty controversy?
8. Why, according to Bedau, aren't we consistent in our application of the principle of retribution (the *lex talionis*)?
9. In what way does Bedau think that the application of the death penalty is biased? Why does this unfairness occur?

THE ANALOGY WITH SELF-DEFENSE

CAPITAL PUNISHMENT, it is sometimes said, is to the body politic what self-defense is to the individual. If the latter is not morally wrong, how can the former be morally wrong? In order to assess the strength of this analogy, we need to inspect rather closely the morality of self-defense.

Except for the absolute pacifists, who believe it is morally wrong to use violence even to defend themselves or others from unprovoked and undeserved aggression, most of us believe that it is not morally wrong and may even be our moral duty to use violence to prevent aggression. The law has long granted persons the right to defend themselves against the unjust aggressions of others, even to the extent of killing a would-be assailant. It is very difficult to think of any convincing argument that would show it is never rational to risk the death of another in order to prevent death or grave injury to oneself or to others. Certainly self-interest dictates the legitimacy of self-defense. So does concern for the well-being of others. So also does justice. If it is unfair for one person to attempt violence on another, then it is hard to see why morality compels the victim to acquiesce in the attempt by another to hurt him or her, rather than to resist it, even if that resistance may involve injury to the assailant.

The foregoing account assumes that the person acting in self-defense is innocent of any provocation of the assailant. It also assumes that there is no alternative to victimization except resistance. In actual life, both assumptions—especially the second—are often false, because there may be a third alternative: escape, or removing oneself from the scene of danger and imminent aggression. Hence, the law imposes on us the so-called "duty to retreat." Before we use violence to resist aggression, we must try to get out of the way, lest unnecessary violence be used to resist aggression. Now suppose that unjust aggression is imminent, and there is no path open for escape. How much violence may justifiably be used to ward off aggression? The answer is: No more violence than is necessary to prevent the aggressive assault. Violence beyond that is unnecessary and therefore unjustified. We may restate the principle governing the use of violence in self-defense in terms of the use of "deadly force" by the police in the discharge of their duties. The rule is this: Use of deadly force is justified only to prevent loss of life in immediate jeopardy where a lesser use of force cannot reasonably be expected to save the life that is threatened.

In real life, violence in self-defense in excess of the minimum necessary to prevent aggression is often excusable. One cannot always tell what will suffice to deter or prevent becoming a victim, and the law looks with a certain tolerance upon the frightened and innocent would-be victim who turns upon a vicious assailant and inflicts a fatal injury even though a lesser injury would have been sufficient. What is not justified is deliberately using far more violence than is necessary to prevent becoming a victim. It is the deliberate, not the impulsive, use of violence that is relevant to the death-penalty controversy, since the death penalty is enacted into law and carried out in each case only after ample time to weigh alternatives. Notice that we are assuming that the act of self-defense is to protect one's person or that of a third party. The reasoning outlined here does not extend to the defense of one's property. Shooting a thief to prevent one's automobile from being stolen cannot be excused or justified in the way that shooting an assailant charging with a knife pointed at one's face can be. In terms of the concept of "deadly force," our criterion is that deadly force is never justified to prevent crimes against property or other violent crimes not immediately threatening the life of a person.

The rationale for self-defense as set out above illustrates two moral principles of great importance to our discussion. One is that if a life is to be risked, then it is better that it be the life of someone who is guilty (in our context, the initial assailant) rather than the life of someone who is not (the innocent potential victim). It is not fair to expect the innocent prospective victim to run the added risk of severe injury or death in order to avoid using violence in self-defense to the extent of possibly killing his assailant. It is only fair that the guilty aggressor run the risk.

The other principle is that taking life deliberately is not justified so long as there is any feasible alternative. One does not expect miracles, of course, but in theory, if shooting a burglar through the foot will stop the burglary and enable one to call the police for help, then there is no reason to shoot to kill. Likewise, if the burglar is unarmed, there is no reason to shoot at all. In actual life, of course, burglars are likely to be shot at by aroused householders because one does not know whether they are armed, and prudence may dictate the assumption that they are. Even so, although the burglar has no right to commit a felony against a person or a person's property, the attempt to do so does not give the chosen victim the right to respond in whatever way he or she pleases in retaliation, and then to excuse or justify such conduct on the ground that he or she was "only acting in self-defense." In these ways the law shows a tacit regard for the life of even a felon and discourages the use of unnecessary violence even by the innocent; morality can hardly do less.

THE DEATH PENALTY AS A CRIME DETERRENT

Determining whether the death penalty is an effective deterrent is even more difficult than determining its effectiveness as a crime preventive. In general, our knowledge about how penalties deter crimes and whether in fact they do—whom they deter, from which crimes, and under what conditions—is distressingly inexact. Most people nevertheless are convinced that punishments do deter, and that the more severe a punishment is the better it will deter. For more than a generation, social scientists have studied the question of whether the death penalty is a deterrent and of whether it is a better deterrent than the alternative of imprisonment. Their verdict, while not unanimous, is fairly clear. Whatever may be true about the deterrence of lesser crimes by other penalties, the deterrence achieved by the death penalty for murder is not measurably greater than the deterrence achieved by long-term imprisonment. In the nature of the case, the evidence is quite indirect. No one can identify for certain any crimes that did not occur because the would-be offender was deterred by the threat of the death penalty and that would not have been deterred by a lesser threat. Likewise, no one can identify any crimes that did occur because the offender was not deterred by the threat of prison even though he would have been deterred by the threat of death. Nevertheless, such evidence as we have fails to show that the more severe penalty (death) is really a better deterrent than the less severe penalty (imprisonment) for such crimes as murder.

If the conclusion stated above is correct, and the death penalty and long-term imprisonment are equally effective (or ineffective) as deterrents to murder, then the argument for the death penalty on grounds of deterrence is seriously weakened. One of the moral principles identified earlier comes into play and requires us to reject the death penalty on moral grounds. This is the principle that unless there is a good reason for choosing a more rather than a less severe punishment for a crime, the less severe penalty is to be preferred.

This principle obviously commends itself to anyone who values human life and who concedes that, all other things being equal, less pain and suffering is always better than more. Human life is valued in part to the degree that it is free of pain, suffering, misery, and frustration, and in particular that it is free of such experiences when they serve no purpose. If the death penalty is not a more effective deterrent than imprisonment, then its greater severity than imprisonment is gratuitous, purposeless suffering and deprivation.

A COST/BENEFIT ANALYSIS OF THE DEATH PENALTY

A full study of the costs and benefits involved in the practice of capital punishment would not be confined solely to the question of whether it is a better deterrent or preventive of murder than imprisonment. Any thoroughgoing utilitarian approach to the death-penalty controversy would need to examine carefully other costs and benefits as well, because maximizing the balance of social benefits over social costs is the sole criterion of right and wrong according to utilitarianism. Let us consider, therefore, some of the other costs and benefits to be calculated. Clinical psychologists have presented evidence to suggest that the death penalty actually incites some persons of unstable mind to murder others, either because they are afraid to take their own lives and hope that society will punish them for murder by putting them to death, or because they fancy that they, too, are killing with justification, analogous to the justified killing involved in capital punishment. If such evidence is sound, capital punishment can serve as a counterpreventive or an incitement to murder, and these incited murders become part of its social cost. Imprisonment, however, has not been known to incite any murders or other crimes of violence in a comparable fashion. (A possible exception might be found in the imprisonment of terrorists, which has inspired other terrorists to take hostages as part of a scheme to force the authorities to release their imprisoned comrades.) The risks of executing the innocent are also part of

the social cost. The historical record is replete with innocent persons indicted, convicted, sentenced, and occasionally legally executed for crimes they did not commit, not to mention the guilty persons unfairly convicted, sentenced to death, and executed on the strength of perjured testimony, fraudulent evidence, subornation of jurors, and other violations of the civil rights and liberties of the accused. Nor is this all. The high costs of a capital trial, of the inevitable appeals, the costly methods of custody most prisons adopt for convicts on "death row," are among the straightforward economic costs that the death penalty incurs. No scientifically valid cost/benefit analysis of capital punishment has ever been conducted, and it is impossible to predict exactly what such a study would show. Nevertheless, based on such evidence as we do have, it is quite possible that a study of this sort would favor abolition of all death penalties rather than their retention.

WHAT IF EXECUTIONS DID DETER?

From the moral point of view, it is quite important to determine what one should think about capital punishment if the evidence clearly showed that the death penalty is a distinctly superior method of social defense by comparison with less severe alternatives. Kantian moralists, as we have seen, would have no use for such knowledge, because their entire case for the morality of the death penalty rests on the way it is thought to provide just retribution, not on the way it is thought to provide social defense. For a utilitarian, however, such knowledge would be conclusive. Those who follow Locke's reasoning would also be gratified, because they defend the morality of the death penalty both on the ground that it is retributively just and on the ground that it provides needed social defense.

What about the opponents of the death penalty, however? To oppose the death penalty in the face of incontestable evidence that it is an effective method of social defense seems to violate the moral principle that where grave risks are to be run, it is better that they be run by the guilty than by the innocent. Consider in this connection an imaginary world in which by executing a murderer the victim is invariably restored to life, whole and intact, as though the murder had never occurred. In such a miraculous world, it is hard to see how anyone could oppose the death penalty on moral grounds. Why shouldn't a murderer die if that will infallibly bring the victim back to life? What could possibly be morally wrong with taking the murderer's life under such conditions? It would turn the death penalty into an instrument of perfect restitution, and it would give a new and better meaning to *lex talionis,* "a life for a life." The whole idea is fanciful, of course, but it shows better than anything else how opposition to the death penalty cannot be both moral and wholly unconditional. If opposition to the death penalty is to be morally responsible, then it must be conceded that there are conditions (however unlikely) under which that opposition should cease.

But even if the death penalty were known to be a uniquely effective social defense, we could still imagine conditions under which it would be reasonable to oppose it. Suppose that in addition to being a slightly better preventive and deterrent than imprisonment, executions also have a slight incitive effect (so that for every ten murders an execution prevents or deters, it also incites another murder). Suppose also that the administration of criminal justice in capital cases is inefficient, unequal, and tends to secure convictions of murderers who least "deserve" to be sentenced to death (including some death sentences and a few executions of the innocent). Under such conditions, it would still be reasonable to oppose the death penalty, because on the facts supposed more (or not fewer) innocent lives are being threatened and lost by using the death penalty than would be risked by abolishing it. It is important to remember throughout our evaluation of the deterrence controversy that we cannot ever apply the principle that advises us to risk the lives of the guilty in order to save the lives of the innocent. Instead, the most we can do is weigh the risk for the general public against the execution of those who are *found* guilty by an imperfect sys-

tem of criminal justice. These hypothetical factual assumptions illustrate the contingencies upon which the morality of opposition to the death penalty rests. And not only the morality of opposition; the morality of any defense of the death penalty rests on the same contingencies. This should help us understand why, in resolving the morality of capital punishment one way or the other, it is so important to know, as well as we can, whether the death penalty really does deter, prevent, or incite crime, whether the innocent really are ever executed, and whether any of these things are likely to occur in the future.

HOW MANY GUILTY LIVES IS ONE INNOCENT LIFE WORTH?

The great unanswered question that utilitarians must face concerns the level of social defense that executions should be expected to achieve before it is justifiable to carry them out. Consider three possible situations: (1) At the level of a hundred executions per year, each additional execution of a convicted murderer reduces the number of murder victims by ten. (2) Executing every convicted murderer reduces the number of murders to 5,000 victims annually, whereas executing only one out of ten reduces the number to 5,001. (3) Executing every convicted murderer reduces the murder rate no more than does executing one in a hundred and no more than a random pattern of executions does.

Many people contemplating situation (1) would regard this as a reasonable trade-off: The execution of each further guilty person saves the lives of ten innocent ones. (In fact, situation (1) or something like it may be taken as a description of what most of those who defend the death penalty on grounds of social defense believe is true.) But suppose that, instead of saving 10 lives, the number dropped to 0.5, i.e., one victim avoided for each two additional executions. Would that be a reasonable price to pay? We are on the road toward the situation described in situation (2), where a drastic 90 percent reduction in the number of persons executed causes the level of social defense to drop by only 0.0002 percent. Would it be worth it to execute so many more murderers at the cost of such a slight decrease in social defense? How many guilty lives is one innocent life worth? In situation (3), of course, there is no basis for executing all convicted murderers, since there is no gain in social defense to show for each additional murderer executed after the first out of each hundred murderers has been executed. How, then, should we determine which out of each hundred convicted murderers is the unlucky one to be put to death?

It may be possible, under a complete and thoroughgoing cost/benefit analysis of the death penalty, to answer such questions. But an appeal merely to the moral principle that if lives are to be risked then let it be the lives of the guilty rather than the lives of the innocent will not suffice. . . . Nor will it suffice to agree that society deserves all the crime prevention and deterrence it can get by inflicting severe punishments. These principles are consistent with too many different policies. They are too vague by themselves to resolve the choice on grounds of social defense when confronted with hypothetical situations like those proposed above.

Since no adequate cost/benefit analysis of the death penalty exists, there is no way to resolve these questions from this standpoint at the present time. Moreover, it can be argued that we cannot have such an analysis without already establishing in some way or other the relative value of innocent lives versus guilty lives. Far from being a product of a cost/benefit analysis, this comparative evaluation of lives would have to be brought into any such analysis. Without it, no cost/benefit analysis can get off the ground. Finally, it must be noted that we have no knowledge at present that begins to approximate anything like the situation described above in (1), whereas it appears from the evidence we do have that we achieve about the same deterrent and preventive effects whether we punish murder by death or by imprisonment. Therefore, something like the situation in (2) or in (3) may be correct. If so, this shows that the choice between the two policies of capital punishment and life imprisonment for murder will probably have to be made on some basis other than social defense; on that basis the two policies are equivalent and therefore equally acceptable.

CAPITAL PUNISHMENT AND RETRIBUTIVE JUSTICE

. . . There are two leading principles of retributive justice relevant to the capital-punishment controversy. One is the principle that crimes should be punished. The other is the principle that the severity of a punishment should be proportional to the gravity of the offense. (A corollary to the latter principle is the judgment that nothing so fits the crime of murder as the punishment of death.) Although these principles do not seem to stem from any concern over the worth, value, dignity, or rights of persons, they are moral principles of recognized weight and no discussion of the morality of capital punishment would be complete without them. Leaving aside all questions of social defense, how strong a case for capital punishment can be made on the basis of these principles? How reliable and persuasive are these principles themselves?

CRIME MUST BE PUNISHED

Given [a general rationale for punishment], there cannot be any dispute over this principle. In embracing it, of course, we are not automatically making a fetish of "law and order," in the sense that we would be if we thought that the most important single thing society can do with its resources is to punish crimes. In addition, this principle is not likely to be in dispute between proponents and opponents of the death penalty. Only those who completely oppose punishment for murder and other erstwhile capital crimes would appear to disregard this principle. Even defenders of the death penalty must admit that putting a convicted murderer in prison for years is a punishment of that criminal. The principle that crime must be punished is neutral to our controversy, because both sides acknowledge it and comply with it.

It is the other principle of retributive justice that seems to be a decisive one. Under the principle of retaliation, *lex talionis*, it must always have seemed that murderers ought to be put to death. Proponents of the death penalty, with rare exceptions, have insisted on this point, and it seems that even opponents of the death penalty must give it grudging assent. The strategy for opponents of the death penalty is to show either (a) that this principle is not really a principle of justice after all, or (b) that although it is, other principles outweigh or cancel its dictates. As we shall see, both these objections have merit.

IS MURDER ALONE TO BE PUNISHED BY DEATH?

Let us recall, first, that not even the Biblical world limited the death penalty to the punishment of murder. Many other nonhomicidal crimes also carried this penalty (e.g., kidnapping, witchcraft, cursing one's parents). In our own recent history, persons have been executed for aggravated assault, rape, kidnapping, armed robbery, sabotage, and espionage. It is not possible to defend any of these executions (not to mention some of the more bizarre capital statutes, like the one in Georgia that used to provide an optional death penalty for desecration of a grave) on grounds of just retribution. This entails that either such executions are not justified or that they are justified on some ground other than retribution. In actual practice, few if any defenders of the death penalty have ever been willing to rest their case entirely on the moral principle of just retribution as formulated in terms of "a life for a life." Kant seems to have been a conspicuous exception. Most defenders of the death penalty have implied by their willingness to use executions to defend limb and property, as well as life, that they did not place much value on the lives of criminals when compared to the value of both lives and things belonging to innocent citizens.

ARE ALL MURDERS TO BE PUNISHED BY DEATH?

Our society for several centuries has endeavored to confine the death penalty to some criminal homicides. Even Kant took a casual attitude toward a mother's killing of her illegitimate child. ("A child born into the world outside marriage is outside the law . . . , and consequently it is also outside the protection of the law.")[1] In our society, the development nearly 200 years ago of the distinction between first- and second-degree murder was an attempt to narrow the class of criminal homicides deserving of the death penalty. Yet those dead owing to manslaughter, or to any kind of unintentional, accidental, unpremeditated, unavoidable, unmalicious killing are just as dead as the victims of the most ghastly murder. Both the law in practice and moral reflection show how difficult it is to identify all and only the criminal homicides that are appropriately punished by death (assuming that any are). Individual judges and juries differ in the conclusions they reach. The history of capital punishment for homicides reveals continual efforts, uniformly unsuccessful, to identify before the fact those homicides for which the slayer should die. Benjamin Cardozo, a justice of the United States Supreme Court fifty years ago, said of the distinction between degrees of murder that it was

> . . . so obscure that no jury hearing it for the first time can fairly be expected to assimilate and understand it. I am not at all sure that I understand it myself after trying to apply it for many years and after diligent study of what has been written in the books. Upon the basis of this fine distinction with its obscure and mystifying psychology, scores of men have gone to their death.[2]

Similar skepticism has been registered on the reliability and rationality of death-penalty statutes that give the trial court the discretion to sentence to prison or to death. As Justice John Marshall Harlan of the Supreme Court observed a decade ago,

> Those who have come to grips with the hard task of actually attempting to draft means of

channeling capital sentencing discretion have confirmed the lesson taught by history. . . . To identify before the fact those characteristics of criminal homicide and their perpetrators which call for the death penalty, and to express these characteristics in language which can be fairly understood and applied by the sentencing authority, appear to be tasks which are beyond present human ability.[3]

The abstract principle that the punishment of death best fits the crime of murder turns out to be extremely difficult to interpret and apply.

If we look at the matter from the standpoint of the actual practice of criminal justice, we can only conclude that "a life for a life" plays little or no role whatever. Plea bargaining (by means of which one of the persons involved in a crime agrees to accept a lesser sentence in exchange for testifying against the others to enable the prosecutor to get them all convicted), even where murder is concerned, is widespread. Studies of criminal justice reveal that what the courts (trial or appellate) decide on a given day is first-degree murder suitably punished by death in a given jurisdiction could just as well be decided in a neighboring jurisdiction on another day either as second-degree murder or as first-degree murder but without the death penalty. The factors that influence prosecutors in determining the charge under which they will prosecute go far beyond the simple principle of "a life for a life." Nor can it be objected that these facts show that our society does not care about justice. To put it succinctly, either justice in punishment does not consist of retribution, because there are other principles of justice; or there are other moral considerations besides justice that must be honored; or retributive justice is not adequately expressed in the idea of "a life for a life."

IS DEATH SUFFICIENTLY RETRIBUTIVE?

Given the reality of horrible and vicious crimes, one must consider whether there is not a quality of unthinking arbitrariness in advocating capital punishment for murder as the retributively just punishment. Why does death in the electric chair or the gas chamber or before a firing squad or on a gallows meet the requirements of retributive justice? When one thinks of the savage, brutal, wanton character of so many murders, how can retributive justice be served by anything less than equally savage methods of execution for the murderer? From a retributive point of view, the oft-heard exclamation, "Death is too good for him!" has a certain truth. Yet few defenders of the death penalty are willing to embrace this consequence of their own doctrine.

The reason they do not and should not is that, if they did, they would be stooping to the methods and thus to the squalor of the murderer. Where criminals set the limits of just methods of punishment, as they will do if we attempt to give exact and literal implementation to *lex talionis,* society will find itself descending to the cruelties and savagery that criminals employ. But society would be deliberately authorizing such acts, in the cool light of reason, and not (as is often true of vicious criminals) impulsively or in hatred and anger or with an insane or unbalanced mind. Moral restraints, in short, prohibit us from trying to make executions perfectly retributive. Once we grant the role of these restraints, the principle of "a life for a life" itself has been qualified and no longer suffices to justify the execution of murderers.

Other considerations take us in a different direction. Few murders, outside television and movie scripts, involve anything like an execution. An execution, after all, begins with a solemn pronouncement of the death sentence from a judge, is followed by long detention in maximum security awaiting the date of execution, various appeals, perhaps a final sanity hearing, and then "the last mile" to the execution chamber itself. As the French writer Albert Camus remarked,

> For there to be an equivalence, the death penalty would have to punish a criminal who had warned his victim of the date at which he would inflict a horrible death on him and who, from that moment onward, had confined him at his mercy for months. Such a monster is not encountered in private life.[4]

DIFFERENTIAL SEVERITY DOES NOT REQUIRE EXECUTIONS

What, then, emerges from our examination of retributive justice and the death penalty? If retributive justice is thought to consist in *lex talionis,* all one can say is that this principle has never exercised more than a crude and indirect effect on the actual punishments meted out. Other principles interfere with a literal and single-minded application of this one. Some murders seem improperly punished by death at all; other murders would require methods of execution too horrible to inflict; in still other cases any possible execution is too deliberate and monstrous given the nature of the motivation culminating in the murder. Proponents of the death penalty rarely confine themselves to reliance on this principle of just retribution and nothing else, since they rarely confine themselves to supporting the death penalty only for all murders.

But retributive justice need not be thought to consist of *lex talionis.* One may reject that principle as too crude and still embrace the retributive principle that the severity of punishments should be graded according to the gravity of the offense. Even though one need not claim that life imprisonment (or any kind of punishment other than death) "fits" the crime of murder, one can claim that this punishment is the proper one for murder. To do this, the schedule of punishments accepted by society must be arranged so that this mode of imprisonment is the most severe penalty used. Opponents of the death penalty need not reject this principle of retributive justice, even though they must reject a literal *lex talionis.*

EQUAL JUSTICE AND CAPITAL PUNISHMENT

During the past generation, the strongest practical objection to the death penalty has been the inequities with which it has been applied. As Supreme Court Justice William O. Douglas once observed, "One searches our chronicles in vain for the execution of any member of the affluent strata of this society."[5] One does not search our chronicles in vain for the crime of murder committed by the affluent. Every study of the death penalty for rape has confirmed that black male rapists (especially where the victim is a white female) are far more likely to be sentenced to death (and executed) than white male rapists. Half of all those under death sentence during 1976 and 1977 were black, and nearly half of all those executed since 1930 were black. All the sociological evidence points to the conclusion that the death penalty is the poor man's justice; as the current street saying has it, "Those without the capital get the punishment."

Let us suppose that the factual basis for such a criticism is sound. What follows for the morality of capital punishment? Many defenders of the death penalty have been quick to point out that since there is nothing intrinsic about the crime of murder or rape that dictates that only the poor or racial-minority males will commit it, and since there is nothing overtly racist about the statutes that authorize the death penalty for murder or rape, it is hardly a fault in the idea of capital punishment if in practice it falls with unfair impact on the poor and the black. There is, in short, nothing in the death penalty that requires it to be applied unfairly and with arbitrary or discriminatory results. It is at worst a fault in the system of administering criminal justice (and some, who dispute the facts cited above, would deny even this).

Presumably, both proponents and opponents of capital punishment would concede that it is a fundamental dictate of justice that a punishment should not be unfairly— inequitably or unevenly—enforced and applied. They should also be able to agree that when the punishment in question is the extremely severe one of death, then the requirement to be fair in using such a punishment becomes even more stringent. Thus, there should be no dispute in the death penalty controversy over these principles of justice. The dispute begins as soon as one attempts to connect these principles with the actual use of this punishment.

In this country, many critics of the death penalty have argued, we would long ago have got rid of it entirely if it had been a condition of its use that it be applied equally and fairly. In the words of the attorneys who argued against the death penalty in the Supreme Court during 1972, "It is a freakish aberration, a random extreme act of violence, visibly arbitrary and discriminatory—a penalty reserved for unusual application because, if it were usually used, it would affront universally shared standards of public decency."[6] It is difficult to dispute this judgment, when one considers that there have been in the United States during the past fifty years about half a million criminal homicides but only about 4,000 executions (all but 50 of which were of men).

We can look at these statistics in another way to illustrate the same point. If we could be assured that the 4,000 persons executed were the worst of the worst, repeated offenders without exception, the most dangerous murderers in captivity—the ones who had killed more than once and were likely to kill again, and the least likely to be confined in prison without imminent danger to other inmates and the staff—then one might accept half a million murders and a few thousand executions with a sense that rough justice had been done. But the truth is otherwise. Persons are sentenced to death and executed not because they have been found to be uncontrollably violent, hopelessly poor parole and release risks, or for other reasons. Instead, they are executed for entirely different reasons. They have a poor defense at trial; they have no funds to bring sympathetic witnesses to court; they are immigrants or strangers in the community where they were tried; the prosecuting attorney wants the publicity that goes with "sending a killer to the chair"; they have inexperienced or overworked counsel at trial; there are no funds for an appeal or for a transcript of the trial record; they are members of a despised racial minority. In short, the actual study of why particular persons have been sentenced to death and executed does not show any careful winnowing of the worst from the bad. It shows that the executed were usually the unlucky victims of prejudice and discrimination, the losers in an arbitrary lottery that could just as well have spared them as killed them, the victims of the disadvantages that almost always go with poverty. A system like this does not enhance respect for human life; it cheapens and degrades it. However heinous murder and other crimes are, the system of capital punishment does not compensate for or erase those crimes. It only tends to add new injuries of its own to the catalogue of our inhumanity to each other.

NOTES

1. Immanuel Kant, *The Metaphysical Elements of Justice* (1797), tr. John Ladd, p. 106.

2. Benjamin Cardozo, "What Medicine Can Do for Law" (1928), reprinted in Margaret E. Hall, ed., *Selected Writings of Benjamin Nathan Cardozo* (1947), p. 204.

3. *McGautha v. California*, 402 U.S. 183 (1971), at p. 204.

4. Albert Camus, *Resistance, Rebellion, and Death* (1961), p. 199.

5. *Furman v. Georgia*, 408 U.S. 238 (1972), at pp. 251–252.

6. NAACP Legal Defense and Educational Fund, Brief for Petitioner in *Aikens v. California*, O.T. 1971, No. 68–5027, reprinted in Philip English Mackey, ed., *Voices Against Death: American Opposition to Capital Punishment*, 1787–1975 (1975), p. 288.

For Further Reflection

1. Is the death penalty "cruel and unusual punishment," thus meriting prohibition under the Eighth Amendment?

2. Do you agree with Bedau that the death penalty "only tends to add new injuries of its own to the catalogue of our inhumanity to each other"?

3. Do you think that long-term imprisonment is an adequate punishment for first-degree murder? Some people think that long-term imprisonment is worse punishment than execution. Do you agree? Explain.

IX.C   Do Animals Have Rights?

Every minute of the day, 24 hours a day, 100 animals are killed in laboratories in the United States. Fifty million animals used in experiments are put to death each year. Some die during testing of industrial and cosmetic products, some are killed after being force fed or after being tested for pharmaceutical drugs. Product testing on animals is required by government before the products are allowed for use by human beings.

Legal requirements that animals be anesthetized are circumvented in many experiments. Recently, at a major university, baboons were strapped down in boxlike vises and had specially designed helmets cemented to their skulls. Then a pneumatic device delivered calibrated blows to the helmet to determine its strength. The blows continued until the baboon's skull was fractured and the animal was brain damaged. Dogs are driven insane with electric shocks so that scientists can study the effects of insanity. Cats are deprived of sleep until they die. Primates have been restrained for months in steel chairs allowing no movement, and elephants have been given LSD to study aggression. Legs have been cut off mice to study how they walk on the stumps, and polar bears have been drowned in vats of crude oil to study the effect of oil spills in polar regions.

Kittens have been blinded, castrated, and rendered deaf so researchers could see what effect these incapacities would have on their sexual development. Civet cats are placed in small cages in dark rooms where the temperature is 110° F and confined there until they die. The musk that is scraped from their genitals once a day for as long as they can survive makes the scent of perfume last a bit longer after each application.

Neither is all well down on the farm. Factory farming with high-tech machinery has replaced free-range agriculture. Farmer McDonald doesn't visit his hens in barns to pick an egg from the comfortable nest. Now, as soon as chicks are hatched, they are placed in small cages. Between five and nine chickens are pressed together in cages about 18 inches by 10 inches where they cannot move around, with thin wire-mesh floors that hurt their feet. They are painfully debeaked so that they cannot attack each other in these unnatural quarters. In other chicken factories, the chickens are hung by their feet from conveyer belts that transport them through automatic throat-slicing machines. Three billion chickens are killed in the United States each year. Likewise, pigs and veal calves are kept in pens so small they cannot move or turn around and develop muscles. They are separated from their mothers so they cannot be suckled and are fed a diet low in iron so they will produce very tender meat.

Do animals have rights? Given the practices just described, do we have a responsibility to improve our behavior toward the animal kingdom? No one disagrees that we should not cause animals *unnecessary* suffering, but those who defend animal factories and animal experimentation argue that human need justifies these practices. On the other side of the controversy, animal rights advocates argue that animals should be accorded equal consideration with humans—that their specific needs should be taken seriously. If this were done, we would become vegetarians, cease to use leather, and cease all (or almost all) animal experimentation.

In our first reading, Peter Singer, the torchbearer of animal liberation, argues that animals should be treated with equal consideration as human beings. Singer says that if a nonhuman and a human are suffering, and we have only enough painkiller for one, it is not clear who should get the painkiller.

Carl Cohen argues in our second reading that the idea of rights does not apply to animals since "rights" is a concept appropriate only to members of the moral community and animals cannot make moral decisions. Humans are of far greater value than animals. Cohen readily admits that gratuitous suffering should be prohibited, but animal experimentation is needed to ameliorate human suffering, and, as such, it is justified.

IX.86   The Case for Animal Liberation

PETER SINGER

Peter Singer is a member of the philosophy department at Princeton University. His book, *Animal Liberation* (1975), from which this selection is taken, is one of the most influential books ever written on the subject and inaugurated the contemporary animal rights movement. Singer argues that animal liberation today is analogous to racial and gender justice. Just as people once thought it incredible that women should be treated as equal to men, or blacks as equal to whites, so now "speciesists" mock the idea that all animals should be given equal consideration. Singer defines "speciesism" as the prejudice (unjustified bias) that favors one's own species over every other. That which equalizes all sentient beings is our ability to suffer. In that, we and animals are equal and deserve equal respect.

Study Questions

1. What is the relationship between the women's rights movement, the civil rights movement, and the animal rights movement?
2. How does Singer define "speciesism"?
3. What is the basis of equality in humans and nonhumans?
4. Does equal consideration mean that we should treat animals exactly as we treat humans?
5. What changes would have to be made in our behavior if we took animal rights seriously?

THIS [VIEWPOINT] IS about the tyranny of human over nonhuman animals. This tyranny has caused and today is still causing an amount of pain and suffering that can only be compared with that which resulted from the centuries of tyranny by white humans over black humans. The struggle against this tyranny is a struggle as important as any of the moral and social issues that have been fought over in recent years.

Most readers will take what they have just read to be a wild exaggeration. Five years ago I myself would have laughed at the statements I have now written in complete seriousness. Five years ago I did not know what I know today. . . .

Reprinted by permission of the author from Animal Liberation *(New York Review of Books, 1975).*

CHANGING PREJUDICIAL ATTITUDES

A liberation movement demands an expansion of our moral horizons. Practices that were previously regarded as natural and inevitable come to be seen as the result of an unjustifiable prejudice. Who can say with any confidence that none of his or her attitudes and practices can legitimately be questioned? If we wish to avoid being numbered among the oppressors, we must be prepared to rethink all our attitudes to other groups, including the most fundamental. . . .

I believe that our present attitudes are based on a long history of prejudice and arbitrary discrimination. I argue that there can be no reason—except the selfish desire to preserve the privileges of the exploiting group—for refusing to extend the basic principle of equality of consideration to members of other species. I ask you to recognize that your attitudes to members of other species are a form of prejudice no less objectionable than prejudice about a person's race or sex. . . .

"Animal Liberation" may sound more like a parody of other liberation movements than a serious objective. The idea of "The Rights of Animals" actually was once used to parody the case for women's rights. When Mary Wollstonecraft, a forerunner of today's feminists, published her *Vindication of the Rights of Women* in 1792, her views were widely regarded as absurd, and before long an anonymous publication appeared entitled *A Vindication of the Rights of Brutes*. The author of this satirical work (now known to have been Thomas Taylor, a distinguished Cambridge philosopher) tried to refute Mary Wollstonecraft's arguments by showing that they could be carried one stage further. If the argument for equality was sound when applied to women, why should it not be applied to dogs, cats, and horses? The reasoning seemed to hold for these "brutes" too; yet to hold that brutes had rights was manifestly absurd; therefore the reasoning by which this conclusion had been reached must be unsound, and if unsound when applied to brutes, it must also be

unsound when applied to women, since the very same arguments had been used in each case. . . .

One way in which we might reply is by saying that the case for equality between men and women cannot validly be extended to nonhuman animals. Women have a right to vote, for instance, because they are just as capable of making rational decisions about the future as men are; dogs, on the other hand, are incapable of understanding the significance of voting, so they cannot have the right to vote. There are many other obvious ways in which men and women resemble each other closely, while humans and animals differ greatly. So, it might be said, men and women are similar beings and should have similar rights, while humans and nonhumans are different and should not have equal rights.

EQUAL CONSIDERATION OF RIGHTS

The reasoning behind this reply to Taylor's analogy is correct up to a point, but it does not go far enough. There *are* important differences between humans and other animals, and these differences must give rise to *some* differences in the rights that each has. Recognizing this obvious fact, however, is no barrier to the case for extending the basic principle of equality to nonhuman animals. The differences that exist between men and women are equally undeniable, and the supporters of Women's Liberation are aware that these differences may give rise to different rights. Many feminists hold that women have the right to an abortion on request. It does not follow that since these same feminists are campaigning for equality between men and women they must support the right of men to have abortions too. Since a man cannot have an abortion, it is meaningless to talk of his right to have one. Since a dog can't vote, it is meaningless to talk of its right to vote. There is no reason why either Women's Liberation or Animal Liberation should get involved in such nonsense. The extension of the basic principle of equality from one group to another does not imply that we must treat both groups in exactly the same way, or grant exactly the same rights to both groups. Whether we should do so will depend on the nature of the members of the two groups. The basic principle of equality does not require equal or identical *treatment;* it requires equal *consideration.* Equal consideration for different beings may lead to different treatment and different rights. . . .

THE BASIS OF EQUALITY

Although, it may be said, humans differ as individuals there are no differences between the races and sexes *as such.* From the mere fact that a person is black or a woman we cannot infer anything about that person's intellectual or moral capacities. This, it may be said, is why racism and sexism are wrong. The white racist claims that whites are superior to blacks, but this is false—although there are differences among individuals, some blacks are superior to some whites in all of the capacities and abilities that could conceivably be relevant. The opponent of sexism would say the same: a person's sex is no guide to his or her abilities, and this is why it is unjustifiable to discriminate on the basis of sex. . . .

It is an implication of this principle of equality that our concern for others and our readiness to consider their interests ought not to depend on what they are like or on what abilities they may possess. Precisely what this concern or consideration requires us to do may vary according to the characteristics of those affected by what we do: concern for the well-being of a child growing up in America would require that we teach him to read; concern for the well-being of a pig may require no more than that we leave him alone with other pigs in a place where there is adequate food and room to run freely. But the basic element—the taking into account of the interests of the being, whatever those interests may be—must, according to the principle of equality, be extended to all beings, black or white, masculine or feminine, human or nonhuman. . . .

When in the 1850s the call for women's rights was raised in the United States, a remarkable black feminist named Sojourner Truth [spoke] . . . at a feminist convention:

> They talk about this thing in the head; what do they call it? ["Intellect," whispered someone near by.] That's it. What's that got to do with women's rights or Negroes' rights? If my cup won't hold but a pint and yours holds a quart, wouldn't you be mean not to let me have my little half-measure full?

It is in accordance with this principle that the attitude that we may call "speciesism," by analogy with racism, must also be condemned. Speciesism—the word is not an attractive one, but I can think of no better term—is a prejudice or attitude of bias toward the interest of members of one's own species and against those members of other species. . . .

Many philosophers and other writers have proposed the principle of equal consideration of interests, in some form or other, as a basic moral principle; but not many of them have recognized that this principle applies to members of other species as well as to our own. Jeremy Bentham was one of the few who did realize this. In a forward-looking passage written at a time when black slaves had been freed by the French but in the British minions were still being treated in the way we now treat animals, Bentham wrote:

> The day *may* come when the rest of the animal creation may acquire those rights which never could have been withholden from them but by the hand of tyranny. The French have already discovered that the blackness of the skin is no reason why a human being should be abandoned without redress to the caprice of a tormentor. It may one day come to be recognized that the number of the legs, the villosity of the skin, or the termination of the *os sacrum* are reasons equally insufficient for abandoning a sensitive being to the same fate. What else is it that should trace the insuperable line? Is it the faculty of reason, or perhaps the faculty of discourse? But a full-grown horse or dog is beyond comparison a more rational, as well as a

more conversable animal, than an infant of a day or week or even a month, old. But suppose they were otherwise, what would it avail. The question is not, Can they *reason?* nor Can they *talk?* but, *Can they suffer?*

In this passage Bentham points to the capacity for suffering as the vital characteristic that gives a being the right to equal consideration. The capacity for suffering—or more strictly, for suffering and/or enjoyment or happiness—is not just another characteristic like the capacity for language or higher mathematics. Bentham is not saying that those who try to mark "the insuperable line" that determines whether the interests of a being should be considered happen to have chosen the wrong characteristic. By saying that we must consider the interests of all beings with the capacity for suffering or enjoyment Bentham does not arbitrarily exclude from consideration any interests at all—as those who draw the line with reference to the possession of reason or language do. The capacity for suffering and enjoyment is *a prerequisite for having interests at all,* a condition that must be satisfied before we can speak of interests in a meaningful way. It would be nonsense to say that it was not in the interests of a stone to be kicked along the road by a schoolboy. A stone does not have interests because it cannot suffer. Nothing that we can do to it could possibly make any difference to its welfare. A mouse, on the other hand, does have an interest in not being kicked along the road, because it will suffer if it is.

NO EXCUSE FOR IGNORING SUFFERING

If a being suffers there can be no moral justification for refusing to take that suffering into consideration. No matter what the nature of the being, the principle of equality requires that its suffering be counted equally with the like suffering—in so far as rough comparisons can be made—of any other being. If a being is not capable of suffering, or of experiencing enjoyment or happiness, there is nothing to be taken into account. So the limit of sentience (using the term as a convenient if not strictly accurate shorthand for the capacity to suffer and/or experience enjoyment) is the only defensible boundary of concern for the interests of others. To mark this boundary by some other characteristic like intelligence or rationality would be to mark it in an arbitrary manner. Why not choose some other characteristic, like skin color?

The racist violates the principle of equality by giving greater weight to the interests of members of his own race when there is a clash between their interests and the interests of those of another race. The sexist violates the principle of equality by favoring the interests of his own sex. Similarly the speciesist allows the interests of his own species to override the greater interests of members of other species. The pattern is identical in each case.

For Further Reflection

1. Has Singer convinced you that animals have rights equal to humans not to suffer needlessly? If Singer is correct, how should we change our social practices?

2. What are the broader implications of Singer's proposal? How far should we go with equal treatment of all animals? Should we kill bacteria or call the exterminator when termites are making a meal of our house? Does his theory lead to a reverence for all life in the manner of Albert Schweitzer?

Albert Schweitzer (1875–1965), the missionary doctor and Nobel Peace Prize winner, combined a Christian and animist view in advocating what he called "Reverence for Life."

I am life which wills to live, and I exist in the midst of life which wills to live. . . . A living world—and life view, informing all the facts of life, gushes forth from it continually, as from an eternal spring. A mystically ethical oneness with existence grows forth from it unceasingly. . . . Ethics thus consists in this, that I experience the necessity of practising the same reverence for life toward all will-to-live, as toward my own. Therein I have already the needed fundamental principle of morality. It is *good* to maintain and cherish life; it is evil to destroy and to check life. A man is really ethical only when he obeys the constraint laid on him to help all life which he is able to succour, and when he goes out of his way to avoid injuring anything living. He does not ask how far this or that life deserves sympathy as valuable in itself, nor how far it is capable of feeling. To him life as such is sacred. . . . He tears no leaf from its tree, breaks off no flower, and is careful not to crush any insect as he walks. If he works by lamplight on a summer evening, he prefers to keep the window shut and to breathe stifling air, rather than to see insect after insect fall on his table with singed and sinking wings.

If he goes out into the street after a rainstorm and sees a worm which has strayed there, he reflects that it will certainly dry up in the sunshine, if it does not quickly regain the damp soil into which it can creep, and so he helps it back from the deadly paving stones into the lush grass. Should he pass by an insect which has fallen into a pool, he spares the time to reach it a leaf or stalk on which it may clamber and save itself.

Ethics is, in its unqualified form, extended responsibility with regard to everything that has life.

How do you react to this passage? Is it consistent with Singer's idea of liberation? If the ideas are not exactly the same, where do they differ? What do you think of the reverence for life principle?

IX.87   The Case Against Animal Rights

CARL COHEN

Carl Cohen is a professor of philosophy at the University of Michigan. Cohen argues that while humans have a duty to treat animals humanely, animals cannot have rights. The idea of rights does not apply to animals since "rights" is a concept appropriate only to members of the moral community and animals cannot make moral decisions. Humans are of far greater value than animals, and the result of not using animals for medical experimentation would be greater human suffering.

Study Questions

1. Why don't animals have rights? What does one need to have in order to have moral rights?
2. What are some philosophical views on the attributes necessary for moral capability?
3. What does Kant say that makes humans members of the moral community?
4. Why does Cohen defend speciesism?
5. What are the "absurd consequences" of the animal rights position?

USING ANIMALS AS RESEARCH subjects in medical investigations is widely condemned on two grounds: first, because it wrongly violates the *rights* of animals, and second, because it wrongly imposes on sentient creatures much avoidable *suffering*. Neither of these arguments is sound. The first relies on a mistaken understanding of rights; the second relies on a mistaken calculation of consequences. Both deserve definitive dismissal.

WHY ANIMALS HAVE NO RIGHTS

A right, properly understood, is a claim, or potential claim, that one party may exercise against another. The target against whom such a claim may be registered can be a single person, a group, a community, or (perhaps) all humankind. The content of rights claims also varies greatly: repayment of loans, nondiscrimination by employers, noninterference by the state, and so on. To comprehend any genuine right fully, therefore, we must know *who* holds the right, *against whom* it is held, and *to what* it is a right.

Alternative sources of rights add complexity. Some rights are grounded in constitution and law (e.g., the right of an accused to trial by jury); some rights are moral but give no legal claims (e.g., my right to your keeping the promise you gave me); and some rights (e.g., against theft or assault) are rooted both in morals and in law.

The differing targets, contents, and sources of rights, and their inevitable conflict, together weave a tangled web. Notwithstanding all such complications, this much is clear about rights in general: they are in every case claims, or potential claims, within a community of moral agents. Rights arise, and can be intelligibly defended, only among beings who actually do, or can, make moral claims against one another. Whatever else rights may be, therefore, they are necessarily human; their possessors are persons, human beings.

The attributes of human beings from which this moral capability arises have been described variously by philosophers, both ancient and modern: the inner consciousness of a free will (Saint Augustine); the grasp, by human reason, of the binding character of moral law (Saint Thomas Aquinas); the self-conscious participation of human beings in an objective ethical order (G. W. F. Hegel); human membership in an organic moral community (F. H. Bradley); the development of the human self through the consciousness of other moral selves (G. H. Mead); and the underivative, intuitive cognition of the rightness of an action (H. A. Prichard). Most influential has been Immanuel Kant's emphasis on the universal human possession of a uniquely moral will and the autonomy its use entails. Humans confront choices that are purely moral; humans—but certainly not dogs or mice—lay down moral laws, for others and for themselves. Human beings are self-legislative, morally *autonomous*.

Animals (that is, nonhuman animals, the ordinary sense of that word) lack this capacity for free moral judgment. They are not beings of a kind capable of exercising or responding to moral claims. Animals therefore have no rights, and they can have none. This is the core of the argument about the alleged rights of animals. The holders of rights must have the capacity to comprehend rules of duty, governing all including themselves. In applying such rules, the holders of rights must recognize possible conflicts between what is in their own interest and what is just. Only in a community of beings capable of self-restricting moral judgments can the concept of a right be correctly invoked.

Reprinted from The New England Journal of Medicine *vol. 315, pp. 864–870, by permission of the editor.* © *1986 Massachusetts Medical Society. All rights reserved.*

Humans have such moral capacities. They are in this sense self-legislative, are members of communities governed by moral rules, and do possess rights. Animals do not have such moral capacities. They are not morally self-legislative, cannot possibly be members of a truly moral community, and therefore cannot possess rights. In conducting research on animal subjects, therefore, we do not violate their rights, because they have none to violate. . . .

Genuinely moral acts have an internal as well as an external dimension. Thus, in law, an act can be criminal only when the guilty deed, the *actus reus,* is done with a guilty mind, *mens rea.* No animal can ever commit a crime; bringing animals to criminal trial is the mark of primitive ignorance. The claims of moral rights are similarly inapplicable to them. Does a lion have a right to eat a baby zebra? Does a baby zebra have a right not to be eaten? Such questions, mistakenly invoking the concept of right where it does not belong, do not make good sense. Those who condemn biomedical research because it violates "animal rights" commit the same blunder.

IN DEFENSE OF SPECIESISM

Abandoning reliance on animal rights, some critics resort instead to animal sentience—their feelings of pain and distress. We ought to desist from the imposition of pain insofar as we can. Since all or nearly all experimentation on animals does impose pain and could be readily forgone, say these critics, it should be stopped. The ends sought may be worthy, but those ends do not justify imposing agonies on humans, and by animals the agonies are felt no less. The laboratory use of animals (these critics conclude) must therefore be ended—or at least very sharply curtailed.

Argument of this variety is essentially utilitarian, often expressly so; it is based on the calculation of the net product, in pains and pleasures, resulting from experiments on animals. Jeremy Bentham, comparing horses and dogs with other sentient creatures, is thus commonly quoted: "The question is not, Can they reason? nor Can they talk? but, Can they suffer?"

BIOMEDICAL RESEARCH MUST STILL PROCEED

Animals certainly can suffer and surely ought not to be made to suffer needlessly. But in inferring, from these uncontroversial premises, that biomedical research causing animal distress is largely (or wholly) wrong, the critic commits two serious errors. The first error is the assumption, often explicitly defended, that all sentient animals have equal moral standing. Between a dog and a human being, according to this view, there is no moral difference; hence the pains suffered by dogs must be weighed no differently from the pains suffered by humans. To deny such equality, according to this critic, is to give unjust preference to one species over another; it is "speciesism." The most influential statement of this moral equality of species was made by Peter Singer:

> The racist violates the principle of equality by giving greater weight to the interests of members of his own race when there is a clash between their interests and the interests of those of another race. The sexist violates the principle of equality by favoring the interests of his own sex. Similarly the speciesist allows the interests of his own species to override the greater interests of members of other species. The pattern is identical in each case.

This argument is worse than unsound; it is atrocious. It draws an offensive moral conclusion from a deliberately devised verbal parallelism that is utterly specious. Racism has no rational ground whatever. Differing degrees of respect or concern for humans for no other reason than that they are members of different races is an injustice totally without foundation in the nature of the races themselves. Racists, even if acting on the basis of mistaken factual beliefs, do grave moral wrong precisely because there is no morally relevant distinction among the races. The supposition of such differences has led to outright horror. The same is true of the sexes, neither sex being entitled by right to greater respect or concern than the other. No dispute here.

Between species of animate life, however—between (for example) humans on the one hand and cats or rats on the other—the morally relevant differences are enormous, and almost universally appreciated. Humans engage in moral reflection; humans are morally autonomous; humans are members of moral communities, recognizing just claims against their own interest. Human beings do have rights; theirs is a moral status very different from that of cats or rats.

SPECIESISM IS NECESSARY

I am a speciesist. Speciesism is not merely plausible; it is essential for right conduct, because those who will not make the morally relevant distinctions among species are almost certain, in consequence, to misapprehend their true obligations. The analogy between speciesism and racism is insidious. Every sensitive moral judgment requires that the differing natures of the beings to whom obligations are owed be considered. If all forms of animate life—or vertebrate animal life—must be treated equally, and if therefore in evaluating a research program the pains of a rodent count equally with the pains of a human, we are forced to conclude (1) that neither humans nor rodents possess rights, or (2) that rodents possess all the rights that humans possess. Both alternatives are absurd. Yet one or the other must be swallowed if the moral equality of all species is to be defended. . . .

Those who claim to base their objection to the use of animals in biomedical research on their reckoning of the net pleasures and pains produced make a second error, equally grave. Even if it were true—as it is surely not—that the pains of all animate beings must be counted equally, a cogent utilitarian calculation requires that we weigh all the consequences of the use, and of the nonuse, of animals in laboratory research. Critics relying (however mistakenly) on animal rights may claim to ignore the beneficial results of such research, rights being trump cards to which interest and advantage must give away. But an argument that is explicitly framed in terms of interest and benefit for all over the long run must attend also to the disadvantageous consequences of not using animals in research, and to all the achievements attained and attainable only through their use. The sum of the benefits of their use is utterly beyond quantification. The elimination of horrible disease, the increase of longevity, the avoidance of great pain, the saving of lives, and the improvement of the quality of lives (for humans and for animals) achieved through research using animals is so incalculably great that the argument of these critics, systematically pursued, establishes not their conclusion but its reverse: to refrain from using animals in biomedical research is, on utilitarian ground, morally wrong.

When balancing the pleasures and pains resulting from the use of animals in research, we must not fail to place on the scales the terrible pains that would have resulted, would be suffered now, and would long continue had animals not been used. Every disease eliminated, every vaccine developed, every method of pain relief devised, every surgical procedure invented, every prosthetic device implanted—indeed, virtually every modern medical therapy is due, in part or in whole, to experimentation using animals. Nor may we ignore, in the balancing process, the predictable gains in human (and animal) well-being that are probably achievable in the future but that will not be achieved if the decision is made now to desist from such research or to curtail it. . . .

THE ABSURD CONSEQUENCES OF ANIMAL RIGHTS

Finally, inconsistency between the profession and the practice of many who oppose research using animals deserves comment. This frankly *ad hominem* observation aims chiefly to show that a coherent position rejecting the use of animals in medical research imposes costs so high as to be intolerable even to the critics themselves.

One cannot coherently object to the killing of animals in biomedical investigations while continuing to eat them. Anesthetics and thoughtful animal husbandry render the level of actual animal distress in the laboratory generally lower than that in the abattoir. So long as death and discomfort do not substantially differ in the two contexts, the consistent objector must not only refrain from all eating of animals but also protest as vehemently against others eating them as against others experimenting on them. No less vigorously must the critic object to the wearing of animal hides in coats and shoes, to employment in any industrial enterprise that uses animal parts, and to any commercial development that will cause death or distress to animals. . . .

Scrupulous vegetarianism, in matters of food, clothing, shelter, commerce, and recreation, and in all other spheres, is the only fully coherent position the critic may adopt. At great human cost, the lives of fish and crustaceans must also be protected, with equal vigor, if speciesism has been forsworn. A very few consistent critics adopt this position. It is the *reductio ad absurdum* of the rejection of moral distinctions between animals and human beings.

For Further Reflection

1. Compare Cohen's argument against animal rights with Singer's argument for animal rights. Which, in your opinion, is closer to the truth? Explain.
2. Examine Cohen's "absurd consequences." How absurd do you think they really are?
3. Cohen doesn't address the problem of suffering caused by factory farming. Given his assumptions, how might he respond to the facts itemized in the introduction to this section? How do you react to them?

IX.D   Do We Have Obligations to the Poor and Hungry?

In our time—as always—the great divide between the haves and the have-nots, the well-fed and the starving, persists as if ordained by God or Nature. Almost half the planet's population subsists on less than $2.50 a day. Of the earth's six billion inhabitants, one billion are hungry, and two billion are undernourished. Each day 25,000 adults and children die from hunger and related causes. Some 80 percent of the world's wealth (measured by gross domestic product) belongs to 17 percent of its people, the citizens of the relatively rich, developed nations. Twenty percent of the wealth is divided among the rest of humankind, the people of developing countries.*

*Statistics from World Bank Development Research Group, "The Developing World Is Poorer Than We Thought," Worldbank.org, August 2008, http://www.worldbank.org/ (11 April 2009); UNICEF, "The State of the World's Children, 2005," UNICEF, 2005, http://www.unicef.org/sowc05/english/sowc05.pdf (11 April 2009); World Bank, "World Development Indicators 2008," Worldbank.org, 2008, http://www.worldbank.org/ (11 April 2009); United Nations Department of Public Information, "Millennium Development Goals: Fact Sheet," 25 September 2008.

What gives these facts ethical import is that the affluent—both individuals and nations—have the wherewithal to ease the suffering of the poor and hungry. Whatever the causes of the gulf between the haves and the have-nots, the haves can do much to bridge it, or at least pull many unfortunates from the brink. What, then, are the moral duties of the rich regarding the needy of the world? What are we—the secure and comfortable denizens of the West—obligated to do for the impoverished, starving, and dying of the Third World?

We can sort those who offer answers to these questions into three groups. Some argue that we have very strong duties to aid the poor and hungry in other countries, duties that demand substantial sacrifices from us. Others deny that we have any such obligations. And many take a middle path, holding that we should help the needy but not if the burden is excessive.

Those in the first group include strong egalitarians who argue that since all persons have equal moral worth, they are all entitled to equal portions of the world's essential goods such as food and water. We are therefore obligated to share the earth's resources with all those in need. The resulting distribution may lower our standard of living, impoverish us, or threaten our survival, but share we must, in the name of equality.

This view, of course, is built on deontological, or nonconsequentialist, premises, but other positions urging strong duties to the needy are utilitarian. Peter Singer offers the most widely discussed argument of this kind as he presses for radical changes in how we the affluent live and how we think about aid to the needy. He contends that if we have the power to prevent a very bad thing from occurring, and if we can prevent it without "sacrificing anything morally significant," then we have a moral duty to do it. Luxuries such as new clothes, for example, are not morally significant, so we should forgo them and give the money to famine relief. This principle, Singer says, establishes a person's obligation to help needy people even if they are far away and regardless of whether the person is the only one giving aid or one among many.

People in the second group hold that we have no duty to feed the hungry in distant lands and, in fact, have a duty *not* to feed them. Like Singer, many of these argue from a utilitarian perspective, but they reach a contrary conclusion. Garrett Hardin, for example, argues that the problems of poverty and starvation are due to uncontrolled population growth. In any inhabited area, the human population naturally increases over time and, if unchecked, eventually outpaces the food supply—the "carrying capacity" of the environment. The result is famine, a decimation of the inhabitants, and a return to a proper balance between population and carrying capacity. This tragic cycle thus "solves" the problem of famine and starvation. According to Hardin, giving the hungry inhabitants food will make the situation much worse by artificially enlarging the population still more, causing it to outstrip the carrying capacity even further. When the inevitable famine finally comes, it will be an even bigger catastrophe—causing an even greater loss of life—than before the food aid arrived. The conclusion to be drawn, Hardin says, is that we should not give food to needy countries where population growth is unrestrained. Doing so leads to suffering and death on a vast scale.

Others in the second group appeal to a restricted notion of rights. A right is a bona fide claim to something, an entitlement that imposes obligations on others. Rights can be either positive or negative. If a person has negative rights, then others have a duty *not to interfere* with her getting something. If she has positive rights, then others have a duty *to help her* get something. Most people assume that we have both negative and positive rights, but some assert that all our rights are negative. A person has no positive rights, they say, and therefore others are not obligated to help him or her acquire anything. Those who take this view would insist that we have no duty to aid poor or starving people in other countries. We of course should not do anything to harm them or to make their plight worse, but we are not obliged to send them food or medicine.

This negative-rights approach to aiding the needy does not, however, rule out charitable acts. Out of the goodness of our hearts, we might decide to help needy, distant people. But, the argument goes, we have no obligation to do so. If we refuse to send aid, we do no wrong.

People in the third group think we should make a reasonable, not exhaustive, effort to aid the needy. They generally recognize a duty of beneficence—the moral obligation to do good to others and avoid harming them—but hold that this duty must be weighed against other obligations or rights.

IX.88   Famine, Affluence, and Morality

PETER SINGER

Peter Singer advocates a fundamental shift in the attitudes of people in affluent countries toward the poor and starving of the Third World. His argument is that (1) suffering and death from lack of food and other necessities are bad; (2) "if it is in our power to prevent something bad from happening" without excessive sacrifice, we have a moral duty to do it; therefore, (3) we have a moral duty to help the poor and starving of the world (regardless of their proximity to us or how many other people are in a position to help). If this argument is sound, it shows that giving to famine relief and similar causes is not an act of charity (and therefore optional)—it is a stringent moral obligation.

The second premise comes in two forms, strong and weak. The strong version says that we have a duty to prevent something bad from happening if we can do it without "sacrificing anything of comparable moral importance." This principle requires us to give aid to the level of "marginal utility"—to the point where we could not give any more without causing as much suffering to ourselves or our families as we would ease by our giving. We must reduce our circumstances almost to the same degree of hardship experienced by those we are trying to aid.

Singer thinks the strong principle is the correct one, but he believes the weak version would also transform how we view our obligations to the needy. According to this less stringent principle, we have a duty to prevent something bad from happening if we can do it without "sacrificing anything morally significant." It requires us not to sacrifice to the point of marginal utility, but to stop spending money on comparatively trivial things. It would have us give money to famine relief instead of spending it on a new car or new clothes.

A common criticism of Singer's view is that the strong principle allows the needs of others to outweigh or overrule our own legitimate rights and needs. Some critics also insist that while we have a duty to help needy people in faraway places, we also have special duties to those close at hand—members of our family, friends, and neighbors.

Study Questions

1. What is Singer's argument for aiding the poor?
2. What are the two forms of Singer's second premise?
3. What does Singer mean by giving aid to the level of marginal utility?

As I write this, in November 1971, people are dying in East Bengal from lack of food, shelter, and medical care. The suffering and death that are occurring there now are not inevitable, not unavoidable in any fatalistic sense of the term. Constant poverty, a cyclone, and a civil war have turned at least nine million people into destitute refugees; nevertheless, it is not beyond the capacity of the richer nations to give enough assistance to reduce any further suffering to very small proportions. The decisions and actions of human beings can prevent this kind of suffering. Unfortunately, human beings have not made the necessary decisions. At the individual level, people have, with very few exceptions, not responded to the situation in any significant way. Generally speaking, people have not given large sums to relief funds; they have not written to their parliamentary representatives demanding increased government assistance; they have not demonstrated in the streets, held symbolic fasts, or done anything else directed toward providing the refugees with the means to satisfy their essential needs. At the government level, no government has given the sort of massive aid that would enable the refugees to survive for more than a few days. Britain, for instance, has given rather more than most countries. It has, to date, given £14,750,000. For comparative purposes, Britain's share of the nonrecoverable development costs of the Anglo-French Concorde project is already in excess of £275,000,000, and on present estimates will reach £440,000,000. The implication is that the British government values a supersonic transport more than thirty times as highly as it values the lives of the nine million refugees. Australia is another country which, on a per capita basis, is well up in the "aid to Bengal" table. Australia's aid, however, amounts to less than one-twelfth of the cost of Sydney's new opera house. The total amount given, from all sources, now stands at about £65,000,000. The estimated cost of keeping the refugees alive for one year is £464,000,000. Most of the refugees have now been in the camps for more than six months. The World Bank has said that India needs a minimum of £300,000,000 in assistance from other countries before the end of the year. It seems obvious that assistance on this scale will not be forthcoming. India will be forced to choose between letting the refugees starve or diverting funds from her own development program, which will mean that more of her own people will starve in the future.[1]

These are the essential facts about the present situation in Bengal. So far as it concerns us here, there is nothing unique about this situation except its magnitude. The Bengal emergency is

From *Philosophy and Public Affairs 1, no. 3, Peter Singer,* © *1972. Reproduced with permission of Blackwell Publishing Ltd.*

just the latest and most acute of a series of major emergencies in various parts of the world, arising both from natural and from man-made causes. There are also many parts of the world in which people die from malnutrition and lack of food independent of any special emergency. I take Bengal as my example only because it is the present concern, and because the size of the problem has ensured that it has been given adequate publicity. Neither individuals nor governments can claim to be unaware of what is happening there.

What are the moral implications of a situation like this? In what follows, I shall argue that the way people in relatively affluent countries react to a situation like that in Bengal cannot be justified; indeed, the whole way we look at moral issues—our moral conceptual scheme—needs to be altered, and with it, the way of life that has come to be taken for granted in our society.

In arguing for this conclusion I will not, of course, claim to be morally neutral. I shall, however, try to argue for the moral position that I take, so that anyone who accepts certain assumptions, to be made explicit, will, I hope, accept my conclusion.

I begin with the assumption that suffering and death from lack of food, shelter, and medical care are bad. I think most people will agree about this, although one may reach the same view by different routes. I shall not argue for this view. People can hold all sorts of eccentric positions, and perhaps from some of them it would not follow that death by starvation is in itself bad. It is difficult, perhaps impossible, to refute such positions, and so for brevity I will henceforth take this assumption as accepted. Those who disagree need read no further.

My next point is this: if it is in our power to prevent something bad from happening, without thereby sacrificing anything of comparable moral importance, we ought, morally, to do it. By "without sacrificing anything of comparable moral importance" I mean without causing anything else comparably bad to happen, or doing something that is wrong in itself, or failing to promote some moral good, comparable in sig-

nificance to the bad thing that we can prevent. This principle seems almost as uncontroversial as the last one. It requires us only to prevent what is bad, and not to promote what is good, and it requires this of us only when we can do it without sacrificing anything that is, from the moral point of view, comparably important. I could even, as far as the application of my argument to the Bengal emergency is concerned, qualify the point so as to make it: if it is in our power to prevent something very bad from happening, without thereby sacrificing anything morally significant, we ought, morally, to do it. An application of this principle would be as follows: if I am walking past a shallow pond and see a child drowning in it, I ought to wade in and pull the child out. This will mean getting my clothes muddy, but this is insignificant, while the death of the child would presumably be a very bad thing.

The uncontroversial appearance of the principle just stated is deceptive. If it were acted upon, even in its qualified form, our lives, our society, and our world would be fundamentally changed. For the principle takes, firstly, no account of proximity or distance. It makes no moral difference whether the person I can help is a neighbor's child ten yards from me or a Bengali whose name I shall never know, ten thousand miles away. Secondly, the principle makes no distinction between cases in which I am the only person who could possibly do anything and cases in which I am just one among millions in the same position.

I do not think I need to say much in defense of the refusal to take proximity and distance into account. The fact that a person is physically near to us, so that we have personal contact with him, may make it more likely that we *shall* assist him, but this does not show that we *ought* to help him rather than another who happens to be further away. If we accept any principle of impartiality, universalizability, equality, or whatever, we cannot discriminate against someone merely because he is far away from us (or we are far away from him). Admittedly, it is possible that we are in a better position to judge what needs to be done to help a person near to us than one far away, and perhaps also to provide the assistance we judge to be necessary. If this were the case, it would be a reason for helping those near to us first. This may once have been a justification for being more concerned with the poor in one's own town than with famine victims in India. Unfortunately for those who like to keep their moral responsibilities limited, instant communication and swift transportation have changed the situation. From the moral point of view, the development of the world into a "global village" has made an important, though still unrecognized, difference to our moral situation. Expert observers and supervisors, sent out by famine relief organizations or permanently stationed in famine-prone areas, can direct our aid to a refugee in Bengal almost as effectively as we could get it to someone in our own block. There would seem, therefore, to be no possible justification for discriminating on geographical grounds.

There may be a greater need to defend the second implication of my principle—that the fact that there are millions of other people in the same position, in respect to the Bengali refugees, as I am, does not make the situation significantly different from a situation in which I am the only person who can prevent something very bad from occurring. Again, of course, I admit that there is a psychological difference between the cases; one feels less guilty about doing nothing if one can point to others, similarly placed, who have also done nothing. Yet this can make no real difference to our moral obligations.[2] Should I consider that I am less obliged to pull the drowning child out of the pond if on looking around I see other people, no further away than I am, who have also noticed the child but are doing nothing? One has only to ask this question to see the absurdity of the view that numbers lessen obligation. It is a view that is an ideal excuse for inactivity; unfortunately most of the major evils—poverty, overpopulation, pollution—are problems in which everyone is almost equally involved.

The view that numbers do make a difference can be made plausible if stated in this way: if everyone in circumstances like mine gave £5 to the Bengal Relief Fund, there would be enough to provide food, shelter, and medical care for the refugees; there is no reason why I should give more than anyone else in the same circumstances as I am; therefore I have no obligation to give more than £5. Each premise in this argument is true, and the argument looks sound. It may convince us, unless we notice that it is based on a hypothetical premise, although the conclusion is not stated hypothetically. The argument would be sound if the conclusion were: if everyone in circumstances like mine were to give £5, I would have no obligation to give more than £5. If the conclusion were so stated, however, it would be obvious that the argument has no bearing on a situation in which it is not the case that everyone else gives £5. This, of course, is the actual situation. It is more or less certain that not everyone in circumstances like mine will give £5. So there will not be enough to provide the needed food, shelter, and medical care. Therefore by giving more than £5 I will prevent more suffering than I would if I gave just £5.

It might be thought that this argument has an absurd consequence. Since the situation appears to be that very few people are likely to give substantial amounts, it follows that I and everyone else in similar circumstances ought to give as much as possible, that is, at least up to the point at which by giving more one would begin to cause serious suffering for oneself and one's dependents—perhaps even beyond this point to the point of marginal utility, at which by giving more one would cause oneself and one's dependents as much suffering as one would prevent in Bengal. If everyone does this, however, there will be more than can be used for the benefit of the refugees, and some of the sacrifice will have been unnecessary. Thus, if everyone does what he ought to do, the result will not be as good as it would be if everyone did a little less than he ought to do, or if only some do all that they ought to do.

The paradox here arises only if we assume that the actions in question—sending money to the relief funds—are performed more or less simultaneously, and are also unexpected. For if it is to be expected that everyone is going to contribute something, then clearly each is not obliged to give as much as he would have been obliged to had others not been giving too. And if everyone is not acting more or less simultaneously, then those giving later will know how much more is needed, and will have no obligation to give more than is necessary to reach this amount. To say this is not to deny the principle that people in the same circumstances have the same obligations, but to point out that the fact that others have given, or may be expected to give, is a relevant circumstance: those giving after it has become known that many others are giving and those giving before are not in the same circumstances. So the seemingly absurd consequence of the principle I have put forward can occur only if people are in error about the actual circumstances—that is, if they think they are giving when others are not, but in fact they are giving when others are. The result of everyone doing what he really ought to do cannot be worse than the result of everyone doing less than he ought to do, although the result of everyone doing what he reasonably believes he ought to do could be.

If my argument so far has been sound, neither our distance from a preventable evil nor the number of other people who, in respect to that evil, are in the same situation as we are, lessens our obligation to mitigate or prevent that evil. I shall therefore take as established the principle I asserted earlier. As I have already said, I need to assert it only in its qualified form: if it is in our power to prevent something very bad from happening, without thereby sacrificing anything else morally significant, we ought, morally, to do it.

The outcome of this argument is that our traditional moral categories are upset. The traditional distinction between duty and charity cannot be drawn, or at least, not in the place we normally draw it. Giving money to the Bengal Relief Fund is regarded as an act of charity in our society. The bodies which collect money are known as "charities." These organizations see themselves in this way—if you send them a check, you will be thanked for your "generosity." Because giving money is regarded as an act of charity, it is not thought that there is anything wrong with not giving. The charitable man may be praised, but the man who is not charitable is not condemned. People do not feel in any way ashamed or guilty about spending money on new clothes or a new car instead of giving it to famine relief. (Indeed, the alternative does not occur to them.) This way of looking at the matter cannot be justified. When we buy new clothes not to keep ourselves warm but to look "well-dressed" we are not providing for any important need. We would not be sacrificing anything significant if we were to continue to wear our old clothes, and give the money to famine relief. By doing so, we would be preventing another person from starving. It follows from what I have said earlier that we ought to give money away, rather than spend it on clothes which we do not need to keep us warm. To do so is not charitable, or generous. Nor is it the kind of act which philosophers and theologians have called "supererogatory"—an act which it would be good to do, but not wrong not to do. On the contrary, we ought to give the money away, and it is wrong not to do so.

I am not maintaining that there are no acts which are charitable, or that there are no acts which it would be good to do but not wrong not to do. It may be possible to redraw the distinction between duty and charity in some other place. All I am arguing here is that the present way of drawing the distinction, which makes it an act of charity for a man living at the level of affluence which most people in the "developed nations" enjoy to give money to save someone else from starvation, cannot be supported. It is beyond the scope of my argument to consider whether the distinction should be redrawn or abolished altogether. There would be many other possible ways of drawing the distinction—

for instance, one might decide that it is good to make other people as happy as possible, but not wrong not to do so.

Despite the limited nature of the revision in our moral conceptual scheme which I am proposing, the revision would, given the extent of both affluence and famine in the world today, have radical implications. These implications may lead to further objections, distinct from those I have already considered. I shall discuss two of these.

One objection to the position I have taken might be simply that it is too drastic a revision of our moral scheme. People do not ordinarily judge in the way I have suggested they should. Most people reserve their moral condemnation for those who violate some moral norm, such as the norm against taking another person's property. They do not condemn those who indulge in luxury instead of giving to famine relief. But given that I did not set out to present a morally neutral description of the way people make moral judgments, the way people do in fact judge has nothing to do with the validity of my conclusion. My conclusion follows from the principle which I advanced earlier, and unless that principle is rejected, or the arguments shown to be unsound, I think the conclusion must stand, however strange it appears.

It might, nevertheless, be interesting to consider why our society, and most other societies, do judge differently from the way I have suggested they should. In a well-known article, J. O. Urmson suggests that the imperatives of duty, which tell us what we must do, as distinct from what it would be good to do but not wrong not to do, function so as to prohibit behavior that is intolerable if men are to live together in society.[3] This may explain the origin and continued existence of the present division between acts of duty and acts of charity. Moral attitudes are shaped by the needs of society, and no doubt society needs people who will observe the rules that make social existence tolerable. From the point of view of a particular society, it is essential to prevent violations of norms against killing,

stealing, and so on. It is quite inessential, however, to help people outside one's own society.

If this is an explanation of our common distinction between duty and supererogation, however, it is not a justification of it. The moral point of view requires us to look beyond the interests of our own society. Previously, as I have already mentioned, this may hardly have been feasible, but it is quite feasible now. From the moral point of view, the prevention of the starvation of millions of people outside our society must be considered at least as pressing as the upholding of property norms within our society.

It has been argued by some writers, among them Sidgwick and Urmson, that we need to have a basic moral code which is not too far beyond the capacities of the ordinary man, for otherwise there will be a general breakdown of compliance with the moral code. Crudely stated, this argument suggests that if we tell people that they ought to refrain from murder and give everything they do not really need to famine relief, they will do neither, whereas if we tell them that they ought to refrain from murder and that it is good to give to famine relief but not wrong not to do so, they will at least refrain from murder. The issue here is: Where should we drawn the line between conduct that is required and conduct that is good although not required, so as to get the best possible result? This would seem to be an empirical question, although a very difficult one. One objection to the Sidgwick-Urmson line of argument is that it takes insufficient account of the effect that moral standards can have on the decisions we make. Given a society in which a wealthy man who gives five percent of his income to famine relief is regarded as most generous, it is not surprising that a proposal that we all ought to give away half our incomes will be thought to be absurdly unrealistic. In a society which held that no man should have more than enough while others have less than they need, such a proposal might seem narrow-minded. What it is possible for a man to do and what he is likely to do are both, I think, very greatly influenced by what people around him are doing and expecting him to do. In any case, the possibility that by spreading the idea that we ought to be doing very much more than we are to relieve famine we shall bring about a general breakdown of moral behavior seems remote. If the stakes are an end to widespread starvation, it is worth the risk. Finally, it should be emphasized that these considerations are relevant only to the issue of what we should require from others, and not to what we ourselves ought to do.

The second objection to my attack on the present distinction between duty and charity is one which has from time to time been made against utilitarianism. It follows from some forms of utilitarian theory that we all ought, morally, to be working full time to increase the balance of happiness over misery. The position I have taken here would not lead to this conclusion in all circumstances, for if there were no bad occurrences that we could prevent without sacrificing something of comparable moral importance, my argument would have no application. Given the present conditions in many parts of the world, however, it does follow from my argument that we ought, morally, to be working full time to relieve great suffering of the sort that occurs as a result of famine or other disasters. Of course, mitigating circumstances can be adduced—for instance, that if we wear ourselves out through overwork, we shall be less effective than we would otherwise have been. Nevertheless, when all considerations of this sort have been taken into account, the conclusion remains: we ought to be preventing as much suffering as we can without sacrificing something else of comparable moral importance. This conclusion is one which we may be reluctant to face. I cannot see, though, why it should be regarded as a criticism of the position for which I have argued, rather than a criticism of our ordinary standards of behavior. Since most people are self-interested to some degree, very few of us are likely to do everything that we ought to do. It would, however, hardly be honest to take this as evidence that it is not the case that we ought to do it.

It may still be thought that my conclusions are so wildly out of line with what everyone else thinks and has always thought that there must be something wrong with the argument somewhere. In order to show that my conclusions, while certainly contrary to contemporary Western moral standards, would not have seemed so extraordinary at other times and in other places, I would like to quote a passage from a writer not normally thought of as a way-out radical, Thomas Aquinas.

> Now, according to the natural order instituted by divine providence, material goods are provided for the satisfaction of human needs. Therefore the division and appropriation of property, which proceeds from human law, must not hinder the satisfaction of man's necessity from such goods. Equally, whatever a man has in super-abundance is owed, of natural right, to the poor for their sustenance. So Ambrosius says, and it is also to be found in the *Decretum Gratiani*: "The bread which you withhold belongs to the hungry; the clothing you shut away, to the naked; and the money you bury in the earth is the redemption and freedom of the penniless."[4]

I now want to consider a number of points, more practical than philosophical, which are relevant to the application of the moral conclusion we have reached. These points challenge not the idea that we ought to be doing all we can to prevent starvation, but the idea that giving away a great deal of money is the best means to this end.

It is sometimes said that overseas aid should be a government responsibility, and that therefore one ought not to give to privately run charities. Giving privately, it is said, allows the government and the noncontributing members of society to escape their responsibilities.

This argument seems to assume that the more people there are who give to privately organized famine relief funds, the less likely it is that the government will take over full responsibility for such aid. This assumption is unsupported, and does not strike me as at all plausible. The opposite view—that if no one gives voluntarily, a government will assume that its citizens are uninterested in famine relief and would not wish to be forced into giving aid—seems more plausible. In any case, unless there were a definite probability that by refusing to give one would be helping to bring about massive government assistance, people who do refuse to make voluntary contributions are refusing to prevent a certain amount of suffering without being able to point to any tangible beneficial consequence of their refusal. So the onus of showing how their refusal will bring about government action is on those who refuse to give.

I do not, of course, want to dispute the contention that governments of affluent nations should be giving many times the amount of genuine, no-strings-attached aid that they are giving now. I agree, too, that giving privately is not enough, and that we ought to be campaigning actively for entirely new standards for both public and private contributions to famine relief. Indeed, I would sympathize with someone who thought that campaigning was more important than giving oneself, although I doubt whether preaching what one does not practice would be very effective. Unfortunately, for many people the idea that "it's the government's responsibility" is a reason for not giving which does not appear to entail any political action either.

Another, more serious reason for not giving to famine relief funds is that until there is effective population control, relieving famine merely postpones starvation. If we save the Bengal refugees now, others, perhaps the children of these refugees, will face starvation in a few years' time. In support of this, one may cite the now well-known facts about the population explosion and the relatively limited scope for expanded production.

This point, like the previous one, is an argument against relieving suffering that is happening now, because of a belief about what might happen in the future; it is unlike the previous point in that very good evidence can be adduced in support of this belief about the future. I will not go into the evidence here. I accept that the earth cannot support indefinitely a population rising at the present rate. This certainly poses a problem for anyone who thinks it important to prevent famine. Again, however, one could accept the argument without drawing the conclusion that it absolves one from any obligation to do anything to prevent famine. The conclusion that should be drawn is that the best means of preventing famine, in the long run, is population control. It would then follow from the position reached earlier that one ought to be doing all one can to promote population control (unless one held that all forms of population control were wrong in themselves, or would have significantly bad consequences). Since there are organizations working specifically for population control, one would then support them rather than more orthodox methods of preventing famine.

A third point raised by the conclusion reached earlier relates to the question of just how much we all ought to be giving away. One possibility, which has already been mentioned, is that we ought to give until we reach the level of marginal utility—that is, the level at which, by giving more, I would cause as much suffering to myself or my dependents as I would relieve by my gift. This would mean, of course, that one would reduce oneself to very near the material circumstances of a Bengali refugee. It will be recalled that earlier I put forward both a strong and a moderate version of the principle of preventing bad occurrences. The strong version, which required us to prevent bad things from happening unless in doing so we would be sacrificing something of comparable moral significance, does seem to require reducing ourselves to the level of marginal utility. I should also say that the strong version seems to me to be the correct one. I proposed the more moderate version—that we should prevent bad occurrences unless, to do so, we had to sacrifice something morally significant—only in order to show that even on this surely undeniable principle a great change in our way of life is required. On the more moderate principle, it may not follow that we ought to reduce ourselves to the level of marginal utility, for one might hold that to reduce oneself and one's family to this level is to cause something significantly bad to happen. Whether this is so I shall not discuss, since, as I have said, I can see no good reason for holding the moderate version of the principle rather than the strong version. Even if we accepted the principle only in its moderate form, however, it should be clear that we would have to give away enough to ensure that the consumer society, dependent as it is on people spending on trivia rather than giving to famine relief, would slow down and perhaps disappear entirely. There are several reasons why this would be desirable in itself. The value and necessity of economic growth are now being questioned not only by conservationists, but by economists as well.[5] There is no doubt, too, that the consumer society has had a distorting effect on the goals and purposes of its members. Yet looking at the matter purely from the point of view of overseas aid, there must be a limit to the extent to which we should deliberately slow down our economy; for it might be the case that if we gave away, say, forty percent of our Gross National Product, we would slow down the economy so much that in absolute terms we would be giving less than if we gave twenty-five percent of the much larger GNP that we would have if we limited our contribution to this smaller percentage.

I mention this only as an indication of the sort of factor that one would have to take into account in working out an ideal. Since Western societies generally consider one percent of the GNP an acceptable level for overseas aid, the matter is entirely academic. Nor does it affect the question of how much an individual should give in a society in which very few are giving substantial amounts.

It is sometimes said, though less often now than it used to be, that philosophers have no special role to play in public affairs, since most public issues depend primarily on an assessment of facts. On questions of fact, it is said, philosophers as such have no special expertise, and so it has been possible to engage in philosophy without committing oneself to any position on major public issues. No doubt there are some issues of social policy and foreign policy about which it can truly be said that a really expert assessment of the facts is required before taking sides or acting, but the issue of famine is surely not one of these. The facts about the existence of suffering are beyond dispute. Nor, I think, is it disputed that we can do something about it, either through orthodox methods of famine relief or through population control or both. This is therefore an issue on which philosophers are competent to take a position. The issue is one which faces everyone who has more money than he needs to support himself and his dependents, or who is in a position to take some sort of political action. These categories must include practically every teacher and student of philosophy in the universities of the Western world. If philosophy is to deal with matters that are relevant to both teachers and students, this is an issue that philosophers should discuss.

Discussion, though, is not enough. What is the point of relating philosophy to public (and personal) affairs if we do not take our conclusions seriously? In this instance, taking our conclusion seriously means acting upon it. The philosopher will not find it any easier than anyone else to alter his attitudes and way of life to the extent that, if I am right, is involved in doing everything that we ought to be doing. At the very least, though, one can make a start. The philosopher who does so will have to sacrifice some of the benefits of the consumer society, but he can find compensation in the satisfaction of a way of life in which theory and practice, if not yet in harmony, are at least coming together.

NOTES

1. There was also a third possibility: that India would go to war to enable the refugees to return to their lands. Since I wrote this paper, India has taken this way out. The situation is no longer that described above, but this does not affect my argument, as the next paragraph indicates.

2. In view of the special sense philosophers often give to the term, I should say that I use "obligation" simply as the abstract noun derived from "ought," so that "I have an obligation to" means no more, and no less, than "I ought to." This usage is in accordance with the definition of "ought" given by the *Shorter Oxford English Dictionary*: "the general verb to express duty or obligation." I do not think any issue of substance hangs on the way the term is used; sentences in which I use "obligation" could all be rewritten, although somewhat clumsily, as sentences in which a clause containing "ought" replaces the term "obligation."

3. J. O. Urmson, "Saints and Heroes," in *Essays in Moral Philosophy*, ed. Abraham I. Melden (Seattle and London, 1958), p. 214. For a related but significantly different view see also Henry Sidgwick, *The Methods of Ethics*, 7th edn. (London, 1907), pp. 220–221, 492–493.

4. *Summa Theologica*, II-II, Question 66, Article 7, in *Aquinas, Selected Political Writings*, ed. A. P. d'Entreves, trans. J. G. Dawson (Oxford, 1948), p. 171.

5. See, for instance, John Kenneth Galbraith, *The New Industrial State* (Boston, 1967); and E. J. Mishan, *The Costs of Economic Growth* (London, 1967).

For Further Reflection

1. Are you persuaded by Singer's argument? If so, why? If not, why not? Do you accept or reject the second premise? Why?

2. Do you believe that Singer's view demands too much of individuals? Does it undercut duties that we have to ourselves? Explain.

3. Does Singer's view emphasize duties to strangers at the expense of our obligations to our friends and loved ones? Why or why not?

Living on a Lifeboat   IX.89

GARRETT HARDIN

Garrett Hardin (1915–2003) was trained as an ecologist and microbiologist and became famous for his theory predicting tragic consequences for aiding poor and hungry nations. In this article, he argues that the affluent should not aid the poor and starving people of the world because doing so will only lead to disaster for everyone, rich and poor. Helping desperately needy, overpopulated countries is morally wrong. He makes his case using several metaphors, the "lifeboat" being the most memorable.

Imagine, he says, that the affluent nations are lifeboats carrying rich people in a sea dotted with the desperately poor, many of them trying to clamber aboard or seize some of the passengers' supplies. Each lifeboat has a limited carrying capacity, just as each rich nation does. For safety's sake, a lifeboat should carry fewer passengers than it can actually accommodate, just as a country should have a population small enough to guarantee excess carrying capacity to offset emergencies such as droughts or crop failures. No lifeboat can take on more passengers or give handouts without risking disaster for everyone. If all those trying to climb aboard are taken into a boat, it will capsize and everyone will drown. If only some of the poor people are let on board—enough to fill the craft to maximum capacity—the safety factor is eliminated and the boat will sink sooner or later. The third option, unthinkable to some, is to turn away all the poor. Many will perish, but the lucky few already on board will survive. Given these cruel realities, the morally right course for affluent nations is clear: Do not aid the people of desperately poor, overpopulated countries.

Hardin bolsters his argument with another metaphor, "the tragedy of the commons." The commons is any land or resource that is open to all to exploit. In any arrangement based on a commons system—such as a public field where all shepherds can freely graze their sheep, or a social system in which all goods are shared alike—it is in each member's self-interest to use the system's resources to the maximum. It is in each shepherd's interest, for example, to graze as many sheep as possible to support his family. There is no incentive for him to think about the common good, to act responsibly so the field is not overgrazed and ruined for everyone. The result is disaster; the field is destroyed. This is the tragedy of the commons: "mutual ruin" from a well-meaning system of sharing.

Hardin claims that in a world where all resources are shared and reproduction in the impoverished countries is uncontrolled, the tragedy of the commons is inevitable. The catastrophe will come when rich countries let the poor inundate their lifeboats or when a world food bank becomes an international commons that shares the earth's food reserves.

Hardin's lifeboat ethics has many detractors. Some accuse his analysis of being simplistic. For one thing, they say, the metaphor implies that the rich lifeboats barely interact with the poor, but in the real world the rich countries have greatly affected the poor ones, and often for the worse. Others question Hardin's assertion that aiding the poor will inevitably increase their suffering.

Study Questions

1. What is Hardin's argument against aiding poor nations?
2. What point is he trying to make with the lifeboat analogy?
3. What is the tragedy of the commons?
4. Why does Hardin think that the World Food Bank is a bad idea?

Susanne Langer (1942) has shown that it is probably impossible to approach an unsolved problem save through the door of metaphor. Later, attempting to meet the demands of rigor, we may achieve some success in cleansing theory of metaphor, though our success is limited if we are unable to avoid using common language, which is shot through and through with fossil metaphors. (I count no less than five in the preceding two sentences.)

Since metaphorical thinking is inescapable it is pointless merely to weep about our human limitations. We must learn to live with them, to understand them, and to control them. "All of us," said George Eliot in Middlemarch, "get our thoughts entangled in metaphors, and act fatally on the strength of them." To avoid unconscious suicide we are well advised to pit one metaphor against another. From the interplay of competitive metaphors, thoroughly developed, we may

From Garrett Hardin, "Living on a Lifeboat," BioScience 24, no. 10, pp. 561–65, 568. © *1974 University of California Press.*

come closer to metaphor-free solutions to our problems.

No generation has viewed the problem of the survival of the human species as seriously as we have. Inevitably, we have entered this world of concern through the door of metaphor. Environmentalists have emphasized the image of the earth as a spaceship—Spaceship Earth. Kenneth Boulding (1966) is the principal architect of this metaphor. It is time, he says, that we replace the wasteful "cowboy economy" of the past with the frugal "spaceship economy" required for continued survival in the limited world we now see ours to be. The metaphor is notably useful in justifying pollution control measures.

Unfortunately, the image of a spaceship is also used to promote measures that are suicidal. One of these is a generous immigration policy, which is only a particular instance of a class of policies that are in error because they lead to the tragedy of the commons (Hardin 1968). These suicidal policies are attractive because they mesh with what we unthinkingly take to be the ideals of "the best people." What is missing in the idealistic view is an insistence that rights and responsibilities must go together. The "generous" attitude of all too many people results in asserting inalienable rights while ignoring or denying matching responsibilities.

For the metaphor of a spaceship to be correct the aggregate of people on board would have to be under unitary sovereign control (Ophuls 1974). A true ship always has a captain. It is conceivable that a ship could be run by a committee. But it could not possibly survive if its course were determined by bickering tribes that claimed rights without responsibilities.

What about Spaceship Earth? It certainly has no captain, and no executive committee. The United Nations is a toothless tiger, because the signatories of its charter wanted it that way. The spaceship metaphor is used only to justify spaceship demands on common resources without acknowledging corresponding spaceship responsibilities.

An understandable fear of decisive action leads people to embrace "incrementalism"—moving toward reform by tiny stages. As we shall see, this strategy is counterproductive in the area discussed here if it means accepting rights before responsibilities. Where human survival is at stake, the acceptance of responsibilities is a precondition to the acceptance of rights, if the two cannot be introduced simultaneously.

LIFEBOAT ETHICS

Before taking up certain substantive issues let us look at an alternative metaphor, that of a lifeboat. In developing some relevant examples the following numerical values are assumed. Approximately two-thirds of the world is desperately poor, and only one-third is comparatively rich. The people in poor countries have an average per capita GNP (Gross National Product) of about $200 per year; the rich, of about $3,000. (For the United States it is nearly $5,000 per year.) Metaphorically, each rich nation amounts to a lifeboat full of comparatively rich people. The poor of the world are in other, much more crowded lifeboats. Continuously, so to speak, the poor fall out of their lifeboats and swim for a while in the water outside, hoping to be admitted to a rich lifeboat, or in some other way to benefit from the "goodies" on board. What should the passengers on a rich lifeboat do? This is the central problem of "the ethics of a lifeboat."

First we must acknowledge that each lifeboat is effectively limited in capacity. The land of every nation has a limited carrying capacity. The exact limit is a matter for argument, but the energy crunch is convincing more people every day that we have already exceeded the carrying capacity of the land. We have been living on "capital"—stored petroleum and coal—and soon we must live on income alone.

Let us look at only one lifeboat—ours. The ethical problem is the same for all, and is as follows. Here we sit, say 50 people in a lifeboat. To be generous, let us assume our boat has a capacity of 10 more, making 60. (This, however, is to violate the engineering principle of the "safety factor." A new plant disease or a bad change in the weather may decimate our population if we don't preserve some excess capacity as a safety factor.)

The 50 of us in the lifeboat see 100 others swimming in the water outside, asking for admission to the boat, or for handouts. How shall we respond to their calls? There are several possibilities.

One. We may be tempted to try to live by the Christian ideal of being "our brother's keeper," or by the Marxian ideal (Marx 1875) of "from each according to his abilities, to each according to his needs." Since the needs of all are the same, we take all the needy into our boat, making a total of 150 in a boat with a capacity of 60. The boat is swamped, and everyone drowns. Complete justice, complete catastrophe.

Two. Since the boat has an unused excess capacity of 10, we admit just 10 more to it. This has the disadvantage of getting rid of the safety factor, for which action we will sooner or later pay dearly. Moreover, *which* 10 do we let in? "First come, first served?" The best 10? The neediest 10? How do we *discriminate*? And what do we say to the 90 who are excluded?

Three. Admit no more to the boat and preserve the small safety factor. Survival of the people in the lifeboat is then possible (though we shall have to be on our guard against boarding parties).

The last solution is abhorrent to many people. It is unjust, they say. Let us grant that it is.

"I feel guilty about my good luck," say some. The reply to this is simple: *Get out and yield your place to others.* Such a selfless action might satisfy the conscience of those who are addicted to guilt but it would not change the ethics of the lifeboat. The needy person to whom a guilt-addict yields his place will not himself feel guilty about his sudden good luck. (If he did he would not climb aboard.) The net result of conscience-stricken people relinquishing their unjustly held positions is the elimination of their kind of conscience from the lifeboat. The lifeboat, as it were, purifies itself of guilt. The ethics of the lifeboat persist, unchanged by such momentary aberrations.

This then is the basic metaphor within which we must work out our solutions. Let us enrich the image step by step with substantive additions from the real world.

REPRODUCTION

The harsh characteristics of lifeboat ethics are heightened by reproduction, particularly by reproductive differences. The people inside the lifeboats of the wealthy nations are doubling in numbers every 87 years; those outside are doubling every 35 years, on the average. And the relative difference in prosperity is becoming greater.

Let us, for a while, think primarily of the U.S. lifeboat. As of 1973 the United States had a population of 210 million people, who were increasing by 0.8% per year, that is, doubling in number every 87 years.

Although the citizens of rich nations are outnumbered two to one by the poor, let us imagine an equal number of poor people outside our lifeboat—a mere 210 million poor people reproducing at a quite different rate. If we imagine these to be the combined populations of Colombia, Venezuela, Ecuador, Morocco, Thailand, Pakistan, and the Philippines, the average rate of increase of the people "outside" is 3.3% per year. The doubling time of this population is 21 years.

Suppose that all these countries, and the United States, agreed to live by the Marxian ideal, "to each according to his needs," the ideal of most Christians as well. Needs, of course, are determined by population size, which is affected by reproduction. Every nation regards its rate of reproduction as a sovereign right. If our lifeboat were big enough in the beginning it might be possible to live *for a while* by Christian-Marxian ideals. *Might*.

Initially, in the model given, the ratio of non-Americans to Americans would be one to one. But consider what the ratio would be 87 years later. By this time Americans would have doubled to a population of 420 million. The other group (doubling every 21 years) would now have swollen to 3,540 million. Each American would have more than eight people to share with. How could the lifeboat possibly keep afloat?

All this involves extrapolation of current trends into the future, and is consequently suspect. Trends may change. Granted: but the change will not necessarily be favorable. If—as seems likely—the rate of population increase falls faster in the ethnic group presently inside the lifeboat than it does among those now outside, the future will turn out to be even worse than mathematics predicts, and sharing will be even more suicidal.

RUIN IN THE COMMONS

The fundamental error of the sharing ethics is that it leads to the tragedy of the commons. Under a system of private property the man (or group of men) who own property recognize their responsibility to care for it, for if they don't they will eventually suffer. A farmer, for instance, if he is intelligent, will allow no more cattle in a pasture than its carrying capacity justifies. If he overloads the pasture, weeds take over, erosion sets in, and the owner loses in the long run.

But if a pasture is run as a commons open to all, the right of each to use it is not matched by an operational responsibility to take care of it. It is no use asking independent herdsmen in a commons to act responsibly, for they dare not. The considerate herdsman who refrains from overloading the commons suffers more than a selfish one who says his needs are greater. (As Leo Durocher says, "Nice guys finish last.") Christian-Marxian idealism is counterproductive. That it *sounds* nice is no excuse. With distribution systems, as with individual morality, good intentions are no substitute for good performance.

A social system is stable only if it is insensitive to errors. To the Christian-Marxian idealist a selfish person is a sort of "error." Prosperity in the system of the commons cannot survive errors. If *everyone* would only restrain himself, all would be well; but it takes *only one less than everyone* to ruin a system of voluntary restraint. In a crowded world of less than perfect human beings—and we will never know any other— mutual ruin is inevitable in the commons. This is the core of the tragedy of the commons.

One of the major tasks of education today is to create such an awareness of the dangers of the commons that people will be able to recognize its many varieties, however disguised. There is pollution of the air and water because these media are treated as commons. Further growth of population and growth in the per capita conversion of natural resources into pollutants require that the system of the commons be modified or abandoned in the disposal of "externalities."

The fish populations of the oceans are exploited as commons, and ruin lies ahead. No technological invention can prevent this fate: in fact, all improvements in the art of fishing merely hasten the day of complete ruin. Only the replacement of the system of the commons with a responsible system can save oceanic fisheries.

The management of western range lands, though nominally rational, is in fact (under the steady pressure of cattle ranchers) often merely a government-sanctioned system of the commons, drifting toward ultimate ruin for both the rangelands and the residual enterprisers.

WORLD FOOD BANKS

In the international arena we have recently heard a proposal to create a new commons, namely an international depository of food reserves to which nations will contribute according to their abilities, and from which nations may draw according to their needs. Nobel laureate Norman Borlaug has lent the prestige of his name to this proposal.

A world food bank appeals powerfully to our humanitarian impulses. We remember John

Donne's celebrated line, "Any man's death diminishes me." But before we rush out to see for whom the bell tolls let us recognize where the greatest political push for international granaries comes from, lest we be disillusioned later. Our experience with Public Law 480 clearly reveals the answer. This was the law that moved billions of dollars worth of U.S. grain to food-short, population-long countries during the past two decades. When P.L. 480 first came into being, a headline in the business magazine *Forbes* (Paddock and Paddock 1970) revealed the power behind it: "Feeding the World's Hungry Millions: How it will mean billions for U.S. business."

And indeed it did. In the years 1960 to 1970 a total of $7.9 billion was spent on the "Food for Peace" program, as P.L. 480 was called. During the years 1948 to 1970 an additional $49.9 billion were extracted from American taxpayers to pay for other economic aid programs, some of which went for food and food-producing machinery. (This figure does *not* include military aid.) That P.L. 480 was a give-away program was concealed. Recipient countries went through the motions of paying for P.L. 480 food—with IOU's. In December 1973 the charade was brought to an end as far as India was concerned when the United States "forgave" India's $3.2 billion debt (Anonymous 1974). Public announcement of the cancellation of the debt was delayed for two months: one wonders why.

"Famine—1974!" (Paddock and Paddock 1970) is one of the few publications that points out the commercial roots of this humanitarian attempt. Though all U.S. taxpayers lost by P.L. 480, special interest groups gained handsomely. Farmers benefited because they were not asked to contribute the grain—it was bought from them by the taxpayers. Besides the direct benefit there was the indirect effect of increasing demand and thus raising prices of farm products generally. The manufacturers of farm machinery, fertilizers, and pesticides benefited by the farmers' extra efforts to grow more food. Grain elevators profited from storing the grain for varying lengths of time. Railroads made money hauling it to port, and shipping lines by carrying it overseas. Moreover, once the machinery for P.L. 480 was established an immense bureaucracy had a vested interest in its continuance regardless of its merits.

Very little was ever heard of these selfish interests when P.L. 480 was defended in public. The emphasis was always on its humanitarian effects. The combination of multiple and relatively silent selfish interests with highly vocal humanitarian apologists constitutes a powerful lobby for extracting money from taxpayers. Foreign aid has become a habit that can apparently survive in the absence of any known justification. A news commentator in a weekly magazine (Lansner 1974), after exhaustively going over all the conventional arguments for foreign aid—self-interest, social justice, political advantage, and charity—and concluding that none of the known arguments really held water, concluded: "So the search continues for some logically compelling reasons for giving aid…" In other words. *Act now, Justify later*—if ever. (Apparently a quarter of a century is too short a time to find the justification for expending several billion dollars yearly.)

The search for a rational justification can be short-circuited by interjecting the word "emergency." Borlaug uses this word. We need to look sharply at it. What is an "emergency?" It is surely something like an accident, which is correctly defined as *an event that is certain to happen, though with a low frequency* (Hardin 1972a). A well-run organization prepares for everything that is certain, including accidents and emergencies. It budgets for them. It saves for them. It expects them—and mature decision-makers do not waste time complaining about accidents when they occur.

What happens if some organizations budget for emergencies and others do not? If each organization is solely responsible for its own well-being, poorly managed ones will suffer. But they should be able to learn from experience. They have a chance to mend their ways and learn to budget for infrequent but certain emergencies. The weather, for instance, always varies and periodic crop failures are certain. A wise and competent government saves out of the production of the good years in anticipation of bad years that are sure to come. This is not a new idea. The Bible tells us that Joseph taught this policy to Pharaoh in Egypt more than 2,000 years ago. Yet it is literally true that the vast majority of the governments of the world today have no such policy. They lack either the wisdom or the competence, or both. Far more difficult than the transfer of wealth from one country to another is the transfer of wisdom between sovereign powers or between generations.

"But it isn't their fault! How can we blame the poor people who are caught in an emergency? Why must we punish them?" The concepts of blame and punishment are irrelevant. The question is, what are the operational consequences of establishing a world food bank? If it is open to every country every time a need develops, slovenly rulers will not be motivated to take Joseph's advice. Why should they? Others will bail them out whenever they are in trouble.

Some countries will make deposits in the world food bank and others will withdraw from it: there will be almost no overlap. Calling such a depository-transfer unit a "bank" is stretching the metaphor of *bank* beyond its elastic limits. The proposers, of course, never call attention to the metaphorical nature of the word they use.

THE RATCHET EFFECT

An "international food bank" is really, then, not a true bank but a disguised one-way transfer device for moving wealth from rich countries to poor. In the absence of such a bank, in a world inhabited by individually responsible sovereign nations, the population of each nation would repeatedly go through a cycle. . . . P_2 is greater than P_1, either in absolute numbers or because a deterioration of the food supply has removed the

safety factor and produced a dangerously low ratio of resources to population. P_2 may be said to represent a state of overpopulation, which becomes obvious upon the appearance of an "accident," e.g., a crop failure. If the "emergency" is not met by outside help, the population drops back to the "normal" level—the "carrying capacity" of the environment—or even below. In the absence of population control by a sovereign, sooner or later the population grows to P_2 again and the cycle repeats. The long-term population curve (Hardin 1966) is an irregularly fluctuating one, equilibrating more or less about the carrying capacity.

A demographic cycle of this sort obviously involves great suffering in the restrictive phase, but such a cycle is normal to any independent country with inadequate population control. The third century theologian Tertullian (Hardin 1969a) expressed what must have been the recognition of many wise men when he wrote: "The scourges of pestilence, famine, wars, and earthquakes have come to be regarded as a blessing to overcrowded nations, since they serve to prune away the luxuriant growth of the human race."

Only under a strong and farsighted sovereign—which theoretically could be the people themselves, democratically organized—can a population equilibrate at some set point below the carrying capacity, thus avoiding the pains normally caused by periodic and unavoidable disasters. For this happy state to be achieved it is necessary that those in power be able to contemplate with equanimity the "waste" of surplus food in times of bountiful harvests. It is essential that those in power resist the temptation to convert extra food into extra babies. On the public relations level it is necessary that the phrase "surplus food" be replaced by "safety factor."

But wise sovereigns seem not to exist in the poor world today. The most anguishing problems are created by poor countries that are governed by rulers insufficiently wise and powerful. If such countries can draw on a world food bank in times of "emergency," the population cycle

. . . will be replaced by the population *escalator*. The input of food from a food bank acts as the pawl of a ratchet, preventing the population from retracting its steps to a lower level. Reproduction pushes the population upward, inputs from the world bank prevent its moving downward. Population size escalates, as does the absolute magnitude of "accidents" and "emergencies." The process is brought to an end only by the total collapse of the whole system, producing a catastrophe of scarcely imaginable proportions.

Such are the implications of the well-meant sharing of food in a world of irresponsible reproduction.

I think we need a new word for systems like this. The adjective "melioristic" is applied to systems that produce continual improvement; the English word is derived from the Latin *meliorare*, to become or make better. Parallel with this it would be useful to bring in the word *pejoristic* (from the Latin *pejorare*, to become or make worse). This word can be applied to those systems which, by their very nature, can be relied upon to make matters worse. A world food bank coupled with sovereign state irresponsibility in reproduction is an example of a pejoristic system.

This pejoristic system creates an unacknowledged commons. People have more motivation to draw from than to add to the common store. The license to make such withdrawals diminishes whatever motivation poor countries might otherwise have to control their populations. Under the guidance of this ratchet, wealth can be steadily moved in one direction only, from the slowly-breeding rich to the rapidly-breeding poor, the process finally coming to a halt only when all countries are equally and miserably poor.

All this is terribly obvious once we are acutely aware of the pervasiveness and danger of the commons. But many people still lack this awareness and the euphoria of the "benign demographic transition" (Hardin 1973) interferes with the realistic appraisal of pejoristic mechanisms.

As concerns public policy, the deductions drawn from the benign demographic transition are these:

1. If the per capita GNP rises the birth rate will fall; hence, the rate of population increase will fall, ultimately producing ZPG (Zero Population Growth).
2. The long-term trend all over the world (including the poor countries) is of a rising per capita GNP (for which no limit is seen).
3. Therefore, all political interference in population matters is unnecessary; all we need to do is foster economic "development"—*note the metaphor*—and population problems will solve themselves.

Those who believe in the benign demographic transition dismiss the [population escalator] in the belief that each input of food from the world outside fosters development within a poor country thus resulting in a drop in the rate of population increase. Foreign aid has proceeded on this assumption for more than two decades. Unfortunately it has produced no indubitable instance of the asserted effect. It has, however, produced a library of excuses. The air is filled with plaintive calls for more massive foreign aid appropriations so that the hypothetical melioristic process can get started.

The doctrine of demographic laissez-faire implicit in the hypothesis of the benign demographic transition is immensely attractive. Unfortunately there is more evidence against the melioristic system than there is for it (Davis 1963). On the historical side there are many counter-examples. The rise in per capita GNP in France and Ireland during the past century has been accompanied by a rise in population growth. In the 20 years following the Second World War the same positive correlation was noted almost everywhere in the world. Never in world history before 1950 did the worldwide population growth reach 1% per annum. Now the average population growth is over 2% and shows no signs of slackening.

On the theoretical side, the denial of the [population escalator] probably springs from the hidden acceptance of the "cowboy economy" that Boulding castigated. Those who recognize the limitations of a spaceship, if they are unable to achieve population control at a safe and comfortable level, accept the necessity of the corrective feedback of the population cycle. . . . No one who knew in his bones that he was living on a true spaceship would countenance political support of the population escalator. . . .

ECO–DESTRUCTION VIA THE GREEN REVOLUTION

The demoralizing effect of charity on the recipient has long been known. "Give a man a fish and he will eat for a day: teach him how to fish and he will eat for the rest of his days." So runs an ancient Chinese proverb. Acting on this advice the Rockefeller and Ford Foundations have financed a multipronged program for improving agriculture in the hungry nations. The result, known as the "Green Revolution," has been quite remarkable. "Miracle wheat" and "miracle rice" are splendid technological achievements in the realm of plant genetics.

Whether or not the Green Revolution can increase food production is doubtful (Harris 1972, Paddock 1970, Wilkes 1972), but in any event not particularly important. What is missing in this great and well-meaning humanitarian effort is a firm grasp of fundamentals. Considering the importance of the Rockefeller Foundation in this effort it is ironic that the late Alan Gregg, a much-respected vice-president of the Foundation, strongly expressed his doubts of the wisdom of all attempts to increase food production some two decades ago. (This was before Borlaug's work—supported by Rockefeller—had resulted in the development of "miracle wheat.") Gregg (1955) likened the growth and spreading of humanity over the surface of the earth to the metastasis of cancer in the human body, wryly remarking that "Cancerous growths demand food; but, as far as I know, they have never been cured by getting it."

"Man does not live by bread alone"—the scriptural statement has a rich meaning even in the material realm. Every human being born constitutes a draft on all aspects of the environment—food, air, water, unspoiled scenery, occasional and optional solitude, beaches, contact with wild animals, fishing, hunting—the list is long and incompletely known. Food can, perhaps, be significantly increased: but what about clean beaches, unspoiled forests, and solitude? If we satisfy the need for food in a growing population we necessarily decrease the supply of other goods, and thereby increase the difficulty of equitably allocating scarce goods (Hardin 1969b, 1972b).

The present population of India is 600 million, and it is increasing by 15 million per year. The environmental load of this population is already great. The forests of India are only a small fraction of what they were three centuries ago. Soil erosion, floods, and the psychological costs of crowding are serious. Every one of the net 15 million lives added each year stresses the Indian environment more severely. *Every life saved this year in a poor country diminishes the quality of life for subsequent generations.*

Observant critics have shown how much harm we wealthy nations have already done to poor nations through our well-intentioned but misguided attempts to help them (Paddock and Paddock 1973). Particularly reprehensible is our failure to carry out post-audits of these attempts (Farvar and Milton 1972). Thus have we shielded our tender consciences from knowledge of the harm we have done. Must we Americans continue to fail to monitor the consequences of our external "do-gooding?" If, for instance, we thoughtlessly make it possible for the present 600 million Indians to swell to 1,200 millions by the year 2001—as their present growth rate promises—will posterity in India thank *us* for facilitating an even greater destruction of *their* environment? Are good intentions ever a sufficient excuse for bad consequences?

IMMIGRATION CREATES A COMMONS

I come now to the final example of a commons in action, one for which the public is least prepared for rational discussion. The topic is at present enveloped by a great silence which reminds me of a comment made by Sherlock Holmes in A. Conan Doyle's story, "Silver Blaze." Inspector Gregory had asked, "Is there any point to which you would wish to draw my attention?" To this Holmes responded:

> "To the curious incident of the dog in the night-time."

> "The dog did nothing in the night-time," said the Inspector.

> "That was the curious incident," remarked Sherlock Holmes.

By asking himself what would repress the normal barking instinct of a watch dog Holmes realized that it must be the dog's recognition of his master as the criminal trespasser. In a similar way we should ask ourselves what repression keeps us from discussing something as important as immigration?

It cannot be that immigration is numerically of no consequence. Our government acknowledges a *net* inflow of 400,000 a year. Hard data are understandably lacking on the extent of illegal entries, but a not implausible figure is 600,000 per year (Buchanan 1973). The natural increase of the resident population is now about 1.7 million per year. This means that the yearly gain from immigration is at least 19%, and may be 37%, of the total increase. It is quite conceivable that educational campaigns like that of Zero Population Growth, Inc., coupled with adverse social and economic factors—inflation, housing shortage, depression, and loss of confidence in national leaders—may lower the fertility of American women to a point at which all of the yearly increase in population would be accounted for by immigration. Should we not at least ask if that is what we want? How curious it is that we so seldom discuss immigration these days!

Curious, but understandable—as one finds out the moment he publicly questions the wisdom of the status quo in immigration. He who does so is promptly charged with *isolationism, bigotry, prejudice, ethnocentrism, chauvinism,* and *selfishness.* These are hard accusations to bear. It is pleasanter to talk about other matters, leaving immigration policy to wallow in the cross-currents of special interests that take no account of the good of the whole—*or of the interests of posterity.*

We Americans have a bad conscience because of things we said in the past about immigrants. Two generations ago the popular press was rife with references to *Dagos, Wops, Pollacks, Japs, Chinks,* and *Krauts*—all pejorative terms which failed to acknowledge our indebtedness to Goya, Leonardo, Copernicus, Hiroshige, Confucius, and Bach. Because the implied inferiority of foreigners was *then* the justification for keeping them out, it is *now* thoughtlessly assumed that restrictive policies can only be based on the assumption of immigrant inferiority. *This is not so.*

Existing immigration laws exclude idiots and known criminals; future laws will almost certainly continue this policy. But should we also consider the quality of the average immigrant, as compared with the quality of the average resident? Perhaps we should, perhaps we shouldn't. (What is "quality" anyway?) But the quality issue is not our concern here.

From this point on, *it will be assumed that immigrants and native-born citizens are of exactly equal quality,* however quality may be defined. The focus is only on quantity. The conclusions reached depend on nothing else, so all charges of ethnocentrism are irrelevant.

World food banks move food to the people, thus facilitating the exhaustion of the environment of the poor. By contrast, unrestricted immigration moves people to the food, thus speeding up the destruction of the environment in rich countries. Why poor people should want to make this transfer is no mystery: but why should rich hosts encourage it? This transfer, like the reverse one, is supported by both selfish interests and humanitarian impulses.

The principal selfish interest in unimpeded immigration is easy to identify: it is the interest of the employers of cheap labor, particularly that needed for degrading jobs. We have been deceived about the forces of history by the lines of Emma Lazarus inscribed on the Statue of Liberty:

> *Give me your tired, your poor*
> *Your huddled masses yearning to breathe free,*
> *The wretched refuse of your teeming shore,*
> *Send these, the homeless, tempest-tossed, to me:*
> *I lift my lamp beside the golden door.*

The image is one of an infinitely generous earth-mother, passively opening her arms to hordes of immigrants who come here on their own initiative. Such an image may have been adequate for the early days of colonization, but by the time these lines were written (1886) the force for immigration was largely manufactured inside our own borders by factory and mine owners who sought cheap labor not to be found among laborers already here. One group of foreigners after another was thus enticed into the United States to work at wretched jobs for wretched wages.

At present, it is largely the Mexicans who are being so exploited. It is particularly to the advantage of certain employers that there be many illegal immigrants. Illegal immigrant workers dare not complain about their working conditions for fear of being repatriated. Their presence reduces the bargaining power of all Mexican-American laborers. Cesar Chavez has repeatedly pleaded with congressional committees to close the doors to more Mexicans so that those here can negotiate effectively for higher wages and decent working conditions. Chavez understands the ethics of a lifeboat.

The interests of the employers of cheap labor are well served by the silence of the intelligentsia of the country. WASPS—White Anglo-Saxon Protestants—are particularly reluctant to call for a closing of the doors to immigration for fear of being called ethnocentric bigots. It was, therefore, an occasion of pure delight for this particular WASP to be present at a meeting when the points he would like to have made were made better by a non-WASP speaking to other non-WASPS. It was in Hawaii, and most of the people in the room were second-level Hawaiian officials of Japanese ancestry. All Hawaiians are keenly aware of the limits of their environment, and the speaker had asked how it might be practically and constitutionally possible to close the doors to more immigrants to the islands. (To Hawaiians, immigrants from the other 49 states are as much of a threat as those from other nations. There is only so much room in the islands, and the islanders know it. Sophistical arguments that imply otherwise do not impress them.)

Yet the Japanese-Americans of Hawaii have active ties with the land of their origin. This point was raised by a Japanese-American member of the audience who asked the Japanese-American speaker: "But how can we shut the doors now? We have many friends and relations in Japan that we'd like to bring to Hawaii some day so that they can enjoy this beautiful land."

The speaker smiled sympathetically and responded slowly: "Yes, but we have children now and someday we'll have grandchildren. We can bring more people here from Japan only by giving away some of the land that we hope to pass on to our grandchildren some day. What right do we have to do that?"

To be generous with one's own possessions is one thing; to be generous with posterity's is quite another. This, I think, is the point that must be gotten across to those who would, from a commendable love of distributive justice, institute a ruinous system of the commons, either in the form of a world food bank or that of unrestricted immigration. Since every speaker is a member of some ethnic group it is always possible to charge him with ethnocentrism. But even after purging an argument of ethnocentrism the rejection of the commons is still valid and necessary if we are to save at least some parts of the world from environmental ruin. Is it not desirable that at least some of the grandchildren of people now living should have a decent place in which to live?

THE ASYMMETRY OF DOOR-SHUTTING

We must now answer this telling point: "How can you justify slamming the door once you're inside? You say that immigrants should be kept out. But aren't we all immigrants, or the descendants of immigrants? Since we refuse to leave, must we not, as a matter of justice and symmetry, admit all others?"

It is literally true that we Americans of non-Indian ancestry are the descendants of thieves. Should we not, then, "give back" the land to the Indians; that is, give it to the now-living Americans of Indian ancestry? As an exercise in pure logic I see no way to reject this proposal. Yet I am unwilling to live by it; and I know no one who is. Our reluctance to embrace pure justice may spring from pure selfishness. On the other hand, it may arise from an unspoken recognition of consequences that have not yet been clearly spelled out.

Suppose, becoming intoxicated with pure justice, we "Anglos" should decide to turn our land over to the Indians. Since all our other wealth has also been derived from the land, we would have to give that to the Indians, too. Then what would we non-Indians do? Where would we go? There is no open land in the world on which men without capital can make their living (and not much unoccupied land on which men with capital can either). Where would 209 million putatively justice-loving, non-Indian, Americans go? Most of them—in the persons of their ancestors—came from Europe, but they wouldn't be welcomed back there. Anyway, Europeans have

no better title to their land than we to ours. They also would have to give up their homes. (But to whom? And where would *they* go?)

Clearly, the concept of pure justice produces an infinite regress. The law long ago invented statutes of limitations to justify the rejection of pure justice, in the interest of preventing massive disorder. The law zealously defends property rights—but only *recent* property rights. It is as though the physical principle of exponential decay applies to property rights. Drawing a line in time may be unjust, but any other action is practically worse.

We are all the descendants of thieves, and the world's resources are inequitably distributed, but we must begin the journey to tomorrow from the point where we are today. We cannot remake the past. We cannot, without violent disorder and suffering, give land and resources back to the "original" owners—who are dead anyway.

We cannot safely divide the wealth equitably among all present peoples, so long as people reproduce at different rates, because to do so would guarantee that our grandchildren—everyone's grandchildren—would have only a ruined world to inhabit.

MUST EXCLUSION BE ABSOLUTE?

To show the logical structure of the immigration problem I have ignored many factors that would enter into real decisions made in a real world. No matter how convincing the logic may be it is probable that we would want, from time to time, to admit a few people from the outside to our lifeboat. Political refugees in particular are likely to cause us to make exceptions: We remember the Jewish refugees from Germany after 1933, and the Hungarian refugees after 1956. Moreover, the interests of national defense, broadly conceived, could justify admitting many men and women of unusual talents, whether refugees or not. (This raises the quality issue, which is not the subject of this essay.)

Such exceptions threaten to create runaway population growth inside the lifeboat, i.e., the receiving country. However, the threat can be neutralized by a population policy that includes immigration. An effective policy is one of flexible control.

Suppose, for example, that the nation has achieved a stable condition of ZPG, which (say) permits 1.5 million births yearly. We must suppose that an acceptable system of allocating birth-rights to potential parents is in effect. Now suppose that an inhumane regime in some other part of the world creates a horde of refugees, and that there is a widespread desire to admit some to our country. At the same time, we do not want to sabotage our population control system. Clearly, the rational path to pursue is the following. If we decide to admit 100,000 refugees this year we should compensate for this by reducing the allocation of birth-rights in the following year by a similar amount, that is downward to a total of 1.4 million. In that way we could achieve both humanitarian and population control goals. (And the refugees would have to accept the population controls of the society that admits them. It is not inconceivable that they might be given proportionately fewer rights than the native population.)

In a democracy, the admission of immigrants should properly be voted on. But by whom? It is not obvious. The usual rule of a democracy is votes for all. But it can be questioned whether a universal franchise is the most just one in a case of this sort. Whatever benefits there are in the admission of immigrants presumably accrue to everyone. But the costs would be seen as falling most heavily on potential parents, some of whom would have to postpone or forego having their (next) child because of the influx of immigrants. The double question *Who benefits? Who pays?* suggests that a restriction of the usual democratic franchise would be appropriate and just in this case. Would our particular quasi-democratic form of government be flexible enough to institute such a novelty? If not, the majority might, out of humanitarian motives, impose an unacceptable burden (the foregoing of parenthood) on a minority, thus producing political instability.

Plainly many new problems will arise when we consciously face the immigration question and seek rational answers. No workable answers can be found if we ignore population problems. And—if the argument of this essay is correct—so long as there is no true world government to control reproduction everywhere it is impossible to survive in dignity if we are to be guided by Spaceship ethics. Without a world government that is sovereign in reproductive matters mankind lives, in fact, on a number of sovereign lifeboats. For the foreseeable future survival demands that we govern our actions by the ethics of a lifeboat. Posterity will be ill served if we do not.

REFERENCES

Anonymous. 1974. *Wall Street Journal* 19 Feb.

Borlaug, N. 1973. Civilization's future: a call for international granaries. *Bull. At. Sci.* 29: 7–15.

Boulding, K. 1966. The economics of the coming Spaceship earth. In H. Jarrett, ed. *Environmental Quality in a Growing Economy.* Johns Hopkins Press, Baltimore.

Buchanan, W. 1973. Immigration statistics. *Equilibrium* 1(3): 16–19.

Davis, K. 1963. Population. *Sci. Amer.* 209(3): 62–71.

Farvar, M. T., and J. P. Milton. 1972. *The Careless Technology.* Natural History Press, Garden City, N.Y.

Gregg, A. 1955. A medical aspect of the population problem. *Science* 121: 681–682.

Hardin, G. 1966. Chap. 9 in *Biology: Its Principles and Implications*, 2nd ed. Freeman, San Francisco.

———. 1968. The tragedy of the commons. *Science* 162: 1243–1248.

———. 1969a. Page 18 in *Population, Evolution, and Birth Control*, 2nd ed. Freeman, San Francisco.

———. 1969b. The economics of wilderness. *Nat. Hist.* 78(6): 20–27.

———. 1972a. Pages 81–82 in *Exploring New Ethics for Survival: The Voyage of the Spaceship* Beagle. Viking, N.Y.

———. 1972b. Preserving quality on Spaceship Earth. In J. B. Trefethen, ed. *Transactions of the Thirty-Seventh North American Wildlife and Natural Resources Conference*. Wildlife Management Institute, Washington, D.C.

———. 1973. Chap. 23 in *Stalking the Wild Taboo*. Kaufmann, Los Altos, Cal.

Harris, M. 1972. How green the revolution. *Nat. Hist*. 81(3): 28–30.

Langer, S. K. 1942. *Philosophy in a New Key*. Harvard University Press, Cambridge.

Lansner, K. 1974. Should foreign aid begin at home? *Newsweek*, 11 Feb., p. 32.

Marx, K. 1875. Critique of the Gotha program. Page 388 in R. C. Tucker, ed. *The Marx-Engels Reader*. Norton, N.Y., 1972.

Ophuls, W. 1974. The scarcity society. *Harpers* 248(1487): 47–52.

Paddock, W. C. 1970. How green is the green revolution? *BioScience* 20: 897–902.

Paddock, W., and E. Paddock. 1973. *We Don't Know How*. Iowa State University Press, Ames, Iowa.

Paddock, W., and P. Paddock. 1967. *Famine—1975!* Little, Brown, Boston.

Wilkes, H. G. 1972. The green revolution. *Environment* 14(8): 32–39.

For Further Reflection

1. Is Hardin's analysis of world hunger and our moral obligations simplistic as some critics say?

2. Will aiding the poor invariably increase their suffering? Are some ways better than others? Explain.

3. Do you have a duty to give aid to the needy in other countries? Why or why not?

Suggestions for Further Reading

Adam Bedau, Hugo. and Paul Cassell, eds. *Debating the Death Penalty*. New York: Oxford University Press, 2004.

Aiken, William. and Hugh LaFollette, ed. *World Hunger and Morality*. Englewood Cliffs, NJ: Prentice Hall, 1996.

DeGrazia, David. *Animal Rights: A Very Short Introduction*. Oxford: Oxford University Press, 2002.

Devine, Philip. *The Ethics of Homicide*. Ithaca, NY: Cornell University Press, 1978.

Midgley, Mary. *Animals and Why They Matter*. Harmondsworth, UK: Penguin, 1984.

Nathanson, Stephen. *An Eye for an Eye?* Lanham, MD: Rowman & Littlefield, 1987.

O'Neil, Onora. *Faces of Hunger: An Essay on Poverty, Justice, and Development*. London: Unwin Hyman, 1986.

Pojman, Louis P. and Francis J. Beckwith, ed. *The Abortion Controversy: 25 Years After Roe v. Wade: A Reader*, 2nd ed. Belmont, CA: Wadsworth, 1998.

Pojman, Louis P. and Jeffrey Reiman, *The Death Penalty: For and Against*. Lanham, MD: Rowman and Littlefield, 1998.

Primoratz, Igor. *Justifying Legal Punishment*. Atlantic Highlands, NJ: Humanities Press International, 1989.

Regan, Tom. *The Case for Animal Rights*. Berkeley: University of California Press, 1983.

Sandel, Michael J. ed. *Justice: A Reader*. New York: Oxford University Press, 2007.

Schwarz, Stephen. *The Moral Question of Abortion*. Chicago: Loyola University Press, 1990.

Scruton, Roger. *Animal Rights and Wrongs*. London: Metro Publishing, 1998.

Sherwin, Susan. *No Longer Patient: Feminist Ethics and Health Care*. Philadelphia: Temple University Press, 1992.

Singer, Peter. *Animal Liberation*, 2nd ed. New York: New York Review of Books, 1990.

Tooley, Michael. *Abortion and Infanticide*. New York: Oxford University Press, 1983.

Appendix

෴

How to Read and Write Philosophy Papers

Reading

In some ways, reading philosophy is like reading the literature of many other fields. It requires a good deal of abstract thought, often involves difficult concepts or extraordinary propositions, and can be intimidating to those who approach the subject for the first time. But in other ways, reading philosophy is fairly distinctive. When you read a philosophical essay, you are not simply trying to glean some facts from it as you might if you were reading a science text or technical report. Neither are you following a storyline as if you were reading a mystery novel (though philosophy papers sometimes contain their share of mysteries). In most cases, you are tracing the steps in an argument, trying to see what conclusion the writer wants to prove and whether she succeeds in proving it. Along the way, you may encounter several premises with their accompanying analyses, clarifications, explanations, and examples. You may even run into a whole chain of arguments. In the end, if you have read well and the writer has written well, you are left not with a new set of data or a story ending, but with a realization—maybe even a revelation—that a conclusion is, or is not, worthy of belief.

The best way to learn how to read philosophy well is to read philosophy often. You will probably get plenty of chances to do that in your current philosophy course. Having a few rules to guide you in your reading, however, may help shorten the learning curve. As you read, keep the following in mind.

1. Approach the text with an open mind

If you are studying philosophy for the first time, you are likely—at least at first—to find a good bit of the material difficult, strange, or exasperating, sometimes all three at once. That's normal. Philosophy is an exploration of the rugged frontiers of our knowledge of fundamental things, so much of this new territory is likely to seem daunting or unfamiliar. There's also an excellent chance that your first visits to this terrain will be vexing, perhaps even infuriating, because you may sometimes disagree with what you read. There is no shame in experiencing any of these reactions. They come with the territory. But if you are to make any headway in philosophy and write good papers, you need to try your best to counteract these attitudes and feelings. Remember, philosophy at its best is a fair-minded, fearless search for truth. Anything that interferes with this noble quest must be overcome and cast aside.

Avoid making a judgment about an essay's ideas or arguments until you fully understand them and have fairly considered them. Make sure you are not reading with the intent to prove the conclusions false (or true). Be open to the possibility that the essay could give you good reasons to change your mind about something.

Try to maintain a neutral attitude toward the writer, presuming neither that she is right nor wrong, neither sinner nor saint. Don't assume that everything a renowned philosopher says must be true, and don't presuppose that everything a philosopher you dislike says must be false. Give the writer the same attention and respect that you would give a friend who is discussing a serious issue with you.

If you are reading the work of a famous philosopher and you find yourself thinking that his or her ideas are obviously silly or ridiculous, think again. The odds are good that you are misunderstanding what you read. It is wiser to assume that the text offers something of value (even if you disagree with it) and that you need to read more carefully.

2. Read actively and critically

Philosophical reading is intense. It cannot be rushed. It cannot be crammed. It cannot be done while your mind is on automatic pilot.

Philosophical reading is *active* reading. Instead of reading just to get through a piece of writing, you must take your time and ask yourself what key terms and passages mean, how the argument is structured, what the central thesis is, where the premises are, how certain key ideas are related, whether the main conclusion conflicts with propositions you know are true, even how the material compares with other philosophical writing on the same subject.

Philosophical reading is also *critical* reading. In critical reading, you ask not what something means but whether a statement is true and if the reasoning is solid. You ask if the conclusion really follows from the premises, whether the premises are true, if the analysis of a term really makes sense, if an argument has been overlooked, if an analogy is weak, whether there are counter-examples to key claims, and whether the claims agree with other things you have good reason to believe.

3. Identify the conclusion first, then the premises

When you first begin reading philosophical texts, they may seem to you like dark thickets of propositions into which you may not enter without losing your way. But your situation is really not that bad. As we have seen, in argumentative writing (the kind you are most likely to encounter in philosophy), you can depend on there being, well, an argument, a conclusion backed by premises. There could, of course, be several arguments that support the main argument, and the arguments could be complex, but these sets of conclusion-plus-premises will all serve as recognizable guideposts. If you want to penetrate the thicket, then, you must first identify the argument (or arguments). And the key to doing that is to *find the conclusion first, then look for the premises.*

When you find the main conclusion, you thereby identify the main point of the essay, and you then have the number-one clue to the function of all the rest of the text. Once you uncover the point that the writer is trying to prove, finding the supporting premises becomes much easier. And when you isolate the premises, locating the text that explains and amplifies the premises gets easier, too. Therefore, the first—and most important—question you can ask about a philosophical essay is, *"What claim is the writer trying to prove?"*

4. Outline, paraphrase, or summarize the argument

Understanding an essay's argument is so important that testing whether you really "get it" is crucial. You can test your grasp of the argument by outlining, paraphrasing, or summarizing it. If you can lay out an argument's premises and conclusion in an outline, or if you can accurately paraphrase or summarize the argument, you probably have a pretty good understanding of it. Very often students who think they comprehend an argument are surprised to see that they cannot devise an adequate outline or summary of it. Such failures suggest that, although outlining, paraphrasing, or summarizing may seem to some to be unnecessary, they are not—at least not to those new to philosophy.

5. Evaluate the argument, and formulate a tentative judgment

When you read philosophy, understanding it is just the first step. You also must do something that many beginners find both difficult and alien: You must make an informed judgment about what you read. Simply reiterating what the writer has said will not do. *Your* judgment is what matters here. Mainly, this judgment is your evaluation of the argument presented by the writer—an assessment of (1) whether the conclusion follows from the premises and (2) whether the premises are true. Only when the answer is *yes* to both these questions can you say that the conclusion of the argument is worthy of acceptance. This kind of evaluation is precisely what your instructor expects when she asks you to critique an argumentative essay in philosophy.

A philosophical text, of course, contains more than just a bare-bones argument. Often a considerable amount of space is devoted to explaining the background or history of the topic being addressed, elaborating on each of the premises, discussing the implications of the argument's conclusion, and answering possible criticisms of the essay's main points. Certainly you must take these into account when you are reading and evaluating a philosophical text. But your primary task is to arrive at an honest and well-reasoned assessment of the text's central claim.

Writing

In conversations, letters to the editor, or online discussions, have you ever taken a position on an issue and offered reasons why your view is correct? If so, then you have defended a thesis. You have presented an argument, giving reasons for accepting a particular thesis, or conclusion. If you elaborate on your argument in a written paper, you create something even more valuable—a *thesis defense* (or *argumentative*) *essay*. In a thesis defense essay, you try to show the reader that your view is worthy of acceptance by offering reasons that support it. Your thesis may assert your position on a philosophical, social, or political issue; on the arguments or claims of other writers (including some famous or not-so-famous philosophers); or on the interpretation of a single work or several. In every case, you affirm a thesis and give reasons for your affirmation.

This type of essay is not merely an analysis of claims, a summary of points made by someone else, or a reiteration of what other people believe or say—though a good thesis defense essay may contain some of these elements. A thesis defense essay is supposed to be a demonstration of what you believe and why you believe it. What other people think is, ultimately, beside the point.

Basic Essay Structure

Thesis defense essays usually contain the following elements, though not necessarily in this order:

  I. Introduction (or opening)
    A. Thesis statement (the claim to be supported)
    B. Plan for the paper
    C. Background for the thesis
 II. Argument supporting the thesis
III. Assessment of objections
IV. Conclusion

Introduction

The introduction often consists of the paper's first paragraph, sometimes just a sentence or two. Occasionally it is longer, perhaps several paragraphs. The length depends on how much ground you must cover to introduce the argument. Whatever the length, the introduction should be no longer than necessary. In most cases the best introductions are short.

If there is a rule of thumb for what the introduction must contain, it is this: *The introduction should set forth the thesis statement.* The thesis statement usually appears in the first paragraph. It is the claim that you hope to support or prove in your essay, the conclusion of the argument that you intend to present. You may want to pose the thesis statement as the answer to a question that you raise or as the solution to a problem that you wish to discuss. However presented, your thesis statement is the assertion you must support with reasons. It is like a compass to your readers, guiding them from paragraph to paragraph, premise to premise, showing them a clear path from introduction to conclusion. It also helps you stay on course. It reminds you to relate every sentence and paragraph to your one controlling idea.

Your thesis statement should be restricted to a claim that you can defend in the space allowed. You want to state it in a single sentence and do so as early as possible.

You may need to add a few words to explain or elaborate on the statement if you think its meaning or implications are unclear.

The other two parts of an introduction—the plan for the paper (B) and background information for the thesis (C)—may or may not be necessary, depending on your thesis and your intent. In more formal essays, you will need not only to state your thesis but also to spell out how you intend to argue for it. You will have to summarize your whole argument—each of your premises and conclusion—or, if your argument is long or complex, at least the most important points. Providing background information for your thesis is a matter of explaining what your thesis means (which includes defining terms and clarifying concepts), what its implications are, why the issue is so important or pressing, or why you have decided to address it. Sometimes the needed background information is so extensive that you must supply much of it after the introduction. At any rate, by adding the right kind of background information, you give your readers good reason to care about what you are saying and to continue reading.

In many philosophy papers, the background information includes a summary or sketch of the views of other philosophers—what they have said that is relevant to the issue or to your thesis. Providing this kind of material can help the reader understand why your topic is worth exploring and why your argument is relevant.

Argument Supporting the Thesis

Between your paper's introduction and conclusion is the *body* of the essay. The basic components of the body are (1) the premises of your argument plus the material that supports or explains them and (2) an evaluation of objections to your thesis. Each premise must be clearly stated, carefully explained and illustrated, and properly backed up by examples, statistics, expert opinion, argument, or other reasons or evidence. You may be able to develop the essay adequately by devoting a single paragraph to each premise, or you may have to use several paragraphs per premise.

Whatever tack you take, you must stick to the central rule of paragraph development: Develop just one main point in each paragraph, embodying that point in a topic sentence. Make sure that each paragraph in turn relates to your thesis statement.

If your essay is a critique of someone else's arguments, you should examine them in the body, explaining how they work and laying out the author's response to any major criticisms of them. Your account of the arguments should be accurate and complete, putting forth the author's best case and providing enough detail for your readers to understand the import of your own argument. After the presentation of the author's side of things, you can then bring in your critique, asserting and explaining each premise.

Some premises, of course, may be so obvious that they do not require support. The determining factor is whether your readers would be likely to question them. If your readers are likely to accept a premise as it is, no backup is required. If they are not, you need to support the premise. A common mistake is to assume that a premise would be accepted by everyone when in fact it is controversial.

Recall that in a good argument the conclusion logically follows from the premises, and the premises are true. Your task in the body of your essay is to put forth such an argument and to do so plainly—to demonstrate clearly to your readers that your premises are properly related to your conclusion and that they are true. You should leave no doubt about what you are trying to prove and how you are trying to prove it. In longer papers, you may want to back up your thesis with more than one argument. This is an acceptable way to proceed, providing you make the relationships between the separate arguments and your thesis clear.

Assessment of Objections

Very often an argumentative essay includes an *assessment of objections*—a sincere effort to take into account any objections or doubts that readers are likely to have about points in your essay. (In some cases, however, there may be no significant objections to assess.) You must show your readers that the objections are unfounded, that your argument is not fatally wounded by likely criticisms. Contrary to what some may think, when you deal effectively with objections in your essay, *you do not weaken it—you strengthen it*. You lend credibility to it by making an attempt to be fair and thorough. You make your position stronger by removing doubts from your readers' minds. If you don't confront likely objections, your readers may conclude either that you are ignorant of the objections or that you don't have a good reply to them. An extra benefit is that in dealing with objections, you may see ways to make your argument stronger.

On the other hand, you may discover that you do not have an adequate answer to the objections. Then what? Then you look for ways to change your arguments or thesis to overcome the criticisms. You can weaken your thesis by making it less sweeping or less probable. Or you may need to abandon your thesis altogether in favor of one that is stronger. Discovering that your beloved thesis is full of holes is not necessarily a setback. You have increased your understanding by finding out which boats will float and which will not.

Conclusion

Unless your essay is very short, it should have a *conclusion*. The conclusion usually appears in the last paragraph. Many conclusions simply reiterate the thesis statement and then go on to emphasize how important it is. Others issue a call to action, present a compelling perspective on the issue, or discuss further implications of the thesis statement. Some conclusions contain a summary of the essay's argument. A summary is always a good idea if the argument is complex, long, or formal.

Writing the Essay: Step by Step

Now we examine the steps involved in crafting a good thesis defense essay. You have the best chance of writing a good essay if you try to follow these steps. Just remember that the process is not linear. You may not be able to follow the steps in the sequence suggested. You may have to backtrack or rearrange the order of the steps. This kind of improvising on the fly is normal—and often necessary. At any stage in the process, you may discover that your argument is not as good as you thought, that you did not take an important fact into account, or that there is a way that you can alter the essay to make it stronger. You may then want to go back and rework your outline or tinker with the draft you are working on—and your essay will be better for it. Rethinking and revising are normal procedures for even the best writers.

Here are the steps:

1. Select a topic and narrow it to a specific issue.
2. Research the issue.
3. Write a thesis statement.
4. Create an outline.
5. Write a first draft.
6. Study and revise your first draft.
7. Produce a final draft.

Step 1. Select a topic and narrow it to a specific issue

This step is first for a reason. It is here to help inexperienced writers avoid a tempting but nasty trap: picking a thesis out of the air and writing their paper on it. Caution: *Any thesis that you dream up without knowing anything about it is likely to be unusable*— and a waste of time. It is better to begin by selecting a topic or issue and narrowing it through research and hard thinking to a manageable thesis.

A topic is simply a broad category of subject matter, such as *human cloning, the mind, capital punishment,* and *God.* Within topics there lurk an infinite number of issues—that is, questions that are in dispute. From the topic of capital punishment, for example, countless issues arise: whether executing criminals deters crime, whether executing a human being is ever morally permissible, whether it is ethical to execute people who are insane or mentally impaired, whether the system of capital punishment in the United States is unfair, whether the death penalty should be mandatory for serial killers, whether executing juveniles is immoral . . . the list could go on and on. The basic idea is to select from the roster of possibilities an issue that (1) you are interested in and (2) you can adequately address in the space allowed.

Step 2. Research the issue

The main reason for researching an issue is to find out what viewpoints and arguments are involved. Often your instructor will suggest good sources to research for a particular writing assignment. Your assigned reading may be the only source you need to check. Otherwise, you can read articles and books, talk to people who have studied the issue or at least thought about it carefully, or go online to review topical or philosophical sites.

Step 3. Write a thesis statement

The conclusion of your selected argument will serve as the basis for your thesis statement. Often the conclusion *is* your thesis statement. Writing a good thesis statement is an essential step because the entire essay is built on it. An imprecise or clumsy thesis statement can lead to an imprecise or clumsy argument, which can wreck any argumentative essay.

At this stage, you should try to get the wording of your statement just right, even though you may revise it later on. Its scope should be restricted to what you can handle in the space you have. It should also be focused on just one idea, not several. A good thesis statement must be clear. No one should have to guess about the meaning of your thesis. The thesis "Same-sex marriages are intolerable," for example, is intolerably vague since there are many ways that something can be intolerable. It gives us very little information about what will be discussed in the essay.

It is possible to devise a thesis statement that is restricted, focused, clear—and trivial. A trivial thesis statement is one that either concerns an insignificant issue or makes an insignificant claim. People generally don't care about insignificant issues, and few would bother to disagree with an insignificant claim. Who cares whether pens are better than pencils, or whether gambling is more fun than beachcombing? And who would care to contest the claim that pleasure is better than pain? An essay built on a trivial thesis statement wastes your readers' time (if they bother to read it at all), and you learn nothing and change nothing by writing it. Thesis statements should be worthy.

Here are some thesis statements that meet these criteria:

- Jeremy Bentham's moral theory known as act-utilitarianism conflicts with our commonsense ideas about human rights.
- The U.S. government should be allowed to arrest and indefinitely imprison without trial any American citizen who is suspected of terrorism.
- Subjective relativism—the view that truth depends on what someone believes—is self-refuting.
- Racial profiling should not be used to do security screening of airline passengers.

Step 4. Create an outline of the whole essay

If you can write out your thesis statement and outline the argument used to defend it, you have already come far. Your argument and thesis statement will constitute the skeleton of your essay. The next step is to flesh out the bones with introductory or explanatory material, responses to objections, and support for the premises (which may consist of subordinate arguments, examples, explanations, analogies, statistics, scientific research, expert opinion, or other evidence). Producing a detailed, coherent outline of the whole essay is the best way to manage this task, and if you already have an outline of your argument, creating an outline for the whole essay will be easy. An outline helps you fill out your argument in an orderly fashion, showing you how the pieces fit together and whether any parts are missing or misaligned. This filling-out process will probably require you to research your thesis further—to check the truth of premises, examine alternative arguments, look for additional evidence, or assess the strength of objections to your argument.

Do not be afraid to alter your outline at any stage. As you write, you may realize that your thesis is weak, your argument flawed, or your premises vague. If so, you should go back and adjust the outline before writing any further. Writing is an act of exploration, and good writers are not afraid to revise when they find something amiss.

When you outline your essay, include your full thesis statement in the introduction. Then as you work on the outline, you can refer to the statement for guidance. The major points of your outline will include the premises, conclusion, objections, and responses to objections.

You will find that as you tweak the outline, you may need to adjust the thesis statement. And as you perfect the thesis statement, you may need to adjust the outline. In the end, you want to satisfy yourself that the outline is complete, accurate, and structurally sound, tracing a clear and logical progression of points.

Step 5. Write a first draft

Good writers revise . . . and revise and revise. They either write multiple drafts, revising in successive passes, or revise continuously as they write. They know that their first tries will always be in need of improvement. Inexperienced writers, on the other hand, too often dash off a first draft without a second look—then turn it in! A much more reasonable approach (and the best one for most students) is to at least write a first draft and a final draft or—better—several drafts and a final one.

In argumentative essays, because of the importance of articulating an argument carefully and the difficulty of writing later drafts of the essay unless the first one is in reasonable shape, the first draft should be fairly solid. That is, in your first draft, you should write a tentative version of each paragraph, and the wording of your thesis statement and all premises should be at least close to final form.

Give your draft a good introduction that lays out your thesis statement, provides background information on the issue, and draws your readers into the essay. Make it interesting, informative, and pertinent to the question at hand. Do not assume that your readers will automatically see that your paper is worth reading.

Every paragraph in your paper should relate to the thesis; every sentence in each paragraph should relate to a topic sentence. Delete any sentence that does not serve the essay's purpose. Ensure that paragraphs appear in a logical sequence and are clearly linked by transitional words and phrases or references to material in preceding paragraphs. Your readers should never have to wonder what the connection is between parts of your paper.

Step 6. Study and revise your first draft

Your first draft is likely to have problems both big and small. At this stage, though, you should scrutinize mostly the big ones. This is no time for proofreading (correcting spelling, fixing punctuation, repairing typos, and the like). This is the time to make substantive changes.

Step 7. Produce a final draft

After completing all substantive changes, you should generate a final draft, the one you will turn in. The final draft should reflect not only the big changes but also the corrections of all minor errors—misspellings, typos, grammatical errors, misplaced words, faulty punctuation, and documentation mistakes. This task should be primarily a proofreading job. At this stage, you should also format the manuscript according to your instructor's requirements.

The key to producing a clean final draft is *down time*—an interim in which you leave the last draft alone and focus on something else. Coming back to your paper after a day or so away from it can help you see errors that passed right by you before. You may be surprised how many mistakes this fresh look can reveal. If you cannot set the essay aside, ask a friend to read it and give you some constructive criticism.

Glossary

absolutism, political   A political system in which the state has immense power over its citizens to ensure peace and security.

anarchism   The political view that the state has no right to violate personal freedom or autonomy.

a posteriori **argument**   An argument with premises that can be known only through experience.

a posteriori **knowledge**   Knowledge that depends entirely on sense experience.

a priori **argument**   An argument that does not depend on premises known only through experience.

a priori **knowledge**   Knowledge acquired independently of or prior to sense experience.

argument   A group of statements—one statement to be supported (the conclusion) and one or more statements trying to support it (the premises).

argument from evil   An argument purporting to show that since there is unnecessary evil, an all-powerful, all-knowing, and all-good God must not exist.

cognitive realism   The view that there is such a thing as objective truth, that there is a way things are independently of how we represent these things to ourselves.

cognitive relativism   The view that truth is relative, that the way things are depends on how we represent them to ourselves.

compatibilism   The view that free actions are compatible with causal determinism.

conclusion   In an argument, the statement to be supported by premises.

conventionalism (cultural relativism)   The notion that moral standards are relative to culture.

cosmological argument   An argument that tries to show that from the fact that the universe exists, God exists.

deductive argument   An argument meant to give logically conclusive support to its conclusion.

democracy   A political system based on the principles of majority decision-making and individual rights.

deontological ethics   Moral theories in which the rightness of actions is determined not solely by their consequences but partly or entirely by their intrinsic nature.

determinism   The doctrine that every event has a cause.

dialectic   A process of reasoning or intellectual conversation in which argument and counterargument, or thesis and counterthesis, are continually juxtaposed in order to discover the truth of a matter.

dualism   The view that the mind (or soul) and the body are two separate things.

dualism, property   The view that mental properties are nonphysical properties arising from, but not reducible to, physical properties.

dualism, substance   The notion that mind and body consist of two fundamentally different kinds of stuff, or substances.

empiricism   The view that our knowledge of the empirical world comes solely from sense experience.

epistemology   The philosophical study of knowledge.

ethical egoism   The view that right actions are those that serve one's own best interests.

ethical objectivism   The view that there exist objective moral standards.

ethical relativism   The view that moral standards do not have independent status but are relative to what individuals or cultures believe.

ethics   The study of morality using the methods of philosophy.

ethics of care   An ethical perspective that focuses on the unique demands of specific situations and the virtues and feelings that are central to close personal relationships—empathy, compassion, love, sympathy, and fidelity.

functionalism   The view that the mind is the functions that the brain performs.

hard determinism   The view that there is no free will.

identity theory   The view that mental states are identical to physical brain states.

indicator words   Words that often accompany an argument and indicate that a premise or conclusion is present.

inductive argument   An argument meant to provide probable support to its conclusion.

inference   The process of reasoning from premises to a conclusion.

inference to the best explanation   A form of inductive reasoning in which we reason from premises about a state of affairs to an explanation for that state of affairs.

liberalism, political   The doctrine that a government should promote both maximum liberty and social equality.

libertarianism   The view that some actions are controlled by persons.

libertarianism, political   The doctrine that people have inviolable personal freedoms and the right to pursue their own social and economic well-being in a free market without interference from others.

logic   The study of arguments, or correct reasoning.

materialism   The view that the mind (or soul) is physical or can be reduced entirely to the physical.

moral absolutism   The view that moral principles are invariable and without exceptions.

moral skepticism   The rejection of ethical objectivism.

ontological argument   An argument that tries to demonstrate God's existence by logical analysis of the concept of God.

philosophy   A discipline that systematically examines life's big questions through critical reasoning, logical argument, and careful reflection.

premise   In an argument, a statement meant to support a conclusion.

principle of fallibilism   The thesis that we are likely incorrect in many of our beliefs and have a tendency toward self-deception and resistance to opinions opposed to our own.

principle of parsimony   The principle that, all things being equal, we should prefer the simpler explanation to the more complex.

property dualism   The view that mental properties are nonphysical properties arising from, but not reducible to, physical properties.

propositional knowledge   Knowledge of a proposition, or *knowing that* something is the case.

rationalism   The view that through unaided reason we can come to know what the world is like.

skepticism   The view that we cannot or do not have knowledge.

subjectivism   The view that moral standards are relative to individuals.

substance dualism   The notion that mind and body consist of two fundamentally different kinds of stuff, or substances.

teleological argument   An argument that tries to show that God must exist because features of the universe show signs of purpose or design.

teleological ethics   Moral theories asserting that the rightness or wrongness of an act is determined by some nonmoral value.

utilitarianism   A moral theory that says right actions are those that result in the most beneficial balance of good over bad consequences for everyone involved.

virtue ethics   A moral theory that focuses on the development of virtuous character.